THE NEW INTERNATIONAL COMMENTARY ON THE OLD TESTAMENT

R. K. HARRISON, *General Editor*

The Book of JEREMIAH

by

J. A. THOMPSON

WILLIAM B. EERDMANS PUBLISHING COMPANY
GRAND RAPIDS, MICHIGAN

255 Jefferson Ave. SE, Grand Rapids, Mich. 49503

Printed in the United States of America
Reprinted, December 1981

Library of Congress Cataloging in Publication Data

Thompson, John Arthur, 1913-
The book of Jeremiah.

(The New international commentary on the Old Testament)
Bibliography: p. 131
Includes indexes.
1. Bible. O.T. Jeremiah—Commentaries. I. Title
II. Series: New international commentary on the Old Testament.
BS1525.3.T47 224'.2'077 79-16510
ISBN 0-8028-2369-6

TO MARION

AUTHOR'S PREFACE

It is many years now since the late Professor E. J. Young invited me to write a commentary on the books of Samuel for this series. On his death there were some changes in his original assignments and I was invited to transfer to Jeremiah. I was more than happy to make the change since I had worked on the Hebrew text of Jeremiah in my student days while studying for both Arts and Divinity degrees, and later, when I became a teacher, it was a continuing delight over some years to teach both the Hebrew text and the English version of Jeremiah to theological students.

Over the years I have set foot in Jerusalem, Shiloh, Bethel, Dan, and other places known to Jeremiah. Archeological work carried out in these and other sites has had a particular fascination for me. The reader will discover many references to archeological discoveries in the pages that follow.

I can still recall quite vividly the first visit I made to the modern Arab village of 'Anata, which must represent the approximate site of Jeremiah's village of Anathoth. The whole village seemed to be a blaze of almond blossoms in every direction. I climbed a high fence and plucked a half dozen almond kernels left over from the last season to take home to Australia as a useful teaching aid. In fancy I saw Jeremiah toiling across the intervening hills on his three-mile walk into Jerusalem to take up his stand in the temple courtyard and preach his Temple Sermon. I have returned again and again to that sermon for my own preaching over the years, but not alone to the Temple Sermon. The whole book still seems alive and is a never ending source of instruction to me, and I would hope to those whom I have taught.

It has been a rare privilege to write the commentary that follows. It is my hope and prayer that readers of this volume may enter a little into the experiences of that lonely figure of the late seventh and early sixth centuries B.C. and to catch something of the deep significance of his call to his own people to be true to their covenant Lord and to live in conformity with his covenant.

Clearly, no writer can produce a commentary without the help of others. Much of the work for this volume was carried out in the University Library in Cambridge, England, where I spent three happy and profitable years on a research project. I knew that few libraries could provide more source material than the Cambridge University Library.

Special thanks are due two who have helped in the preparation of the manuscript, Mrs. Pat Johnson of the Department of Middle Eastern Studies at the University of Melbourne, and my wife, who has been critic and proofreader of the numerous manuscripts I have written during nearly forty years. She has once again shown patience and understanding as I have devoted the long hours necessary to complete such a task. If my readers can enter in some measure into the profound thinking of Jeremiah, our toil will not have been in vain.

J. A. THOMPSON

CONTENTS

INDEXES

PRINCIPAL ABBREVIATIONS

ADAJ	*Annual of the Department of Antiquities of Jordan*
AJSL	*American Journal of Semitic Languages*
Akk.	Akkadian
ANET(S)	J. B. Pritchard, ed., *Ancient Near Eastern Texts* (^{2}1955, ^{3}1969); Supplement (1969)
Arab.	Arabic
ARAB	D. D. Luckenbill, *Ancient Records of Assyria and Babylonia*, 2 vols. (1926–27)
ARM	*Archives Royales de Mari*
ATD	*Das Alte Testament Deutsch*
AV	Authorised (King James) Version of the Bible
BA	*Biblical Archaeologist*
BASOR	*Bulletin of the American Schools of Oriental Research*
BHS	*Biblia Hebraica Stuttgartensia*
BJRL	*Bulletin of the John Rylands Library*
CAD	*The Assyrian Dictionary of the Oriental Institute of the University of Chicago*
CBQ	*Catholic Biblical Quarterly*
EQ	*Evangelical Quarterly*
E.T.	English Translation
FRLANT	Forschungen zur Religion und Literatur des Alten und Neuen Testaments
GNB	Good News Bible
HAT	Handbuch zum Alten Testament
HUCA	*Hebrew Union College Annual*
IB	*Interpreter's Bible*
ICC	International Critical Commentary
IDB	*Interpreter's Dictionary of the Bible*
IEJ	*Israel Exploration Journal*
JA	*Journal Asiatique*
JAOS	*Journal of the American Oriental Society*
JBC	*The Jerome Bible Commentary* (1969)

JBL	*Journal of Biblical Literature*
JCS	*Journal of Cuneiform Studies*
JNES	*Journal of Near Eastern Studies*
JPOS	*Journal of the Palestine Oriental Society*
JQR	*Jewish Quarterly Review*
JSS	*Journal of Semitic Studies*
JTS	*Journal of Theological Studies*
KB	Koehler and Baumgartner, *Lexicon in Veteris Testamenti Libros*
LXX	Septuagint
MT	Masoretic Text
NBD	J.D. Douglas, ed., *The New Bible Dictionary* (1962)
NEB	The New English Bible
NICOT	New International Commentary on the Old Testament
OTS	*Oudtestamentische Studiën*
PEQ	*Palestine Exploration Quarterly*
RB	*Revue Biblique*
RHPR	*Revue d'Histoire et de Philosophie Religieuses*
RSV	Revised Standard Version of the Bible
RV	Revised Version of the Bible
SVT	Supplements to *Vetus Testamentum*
Syr.	Syriac
UF	*Ugarit-Forschungen*
Ugar.	Ugaritic
UT	C. H. Gordon, *Ugaritic Textbook*
VT	*Vetus Testamentum*
Vulg.	Vulgate
WMANT	Wissenschaftliche Monographien zum Alten und Neuen Testament
ZAW	*Zeitschrift für die alttestamentliche Wissenschaft*

The Book of
JEREMIAH

INTRODUCTION

I. JEREMIAH AMONG THE PROPHETS

It is not an empty truism to say that Jeremiah was one of the prophets of Yahweh in Israel, of whom there were a great number. The canonical books of the OT have preserved the memory of only a small number of them. But the biblical references to prophets are persistent over many centuries.

Leaving aside Moses, the first clear picture of prophecy in Israel comes from the age of Saul, some four hundred years before Jeremiah. In those years there were groups of prophets who travelled about delivering oracles at the request of those who sought them out (1 Sam. 10:5–13).[1] The behavior of these prophets seems to have been unusual, for they danced around to the accompaniment of music. Saul himself was seized by the Spirit and began to "prophesy" in their midst (1 Sam. 19:18–24). It was an ecstatic manifestation which was unusual and in later times was virtually unknown. Perhaps these were men who were stirred up in order to urge the nation to fight Yahweh's holy war against his foes.[2]

1. See Simon John DeVries, *Prophet Against Prophet* (Grand Rapids, 1978), pp. 54, 57, 149. This volume provides helpful insights into certain aspects of the prophetic movement but notably the conflict that often arose between a prophet and his fellow prophets.

2. We do not propose to attempt a study of possible precursors of Israelite prophecy outside Israel; indeed it is entirely possible that the phenomenon in Israel was quite indigenous. The human spirit is capable of being stirred by a wide variety of influences. In the area of religion it seems that wherever men reach out to a deity they pray, offer some form of sacrifice, and sense the divine presence. They have their cult officials to administer the cultic rites and to speak in the name of the deity. Sometimes there are ecstatic manifestations as well (this continues till today in a Christian environment). It is possible to point to a variety of phenomena outside Israel where it is evident that prophecy of some kind was practiced, e.g., the prophets

Samuel himself is described as a "man of God" (1 Sam. 9:6–10) and a "seer" (*rō'eh,* 1 Sam. 9:9). In the same general period we meet a "man of God" who came to Eli with a message from Yahweh (1 Sam. 2:27). By the age of David it is clear that a prophet like Nathan could rise to some prominence and become involved in the affairs of the nation. Nathan's oracle to David (2 Sam. 7) promising him divine support and the establishment of his descendants on the throne of Israel was important for the whole future of Israel. Nathan also rebuked the king in the matter of Bathsheba (2 Sam. 12) and took part in the anointing of Solomon (1 K. 1:38–39). His contemporary, Gad, likewise brought an oracle from Yahweh to David (2 Sam. 24:10–19). In the days of Jeroboam I (*c.* 922–901 B.C.), Ahijah of Shiloh spoke of Jeroboam's future position as a ruler of the northern part of the Israelite state, an encouragement to rebellion (1 K. 11:29–39). A nameless "man of God" also delivered a word from Yahweh to Jeroboam (1 K. 13), while in Judah Shemaiah, a "man of God," forbade Rehoboam to fight Jeroboam (1 K. 12:22). Elijah and Elisha in the ninth century continued the tradition. Elijah appeared as the champion of Yahweh to challenge the priests of Baal (1 K. 18) at a time when Jezebel the queen sought to slay the prophets of Yahweh (1 K. 18:3, 4, 13). In those days the prophet Micaiah ben Imlah[3] stood in Ahab's court and prophesied disaster in sharp contrast to all the other prophets who prophesied victory for Ahab (1 K. 22:5–28). Elisha, who was Elijah's protégé and successor, was a strong nationalist at a time when Israel was beset by constant border clashes with the Arameans (2 K. 6:8–23; 13:14–19). Both he and Elijah were the leaders of bands of prophets (*b^e nê hann^e ḇî'îm,* 2 K. 2:1–5; 9:1).

All these references are to "prophets" or "men of God" who

of Baal and Asherah (1 K. 18:19; 2 K. 10:19); Akkadian prophecies (see *ANET*[3], pp. 604–607); "prophecy" in Egypt (SVT 9 [1963], pp. 47– 65); the Wen Amon incident (*ANET*, pp. 25–29); the Zakir Stele (*ANET,* pp. 655f.); and in particular, prophecy in Mari (H. B. Huffmon, "Prophecy in the Mari Letters," *BA* 31/4 [1968], pp. 101–124; W. L. Moran, "New Evidence from Mari on the History of Prophecy," *Biblica* 50 [1969], pp. 15–56). But whether all this data tells us more than that in other religions as well as Yahwism men sought to discover and proclaim the mind of the deity seems to be a very open question. We are certainly safe in claiming that in Israel some devout men were open to the call of Yahweh, Israel's God, and were bold enough to declare what were often unpalatable messages. For a succinct recent discussion see Georg Fohrer, *History of Israelite Religion* (1968, E.T. 1972).

3. See S. J. DeVries, *Prophet Against Prophet.* The whole volume is a development of the conflict between Micaiah and the prophets of his day. See the Index (p. 160) for many references.

addressed a word from Yahweh to the people of their day, often to men of importance like kings. It seems clear that there were numerous unnamed prophets as well as large groups of prophets who constituted a body of supporters of the Yahwistic religion. This was not unique; Baal too was served by groups of prophets (1 K. 18:19). But Yahweh's prophets were quite specifically the spokesmen of Yahweh to his people.[4] The question of whether they had some connection with the official cult in Israel need not occupy us here except to say that some like Ezekiel were priests, some may have had intercessory or teaching functions in the official cult, but many of them like Amos were free agents. Presumably they all regarded their work as a divine vocation and believed that they had been called to it, whether through some religious experience or as a consequence of family background. The precanonical prophets we have referred to above spoke to the people in terms both of salvation and judgment. One significant feature about these early prophets was that they established the principle that it was part of the prophetic calling to criticize the king and his policies in the light of ancient traditional beliefs and to seek to correct them, by political action if necessary. Nathan rebuked David (2 Sam. 12:1–14). So did Gad (2 Sam. 24). Ahijah was outraged by Solomon's tyrannical practices and religious laxity and announced to Jeroboam the destruction of his kingdom (1 K. 11:26–40). Elijah challenged Ahab time and again and Elisha and his associates were implicated in the Jehu revolution (2 K. 9–10). By contrast, some of the prophets surrendered their independence and spoke to the king only the things that pleased him (e.g., 1 K. 22:5–6). As a result it sometimes happened, as it did in the case of Jeremiah, that prophet spoke against prophet (ch. 28). It would seem that the prophetic orders very often surrendered their original function and it was left to individuals to declare the word of Yahweh. This was true no less in the days of the precanonical prophets than in the days of the canonical prophets.

About the middle of the eighth century B.C., approximately a century before Jeremiah began his ministry, the prophetic movement in Israel entered a new phase. Henceforth prophets ministered

4. The etymology of the noun *nāḇî'*, "prophet," and the verb **hiṯnabbē'*, "to prophesy," is not certain. Many have argued for a connection with Akk. *nabû*, "to call, announce," and think of the noun as active, "caller, announcer," or passive, "one who is called," of the same structure as several Hebrew nouns, e.g., *pāqîḏ*. See W. F. Albright, *From the Stone Age to Christianity* (New York, [2]1957), p. 305; A. R. Johnson, *The Cultic Prophet in Ancient Israel* (Cardiff, 1944), p. 24, nn. 6–8.

to Israel but their words were carefully recorded, at least in part. In the first group of "classical" prophets were Amos and Hosea, whose ministry was largely to Northern Israel. These were followed after a short time by Isaiah and Micah, who preached mainly to Judah. None of these could be classed as a representative of the prophetic orders that had functioned up till then. Clearly Amos regarded himself as a prophet although he did not identify with any prophetic guild (Amos 7:14–15).[5] Yet in a real sense Amos and his contemporaries continued an ancient tradition. They were not ecstatics but they sometimes performed symbolic acts. Isaiah gathered disciples (e.g., Isa. 8:16) but preached independently. They preached at sanctuaries, Amos at Bethel, Isaiah at Jerusalem. They may have used the language of the cult at times, but they did not speak officially in the name of the cult. They rebuked kings, as did Nathan and Elijah, for their crimes against the people. They attacked the worship of other gods than Yahweh as Elijah had done, and like him deplored empty rituals. It is clear that both Amos and Hosea held the tradition that Israel had become the people of Yahweh through divine election at the Exodus, and referred at times to the wilderness period (Amos 2:9–10; 9:7; Hos. 11:1; 12:9; 13:4; cf. Hos. 7:16; 8:13; 9:3, 10; 11:5). Both Hosea and Amos understood their own mission in the light of the particular privileges and responsibilities of Israel, the people to whom they preached. There was evidently no need to teach the people these facts as though they had never heard them. And when the prophets castigated the people because of their disloyalty and neglect of the obligations which lay upon them because of their privileged position, they were not preaching in a vacuum. Rather, the people were reminded of what they knew, or should have known.

Isaiah and Micah stressed another aspect of election, the divine choice of David and his dynasty to rule Yahweh's elect people and the related choice of Mount Zion as the place where the Ark of the Covenant rested, the place where Yahweh's dwelling place was to be found. Amos was not unaware of these traditions (Amos 1:2; 9:11–12).[6] Isaiah, however, made a good deal of reference to them. Yahweh's presence in Jerusalem was the hope for the future of Israel and the nations (Isa. 2:2–4). He would fight for Israel from Mount

5. See R. E. Clements, *Prophecy and Covenant* (1965), pp. 36ff.

6. Both these passages have been regarded by at least some writers as editorial expansions, but 9:11–12 at least may be regarded as authentic. See R. E. Clements, *Prophecy and Covenant,* p. 49, n. 1.

Zion (Isa. 14:32; 17:12–14; 28:14–18; 29:5–8). At the same time Isaiah could preach judgment against Judah (Isa. 1:21–26) and against Jerusalem (Isa. 29:1–4), a theme taken up by Micah (Mic. 3:9–12). The use by these eighth-century prophets of these traditions with their stress on the Exodus and on the covenant between Yahweh and the house of David points to ancient traditions which they inherited. There was, in fact, a double tradition of a covenant, the covenant of Sinai which brought Israel into its privileged position and laid a heavy obligation upon her, and the covenant which Yahweh made with the house of David (2 Sam. 7).[7] Even though the term "covenant" is seldom used there is no escaping its reality, with its emphasis on the divine grace which originated it and the privilege and obligations resting on those who regarded themselves as members of the covenant family. The two covenants were not unrelated. In the age of David the older Sinai Covenant tradition was extended to provide a divine authorization for the new state with its territorial and political claims. The dual election of the Davidic house to rule over Israel and of Mount Zion to be Yahweh's dwelling place was not intended to overshadow the Sinai Covenant. Indeed, the presence of the Ark of the Covenant in Jerusalem was a permanent reminder of the obligations of Israel to acknowledge Yahweh's lordship and to obey his covenant law. There was uneasiness about the covenant between Yahweh and David, and also about the unique claims of Jerusalem among the northern tribes, because the doctrine seemed to overshadow the Sinaitic covenant. In Judah the two covenants existed side by side and had done so since David's time. But the double tradition was the cause of a great deal of tension over the centuries, and part of the prophetic task was to remind the people of the primacy of the Sinai Covenant.[8]

There was another aspect to the doctrine of covenant which loomed large in the prophets of the eighth century, namely, the obligations imposed upon the nation and upon individuals in the nation. These were expressed in the basic covenant law. Behind these prophets we must certainly recognize the existence of a well-developed tradition of law which embraced the whole area of Israelite life. There were ethical claims upon Israel of the strongest kind. When

7. The question of whether a secular parallel to the covenant can be found in the ancient Near Eastern treaties is discussed further on pp. 59-67.

8. For a succinct summary of the main points at issue and bibliography see R. E. Clements, *Prophecy and Covenant,* pp. 45–68. See also John Bright, *Covenant and Promise* (Philadelphia, 1976).

that law was held lightly and openly disregarded, Israel placed herself under the judgment of that law. Failure to fulfil the demands of the covenant law would result in the divine judgment falling on the offenders. Instead of the law being a guide to national welfare and happiness it became a curse and a threat to national existence.

The greatest offense of all was the rejection of Yahweh himself as Israel's sovereign Lord. There could be no shared allegiance between Yahweh and any other god. The cry of Elijah was "If Yahweh be God, follow him" (1 K. 18:21). The spirit of that cry, if not the exact words, is found again and again in the prophets of Israel. To worship any other god was to violate Yahweh's covenant and to lay oneself open to Yahweh's wrath. All the eighth-century prophets gave warning of judgment to come, not in some distant future but in the context of historical events. At the same time they looked beyond judgment to a better future.

It was against the background of a long prophetic tradition that Jeremiah was called to preach. Like his predecessors he had a profound sense of divine vocation, of being called even before his birth. He felt the divine hand upon his life and knew that the divine word had been placed in his mouth. When he spoke he could say, "This is what Yahweh has said," or he even spoke in Yahweh's name using the first person "I." Like his contemporaries and predecessors he drew upon the great traditions of the past such as Israel's election in the Exodus period (2:2–8; 7:21–22; 16:14–15; 23:7–8; 31:31–34) and Yahweh's covenant with the house of David (23:5–6; cf. 22:30). He was deeply aware of the demands of the covenant and the dangers that lay in the breach of covenant law. For him there was no God but Yahweh. Any kind of syncretism was intolerable and fraught with great peril, the peril of divine judgment. He rejected every glib attitude, every wanton disregard of the divine law, every false and immoral trust in a cult or a temple (7:1–15; 25:1–29). He took up much of the symbolism of Hosea. Like Hosea[9] he depicted the relationship between Yahweh and Israel as a marriage relationship (2:2; 3:6–14) and called Israel Yahweh's sons (3:19, 22; 4:22). Like Hosea he traced this relationship back to the Exodus and the deliverance from Egypt (2:6). Like Hosea he limited the period of unclouded fellowship between Israel and Yahweh to the days of Moses and the desert period (7:22). It was in the land that apostasy

9. For the special relationship between Jeremiah and Hosea see IV.G below, "The Debt of Jeremiah to Hosea," pp. 81–85.

began (2:7), and he described that apostasy in natural rather than historical terms (2:2–3, 7–8; 3:19–20; 8:4–7). Like his predecessors he saw that the only possibility of escape from the impending disaster lay in repentance and return to Yahweh (e.g., 3:6–13; 3:21–4:2; 4:3–4; 23:3–7).

There is much else that might be said about Jeremiah and this will emerge in the commentary. He was a prominent representative of one of the most remarkable groups of men in the whole of history, the prophets of Israel, whose words have come down the centuries. Though addressed to specific situations in an ancient past, their words still nurture the faith of many and bring instruction, courage, and inspiration to a better life. Somehow the specific words of Jeremiah, addressed to specific situations at the end of the seventh and the early part of the sixth centuries B.C., come alive as guidelines for believers in every age. It is a fruitless endeavor to try to defend the proposition that Jeremiah spoke a true word from God. For Jeremiah there was no doubt. If we would understand him we need to take up a position alongside him and read his utterances with both empathy and sympathy.

II. JEREMIAH IN HIS HISTORICAL SETTING

The prophets were not merely religious teachers or philosophers in the abstract, but saw themselves as the messengers of God commissioned to convey to the people of their own day the word that God had given them. They had a specific message to a specific people at a specific point in history. It was a message which would interpret the events through which their people were passing, or would pass, in the light of the demands and promises which God had given to their people. Clearly, this dimension of a prophet's ministry cannot be understood unless the historical background of his times is known.

The book of Jeremiah makes contact with historical events at many points. In many cases precise dates and otherwise known events are referred to. It was Jeremiah's responsibility to proclaim a message about nations and kingdoms, "to pluck up and to break down, to destroy and to overthrow, to build and to plant" (1:10). It was an age of crises. As Jeremiah began to preach, the Assyrian empire was in decay. At the collapse of Assyria, Egypt, and then Babylon, the kingdom of the Medes stood waiting to pick the spoils of war. Judah herself was caught up in the drama. To begin she was nominally a vassal of Assyria, then for a brief period independent, then a vassal of Egypt, and finally a vassal of Babylon, under whom Judah lost even her identity as a nation when Nebuchadrezzar took her king into exile and destroyed her city and temple. Jeremiah lived through all this, and much of the drama of those years is reflected in his book. It was a time of agony for Jeremiah himself and for his people. Anyone who attempts to read the book without knowing something of the times will be more bewildered than ever. The arrangement of the book is complex and the variety of materials is considerable. If one lacks any sort of historical anchorage as well, the book is a bewildering one.

We have a good deal of biblical material to help fill in some of the historical background to Jeremiah. There are the narratives in 2 K. 21–25, supplemented by the account in 2 Chr. 33–36. Further material is available from the books of contemporary prophets Zephaniah, Nahum, Habakkuk, and Ezekiel. Then we have the Babylonian Chronicle for the years 617 B.C. on. Archeological discoveries of one kind and another, including some small but important written items, add to our knowledge. There are, alas, many gaps in our knowledge in spite of these sources, but such information as we have enables us to make some headway in understanding the period.

It will help our understanding of this complex period if we systematize our discussion under six sections: (i) Judah up to the accession of Josiah in 640 B.C.; (ii) the nations at the time of Assyrian power; (iii) Josiah's reign 640–609 B.C. and the final collapse of Assyria; (iv) from Josiah's death to the fall of Jerusalem in 597 B.C.; (v) the period 597–587 B.C.; (vi) post–587 B.C.

A. JUDAH UP TO THE ACCESSION OF JOSIAH IN 640 B.C.

If the date at which Jeremiah commenced his ministry[1] was the

1. The date of Jeremiah's birth and hence the date at which his ministry began is disputed, but most scholars accept 627 B.C. as the date when he commenced his ministry. A few, however, accept the thirteenth year of Josiah both as the year of his birth and also as the year of his call, since he was called from the womb. See W. L. Holladay, *Jeremiah: Spokesman Out of Time* (1974), pp. 18–23; "The Background of Jeremiah's Self-Understanding," *JBL* 83 (1964), pp. 153–164, esp. p. 161; J. P. Hyatt, "Jeremiah," *IB* V, p. 779.

thirteenth year of Josiah (1:6), i.e., 627 B.C. when he was a mere lad of 16 to 18 years of age, his birth may be set toward the end of the reign of the notorious Manasseh (687–642 B.C.). He would have known nothing at first hand about Manasseh, of whom the writer of 2 Kings said that "he did what was evil in the sight of the Lord, according to the abominable practices of the nations whom the Lord drove out before the people of Israel" (2 K. 21:2). In many ways Manasseh, the grandfather of Josiah, was the catalyst to many of the evils in Judah to which Jeremiah drew attention in his preaching. In his day Judah was a vassal state of Assyria, and had been since 732 B.C. A brief review of the history of Judah from the death of Solomon in about 922 B.C. to the accession of Josiah in 740 B.C. will help to explain how it was that Manasseh behaved as he did and why it was that Josiah was seen in such sharp contrast.

After the death of Solomon his kingdom fell apart into two rival states, Israel and Judah, with two capitals, Samaria and Jerusalem, two administrations, two armies, and two kinds of religious practice. Of the two, Israel was the larger and the wealthier state. The two states were kingdoms so that there were two kings in this tiny area. For almost two hundred years they coexisted, sometimes at war and sometimes living on peaceful terms. They lived independently and fought their own wars with their neighbors. Sometimes they had to pay dearly because of enemy invasion but maintained their independence till the middle of the eighth century. Both experienced an Egyptian invasion. Israel suffered from the Arameans a good deal. Judah was troubled by Edomites, Israel by Moab. But it was a world in which no great empire forced its control on Western Asia. Only Assyria gave signs of rising to become a great power, and during the ninth century probed into areas to her west to be resisted by coalitions of small states. King Ahab of Israel was involved in the battle of Qarqar with eleven other kings in 853 B.C., against Shalmaneser III (859–825 B.C.).[2] During the first half of the eighth century B.C., a period of Assyrian withdrawal to defend her own frontiers to the north and a time when Aramean states to Israel's northeast were at war with one another, both Israel and Judah prospered greatly. The prophet Amos was active toward the end of this period.

But all changed with the rise of the Assyrian Tiglath-pileser

2. See *ANET*, pp. 278f.

III (745–727 B.C.) just over a century before Jeremiah lived. It was a vital century which saw the introduction into Israel and Judah of a great many political and religious problems. When Tiglath-pileser turned westward the small nations tended to group as of old into coalitions. One such coalition was formed by Rezin of the Aramean state of Damascus and Pekah ben Remaliah (737–632 B.C.), who had usurped the throne of Israel from the previous king. These two sought to draw Ahaz king of Judah (735–715 B.C.) into the coalition. Ahaz refused and his land was invaded. His throne was threatened, for Pekah and Rezin planned to replace him with a certain Tabeel. In his helplessness he appealed for help to Tiglath-pileser against the advice of Isaiah (Isa. 7:1–8:18). Ahaz persisted in his plan and sent a large gift to the Assyrian king (2 K. 16:7–8), who acted promptly. He fell upon the coalition, marched into Israel, overran Israelite lands in Galilee and Transjordan and turned them into three Assyrian provinces, and finally destroyed Damascus in 732 B.C. But Judah thereby became a vassal of Assyria and remained so till Assyria herself collapsed.

As a result of Ahaz' policy Judah was compelled to undertake the obligations of a normal vassal, which involved the paying of tribute and the recognition of Assyria's gods in the temple in Jerusalem. Ahaz was obliged to appear before Tiglath-pileser in Damascus and to pay homage to the Assyrian gods at a bronze altar that stood there. A copy of this altar was then made and set up in the Jerusalem temple (2 K. 16:10–15). It was a humiliating position and not likely to win the approval of the people of Judah. But Judah was spared military occupation and even loss of their territory as had happened to Israel and Damascus. Perhaps this submission helped Judah escape the fate of Samaria in 722/1 B.C. when, because of renewed rebellion, Tiglath-pileser's successor Shalmaneser V (727–722 B.C.) invaded Israel.

Ahaz' son Hezekiah (715–687 B.C.) probably reflected the discontent of many in the nation and he took steps to reverse his father's policy, undertaking sweeping religious reforms and making a sufficient display of his desire to regain the independence of Judah to draw the attention of the Assyrian ruler Sennacherib (705–681 B.C.) in 701. Hezekiah was encouraged by unrest all over the empire and seems to have joined a coalition of states in open rebellion. In a strong campaign, his third to the west, Sennacherib ousted the opposition, besieged Jerusalem, forced Hezekiah's surrender, and laid a heavy tribute on Judah (2 K. 18:9–19:37). Hezekiah's efforts to break free from Assyria failed. After his death, his son Manasseh (687–642 B.C.) once again led Judah to the position of a loyal vassal state of Assyria. He probably had no choice. During the period of his reign Assyria attained her height. Sennacherib's successors Esarhaddon (681–669 B.C.) and Ashurbanipal (669–627 B.C.) were able to invade Egypt and even to sack the ancient capital Thebes in 663 B.C.

Manasseh in Judah returned to the pro-Assyrian policy of his grandfather Ahaz. This involved not merely political subservience but also some recognition of the gods of Assyria. But he went much further than this and seems to have opened the door to all kinds of religious practices of an irregular kind. He cancelled the reform measures of Hezekiah, allowed the restoration of local shrines, gave full rein to pagan practices of all kinds, tolerated the fertility cult with its sacred prostitution in the very temple precincts (2 K. 21:4–7; Zeph. 1:4–5). Even the cult of Molech which practiced human sacrifice was allowed (2 K. 21:6). Old Canaanite practices, the worship of Baal, the erection of an Asherah, the worship of astral deities, and a host of other practices which were an offense to all true Yahwists were unleashed in Judah once again. All this led to a blurring of the distinction between Yahwism and paganism, and to a wholesale disregard of covenant law. Indeed, the tolerance of all these pagan practices was tantamount to a rejection of the sole sovereignty of Yahweh, Israel's covenant God. Once the law of the covenant was rejected violence and injustice abounded (2 K. 21:16). The later editors of the books of Kings saw in the enormity of Manasseh's misdeeds an adequate explanation for the judgment that befell the nation (2 K. 21:9–15; 24:3–4).

It was conditions like these which prevailed when Jeremiah was called to preach. Manasseh's long reign ended in 642 B.C. His son Amon evidently followed his father's policy but reigned only briefly (642–640 B.C.) before being assassinated, probably by high officials who may have been trying to organize an anti-Assyrian revolt. The assassins were executed and the eight-year-old Josiah, grandson of the notorious Manasseh, was placed on the throne. In his day Judah's independence became a fact. The accession of Josiah heralded a new age in all kinds of ways. It was, in particular, the period when Jeremiah commenced his ministry.

B. THE NATIONS IN THE DAYS OF ASSYRIAN POWER

Assyria's power began to wane after the death of Ashurbanipal in 627 B.C., the year in which Jeremiah began his career as a prophet.[3] But it is important to understand something of the story of other nations during the seventh century B.C., since this may throw light on some of the references to these nations in the book of Jeremiah, particularly in the section comprising oracles addressed to the nations—Egypt, Philistia, Moab, Ammon, Edom, Damascus, Arab tribes, Elam, and Babylon (chs. 46–51).

At her greatest extent Assyria held sway from Egypt to Lake Van and Lake Urmia and from the Mediterranean Sea to regions to the east of the Tigris River. Such a vast area was beyond her control permanently, and it is little wonder that at about the time of Jeremiah's birth there were signs of collapse. Peoples on her northern and eastern frontiers had become a major threat.

To the northwest lay the Gimirrai people of whom we hear nothing in Jeremiah. The Urartu people in the region of Lake Van were a continuing problem. Late in the ninth century, Shamshi-adad I (824–812 B.C.) had to withdraw from activities to the west to contain the Urartu people. It was continuing pressure from the Urartu that kept Assyria away from the Aramean and Phoenician and Israelite areas early in the eighth century. The Urartu were expanding to the east and to the west and trying to extend southward into northern Syria. It was Tiglath-pileser (745–727 B.C.) who crushingly defeated the Urartian king Sardur II and besieged his capital. The Urartu people ceased to be a rival to Assyria when Sargon II (721–705 B.C.) broke their power completely. In doing so he removed a useful buffer between Assyria and the Indo-Aryan barbarians, the Cimmerians, who were moving down from the Caucasus. There is a reference to Urartu under the name Ararat in 51:27.[4]

A second group that became a serious problem was the Medes (51:11, 28), one of the more significant of the Indo-Aryan peoples. The annals of Shalmaneser III (859–825 B.C.) and Shamshi-adad V

3. That is, following the normal understanding of chronology. The views of W. L. Holladay and J. P. Hyatt that Jeremiah's ministry did not commence till the reign of Jehoiakim when there was a reversion to conditions like those that obtained in the days of Manasseh have not won general acceptance. But see below, pp. 50–56.

4. See *Cambridge Ancient History* III, *The Assyrian Empire* (1929), pp. 26, 34, 51, etc. See index; D. J. Wiseman, *Chronicles of Chaldaean Kings* (1956), pp. 13ff., 36, 39, 44f., 57.

(824–812 B.C.) give the first references to the Medes, who settled in the area of northwestern Iran. Tiglath-pileser III (745–727 B.C.) campaigned against the Medes in northern Iran as far as Mount Demavend, south of the Caspian Sea. Sargon II (721–705 B.C.) had troubles with Medean chiefs southeast of Lake Urmia. According to 2 K. 17:24 he deported some of the people of Samaria to Media. Tiglath-pileser (745–727 B.C.) had further campaigns in northwestern Iran and established Assyrian control there. The Medes were to play a prominent role in the destruction of Assyria before another century had passed. The last important king of Assyria, Ashurbanipal (668–627 B.C.), actually allied with the Scythians against the Medes and the Cimmerians.

The Cimmerians and Scythians were two other barbarian groups. The Cimmerians were an Indo-Aryan group who moved down from the Caucasus in the late eighth century B.C. and settled in large parts of eastern Anatolia. They ravaged Urartu in the reign of Sargon II (721–705 B.C.), then pressed on into Asia Minor and destroyed the kingdom of Midas in Phrygia. Other Cimmerians settled in northwestern Iran. Both Esarhaddon and Ashurbanipal had campaigns against them, but they remained as a threat on the borders of Assyria.

The Scythians are of particular interest since earlier commentators on Jeremiah identified the "foe from the north" in the early chapters of the book with this group. Esarhaddon (680–669 B.C.) allied with Scythians to contain the Cimmerians and Medes. The Greek historian Herodotus[5] tells of a Scythian invasion of Western Asia, probably about 625 B.C., at the time when Assyria was starting to collapse. But the significance of Herodotus' remark is not at all clear, and even if there was a Scythian irruption into Palestine the description of the "foe from the north" in the early chapters of Jeremiah is far too orderly for a marauding horde of barbarians.[6] The Scythians helped the Assyrians beat off a Medean attack in about 625 B.C. The Ashkenaz (= Ashguzai) of 51:27 may have been the Scythians.[7]

The Elamites (49:34–39) constituted a problem to the east of Babylonia. Already in the third millennium B.C. they were a power

5. *Hist.* i.103–106.
6. See H. Cazelles, "Sophonie, Jérémie, et les Scythes en Palestine," *RB* 74 (1967), pp. 24–44; A. Malamat, "The Historical Setting of Two Biblical Prophecies on the Nations," *IEJ* 1 (1950/51), pp. 154–59.
7. So J. Bright, *Jeremiah* (1965), p. 357 on v. 27.

to be reckoned with. They enter the horizon of this review in the days of Sargon II (721–705 B.C.) about a century before the fall of Nineveh. The Chaldean prince Marduk-apal-iddina, the Merodach-baladan of the Bible (2 K. 20:12; Isa. 39:1), had the help of Elam in his revolt against Assyria. It was some years before the Assyrians could drive him out of Babylonia. In about 694/3 B.C. there was another revolt, again with the assistance of Elam, and when Sennacherib moved to quell it in 691 B.C. he was met with a coalition of Babylonians, Elamites, and others, who defeated him in battle. The incident may have encouraged others in the empire to revolt, e.g., Hezekiah (2 K. 18:9). At the same time Egypt was in revolt to the west. Later, Ashurbanipal (668–627 B.C.), after quelling yet another revolt in Babylonia, turned on Elam, took Susa the capital, and brought the Elamite state to an end about 640 B.C., deporting and resettling some of the citizens in Samaria (Ezra 4:9ff.).[8]

Further west the Arab tribes were likely to pose a problem at any time (49:28–33). Assyrian records show that Sargon, Sennacherib, and Esarhaddon all had contact with Arab tribes and took away their gods and booty.[9] When Ashurbanipal's brother, who ruled in Babylon, rebelled in 642 B.C., Arab tribes of the Syrian desert seized the opportunity to overrun Assyrian vassal states in eastern Palestine from Edom and Moab northward, spreading havoc everywhere. It was a disaster from which Moab seems never to have fully recovered. Some of the poems of ch. 48 may have been produced at the time and were re-used later.

Moab, Edom, and Ammon were within the orbit of Assyrian control and are referred to in Assyrian texts[10] from the time of Adad-nirari III (801–783 B.C.) to Ashurbanipal (668–627 B.C.). They, too, were likely to be drawn into anti-Assyrian coalitions, and later, anti-Babylonian coalitions (ch. 27).

One of the most troublesome of the nations that lay on the frontiers of Assyria's empire was Egypt. Over the centuries Egypt regarded Western Asia as an area in which she might exercise some control, and she encouraged many revolts in this area. An Egyptian army was lurking on the borders of Palestine not long after the fall of Samaria, and in 720 B.C. Sargon crushed an Egyptian force which had come to assist the Philistine city of Gaza. By 716 B.C. an Ethi-

8. Both Esarhaddon and Ashurbanipal (Osnappar) settled deportees in Samaria according to Ezra 4:2, 9ff.
9. *ANET*, pp. 286, 291, 292.
10. *ANET*, pp. 281f., 287, 291, 294, 298, 301.

opian founded the Twenty-fifth Dynasty in Egypt, and by 710/9 B.C. all Egypt was united under his control. This gave Assyrian vassals of the west some hope of Egyptian help in case of an uprising. Ashdod rebelled in 714 B.C. but was soon crushed. Egypt provided no help. When Hezekiah of Judah was under attack from Sennacherib in 701 B.C. Tirhakah of Egypt marched to help him (2 K. 19:9). The result of the encounter of Assyria with Egypt is not known, but Jerusalem was preserved and Sennacherib returned home where he was later murdered (2 K. 19:37).[11] A younger son, Esarhaddon (680–669 B.C.), returned to deal with Egypt, which was still encouraging rebellion in Western Asia. Eventually in 671 B.C. his troops routed Tirhakah and occupied Memphis. Local Egyptian princes accepted Assyrian overlordship. Tirhakah stirred up more trouble and Ashurbanipal (668–627 B.C.) crushed the rebellion in 667 B.C., took Egyptian princes to Nineveh as captives, but spared Necho of Sais and his son Psammetichus. When trouble broke out again the Assyrians marched south as far as Thebes, the ancient capital, and destroyed it in 663 B.C. (cf. Nah. 3:8). This display of Assyrian might made Manasseh king of Judah (687/6–642 B.C.) less inclined to rebel. He lived through those years. But the days were drawing in for Assyria. In Egypt, when Psammetichus I (664–610 B.C.), whom Assyria spared as a boy, became a local ruler, he extended his control gradually and about 655 B.C. withheld tribute; and Ashurbanipal was in no position to deal with him because of troubles nearer home. The son of Psammetichus, Necho II (610–594 B.C.), was to prove a friend to Assyria in her dying agonies.

Finally we should take a brief glimpse at events in Babylonia, which had been under Assyrian domination. It was Tiglath-pileser III (745–727 B.C.) who brought Babylonia under Assyrian control. In 729 B.C. he took the throne of Babylonia himself and ruled under the name Pulu (2 K. 15:19). Sargon II (721–705 B.C.) had scarcely ascended the throne of Assyria when the Chaldean prince Marduk-apal-iddina (Merodach-baladan, 2 K. 20:12; Isa. 39:1), assisted by Elam, seized Babylonia and defeated Sargon's army so that Assyria lost control for a dozen years before Sargon regained control. Then under Sennacherib (704–681 B.C.) Marduk-apal-iddina again seized Babylon with the help of Elam until he was thrown out in 702 B.C. In such uncertain years revolt was in the air. Hezekiah of Judah also rebelled. In the days of Manasseh of Judah, Esarhaddon the Assyr-

11. See *ANET*, p. 289 for the Assyrian texts.

ian ruler (680–669 B.C.) stabilized the situation in Babylon and restored the city and the temple of Marduk destroyed by his father. But unrest continued in Babylonia. In the days when Shamash-shum-ukin ruled as deputy for his brother Ashurbanipal, he rebelled with the support of the Chaldean population of the area, the Elamites, and others. The revolt was quelled by Ashurbanipal in 648 B.C. after a two-year struggle. On the surface it seems that Ashurbanipal's campaigns during these years reduced Babylon, Elam, and the Arab tribes, and Assyria was able to enjoy a measure of peace for a few years. But when he died in 627 B.C. Assyria failed rapidly. These were critical years in Judah. Manasseh (687/6–642 B.C.) had proved a loyal vassal of three Assyrian kings. His son Amon (642–640 B.C.) followed in his steps. Josiah (640–609 B.C.) was cast in a different mold. He was only eight years old when he became king. When Ashurbanipal died in 627 B.C., Josiah was twenty-one and ready to lead Judah to independence from Assyria, whose far-flung empire was collapsing everywhere.

C. JOSIAH'S REIGN, 640–609 B.C., AND THE FINAL COLLAPSE OF ASSYRIA

Josiah quickly became emboldened to express his independence of Assyria. Ashurbanipal's son Sin-shar-ishkun was co-regent with his father 629–627 B.C. When his father died there was general rebellion and civil war in Assyria, which seems to have lasted about four years (627–624 B.C.). This weakened Assyria still further. The Medes made an assault on Nineveh which was repelled with the help of the Scythians. The Median king Phraortes was slain. Within a few years his son Cyaxares (*c.* 625–585 B.C.) defeated the Assyrian army near Babylon and seized the throne. Hence by about 625 B.C. it was clear that Assyria could no longer survive.

In Judah we may assume that a Council of State cared for the affairs of state while Josiah was a child. In the eighth year of his reign he "began to seek the God of David his father" (2 Chr. 34:3a), that is, when he was sixteen. This may be an indication of his intention to change the direction of national policy in Judah as soon as he was able. In the twelfth year of his reign (629/8 B.C.) he began to act by commencing some sweeping reforms (2 Chr. 34:3b–7). This would coincide in time with the accession of Sin-shar-ishkun to the throne of Assyria. Josiah moved into areas which had been Assyrian provinces for a century or more, namely, Samaria and Gilead, and even reached the Mediterranean Sea.[12] But there was no Assyrian resistance.

The account of Josiah's reform is given in 2 K. 22–23 and 2 Chr. 34–35. The accounts differ somewhat and the exact chronology of events escapes us, although the reform no doubt took some time. The reform was already well in progress before the law book was found in the temple in 622 B.C. This discovery did not spark off the reform but certainly gave impetus to the program.

In its initial stages the reform was concerned with the purging of foreign cults of all kinds both in the Jerusalem temple and further afield. The repairs to the temple (2 K. 22:3–7) no doubt involved the removal of evidences of Assyrian religion, notably the bronze altar (2 K. 17:12–16). But all the paraphernalia of the foreign cults and practices, the solar and astral cults largely of Mesopotamian origin (2 K. 23:4–5, 11–12), the native pagan cults, some introduced by Manasseh (2 K. 23:6, 10) and some more ancient (vv. 13–14), were removed. The personnel associated with these cults were put to death. Divination and magic were banned. The cult places in Northern Israel were likewise destroyed (2 K. 23:15–20) as far north as Galilee (2 Chr. 34:6). In Judah itself Yahweh shrines throughout the land were closed and all public worship was centralized in Jerusalem. Country priests were invited to come to Jerusalem and take their place among the priests there (2 K. 23:8).

It was in the course of these sweeping reforms that the "book of the law" was found in the temple in Jerusalem. There is good reason to think that this book was some form of the book of Deuteronomy[13] or of the Covenant Law, since a number of Josiah's actions are consistent with the requirements of Deuteronomy: centralization of the cult, the concentration of the priests at the central sanctuary (e.g., Deut. 12:13–14, 17–18; 18:6–8), the rejection of idolatry (Deut. 13) and the operation of the death penalty for idolaters, Josiah's concern about curses that may fall on the nation (2 K. 22:11–13). We ought not to accept the view that the teaching of Deuteronomy was something new. Even if it reached its final form in the period preceding the reform, its teaching and much of its content were ancient. It would be impossible to say how this homiletical presentation of covenant law came into being since it was the

12. See J. Bright, *A History of Israel* (^{2}1960), p. 316, n. 21.
13. See H. H. Rowley, "The Prophet Jeremiah and the Book of Deuteronomy" (1950; repr. in *From Moses to Qumran* [London, 1963], pp. 187–208).

result of a long period of transmission. Some have argued[14] that it stemmed originally from Northern Israel and had come to Jerusalem after the fall of Samaria, where, at some time between the reigns of Hezekiah and Josiah, it was completed. The truth of the matter cannot be known. But the heart of Deuteronomy was not a completely new law. It was known in Israel for centuries past with roots going back to Moses. It was the covenant law of Yahweh, who alone was Israel's sovereign Lord. Israel must worship him alone and no other. She must obey his law or face destruction.

The reform was comprehensive and far-reaching. But there were other factors than the religious one. The reform was a principal expression of a resurgent nationalism. Subservience to the Assyrians resulted in the syncretism of Ahaz and Manasseh. Nationalists like Hezekiah and Josiah sought to reverse Assyrian domination, and as part of that to remove religious symbols from the temple which reminded the people of their subservience to Assyria. Josiah's annexation of Northern Israel gave political expression to a renewed nationalism. Political unification and cultic unification went hand in hand. There may have been another factor too in the form of a general world anxiety and a sense of impending doom.[15] Perhaps the revival of prophetic preaching after a comparatively long gap had something to do with the unease of the times. The nations were passing through a period of unrest. Some, at least, in Judah were well aware of the religious apostasy and syncretism of the times. We sense that there were those in the nation who kept alive the pure faith of Yahweh. In that setting the canonical prophets Jeremiah, Zephaniah, Nahum, and Habakkuk arose. Our present concern is with Jeremiah, but his contemporary Zephaniah also attacked Judah for the religious and moral decay which Manasseh had allowed to flourish. It was a rebellion against Yahweh which could only result in a display of his wrath (e.g., Zeph. 1:4–6, 8–9, 12; 3:1–4, 11). Judgment was at hand (1:2–3, 7, 14–18) and repentance was called for (2:1–3). The reforms of Josiah gave hope of a change, and both Zephaniah and Jeremiah were in favor of the reform program, even though Jeremiah discovered later that it was all too temporary and superficial.

14. See G. von Rad, *Studies in Deuteronomy* (SCM, 1953), pp. 68f.; G. E. Wright, "The Book of Deuteronomy," *IB* II, pp. 325f.; A. C. Welch, *The Code of Deuteronomy* (1924), *passim*.

15. On this point see W. F. Albright, *From the Stone Age to Christianity* (^{2}1957), pp. 316–19.

Josiah's reforms went on while Assyria slowly collapsed. Unfortunately we have little information about the latter years of Josiah's reign between the finding of the "book of the law" in 622 and his death in 609 B.C. The prophets Zephaniah, Nahum, and Habakkuk give a glimpse of prophetic activity and most commentators allow that at least some of Jeremiah's preaching came from Josiah's day.[16] But externally things moved rapidly. Nabopolassar the Chaldean, who drove the Assyrians from Babylon in 626 B.C.,[17] was ready to attack the heart of the Assyrian homelands by 616 B.C., and he advanced far up to the Euphrates and defeated the Assyrians in that year. At that stage the Egyptian ruler Psammetichus I (664–610 B.C.), who had once been spared by the Assyrians, and probably fearing that the rising Babylonians and Medes would be a greater danger than a weak Assyria, determined to help Assyria. By 616 B.C. there was an Egyptian army in Assyria in time to check Nabopolassar's further advance.

By then the Medes began to press in on the east and in 614 B.C. Cyaxares took Ashur, the ancient Assyrian capital. Nabopolassar's army arrived too late to help but the two rulers made a formal treaty. Two years later in 612 B.C. the two allies attacked Nineveh and took it after a three-month siege. The new Assyrian ruler Ashur-uballit II fled west to Haran after Sin-shar-ishkun had perished in the flames of the burning city. In 609 B.C. the Babylonians, assisted by the Umman Manda peoples (possibly the Scythians and other Indo-Aryan groups) took Haran despite the Egyptian presence. Ashur-uballit retired beyond the Euphrates to the Egyptians. An attempt to retake Haran in 609 B.C. failed. Assyria's days were over.[18]

We know virtually nothing concerning Judah during these dramatic years. What steps Josiah took to maintain the momentum of the reform we do not know. Presumably he preserved all his gains while he lived. But it was, of course, an imposed reform, and we may well wonder whether the great bulk of the people underwent any change in heart at all. To judge from Jeremiah's later preaching many of them did not, and once Josiah passed from the scene they reverted to their old ways under Jehoiakim. One cannot change peo-

16. See the discussion on pp. 54–56. Unfortunately the Babylonian Chronicle on which we are dependent for details of the period is lacking for 622–617 B.C.

17. See Babylonian Chronicle in D. J. Wiseman, *Chronicles of Chaldaean Kings*, pp. 5–9, 43, 53.

18. For these years see D. J. Wiseman, *Chronicles of Chaldaean Kings*, pp. 18ff., 61ff.

ple's hearts by government regulation. No doubt there were many good results in areas of national morality and justice. The abolition of pagan cults would have been a moral and spiritual benefit. But there were, no doubt, problems too. The closing of the country shrines created problems for the country priests, and many village people were deprived of at least some form of public worship. The temple in Jerusalem gained in prestige, but participation in the official services in the temple led to complacency and under the cover of religious observances many people indulged in blatant violations of covenant law (7:1–15, cf. vv. 21–31). A man like Jeremiah saw through the whole sham of external conformity without inward change, and as the years went by he became disillusioned. Alongside increased cultic activity (6:16–21) was ingrained rebellion (7:1–5; 8:4–9). There was also a smug complacency arising out of Yahweh's having given the people a new independence and having preserved the temple, the king, and the state. Somehow they believed that the whole scandalous eclipse of religion and state hardly mattered since Yahweh guaranteed the inviolability of both temple and state. The death of Josiah came as a rude shock, but not of such a kind as to lead the nation to repentance.

D. FROM JOSIAH'S DEATH TO THE FALL OF JERUSALEM IN 597 B.C.

For reasons that are not clear, Josiah opposed the passage of Pharaoh Necho II through Palestine on his way to bring help to the Assyrians (2 K. 23:29–30; 2 Chr. 35:20–24). At Megiddo, now part of the territory of a reunited Israel, Josiah was killed in battle. Perhaps he feared an Assyrian-Egyptian victory which would have placed him at the mercy of Egypt. Necho marched on Carchemish on the Euphrates to help Ashur-uballit in his attempt to recapture Haran from the Babylonians. What Josiah feared took place. Judah fell under Egyptian control. As for Assyria, she could not be saved. Her great empire was carved up as the Medes extended their control through areas to the north and east of Assyria in Iran, Armenia, and Asia Minor, Babylon took the whole of the Mesopotamian plain, and Egypt held areas to the west of the Euphrates including Palestine.

On Josiah's death his son Jehoahaz became king (2 K. 23:31). After three months he was summoned to Riblah by Necho, and sent in bonds to Egypt (22:10–12; 2 K. 23:31–35). His brother Eliakim, assuming the throne name Jehoiakim, was set in his place as an

Egyptian vassal. Judah was laid under heavy tribute (2 K. 23:34–35). Judah's short independence of twenty years was ended.

Pharaoh Necho was able to hold his position in Western Asia for a few years until the Babylonians were ready to challenge him. During 608/7 and 607/6 B.C. Nabopolassar campaigned in the Armenian mountains, no doubt to secure this northern flank. Egyptians and Babylonians made raids across the Euphrates on one another, the Egyptians seeking a bridgehead north of Carchemish from which to attack the Egyptians and the Egyptians counterattacking to prevent this.

Meantime Jehoiakim remained a loyal vassal of Egypt. He was a poor replacement for Josiah. He was personally extravagant and built a fine palace with forced labor (22:13–19).[19] He allowed Josiah's reform to lapse and played into the hands of those who had always opposed it. There may not have been the excesses of Manasseh's reign but popular pagan practices were introduced again (7:16–18; 11:9–13; Ezek. 8). Public morality deteriorated (5:26–29; 7:1–15). Prophets who resisted these tendencies were harassed and even put to death (26:20–23). Despite this, priests and prophets continued to assure the people that all was well (5:12; 7:4; 14:13; etc.). Jeremiah's exposure of the evil of all this led him into deep personal persecution, even in his own village Anathoth (11:18–23).

In 605 B.C. Judah was again at the crossroads. In that year Nebuchadrezzar fell upon the Egyptian garrison at Carchemish and routed it (46:2ff.). The Egyptians fled, pursued by the Babylonians. They were defeated again at Hamath[20] and the way lay open to Syria and Palestine. Nebuchadrezzar could not take advantage of the opportunity at once since his father's death in August 605 B.C. required his return to Babylon to assume the throne. By the end of 604 B.C. the Babylonians were in the Philistine plain where they took and destroyed Ashkelon (47:5–7) and deported leading members of the city's population. Consternation overtook Judah, and the fast of December 604 B.C. (36:9) may have been one result. But some of the prophetic utterances of the day also throw light on Judah's concern (5:15–17; 6:22–26; Hab. 1:5–11; etc). Jehoiakim transferred his allegiance to Nebuchadrezzar and became his vassal (2 K. 24:1). Once again Judah was subject to a Mesopotamian power. It seems clear

19. Possibly at Ramat Raḥel south of Jerusalem. See Y. Aharoni, "Excavations at Ramat Raḥel," *BA* 24 (1961), p. 118.
20. D. J. Wiseman, *Chronicles of Chaldaean Kings*, pp. 23, 28, 46f., 67ff.

that Jehoiakim's loyalty was not with Nebuchadrezzar, however. He hoped for rescue from Egypt but lay quiet meanwhile. Later in 601 B.C. Nebuchadrezzar moved against Egypt but suffered badly in a battle against Necho near the Egyptian border and did not campaign the next year, 600/599 B.C., at least in that area. Jehoiakim rebelled (2 K. 24:1) and Nebuchadrezzar sent a punitive force of some Babylonians along with guerrilla bands (35:11; 2 K. 24:2). But in December 598 B.C. the Babylonian army set out again. That very month Jehoiakim died; since he was a rebel against Babylon he may have been assassinated (22:18–19; 36:30) in the hope that Judah might be treated lightly. Perhaps she was, for the capital city was not destroyed. The new king, the eighteen-year-old Jehoiachin (2 K. 24:8), was taken captive after a mere three months on the throne, along with the queen mother, state officials and leading citizens, and a vast booty (2 K. 24:10–17). The king's uncle Mattaniah (Zedekiah) was installed as ruler (2 K. 24:17–18). The exact date of the fall of Jerusalem is attested in the Babylonian Chronicle. It was the second day of Adar, 15/16th March 597 B.C.[21] Had Judah learned her lesson then, she might have been spared the disaster of 587 B.C.

E. THE PERIOD 597–587 B.C.

Zedekiah's reign (597–587 B.C.) proved that Judah had not learned her lesson, and within ten years she was destroyed. Babylon was too powerful to permit any light assessment of Judah's obligations to her. The deportation of 597 B.C., though not large, was significant, for it removed many of Judah's key personnel.[22] Those who now led the government were ultranationalists lacking in both experience and caution. Zedekiah was young (2 K. 24:18) and may have wished for better things; more than once he consulted Jeremiah (37:17–21; 38:7–28; cf. 21:1–7; 37:3). But he was too weak to control the officials and too fearful of public opinion (38:5, 19, 24). Moreover, it seems clear that many in Judah still regarded Jehoiachin as king[23] and hoped for his speedy return (ch. 27). Prophets forecast that the exile would be over in two years (28:2–4). Jeremiah spoke of seventy years.

21. *Ibid.*, pp. 32–35, 73.
22. The figures in 2 K. 24:14, 16 are 10,000 and 8,000, while Jer. 52:58 gives 3023. We are not certain of how the count was made. The first two are round figures. The third may represent males only, or the number of those who survived.
23. See W. F. Albright, "King Joiachin in Exile," *BA* 5 (1942), pp. 49–55.

Plots were the order of the day. In 595/4 B.C. there had been an uprising in Babylon[24] in which some of the exiles may have been implicated (29:20–23). Then in 594/3 B.C., in Zedekiah's fourth year, plans for revolt were discussed among the small states in the west, Edom, Moab, Ammon, Tyre, Sidon, and Judah (27:3). Prophets in both places were encouraging revolt (29:20–23; 28:2–4). The plans for rebellion in the west were abandoned, and it seems possible that Zedekiah sent envoys to Babylon (29:3) or even went himself (51:59) to assure Nebuchadrezzar of his loyalty. But this was not the end of plans for rebellion. By 589 B.C. Judah was again speaking of revolt. They may have been encouraged by some alliance with Pharaoh Hophra (Apries, 589–570 B.C.), who was again interfering in Asia. It may be that Tyre and Ammon were involved, for Nebuchadrezzar attacked Tyre after the fall of Jerusalem and Ammon's involvement may be inferred from Ezek. 21:18–32 and Jer. 40:13–41:15. Edom was not involved since she was an ally of Babylon (Obad. 10–14). Finally Zedekiah rebelled (2 K. 25:1).

The response of Babylon was prompt. By autumn of 589 B.C. their army was in Palestine and by January 588 B.C. Jerusalem was under siege. The Babylonians did not attack the city at once but slowly eliminated the fortified cities throughout Judah. We have two glimpses into the progress of the action in the country areas. From 34:6–7 we learn that only Lachish (Tell ed-Duweir) and Azekah (Tell ez-Zakariyah) remained. And from ostraca found in excavations at Lachish,[25] ostracon IV seems to indicate that only Lachish remained when this letter was written. Ostracon VI, incidentally, refers to the fact that officials in Jerusalem had "weakened the hands (i.e., the morale) of the people"; cf. 38:4.

Hope of relief came in the summer of 588 B.C. when an Egyptian army entered the land. Another Lachish letter (III) tells of the visit of the commander of the Judean army to Egypt about that time. At Jerusalem the Babylonians raised the siege in order to meet the Egyptian threat (37:5). One senses in Jeremiah that hopes were high in the city (34:8–11; 37:3–10). Jeremiah warned the people against undue optimism since the city was doomed. In a very brief time, perhaps only a few weeks, the siege was resumed. Jerusalem hung out for approximately another year. Jeremiah urged surrender and Zedekiah was willing (38:14–23) but feared to do so. Finally in July

24. D. J. Wiseman, *Chronicles of Chaldaean Kings*, pp. 36f.
25. *ANET*, pp. 321f.

587 B.C. (52:5) the walls of the city were breached just as the supply of food ran out. Zedekiah and his family with some Judean troops managed to flee by night toward the Jericho plains (52:7ff.; 2 K. 25:3ff.), but they were captured near Jericho and taken to Nebuchadrezzar's headquarters at Riblah in central Syria. Zedekiah's sons were slain before his eyes, and he was blinded and taken in chains to Babylon where he died. A month later (52:12ff.; 2 K. 25:8ff.) Nebuzaradan the commander of the royal bodyguard, acting under Nebuchadrezzar's orders, burned the city and broke down its walls. At the same time he rounded up many priests, military personnel, and state officials as well as some of the citizens. Some were taken to Nebuchadrezzar at Riblah and executed, and others were deported to Babylon.[26]

Jerusalem and the walled cities of Judah were left in ruins. Modern archeological work demonstrates how complete the devastation was. Most of the towns were not rebuilt for a long time, and some never. Only in the Negeb and in the area north of Jerusalem were the towns spared.

F. POST–587 B.C.

After such terrible destruction the Babylonians organized Judah into their provincial system. It was, in any case, not likely to cause trouble for a long time to come since the population remaining consisted largely of poor peasants (52:16; 2 K. 25:12). Gedaliah ben Ahikam was appointed governor. His father had once saved Jeremiah's life (26:24), and his grandfather Shaphan was one of Josiah's high officials (2 K. 22:3) and gave strong support to Josiah's reform. Gedaliah himself had been one of Zedekiah's chief officials. Since Jerusalem was uninhabitable,[27] the seat of government was placed at Mizpah (probably Tell en-Nasbeh).

But even this plan failed, though Gedaliah tried hard to conciliate the population (40:7–12). After a time (we are not told how long in 41:1 or 2 K. 25:25) a certain Ishmael, a member of the royal house who must have escaped from the Babylonians, with backing from the king of Ammon assassinated Gedaliah, who, though warned, would not believe the warning. Ishmael and his fellow conspirators

26. 52:29 gives a figure of 832. This may refer only to those taken from Jerusalem itself, but we are not at all certain of how the count was made.
27. See K. M. Kenyon, *Jerusalem* (1967), pp. 78–104, 107f. for text and vivid photographs.

also slew the Babylonian garrison and innocent people who were present. The news of this dastardly act reached Johanan ben Kareah, who was absent from Mizpah at the time, and he pursued Ishmael with a band of armed men. Ishmael escaped to Ammon. Gedaliah's friends in Mizpah, fearing repercussions from Nebuchadrezzar, determined to flee to Egypt, taking with them an unwilling Jeremiah (ch. 42). Whether because of this senseless massacre or for some other reason there was a third deportation in 582 B.C. (52:30).

What happened to Judah thereafter we are not told. It may have been incorporated into Samaria but that is uncertain. Nothing more is heard of the land of Judah for over forty years, although we know a little about those who fled to Egypt (ch. 44), and a little more about the exiles in Babylon. The story does not resume till the Babylonian empire itself was destroyed by Cyrus the Persian and exiled Jews were repatriated to resume their life in their homeland.

III. THE BOOK OF JEREMIAH

A. STRUCTURE

The manner in which the book of Jeremiah was arranged by those who brought it together remains something of a puzzle. Part of the problem is that the book of Jeremiah, like other prophetic books, is not a book in the modern sense but rather a collection of prophetic oracles and other materials which have passed through a long and complex history of transmission. It would help the modern exegete and interpreter a great deal if he could discern the structure imposed on the great variety of available materials by those who brought them together.[1]

As a start it is possible to discover evidence of what seem to have been originally shorter "books" with some unifying feature about them. There are several of these collections.

1. Chapters 1–25: Divine Judgment upon Judah and Jerusalem

The first collection appears to conclude with the segment 25:1–13a, ending with the words "all that is written in this book." The Sep-

1. W. L. Holladay, *The Architecture of Jeremiah 1–20* (1976), has attempted this with some success for the first twenty chapters.

tuagint (LXX) concludes the section at this point and, omitting v. 14, inserts chs. 46–51 which comprise prophecies about the nations before resuming at v. 15. The original scope of this collection of material is set out in 25:1–3, which refers back to the beginning of Jeremiah's ministry in 627 B.C. There are several striking verbal similarities between 25:3–9 and ch. 1 (esp. vv. 15–19). There is thus some reason to think that ch. 1 was the beginning and 25:1–13a the conclusion to a collection of material covering the period between 627 and 605 B.C. (the fourth year of Jehoiakim). It may be that in its present form it contains some material which was preached after 605 B.C., but this later Jeremiah material could have been inserted into an originally separate collection of Jeremiah's oracles.

Inside the broad range of chs. 1–25 there is evidence of some shorter "books." Thus 14:1–15:4 commences with a formula "The word of Yahweh that came to Jeremiah concerning (*'al*) the drought."[2] Another collection which appears in 21:11–23:8 had the title "To the Royal House of Judah." Utterances about the royal house of Judah are drawn together, and Jehoahaz (Shallum), Jehoiakim, and Jehoiachin (Coniah) are passed in review following a basic statement of the obligations of the royal house. But again, the collection is complex and comprises material in both prose and poetry. A further collection with a title occurs in 23:9–40, addressed "To the Prophets."

There are yet other segments inside the broad collection in chs. 1–25. Thus within chs. 11–20 are to be found Jeremiah's "Confessions," which give a very personal insight into the inner turmoil and struggle of the prophet in the face of all the problems and dangers his ministry brought to him. Each of these was originally an independent segment. They comprise 11:18–23; 12:1–6; 15:10–21; 17:14–18; 18:18–23; 20:7–13, 14–18.[3] At present these are embedded in other kinds of material.

It may be conjectured that chs. 2–6; 8:4–10:25; 12:7–17; 13:15–27; 15:5–9; 16:19–21; 17:1–11; and 18:13–17 may once have formed small groups of passages related in date, or origin, or content, or

2. MT reads lit. "concerning matters of droughts" although the context refers to only one drought. This whole unit 14:1–15:4 is itself composite and consists of both poetry and prose. The segment which relates to the drought would have included vv. 2–10, 19–22.

3. The list we give is basically that in O. Eissfeldt, *The OT: An Introduction* (^{3}1964, E.T. 1965), pp. 356ff. This list provides an excellent statement of the complexity of these chapters. But see below, "The 'Confessions' of Jeremiah," pp. 88–92.

form. The theme of the "foe from the north" occurs in 4:5–8, 11–13, 15–17; 5:10–17; 6:1–8; 8:16–17. Then 9:20–21 is a funeral dirge in Qinah measure.

It is clear that this first large collection in the book of Jeremiah is an extremely complex one which is concerned largely with the divine judgment upon Judah and Jerusalem. Much of it seems to consist of oracles that Jeremiah delivered prior to 605 B.C. (cf. 25:1–13), but it contains also materials from a later date.

2. Chapters 30–33: The Book of Consolation

This section deals with hopes of restoration for Jerusalem. Here too, sayings and other literary units dwell on a theme which was as integral to Jeremiah's preaching as his oracles on judgment. He looked beyond judgment to a new beginning for Israel. Chs. 30–31 are closely linked around the theme of restoration and are largely in verse. Chs. 32–33 are in prose and may well have been linked to the other chapters because of the significance of the historical incident in which Jeremiah bought a field even as the Chaldean armies were at the gates of Jerusalem. It was his symbolic way of expressing his belief in the future restoration of Israel.

3. Chapters 46–51: Oracles against the Nations

These chapters comprise a separate "book" within the larger book of Jeremiah, as we learn from 46:1. Blocks of prophecies against the nations are known in other prophetic books.[4] In LXX these chapters follow 25:13 (24:14 is omitted), and 25:13–38 is given as the conclusion to the whole. Further, they appear in a different order in LXX. Such differences between the Hebrew text and LXX suggest that these chapters had a different history of transmission in Hebrew and Greek.

The three "books" we have been discussing suggest themselves very readily as forming significant areas in the total book of Jeremiah: 1:1–25:13a, chs. 30–33, and 46–51. There remain two other blocks of material, chs. 26–29 and 34–45, which appear in the gaps between the other three blocks. They are for the most part related to biographical narratives referring to incidents in the life of Jeremiah. Their present arrangement is not in any way chronological. In an attempt to provide chronological order John Bright groups the

4. Isa. 13–23; Ezek. 25–32; Amos 1:3–2:3; all of Nahum and Obadiah; Zeph. 2:4-15.

incidents together, and for the sake of completeness includes here parts of chs. 19, 20, 21, and 24[5] under the heading "Incidents from the life of Jeremiah." In doing this he has destroyed the original arrangement and accommodated his commentary to the chronological demands of the modern reader. This contributes to our modern understanding of the sequence of events, but it may well obscure some important intention of the compilers which may be more significant for interpretation than mere chronology.

E. W. Nicholson[6] groups chs. 26–36 together as a collection of oracles and sayings presented for the most part within a narrative framework. The section as a whole is seen as a history of the word of God proclaimed by Jeremiah and rejected by the nation. Ch. 26 reintroduces the theme of the Temple Sermon and its rejection by the people and the state officials, while ch. 36, the closing chapter and the climax, shows the king not merely rejecting the word of Yahweh but burning Jeremiah's scroll, partly as an act of defiance but perhaps also in an attempt to nullify the prophetic word. This proposal of Nicholson is attractive and has much to commend it. If it represents the original editor's intention, then the so-called "Book of Consolation" becomes a collection gathered up into a larger unit in much the same way as smaller units were gathered into chs. 1–25.

Chapters 37–45 cover the period of Jeremiah's life and ministry from the siege and fall of Jerusalem in 587 B.C. down to the last recorded episode in his ministry in Egypt. In 37:1–40:6 Jeremiah is seen suffering severely at the hands of his fellow countrymen because of his preaching. In the end he was vindicated and his preaching was fulfilled. In 40:7–44:30 we are given the story of the community left in Judah by the Babylonians. Following the assassination of the governor Gedaliah they fled to Egypt. But it is clear that the true "remnant" of the nation through whom renewal would come was not those in Egypt but the exiles in Babylon.

The book ends with a historical appendix (ch. 52) based on 2 K. 24:18–25:30, although it includes information not found there or elsewhere.

When we come to inquire whether any principles of arrangement can be observed in the book of Jeremiah, we have to admit that any consistent principles escape us. Clearly there arose a num-

5. J. Bright, *Jeremiah* (1965), pp. viii, 167–266.
6. E. W. Nicholson, *Jeremiah 1–25* (1973); *Jeremiah 26–52* (1975), p. 14 in each case.

ber of small groupings of material which seem to have been of a topical kind, e.g., chs. 30–33 are concerned with a message of hope; 21:11–23:8, oracles against the kings of Judah; 23:9–40, oracles against the prophets. These were ultimately brought into larger collections which seem to have been broadly topical, but not entirely so. Thus chs. 1–25 seem to gather together oracles of warning and judgment, but there are segments here which are concerned with hope (e.g., 3:11–18; 16:14–15; 23:1–8). And even in the Book of Consolation, chs. 30–33, which is mostly concerned with hope, there are words of doom (32:28–35). Principles of arrangement are not much easier to follow even when a topical arrangement is clearly intended, e.g., in the oracles against the nations (chs. 46–51). The order in which they are presented in the Hebrew Bible, Egypt, Philistia, Moab, Ammon, Edom, Damascus, Arab tribes, Elam, Babylon, is roughly in geographical progression from south to north and west to east, but this is not exact. Nor could it be argued that they are presented in the order of their importance. LXX does not help in providing a solution, for the arrangement there seems to be in the order of political importance. But while this is so in some areas of the list, it cannot be applied completely. We have to confess that the plan employed by the editors finally escapes us.

Our uncertainty is increased by the fact that the book of Jeremiah is partly in prose and partly in poetry, these being present in approximately equal proportions. But there is no attempt to keep the prose and the verse separate since both appear side by side in many parts of the book. Nor does any help come from the fact that Jeremiah sometimes speaks for himself in the first person, sometimes in the name of Yahweh in the first person, and is sometimes spoken of in the third person. He refers to the people as "you" or "they" or "she." The three major blocks of material, poetic sayings, biographical prose, and prose discourses, do not furnish any clue to the arrangement of the book either.

It seems that in some areas keywords may have been used to link smaller oracles or sayings into larger segments. Thus ch. 2 refers to "youth" as an abstract noun (*n^{e}'ûrîm,* 2:2) which is related to the noun (*na'ar*) in 1:7. Hence ch. 1 could be linked with the first section of ch. 2. Then in 2:2 the phrase "bridal love" occurs, while in 2:32 the noun "bride" occurs. Further, ch. 3 begins and ends with "youth" (vv. 4 and 24, *n^{e}'ûrîm*), which draws ch. 3 into the same grouping.

In the same context are sections on the harlotry of the nation in chs. 2 and 3. There thus seems to be a linking together of poetic material on the basis of keywords with associated ideas.[7]

Another good example comes in the cycle of war poems, all of which have the theme of war and the foe from the north. The cycle is linked to ch. 3 by reason of the verb "turn" or "return" (*šûḇ*) in 3:22; 4:1, a term which occurs again at 8:4 (ch. 7 is in prose).

Some of the linking words and ideas may escape us, but there are enough of them to suggest that we may have here another clue to the arrangement of the materials in the book of Jeremiah.

The one thing that does become clear is that the book of Jeremiah as we have it today was the result of a long and complex process. It is a collection of collections which were brought together by more than one hand over a period of time. Some of the material was written, as for example Jeremiah's first and second scrolls (ch. 36).[8] Some of it was orally transmitted for a time. It seems probable that a written tradition and an oral tradition existed side by side and the two interacted, "the oral tradition sifting, shaping, grouping and supplementing material, the written tradition serving as a control on the vagaries of the oral."[9] The oral tradition, however, grew by the application of exegetical and homiletical principles which sought not merely to preserve the message of Jeremiah but also to show its continuing applicability as the years went by, during his lifetime and after his death.[10] All these factors have contributed to the making of the book of Jeremiah. The very complexity of the process accounts for the seeming disarray of the book to our modern logic-orientated thinking. Nevertheless we can go a long way in interpreting and understanding the smaller segments of the book, and the word of God which Jeremiah brought to the people of Judah in the late seventh and early sixth centuries can be read and understood against a background which is remarkably well attested.

7. The main thrust of W. L. Holladay's argument in *The Architecture of Jeremiah 1–20* is that it is possible to discern these linking words. On that basis 2:2–3 is seen as the seed oracle for two cycles which he calls "The Harlotry Cycle" (2:5-37; 3:1–5, 12b–14a, 19–25) and "The Foe Cycle" (4:1–6:30; 8:4–10a, 13). His thesis is of considerable significance.

8. For a discussion of the composition of these see below, "Jeremiah's First and Second Scrolls," pp. 56–59.

9. J. Bright, *Jeremiah,* p. lxiii.

10. This theme is taken up in more detail in the following section.

B. COMPOSITION

It is proper to ask in reference to any one of the prophetic books a number of questions. What kinds of material were drawn into the book? What were the sources of this material? Was the prophet himself responsible for the whole of the book, and if not, whence came the other material? Is the underlying purpose of the book as we have it historical, theological, homiletical, or what? Did the book come to its present shape as a result of purely literary activities or were there other creative processes at work? Discussion of such issues has ranged over a wide field during the past century and continues unabated. It will help us to arrive at the conclusions which this commentary will assume if we review the progress of debate since about A.D. 1900.

In ch. 36 reference is made to the dictation of a scroll of oracles by Jeremiah to his scribe and companion Baruch in the fourth year of Jehoiakim (605/4 B.C.) "concerning Israel and Judah and all the nations" (36:2) since the beginning of his prophetic ministry. That scroll was eventually read first in the temple courtyard, then to the royal and state officials, and finally to the king, who destroyed it by fire. The oracles were rewritten and "many similar words" were added. The narrative makes it clear that on Jeremiah's initiative there came into existence a written collection of oracles and sayings which he delivered during the early years of his ministry, that this original collection was supplemented later, and that Baruch the scribe was associated with Jeremiah in the project. On the basis of this narrative several generations of scholars have argued that the poetic oracles in the first part of the book represent Jeremiah's original sayings, while the historical and biographical narratives are due to Baruch.[11] In addition to these materials, however, there is a very considerable amount of sermon and discourse material scattered throughout the book and interspersed between poetic and biographical materials.[12] The origin of this material has been a subject of considerable debate, some scholars accepting it as basically authentic Jeremianic material, some regarding the passages as compositions of Baruch or of some of Jeremiah's other followers, and yet others regarding them as deriving from the Deuteronomists, that is,

11. There have been notable exceptions, e.g., B. Duhm, *Das Buch Jeremia* (1901) (see below).

12. For example, 7:1–8:3; 11:1–17; 13:1–14; 14:11–16. The biographical passages like chs. 28, 29, 34, and 35 also contain prose discourse material.

men who wrote under the influence of the book of Deuteronomy and who were inheritors of the language and style of that book.

The majority of modern scholars, with a lot of variation in detail, regard the book of Jeremiah as commencing with the original scroll (*Urrolle*) in 604 B.C. It was then expanded by Baruch and given its final shape by an editor or series of editors who added further materials.[13] Much of the work of the earlier scholars placed considerable emphasis on literary considerations and concluded that the book of Jeremiah owed its present form largely to the scribal and literary activity of Baruch and other authors and editors. In recent years a larger place has been given in discussions to the possibility that "the book represents substantially the final literary expressions and deposit of a tradition which grew and developed at the hands of a body of people who sought not only to transmit the prophet's sayings but to present an interpretation of his prophetic ministry and preaching on the basis of theological concerns and interests which were of vital importance for them in the age in which they lived."[14]

We shall return to this view of E. W. Nicholson, which lays stress on another dimension in the discussions, but it ought to be said in passing that at least some of the earlier commentators were not unaware of the theological, exegetical, and homiletical emphases which Nicholson rightly says are of great importance, although they may have applied these in different ways than he does.[15]

Before taking up the work of J. Bright and E. W. Nicholson in some detail, it will be of value to review some of the earlier work on Jeremiah, since this will help us to see where the issues lie.

The commentary of B. Duhm in 1901 provides a starting point. He argued that the book resulted from the gathering together of the authentic writings of Jeremiah, the biographical narratives of Baruch, and a considerable body of material which represented expansions by the Deuteronomistic redactors who in exilic and postexilic periods continued to espouse the theology of Deuteronomy and the reform of Josiah. Duhm limited the authentic oracles of

13. This view is expressed by such people as B. Duhm, *Das Buch Jeremia*; W. Rudolph, *Jeremia* ([3]1968); A. Weiser, *Das Buch des Propheten Jeremia. ATD* 20–21 (1952/55); J. B. Hyatt, "The Book of Jeremiah," *IB* V (New York, 1956); and J. Bright, *Jeremiah.*

14. E. W. Nicholson, *Preaching to the Exiles* (1970), p. 4.

15. Thus, it could hardly be argued that J. Bright in his commentary on Jeremiah was unaware of theological and homiletical issues. See J. Bright, *Jeremiah,* pp. lxiii–lxxiii.

Jeremiah to part (280 verses) of the poetic sections cast, for the most part, in the 3:2 Qinah rhythm. The only prose he would allow to Jeremiah was his letter to the exiles in ch. 29.

Duhm's work was carried a stage further by S. Mowinckel,[16] who concluded that the complex character of the book, which in some areas appears to be ordered and in other areas rather confused, was due to its having passed through a long process of editorial compilation and redaction. Of particular interest to Mowinckel were the prose passages, which seemed to him to be profoundly influenced by the theological emphasis of Deuteronomy. Under the influence of the Scandinavian OT scholars, Mowinckel laid greater stress on oral tradition than did Duhm.[17] As a first step toward understanding the book he analyzed out three major collections of material which he designated Types A, B, and C.

The Type A material comprises authentic prophetic oracles of Jeremiah which had been recorded without either introductory material or concluding formulas. These oracles were cast in the metrical form which the prophet used for his public proclamations of the word of Yahweh. Much of this verse material occurs in chs. 1–25. Prose passages like chs. 7, 19, and perhaps 24 are excluded. The poetic rhythm and style follow standard patterns on the whole, although there is some variety. For the most part Yahweh is presented as speaking through the prophet's mouth. The oracles are introduced by characteristic formulas such as "this is what Yahweh has said." The "I" of these passages is Yahweh. Typical passages are 2:2b–3, 5–37; 4:1–2, 3b–4, 5b–8.[18]

One important section of the poetic material is concerned with Jeremiah's own personal heart-searching, the so-called "confessions."[19] Jeremiah seems to have been prone to this kind of introspection and to the laying bare of his heart, not merely in longer sections like 11:18–12:6; 15:10–11, 15–21; 17:14–18; 18:18–23; 20:7–

16. S. Mowinckel, *Zur Komposition des Buches Jeremia* (Kristiana, 1914).

17. A brief survey of the Scandinavian scholars in question is given by C. R. North in *The OT and Modern Study,* ed. H. H. Rowley (1951), pp. 76–81, and G. W. Anderson, "Some Aspects of the Uppsala School of OT Study," *Harvard Theological Review* 43 (1950), pp. 239–256.

18. It is never easy to decide whether a particular section represents an oracle delivered at one particular time since it is not impossible that oracles or fragments of oracles were linked together in the editorial process (e.g., ch. 2). For interpreting long passages some attempt should be made to isolate shorter units which have a particular theme.

19. See below, "The 'Confessions' of Jeremiah," pp. 88–92.

13, 14–18, but in numerous shorter segments where he spoke in the first person (e.g., 4:19–21; 5:3–5; 8:18–23 [Eng. 9:1]). The "I" of these passages is Jeremiah, not Yahweh.[20]

Mowinckel's Type B consists of personal and historical material of a biographical kind. The bulk of this material occurs in chs. 26–29, 34–45, where he found a wealth of circumstantial detail often introduced by precise chronological data (e.g., 26:1; 28:1; 36:1) and written in the third person. Many of these accounts include longer or shorter addresses given by the prophet on the occasion referred to.[21] At times snatches of autobiography occur also (e.g., 32:6–15, 16–35), which suggests that the biographer was drawing on personal reminiscences of the prophet.

In his early work Mowinckel did not regard Baruch as the writer of this biographical material but held that it came from an Egyptian background during the period 550–450 B.C., after the death of Jeremiah. At first he regarded Baruch simply as a public scribe who undertook such work as he was asked to do, to write the scrolls referred to in ch. 36, to write the deeds of transfer of property in ch. 32, and so on. Although he may have been held suspect for accepting work from Jeremiah, he was merely a public scribe and in no way implicated in Jeremiah's activities. More recently Mowinckel has revised his opinion of Baruch's role and now supports the view that Baruch made an important contribution to the formation of the book.[22]

While modern scholars recognize the usefulness of Mowinckel's Type B, there is considerable variety of opinion both as to who the "biographer" was and as to the historical value of the material.[23]

The third group of materials, Type C, has given rise to one of the major critical problems of the book of Jeremiah. It comprises the prose discourses of the book, which are presented in a verbose, repetitious, monotonous, and highly rhetorical style and include many stereotyped expressions. Mowinckel argued that this material

20. An interesting question about such material is whether Jeremiah revealed such thoughts publicly or only to his friends. The latter seems more likely. But as the book has come down to us the compiler(s), not wishing to leave out any of the prophet's words that had been preserved, put them all into the anthology. An original connection between such material and the context in which they now lie seems unlikely (unless they were asides or uttered *sotto voce*).

21. Mowinckel allotted such prose discourses to his Type C.

22. S. Mowinckel, *Prophecy and Tradition* (Oslo, 1946), pp. 61f.

23. The point is taken up again on pp. 38–43.

bore many resemblances to the language of Deuteronomy. It is normally presented in an "autobiographical" framework and is often introduced by some such formula as "The word which came to Jeremiah from Yahweh" instructing him what he was to say or do (e.g., 7:2, 16, 27–28; 16.1–13; 18:1–12; 19:1–13). Sometimes a dialog ensues (11:1–17), and sometimes the word of Yahweh comes without an introductory formula (e.g., 16:14–18; 31:27–34, 38–40). Such material is scattered throughout the book, sometimes introduced into poetic sections (e.g., throughout 1–25 and 30–31) and sometimes inserted into the biographical sections (e.g., ch. 27; 29:16–20; 32:17–44; 34:12–22; 35:12–17).

It was Mowinckel's view that this prose material was not from Jeremiah but was the literary composition of later editors and redactors.

While Mowinckel's influence was far-reaching, there have been criticisms of his work, notably of his views about Type B and Type C. The poetic sections of Type A have been generally accepted as authentic Jeremiah material although there have been disagreements about how to designate certain passages. Editorial processes may have obscured the poetic nature of some passages so that they take on the appearance of prose. Several of these will be discussed in the course of the commentary.[24] In some cases, by ignoring introductory material and words that are absent in LXX it has been possible to reconstruct a poetic oracle.[25] The view of Duhm that the only authentic oracles of Jeremiah were those written in the 3:2 Qinah rhythm was far too circumscribed to command general acceptance since it seems beyond doubt that Jeremiah employed other patterns of stress in his poetic oracles. If we wish to recognize verse as a literary category in Jeremiah, it is probably a wiser procedure to group under this caption all the verse and designate it as Type A. Analysis of its source and nature can proceed after that. The authentic Jeremiah material will form the bulk of it. But Jeremiah is hardly to be confined to a literary strait jacket so that he could produce only verse in the Qinah rhythm. He was capable of flexi-

24. See pp. 500, 503–505, 576f., 601f., 736f., etc.

25. E.g., 34:1–7, which is given as prose in RSV, NEB, GNB, J. Bright, *Jeremiah.* But see E. Lipiński, "Prose ou poésie en Jer. xxxiv:1–7?" *VT* 24 (1974), pp. 12f. Other passages which may be seen as poetic are 23:25–32, 33–40; 31:23a, 26; 33:15–16; 50:17–20; 51:24. These will be discussed in the commentary below. A valiant attempt to see a considerable amount of poetic material in the book of Jeremiah is that of A. Condamin, *Le Livre de Jérémie* ([3]1936).

bility and was too free a spirit to be confined in this way. On the other hand it must be allowed that the book of Jeremiah may well contain later and anonymous poetic material which was drawn into the final shape of the book. We shall refer to the nature of the poetic material before us in the commentary on a number of occasions.[26]

Discussion has arisen on the nature of the "Confessions of Jeremiah," which, though classified by Mowinckel as authentic Jeremiah material of Type A, should probably be regarded as a separate kind of authentic material since they are virtually peculiar to Jeremiah. No other prophet revealed the inner turmoil of his heart so much as Jeremiah.[27] But some commentators have interpreted these passages in terms of cultic rites and so have deprived them of their significance as authentic expressions of Jeremiah's personal experience. This trend in some areas of OT study has not found universal acceptance with scholars and is rejected, at least in its more radical form, by many.[28] Other studies which have tended to minimize or even negate the biographical value of these confessions have followed a different line.[29]

In regard to the biographical and historical material, classified by Mowinckel as Type B, there have been significant discussions along several lines. Mowinckel's earlier view that this material came from an Egyptian background in the century after Jeremiah's death, say 580–480 B.C., effectively ruled out Baruch as the writer of the narratives concerned. The view was contrary to the centuries-old opinion that Baruch was not merely the writer of the biographical material in Mowinckel's Type B material but may even have been the compiler of a great deal more, and was largely responsible for the final shape of the book. That view was, no doubt, too wide-sweeping, but even if one refers to the writer of this material as the "Biographer" it would seem to be altogether unlikely that he was other than a contemporary, and perhaps even an eyewitness of the events recorded.

Otto Eissfeldt as late as 1964[30] argued persuasively that the assigning of these narratives to Baruch follows from the generally

26. J. Bright, *Jeremiah,* p. lxiv, n. 13 touches on the point. It is a pity he did not develop these observations further.
27. For further discussion see below, "The 'Confessions' of Jeremiah," pp. 88–92.
28. J. Bright, *Jeremiah,* p. lxiv, n. 13. Cf. G. Fohrer, "Remarks on the Modern Interpretation of the Prophets," *JBL* 80 1961), pp. 309–312.
29. E. Gerstenberger, "Jeremiah's Complaints: Observations on Jer. 15:10–21," *JBL* 82 (1963), pp. 393–408.
30. O. Eissfeldt, *The OT: An Introduction* (^{3}1964, E.T. 1965).

accepted and probable assumption that the man who is mentioned as being closely bound up with Jeremiah's fortunes, and who appears as his secretary in ch. 36, is likely to have had a share in the book as we now have it.[31]

He concludes that there is much to be said in favor of tracing back to Baruch the biographical narrative work.[32] He also gives a useful outline of the scope of Baruch's work and suggests reasons why chs. 36, 45, and 51:59–64 now appear at points in the book which are chronologically out of order.

One of the obvious difficulties with Mowinckel's theory of a later date for the Type B narratives is that it fails to explain how anyone other than Jeremiah or Baruch could have been responsible for such material in Egypt. According to the narrative Jeremiah stirred up animosity among the Jews in Egypt by his severe condemnation of their way of life (44:1–2), and it is difficult to see who else would have been sufficiently sympathetic toward Jeremiah to record such narratives about him. Admittedly several of them show him in conflict with the authorities, but the total impression created on a reader today is one of admiration for such persistence and sincerity of purpose.

Other writers besides Eissfeldt reject Mowinckel's earlier view and would attribute to Baruch an even more extensive part in the formation of the whole book. Thus P. Volz[33] traces the basic form of chs. 1–45 back to Baruch and assumes that it was he who gave shape to the three major sections of the book, chs. 1–25, 26–36, and 37–45, concluding each with a reference to the dictation of a scroll (25:1–14; ch. 36; ch. 45). R. H. Pfeiffer[34] also held the view that Baruch not only wrote material himself but was responsible for preparing an edition of the book of Jeremiah in which he combined the prophet's book with his own, but revised or rewrote many of his

31. *Ibid.*, p. 355.

32. The material of Type B has been variously classified. Thus Eissfeldt (*Introduction*, pp. 354f.) includes 19:2, 3–9, 11b–15; 20:1–6; chs. 26; 28–29; 51:59–64; 34:8–22; chs. 36, 37–44, 45; while J. Bright, *Jeremiah*, p. viii under his large section "Incidents from the Life of Jeremiah" includes in chronological order, 26:1–24; 19:1–2, 10–11, 14–15; 20:1–6; 36:1–32; 45:1–5; 35:1–19; 24:1–10; 27:1–22; 28:1–17; 29:1–5, 21–23, 16–20, 24–32; 51:59–64b; 21:1–10; 34:1–7; 34:8–22; 37:1–10; 37:11–21; 38:1–28a; 39:15–18; 32:1–15; 39:1–2, 4–10; 38:28b; 39:3, 14, 11–13; 40:1–6; 40:7–16; 41:1–18; 42:1–18; 43:1–3; 42:19–22; 43:4–7; 43:8–13; 44:1–30.

33. P. Volz, *Der Prophet Jeremia* (1922).

34. R. H. Pfeiffer, *Introduction to the OT* (1948), p. 505.

master's speeches in his own Deuteronomistic style sometime after the death of Jeremiah.[35]

A different view was presented by H. G. May in 1942.[36] He too rejected Baruch as the biographer of Jeremiah and regarded him merely as his amanuensis. In his view the extant prophecy was the work of an anonymous biographer who lived no earlier than the first half of the fifth century B.C.

May rejected the view of many of his predecessors that the book of Jeremiah had been compiled by a "school" of writers, the so-called Deuteronomic School. He would reject out of hand the view represented by J. Skinner that "there is no doubt that the prophecies of Jeremiah passed through the hands of the Deuteronomic School, and were freely edited by them."[37] Instead, May argued that it was not a school but a particular individual, not Baruch but the "Biographer" who had undertaken the task of compiling all the relevant material from a number of sources including oracles of Jeremiah, Jeremiah's memoirs, and other materials which the tradition of the time of the Biographer seems to have ascribed to Jeremiah. Nor did the Biographer hesitate to place in the mouth of Jeremiah long speeches or oracles which were entirely his own composition.[38] The dominant interest of the "Biographer" was the return of both Israel and Judah from exile, but in particular, the restoration of the Davidic monarchy, which in the Biographer's day had not taken place.[39] He imitated the biographical style of Jeremiah's memoirs, but the net result of his work was to obscure the historical Jeremiah. May regarded his own work as "the first spade work for a more important task, namely, the recovery of the historical Jeremiah."[40] May's work has been severely criticized, and rejected by J. Bright on the grounds that the stylistic analysis on which he based his argument simply does not tally with the facts.[41] A

35. The nature of this Deuteronomistic style is discussed below, pp. 43–46.

36. H. G. May, "Towards an Objective Approach to the Book of Jeremiah: The Biographer," *JBL* 61 (1942), pp. 139–155.

37. J. Skinner, *Prophecy and Religion: Studies in the Life of Jeremiah* (1922; paperback ed. 1961), p. 102.

38. E.g., 17:19–27; 30:2–3; 32:17–24.

39. Part of May's argument turns on the language used by the Biographer, which, in his view, is more suitable to a period considerably later than Jeremiah, at the earliest in the first half of the 5th century B.C. (May, *art. cit.*, p. 152). But the argument is more relevant to the discussion of Mowinckel's Type C, which follows on pp. 43–50.

40. *Ibid.*, p. 153.

41. J. Bright, "The Date of the Prose Sermons of Jeremiah," *JBL* 70 (1951), pp. 15–35.

fundamental weakness of his proposal is that it credits too little of the written material to Jeremiah himself. While the exact extent of authentic Jeremiah material cannot be ascertained with any degree of certainty, the extant book suggests that a significant portion of the underlying sources was available in written form in the lifetime of Jeremiah. May's view ignores the significance of Baruch's reputation (43:3) and fails to deal adequately with the complexity and diversity of the literary types in the extant prophecy.

J. Bright in his commentary on Jeremiah[42] seems to follow a traditional view, namely that the biographical prose sections are basically attributable to Baruch. The accounts bear on their face the stamp of authenticity and must have been set down by Baruch or another who was a contemporary and an intimate of the prophet. He rejects the idea that we have a "biography" but thinks rather of a series of disconnected narratives, not in chronological order, which deal with critical incidents in Jeremiah's life. These were probably produced separately and at first circulated separately. But the Biographer's work was in written form from the beginning although doubtless based on oral accounts of eyewitnesses and the Biographer's own memory. Even after having been committed to writing, stories continued to be told and may have been expanded verbally or linked with other material until finally the whole, written tradition and oral tradition, was reduced to writing.

Bright's discussion does not seem to provide any indication of the underlying reason why this material was gathered together, apart perhaps from the historical reason that it was felt to be important to preserve a picture of the prophet's work and ministry.[43] It may be, of course, that the issues raised by the so-called Deuteronomic editors were none other than those raised by Jeremiah himself, so that Bright has no case to answer.

One other view about the materials of Type B, that is, the "biographical" materials, is that far from being a biography[44] they

42. J. Bright, *Jeremiah,* p. lxx.

43. This is in contrast to the proposal of E. W. Nicholson that there were didactic, exegetical, and homiletical reasons why this work should be preserved. See below, p. 42.

44. In fact, these materials cover only a limited part of Jeremiah's life and neglect many important areas of his career, notably the early years during Josiah's reign. See S. Mowinckel, *Zur Komposition des Buches Jeremia,* p. 25. These narratives were not written to tell us something about Jeremiah, or even to provide material for his biography, but because the events and situations described were the occasion for some of the prophet's memorable words.

should be seen as a kind of "passion narrative" (*Leidensgeschichte*) describing Jeremiah's sufferings as Yahweh's spokesman in the troublous years which preceded Judah's collapse.[45] The proposal has something to commend it although many of the narratives have little to do with Jeremiah's suffering but touch on a variety of issues: the manner in which prophets declared Yahweh's word (chs. 26, 36); the problem of false prophecy (chs. 27, 28, 29); the future hope (chs. 32, 33); the breach of Yahweh's law (ch. 33); the faithfulness of the Rechabites in comparison with Israel's faithlessness (ch. 35). The emphasis of these chapters is better understood as didactic and perhaps only incidentally biographical or historical, and almost certainly not part of a "passion narrative." According to E. W. Nicholson these chapters are best understood as "edifying stories which owe their origin to a circle of traditionists who have sought to draw out the implications of various incidents in the prophetic ministry and teaching of Jeremiah, on matters with which they were vitally concerned, such as the authority of the prophetic word, the problem of false prophecy, and disobedience to the requirements of the law."[46] The later chs. 37–44 may be interpreted in a similar way, not as the work of Baruch or some other "biographer," but as the work of a circle of traditionists with a theological and didactic purpose.[47]

But we have already embarked on a discussion of the views of E. W. Nicholson,[48] which likewise call into question the traditional view about Baruch and raise serious doubts about Mowinckel's Type B. For Nicholson, both of the categories Type B and Type C coalesce into one, although they cover different kinds of material from a literary point of view. Both the "biographical" material (Type B) and the "sermon" material (Type C) are seen as originating from a circle of men who were responsible for the prose material in the book of Jeremiah, which in its final form represents the final expression of a tradition which grew and developed around the ministry and teaching of Jeremiah, in response to the needs of the community in which those responsible for the tradition lived and worked.[49]

45. W. Rudolph, *Jeremia,* pp. xix, 195ff.; H. Kremers, "Leidensgemeinschaft mit Gott in AT. Eine Untersuchung der 'biographischen' Berichten in Jeremiabuch," *Evangelische Theologie* 13 (1953), pp. 122ff.
46. E. W. Nicholson, *Preaching to the Exiles,* p. 17.
47. *Ibid.,* p. 18.
48. *Ibid.*
49. *Ibid.,* p. 20.

Some conclusions should be reached in reference to the material of Type B as far as the present commentary is concerned, since we shall need to have a "point of view" from which to approach the commentary. We shall assume that the basic historical material came from a "Biographer" of some kind who was contemporary with the events and perhaps an eyewitness. The best candidate for such a biographer is Baruch. It is possible that Baruch simply provided basic material which was then available to men who had been deeply influenced by the reforms of Josiah and by the book of Deuteronomy and who, like Jeremiah himself, were inheritors of a literary prose style which came to expression in various ways during the seventh and early sixth centuries B.C., in these Jeremianic narratives, in the Deuteronomistic history (Joshua to II Kings), and in the Sermons of the book of Jeremiah (Mowinckel's Type C). Clearly, however, Baruch himself would have been an inheritor of the same traditions. In any case, the "Biographer's" narrative material was taken up and used to serve an important didactic, theological, exegetical, and homiletical purpose, namely, to preserve the teaching of Jeremiah and to show how his ministry of judgment and hope need not die with him but could continue to be relevant to the people of Israel after the fall of Jerusalem. It is quite impossible to say when the particular treatment of the narratives was given a fixed form in writing, although this need not have been very late in the exilic period. The particular emphases which are evident in these narratives were already current in Jeremiah's own day.[50] For the present we shall not attempt to define this circle of tradition further but will return to the question later in this section.[51]

We turn now to the third of Mowinckel's categories, Type C, which included the prose sermons in the Deuteronomic style and with the Deuteronomic outlook. These, according to Mowinckel, were transmitted for a period after Jeremiah's death until they were

50. In the exegesis of ch. 36, a representative narrative of this type, we will seek to demonstrate what a simple historical narrative became in the hands of men trained in this tradition.

51. See the discussion on pp. 48–50. E. W. Nicholson, *Preaching to the Exiles,* understands it as the attempt of the Deuteronomists to present a theological interpretation of the prophetic teaching and ministry of Jeremiah. But if the present writer understands him aright, the circle responsible for both the narratives and the sermons in their final form were working on the basis of genuine Jeremianic material so that they are shot through with elements of original material and even a substratum of the original language which Baruch or Jeremiah used (see *ibid.,* p. 30, etc.).

finally gathered up into the completed book.[52] The major question which arises from these sermons and discourses in the book of Jeremiah is that they appear to be written in a type of Hebrew prose which is closely akin to that of the Deuteronomic histories (Joshua–II Kings) and Deuteronomy. Several explanations of this phenomenon have been offered.

Some earlier writers held that Jeremiah himself employed, if he did not actually create, the style.[53] A variant of this view is that the prophet first used this style, which was then used during the exilic or early postexilic period to produce Deuteronomy.[54] These views are no longer acceptable. Rather, it is widely recognized today that Jeremiah was directly influenced by the style of Deuteronomy,[55] which probably formed part of his early training at Anathoth.[56] One variant of this view is that Jeremiah was indebted to the form of the sermon which was widely used by prophets and priests in the seventh century B.C.,[57] sometimes in the context of liturgical celebration.[58] All these latter views assume that Jeremiah employed this prose style himself so that passages in the book of Jeremiah which use the style could well come from the prophet himself, at least to some degree.

A significant attempt to recognize the prose sermons as for the most part genuine speeches of Jeremiah has been made by John Bright. He argued this point theoretically and has used it in a commentary.[59] His approach has been taken up and developed by J. W. Miller.[60] Bright undertook a detailed study of the characteristic expressions of the prose of Jeremiah and identified forty-seven typ-

52. S. Mowinckel, *Prophecy and Tradition,* pp. 62f.

53. Useful surveys of the origins of Deuteronomy are given in E. W. Nicholson, *Deuteronomy and Tradition* (Oxford, 1967), esp. pp. 58ff., 83ff.; H. H. Rowley, "The Prophet Jeremiah and the Book of Deuteronomy" in *Studies in OT Prophecy,* ed. H. H. Rowley (Edinburgh, 1950), pp. 157–174; S. Loersch, *Das Deuteronomium und seine Deutungen* (Stuttgart, 1967).

54. R. H. Kennett, "The Date of Deuteronomy," *JTS* 7 (1906), pp. 481–500; J. N. Schofield, "The Significance of the Prophets for Dating Deuteronomy" in *Studies in History and Religion,* ed. E. A. Payne (London, 1942), pp. 44–60.

55. S. R. Driver, *Deuteronomy.* ICC (1902), pp. xviiff., was an early exponent of this view.

56. Y. Kaufmann, *The Religion of Israel* (London, 1961), pp. 416ff.

57. Cf. O. Eissfeldt, *The OT: An Introduction,* pp. 15f., 352.

58. Cf. A. Weiser, *Introduction to the OT* (London, 1961), pp. 217f.

59. J. Bright, "The Date of the Prose Sermons of Jeremiah," *JBL* 70 (1951), pp. 15–35; *Jeremiah*, pp. lxx–lxxiii.

60. J. W. Miller, *Das Verhältnis Jeremias und Hesekiels sprachlich und theologisch Untersucht* (Assen, 1955).

ical expressions. At the same time he traced the occurrence of these expressions in the Jeremiah verse, in exilic and postexilic books, and in the books of Deuteronomy and the Deuteronomistic histories. He was able to rule out any dependence on stylistic or other grounds on the literature of the exilic or postexilic period[61] as H. G. May had proposed.[62] But more pertinent to our present discussion are his conclusions about the prose passages of Jeremiah in comparison with Deuteronomy and the Deuteronomistic histories. He concluded that although there are many points of resemblance both in style and ideas between the Jeremiah prose and Deuteronomy and the Deuteronomistic histories, there are also many points of difference. Of a total of fifty-six expressions in the Jeremiah prose, twenty-three do not occur at all in Deuteronomy, and of the thirty-three that do occur, only thirteen occur in all that literature and none more than twice.[63] Most of these occur in earlier literature anyhow. The usage of the phrases in the Jeremiah prose passages outnumbers the Deuteronomic usage on the average by seven to one. On that basis Bright argues that it is too risky to talk of any sort of dependence of the Jeremiah prose passage on Deuteronomic models.[64] Conversely a host of clichés which are common in the Deuteronomic literature rarely occur in the Jeremiah prose,[65] although there are marked resemblances between the Jeremiah prose passages and 2 K. 17, 21, 22. Further, of the thirty-three entries common to Jeremiah and Deuteronomic prose, only fifteen occur in Deuteronomy five or more times and are characteristic of Deuteronomy, but not one is exclusively from the Deuteronomistic histories. Most of these occur in earlier literature anyhow, but the incidence in Jeremiah far exceeds that in the Deuteronomic literature. Finally, twenty-nine of the expressions occur in both the prose and poetry sections in Jeremiah. To sum up, while there are profound resemblances between the Jeremiah prose and Deuteronomic prose, there are differences almost as marked as the similarities.[66] Thus the prose of Jeremiah is a style in its own right akin to that of the Deuteronomic writings but by no means an imitation of it. Deuteronomy, the Deuteronomistic histo-

61. Bright, *JBL* 70, pp. 15–35, esp. pp. 17–25.
62. H. G. May, *JBL* 61 (1942), pp. 139–155.
63. Bright, *JBL* 70, p. 25.
64. *Ibid.*, p. 26.
65. Bright makes use of the list of Deuteronomic expressions in S. R. Driver, *Introduction to the Literature of the OT* ([9]1913), pp. 99ff., 200ff.
66. Bright, *JBL* 70, p. 26.

ries, and the Jeremiah prose may each be regarded as examples of the rhetorical prose of the late seventh and early sixth centuries in Judah.[67] This view does not minimize the influence of Deuteronomy on Jeremiah and his whole generation but it makes us cautious about explaining all similarities of diction and idea in terms of literary dependence.

The discussion in which we have been engaging shows that there is little unanimity among the scholars who have occupied themselves with trying to elucidate the book of Jeremiah and the character of the prophet of whom the book speaks. But in the purely literary realm it seems proper to raise the question as to whether scholars have been making too fine a distinction between the prose of Jeremiah and that of his contemporaries on the one hand, and between the poetry and the prose of Jeremiah himself on the other hand. Some of the prose passages in the book are almost poetic in character and may be described as "elevated prose." Perhaps the distinction between prose and poetry in the prophetic books is not as clear-cut as many scholars have assumed. It is possible that we have been asking the wrong questions and working with wrong literary categories. Should we not rather have been giving close attention to a category of *prophetic discourse*? If we were to postulate such a category we could account more readily for the fact that in the book of Jeremiah we cannot be certain always whether we are dealing with prose or poetry since "elevated prose" is very close to poetry and contains similar phrases and elements of vocabulary.[68] Modern literary analysis recognizes the art of discourse analysis[69] with important results for the understanding of certain types of literature.

We return then to the question of the prose sermons in Jeremiah (Mowinckel's Type C). Did Jeremiah himself produce such material? We need not assume on any *a priori* grounds that the prophet was confined to what we have normally regarded as po-

67. The view is expressed also in W. O. E. Oesterley and T. H. Robinson, *Introduction to the Books of the OT* (London, 1934), pp. 304f.; see also G. P. Couturier, "Jeremiah," *JBC*, p. 302.

68. Perhaps some of the attempts made in the present commentary to give poetic form to prose passages are unnecessary. See 23:25–32, 33–40; 31:23a, 26; 33:15–16; 50:17–20; 51:24.

69. Keith R. Crim, "Hebrew Direct Discourse as a Translation Problem," *The Bible Translator* 24 (1973), 311–16; E. A. Nida and C. R. Taber, *The Theory and Practice of Translation* (Leiden, 1969), pp. 112, 131–33, 152–59.

etry.[70] This is not to rule out the possibility that editorial processes gave rise to some prose elements in these sermons in the form of verbal expansions. But we have good reason to assume that the so-called prose sermons were already well developed in Jeremiah's lifetime.[71]

A related question in reference to these prose sermons is whether they represent, in any sense, Jeremiah's authentic message or whether there is such a high degree of distortion in them as to obscure Jeremiah's teaching.[72] John Bright, while not arguing that we have the *ipsissima verba* of Jeremiah in these prose sermons, does argue that there is no general distortion of the prophet's message.[73]

Bright's view is important and compels a reassessment of a good deal of earlier work. Some helpful, constructive criticism of his view has been offered by E. W. Nicholson,[74] who has argued that Bright's proposal that differences in vocabulary between the prose in Jeremiah and that in the Deuteronomistic literature render untenable the view that the Jeremiah prose was composed by the Deuteronomists, may not be as conclusive as it appears. The peculiarly Jeremianic vocabulary of these sermons may well represent authentic Jeremiah material which was taken up by the Deuteronomists and used as the basis of their own work, which was not designed to obscure or falsify Jeremiah's message but merely to press home the implications already present.[75] Nicholson claims further that although there are points of correspondence between the vocabulary of Jeremiah's verse and prose, there are also many points

70. John Bright wryly observes that even Shakespeare wrote prose at times! See *JBL* 70, p. 27.

71. The date of Jeremiah's death is not known. It was certainly post–587 B.C. Hence the fixation of the prose sermons would have taken place some time later though perhaps not more than a few decades. See J. Bright, *Jeremiah*, p. lxxi.

72. Such is the view of B. Duhm, *Das Buch Jeremia*, pp. xviif. and S. Mowinckel in his earlier work *Zur Komposition des Buches Jeremia*, p. 57, where he stated that the Jeremiah of Type C bears little relationship to the real Jeremiah. Cf. G. Hölscher, *Die Propheten* (Leipzig, 1914), pp. 379f.; F. Horst, "Die Anfänge des Propheten Jeremia," *ZAW* 41 (1923), pp. 94–153. All of these writers placed these prose sermons in the postexilic period. More recently H. G. May, as we have seen, proposed that the book as a whole was the work of a biographer of the prophet, not Baruch, who lived not earlier than 500 B.C. See *JBL* 61 (1942), pp. 139–155. May holds that the Biographer inserted into the book speeches which he himself composed even though he used genuine material as well.

73. J. Bright, *Jeremiah*, pp. lxxif.; *JBL* 70, pp. 28f.

74. E. W. Nicholson, *Preaching to the Exiles, passim,* but note pp. 11–14, 25–37.

75. *Ibid.*, pp. 25f.

of difference (the reversal of Bright's argument), which raises the question of whether Jeremiah was entirely responsible for both. In fact, there may have been more differences than appear on the surface. W. L. Holladay[76] has recently added a new dimension to the debate. He has urged that only a wide-ranging study of the phrases in both the verse and prose of the book of Jeremiah and in all the parallel passages outside Jeremiah, without any *a priori* assumption as to whether the style is "Deuteronomic" or not, or as to whether it was written by Jeremiah, or Baruch, or whoever, can yield the basic evidence needed to draw firm conclusions on the basis of vocabulary. Holladay has pointed out that certain phrases which occur repeatedly in Jeremiah's prose have a prototype in the poetic oracles. In some cases the prototype is a striking turn of phrase without parallel in pre-Jeremianic literature, so that Jeremiah seems to have been the originator of the phrase which was subsequently taken up and used by the author(s) of the prose in the book.[77] Such parallels between the prose and poetic oracles in Jeremiah indicate that whoever was responsible for the sermons was in possession of a collection of the prophet's oracles and sayings. It may also be that some of the prose usages go back to sayings of Jeremiah which are not in the poetry but were in the actual sayings or speeches of the prophet upon which the sermons are based. In fact, the presence of non-Deuteronomistic language and material in the prose sermons of Jeremiah is not incompatible with their having assumed their present shape at the hands of a circle of men who knew Jeremiah and his work, whether they were his intimates or the Deuteronomists. These designations need not be mutually exclusive.[78] Nicholson would argue that the circle that produced the prose sermons was, in fact, the Deuteronomists, because the manner in which they handled the original prophetic material is precisely the way in which similar material was handled in the Deuteronomistic literature.[79] In his com-

76. W. L. Holladay, "Prototype and Copies: A New Approach to the Poetry-Prose Problem in the Book of Jeremiah," *JBL* 79 (1960), pp. 351–367; "Style, Irony and Authenticity in Jeremiah," *JBL* 81 (1962), pp. 44–54.

77. E.g., "the gates of Jerusalem" occurs in poetry in 1:15; 22:19; in prose, 17:19, 21, 27; "deliver from the hand of the oppressor him who has been robbed" in poetry in 21:12; in prose, 22:3.

78. J. Bright, *JBL* 70, p. 27.

79. E. W. Nicholson, *Preaching to the Exiles*, p. 32. But the whole volume is a development of this thesis. The argument follows the lines developed by E. Janssen, *Juda in der Exilszeit.* FRLANT 69 (1956), and in a broad sense the interpretation of P. R. Ackroyd, "The Vitality of the Word of God in the OT," *Annual of the Swedish Theological Institute in Jerusalem* 1 (1962), pp. 7–23.

mentary on Jeremiah[80] Nicholson seeks to apply to the exegesis of the book the principles marked out in his more technical treatment,[81] namely, that the prose sermons of the book of Jeremiah were the work of Deuteronomic authors who lived and worked in the shadow of 587 B.C., and whose main purpose was twofold: first to explain why Israel, God's chosen people, had suffered the terrible disasters of 722 and 587 B.C., and second, to hold out hope for the future of the people now deprived of their land and living in exile. In Nicholson's view the same position obtained for the autobiographical narratives.

We must now state the basis from which our exegesis in the present commentary will proceed. It recognizes the exegetical principle that the truth with which the Word of God confronted men in one age may come alive as guidelines for believers in every age.[82] The relevance of Jeremiah's preaching did not die with him but the same Word of God had an enduring vitality for those who lived after him, so that it was applicable to people in the post–587 B.C. years. We incline to the dynamic view of E. W. Nicholson that preachers were active among the exiles pressing home the message of Jeremiah. But we admit a degree of sympathy with the views of John Bright that the prose sermons of Jeremiah may have owed a great deal more to his inspiration than has been acknowledged by many of the scholars. Bright allows for a re-presentation of the Jeremiah prose tradition by his intimates who may also have been influenced by Deuteronomic emphases. Perhaps the weakness of Bright's commentary is that he fails to stress sufficiently the dynamic nature of Jeremiah's preaching, so that its relevance to the post–587 B.C. people of Judah is not drawn out clearly enough. However, Bright does indicate clearly what was the main thrust of Jeremiah's own preaching for the people of Judah in his day, and this is of very great importance to any exegete. A proper understanding of the way in which the Word of God came to people in the historical setting of a particular epoch and of a particular place is the stuff from which the exegete of any age may discover divine truths applicable to his own age. By stressing overmuch the special relevance of at least some sections of Jeremiah for the people of Judah in the post–587

80. E. W. Nicholson, *Jeremiah 1–25; Jeremiah 26–52* (The Cambridge Bible Commentary on the New English Bible).

81. E. W. Nicholson, *Preaching to the Exiles*.

82. The phrase is taken from Leslie C. Allen, *The Books of Joel, Obadiah, Jonah and Micah.* NICOT (1976), p. 266, although the idea is a very old one.

B.C. period, one may miss the importance of Yahweh's word through Jeremiah to the people of Judah in the pre–587 period. Both aspects of the implications of Jeremiah's preaching are important.

That the biographical narrative materials are based on authentic historical events need not be doubted. Nor need it be doubted that the prose sermons were firmly based on utterances once made by Jeremiah. The important difference between Bright and Nicholson lies in the fact that Nicholson sees the sermons[83] as reaching their final form in a situation that demanded a continuation of the theological emphases of Jeremiah. They were thus a homiletical and exegetical development of the prophet's original sayings or of certain aspects of his teaching.[84]

Whether we must identify these preachers as "Deuteronomists" or as intimates or successors of Jeremiah may be a question of opinion. But they were inheritors of an exegetical and homiletical tradition which they could turn to good effect and were thus able both to preserve the authentic history and preaching of Jeremiah (a historical exercise) and to demonstrate the relevance of his preaching in the decades after his death (an exegetical and homiletical exercise).

IV. SOME IMPORTANT ISSUES FOR EXEGESIS

A number of questions which bear on our approach to the book of Jeremiah call for some discussion and some decision, even if tentative. What was the date of Jeremiah's call? What were the contents and nature of Jeremiah's first and second scrolls? What was the attitude of Jeremiah to the covenant and to the cult? What was the significance of the many symbolic actions which the prophet used in the course of his ministry? What was the particular significance of Jeremiah's interest in the root *šûḇ?* What was the relationship between Jeremiah and Hosea? What was the significance of Jeremiah's "Confessions"?

A. THE DATE OF JEREMIAH'S CALL

According to 1:2 the word of Yahweh came to Jeremiah in the days of Josiah ben Amon king of Judah in the thirteenth year of his reign,

83. Presumably Nicholson would agree that much of the verse material in Jeremiah had a particular relevance to the pre–587 B.C. people of Judah.
84. E. W. Nicholson, *Preaching to the Exiles,* p. 20.

which would be 627 B.C., five years prior to the finding of the Book of the Law in Josiah's eighteenth year in 622 B.C. Reforms had already been initiated. Josiah's decision to repudiate the official Assyrian cult may well have been made as early as Josiah's eighth year, when he was sixteen, when he "began to seek the God of David his father" (2 Chr. 34:3), but by his twelfth year, when he was twenty, i.e., 629/8 B.C., the year that Sin-shar-ishkun came to the throne of Assyria, he began a radical purge of all kinds of idolatrous practices both in Judah and in Northern Israel. Those are the historical facts surrounding the reference in 1:2.

The question arises as to how to interpret the phrase "to whom the word of Yahweh came." On the surface it would appear that a word from Yahweh was given to a mature boy (*na'ar,* 1:7) who was commanded to proclaim it. "Yahweh stretched out his hand and touched my mouth and said: 'There! I have put my words in your mouth.' " But the time to which these words applied has been variously interpreted. On one view, even before Yahweh had formed Jeremiah in the womb he knew him and set him apart (*hiqdîš*) and appointed (*nāṯan*) him a prophet to the nations, so that from the moment of his birth Jeremiah was called to preach. The year 627 B.C. was therefore the date of his birth. Josiah's reforms would have been beginning about the time of Jeremiah's birth so that he would hardly have been aware of what was taking place. At the time of the finding of the Book of the Law he would have been only five, although he might well have been described as a "boy" (*na'ar*) since the word is very flexible in its meaning.[1] But any kind of effective ministry must have been delayed for at least another decade until say about 610, somewhere about the time of Josiah's death or early in the reign of Jehoiakim (609–578 B.C.).

On another view, the date 627 refers to the date at which the divine intention began to be realized in a lad, say about sixteen years old. His birth then would have been about 643 B.C., at the end of Manasseh's reign. Jeremiah was already fifteen or sixteen at the time Josiah was commencing his reforms. The finding of the Book of the Law would have meant something to him, and he would have lived through those days of reform and national reorientation. He might even have begun to preach. But even on this view the question must be asked: When did Jeremiah commence his ministry? The fact that in 1:1–3 reference is made to the period from Josiah to

1. KB, p. 623.

Zedekiah and the deportation of Jerusalem's population may represent little more than a general identification of a period rather than a specific statement of a precise range in time.

A third view which has not won general acceptance is that the thirteenth year is a scribal error for the twenty-third year, since *š^{e}lōš 'eśrēh* (=13) is very close to *š^{e}lōš w^{e}'eśrîm* (=23). If this could be supported, Jeremiah's preaching began in 617/6 B.C., about the time Nabopolassar began his attack on Assyria and Babylonian power was growing. Such textual confusions are possible, but there is no textual support for the proposal.[2]

The dominant view up to the present has been that at the time of his call in 627 B.C. Jeremiah was already a lad of about sixteen. The precise date at which he began his preaching is, to some extent, a matter of conjecture.

In recent years a small group of scholars has been enthusiastically presenting the second of the above views, namely, that Jeremiah did not begin to preach till Jehoiakim's reign. Because the point is important exegetically we need to explore this view in some detail.

W. L. Holladay has argued recently[3] that the generally accepted view, that Jeremiah's career as a prophet began in 627 B.C. when he began to declare God's word to his fellow citizens, presents three major difficulties: (a) we find no oracles of Jeremiah which can confidently be assigned to the time of Josiah. This evidence is negative. The only clear reference to Josiah is in 22:15–16, but the passage deals with King Jehoiakim and contrasts him with his noble father. If there is truth in the assumption that Jeremiah's early oracles are to be found in chs. 2–10, the picture given there is quite unlike what we should expect from the fact that Josiah's reforms commenced in 628 B.C. (2 Chr. 34:3). Nor is there any reference to the death of Josiah, which must have sent a deep shock throughout the land. In short, nothing that we know from the time of Josiah seems to fit anything we can learn from the book of Jeremiah. (b) There is no direct word from Jeremiah about the reform of Josiah (2 K. 22:3–23:24; 2 Chr. 34:14–35:19). In particular there is no direct reference to the finding of the Book of the Law. Jeremiah's reaction

2. T. C. Gordon, "A New Date for Jeremiah," *Expository Times* 44 (1932/33), pp. 562–65.

3. W. L. Holladay, *Jeremiah: Spokesman Out of Time* (1974), pp. 18–24; "The Background of Jeremiah's Self-Understanding," *JBL* 83 (1964), pp. 153–164; "Jeremiah and Moses: Further Observations," *JBL* 85 (1966), pp. 17–27.

is not declared. There is insufficient information to show whether it was positive or negative. The reference to "covenant" in 11:1–13 refers more likely to the Sinai Covenant. (c) There is no good candidate for the "foe from the north" in 627 B.C. The Assyrians had stopped moving west. The Babylonians had not yet commenced their drive. The older solution that was offered, that the foe referred to is the Scythians, is of very doubtful validity.

However, argues Holladay, if Jeremiah began to preach much later, in the early part of Jehoiakim's reign (609–598 B.C.), when there was a reversion to the religious practices outlawed by Josiah (cf. 7:16–18), when the reform was many years in the past, and when the foe from the north was clearly Babylon (5:15–17; 2 K. 24), the above three difficulties disappear. In reference then to 1:5, the thirteenth year of Josiah becomes the date of Jeremiah's birth, the date when God set him apart for his ministry. Further, 15:16 may be drawn in to support this view.[4] The phrase "thy words were found" is a poetic reference to the finding of the scroll in the temple in 621 B.C., while the phrase "and I ate them" refers to Jeremiah's acceptance of God's call (cf. 1:9). According to this view of 15:16, Jeremiah must have accepted the call *after* the finding of the scroll in 621 and not before, that is, not in 627. It is of some interest that apart from the enigmatic reference in 1:5, the first dated event found in the biographical material in Jeremiah is the preaching of the Temple Sermon "in the accession year of Jehoiakim" (26:1), that is, in 609 B.C., after the death of Josiah.

J. P. Hyatt[5] likewise disagrees with the traditional chronology and comes to a solution similar to that of Holladay and on similar grounds. He too takes 627 B.C. as the date of Jeremiah's birth. He argues that the foe from the north is Babylon rather than the Scythians. The descriptions of this foe in 4:13, 16; 5:15; 6:6, 23 suit the Babylonians rather than a nomadic foe like the Scythians. Further, not only is there a lack of evidence about the reform, or about any support Jeremiah might be expected to give, but there are passages which suggest that he opposed it,[6] and finally there are no passages that can be attributed with confidence to Josiah's reign. It may be

4. Holladay, *JBL* 85, pp. 21–24.
5. J. P. Hyatt, "Jeremiah," *IB* V, pp. 779f., 797f.; "Jeremiah and Deuteronomy," *JNES* 1 (1942), pp. 146–173; "The Peril from the North in Jeremiah," *JBL* 59 (1940), pp. 499f.
6. See Hyatt, *JNES* 1, pp. 162f., where Jer. 2:8; 6:20; 7:21–33; 8:8, 9, 13; 11:15 are cited in support.

that Jeremiah had sympathy with the aim of those who sponsored the reform when these concerned social injustice and corrupt business practice, but it is difficult to believe that he was concerned about such matters as the centralization of sacrificial worship at the Jerusalem temple or the reform of rituals. Because the Deuteronomists were the final editors, affinities between Jeremiah's and their viewpoint seem closer than they were in fact. By placing the date at which Jeremiah began his ministry in Jehoiakim's reign, all these difficulties are overcome.

Contrary to this view the majority of scholars hold that Jeremiah began his active ministry in 627 B.C. The important element in this viewpoint is the chronological reference, where it is explicitly stated that the word of Yahweh came to Jeremiah in the thirteenth year of the reign of Josiah (1:2; 25:3; cf. 3:6). This statement occurs in the prose sections, which are often held suspect though probably without adequate reason. But granted the authenticity of the chronological reference, we have to come to a decision about its meaning. In support of the view that Jeremiah began to preach in 627 B.C. are the two chronological items noted (1:2; 25:3), the specific reference in 3:6–14 to a message from Josiah's day, and the presumption in 2:18 that Assyria was still in existence, which no longer obtained in Jehoiakim's day.[7]

What then should be said about the problems raised by Holladay and Hyatt? It might be replied that the "foe from the north" is not defined specifically, and that the phrase was almost a traditional one and pointed to yet another invader from the region from which invasions came many times over the centuries. On the other hand some of the material of chs. 4–6 may have come from rather late in Josiah's reign or from the reign of Jehoiakim. By that time the "foe from the north" was clearly Babylon. As to Jeremiah's silence about the reform, it has been argued that some of his early preaching came from days before Josiah's reforms had begun, at which time he would have had much to accuse the people about in the cultic, moral, and political realms. Failure in all these areas moved him to pronounce judgment and to call the people to repentance through which alone there could be deliverance. According to some scholars it was when Jeremiah realized that his preaching was fruitless that he considered his mission was ended and left matters

7. H. H. Rowley, "The Early Prophecies of Jeremiah in Their Setting," *BJRL* 45 (1962/63), pp. 198–234.

in Yahweh's hands (6:10–11, 27–29). According to other scholars Jeremiah was either embarrassed because his prophecies of gloom were not fulfilled and there was no "foe from the north" to give substance to his prophecies, or he was discredited and ceased preaching. According to yet other scholars, once Jeremiah saw that Josiah's reform was having a useful effect he entered on a period of silence which lasted through most of Josiah's reign. Whether he actively supported the reforms or remained silent because he felt the task was being done well enough, or whether he gave initial support but soon rejected the program because of its superficiality and withdrew from the arena, is difficult to say. Each possibility has found support from some commentators. Some even propose that he rejected the program from the outset.[8] In view of the paucity and ambiguity of the data it is unlikely that complete agreement about Jeremiah's attitude to the reform of Josiah will ever be reached. It seems on the whole likely that initially there was much in the reform he could accept. If he later became dissatisfied, it was because it dealt with externals and did not reach into areas of personal conviction for the majority of the people. But it seems difficult to believe that one who was so outspoken on so many issues during his lifetime would have remained silent in the face of shallowness and superficiality. The theory of complete silence seems to be out of character, and even if we are unable to identify much from these years, at least a few poetic passages can be readily understood as belonging to the period after the reform.[9] Once the reform lost its momentum and the people grew careless and indifferent, there was scope for Jeremiah's preaching. It was one thing for Josiah to centralize worship and forbid pagan practices. It was quite another thing to police the nation in this respect. The fact that reversion to former practices took place so rapidly after Josiah's death is an indication that these were merely dormant or practiced under cover.

Those who adhere to a date of 627 B.C. for the call of Jeremiah and his preaching task are able to defend their position, and apart from one or two dissenters the view is still widely held.[10] Probably the objections of Hyatt and Holladay can be met reasonably well. But it is best to avoid dogmatism. The easiest course is

8. Hyatt, *JNES* 1, pp. 156–173; H. G. May, "The Chronology of Jeremiah's Oracles," *JNES* 4 (1945), pp. 217–227.

9. See J. Bright, *Jeremiah,* p. cv.

10. The view of J. Bright, *Jeremiah,* pp. lxxii–lxxxi, is representative of many modern commentators, at least in a general way.

to take each small segment in chs. 1–6 and seek to identify it. This we shall do. These chapters are in any case composite and contain material dating over a considerable span of time, say from 627 B.C. till well on in Jehoiakim's reign. On the assumption that Josiah's earliest reforms were only a beginning and were to be extended in scope and depth in due course, considerable portions of chs. 2 and 3:1–4:4 would suit a period when the nation was still suffering from the evil legacy of Manasseh's reign.[11] Some time elapsed before Josiah's reform began to take effect. Jeremiah could well have commenced his preaching task in 627 B.C., and we would expect, in that case, to find evidence of his strong reaction to the current evils. We shall explore the various possibilities in the commentary that follows.

B. JEREMIAH'S FIRST AND SECOND SCROLLS

The narrative of ch. 36 tells us that in the fourth year of Jehoiakim (605 B.C.) Yahweh commanded Jeremiah to obtain a scroll and write on it everything concerning Israel and Judah and all the nations since Yahweh first spoke to him in the days of Josiah. The tantalizing question is: What was the content of this scroll, and also of the expanded scroll which Jeremiah and Baruch produced when King Jehoiakim burned the first one leaf by leaf? We can do little more than speculate since we do not really know the truth of the matter. Some things are clear. We may accept 605 B.C. as the date when the first scroll was read. Hence we may limit the contents of the scroll to Jeremiah's ministry before that date. Then we may accept the proposition that the scroll was relatively short, since it was read aloud three times in a single day to different audiences and with an interval between the various readings (36:10, 15, 21). However, it seems to have contained several multiples of three or four columns of writing, since Jehoiakim is pictured as destroying these as they were cut off section by section (v. 23). Further, the contents were of such a character that the people might be led to abandon their evil ways (v. 3).

A variety of answers has been proposed. A brief look at some of these will show how varied these proposals have been. But as a general statement most scholars would seek the contents of the

11. Those who argue for a later date for the commencement of Jeremiah's ministry would reply that such preaching suited the conditions in Jehoiakim's reign.

scroll among the poetic oracles of Jeremiah,[12] although there are those who would seek for it among the prose discourses.[13]

W. L. Holladay (1974),[14] who, as we have noted, holds that Jeremiah did not begin his ministry till early in the reign of Jehoiakim, in 609 B.C., proposes that the first scroll consisted of 1:1–6:30, which in Kittel's *Biblia Hebraica* covers some sixteen pages. In his view the second scroll consisted of the contents of the first plus three additional sections represented by 8:14–9:9; 9:17–22, and 10:17–25. Other material in this area was, in Holladay's view, placed here later on the basis of word association.

W. O. E. Oesterley and T. H. Robinson (1934)[15] conjectured that the first scroll comprised largely the first person prose material (Mowinckel's Type C) written by Baruch at Jeremiah's dictation in 605 B.C., and that it was couched in the rhetorical prose of the age with chronological headings added (7:1; 18:1; 21:1–2). Later material of this type belongs to the post–605 B.C. period of Jeremiah's preaching and comprised the "many like words."

R. H. Pfeiffer (1948)[16] made a tentative suggestion as follows. The first scroll included 1:11–16 from 626 B.C.; 11:1–17 in support of the 621 reform of Josiah; 22:10–12 concerning Shallum from 609; 7:1–8:3 and 8:4–9, the Temple Sermon from soon after 609; and 8:18–9:11; 9:15–22 in their original form from about 605 but rewritten after 605. He agrees that some of this material may represent editorial work. After a space of seven years during which Jeremiah remained in hiding, he produced a second edition of the scroll for which Pfeiffer also proposed a tentative reconstruction.[17] How close these conjectures are to the truth we cannot tell. The decision must, to some extent, be a subjective one. It is of interest that Pfeiffer includes both prose and verse material in his proposed scroll.

Otto Eissfeldt (1964)[18] likewise includes basically prose material. He considers that the first scroll was a record, rather like a diary, with the various sections in the first person, couched in a parenetic prose style similar to the diction of Deuteronomy. It in-

12. Mowinckel's Type A; see pp. 35f.
13. Mowinckel's Type C; see pp. 36f.
14. W. L. Holladay, *Jeremiah: Spokesman Out of Time*, pp. 555f.; *The Architecture of Jeremiah 1–20* (1976), pp. 169–174.
15. W. O. E. Oesterley and T. H. Robinson, *Introduction to the Books of the OT* (1934), p. 306.
16. R. H. Pfeiffer, *Introduction to the OT* (1948), p. 500.
17. *Ibid.*
18. O. Eissfeldt, *The OT: An Introduction* (^{3}1964, E.T. 1965), pp. 350–54.

cluded the accounts of the visions and auditions in ch. 1 as an introduction and then 3:6–13; 7:1–8:3; 11:6–14; 13:1–14; 16:1–3; 17:19–27; 18:1–12; 19:1–2, 10–11; 22:1–5, 25. In the second scroll there were added chs. 24, 27, 32, and 35. This material corresponds in large measure to speeches of Jeremiah which, in the view of other scholars, were Deuteronomistic redactions and thus could not be in the original scroll.

W. Rudolph[19] thinks that the first scroll consisted primarily of sayings directed against Judah and Jerusalem, represented for the most part in 1:4–6:30 (except 3:14–18; 5:18–20); 8:4–9, 13–17; 9:1–7; 13:1–11, 20–22, 25–27; 14:1–15:3; 23:9–12, as well as some prophecies against the nations, 25:15–38; 46:1–49:33 (insofar as these are from Jeremiah). He included also possibly 9:9–10, 16–21, 24–25; 11:15, 16; 13:23–24; 16:16–17; 17:1–4; 18:13–17. The second scroll added 10:17–27; 12:7–14; 13:12–19; 15:5–9; 23:33; chs. 24, 27; 49:34ff.

Rudolph's scroll has been criticized as being too comprehensive, apart from the exegetical question of whether many of these texts really go back to Jeremiah, and Eissfeldt's scroll has been criticized as too one-sided in view of the model of ch. 25.

One last proposal might be mentioned, that of J. P. Hyatt.[20] Working on the assumption that Jeremiah did not commence his preaching ministry till Jehoiakim's reign and that his earliest messages came from the years 609–598 B.C., he conjectures that the original scroll contained 1:1–14, 17; 2:1–37; 3:1–5, 19–25; 4:1–8, 11–22, 27–31; 5:1–17, 20–31; 6:1–30, and perhaps 8:4–9:1. He regards 8:18–9:1 an excellent conclusion to a scroll on a fast day called because of a drought. He would add to this material in the second scroll the "confessions," the lamentation of 12:7–13 and perhaps others, and probably 9:10–11, 17–22, the story of the Rechabites in 35:1–19, the parables, acted or spoken in 13:1–10, 12–14; 18:1–6, and the proverb of 9:23–24.

Quite an influential group of commentators express serious reservations about identifying the contents of the scroll at all, maintaining that it is impossible now to reconstruct it with any assurance. Thus A. Weiser[21] agrees that the first scroll must have been very short since it was read three times in one day and consisted of

19. W. Rudolph, *Jeremia* (1958), pp. xviif.
20. J. P. Hyatt, "Jeremiah," *IB* V, p. 787.
21. A. Weiser, *Introduction to the OT* (^{4}1957, E.T. London, 1951), p. 212.

oracles delivered from 626 to 605 B.C. The second edition included the first with later additions, but in no case is it possible to specify the scope of the two rolls.

John Bright[22] thinks that it is futile to speculate regarding the precise contents of the first scroll. All that one can say with assurance is that it contained a selection of the prophet's words uttered between 627 and 605 B.C. or a digest of them, and that in comparison with the length of the present book it was relatively short.

Finally Georg Fohrer (1965)[23] agrees that it is probably hopeless to try to reconstruct an original scroll, and just as difficult to separate out from extant material an original scroll and the added material in a second scroll. Fohrer does, however, suggest that much of chs. 2–6 came from the first period of Jeremiah's ministry, while parts of chs. 7, 8, 9, 11, 13, 14, 18, 25 came from the second period. Perhaps 25:15ff. and part of ch. 46 belonged here, and also the symbolic acts in chs. 13 and 16. As a general statement Fohrer thinks that most of the scroll is still to be found in chs. 2–9, but this is interrupted by interpolations. These chapters are by and large continuous and generally in chronological order. Only a comparatively few sayings were later displaced to chs. 13, 14, 18, 25, and 46. It is evident from this brief review that there is considerable disagreement among scholars. On the whole recent opinion inclines to the view that it is impossible to reconstruct the scroll referred to in ch. 36, although most are agreed that its material is embedded somewhere in chs. 1–25 and probably in the early chapters. It was, in any case, rather short, capable of being read three times in one day, and was concerned largely with divine judgment on a rebellious nation.

C. JEREMIAH AND THE COVENANT

Even a cursory reading of the book of Jeremiah will indicate its deep interest in the covenant between Yahweh and Israel. The word "covenant" (*b^erîṯ*) occurs some twenty-three times, most of these in reference to Yahweh's covenant with his people, whether the Mosaic Sinai Covenant or the New Covenant,[24] but five times in connection with the covenant that Zedekiah made with the people

22. J. Bright, *Jeremiah,* p. lxi.
23. Georg Fohrer, *Introduction to the OT* (10th ed. of E. Sellin, revised and rewritten, 1965, E.T. London, 1968), pp. 393f.
24. 11:2, 3, 9, 10; 14:21; 22:9; 31:31, 32, 33; 32:40; 33:20, 21; 50:5.

to liberate their slaves.[25] Even where the term "covenant" is not used we cannot help sensing that the background to much of Jeremiah's thinking is the covenant between Yahweh and Israel, perhaps chiefly the fact that Yahweh's judgment will fall on his people for their rebellion and disobedience to his laws. Terms like "listen" (obey), "not to listen" (disobey), "law," "commandments" reflect covenant thinking. The many references in Jeremiah to the Exodus show that he was fully aware of the tradition of Israel's election at the time of the Exodus, and the idea is given great prominence.[26] Jeremiah was also aware of Yahweh's covenant with the house of David,[27] and no doubt he must have wrestled with the problem of how to reconcile the two. Certainly he would not allow any belief in the covenant of Yahweh with the descendants of David to take precedence over the ancient and more fundamental covenant with the whole nation, particularly since most of the kings he knew were guilty of many breaches of the Mosaic covenant (21:11–23:8). A number of questions arise out of this clear concern of Jeremiah with the covenant idea. What was Jeremiah's opinion of the reforms of Josiah which were given such impetus after the discovery of the Book of the Covenant (2 K. 23:2–3) in the temple? To what extent is the view valid that Jeremiah was indebted to ideas he had inherited in which the covenant was formulated in accordance with the pattern of ancient Near Eastern treaty documents? On this view Yahweh was the divine suzerain of Israel, who was bound to Yahweh in a relationship akin to that of a vassal to his imperial overlord. Can Jeremiah's views on judgment and blessing be related to such a pattern or can they be explained on some other basis?

On the view that Jeremiah began his preaching ministry in 627 B.C., the reforms of Josiah were but recently launched (629/8 B.C.). To begin with, it was an independence reform movement concerned to purge Judah of foreign cults of all sorts. It was in 622 B.C. that the Book of the Covenant was found in the temple, and this gave the reform some direction and a new intensity. Josiah summoned the elders, read the law to them, and entered with them into a solemn covenant before Yahweh to obey it (2 K. 23:1–4). The "Book of the Covenant" is generally held to have been some form

25. 34:8, 10, 13, 15, 18.
26. 2:2–7; 7:21–22; 16:14–15; 23:7–8; 31:31–34.
27. 23:5–6; cf. 22:30.

of the book of Deuteronomy.[28] Certainly much of Josiah's later reform program corresponds to the demands laid down in Deuteronomy, e.g., the centralization of the cult in Jerusalem (cf. Deut. 12:13–14, 17–18; 18:6–8). The law of Deut. 13 also speaks strongly against idolatry, which it regards as a capital crime.

One of the crucial sections in discussions about Jeremiah's relation to the covenant is 11:1–17. The chapter is largely in prose, except possibly for vv. 15–16, and it has been argued that the style is "Deuteronomic" and therefore reflects the Deuteronomic method of thinking. Even if this were so, there is no necessity to doubt that the passage reflects Jeremiah's actual thinking.[29] The thrust of the section is to urge obedience to "this covenant" and then to castigate the people for their breach of it. But what does "this covenant" refer to? Was it the covenant made under Josiah, or simply the ancient Mosaic covenant? Perhaps no sharp distinction need be drawn since Josiah's covenant may have been understood merely as a restatement and renewal of the Mosaic covenant. To be sure the expression "this covenant" occurs a number of times in Deuteronomy (5:3; 29:9, 14 [Eng. 8, 13]) and is used of the Josianic covenant in 2 K. 23:3. But even if Jeremiah picked up words that were well known, his reference point was still back to this Sinai Covenant. He was urging people to take heed to the demands of that ancient, fundamental covenant. There is no need to assume that Jeremiah gave his full support to everything that was done during Josiah's reform program. Indeed he may have preached these words after the program had been established. But his point was that Judah was called upon to obey the terms of the covenant of Moses, and he castigated the people for their failure to do so.[30]

What then was Jeremiah's attitude to the covenant? The covenant of Moses was, of course, fundamental to his whole thinking. We may well believe that he was instructed carefully in the ancient traditions of Israel and that even as a boy he developed a distaste for much that went on in the religious and social environment in

28. See H. H. Rowley, "The Prophet Jeremiah and the Book of Deuteronomy" in *Studies in OT Prophecy* (1950; repr. in *From Moses to Qumran* [1963]), pp. 187–208.
29. E. W. Nicholson, *Jeremiah 1–25*, pp. 108f., regards only vv. 15–16 as Jeremiah's. The whole of the section is a Deuteronomic composition. If there is any genuine Jeremianic saying behind the utterance it has been so recast that the words of Jeremiah have disappeared.
30. J. Bright, *Jeremiah*, p. 89, thinks that ch. 11 may relate in the main to Jehoiakim's reign when the reform was lapsing. It is of interest that LXX omits all of vv. 7–8 except the last two words. These verses may be a later editorial expansion.

which he grew up. The vehemence of his attack on national sin can scarcely be exaggerated. He was an ardent contender for the ancient faith of Israel, for the "ancient paths" (6:16). There is no indication that he played any part in the implementation of Josiah's reforms. It is reading too much into 11:6 to argue that he became an itinerant preacher up and down the land in support of the reform. In any case it was a royal decree and did not need the support of a young prophet. But we cannot think that Jeremiah would have opposed Josiah's efforts to rid the land of so many pagan cults or to revive in the nation the ancient Mosaic covenant. Jeremiah was later to express profound admiration for Josiah (22:15–16). In later years also, it was the men who supported the reform and their sons who defended Jeremiah in some critical situations (26:24; ch. 36; etc.). What seems to have concerned the prophet as the years passed was that for many people the reform was superficial. Merely to destroy pagan cult shrines and forbid their cult practices, merely to centralize and regularize worship in Jerusalem, merely to reactivate the annual passover and other formal aspects of worship did not really touch the basic problem. The reforms had by no means satisfied Yahweh's demands or brought the nation into conformity to his will. Deep repentance, inward and sincere acceptance of the obligations of the covenant would alone fulfil the requirements of Yahweh. One could recite "The temple of Yahweh, the temple of Yahweh, the temple of Yahweh" (7:4) and still tolerate all kinds of personal evils and breaches of the covenant (7:5–10). If the reform led men only to superficial areas of the national life, then it had not succeeded. Clearly it was of value to rid the nation of pagan cults and to improve, at least temporarily, public morality and the administration of justice. But official policies stop short with external measures, and no officially sponsored measure ever changed the inward character of individuals. If, therefore, Jeremiah showed any disillusionment about the reform, it was not for what it had achieved but for the vast areas of personal and national life which it did not, and could not touch, the areas of deep personal repentance and strong personal commitment to the covenant which would transform people and perhaps, through individuals, the nation. Jeremiah's personal commitment to the covenant, the Mosaic covenant, was unswerving. But he could hardly be committed to the view that in following official policies one had fulfilled the demands of the covenant. That view had to be exposed and rebuked. It would lead only to judgment at the last.

The second question we have to ask is whether Jeremiah's thinking and modes of expression owed something to secular covenant formulations or whether there were other kinds of covenant formulation. At the outset it must be stated that the issue is an extremely complex one.[31] The prophets did not use the term "covenant" (*b^e rîṯ*) a great deal. But despite that, their thinking was strongly covenantal. What concept of covenant did they, and in particular Jeremiah, have in mind? A lot of recent investigation has revealed analogies between some parts of the OT and the literature of the ancient Near East. In particular, largely following the work of George E. Mendenhall,[32] an analogy has been proposed between some areas in the OT and ancient Near Eastern treaties between sovereigns and vassals. Mendenhall argued that the underlying literary structure of Exod. 20, Deut. 5, Josh. 24, and the whole book of Deuteronomy resembled the structure of a Hittite treaty, which included the following elements:

1. Preamble introducing the Sovereign
2. Historical Prologue describing previous relations between the parties
3. The stipulations which outline the nature of the community established by the covenant
4. The document clause providing for the preservation and regular rereading of the treaty
5. The list of gods who witnessed the treaty
6. The curse and blessing formulas, curses for infidelity and blessings for fidelity to the covenant

The parallels with the OT are never complete, partly because they lie in a narrative or a parenetic setting. But clearly Israel did speak of "statutes and laws," witnesses, curses and blessings, a covenant document, etc. The evidence that Israel made use of such a literary form in some, at least, of its religious literature to describe its special relationship with Yahweh seems clear enough, and many studies have arisen which are based on an extension of Mendenhall's proposal. There is a very considerable literature on the subject.[33] Some

31. See D. J. McCarthy, "Covenant in the OT: The Present State of Inquiry," *CBQ* 27 (1965), pp. 217–240; R. E. Clements, *Prophecy and Tradition* (1975), pp. 8–23.

32. G. E. Mendenhall, *Law and Covenant in Israel and the Ancient Near East* (Pittsburgh, 1955) = *BA* 17 (1954), pp. 26–46, 49–76. Mendenhall based his work on that of V. Korošec, *Hethitische Staatsvertrage* (Leipzig, 1931).

33. James Muilenburg, "The 'Office' of the Prophet in Ancient Israel" in *The Bible in Modern Scholarship,* ed. J. P. Hyatt (London, 1966), pp. 74–97 gathers up a lot of

of the proposals are quite revolutionary, as for example that of N. Lohfink, who has proposed that the document found in the temple in Josiah's reign was not Deuteronomy but some other covenant document, akin, perhaps, to the "testimonies" (*'ēḏûṯ*) handed to King Joash at the time of his coronation (2 K. 11:12). Others throw new light on particular items of vocabulary, as for example the proposal of W. Moran that the term "love" (*'āhēḇ*) so widely used in Deuteronomy can be related to the treaty tradition. The vassal was called upon to "love," that is, to be faithful, to dedicate himself to the service of his overlord. In this sense "love" is essentially obedience and fidelity, a love that could be and was commanded.[34]

Despite this wide use of the concept of covenant in OT research, a number of scholars have rejected the idea in whole or in part. That is not to deny that there are some features in common between the Hittite treaty and some areas of OT literature and even of OT covenant thinking. In particular the sequence of events in some rituals is close to the sequence of items in a Hittite treaty.[35] But criticism has come in a number of specific areas. One of the prominent features of the ancient Near Eastern treaties was that of the curses. Detailed comparisons between OT curses and curses found in the treaties have been undertaken, and some remarkable parallels have been pointed out.[36] There can be no doubt about the occurrence of such curses in the OT and in the Near Eastern treaties. But similar curses are to be found in a wide variety of texts which show that there was a large general tradition of cursing in the ancient Near East, so that one needs to exercise caution in drawing conclusions.[37]

---

relevant discussion on the question. See also D. J. McCarthy, *CBQ* 27 (1965), pp. 217–240, for bibliography.

34. W. L. Moran, "The Ancient Near Eastern Background of the Love of God in Deuteronomy," *CBQ* 25 (1963), pp. 77–87; cf. N. Lohfink, "Hate and Love in Osee 9:15," *CBQ* 25 (1963), p. 417; J. A. Thompson, "The Significance of the Verb *Love* in the David-Jonathan Narratives in I Samuel," *VT* 24 (1974), pp. 334–38.

35. J. J. Stamm, *The Decalogue in the Light of Recent Research* (E.T. London, 1962).

36. F. C. Fensham, "Malediction and Benediction in Ancient Near Eastern Vassal-Treaties and the OT," *ZAW* 74 (1962), pp. 1–9; "Salt and Curse in the OT and the Ancient Near East," *BA* 25 (1962), pp. 48–50; "Common Trends in Curses of the Near Eastern Treaties and *kudurru*-Inscriptions Compared with the Maledictions of Amos and Isaiah," *ZAW* 75 (1963), pp. 155–175; D. Hillers, *Treaty-Curses and the OT Prophets*. Biblica et Orientalia 16 (1964).

37. D. J. McCarthy, *Treaty and Covenant; A Study in Form in the Ancient Oriental Documents and in the OT.* Analecta Biblica 21 (1963) explores a wide range of treaties, Hittite, Syrian, Mesopotamian, over the period from the 18th century B.C. to the 7th century B.C. and issues some cautions about overenthusiastic deductions.

A related area of research has been the study of the covenant lawsuit, the *rîḇ* form.[38] The accused is summoned before the divine judge and called to account for his violation of the covenant in the presence of witnesses (including heaven and earth). Such a procedure is known in the ancient Near East where vassals are called to account by their overlords.[39]

There can be no doubt that the prophets issued their indictments and judgments against Israel along lines very similar to those of a treaty, and it is very difficult not to come to the conclusion that somewhere in their tradition lay an awareness that just as a breach of treaty in the secular world brought curses upon the offenders, so a breach of Yahweh's covenant brought judgment on Israel. Whether one needs to argue that the prophets were closely dependent on the model of the Near Eastern treaty is open to discussion. But that the prophets spoke in terms of judgment for breach of covenant is clear. It seems unlikely that the similarities of content and expression such as occur in the *rîḇ* form are only accidental. The basic elements in that pattern, namely, the call to witnesses, the statement of the case at issue by the divine judge, an account of the benevolent acts of the divine suzerain, the indictment, and the sentence,[40] certainly have a strong parallel with their secular counterpart.[41]

It will probably be agreed that the covenant form should not be offered as a panacea for all our theological problems.[42] The covenant idea in the OT is a complex one, and there are important elements of the OT which are concerned with a covenant between Yahweh and his people but express it in terms other than those which occur in the covenant or treaty form. Covenant was also of concern in the cult. It was religious and not purely secular or legalistic. The covenant was made, reaffirmed, and renewed in the cult.[43]

38. H. B. Huffmon, "The Covenant Lawsuit in the Prophets," *JBL* 78 (1959), pp. 285–295; J. Harvey, "Le 'Rîb-Pattern', réquisitoire prophétique sur la rupture de l'alliance," *Biblica* 43 (1962), pp. 172–196; G. E. Wright, "The Lawsuit of God: A Form-critical Study of Deuteronomy 32," *Muilenburg Festschrift* (New York, 1962), pp. 26–67.
39. J. Harvey, *art. cit.,* pp. 182–88.
40. See Deut. 32; Isa. 1:2–3, 10–20; Mic. 6:1–8.
41. R. E. Clements, "The Prophets and the Covenant" in *Prophecy and Tradition,* is a critical review of the issues we have been raising but probably unnecessarily cautious.
42. The expression is used by D. J. McCarthy, *CBQ* 27, p. 234.
43. C. Baltzer, *Das Bundesformular* (WMANT 4; Neukirchen, 1960), pp. 48–70, and D. J. McCarthy, *Treaty and Covenant,* pp. 152–167, 173–77 make this point clearly.

But there are other analogies than that of the treaty to describe the relationship between Yahweh and his people, namely, the marriage analogy and the father-son analogy. Hosea in particular made much of the marriage analogy with Israel, who was pictured as the faithless wife of Yahweh whom Yahweh was unwilling to abandon for ever. She would be restored after chastisement. Jeremiah (31:32) described Yahweh as a husband (*ba'al*) toward Israel,[44] and thus carried on the image of the husband-wife relationship between Yahweh and Israel. But this relationship was also a contractual one. The same chapter in Jeremiah is concerned with both the old covenant which was broken and the new covenant to be restored.

The other analogy, that of father-son, is not normally contractual, but when Israel is an adopted son the relationship is contractual and is described in terms which are identical with those used to describe the covenant-love relationship between Yahweh and Israel in Deuteronomy. The father-son relationship is essentially that of the covenant, and there is no doubt that covenants, even treaties, were thought of as establishing a kind of family unity.[45]

What then are we to conclude about Jeremiah in reference to any possible dependence on secular covenants to give expression to his own ideas? Probably he did not consciously strive to accommodate his preaching to such models. But he was the inheritor of a tradition which may be traced in his predecessors. Whether his constant declaration of judgment on covenant-breakers owed something to secular models can neither be proved nor disproved. Curses for breach of obligation were widely known both inside and outside the treaty models. Jeremiah might well have known of the summons of a vassal before his overlord and of the indictment and judgment in such cases. He might even have thought of himself as an emissary from Yahweh to the people to identify their rebellious acts, to call them to repent, or to speak of judgment if they did not repent. He certainly saw himself as Yahweh's messenger, one who spoke for Yahweh and proclaimed Yahweh's covenant demands continually. There is some evidence that he regarded himself as in a sense a successor to Moses.[46] But whatever the source of his language there

44. J. Coppens, "La nouvelle alliance en Jer. 31:31–34," *CBQ* 25 (1963), pp. 14f.
45. D. J. McCarthy, "Notes on the Love of God in Deuteronomy and the Father-Son Relationship between Yahweh and Israel," *CBQ* 27 (1965), pp. 144–47.
46. W. L. Holladay, "The Background of Jeremiah's Self-Understanding," *JBL* 83 (1964), pp. 153–164; cf. James Muilenburg, "The 'Office' of Prophet in Ancient Israel," in *The Bible in Modern Scholarship,* pp. 74–97.

can be no escaping the fact that he saw Israel as a covenant-breaker. Despite the divine election, the gracious provision by Yahweh of his commandments as a guide to life, the definition of the relationship between Yahweh and his people and Yahweh's unbounded favor toward Israel over the centuries, they cast all that back in his face and rejected not merely his sovereignty but his grace. All that provided grounds enough for Yahweh's judgment.

D. JEREMIAH AND THE CULTUS

One of the most controversial aspects of Jeremiah's preaching is his attitude to the official cultus, that is, the whole range of activities, objects, and official personnel involved in the public practice of Israel's religion. From his oracles we are able to learn something of his views on the temple itself, the sacrificial system, the Ark of the Covenant, circumcision, and the sabbath, and are also able to gain some idea of the practices of at least some of the people in relation to pagan cults. As a general statement we may say that Jeremiah recognized the value of much that went on in the public practice of religion as an aid to worship, provided only that it was undertaken by obedient people. He was no enemy of the externals of religion as such, but insisted that God, who is spirit, could not be worshipped by the material and the external, which at best were only pointers to spiritual realities. Where men rested content with externals these became worthless and, in fact, dangerous.

First, in regard to the temple, it was Jeremiah's view that when the people uttered the formula "The temple of Yahweh, the temple of Yahweh, the temple of Yahweh," they were uttering lying and deceptive words (7:4). He was not questioning the expression as a proper description of the sanctuary. The temple was a means by which Yahweh could show his grace to Israel but had no value in itself if that grace was not being communicated. If we take the book of Jeremiah as a whole, it would appear that the prophet had come to the conclusion that the temple was not essential to the communion of the man of Israel with his God. But the time of liberation had not yet come (cf. 31:31–33). In other passages in Jeremiah there is complete lack of hostility to the venerable shrine. In the oracles of restoration like 31:6, 12 the existence of the temple seems to be implied. There is no doubt about such an inference in 33:11. In addition, in 17:26 the temple is depicted as a focus for divine blessing.[47] It is probably best to think of Jeremiah as not being opposed to the temple as such but only to its misuse. It is not possible to say whether the prophet came to his profound understanding of the true nature of worship because of the temple or in spite of it. One suspects that his emphasis on the spiritual as over against the material would have been the same even if there were no temple. His emphasis was linked neither to the temple nor to the cultus but to Yahweh himself and his covenant with Israel.

We must come to a similar conclusion about Jeremiah's attitude to the sacrificial system. A key passage is 6:16–21 where two sins of omission are condemned. The people refused to learn from the past (v. 16) or from prophecy (v. 17). For that reason judgment would fall on them (vv. 18, 19). It is in this setting that v. 20 occurs. Here Yahweh declares that of sweet-smelling cane from a distant land, incense from Sheba, burnt offerings and sacrifices, not one of them is acceptable to him. Obedience is better than sacrifice.[48] At no time in Israel's history was sacrifice, divorced from the obedience demanded by the covenant, regarded as something acceptable to Yahweh.

Another key passage is 7:21–23 (see Exegesis). What the passage seems to be saying is that God is completely indifferent to the way in which the people bring their sacrifices if obedience is absent. They may even commit the cultic enormity of eating the whole burnt offering as though it were a peace offering. If the basic ingredient of obedience is lacking, God refuses to regard the goings-on in the temple as a sacrifice to him. Sacrifice does not create a relationship between Israel and Yahweh but sustains it. If the relationship has been destroyed by disobedience, sacrifice cannot restore it. The main thrust of Yahweh's words in the days of the Exodus was not that Israel should be taken up with the details of burnt offerings and sacrifices, for Yahweh did not speak about the details (*'al diḇrê*) of these things but rather about obedience to the covenant. However, Jeremiah's interest seems not to have been in destroying the cultus as such but in persuading Judah to return to its covenant obedience. Merely to destroy the worship of the cultus would not necessarily

47. We are dogged in many of the prose passages in Jeremiah with the view that they are Deuteronomic in character and may not represent Jeremiah's words. Even if we allow some free reporting of Jeremiah's words or some editorial work, in many cases it is difficult to deny that an oracle of Jeremiah lies behind the prose passages. Each passage must be treated separately on its merits.
48. Cf. 1 Sam. 15:22; Ps. 50:13, 14.

turn the people's hearts to Yahweh. It may only make them search about for a substitute.

One of the most important of the cult objects was the Ark of the Covenant. The reference to the Ark in 3:16 is taken by some commentators as an editorial composition. But it could hardly be agreed that the ideas expressed are inconsistent with Jeremiah's own thinking, and he may well have made such a statement on some occasion. The Ark was the symbol of the reality of Yahweh's presence among his people. But if the Ark were ever to disappear, Yahweh would not vanish. Here too Jeremiah should not be seen as the enemy of the material objects used in worship, for these were only symbols. The great reality was Yahweh himself. The day would come when men would understand that and the Ark would not be missed or remade.

There is a brief reference to circumcision in 9:25–26 (Eng. 24–25). Though the historic setting is unknown and the text is difficult, the main thrust is clear and the passage reflects Jeremiah's spirit authentically (cf. 4:4; 6:10 and 9:26 [Eng. 25]; etc.). Circumcision as a ritual act was not unique to Israel but was widely practiced in areas around Israel. But those who lived in lands adjoining Israel, though circumcised, were uncircumcised, presumably because they were all, like Judah, uncircumcised in their hearts. No doubt Judah laid great store by this cultic rite. It was the sign of the covenant, and provided for the people of Judah a reason why God should not forsake his people. But the argument was futile since it might have applied to others too. Here again Jeremiah was not attacking circumcision as such. Jeremiah was neutral in respect to the ceremony. But when the ceremony was divorced from spiritual reality it represented a worthless ritual.

There is an extended reference to the sabbath in 17:19–27. The passage is in prose and on the surface seems to be asserting that the keeping of the sabbath is a condition of the nation's continued existence. It is often rejected as genuinely Jeremianic material simply because a concern about sabbath keeping is held to be a postexilic concern. But presumably Jeremiah had a view about the sabbath and would have wished the sabbath to be observed. He did, in fact, single out some other specific laws for comment (7:9). Sabbath observance no less than stealing, murder, adultery, or perjury was part of the covenant law. Obedience to the covenant law was obedience to Yahweh, and the nation's future depended on obedience. In a sense, then, particular reference to the sabbath was an interest in *pars pro toto*. But here again, true sabbath keeping was not meant to be a mere ritual observance but an indication of the involvement of the whole man in the covenant. There is an emphasis precisely on obedience in vv. 24, 27. This means that 17:19–27 is not in conflict with what we have argued above but may very well support the argument. Also, v. 26 may serve as a warning against too radical an interpretation of 7:21–23.

In general, therefore, we sense that Jeremiah was not the enemy of the material and external aspects of religion, but more than anyone in his age (and perhaps among all the prophets of Israel) he asserted that God, who is spirit, cannot be worshipped by the material, whether sacrifice, circumcision, temple, cultic furniture, etc., unless these are the means to point the worshipper to God. If that were so, they served a useful though not an essential purpose. Otherwise they were a worthless hindrance and positively dangerous because men might be content with them and put their trust in them. Jeremiah's own relationship with God was intensely private and inward. When he realized that the national cult had become an empty parade in which he could not participate, he seems to have rejected it.

A further problem was that the cult became a screen for lawbreaking (cf. 7:1–15) and lent support to a theology which laid stress on such doctrines as Yahweh's eternal covenant with David (cf. 2 Sam. 7:4–17; 23:1–7; etc.) and his choice of Zion and its temple as his earthly abode. The first of these with its affirmation of the everlasting rule of the Davidic dynasty led to complacent views about the ruling kings of the day. Even though it was understood that the king might bring judgment on himself and his people because of his sins, yet because of the permanent character of the dynasty, it would finally triumph over its foes. As to Zion, the Holy City Jerusalem, many believed in its inviolability to such an extent that they believed a powerful ruler like Nebuchadrezzar could be defied. Yahweh would deliver them as he had done earlier in the days of Hezekiah when both the king and the city were delivered from Sennacherib. But such doctrines gave a false hope to the nation as though Yahweh were committed unconditionally to the defense of the nation, the temple, and the dynasty, whether or not the king and the people gave heed to the more basic demands of the Mosaic covenant.

Jeremiah, therefore, though not wishing to advocate the destruction of the cult as such, could not but recognize that as it was practiced in his day it was a positive hindrance to true heart religion.

What had been provided for Israel as a useful and meaningful apparatus for worship by an obedient people had become a hollow sham which served only as a hindrance to the attainment of true spiritual worship.

E. SYMBOLIC ACTIONS IN JEREMIAH

Jeremiah made a good deal of use of the symbolic action. This was an action which accompanied the spoken word, partly to emphasize a particular message that was being declared by providing a vivid visual illustration, but partly also to provide a supporting "visible word." The noun *dāḇār* in Hebrew means "word," "thing," "action," "event." The "word of God" is an expression of the divine mind, what God thinks and plans, says, does, purposes. Hence a spoken word plus a visible "word" could convey the divine mind very forcefully.

There are examples in the OT of such symbolic actions both before and after Jeremiah's day. In the ninth century in the days of King Ahab a prophet Zedekiah ben Chenaanah made horns of iron for himself and declared to Ahab of Israel and Jehoshaphat of Judah, "with horns like these you shall gore the Arameans and make an end of them" (1 K. 22:11). In Elisha's day, the prophet told Jehoash king of Israel to shoot arrows in the direction of Syria to symbolize Israel's forthcoming victory over the Arameans (2 K. 13:14–19).

In the eighth century B.C. symbolic actions were associated with both Isaiah and Hosea. Thus Isaiah went naked and barefoot, i.e., without a loincloth[49] and sandals, as a sign and symbol to indicate that the Assyrian king would lead Egyptians and Ethiopians barefoot and with buttocks uncovered to Assyria. Hence Israel ought not to trust in an alliance with Egypt (Isa. 20). Even the naming of his children with symbolic names was a kind of symbolic act. The names Shear-jashub (7:3, "a remnant shall return") and Maher-shalal-hashbaz (8:1, "spoil hastens, booty hurries") refer to events in the future, and the name Immanuel ("God with us," 8:8, 10) symbolized the divine presence with his people.

Hosea's marriage to Gomer was a symbolic enactment of the

49. The noun is *śaq,* generally translated "loincloth" or "sackcloth" (cf. Jer. 13). It was woven of goat's hair and formed part of the special dress of a prophet. The fact that Isaiah took off his loincloth did not mean that he was naked; he probably wore a mantle (*'adderet*). Cf. Mic. 1:8 where Micah went barefoot and "naked" but as a sign of grief. See J. Lindblom, *Prophecy in Ancient Israel* (1962), p. 169, nn. 10f.

relationship of Israel to Yahweh. The precise character of the story has been the subject of a good deal of debate, but the main thrust of its message is clear. Hosea the faithful husband symbolizes Yahweh, and Gomer the unfaithful wife symbolizes Israel.[50] The names of Hosea's children are likewise symbolic of the judgment of Yahweh on Israel: Jezreel ("God sows") indicating that Yahweh would soon demand from the house of Jehu "the blood of Jezreel" and the massacre of the royal family recorded in 2 K. 9–10; Lo Ruhamah ("She who is unpitied") symbolizing that Yahweh would have no pity on the house of Israel; Lo 'Ammi ("Not-my-people") symbolizing Yahweh's rejection of his people.

Ezekiel employed symbolic actions on several occasions. He sketched the siege of Jerusalem on a large mud brick (4:1–2). He lay on his side like one paralyzed for a long period to symbolize the guilt of Israel and its punishment (4:4–8). The lack of provisions in Jerusalem during the siege was symbolized by Ezekiel taking only small quantities of bread and water (4:9–12); and the life in exile was symbolized by his eating unclean food (4:12–17). Ezekiel shaved off his hair and beard, then burned, smote, and scattered it to the winds to symbolize the fate of the inhabitants of Jerusalem (5:1–17). He used other symbolic actions to symbolize the advance of the Babylonian army (12:1–20), the distress of the inhabitants of Jerusalem during the siege (21:24–28 [Eng. 19–23]), the paralyzing grief of the Jews in Babylonia at the fall of Jerusalem (24:1–14), the second deportation of the people of Judah (24:15–27), the reunion of the two kingdoms into one in the age to come (37:15–28).

The later prophet Zechariah was commanded to take silver and gold and make a crown to place on the head of Joshua symbolically pointing to the coming Messiah (Zech. 6:9–15).

When we come to Jeremiah specifically and find that he too performed symbolic actions, it is evident that he was in a long tradition which continued after his death. Thus he gave Pashhur the priest the symbolic name *māgôr missāḇîḇ* ("terror all around"). But he accompanied this symbolic naming by a verbal statement foretelling the disaster that would befall Pashhur, his friends, and his people (20:3).

Jeremiah did not marry, at Yahweh's command. This prohibition was a way of proclaiming that in the day of divine judgment

50. See H. H. Rowley, "The Marriage of Hosea," *BJRL* 39 (1956), pp. 200–233; J. Lindblom, *Prophecy in Ancient Israel,* pp. 165–69.

parents as well as children would perish. But his symbolic celibacy was accompanied by a verbal explanation (16:1–3). At the same time Jeremiah stood apart from the common funeral observances in his village. This was explained verbally as a declaration that in the day of Judah's judgment mourning practices would be impossible (16:5–7). Jeremiah was also forbidden to participate in the ordinary festivities of life, eating and drinking, because "the sound of mirth and the sound of gladness, the voice of the bridegroom and the voice of the bride" would be heard no more in the land (16:8–9).

The potter provided Jeremiah with a powerful symbolic action. One day the prophet bought an earthenware jar and, taking with him some elders and priests, went out to the Potsherd Gate, where he smashed the bottle before their eyes, saying as he did so, "Thus says Yahweh of Hosts, 'As a potter's vessel is broken and cannot be mended again, so will I break this people and this city' " (19:10–11).

The incident with the Rechabites (ch. 35) was a kind of symbolic action. This unusual group held to nomadic customs and protested against the agricultural and urban mode of life in Palestine. One of their strong tenets was not to drink wine. Down the centuries they adhered rigidly to the instructions of their ancestor and founder Jonadab. One day Jeremiah summoned them to the temple in Jerusalem and set wine before them with an invitation to drink. They refused and stood by their principles and the command of their ancestor. The obedience of the Rechabites to their founder's charge was presented by Jeremiah as a model of faithfulness and a rebuke to the people of Judah and Jerusalem for their disobedience and unfaithfulness to Yahweh. Again, the symbolic act was accompanied by the prophet's word.

At the time of a visit to Jerusalem by messengers from Edom, Moab, Ammon, Tyre, and Sidon to plot a rebellion against Nebuchadrezzar, Jeremiah made a yoke and carried it on his own neck and shoulders and thus proclaimed in a striking way that these nations, as well as Judah, had to bring their necks under the yoke of the king of Babylon if they wished to survive. The symbolic act was accompanied by the prophetic word (27:1–15). Later a false prophet Hananiah took the yoke from Jeremiah's neck and broke it, declaring that Yahweh would break the yoke of the king of Babylon from off the neck of these nations (28:1–4). He too performed a symbolic action and spoke his own prophetic word. The story shows that other prophets as well as the canonical prophets performed such actions. Sometime later Jeremiah appeared again to declare that the yoke of Yahweh was not wooden but iron and that his word would be fulfilled (28:12–14).

During the siege of Jerusalem, when Jeremiah was shut up in the court of the guard, he bought a field at Anathoth according to the standard purchasing procedures. The act was a symbolic one. Jeremiah gave the accompanying prophetic word, "Thus says Yahweh of Hosts, the God of Israel: 'Houses and fields and vineyards shall again be bought in this land' " (32:15).

The command to Seraiah ben Neriah, who went to Babylon with King Zedekiah, that he was to cast into the Euphrates a scroll containing a statement of all the evil that Yahweh purposed for Babylon, saying as he did so, "Thus shall Babylon sink, to rise no more, because of the evil I am bringing upon him" (51:64), is a further example of a symbolic action accompanied by a spoken word.

Finally, when Jeremiah arrived in Egypt with the refugees after the massacre of Gedaliah, he took some large stones and buried them at the entrance to the government building in Tahpanhes as a symbolic demonstration that one day the king of Babylon would come and set his royal throne just above these stones (43:8–13). The symbolic act was accompanied by the prophetic word.

This is an impressive list of symbolic actions, and shows that Jeremiah had something of a penchant for this kind of preaching in which a symbolic action was associated with the prophetic spoken word.

There is a second group of phenomena which should properly be associated with the symbolic action, namely, the symbolic perception in which a real, objective object in the physical world was conceived of as symbolic of something else. The phenomenon occurs several times in Jeremiah. It is represented earlier in Amos' perception of a basket of summer fruit, perhaps ripe figs, which became a symbol of the end of Israel. In this case the connection is based on a pun rather like that in Amos 8:1–2, where "summer fruit" (*qayiṣ*) and "end" (*qēṣ*) sounded very much alike. The formula "What do you see, Amos?" leads on to the symbolic perception beyond the physical object.

There are four similar incidents in Jeremiah. The confirmation of Jeremiah's call came through his noticing one day a branch of an almond tree (*šāqēḏ*). By word association this was transformed to *šōqēḏ,* "a watcher." The experience was accompanied by the question "Jeremiah, what do you see?" On reporting what he saw he received Yahweh's word, "I am watching over my word to perform it" (1:11–12).[51]

The second of these symbolic perceptions in Jeremiah comes in 1:13–14 where Jeremiah's attention was drawn to a cauldron placed on a fire blown by a strong wind from the north, but as it was slightly tilted to the south it boiled over toward the south. The phrase "What do you see?" occurs again here. What Jeremiah saw physically led on to a symbolic perception of judgment coming from the north and spilling over toward the south, that is, toward Judah.

The two baskets of figs (ch. 24) belong to the same general category. These became to Jeremiah, as he saw them standing there, symbols of something else, namely, two groups in Judah; good figs which symbolized the exiles, and bad figs which symbolized those who remained in the land. It was the exiles who would be the bearers of the age of renewal and restoration.

Finally there was the incident in the potter's house recorded in ch. 18. As Jeremiah watched the potter at work he observed that it lay in the potter's power to refashion spoiled vessels which for some reason would not conform to the potter's original plan. The potter did this according to his own pleasure. But as Jeremiah looked, he saw beyond the physical happening in front of him to the work of Yahweh with his people, or with any people for that matter. A people destined for judgment might be granted deliverance in the potter's hand (ch. 18). In this case the whole incident was understood as "The word that came to Jeremiah from Yahweh" (18:1), and Yahweh's word was added alongside the symbolic action which lay before the prophet.

In these examples of symbolic perception a physical object remains a physical object but it is interpreted by a spontaneous act of reflection into a symbol of an idea of a higher character.

A number of general observations may be made. The symbolic action and the symbolic perception were evidently part of the prophetic preaching tradition. Jeremiah was neither the originator of these nor the last to use them. In every case they centered upon normal physical events or objects. In no sense were they illusions in which something real was seen but was transformed in error by some hallucinatory mental process. Each of the physical objects

51. One wonders whether the almond stick may not have been an allusion to Aaron's rod in Num. 17. So W. G. Williams in "Jeremiah's Vision of the Almond Rod," in *A Stubborn Faith*, ed. E. C. Hobbs (Dallas, 1956), pp. 91ff.

became a symbol of some higher idea while the prophet remained in full possession of his faculties.

Further, the symbolic action and the symbolic perception did not stand alone. There was in every case an accompanying word. Both the symbolic action and the symbolic perception constituted a form of the divine word. It was a "visible word" but shared in all the qualities of the spoken word. As such, once it was performed, being a word of Yahweh it had effective power to be fulfilled. The symbolic action not only served to represent and make evident to those who saw it the particular truth it portrayed, but being Yahweh's word it initiated the event it portrayed. The reason that Jeremiah and others made use of both the prophetic word and the symbolic action may serve to underline the fact that in that ancient world audiences responded equally to both.[52]

It must be insisted that in the symbolic action the prophets were not dealing in magical actions, which are well known in more primitive cultures. The magical action was thought to be dependent on the inner power connected with it and its performance in accordance with certain definite magical laws. But nothing of this is to be found in the prophet's use of the symbolic action. The power of both the prophetic word and the symbolic action derived from Yahweh alone and was directed to the fulfilment of Yahweh's plans and purposes concerning his elect people Israel, or sometimes the pagan nations who also lay in his power. The prophets who made use of the symbolic action emphasized that these actions were carried out by Yahweh's command. What was done served to reinforce what was said.

F. THE USE AND SIGNIFICANCE OF THE ROOT *šûḇ* IN JEREMIAH

Jeremiah with his profound concern about the covenant had a particular interest in the Hebrew root *šwb,* which occurs in the verb *šûḇ,* "to turn."[53] The verb is a remarkable one in several ways. It occurs frequently in the OT (some 1059 times). It has a rich variety of meanings and a deliberate specialized ambiguity as well. The

52. The use of the symbolic act in the 20th century A.D. is often confined to communication with children, a good indication that the modern, Western adult has lost an important dimension in communication, although certain kinds of modern advertising depend a great deal on visual images.

53. See W. L. Holladay, *The Root šûbh in the OT* (1958).

subtle nuances of the verb were seized upon by Jeremiah as by no other prophet. The problem of the verb is evident from its use in 8:4.

> "You shall say to them: 'Thus says Yahweh:
> Do they (i.e., does one) fall and not rise (again)?
> Does one turn (away) and not turn (back)?' "

The last line in Hebrew reads:

> *'im-yāšûḇ wᵉlō' yāšûḇ*

As it is written it involves a double ambiguity, first of direction, since the verb can mean "turn back" (from someone or something) or "return" (to something or someone). The previous line indicates that we are concerned with opposites. The second ambiguity is that Jeremiah is using the verb to cover both physical movement and religious relation.

The next verse reads:

> "Why, then, has this people turned back (*šôḇᵉḇâ*) in perpetual apostasy (*mᵉšūḇâ*)? They hold fast to deceit, they refuse to return (*lāšûḇ*)."

Here the root *šûḇ* shows ambiguity of direction, but in terms of faithlessness and faithfulness on the part of Israel to Yahweh. Such a juxtaposition of two ideas is typical of what Holladay calls the "covenantal" usage of the verb.[54] Normally the verb is a verb of motion, but in the prophetic books of the OT in particular it assumes this "covenantal" sense expressing a change of loyalty on the part of Israel or God, each for the other. In this sense it occurs 164 times in the books of the OT.[55] The related nouns and adjectives occur with relative infrequency.

A glimpse at its verbal usage shows that in the book of Jeremiah there are forty-eight instances of the covenantal use of *šûḇ*.[56] No other book in the OT has this concentration on the verb. Before we discuss these in a little more detail, and in order to provide a contrast with Jeremiah, it is to be noted that the eighth-century prophets used the verb in this sense but not nearly as much as Jeremiah. The covenantal usage appears five times in Amos 4 in the stylized phrase, "but you have not returned to me."[57] In Hosea there are nine instances of the covenantal usage. Although there is disagreement about the authenticity of some of the passages there is general agreement about Hos. 5:4; 11:7 and reasonable agreement

54. *Ibid.*, p. 1.
55. *Ibid.*, p. 2.
56. *Ibid.*, p. 128.
57. *Ibid.*, p. 120.

about 6:1 and 11:5 (twice).[58] In Micah there is but one occurrence in 2:4,[59] and in Isaiah six occurrences of the verb and one of the noun *šûḇâ* in chs. 1–39.[60] All these eighth-century examples are Qal with the sense "return," and they include the phrase "to God" in each occurrence.

In the Pentateuch and the Former Prophets there are only twenty-four instances of the covenantal use of *šûḇ*.[61] In the non-Deuteronomistic passages there are seven instances which exhibit the idiom *šûḇ mē'aḥªrê* plus God, in the speeches of Moses and others. In the Deuteronomistic passages there are seventeen instances of the covenantal use of *šûḇ* in Deuteronomy and thirteen in the historical books Joshua, 1 Samuel, 1 and 2 Kings. In every case the verb form is Qal, although there is variety in the use with Israel as subject fifteen times and God as subject twice.

It will be helpful to review the categories of Holladay[62] before we discuss the case of Jeremiah, where there is a remarkable change in the usage from the period before Jeremiah. Holladay recognizes eight clear categories in which the various nuances of *šûḇ* are used with some sense of "turn," "turn to" or "turn from" Yahweh, "turn to" or "turn from" evil, "turn back to" or "turn back from" Yahweh or evil, etc. In outline the categories are:

(a) "Change one's loyalty," subject Israel, e.g., Jer. 4:1: "If you turn (change your loyalty), O Israel, return to me."

(b) "Return" (to God), often "repent," subject generally Israel. There are sixty-two examples, many of which include a prepositional phrase with *'el, ʿad, ʿal,* or *lᵉ*.[63]

(c) "Turn back" (from evil), i.e., "repent" from evil, subject Israel. There are thirty-eight instances, mostly with the preposition *min*.[64]

(d) "Withdraw" (from following God), "become apostate," subject Israel. There are ten instances only one of which occurs in Jeremiah, at 3:19.

(e) "Turn back" (from good, the covenant, etc., to evil), "become apostate," subject Israel. There are eleven occurrences, of which

58. *Ibid.*, pp. 120–24.
59. *Ibid.*, p. 125.
60. *Ibid.*, pp. 124f.
61. *Ibid.*, p. 126.
62. *Ibid.*, pp. 78–81.
63. *Ibid.*, p. 79. In Jeremiah we have 3:1, 7, 10; 4:1; 24:7 with a preposition, and 3:12, 14, 22; 5:3; 8:4, 5; 15:19; 34:15 without a preposition.
64. *Ibid.*, p. 80. The instances in the book of Jeremiah are 15:7; 18:8, 11; 23:14; 25:5; 26:3; 35:15; 36:3, 7; 44:5.

Jeremiah has four in 8:4, 6; 11:10; 34:16. The prepositions vary. In 11:10 it is *'al,* in 8:6 it is b^e (an unusual passage).

(f) "Change relationship within the covenant," subject God. There are no examples in Jeremiah.

(g) "Return" (to Israel), subject God. There are no examples in Jeremiah.

(h) "Withdraw" (from Israel), subject God. There are only two instances, one of which is at 32:40, "And I shall make with them an everlasting covenant in which I shall not withdraw from them."

(i) Uncertain. In 31:19 there is an expression "For after I returned (or turned back), I repented."

When we come to the question of how and where these various nuances appear in Jeremiah we are confronted at once with the question of the various types of material in Jeremiah. Taking Mowinckel's types as a useful guide without necessarily being committed to Mowinckel's view completely, we should ask how the root *šûḇ* is used in each of the Types A (poetic passages), B (biographical passages), and C (Deuteronomistic passages). In the biographical material the covenantal use of *šûḇ* is rare, so it is basically a question of the distribution of the root in its covenantal use among the poetic segments and the Deuteronomistic prose material.

Of the forty-eight instances of covenantal *šûḇ* there is wide agreement as to how twenty-nine of these should be assigned: to Jeremiah twenty instances[65] and to the Deuteronomist nine.[66] The other nineteen instances are variously distributed by scholars.[67] Holladay's own view is that twenty-four of the occurrences belong to Jeremiah, nineteen to the Deuteronomist, and five are uncertain.[68] His general conclusion is that both Jeremiah and the Deuteronomist display variety of usage with the covenantal *šûḇ*. In general, God is not the subject of the Qal (none in Jeremiah, one in the Deuteronomist). The Deuteronomist is dependent on Jeremiah for many special uses. But there are striking differences between the two in their treatment of covenantal *šûḇ*. The imperatives in Jeremiah are all of the type "repent" (3:12, 14, 22), while the im-

65. 2:19; 3:1, 19, 22 (three); 4:1 (twice); 5:3, 6; 8:4 (twice), 5 (three), 6; 15:7, 19 (twice); 23:14.

66. 11:10; 18:8, 11; 25:5; 32:40; 34:15, 16; 35:15; 44:5.

67. 3:7 (twice), 10, 12 (twice), 14 (twice); 14:7; 23:22; 24:7; 26:3; 31:19, 22; 36:3, 7; 44:4.

68. W. L. Holladay, *The Root šûbh in the OT,* pp. 139f.

peratives of the Deuteronomist are of the type "turn from evil" (18:11; 25:5; 35:15).

Jeremiah is fond of the type (b), "return" (to God), but of the twelve instances seven are without the preposition whereas the Deuteronomist uses the type five times only and only once without the preposition.[69] On the other hand Jeremiah uses type (c) only twice while the Deuteronomist uses it eleven times.[70] Of other types[71] the occurrences are not frequent except for the nouns.[72] Jeremiah uses the noun *m^e^šûḇâ* with Israel in 3:12, without Israel in 8:5, and in the plural with personal suffixes in 2:19; 3:22; 5:6. The Deuteronomist uses this noun with Israel in 3:6, 8, 11. Only Jeremiah uses *šôḇāḇ* in 3:14, 22.

There are a number of what Holladay calls miscellaneous occurrences which he does not classify.[73]

There is no doubt, therefore, about the considerable use of the root *šwb* in the book of Jeremiah, whatever conclusions one may come to about the areas in which the various usages occur. The main emphasis seems to lie with the ideas of "return" (to God), "repent," and "turn back" or "repent" from evil. In many ways the root *šûḇ* embodies the germ of Jeremiah's message. He employed the verb in several original ways and was the conscious master of it, able to use its varied nuances skillfully to make his point. It is arguable that the Deuteronomistic tradition followed the lead of Jeremiah but with its own particular emphasis. Holladay argues that the Deuteronomistic material in the book of Jeremiah is not in all respects identical with that outside Jeremiah, and asserts that the Deuteronomist in Jeremiah was no innovator but given rather to stereotyped expression and completely lacking the originality of Jeremiah.[74]

One way or another, it would seem that the influence of the

69. Jeremiah, with the prepositional phrase, 3:1; 4:1; without the prepositional phrase, 3:12, 14, 22; 5:3; 8:4, 5; 15:19; imperative, 3:12, 14, 22; the Deuteronomist, with the prepositional phrase, 3:7, 10; 24:7; with a prepositional phrase nearby, 3:7; without the preposition phrase, 34:15. See Holladay, *ibid.,* p. 137.
70. Jeremiah, with *'îš*, 23:14; without *'îš*, 15:17; Deuteronomist, with *'îš*, 18:11; 25:5; 26:3; 35:15; 36:3, 7; without *'îš*, 18:8; 44:5; and three imperatives, 18:11; 25:5; 35:15.
71. Jeremiah uses (d) in 3:19; (e) in 8:4, 5; Hiphil in 15:19, and Polel in 8:5; the Deuteronomist uses (e) in 11:10; 34:16; (h) in 32:40.
72. For nouns see W. L. Holladay, *The Root šûbh in the OT,* p. 138.
73. See *ibid.,* pp. 139f.
74. See *ibid.,* pp. 152ff. for a valuable discussion about the two areas in Jeremiah. The whole character of these so-called Deuteronomistic passages is, of course, in question. See above under "The Book of Jeremiah: Composition," pp. 33–50.

book of Jeremiah passed on to the prophet Ezekiel, although he made use largely of type (c), "turn back from evil," and type (e), "turn back from righteousness."[75] But the expressions are used in an unoriginal and monotonous fashion. The covenantal use of *šûḇ* occurs also in other exilic and postexilic literature, but there was never to be such a flowering of its use as there was at the hands of Jeremiah.

G. THE DEBT OF JEREMIAH TO HOSEA

A succession of commentators over the years has recognized the close relation between Jeremiah and Hosea. The resemblance between the two prophets appears not only in the use of language and figures but extends to fundamental ideas on God and his relation to Israel. We may conjecture how this came about. Hosea was a prophet of Northern Israel. Anathoth, the birthplace of Jeremiah, lay north of Jerusalem and not very far from the southern border of Israel. Moreover, Jeremiah's family was probably descended from Eli, the priest of Shiloh.[76] There were thus both family and geographical links to the north, and Hosea, the finest flower of North Israelite piety, may well have played a significant part in his early training. Either his father or some godly teachers conveyed to Jeremiah the great traditions of Israel's faith and her unique relationship to Yahweh in the covenant, her election, and the profound obligations laid on her because of this. That tradition shines through Jeremiah's preaching.[77]

It is particularly in the oracles recorded in chs. 2 and 3 of Jeremiah that we become aware of links with Hosea both as to vocabulary and also in regard to ideas.

One of Hosea's great words was *ḥeseḏ,* "loyalty," "faithfulness." It was Yahweh's complaint against Israel that there was no *faithfulness (ḥeseḏ)* in the land (Hos. 4:1). He desired "steadfast love" (*ḥeseḏ*) more than sacrifice (Hos. 6:6), but alas, Israel's "love" (*ḥeseḏ*) was like a cloud that vanishes early (Hos. 6:4). She needed to sow righteousness and reap the fruit of "steadfast love" (Hos. 10:12) and hold fast to "loyalty" (Hos. 12:6). In days of restoration

75. *Ibid.,* pp. 139f.
76. See p. 95.
77. The remark in 28:8 is witness to Jeremiah's debt to the prophets of the past. Even those who would regard ch. 28 as the composition of Deuteronomic editors do not deny the basic historicity of the story.

Yahweh would betroth her again to himself in "faithfulness" (*ḥesed*, Hos. 2:21 [Eng. 19]). Jeremiah spoke of the happy days when Israel first followed Yahweh into the wilderness, into a land not sown, and recalled the "devotion" (*ḥesed*) of her youth, her love as a bride (2:2). For both Jeremiah and Hosea the days of Israel's faithfulness were during the period of settlement in the land. Yahweh would one day take his people back to the wilderness to woo them all over again (Hos. 2:16, 17 [Eng. 14, 15]). Yahweh's own faithfulness is referred to in the liturgical refrain in Jer. 32:18 and 33:11 and in the threat of 16:5 and the wisdom saying of 9:24.

The picture in 3:1–5, 20 of Israel as an unfaithful wife who had turned away to lovers is strongly reminiscent of Hosea's favorite figure of the relation between himself and his wife Gomer, which was an illustration of the relation between Yahweh and Israel. Jeremiah asked whether it was proper that a man who had divorced his wife who had left him for another man should take her back. Israel had gone after many lovers (cf. Hos. 2:4–7 [Eng. 2–5]). One needed only to look around at the heights to see altars set up for strange gods (3:2). Israel had the forehead of a "harlot" (*zônâ*), had "played the harlot" (*zānâ*) with many lovers. These same terms "play the harlot" (*zānâ*), "harlot" (*zônâ*), and "harlotry" (*z^e^nûnîm*) occur in both Jeremiah and Hosea.[78]

Even in such circumstances the people continued to call Yahweh "my husband"[78a] and "the friend of my youth." It was an odd way of thinking for Israel to follow. There seemed no incompatibility in their thinking of Yahweh as the friend of their youth while at the same time recognizing other gods. And like Hosea's wife, Israel felt she could change her allegiance at will (Hos. 2:9 [Eng. 7]). Both Jeremiah and Hosea understood that the covenant demanded complete unshared allegiance to Yahweh. Hosea taught that Gomer his wife owed everything to his own love (Hos. 2:10 [Eng. 8]). Jeremiah taught the same truth (2:4–8, 13). Both Hosea and Jeremiah were persistent in their appeals to Israel to repent. It is possible that Jeremiah's expression in 4:3:

> "Break up your fallow ground
> And sow not among thorns"

78. *Zônâ*, "harlot," in 2:20; 3:3; 5:7; *z^e^nûṯ*, "harlotry," in 3:2, 9; 13:27; *zānâ*, "You have played the harlot" in 3:1; cf. *z^e^nûnîm*, "harlotry," Hos. 1:2; 2:6 (Eng. 4); 4:12; 5:4; *zānâ*, "she played the harlot," Hos. 2:7 (Eng. 5).

78a. The word *'āḇî*, "my father," may denote "my husband" in some cases. See A. C. Welch, *Jeremiah: His Time and His Work* (1955), p. 59, n. 3.

is a quotation from Hos. 10:12. In both cases the expression, which may have been a well-known saying, is applied in an appeal to seek Yahweh, although with Hosea the appeal leads on to a promise of Yahweh's salvation and with Jeremiah a warning of impending judgment. But as a general statement, Jeremiah, like Hosea, coupled with his bitter censure of Israel many moving pleas to repentance (e.g., 3:19–4:2). In the commentary that follows it will become evident that there lay in Jeremiah's mind right to the end the hope that his people might repent of their evil ways (e.g., 38:17–23).

Jeremiah used the metaphor of "son" for Israel. It was in Yahweh's mind to treat Israel as a son (3:19) and having redeemed him from Egypt to give him a pleasant land and a beautiful heritage. The figure has a parallel in Hos. 11:1. When Israel was a child (*na'ar*) Yahweh loved him, called him from Egypt, and nurtured him despite his rebellious ways. Jeremiah's development of the theme is essentially the same. Yahweh had hoped that Israel would call him "My Father," but as a faithless wife deserts her husband so Israel proved faithless. Jeremiah combined the metaphors of son and wife in 3:19, 20, 22 (cf. 4:22).

Another idea that Jeremiah held in common with Hosea was the "knowledge of God." It was Hosea's complaint that there was no knowledge of God (*da'aṯ 'ᵉlōhîm*) in the land (Hos. 4:1) and that Yahweh's people were destroyed because of lack of knowledge (Hos. 4:6). Jeremiah likewise complained on Yahweh's behalf, "Those who handle the law do not know (*yāḏa'*) me" (2:8). Again, "My people are foolish, they do not know me, they are stupid children, they have no understanding" (4:22). To "know" Yahweh was to be committed to him with a profound personal commitment which touched the whole of one's life. In the days of the New Covenant "all will know me from the least to the greatest" (31:34). Hosea likewise envisaged a day when Yahweh would betroth his people to himself in faithfulness and they would "know" him (Hos. 2:22 [Eng. 20]).

The picture of Yahweh's controversy (*rîḇ*) against Israel appears in Hos. 4:1–3. The covenant lawsuit is a well-known feature in the OT.[79] Hosea pictured Israel as being called upon to answer Yahweh in the matter of certain failures on her part to observe the demands of the covenant, and names lack of "faithfulness" (*'ᵉmeṯ*),

79. See above under "Jeremiah and the Covenant," pp. 59–67.

"loyalty" (*ḥeseḏ*), and "knowledge of God" (*da'aṯ *'*ᵉlōhîm*). Jeremiah too uses the term (*rîḇ*), though sometimes in a slightly different sense. Yahweh had a lawsuit against the nations (25:31). Jeremiah under great pressure from his foes committed his own case (*rîḇ*) to Yahweh (11:20; 20:12; cf. 50:34; 51:36). But even if the formal expression is not used it is clear that Jeremiah was laying a charge against Israel throughout his ministry (15:10) and issuing a threat of judgment against them in which the land itself would share (cf. Hos. 4:1–3). Hosea spoke in particular about Yahweh's lawsuit against the priests (Hos. 4:4–10). Jeremiah, too, had strong things to say against the priests (2:8, 26–27; 4:9; 5:31; 13:13; etc.).

Both Hosea and Jeremiah express wonderment that Israel could have turned aside from Yahweh in the face of all he had done for them. According to Hosea, no sooner had Israel reached the land, the home that Yahweh had prepared for his bride, and there discovered that love meant loyalty, than she rebelled (Hos. 2:7–10 [Eng. 5–8]; 9:10). It was a puzzle to Yahweh to know what to do with his people whose loyalty was no more substantial than the morning cloud (Hos. 6:4). Jeremiah took up the same question but took it further. To him Israel's disloyalty required an explanation, and all the more so because pagan peoples to the west and to the east were not guilty of changing their gods as Israel had done. Israel had put in place of Yahweh a helpless idol (2:10–11). The remarkable thing was that any of these peoples might have changed their gods without loss, for they were all powerless. But for Israel to desert Yahweh was to leave aside a running spring and dig a cistern which merely collected water and was prone to lose its water (2:12, 13).

Both Jeremiah and Hosea idealized the wilderness period as a time when Israel's faith was uncontaminated by the corrupting influence of Canaanite Baalism (2:1–3; Hos. 9:10; 11:1). It was the enormity of Israel's declension from that former state of bliss to her present squalid state that provoked wonderment in the two prophets. Such apostasy could not but affect the very foundations of family morality (Hos. 4:14). Jeremiah, like his predecessor, emphasized the essential incongruity between the inherent sensuousness of this false worship and the ethical motives of love, trust, and gratitude which a right relation with Yahweh demanded and produced. And the tragic thing was that Baalism was empty and unreal (2:5, 11, 13; Hos. 9:10).

Both Jeremiah and Hosea struck a strong note of repentance. Three passages in Jeremiah, 3:22–25; 14:7–10; and 14:19–22, represent "confessions of sin" of the type Jeremiah believed the people should make. Israel is pictured as confessing to Yahweh that the hills were a delusion and that the salvation of Israel was to be found only in Yahweh; that their iniquities testified against them and that Yahweh alone was the hope of Israel and her savior in a time of trouble; and asking Yahweh why he had rejected them. They acknowledged their wickedness and asked him not to break his covenant. Such confessions are strongly reminiscent of Hos. 6:1–3 and 14:2–3 where Israel is pictured as saying "come, let us return to Yahweh," confessing that "Assyria would not save them," and asking Yahweh to take away their iniquity.

There are further points of comparison (or contrast) between Jeremiah and Hosea. Thus, in respect to marriage, Hosea's tragic marriage became symbolic of the relationship between Yahweh and Israel. It was a marriage that was commanded by Yahweh (Hos. 1:2). But, by contrast, Jeremiah was commanded *not* to marry (16:1–2). His enforced celibacy was also symbolic.[80] It would be too much to claim that Jeremiah's celibacy was in any way related to what he knew of Hosea, although, if he knew Hosea's life and teaching so well, he can hardly have been unaware of his predecessor's tragedy and of its significance. In the matter of symbolic actions, however, there was a long tradition of these in national history, so that his own actions may have been carried out quite independently of anything he learned from Hosea.

On the other hand the Decalog-type list of offenses in Hos. 4:2, "swearing, lying, killing, stealing, committing adultery, murder," has a strange resemblance to Jeremiah's list of offenses in the Temple Sermon: stealing, murder, committing adultery, false witness (7:9).

The present discussion is not exhaustive but only suggestive. The subject has been studied in some depth by K. Goss.[81] It is difficult to avoid the conclusion that Hosea exercised a considerable influence on Jeremiah both in the area of specialized vocabulary and also in the realm of ideas.

80. See under "Symbolic Actions in Jeremiah," pp. 71–76.
81. K. Goss, *Die literarische Verwandschaft Jeremias mit Hosea* (diss., Berlin, 1930); *idem,* "Hoseas Einfluss auf Jeremias Anschauungen," *Neue Kirkliche Zeitschrift* 42 (1931), pp. 241–265, 327–343. Unfortunately these works were not available to the present writer.

H. THE FOE FROM THE NORTH

In the early chapters of Jeremiah there are several sections which refer to the coming of a foe from the north who would bring judgment on Judah, namely, 1:13–16; 4:5–8, 13–22, 27–31; 5:15–17; 6:1–8, 22–26; 8:14–17. Older commentators regarded these passages as referring to the Scythians who had come into Palestine about the time Jeremiah began to prophesy. This hypothesis was popularized by B. Duhm in 1901 but was later accepted and expounded by A. S. Peake, G. A. Smith, and T. Skinner.[82] The hypothesis was based on a statement in Herodotus[83] that after the death of Phraortes, king of the Medes, in his abortive attack on Nineveh the Assyrian capital, the Scythians dominated Western Asia for twenty-eight years. They pressed on to the very borders of Egypt, where Pharaoh Psammetichus fought them off. The argument runs that this invasion of the Palestine area must have taken place in the early years of Jeremiah's ministry. In defense of the theory is the proposal that following the death of Ashurbanipal in 627 B.C. and the struggle between two rivals to the Assyrian throne, Sin-shar-ishkun and Ashur-etil-ilani, for some years (about 622–624 B.C.) before the former finally triumphed there was a period when Assyria lost control all over the Empire. In that period the attack of the Medes in which Phraortes lost his life, and which is mentioned by Herodotus,[84] took place. The Medean attack was beaten off with the help of the Scythians. If the Scythian irruption into Western Asia took place at all, it may have taken place in the troubled years after about 625 B.C. coincident with the closing stages of Assyria's existence.[85] But the matter is too uncertain, and even Herodotus does not connect the Scythians with Judah.

But against the theory, several of the descriptions of the "foe from the north" offered in the relevant passages do not suit a wild, disorganized group such as the Scythians seem to have been. The expression "an enduring nation, an ancient nation" (5:15) would not

82. A. S. Peake, *Jeremiah* (1910–12); George Adam Smith, *Jeremiah* ([4]1929); J. Skinner, *Prophecy and Religion* (1922).
83. *Hist.* i.104–106.
84. *Hist.* i.102.
85. See R. Labat, "Kastariti, Phraorte et les débuts de l'histoire mède," *Journal Asiatique* 249 (1961), pp. 1–12, who argues that Herodotus intended to include the years of the Scythian domination of which he speaks within the reign of Cyaxares, the successor of Phraortes who was killed in 625 B.C. Cf. H. Cazelles, *RB* 74 (1967), pp. 24–44; A. Malamat, *IEJ* 1 (1950/51), pp. 154–59.

have been understood of the Scythians but it would suit the Babylonians. The mention of "chariots" (4:13), the references to siege warfare (4:16; 6:5) and to an army set in array (6:23), the description of the foe as "lovers" of Jerusalem (4:30), all suit the Babylonians but not the Scythians. Certainly in 13:20 and 25:9 the "foe from the north" is the Babylonians (cf. 46:24). There is thus great uncertainty about referring these poems in Jeremiah to Scythians at an early period in his ministry. If there was a Scythian irruption it is more likely that it took place following the collapse of Assyria. The Scythians were giving some help to Assyria at the time as they had done earlier.[86]

But in view of the considerable uncertainty it is better to abandon the Scythian proposal and regard the Babylonians as the foe from the north. This would require that these poems come from later in Jeremiah's ministry, perhaps some from well on in Josiah's reign when Babylon was already rising, and others from the reign of Jehoiakim. The chapters in which these poems lie are, in any case, composite and contain material early and late. The poems may reflect something of the terror of the Scythians and Medes as they joined in the final attack on Assyria, but it is more likely that the Babylonians were more clearly in view. This is not to rule out the possibility that some of the poems, couched as they are in fairly conventionalized imagery, may have come from early in Jeremiah's ministry when the "foe from the north" was a vague description of the agent of Yahweh's judgment when the day of Yahweh arrived. The "north" was the area from which troubles had come over the centuries. As the years passed, the vague picture took on clear definition as the Babylonians emerged.[87] There is no necessity to argue that Jeremiah as a young man became stirred up over a Scythian invasion which failed to materialize so that he suffered severe criticism and went into temporary retirement because of his error.

The viewpoint adopted in this commentary, while allowing other possibilities, is that the poetic material dealing with the foe from the north comes from a period dating late in Josiah's reign to well on in the reign of Jehoiakim, when the Babylonian menace was clearly a present threat or had even begun to be a reality.

86. This is the view of A. Malamat, *loc. cit.*
87. A. C. Welch, *Jeremiah: His Time and His Work,* pp. 97–131, expounds this view. See J. Bright, *Jeremiah,* p. xxxvii; J. P. Hyatt, "The Book of Jeremiah," *IB* V (1956), p. 229; A. S. Peake, *Jeremiah,* p. 11.

I. THE "CONFESSIONS" OF JEREMIAH

The book of Jeremiah is unique among the prophetic books because of a remarkable group of utterances which are usually referred to as the "Confessions" of Jeremiah. Broadly speaking these comprise 11:18–23; 12:1–6; 15:10–12, 15–21; 17:14–18; 18:18–23; 20:7–13, 14–18, although some scholars differ in detail. The term "confession" is probably not an apt one since the passages consist of prayers or laments, monologs, dialogs, and disputes with Yahweh. They could all be described as "Dialogs with Yahweh, Personal lyrics." In the case of three of these dialogs Yahweh's reply to Jeremiah's complaint is recorded in the latter part of the section (11:18–23; 12:1–6; 15:15–21). In each passage the reference is clearly to Jeremiah, and the pronouns "I," "me," "my" are met numerous times. To be sure there are other passages where Jeremiah speaks in the first person and gives expression to his anguish or tells his thoughts (e.g., 4:19–21; 5:3–5; 8:18–23 [Eng. 9:1]). All of these passages combine to give a remarkable picture of the personality of Jeremiah and reveal something of the inner struggles of the prophet. Perhaps these "confessions" might be expected of the kind of man Jeremiah is shown to be. His call was evidently a traumatic experience (1:4–10). His task was to be an assayer and a tester of his own people (8:18–23 [Eng. 9:1]). But he was a sensitive soul who could be deeply moved by some national disaster. He was denied a normal life by Yahweh (16:1–13). In a sense he was an unwilling prophet (1:4) and unlike some who had accepted their calling without question and with deep awe (e.g., Isa. 6:1–8). Like Moses, with whom he sensed a deep affinity, he entered into a dialog with Yahweh about his call. He was only a lad (*na'ar*). He would have Yahweh convince him that he should become a prophet. He was convinced, although he was later to say that it was under compulsion, for Yahweh was stronger than he and had prevailed over him (20:7). In this encounter Jeremiah revealed an independent spirit which was to come to the surface many times in his encounters with Yahweh and with his contemporaries.

It becomes evident also that Jeremiah was deeply conscious of his own human existence. He was very much a human being, although a sensitive one who felt deeply about the sufferings of his fellows. But he was also deeply aware of his own calling to the prophetic office. As a result his life was one of continuous tension between Jeremiah the man and Jeremiah the prophet. This led him into the kind of controversy with Yahweh that becomes clear in the so-called "confessions."

One of Jeremiah's deepest tensions was that between his natural human desires and his prophetic task. His call to be a prophet thrust him into the rough and tumble of life, not as one committed to deep and happy involvement in the affairs of men, but as one who became aware of the great sin of the nation. He was filled with a passionate spirit of condemnation so that he pronounced alarm and destruction continually. This meant that his friends shunned him and hated him. The people of his own village of Anathoth plotted against him (11:18–19). Later, the officials sought to cut short his life by putting him in a cistern (38:1–6). As a young man he might have married, but this was denied to him by Yahweh as was any participation in the joys or sorrows of village life (16:1–9). There was a grim symbolism in these unusual withdrawals from life. This made Jeremiah seem the odd man out, and he declared in one of his dialogs with Yahweh:

"I did not sit in the company of merrymakers,
Nor did I rejoice;
I sat alone, because thy hand was upon me,
For thou hadst filled me with indignation." (15:17)

This unusual behavior left Jeremiah open to ridicule, insult, and even physical assault on occasion. And for a man who loved people and craved their friendship and companionship, the prophetic office brought loneliness and deep anguish, which came to expression in such words as,

"Why is my pain unceasing,
My wound incurable,
Refusing to be healed?" (15:18a)

It was on that occasion that Jeremiah cast in Yahweh's face the accusation:

"Wilt thou become like a deceitful brook,
Like waters that fail?" (15:18b)

In other circumstances he charged Israel with forsaking Yahweh "the fountain of living waters" in favor of broken cisterns that can hold no water (2:13).

These experiences were accompanied by deep anguish, for Jeremiah felt deeply for his people. On one occasion in an hour of national disaster he mourned for the people, and was seized with dismay, and wished that his head were water and his eyes a fountain of tears so that he might weep day and night for the slain among his people (8:23 [Eng. 9:1]). He wept on other occasions too, and called upon others to mourn (9:9–10, 16–21 [Eng. 10–11, 17–22]; 10:19–21; 14:2–6).

Yahweh sometimes replied in the dialog, and on the occasion when Jeremiah charged Yahweh with being a deceitful brook (15:18) the reply to this virtually blasphemous charge was that Jeremiah was in need of repentance, for he was forsaking his prophetic calling. Only by returning to Yahweh and to his call, and by offering what was precious instead of what was worthless, could he continue to act as Yahweh's spokesman and enjoy Yahweh's protection (15:19, 20).

It was a continuing source of grief to Jeremiah that his preaching provoked such violent opposition from his enemies so that he became a laughing-stock all the day long and everyone mocked him. Yahweh's work had become for him a reproach and a derision (20:7). The prophet blamed Yahweh and charged him with seducing him. The accusation of 20:7 contains all the bitterness of a deceived man. The same verb "seduce" (see commentary) is used in Exod. 22:15 (Eng. 16) for seducing a virgin. Jeremiah saw himself as a young, inexperienced lad being enticed with promises and then being overwhelmed by one who was mightier than he (20:7a). The word of God which he preached deprived him of the normal happy relationships of life and made him an object of derision. He decided to leave his prophetic office only to find that Yahweh's word burned like a fire in his heart (20:9). Here was a terrible dilemma. He was caught between two powerful urges: the desire to be normal and win the friendship and approval of his fellows or to pursue his duty to Yahweh and lose his friends.

This brought him to the lowest point of his inner conflicts and struggles. He cursed the day of his birth, which by implication, since he was appointed to his task before birth (1:5), was tantamount to cursing his prophetic call (20:14–18; cf. 15:10). So despondent did he become on another occasion with the wickedness and dishonesty of his fellows that he could have wished to leave his fellow countrymen and escape to some wayfarer's lodge in the desert (9:1–2 [Eng. 2–3]).

His suffering at the hands of his "enemies" caused him at times to call upon God to visit them with vengeance (11:20; 12:3; 15:15; 17:18), and on one occasion he asked God to deliver up their children to famine and give his foes over to the sword so that their wives might become childless and widowed. It was a grim cry from a man in deep despair (18:21–23). All that can be said in the prophet's favor is that he had become so identified with the cause of Yahweh that he saw in his own enemies the enemies of Yahweh. It was not Jeremiah's words that were being rejected but the words of Yahweh. And yet, he prayed for his enemies and sought their welfare (15:11; 18:20).

There were evidently times when the prophet found joy in his task. On one occasion he spoke of how he found Yahweh's words and ate them and found them to be a joy and a delight to his heart (15:16). There were times too when he knew Yahweh was his deliverer, a strong warrior who caused his persecutors to stumble (20:11). These times of joy and confidence stood in sharp contrast to times of deep heart-searching and a sense of having been abandoned by Yahweh.

It was not easy to determine when the dialogs and monologs which are the subject of this section were produced. It is most unlikely that they were declared publicly. They may have been revealed to Baruch or to some intimate friends or even committed to writing. Most of them would seem to reflect the severe tensions of the prophet's life in the days of Jehoiakim. On one theory, after an initial period of preaching followed by persecution and rejection, Jeremiah passed through a period of comparative silence during which he gave expression to the "confessions" of 11:18–23; 12:1–3, 4–6. Following the traumatic experience at Anathoth when he was still a young man (11:19), when his own family and friends turned against him, he debated the matter with Yahweh. The three passages here referred to may represent three independent utterances. In the years that followed, Josiah's reforms took root and Jeremiah seems to have had little to say.

With the death of Josiah and the advent of Jehoiakim to the throne, things in Judah returned to the pre-reformation standards in religion and social practice. Jeremiah began to preach again. This resulted in oracles such as those declared in the Hinnom Valley and in the temple court (19:1–13, 14–15). Pashhur, the priest-overseer of the temple, had him whipped and put in stocks (20:2). On this sorrowful occasion Jeremiah gave expression to his feelings in 20:7–9 and 20:14–18. Possibly 17:14–18 belongs here also. Thereafter the antagonists of Jeremiah "watched for a slip" (20:10). They found their opportunity at the delivery of the Temple Sermon (7:1–15; 26:2–6). Jeremiah was seized and brought before the king's ministers, and only the support of Ahikam ben Shaphan prevented his death (26:24). To this period may belong the two utterances in 20:10–13 and 18:18–23. Jeremiah was forbidden to speak, and embarked on a second period of silence which lasted till the fourth or fifth year of Jehoiakim. The dialog of 15:15–21, comprising the complaint of Jeremiah (vv. 15–18) and the answer of Yahweh (vv. 19–21), probably took place at this time. Perhaps also at this time the prophet uttered 15:10–11 and received the reply in 15:13–14, but later rather than earlier in the period.

With the death of Jehoiakim in 598 B.C. Jeremiah saw clearly that the die was cast for Judah, and he entered upon his final period of preaching, evidently no longer doubting his call, although continuing a sensitive soul to the end.

Such a reconstruction is necessarily conjectural but it may provide a setting in which to study these remarkable monologs and dialogs.

J. THE "SEDITIOUS" UTTERANCES OF JEREMIAH

In a number of passages in the book, Jeremiah appears to be speaking in a manner so different from the authorities that his words might appear to point to his being seditious. These utterances seem to have been particularly common during the last days of Judah.

The events of 598/7 B.C., which included the surrender of Jerusalem to Nebuchadrezzar and the deportation of the king and the leading citizens, seemed to be a vindication of Jeremiah's predictions of judgment. But the citizens who remained did not understand the warning. After all, the city had been spared and a king of David's line was on the throne. Loyalty seemed to require the people of Judah to continue their struggle for independence. The hope of a coalition with other nations who opposed Babylon was always present. But the policy was a foolhardy one even though it may have been based on some strongly held theological concepts, chiefly a belief in the inviolability of Zion, the temple, and the Davidic kingship.

Jeremiah saw the truth more deeply than the national leaders, whom he regarded as bad figs (ch. 24). While not denying the validity of the divine promises to David, he did not expect these to be fulfilled in Zedekiah (23:5–6) and he did not anticipate that the deported Jehoiachin and his sons would ever sit on the throne of Judah again (22:24–30). The enthusiastic promises of contemporary prophets that the exile would be over in two years (28:2–4) was to be rejected out of hand. Not two years, but seventy years (25:11, 12). The attempt to form a coalition with neighboring kings of Edom, Moab, Ammon, Tyre, and Sidon in 594/3 B.C. (27:3) and the activities of nationalistic prophets in Babylon (29:20, 21) seemed to Jeremiah to be both foolhardy and contrary to the will of God. He strongly opposed all such talk. Putting an ox-yoke on his neck, he appeared in public to tell the visiting ambassadors to return to their rulers with a warning that they must all wear the yoke of Nebuchadrezzar or suffer destruction (27:2–11). He spoke in the same terms to King Zedekiah (27:12–15), and repeated the warning in the temple precincts (27:16–22). At the same time he wrote to the exiles already in Babylon urging them to disregard the prophets who held out to them empty promises (29:1–14, 22–23). It was talk such as this that seemed to the people of Jerusalem seditious. He was suspected of being in league with the Babylonian army itself (37:11–15). Such accusations were groundless since Jeremiah spoke also about the doom of Babylon (51:59–64). Nor would it be correct merely to say that Jeremiah was a pragmatist who saw that in the circumstances of the time surrender to Babylon was the best policy to follow in the hope that present troubles would soon be past. The prophet's conviction was much deeper. Judah stood in danger of divine judgment which became inevitable as the years went by even if there may have been some hope of repentance earlier. In the execution of his purposes of judgment Yahweh the Creator and Lord of the whole earth had chosen to give the earth into the hands of Nebuchadrezzar. To resist Nebuchadrezzar was, therefore, to resist Yahweh (27:5–8). One might even say that Jeremiah was the most loyal nationalist of them all since Judah's national existence depended on her adherence to her covenant with Yahweh. Strong nationhood was based on deep national and personal commitment to Yahweh, and in a sense nationalistic considerations far from being of secondary importance were of prime importance. Yet, to his contemporaries who did not have Jeremiah's penetrating understanding of the true character of nationhood, the prophet seemed to be a traitor and a seditious, anti-nationalist individual. Despite discouragement Jeremiah persevered to the last in his insistence that the only thing to do was to acknowledge Yahweh's hand of judgment in the activities of Nebuchadrezzar and to surrender to him. Soon after the Babylonian attack began and before the siege of the city became effective, Jeremiah urged Zedekiah the king to surrender (21:1–7). Indeed Yahweh himself was fighting with the Babylonians against Judah. Jeremiah's advice on each occasion of his meeting with the king was that he should surrender (34:1–7).

Even when the siege was lifted temporarily Jeremiah warned the king that it would be resumed, and even if the Babylonian army consisted only of wounded men they would capture the city (37:3–10). When some of the people who had released slaves brought these slaves back into bondage when the siege was lifted, Jeremiah castigated them severely (34:8–22) and declared their final doom. So convinced was Jeremiah of the outcome that he advised people to desert and surrender to the Babylonians (21:8–10). As the situation deteriorated, many of them did so (38:19; 39:9). Little wonder that the people looked on Jeremiah as a defeatist and a traitor. On their part they were convinced nationalists and no doubt felt that their course of action was for the best. But in the event Jeremiah was right. Judah was overwhelmed, Jerusalem and the temple were destroyed, and Zedekiah had his eyes taken out and was taken into exile. Given the choice of going to Babylon or remaining in the land, Jeremiah opted to remain (40:1–6). He had no love for the Babylonians, he was no collaborator and had no sympathy for the Babylonian cause as many of his fellow-countrymen believed (28:2–4; cf. 32:3–5). Nor was he a coward, for he did not run away from the city but was there when it fell. His sole motivation in speaking as he did was that he had received Yahweh's word and was convinced that the Babylonians were the instrument of Yahweh's judgment upon Judah for her breach of covenant. Yahweh had spoken. He could but warn them that to resist the Babylonians was to resist Yahweh and to be destroyed.

V. THE LIFE OF JEREMIAH

Jeremiah is unique among the prophets of the OT in several respects. We know far more about his life than we do about the life of any other prophet, although this does not mean that we are in a position to write anything approaching a full biography. We also know far more about the personal feelings of Jeremiah than we do for any other prophet. Others delivered their oracles without disclosing much of their inner selves, whereas Jeremiah laid bare the emotional conflicts of a man who was chosen to be a spokesman for God to his own generation but very much against his personal inclinations. He suffered both physically and emotionally probably more than any other prophet. He spent a night in the stocks and several periods in cisterns and prisons of various sorts. He experienced a plot against his life by the people of his own village. In addition he suffered the ostracism and misunderstanding of priests, prophets, officials, and ordinary people over many years.

And yet, despite the fact that we know so much about Jeremiah, we know very little about his career before the year 609 B.C.; and although there are valuable chronological notes for the years after that date, a lot of his oracles are undated. As a result of this there are numerous areas of uncertainty and disagreement, especially in details. We can, however, attempt a general reconstruction of his career on the understanding that we may be in error in a number of places.

He was born into a priestly family at Anathoth some 3 miles northeast of Jerusalem. His father was a certain Hilkiah, and though proof is lacking, may have been descended from the line of Abiathar, one of David's priests who fell into disfavor in Solomon's day (1 K. 2:26f.).[1] Abiathar himself was a descendant of Eli (cf. 1 Sam. 14:3; 22:20; 1 K. 2:27), who cared for the Ark at Shiloh in the days before the monarchy. It is possible that the interest of Jeremiah in the shrine at Shiloh and its fate (7:14; 26:6) stems from this ancient family connection with that town.

The date of Jeremiah's birth is a matter of dispute[2] simply because of a certain obscurity attaching to the enigmatic words in 1:2, "in the thirteenth year" of the reign of Josiah, which is given as the date of his call. Josiah began his reign in 640 B.C. so that the thirteenth year of his reign was 627 B.C. In the opinion of most scholars this is the date when Jeremiah, described as a youth (*na'ar*), began his public ministry. Assuming he was then sixteen to eighteen years of age, his birth would have been just before 640 B.C.,[3] that is, just at the close of the reign of the notorious Manasseh (687/6–642 B.C.). The precise date depends on how old the "youth" (1:6) was, but we shall assume this date in the commentary while recognizing the alternative view that the "thirteenth" year may represent the date of his call at birth (1:5).

We are in complete ignorance about Jeremiah's childhood, but in view of his later ministry we may conjecture that he was carefully trained in the great traditions of Israel's faith and history.

1. See the commentary at 1:1.
2. See "The Date of Jeremiah's Call," pp. 50–56.
3. In the course of this brief outline we shall attempt to indicate the approximate age of Jeremiah at each stage of his career, and propose to base these ages on the assumption that in 627 B.C. he was 17 years old.

There is no evidence that the boy was trained for the priesthood or that he ever functioned as a priest. Yet he probably became aware of priestly duties quite early, for he knew about the responsibilities of priests in the matter of the law and the flagrant way they neglected them (2:8). Indeed, so far from interpreting the obligations of the covenantal relationship for the people, the priests had supported the pagan worship which flourished under Manasseh and Amon (cf. 2 K. 21:1–22). Small wonder that Jeremiah held them to be largely responsible for the spiritual decay of Judah.

But there were other influences on the boy's life. He seems to have become familiar with many of the great stories of the past and to have been introduced to the sayings of earlier prophets, notably Hosea, who greatly influenced his early preaching in particular, both in language and thought.[4] In addition to his training we must recognize his own sensitive nature and early response to Yahweh. With such a traditional and conservative background he must have begun to form convictions at an early age about the pagan practices which he found all around him and even in the temple itself. When the call of Yahweh came to him, it came to one in whose heart there were already many thoughts about many things. It came as seed into ground prepared.

Jeremiah, like Isaiah and Ezekiel and others, entered upon his work following a definite experience of a call (1:4–10). This was in the year 627 B.C., a very significant year in the ancient Near East. Ashurbanipal (668–627 B.C.) died after a long reign and the collapse of Assyria began at once. By 609 Assyria was to have vanished for ever. Nabopolassar the Chaldean prince seized Babylon from the Assyrians in 626 and could not be dislodged. Assyria's successor was already in place and in less than twenty years was to occupy Assyrian domains as far as the borders of Egypt.

Like Moses, Jeremiah sought to escape from Yahweh's call, arguing that he was too young. He may have had other reasons to balk at the call. Perhaps he sensed the cost such a calling might involve. Only the assurance of divine aid (1:17–19) made him accept the call. Somehow it was inescapable, and in later years he was to describe Yahweh's powerful hand prevailing over him (20:7). Despite his unease and his unwillingness, Yahweh placed his word in Jeremiah's mouth and he went out to declare it as long as he lived, to the accompaniment of great agony of soul. He seems to have had

4. See above, "The Debt of Jeremiah to Hosea," pp. 81–85.

a continuing conviction that his people and his land were marked down for judgment. The anguished cry of his confession in 20:7–18, although it came somewhat later, gives a clue to the burden of his ministry, and the vision of 1:11–16, though this too may be a later experience, warned him of the terrible foe from the north that would bring judgment on Jerusalem.

As a young man following the custom of his day he should have married, but did not because of a divine constraint upon him (16:1–4). His failure to marry was a symbolic action, for it pointed to days when parents would be bereft of children and old people would have no one to bury them at death. He likewise eschewed the joyous experiences of the life of a young man and even cut himself off from sharing in the sorrows of his village people at the death of a loved one (16:5–9). Both attitudes were symbolic actions which pointed to the cutting off of happiness and joy from the land and the dark days ahead when men would not have opportunity to enter into their griefs adequately, if at all.

In Jeremiah's very early days as a preacher, Manasseh's evil influence was still being felt and Josiah's reforms had hardly begun. The youthful preacher spoke vividly about the paganism, the apostasy, and the sheer ingratitude of the people to Yahweh. We probably have examples of his early preaching in ch. 2[5] and 3:1–4:1. Jeremiah was appalled at the prevailing apostasy. The bitter attack in these chapters on the nation's "harlotry" and its worship of pagan gods, especially the Canaanite god Baal, would suit these early years. Along with his attack on apostasy the prophet made an impassioned appeal to the people to turn again to Yahweh (3:12–13, 19–22; 4:1–9). One of Jeremiah's deep concerns in these years was the gross ingratitude of the people, the like of which was unknown among the pagan nations (2:4–13) and was contrary to nature (cf. 5:20–25; 18:13–17). Judah had pursued these strange gods with the burning passion of a wild ass in heat (2:23–25). The nation was stained so deeply that nothing could erase the stain (2:20–22). None of her handmade idols (2:26–28) nor her political alignments could save her (2:18–19). Judah was an adulterous wife who had betrayed her husband again and again but counted on his forgiveness (3:1–5).[6] Indeed, Yahweh would forgive if Israel turned back to him

5. The present form of ch. 2 comes from Jehoiakim's reign so that it probably contains a range of oracles from 627 to 609 B.C.

6. The idea may have come from Hosea. See above, "The Debt of Jeremiah to Hosea," pp. 81–85.

(3:19–4:2). In that case, once truth, justice, and uprightness were restored the nations would bless themselves in Israel (4:2; cf. Gen. 18:18; etc.). We almost sense in the promise of 3:12ff., evidently addressed to Northern Israel, that Josiah had already begun to press his initial reform program in the north, which had been under Assyria since 721 B.C. (cf. 31:2–6, 15–22).

During these years Josiah's reform pressed ahead. It began when the king was in the twelfth year of his reign, that is, about 629/8 B.C. (2 Chr. 34:3–4). What Jeremiah's attitude was to the reform is by no means clear.[7] He could hardly not approve of official measures which brought an end to pagan cult centers and undertook important measures in the administration of justice, although it would seem unlikely that he took any particular part in the reform. It was in any case initiated by royal decree and presumably executed by state officials, so that in a sense Jeremiah was not called upon to do anything at all. But it seems reasonable to assume that though he was not in favor of everything the king did, he could support his general aims. He certainly held Josiah in high esteem (22:15–16). Such reservations as he may have had lay not so much in his opposition to the reform, but in his insistence that such superficial and external measures did not touch the area of personal commitment to Yahweh and his covenant.

The climax to the reform came with the finding of the "Book of the Covenant" in 622 B.C. when Jeremiah was about twenty-two years old. That Jeremiah did not criticize the reform and make himself thereby an enemy of the king and his supporters is suggested by the fact that in later years it was the men who assisted in carrying the reform through and their sons, men like Ahikam ben Shaphan (26:24), Gemariah ben Shaphan, Elnathan ben Achbor (ch. 36), who protected the prophet. It was true, however, that Jeremiah insisted that external practice is no substitute for inward obedience. We are completely in the dark about Jeremiah's ministry over the years 622–609 B.C., that is, for the latter part of Josiah's reign. No dated oracles from these years have been preserved, although there may be material here and there in the book which fills in the gap. We next hear of Jeremiah at the beginning of the reign of Jehoiakim (26:1). The tragic death of Josiah at Megiddo in 609 B.C., and the quick removal of his son Jehoahaz (Shallum) to Egypt by Pharaoh Necho, brought Jehoiakim to the throne. Jeremiah was then thirty-five years old. Some

7. See above, "Jeremiah and the Covenant," pp. 59–67.

have argued for a period of silence when Jeremiah ceased preaching after the busy years of his early ministry.[8] The prose tradition of Jeremiah (25:3) suggests that he had preached persistently to the people for twenty-three years; and the narrative about the writing of the scroll suggests that Jeremiah had preached "from the days of Josiah until now," that is, the fourth year of Jehoiakim (605 B.C.). It is possible that during those years Jeremiah spoke much about the failure of the nation to fulfil the high hopes of the reform. The flagrant violations of covenant law against which Jeremiah inveighed in the Temple Sermon (7:2–15) did not develop overnight. The short message in 3:6–10 dated in the days of Josiah may refer to the post-reform years, and if so, the picture is a sad one. One wonders whether, with the rise of Babylon at this time, Jeremiah's vision of 1:11–16 should not be dated to this period and perhaps also some of the passages dealing with the "foe from the north" in chs. 4–6, although most of these are best understood as coming from the days of Jehoiakim.

But with the evident collapse of the reform it would be out of character for Jeremiah to remain silent before such irregularities.

With the Temple Sermon we begin to obtain clear information about Jeremiah, and from 609 to 587 B.C. or a little after, we have a good deal of information. It is clear from the Temple Sermon that whatever good effects the reform of Josiah may have had in the beginning, their results were temporary. As the years passed the reform was largely forgotten, and it would appear from 2:16 that the calamity brought about by "the men of Memphis and Tahpanhes" (Egypt) had been brought about by Judah herself, who had forsaken Yahweh.

The immediate background to the Temple Sermon was the state of the nation under the willful, selfish, and arrogant young king Jehoiakim, who abandoned the reforms of his father Josiah and permitted a return to the paganism of his great-grandfather Manasseh. Non-Yahwistic cults and their religious practices reappeared in the land (7:6, 9, 16–20) along with all kinds of social ills. The king himself built a grand palace thinking to gain prestige thereby. Lacking the public funds to pay for it because of heavy tribute payable to Egypt (2 K. 23:33, 35), he undertook his building program by forced labor. Jeremiah summed up the king's misdeeds in a trenchant crit-

8. See above, "The Date of Jeremiah's Call," pp. 50–56.

icism of him (22:13–19), and foretold a shameful death for him and a donkey's burial. His outlook became evident early in his reign, and already in his accession year (609 B.C.) Jeremiah, then aged about thirty-five, delivered his Temple Sermon (7:2–15; 26:1–6). The causes for Jeremiah's complaint are clear. There were many instances of social evil and evidence of a low state of personal morality (7:5, 6, 9). Alongside this lay a smug complacency in religious matters. The people seem to have come to accept the inviolability of the temple as an axiom of life (7:11) because of Yahweh's promises to the Davidic dynasty (2 Sam. 7) and his choice of Jerusalem as the place where he would manifest himself to his people. Small wonder that when Jeremiah commanded the people to amend their ways, and declared that the temple would become like Shiloh (7:12–14) and the nation would be cast out, there was a violent reaction from the priests, the prophets, and the people, who would have done Jeremiah to death there and then (26:7–9). The state officials set up a trial and took evidence from the priests and prophets and from Jeremiah (26:10–15). Jeremiah was acquitted of any capital charge (26:16–18), but the incident nearly cost the prophet his life. Some of the state officials, notably Ahikam ben Shaphan (26:24), one of the leaders in Josiah's reform and perhaps a son of the Secretary of State in Josiah's day (2 K. 22:12), were able to rescue him. Another prophet, Uriah, met his death at the hands of Jehoiakim about the same time (26:20–23).

The incident of 19:14–20:6 seems to have taken place between 609 and 605/4 B.C. (see discussion in commentary). One may conjecture that after the Temple Sermon and the failure of the priests and prophets to secure Jeremiah's persecution, they were on the lookout for a chance to silence him. Jeremiah's symbolic action performed at the Potsherd Gate (19:1–13), before witnesses, provided the opportunity for Pashhur ben Immer the temple overseer to arrest Jeremiah and hold him in the stocks for a night. Jeremiah's response was to assign a new symbolic name to Pashhur, Magormissabib ("terror all around") (20:1–6). This further alienated Jeremiah from the religious leaders, and he seems to have been forbidden to preach in the temple area as a result. Whether this is the explanation or not, by 605/4 B.C. Jeremiah could not enter the sacred area (cf. 36:5). A number of significant oracles may well have been delivered in the years 609–605 B.C., but as they are undated we can only conjecture. Jeremiah may well have pronounced sentence on the Davidic dynasty when he witnessed the misdeeds of Jehoiakim

(21:11–22:9). The abandonment of the covenant was seen as revolt against Yahweh (11:9–13), and no amount of cultic activity could save the nation (11:14–17). The exile of Jehoahaz was a grief to Jeremiah (22:10–12). During the years following the death of Josiah in 609 B.C. the menace of the Babylonians became clearer, and there are good reasons to think that several, if not all, of the poems dealing with the "foe from the north" in chs. 4–6 came from this period. Woven into some of these poems was a call for repentance (4:14). Priests and prophets who denied the coming judgment were speaking falsehood (4:9–10; 5:10–14).

There was a growing resentment to Jeremiah. On one occasion the people of his own village Anathoth planned to take his life (11:18–23), and even members of his own family were implicated in the plot (12:6).[9] His unpopularity grew, and brought upon him jeering, ostracism, and cursing (15:10–11, 17; 17:15; 20:7). It may well be that some of Jeremiah's "confessions" came from these years, although none of them is dated.[10] These "confessions" reveal something of the prophet's heart. He called upon Yahweh to espouse his cause and to bring judgment upon his enemies (11:20; 12:3; 15:15; 17:18; 18:18–23; 20:12). He was prepared to give up his prophetic task (9:1 [Eng. 2]; 15:10–11, 17–18; 20:9). He declared that at no time did he desire or wish to speak about the coming disaster (17:14–18), and accused Yahweh of prevailing over him in his great strength and forcing him to continue (20:7–10). Yahweh had, in fact, "seduced" him (15:15–18; 20:7). Once he likened Yahweh to a dry brook (15:18; cf. 2:13). And yet he could not tolerate the facile preaching of other contemporary prophets (23:16–22). Finally, in anguished despair he cursed the day of his birth because it brought only agony to him (20:14–18). The remarkable thing is that though he determined to give up preaching he could not bear holding in the prophetic word (20:9), which was like a fire burning within him. So he preached on, down the years, through the tragic events of the first and second falls of Jerusalem and finally in exile in Egypt. We can only conclude that oftentimes in his hours of despair and loneliness, with hatred all about him, he recalled the promise Yahweh had made to him when he was called: "They will fight against you, but they shall not prevail against you, for I am with you to deliver

9. These events may have occurred early in his career. See above under "The 'Confessions' of Jeremiah," pp. 88–92.
10. *Ibid.*

you" (1:19). Strange too that he knew full well that Yahweh would have none of his complaints, which were altogether unworthy of a man called to the prophetic office (12:5; 15:19–21). And despite his frequent calls on Yahweh to bring judgment on those who persecuted him, he seems to have interceded for his people continually (15:10–11; 18:20; cf. 7:16; 11:14; 14:11). Admittedly a good deal of what we have just said can be referred to the days of Jehoiakim only by conjecture, but wherever these facts fit into the prophet's life they serve to indicate the character of this lonely, dedicated servant of God.

The next securely dated event in Jeremiah's life was in the fourth year of Jehoiakim's reign, i.e., in the year 605 B.C. when Jeremiah was about thirty-nine or forty years old. He may have sensed impending doom as never before. Nebuchadrezzar had crushed the Egyptians at Carchemish that very year (46:2–12), and although he could not at once press his advantage into Egypt because he was suddenly called back to Babylon to assume the throne on the death of his father, it was only a matter of time before he would be in Judea. Clearly, here was the "foe from the north." By the end of 604 B.C. the Babylonian army had moved into the Philistine plain where Ashdod was taken and destroyed (cf. 47:5–7). A day of national fasting was set aside (36:9). Jeremiah was ready to take advantage of the occasion. In response to the events of 605 B.C. and on the instructions of Yahweh, he summoned Baruch ben Neriah the scribe and dictated to him a summary of his preaching for the last twenty-three years.[11] It was important that the nation should know that his prophecies were about to be fulfilled. And if it should happen that he himself were to die in the calamity, his message would not be lost. It seems to have been a year later that Baruch was sent to read the scroll[12] in the temple courtyard on the fast day, since Jeremiah was forbidden to enter the temple precincts.

When Gemariah ben Shaphan and Elnathan ben Achbar, sons of men who supported Josiah's reform (2 K. 22:12), and others of the king's officials heard the reading, they determined to bring the matter to the attention of the king. Baruch was sent into hiding with Jeremiah (36:19), for the officials feared the outcome (36:26). As the king heard the contents read, he cut off segments of the scroll and threw them into the fire burning in the brazier, despite pleas from

did he recall it? He no doubt kept notes or outlines over the years.

ve, "Jeremiah's First and Second Scrolls," pp. 56–59.

his officials (36:25). It was a total rejection by the king of Yahweh's word, and must have been a blow to Jeremiah. Jeremiah, in hiding, had Baruch write a second scroll and added material which was not in the first. We have no means of knowing the contents of this second scroll or when it was completed. No doubt some of the oracles scattered here and there through chs. 1–25 represent some of the new material. But we may suspect that Jeremiah pressed his message even if he felt that there was little response.

The king's change of allegiance from Egypt to Babylon was less than sincere. Judah's hope seemed to lie with Egypt, particularly after Nebuchadrezzar's attempted invasion of Egypt in late 601 B.C. resulted in a severe mauling of his army and a year's delay before he ventured again (600–599 B.C.). In that space of time Jehoiakim rebelled (2 K. 24:1). A punitive expedition of Nebuchadrezzar's vassals quelled him (2 K. 24:2), but in 598/7 B.C. Nebuchadrezzar's armies subdued Judea and captured Jerusalem, taking the king, the queen mother, and key officials into exile (2 K. 24:10–17). Jehoiakim did not live to see that day. He may have been assassinated. His son Jehoiachin became king but was taken to exile. The two short oracles in 13:18–19 and 22:24–30 come from this period. Jeremiah spoke of the sad fate of the young Jehoiachin and the queen mother. We may suspect that other segments of ch. 13, namely vv. 15–17 and 20–27, come from this period also. They were uttered just prior to Jerusalem's surrender in 597 B.C.

Alas, Judah seemed incapable of change, and in that respect was like the Ethiopian and the leopard (13:23). For their evil actions Yahweh would scatter them (13:24–27). The tragedy was Yahweh's righteous judgment on the nation. The young king who was sent to exile was only eighteen years old (2 K. 24:8). By that time Jeremiah was already forty-seven. Was it on this occasion, when the "hot wind from the bare heights" blew toward his people, that Jeremiah uttered the anguished words of 4:11–31 or 8:18–23 (Eng. 9:1)? If so, Jeremiah's grief was profound.

With the appointment of Zedekiah, the uncle of the young Jehoiakim and himself a very young twenty-one years (2 K. 24:18), the stage was set for the last tragic scenario in which Jeremiah himself suffered a good deal. Zedekiah was dominated by inexperienced and incautious nationalists, since the best leaders had gone to exile. These men could not perceive that a blind nationalism at that time would end in disaster. A wiser policy would have been to bide their time for a better day. Nebuchadrezzar had showed relative leniency in 597 B.C. by not destroying the city. But the leaders seemed unable to assess the realities of the situation. One of the things that seems to have possessed them was the belief that Jerusalem was inviolable. Had it not been delivered once again in 597 as it had in the days of Hezekiah when Sennacherib the Assyrian laid it under siege (cf. Isa. 37:21–35)? These men felt that there was hope for the future. Jeremiah sought to persuade them otherwise. They were the bad figs. The good figs had gone to exile (ch. 24). There was no hope in Zedekiah (23:5–6), nor for that matter in the exiled Jehoiachin (22:24–30). To be sure, there was a hope of restoration one day but not in the near future. In the succeeding years Jeremiah clashed more than once with the other prophets, who held out hope of a speedy end to the exile and a restoration of the nation. Prophets in Babylon and in Judea alike spoke in these terms (29:8, 9, 15; 28:3, 4).

In the year 594/3 B.C. in Jeremiah's fiftieth year, Judah very nearly came to a premature end. Barely four years after the events of 597 Zedekiah entertained ambassadors from Edom, Moab, Ammon, Tyre, and Sidon (27:3), who were plotting rebellion against Nebuchadrezzar. Nationalistic prophets were pressing the point that within two years the exile would be over (28:2–4). Jeremiah spoke strongly against the idea and performed one of his striking symbolic actions. He appeared before the visiting ambassadors wearing an ox-yoke on his neck and bidding them to return to their rulers and tell them to submit to Babylon (27:2–11). He spoke in the same terms to Zedekiah (27:12–15), and declared the same in public in the temple area (27:16–22). Evidently after the death of Jehoiakim he could range abroad once again. In this context we may read the letter Jeremiah wrote to the exiles in Babylon, who were being fed by prophets there on the same false notions (29:1–14, 21–23). Wild promises of a quick return were false. The exiles must settle down for seventy years, although at length there would be restoration. When Zedekiah went to report to Nebuchadrezzar, possibly about the events of 594/3 B.C., Jeremiah instructed one of the officials Seraiah to read a scroll containing an oracle of doom against Babylon and then bind a stone to it and cast it into the Euphrates (51:59–64). This makes it clear that Jeremiah was not pro-Babylonian, but he understood that to resist Nebuchadrezzar was to resist Yahweh (27:5–8).

The reply of the false prophet Hananiah to Jeremiah's symbolic action of wearing the yoke was to declare that the exile would be over within two years (28:2–4) and to break the yoke from Jeremiah's neck (28:10–11). Jeremiah's reply after a short delay was that Yahweh's yoke was not of wood but of iron (28:12–14) and that Hananiah himself would perish. Clearly Jeremiah was in sharp conflict with the other prophets. He may have given expression to some of the ideas in 23:9–40 in such a context, although there is no indication of date in this passage.

We know nothing of the activity of Jeremiah following the events of 594 B.C. The next group of incidents took place as the end of Judah was at hand. Zedekiah intrigued with Egypt, presumably in 589 B.C. Jeremiah was then fifty-five years old. The Babylonian response was quick, and by the autumn of 589 the armies of Nebuchadrezzar were already in Palestine (52:4). We may date the incident of 21:1–10 to this time. Zedekiah consulted Jeremiah about the meaning of events, hoping, it seems, for a reply that would assure him that the Babylonians would go. There was no such assurance, only the threat of doom. It was Yahweh himself who was fighting against the king and the people, and the end was at hand. Jeremiah, in fact, advised the people to surrender to the Babylonians (21:8–10). A second word came to the king from Jeremiah at this time as the initial stages of Nebuchadrezzar's campaigns were drawing to a close. Jerusalem was under siege, and all the provincial towns except Lachish and Azekah had fallen (34:1–7). Zedekiah was promised that his own life would be spared although the city would be captured. The arrival of an Egyptian army caused the siege to be lifted for a short space (37:5). It was in that brief space that a number of incidents took place. The inhabitants of Jerusalem had released their slaves as the siege was pressed but took them back when the siege was lifted. Jeremiah castigated them severely for their perfidy (34:8–22). At the same time Zedekiah sent a messenger to ask the meaning of the arrival of the Egyptian army, only to be told that the respite was only brief and that soon the Chaldeans would return (27:1–10). It was during this brief interval also that Jeremiah was cast into the cistern as he attempted to visit Anathoth to settle some family business (37:11–15). Zedekiah again sought an interview after having Jeremiah released from the cistern (38:1–23). Jeremiah's reply was the same. The city was doomed. The only safe and wise action was for the king to surrender (38:17–19). Zedekiah was afraid both of his officials and of deserters outside the city, and retired to the palace. In those weeks Jeremiah in prison arranged to purchase his cousin's field in Anathoth as a promise that one day houses and fields and vineyards would be bought in the land (32:1–16). The officials felt that Jeremiah was a traitor and a Babylonian sympathizer (38:2–4; cf. 32:3–5). This may account for their desire to cast him into prison. He might have perished in the cistern without any shedding of his blood (38:6), but Ebed-melech rescued him (38:7–13) and they had to be content to keep him under arrest in the court of the guard.

Jerusalem held out with heroic stubbornness until the following summer. Zedekiah wished to surrender (38:14–23) but feared to do so. In July 587 B.C. (52:5–6; 2 K. 25:2–3), just as the city's food supply ran out, the Babylonians breached the walls and entered the city. The story of Zedekiah's escape, capture, and punishment has been told (2 K. 25:3–4; Jer. 52:7–8).[13]

Jeremiah survived the siege. He was then fifty-seven years of age and had completed forty years of preaching. He was allowed to remain, at his own choice, in the land with Gedaliah ben Ahikam, whose father had once saved his life (26:24). The story of Gedaliah's brief period as governor has been told.[14] When Gedaliah was assassinated (chs. 40–41) Jeremiah was taken to Egypt by those who feared further Babylonian reprisals. Even before they fled they asked Jeremiah to seek some word from Yahweh (42:1–43:7). Jeremiah declared that the plan did not have Yahweh's blessing and that they should remain in the land. Heedless of this advice they found asylum at Tahpanhes just inside the Egyptian frontier. The last words we have from Jeremiah's lips were words of condemnation for the apostasy and lack of faith of this group also. The prophet declared that Yahweh would bring judgment upon them even there (43:8–13; 44). It is the last we hear of Jeremiah. He was about sixty years old and may not have survived many more years. But whether he died there soon after his arrival or later we do not know.

It has often been remarked that Jeremiah's life was finally a failure. He was alone for most of his ministry. It seemed that no one gave any heed to his words. He was dragged off finally to live his last days in exile against his own will. He was a failure as the world judges human achievement. But a more balanced assessment of him would be that his very words of judgment saved Israel's faith from disintegration, and his words of hope finally helped his people to gain hope in God's future for them.

13. See above, "Jeremiah in His Historical Setting," p. 26.
14. *Ibid.*, pp. 26f.

VI. THE MESSAGE OF JEREMIAH

Jeremiah, like the other prophets, was not a systematic theologian or even a systematic thinker. His theology and his thinking came out of life and from what he had learned at the feet of those who taught him of Israel's traditions. But, clearly, he had to deal with many problems that were basically theological, and his whole message had a theological basis. Jeremiah's contribution in these areas was twofold. First, he made his particular contribution to his own age as his ideas about God, the nation, the individual, sin, repentance, the future hope were proclaimed over a period of some forty years. But second, his teaching made a contribution to the future generations and especially to those in exile. The men who edited Jeremiah's oracles were at pains to let them speak their own message to men in the restricted life of the exiles. In particular, the prose passages of Jeremiah represent, at least to some degree, the free reconstructions of Jeremiah's sayings by those who transmitted his teaching to the next generation.[1]

A. THE MESSAGE OF JEREMIAH TO HIS OWN GENERATION

While Jeremiah himself would never have organized his theological beliefs under the categories one finds in modern "Theologies," there is some value for those who would seek to obtain a picture of his views about the great issues of theology in following the systematic categories of the textbooks. His was a dynamic theology which prompted him to action, gave direction to his preaching, and sustained him in the many hours of crisis. At the risk then of systematizing Jeremiah's thoughts in ways he would never have dreamed of, we turn to a brief study of his views about God, Israel, the Nation and the Individual, Sin and Repentance, the Future Hope.

1. God

Jeremiah's ideas of God came partly from his boyhood training at Anathoth, where he learned the great traditions of Israel's faith passed on through the generations. In particular, he seems to have owed much to Hosea.[2] But much of Jeremiah's theology must have

1. See "The Book of Jeremiah: Composition," pp. 33–50.
2. See "The Debt of Jeremiah to Hosea," pp. 81–85.

come from his own encounters with Yahweh in the rough and tumble of life.

For Jeremiah, Yahweh was the "Fountain of living waters" (2:13), the sure source of the life and sustenance of his people Israel. He was a Potter who stood as a free Person over against men who were also free persons (18:1–12). He was the Creator of the world who had set up the natural order of things (5:22; 8:7; 10:12, 13; 27:5–6; 31:35–36). He was the Lord of history who directed Israel's history from the time of her election (2:1ff.) but who also controlled the nations. Nebuchadrezzar king of Babylon was his "servant" (27:6), and he formed purposes for all men and nations. Thus he gave Edom, Moab, Ammon, Tyre, and Sidon, as well as Judea, into the power of Nebuchadrezzar (27:2–8). He knew the hearts of men and tried them and rewarded men according to their deeds (11:20; 16:17; 18:10; 20:12; 29:23). In 23:23–24 a doctrine of divine transcendence and divine immanence is declared. Yahweh was a God both "near" (*miqqārōḇ*) and "far off" (*mērāḥōq*), that is, he was personally involved in human affairs, Israel's affairs, the affairs of the nations and the affairs of individuals like Jeremiah. As one who was near he displayed his love for his people. Jeremiah made use of warm personal figures like "husband" (2:2) and "father" (3:19) to describe Yahweh's relationship to Israel, while Israel was described as "son" (3:19, 21; 4:22). Toward his people Yahweh was "merciful" (*ḥāsîḏ*, 3:12), that is, he displayed "loyalty" (*ḥeseḏ*).[3] The noun "loyalty," "steadfast love," "steadfast loyalty" is used of Yahweh in 9:23 (Eng. 24); 32:18; 33:11. This love of Yahweh for Israel is implied in passages which express his pain and consternation that Israel should turn away from him in her sinfulness (2:5, 31–33). He had loved Israel with an "everlasting love" (*'ahaḇaṯ 'ôlām*), and despite her rebellion he had prolonged his unfailing faithfulness (*ḥeseḏ*) to her (31:3). There is something of a paradox in such teaching, for Jeremiah experienced another side of Yahweh's nature. Despite his faithfulness to his call, he had suffered pain unceasing and an incurable wound which would not be healed (15:18). Yahweh seemed to have deceived him and to have compelled him to undertake his difficult task against his will (20:7). It may have been difficult sometimes to see Yahweh's love displayed in his own life.

We gain a significant insight into Jeremiah's view of God in

3. The term *ḥāsîḏ* is used only in 3:12 and Ps. 145:17 of God in the OT, but it is often used of men, Ps. 4:4 (Eng. 3); 30:5 (Eng. 4); 32:6; etc.

the area of man's relationship to God and the divine requirements. Yahweh did not require from men sacrifices and ritual observances which the priests and temple prophets would require, but repentance and obedience. God dealt with men in the immediacy of personal relationship, which excluded any necessity for the intervention of the priests and the cult or their mistaken trust in cultic activities (6:20; 7:1–31; 11:15; 29:12–14; 31:34). In the context of a personal relationship, obedience to Yahweh's laws which would issue in social and personal ethics was demanded (2:34; 6:7; 21:11–12; 34:8–22). The divine requirements are summed up in 9:24. Yahweh himself practices loyalty (*ḥeseḏ*), justice (*mišpāṭ*), and righteousness (*ṣᵉḏāqâ*), and in these he delights.

Jeremiah was, of course, a monotheist. He speaks of the gods of the nations in contemptuous terms such as "worthlessness" (2:5), "no gods" (2:11), "broken cisterns" (2:13), powerless to help men in the hour of trouble (2:28). Yahweh's power to control the nations who neither know him nor recognize him shows his superiority over their lifeless and powerless "no gods."

2. *Israel, the Nation, and the Individual*

Jeremiah had a noble view of Israel and explored a number of striking metaphors to describe her. Following his predecessors among the prophets and in line with ancient traditions, he saw Israel as God's elect people. Yahweh once chose (*bāḥar*) the two families, Judah and Northern Israel (33:24). The verb is used only here but the idea is presented in various ways. Israel was Yahweh's "firstfruits" (2:3), a "choice vine" (2:21), the "beloved" of Yahweh (11:15; 12:7), Yahweh's own "heritage" (*naḥᵃlâ*, 12:7–9), his "vine-yard" (12:10), and his "flock" (13:17) whom he loved with an everlasting love (31:3). Like Hosea before him, Jeremiah described the relationship between Yahweh and Israel as a marriage relationship (2:2; 3:6ff.). Sometimes he mixes the metaphor and speaks of Israel as "sons" (3:19, 22; 4:22). That relationship began with the deliverance from Egypt (2:6) and it arose out of Yahweh's love. However, that pristine pure relationship was limited to the period of desert wandering (2:2). Entrance into the settled land of Canaan marked the beginning of apostasy from Yahweh (2:7), which Jeremiah depicts in figures drawn from nature (8:6–7). Israel was like a "restive young she-camel" or "a wild ass used to the wilderness" (2:23–24). Because Israel had left her first love and had turned aside to worship false gods, and had even attempted to worship Yahweh with pagan rites, Israel was depicted under the figures of "adultery" or "harlotry," following Hosea's descriptive terms. Yahweh through his servants the prophets called on the people continually to return to him. Yahweh afflicted them by way of correction (*mûsār*), but they refused his correction (2:30; 5:3; 17:23; 32:33; 35:13). In that context rebellious Israel would suffer judgment. Their state was one of imminent disaster. False priests and prophets healed their wound lightly saying "Peace, peace" when there was no peace (6:14). There was no hope for Israel but to repent (25:1–14; see the next section). Yet even if judgment came, it was not to be the end of Yahweh's people. There would be an assured restoration after the judgment, and a new covenant based on the foundation of the forgiveness of sins and a new heart (24:7; 31:31–34; see below under "Future Hope").

So much for the nation. The nation, however, was composed of individuals, and Jeremiah understood better than most that God works with the individual. Jeremiah's teaching on the individual comes more by implication than by direct statement. He had much to say about the "heart," which in the psychology of the time represented the inclinations and attitudes of men. Yahweh tries the heart and the mind (11:20; 17:10; 20:12). The heart of man is the source of evil, "deceitful above all things and desperately wicked" (17:9). In the heart of false prophets was deceit (23:26). In the day of restoration Yahweh would give men a new "heart" (24:7).

Jeremiah's view is that a man's acceptance with God is not dependent on the temple and its rituals (7:1–15; 26:1–24), or circumcision (9:24–25 [Eng. 25–26]). Nor does a man need to live in the land of Judah, for Yahweh may be worshipped and served in exile (29:1–14). Wherever men are, they may seek Yahweh with all their heart (29:13, 14). When Yahweh restored his people and established a New Covenant with the nation, the law would be in the hearts of men, that is, the emphasis is on personal acceptance of the law and personal obedience to it (31:31–33). Jeremiah's own deep personal experience with Yahweh was testimony enough to the importance of the individual.

3. Sin and Repentance

We may be pardoned for thinking that Jeremiah placed an enormous emphasis on the sins and misdeeds of Israel. He drew into his vocabulary a wide range of terms to describe the misdeeds of Israel.

Among these we find *ʿāwōn*, "guilt" or "iniquity,"[4] *pešaʿ*, "rebellion,"[5] *ḥaṭṭāʾṯ*, "sin,"[6] *rāʿâ*, "evil."[7] The source of this wickedness in Israel is the hearts of the people (4:14; 5:23; 17:1, 9). The people are described as having a stubborn and rebellious heart. The phrase "the stubbornness of their hearts" (*šᵉrirûṯ libbām*) occurs several times.[8]

The evil deeds in which Israel was involved were of two broad classes—the worship of false gods, and the perpetration of personal and social sins of an ethical and moral kind. To worship false gods was to commit an abomination (*tôʿēḇâ*).[9] The ethical sins touched on matters of justice, honesty, purity, etc. (7:5, 8). All such evil deeds were offenses against Yahweh's law and represented a breach of the covenant. Obedience to the covenant demands was incumbent on Israel (7:5, 6; 11:3, 4, 7; 21:11, 12; 34:8–22; etc.). Yet sin was not simply a matter of casual, or even habitual breach of the covenant laws. It was a basic attitude in Israel in regard to Yahweh (2:22; 5:3, 5; 36:7). And yet, to Jeremiah such acts of wickedness seemed to be unnatural. Even the nations did not forsake their gods (2:10, 11), nor leopards change their spots, nor Ethiopians their skin (13:23). Likewise the birds and animals held to the laws of nature (5:22–23; 8:7; 18:13–17). It became clear to Jeremiah that Israel's only hope lay in repentance and the turning of the whole person to Yahweh (3:1–4:4; 8:4–7; 15:19; 36:7). No prophet explored the meaning of the root *šûḇ* more than Jeremiah.[10] When Israel *turned from* their evil ways and *turned to* Yahweh with all their hearts they would find that Yahweh yearned for them and would have mercy (*riḥam*) on them (31:20). There were profound possibilities of forgiveness in Yahweh. Any purpose of his to bring

4. 2:22; 3:13; 11:10; 13:22; 14:7, 10, 20; 16:10, 17, 18; 18:23; 25:12; 30:14, 15; 31:30, 34; 32:18; 33:8; 36:3, 31; 50:20; 51:6.
5. It is strange that this noun occurs only in 5:6 since the root *pšʿ* seems to be a very appropriate one to use to describe Israel's behavior. The verb is used more frequently.
6. The noun is not in fact used. The verb occurs in 2:35; 3:25; 8:14; 14:7, 20; 33:8.
7. The noun in its singular absolute and construct forms and the adjective occur more than a hundred times. The verb is used infrequently. One needs to distinguish between the two senses of *rāʿâ*, "evil" and "calamity." The use of *rāʿâ* as an adjective with a variety of nouns is common, "evil way" (25:5; 26:13; 35:15; 36:3, 7). As the noun "evil" it occurs in 1:16; 2:19; 3:5; 9:2 (Eng. 3); 11:17; 14:16; 33:5; 41:11; 44:3, 9; etc.
8. "Their hearts" in 3:17; 7:24; 9:13 (Eng. 14); 13:10; "his heart," 16:12; 18:12; 23:17.
9. 2:7; 6:15; 7:10; 8:12; 16:18; 32:35; 44:22. The alternate term *šiqqûṣ* is used in 4:1; 7:30; 13:27.
10. See "The Use and Significance of the Root *šûḇ* in Jeremiah," pp. 76–81.

judgment on his people for their sins might be transformed into a purpose to forgive on the basis of a response of repentance.[11]

Hence Jeremiah summoned his people to turn aside (repent) from their evil ways and turn again to Yahweh to live in obedience to his laws (3:12–14; 4:1–4; 18:11; 31:18–19). It is altogether consistent with his own preaching that when Jeremiah behaved in a rebellious and complaining fashion Yahweh called on the prophet himself to repent (15:19).

As the years went by, it would seem that Jeremiah was less and less persuaded that the people would or could repent. It was not that Yahweh was unable to forgive or unwilling to restore the repentant man of Israel to fellowship with himself, but rather that Israel by habit and custom would not repent.

"My people are foolish, they know me not;
They are stupid children, they have no understanding.
They are skilled in doing evil, but how to do good they know not." (4:22)

Following Hosea (Hos. 6:1–3; 14:2–3), Jeremiah proposed some appropriate expressions of forgiveness to be uttered by a repentant Israel (3:22–25; 14:7–10, 19–22).

Once repentance and return to Yahweh had been shown to be impossible, the judgments of Yahweh on the people's sins became inevitable. Jeremiah pressed the point more and more. At the end he could hold out no hope to the apprehensive King Zedekiah (38:17–23).

4. The Future Hope

Jeremiah's message pointed men beyond judgment to a future hope when Israel's fortunes would be restored. Several significant passages indicate his views. When he purchased the field of his cousin Hanamel in Anathoth, with the Babylonians already overrunning the land having only recently lifted the siege of Jerusalem and with every prospect of renewing it, he wanted to demonstrate his faith in Yahweh's plans for future restoration. "Thus says Yahweh of hosts the God of Israel: Houses and fields and vineyards shall again be bought in this land" (32:15). Again, his letter to the exiles in Bab-

11. The verb *niḥam* occurs in 8:6 and 31:19 of a man "repenting" of his wickedness. But the verb is used more frequently in Jeremiah of Yahweh changing his purpose in response to some change in attitude in men, 4:28; 15:6; 18:8, 10; 20:16; 26:3, 13, 19; 42:10. In these cases the translation "repent" is hardly appropriate.

ylon (ch. 29) contains a promise that when seventy years had been completed Yahweh would visit his people and bring them back to their land and restore their fortunes. Part of that vision saw Israel seeking Yahweh with all their heart (29:10–14). Other passages appear in 31:2–6, 15–22, both of which seem to have been directed to Northern Israel, possibly from the early years of Jeremiah's career. These views breathe a spirit of hope.[12]

In the famous passage in 31:31–34 describing the New Covenant, Jeremiah reached the apex of his thinking on the new hope. One day God would give his people a covenant, not like the one they had broken during the centuries but one in which his law would be written on people's hearts. The New Covenant would be with the nation, but since it was to be written on the hearts of the people it would also be with individuals. The authenticity of the passage has been questioned by some scholars but without reason. Even if in its present form it may not preserve Jeremiah's *ipsissima verba,* it seems to be unnecessarily critical to deny that Jeremiah could rise to such noble heights, since in other areas he showed himself capable of profound thoughts which penetrated to new horizons.

Jeremiah also gave expression to messianic hopes. God would raise up a "righteous Branch for David," who would deal wisely and perform justice and righteousness in the land (23:5–6; 33:15–16). Jeremiah, like some of his predecessors, gave him the symbolic name "Yahweh our Righteousness." He would be an earthly king of the Davidic dynasty who would reign as an ideal monarch. The picture Jeremiah gives is a realistic, earth-centered one lacking the highly speculative and imaginative pictures of some later Jewish writers. For Jeremiah, restoration would take place in the land under wise and good government, with king and people renewed in heart, so that all men would avow Yahweh and obey him by nature (31:31–34).

B. THE MESSAGE OF JEREMIAH TO THE EXILES AND FUTURE GENERATIONS

Jeremiah's message contained within it significant elements which would serve to explain to the exiles the reason for the calamity that

12. There are many other passages where hope for the future is expressed (cf. 3:15–16; 4:9–10; 12:14–17; 16:14–15; 23:3–4, 7–8; 30:8–11, 16–24; 31:1, 7–14, 23–28, 35–40; 33:6–26), which are disputed by some scholars. But each passage has to be treated separately. See the commentary in each case.

had befallen the nations, and to foster in the hearts of the exiles, who may have been inclined to despair, hopes for a future restoration. Jeremiah's ministry in this regard is clear from the oracles, the narrative material, and the prose sermons, which were cast in their present shape by an editor or editors.

The fall of Jerusalem and the exile that followed was more than a political catastrophe. Inasmuch as the people of Judah had been led to think that the Davidic dynasty based on Yahweh's eternal covenant with David (cf. 2 Sam. 7:4–17; 23:1–7) was inviolable and that the city of Jerusalem, the temple (the symbol of Yahweh's presence among men), and indeed the people of God themselves were likewise inviolable, the destruction of all three left the survivors of the holocaust bewildered. It was simply not true that Yahweh was committed unconditionally to the defense of the nation, the city, the temple, and the Davidic dynasty. They might have had hints of this after 597 B.C., and certainly Jeremiah had warned them of the possibility that what they complacently believed could not happen, would happen. It seems clear both from 31:29 and from remarks made by some of the survivors early in the exile (Ezek. 18:2, 25; Lam. 5:7) that Yahweh's very justice was doubted, and we may believe that there were even those who had come to believe that Yahweh was powerless before the gods of Babylon.[13] It is clear also from some passages in Ezekiel that a spirit of despair had overtaken some of the exiles (Ezek. 33:10; 37:11). What was the meaning of the tragic events which came to a climax in 587 B.C.? The meaning had already been spelled out over many years by Jeremiah. Those tragic events were judgment on the people for their rebellion against Yahweh; their source was in Yahweh himself and represented his righteous judgment on the nation for its sin. Every false hope of Israel had to be destroyed before they could be brought to repentance and a new life. Dependence on the temple and its rituals, belief in the inviolability of Jerusalem and the Davidic dynasty, pride in their being the people of Yahweh were all, in the final count, false bases for hope. Had they been a true basis for hope faith itself would have been destroyed. Jeremiah's preaching of judgment and his insistence on personal commitment to Yahweh and his covenant in place of every other false hope made it clear to the people, once they had recovered from their numbing experience, that Yahweh

13. Some of the oracles of Second Isaiah were designed in part, it seems, to expose the emptiness of these gods.

was unimpeachably just, and even in the midst of judgment remained in sovereign control.

But there had to be more if the nation was to survive. There had to be hope if the nation was to survive as a people beyond the destruction of 587 B.C. Clearly it could not continue as it had gone on for centuries past. Ideally, its statehood involved the kinds of rights and responsibilities that were envisaged under the old covenant law. Jeremiah, like his predecessors Amos and Micah, made it clear that the covenant law had been neglected and, instead, men had come to depend on a corrupt religious system, which was at best an aid to worship but no substitute for obedience (6:16–21; 7:2–15, 21–23). If there was to be survival it would require a community based on the loyalty and personal commitment of each individual to Yahweh himself, and that was something inward and not external. Jeremiah's own deep experience with Yahweh taught him that. Without such commitment, no external structure for national life could succeed. Hence Jeremiah offered no blueprint for the external structure and organization of a new state. But he did speak of a positive hope for the future.

Unfortunately critical studies over the past century have tended to minimize the authentic Jeremianic material dealing with hope, of which many are in fact open to debate. But there are some passages which are widely accepted, e.g., chs. 29 and 33 and passages directed to Northern Israel like 3:12–13; 31:2–5, 15–22. The so-called "Book of Consolation" (chs. 30–33) contains other widely accepted material. But it is unthinkable that Jeremiah would have left the people without hope. His very call (1:10) contained two broad emphases, judgment ("uproot" and "tear down") and promise ("build" and "plant"), that is, his ministry was to serve a two-fold purpose, first of judgment, then of restoration. His preaching of judgment had an undertone of being conditional, at least until late in his ministry (cf. 18:1–10), and he spoke more about repentance than any other before him or after him. He assured loyal groups like the Rechabites that they would survive (ch. 35). Perhaps it was Jeremiah's confidence in Yahweh's final purposes of good for the people and the land that made him remain in the land after the collapse of 587 B.C. (40:1–6). This also explains his opposition to any flight to Egypt (42:7–22).

The greatest passage of all is, of course, the "New Covenant" passage in 31:31–35, which we regard as authentic, if not in precise wording then in substance. It is altogether characteristic of Jeremiah. It is not based on any of the standard formulations, e.g., in terms of the promise to the Davidic dynasty, or on the choice of Jerusalem as Yahweh's "dwelling place" and the site of the temple, but reaches back to fundamentals. Yahweh would undertake a new act of divine grace and restore the ancient covenant relationship by writing the law in people's hearts, forgiving their sin, and restoring the basic personal relationship "their God—my people." In Jeremiah it was unthinkable that Yahweh would cast away his people for ever, as unthinkable as that the fixed order of sun, moon, and stars should cease to be (31:35–37).

It would have taken time for the exiles to combine the two aspects of Jeremiah's ministry. But with the help of Ezekiel they did, and came to understand both the reason for the tragedies of 597 and 587 B.C. and the grounds for hope. In due course a community was preserved and prepared to build again.

Before we leave our discussion of the teaching of Jeremiah something must be said about the editors of the final edition of the book of Jeremiah, and in particular about the prose sermons in the book, which are couched in a style and language and expound a theological outlook which has been recognized as Deuteronomistic. A widely held view about these passages is that most of them are based on Jeremiah's original sayings, which were transmitted by men who expanded, developed, and even supplemented the prophet's own message so as to relate it more significantly to the needs of the nation at a time later than Jeremiah and to draw out its significance for that time.[14] On this view the book of Jeremiah in its final form is seen as covering a longer period than that covered by Jeremiah's own ministry of forty years or so, and as containing much which originated during the period of the Exile, when the Deuteronomic authors were at work seeking to revive and renew the nation's life after the catastrophe of 587 B.C. The commentator E. W. Nicholson draws the biographical narratives into the same theory and claims that the Deuteronomic editors bent these also to serve their purpose.

There may be a degree of truth in the contention of writers like Nicholson, but it seems to the present writer that their case is

14. The view has been recently defended and worked out in considerable detail by E. W. Nicholson, *Preaching to the Exiles: A Study of the Prose Tradition in the Book of Jeremiah* (1970), and then applied in some detail in his commentary on Jeremiah in the Cambridge Bible Commentary series, *Jeremiah 1–25* (1973) and *Jeremiah 26–52* (1975). There is much that is valuable in these two commentaries. Unfortunately limited space prevented Nicholson from developing his thesis more adequately.

overdone. Undoubtedly Jeremiah's oracles and the stories about him had to be edited. And no doubt, the present arrangement of the material was intended to serve a theological purpose and to highlight areas of his teaching which were relevant to people who lived in the post–587 B.C. era. But that this requires a wholesale rewriting, expansion, and supplementation of Jeremiah's work as proposed by Nicholson and others is open to question. It would seem that even if the editors had merely collected Jeremiah's own poetic material, such biographical material as was available, and such additional material as may have been preserved comprising other sayings of the prophet as they were remembered, understood, and repeated by friends who heard them, there would have been adequate information to achieve the result proposed. Those who discerned the import of Jeremiah's teaching on judgment and restoration had abundant source material to use. The real question is whether the biographical passages and prose sermons comprise "Preaching to the Exiles" or a recording for posterity of what were basically the utterances of the prophet and the record of certain critical incidents in his life.[15] It would seem that it is impossible to arrive at firm conclusions either way, and dogmatism is certainly to be avoided.

VII. THE TEXT

One of the striking features about the text of Jeremiah is that the Hebrew Masoretic Text (MT) is considerably longer than the Greek text (LXX).[1] In fact, statistically the Greek text is one-eighth shorter than the Hebrew text, since there are some 2700 words which are present in the MT but absent in LXX. The Greek omissions comprise single words, phrases, sentences, and some entire passages, of which the longest is about 180 words and some others are quite sizable, e.g., 33:14–26; 39:4–13; 51:44b–49a; 52:27b–30. In addition to these textual variants there is a major difference in the order of

15. See above under "The Book of Jeremiah: Composition," pp. 33–50.

1. The so-called Septuagint translation of the Hebrew Bible into Greek is thought to have been made in Egypt in the course of the last three centuries B.C. The Jeremiah translation was probably made in the second century B.C. and its Hebrew counterpart must have been somewhat earlier, perhaps a century. Later forms of the Greek text include Codex Alexandrinus (A), Codex Vaticanus (B), Codex Lucianus (L), and Codex Sinaiticus (S).

the oracles against the nations, which in the MT are at the end of the book but in LXX are in the middle, inserted after 25:13 (v. 14 is lacking in LXX). Moreover, the order is different. MT has the order, Egypt (46:2–28), Philistia (47:1–7), Moab (ch. 48), Ammon (49:1–6), Edom (49:7–22), Damascus (49:23–27), Kedar (49:28–33), Elam (49:34–39), Babylon (chs. 50, 51). LXX has the order Elam, Egypt, Babylon, Philistia, Edom, Ammon, Kedar, Damascus, Moab.

These differences between LXX and MT raise several important questions and call for an explanation. Over the past century and a half a variety of proposals have been made.[2] Some of the differences can probably be accounted for by homoioteleuton, as in 39:4–13; 51:44b–49a, and in a whole series of shorter omissions. Others may go back to the efforts of the translator to lighten the text of his original, which seemed to be overloaded and unwieldy, as perhaps 17:1–5a. It may be that in some cases particular passages were not in the Hebrew text on which the translation was based, e.g., 33:14–26. Of the explanations offered for this we have a great variety:[3] the two text traditions originated in successive editions of Jeremiah himself, the second being an expanded copy of the first; the translator deliberately omitted passages, particularly those which occurred a second time in the Hebrew text; the Greek was an older text than the current Hebrew text and is to be preferred since the additional materials in MT are secondary glosses; the Greek text was a mutilated and corrupted form of the Hebrew text which is extant today, the mutilations and corruptions being due to the translators (a view that is representative of those who uphold the superiority of MT); that LXX was a translation of a different basic text.

The wide variety of views suggests that we are not yet in possession of the kind of information that will allow a definitive solution. In recent years two important tools for research have given some prospect of finding an acceptable solution. First, a critical edition of the LXX published in 1958, with a commentary on the text families and recensions, has made possible a new level of precision in analysis.[4] Second, new manuscript evidence for the Hebrew text of Jeremiah has come from the caves of Qumran.[5]

2. The most recent standard discussion is that of J. Gerald Janzen, *Studies in the Text of Jeremiah*. Harvard Semitic Monographs 6 (1973).
3. See *ibid.*, pp. 2–9.
4. J. Ziegler, *Septuaginta: Vetus Testamentum Graecum* (Göttingen, 1958).
5. Until the definitive publication of the Jeremiah materials from Cave IV at Qumran becomes available we are dependent on preliminary discussions. F. M. Cross, *The Ancient Library of Qumran* (New York, 1958, new ed. 1961), p. 187, gives a fragment

Current studies based on these biblical manuscripts from Qumran are providing a new picture of the history of the biblical text in its broad outlines and are giving support for the view that there was a text tradition at times substantially divergent from MT and closer to LXX. Thus the Hebrew manuscript for Jer. 10 omits four verses and shifts the order of a fifth in agreement with LXX. Although the fragment is small and contains only the left portion of a column of text, the ends of lines are preserved for Jer. 9:22–10:8. In the critical area lines 5, 6, and 7 on the fragment preserve vv. 4, 9, and 11 of ch. 10, and reconstruction demonstrates what can be seen even with a casual comparison of MT and LXX, that this new text (denoted by the symbol 4QJer[b]) transposes v. 5 to after v. 9 and omits vv. 6–8 and 10. Even inside v. 4, words are transposed so that MT *bmsmrwt wbmqbwt* reads *bmqbwt [w(b) msmrwt]* with LXX, i.e., "with nails and hammer" has become "with hammer and nails."

On the other hand the MT tradition is preserved on other fragments which seem to agree with MT as against LXX.[6] It seems clear that the group of fragments denoted as 4QJer[b] which comprise portions of 9:22–10:18; 43:3–9; 50:4–6 give clear, if not complete support to the view that the background to LXX was a form of the Jeremiah shorter Hebrew text; or, to state the case the other way round, the Greek text is clearly, if not perfectly, a witness to a short Hebrew text of the book of Jeremiah.[7] Thus the textual tradition of Jeremiah is at least twofold. It now seems clear from Qumran that both the longer and shorter forms of the text were available in the Qumran community and that the MT and LXX of Jeremiah are based on different recensions of the Hebrew text of the book. It is not possible to say at what point the Hebrew tradition on which LXX was based diverged from that on which MT was based. It may be that both traditions had relatively long histories of scribal transmission. Where they diverge it is not possible always to decide which reading is to be preferred. One might ask whether the MT traditions added material or the LXX tradition subtracted material. Perhaps

---

of Jer. 10 in Hebrew in the shorter forms and following the transposed order of LXX. Cf. M. Baillet, J. T. Milik, and R. de Vaux, *Discoveries in the Judaean Desert, III: Les 'Petites Grottes' de Qumrân* (1962), pp. 62–69. In the meantime Appendix D to Janzen, *Studies in the Text of Jeremiah,* pp. 173–184 gives transcriptions of most of the extant fragments of the Qumran Jeremiah, 4QJer[a] and 4QJer[b].

6. Fragments for chs. 42–49 (2Q13) in M. Baillet, J. T. Milik, and R. de Vaux, *Discoveries in the Judaean Desert, III,* pp. 62–69.

7. So Janzen, *Studies in the Text of Jeremiah,* p. 173.

both processes were at work. It seems, particularly in the MT prose tradition, that conflation took place and that the shorter LXX is more original. In the commentary that follows we will point out a good number of LXX omissions but by no means all.[8]

VIII. POETIC FORMS

Jeremiah inherited from his society both his prose style and his poetic forms, though no doubt both took on certain personal characteristics. Hebrew poetry, unlike Western poetry, does not depend on rhythm, although occasionally the occurrence of identical sounds at the end of lines where the same verbal ending or pronominal suffix occurs looks like Western poetry, e.g.,

b^{e}*ṭerem 'eṣṣār*^{e}*ḵā, ḇabbeṭen y*^{e}*ḏa'tîḵā*
ûḇ^{e}*ṭerem tēṣē' mēreḥem hiqdaštîḵā*

in 1:5 has endings which appear to rhyme. But this was probably fortuitous and was not a normal part of the Hebrew poetic system. Moreover, Hebrew poetry does not follow the system of regular accented and unaccented syllables which are a part of Western poetry.

There are two basic characteristics of Hebrew poetry: parallelism of some kind between the lines of a poem, and the more or less regular recurrence of accent patterns from line to line. To be sure, the way in which accent patterns are to be recognized is disputed. On the classical view only the accented syllables matter; unaccented syllables may vary in number but are not determinative. A different view is that both accented and unaccented syllables are to be taken into consideration.[1]

The classical view will be the basis of the discussion that follows, although it is recognized that problems abound and the matter has by no means been settled finally.

A line of Hebrew poetry normally contains shorter metrical units or "cola." A line with two such units is a "bicolon," a line of three units is a "tricolon." Normally, though not always, the unit of syntax (sentence, clause, phrase) coincides with the metrical unit

8. The commentary of D. F. Giesebrecht, *Das Buch Jeremia* (1907), pp. xix–xxxiv provides a detailed list of most, if not all, of the variants.

1. The view is proposed by S. Mowinckel, *The Psalms in Israel's Worship* (E.T. New York, 1962), II, pp. 159–175, 261–66, among others.

or colon.[2] Within the line the cola stand in some kind of parallel relation as regards their thought. Often one line is parallel to the next. Sometimes the first and fourth cola form one parallel, and the second and third another. But there are many variations.

In a pair of lines such as occur in Ps. 19:8 (Eng. 7) we have a case of synonymous parallelism:

The-law-of-the-Lord (is) perfect reviving-the-soul,
The-testimony-of-the-Lord (is) sure making-wise-the-simple.[3]

The second colon reinforces the first.

Sometimes the parallelism is antithetical (Prov. 15:1):

A-soft-answer turns-away wrath,
But a-harsh-word stirs-up anger.

Sometimes there is not strict parallelism but a development of the thought as in Ps. 14:1:

The-fool says in-his-heart
There-is-no-God.

Many other kinds of parallelism have been proposed.[4]

Another possible classification is in terms of whether the parallelism is complete or incomplete. On this basis a very considerable variety of forms can be detected.[5] In one simple case words in one colon are balanced by words in the next. Thus in Ps. 19:8 (Eng. 7) quoted above we have a pattern

a	b	c
a'	b'	c'

A variation of this simple form is to omit one element in the second colon as in Isa. 40:2,

Speak-ye	comfortably	to-Jerusalem
And-say		unto-her
a	b	c
a'		c'

or, omit one element and introduce a new one as in Ps. 75:7 (Eng. 6),

For not from-the-east nor from-the-west

2. W. L. Holladay has proposed a theoretical basis for describing the elements of Hebrew poetry and has shown how the application of these principles made possible the discovery of some poetry now disguised as verse. W. L. Holladay, "The Recovery of Poetic Passages of Jeremiah," *JBL* 85 (1966), pp. 401–435.

3. The hyphens link together all the English words which appear in Hebrew as a single idea.

4. See W. O. E. Oesterley, *The Psalms* (London, 1953), pp. 20f.

5. See George Buchanan Gray, *The Forms of Hebrew Poetry* (London, 1925), pp. 37–83.

Nor from-the-wilderness (comes) uplifting.

a b c

a' b' d

One of the more complex patterns comes from Ps. 29:1–2,

Give to-Yahweh ye-sons-of the-gods
Give to-Yahweh glory and-strength
Give to-Yahweh the-glory-of his-name

which might be represented by

a	b	c	d			
a	b			e	f	
a	b			e		g[6]

This arrangement has a parallel in Ugaritic literature, from which Ps. 29 may well have been adopted.

An example from Jeremiah comes from 1:5:

Before	I-formed-you	in-the-womb	I-knew-you
Before	you-came	from-the-womb	I-consecrated-you
A-prophet	to-the-nations		I-appointed-you

The verse is a tricolon. The first two cola are in synonymous parallelism and complete, since each word in the first is balanced by a word in the second. The scheme is a b c d / a' b' c' d'. The third colon simply carries the thought forward and only the verb is parallel. Hence it might be described as e f d''.

Similarly, 2:2:

I-remember	concerning-you	the-devotion-of	your-youth
		the-love-of	your-bridal-days

This may be described as a b c d / c' d'.

And again in 2:15,

The lions	have-roared	against-him	
	They-have-given-forth		their-voice
a	b	c	
a	b'		d

The second colon is peculiar, since the whole phrase means "they have roared" but formally there is another word. For an example of antithetic parallelism we may take 12:2b:

Near	art-thou	in-their-mouth
But far		from-their-heart

a b c / a' - c'

As to rhythm, the meter is decided on the basis of accented syllables

6. Numerous examples are given in Gray, *ibid.*, pp. 60–83; T. H. Robinson, *The Poetry of the OT* (1947), pp. 26–29; W. O. E. Oesterley, *The Psalms,* pp. 21–24.

within the cola of each line. Thus, if a line has two cola (bicolon) and each has three accented syllables, the meter is described as 3/3. If the first colon has three accented syllables and the second, two, the meter is 3/2. In Hebrew verse the 3/3 and 3/2 meters are the most common, but there are many combinations of two, three, and four beats (2/2, 4/4, 4/3, 2/3 , etc.). In the case of a tricolon there are other combinations: 3/3/3, 3/2/2, 4/4/3, etc. Unlike a lot of Western poetry, however, Hebrew poetry shows very wide flexibility. In the verse of Jeremiah, for example, it is unusual for the meter to continue unchanged throughout an entire poem.

One of our problems is that we are not entirely certain how the poet stressed his words when he spoke them. A few illustrations will help to clarify the point. Thus in 1:5 we have,

b^{e}ṭérem   ’eṣṣā́r^{e}ḵā   ḇabbéṭen   y^{e}ḏa‘tíḵā
ûḇ^{e}ṭérem   tēṣḗ’   mēréḥem   hiqdaštíḵā
nāḇî́’   laggôyím   n^{e}ṯattíḵā

The verse is a tricolon. The first two cola have four accented syllables each and the third has three. The meter is thus 4/4/3.

Again in 4:1, 2 we have,

(1) ’im-tāšûḇ   yiśrā’ēl   n^{e}’um-yhwh
’ēláy   tāšûḇ
w^{e}’im-tāsîr   šiqqûṣéyḵā   mippānáy
w^{e}lṓ’   ṯānûḏ
(2) w^{e}nišbá‘tā   ḥay-yhwh   be’^{e}méṯ
b^{e}mišpā́ṭ   ûḇiṣ^{e}ḏāqā́
w^{e}hiṯbā́r^{e}ḵû   ḇṓ   gôyím
ûḇṓ   yiṯhallālû́

Here we have four lines of Hebrew poetry, each a bicolon and each having a meter of 3/2. Thus the whole metric scheme is 3/2, 3/2, 3/2, 3/2. A more complex example comes from 2:6.

(6) w^{e}lṓ’   ’ām^{e}rû́,   ’ayyḗh   yhwh
hamma‘^{a}léh   ’ōṯā́nû   mē’éreṣ   miṣrā́yim
hammôlíḵ   ’ôṯā́nû   bammiḏbā́r
b^{e}’éreṣ   ‘^{a}rāḇā́   w^{e}šûḥā́
b^{e}’éreṣ   ṣiyyā́   w^{e}ṣalmā́weṯ
b^{e}’éreṣ   lō’-‘ā́ḇar   bā́h   ’î́š
w^{e}lṓ’-yāšáḇ   ’āḏā́m   šā́m
(7) wā’āḇî́’   ’eṯ^{e}ḵém   ’el-’éreṣ   hakkarmél
le’^{e}ḵṓl   piryā́h   w^{e}ṭûḇā́h
wattāḇṓ’û   watt^{e}ṭamm^{e}’û́   ’eṯ-’arṣí
w^{e}naḥ^{a}lāṯî́   śamtém   l^{e}ṯô‘ēḇā́

The meter may be 4/4, 3/3/3, 4/3, 4/3, 3/3. But there is room for a difference of opinion in some lines since we are not certain how quickly a speaker would pass over some small words but emphasize others. Thus the last two cola of v. 6 might be described as 3/3 rather than 4/3 if we absorb the element *bāh* into the verb, and the first line of v. 6 may be 3/3 if we do not accent *w^{e}lō'*, and absorb the accusative *'ōṯānû* into the first verb. Also the *'eṯ^{e}ḵem* of the first line of v. 7 may be absorbed into the verb. If these changes are made we have a passage that has three stresses to every colon throughout.

These remarks are not designed to be exhaustive but merely to introduce the reader to some of the main features of Hebrew poetry.

Because of our uncertainty about meter it may be that there remains hidden behind some apparently prose passages what was originally poetry. It is not always easy to recognize the difference between verse and rhythmical prose. But perhaps they were so close as to be indistinguishable.[7] Some recent studies of passages in Jeremiah have endeavored to define as verse some areas of the book previously understood to be prose.[8] The point may be important exegetically since many scholars will accept poetic material as authentic Jeremiah material where they find difficulty with prose.

The discovery of important texts from Ras Shamra, the ancient Ugarit, on the Syrian coast, by C. H. Schaeffer in the years following 1929 have added a new dimension to the study of ancient Hebrew poetry, since both in formal language and in the poetic structure a growing volume of parallels has been demonstrated.[9] Many advances in the study of this ancient Western Semitic dialect and its literature have had a significant impact on the study of Hebrew poetry.[10] The last has not been heard, therefore, on the poetic portions in the book of Jeremiah.

7. Some modern poetry lacks the formal structure of classical poetry but consists of a collection of vivid pictures and ideas expressed in elevated language. If the poetic appearance in which it is presented is destroyed and it is allowed to run on, it might be regarded as elevated and often rhythmical prose. The problem is an ancient one, however.

8. See pp. 606f. where the work of E. Lipiński is mentioned. But W. L. Holladay has recently proposed other areas which are probably poetic. See p. 48.

9. For an older but still valuable discussion see W. F. Albright, "The OT and Canaanite Language and Literature," *CBQ* 7 (1945), pp. 5–31.

10. The three volumes of M. Dahood on *Psalms* in the Anchor Bible make continual reference to insights provided by Ugaritic.

IX. ANALYSIS OF CONTENTS

Any analysis of contents has a certain artificiality about it. It is an attempt to arrange the text of a particular book into manageable sections for study. The students of the book of Jeremiah have sought for centuries to understand the structure of the book as it left the hands of its final editors. He would be a bold man who would claim to have discovered the organizing principles, although many have made a valiant attempt to do so. The present analysis makes no claim to originality but perhaps it may provide the student with a helpful guide to the contents of the book.

SUPERSCRIPTION (1:1–3)

I. THE CALL OF JEREMIAH AND THE TWO VISIONS (1:4–19)

- (i) The Call of Jeremiah (1:4–10)
- (ii) The Two Visions (1:11–16)
- (iii) The Divine Charge and Promise (1:17–19)

II. THE DIVINE JUDGMENT ON JUDAH AND JERUSALEM (2:1–25:38)

A. ISRAEL'S GUILT AND PUNISHMENT (2:1–6:30)

1. Israel Indicted for Her Sins (2:1–37)
   - (i) The Faithfulness of Israel's Youth: Her Ideal Status (2:1–3)
   - (ii) Israel's Apostasy (2:4–13)
   - (iii) The Consequences of Israel's Apostasy (2:14–19)
   - (iv) The Fascination and Futility of Baal Worship (2:20–28)
   - (v) Israel Deserves Judgment (2:29–37)
2. A Plea for Israel's Repentance (3:1–4:4)
   - (i) The Alarm—Invasion Is Threatened (4:5–10)
   - (ii) Apostate Israel and Faithless Judah (3:6–11)
   - (iii) Israel Summoned to Repent. Future Promises (3:12–18)
   - (iv) The Need for True Repentance (3:19–4:4)
3. The Coming Judgment (4:5–6:30)
   - (i) The Alarm—Invasion is Threatened (4:5–10)
   - (ii) The Scorching Hot Wind of Judgment (4:11–18)
   - (iii) Jeremiah's Anguished Cry (4:19–22)
   - (iv) A Vision and an Oracle about the Coming Destruction (4:23–28)
   - (v) The Death Agony of Zion (4:29–31)
   - (vi) The Unpardonable Sin and Moral Depravity of Jerusalem (5:1–9)
   - (vii) False Security in the Face of a Terrible Foe (5:10–19)
   - (viii) Yahweh Warns a Foolish, Rebellious, Complacent People (5:20–31)
   - (ix) Jerusalem under Siege (6:1–8)
   - (x) Judgment Falls on a Corrupt People (6:9–15)

(xi) Elaborate Ritual No Substitute for Obedience (6:16–21)
(xii) The Terrible Foe from the North (6:22–26)
(xiii) Jeremiah, the Assayer of His People (6:27–30)

B. FALSE RELIGION AND ITS PUNISHMENT (7:1–10:25)
1. The Temple Sermon and False Religion (7:1–8:3)
(i) The Temple Sermon (7:1–15)
(ii) The Cult of the Queen of Heaven (7:16–20)
(iii) Obedience rather than Mere Sacrifice (7:21–28)
(iv) Sinful Deeds in the Valley of Hinnom (7:29–34)
(v) Astral Worship and its Awful Punishment (8:1–3)
2. An Incorrigible People and Their Fate (8:4–10:25)
(i) Blindly Complacent and Heading to Ruin (8:4–12)
(ii) No Grapes on the Vine (8:13–17)
(iii) The Prophet's Passionate Grief over Jerusalem (8:18–23 [Eng. 9:1])
(iv) A Depraved People and Yahweh's Judgment (9:1–8 [Eng. 2–9])
(v) Jerusalem's Ruin (9:9–15 [Eng. 10–16])
(vi) A Dirge over Jerusalem (9:16–21 [Eng. 17–22])
(vii) Man's Only Grounds for Boasting (9:22–23 [Eng. 23–24])
(viii) The Worthlessness of Circumcision (9:24–25 [Eng. 25–26])
(ix) A Satire on Idolatry: Yahweh and the Idols (10:1–16)
(x) The Coming Exile: Lament and Intercession (10:17–25)

C. WARNINGS AND JUDGMENT (11:1–15:9)
1. The Broken Covenant and Warnings of Judgment (11:1–13:27)
(i) The Broken Covenant (11:1–17)
(ii) A Plot against Jeremiah's Life (11:18–12:6)
(iii) Yahweh Laments His Ravaged Inheritance (12:7–13)
(iv) Yahweh's Conditional Promise of Death or Life for Israel's Neighbors (12:14–17)
(v) The Linen Waistcloth: A Symbolic Act (13:1–11)
(vi) The Parable of the Wine Jars (13:12–14)
(vii) A Plea and a Last Warning (13:15–17)
(viii) A Lament over the King and the Queen Mother (13:18–19)
(ix) Jerusalem's Incurable Sickness and Punishment (13:20–27)
2. Laments in a Time of Drought and National Defeat (14:1–15:9)
(i) Lament, Supplication, and Divine Response in a Time of Drought (14:1–16)
(ii) A Further Lament and Supplication in a Time of Defeat and Famine (14:17–15:4)
(iii) Jerusalem's Terrible Fate (15:5–9)

(d) The dream and God's word contrasted (23:23–32)
(e) The burden of Yahweh (23:33–40)

3. Two Visions and a Summary (24:1–25:38)
(i) The Two Baskets of Figs (24:1–10)
(ii) A Concluding Summary (25:1–14)
(iii) Judgment on the Nations—Yahweh's Cup of Wrath (25:15–29)
(iv) The Universal Judgment of Yahweh (25:30–38).

III. JEREMIAH'S CONTROVERSY WITH FALSE PROPHETS (26:1–29:32)

A. THE TEMPLE SERMON AND ITS CONSEQUENCES (26:1–24)

B. JEREMIAH AND THE FALSE PROPHETS (27:1–29:32)
(i) Jeremiah Warns against a Coalition against Nebuchadrezzar (27:1–22)
(ii) Jeremiah against Hananiah: Prophecy against Prophecy (28:1–17)
(iii) Correspondence with the Exiles (29:1–32)

IV. THE BOOK OF CONSOLATION (30:1–33:26)

A. THE RESTORATION OF ISRAEL AND JUDAH (30:1–31:40)
(i) Superscription (30:1–3)
(ii) Jacob's Distress and Deliverance (30:4–11)
(iii) The Healing of Zion's Wounds (30:12–17)
(iv) The Restoration of Jacob (30:18–22)
(v) The Divine Judgment: A Fragment (30:23–24; 31:1)
(vi) Further Promises to Ephraim and Judah (31:2–6)
(vii) Israel's Homecoming (31:7–14)
(viii) The End of Rachel's Mourning (31:15–22)
(ix) The Restoration of Judah (31:23–26)
(x) Two Short Sayings (31:27–30)
(xi) The New Covenant (31:31–34)
(xii) The Inseparable Bond between Yahweh and Israel (31:35–37)
(xiii) The New Jerusalem (31:38–40)

B. THE RESTORATION OF JUDAH AND JERUSALEM: A PROSE COLLECTION (32:1–33:26)
(i) Jeremiah's Purchase of Land at Anathoth (32:1–15)
(ii) Jeremiah's Prayer (32:16–25)
(iii) Yahweh's Reply to Jeremiah (32:26–35)
(iv) Yaweh's Reply, continued (32:36–44)
(v) Jerusalem and Judah Restored (33:1–13)
(vi) The Dynasty of David and the Levitical Priests (33:14–26)

V. INCIDENTS FROM THE DAYS OF JEHOIAKIM AND ZEDEKIAH (34:1–39:18)

(i) A Message to Zedekiah (34:1–7)
(ii) Treachery against Slaves (34:8–22)
(iii) Jeremiah and the Rechabites (35:1–19)
(iv) Jeremiah's Scrolls (36:1–32)
(a) The writing of the scroll: Yahweh's word recorded (36:1–8)
(b) The reading of the scroll: Yahweh's word heard (36:9–20)
(c) Jehoiakim destroys the scroll: Yahweh's word rejected (36:21–26)
(d) The scroll is rewritten: Yahweh's word preserved (36:27–32)
(v) Zedekiah Consults Jeremiah: First Account (37:1–10)
(vi) Jeremiah's Arrest and Imprisonment (37:11–21)
(vii) Zedekiah Consults Jeremiah: Second Account (38:1–28a)
(a) Arrest and imprisonment (38:1–6)
(b) Jeremiah rescued from the miry cistern (38:7–13)
(c) Zedekiah's last interview with Jeremiah (38:14–28a)
(viii) The Fall of Jerusalem (39:1–10)
(ix) Jeremiah's Release: First Account (39:11–14)
(x) Hope for Ebed-melech (39:15–18)

VI. JEREMIAH'S EXPERIENCES AFTER THE FALL OF JERUSALEM (40:1–45:5)

A. IN JUDAH (40:1–43:7)
(i) Jeremiah's Release: A Second Account (40:1–6)
(ii) Gedaliah and the Community in Judah after 587 B.C. (40:7–12)
(iii) The Assassination of Gedaliah (40:13–41:3)
(iv) Further Atrocities (41:4–18)
(v) The Flight to Egypt: Jeremiah's Warning Rejected (42:1–43:7)
(a) Jeremiah is consulted (42:1–6)
(b) Yahweh's answer to Jeremiah's prayer (42:7–22)
(c) Jeremiah and the community go to Egypt (43:1–7)

B. IN EGYPT (43:8–45:5)
(i) Nebuchadrezzar's Invasion of Egypt Foretold (43:8–13)
(ii) Jeremiah's Last Known Words (44:1–30)
(a) No remorse for sin and no reverence for Yahweh (44:1–14)
(b) Idolatry in Egypt (44:15–19)
(c) Jeremiah's final condemnation (44:20–30)

(iii) A Parenthesis: Baruch's Despair and Consolation (45:1–5)

VII. ORACLES AGAINST THE NATIONS (46:1–51:64)

(i) Egypt (46:1–28)
- (a) The defeat of Egypt at Carchemish (46:1–12)
- (b) Nebuchadrezzar's conquest of Egypt (46:13–24)
- (c) Two fragments: Egypt humiliated; Israel delivered (46:25–28)

(ii) The Philistines (47:1–7)

(iii) Moab (48:1–47)
- (a) The destruction of Moab (48:1–10)
- (b) Moab's complacency ended (48:11–17)
- (c) Catastrophe for Moab's cities (48:18–28)
- (d) A lament over Moab (48:29-39)
- (e) Moab's doom—and final mercy (48:40–47)

(iv) Ammon (49:1–6)

(v) Edom (49:7–22)

(vi) Damascus (49:23–27)

(vii) Arab Tribes (49:28–33)

(viii) Elam (49:34–39)

(ix) Babylon (50:1–51:64)
- (a) Babylon's fall and Israel's release (50:1–10)
- (b) Babylon's fall (50:11–16)
- (c) Israel's return (50:17–20)
- (d) God's judgment on Babylonia (50:21–40)
- (e) The agony of Babylon (50:41–46)
- (f) Again—the judgment of Babylon (51:1–14)
- (g) A hymn of praise to God (51:15–19)
- (h) Yahweh's hammer and its end (51:20–26)
- (i) The nations ally against Babylon (51:27–33)
- (j) Judah's complaint against Babylon and Yahweh's requital (51:34–40)
- (k) Babylon's fate (51:41–48)
- (l) Yahweh's message to the exiles in Babylon (51:49–53)
- (m) Babylon is finally repaid in full (51:54–58)
- (n) A symbolic action against Babylon (51:59–64)

VIII. APPENDIX—THE FALL OF JERUSALEM (52:1–34)

(i) The Fall of the City and the Capture of Zedekiah (52:1–16)

(ii) The Sacking of the Temple (52:17–23)

(iii) The Numbers Deported to Babylon (52:24–30)

(iv) The Release of Jehoiachin from Prison (52:31–34)

X. SELECT BIBLIOGRAPHY

An enormous quantity of secondary literature has appeared in recent years on the book of Jeremiah, both books and scholarly articles. The bibliography that follows is necessarily selective, and the serious student or scholar will want to consult those works marked with an *asterisk* for additional extensive bibliographies.

A. *Commentaries and Books*

Aharoni, Y., *The Land of the Bible* (London, 1967).
Albright, W. F., *Archaeology and the Religion of Israel* (Baltimore, 1946).
Idem, From the Stone Age to Christianity, 2nd ed. (Baltimore, 1957).
Idem, The Archaeology of Palestine (London, 1960).
*Bright, J., *Jeremiah* (New York, 1965), Anchor Bible 20.
Idem, A History of Israel, 2nd ed. (Philadelphia, 1972).
Brueggemann, W., *Tradition for Crisis* (Richmond, 1968).
Clements, R. E., *Prophecy and Covenant* (London, 1965).
Condamin, A., *Le Livre de Jérémie*, 3rd ed. (Paris, 1936).
Couturier, G. P., "Jeremiah" in *JBC* (London, 1968).
Cowley, A., *Aramaic Papyri of the Fifth Century B.C.* (Oxford, 1923).
Cunliffe-Jones, H., *Jeremiah* (London, 1960), SCM Torch.
*Dahood, M., *Psalms I, II, and III* (New York, 1966–70), Anchor Bible 16, 17, 17A.
Driver, G. R., *Canaanite Myths and Legends* (Edinburgh, 1956).
Driver, S. R., *The Book of the Prophet Jeremiah* (London, 1906).
Duhm, B., *Das Buch Jeremia* (Tübingen, 1901).
Eissfeldt, O., *The Old Testament: An Introduction,* 3rd ed. (Oxford, 1965).
Giesebrecht, D. F., *Das Buch Jeremia* (Göttingen, 1907).
Glueck, N., *Ḥesed in the Bible* (Cincinnati, 1967), trans. by A. Gottschalk.
Gray, J., *I and II Kings,* 2nd ed. (London, 1970).
Idem, The Legacy of Canaan, 2nd ed., SVT V (Leiden, 1965).
Harrison, R. K., *Jeremiah and Lamentations* (London, 1973).
Heaton, E. W., *The Old Testament Prophets* (London, 1961).
*Hillers, D., *Treaty-Curses and the Old Testament Prophets* (Rome, 1964).
Holladay, W. L., *The Root šûbh in the Old Testament* (Leiden, 1958).
Idem, Jeremiah: Spokesman Out of Time (Philadelphia, 1974).
**Idem, The Architecture of Jeremiah 1–20* (Lewisburg, 1976).
Hyatt, J. P., "*Jeremiah*" in *IB* V (New York, 1956).
Kenyon, K. M., *Jerusalem. Excavating 3000 Years of History* (London, 1967).
Leslie, E. A., *Jeremiah* (New York, 1954).
Lindblom, J., *Prophecy in Ancient Israel* (Oxford, 1962).
Mowinckel, S., *Zur Komposition des Buches Jeremia* (Kristiana, 1914).
*Nicholson, E. W., *Preaching to the Exiles* (Oxford, 1970).

Idem, Jeremiah 1–25 (Cambridge, 1973).
Idem, Jeremiah 26–52 (Cambridge, 1975).
Noth, M., *The History of Israel*, 2nd ed. (Oxford, 1960).
Nötscher, F., *Das Buch Jeremias* (Bonn, 1934).
Overholt, T. W., *The Threat of Falsehood* (London, 1970).
Paterson, J., "*Jeremiah*" in *Peake's Commentary on the Bible*, rev. ed. (London, 1962), pp. 537–562.
Peake, A. S., *Jeremiah*, 2 vols. (Edinburgh, 1910–12).
Rudolph, W., *Jeremiah*, 3rd ed. (Tübingen, 1968), HAT.
Saggs, H. W. F., *The Greatness that was Babylon* (London, 1962).
Skinner, J., *Prophecy and Religion* (Cambridge, 1922).
Smith, G. A., *Jeremiah*, 4th ed. (Cambridge, 1929).
Steinmann, J., *Le prophète Jérémie* (Paris, 1952).
Streane, A. W., *Jeremiah and Lamentations* (Cambridge, 1899).
Thomas, D. W., ed., *Archaeology and Old Testament Study* (Oxford, 1967).
Thompson, J. A., *The Vocabulary of Covenant in the Old Testament* (Unpub. Ph.D. thesis, Cambridge, 1963).
Idem, Deuteronomy (London, 1974).
deVaux, R., *Ancient Israel* (London, 1961).
Volz, P., *Der Prophet Jeremia* (Leipzig, 1922).
Weiser, A., *Das Buch des Propheten Jeremia* (Göttingen, 1960).
Welch, A. C., *Jeremiah: His Time and His Work* (Oxford, 1928).
Wiseman, D. J., *Chronicles of Chaldaean Kings (626–556 B.C.) in the British Museum* (London, 1956).

B. Articles

Ackroyd, P. R., "Jeremiah x:1–16," *JTS* N.S. 14/2 (1963), pp. 385–390.
Aharoni, Y., "Excavations at Ramat Raḥel," *BA* 24 (1961), pp. 98–118.
Idem, "Arad: Its Inscriptions and Temple," *BA* 31/1 (1968), pp. 2–32.
Idem, "The Horned Altar of Beersheba," *BA* 37/1 (1974), pp. 2–6.
Albright, W. F., "King Joiachin in Exile," *BA* 5 (1942), pp. 49–55.
Avigad, N., "Two Newly Found Hebrew Seals," *IEJ* 13 (1963), pp. 322f.
Bailey, K. E., and W. L. Holladay, "The 'Young Camel' and 'Wild Ass' in Jer. 2:23–25," *VT* 18 (1968), pp. 256–260.
Bergman, A., "Soundings at the Supposed Site of OT Anathoth," *BASOR* 62 (1936), pp. 22–26.
Biran, A., "Tel Dan," *BA* 37/3 (1974), pp. 26–51.
Blair, E. P., "Soundings at 'Anâtā (Roman Anathoth)," *BASOR* 62 (1936), pp. 18–21.
de Boer, P. A. H., "An Enquiry into the Meaning of the Term *maśśa'*," *OTS* 5 (1948), pp. 197–214.
Bright, J., "The Date of the Prose Sermons of Jeremiah," *JBL* 70 (1951), pp. 15–35.

Idem, "The Book of Jeremiah, Its Structure, Its Problems, and their Significance for the Interpreter," *Interpretation* 9 (1955), pp. 259–278.
Idem, "A New Letter in Aramaic Written to a Pharaoh of Egypt," *BA* 12 (1949), pp. 46–52.
Carroll, R. P., "A Non-cogent Argument in Jeremiah's Oracles against the Prophets," *Studia Theologica* 30 (1976), pp. 43–51.
Idem, "Ancient Israelite Prophecy and Dissonance Theory," *Numen* 24 (1977), pp. 129ff.
Clines, D. J. A., and D. M. Gunn, "Form, Occasion and Redaction in Jeremiah 20," *ZAW* 88 (1976), pp. 390–409.
Corney, R. W., "Abiathar," *IDB* I, pp. 6–7; "Eli," *IDB* II, p. 85.
Dahood, M., "Denominative *riḥḥam,* 'to conceive, enwomb,'" *Biblica* 44 (1963), pp. 204f.
Idem, "Two Textual Notes on Jeremiah," *CBQ* 23 (1961), pp. 462–64.
Idem, "Hebrew-Ugaritic Lexicography I," *Biblica* 44 (1963), pp. 289–303.
Idem, "The Metaphor in Jeremiah 17:13," *Biblica* 48 (1967), pp. 109f.
Idem, "Philological Notes on Jer. 18:14–15," *ZAW* 74 (1962), pp. 207–209.
Idem, "Ugaritic Studies and the Bible," *Gregorianum* 43 (1962), pp. 55–79.
Driver, G. R., "Linguistic and Textual Problems: Jeremiah," *JQR* 28 (1937/38), pp. 97–129.
Idem, "Birds in the OT—II," *PEQ*, 1955, pp. 139f.
Idem, "Two Misunderstood Passages of the OT," *JTS* N.S. 6 (1955), pp. 82–87.
Idem, "Difficult Words in the Hebrew Prophets," *Studies in OT Prophecy,* ed. H. H. Rowley, presented to T. H. Robinson (1950), pp. 52–72.
Ellison, H. L., Series of articles on "The Prophecy of Jeremiah," *EQ*, 1959–1968.
Ginsberg, H. L., "An Aramaic Contemporary of the Lachish Letters," *BASOR* 111 (1948), pp. 24–27.
Goldman, M. D., "Was Jeremiah Married?" *Australian Biblical Review* 2/1–2 (1952), pp. 42–47.
Greenberg, H., "Stocks," *IDB* IV, p. 443.
Haran, M., "The Disappearance of the Ark," *IEJ* 13 (1963), pp. 46–58.
Harvey, J., "Le 'Rîb-Pattern,' réquisitoire prophétique sur la rupture de l'alliance," *Biblica* 43 (1962), pp. 172–196.
Hobbs, T. R., "Some Remarks on the Structure and Composition of the Book of Jeremiah," *CBQ* 34 (1972), pp. 257–275.
Holladay, W. L., "The Background of Jeremiah's Self-Understanding: Moses, Samuel, and Psalm 22," *JBL* 83 (1964), pp. 153–164.
Idem, "Jeremiah and Moses: Further Observations," *JBL* 85 (1966), pp. 17–27.
Idem, "On Every High Hill and Under Every Green Tree," *VT* 11 (1961), pp. 170–76.

Idem, "Prototype and Copies: A New Approach to the Poetry-Prose Problem in the Book of Jeremiah," *JBL* 79 (1960), pp. 351–367.

Idem, "Style, Irony, and Authenticity in Jeremiah," *JBL* 81 (1962), pp. 44–54.

Idem, "The so-called 'Deuteronomic Gloss' in Jer. 8:19b," *VT* 12 (1962), pp. 494–98.

Idem, "'The priests scrape out on their hands', Jeremiah V:31," *VT* 15 (1965), pp. 111–13.

Idem, "Jeremiah's Lawsuit with God," *Interpretation* 17 (1963), pp. 280–87.

Idem, "The Recovery of Poetic Passages of Jeremiah," *JBL* 85 (1966), pp. 401–435.

Huffmon, H. B., "The Treaty Background of Hebrew *Yāda',*" *BASOR* 181 (1966), pp. 31–37.

Idem, "Prophecy in the Mari Letters," *BA* 31/4 (1968), pp. 101–124.

Hyatt, J. P., "The Deity Bethel and the OT," *JAOS* 59 (1939), pp. 81–98.

Irwin, W. A., "An Ancient Biblical Text," *AJSL* 48 (1931), p. 184.

Kessler, M., "Form-critical Suggestions on Jer. 36," *CBQ* 28 (1966), pp. 389–401.

Idem, "From Drought to Exile, A Morphological Study of Jer. 14:1–15:4," *Proceedings of the Society of Biblical Literature*, 1922, pp. 501–525.

Idem, "Jeremiah Chapters 26–45 Reconsidered," *JNES* 27 (1968), pp. 61–88.

Kjaer, H., "The Excavation of Shiloh 1929," *JPOS* 10/2–3 (1930), pp. 87–114.

Lambdin, T. O., "Migdol," *IDB* III, p. 377.

Idem, "Put," *IDB* III, p. 971.

Lambert, W. G., "Celibacy in the World's Oldest Proverb," *BASOR* 169 (1963), pp. 63f.

Landes, E. M., "The Fountain of Jazer," *BASOR* 144 (1956), pp. 30–37.

Idem, "The Material Civilization of the Ammonites," *BA* 24 (1961), pp. 66–86.

Lehmann, M. R., "A New Interpretation of the Term *šdmwt,*" *VT* 3 (1953), pp. 361–371.

Lipiński, E., "*b^{e}'aḥ^{a}rîṯ hayyāmîm* dans les textes préexiliques," *VT* 20 (1970), pp. 445–450.

Idem, "Prose ou poésie en Jer. xxxiv:1–7?" *VT* 24 (1974), pp. 112f.

Lofthouse, W. F., "Ḥen and Ḥesed in the OT," *ZAW* 51 (1933), pp. 29–35.

Long, Burke O., "The Stylistic Components of Jeremiah 3:1–5," *ZAW* 88 (1976), pp. 386–390.

Malamat, A., "The Historical Setting of Two Biblical Prophecies on the Nations," *IEJ* 1 (1950/51), pp. 154–59.

May, H. G., "Some Cosmic Connotations of *mayim rabbîm*, 'Many Waters,'" *JBL* 74 (1955), pp. 9–21.

McCarthy, D. J., "Covenant in the OT: The Present State of Inquiry," *CBQ* 27 (1965), pp. 217–240.

Moran, W. L., "The Ancient Near Eastern Background of the Love of God in Deuteronomy," *CBQ* 25 (1963), pp. 77–87.

Idem, "Ugaritic *ṣîṣûma* and Hebrew *ṣîṣ,*" *Biblica* 39 (1958), pp. 69–71.

Nicholson, E. W., "The Meaning of the Expression *'am hā'āreṣ* in the OT," *JSS* 10 (1965), pp. 59–66.

Idem, "Blood-spattered Altars?" *VT* 27 (1977), pp. 113–16.

Olley, J. W., "A Forensic Connotation of *bôš,*" *VT* 26 (1976), pp. 230–34.

Orr, A., "The Seventy Years of Babylon," *VT* 6 (1956), pp. 304–306.

Overholt, T. W., "The Falsehood of Idolatry: An Interpretation of Jer. X:1–16," *JTS* N.S. 16 (1965), pp. 1–12.

Soggin, J. A., "Jeremias 6:27–30," *VT* 9 (1959), pp. 95–98.

Swetnam, J., "Some Observations on the Background of *ṣaddîq* in Jeremias 23:5a," *Biblica* 46 (1965), pp. 29–40.

Thomas, D. W., "*Ṣalmāweṯ* in the OT," *JSS* 7 (1962), pp. 191–200.

Idem, "A Note on *weᵉlō' yāḏā'û* in Jeremiah 24:1," *JTS* N.S. 3 (1952), p. 55.

Idem, "A Note on *mû'āḏîm* in Jeremiah 24:1," *JTS* N.S. 3 (1952), p. 55.

Idem, The "Prophet" in the Lachish Ostraca. Tyndale Monograph (1946).

Thompson, J. A., "The Root *'-l-m* in Semitic Languages and Some Proposed New Translations in Ugaritic and Hebrew," *Festschrift A. Vööbus* (1977), pp. 301–308.

Idem, "The Significance of the Verb *Love* in the David-Jonathan Narratives in I Samuel," *VT* 24 (1974), pp. 334–38.

Idem, "Israel's 'Lovers,'" *VT* 27 (1977), pp. 475–481.

Tsevat, M., "Alalakhiana," *HUCA* 29 (1958), pp. 125f.

de Vaux, R., "Mélanges: Le sceau de Godolias, maître du palais," *RB* 45 (1936), pp. 96–102.

Vogt, E., "70 anni exsilii," *Biblica* 38 (1957), p. 236.

Idem, "Vox *bᵉrît* concrete adhibita illustratur," *Biblica* 36 (1955), pp. 565f.

Weinfeld, M., "Jeremiah and the Spiritual Metamorphosis of Israel," *ZAW* 88 (1976), pp. 17–56.

Wernberg-Møller, P., "The Pronoun *'tmh* and Jeremiah's Pun," *VT* 6 (1956), pp. 315f.

Whitley, C. F., "The Term Seventy Years Captivity," *VT* 4 (1954), pp. 60–72.

Idem, "The Seventy Years Desolation—A Rejoinder," *VT* 7 (1957), pp. 416–18.

Wiseman, D. J., "The Vassal-Treaties of Esarhaddon," *Iraq* 20 (1958), pp. 1–90.

Idem, "Abban and Alalakh," *JCS* 12/4 (1958), pp. 124–129.

Wright, G. E., "Solomon's Temple Resurrected," *BA* 4/2 (1941), pp. 17–31.

Yadin, Y., "Expedition D—The Cave of Letters," *IEJ* 12 (1962), pp. 227–267.

Yaure, L., "Elymas—Nehelamite—Pethor," *JBL* 79 (1960), pp. 297–314.

Zayadine, F., "Recent Excavations on the Citadel of Amman," *ADAJ* 17 (1973), pp. 17–53.

Zevit, Z., "The Use of *'eḇeḏ* as a Diplomatic Term in Jeremiah," *JBL* 88 (1969), pp. 74–77.

TEXT AND COMMENTARY

SUPERSCRIPTION (1:1–3)

1 *The message of Jeremiah*[1] *ben Hilkiah, one of the priests at Anathoth in the land of Benjamin,*
2 *to whom the word of Yahweh came in the thirteenth year of the reign of Josiah ben Amon king of Judah,*
3 *and also during the reign of Jehoiakim ben Josiah king of Judah, until the end of the eleventh year of Zedekiah ben Josiah king of Judah, that is, until the deportation of the people of Jerusalem in the fifth month.*

1 The editorial introduction to the book of Jeremiah gives three important pieces of information which are basic to the understanding of the book as a whole: some personal details about the prophet, the divine source of the messages of Jeremiah, and the period during which Jeremiah's ministry was exercised.

The prophet is introduced by name, family, status, and place of origin, which is a reasonably comprehensive introduction[2] and much more complete than that given for some other prophets.[3] Jeremiah was the son of a certain Hilkiah, who is otherwise unknown. The name *Jeremiah* was common in Judah. It occurs several times in the OT. At the time of David there were two, and possibly three Jeremiahs among David's mighty men (1 Chr. 12:4, 10, 13). In the book of Jeremiah there are two other individuals who bore the same name, one a Rechabite referred to in 35:3, and the other the maternal grandfather of King Zedekiah (52:1; 2 K. 24:18). The meaning of the name is uncertain, but two proposals have been made, either "Yahweh loosens (the womb)" or "Yahweh exalts."

1. LXX reads "The word of God which came to Jeremiah." The same information comes in v. 2 in MT.
2. Cf. Isa. 1:1; Hos. 1:1; Amos 1:1; Mic. 1:1; Zeph. 1:1.
3. Cf. Ezek. 1:3; Obad. 1:1; Jon. 1:1; Nah. 1:1; Hab. 1:1; Hag. 1:1; Zech. 1:1; Mal. 1:1.

The name of Jeremiah's father, *Hilkiah*, was also a common name. The most famous of the men who bore this name was the priest who found the "book of the law" in the temple in 622 B.C. (2 K. 22:8). It is most unlikely that Jeremiah's father was the same man. However, Hilkiah was a member of a priestly family that lived, not in Jerusalem, but at Anathoth some 3 miles northeast of Jerusalem. It has been suggested that Jeremiah's family may have descended from Abiathar, who was David's priest but was deposed by Solomon in favor of Zadok and banished to his home in Anathoth (1 K. 2:26–27). His complicity in the attempt of Adonijah to usurp the throne (1 K. 1:5–19) lends support to this view. Solomon might have put him to death but spared him because he shared in David's affliction and carried the Ark in David's time (1 K. 2:26). There is no evidence that Jeremiah himself ever functioned as a priest and, indeed, he was often in opposition to the priests (2:26; 4:9; 5:31; 13:13; 19:1; etc.). His whole outlook and his oracles lack the priestly background which comes through clearly in Ezekiel. However, if Jeremiah did not perform priestly functions, one wonders whether, in the days preceding Josiah's great reforms, his father may not have had priestly duties like instructing the local community in the "law" and handing on the old covenant traditions. He might even have presided over certain sacrifices offered in the village by the villagers. Josiah's reforms would change all that. The ancient sanctuary of Shiloh was a mere 20 miles away to the north, and Jeremiah's father, probably a descendant of Abiathar, may have had strong links with Eli the priest some centuries earlier (1 Sam. 14:3; 22:20; 1 K. 2:27). Such an ancestry would explain Jeremiah's deep feeling for Israel's ancient traditions, his special interest in Shiloh and its fate (7:14; 26:6), his genuine concern for the people of Northern Israel, and his affinity with Hosea, the great prophet to the people of Northern Israel in the eighth century B.C.[4]

His village was *Anathoth*[5] in the land of Benjamin, in the general area of the present-day Arab village of 'Anata, which preserves the ancient name. Anathoth is mentioned in a list of Levitical cities in Josh. 21:18 dating back to at least the tenth century B.C. There are, however, problems of identification since the Anathoth of Jeremiah's day is not the same as the modern 'Anata. One pro-

4. See R. W. Corney, "Abiathar," *IDB* I, pp. 6–7; "Eli," *IDB* II, p. 85; cf. J. Bright, *Jeremiah* (1965), pp. lxxxvii–lxxxviii.
5. See 11:21, 23; 32:7–9.

posed identification is *Ras el-Kharrabeh* near the modern village.[6] Anathoth was situated in the land of Benjamin which lay on the northern frontier of Judah. Three passages in the book of Jeremiah refer to the gate of Benjamin,[7] which must have been situated on the northern side of the city. From vantage points in Anathoth one could clearly see the walls of Jerusalem. Jeremiah grew up not *in* the great capital but within sight of it. The modern visitor to ʿAnata can visualize the whole scene of Jeremiah's frequent visits to Jerusalem across the intervening hills about an hour's walk away.

2–3 The claim is made that *the word of Yahweh came* to Jeremiah over a period of time. It was a claim that Jeremiah himself often made. His oracles had a supernatural origin. He did not speak out of his own understanding of the ways of Yahweh, but he had stood in the council *(sôḏ)* of Yahweh (23:18, 22) and knew the mind of Yahweh as other prophets did not (23:22). He based his claim to be Yahweh's servant on the fact that his words would be fulfilled since they were Yahweh's words. That inspiration was a warrant for the preservation of Jeremiah's words, and there were those like Baruch who carefully preserved them for posterity.

The period of Jeremiah's ministry extended from the thirteenth year of Josiah's reign, i.e., 627 B.C., to the time of the second deportation, 587 B.C., thus during the last part of the seventh and the early part of the sixth century B.C. There is particular significance in the reference to the *deportation (gālûṯ)* of Jerusalem. This event was a climax to Jeremiah's preaching and a demonstration of his authenticity as a genuine prophet of Yahweh, for in that event the basic thrust of his prophecy was fulfilled. He had spoken of judgment over many years and had referred specifically to the overthrow of the kingdom of Judah and the destruction of Jerusalem. When this happened the real culmination and climax of his message was reached. The short period of renewed activity recorded in chs. 42–44, though significant in itself, is something like an appendix to his ministry and had relevance mainly to the group of exiles who fled to Egypt. It did, of course, serve to emphasize that the future hopes of a restored Israel lay elsewhere than with the exiles to Egypt.

The range of years given in v. 3 is very general. We have

6. P. Blair, "Soundings at ʿAnâtā (Roman Anathoth)," *BASOR* 62 (1936), pp. 18–22; A. Bergman, "Soundings at the Supposed Site of OT Anathoth," *ibid.*, pp. 22–26.
7. 20:2; 37:13; 38:7.

already discussed the date when Jeremiah began his ministry.[8] There is some debate as to how much of his ministry actually took place in Josiah's reign. At the other end of his life he certainly continued preaching after the commencement of the Exile since he was taken to Egypt with a group of refugees, and at least some of his preaching there is given in chs. 42–44. Hence the statement in v. 3 should be understood as being a somewhat loose reference to the period of Jeremiah's ministry. But the historical framework is intended to indicate that the words of Jeremiah were given in a historical context. For a proper understanding of the import of his words a knowledge of the historical, geographical, and cultural background is essential. We shall be at pains throughout this commentary to bring these features to the fore. The transfer of great truths from Jeremiah's age to another age may be made by searching for parallels and differences between his and a later age. The truths that confronted men in Jeremiah's day and in his historical, cultural, and religious setting may provide guidelines for believers in every age.

8. Introduction, "The Date of Jeremiah's Call," pp. 50–56.

I. THE CALL OF JEREMIAH AND THE TWO VISIONS (1:4–19)

(i) The Call of Jeremiah (1:4–10)

4 *The word of Yahweh came to me*[1] *thus:*
5 *"Before I formed you in the womb I knew you intimately;*[2]
Before you were born[3] *I set you apart,*[4]
And appointed[5] *you a prophet to the nations."*
6 *Then I answered, "Ah, my Lord Yahweh! Look! I don't know how to speak; I am only a boy!"*
7 *But Yahweh answered me,*
"Don't say, 'I am a boy';
For you will go to everyone to whom I send you[6]
And you will tell them everything I command you to say.
8 *Don't be afraid of them!*
For I am with you to rescue you[7]*—Yahweh's word."*

1. LXX reads "to him" in narrative style.
2. A strong element of personal commitment is conveyed by the verb *yāḏa'* in Hebrew; hence NEB "I knew you for my own"; J. Bright, *Jeremiah*, p. 3, "I chose you."
3. Lit. "Before you came forth from the womb."
4. The Hiphil *hiqdîš* partakes of the meaning of the root *qdš* which denotes being "separated," "set apart," generally for some sacred purpose. The Hiphil as a causative denotes "to cause someone or something to be set apart." It is therefore often translated "consecrate" or "dedicate." See KB, p. 825, for the range of meanings. NEB and RSV translate "consecrate," GNB "selected you," J. Bright, p. 3, "set you apart."
5. Lit. "I gave you." But frequently the verb has the sense of "appoint" or "set."
6. Lit. "upon whatever (or, to whomever) I send you," or, since the prepositions *'al* and *'el* seem to be interchanged frequently in the book of Jeremiah, "to whomsoever I send you" or "to whatever place I send you."
7. The root *nṣl* means "to snatch away." The Hiphil here means "rescue," "protect," "deliver."

9 *Then Yahweh stretched out his hand*[8] *and touched my mouth, and*
Yahweh said to me:
"Look![9] *I have put my words in your mouth.*
10 *See! I have given you authority*[10] *this day*
Over nations and kingdoms
To uproot and to pull down,
To destroy and to demolish,
To build and to plant."

The rest of ch. 1 is concerned with experiences associated with Jeremiah's call to the prophetic office, the confirmation of the call, and some definition of his task. The material undoubtedly came from Jeremiah himself. But despite the fact that the whole chapter is concerned with Jeremiah's call, it is a gathering together of several experiences and combines words which were spoken on a number of occasions. The call itself in vv. 4–10 is in the form of a dialog[11] between Jeremiah and Yahweh. The two visions in vv. 11–12 and 13–16 were probably given somewhat later, though the experiences may still have happened quite early in Jeremiah's ministry. These too are in dialog form, and the fact that the second vision is introduced with "The word of Yahweh came to me a second time" suggests that it was later than the first. This expression occurs in vv. 4, 11, and 13, suggesting separate experiences. At some time future to these experiences the material was brought together and placed at the beginning of the book after the superscription. It is not impossible that Jeremiah himself was responsible for such an arrangement. It may even be that this material formed the introduction to the scroll he dictated in 605 B.C. (see ch. 36) since it provides the sort of authentication of Jeremiah's right to speak in Yahweh's name that both he and his hearers needed. Indeed with this material as an introduction and the material in 25:1–13a which came from the fourth year of Jehoiakim (605 B.C.) as a conclusion, the oracles of Jeremiah's first collection would have been set in a significant framework.

4 The expression *the word of Yahweh* (cf. v. 1 and *passim* in Jeremiah), which opens the account of Jeremiah's call, is signif-

8. LXX adds "to me."
9. Heb. *hinnēh* is difficult to translate. The AV renderings "Behold!" "Lo!" are archaic. Depending on the context some such exclamation as "Look!" "See!" "There!" "Come!" "See here!" "Listen!" may be used.
10. Lit. "I have appointed you," Hiphil of *pqd*. The noun *pāqîḏ*, "overseer," describes Pashhur in 20:1, "overseer of the house of Yahweh."
11. The dialog has been recognized in recent years as a widely used literary form in biblical literature.

icant. The noun *dāḇār* in Hebrew means "word," "thing," "action," etc. For the ancient Israelite, "word" and "event" were part of the same experience. What a person thinks or plans, what he says and what he does are all part of the same event. During his ministry Jeremiah both preached and performed symbolic acts (chs. 13, 18, 19; 51:59–64); both these activities were means of declaring the word of Yahweh.

5 The clear consciousness of a call came to Jeremiah in the form of a dialog. That was not an unusual occurrence in Israel. Isaiah's call involved a dialog (Isa. 6) as did the call of Ezekiel (Ezek. 1–3). It was important for Jeremiah to be able to claim that his call had come direct from Yahweh since he was to encounter other prophets during the long years of his ministry. Of particular importance to Jeremiah was the awareness that he had been predestined to occupy the prophetic office since his birth, indeed before his birth. Yahweh's word was,

Before I formed you in the womb I knew you intimately;
Before you were born I set you apart,
And appointed you a prophet to the nations.

This opening word of the dialog is deeply significant. If ever Jeremiah in later days were overtaken by despair he could know that the divine purpose for him reached back before his birth. The three verbs used here are also significant. The verb *yāḏaʿ*, "know," often carried considerable depth of meaning in the OT, for it reached beyond mere intellectual knowledge to personal commitment.[12] For this reason it is used of the intimate relations between a man and his wife (Gen. 4:1). It was used of Yahweh's commitment to Israel: "You only have I known of all the families of the earth" (Amos 3:2). It was Yahweh's deep sorrow that there was no knowledge of God among his people (Hos. 4:1), for the knowledge of Yahweh was far more important than burnt offerings (Hos. 6:6). Yahweh's deep commitment to his servant, then, reached back before his birth.

The second verb, "set apart" *(hiqdîš)*, gathers about it another aspect of commitment. Basically the root *qdš* is concerned with setting something apart from all other uses to a specific use. It is therefore of significance in the religious sphere where persons, places, things, days, seasons can be set apart (consecrated) for

12. The verb was taken up on the political scene to denote the commitment of a vassal to his overlord. See H. B. Huffmon, "The Treaty Background of the Hebrew *yāḏaʿ*," *BASOR* 181 (1966), pp. 31–37.

Yahweh. Once set apart, these items were for the sole use of Yahweh, and it was an act of blasphemy to remove them from Yahweh's sovereign right to them. Jeremiah made use of the noun *qōḏeš*, "holiness," in reference to Israel's early acceptance of Yahweh's covenant (see comments on 2:2). Israel by that act had been set apart for Yahweh alone. She was his very own portion. Jeremiah understood himself in a similar light.[13] Yahweh had set him apart for a particular task. That awareness was to sustain him in many dark hours, and when he cursed the day of his birth he was really casting doubts upon his call (cf. 20:14–15).

The third verb, "appoint" *(ntn)*, refers to the specific assignment of Jeremiah to a particular task, that of being *a prophet to the nations*. A more normal verb would have been *pqd*, but the verb *ntn* is used in a number of important passages in the OT to describe this sort of special appointment (cf. Gen. 1:17; 17:5; Exod. 7:1; Isa. 49:6). Jeremiah's special appointment was to the nations (plur.), not simply to Judah alone. There were no limits to Yahweh's sovereignty and therefore there were no limits to the scope of Jeremiah's ministry. In the book of Jeremiah a large section is devoted to his oracles to the nations (chs. 46–51). Other prophets took the nations within the ambit of their concern, for example Amos (chs. 1–2), Isaiah (chs. 13–23), Ezekiel (chs. 25–32), Obadiah, Jonah, Nahum, Habakkuk. These last four had only a single nation in focus. But it would be generally true that all the prophets had some reason to refer to the nations. Clearly, if Yahweh was the God of the whole earth one would expect some of Yahweh's servants to express Yahweh's mind about the nations. It was an essential aspect of a monotheistic theology. It was a formidable task for a young man like Jeremiah, and it is little wonder that he hesitated.

But before taking up Jeremiah's response to Yahweh's call, reference must be made to the question of the date of the call. Two aspects of the call are clear. Yahweh had chosen and set apart Jeremiah from his birth. In a sense, then, his call could be dated from the time of his birth. But since a call can be recognized only once a person has reached a degree of maturity, Jeremiah did not respond to the divine purpose for him till he was a youth, although he was probably aware that Yahweh had a task for him to do even before he responded in a specific way. From which time, then, should his

13. The verb is the Hiphil of *qdš*. See KB, pp. 825f. for passages where this verb is used. The Piel of the same verb has a similar range of uses.

call be dated? The statement of v. 2 is that the word of Yahweh came to him in the thirteenth year of Josiah, which was 627 B.C. This could mean either that 627 B.C. was the year of his birth, since he was set apart at birth, or that he was already a youth (*na'ar*, v. 6) at that date. Both dates seem possible and commentators are sharply divided on the issue. If the call is to be dated at his birth, he would have known little about some of the great events of Josiah's day. Thus he would have been a small boy in the year when the "book of the law" was found in the temple and during the period of Josiah's reform (2 K. 22:3–23:27). It has been argued, indeed, that the reference in 15:16,[14] "Thy words were found and I ate them," deals with two events—the first, the finding of the scroll in the temple in 621 B.C., and the second, Jeremiah's own acceptance of the call many years after that event, perhaps at the end of Josiah's reign or even after his death. Alternatively, Jeremiah's call came in 627 B.C., and he was already a young man when the book of the law was found and the reforms took place. The answer we give to a number of questions in the book depends on the answer we give to this question.[15]

6 Jeremiah's response was hesitant and brief. Small wonder, since the great nations like Assyria, Babylon, Egypt were enough to cause consternation to a mere boy. But even smaller nations like Moab, Edom, Damascus, Philistia, and Ammon had a long history of violent activity against Israel. *I don't know how to speak* was a simple confession, not of dumbness, but of lack of training to speak confidently about any one of the nations. Equally disconcerting was the fact that Jeremiah was a mere *boy (na'ar)*. The exact meaning of the Hebrew word is difficult to determine, but in normal usage it refers to boys and youths.[16] On the two grounds then of inexperience and youth, Jeremiah hesitated to accept Yahweh's call.

The way in which a call from God came to a potential prophet is impossible to define, since God makes his approach in very personal ways. Often a good deal of preliminary activity goes on before a man responds. The experiences of life, the influence of other people, the personal cultivation of one's communion with God all contribute. It is difficult to avoid the conclusion that some in Jeremiah's

14. See commentary *in loc*.
15. See the Introduction, "The Date of Jeremiah's Call," pp. 50–56.
16. See KB, p. 623. The word means "child" or "infant" in Exod. 2:6; 1 Sam. 4:21, and also "young man" (Gen. 14:24; 22:3; 34:19). The sense here seems to be "youth" (cf. Judg. 8:14).

circle who were sincere adherents of the ancient covenant precepts influenced the growing boy. Possibly he had early contact with the "book of the law," almost certainly some form of the ancient covenant law and perhaps a form of the book of Deuteronomy. The proposal that Jeremiah's sense of God's pressure upon his life was influenced by such a passage as Deut. 18:18 has considerable merit.[17] Indeed, some of the actual phrases in that passage, which refers to another prophet, like Moses, whom God would raise up to continue the work of Moses, reappear here in vv. 7 and 9 only slightly modified. Deut. 18:18 reads, "I will put my words in his mouth, and he shall speak to them all that I command him." Probably no other account of a prophetic call in the OT resembles Deut. 18:18 so closely. It is altogether likely that Jeremiah formed the conviction that he was himself the prophet like Moses.

In several particulars Jeremiah was much like Moses. He shrank from God's call as Moses did. The narrative in Exod. 4:1–17 reveals Moses presenting excuse after excuse to God in answer to God's call. The people did not believe him. He was not eloquent but was slow of speech and tongue. Jeremiah also complained that he did not know how to speak. The prophet Isaiah like Moses and Jeremiah pleaded his unworthiness to undertake the task to which he was called (Isa. 6:5). In all three instances God rejected their protestations, and as their life-stories unfold it is clear they were commissioned for their task and duly undertook it.

7–9 Human inadequacy and inexperience provide the occasion for divine enablement. It was so in the case of Moses and Isaiah and it was the experience of Jeremiah. Yahweh rejected all excuses with a simple instruction, *"Don't say, 'I am a boy'; for you will go. . . ."* There was no choice of audience for Jeremiah. He was to go to anyone and everyone to whom Yahweh might send him. Nor did he have a choice of message. He was to tell his audience all that Yahweh commanded him (cf. Deut. 18:18).[18] It was a continuing conviction of Jeremiah's that he was simply speaking the word Yahweh had given him, and he declared this at times of extreme peril or at times when it might have been to his advantage

17. W. L. Holladay, "The Background of Jeremiah's Self-Understanding," *JBL* 83 (1964), pp. 153–164; "Jeremiah and Moses: Further Observations," *JBL* 85 (1966), pp. 17–27.

18. Deut. 18:18 reads *wᵉḏibber 'ᵃlêhem 'ēṯkol-'ᵃšer 'ᵃṣawwennû,* which is to be compared with v. 7, *wᵉ'ēṯ kol-'ᵃšer 'ᵃṣawwᵉḵā tᵉḏabbēr.* The basic difference is that Deut. 18:18 is in the 3rd person while v. 7 is in the 2nd person.

to modify Yahweh's word. Thus when Zedekiah asked, "Is there a word from Yahweh?" Jeremiah could only reply, "There is: you shall be delivered into the hand of the king of Babylon" (37:16–17; 38:14–18).

But coupled to that imperious word was a strong word of reassurance. It may be sound theology to say, "One man with God is a majority"; but when that one man faces the crowd, in the hour of actual confrontation he needs more than theoretical theology. Nothing less than the deepest conviction that God will be with him will suffice. The reassuring word that Jeremiah received, *Don't be afraid of them! For I am with you to rescue you,* was a necessity. In the years that followed he needed to commit his cause to Yahweh (cf. 20:12). His charge was a comprehensive one and somewhat ambiguous. He was to go "upon whatever errand he was given," "to whomsoever he was sent," or "wherever he was sent" (see textual note). Only the strong reassurance of Yahweh's abiding protection would suffice. There was no need to be afraid, for Yahweh would *rescue (hiṣṣîl)* him. If Jeremiah knew the Exodus story, and there is every reason to believe he did, he would have known that Yahweh "rescued" his people from Egypt.[19] But the verb was used in other well-known narratives, e.g., the rescue of David from the paw of a bear or a lion (1 Sam. 17:37),[20] and was employed in the songs sung in temple services with a much wider meaning than mere physical deliverance.[21] If then Jeremiah was to speak for Yahweh, he had Yahweh's assurance that no harm would befall him. At times, Jeremiah felt bowed down by the pressures of his persecutors and seems almost to have doubted Yahweh's assurance (20:7–18). But it was only a temporary doubt in every case, and his persistence in his calling even beyond the fall of Jerusalem bears witness to his own deep conviction about Yahweh's promise.

Yahweh's touching his mouth was reminiscent of the promise of Deut. 18:18, "I will put my words in your mouth."[22] The identification of Jeremiah with that promised successor to Moses must have increased the prophet's reassurance. The anthropomorphism *Yahweh stretched out his hand and touched my mouth* was a pow-

19. Ex. 3:8; 5:23; 6:6; 12:27; 18:4, 8–10; 1 Sam. 10:18.
20. See KB, p. 630; G. Lisowsky, *Konkordanz zum hebräischen AT* (Stuttgart, 1958), pp. 950f.
21. G. Lisowsky, *ibid.*
22. Deut. 18:18 reads: *wᵉnāṯattî ḏᵉḇāray bᵉpîw.* The only difference in v. 9 is in the last word *bᵉpîḵā,* "in your mouth."

erful way of saying that Yahweh was to be personally involved and identified with all that Jeremiah would undertake. The same motif occurs in Isaiah (6:6–7), whose lips Yahweh is said to have touched. Ezekiel, too, had Yahweh's words placed in his mouth (Ezek. 2:9–3:3).

The question has been raised by commentators as to whether the accounts of Jeremiah's call have been edited by a Deuteronomic author who wished to show that Jeremiah was a prophet who stood in the succession of Moses, demanding Israel's obedience to Yahweh's laws (e.g., 7:1–15; 11:1–18; 17:19–27; 34:8–22; ch. 35).[23] The proposal is argued persuasively and bears a certain plausibility. Part of the argument turns on the supposed differences between the prose and poetic passages in the book of Jeremiah.[24] Even if one allowed, however, that editorial processes brought the book of Jeremiah into its present form, which is undoubtedly the case, the mere fact of editing Jeremiah's oracles does not necessarily deny that Jeremiah believed himself to be the successor to Moses spoken of in Deut. 18:18. Jeremiah's persistence in his task over the years is more readily understandable if he understood his task in terms of this passage. We shall have cause to take up a number of similar suggestions in the course of the commentary and will argue, in general, that many of the insights allowed to the Deuteronomic editors should not too readily be denied to Jeremiah. The prophet showed himself to be a man of deep theological insight again and again, and it is hardly necessary to allow to others powers of theological interpretation beyond those of Jeremiah.

10 The specific task of Jeremiah is here spelled out in general terms which are nevertheless given a degree of particularity. Jeremiah was given authority[25] over nations and kingdoms in two directions. He was to proclaim oracles about their overthrow or their restoration. It is impossible for us to know how such convictions came to the prophet. He himself would not allow any other source than Yahweh. There is no doubt that in particular reference to Judah and Jerusalem he delivered strong messages of judgment; but also, later in his ministry, he spoke of restoration. The question

23. A recent proponent of this view is E. W. Nicholson, *Jeremiah 1–25* (1973), pp. 25f.

24. See Introduction, "The Book of Jeremiah: Composition," pp. 33–50.

25. The verb is the Hiphil *hipqîḏ* of the verb *pāqaḏ* which has so many varieties of meaning in the OT (see KB, p. 773), one of which is "appoint to a position of authority." The noun *pāqîḏ* means "overseer."

is raised by some commentators as to the exact character of v. 10, which seems to be a reflection of the prophecies addressed to the foreign nations in chs. 46–51. The particular combination of words used here occurs in more or less the same form in other places in Jeremiah, all of which are in prose (12:14–17; 18:7–9; 24:6; 31:28, 40; 42:10; 45:4). Clearly there have been changes in some original utterances since not only does the order of the verbs change, but the number of the verbs changes and also their form.[26] What the meaning of this variety may be is open to different interpretations. If Jeremiah spoke in prose as well as poetry he may himself have tried to ring the changes when he drew on the phraseology he used in a poetic prototype and re-used it in prose with variations. On the other hand some commentators have argued that the prose passages represent the work of editors who gave expression to Jeremiah's preaching in free prose. The question of the relationship between poetry and prose in the book is again raised.[27] The fact that the verbs of v. 10 anticipate the whole message of the book of Jeremiah is only to be expected in a chapter which is given as the introduction to the whole book. Perhaps the literary editor of the verse (and for that matter of all of the introduction) in its present form cannot be determined. But there is no reason to doubt that the material derives from Jeremiah's own reminiscences and may even have been brought together by him in a succinct and summary form to introduce the large body of oracles that followed.

Jeremiah would clearly have preferred not to speak about uprooting, pulling down, destroying, and demolishing the nation, and at times he clearly wished to escape that task (cf. 20:7–9). A far more agreeable task would have been to speak of building and planting. But he did comparatively little of this constructive preaching and a great deal of the destructive kind.

(ii) The Two Visions (1:11–16)

11 *The word of Yahweh came to me thus: "What do you see, Jeremiah?"*
I said, "A branch of an almond tree."

26. W. L. Holladay, "Prototype and Copies: A New Approach to the Poetry-Prose Problem in the Book of Jeremiah," *JBL* 79 (1960), pp. 351–367.
27. See Introduction, "The Book of Jeremiah: Composition," pp. 33–50.

12 *Then Yahweh said to me, "You see correctly![1] For I am watching[2] to carry out my word."[3]*
13 *The word of Yahweh came to me a second time: "What do you see?"[4]*
And I said, "I see a boiling[5] cauldron tipped away[6] from the north."
14 *Then Yahweh said to me:*
"From the north disaster will be loosed
Upon all who live in the land.
15 *For see! I am calling*
All the clans[7] and kings[8] of the north—Yahweh's word;
And they will come and each one will set up his throne
Before the very gates[9] of Jerusalem,
Against all her surrounding walls,
And against all the cities of Judah.
16 *And I will pass sentence[10] upon them*
For all their wrongdoing in forsaking me,
In burning offerings to other gods
And in worshipping the work of their own hands."

The two visions recorded in vv. 11 and 13 are of a type known elsewhere in the prophetic literature in the OT. A familiar object or event provides the imagery for an oracle. By means of some visual

1. Lit. "You have done well in seeing."
2. In Hebrew the words for *almond (šāqēḏ)* and *watching (šōqēḏ)* provide a neat wordplay difficult to capture in English.
3. Lit. "I am watching over my word to do it."
4. LXX adds "Jeremiah" as in v. 11.
5. Lit. "a cauldron blown upon (passive participle *nāp̱ûaḥ*)," i.e., a draft was applied to the fire beneath the pot which caused the pot to boil.
6. MT *ûpānāyw,* lit. "and its face (surface)" is from the north. By a slight emendation we may read *ûp̱ānûy,* "and it is turned (tipped)" away from the north. See G. R. Driver, "Linguistic and Textual Problems: Jeremiah," *JQR* 28 (1937/38), pp. 97–129, esp. p. 97. The emendation is probably not necessary; the prophet seems to have envisaged a cauldron boiling over and tipping slightly so that its contents spilled in a southerly direction, and the sense is the same by either reading.
7. LXX omits *clans*. Some commentators omit the word both on that basis and because it adds to the length of the colon and disturbs the meter. We retain it because it is possible to treat the line even so as two colons of three stresses each. The final *Yahweh's word* is extrametrical.
8. The term *mamlᵉḵôṯ (mmlkt)* is usually translated "kingdoms," but it probably has the meaning *kings* here since the next colon speaks of each setting up his throne. The word *mmlkh* can mean "king" both in Phoenician (Z. S. Harris, *A Grammar of the Phoenician Language* [New Haven, 1936], p. 118) and in Hebrew (W. F. Albright, "A Catalogue of Early Hebrew Lyric Poems [Psalm LXVIII]," *HUCA* 23 [1950/51], p. 34); cf. 1 Sam. 10:18.
9. Lit. "at the entrance of the gates of Jerusalem."
10. MT *wᵉḏibbartî mišpāṭay 'ôṯām,* "and I will speak my judgments (against) them." The last word may be emended to *'ittām* without any change in consonants. The sentence then reads, "And I will speak my judgments with them," an idiom meaning *pass sentence* on them.

impression the prophet, like Amos (1:1; 8:1–2) and Isaiah (2:1), was able to show how the divine word came to him at this stage in his ministry. The two incidents occurred early in his ministry though there is no indication of when, or how far apart. They may have been quite separate, and separate again from the call recorded in vv. 4–10. But the several incidents taken together helped to authenticate Jeremiah's commission both to himself and to others. And the collection of experiences welded into a thematic unit in ch. 1 provided an excellent introduction first of all to Jeremiah's first roll and later to the book as a whole.

11–12 Jeremiah's first vision was of a branch of an almond tree, the first tree to bud in spring. Anathoth remains to this day a center for almond growing. The modern visitor to the area in the very early spring is promised the memorable and unforgettable sight of almond trees in bloom and in great profusion around the village of 'Anata. There is nothing in the text to say that the almond tree was in bloom at the time. Indeed it is not essential that it should have been. As Jeremiah looked at an almond stick the closely related word *watching* came to his mind by association. Unfortunately we cannot capture in English the wordplay in the Hebrew (see text note). It was Yahweh's assurance and promise that he was watching over his word proclaimed by Jeremiah, to bring it to pass. Perhaps there was a further overtone, as neatly conveyed by the NEB "I am early on the watch *(šōqēḏ)* to carry out my purpose."[11] Yahweh would be prompt to fulfil his word as Jeremiah declared it. Just as the early bursting into leaf and bloom of the almond tree heralded the springtime, so the spoken word pointed to its own rapid fulfilment. It was not an unusual thing for a prophet to discover that nature was often the mouthpiece of God (cf. 2:24; 8:7; 12:8–13; 14:4–6; etc.). The books of Isaiah, Amos, Ezekiel, and others are rich in references to nature, which provided the prophets with illustrations for their preaching.

Verses 11–12 summarize the theme of the inevitable fulfilment of Yahweh's purposes of judgment for Judah and for the nations. It is, perhaps, the central theme of the whole book.

13–14 The second vision was more sinister and may have been separated from the first by an interval of time. Again, the

11. Cf. the wordplay in Amos 8:1–3. Amos saw a basket of summer fruit (*qāyiṣ*). By association the word of Yahweh was, "The end (*qēṣ*) has come upon my people Israel." See also Mic. 1:6–7, 10–13 for extensive use of associative wordplay.

prophet "saw" a specific object which conveyed a message to him. At the time the full details of the message were not clear. They were to be given clearer definition as the years went by. Jeremiah saw a large pot or *cauldron (sîr)* set on a fire which was well fanned by a good wind (*sîr nāp̄ûaḥ,* "a cauldron blown upon"), which apparently caused the cauldron to boil over. The fact that it was slightly tilted caused the liquid to overflow in a southerly direction (*from the north*). It was a scene which Jeremiah might have witnessed any day in his village at Anathoth. The explanation of the simple visual impression was that just as the boiling liquid boiled over in a southerly direction, so disaster (*rā'â*) would be let loose from the north. The full significance of that may not have been clear at once. If Jeremiah began preaching in 627 B.C., the meaning must have been rather ill defined. Many of Israel's troubles had originally come from the north over the centuries, from the Philistines, the Assyrians, and the Arameans. The *north* was a symbol for dark powers often of uncertain origin. If, however, Jeremiah did not begin to preach till right at the end of Josiah's reign,[12] the foe from the north was already identified as Babylon. In the completed book as it now stands there is no doubt that the Babylonians were that foe.

15–16 Some details are now supplied in a text which has suffered somewhat in transmission. Yahweh was calling powers from the north. It makes little difference whether we read simply "all the kings of the north" and omit "clans" with LXX[13] or accept the longer Hebrew text, for in either case the language hints at a massive invasion of Judah from the north. The setting up of thrones at the gates of Jerusalem would be a symbol of conquest and subsequent rule over the land. Such a prophecy would have provoked great resentment in Jerusalem at any time during Jeremiah's ministry. Even after the fall of Jerusalem in 597 B.C. there were many who could not accept the rule of the Babylonians, and even after 586 B.C. when the position had become absolutely clear there were many who regarded it as only a temporary setback.

The reason Yahweh passed such a sentence and warned of such a disaster was that his covenant people had forsaken him, offered sacrifices to other gods, and worshipped the work of their own hands. It was a clear case of breach of covenant. The theme of the

12. See Introduction, "Some Important Issues for Exegesis: The Date of Jeremiah's Call," pp. 50–56.
13. Cf. 25:9, where the text reads, "I will send for all the tribes (*mišpᵉḥôṯ*) of the north."

covenant lies close to the surface in many of the passages in the book of Jeremiah. Yahweh was Israel's sovereign Lord, who had performed many gracious acts for them in days past, but supremely in the days of the Exodus, when he liberated his people and took them into a covenant with himself. That covenant involved the acknowledgment of Yahweh as their sole and unique Lord to whom they were obligated by covenant stipulations, the observance of which would bring blessing to them and the rejection of which would bring a curse. Once the people sought to share their allegiance to Yahweh with other deities they were guilty of a breach of covenant. In such a state the curses of the covenant would operate and disaster would befall them. The evidence of breach of covenant was twofold. They neglected to obey the covenant stipulations, and they forsook Yahweh by offering sacrifices (*qiṭṭēr*) to other gods[14] and prostrating themselves before (*worshipping, hištaḥ[a]wâ*) the symbols of those deities, which were the work of their own hands. We shall return again and again to this theme in the course of the commentary. Jeremiah himself had a very clear understanding of the nature of the covenant and of the heinousness of Israel's rejection of Yahweh and his covenant demands. It is important to grasp these facts clearly. Jeremiah certainly had some sound early training in the ancient covenant traditions and could readily understand both what was taking place in Israel's religious life and what would be the inevitable outcome of Israel's breach of covenant.

(iii) The Divine Charge and Promise (1:17–19)

17 *"As for you—brace yourself.*[1]
Stand up and speak to them
Whatever I tell you to say.
Don't be fearful[2] *before them*
Lest I make you fearful in their presence.

14. The verb *qiṭṭēr* is translated "burn incense" in most English versions. This meaning is frequently correct. But the verb is also used in the OT for the burning of offerings of the fat of animals (1 Sam. 2:16; Ps. 66:15) or of meal (Amos 4:5). The verb may even have the more general meaning of "burning sacrifices" (so NEB).

1. Lit. "gird your loins."

2. There is a play on words here. The root *ḥāṭāṭ* has a range of meanings in English in the Qal: "to be terrified," "to be dismayed," "to be confounded," "to be fearful." In the Hiphil it means "to terrify," "to confound," "to put to shame," "to make fearful." Translators generally endeavor to preserve the related senses. The Berkeley Version gives "Do not be undone by their faces, lest I ruin you in their presence."

18 *And for my part, look! this day I have made*[3] *you*
A fortified city,
An iron pillar,[4]
A wall of bronze
Against the whole land:
Against Judah's kings and state officials,[5]
Its priests and the people of the land.[6]
19 *They will make war on you but will not overcome you,*
For I am with you and will rescue you—Yahweh's word."[7]

In terms of the whole chapter these verses may be taken as independent of the two visions of vv. 11–16 and seem either to point back to the call narrative in vv. 4–10, of which they originally formed the conclusion, or perhaps to be a separate fragment in which Yahweh gave Jeremiah a charge and a promise in the light of all the experiences which combined to constitute the complete call experience.

17 The charge to Jeremiah was threefold: Brace yourself; speak Yahweh's word; don't be dismayed. Jeremiah felt apprehensive about Yahweh's call to one so young. The charge is reminiscent of that to Joshua in Deut. 31:6–8 and Josh. 1:6–9, "Be strong and of good courage, do not fear or be in dread of them: for it is the Lord your God who goes with you; he will not fail you or forsake you." There is no disguising the torrid experiences that lay ahead. These needed to be faced as resolutely as a man preparing for battle faced possible dangers, or with the determination of one who faced a task which involved physical exertion. Long flowing dress which would hinder freedom of movement needed to be tied up around one's waist. With loins girded men were prepared for the challenge ahead.

The NEB renders the lines as "Do not let your spirit break at the sight of them, or I will break you before their eyes." The GNB translates "Do not be afraid of them now, or I will make you even more afraid when you are with them." John Bright (p. 4) renders "Don't lose your nerve because of them, lest I shatter your nerve right before them."

3. The verb is *nāṯan,* "give," "place," as in v. 5.

4. Lacking in LXX.

5. Heb. *śārîm* is traditionally rendered "princes." The term is used nearly fifty times in Jeremiah and in most cases the translation *state officials* suits the context. The king was surrounded by these high officials, who were not necessarily royal princes. Indeed in 39:6 when the king's sons, the royal princes, are specifically mentioned they are called "the sons of Zedekiah."

6. The expression *'am hā'āreṣ* has sometimes been understood to refer to the landed gentry. But its real meaning was fluid and varied from context to context. See E. W. Nicholson, "The Meaning of the Expression *'am hā'āreṣ* in the OT," *JSS* 10 (1965), pp. 59–66.

7. Transposed from the middle of the colon.

Then Yahweh's word had to be declared. Jeremiah would need to stand up and speak. But it was not that he was to speak from his own heart (as the false prophets did). He was to speak only what Yahweh had commanded him to speak.

And third, in order that God might conquer the last hesitations of Jeremiah after the calm advice of v. 17a, he added in v. 17b the brief and almost harsh warning. If Jeremiah draws back in fear and flees from his mission, he will encounter not merely men as adversaries, but God himself (cf. 12:5, 6; 20:9). If Jeremiah was afraid before men, and lacked trust in his divine commissioner, he would be defenseless. A man who fears man has also God to fear.

18 Yahweh's promise, to which Jeremiah must often have returned, was strong and reassuring, and made use of military symbolism. Yahweh promised to make Jeremiah as impregnable as a fortress, as irresistible as a fortified city, as strong as an iron pillar (cf. Judg. 16:29), and as resistant to attack as a bronze wall, in his stand against the whole land. Jeremiah's opponents would be largely the members of the establishment, Judah's kings, state officials, and priests, but ordinary citizens would also oppose him. In fact, he encountered the influential groups throughout his ministry, although the ordinary citizens played a part in the persecution of Jeremiah, e.g., the citizens of Anathoth plotted to take his life (11:18–23). But finally, authority lay in the hands of the ruling classes, and it seems that we have a grouping together of these influential national leaders in this verse.

19 Yahweh's final word to Jeremiah was one of strong assurance which did not hide the truth. In the task which lay ahead of the prophet, powerful and influential groups would *make war* on him, but would not overcome him because Yahweh was with him to *rescue*[8] him from their power. There was something strong and reassuring about such a promise, since Yahweh had always engaged in such rescuing and delivering activity, at no time more convincingly than in the days of the Exodus in the face of a powerful opponent like the pharaoh. Jeremiah seems to have had a sense of deep kinship with Moses and understood himself to be his successor in his own age. Moses too had seen Yahweh's strong arm stretched out to save his people. The Exodus story calls on this verb again

8. The verb is the Hiphil of *nṣl, hiṣṣîl,* a word that could call up in Jeremiah's mind many memories of divine deliverance. See p. 143, n. 7; p. 399, n. 13; KB, p. 630.

and again to depict the power of Yahweh to snatch his people away from a powerful foe (Exod. 3:8; 18:4, 8, 9, 10; etc.).

With hindsight we now know how the story unfolded. And to the compiler of the materials of ch. 1, whether Jeremiah or Baruch or whoever it may have been, the end of the story was known. But to Jeremiah at the beginning there was only the appalling prospect of a task before him for which he felt ill equipped. Only turmoil and apprehension filled the mind of such a youthful ambassador for Yahweh. Yet Jeremiah sensed the need for a prophet like Moses to continue the work of keeping Yahweh's word alive among a people who had grown careless and apostate. He accepted the task, strengthened by the strong conviction that Yahweh his God would be early on the watch to carry out his purposes and to stand by his servant who spoke Yahweh's word to the men of his age.

II. THE DIVINE JUDGMENT ON JUDAH AND JERUSALEM (2:1–25:38)

A. ISRAEL'S GUILT AND PUNISHMENT (2:1–6:30)

1. ISRAEL INDICTED FOR HER SINS (2:1–37)

(i) The Faithfulness of Israel's Youth: Her Ideal Status (2:1–3)

1 *The word of Yahweh came to me as follows:*
2 *"Go, cry in the ears of Jerusalem, and say: This is what Yahweh has said:*[1]
I remember the unfailing devotion of your youth,
The love of your bridal days;
You followed me in the wilderness
Through a land that had not been sown.
3 *Israel was set apart for Yahweh alone,*
The first yield of his harvest.
Anyone who eats of it is held guilty;
Evil will overtake them—Yahweh's word."

Some general comments on ch. 2 as a whole should first be made. The whole chapter has strong reminiscences of a legal form which was well known in the secular world, the so-called *rîḇ* pattern.[2] When lesser kings offended their overlords in some act of rebellion, the overlord sent a written message by the hands of a messenger. Several of these documents are extant today. It seems clear that there was a proper legal form in which to lay a charge against a rebel. The shape was as follows: (i) an appeal to the vassal to pay heed, and a summons to the earth and the sky to act as witnesses; (ii) a series of questions each of which carried an implied accusation;

1. LXX to this point in ch. 2 has only, "And he said, 'Thus says the Lord.' "
2. J. Harvey, "Le 'Rîb-Pattern', réquisitoire prophétique sur la rupture de l'alliance," *Biblica* 43 (1962), pp. 172–196.

(iii) a recollection of past benefits bestowed on the vassal with some statement of the offenses by which he had broken his treaty (covenant); (iv) a reference to the futility of ritual compensations, recourse to foreign cults, or other kinds of aid; (v) a declaration of culpability and a threat of judgment.[3]

This pattern is discernible in ch. 2, although it has been transformed and partly obscured by the present literary form. We shall propose that the chapter consists of a literary arrangement of several originally independent segments brought together to serve a theological purpose. The chapter is dominated by the prophet's charge of flagrant, inexcusable, and incomprehensible apostasy. Israel is, as it were, in the law court being arraigned by Yahweh in a lawsuit (*rîḇ*). The case is not formally set out here, but overtones of the secular lawsuit keep appearing behind the present literary form. Yahweh has a case against Israel. This is stated (vv. 9–11) and is argued out with warning, pleading, and threat. The theological thrust is that Yahweh's elect people have offended against the covenant and stand under judgment. It is a theme to which Jeremiah returned again and again throughout his ministry and which was relieved only occasionally by the opposite theme of hope. The two themes have already appeared in ch. 1 with the charge to Jeremiah on the one hand to uproot, tear down, destroy, and raze, and on the other hand to build and to plant. In the present chapter the theme of judgment has for its *Sitz im Leben* the covenant lawsuit. Its occurrence at the beginning of Jeremiah's ministry places it historically at the point when Judah, in grave political peril, broke her covenant with Yahweh and entered into forbidden alliances, both with neighboring nations and with pagan deities. Such a state of affairs in the secular realm would have resulted in the despatch of a warning letter from the great king. In the case of Yahweh and Israel, Yahweh sent his prophet. In terms of the *rîḇ* pattern set out above, the following comparisons may be made:[4]

(i) v. 12, (ii) vv. 5–6, (iii) vv. 7–11, 13, 14–19, 20–28, 29–30, (iv) vv. 26–28, (v) vv. 31–37.

The details of these sections will become clear in the exposition.

Some further matters call for comment. The chapter contains a variety of segments and topics. Thus in vv. 2–3 which initiate the present line of thought, the person of address is second feminine

3. See Mic. 6:1–8 for a fine biblical example.

4. See J. Harvey, *art. cit.*, p. 178. There is some overlapping of verses.

singular. The same obtains for vv. 14–19. By contrast vv. 4–13 are couched in the second masculine plural. While it is not impossible that Jeremiah should have alternated his mode of address in this way, it is arguable that vv. 2–3 and 14–19 belong together and belong to one particular occasion, while vv. 4–13 belong to another occasion.

Further, vv. 20–28 which refer to Judah's passion for foreign gods divide readily into three segments, vv. 20–22, 23–25, and 26–28, while vv. 29–37 which refer to the fate that awaits Judah divide readily into vv. 29–32 and 33–37. Again, while it is possible that a man with literary ability like Jeremiah would ring the changes in his literary forms, it seems more likely that each of these segments represents an independent saying of Jeremiah dealing with a single theme. Later these were brought together here by an editor.[5] All of them, in any case, would suit an early period in his preaching. If this is so, they may have assumed their present shape in 605 B.C. when, in the fourth year of Jehoiakim's reign, after the king had burned the scroll containing Jeremiah's writings, Jeremiah dictated his prophecies afresh to Baruch the scribe (ch. 36). This may have given him the opportunity to update his original words here and there (e.g., v. 16).

It is impossible to be certain about the exact nature of the editorial processes that took place in bringing together the separate fragments, although the book of Jeremiah gives many evidences that these took place. Certainly in all such cases the final shape in which a particular chapter now appears must reflect some topical, literary, or theological intention and perhaps all three. In ch. 2 there is a clear thematic unity and a skillful arranging of material which gives a remarkable coherence and artistry to the whole.

In ch. 1 Jeremiah was called and commissioned to preach to rebellious Judah. Ch. 2 opens with Jeremiah's preaching in Jerusalem in response to the divine call. The whole chapter is a powerful indictment of the nation's rebellion, delivered with some passion. It may be taken as representing Jeremiah's early preaching either prior to the commencement of the reforms of Josiah or early in the reform program. The rhetorical nature of the chapter with its vivid and rapidly changing figures and metaphors portrays a preacher with a

5. It is even possible that some of this editorial work was done by Jeremiah in his first scroll.

burning heart. This may account for changes in meter and in the person of address.

1 The syntax of the first phrase following immediately on 1:19 suggests that what follows was the consequence of the call referred to in ch. 1. No indication is given as to how the word of the Lord came to Jeremiah, but like other prophets he had a strong sense of conveying the mind of God to his people. The prophetic oracle was conveyed through the personality of the sanctified speaker. The weight and authority of the message was not invalidated or minimized by this fact. It was the way divine revelation came to men. "Holy men of God spoke as they were moved by the Holy Ghost."[6]

2 Although the first part of this verse is lacking in the Greek text, there is no reason to doubt that the message was delivered originally in Jerusalem. Presumably Jeremiah walked the 3 miles into the city across the hills from Anathoth (near the modern 'Anata). The vivid expression *cry in the ears of* Jerusalem is not unknown elsewhere in Jeremiah and in the OT.[7] It was Yahweh's intention that his word should be heard, for there had developed a sad contrast between what had obtained long ago, in the days of Israel's first enthusiastic acceptance of Yahweh's sovereignty, and what now obtained. The mind of Yahweh went back in memory to the days of Israel's youth when she first entered into a covenant with him. He intended that Israel too should *remember (zāḵar)*. Her great religious festivals, the Passover, the feasts of Tabernacles and Firstfruits, etc., were designed to keep alive that memory. Many of Israel's cult celebrations were centered around the recollection of the mighty acts of Yahweh on her behalf and of the covenant into which she had entered and the salvation she enjoyed. In the present context Yahweh recalled the loyalty (or *unfailing devotion, ḥeseḏ*) of Israel in her honeymoon period in the desert following upon her acceptance of his covenant. The Hebrew word *ḥeseḏ* has a rich connotation in the OT and is used in reference both to God and to man.[8] It describes the manner of response to a covenantal relationship which goes beyond mere legal requirements. It is a particularly powerful term in reference to the *ḥeseḏ* of Yahweh which can

6. 2 Pet. 1:21.
7. Exod. 24:7; Deut. 31:11; Judg. 7:3; 2 K. 23:2; 2 Chr. 34:30; Neh. 13:1; Ezek. 8:18; 9:1. Jeremiah uses it in 2:2; 36:10, 13, 15, 21.
8. N. Glueck, "Das Wort *ḥeseḏ* im alttestamentlichen Sprachgebrauch," BZAW 47 (1961); *Ḥesed in the Bible* (E.T. 1967).

overleap Israel's gross neglect of the covenant, love them despite everything, and plan for their restoration to fellowship with himself. Yahweh's *ḥeseḏ* surpasses immeasurably any quality of *ḥeseḏ* shown by a man to Yahweh, or one man to another, although at high points in such relationships one may sometimes catch glimpses of the depths to which *ḥeseḏ* will reach. The point that is here made is that when Israel was young and a new bride one could speak of "the devotion of your youth" (RSV), or "youthful devotion" (Bright).

Another feature of those days was Israel's "bridal love" (Bright), or "love as a bride" (RSV), or *the love of your bridal days* (NEB). The Sinai relationship is depicted in terms of a marriage where the bride accepts her husband in full confidence and follows him into a new life. One is reminded at once of the imagery of Hos. 1–3 where the husband-wife relationship between Hosea and Gomer is a picture of the relationship between Yahweh and Israel. In the days of the wilderness wandering Israel was Yahweh's bride. She was loyal to him and displayed deep love and devotion.

The term *love ('ahᵃḇâ)* may carry a slight political overtone as well. While it appears to be set firmly in a husband-wife relationship, the Hebrew verb "love" (*'āhēḇ*) sometimes has a political connotation. It is arguable that in some other passages in Jeremiah the term points to political involvements and that Israel's *lovers* are the nations round about.[9] In the early days of Israel's covenant (treaty) with Yahweh she was as loyal as a bride. This was to be remembered. Later she entered into other alliances both political and religious. In the world of Jeremiah's day religious loyalties were often involved in a political alliance because the vassals of great kings were required to indicate at least a token acknowledgment of the deities of the overlord (cf. 2 K. 16:10–16).

The measure of Israel's loyalty and devotion in those early days was that she ventured into the wilderness, an open area that had never been tilled. This was in contrast to what she had known in Egypt with its tilled lands and abundant crops. But strong confidence in Yahweh led Israel to follow him into such unfamiliar paths, so deeply did she trust him.

9. See vv. 25, 33; 20:4, 6; 22:20, 22. Cf. J. A. Thompson, "The Significance of the Verb *Love* in the David-Jonathan Narratives in I Samuel," *VT* 24 (1974), pp. 334–38; "Israel's 'Lovers,' " *VT* 27 (1977), pp. 475–481.

The contrast between this beautiful state and the sad unfaithfulness of the years that followed is drawn in vv. 4–13.[10]

3 The sovereign rights of Yahweh are now drawn out by reference to the ancient law of firstfruits (Lev. 23:10, 17; Deut. 25:1–11). In those early years Israel was "holiness (*qōḏeš*) to Yahweh," that is, she was something *set apart* for his enjoyment alone. She is defined, indeed, as the firstfruits (*rē'šîṯ*) of his harvest. According to biblical law the first yield of the harvest was assigned to God as his own portion. In this way Israel acknowledged all of earth's produce as having come from God.[11] The firstfruits were a token of the bounty that God would bestow at full harvest. As with the harvest, so in the world of man, Israel comprised God's portion of the harvest of the nations that would one day be realized. Because Israel was Yahweh's own portion[12] just as the firstfruits were, she was under his special protection. Hence anyone who touched her, touched God's peculiar possession and would suffer the consequences. All who ate of her were held guilty, and punishment would come upon them.[13] In Jeremiah's time, of course, Judah was bruised and humbled, Israel had been eliminated, many of her people were in exile, and her lands had been an Assyrian province since 722 B.C. It may have appeared to the people of Jeremiah's day that Yahweh had forgotten them. They, in fact, had forgotten him; and the long years of Manasseh's reign with the gross apostasy which he allowed added weight to the feeling that Yahweh either was powerless to help them or had cast them off. But that was far from the truth. Jeremiah began his ministry with the strong assurance that fundamentally Israel was Yahweh's treasured possession and in the end all who touched her could expect Yahweh's judgment. There is perhaps another overtone. In the world of Jeremiah's day and earlier, great kings held their vassals as their own peculiar possession. Revolt on the part of the vassal merited judgment. But encroachment on the territory of

10. Despite Ezekiel's stress on the fact that Israel's corruption went back to its beginning in Egypt and continued in the wilderness (Ezek. 20:5–26), he still portrays the wilderness period as a time of close fellowship with God (Ezek. 16:8–14).

11. *Harvest*— Heb. *tᵉḇû'â* means lit. "that which goes forth," i.e., "produce."

12. The special term *sᵉgullâ* is not used here. It occurs in other OT passages to denote God's peculiar and special possession. See Exod. 19:5; Deut. 7:6; 14:2; 26:18; Ps. 135:4; Mal. 3:17.

13. The first sentence of v. 3 is a nominal sentence without a verb, "Holiness to Yahweh, Israel: the firstfruits of his harvest." The second sentence reads, "All eating him will be held guilty, punishment will come upon them." The syntax suggests that Jeremiah had in view the contemporary scene, however much the principles may have been true in the past as well.

the vassal by another ruler brought an attack by the great king on the offender. The verb "eat" sometimes represents such an unauthorized invasion in Akkadian texts.[14]

In any case, anyone who encroached on Israel would merit the judgment of Yahweh on him. Here was hope for the people of Jeremiah's day if only they would heed his words. In order to press his point Jeremiah expounded in some detail the sad contrast between present apostasy and the noble picture of those early years. Jeremiah idealized the desert period in much the same way as did Hosea (9:10; 11:1).[15] What both Jeremiah and Hosea may have had in mind was the later corrupting influences of Canaanite Baalism.[16] There was a strong contrast, even contradiction between God's estimate of Israel and the reality of things as demonstrated by her repeated failures.

(ii) *Israel's Apostasy (2:4–13)*

4[1] *Listen to the word of Yahweh, people*[2] *of Jacob,*
All the tribes[3] *of Israel's stock.*
5 *This is what Yahweh has said:*
"What did your fathers find wrong in me
That they wandered far away from me,
And followed 'The Delusion' and became deluded?
6 *They did not ask, 'Where is Yahweh*
Who brought us up from the land of Egypt,
Who led us through the wilderness,
Through a land of desert and ravine,
Through a land of drought and danger,[4]
Where no man has ever trod
And where no human being lives?'
7 *I brought you to a fertile land*
To enjoy its harvests and its bounty.
But when you came in you defiled my land
And turned my heritage into something loathsome.

14. See *CAD*, IA, Part 1, p. 254, col. 2.
15. See the Introduction, "The Debt of Jeremiah to Hosea," pp. 81–85.
16. See J. Skinner, *Prophecy and Religion: Studies in the Life of Jeremiah* (1922, 1961), pp. 64f.

1. This verse is here regarded as part of the poem. The parallelism allows this possibility. Most translators take it as prose; cf. RSV, NEB, GNB. There is a normal 3:2 stress pattern.
2. Lit. "house." The reference is not here to a dynasty but to the people as a whole. The noun recurs in the next line where we translate *stock*.
3. Lit. "families." J. Bright, *Jeremiah*, p. 10 translates "clans."
4. The noun *ṣalmāweṯ* means lit. "deep darkness" but it often denotes distress or *danger,* e.g., Ps. 23:4; 44:20 (Eng. 19). LXX reads "barren" (Heb. *galmûḏâ*). Cf. D. Winton Thomas, "*Ṣalmāweṯ* in the OT," *JSS* 7 (1962), pp. 191–200.

8 *The priests did not ask 'Where is Yahweh?'*
Those skilled in the law did not know me,
The rulers rebelled against me,
And the prophets prophesied in Baal's name
And followed 'the useless ones.'
9 *And so I must state my case against you once more—*
Yahweh's word—
To your children's children I will bring my charge.
10 *Yes, indeed,*[5] *cross over to the western isles*[6] *and look!*
Send someone to Kedar and take special notice
And see whether anything like this has ever happened.
11 *Has ever a nation changed gods*
(even though they are not gods)?
But my people! They have exchanged me[7]
For 'The Useless One.'
12 *Be appalled at this, you heavens,*
Shudder and shudder again[8]*—Yahweh's word.*
13 *For my people have committed a double evil:*
Me, they have forsaken,
A spring of living water,
To hew cisterns for themselves,
Cracked cisterns
That cannot hold water."

As we have pointed out above,[9] the present section employs throughout the second masculine plural. Whatever the origin of this passage, it certainly follows the statements of vv. 1–3 in the unfolding of the argument and no doubt represents an editorial arrangement of available materials. The material in these verses seems to reflect the prereformation conditions known to Jeremiah before the many abuses that had grown up under Manasseh had been put away. But even after Josiah's first attempts at reform had been initiated, it would have taken some time to extend control into all areas of national life.

In the context of the whole chapter, vv. 4–13 form a bridge between the statement of Israel's early devotion to Yahweh (vv. 2–3) and the description of her present sad state of bondage to Assyria

5. Heb. *kî* is here taken as asseverative.
6. Lit. "the isles of Kittim (Cyprus)." But the expression is a general one.
7. Lit. "his glory." A marginal note in *BHS* advises that this is a case of *Tiqqun sopherim*, a deliberate alteration of the text from "my glory" to "his glory" in order to avoid what was regarded as a blasphemous utterance of the divine name in some way. The word, in any case, stands for Yahweh.
8. Read *harbēh* for MT *ḥārᵉḇû*, following LXX; cf. J. Bright, pp. 11, 15.
9. See p. 61.

(vv. 14–19). Thus we have a sequence: Israel's early devotion (vv. 2–3); Israel's apostasy (vv. 4–13); the tragic results of apostasy (vv. 14–19). And even if these three segments were originally independent, skillful editing has arranged them into steps in an argument.

4 At a later period in Jeremiah's ministry after Josiah had extended his authority over the remnants of the northern tribes which formerly made up Israel, he could speak of Israel in a wider sense. But the present oracle may have been spoken at some covenant festival where members of Judah, the southern kingdom, were addressed as representing "all the tribes of the house of Israel." The twice-repeated formula "Where is the Lord?" (vv. 6, 8) is possibly a liturgical formula used at such festivals but taken up here to serve Jeremiah's purpose.

5 The expression "Thus saith the Lord" or *This is what Yahweh has said* is quite characteristic of the prophets, who regarded themselves as recipients of divine revelation and spoke with a sense of authority. Jeremiah now begins to expound Israel's apostasy. It was not merely something in the immediate past, that is, in the days of Manasseh's apostasy (2 K. 21), but rather something that had begun as long ago as the days of the Conquest (v. 7) and had continued ever since. The question "What wrong (*'āwel*) did your fathers (2nd masc. plur.) find in me?" carries the implication that some "fault" or "wrong" in Yahweh caused Israel to depart from him and to wander far from him. But there was none. The question called for a negative answer. On the contrary, Israel had gone after an empty "phantom." The text here uses the noun *heḇel*[10] and the cognate verb. Various attempts have been made to render this in English: "pursuing empty phantoms and themselves becoming empty" (NEB); they "went after worthlessness, and became worthless" (RSV); "following 'Lord Delusion,' deluded they became" (Bright). The noun *heḇel* may be a play on "Baal," the principal deity of Canaanite worship. Israel's deep sin lay in her disloyalty to Yahweh. It is of some interest that in the secular treaties of the day a rebel vassal who "went after" some other ruler was understood to have renounced allegiance to his overlord. Indeed the expression "go after" meant "serve as a vassal."[11] Whether Jeremiah had the secular parallel consciously in mind may be hard to demonstrate.

10. This is the noun which occurs so often in Ecclesiastes, "Vanity of vanities, all is vanity."

11. See W. L. Moran, "The Ancient Near Eastern Background of the Love of God in Deuteronomy," *CBQ* 25 (1963), pp. 77–87, for examples.

But the parallel is close. Israel forsook Yahweh her Lord and thereby broke her covenant when she followed "The Delusion" (*heḇel*).

6–7 The result of such apostasy was that Israel forgot the gracious delivering activity of Yahweh, who had brought them up from the land of Egypt and guided them in the wilderness, through a land of *desert ('ᵃrāḇâ)* and *ravine (šûḥâ),* and through a land of drought and danger where no human beings dwelt.

Yahweh, unlike Israel, was true to his word. He cared for Israel right through the wilderness wanderings and brought them to the promised land of great bounty. The expression *fertile land*, or "plentiful land" (RSV) or "land of Carmel" (Heb. *'ereṣ hakkarmel*), would remind Jeremiah's hearers of the luxurious growth of the Mount Carmel area (cf. Amos 1:2; 9:3; Mic. 7:14; Nah. 1:4). Alas, the natural beauty of the land was soon polluted and Yahweh's *heritage (naḥᵃlâ)* became an abomination (*tô'ēḇâ*). In Jeremiah's view there was a close correlation between a nation's sins and the lack of prosperity of the land.[12]

8 Four classes of leaders are now castigated and charged with some measure of responsibility for the prevailing idolatry and apostasy—the priests, the legal authorities, the rulers, and the prophets. The *priests* were not only responsible for the sacrifices but were interpreters of the law and also had charge of the divine oracle through the proper use of the ephod (*'ēpôḏ*) and the Urim (*'ûrîm*) and Thummim (*tummîm*).[13] These means were mechanical to a degree, but were operative in certain cases. They had evidently been neglected or were wrongfully used. Moreover, the priests were sometimes inclined to issue instructions to people for payment.[14] By thus becoming specialists in the law but without deep commitment to Yahweh, their "knowledge of Yahweh," that is, their whole religion, was reduced to nothing (cf. Hos. 4:4–10). They are here described as "those who handle the law" or *those skilled in the law*, a phrase which probably includes in it a reference to the Levites also. Both groups were intended to be interpreters of the law (cf. Mal. 2:5–8). In any case Jeremiah expressed the view that they *did not know* Yahweh. The Hebrew verb *know (yāḏa')* had a much deeper sense than mere intellectual knowledge. It carried an emotional and

12. The view is found elsewhere in the OT, e.g., Amos 4:6–10; Hag. 1:7–10; cf. Jer. 8:12–13, etc.

13. 18:18; Ezek. 7:26; Mic. 3:11; Mal. 2:5–8. See R. de Vaux, *Ancient Israel: Its Life and Institutions* (1961), pp. 349–355.

14. Cf. Ezek. 34:3; Mic. 3:11; etc.

volitional emphasis as well. To "know" Yahweh was to enter into deep personal commitment to him. The priests and those skilled in the law acted too much on a purely ritual and mechanical level.

The *rulers* (lit. "shepherds") were themselves rebels against the Lord (Heb. verb *pāšaʿ*). The term "shepherd" (*rôʿēh*) was commonly used to describe political leaders in OT times[15] and was also known in non-Israelite areas. The temporal rulers were as disobedient and blameworthy as the priests from whom they may have taken their lead.

Finally, the *prophets prophesied in Baal's name* and followed after "*the useless ones.*" The Hebrew of this latter phrase means literally "they do not profit" (*lōʾ yôʿilû*). A play on the name Baal seems to be intended (cf. vv. 5, 23). It was not from Baal that a prophet should draw his inspiration but from Yahweh the God of Israel. Despite reformations at various times in Israel (e.g., under Asa and Hezekiah) the people reverted to the deities and rituals of Canaan.[16] Throughout his ministry Jeremiah was in conflict with such prophets. Perhaps, indeed, this was Jeremiah's chief complaint against the nation. The prophets gave themselves up to the leading of the strange psychic powers within nature rather than to Yahweh.

9 As the argument continues, the point is reached where Yahweh can declare against this sad background of apostasy, "So, once more, I must state my case (or, bring a charge) against you."[17] Indeed, Yahweh would bring his case also against the descendants of these people. In any such lawsuit Israel stood to lose the case, for she had violated her covenant obligations on many occasions. On the secular scene, vassals who broke their treaty were punished severely by their overlords. The people of Jeremiah's day well understood the implication of his words. In 597 B.C. Nebuchadrezzar of Babylon was meting out judgment on Judah for precisely this political offense (2 K. 24:1–2). It was to happen again in 598 B.C. (2 K. 24:10–17) and in 587 B.C. (2 K. 25). The implication of Jeremiah's

15. 2 Sam. 5:2; 7:7; Ezek. 34:2, 5, 7–12; 37:24; Nah. 3:18; Zech. 10:2–3. Jeremiah uses the term in this metaphorical sense, e.g., 3:15; 10:21; 12:10; 23:1, 2, 4; 25:34–36.

16. For the religion of Canaan see W. F. Albright, *Archaeology and the Religion of Israel* (1946), pp. 76ff.; *From the Stone Age to Christianity* (1957), pp. 231ff.; R. K. Harrison, *Introduction to the OT* (Grand Rapids, 1969), pp. 363ff.; John Gray, *The Legacy of Canaan* (^{2}1965).

17. The root of the verb is *ryb*. The use of this verb suggests that ch. 2 may contain a hidden covenant lawsuit. See above, pp. 159f.

words in the religious realm was that Yahweh, Israel's sovereign Lord, would visit her with judgment.

10–11 After this declaration of the divine intention to enter into legal proceedings with Israel, the prophet reflects on the enormity of the crime, for which there was no parallel in the lands around Israel. No nation had ever changed its ancient gods, even if its gods were not real gods. Whether one travelled to *the western isles* (lit., the isles or shores of the Kittim[18]) or to the Arab tribes of the desert away to the east (cf. 49:28–33), such a phenomenon would never be observed. There was a certain literalness in this claim. While over the centuries polytheists changed the names of their deities, or their relative importance within the pantheon, due to syncretistic contacts with their neighbors or due to the infiltration of foreigners, the changes were not fundamental since their deities were personifications of aspects of nature and remained basically the same. But Yahweh stood outside of the whole universe, and to bring him down to the level of a nature deity and attempt to subordinate him to the laws and limitations of nature was to make him a radically different deity, however much his names and titles were retained. By tragic contrast with the nations around Israel, Yahweh's people had abandoned him, the Living God, her "Glory," for *"The Useless One."* The word "glory" (*kāḇôḏ*) denotes Yahweh. The expression "the glory of the Lord" occurs numerous times in the OT and refers to the effulgence of the divine presence, the *k*ᵉ*ḇôḏ Yahweh* who was enthroned in the temple.[19] The other expression, literally "that which does not profit" (*b*ᵉ*lō' yô'îl*), is evidently a play on the name Baal (cf. vv. 5 and 23).[20]

12–13 Such shameful and sacrilegious behavior would provoke the heavens, which had been invoked as witnesses, to be appalled.[21]

The two grave offenses of Israel are now spelled out. On the one hand she had abandoned Yahweh the *spring of living water,* and

18. The name Kittim derives from the Phoenician colony of Kittim on Cyprus. The name came to denote the inhabitants of Cyprus as a whole and later, by extension, islands and coastlands further to the west.

19. 1 Sam. 4:4; 1 K. 8:11–12; Ps. 27:4; 45:7 (Eng. 6); 76:3 (Eng. 2); Isa. 6:1–4; Ezek. 43:7; etc.

20. J. Bright, *Jeremiah,* p. 11, translates "They've traded my Presence for 'Lord Useless.' "

21. For the summoning of the heavens as God's witnesses, see Deut. 32:1; Isa. 1:2; Mic. 6:1; etc.

on the other she had hewed out cisterns that were cracked and unable to hold water. The symbolism was clear to the people of Judah. Every landowner could wish to have a flowing spring on his property, which would obviate his having to dig a cistern in the limestone hills. To ensure that it held water he had to plaster inside with lime plaster. He would then direct rainwater into it when the rain came. But such cisterns built into limestone rock developed cracks and the water seeped out, leaving the farmer without the precious life-giving commodity. In like manner Israel, who had available the full resources of their God Yahweh, the spring of living water, turned aside to worthless substitutes, to trust themselves to powerless deities which, in the end, could not meet their deep spiritual needs.

(iii) The Consequences of Israel's Apostasy (2:14–19)

14 *"Is Israel a slave?*
Was he born into slavery?[1]
Why then has he become a prey
15 *Over which lions roar*
And clamor aloud?[2]
They have laid waste his land;
His cities lie in ruins and abandoned.
16 *Yes, men of Noph and Tahpanhes*
Have cracked your skull.[3]
17 *Did you not do this to yourself*
By forsaking Yahweh your God
While he was leading you in the way?[4]
18 *And now what advantage is it to you to go to Egypt*
To drink water from the Nile?
What advantage is it to you to go to Assyria
To drink water from the Euphrates?

1. Lit. "Or a house-born one?" Bright, p. 9, proposes "A house-born slave, perhaps?"
2. Lit. "They give forth their voice." This is aptly rendered by Bright, p. 14, "roar with clamorous din." The phrase seems to add emphasis to the first expression.
3. Reading *y^{e}rō'ûḵ* from the root *r''*, "fracture," for MT *yir'ûḵ*, "they graze" or "they graze upon." Another proposal is *y^{e}'ārûḵ,* "they shave you," "they lay you bare," hence "they shave your skull."
4. MT has this third colon "at the time of one leading you in the way," which is omitted in LXX and by NEB and J. Bright. It can be made to give good sense, however. Those who omit the phrase suggest a dittography with v. 18, where the consonantal text reads *mhlk ldrk* compared to *mwlkk bdrk* here.

19 *It is your own wickedness that will punish you*
And your apostasy that will condemn you.
Consider and take note what a bitter and evil[5] *thing it is*
To forsake Yahweh your God
So that you have no reverence for me[6]*—*
The word of the Lord, Yahweh of Hosts."

The Hebrew text in these verses reverts to the second feminine singular as in vv. 2–3. It has been proposed, therefore, that these two groups of verses once comprised a separate poem distinct from the poem in vv. 4–13, where the person of address is second masculine plural. While such a proposal has something to commend it, the present arrangement of verses provides a certain logical development in thought. If once there were two separate poems, the editor[7] in presenting his material rearranged the material into the present form.

The logic of the argument is clear. Judah, indeed all Israel, whose early devotion is spoken of in vv. 2–3, had rejected Yahweh's claims upon them. As a consequence she had fallen prey to lions and had been drawn into compromising and dangerous alliances. The apostasy described in vv. 4–13 had led to the description of the evil consequences referred to in vv. 14–19.

14–16 For a long time now Israel had been in bondage. First, the northern kingdom fell to Assyria in 722 B.C. Was Israel really a *slave* (MT *'eḇeḏ*), or perhaps a house-born slave (*yᵉlîḏ bayiṯ*), that is, one who had been born in the household of the master and was therefore his personal property? Slaves were normally bought, but their children belonged to the same master.[8] It seemed to Jeremiah that some freeborn Israelites were already slaves and others were about to become slaves. If that were not so, why had she become like a prey over which lions roared and growled aloud?

It is important to identify the historical background to these verses. It would appear from the reference to Assyria in v. 18 that Assyria was still a world power to be reckoned with, so that the poem must originally have been composed at the very beginning of

5. J. Bright, *Jeremiah,* p. 10, takes the Hebrew expression as a hendiadys and translates "how bitterly evil it is."

6. This colon is omitted by some translators because its meaning is not clear. It reads "and my fear (?) was not in you." The translation depends on the meaning assigned to the noun *paḥdâ,* which may be related to *paḥaḏ,* "fear," perhaps *reverence* (AV, NEB, RSV). LXX reads "I have no pleasure in you."

7. Was this Jeremiah himself?

8. See *NBD*, pp. 1195ff. *s.v.* "Slave, Slavery" (K. A. Kitchen).

Jeremiah's ministry before Assyria began to show signs of collapse, which, as we have seen, did not commence till the death of Ashurbanipal in 627 B.C.[9] The reference to the Egyptians in v. 16 seems to allude to Judah's suffering at the hands of Egypt in 609 B.C. This would seem to indicate that the earlier poem was enlarged at this point to allow for this event, so that the poem did not reach its final form till early in the reign of Jehoiakim.

If then the Assyrians are represented by the roaring lions of v. 15, the devastation of the land and the destruction of the cities and their subsequent abandonment may refer to any one of a number of Assyrian campaigns from the days of Tiglath-pileser III (745–727 B.C.), Shalmaneser V (726–722 B.C.), Sargon II (721–705 B.C.), Sennacherib (704–681 B.C.), Esarhaddon (680–669 B.C.), and Ashurbanipal (668–627 B.C.), each of whom had campaigns which touched on the territory of Israel at some point.[10]

As to the references to Egypt in vv. 16 and 18, we have proposed that v. 16 represents a later comment[11] to include the activities of the Egyptians, who also turned the people of Israel into servants. However, v. 18 may be a comment on Israel's propensity to turn to Egypt for help. She had done it often in the past and might well do it again.

Noph is Memphis, the ancient capital of Lower Egypt, located about 13 miles south of the modern Cairo. *Tahpanhes* is the later Greek Daphne, represented today by Tell Defneh, situated near Lake Manzaleh in northeastern Egypt (cf. 43:7; 44:1; 46:14).

There is some ambiguity about v. 16. The fact that Noph and Tahpanhes are mentioned and not Egypt as such may suggest that at the time the poem was written Egypt was a vassal of Assyria, and these two towns would then represent places which were severely mauled by the Assyrians in the campaigns of Esarhaddon (681–669 B.C.) and Ashurbanipal (669–627 B.C.). In that case the verse might be translated: "The men of Noph and Tahpanhes will crack your skulls" (NEB), i.e., it is a prophecy that these places will yet arise to deal a blow against Judah from the south. However, it is arguable that whatever the original form of the poem may have been, Jeremiah has drawn into an enlarged version of the original a reference to the

9. For the wider historical background see the Introduction under "Jeremiah in His Historical Setting," pp. 9-27.
10. *Ibid.*
11. It may well have been Jeremiah's own comment.

campaign of Pharaoh Necho in 609 B.C. as he passed through the land on his way to bring help to the Assyrians.[12]

In any case the main thrust of the verse is that both Assyria and Egypt have brought only desolation to the land in the past, and no good purpose could be served by continuing to seek political alliances with those who have only brought trouble to Israel, whose greatest need was not ability in political maneuvering but renewal of her covenant with Yahweh.

17 The real cause of Judah's trouble was plainly that she had forsaken Yahweh her God. She had broken his covenant and had entered into other alliances. The point is made that the people were responsible for all the trouble that had befallen them. "Is it not your desertion of Yahweh your God that brings all this upon you?" (NEB). This is a theme to which Jeremiah returned again and again. He saw all Israel's calamities as Yahweh's judgment on his people because of their breach of covenant. And, in the present context, this was the reason why Israel had become slaves.[13]

18 Jeremiah makes use here of a theme used by other prophets, namely, that it is futile for Judah to rely upon Egypt or Assyria or any other nation (cf. Isa. 30:1–5). The motif is part of the *rîḇ* pattern.[14] The reference is evidently to overtures of a political nature made by the two politically oriented groups in Judah, the pro-Egyptians and the pro-Assyrians.[15] In the early period of Jeremiah's ministry these two great nations held the balance of power in the Middle East. After the collapse of Assyria in 609 B.C. this no longer obtained. Indeed, after the death of Ashurbanipal c. 627 B.C. Assyria began to wane. We have here a pointer to the early date of this passage. It must have at least predated 612 B.C., the year of Assyria's collapse. The terms *Nile* and *Euphrates* here represent the nations Egypt and Assyria. The Nile is referred to as *šiḥôr* (lit. "blackness"), possibly with the intention of denigrating the river which was one of the important Egyptian gods. The Euphrates is here referred to as *"the River,"* as elsewhere in the OT.[16]

12. See the Introduction under "Jeremiah in His Historical Setting," pp. 9-27.
13. The noun *'eḇeḏ*, "slave," can also mean "vassal" in the political sphere. Israel was enslaved both to foreign powers and to foreign gods, even though she was born free.
14. See above, pp. 159f.
15. See the Introduction, "Jeremiah in His Historical Setting," pp. 9–27.
16. Deut. 1:7; 11:24; 1 K. 4:21; Neh. 2:7, 9; Isa. 7:20; etc.

19 The outcome of Judah's wickedness (*rā'â*) would be that she would be punished. By means of an apt figure Jeremiah declares, "Your wickedness will chasten you" (RSV).[17] In terms of the Near Eastern treaty pattern, breach of covenant brings upon the rebel the curses of the covenant.[18] An alternative translation is, "Your apostasies reprove you." The term "apostasy" (*m^e šûḇâ*) is a derivative of the root *šûḇ*. Jeremiah rings the changes again and again in the use of derivatives of *šûḇ*, "to turn," "turn aside," etc. One may turn to or away from Yahweh, and one may turn to and away from other allegiances. No book in the OT contains so many nuances of this idea as Jeremiah.[19] The term "backsliding" is a useful one to describe Judah's apostasy from Yahweh (cf. 2:19; 3:6–8, 11–12, 14–22; 5:6; 8:5; 14:7; 31:22). It was Judah's sin and her apostasy that brought troubles upon her. In a sense neither Egypt nor Assyria was responsible for the coming disasters. They were but the agents of Yahweh, who had decreed their invasions as a judgment for the nation's sin. It was a high price to pay for the breach of her covenant. It was for Judah now to consider how bitter and how evil a thing it was to forsake Yahweh her God. As a result Judah had lost her sense of awe of Yahweh. She seemed rather to have shown respect and awe for treacherous earthly rulers than for Yahweh the immutable God.

The brief passage in vv. 14–19 which describes the fruit of apostasy concludes with the expression *Word* (oracle) *of the Lord, Yahweh of Hosts*, which may indicate that this once had an independent existence before it was woven into the present context.

(iv) The Fascination and Futility of Baal Worship (2:20–28)

20 *"Long ago you broke away from your yoke,*
You snapped[1] *your traces,*
And you said, 'I will not be a slave.'
Indeed, on every high hill
And under every green tree
You sprawled in sexual vice.

17. J. Bright, *Jeremiah*, p. 10, "will get you a flogging."
18. See the Introduction under "Jeremiah and the Covenant," pp. 59–67.
19. W. L. Holladay, *The Root šûbh in the OT* (1958). Note Art. 29, pp. 128–139.

1. MT preserves the old fem. ending *-tî*, which later became *t;* cf. 2:33.

21 *But I planted you a Sorek vine*
Of thoroughly good stock.[2]
Then how have you turned into something foul-smelling,[3]
A wild vine?
22 *Even if you scrub yourself*[4] *with soda*
And use much soap on yourself[5]
The stain of your wickedness is before me—
Word of the Lord Yahweh.
23 *How can you say, 'I have not defiled myself,*[6]
I have not followed the Baals'?
Look at your behavior in the Valley!
Understand what you have done!
You are a fast she-camel
Crisscrossing her tracks;
24 *A wild ass used to the desert,*[7]
Sniffing the wind in her lust!
Who can restrain her when she is in heat?
No male pursuing her need tire himself out;
In her season they will find her.
25 *Spare your feet from wearing out*
And your throats from thirst.
But you said, 'It's no use! No!
For I love strange gods,
And I must go after them.'
26 *As a thief is ashamed when he is found out,*
So the people of Israel[8] *feel ashamed,*
They, their kings, their officials,[9]
Their priests, and their prophets,

2. Lit. "all of it, good stock." MT *klh* need not be emended since the final *h* represents the old masc. sing. suffix which is still preserved in Syriac.
3. In place of MT *lî sûrê haggep̄en* we read *lᵉsôriyyâ gep̄en*. The consonantal text remains the same but is redivided. The proposed noun is not known in texts but would be a normal derivative from the root *sûr.*
4. The translation attempts to capture the intensive (Piel) form of the verb.
5. Lit. "You increase soap for yourself."
6. Reading the Niphal reflexively.
7. MT *pereh,* or *pere'* as many texts read, "a wild ass (or heifer)," seems to break the metaphor of a she-camel. Some commentators take it as a gloss. Others emend *pereh limmuḏ miḏbār* to *pōrᵉṣâ lammiḏbār,* "breaking loose into the desert"; cf. L. Köhler, *ZAW* 29 (1909), pp. 35ff. But see the commentary for the appropriateness here of *wild ass*. The noun *pereh* and the adjective *limmuḏ* are masc. while the following verb is fem. as are most suffixes in the verse. Possible *pere'* serves both for masc. and fem. and the adjective is then left masc. In the next line *nap̄šû* may be read with Qere and LXX *nap̄šāh, her lust*. Apart from that MT may be retained.
8. LXX reads "sons of Israel," MT "house of Israel."
9. LXX reads "sons."

27 *Who say to a tree, 'You are my father!'*
And to a stone, 'It was you who gave me birth!'
But they have turned their backs on me
And not their faces.
In the hour of trouble they say,
'Rise up and save us!'
28 *But where are your gods which you made for yourself?*
Let them rise up, if they can save you in your hour of trouble.
For as numerous as your cities
Are your gods, O Judah."

By comparison with the *rîḇ* pattern these verses may be equated with the section that refers to the futility of ritual compensations or allegiance to other powers whether secular or religious.[10] Such subterfuges will avail nothing but only increase the severity of the judgment which attends a broken covenant. The passage deals with Judah's lust after foreign gods. Some of the pictures are very sexually loaded. All of them are extremely apt and depict Judah's apostasy under a variety of figures.

20 The first figure is of a beast that had broken free from its yoke. It was no new thing for Judah to abandon the covenant. It happened *long ago.* As an ox breaks its yoke, so Judah had snapped Yahweh's yoke and broken the fetters which bound her to him, that is, Israel had cast off all restraints that bound her to Yahweh her sovereign Lord, declaring, "I will not serve." The verb *'āḇaḏ,* "serve," *be a slave,* is also used to describe the action of one who is a vassal. The context thus points to the covenant. The servant who had broken with his overlord now surrenders to another lord, namely, Baal, and indulges in the sexual rituals of sacred prostitution which were a part of the fertility rites performed at local sanctuaries. These were located on hilltops, possibly so that they were nearer to the cosmic deity Baal and other members of the Canaanite pantheon. Here, lying sprawled out under the leafy trees, God's people indulged in sexual acts like a common harlot.[11] The reference may be to the physical activities involved in these rituals as well as to the spiritual involvement with a pagan deity. Participation in the cultic activities of ritual prostitution was idolatry. But Israel had been so enchanted and seduced by Canaanite religious practices that

10. See pp. 159f.; cf. Mic. 6:6.
11. J. Bright, *Jeremiah*, p. 11 gives a vigorous translation, "There you sprawled, a-whoring."

she refused to accept the obligations of the Sinai Covenant any longer.

21 The *Sorek vine* provided a second picture for Jeremiah. This vine was a high-quality red grape grown in the Wadi al-Sarar between Jerusalem and the sea (cf. Isa. 5:2). God has planted his people a thoroughly reliable stock hoping to gather a rich harvest of choice grapes. But she became a strange wild vine, a foul-smelling thing.

22 The third picture is of a *stain* that will not wash off. The stain of her guilt would not respond to scrubbing with lye or washing with soap. Judah's iniquity was so ingrained that no amount of treatment with normally reliable detergents would remove it.

23–25 The figure changes to one that is vividly sexual, the lust of a *she-camel* in heat. Here is a picturesque reference to the practices associated with the fertility cult of the Baals. The use of the plural *Baals* refers to the fact that Baal was worshipped in many centers in Canaanite practice, so that it was possible to refer to the Baal of the particular place.[12] Jeremiah here refers to the claim by some in Israel that they had not followed the Baals and were not defiled by practices associated with the fertility cult, among which sacred prostitution played a central part. The particular emphasis here is partly on the character of the pagan cult rites but partly on the behavior of the two animals to be used in the illustration which follows, namely, the young she-camel[13] and the wild ass. An understanding of the text involves an understanding of the behavior of these two animals. Young female camels are altogether unreliable, ungainly, and easily disturbed, so that they dash about in an apparently disorganized fashion. The expression "interlacing her tracks" (RSV) or *crisscrossing her tracks* (Bright) is an accurate description of a young camel. Jeremiah had before him a perfect illustration of the fickleness and unreliability of Israel.[14]

12. This practice is evident in the pages of the OT. Several place names containing the element Baal probably represented particular centers of Baal-worship. Note, among other references, Baal-gad (Josh. 11:17; 12:7; 13:5); Baal-hanan (Gen. 36:39); Baal-hazor (2 Sam. 13:23); Baal-hermon (Judg. 3:3; 1 Chr. 5:23); Baal-meon (Num. 32:38; 1 Chr. 5:8; Ezek. 25:9); Baal-peor (Num. 25:3, 5; Deut. 4:3; Hos. 9:10); Baal-perazim (2 Sam. 5:20; 1 Chr. 14:11); Baal-shalisha (2 K. 4:42); Baal-tamar (Judg. 20:33); Baal-zephon (Exod. 14:2, 9; Num. 33:7).

13. The fem. *biḵrâ* is used in this sense only here. The feminine verbs and pronominal suffixes in vv. 16ff. are in agreement.

14. K. E. Bailey and W. L. Holladay, "The 'Young Camel' and 'Wild Ass' in Jer. 2:23–25," *VT* 18 (1968), pp. 256–260; W. L. Holladay, *Jeremiah: Spokesman Out of Time* (1974), p. 41.

The female camel in heat is very mild and gives little evidence of the fact. By contrast the female *ass* in heat is almost violent. She sniffs the path in front of her trying to pick up the scent of a male (from his urine). Then she races down the road in search of the male. One Arab proverb runs, "She is intoxicated with the urine of the male." Under such circumstances the males need not weary themselves chasing the she-ass, because she is bent on chasing them. The description of Israel as a wild ass is thus an extremely vivid description of Israel's lusting after the Baals.

The two pictures then combine to describe Israel as unreliable in the extreme and captivated, enslaved, and driven on by a fierce passion to seek the gods of Canaan. She is like a young female camel that cannot walk straight and also like the female wild ass that cannot be diverted from racing straight to her sexual goal. Neither is responsible or reliable.

In Israel's case the particular practices which called forth this vivid picture took place in *the Valley*, that is, the valley of Ben-hinnom, the deep gorge which skirts the west and south of Jerusalem and joins the Kidron Valley at the southeast corner of the city. Here all sorts of heathen rites were practiced, including the worship of Baal and the worship of Molech (cf. 7:31–32; 2 K. 23:10).

The prophet warns Israel not to chase after false gods with the words *Spare your feet from wearing out and your throats from thirst,* that is, they are to refrain from running after these gods till their shoes wear out and they faint with thirst. Evidently Israel was ready to acknowledge the correctness of Jeremiah's analysis of her state but, like the alcoholic or the drug addict, declared that she was incurable—*It's no use! No! For I love strange gods, and I must go after them.* In fact, in a strangely literal way, Judah eventually suffered the judgment spoken of by Jeremiah and went off shoeless and thirsty into captivity to Babylon. It was only when a remnant of these people returned from exile by the miracle of a second exodus that the infatuation with the fertility cult was finally rooted out.

26–27 Earlier in the present chapter four groups in the nation were charged with the responsibility for Israel's declension from allegiance to Yahweh: the priests, those who handle the law, the rulers, and the prophets (v. 8). Jeremiah now returns to castigate them once more, likening them to a professional thief who is embarrassed when caught in the act of stealing. He declares that the day will come when the whole house of Israel along with their leaders will likewise be embarrassed and put to shame. Jeremiah proceeds to make a mocking reference to the practices of Canaanite worship. The people say to a tree (probably the Asherah or wooden pole representing the female Canaanite deity), *You are my father!*, and to a stone (probably the *maṣṣēḇâ* or standing stone pillar representing the male Canaanite deity), *It was you who gave me birth!* These stone pillars (*maṣṣēḇôṯ*) have been found in excavations in Palestine.[15] All that remains of the wooden poles (*'ᵃšērîm*) is a posthole in which the rotted timber has left a differently colored soil. There is enough archeological evidence for these to indicate a widespread usage. There is strong satire here, for it is the female symbol that is called *Father* and the male symbol that is called *You who gave me birth.* Israel was confused about what she was worshipping when she ascribed to the gods of fertility her very existence. Even if such symbols, borrowed as they were from the Canaanites, were regarded by some as harmless expressions of an essential truth, they could, and did, become objects of trust and worship and were therefore to be rejected.[16] But all such practices were regarded by Jeremiah as tantamount to a rejection of Yahweh—*they have turned their backs on me and not their faces.* It was only when calamity struck that Israel realized the futility of depending on gods of Canaan who were powerless to deliver them. They needed a deity to *save (hôšîa')*[17] them, and only Yahweh the God of the covenant, the God of Sinai, could do that.

28 With telling irony Jeremiah suggested that Israel should be asking help of the gods they had fashioned for their cities. The strong inference is that such gods, being the work of men's hands, were powerless to help in the hour of crisis (cf. Isa. 40:19–20; 44:9–20). LXX adds another phrase at this point (cf. 11:13), "and as many

15. G. E. Wright, *Shechem, the Biography of a Biblical City* (London, 1965), pp. 84–86; Figs. 36, 37, 38, 39. These date from the Late Bronze Age, i.e., c. 1550–1200 B.C.

16. It has been argued that the golden calf of Exodus or the calves of Amos were mere symbols of Yahweh, rather like the animals in processions of Hittite deities, some of which carry deities on their back, and others of which carry no deity but may have been regarded as symbols of the deity. See O. R. Gurney, *The Hittites* (London, 1952), ch. 7, "Religion," pp. 132–169. Note p. 137, Fig. 7; pp. 142f., Fig. 8.

17. This verb has a wide range of uses in the OT ranging from mere physical deliverance to deliverance of a spiritual kind. See KB, pp. 412f.

as is the number of Jerusalem's streets, so many are the altars of Baal." These additional words are certainly in the spirit of the passage and bring the oracle into the context of Jerusalem.

The passage should probably not be taken literally. When men worship the powers of nature they vary in their interpretation of these powers, although they acknowledge the one underlying power. A unitary and coherent picture of deity such as is taught in Israel's faith was lacking in nature religions, where the deity was interpreted differently at each local sanctuary. Jeremiah seems to be mockingly calling each local concept of the deity a separate deity.

(v) Israel Deserves Judgment (2:29–37)

29 *"Why argue your case to me?*
You have all rebelled against me—Yahweh's word.
30 *In vain have I struck down your sons;*
They did not take correction.
Your sword devoured your prophets
Like a raging lion.
31[1] *Have I been a desert to Israel*
Or a land of darkness?
Why do my people say, 'We are free;[2]
We will never come back to thee'?
32 *Will a young bride forget her jewelry*
Or a bride her sash?
But my people have forgotten me
Days without number.
33 *How well you set your course*
To seek for 'love,'
So that even to evil women
You have taught your ways![3]

1. MT has an opening line, "You, O generation, see the word of the Law," which LXX reads differently, "Hear the word of the Lord. Thus says the Lord." The line may be a marginal comment by a later reader which became incorporated into the text. It is omitted here.
2. The meaning of the verb translated *We are free* is uncertain. LXX translates "We will not be ruled over." The root *rdy* can mean "subdue," "rule," "oppress," "have dominion." The notion of having the power to carry out one's own will seems to be basic.
3. There is a translation problem here. MT may be translated, "So that even to wicked women you have taught your ways" (RSV). However, the fem. plur. *rā'ôṯ* can mean also "wicked deeds," and the Piel form of the verb may mean "to instruct" so that we may translate "you have schooled your ways with (or, to) sinful deeds" (cf. Bright, p. 13).

34 *Even on your skirts*[4] *one finds*
The lifeblood of poor innocent men.[5]
You did not catch them housebreaking.
Yet in spite of all these things[6]
35 *You say, 'I am innocent;*
Surely his wrath has turned away from me!'
But see here! I will bring you to judgment
Because you say, 'I have not done evil.'
36 *How very cheaply you regard it*
To alter your course!
But you will be disappointed by Egypt
Just as you were by Assyria,
37 *And you will also come away from her*
With your hands on your head;
For Yahweh has rejected those in whom you've trusted;
They will not bring you any success."

The last group of verses in this chapter presents a series of pictures of irresponsibility and corruption. There are two sections, which may have had a separate origin because they have a different person of address. In the first part, vv. 29–32 are in the plural and vv. 33–36 in the singular.

29 Once again we have law-court terminology. The expression *argue your case (rîḇ)* is a legal word[7] and suggests that the people wished to bring a legal suit against Yahweh, though the grounds for such a suit are not specified. Yahweh will not accept the validity of the suit but takes up his own *rîḇ* against Israel again. The truth was, *You have all rebelled (pāšaʿ) against me*.

30 In the secular realm when a great king visited an erring vassal with some kind of punishment the vassal would come to heel, at least in the normal case. But in the case of Israel the divine visitation in some form of judgment was in vain. The people would

4. LXX and Syr. read "on your palms," i.e., hands. The change is only slight and involves the dropping of a consonant: MT *knpyk* became *kpyk*.
5. Some commentators would omit the substantive *poor*, which is lacking in LXX. But MT has both words, which may be taken as two separate nouns or grouped into one phrase, "the innocent poor."
6. The last phrase in MT reads lit., "but upon (or, because of) all these," which is not easy to interpret unless the phrase points forward to the next verse as in our translation (following RSV). *BHS* suggests that a haplography has obscured the sense, and instead of MT *kî ʿal kol ʾēlleh* we should read *kî ʿālayiḵ lᵉʾālâ ḵol ʾēlleh*, i.e., "but upon you as a curse are all these things." NEB understands *ʾēllâ*, "oak," for *ʾēlleh* with LXX and translates "but, at every oak," i.e., "but by your sacrifices at every oak." But the passage is admittedly difficult and J. Bright, p. 13, does not attempt to translate it.
7. See comments on vv. 1–3.

not accept correction. Rather, they turned on Yahweh's representatives and spokesmen the prophets and destroyed them. The reference may be something more than a metaphor and may well refer to the vicious attack on innocent people during Manasseh's reign (2 K. 21:16; cf. Neh. 9:26). Prophets may have been included among these innocent ones. The viciousness of the attack is compared to that of a destructive lion. During Jeremiah's lifetime King Jehoiakim slew a prophet (26:20–23).

Devoured—The picture of a sword devouring is a well-known one. A quaint but gruesome expression is "to smite to the mouth of the sword (*l^e pî ḥereḇ*)." Swords discovered in excavations often have an animal's head at the top of the blade, the blade being the tongue of the beast.[8]

31 In contrast to Israel's rebellious ways Yahweh asks whether he has been inhospitable (lit. *a desert*) to Israel or a land of dark despair. The picture was no doubt intended to point the people back to the period of wandering in the wilderness after the Exodus, the theme with which the present chapter opened. In those days the people travelled through the inhospitable desert, through a land of thick darkness (cf. Deut. 8:15), but Yahweh had led them through to the land of promise. The people had been dependent on him to lead them and deliver them. In those days, fresh from their acceptance of the covenant, they were like a young bride venturing forth with her husband (2:2), and the obligations of the covenant did not seem a burden but a gracious delineation of the will of Yahweh for their peace. Yet, although Yahweh was the source of victory, hope, and confidence, Israel had turned away and desired to be free, carrying through her own will and determining her own course of action. The defiant words *We will never come back to thee* emphasize the mood of the covenant people. Such waywardness was incomprehensible in the light of all Yahweh's activity on behalf of his people. The ideas hark back to the thought of vv. 4–8.

32 The seemingly impossible had happened. In a vivid figure Jeremiah observes that it is altogether unlikely that a young

8. See T. J. Meek, "Archaeology and a Point of Hebrew Syntax," *BASOR* 122 (Apr. 1951), pp. 31–33. Akk. *akālu*, "eat," is sometimes used of the action of an invader devouring a land. The same verb is used for "destroy" or "raze" a city, and of the action of gods, fire, pestilence, wild animals. See *CAD*, Vol. I, A, part 1, pp. 253f.

bride (*b^eṯûlâ*) should forget (*šāḵaḥ*) her *jewelry*[9] or more particularly the *sash* or girdle which proclaimed her status as a married woman (cf. Isa. 3:20). Yet Israel had forgotten precisely those things which marked her out as Yahweh's covenant people, notably the covenant itself, which involved her in a total unshared loyalty to Yahweh. The heinousness of forgetting all that he had done for his people is a theme to which the prophets and writers of Israel returned again and again (cf. Deut. 8:11, 19; 32:18; Ps. 78:11; 106:13, 21; Isa. 17:10, etc.). It was reprehensible to forget Yahweh's past favors and divine calling. Israel was called upon to remember who Yahweh was and who they were. One important purpose of Israel's rituals was to keep fresh in the memory of the people the saving activity of Yahweh in their past history. Yet there was something more important than ritual observances, for these could be performed externally without any deep inward commitment. Indeed, it was possible to carry out these rituals while being involved also in the worship of Baal. Nor was it that Israel lapsed occasionally. She forgot Yahweh *days without number.*

This verse provides an illustration of a well-known "disputation" literary form comprising a rhetorical question and an indictment (cf. 3:1–5;[10] 8:14–15; 13:23; 44:15–25; Mal. 2:10–11; Job 15:2–6; 22:2–11; etc.).

33 With v. 33 there is a change in the number of the person of address from plural to second singular feminine. It may be that vv. 33–37 represent another independent segment of Jeremiah's preaching, but it is also possible that the more general plural has become pointed as a second singular. In any case attention is now directed to Israel's tendencies to harlotry. She had set her course to seek *love ('ahᵃḇâ)*. Her proper course would have been to remain loyal to Yahweh her husband. But she sought other lovers, presumably the fertility gods and their immoral rites. The use of sexually loaded terms like "love," "lover," "harlot" is frequent in the prophets (cf. 3:1, 6, 8; 4:30; 22:20; Hos. 2:2–13; 3:3; 4:15; Ezek. 16:15, 16, 28, 31–34, 35–37, 39, 41; 23:5, 19, 44). It is not always clear

9. The term *'ᵃdî* is generally translated "jewels," but it may denote the whole of the special bridal attire, unless, of course, the reference is to a particular item in the bridal attire which marked the woman as married. Such a token would be cherished throughout life.

10. Burke O. Long, "The Stylistic Components of Jeremiah 3:1–5," *ZAW* 88 (1976), pp. 386–390. Note that the passage in 44:15–25 is in prose, but we have the rhetorical question in v. 21, the explanation of calamity in v. 23, and the sarcastic reproach in v. 25.

whether Israel became involved in physical sexual activity, but since this formed part of the Canaanite cult the reference may well have been both to the act of deserting Yahweh and to physical participation in cult activities. Jeremiah asserts that the people have "set their course" to seek lovers, that is, they had carefully planned to accomplish their evil purpose. Moreover, they had *taught* or "schooled" their ways to wicked deeds, or alternately, they had taught their ways to wicked women. If the latter translation is followed, the sense is that Israel had become so skilled in doing evil that she had things to teach even experienced prostitutes.

34–35 Another facet of their evil living is that they had become involved in shedding the blood of innocent men, a statement to be taken literally in all probability (cf. 26:20–23; 1 K. 21:16; Neh. 9:26). The murder of *poor innocent men* (or, "guiltless poor," RSV) had left blood on their garments (or on their hands, see textual note), and there was something terribly wicked about these murders.

You did not catch them housebreaking—An ancient law (Exod. 22:1–2 [Eng. 2–3]) decreed that when a burglar was caught breaking into and entering a house, anyone who killed him in the act was guiltless. The inference here is that the people responsible for these murders had no excuse and deserved all that might come to them by way of divine judgment despite their claim *I am innocent; surely his wrath has turned away from me*. Yahweh would bring them to judgment for saying *I have not done evil*.[11] The verb (*ḥāṭā'*) means basically "miss the mark," that is, to err from the path of right and duty. This was precisely Israel's trouble. There was a path of duty laid down by the covenant. Israel had missed that path deliberately.

36–37 Israel was capricious and had acted in a thoughtless fashion by changing her ways[12] (cf. vv. 10, 11). But Jeremiah asked whether it was proper for them to change their course at will with impunity and with no regard to the consequences. In fact none of those to whom they turned as they gadded about was steadfast or reliable, whether the pagan gods or the nations. Both Egypt and Assyria were fickle and treacherous and would only bring shame, humiliation, and despair on Judah. Already Assyria had brought shame on the northern kingdom, and had laid Judah under heavy tribute also in fairly recent times. Egypt would do the same.

11. There is another way of translating the Hebrew text. The verb *nišpāṭ* might be understood as "challenge a claim." Hence, "I will challenge your claim that you have not sinned."

12. NEB: "Why do you so lightly change your course?"

Commentators are not agreed about the exact historical events lying behind these assertions. It would appear that Assyria was no longer in a position to help Judah. In that case some have seen in v. 36a a reference to Egyptian troubles in Jehoiakim's reign and have regarded these verses as editorial additions, perhaps by Jeremiah himself, in Jehoiakim's time, even though the bulk of the chapter dates to Josiah's time. But other commentators propose a different background since it appears that Judah had turned to Egypt voluntarily, rather than by any military compulsion. Hence a historical situation in which Judah was involved in some unknown political maneuver in Josiah's reign (perhaps after Assyria had ceased to be of any great significance) is possible. In either case such a turning aside from Yahweh's sovereignty was doomed to disaster, and could result only in a curse and not in a blessing. Egypt would fail her in the end. She would retrace her steps, *with your hands on your head* (cf. 2 Sam. 13:19), that is, displaying signs of grief. There was no help for Judah in either of those quarters, for Yahweh who ruled the course of history had rejected those in whom Judah trusted. When he decided to use a nation to help his people, Israel would be blessed (e.g., Persia and its ruler Cyrus, Isa. 44:27–45:7). Otherwise he might use the nations to bring judgment on his rebellious people.

In its final form ch. 2 carries forward the thought of ch. 1 and is a transition to the somber outlook of 3:6–4:4. There is, as we have been arguing, a strong background of covenantal thinking to ch. 2. If, indeed, the basic material of the chapter represents Jeremiah's early preaching it represents the kind of message he was delivering as Josiah's reformation was gradually gaining momentum. The reformation had begun before the finding of the law book in the temple in 621 B.C. Possibly its earliest reforms were made as early as 629 B.C. before Jeremiah began his prophetic ministry (2 K. 23:5–20; 2 Chr. 34:3b–7).[13] By the time Jeremiah began to preach in 627 B.C. the reform was well under way. It was directed partly against high places, astral cults, and all forms of idolatry both in Samaria and in Judah and Jerusalem. It is clear that both Josiah and Jeremiah were motivated by very strong covenant traditions whose origins go back to Mosaic traditions. The idea of covenant was certainly not an invention of the eighth-century prophets but had roots much more ancient.[14] Any reform which set out to restore among the covenant

13. D. W. B. Robinson, *Josiah's Reform and the Book of the Law* (London, 1951).
14. R. E. Clements, *Prophecy and Covenant* (1965).

people a proper recognition of the sovereignty of Yahweh and to destroy allegiance to other gods would have enjoyed Jeremiah's support. The current apostasy was a breach of the covenant and would lead to judgment, defined on the covenant document as the curses of the covenant (Lev. 26:14–39; Deut. 28:15–68). This emphasis on the covenant is evident in a great deal of Jeremiah's preaching, as we shall see in the course of the commentary. The only way for Israel to enjoy peace and blessing was to be obedient to the covenant demands of Yahweh. In the end Jeremiah despaired of Judah ever recognizing the final and total sovereignty of Yahweh in the nation and lifted his eyes to the day when there would be a New Covenant (31:31–34).

2. A PLEA FOR ISRAEL'S REPENTANCE (3:1–4:4)

(i) Israel, the Faithless Wife (3:1–5)

1 *(The word of Yahweh came to me)*[1] *as follows:*
"Suppose[2] *a man divorces his wife,*
And she leaves him
And becomes the wife of another man.[3]
May he go back to her again?
Would that not completely defile
That land?[4]
Yet you have played the harlot with many lovers,
And you would return to me?—Yahweh's word.
2 *Look up at the bare hilltops*[5] *and see!*
Where have you not acted like a prostitute?
You sat by the roadside waiting for them[6]

1. MT commences merely with "Saying" (*as follows*). LXX and Syr. begin at once on the poem. The full sentence is restored here by comparison with several other passages; cf. W. Rudolph, *Jeremia* (1958), p. 33.
2. Heb. *hēn*; cf. Aramaic.
3. MT reads simply "She becomes another man's."
4. LXX reads "the woman." Read MT; cf. v. 2b; 3:9; Deut. 24:4.
5. The Hebrew noun *š^epî* occurs at 3:2, 21; 4:11; 7:29; 12:12; 14:6. In each case it seems to refer to the high points in the land where the cult of Baal was practiced. Either from the rocky nature of these hills or from the constant traffic of worshippers to and fro, these areas were bare. They would normally be wind-swept and bare. We have used a variety of translations, largely for variety and with no set plan, so that in 3:2, 21 we translate *hilltops*; 4:11, "bare desert heights" because of the reference to scorching winds blowing in from the east; 7:29, "heights"; and 12:12 and 14:6, "bare heights."
6. MT reads simply "for them," but the sense is that Israel was waiting for "lovers" (RSV).

Like an Arab[7] *in the desert,*
And you have defiled the land
With your fornication and your wickedness.[8]
3 *Therefore the showers were withheld*
And the spring rains failed.
Yours was the brow of a harlot woman;
You refused to be ashamed.
4 *Not long ago*[9] *you called to me, 'My Father!*
You were my friend in youth!
Will he be angry for ever,
5 *Will he be cross with me always?'*
This is how you have spoken,[10] *but you have done*
All the evil you could."

In the editorial process the collection of material in this section serves to carry forward the thought of ch. 2. Following a further vivid description of Israel's unfaithfulness under the figure of adultery, there is a passionate plea for repentance and the promise of Yahweh's forgiveness and mercy. It is a theological emphasis to which Jeremiah returned again and again. Israel had turned away. She could turn back and enjoy divine forgiveness and restoration.

The section contains both poetic and prose material, with the poetry interspersed among the prose. The question of the nature of the poetry and the prose arises at once. It has been widely argued that the poetry is Jeremiah's and the prose is either the work of Jeremiah's friends or later Deuteronomic writers. But it is legitimate to ask also whether Jeremiah presented his message in both prose and poetry (as Shakespeare did).[11] The answer to this question constitutes one of the important critical questions of the book. That Jeremiah was capable of writing or preaching both in prose and in poetry need not be doubted. But exactly how much of the present section is genuinely Jeremianic may be impossible to decide. Editorial work certainly formed part of the process of producing the present book. But the possibility that Jeremiah had wide literary

7. LXX reads "like a raven," reading Heb. *'ōrēḇ* instead of MT *'ᵃrāḇî*.
8. Or, "with your wicked fornication," regarding the two nouns as a hendiadys. Cf. J. Bright, *Jeremiah*, p. 19, "Your whorish depravity."
9. MT reads "Did you not from now (*mē'attâ*) cry to me?" i.e., from the time when the drought began.
10. MT reads *hinneh*, "behold." By revocalizing we obtain *hēnnâ*, "these things," i.e., "these things you said." The rest of the sentence reads "you did evil things and were able," i.e., "you have done all the evil you could."
11. See the Introduction, "The Book of Jeremiah: Structure," pp. 27–32. See J Bright, "The Date of the Prose Sermons of Jeremiah," *JBL* 70 (1951), p. 27.

skills should not be minimized. As the chapter stands, it would seem that the material collected here was chosen because of the marked similarities in theme and language which existed between the various poetic and prose segments. Both the prose and the poetry are dominated by the charge of apostasy, which is characterized as "adultery."[12] The other central idea in both the prose and the poetry is defined by the Hebrew verb *šûḇ,* which means basically "to turn," but can mean "turn away" (apostatize) or "turn back" (repent).[13] The root is played upon in a variety of ways (cf. 3:1, 7, 10, 12, 14, 19, 22; 4:1). Details will be given in the commentary that follows.

The poetic material occurs in 3:1–5, 12–15, 19–25, and 4:1–4, while the prose occurs in 3:6–11, 16, 18. It is arguable that the poetry in 3:1–5, 19–25; 4:1–4 forms a single unit which represents Jeremiah's early preaching prior to 622 B.C. Similarities to Hosea, which seem to be very common in the early writing of Jeremiah, include the theme of adultery, and some verbal similarities (3:22; 4:3). The prose passages seem to interrupt the flow of the poem. If this is so, they must have been inserted during the editing process. There seems little reason to deny the short segment dealing with Josiah's day (vv. 6–15) to Jeremiah in his early period. Some commentators have raised questions about other parts of the prose. But nothing in the whole section is inconsistent with Jeremiah's thought in general. Even passages which seem to refer to exiles may well have had the exiles from Northern Israel in mind. But it is not impossible that Jeremiah envisaged a similar exile for Judah and spoke with that in mind. These issues will be taken up in the commentary.

In vv. 1–5 Israel is depicted as a wife who has been faithless to her husband, so that the question of divorce arises. The faithlessness in question refers to Israel's involvement with the worship of the Canaanites whereby she had attempted to share her allegiance to Yahweh with allegiance to other deities. The figure is strong in Hosea but occurs also in other prophets. A concomitant of this involvement in fertility rites was that the people became involved in physical sexual activity as well.

The literary form of these verses is interesting. It comprises

12. The theme was a favorite one with Hosea. See the Introduction, "The Debt of Jeremiah to Hosea," pp. 81–85.

13. See W. L. Holladay, *The Root šûbh in the OT*, esp. pp. 1f., 128–139, 152f. See the Introduction, "The Use and Significance of the Root *šûḇ* in Jeremiah," pp. 76–81.

a rhetorical question in v. 1, and an indictment in vv. 2–5. In this respect the passage resembles other passages in Jeremiah, 2:11–12, 32; 8:4–5; 13:23; 18:14–15. The accusation is sometimes in the second person (13:23), sometimes there are two questions (18:14–15),[14] and sometimes three questions (8:4–5).[15] In 3:1–5 we have a similar pattern, which is really a disputation with a strong juridical flavor.[16]

1 In interpreting the short poetic segment introduced by v. 1, it is important to try to locate it in an appropriate historical situation. Ch. 2 can be readily understood as coming from the days when Josiah's reformation was gaining momentum during the years following 629/8 B.C. After the law book was discovered and accepted by the people in 621 B.C. (2 K. 22:3–23:3), it became evident that its acceptance was far too formal and superficial. It seemed to Jeremiah that some deep evidence of heart repentance was necessary. It was all too easy to go through a form of repentance and reach out for forgiveness. The evidence of centuries of apostasy and rebellion shrieked aloud. Could this be glibly and casually overlooked?

Jeremiah raised the question of divorce in making his point. The whole section is caustic comment on the superficial character of the repentance. In fact, not many years passed before Judah returned to her old ways.

The discussion harks back to Deut. 24:1–4. The statute forbade a man who divorced his wife to remarry her if she had married some other man in the interval. The particular case discussed in the passage in Deuteronomy concerns the action to be taken if the second husband grew tired of her and divorced her, or perhaps died leaving her free to marry again. In no circumstances was her former husband permitted to take her again as his wife, for she had been defiled (lit., caused to miss the way, caused to err). To take her back would be an abomination (*tôʿēḇâ*) before Yahweh.[17] The precise reasons for this ancient law may have been various, among them being an attempt to preserve the second marriage.[18] But whatever the reason, there was no possibility of the first husband reclaiming her. Jeremiah's language makes it clear that quite apart from Yahweh's condemnation of the practice, Jeremiah's contemporaries them-

14. Introduced respectively by *hᵃ-* and *'im*.
15. Introduced respectively by *hᵃ-*, *'im*, and *maddûaʿ*.
16. See B. O. Long, "The Stylistic Components of Jeremiah 3:1–5," *ZAW* 88 (1976), pp. 386–390.
17. See J. A. Thompson, *Deuteronomy* (1974), pp. 244f.
18. *Ibid*. Cf. R. Yaron, "Restoration of Marriage," *JJS* 17 (1966), pp. 1–12.

selves regarded remarriage to a woman who had already been divorced and remarried to another as something particularly abominable. Hence his words would come to his hearers with considerable emphasis.

Suppose a man divorces his wife,
And she leaves him
And becomes the wife of another man.
May he go back to her again?[19]

Jeremiah's contemporaries would have replied emphatically—No! There is a beautiful reminder here of the strength of Hosea's love for Gomer, for he sought for her among her strange lovers and brought her back home (Hos. 2:14–3:3).

There is an interesting difference here between MT and LXX. The latter text reads, "Can she return to him . . . ?" as against the Hebrew text, "Can he return to her . . . ?" which corresponds to the language of Deut. 24:1–4, where it is stated that "the former husband, who sent her away, may not take her again to be his wife after she has been defiled" (v. 4). The initiative in marriage, as in divorce, was the man's.

Against this background Yahweh can be seen as the one who took the initiative in taking Israel as his wife. But Israel took the initiative in turning aside from Yahweh. Under the circumstances, and in the light of the legal prohibition, what right had Judah, frightened by the consequences of her evil deeds, to take the initiative in seeking to return to Yahweh? If that were ever possible, then it could only be on the basis of a profound repentance and a strong initiative from Yahweh himself. There was, perhaps, a loophole in the law. Israel had not, in fact, married a particular lover but was a prostitute to several lovers, in much the same way as Gomer. But there were abundant grounds for divorce in either case, although the husband had not issued a document (cf. Isa. 50:1).

There was a further problem. In OT thought there was a close link between the land and the people. Sin or evil in the people had repercussions on the land (e.g., Lev. 18:25, 28; 19:29; Deut. 24:4; Hos. 4:2, 3; Amos 4:6–10). Behavior such as is suggested here would result in great pollution upon the land where such an iniquitous thing was allowed.

Jeremiah then makes the charge, *You have played the harlot*

19. Cf. J. Bright, *Jeremiah,* pp. 19, 23.

with many lovers,[20] and asks incredulously, *You would return to me?* AV and RV translate the Hebrew text here as an imperative, "Yet return again to me." This is possible grammatically but is out of harmony with the whole tenor of the passage. The question at issue is whether Israel, who has sinned so deeply, may lightly decide to return to Yahweh as though nothing had happened. The verb *return* (MT *šûḇ*) with the sense of turning to God appears again in vv. 12, 14, and 22 where Yahweh calls upon Israel to repent. There *was* a place for forgiveness, on the basis of true repentance for past sins and a proper confession of iniquity, springing from a contrite spirit and a determination to follow the commandments of God. But Jeremiah needed to be persuaded of Judah's sincerity in the matter. We judge that what he had seen up to that point was hardly convincing.

2 So profligate had the nation become that the evidence of her apostasy was to be seen on the bare hilltops, where shrines abounded for the practice of the immoral rites of the fertility cult. *Where have you not acted like a prostitute?* the prophet asked. The people's preoccupation with the evil rites of the Canaanites was likened to the activities of Arabs of the desert waiting in ambush for some caravan to rob. So Israel eagerly awaited the opportunity to commit some adulterous act (cf. Gen. 38:14; Prov. 7:12–15; Ezek. 16:25). It was behavior like this that polluted the land, as v. 3 indicates.

3 These accompaniments of the harlotry of the people are typical (cf. Amos 4:7). The two kinds of rain mentioned are the *showers (rᵉḇîḇîm)* and the late rain (*malqôš*) which fell in March and April. The earlier rain (*yôreh*) fell in October and November (cf. 5:24). Despite that, Judah had a "harlot's brow" and refused to be ashamed. It is possible that Jeremiah here referred to some period of drought during these early years of his ministry. There were droughts also later in his ministry (cf. 8:18–21; 14:1–6).

4–5 When the drought struck the land, Israel, who had neglected Yahweh over the years, began to call upon him and to address him in the endearing terms she knew in her happier days, *"My Father! You were my friend in youth!"* The term used for *friend ('allûp̱)* has a variety of meanings—tame animal, ox, friend, companion, husband, head of family or tribe. It may have been chosen advisedly by Jeremiah, for it conveyed the wide range of functions that Yahweh had served since Israel's youth (*nᵉʿûrîm*). That Israel

20. The Heb. verb *zānâ* is regularly used in this connection.

had forgotten, or failed to act according to what she knew, made her apostasy all the more heinous. If they sought Yahweh when the drought struck, one might ask why they had not sought him in the past.

Israel's plea continues:
"Will he be angry for ever,
will he be indignant to the end?" (RSV)

The shallow belief seems to have been that after their pleas and protestations a merciful God would come quickly to rescue his people, closing his eyes to the enormity of their sin. To be sure, he was willing to forgive, but not in the face of a grave disparity between what his people professed and how they acted. Judah spoke fair words but perpetrated evil deeds.

This is how you have spoken, but you have done
All the evil you could.

Fine words were not matched by corresponding deeds.

It has been argued that logically there is an easy transition at this point to v. 19, and some commentators have grouped the poetic portions together to preserve this continuity.[21] While such a device may preserve logic according to Western modes of thinking (and it may be of some help for that reason), the thought patterns of ancient Israel did not always follow Western logic. It is not uncommon to find arguments interrupted by digressions and resumed later.[22] The prose passage 3:6–18 (with its brief poetic insertion in vv. 12–15) gives some details about the apostasy of the northern kingdom which provide a reinforcement for 3:1–5. The divine intention which is stated in vv. 19–20 is thus seen against a much more detailed background. We suspect that vv. 6–18 were added at this point for this reason. The dilemma of Yahweh given in vv. 19–20 is thus highlighted.

(ii) Apostate Israel and Faithless Judah (3:6–11)

6 *In the days of King Josiah Yahweh said to me, "Have you not seen what apostate Israel did? She went up onto every high hill and under every spreading tree, and played the harlot there.*
7 *Even after she had done all this, I thought*[1] *she would come back to me. But she did not come back. Her faithless sister Judah saw this.*

21. E.g., J. Bright, *Jeremiah*, pp. 19, 20, 23 (note on v. 5).
22. Paul in the NT is a striking example of such processes of thinking.

1. Lit. "I said," i.e., "I said to myself."

8 *She saw*[2] *too that it was because apostate Israel had committed adultery that I put her away and gave her a document of divorce. Yet faithless Judah her sister was not afraid but went and played the harlot also.*

9 *And because her adultery mattered so little, she defiled the land and committed adultery with stones and trees.*

10 *And further, in spite of all this, faithless Judah, her sister, did not return to me in sincerity of heart*[3] *but only in pretense*[4]*—Yahweh's word."*

11 *Then Yahweh said to me, "Apostate Israel has proved herself to be better*[5] *than faithless Judah."*

The material in this prose section consists of a monolog in which Yahweh addresses Jeremiah (vv. 6–11) preparatory to giving him words to speak to Northern Israel, bidding them to return to Yahweh (vv. 12–14).

The historical background to the oracle (3:6–11) was that Judah did not seem to have entered quite so deeply into the idolatrous practices known in the north until after the fall of Samaria (722 B.C.), i.e., in the days of Manasseh (2 K. 21:1–18). Despite the reforms of Hezekiah, Judah declined seriously after his death in 687 B.C. During the long reign of Manasseh (687–642 B.C.) things went from bad to worse. Apostasy was still rampant in the early part of Josiah's reign (640–609 B.C.). Two adulterous (apostate) sisters, Israel and Judah, are here compared, very much to the disadvantage of Judah. Jeremiah's thinking is a development of Hosea's theme of the adulterous wife. The same picture occurs in Ezek. 16 and 23 in a slightly different form. The many affinities between this prose passage and the poetic passages of Jeremiah suggest interesting questions about the character of the prose here.[6]

2. MT reads "I saw," which does not suit the context. We follow LXX mss., Syr.; see *BHS*.

3. Lit. "with all her heart."

4. Lit. "in falsehood."

5. Lit. "has justified herself more than."

6. In a close analysis of the vocabulary of 3:6–12a John Bright comes to the conclusion that this passage has qualities of its own. It is quite without the clichés of the Jeremiah prose and exhibits only one characteristic of the Deuteronomic literature. On the other hand its diction is quite close to the poetic passages in Jeremiah and to Hosea (J. Bright, "The Date of the Prose Sermons of Jeremiah," *JBL* 70 [1951], pp. 21, 35). This raises the question as to whether a poetic prototype lies behind the prose here. See W. L. Holladay, "The Recovery of Poetic Passages of Jeremiah," *JBL* 85 (1966), pp. 401–435. The remark of E. W. Nicholson, *Jeremiah 1–25* (1973), p. 44, that "the passage is composed in the characteristic prose style of the book

6–7 Here the apostate northern kingdom is described literally as "Apostasy (*m^e^šuḇâ*) Israel." The same name appears in vv. 8, 11, and 12, that is, Israel is seen as Apostasy personified. The reason for naming Israel in this way is given immediately: *She went up onto every high hill and under every spreading tree, and played the harlot there.*[7] The reference is to her involvement with the fertility cult (2:20; 3:2, 8, 21; etc.). The hilltops and the leafy trees seem to have held a special attraction for those who practiced fertility rites.

The deeply ingrained commitment of Israel to such practices is here emphasized. One might think that after some trial of the fertility cult Israel might have become disillusioned and returned (*šûḇ*)[8] to Yahweh. But not so. She was too deeply committed to it.

An interested spectator of Israel was her sister Judah, here described as *faithless* (NEB) or "false" (RSV).[9] What would be the reaction of Judah to her northern sister?

8 The historical fact is that in 722/1 B.C. Samaria fell to the Assyrians (2 K. 17:1–18). But even before this, parts of the kingdom of Israel had been lopped off by Assyria (2 K. 15:29). In fact, the Assyrians in the days of Tiglath-pileser III (745–726 B.C.) formed three Assyrian provinces from all the territory north of the plain of Jezreel and the Israelite lands in Transjordan, namely, Megiddo, Karnaim, and Gilead. The upper strata of the population were de-

---

and is probably the work of a Deuteronomic editor," seems to be too sweeping. His further remark that this prose segment "serves the purpose of rounding off the complex of sayings which precede it and to which it is clearly closely linked in content, whilst at the same time forming an introduction to the material which follows," is very helpful as a comment apart from the preceding statement.

7. The verb is *zānâ* (root *zny*) as in many other passages.

8. The significant Heb. verb *šûḇ* appears here. In a natural sense it means "turn" but can also mean either "turn away" from Yahweh ("apostatize") or "turn back" to Yahweh ("repent"). Jeremiah made considerable use of the verb in several nuances. In the section 3:1–4:4 alone there are some eight occurrences of it (3:1, 7, 10, 12, 14, 19, 22; 4:1). See the Introduction, "The Use and Significance of the Root *šûḇ* in Jeremiah," pp. 76–81.

Here the sense is "turn back to Yahweh"—*she would come back to me.*

There is some variation in the translation of the verb in this passage. LXX, Syr., AV, and NEB take the verb to be equivalent to an imperative, "Turn back to me." RSV adopts the view that the verb has a future idea, "She will return to me"; so also J. Bright, *Jeremiah*, p. 21. This seems preferable. A willful Israel would not answer to a command but she may, at her own convenience or as a result of a sad experience, return of her own will as it were.

9. MT reads *bāḡôḏâ*. For a helpful discussion of the meaning of this root see G. J. Botterweck and H. Ringgren, eds., *Theological Dictionary of the OT* I (E.T. 1974), pp. 470–73 (S. Erlandsson).

ported and replaced by colonists from distant lands (2 K. 15:29). It was a high price to pay for her apostasy. What should have been clear to faithless Judah was that "Apostate Israel" had been punished because of her adulterous conduct. Indeed Yahweh had sent her away with a divorce document (*sēp̄er kerîṯuṯ*). Despite the clear evidence of divine judgment on Israel, however, her *faithless (bōg̱ēḏâ)* sister Judah was in no way fearful of what she saw but went and played the harlot (*zānâ*) herself also.

9 The explanation of Judah's behavior was simple. Her apostasy was so great that her sensitiveness to the demands of her covenant with Yahweh had become dulled so that she regarded adultery as something insignificant. The Hebrew text reads literally "through the lightness of[10] adultery"; that is, adultery mattered so little to her that she participated in the same evil practices as her sister Israel and polluted[11] the land. The connection between Israel's sin and the occurrence of natural calamities has already been noted.[12] The stones and the trees were significant instruments in the fertility cult (cf. 2:27).

10 The sum of the matter was this. Despite all the evidence before treacherous Judah that her sister Israel had suffered judgment because of the broken covenant, Judah did not turn (*šûḇ*) to Yahweh in complete sincerity (lit. "with all her heart") but *only in pretense* (*šeqer*). Judah was not merely apostate, but false also. What may have been in Jeremiah's mind was a reference to Josiah's reformation.[13] If so, the present form of the passage dates from after 622 B.C.[14] Judah seems to have been less extreme in her idolatrous ways than Israel until the reign of Manasseh, that is, after Samaria had fallen. Thereafter the declension in Judah was severe. Then came Josiah's reformation with some show of a return to right ways. But it became clear to Jeremiah that there was neither depth nor sincerity in the return, at least for many of the people. While the

10. The noun *qōl* seems to derive from the root *qll*, "to be small, be light"; cf. W. Holladay, *A Concise Hebrew and Aramaic Lexicon of the OT* (1971): "lightheartedness."

11. MT has the qal form of the verb, "be polluted, desecrated." The Hiphil would suit the context, that is, "cause to be polluted" or "pollute." This is suggested by various versions, Aquila, Theodotion, Syr., Targ., and Vulgate. The reading "she polluted the land" seems more appropriate than the MT "she was polluted with the land."

12. See above on v. 1.

13. See the Introduction, "Jeremiah and the Covenant," pp. 59–67.

14. It is not impossible, however, that we have here a reference to earlier efforts at reform such as that of Hezekiah, which were abortive.

reform may have had some beneficial results, it seems clear that it produced no profound change in the national character but tended to stop short with external measures. Religious activity may have increased but true repentance was lacking, and Jeremiah was thoroughly disillusioned (cf. 5:20–31; 6:16–21; 7:1–15). As to the date of these words, they can easily be understood as having been uttered originally before the finding of the law book, consequent upon which Josiah intensified his reforms (2 K. 22:8–23:14), even extending them into the areas of the old northern kingdom (2 K. 23:15–20). However, there remains some uncertainty about the historical background to the picture we have in v. 10. The reference may be to abortive attempts at reform between 627 and 622 B.C., or even to the post-622 B.C. period. The main emphasis remains the same.

11 The argument moves on to a comparison between Judah and Israel at another level. Apostate Israel had shown herself less guilty than faithless Judah. Although Israel had been apostate and had suffered the consequences, she could plead that she had no example to follow. But Judah, warned by the events in the northern kingdom, stood condemned for not changing her ways, and thus Israel "came nearer to justifying herself" (Bright) than did Judah. In such circumstances Jeremiah was commanded to preach to the apostate northerners.

(iii) Israel Summoned to Repent. Future Promises (3:12–18)

12 *"Go and proclaim this message*[1] *to the North and say:*
'Come back, apostate Israel—Yahweh's word.
I will not look on you in anger,[2]
For I am merciful[3]*—Yahweh's word.*
I will not be angry for ever.
13 *Only acknowledge your wrongdoing,*
That you have rebelled against Yahweh your God
And that you have lavished your favors[4] *on foreign gods*
Under every spreading tree,
And you have not listened to my voice—Yahweh's word.

1. Lit. "these words."
2. Lit. "I will not let my face fall upon you."
3. Heb. *ḥāsîḏ,* i.e., one who displays *ḥeseḏ,* "loyalty," "steadfast loyalty," "loving kindness," etc. The word is difficult to translate into English. Cf. "merciful" (RSV, GNB), "love unfailing" (NEB), "gracious" (J. Bright).
4. Lit. "you have scattered your ways." There is an underlying sexual sense. Israel had been involved in "promiscuous traffic" (NEB) with pagan deities. W. Rudolph, *BHS*, proposes reading *dôḏayiḵ,* "your lovers," in place of MT *d*e*rāḵayiḵ,* "your ways"; but there is no textual support in the Versions.

14[5] *Turn back, backsliding people*[6]*—Yahweh's word;*
For I myself am your Lord.
And I will take you one from each city and two from each clan,
And I will bring you to Zion.
15 *Then I will give you shepherds after my own heart,*
And they will rule you with wisdom and understanding.
16 *And when you have multiplied and become fruitful in the land, in*
those days—Yahweh's word—they will no longer say "The Ark of the
Covenant of Yahweh!" It will not enter their thoughts and they will
neither call it to mind nor ask[7] *for it, nor will another one ever be*
made.
17 *At that time Jerusalem will be called Yahweh's throne, and all nations*
shall be gathered there to honor Yahweh's name in Jerusalem,[8] *and*
no longer will they follow their own stubbornly wicked inclinations.[9]
18 *In those days the house of Judah will join the house of Israel, and*
together they will come from the north country to the land which I
gave to your[10] *fathers as an inheritance.' "*[11]

5. Verses 14 and 15 are here taken as poetry, scanning as follows:
14 Turn'-back unfaithful' people'—Yahweh's' word
For' I-myself' am'-Lord among you'
And-I-will take' you' one' from-a-city' and-two' from-a-tribe'
And-I-will-bring' you' to Zion'
15 And-I-will-give' to-you' rulers' according-to-my-heart'
And-they-will-rule' you' with-knowledge' and-with-wisdom'

There is contrastive parallelism in the first colon of v. 14, the people and Yahweh, Yahweh's lordship and their disloyalty. In the second colon there is also parallelism, take–bring, from afar–to Zion. In v. 15 there is contrastive parallelism, I will give–they will rule, plus the parallelism "rulers according to my heart," "rulers who rule with knowledge and wisdom."

This brings vv. 12–15 together as a single poetic unit addressed to Northern Israel.

6. Lit. "sons," *bānîm*.

7. The root *pqd* has a variety of uses, e.g., "order," "command," "appoint." RSV translates "it shall not be missed."

8. MT reads "to the name of Yahweh to Jerusalem," which has been taken as a gloss by some writers. LXX omits. We have kept the words because they seem to convey an important idea which is known elsewhere in the OT, viz., the coming of the nations to Jerusalem to worship Yahweh, e.g., Isa. 2:2–3; 56:6–8; 60:11–14; Zech. 8:20–23.

9. Lit. "the stubbornness of their wicked heart." The heart denotes the seat of the thoughts or inclinations.

10. LXX, Syr., Targ., and some mss. read "their fathers"; but MT may be original. There was less concern about consistency of personal endings in Hebrew than we have in English. The speaker might, at times, forsake address in the 3rd person and apparently address the audience before him directly. Here, the 2nd person may be an adaptation to the form of address in vv. 14–15 (cf. v. 16a).

11. MT *naḥ*ᵃ*lâ*, "patrimony." The term is used in several senses in Jeremiah, cf. 2:7; 10:16; 12:7, 8, 9, 14; 16:18; 17:4; 50:11; 51:19.

The material in vv. 12–18 is partly poetic (vv. 12–15) and partly prose (vv. 16–18). Following the description of the two sisters, apostate Israel and faithless Judah, there comes the call to Israel (northern) to repent (vv. 12–14a) and a promise of restoration (vv. 14b–15). These words, addressed specifically *to the North* (v. 12), that is, to the exiles of the former northern kingdom of Israel, are to be compared with material in 31:2–6, 15–22. Such appeals to the North may well have arisen in the days when Josiah was expanding into the territories formerly occupied by Northern Israel but recently under Assyrian domination. Some commentators see in the word *Israel* (v. 12) an address to the whole people of Yahweh and not specifically to the Northern Israelites in exile (cf. 2:14, 26, 31; 3:21; 6:9; 7:12; 12:14; 18:13; etc.).[12] This view minimizes Jeremiah's own deep interest in the North.[13] He cherished the hope that one day the people of Yahweh in exile would return and be reunited with Judah. That hope finds expression in vv. 12–15, which conclude with a picture of the reunification of the whole nation of Israel, the renewal of worship in Zion, and the replacement of ineffective and bad rulers with wisdom and understanding.

Verses 12–15 fit readily into the earlier period of Jeremiah's ministry, long before Judah herself went into exile. The prose segment that follows (vv. 16–18) seems to have a wider perspective and might even, though not necessarily, presuppose an exile for Judah as well. The Ark of the Covenant may have been removed[14] and Jerusalem may have suffered. It is not unlikely that vv. 16–18 represent a state of affairs somewhat later than the early years of Josiah's reign, and that when the book of Jeremiah was finally edited these were inserted here to provide a rounding out of Jeremiah's earlier message to the northern exiles. But dogmatism is to be avoided. The verses express hopes for the future, and these may well have antedated the fall of Judah by many years. The division between Judah and Israel and the exile of Israel would have been sufficient to give rise to such hopes. In general, we are hardly in a position to assert what Jeremiah might or might not have thought about a whole range of topics.

12. E. W. Nicholson, *Jeremiah 1–25*, pp. 45f. is representative of this view.
13. See the Introduction, "The Life of Jeremiah," pp. 95–106.
14. M. Haran, "The Disappearance of the Ark," *IEJ* 13 (1963), pp. 46–58 argues that Manasseh had removed the Ark before the fall of Jerusalem. However, 2 Chr. 35:3 suggests that the Ark was in the temple in Josiah's day.

It seems likely that we have in these final three verses three separate sayings, each introduced either by "in those days" (vv. 16, 18) or "at that time" (v. 17). There is nothing in any of these sayings which is inconsistent with Jeremiah's thinking in other places.[15]

However, while vv. 12–15 may have been written originally for Northern Israel, they could easily have been taken up again later and set in a wider context. If Yahweh's grace could be effective for Israel under conditions of exile, it would avail for Judah in similar circumstances when she too went to exile. If the prose vv. 16–18 have as a background some actual or anticipated exile of Judah as well as Israel, it is possible to see how the whole section vv. 12–18 came to have significance also for Judah, or for that matter, for the total Israel. What is not certain now is whether the Ark had actually been taken and whether Jerusalem had fallen. As to the Ark, the text does not necessarily require that the Ark had been taken but only that it will no longer be of central significance. Nor do the verses require Jerusalem to have fallen, although this has sometimes been inferred. Helpless Jerusalem would become the center where all nations would worship Yahweh. But when that day came, Yahweh's people would be united once again.

12 *Come back, apostate Israel*—There is a neat play on two derivatives of the root *šûḇ* here which J. Bright has attempted to capture in his translation "Come back, backslidden Israel."[16] The "backslider" (turn away) is invited to "come back" (turn back). There would be a welcome for her. Yahweh would not look upon her in anger because he is merciful and does not retain his anger for ever. Here is a beautiful statement of the divine concern that his people should repent and of his willingness to receive the penitent.

The thought can hardly be that Israel may be pardoned because Judah is worse than she. Nor is there any suggestion that the judgment that fell on Samaria was either too severe or unmerited. The point was that if God had borne with Judah so long in spite of her sins, then Israel, disadvantaged by having no example before

15. Verses 14–18 are sometimes regarded as an editorial composition prompted by the poetic oracle of vv. 12–13 and deriving from a Deuteronomic author who wrote in the characteristic prose style of the book. The argument we have presented should at least indicate the possibility of genuine Jeremianic material lying behind vv. 14–16. See E. W. Nicholson, *Jeremiah 1–25,* pp. 45f. On the question of the character of the prose in Jeremiah see the Introduction, "The Book of Jeremiah: Composition," pp. 33–50.

16. J. Bright, *Jeremiah,* p. 22.

her, might expect divine acceptance if she returned. In either case there needed to be proper recognition of the enormity of her sin and a corresponding outward expression of this in confession and repentance.

13 The call to Judah's wayward sister Israel contained several elements. She was required to acknowledge (lit. "know") her *wrongdoing* (MT *'āwôn*) in that she had rebelled (*pāša'*) against Yahweh. She had "lavished her favors" on strangers, that is, on *foreign gods,* beneath every leafy tree (cf. v. 6). The final charge is that Israel had *not listened to* Yahweh's voice. The expression here translated "listen to" is literally "hear into," as though to emphasize that Israel was not merely to hear words but to commit herself to the words in obedience. The background to such a charge is still the covenant with Yahweh which called for acceptance and obedience (cf. 7:22–26; Exod. 19:5). The theme is writ large in the OT. Obedience is a basic requirement for Yahweh's covenant people. In no other way could Israel remain the covenant people. Obedience leads to blessing and disobedience to cursing (judgment). The theme is present with considerable emphasis in Deuteronomy (e.g., Deut. 28:1, 2, 15).

14 The interpretation of the verb *šûḇ* is important here. In context it would seem that it means simply "return," that is, from exile. There is a further play on words. It is the *backsliding (šôḇā-ḇîm̱)* "sons" (or faithless children) who are bidden to return (cf. v. 22) to Yahweh. The verb *bā'al*, "to be master (husband, lord)" is here used with the pronoun "I" in an emphatic position. *I myself am your Lord* (or husband, or master). The use of this verb is significant. In the setting of the covenant, it is the sovereign Lord of the covenant who calls to Israel his servant. The One who called her to be his bride is her husband (2:2; cf. Hos. 2:2, 16). But there is further play on the word. Yahweh is Israel's true *ba'al*, not Baal.

The reference to taking the people from here and there and bringing them back to Zion suggests an exile, in this case the exile of Northern Israel. There does not seem to be any suggestion of a total return but *one from each city and two from each clan* (or district).[17] Thus there would be a return from exile but only a remnant. There is significance too in that the exiles from the North will be

17. Heb. *mišpāḥâ* is properly a subdivision of a tribe or clan and hence may denote a "district," which is parallel here to "city."

brought to Zion. In the days of the united monarchy, Zion (Jerusalem) was the symbol of unity both of the state and the cult. When the North returned to Zion, the whole of Israel would again be united and in place of rival sanctuaries there would be one. The external indications of division would then be removed and there would be one people, and one Lord.

15 One of the important features about the days of restoration would be that Yahweh's people would have rulers (*rō'îm, shepherds*) after Yahweh's own heart, that is, who would rule in accordance with his will (cf. 23:1–4; Ezek. 34:23; 37:24). Such rulers would be in contrast with those who had ruled them over the centuries, few of whom "walked in the ways of David."[18] This new line of kings would *rule* (*rā'â,* "shepherd, pasture") the people with knowledge and understanding, that is, wisely and well. Here Jeremiah passes from the picture of judgment to one of grace. He could be a prophet of grace just because he took God's judgment seriously. Lesser prophets, the optimistic popular prophets, did not accept the fact of judgment and so could not understand the operation of grace after judgment (cf. 27:16; 28:2–4). For them there was no judgment but the continual operation of "cheap grace."[19]

16 The picture of the days of restoration is now enlarged. There will be material prosperity (*when you have multiplied and become fruitful in the land*) and true religion (*they will no longer say "The Ark of the Covenant of Yahweh"*).[20] This latter statement reveals remarkable insight into the nature of true religion. It was not that Jeremiah was opposed to symbols in Israel's worship. Material items, whether sacrifices, circumcision, or cultic furniture, were only pointers to spiritual realities and were of value only as long as they led men to the spiritual. Where men remained content with the material items, these became worthless and even dangerous (cf.

18. The writer of the books of Kings assessed the value of the various kings in these terms, but few measured up to the standard. In Jeremiah's day this could be said of Josiah (2 K. 22:2), but of no other contemporary kings. Cf. Hos. 8:4, which depicts the kings of Northern Israel. By contrast cf. the character of the ideal ruler in Isa. 11:2.

19. The expression "cheap grace" is used very effectively in one of the sermons of Dietrich Bonhoeffer, *The Cost of Discipleship* (E.T. 1955), pp. 37–49.

20. There is a change in person in v. 16. It commences in the 2nd plur., *when you have multiplied* . . . , and continues in the 3rd person, *they will no longer say* . . . , for the rest of the sentence. The 3rd plur. verb may, however, be taken as impersonal, i.e., people will not say.

7:22–23). Jeremiah here pictures a day when that very significant material item, the Ark of the Covenant of the Lord, would not enter men's minds. They would neither ask for it, nor call it to mind, nor fashion another. The passage does not necessarily presuppose the disappearance of the Ark. According to 2 Chr. 35:3 it was still in existence in Josiah's day. But if the text implies that the Ark was no longer in existence, then the original words of v. 16 should be dated either to the days of Zedekiah or shortly after the destruction of Jerusalem and the temple. It is not clear just what items of temple furniture were carried away by Nebuchadrezzar at his first assault on Jerusalem (2 K. 24:13). Hence v. 16 may be understood as one of Jeremiah's later oracles inserted here during the compilation of this chapter. It is arguable that vv. 16, 17, and 18 each represent an independent saying since each contains either the phrase "in those days" (vv. 16, 18) or "at that time" (v. 17).

17 The verse continues the picture of true religion. The function formerly played by the Ark, that is, Yahweh's throne, the symbol of Yahweh's presence (Lev. 16:2, 13; 2 K. 19:15; Ps. 80:2 [Eng. 1]), will be played by Jerusalem itself (cf. Ezek. 48:35). Jerusalem, in virtue of its new splendor, will become the focal point for the worship of the nations (cf. Isa. 2:2–3 = Mic. 4:1–2; Isa. 56:6–8; 60:11–14; etc.). In these days the nations will cease stubbornly following their own wicked ways (or *their own stubbornly wicked inclinations*).[21]

18 The passage closes with a third short oracle introduced by *In those days*. The promise of the reunion of Northern Israel and Judah, a theme that had already been announced by the eighth-century prophets (Hos. 3:5; Mic. 2:12), is renewed. Here, however, the reunification is seen as coming to pass only after both groups had undergone exile (cf. Ezek. 37:15–28; Isa. 11:10–16). Some commentators have regarded this verse as a very late postexilic insertion. However, the vocabulary and the thought are not out of keeping with Jeremiah's thought (cf. 23:1–8).[22] The return would be *from the north country* (i.e., from lands to the north) to the land which the Lord gave to their fathers as an inheritance. This expectation

21. J. Bright, *Jeremiah*, p. 22.
22. See commentary at 23:1–8. The passage is generally regarded as prose, but we shall argue that some of it at least is poetic and therefore more likely to be genuinely Jeremianic.

was one of the numerous elements in Israel's hope for the future, when all that harmed the unity and welfare of Yahweh's elect people would be removed and they would be restored to a state of "peace" (*šālôm*), in the totality of well-being under the beneficent rule of the Lord's chosen King, the Messiah (cf. Isa. 11; Ezek. 37; Zech. 8; etc.), with all divisions done away (cf. Hos. 1:11; Isa. 11:12–14; Ezek. 37:15–28).

(iv) The Need for True Repentance (3:19–4:4)

19 *"Then I said to myself,*[1]
'I would treat you as a son[2]
And give you a delightful land,
The most beautiful patrimony[3] *in all the world';*
I said, 'You must call me, My Father,
And not turn back from following me.'
20 *But like a woman who is false to her lover*[4]
You have been false to me, house of Israel—Yahweh's word."
21 *A cry is heard on the bare hilltops,*
The weeping entreaties[5] *of the people of Israel,*
Because they have perverted their ways,
They have forgotten Yahweh their God!
22 *"Turn back, backsliding sons,*
I will heal your backslidings!"
"Yes, we are coming to thee,[6]
For thou art Yahweh our God.
23 *Truly the hills are false,*[7]
The clamor on the heights;
Truly in Yahweh our God
Is Israel's help.

1. The verb "I said" is prefixed by the pronoun "I" with some such sense as "I, for my part, said." The translation offered is another way of expressing emphasis.
2. LXX treats Heb. *'êḵ* as an abbreviation for "May it be, Lord, that . . ." (*'āmēn YHWH kî*). This is possible but hardly necessary. The expression *as a son* is lit. "among sons."
3. See the commentary below.
4. MT reads *'āḵēn bāgᵉḏâ 'iššâ*, "surely a woman has played false." LXX and Vulg. imply *'aḵ kiḇᵉgōḏ 'iššâ*, "Ah, like a woman playing false."
5. Lit. "The weeping of the entreaties of. . . ."
6. LXX reads "Lo! we are your servants," which would suggest Heb. *hinnēh 'ᵃnaḥnû lᵉḵā*. We follow MT.
7. Following LXX, Syr. MT "Truly in vain, from the hills" is difficult. If the *m* before "hills" is taken as an enclitic from the last word, then MT agrees with LXX. Also the *l* may be taken as an emphatic *lameḏ*. See F. Nötscher, "Zum emphatischen Lamed," *VT* 3 (1953), pp. 372–380.

24 *But the Shameful Thing has devoured*
All the fruit of our fathers' toil from our youth;
Their flocks and herds,
Their sons and daughters.
25 *Let us lie down in our shame,*
Let our dishonor wrap us round;
For we have sinned against Yahweh our God,
We and our fathers,
From our youth until this day.
We have not obeyed Yahweh our God."
4:1 *"If you will turn back, Israel—Yahweh's word—*
If you will return to me,
If you will put aside your loathsome idols
And will not[8] *wander away from me,*
2 *If you will swear 'As Yahweh lives,'*
Truthfully, justly, and rightly,
Then the nations will bless themselves in him[9]
And in him they will exult."
3 *Yes,*[10] *this is what Yahweh has said to the men of Judah and the citizens of Jerusalem:*
"Plough up your unploughed ground;
Do not sow among thorns!
4 *Circumcise yourselves to Yahweh,*
Remove the foreskin of your hearts,
Men of Judah and citizens of Jerusalem,
Lest my wrath come forth like fire
And burn so that none can put it out,
Because of the wickedness of your deeds."

All the verses in this section are in poetry, and have been accepted by many commentators as having once been part of a longer poem, which commenced at 3:1–5 but was interrupted by the insertion of 3:6–19. Both the prose and poetic material are characterized by similar vocabulary and similar thought. The root *šûḇ* ("turn") features in both, as does the figure of "adultery." After the strong condemnation of 3:1–5, the poem resumes in vv. 19–22a, where Yahweh expostulates with his faithless people and pleads for sincere repentance so that he may fulfil his promises to them. Then in vv.

8. Read with LXX, Syr., Targ., and several mss. *lō'* for MT *wᵉlō'*. The point is important in exegesis; see below.
9. Apparently the writer has abandoned the 2nd person mode of address for the 3rd person, *in him,* i.e., in Israel; see the commentary below.
10. MT *kî* is emphatic. MT has only "the men of Judah and Jerusalem," but five mss., LXX, Syr., Targ. add *the citizens of*; see also v. 4a.

22b–25 Jeremiah offers a liturgy of repentance in which Israel is pictured making a sincere and heartbroken confession of their sin. To this Yahweh replies in 4:1–2 with the promise that the people may "return" if they "turn" from their evil ways. The closing vv. 3–4 spell out the character of repentance Yahweh expects. It must be repentance at a deep level lest Yahweh's burning and unquenchable wrath be poured out on them.

19–20 It was ever Yahweh's intention that his people should live in obedience to him and within the bounds of their covenant obligations. That way lay the promise of blessing (Deut. 28:1–6; 30:9–10, 19–20; etc.). It is an important theme in the OT that God would be a father to his son Israel (Hos. 11:1). In v. 19 there is a strong emphasis on the pronoun *I* in the Hebrew text. Yahweh's people in the day of their calamity cried "My Father" (3:4) but did not act according to their cry (v. 5). By contrast, Yahweh had intentions of good: "I, for my part, said . . ." (v. 19), or, as we have translated, *Then I said to myself.* The MT as it stands suggests that Israel is regarded as a daughter, for the pronoun *you* is second feminine.[11] If this is correct, then it was the desire of Yahweh to give Israel as daughter an inheritance among sons, or perhaps like that of sons. Daughter inheritance was rare in Hebrew practice although not unknown in special cases (Num. 27:1–8; Job 42:15). However, in view of the use of *bānîm,* "sons," in v. 19, the revocalization of these words to give a masculine reference seems more acceptable. If v. 19 is seen as a continuation of v. 5, the pronouns could be taken as masculine and the verse translated, "I would set you among the sons, and give you a delightful land. . . ." The masoretes may have overlooked the link of v. 19 with v. 5 and interpreted it in the light of v. 20, changing the masculine to feminine and the plural to singular as the Qere suggests. The thought of v. 19 is reminiscent of that in Exod. 19:5. It may not therefore be a question of a daughter being given the status of a son[12] but rather of a favorite son being raised above the other sons.

There is, to be sure, some difference of opinion about the interpretation and translation of v. 19. Thus RSV translates:

11. The verb *'ᵃšîṯēḵ* means "I will set you (fem.)" and *'etten-lāḵ,* "I will give you (fem.)." Emendations are suggested to make these pronoun endings masc., *'ᵃšîṯᵉḵā* and *'etten lᵉḵā*, because of the noun *bānîm*, "sons." See W. Rudolph, *Jeremia*, p. 26, and *BHS*.
12. A widely held interpretation, rejected by W. Rudolph, *Jeremia,* p. 27.

"I thought
how I would set you among my sons,
and give you a pleasant land,
a heritage most beauteous of all nations.
And I thought you would call me,
My Father,
and would not turn from following me."

In contrast to our translation, RSV translates *I said* as "I thought" and follows our translation except for a difference of language until the last two colons when we suggest a note of command, *You must call me, My Father,* etc. The RSV suggests reported speech and not a command from Yahweh. In many cases the commentator is called upon to decide between two or more possibilities. It seemed to the present commentator that Yahweh was indeed commanding Israel to call him *My Father.* The RSV interpretation may follow on the translation of the verb as "thought," whereas we have decided to follow the literal meaning *said.* Once that decision is made, the verb form "you will call" can just as easily be translated as *You must call.*[13]

There is some ambiguity of reference in these verses. In 3:1–5, 19, 20 Israel's sin is expressed constantly in terms of adultery. But God is not always referred to as husband; he is also father. The metaphors overlap. The main thrust of the argument is the same. Jeremiah wanted to indicate to the people that God had a special desire to give them the best, *a delightful land, the most beautiful patrimony in all the world.*[14] But if that were to be the case, Israel would need to call Yahweh *My Father* in utter sincerity and not turn back.[15] That is what Yahweh hoped for, but in fact things were quite otherwise. Returning to his metaphor of Israel the unfaithful in v. 20, Jeremiah likens the house of Israel to "a woman playing false (*bāgaḏ*) with her lover."

Verses 21–25, which bear some resemblance to a similar passage in Hos. 14, have been taken by some commentators to repre-

13. The MT reads *'āmartî*, "I said," in the first usage and *wā'ōmar* in the second.
14. Lit. "A heritage of the beauty of beauties (or, ornament of ornaments) of the nations." The expression "beauty of beauties" is a Hebrew superlative. Compare "Song of Songs" (the greatest or most beautiful song), "Lord of lords" (the highest of all lords). Heb. *ṣiḇ'ôṯ* is best understood as the construct plur. of *ṣ^eḇî* (cf. Ezek. 7:20), *contra* LXX which reads "the patrimony of the Lord of Hosts (*ṣ^eḇā'ôṯ*)."
15. The root *šûḇ* here carries the sense "turn back." The preposition "back" is added to the verb, lit. "from after me."

sent a psalm of repentance.[16] The question may be asked whether Jeremiah presented here a typical psalm of repentance which was then followed by Yahweh's demand for true repentance (4:14), or whether Jeremiah was hopefully offering the people a penitential prayer which they might use. The answer to the question would depend on whether Jeremiah had any hope of real repentance in Israel until after divine judgment had passed over them. There is much in the book to suggest that Jeremiah soon lost all hope of repentance among his people. One reasonable interpretation of these verses is that they represent an expansion of vv. 4–5a. Josiah's reformation would have produced many a penitential response on the formal level. But Yahweh rejects the empty mouthing of penitential phrases without true heart repentance. The verses before us draw the contrast between a repentance in word and a repentance in deed.

21 The opening words may well represent Jeremiah's contemptuous and mocking portrayal of the facts of the case. Here was an odd piece of behavior. The people are pictured as being gathered on the heights where hilltop sanctuaries offered them the opportunity to pursue their nefarious cult practices. In a time of need there was deep anguish in their cry (lit. "weeping, the pleadings of the people of Israel").[17] Their cry may have been directed to Yahweh (cf. v. 4), but their cultic practice followed the ways of the Baal-worshippers. There was no answering cry from Yahweh. They had *perverted* (twisted) *their ways,* and had *forgotten Yahweh their God.*[18] There could be no true worship of Yahweh on those *bare hilltops* either, because the whole thing was a vain and empty exercise carried out on behalf of nonexistent gods, or possibly because Josiah's reform had destroyed the actual sanctuaries that were once there (2 Chr. 34:3–7), making the heights bare. Yet those bare heights still had a strong attraction for the people and the lure of these places still possessed them.

22 At this point Jeremiah presents a liturgy of repentance. It is introduced by the brief but deeply significant call of Yahweh to

16. H. L. Ellison, "The Prophecy of Jeremiah," *EQ* 32/4 (1960), pp. 214f.

17. The "weeping entreaties of Israel's folk" (Bright); "Israel's people pleading for mercy" (NEB); "the weeping and pleading of Israel's sons" (RSV).

18. The verbs "forget" and "remember" are significant in various parts of the OT, e.g., Deut. 8:2, 11, 14, 18. They portray the attitudes of the obedient keeper of Yahweh's covenant and the disobedient covenant-breaker respectively.

his people to turn back to him. This is followed by an abject, heart-broken confession of sin (vv. 22b–25). To this Yahweh responds that if their repentance is sincere they may return (4:1, 2). However, repentance must be from the heart lest Yahweh's wrath fall on the people (4:3–4).

An alternative interpretation of the confession in vv. 22b–25 sees in them a rhetorical device in which Jeremiah gives expression to an appropriate ideal confession which Israel might be expected to give when she came to repentance. It was the kind of confession which Yahweh longed to hear and which the prophet hoped for. He even suggested the form of words which the people might use.

Yahweh's call to Israel contains a strong play on the root *šûḇ* ("return").

Turn back, backsliding sons,
I will heal your backslidings.[19]

The reply commences with the words:

Yes, we are coming to thee,
For thou art Yahweh our God.

Such a call and response would be expected in the case of truly obedient worshipping people. Yahweh would call and his people would answer. The complete answer is comprehensive and far-reaching.

23 The first element in the confession is a declaration that the hills were false[20] and the activities at the high places a mere din, clamor, hubbub. The only source of Israel's salvation is declared to be in Yahweh. Here is the beginning of a proper understanding of the cause of Israel's present plight. She had been deceived and needed to confess again her basic creed that Yahweh was her only God (Exod. 20:2–6; Deut. 5:6–10; 6:4). Such an acknowledgment would bring her once again to the recognition of Yahweh as her sovereign Lord, which would be tantamount to a renewal of her covenant with him, for such a confession would carry with it a willingness to accept Yahweh's covenant demands. The confession is spelled out further in vv. 24 and 25.

24 *The Shameful Thing*—As the confession proceeds, Baal is referred to under the substitute name *bōšeṯ,* "shame." This prac-

19. Heb. *šûḇû bānîm šôḇāḇîm 'erpâ mešûḇōṯêḵem.* There are strong parallels here with Hos. 14:2, 5 (Eng. 1, 4), suggesting that Jeremiah knew and drew on Hosea.
20. J. Bright, *Jeremiah,* p. 20, "A swindle."

tice is known elsewhere in the OT.[21] The same word "shame" reappears in v. 5. The penitents here declare that "Shame" (Baal) had devoured all that the labors of their fathers had produced since the people were children. The reference here may point back to Israel's childhood as a nation when Yahweh called them from Egypt. Already in ch. 2 there is a reference to Israel's *youth,* where the same word (*nᵉʿûrîm*) is used (2:2). The occupation with Baal-worship and participation in the cult practices of the high places had only served to impoverish the nation. Its flocks and herds, its sons and daughters had been swallowed up.

25 The penitential statement finally declares:

Let us lie down in our shame (bōšeṯ),
Let our dishonor wrap us round.

The crux of the confession touches the vital point of obedience. Both the present generation and their forefathers before them from their early days (*youth, nᵉʿûrîm,* cf. 2:2; 3:24), that is, as far back as the days of the Exodus, had failed to give heed to the voice of Yahweh their God.

It was a point to which Jeremiah returned again and again (cf. 7:23–28). True repentance arises from the recognition that men have sinned (Heb. *ḥāṭāʾ*) and have not been obedient to God's word to them. In the case of Israel this had meant the rejection of Yahweh's sovereignty and of his covenant demands. There was something contingent about the appeal at Sinai (Exod. 19:5), "If you will obey my voice and keep my covenant, you shall be my own possession among all peoples."

The words of vv. 22b–25 constitute a noble confession indeed. And yet, it would appear from the divine answer which is given in 4:1–4 that, if such a confession was in fact made, there was a lack of genuine heart repentance, so that there was no correspondence between the formal declaration of repentance, albeit in fine and proper words, and the actual behavior of the people.

God's answer to the penitential statement of 3:22b–25 falls

21. Cf. the name of Saul's son Ish-bosheth (2 Sam. 2–4), which was almost certainly Ish-baal. In Jer. 11:13 the "Shame of Israel" is declared specifically to be Baal, in an interesting parallelism:

"You have set up altars to Shame (*bōšeṯ*),
Altars to burn incense to Baal."

See the commentary at 11:13.

It is possible that Jeremiah originally had "Baal has devoured all for which our fathers labored." The word *bōšeṯ* in MT would then represent scribal alteration. See *BHS*.

into two parts. In 4:1–2 God spells out the meaning of true repentance and provides an answer to the question of 3:1: "If a man divorces his wife, and she leaves him and becomes the wife of another, may he go back to her again?" Yes, he may, that is, in the present context Yahweh *may* take Israel back on certain conditions which are stated in vv. 1–2. In the second part of God's answer in vv. 3–4 the conditions demanded by Yahweh are expanded.

1 There is a slight ambiguity in the verse, particularly at the end of the first line in the Hebrew text. The question is whether the *if ('im)* with which the verse begins may be regarded as being repeated in the second part of the line, or whether we have here an affirmation.

Thus two translations have been proposed. One possibility is to translate:

"If you will but come back, O Israel,
(If) you will but come back to me. . . ."[22]

The other possible translation:

"If you return, O Israel,
To me you should return[23] (or, you may return)."

The Hebrew text would allow both. Again here the root *šûḇ* is pressed into service. It is possible that it carries two senses:

"If you *turn (šûḇ),* O Israel,
To me you should (or may) *return,*"

that is, if the tragic circumstances of her present life were causing Israel to reflect on her ways so that she was prepared to turn from her ways to another way, then she would return to Yahweh. But on this reading there is a further decision necessary when translating the Hebrew verb form used here, since the same form might be expressed by English "will," "may," or "should." Thus any one of the following might be possible:

You *may* return; you *should* return; (if) you *will* return.

There is thus some ambiguity. On the whole it would seem preferable to take vv. 1 and 2 as listing a series of conditionals. This position is taken in the translation above. But in any case Yahweh was anxious for his people to renew their covenant. A gracious expression of *his* willingness to receive his people back is implied in each case. But Yahweh's willingness to do this is based on sincere and lasting repentance represented not by the recitation of a formula

22. So NEB.
23. So RSV; J. Bright, *Jeremiah,* p. 21; W. Rudolph, *Jeremia,* p. 26.

(such as may have been used often during the days of Josiah's reform movement) but by a specific rejection of every other allegiance, so that the sovereignty of Yahweh alone is recognized. A radical change in national and personal life was demanded which did not necessarily accompany any formal recitation of the words in 3:22b–25. The radical change which Yahweh expected is here spelled out under clear directives. The performance of these would demonstrate the reality of the people's repentance.

They must return to Yahweh. They must abandon their previous apostasy by putting away their *loathsome idols* ("vile things," Heb. *šiqqûṣ*). They must cease from wandering away from Yahweh's presence.[24] The term *šiqqûṣ,* "abomination," is widely used in the OT. It denotes filthy garments (Nah. 3:6), meats offered to idols (Zech. 9:7), but especially pagan deities (1 K. 11:5; 2 K. 23:13, 24; 2 Chr. 15:8; Isa. 66:3; Ezek. 20:7, 8; etc.), and even men who associate with false gods (Hos. 9:10). In the present context, the reference is to the false gods of Canaan. These must be *put aside.*[25] The contrast is clear. Israel must "turn to" Yahweh. But she must "turn away from" abominations. There were no grounds of compatibility between Yahweh and other gods. There could be no divided loyalty. The point is further stressed by the expression "if you do not wander (MT *nûḏ*) from my presence."

2 Here we meet with another problem of translation. If the first line of this verse is understood to be a further condition despite the absence of *if*, then we have to translate "and if you swear . . ." (NEB, RSV). Alternately, we may understand the Hebrew text as saying "Then you may swear 'As Yahweh lives,' truthfully, justly, and rightly" (Bright). In this latter case the prophet was declaring that only those who acknowledge Yahweh as God are entitled to take an oath in his name and provide the nations with grounds for exalting in Yahweh.

As Yahweh lives was the usual formula for an oath in ancient Israel. But it was never intended for use by those who rejected Yahweh's sovereignty. Indeed one of the Ten Commandments for-

24. By confining the first part of the verse to the words *If you will put aside your loathsome idols,* and reading the last part of the verse as "(if) you do not wander (stray) from my presence," we obtain a line with three beats in each part to give a 3:3 pattern. The *if* is regarded as serving a double function as in v. 1. Cf. NEB, which reads differently.

25. The Hebrew verb used here is the causative (Hiphil) of the root *sûr,* "to turn aside, turn away, depart." It is related semantically though not etymologically to *šûḇ*, "to turn." There may even be something of a play on the two words.

bade Israel to take Yahweh's name as an empty thing (Exod. 20:7; Deut. 5:11). These words were intended to be uttered *truthfully* (in truth), *justly* (in justice), and *rightly* (in righteousness). The three nouns truth (*'ᵉmeṯ*), justice (*mišpāṭ*), and righteousness (*ṣᵉḏāqâ*) occur many times in the OT and particularly in prophetic literature. The basic roots *'mn, špṭ,* and *ṣdq* gather about them a wide range of ideas[26] which combine to give definition to the covenant demands and would have enabled Israel to understand the kind of life God expected of those who would live in fellowship with him. In the present context these roots appear as nouns each with the preposition *bᵉ*, "in." The sense of the passage therefore is that the one who takes the oath *As Yahweh lives* must do so from within the covenant and as one who acknowledges the sole and complete sovereignty of Yahweh. Clearly that was not possible for one who had wandered from Yahweh's presence or had dealings with "abominations." Allegiance like this and deep commitment of the life to Yahweh's sovereignty would, in the terms of the covenant, result in Israel's enjoyment of the blessings of the covenant.[27] But further, the nations observing the blessing that attended Israel's way would seek such blessings for themselves, only to discover that these flow from a surrender of themselves to the sovereignty of Yahweh, Israel's God. The expression *the nations (gôyîm) will bless themselves in him*—that is, they will discern in the example of Israel that the source of true blessing lies in Yahweh and that he dispenses his blessings to those who are obedient to his covenant—is a variant of a statement that occurs elsewhere in the OT.[28] A related response from the nations is that they will *exult* (glory, boast, Heb. *hiṯhallēl*) in Yahweh.[29]

It becomes clear that true repentance on Israel's part would have far-reaching consequences not merely for Israel but also for mankind in general (cf. Isa. 42:6; 49:6).

26. See N. H. Snaith, *The Distinctive Ideas of the OT* (1944).
27. See Deut. 28:1–6.
28. See Gen. 12:3; 18:18; 22:18; 26:4, etc., where the promise of Yahweh to the patriarchs is "In you shall all the families of the earth bless themselves." *BHS* and NEB propose an emendation of the Hebrew text to "in you." This does not seem necessary and in any case has no support in the Versions. Even the texts which read "in you shall all the nations of the earth bless themselves" must have an ultimate reference to Yahweh, as though the nations would say "May I be blessed as Israel is blessed." But such a blessing is ultimately the blessing of Yahweh. The Hithpael form of the Hebrew verb is used here as in Gen. 22:18; 26:4. The Niphal occurs in Gen. 12:3; 18:18; 28:14 with a reflexive sense (KB, pp. 153f.).
29. There is no need to change the reference to "in you"; see the previous note.

3–4 These two verses appear to be a separate oracle with a short prose introduction addressed *to the men of Judah and the citizens of Jerusalem.* The question arises whether the people addressed here are different from the Israel of v. 1. Some commentators have proposed that the term "Israel" refers to the northern kingdom, now in exile, and already a subject of 3:6–13.[30] The term is ambiguous. Judah never ceased to be part of the whole people Israel, whatever the northern kingdom might call itself. With the fall of Samaria and the transformation of the northern kingdom into Assyrian provinces, Judah was all that remained of Israel as far as the worship of Yahweh was concerned, and for that matter, as far as the recognition of the entity Israel by men was concerned. Moreover, in general Jeremiah refers to the northern kingdom as "the house of Israel" or "Ephraim."[31] Hence it seems possible to regard vv. 3–4 simply as an expansion of vv. 1–2, both addressed to the remnant of the complete Israel, that is, "Judah and the citizens of Jerusalem." It was not due to any merits in Judah that this was so, but because of the sins of the north. Judah might plead for God's favor as Israel, the people of God, but the fact was that in the end God would deal with them as the historic state of Judah with its own record of evil deeds, and particularly the great evil of recent days during the reign of Manasseh.

What then is required of Israel, now represented by the sin-stained Judah? Repentance! Not the superficial repentance conveyed by formulas and liturgical utterances mouthed during a reform movement, but repentance of the kind outlined in vv. 1–2, a deep and radical repentance which was not a working over of old ground but was demonstrated in the opening up of new ground—new wine in new bottles (cf. Matt. 9:17; Mark 2:22).

The people are invited to *plough up your unploughed ground.* The instruction does not refer to ground that has lain untilled for a long time and has grown hard so that it must be broken up again.[32] The Hebrew verb and its cognate noun refer to virgin soil.[33] The command is therefore to break new soil, no easy task on the rocky slopes of Judea. There was a further problem. Tilled ground en-

30. A. W. Streane, *Jeremiah* (1899), p. 33; A. C. Welch, *Jeremiah: His Time and His Work* (1928), p. 70.
31. Even in 31:2–6 the mention of "the mountains of Samaria" makes it clear that the northern kingdom is intended.
32. See A. S. Peake, *Jeremiah* (1910), pp. 116f.
33. Heb. *nîrû lāḵem nîr.* See KB, p. 615.

couraged the growth of thorns and thistles. It was normal to collect and burn the tinder-dry thorns after the harvest had been gathered in.[34] But at sowing time, sowing preceded ploughing. The farmer scattered his seed over the unploughed stubble, on the path, among the thorns, on rocky ground, etc. (Mark 4:3–8). The whole was then ploughed in. This may seem bad farming to the Western mind but it was the custom of centuries in Palestine.[35] The fact was that the ground was infested with thorn seeds despite the fire following the previous harvest, and these were all the more abundant because of years of strong growth in good ground.

Against this background we begin to understand Jeremiah's picture. Judah's own field was so infested with the thorn seeds of past evil deeds that her only hope was to reclaim new ground.[36] The whole future was threatened by the legacy of the past, and only a complete and radical new beginning would suffice to save the nation. Historically, this needed the collapse of Judah and the Babylonian exile, although finally even this was inadequate. Only the new covenant of 31:31–34 would suffice.

4 *Circumcise . . . your hearts*—The radical change necessary in Israel is made much clearer by the call to a circumcision of the heart (v. 4). It is a change of image but touches profoundly on the covenant itself. Circumcision was not unique to Israel (cf. 9:24, 25 [Eng. 25, 26]), but in Israel it was a sign that this people belonged to Yahweh.[37] The rite was given to Abraham as the sign of the covenant (Gen. 17:10–14). It was never intended as a mere outward sign, but as a witness to an inward reality, the surrender of the whole life to the sovereignty of Yahweh (Deut. 10:16; 30:6). It was not the removal of the loose foreskin that covered the extremity of the male organ that was significant, but the removal of the hard excrescence of the heart. The "heart" in this context refers not to the physical heart, nor to the intellect or will or emotions alone, although in some contexts these provide a suitable translation. The reference here seems to be to the totality of man's inner life. Israel is called upon to "circumcise herself" to Yahweh,[38] that is, for

34. See W. M. Thomson, *The Land and the Book* (London, 1910), ch. 23. Cf. Heb. 6:7, 8.
35. Joachim Jeremias, *The Parables of Jesus* (^{3}1972), pp. 11f.
36. There may be a reference here to Hos. 10:12, further evidence of Jeremiah's dependence on Hosea's thinking.
37. R. de Vaux, *Ancient Israel* (1961), pp. 46–48.
38. The Heb. verb is Niphal, which originally had a reflexive sense. LXX has "to God."

Yahweh's benefit or for obedience to him (NEB "to the service of Yahweh"). The physical rite of circumcision could never realize the purpose of the covenant if the heart remained foreign to it. The interior dispositions of the people were more significant than any external practices, and the total commitment of the life (heart) to Yahweh by the removal of every inhibiting element was the only response acceptable to Yahweh. The conversion demanded of Israel was very much more than the restoration of neglected practices. To be sure, Israel must forsake her idols as a prerequisite to true conversion. But the essence of Jeremiah's demand rested on the concept of a new Israel and a new Covenant.

The present section closes on a stern note emphasizing the consequences of the broken covenant. Both in the secular and in the religious realms the sanctions of the covenant/treaty (Heb. *bᵉrîṯ)* included blessings and curses, blessings for those who keep the covenant and curses for those who breach it (Deut. 28; Lev. 26). Once a breach of covenant was noted by the great king and warning was given, failure on the part of a vassal to amend his ways resulted in a punitive visit. The picture was well understood by Israel from the secular realm, and the transfer to the religious realm would not have been difficult. Yahweh was Israel's sovereign lord. The breach of Israel's covenant with him would result in divine visitation in judgment. Thus Jeremiah could conclude his strong appeal to the people to repent with the words:

> *Lest my wrath come forth like fire*
> *And burn so that none can put it out,*
> *Because of the wickedness of your deeds.*

Theologically, chs. 2 and 3 belong together. Ch. 2 begins with the poignant question of the hurt lover, "What wrong did your fathers find in me?" (2:5). Ch. 3 gives expression to Yahweh's appeal for genuine repentance: "Return, faithless Israel, . . . only acknowledge your guilt" (3:12–13), "Return, O faithless sons, I will heal your faithlessness" (3:22). After the moving picture of Israel's faithfulness in her youth and the description of her ideal status (2:1–3), Jeremiah moved into a description of the sin of Israel's ancestors and spoke of the fascination and the futility of Baal-worship which led to Israel's refusal to worship Yahweh. All of this pointed to Israel's rejection of Yahweh as her sovereign Lord. Her rejection of his covenant brought her to a place where judgment was merited. There could be no lighthearted view that Yahweh would overlook her sin. Only deep repentance from the heart would suffice. An oracle once addressed to Northern Israel was gathered into a larger unit when the book was edited, so that the call to Northern Israel to repent became part of a call for the whole of Israel to repent.

The themes of "adultery" and "return" (verb *šûḇ*) recur again and again. The one is concerned with the indictment of Israel for her sin (largely ch. 2), the other with a plea for repentance (largely ch. 3). Both themes were taken up early in Jeremiah's ministry, and despite later editing we have here the burden of his early preaching. Both themes characterized his whole ministry, although it became clear as the years passed that repentance would not take place and that judgment was inevitable. The theme of judgment is the emphasis of the next section, 4:5–6:30.

The likening of Yahweh's judgment to a fire that could not be quenched was evidently a well-known metaphor in Israel (7:20; 17:27; 21:12; Isa. 1:31; Amos 5:6). As far as Jeremiah was concerned, God would deal with Judah as he had with Israel. She was, indeed, more guilty than her sister (3:11), and her judgment was at the door.

3. THE COMING JUDGMENT (4:5–6:30)

(i) The Alarm—Invasion Is Threatened (4:5–10)

5 *Proclaim it in Judah!*
Make it known in Jerusalem! Say:
"Blow the trumpet throughout the land!
Shout loud and clear![1]
Give the command! 'Band together and let us go
To the fortified cities!'
6 *Raise the signal*[2]*—To Zion!*
Run for safety! Do not wait!
For I am bringing disaster out of the north
And great destruction.
7 *A lion has come up from his hiding place,*
The destroyer of nations has set out;
He has left his base[3]
To make your land a ruin;
Your cities will be laid waste and uninhabited.

1. Lit. "Call aloud, fill up."
2. LXX reads "Flee," evidently from a Heb. text *nûsû*, which preserves the same consonants as MT *nēs*, *signal*. The colon would read: "Announce (lift up the voice)—Flee to Zion."
3. Lit. "place."

8 *So put on sackcloth,*
Wail and howl,
For the fierce anger of Yahweh
Has not turned away from us."
9 *"On that day—Yahweh's word—*
The king and the officials will lose their courage,[4]
The priests will be horror-struck
And the prophets dumbfounded."
10 *Then I said, "Ah, Lord Yahweh,*
You have completely deceived
This people and Jerusalem,
Telling them 'You shall have peace';
But a sword is laid on our throats."

The theme of judgment hinted at in the first three chapters of Jeremiah and announced so dramatically in 4:3–4 is now spelled out in some detail, providing the central theme of the next major section, 4:5–6:30. Jeremiah had pleaded earnestly for repentance, and had given warning that repentance of a deep and complete character, accompanied by a radical change in the national and individual life and a circumcision of the heart, needed to take place. This repentance had not taken place, it seems. Hence, the day of judgment was at hand. The material collected in the section before us may be regarded as a direct or indirect fulfilment of the vision of the boiling pot (1:13–16). Judgment is to be realized by a swift invasion from the north.

Interesting questions arise about the dating of the oracles in 4:5–6:30. As a general statement it is probably true that none of the material can be dated with precision. Commentators have differed widely in their opinions, and dates ranging from Josiah's reign to the reign of Zedekiah have been proposed for various portions of the section. One of the criteria for the dating of at least some parts is that the descriptions are so graphic that one might suppose that they represent an eyewitness account of some event. This may or may not be an adequate criterion. Jeremiah thought a great deal in vivid symbolism and imagery. He seems to have been haunted over a long period by a premonition of doom. Nor would he have been unaware of the nature of an invading army. Hence many of the segments may have been composed before the approach of Nebuchadrezzar's army, first in 605/4 B.C. and later in 578/7 B.C. Even the segments that reveal the anguish of the prophet's heart (4:19–21) were not neces-

4. Lit. "heart."

sarily wrung from his heart precisely as the invasion struck, but may have come from a time when he was deeply moved by the vividness of his vision.

There is another fact to be noted. It would appear that this lengthy section is a compilation of a number of shorter segments, some of which may have been re-used in a new situation over a period of time and later collected together in order to provide the material to illustrate the threat of 4:3–4. It is altogether likely with a visionary like Jeremiah that in some areas of this section we have visions clothed in poetic language. It was the prophet's task to render his vision into suitable words. Sometimes the vision became something into which the prophet entered at a deep personal level, sharing some disaster with his own people in all its anguish (cf. 4:19–21). However, it would make a good deal of sense if at least some of these prophecies about the foe from the north[5] were uttered in the shadow of the rising power of Babylon from late in Josiah's reign and well on into the reign of Jehoiakim when the Babylonian menace was clearly a present threat or had begun to be a reality. The older theory that the foe from the north was the Scythians, who invaded Western Asia in the years following the death of Ashurbanipal, the Assyrian ruler, in 627 B.C., has been abandoned.

In the following pages we shall suggest a date for at least some of the sections. Not all of the material deals directly with the foe from the north. Such segments as 5:1–14, 20–31, for example, revert to the questions already raised in chs. 2 and 3. But they are essential elements in the development of Jeremiah's message of doom. It may be that some part of 4:5–6:30 can be ascribed to the reign of Josiah whether earlier in his reign or later. Further, we ought not to argue that the material of this section is necessarily to be dated after the material of chs. 2 and 3. In general, the call to repentance precedes the message of judgment. But once judgment is imminent, or indeed even as it is operating, there is no reason to imagine that the call to repentance ceases. In the book of Jeremiah, as in all the prophetic writings, we are confronted with the literary device of grouping similar oracles together; and while, in general, the call to repentance so strongly uttered in ch. 3 would have preceded the day of judgment, there must have been an overlapping and intermingling of the two facets of the message of the prophet at virtually every stage of his preaching.

5. See the Introduction, "The Foe from the North," pp. 86f.

Like a clap of thunder a note of alarm is sounded as the approach of an unidentified army is heralded. In the present arrangement this section is introduced by the cry of a herald and concludes (4:31) with the anguish of a woman in childbirth. In this respect the section resembles ch. 6 (cf. 4:5 with 6:1; and 4:31 with 6:24–26). There are a number of apparently distinct literary elements here which are woven together into a vivid whole. There is no clue within these verses about the date, so that they would suit almost any period of Jeremiah's ministry.

5–6 These verses constitute a single segment, the content of the herald's cry which is to be made known in Judah and Jerusalem. It echoes a similar alarm raised by Hosea in the days of the Syro-Ephraimite war (735–734 B.C.; Hos. 5:8; cf. 2 K. 16:5–6) and a similar call to be sounded later by the prophet Joel (Joel 2:1). The blowing of the horn (*šôpār*) announced a state of emergency (cf. Amos 3:6). Hearing it citizens would flee for safety behind the walls of their fortified city. In the present case the trumpet was to be blown throughout the land, no doubt because the invader was expected to move swiftly. The herald's cry consists of short staccato utterances.[6]

Blow the trumpet throughout the land!
Shout loud and clear!
Give the command! Band together and let us go
To the fortified cities!
Raise the signal—To Zion!
Run for safety! Do not wait!

It is not clear precisely what *signal* was to be raised. The Hebrew word *nēs* means both "standard" and "signal." Possibly the reference is to a fire signal which was lighted on a height for transmission of the news of a state of emergency to areas farther on (cf. Isa. 13:2; 18:3). One of the letters found in the excavations at Lachish also refers to the state of emergency in southern Judah at the time of Nebuchadrezzar's invasion of 587/6 B.C. The scribe declares, "We are watching for the signals of Lachish according to all the indications which my lord has given, for we cannot see Azekah."[7] This record refers to a time slightly later than that of Jer. 34:7 when both Lachish and Azekah were still standing. Fire signals provided a swift means of communication.

6. The NEB translation captures the note of urgency.
7. *ANET*, p. 321.

The reason for such alarm was that Yahweh was bringing calamity (*rā'â*) out of the north (cf. 1:13–15), described vividly as "a shattering disaster"[8] (*šeḇer gāḏôl*).

7 The invader is described as a *lion* from his *hiding place* (*s^e^ḇōḵ*, "thicket"). He is not named precisely, and this constitutes one of the problems about this passage. Who exactly was the foe from the north? He has been variously identified as the Scythian armies, the Assyrian armies, the Babylonian armies. But it may be that in this passage Jeremiah, with his eschatological visions of doom, was not concerned with the identity of those he saw in his visions because they were not purely historical in character.[9] What mattered to Jeremiah was that God's people because of their sin and their failure to repent were heading fast for judgment. The "lion from his thicket" (whoever he was) is also described as a *destroyer (mašḥîṯ) of nations*,[10] who has set out, left his base (NEB "struck his tents"), and set forth to make Judah a shambles and to lay waste her cities so that no inhabitants remain—a vivid description of the devastation caused by war. The general picture must have been part of Jeremiah's own experience since it was an age of invasions.

8 At such terrifying news men would put on *sackcloth*, a coarse linen garment donned by mourners (6:26; 49:3; Isa. 15:3; 22:12; Lam. 2:10; Ezek. 7:18; 27:31; Joel 1:8; etc.), and would lament and howl. Despite the hope that Israel had expressed that Yahweh's anger might turn away (be averted: *šûḇ*), it had, in fact, fallen on the people, and in the intense form described here literally as the heat of the anger of Yahweh.

9 The response of the nation to this announcement will be one of dismay. The classes of people who had been castigated by Jeremiah earlier (2:8, 26) are singled out for comment. The hearts of the king and his officers fail them, the priests are struck with horror, and the prophets are dumbfounded. The national leadership would collapse because it had no secure basis for hope and security. All it had was the false hopes propounded by false prophets and the empty security offered by apostate priests.

10 Even Jeremiah himself was deeply affected by his own vision (cf. v. 19). There was a side of Jeremiah's character which becomes clear in his many dialogs with God, namely, that he not

8. J. Bright, *Jeremiah*, p. 28; cf. NEB "dire destruction."
9. See the Introduction, "The Foe from the North," pp. 86f.
10. George Adam Smith, *Jeremiah* (1929), p. 112.

merely declared his visions but felt them deeply. The present vision of the coming of the foe from the north wrung from his anguished heart these words.[11] At first glance Jeremiah's comments appear to be blasphemous. Dare a mere man speak thus to God? Well might we ask with Paul, "Who are you, sir, to answer God back? Can the pot speak to the potter and say, 'Why did you make me like this?' Surely the potter can do what he likes with the clay" (Rom. 9:20–21; cf. Isa. 45:9; 64:8). And yet Jeremiah was far from being a blasphemer. He had a deep conviction that God was sovereign and would work his purposes out. Rather must we see in such an utterance not so much a considered judgment, but the spontaneous reaction of a man who felt deeply about the tragedies of life, whether his own or those of others. The same tendency recurs in Jeremiah's later outpourings of soul before God.

But one important aspect of the question here is the source of the widely held view that all was well in Israel. It did not come from Jeremiah himself but from the false prophets (6:14; 14:13; 23:16–17). Jeremiah protests that the words of the false prophets, which supposedly came from Yahweh and which he had allowed them to speak, had misled the people. They had declared *You shall have peace,* but the facts were that the sword was already laid to their throats.[12] Prophets who spoke thus were always a puzzle to Jeremiah. Some years later when Jeremiah was confronted by Hananiah ben Azzur's flat denial of his words, Jeremiah seems to have been somewhat uncertain, although he expressed doubt about Hananiah's words, perhaps hoping against hope that he may have been correct (ch. 28). And even when it had become clear that God's instrument of judgment would be Nebuchadrezzar and the first exile had already taken place, Jeremiah was prepared to hope that his own message might not be completely fulfilled. Hence at an earlier stage, at the height of Josiah's prosperity, with Assyria nearing its end, he

11. A fifth-century text of the LXX (Codex Alexandrinus) and a tenth-century Arabic text have the reading "and they (the priests and prophets) will say." This is accepted by some commentators, but such textual evidence is very weak, and there is evidence elsewhere in the book that Jeremiah spoke like this to God, however strange it may appear to modern ears. Cf. 20:7.

12. Lit. "A sword has reached as far as the throat." The Hebrew word here is *nepeš,* which more commonly means life. But the meaning "throat" is attested in Ugaritic (G. R. Driver, *Canaanite Myths and Legends* [1956], p. 167) and is required also in some biblical passages, e.g., Isa. 5:14. For full discussion on the use of this term see L. Durr, "Hebrew *nepeš* = Akk. *napištu* = Gurgel, Kehle," *ZAW* 43 (1925), pp. 262–69. Note p. 267 for this particular use.

may have supposed that the words of other prophets contained some truth. As a younger prophet he may still have been open to the influence of his fellow prophets, even though he criticized them at times, believing that despite some aberrations they were not entirely false. To prophesy falsely was "an appalling and horrible thing" (5:30). And even if he dismissed the popular prophets by saying that they prophesied by Baal (2:8), he may have felt that they were as much under God's control as were the prophets of Ahab when faced by Micaiah (1 K. 22). Jeremiah stood in a dilemma. The prophets of the day spoke of peace. Jeremiah saw judgment unfolding, either before his inner eyes in a vision or with a deeper understanding of the Babylonians than they had at the time. What he saw he declared. Perhaps his declaration may have been hindered for a time as he hoped that the danger might pass as it had in the days of Hezekiah. But his inner heart told him otherwise. Anything else was false. And if Yahweh had given the word to his contemporary prophets, it was a "lying word" that he had given (cf. 1 K. 22:19–23).

If that case is arguable, then there may well be parts of 4:5–31, such as vv. 5–10, which were preached quite early in Jeremiah's ministry, even before the strong pleas for repentance in ch. 3. Indeed, a strong awareness of coming judgment may have provoked the strong calls to repentance which are recorded in ch. 3.

(ii) The Scorching Hot Wind of Judgment (4:11–18)

11 *At that time it will be said to this people and to Jerusalem:*
"A scorching wind from the bare desert heights
Sweeps down toward[1] *my daughter—my people,*[2]
Not to winnow, not to sift;
12 *A wind stronger than that*[3]
Will come at my bidding;[4]
And now it is I who will declare
Judgments upon them."
13 *Look! like a bank of clouds,*
Like a whirlwind, he climbs into his chariots;
Swifter than eagles are his horses;
Alas,[5] *we are ruined!*

1. Lit. "the way of" (*derek*) with no verb. See the commentary below.
2. We follow J. Bright, *Jeremiah*, p. 29 in the translation; see the commentary below.
3. LXX reads simply "a full wind," i.e., a strong wind, and omits the comparative, suggesting that MT may have a dittography.
4. Lit. "for me."
5. Lit. "Woe to us."

14 *Wash the wickedness from your heart*
So that you may be saved.
How long will sinful thoughts
Find lodging within you?
15 *Listen! a messenger*[6] *from Dan*
And evil tidings from Mount Ephraim!
16 *Report these things to this nation,*[7]
Spread the news around Jerusalem:
"Enemies[8] *come from a distant land*
Raising a shout against the cities of Judah.
17 *Like men guarding a field*
They have surrounded her,
Because it was against me that they rebelled—Yahweh's word.
18 *Your own behavior and your own actions*
Have brought all this upon you.
This misery of yours is bitter indeed;[9]
It has touched you to the very heart."

The short segment 4:11–18 opens with a short oracle (vv. 11–12) announcing the catastrophe that will strike Judah under the figure of a hot wind blowing in from the desert. The figure merges into a military picture which is a short poem in itself (vv. 13–17), although a further call to repent comes in v. 14. The segment concludes with a comment which explains that the judgment has been brought about by the people's sin. This brief passage leads into Jeremiah's own anguished cry (vv. 19–22). Thereafter other terse descriptions of the coming calamity follow. The whole section vv. 11–31 creates an impression of a rapidly approaching catastrophe.

11–12 The *scorching wind from the bare desert heights* was the sirocco, which is here used as a metaphor for destruction. *Not to winnow*—It is too strong a wind for winnowing the grain on the threshing floor, since it carries away both the grain and the chaff, that is, the coming judgment will not discriminate the good from the

6. Lit. "For a voice declaring."
7. MT reads *hazkîrû laggôyim hinnēh*, "Report to the nations, behold," which suggests an error in textual transmission. Among the emendations suggested are *hazhîrû* *l*ᵉ*ḇinyāmîn,* "Warn Benjamin," and *haggîḏû ḇîhûḏâ,* "Tell Judah." Both are conjectural. One plausible proposal is to treat the *m* of *gôyîm* as enclitic, emend *hinnēh* to *hazzeh,* and translate "Report it to this nation." NEB reads *hēnnâ,* "these things," i.e., "Tell these things to the nations."
8. MT reads *nōṣ*ᵉ*rîm,* "watchers," which RSV translates as "besiegers," an unusual usage. LXX suggests *ṣārîm, enemies,* which involves dropping the *n.*
9. Reading *kî* in an asseverative sense to emphasize *bitter.* The proposal of *BHS* to read *meryēḵ* for *mār kî,* followed by NEB, is hardly necessary.

bad but will engulf both alike. It bears down upon *my daughter—my people.*[10] This unusual expression affirms Jeremiah's sense of God's kinship with Israel. In fact, both *my daughter* and *my people* are well-known designations in the OT.

The point is made that the wind comes at the behest of Yahweh (MT "for me"), who now speaks sentence (*judgments, mišpaṭîm*) against his people. The following verses give definition to the hot wind.

13 The approaching foe is like a rising bank of storm clouds (cf. Joel 2:2). His chariot army is like the storm-wind. His horses are swifter than eagles. The vision is altogether terrifying. Little wonder that Jeremiah was to utter the anguished cry of vv. 19–21. Such language is known elsewhere in the OT. The enemy is compared to a bank of storm clouds in Ezek. 38:16, to a cyclone in Isa. 5:28; 66:15, and to eagles in Hab. 1:8. The panic-stricken response of the people is *Alas, we are ruined!* The particular description used here is too general and too vague to enable a specific identification, and may well be as vague as the apocalyptic language which occurs in other passages in the OT. There is no strong case to argue on this passage alone for Scythians, Assyrians, or Babylonians. Once persuaded of the certainty of judgment, Jeremiah had descriptive language ready to hand.

14 If Jerusalem wished to be saved she must wash her heart of evil (*rā'â*). No longer must evil schemes lodge within her. The two terms used here for evil, *rā'â* and *'āwen,* are among a variety of terms used to define "sin" in the OT.[11] The insertion of this call to repentance is quite in keeping with Jeremiah's pleas in ch. 3. Even though judgment was at the doors, it would seem that Jeremiah never thought an appeal to repent was too late.

15–17 There is a fine sense of urgency here. We picture a messenger from Dan passing on the news southward. *Dan*, now identified with Tell el-Qadi, lay at the northern limit of Palestine

10. So J. Bright, *Jeremiah,* p. 29. AV, RV, RSV have "daughter of my people." MT has "daughter—my people." The terms *daughter* and *my people* are in apposition, and the phrase might be translated "my daughter—people," unless the pronoun suffix serves both nouns as J. Bright proposes. The expression is, in any case, poetic and serves as an endearing personification of the people. It is used elsewhere by Jeremiah (8:19, 21, 22; 9:1; 14:17; cf. Lam. 2:11; 3:48; 4:3, 6, 10).

11. E. Jacob, *Theology of the OT* (E.T. 1958), pp. 281f.; T. C. Vriezen, *An Outline of OT Theology* (E.T. 1958), pp. 211f.; G. von Rad, *OT Theology,* I (E.T. 1965), pp. 263f., 266f., 268f., 285f., 385f.

near the headwaters of the Jordan. It was a significant city in Jeremiah's day, as modern excavations have shown.[12] The verbs here are participles, suggesting that the action was taking place at the time of the writing, or, if the passage is visionary, as the prophet witnessed the vision. The voice of a runner is "making known" the news from Dan, and is "causing Israel to hear" evil tidings from Ephraim's hills. The command is given, *Report these things to this nation, spread the news around Jerusalem.* One can picture the foe from the north striking first at Dan as he descended from the Golan Heights and pressed on to *Mount Ephraim*, the name of the mountainous region stretching from about Shechem to Bethel.[13] Before long it would reach Judah and the very heart of the kingdom, Jerusalem itself. These very foes themselves coming from a distant land raise a cry against the cities of Judah,[14] and like men guarding their crops in their fields they settle down to occupy and lay siege to the land. The picture is an apt one since a largely rural population was very familiar with the small shelters or booths erected by shepherds and farmers to protect their flocks and crops (cf. Isa. 1:8). The verb in v. 17 (*šāmar*) is used in 2 Sam. 11:16 of besieging a city. One is reminded at once of Jeremiah's vision in 1:13–15 where the kings of the north come to set up their thrones right in front of Jerusalem's gates, against her surrounding walls and against each of Judah's towns.

The segment closes with the pointed and instructive words "It was me[15] she defied—Yahweh's word."

18 Once again the depth of Israel's wickedness is stressed. What had brought about the sudden calamity? Her own behavior and her own actions. What was happening—her *misery*—was only the punishment[16] for her rebellion. The curses of a broken covenant

12. Until the definitive report appears we have to be content with the interim reports published by A. Biran in *IEJ:* 19 (1969), pp. 121, 139; 20 (1970), pp. 118; 22 (1972), p. 164; 23 (1973), p. 110; 24 (1974), pp. 262–264; 26 (1976), pp. 54–55, and also in *RB* 82 (1975), pp. 562–66; 83 (1976), pp. 278–281, etc.
13. F. M. Abel, *Géographie de la Palestine,* Vol. 1, p. 357; Vol. 2, p. 302; Y. Aharoni, *The Land of the Bible* (1967), pp. 26, 276–78.
14. NEB translates, "Hordes of invaders come from a distant land, howling against the cities of Judah. Their pickets are closing in all about her," an apt and vivid translation.
15. The pronoun is in an emphatic position at the head of the sentence.
16. The noun *rāʿâ* means "evil," but often in the OT it carries the extended meaning of "the consequences of evil."

had become operative.[17] All this had touched the people because of their rebellion. One may sense here the courage and objectivity of Jeremiah, who placed the responsibility for the calamity where it properly belonged. For this kind of utterance he suffered.

(iii) Jeremiah's Anguished Cry (4:19–22)

19 *O my anguish, my anguish!*[1] *I writhe!*
O the walls of my heart!
My heart is beating wildly;
I cannot keep silence.
I hear[2] *the sound of the trumpet,*
The shouts of battle.
20 *Disaster follows disaster;*
The whole land is left in ruins.
Suddenly my tents are destroyed,
In a moment my curtains.
21 *How long must I see the standard*
And hear the trumpet blast?
22 *"Ah, my people are stupid,*
Me they do not know.
Foolish children they are;
They are without understanding.
They are clever at doing evil
But know nothing about doing what is good."

These verses contain one of Jeremiah's "Confessions" (vv. 19–21),[3] to which Yahweh's lament over the stupidity of his people is added.

17. Both in Jeremiah and in most of the prophets, covenant thinking included this concept. The many references to judgment in the prophets are only a concomitant of their frequent thinking in terms of the covenant. See the Introduction, "Jeremiah and the Covenant," pp. 59–67.

1. Lit. "O my bowels, my bowels, I writhe! O the walls of my heart!" (cf. Bright, *Jeremiah*, p. 30). The terms for "bowels" and *walls* used here are difficult to translate into English since they represent an ancient psychology. GNB in an attempt to provide a dynamic equivalent translates:
"My pain! I can't bear the pain!
My heart! My heart is beating wildly!"
NEB renders:
"Oh, the writhing of my bowels,
And the throbbing of my heart."

2. The Qere reads thus. The Ketib suggests 2nd person, with the archaic fem. which preserves the *y* (cf. v. 30; 2:20; etc.). The translation turns on how to deal with *napšî.* If it is understood as simply *I,* we translate "I have heard," or "I hear." Some commentators take *napšî* as "my soul" and translate "You have heard, O my soul" (J. Bright, *Jeremiah*, p. 30). Whichever is followed, the sense is the same.

3. To this classification belong 11:18–23; 12:1–6; 15:10–11, 15–21; 17:14–18; 18:18–23; 20:7–13, 14–18 and perhaps 5:3–5; 8:18–23 (Eng. 9:1). See the Introduction, "The 'Confessions' of Jeremiah," pp. 88–92.

19–21 The vision could not remain with Jeremiah as something visionary or theoretical. It was not merely something seen but something to be realized and something to be shared. In fact, Jeremiah lived through the sad years of Nebuchadrezzar's attacks on Jerusalem and suffered along with the people. But the thought of such a possibility wrung from his anguished heart the words that are preserved in vv. 19–21. By vocation Jeremiah was called upon to announce destruction and judgment (1:9, 10), but by nature he had a deep love for his own people. His whole life was therefore a painful paradox.[4] Little wonder that at times he burst into such anguished utterances as we have here.

The expression "my bowels" (AV) is hardly an appropriate one in modern terms, however appropriate it may have been to ancient psychology where the organs affected by emotional experiences were regarded as entering more deeply into the experience than modern psychologists allow. The reaction of certain organs is the end-point of mental processes. Hence modern translators sometimes substitute for all such words modern words like *anguish* (RSV), or "agony."[5] But there is some value in preserving these ancient expressions since, in any case, the physical organs are a sounding board for other processes.

The prophet was clearly in a very disturbed condition due to an emotional shock. He knew that before long the whole nation would share his anguish.[6] But for Jeremiah the pressures were such that he could not remain silent (cf. 20:9). His innermost being[7] had heard the sound of the trumpet (*šôpār*), the trumpet blast for battle and the battle cry. His ears were attuned to the din of war. Disaster followed on disaster and the whole land was devastated. A deep sense of defenselessness possessed the prophet. Suddenly, in an instant, his flimsy shelter was thrown down and its curtains torn to shreds. He was isolated and swallowed up in the storm which he had called upon the land in God's name. He wondered how much longer he could stand the emotional strain of it all, witnessing the standard of the enemy raised high and hearing the sound of the trumpet blasts.

22 Yahweh's word penetrates the tumult of battle but it brings

4. See the Introduction, "The Life of Jeremiah," pp. 94–106.
5. H. L. Ellison, "The Prophecy of Jeremiah," *EQ* 32/4 (1960), p. 219.
6. See Lamentations for the reaction of some of the poets in the days following the fall of Jerusalem.
7. Heb. *nepeš*; see the textual note.

no hope. His people are fools. With emphatic words Yahweh declared, *Me*[8] *they do not know.* The knowledge of God touches the whole man—mind, emotion, and will. It is a total commitment to and response to God of one's whole being. Their knowledge was altogether superficial. For that reason they were *foolish (sāḵāl)* and without understanding. It is only the knowledge of Yahweh that makes men wise and understanding. So perverse were they that their only skills lay in doing evil. Of doing right they knew nothing. Ignorance and stupidity lay behind the coming judgment, which was appropriate and deserved.

(iv) A Vision and an Oracle about the Coming Destruction (4:23–28)

23 *I saw the earth—it was a barren waste;*[1]
The heavens—there was no light.
24 *I saw the mountains—they were shaking,*
And all the hills rocked to and fro.
25 *I looked, and there was no human being;*
Even the birds of the sky had taken flight.
26 *I looked—and the fertile land was desert,*
And all its cities lay in ruins
Before Yahweh,
Before his fierce anger.
27 *For this is what Yahweh has said:*
"The whole land shall be a waste,
Though I will not make a complete end of it.
28 *For this reason the earth will mourn,*
The sky above will turn black,
Because I have spoken, I have decided,
I will not change my mind and will not turn back."[2]

In a passage filled with striking imagery, the judgment that is to fall on Judah takes on the aspect of a cosmic conflagration. Jeremiah experiences a dramatic glimpse into the outpouring of divine anger upon Judah. The earth and the heavens (v. 23), the mountains and the hills (v. 24), humanity and the birds (v. 25), the fields and the cities (v. 26), all were to feel the weight of Yahweh's wrath. To a degree the language is Oriental hyperbole, but Jeremiah uses im-

8. The pronoun is placed first in the sentence.
1. Heb. *ṯōhû wāḇōhû,* lit. "without form and void" (cf. Gen. 1:2).
2. LXX has a different order for these four verbs:
"I have spoken and not relented,
I have decided and will not turn back."

agery and phraseology which his predecessors used in their references to the divine judgment (cf. Isa. 2:12ff.; Hos. 4:3). The range of disturbance was thus so great that it seemed to represent a return to primeval chaos. Little wonder that Jeremiah was filled with anguish and amazement. None of the other contemporary prophets spoke of the coming doom in such powerful terms.

23 Jeremiah made use of a phrase known from Gen. 1:2, *tōhû wāḇōhû*, "without form and void" (AV), that is, primeval chaos, the formless void that existed before God began to work on the newly created earth. The picture is of a reversal of the story of Gen. 1. Men, beasts, plants have all gone, the mountains reeled, the hills rocked to and fro, light vanished from the heavens, farm lands reverted to desert, towns were levelled to the ground. It was as if the earth had been "uncreated" and reverted to its erstwhile primeval chaos. Order seemed to return to confusion. Imagery something like this, referring to the Day of the Lord, is known elsewhere in the prophets (cf. Joel 2:1–11; Amos 8:9–10; Nah. 1:2–8; Zeph. 1:2–3). Jeremiah's description here is one of the most dramatic of its kind in the entire OT.

24–26 Cosmic disturbances are matched by disturbances on earth. The *mountains* and the *hills,* symbols of stability and strength, reel. Mankind (*'āḏām*) flees the scene, and even the *birds* fly away. *The fertile land (karmel)* turned back to *desert*,[3] and all its cities were razed to the ground *before Yahweh, before his fierce anger.* Solitude and desolation stood in sharp contrast to the former fruitfulness (cf. 2:7).

27–28 Lest the impassioned words of vv. 23–26 be dismissed as poetic imagery lacking real substance they are reinforced by a final word from Yahweh himself. Yes indeed, the whole land would become *a waste (šᵉmāmâ).* The next phrase has occasioned much discussion. MT reads, *though I will not make a complete end,* that is, although the land will become a waste this will not be the *complete end* described in vv. 23–26. Interpreters have understood this to mean that Jeremiah found hope in the midst of judgment. A remnant of God's people would survive the disaster, a view held by other prophets also. An alternate translation offered by many commentators is based on a minor emendation of *lō'* ("not") to *lāh* ("for

3. Both these nouns carry an article as though a specific example of each was in mind, perhaps the finest of fertile lands contrasted with the most desolate of lands like Sinai.

her") to give a reading "I will make her a total destruction (*kālâ*)." This would provide a parallel to the noun *š^emāmâ, waste,* in the first half of the line and would fit the statement made in v. 28b,

I have spoken, I have decided,
I will not change my mind[4] *and will not turn back.*

The latter interpretation would suit one facet of Jeremiah's preaching, namely, that judgment was determined. The root *šûḇ* is used here in a particular sense though it carries the general meaning of "turn," "turn from one's purpose."

The personification of the earth which will *mourn,* and of heaven which will *turn black,*[5] was a stylistic feature known elsewhere in the OT. Jeremiah himself addressed the heavens (2:12), as did prophets before him (Mic. 6:2).

Thus Yahweh's word sets the seal on what Jeremiah had been saying. Judgment was indeed coming and he would not relent from his purposes.

(v) *The Death Agony of Zion (4:29–31)*

29 *At the noise of the horsemen and bowmen*
The whole land[1] *takes to flight.*
They run into the thickets,[2]
They climb up among the rocks.
Every town[3] *is deserted;*
No one lives in them.
30 *But you are despoiled.*[4] *What are you doing*
That you dress yourself in scarlet,
That you adorn yourself with ornaments of gold
And paint your eyes with antimony?
You are making yourself beautiful for nothing.
Your lovers reject you;
It is your life that they want.

4. The verb *niḥam* has several meanings: "have compassion," "pity," "comfort oneself," "repent." In some passages it is translated "repented," a translation which raises the question of whether God can repent. The point here is clear. God has made a decision and will not change his mind (relent).
5. Cf. J. Bright, *Jeremiah,* p. 31: "don mourning."

1. MT reads "The whole city." We follow LXX since v. 30 shows that Jerusalem did not flee but enticed the foe.
2. LXX adds another colon before this: "They creep into caves."
3. Following LXX. MT reads "all the city."
4. There is some uncertainty about this colon. The pronoun is fem., the adjective is masc. and is lacking in LXX.

31 *Ah, I have heard a cry like a woman in labor,*
A scream like a woman bearing her first child.
It is the cry of daughter Zion, gasping for breath,
Stretching out her hand:
"Ah me! I am fainting
Before the slayers."

The figure changes again: Yahweh's daughter Zion is pictured as a harlot decked out to offer herself to lovers (the advancing foe) who loathe her and do her to death.

29–30 At the noise of the approaching horsemen and bowmen the whole land takes to flight and hides in many supposedly secure places. They creep into caves, crouch in thickets, and climb up into cliffs. The picture is not unfamiliar among the prophets (Isa. 2:19–21; cf. Rev. 6:15, 16).[5] This wholesale flight leaves every city deserted.

By contrast Jerusalem, here called "*daughter Zion*" (v. 31), welcomes the coming of the foe. She dresses herself in scarlet, decks herself with gold ornaments, and enlarges her eyes with *antimony.*[6] It is the way of the harlot, who attires herself to seduce any willing male.[7] Normally such behavior would attract clients. But now it was to no purpose that the harlot beautified herself, for the lovers who come are bent on destruction as the agents of Yahweh. It is her life they seek.

Presumably Jeremiah was trying to make it clear that no last-minute compromise with the invading foe would serve to placate them. Having rejected her true spouse (3:1), only desolation and destruction would follow in the wake of her attentions to adulterous paramours like Assyria, Egypt, or Babylon (cf. 2:35–36).

31 The figure changes slightly. The harlot appears as a *woman in labor* trying to bring forth her first child. In his vision Jeremiah hears her cry and her screams.[8] That cry and those screams

5. Caves in biblical times were regularly places of refuge. See 16:16; Judg. 6:2; 1 Sam. 13:6.
6. The verb is "tear" (*qāra'*), lit. "you tear your eyes with antimony." The practice continues in the East today: the eyes are painted with antimony to make them seem larger and more glamorous. But the custom is ancient and Egyptian women are depicted in early paintings with such decoration. Sculptures and paintings in temples and tombs, and numerous small alabaster and pottery vessels containing remains of the black material antimony, have been found in ancient tombs and excavations.
7. The same picture appears in Ezek. 16:26–29; 23:5–34.
8. MT has the noun *ṣārâ,* "anguish," where LXX has the noun *stenagmos*, "screaming," which would suggest either a Heb. noun *ṣeraḥ* or perhaps *ṣᵉwāḥâ,* "cry of sorrow."

come from *Bath-Ṣiyyôn, daughter Zion,* as she lies gasping, stretching out her hands (or clenching her fists) in the agonies of death, and crying out, "Woe is me! For I am fainting before the slayers," meaning perhaps the murderers were taking her life. Wanton Judah, playing the harlot over the years, had reached the climax and had paid the price of her iniquity.

(vi) The Unpardonable Sin and Moral Depravity of Jerusalem (5:1–9)

1 *"Go up and down*[1] *through the streets of Jerusalem!*
Look around; see for yourselves!
Search through her marketplaces!
Can you find a single person,
One man who acts justly,
Who strives to be faithful,[2]
So that I may forgive her?[3]
2 *Though they swear*[4] *'By the life of Yahweh'*
They are really[5] *swearing falsely."*
3 *Thine eyes, O Yahweh,*
Do they not look for faithfulness?
Thou didst strike them down,
But they felt no pain;
Didst pierce them through—
They refused to accept correction.
They set their faces harder than flint;
They refused to come back.
4 *I myself said, "What poor people;*[6]
They act like fools.
Indeed, they do not understand the way of Yahweh,
The demands of their God."
5 *I will go to the leaders*
And speak with them,
For they will understand the way of Yahweh,
The demands of their God.
But they all have broken the yoke
And snapped their traces.
6 *And so, a lion from the forest will strike them down,*
A wolf from the desert will tear them to pieces,
A leopard will prowl about their cities.
Anyone who goes out will be torn apart,
Because their rebellious deeds are many,
Their backslidings are countless.

1. The verb is plural and is addressed to the people of the city.
2. Lit. "who seeks faithfulness."
3. LXX adds "Yahweh's word" to make the point that Yahweh is the speaker.
4. Lit. "though they say."
5. Read *'āḵēn* with Syr. and various mss. MT reads *lāḵēn,* "therefore."
6. Heb. *'aḵ-dallîm*; see the commentary below.

7 *"Why should I forgive you for this?*
Your sons have abandoned me
And sworn by gods that are no gods.
Though I gave them their fill,[7] *they committed adultery,*
And spent their time[8] *at the harlot's house.*
8 *They are like well-fed and lusty stallions;*
Each man whinnies after his neighbor's wife.
9 *Shall I not punish them for these things?—Yahweh's word.*
On a nation such as this
Shall I not take vengeance?"

Before the theme of the foe from the north is resumed in 5:15, there is a further discussion of the reasons for the coming judgment, a subject that has already been dealt with in ch. 2. Israel's blatant rejection of the sovereignty of Yahweh and of his covenant was the basic cause. Once she had abandoned Yahweh and acknowledged some other sovereignty over her life it was inevitable that the curses of the covenant should become operative. If the people would not see this, Jeremiah, at least, understood the painful truth. There is, perhaps, a greater emphasis in ch. 5 on moral evils than in ch. 2. But moral and religious evils are finally inseparable since they stem from a common cause.

The apparent editorial intrusion of 5:1–14 into a sequence of prophecies about the foe from the north is not irrelevant. Yahweh's imminent judgment on his people is declared in ch. 4. The reason for that judgment is declared in ch. 5, albeit with a brief glimpse at judgment in 5:15–19. Then the theme of judgment is resumed in ch. 6. However, it is this theme of the judgment that is about to come on the nation that provides the unifying theme which holds together a variety of literary elements. It is no easier to date the material of ch. 5 than it is for ch. 4. The first segment 5:1–9 certainly seems to presuppose that disaster, although certain, is not imminent and is still theoretically avoidable. Hence 5:1–9 would seem to be dateable to Josiah's reign or very early in Jehoiakim's reign. The

7. A few mss., perhaps influenced by the previous colon, read *š* instead of *ś* for the verb here, i.e., "I caused them to swear" or "I took their oath," a reference to the covenant between Yahweh and Israel, possibly the covenant under Josiah in 2 K. 23:1–3. See A. Weiser, *Das Buch des Propheten Jeremia* (1960), p. 42.

8. MT *yiṯgōḏāḏû,* "they gash themselves" (cf. 16:6; 41:5), is possible. It would refer to participation in Canaanite cult practices. LXX points to a reading *yiṯgôrārû,* "to tarry," "to haunt," "to frequent." Confusion between *d* and *r* is common since the letters are similar. AV, RV, and RSV suppose a derivative of the noun *gᵉḏûḏ,* "troop," i.e., they "trooped to the houses of harlots." This is not otherwise attested.

next segment 5:10–19 is likewise difficult to date. At one point (vv. 15–17) the foe that is coming from afar could be the Babylonians. But since they had not yet come, the material may date from early in Jehoiakim's reign. The brief prose segment (vv. 18–19) may represent an editorial note coming from the time when the oracles of Jeremiah were collected and arranged. Finally, 5:20–31 comprises material which could well be early. Judgment is declared to be certain but is not defined apart from a reference to a drought (cf. 3:3 which is pre–622 B.C.). The abuses referred to in vv. 26–31 are similar to those denounced in the Temple Sermon in 7:2–15, which comes from early in Jehoiakim's reign. Hence they may have been composed at the same time or even toward the end of Josiah's reign. In general, then, there are no strong grounds for proposing any date later than Josiah's reign or, at the latest, early in Jehoiakim's reign.

But the point may be pressed further. The atmosphere of ch. 5 is different from that of ch. 2 where idolatry and false religious practice are highlighted. The emphasis here seems to be on social and personal morality. The question may be asked whether we are moving in ch. 5 in a post-reformation atmosphere after the cult centers had been destroyed and the grosser elements of Baal-worship had been eliminated. Yet loyalty to Yahweh and the acknowledgment of his complete sovereignty over the people required not merely purity in worship but careful adherence to the stipulations of the covenant, which were moral as well as religious. It was not sufficient to destroy the cult centers. People could become used to the fact that they no longer existed. The initial excitement could be lost and the new way (which was the old way) would be accepted as a commonplace. What Jeremiah saw was that the obligations of a covenant people reached to the very roots of personal and social morality. How much time elapsed after the reforms of Josiah before Jeremiah felt it necessary to speak in these terms may be impossible to determine. However, while on the one hand the dating of these oracles cannot be too early,[9] they need not be dated very late since the tendencies suggested by ch. 5 could have become evident in the decade following Josiah's reform.

There is one other uncertainty about the material, namely, the extent to which the various literary units were originally related to one another. It is always open to a preacher to vary the literary forms he uses in a given sermon. Presumably an artist like Jeremiah

9. See G. A. Smith, *Jeremiah* (1929), p. 118.

had the same liberty as any modern preacher. However, we must recognize that we have also to do with the fact of editorial processes in which originally separate sayings and oracles are grouped into new complexes around some central theme—here, the foe from the north, the agent of divine judgment.

It will be assumed in the discussion that follows that most of the material in ch. 5 comes essentially from Jeremiah himself, probably during the days of Josiah, although some may have come at the latest from early in Jehoiakim's reign.

In 5:1–9 we have a segment in which Yahweh and Jeremiah are both spokesmen. It develops as follows: Yahweh (vv. 1, 2); Jeremiah (vv. 3–6); Yahweh (vv. 7–9). The general theme is centered on the question: Can this people be forgiven? The commands in 5:1–2 are quite general, and being in the plural may be understood as a brief oracle addressed to the people either by Jeremiah or Yahweh. Then vv. 3–6 represent Jeremiah's statement of the facts to Yahweh while vv. 7–9 give Yahweh's reply.

1 The people are invited to undertake a search[10] specifically in Jerusalem's open places and streets for one single man who *acts justly* (Heb. *'ōśeh mišpāṭ*) and seeks after faithfulness (*'ᵉmûnâ*). The combination of justice and faithfulness is one that should characterize a man who is faithful to the covenant. In the prophetic literature in general these two terms denote covenantal qualities which govern the relations between men and God and between men and their fellows. They are often linked with the term *ṣᵉḏāqâ* (right action, righteousness) and *ḥeseḏ* (loyalty, faithfulness).[11] In the event that a single man with these qualities should be found God would forgive the city.[12] Comparison with Gen. 18:23–32 indicates that whereas in the days of Abraham God would have spared Sodom for ten men, he offers easier terms by far to Jerusalem even though Jerusalem's sins exceeded those of Sodom (cf. 15:1–4; Ezek. 16:48).

2–3 Our notion of logical arrangement might expect v. 2 to follow the first phrase of v. 3, thus:

10. The verb (*šûṭ*) is here imperative plural in form. It has the meaning "twist," "weave"; hence RSV "run to and fro," NEB "go up and down," J. Bright, "range through."

11. Cf. Hos. 2:21, 22 (Eng. 19, 20); Ps. 36:6, 7 (Eng. 5, 6); 88:12 (Eng. 11); 89:2, 3 (Eng. 1, 2); etc.

12. The clause *so that I may forgive her* has been regarded as an addition by some commentators, but there do not seem to be adequate grounds for omitting it. See G. A. Smith, *Jeremiah,* p. 119; J. Skinner, *Prophecy and Religion* (1922), p. 138.

"O Lord, are thine eyes not set upon the truth?
Men may swear by the life of the Lord,
but they only perjure themselves." (NEB)

However, modern Western logic and the logic of the seventh-century B.C. prophet do not always agree, nor are rearrangements of biblical texts to suit modern logical patterns always necessarily in keeping with ancient methods of expressing an argument. To be sure, the eyes of Yahweh are directed toward *faithfulness* (*'emûnâ*).[13] In the present context the question concerns a man's faithfulness to his oath. To swear by Yahweh is to invoke his name as the guarantor of any obligation which a man may take upon himself. In the event of a breach of any undertaking or agreement Yahweh would be expected to visit the covenant-breaker with judgment. But in a seventh-century B.C. context such oaths were empty and men did nothing but perjure themselves. The adherence of a man to his oath is entirely to be expected of one who is faithful to his covenant with Yahweh (cf. Ezek. 17:15–20). But Israel had broken her covenant and the curses of the broken covenant had fallen on them. Yahweh himself had visited them in judgment:

"Thou didst strike them down, but they took no heed;
Didst pierce them to the heart, but they refused to learn.
They set their faces harder than flint and refused to
come back." (NEB)

One might have expected that when some punishment fell on a man because of his breach of covenant he would learn a lesson and mend his ways. That was the divine intention. But stubborn Jerusalem had refused to *come back* (*šûḇ*).[14]

4 The interpretation of this verse depends on the meaning of the noun *poor* (Heb. *dallîm*). In the context it lies parallel to *they act like fools*.[15] The further statement is made that *they do not understand the way of Yahweh, the demands*[16] *of their God*. The reference seems, therefore, to poverty of knowledge and understanding rather

13. The exact translation turns on the meaning of this word. Its commonest meaning is *faithfulness*, and it is arguable that what Yahweh approves in men is faithfulness to the covenant and to the Lord of the Covenant. Truth is one aspect of a man's faithfulness.

14. Once again Jeremiah used the verb *šûḇ*, this time to refer to a turning back to God.

15. The root *yā'al* is used in the Niphal *nô'al*, "to be foolish, act foolishly."

16. Heb. *mišpāṭ*. The term is often legal but sometimes carries the sense of "the manner of acting" (cf. 1 Sam. 8:11) or even the "claims," "demands," or "ordinances" of someone superior, in this connection God.

than poverty of an economic kind. This view gains support from v. 5 where these poor are contrasted with the great *(g^e^ḏōlîm),* the men of high station who are expected to know. Who then were the *poor* Jeremiah had in mind? The reference may well be to the citizens of Jerusalem, who were insensitive to God's chastenings and unable or unwilling to read the signs of the times because of their preoccupation with their own affairs, which required them to enter into agreements with an appropriate oath. There was no intention on their part to submit their lives and their business dealings to God's scrutiny. They hardly believed that God would care. God was not in their thoughts or in their hearts although they took his name constantly on their lips. It must have come as a shock to Jeremiah to discover that despite Josiah's reformation, which removed the outward signs of false worship and swept and garnished the house of Judah, the house was empty (cf. Luke 11:24–25). The true religion of the citizens of Jerusalem was very shallow (cf. 7:4; 26:1–10). To them Yahweh was a God who was concerned primarily with his temple and its purity. There was protection for the people who lived in the shadow of the temple. But of ethical religion and wholehearted commitment to the covenant the people knew nothing.

5 The *leaders* or "great ones" (men of high station, Heb. *g^e^ḏōlîm*) are described as those who *understand the way of Yahweh, the demands (mišpāṭ) of their God.* However, in contrast to the poor who were ignorant and insensitive, these are described as men who have *broken the yoke* "to a man" (*yaḥdāw*) and *snapped their traces* (NEB). The picture is one of rebellion and defiance and seems to have in mind the ox, who is normally yoked to his plough and draws the plough with the aid of its traces. The picture changes to one who is not only an unwilling servant but actively rebels, breaking the yoke and bursting the thongs (cf. 2:20). This description of the leaders comes as a surprise in the light of Josiah's reformation. Clearly, whatever the reformation achieved externally it did not touch the lives of the "great ones" so deeply that they accepted the yoke of allegiance to Yahweh and his covenant gladly. It seems evident that they had, in fact, rejected the covenant, so that the curses of the covenant would fall on them.

6 The consequences following on a breach of covenant are depicted under the symbolism of attacks of wild animals. These wild animals must be none other than the invaders referred to in chs. 4 and 6 (cf. 2:15; 4:7; Hos. 13:7–8; Hab. 1:8; Zeph. 3:3). Either Yahweh or Jeremiah may be taken as speaker. In either case, the figure of an ox that has broken loose from his yoke and traces is carried forward. Not merely has he escaped his master's yoke but he has by that very act escaped from his protection to be attacked by lions from the forest, wolves from the desert, or by prowling[17] leopards. The ox forsaking his stall to roam abroad will suffer a fate similar to God's people venturing away from his protection. All who venture forth will be torn.

The point is emphasized again that the *rebellious deeds* (Heb. *peša'*) of God's people have been many and their *backslidings* (apostasies, *m^ešûḇâ*) have been *countless*.[18] The covenant undertaking has been broken, the covenant obligations rejected. There is no sign of repentance. Under such circumstances judgment is inevitable, as the following verses show (cf. Deut. 28:15–46).

7–9 These verses are framed between two questions: *Why should I forgive you?* (v. 7) and *Shall I not punish them for these things? . . . Shall I not take vengeance?* There is much to be said for the view that the words were still being addressed to the leaders.[19] Two other features of their life are noted. They swear by gods that are no gods and frequent harlots' houses.

7 The first of these may provide a hint of the kind of thing that Ezekiel saw in his vision of the sinister activities being perpetrated in the temple precincts (Ezek. 8:7–12) by "the seventy men of the elders of the house of Israel" (Ezek. 8:11). Precisely what Ezekiel's words meant may not be clear. But they suggest that "great ones" associated with the court had rejected Yahweh's rule in their hearts and lives and had entertained a secret heart-worship of other gods. When Yahweh's people forsook him he ceased to be regarded by them as the guarantor of their oaths, and his place was usurped by *no gods (b^elō' 'ᵉlōhîm)*. Despite the reforms of Josiah, the extremes of Manasseh's apostasy had taken deep root in the hearts of the leaders. It is arguable that the picture refers primarily to the "great ones," the elders, and that it was essentially a phenomenon

17. *Prowl*—The Heb. root is *šqd*. It appears in 1:12 where Yahweh is described as "watching" over his word, "prowling around," "lurking about" so as to keep his word under surveillance.

18. The Heb. root *'ṣm* expresses a range of ideas: "be strong, powerful, mighty," here an "enormous" number.

19. See H. L. Ellison, "The Prophecy of Jeremiah," *EQ* 33/1 (1961), pp. 30–32. There is, in fact, some element of doubt as to whether vv. 7–9 refer entirely to the "great ones." They may have a more general reference to the people as a whole. In that case swearing by false gods and spending time with harlots were widespread practices throughout the nation.

of the court circles. These were the rebels, acting not so much in ignorance of Yahweh's will, but in defiance of it.

The second feature about the "great ones" is that they lingered at the harlot's house despite the fact that Yahweh satisfied them and gave them all they needed.[20] One is reminded of the picture of Hos. 2 in which Gomer, wife of Hosea, went after lovers, refusing to recognize that her husband had provided her with all she needed. The picture is a symbol of Yahweh and his people. The question arises as to whether the reference to adultery is merely religious symbolism or whether perhaps it refers to physical acts as well. The language seems to be rather too definite to allow us to think that the reference is purely to idolatry here described in metaphorical language. The reference seems to be both to apostasy and to the literal immorality which resulted (v. 8).

8 The words of this verse seem to add weight to the view that literal physical immorality is involved. The picture is a vigorous one: *like well-fed and lusty stallions, each man whinnies after his neighbor's wife*. If, in fact, the reference is to wholesale participation in immoral conduct, we may ask whether this was something unusual. There was a sexual aspect to religion throughout the Fertile Crescent, although the goddesses of fertility played a much greater role among the Canaanites than among any other ancient people.[21] Sacred prostitution was an almost invariable accompaniment of the cult of the fertility-goddesses in Phoenicia and Syria.[22] These practices were known in Israel, for the prophets denounced them, although details are not given. They preferred to call the temple prostitute a *zōnâ* (profane harlot) rather than use the Canaanite term *qᵉḏēšâ* (holy woman). Certainly we may suspect that in the days of Manasseh, cult-prostitution was widely practiced. Josiah swept this all away, but the fires of passion which the practice had kindled may have burned on. We may suspect that what had begun in the sanctuaries continued thereafter in the brothels, and the same women who had been put out of business by the reforms found a new means of livelihood. While fornication (that is, sexual relations between a man and an unmarried woman) is regarded in the OT as blindness to true values and true manhood, and is the result of deeper evils, it does not seem to have been regarded in the same way as adultery,

20. See the textual notes on v. 7.
21. W. F. Albright, *From the Stone Age to Christianity* (²1957), p. 233.
22. *Ibid.*, p. 235.

which was held to be a most grievous sin punishable by death. It was a destruction of the covenant basis of the family and society.[23]

The picture in vv. 7 and 8 is of men who began with irregular sexual relationships in the harlot's house and then moved on to adultery. Jeremiah was depicting a crumbling society in open revolt against both the commandments of Yahweh and the fundamental laws of conscience.

9 Such evils could not escape the divine visitation. God would *take vengeance* (or avenge himself) on such a nation as this. Divine judgment was the inevitable consequence of such wanton defiance of Yahweh and such open revolt against the covenant.

(vii) *False Security in the Face of a Terrible Foe (5:10–19)*

10 *"Go up through her rows of vines and cut them down,*
But do not make a complete end of them.
Strip away her green branches,
For they are not Yahweh's."
11 *"The people of Israel and Judah*
Have been utterly faithless to me—Yahweh's word."
12 *"They have denied Yahweh*
And have said, 'Not he!
Misfortune will not overtake us.
We shall not see sword or famine.'
13 *The prophets are full of wind,*
The word is not in them."[1]
14 *And so this is what Yahweh, God of Hosts, has said:*
"Because they[2] *speak in this way,*[3]
This is what will happen to them.[4]
Look! I will make my words
A fire in your mouth
And this people as wood;
It will burn them up.

23. The writer recalls a visit to the ancient Jewish community in Shiraz, Iran, in 1956 when the guide (a Jewish woman) drew attention to several brothels. It was her view that it was thought to be acceptable behavior for men to visit brothels even though adultery was regarded as a great evil.

1. LXX and some mss. read *The word* in place of MT "Has he spoken?" The consonants are the same.
2. MT reads "you." The context seems to require *they,* although the prophets in general seem to have changed the person of address frequently. It is possible that Jeremiah speaking in the 3rd person lifted his eyes in the direction of some of the prophets standing by and spoke to them as "you."
3. Lit. "this word."
4. In MT this phrase occurs at the end of v. 13. It is lacking in LXX. The phrase would fit neatly into v. 14 after the first line. See J. Bright, *Jeremiah,* p. 32.

15 *See! I am bringing against you*
A nation from afar, O house of Israel—Yahweh's word.
An enduring nation it is,[5]
A nation that is ancient,
A nation whose speech you will not understand,
Nor will you hear what they say.
16 *Their quiver is an open grave,*[6]
They are all warriors!
17 *They will devour your harvest and your food,*
They will devour your sons and your daughters,
They will devour your flocks and your herds,
They will devour your vines and your fig trees;
They will demolish your fortified towns,
In which you trust, with the sword."
18 *"Yet even in those days—Yahweh's word—I will not make a complete end of you.*
19 *And when they*[7] *say, 'Why has Yahweh our God done all this to us?' you shall say to them, 'Just as you forsook me and served alien gods in your own land, so you shall serve foreigners in a land that is not yours.' "*

The section 5:10–19 is introduced and concluded by the theme ". . . not a complete end" (vv. 10 and 18). In the first part of the section (vv. 10–14) a terrible judgment on Judah because of her faithlessness to Yahweh and her complacency is announced. In the second part (vv. 15–17) the foe from the north who would bring judgment is once again described. Whether these two segments were originally part of the one address or whether we have here an editorial arrangement of two poems or even of several fragmentary pieces is probably impossible to decide. The invader in question may well have been the Babylonians (v. 15), in which case the material could date from early in Jehoiakim's reign.

There is another problem, that of assigning the various verses to addressees. It is possible that a number of originally short sayings have been brought together here rather loosely. Verse 10 points back to 2:21, where Israel is described as a choice vine. The reference to faithless Israel and Judah is reminiscent of 3:6–11. Verses 12 and 13 may belong together and refer to the contemptuous comments of the people about individuals like Jeremiah. On the other hand v. 13

5. This colon and the next are lacking in LXX.
6. Lacking in LXX.
7. MT "you" does not seem to suit the context, which requires some impersonal sense: "when people say . . . ," i.e., to Jeremiah.

may be quite unrelated to v. 12 but have reference to the false prophets that misled the nation. In contrast to such prophets who do not have God's word, the true word will come through Jeremiah, in whose mouth Yahweh's word will be as a fire to consume the people (v. 14).

10 An invitation is extended by Yahweh to some unspecified destroyer to go up through the vine rows in God's vineyard, Judah (cf. Isa. 5:1–7), to prune away branches which do not belong to Yahweh. The heavenly Husbandman permits an enemy to undertake a severe pruning of his choice vine now become a degenerate wild vine (2:21). All rank growth is to be torn away, although the vine itself is not to be completely destroyed.[8]

11–13 These verses pose problems for the interpreter since they seem to be isolated fragments brought together by an editor. Assuming v. 10 to be addressed to an unnamed destroyer, v. 11 may be understood as Yahweh's comment about his people in the style of 3:6–11, spoken either to the destroyer to explain the divine intention in permitting the pruning of the choice vine, or perhaps as Yahweh's own aside. The charge is clear. Both Israel and Judah, that is, the whole of Yahweh's people, have been utterly faithless.[9] Verse 12 is a development of the theme of faithlessness. This people had spoken falsely about Yahweh and declared, *Not he!*[10] that is, Yahweh would not punish them. Neither famine nor sword would touch them. Here was blind complacency. The people, forgetful that breach of covenant would result in the operation of the curses of the covenant, that is, divine judgment, and stressing rather the privileges of covenant membership than its obligations, had deluded themselves into thinking that somehow the God of the covenant would overlook breaches of the covenant. Perhaps the people were led into

8. Some commentators believe that the negative here is not original and that it represents an attenuation of the command to destroy utterly (cf. 4:27). That may be so, although a severe pruning that would strip away rank and unproductive growth would still be far from a complete destruction. See comments at 4:27. For the view that the negative here is not original see J. Bright, *Jeremiah,* pp. 39f.; W. Rudolph, *Jeremia* (1958), p. 34; F. Nötscher, *Das Buch Jeremias* (1934), p. 67; A. S. Peake, *Jeremiah* (1910), pp. 124, 130; G. A. Smith, *Jeremiah*, p. 120; G. P. Couturier, "Jeremiah" in *JBC* (1968), p. 309; etc.
9. The finite verb is intensified by the infinitive absolute.
10. NEB understands the words *lōʾ hûʾ* as meaning "he does not exist." RSV translates "He will do nothing." The effect is the same.

such complacency by the words of the false prophets who were saying that misfortune would not overtake them (cf. 14:13–15). Jeremiah's rejoinder to such false utterances was: *The prophets are full of wind,*[11] *the word is not in them* (v. 13).

14 The true word of God is shown to be with Jeremiah, who spoke on behalf of *Yahweh, God of Hosts.* This expression is not easy to interpret and its meaning is disputed. Yahweh is sometimes referred to as the "God of the armies of Israel" (1 Sam. 17:45). The concept of God as a warrior-God who accompanied the armies of Israel to battle is an important one in the OT.[12] The title "Lord of Hosts" was used a number of times by Isaiah (3:1; 5:16; 6:3) and was very frequently used in Second Isaiah. In Isa. 44:6, Yahweh is seen as discrediting the hosts of sun, moon, and stars worshipped by the Babylonians. He thus displays a cosmic sweep of power. Israel is seen as an army battling for God and the establishment of his kingdom. It would seem that the expression underwent changes in the course of the centuries. Early references suggest that it referred to the armies of Israel. But later the expression is used for the "host of heaven" (the heavenly bodies or even the angels) or "the hosts of heaven and earth" (the created universe). This latter sense seems closest to the prophetic usage, where the reference seems to be not so much to some concrete entity, but to the fullness of Yahweh's power and authority throughout the creation. The phrase *Yahweh, God of Hosts* thus gathered up a considerable range of ideas and presented Yahweh as the ultimate power and authority in the universe.

It was in the name of this God that Jeremiah spoke in a day when the men of Judah had ceased to distinguish God's true servants from the prophets of Baal. There was a complete identity between Jeremiah's words and God's word to Judah. The words of the other prophets were only wind. Yahweh's word was not in them. Jeremiah's word to them on Yahweh's behalf was a solemn one. He reported Yahweh's word to himself:

I will make my words a fire in your mouth,
And this people as wood. It will burn them up.

11. Lit. "will become wind," that is, they will be shown to be windbags who have no substance to their words. The term *rûaḥ* means "wind" and "spirit." There is a play on the two senses here: prophets should have been guided by the (divine) "spirit," but these proved to be mere *wind.*

12. D. N. Freedman, "The Name of the God of Moses," *JBL* 79 (1960), p. 156; R. Abba, "The Divine Name Yahweh," *JBL* 80 (1961), pp. 320–28.

The verses that follow underline Jeremiah's conviction that his mission (1:9–10) would be fulfilled, and the invasion of the land by a nation from afar would be a proof of the authenticity of his preaching. Jeremiah's prophetic oracles were like *fire* in his mouth and the nation was as *wood* which would be consumed in the encounter. The true prophetic word in Jeremiah's mouth was as a destroying fire.

15–16 The invader is still not identified clearly, although the description would suit the Babylonians. The nation in question is ancient, enduring, speaking an unknown tongue, altogether alien in culture and religion, all mighty warriors. Their arrows are deadly *(Their quiver is an open grave).*[13]

17 The outcome of the invasion is depicted in vigorous language which is both realistic and authentic. Harvests and food, flocks and herds, vines and fig trees, sons and daughters would all be destroyed. Even the fortified cities in which they trusted would be demolished. Within a few years Jeremiah's words were vindicated.[14]

18–19 These verses are in prose and make the point again that although the devastation caused by the foe will be great, this will not be the complete finish of the nation *(not . . . a complete end).* The effect is to weaken the intensity of the previous threats (cf. 4:27; 5:10). Many commentators regard this passage as the prose comment of an editor of the exilic age, a view that has something to commend it. It must not be forgotten, however, that the doctrine of a remnant was propounded in the previous century by Isaiah, and is not lacking in other areas of Jeremiah. In reference to the statement in v. 19 it might be argued that these words could represent a comment from an editor in exile. But we ought not abandon too

13. An unusual figure, lacking in LXX and very elliptical. It seems to mean that their quiver provides the means of filling graves. But NEB translates "Their jaws are a grave, wide open to devour your harvest and your bread." The first Hebrew word in v. 16, *'ašpāṯô,* is emended slightly to read *śᵉpāṯô,* "his lips," or *'ᵃšer pîhû,* "whose lips." But these are conjectural and lack textual evidence.

14. The effectiveness of the subsequent destruction of the cities of Judah by the armies of Nebuchadrezzar in 586 B.C. is borne out by archeological evidence. See W. F. Albright, *The Archaeology of Palestine* (1949), pp. 141f.: "Many towns were destroyed at the beginning of the sixth century B.C. and never again occupied; others were destroyed at that time and partly reoccupied at some later date; still others were destroyed and reoccupied after a long period of abandonment."

readily the view that they enshrine some word of Jeremiah which reflected his own conviction that an exile was altogether to be expected if an invasion such as he spoke about were to take place.

(viii) Yahweh Warns a Foolish, Rebellious, Complacent People (5:20–31)

20 *"Tell this to the people of Jacob,*
Proclaim it in Judah and say:
21 *Hear this now,*
You foolish and senseless[1] *people,*
Who have eyes but do not see,
Ears but cannot hear.
22 *Have you no reverence for me?—Yahweh's word.*
Do you not tremble before me
Who have placed the sand as the boundary of the sea,
An everlasting decree it may not transgress?
It may toss,[2] *but it cannot prevail;*
Its billows may roar but they cannot break through.
23 *But this people has a rebellious and stubborn heart;*
They have turned aside and gone away.
24 *They did not say to themselves,*
'Let us reverence Yahweh our God,
Who gives us rain,
The autumn rain and the spring rain in season,
And the weeks appointed for harvest
He secures for us.'
25 *But your misdeeds have turned these away,*
Your sins have kept back these blessings from you.
26 *For among my people there are wicked men*
Who lay snares like a fowler's net.[3]
They set deadly traps:
It is men they catch.
27 *Like a cage full of birds*
Their houses are full of treachery.
For that reason they have grown great and rich,

1. Lit. "with no heart (mind)."
2. LXX, Syr. read singular. Hebrew has plural verbs but no subject, unless it is *billows* in the next colon or perhaps an unstated subject like "waters." NEB reads "its waves heave and toss but they are powerless." It is not impossible that *gallîm* serves as subject for three verbs, but it is also possible that *yām (sea)* in the previous line is the intended subject.
3. MT reads *yāšûr k^{e}šaḵ y^{e}qûšîm,* "they watch (lie in wait) as fowlers lie in wait." But the Hebrew is not easy since the verbs are singular and the subject plural. Hence various emendations have been proposed, e.g., *BHS, ad loc., yiśr^{e}ḵû ś^{e}ḇāḵâ ḵ^{e}yôq^{e}šîm,* "they set a net like fowlers"; cf. NEB "who lay snares like a fowler's net," which assumes a text *yiśr^{e}ḵû śēḵ yōq^{e}šîm.*

28 *They are fat and well fed.*[4]
There is no limit to their wicked deeds.
They do not bring to judgment
The cause of the orphan, to win it,
Nor grant justice to the poor.
29 *Shall I not punish them for this?—Yahweh's word.*
On such a people
Shall I not take vengeance?"
30 *An appalling thing, a shocking thing*
Has occurred in the land.
31 *The prophets prophesy falsehood,*
The priests rule at their direction,
And my people love it that way.
But what will you do at the end of it all?

After a characteristic formula of introduction there is a poetic section which reflects upon the folly and unnatural behavior of a people who rebel against Yahweh and do not reverence him or acknowledge that he is the source of their life and sustenance (vv. 21–25). Some specific crimes are then detailed and the formula used in v. 9 follows (vv. 26–29). A final section expresses shock at the behavior of the religious leaders, prophets and priests (vv. 30–31).

20 If some doubts have been expressed as to whether the previous vv. 18–19 are genuinely from Jeremiah rather than perhaps editorial, the segment that follows is widely accepted as part of Jeremiah's preaching.[5] The Ruler of the universe addresses the nation through his spokesman Jeremiah.

21 A foolish and senseless people is bidden to listen.[6] There may be a hint in vv. 24, 25 that there had been a drought. But whether or not this is so, Yahweh's people were insensitive to the many evidences of Yahweh's lordship and power. Jeremiah castigates the people for not discerning Yahweh's control of nature and history as well as his power to visit his people in judgment. They have eyes but see nothing, ears and hear nothing (cf. Isa. 6:9–10; Matt. 13:14–15; John 12:40; Acts 28:26).

22 The stupidity and senselessness of the people consisted in the fact that they did not *reverence* (Heb. *yārē'*) Yahweh or *trem-*

4. The meaning of the verb *'āšeṭû* in MT is uncertain. The phrase is lacking in LXX. Emendations have been proposed, e.g., *šāmenû 'āḇû kāśû,* "they are fat, thick, and sleek"; cf. Deut. 32:15. See J. Bright, *Jeremiah,* p. 40.
5. W. Rudolph, *Jeremia*, p. 38; G. P. Couturier, "Jeremiah" in *JBC*, p. 309; A. Weiser, *Das Buch des Propheten Jeremia,* p. 48, etc.
6. The verbs are in the plural.

ble[7] in his presence. The pronoun *me* is in the emphatic position in the first colon; in the second it is the phrase *before me*. By contrast, presumably, either they showed reverence for other deities like Baal or simply neglected Yahweh. Such insensitiveness to the facts was incomprehensible since it was Yahweh who controlled the mighty seas. The choice of the *sea* in making the point was an apt one. In the mythology of the peoples of the ancient East there was perpetual conflict between the gods and the chaos monster. But Yahweh stood outside of such considerations. In creation he set bounds to the waters and set apart the dry land (Gen. 1:6–10; Job 38:8–11; Ps. 104:5–9). The law that the sand should make the bounds of the sea was an everlasting decree (*ḥoq-'ôlām*) which the mighty seas were unable to transgress. The waves may toss and heave but they are powerless. The billows may roar but they can not cross the sand-barrier. While these words reveal something of the fear that the people of Israel had for the sea, they carry a strong assurance that the thing they feared had no power over them because it was in the control of Yahweh. What Baal could not control, Yahweh could. It was therefore a cause for astonishment that the people should fail to bring to Yahweh the profound reverence that was due him.

23 By contrast, whereas the mighty seas recognized their bounds set by an everlasting decree, Israel recognized no master (cf. Isa. 1:3). The people had a rebellious and defiant heart. They turned aside and went their own way,[8] that is, they broke the barriers set by the covenant, barriers that were voluntarily and solemnly accepted by their forefathers (Exod. 19:4–8; 24:4–7; Josh. 24:14–18, etc.).

24 Nor did this people acknowledge that it was Yahweh who controlled the rains and the seasons. In the religion of Canaan these aspects of nature lay under the control of Baal. Jeremiah thus touches on another sensitive area. It was Yahweh who should be reverenced (Heb. *yārē'*), for he was the giver of the rains in their season, the *autumn rain (yôrēh)* and the *spring rain (malqôš)*. Moreover, it was he who secured for his people *the weeks appointed for harvest,*[9] that

7. Heb. **hēḥîl,* Hiphil of *ḥwl*.
8. Some commentators have proposed here for the verb "go" (*yēlēḵû*) the verb "prevail" (*yuḵālû*), by transposing two consonants. This latter verb occurs in v. 22. The sense would then be "they revolted successfully" (they turned aside and prevailed). See W. Rudolph, *Jeremia,* p. 36.
9. We are reminded of the story of Gomer in Hos. 2:8–11. Gomer failed to recognize in Hosea the source of her sustenance and attributed it to her lovers.

is, the seven weeks which intervened between the Feast of Passover and the Feast of Weeks. At Passover, on the day after the Sabbath, the priest presented the first sheaf of the harvest as a special gift to Yahweh (Lev. 23:10). The same ritual was carried out at the Feast of Weeks when a grain offering from the new crop was presented to Yahweh (Lev. 23:17). The first offering was of barley and the second of wheat. The activity of Yahweh in making possible the maturing of the crop was thereby acknowledged, for it was he who gave Israel her grain.

25 It seems that a period of drought provided Jeremiah with a talking point. In common with other prophets who held that such phenomena as droughts, plagues, pestilences, etc. were divine judgments (cf. Amos 4:6–9), Jeremiah asserted:

Your misdeeds (Heb. *'āwôn) have turned these away,*
Your sins (Heb. *ḥaṭṭā'ṯ) have kept back these blessings*[10]
from you.[11]

The two words used here for Israel's breaches of covenant are common in the OT,[12] but they may have some special point here. The first, *'āwôn,* is related to a root which means "to wander, err," and the second, *ḥaṭṭā'ṯ,* to a root meaning "to miss the mark." Israel had both wandered away from Yahweh and failed to reach the goal set for her. Her actions arose from a contumacious and rebellious heart (v. 23).

In vv. 26–31 a number of specific evils are outlined which are very similar to those denounced in the Temple Sermon (7:2–15). There is therefore no need to regard these verses as being later than the beginning of Jehoiakim's reign (cf. 26:1). They may even have come from the latter part of Josiah's reign.

26–29 Yet another word for wickedness appears in this verse, translated *wicked men (rāšā').* Although there are textual problems[13] in the verse, the general drift is clear. These *wicked men* set out to trap their fellows. The metaphor of the bird-catcher runs through the passage. As the fowler's basket is filled with birds, so the houses of these wicked men are filled with *treachery* or "deceit" (Heb.

10. Heb. *ṭôḇ,* "good."
11. NEB: "Your wrongdoing has upset nature's order and your sins have kept from you her kindly gifts."
12. T. C. Vriezen, *An Outline of OT Theology* (E.T. 1958), pp. 211f.
13. See textual note on v. 26.

mirmâ). The reference seems to be to the ill-gotten gains which follow from their fraud and deceit. As a result they had grown rich and grand, fat and sleek.[14]

And, as if that were not a great enough crime, there was no limit to their wicked deeds.[15] They failed to plead the cause of the fatherless and thus bring about a just settlement of their case. The claims of the poor were neglected. The charge seems to be directed against the men in whose power it lay to bring aid to such needy people. In the Jerusalem of Jeremiah's day not many could do this with any real effect. Those who cared were precisely the rich "officials" who could recite "This is the temple of the Lord, the temple of the Lord, the temple of the Lord" (7:4), while ignoring gross injustice in the land. By virtue of their high position and reputation for piety the weak and helpless came to them for help, but the impression we gain from this passage is that any help they gave was a means to filling their own coffers. The rewards of "justice" remained with them while they gained power and control over those whom they aided. The leaders had somehow been able to fit in with Josiah's reforms on the religious level, so that they attended the temple and ceased to attend the shrines while avoiding the deep ethical implications of the reform. The shrines were destroyed in order to minimize the nation's allegiance to Baal and to direct the people's loyalty once again to Yahweh and his covenant with Israel. But there were deeper implications. Yahweh was Lord of Israel's entire life. His will for his people found expression in the Decalog or Ten Commandments. If Yahweh was not Lord of all, he was not Lord at all.

Such a state of affairs drew from Jeremiah the words of v. 29, a refrain that appears also in v. 9.

30–31 Another sign of the sad state of affairs in Judah was the unholy alliance between priests and prophets. The discovery of the law book in the temple (2 K. 22:8–23:3) touched King Josiah personally and deeply. Here was an objective standard by which tradition could be checked. There were, no doubt, long-cherished

14. See textual note on v. 28.

15. The Hebrew is variously understood. NEB reads "Their thoughts are all of evil," RSV "They know no bounds in deeds of evil"; J. Bright, *Jeremiah,* p. 40, takes the verb *ʿāḇar* to mean "overlook," "excuse," as in Prov. 19:11; Amos 7:8; 8:2; Mic. 7:18. We understand it as lit. "Deeds of wickedness pass over (some limit)," though "they overlook evil" fits the context well.

privileges enjoyed by priests and princes, which were now in danger of being exposed. Any prophet's oracle might provide important clues to the proper interpretation of the law. The true prophet had no regard for vested interests or long-cherished privileges. His task was to declare the mind of Yahweh. Lesser prophets could give oracles which supported the status quo. Jeremiah addressed himself to a situation where the other prophets connived with the priests and spoke of "an appalling and shocking thing in the land," namely, that *the prophets prophesy falsehood, the priests rule at their direction* (or "go hand in hand with them"[16]). But whether the priests worked at the direction of the prophets, or functioned by their own priestly authority with the connivance of the cultic prophets, the result was the same. They gave support to the popular element in contemporary religious life which was happy to pay lip-service to Yahweh and support the reforms at a surface level, but were unwilling to enter into the deep commitment of life which should have characterized the covenant people. It was against this superficial understanding of true religion that Jeremiah strove. But Judah (*my people*) loved it that way despite the prophet's earnest pleas. *What will you do at the end of it all?* asked Jeremiah. Presumably he referred to the coming judgment, when the false teaching of the other prophets and the lies of the priests would be exposed for what they were. The people loved to believe that the words of the priests and the prophets gave the correct perspective. In the day of truth they would be disillusioned and under judgment. The day of repentance would be past. What indeed would they do? A dreadful question mark lay over the future.[17]

What then of Jeremiah's quest for one man who acted justly or sought the truth (5:1)? We do not discern in the words of the chapter any indication whatever that such a man was to be found. For three and a half centuries the ark had rested at Jerusalem, the place where Yahweh willed that his glory should dwell. Here too lived and ruled the line of kings descended from David. There were many reasons why things might have been different. But Jeremiah

16. NEB. The Hebrew text reads lit. "rule at their hands," which can mean "at their side" or "at their (the prophets') direction," or "on their (the priests' own) authority." The sense is thus ambiguous, but some connivance seems to be indicated.
17. See J. Skinner, *Prophecy and Religion: Studies in the Life of Jeremiah* (1922), pp. 138–164 for a moral evaluation of Judah during Jeremiah's day.

looked in vain for one such man. Finally all he could do was to declare a message of doom. The theme of impending judgment which dominates chs. 4 and 5 is still at the fore in ch. 6.

(ix) *Jerusalem under Siege (6:1–8)*

1 *People of Benjamin, run for safety*
Out of Jerusalem!
Blow the trumpet in Tekoa!
On Beth-hakkerem light the fire signal!
For disaster peers down from the north,
And great destruction.
2 *Daughter Zion, are you like*[1]
A beautiful pasture
3 *To which shepherds come*
With their flocks?
They pitch their tents all around her.
They graze each one his own area.[2]
4 *"Prepare*[3] *for the battle against her.*
Up! Let us attack at noon."
"Oh, bother! the day is almost over;
The evening shadows are lengthening."
5 *"Then up! We'll attack by night,*
We'll destroy her fortresses!"
6 *This is what Yahweh of Hosts has said:*
"Cut down her trees! Throw up
Siege-mounds against Jerusalem!
Ah, the city of falsehood,[4]
Everything is oppression within her.
7 *As a well keeps its water fresh*
So she keeps her evil fresh.
'Violence! Robbery!' is heard within her;
Sickness and wounds are continually before me.

1. MT *dāmîṯî* should probably be treated as 2nd fem. sing. with the archaic *y* ending, very common in Jeremiah. Alternately, if the consonants *dmt* are vocalized as Piel *dimmîṯî*, we may translate "I have likened." A further problem rises from the ambiguity of the verb *dāmâ,* which sometimes means "be silent," as in death; hence NEB "Zion, delightful and lovely, her end is near." Some commentators regard the sentence as a question and take the first *h* as the interrogative enclitic (see J. Bright, *Jeremiah,* p. 43, and cf. *BHS*): "Are you like a pleasant pasture . . . ?" or "Have I compared you to a pleasant pasture?"
2. Lit. "his hand"; cf. 2 Sam. 19:44 (Eng. 43); 2 K. 11:7; etc. for a similar sense.
3. Lit. "Sanctify" (Heb. *qaddēš*).
4. MT *hî' hā'îr hopqaḏ,* usually translated "This is the city to be punished," which poses grammatical problems since *city* is fem. and the verbal participle is masculine. Moreover, in the next phrase *kullāh,* "her all," is feminine. LXX makes good sense suggesting an underlying Heb. text *hôy 'îr haššeqer.*

8 *Be warned, Jerusalem,*
Lest my heart be alienated from you,
Lest I make you a desolate waste,
A land where no one lives."

Chapter 6 opens with a vivid poem describing the coming of the foe from the north (vv. 1–8). A dialog between the prophet and Yahweh in which national complacency is exposed (vv. 9–15) is followed by a clear statement that elaborate rituals are no substitute for obedience (vv. 16–21). Then, once again the invader from the north is presented (vv. 22–26). The chapter closes with a further dialog between Yahweh and Jeremiah in which Jeremiah is designated an assayer of the people (vv. 27–30). With the conclusion of ch. 6 we turn to another group of oracles many of which come from the day of Jehoiakim.

The certainty of Jerusalem's fall before the onslaught of the enemy is now declared. The people's only hope is to flee the city. Yet even with the foes at the gates, Jeremiah still held out hope. Disaster could still be avoided (v. 8). Such words may point to a period in Jeremiah's preaching before any of Nebuchadrezzar's invasions from the north. However, the section does convey the impression that the doom about which Jeremiah had spoken was at hand.

1 The warning comes to Jeremiah's own tribe. The town of Anathoth where Jeremiah lived lay about 3 miles northeast of Jerusalem on the outskirts of the modern village of 'Anata, probably Ras el-Kharrabeh.[5] The foe seems to have reached a point close enough to the area of Benjamin to warrant this urgent cry. The men of Benjamin are urged to flee to safety from the midst of Jerusalem. The warning *trumpet (šôp̄ār,* ram's horn) is to be sounded in *Tekoa,*[6] the village of Amos (Amos 1:1), some 5 miles south of Bethlehem. In *Beth-hakkerem* (possibly 'Ain Kārim west of Jerusalem or alternately Ramat Rachel on the road from Jerusalem to Bethlehem, cf. Neh. 3:14)[7] the *fire signal* was to be lit.[8] Each of these places is in the neighborhood of Jerusalem, northeast, west, or southwest.

5. See Y. Aharoni, *The Land of the Bible* (1966), p. 340.
6. There is a fine assonance in Hebrew here, not easily captured in English, *biṯqôa' tiqᵉ'û.*
7. Y. Aharoni, "Excavations at Ramat Raḥel," *BA* (1961), pp. 98–118; D. W. Thomas (ed.), *Archaeology and OT Study* (1967), pp. 171ff.
8. There is assonance here also in *śᵉ'û maś'ēṯ.* The word for *signal,* here *maś'ēṯ,* appears in Lachish Letter IV:10; cf. Judg. 20:38, 40.

The message is that a shattering calamity (*rā'â*) is already glaring down at the city from the north.[9] The fire signals south of Jerusalem may indicate that the foe will head southward, or perhaps it marked the direction in which the inhabitants of Jerusalem would flee.

2–3 Jerusalem (*Daughter Zion*) is described as a delightful meadow (*beautiful pasture*) to which *shepherds* (enemy kings with their troops) come and where they pitch their tents to graze, each one in his own segment. In the minds of the people and, naturally, of Jeremiah, Jerusalem was altogether desirable, all the more so because it was the place where the temple stood (Isa. 2:2–3; Ezek. 24:21; Hag. 2:6–7; etc.). But the foe from the north would come to lay siege to the beautiful city.

4–5 The exact time or the manner in which Yahweh's judgment would come against the city was as yet unclear. There is an ambiguity about vv. 4 and 5, along with an undertone of certain triumph by the enemy however long it might take. The enemy cried out *Prepare for the battle against her.* The Hebrew verb for *Prepare (qaddᵉšû)* may suggest the religious rituals preceding a battle in the ancient institution of the holy war. This would lay special stress on the serious purpose of the invaders and therefore of Yahweh.[10]

It was quite normal in the ancient Near East to call in the staff astrologers attached to the army to consult the oracles and offer ritual sacrifices before any decision was made to begin the battle. The normal time to begin a battle was in the morning. The battle would continue throughout the day until nightfall, when the combatants would rest. Night attack was unusual, though presumably possible under certain circumstances. Here the enemy are impatient to get on with the task, but frustrated in that time has run out for a normal daytime attack. So, *Up! We'll attack by night, we'll destroy her fortresses!* was the cry.

6 We catch a glimpse here of an aspect of siege warfare. In order to run battering rams up to the weaker parts of the walls some distance above the ground, a sloping ramp (Heb. *sōlᵉlâ*) was built with a foundation of trees and large stones. (Perhaps some of the devastation of the hills of Palestine arose from this practice of destroying the trees, either to build ramps or for fuel.) The fall of the

9. The verb **šāqap* means "look out (down, forth)," "peer."

10. However, the verb is used at times in an attenuated sense (e.g., Mic. 3:5), and possibly the sense here is simply "prepare war." On the holy war, see G. von Rad, *Studies on Deuteronomy* (E.T. 1953), pp. 45–59; *Der heilige Krieg im alten Israel* (Zürich, 1951); R. de Vaux, *Ancient Israel* (1961), pp. 258–267, 461–67.

city was inevitable because it was a *city of falsehood* with nothing but *oppression ('ōšeq)* within.

7–8 By way of elucidation a comparison is made between a well which keeps producing fresh water and the city of Jerusalem which keeps producing *evil (rā'â)* from her midst. There was a constant cry of *Violence! Robbery!*—the cry of men set upon by robbers. The Lord had before him constantly a vision of *sickness and wounds*. Hence Jerusalem was urged to let herself be *warned*[11] lest the Lord turn away from her and make her a desolation, a land without inhabitants. The *heart* of God (Heb. *nepeš*) would be *alienated* (Heb. *yāqa'*) and turned away in revulsion from those who claimed to worship him alone but denied him by their breach of his moral laws. Despite the reform and the high personal integrity of King Josiah, it would seem that behind a facade of royal justice lay a great deal of unchecked evil, which was to break out more fiercely after the death of Josiah. However, it appears that at the time represented by v. 8 the hope of avoiding disaster was still being held out to the people, so that the segment 6:1–8 may represent one of the earlier poems dealing with the "foe from the north."

(x) Judgment Falls on a Corrupt People (6:9–15)

9 *This is what Yahweh of Hosts has said:*
"Glean thoroughly[1] *like a vine*
The remnant of Israel;
Pass your hand once again[2] *like a vintager*
Over the tendrils."
10 *"To whom can I speak*
And give solemn warning so that they will listen?
But alas, their ears are uncircumcised
And they cannot listen.
See how Yahweh's word has become to them
A reproach in which they find no pleasure.

11. Heb. *yāšar* in the Niphal can sometimes have a reflexive sense as here, *Be warned,* i.e., "let yourself be admonished."

1. MT *'ôlēl yᵉ'ôlᵉlû,* "they shall thoroughly glean," seems to need emendation since the passage is addressed to Jeremiah (cf. v. 9b). It is generally proposed to read *'ôlēl 'ôlēl* (infinitive and imperative). It is possible, however, to read MT as giving a divine pronouncement which is followed by an instruction to Jeremiah. GNB in a dynamic equivalent reads, "Israel will be stripped clean like a vineyard from which every grape has been picked. So you must . . . ," i.e., the enemy will glean the vine, but before he comes Jeremiah must gather up any remnant.
2. Lit. "return your hand," another use of *šûḇ*.

11 *So I am filled with the wrath of Yahweh;*
I am weary of holding it in."
"Pour it out on the children in the streets
And on the bands of youths as well.
For both husband and wife will be taken,
The old man and the very old.
12[3] *Their houses will be turned over to others,*
Their fields and their women alike,
When I stretch out my hand[4]
Against the people of the land—Yahweh's word.
13 *From the least to the greatest,*
All of them are greedy for gain;
The prophet and the priest,
Everyone practices falsehood.
14 *They treat my people's fracture superficially*
And say 'All is well!'
But nothing is well.
15 *Were they ashamed*[5] *because they did these disgusting things?*
Not they! They were not ashamed at all;
They don't know how to blush.[6]
And so they will fall as others fall;
At the time of their reckoning[7]
They will be brought down—Yahweh's word."

Verses 9–15 take the form of a dialog between the prophet and Yahweh. MT suggests Yahweh's command to Jeremiah was given as a result of the impending "gleaning" activities of the invading foe. Jeremiah was to glean first in much the same way as a grape-gatherer gleans the vines after the main gathering has taken place. In vv. 10–11a Jeremiah protests that the people will not listen to the divine word which he was commissioned to proclaim. He had held the word back but became weary of holding it in. To this complaint Yahweh's reply was that he should hold back the word no longer

3. Verses 12–15a are parallel to 8:10–12 with some variations and omissions.
4. "Stretch out the hand" is an idiom for striking someone; cf. 15:6; Isa. 5:25; etc.; J. Bright, *Jeremiah,* p. 48. The phrase is lacking in 8:10 where the context is very similar.
5. Vocalize *h*^{a}*ḇôšû*. MT has *hōḇîšû,* "They ought to have been ashamed." The sense is not affected.
6. Vocalize *hklm* as *hikkālêm,* "to be ashamed," "to blush," as in 8:12. MT reads *haḵlîm*.
7. Read *p*^{e}*quddāṯām*, as in 8:12. MT reads *p*^{e}*qaḏtîm,* "at the time when I have punished them."

but pour it out on the people, young and old alike (vv. 11b–12). The general corruption of the people is then further exposed and attacked (vv. 13–15).

9 The call to Jeremiah to undertake the task of gleaner may have come in response to some unrecorded complaint by Jeremiah, or perhaps in response to Yahweh's word concerning the activities of the invader. Yahweh's response to Jeremiah's prayer was, *Glean thoroughly like a vine the remnant* (Heb. *šᵉ'ērîṯ*) *of Israel*. Here *the remnant of Israel* may have been used not so much in the technical sense found elsewhere in the prophets for those who survive judgment or return from exile, but in a metaphorical sense. All of Jeremiah's prophetic ministry, however fruitless it seemed, was a kind of grape harvesting, a gleaning of the vine of Israel. Jeremiah's task was to glean Israel. Once more he must return (*šûḇ*) to the task to make certain that there was none remaining who had not heard his message. But the gleaning hand could find no fruit (cf. 5:1) on the vine tendrils.

10–12 The question in Jeremiah's mind was a simple one: To whom could he speak? To whom could he give solemn warning? Who would hear? The disposition of the people was quite otherwise. Their ears were closed (lit. *uncircumcised*). The use of the word *uncircumcised* (*'ᵃrēlâ*) of the ear is unusual (cf. Acts 7:51), although it is elsewhere used of the lips (e.g., Exod. 6:12, 30) and the heart (e.g., Lev. 26:41). In each case the term denotes something which brought about the closing up of the organ. To the closed ear all admonitions were in vain. The people were insensitive and lacked the insight or understanding to comprehend the divine word (cf. 4:4). Yahweh's word was, in fact, a *reproach* (*ḥerpâ*) in which they found no pleasure. Under such circumstances the whole being of Jeremiah was as though united with the being of Yahweh, so that he sensed the wrath of Yahweh and could no longer restrain his anger. He was weary with holding it back. Yahweh's word made plain the comprehensiveness of the coming judgment. It would reach young and old alike—the *children* (Heb. *'ôlāl*)[8] *in the streets,* the gatherings

8. The noun *'ôlāl* derives from the root *'wl*, "to suckle," "to give milk," and might be thought to refer to mere babies. But in Middle Eastern society where children were kept much longer at the breast, the noun may well have referred to small children able to run about in the streets. J. Bright, *Jeremiah,* p. 44, translates "the tots in the streets."

of young men, husbands and wives, greybeards and patriarchs. When judgment fell finally it would involve all, regardless of sex or age. Houses, fields, womenfolk would be handed over to others when Yahweh lashed out and struck[9] the inhabitants of the land.

13–15 The inner greed of the nation touched all, from the least to the greatest. Such greed (*beṣa'*) extended to the prophets and the priests also, all of whom practiced fraud. At a time when religious leaders might have been expected to utter some words of warning, all they could say was *All is well!* The truth was that nothing was well. The people's hurt was severe. There was a serious breach in the relationship between Yahweh and Israel which required urgent and radical treatment instead of superficial treatment with empty and untrue words. The religious leaders treated the people's wound superficially while all the time their rebellious acts and continued breaches of the covenant only beckoned the forces of judgment to hasten on.

We are reminded of Jeremiah's appeal in 4:3–5. Judah needed a radical transformation. She needed to break new ground. If she merely sowed among the thorns, she would produce more thorns. She needed an inward circumcision of the heart, not an external circumcision. See comments on 4:3, 4.

The prophets and priests of the day dressed the nation's wounds, but skin-deep only. Nor did they have any sense of shame for the loathsome deeds they perpetrated. They neither felt shame nor did they know how to blush. They had become completely insensitive to the evils in which they and their nation were immersed. But continued active involvement in evil has a way of dulling the conscience until a point is reached when all awareness of evil is lost. Thereafter leaders fall with the rest of those who fall. In the day of divine reckoning they too would go down, for it would be the day of their own doom.

Some commentators[10] have seen in v. 14 a reflection of post-reformation complacency, when priests and people imagined that by undertaking reforms they had achieved acceptance with Yahweh as

9. See the textual note on "stretch out the hand" in v. 12.
10. Cf. J. Bright, *Jeremiah*, p. 50.

well as lasting peace for themselves. There is some value in the suggestion. In that case the passage could have come from any period after 621 B.C. but prior to the attacks of Nebuchadrezzar.

(xi) Elaborate Ritual No Substitute for Obedience (6:16–21)

16 *This is what Yahweh has said:*
"Stand at the crossroads and look.
Ask for the ancient[1] *paths.*
Which way is the good way? Take that,
And you will find a place of rest for yourselves.
But they said, 'We will not go!'
17 *So I appointed over them*[2] *watchmen:*
'Give heed to the blast of the trumpet!'
But they said, 'We will not heed it.'
18 *Therefore hear, you nations,*
And learn as a witness
What will happen to them.[3]
19 *Hear, O earth!*
Look! I will bring disaster
To this people,
The harvest of their scheming,[4]
For they have paid no attention to my words,
And as for my instruction they have rejected it.
20 *What do I care for incense that comes*[5] *from Sheba,*
Sweet cane from a distant land?
Your whole burnt offerings are not acceptable
And your sacrifices do not please me.

1. MT *'ôlām* is to be translated "ancient, everlasting, of old" in most cases. But the root *'lm* in Ugaritic, Arabic, and some other Semitic languages sometimes has the sense of "learn," "teach," "be wise," etc. Some Arabic derivatives emphasize the idea of "wisdom." It is possible that in the present phrase we have such a usage. Israel is being invited to ask for the "ways of wisdom." See J. A. Thompson, "The Root *'-l-m* in Semitic Languages and Some Proposed New Translations in Ugaritic and Hebrew," *Festschrift for Arthur Vööbus* (1977), pp. 301–308.
2. MT reads "over you," which is awkward in the context of 3rd person plur. verbs. If it is retained we recognize here another example of the tendency to interchange persons without any obvious reason. Such a practice is unacceptable to modern Western grammatical logic, though it may have posed no problem to the people of Jeremiah's time.
3. The latter part of this verse is difficult. J. Bright, *Jeremiah,* p. 45, abandons the verse and offers no translation. MT appears to read lit. "And know, O congregation, (witness) what is in them." The noun *'ēḏâ* may be taken as the feminine of *'ēḏ,* "witness," applied as a collective to "nations." The last three words *'eṯ 'ašer bām* may be taken as an apocopated form for some such phrase as "that which (I will do) to them." The next verse calls on the earth to witness the divine judgment on Judah.
4. LXX reads "their backsliding." MT reads "their thoughts."
5. LXX, Syr. suggest "that you bring," emphasizing the personal endeavor of the people to elaborate their rituals.

21 *So this is what Yahweh has said:*
'Look! I will place before this people
Obstacles over which they will stumble;
Fathers and sons together,
Neighbor and friend will perish.' "[6]

The segment vv. 16–21 raises a number of questions. There is disagreement among the commentators as to whether it is prose or poetry. John Bright and RSV treat it as poetic, as we do in this commentary, because of the many parallelisms. NEB and GNB regard it as prose except for v. 21. E. W. Nicholson agrees that it has an unmistakable poetic character.[7] The question of whether poetic material is, on the whole, to be attributed to Jeremiah, and prose, on the whole, to a Deuteronomic editor is raised here in a pointed way; and Nicholson, who holds a considerable brief for the work of the Deuteronomic editor, argues that "it is possible that an original poetic saying of the prophet has been slightly worked over by a Deuteronomic editor for whom its contents would have been of particular significance."[8] This passage underlines the possibility that Jeremiah himself said many of the things that are supposed to have been of particular interest to the Deuteronomic editor.[9]

A further question is that of the date. The passage would fit a situation just after Josiah's strengthened reform program, i.e., after 622 B.C. It makes the point that the people have rejected two of the features of the Deuteronomic reform, the summons to return to the Mosaic covenant as set out in Deuteronomy and the warnings expressed in the "book of the law." They have rejected Yahweh's law and have imagined that Yahweh would accept a more elaborate ritual in place of obedience to the covenant law. Hence a date in the latter part of Josiah's reign would seem to be indicated.

16–17 Whether these words were originally uttered at the same time as the oracle presented in vv. 9–15 or were uttered in another setting and were placed here by an editor, they suit the present context well. Jeremiah here makes an appeal to his audience to study the traditions of the nation to discover what conduct was pleasing to Yahweh. Israel had reached a point in its spiritual history

6. Read *yō'bĕḏû* for MT *yᵉ'āḇāḏû*.
7. E. W. Nicholson, *Jeremiah 1–25* (1973), pp. 70f.
8. *Ibid.*
9. See the Introduction, "The Book of Jeremiah: Composition," pp. 33–50.

when it did not need a new revelation from God so much as the will to respond to the revelation already given. This was a theme well known from earlier prophets who, like Jeremiah, were not innovators but men deeply attached to ancient traditions which ran back to the covenant established between Yahweh and Israel at Sinai.[10] Hence, Jeremiah exhorted the people to *stand at the crossroads and look. Ask for the ancient paths. Which way is the good way?* It was this way that Israel should take. This way lay a resting place for themselves.

The importance of the covenant for Jeremiah cannot be overrated. For him the covenant was fundamental to Israel's very life, involving as it did the acknowledgment of Yahweh as Israel's only sovereign Lord, and the glad acceptance of the covenant obligations. When Israel took this way she followed the ancient paths, the good way, and found rest. It was a theme to which Jeremiah returned again and again (7:22–23; 11:1–13; etc.). Alas, Israel would not follow the way of obedience but said, *We will not go* (in it).

God, however, was not willing that his people should perish, and set over them *watchmen,* that is, prophets who would warn them of the dangers that attended such calculated and deliberate rejection of Yahweh's sovereignty over his people (cf. Ezek. 3:16–21). The prophetic voices represented here by Jeremiah were appointed by Yahweh to proclaim: *Give heed to the blast of the trumpet,* that is, to the note sounded on the *shophar* or ram's horn, which warned of imminent battle. Ever and anon Israel's response was *We will not heed it!* Men who would not obey the summons to return to the ancient ways were hardly likely to heed warnings about the dangers that attended a breach of the covenant. And they did not.

18–19 The nations and the earth are summoned to witness the judgments that would fall upon a rebellious people. The latter part of v. 18 is not easy to translate[11] but the broad sense of the two verses seems clear. God called for witnesses to hear the sentence of judgment he was about to pronounce against a people who had rejected his covenant.[12] Then in plain words Jeremiah declared—

10. R. E. Clements, *Prophecy and Covenant* (1965).
11. See textual note.
12. Cf. Mic. 6:1–2 where the mountains and hills are called as witnesses.

they have paid no attention to my words, and as for my instruction they have rejected it. The *instruction (tôrâ)* referred to is the Law of Moses as set out in the book of Deuteronomy. In 8:8, 9 the law of Yahweh is set in parallelism to the word of Yahweh. This they spurned, but then sought to satisfy the demands of the covenant by preoccupation with costly temple rituals (v. 20). But these would be of no avail. The coming *disaster (rāʿâ)* would be the fruit of such scheming.

20 Jeremiah was not alone in his affirmation that God would not accept costly offerings as a substitute for obedience (Isa. 1:11–14; Amos 5:21; Mic. 6:6–8). His particular reference here is to *incense* imported from *Sheba,* a country in southwest Arabia, a center of trade in incense and spices (Ezek. 27:22), and to *sweet cane* which may have come from India. Nor would God find pleasure in their *whole burnt offerings (ʿôlâ),* offerings where the entire animal was consumed on the altar, or in their *sacrifices (zeḇaḥ),* in which only choice portions were offered on the altar and the rest was consumed by worshippers.

Such statements seem, at first sight, to amount to a rejection of the whole sacrificial system as practiced in the temple (cf. 7:21–22; Isa. 1:11–14; Amos 5:21; Mic. 6:6–8). This was not the case. The words belong to a manner of speaking which is common both in the OT and in the ancient Near East. Such negative expressions served to call attention to some point of criticism of the subject matter under discussion. The point being made by Jeremiah was that ritual performances divorced from an attitude of obedience and faith were worthless in God's sight (cf. 1 Sam. 15:22; Isa. 1:11; Mic. 6:7, 8; etc.). All exterior practices of religion without the accompanying inner attitudes and dispositions were to be rejected. It was not the cult as such that the prophets rejected, but the cult without proper moral attitudes. Indeed, in the ancient Near East, Israel included, a religion without a cult would have been unthinkable. That concept developed only slowly and in later times.

21 Here then was Yahweh's word through his servant Jeremiah. He would set in front of this people *obstacles* over which they would *stumble*. These obstacles are not defined. They may have been obstacles of their own making, their own apostasies. On the other hand the reference may be to the threatened invader. In either case, *fathers and sons together, neighbor and friend* would perish.

(xii) *The Terrible Foe from the North (6:22–26)*

22 *This is what Yahweh has said:*
"Look! a people is coming
From a country in the north,
A great nation is stirring
From earth's farthest bounds.
23 *They have armed themselves with bow and spear;*
Cruel they are, and pitiless.
They sound like the roaring sea
And ride on horses,
Lined up in battle array
Against you, daughter Zion!"
24 *We have heard the report,*
Our hands hang limp.
Anguish seizes us,
Pangs as of a woman in labor.
25 *Do not go out into the field*
Nor walk by the roadway,
For the enemy has a sword.
There is terror everywhere.
26 *My daughter—my people, gird on sackcloth,*
Sprinkle ashes on yourself,
Mourn as for an only son
With bitter lamentation,
For suddenly
The destroyer[1] *will be upon us.*

Once more we meet the terrible invader from the north. We have here another vivid poem describing the approach of the "foe from the north."[2] The fact that part of this poem (vv. 22–23) appears also in 50:42 suggests that it may have been a poetic fragment which was put to use in more than one situation. Its usage in ch. 50 is secondary. There are also several parallels between these verses and 4:29–31 (see comments *in loc.*).

22–23 The people coming from the land of the north, the nation stirring from earth's farthest bounds, is still not named but their description would fit the Babylonians. They are here described as being armed with *bow (qešeṯ)* and *spear (kîḏôn).* The *spear* or

1. LXX suggests *haššōḏ,* "destruction."
2. See the Introduction, "The Foe from the North," pp. 86f.

blade has generally been taken to be a javelin of some kind. The same word is used in one of the Dead Sea Scrolls for a sword 68.7 cm. long, rather like a Roman *gladius*.[3] This cruel, ruthless foe comes on relentlessly, mounted on chargers, drawn up in battle array, making a din like the roaring of the sea. It is a terrifying picture. One almost senses Yahweh's own anguish that this relentless foe is arrayed against his daughter Zion. The one objective of that ruthless army is the destruction of the nation.

24 The panic that will grip the people is portrayed in striking terms in this verse. The report of the arrival of the foe causes physical weakness to possess the inhabitants of the land. The mental agony and the inward pangs that grip them all are likened to the experience of a woman in childbirth. Jeremiah may well have had in mind the plight of women in conquered lands which was altogether desperate. His use of the phrase *daughter Zion* adds poignancy to the whole crisis. Judah was as unequal to the encounter as a weak, defenseless woman in the pangs of childbirth before a powerful, fully equipped soldier.

25 There is no protection anywhere. Often at the approach of an enemy people took to the roads or the fields as they fled before his advance. But in Judah's coming judgment such a reaction would be futile, for the enemy, sword in hand, was terror let loose. There was no protection anywhere, in the home, or in the fields. The expression *terror is everywhere (māḡôr missāḇîḇ)* was another of Jeremiah's watchwords. He gave it as a name to *Pashhur,* the priest who beat him (cf. 20:3, 10).

26 The only thing left for Judah, here described as *My daughter—my people* (see above at 4:11), was to *gird on sackcloth* and *sprinkle ashes* on herself, that is, to adopt the posture of one who mourns for the death of an only son. The death of *an only son* (*yāḥîḏ*) meant that descendants were thus denied to the parents, which in the East and in Israel was a terrible catastrophe (cf. Amos 8:10; Zech. 12:10). It was the hope of every man of Israel to have a son who would guarantee the perpetuation of the family name. The death of such a son was a grievous calamity and was accompanied by *bitter lamentation*. Such lamentation was called for also

3. Cf. Y. Yadin, *The Scroll of the War of the Sons of Light against the Sons of Darkness* (1962), pp. 124–131. NEB translates "sabre."

in the circumstances about to overtake Judah, which would cut off descendants from many families, and, as far as they knew, might spell the end of the whole nation.

(xiii) Jeremiah, the Assayer of His People (6:27–30)

27 *"I have appointed you an assayer of my people,*
Whom you will know how to test[1] *and whose*
Conduct you shall assay."
28 *"All of them are rebels in revolt,*[2]
Going about as slanderers,
Corrupt to a man.[3]
29 *The bellows puff,*[4] *the fire is ready,*[5]
lead, copper, iron. . . .[6]
In vain does the refiner[7] *smelt (them),*
And the ore[8] *is not separated out.*

1. MT is difficult. The word *miḇṣār,* "fortress," is added after *bāḥôn, assayer,* evidently as a gloss. One proposal is to revocalize *mbṣr* as a Piel participle *m*ᵉ*ḇaṣṣēr* (KB, p. 142), which can mean "one who searches through," i.e., "a tester" (so RSV). NEB, following G. R. Driver, "Two Misunderstood Passages of the OT," *JTS* N.S. 6 (1955), pp. 82–87, redivides the consonants of *mbṣr wtd'* to read *mbṣrw td'*, i.e., *m*ᵉ*ḇaṣṣ*ᵉ*rô tēḏa'*, "its testing you know." The sing. suffix agrees with *'ammî, my people,* although in the next line *darkām* is a plur., representing the collective *people*.
2. The expression *sārê sôr*ᵉ*rîm* may be taken as a superlative expression like "Song of Songs," "King of Kings," and hence "rebel of rebels," i.e., "The most stubborn of rebels" (J. Bright). NEB, following G. R. Driver, *loc. cit.,* sees the juxtaposition of two homonyms from distinct roots to heighten the effect with *sôr*ᵉ*rîm,* "disobedience, revolt," an abstract noun of a known type. The phrase would mean "persons turning aside in/from disobedience." LXX has one word only and omits the first, although other versions have two words.
3. We have transferred *n*ᵉ*ḥōšeṯ ûḇarzel*, *copper and iron,* to the next verse. See n. 6.
4. Heb. *nāḥar* (Qal), "snort," related to Akk. *naḫāru*, "snore," Arab. *naḫara*, and other cognates, describes the noise made by bellows working at full blast. The *m* of *mē'ēštam* is to be taken with the preceding word *mappuaḥ* to form a dual *mappuḥaim, bellows* (cf. Ugar. *mpḫm*).
5. Subdivide the word *mē'ēštam* into *-m 'ēš tām,* hence "the fire is perfect (*ready*)."
6. The words *copper* and *iron* seem to fit awkwardly into the context of v. 28 in MT, which is describing the character of God's people. If they are retained here they must have some kind of metaphorical use, copper denoting brazen, and iron denoting obstinate. But this interpretation seems to be out of character with the passage, which is concerned with a metallurgical picture. In the section the three words *copper, iron,* and *lead* belong together. These items constitute the non-silver material which has to be removed from the ore. We propose to bring the noun *'ōpāreṯ* from the next line and add it to the words *n*ᵉ*ḥōšeṯ ûḇarzel* to form the line *lead, copper, iron. . . .* See G. R. Driver, "Two Misunderstood Passages of the OT," *JTS* N.S. 6 (1955), pp. 82–87.
7. Read *ṣārôp̄* as *nomen agentis (refiner)* like *bāḥôn* ("assayer," v. 27) of the *qāṭôl* type.
8. Read *rā'îm* as *ore*; cf. Arab. *ru'āmu,* "soft earth, fine dust."

30 *Call*[9] *them spurious silver,*
For Yahweh has rejected them."

These final verses of ch. 6 portray Jeremiah still searching for precious metal among the dross of Judah's population. We have here a brief dialog between Yahweh and Jeremiah. Yahweh appoints Jeremiah as an assayer of his people (v. 27), and in due course the assayer gives his verdict (vv. 28–30). The date of these verses is not given, but they could well come from the calamitous events of the year 609 B.C. when Josiah lost his life. This brief oracle appears to be a deliberate epilog to chs. 1–6. Textually the passage presents a number of difficulties, although the general sense is clear.

27 The impending judgment is described in terms of the work of a metallurgist whose task it is to assess the quality of the ore. Yahweh appoints Jeremiah an *assayer (bāḥôn)* of Judah. He is to test and assay their *conduct* (lit. "ways"). Jeremiah was thus not merely an "overseer" over the nations (1:10) but also an assessor of his own people.

28 The remainder of this brief section may be regarded as Jeremiah's report back to God on the completion of his task as assayer. Alternately it may be regarded as a continuation of v. 27 so that the whole segment (vv. 27–30) may be taken as God's oracle to Jeremiah. In either case these verses present a true assessment of the character of Judah. The people are described as *rebels in revolt* or "the most stubborn of rebels,"[10] *going about as slanderers, corrupt* to the last man. Comparison with 5:1, where God asked Jeremiah to run to and fro through the streets of Jerusalem to see whether he could find anyone who acted justly or who sought truth, is striking. Not only did Jeremiah fail to find men of justice and truth, but when he tested the citizens of Jerusalem more closely he found that the truth of the matter was appalling. Breaches of the covenant were discovered on every hand. Rebellion, evil speaking, and corruption had altogether replaced justice and truth.

29–30 The ancient metallurgical process is described in these verses.[11] When lead was placed in a crucible with silver ore and heated, the lead became oxidized and served as a flux to collect

9. Read the imperative *qirᵉʾû* with LXX, Vulgate.
10. See textual notes.
11. See J. Bright, *Jeremiah,* p. 49. Note also the discussion in J. A. Soggin, "Jeremias 6:27–30," *VT* 9 (1959), pp. 95–98; and G. R. Driver, *art. cit.,* pp. 84ff.

impurities. The bellows blew fiercely to give a high temperature, but out of the heat came only lead, copper, and iron.[12] The ore was so impure that the whole procedure failed. The alloys were not removed and the silver, if there was any, was not recovered.

The picture is clear. Jeremiah felt that his task was similar to that of the silver refiner (cf. Mal. 3:3), but the prophetic *fire* had been unable to remove the impurities from Israel and set free the pure silver. The refining process might succeed in the realm of metallurgy, but among the rebellious and corrupt men of Judah, who were professional covenant-breakers, no refining process was adequate to deal with their intractable wills. The people of Judah were hopelessly impure metal, altogether slag, and beyond the refining process. It was useless to go on refining, for the wicked were not being removed. The final assessment was that the people were *spurious silver*, which Yahweh rejected.

With the failure of the refining process we presume that judgment fell. When purification of the national character was shown to be impossible, the day of judgment had arrived.

Review of Chapters 1–6

It is widely agreed that chs. 2–6 preserve many of the early oracles of Jeremiah delivered in the days of Josiah (640–609 B.C.) or early in the reign of Jehoiakim (609–598 B.C.), although commentators may differ in their view about the exact assignment of many sections in these chapters to a specific date. It is clear that the material collected here is somewhat complex and represents a wide variety of oracular utterances made during the years 627/6 to 609 B.C. or a little later. That some is in prose and some in poetry raises further questions.[1]

Whatever may have been the origin of particular sections of these chapters, it seems evident that they have been brought together into a literary whole with a careful interweaving of themes and elements of vocabulary, so that finally we have to do with a single piece of literature. It may be too much to claim that these chapters were prepared originally for reading, a proposal that has been made about

12. Assuming that the words *copper* and *iron* are to be read after *lead*.

1. See the Introduction, "The Book of Jeremiah: Composition," pp. 33–50. The bulk of chs. 2–6 we have read as poetry, the only exceptions being 2:1–2a, 16–18.

other areas of the prophetic literature.[2] But if they represent the distillation of what were originally spoken oracles, the shape they assume in these chapters is certainly of a kind that is meant to be read as literature.[3] One may liken chs. 1–6 to a musical symphony in which a number of themes are introduced in ch. 1 and then developed and restated as the symphony unfolds. In the last telling section, 6:27–30, the failure of the refining process makes clear the inevitability of judgment.

In ch. 1 a number of themes are introduced. God calls Jeremiah as a prophet to the nations (*gôyîm*) and appoints him over nations and kingdoms (*mamlākôṯ*):

to uproot (*nāṯaš*)[4] and to tear down (*nāṯaṣ*),
to destroy (*'āḇaḏ*) and to raze (*hāras*),
to build (*bānâ*) and to plant (*nāṭa'*),

that is, Jeremiah was called upon to declare both judgment and restoration. Yahweh promised to watch over (*šāqaḏ*) his word to perform it.

The means of the divine judgment is revealed as disaster (*rā'â*) from the north, tribes and kingdoms arrayed against Jerusalem.

The reason for the divine judgment is the wickedness (*rā'â*) of Judah, who had forsaken (*'āzaḇ*) Yahweh, made offerings (*qiṭṭēr*) to other gods, and bowed down (*hištaḥᵃwâ*) to their own handiwork.

The particular subjects of the coming judgment were the kings, officials (*śārîm*), priests (*kōhᵃnîm*), and the people of the land (*'am hā'āreṣ*).

In the face of such a judgment Jeremiah would know the divine protection and enablement.

These themes recur throughout the book of Jeremiah, but they are clearly woven into chs. 2–6.

Thus the theme of judgment meets us again and again. The term *nation (gôy)* occurs thirteen times in these chapters in slightly different senses.[5] But in particular it is used of the agent of judg-

2. J. Lindblom, *Prophecy in Ancient Israel* (1962), pp. 159f., 163ff., 263f., 278f.; G. Widengren, *Literary and Psychological Aspects of the Hebrew Prophets* (Uppsala, 1948).

3. In 36:1–3 the prophet himself is pictured as dictating "all the words I have spoken against Israel and Judah and all the nations, from the day I spoke to you, from the days of Josiah until today" (36:2). It was this material, written on a scroll, that was read to the king's officers and to the king (36:12, 21, etc.).

4. This root occurs only 21 times in the OT, of which 13 are in Jeremiah.

5. 2:11; 3:17, 19; 4:2, 7; 5:9, 15(4x), 29; 6:18, 22. The total in Jeremiah is upward of 80.

ment, the foe from the north (3:17; 4:7; 5:15 [4 times]; 6:22). Twice the term is used, almost in contempt, of the people of Judah (5:9, 29).

The sin of Judah is described in various ways. The term *wickedness (rā'â)* is used in a double sense. It denotes both the wickedness of Judah[6] and the calamity which would befall evil-doers.[7] Derivatives of the root *zny*, "play the harlot," occur a number of times in these chapters as another descriptive term for Judah's sin. The root *'zb*, "forsake," also occurs a number of times.[8] The root *šûḇ*, which is used in a wide range of nuances in Jeremiah,[9] is frequently pressed into service to describe both Judah's turning aside from Yahweh and her turning to other gods.[10] Both Judah and her sister Israel are described as *faithless (mᵉšuḇâ)*.[11] The root *pš'*, "transgress," is also used several times to define Judah's rebellion.[12] This list is not exhaustive but will suffice to show that certain key terms are used again and again in these chapters.

But there is evidence of some broad patterns in the arrangement of the material. Thus in 2:8–25 we have the following pattern:

2:8, priests, lawyers, rulers, prophets are castigated for misdeeds; 2:9, God threatens a legal process (*rîḇ*); 2:10–13, Judah's rebellion against Yahweh is compared with the behavior of the nations; 2:14–17, a reference is made to the attacks of Assyria and Egypt on Judah; 2:18, astonishment is expressed that Judah persists in going after Assyria and Egypt in a display of independence; 2:19, judgment is announced on Judah because she has forsaken Yahweh; 2:20–25, rebellious Judah is depicted as a breaker of her bonds, a wild ass, and a young female camel in heat upon whom despair has settled.

A similar pattern may be discerned in 2:26–37, although the space devoted to each of the items varies. Thus in 2:26–28 reference is made to kings, princes, priests, and prophets; 2:29a, Judah's legal process (*rîḇ*) against Yahweh; 2:29b, Judah's rebellion; 2:30, Yahweh's judgment; 2:31–32, Judah's bid for independence and her wicked deeds; 2:35, announcement of judgment, 2:36–37, Judah's fickleness

6. 1:16; 2:19; 3:2, 17; 4:4, 14; 5:28; 6:29.
7. 1:14; 2:3, 27; 4:6, 18; 5:12; 6:1, 19.
8. 1:16; 2:13, 17, 19; 5:7.
9. W. L. Holladay, *The Root šûbh in the OT* (1958), pp. 128–139, 152–54.
10. 3:6, 8, 11, 12, 14, 22; 5:6.
11: 3:6, 8, 11, 12; 5:6.
12. 2:8; 3:13; 5:6.

and ensuing judgment and the tragedy of her shame and rejection by Yahweh.

It is thus apparent that the segments 2:8–25 and 2:26–37 have been arranged in approximately similar patterns. This would suggest a literary arrangement of existing material rather than the spontaneous utterances of a preacher. The individual who arranged the material as we now have it is not clearly identifiable, although Jeremiah himself is described as undertaking some editing and re-presentation of his earlier preaching in 36:1–3. But Baruch acted as his scribe in the execution of this task (36:4). It is conceivable that either or both of these in cooperation were responsible for the literary presentation of material once preached by Jeremiah. After the destruction of the first scroll by King Jehoiakim the work was rewritten "and many similar words were added to them" (36:32). There is a third possibility, namely, that at least some of the redactional work was undertaken by later compilers. The precise answer to the question is impossible to obtain, although speculation is not lacking in the commentaries.

The material in 3:1–4:4 may likewise be regarded as a literary unit comprising poetic material in 3:1–5, 19–25, and 4:1–4, broken by the insertion in 3:6–18 which is partly verse and partly prose. The general theme of the whole segment is a call to repentance. The exact origin of the poetry and the prose is not possible to decide, but both are concerned to stress the nation's apostasy, and in both the figure of "adultery" is characteristic (cf. 3:1, 2, 3 with 3:6, 8, 9). Alongside this figure is the oft-repeated keyword *šûḇ* and its derivatives, which serve to denote both "turning away" (apostasy) and "turning back" (repentance). The root is brought into play several times in both the poetic section (3:1, 19, 22; 4:1) and the prose insertion (3:7, 10, 12, 14). The whole section serves both to reinforce the charge of unfaithfulness which was pressed in ch. 2, and also to add a strong plea for the nation to repent. The assurance of Yahweh's forgiveness and mercy is affirmed.

Finally the section 4:5–6:30 is focused largely around the theme of the "foe from the north," Yahweh's agency of judgment. The whole section may be regarded as an explanation of the last phrases of 4:4:

Lest my wrath come forth like fire
And burn so that none can put it out.

No doubt Jeremiah referred more than once to the "foe from the north," at times in very general terms (cf. 4:23–28) and at times with some more specific attack in view such as the approach of the Chaldean army (cf. 4:5–18; 6:1–8, 22–26). Some of this material may come from quite early in Jeremiah's ministry and could thus have given a theme around which later, somewhat different expressions of the same theme could be woven into a literary whole. References to the foe who would bring disaster are interrupted at one point by Jeremiah's anguished cry (4:19–22), at another by further reference to Judah's sins (5:10–31), and at another by an appeal to the people to stand by the old ways rather than depend on expensive rituals (6:16–21). The theme of judgment is to be understood against the background of a broken covenant which would inevitably bring into operation the curses (judgments) which attended breach of covenant. It was no mystery to Jeremiah, even if it was painful to declare the fact or to contemplate its consequences for his people, that divine judgment would follow the rejection of Yahweh's covenant.

B. FALSE RELIGION AND ITS PUNISHMENT (7:1–10:25)

1. THE TEMPLE SERMON AND FALSE RELIGION (7:1–8:3)

(i) The Temple Sermon (7:1–15)

1 *The word that came to Jeremiah from Yahweh:*
2 *"Stand in the gate of Yahweh's house and proclaim there this word.*[1] *Say, Hear the word of Yahweh, all you of Judah who come through these gates to worship Yahweh!*
3 *This is what Yahweh of Hosts, the God of Israel, has said: Reform your way of life and your actions and I will allow you to remain in this place.*[2]
4 *Do not put your trust in the words of The Lie and keep saying, 'This*[3] *is Yahweh's temple, Yahweh's temple, Yahweh's temple!'*

1. The material up to this point is lacking in LXX.
2. MT uses the Piel of *škn,* "I will cause you to dwell (or, let you live) in this place." There is uncertainty about the meaning of *place,* whether it refers to the temple (v. 12) or more generally to Jerusalem or the land. AV, RSV, NEB, and GNB follow MT. Aquila and Vulg. suggest an alternative, vocalizing MT *wa'ᵃšakkᵉnâ 'eṯᵉḵem* as *wᵉ'eškᵉnâ 'ittᵉḵem,* "and I will dwell with you" (so J. Bright). See comments. It is to be remembered that the OT text was originally transmitted as a consonantal text. Vowel signs were added much later, and even the most conscientious attempts to preserve traditional vocalizations may have deviated here and there from the original intent.
3. MT reads *hēmmâ,* "they," which may refer to the total complex of the temple and its related structures. Targ. and Syr. suggest "you." *BHS* proposes an abbreviation *hm h, hammāqôm hazzeh,* "this place."

5 *Only*[4] *if you truly reform your way of life and your actions, if you really act justly with one another,*
6 *do not oppress the resident alien, the orphan, and the widow, shed no innocent blood in this place, and do not run after other gods to your own ruin,*[5]
7 *then I will let you remain*[6] *in this place, in the land that I gave to your fathers of old for all time.*
8 *But look, you are putting your trust in the words of The Lie to no good purpose.*
9 *Can you steal, murder, commit adultery, swear falsely, burn sacrifices to Baal, run after other gods which you have not known,*
10 *and then come and stand before me in this house which bears my name and say 'We are safe!'—just so that you may continue doing all these abominable things?*
11 *Has this house which bears my name become a robbers' cave in your eyes? But look! I myself have seen—Yahweh's word.*
12 *But go, if you will, to my place of worship*[7] *which used to be at Shiloh, where I first established a dwelling place for my name, and see what I did to it because of the wickedness of my people Israel.*
13 *And now because you have done all these things—Yahweh's word*[8]*—though I spoke to you with great earnestness*[9] *you did not listen, and though I called you did not answer,*
14 *I will treat this house which bears my name, and in which you trust, the place which I gave to you and your fathers, as I treated Shiloh.*
15 *I will cast you out of my sight as I cast out all your kinsfolk, the entire progeny of Ephraim."*

The section 7:1–8:3 consists of several originally independent prose passages apart from a brief poetic piece in v. 29. But there is a unity of theme since all the material is concerned with aspects of the religious practices which were current in Judah at the end of the seventh century B.C, all of them abuses of some kind, whether the practice of some pagan rite or the misuse of the official temple cult. The whole is brought together into a framework in which Yahweh instructs Jeremiah three times what he has to say (7:1–2a, 16–19, 27–28). There are five separate sections: (i) the Temple Sermon (7:1–

4. The *kî* has an asseverative sense.
5. Some archeological evidence of the worship of other deities seems to have been discovered by Kathleen Kenyon in a small "shrine" during her excavations in Jerusalem. See K. M. Kenyon, *Jerusalem. Excavating 3000 Years of History* (1967), pp. 64–66, plates 33–35.
6. See note on v. 3.
7. Lit. "place."
8. This phrase is lacking in LXX.
9. Lit. "rising early and speaking." The expression *haškēm*, "rising early," occurs several times in Jeremiah although with a number of different verbs; 7:13, 25; 11:7; 25:4; 26:5; 29:19; 32:33; 35:14, 15; 44:4.

15); (ii) an attack on the worship of the Queen of Heaven (vv. 16–20); (iii) an oracle condemning the attitude that regarded the offering of sacrifice as a substitute for obedience (vv. 21–28); (iv) an oracle condemning child sacrifice and other evil practices in the Hinnom Valley (vv. 29–34); (v) a condemnation of the worship of astral gods (8:1–3).

We meet here for the first time in the book a considerable segment of prose, which has a characteristic style. The question of the nature of the prose discourses in the book of Jeremiah is one of the most important critical problems of the book. A fuller discussion is taken up in the Introduction,[10] but we may make a number of observations here. The style is stereotyped and is found time and again in prose passages throughout the book. Many scholars argue that it is closely akin to a similar language found in the Deuteronomic corpus of literature, that is, the large block of literature from Deuteronomy to 2 Kings, and go on to postulate a body of Deuteronomic editors and authors who drew on authentic sources to present Israel's history against the theological background of the book of Deuteronomy. One aspect of this Deuteronomic literature is the profound interest of the editors in the prophetic voices who continued the work of Moses, proclaiming Yahweh's law and exhorting and admonishing Israel to obey it (2 K. 17:13).[11] In the case of a book like Jeremiah, it is likely that some of Jeremiah's friends captured his words and enshrined them in "sermons"; thus perhaps the prose sermons in the book are not in their entirety the *ipsissima verba* of the prophet, nor is it possible to isolate the precise Jeremianic content. But we have to recognize the possibility also that Jeremiah sometimes spoke in prose, and when he did he would presumably use the prose of his day, which was the Deuteronomic type of prose.

It cannot be questioned that in 7:1–15 we are dealing with an authentic incident in Jeremiah's life or that the sermon is based on some authentic words of the prophet. A similar account in ch. 26 preserves some of the same words. In particular there are a number of striking expressions, such as the threefold cry "the temple of Yahweh" (v. 4), the simile of the "robbers' cave" (v. 11), the list of offenses so reminiscent of the Decalog (v. 9).

10. See "The Book of Jeremiah: Composition," pp. 33-50.
11. See E. W. Nicholson, *Preaching to the Exiles* (1970) for sustained presentation of this view for the book of Jeremiah.

A further point to note is the structure of the sermon, which follows a particular pattern: (a) the proclamation of Yahweh's word and law (7:1–7); (b) the description of the nation's apostasy and her rejection of Yahweh's word and law (vv. 8–12); the announcement of the judgment (vv. 13–15). It is a pattern that recurs in other sermons like 11:1–17; 17:19–27; 34:8–22.

As to the date of the material, it would seem in the main to relate to Jehoiakim's reign. Certainly the Temple Sermon was delivered shortly after Jehoiakim came to the throne in the autumn of 609 or the winter of 609/8 B.C. (26:1). The attack on empty sacrifices (7:21–26) could well have come from about the same period, although its similarity to 6:16–21 may suggest a date in the latter part of Josiah's reign. The other sayings, 7:16–20, 29–34, and 8:1–3, would suit a period after 609 B.C. when Jehoiakim permitted the return of pagan practices.

There is, in any case, a unity of theme which is concerned with a variety of cultic abuses, from wrong emphases of the temple officials to the tolerance of pagan rites. The parallel narrative in ch. 26 reduces the Temple Sermon to its essentials and excludes the materials here presented in 7:16–8:3.

It becomes clear that there was a view abroad that the temple itself was a guarantee of Jerusalem's inviolability.[12] There was evidently a very great preoccupation with the activities of the cult, but a minimal concern with the ethical demands of the covenant. In Jeremiah's view such an outlook was little more than empty superstition. The presence of a temple made with timber and stone in which ritual activities were performed could be no guarantee of the divine presence and protection when the people despised the moral demands of the covenant. Nothing less than a deep and radical repentance and a profound spiritual renewal would avail to deliver the people from inevitable judgment, that is, from the operation of the curses of the covenant. It was to such a state of affairs among his own people that Jeremiah addressed himself.

1–2 According to the parallel account in 26:1, *the word . . . to Jeremiah from Yahweh* came shortly after Jehoiakim became king, in the autumn of 609 or the winter of 609/8 B.C. According to the Hebrew text Jeremiah was commanded to stand in the *gate*

12. See J. Bright, *Covenant and Promise* (Philadelphia, 1976), ch. 2, pp. 49–77 for an interesting treatment of the theme; see also R. E. Clements, *Abraham and David* (London, 1967).

(šaʿar) of the Lord's *house* (the temple)[13] and *proclaim (qārāʾ)* the word which Yahweh gave him. The Temple Sermon is thus set in the framework of a direct word from Yahweh.

The Hebrew verb *worship (hištaḥ^{a}wâ)* brings to mind a significant picture. The verb arises from a metaphor, namely, that of bowing down or prostrating oneself[14] before someone whose high state is thereby acknowledged and to whom allegiance should be offered. When the Hebrew text was rendered into Greek, an equally expressive word was used to translate it, *proskunéō,* which likewise denotes the physical act of bowing down.[15] A term that was used in the secular context of a vassal bowing down before his suzerain is thus pressed into a cultic and religious use. The great majority of the occurrences of the term in the OT refer to the veneration and worship of Yahweh or to that of false gods, although the secular use occurs sufficiently often to point to the origin of the idea.[16] This powerful figure is a peculiarly apt one to describe the proper attitude of the man of Israel to Yahweh. When the man of Israel came to *worship* Yahweh, he acknowledged on the one hand Yahweh's high status and his complete and sole sovereignty over the worshipper's life, and at the same time he recognized his own dependent status and the need for personal submission to his sovereign Lord, Yahweh. Worship thus involved him in the willing acknowledgment of Yahweh's Lordship and the glad acceptance of his covenant demands. He was therefore obligated to obedience to the commandments, the laws, and the statutes in which the covenant demands came to expression. There were thus powerful ethical demands laid upon every worshipper who came to the temple. In the case where the worshipper sought to perform some ritual act without the intention to obey the covenant stipulations, it was altogether fitting that Yahweh's prophet, who was in any case the guardian of the covenant, should address him in strong words: *This is what Yahweh of Hosts, the God of Israel, has said* (v. 3a).

3 Jeremiah's message that day was simple and direct. *Re-*

13. The exact position of the gate is not clear. The medieval commentator Kimchi says there were seven gates in all. It is clear, however, that it was the gate through which worshippers entered the sacred precincts. In fact, the verse refers also to *these gates* (plur.).

14. The root *ḥwy* is known also in Ugaritic with a similar meaning. See Cyrus Gordon, *Ugaritic Textbook* (Glossary), p. 395, No. 847.

15. Of 171 instances of *hištaḥ^{a}wâ* in MT, 164 are rendered by *proskunéō* in LXX. See *TDNT* VI, p. 760, article by H. Greeven.

16. *Ibid.,* pp. 760–62.

form your way of life and your actions (lit. "make good your ways and your doings").[17] The whole direction of the worshippers' lives and the deeds that flowed from their wrong outlook needed to be transformed, amended, reformed. It was a strange demand to make specifically of worshippers, who of all people might be expected to walk in the right way (cf. 6:16) and to act correctly.

What Jeremiah said next has been variously understood. The Masoretic Text, representing the tradition current in the early Christian centuries, is generally translated as *I will allow you to remain in this place,* that is, Jeremiah indicated to the people that consequent upon their repentance and the amendment of their ways, Yahweh would allow them to remain in Jerusalem or in the land. Some of the versions understand the text to mean "and I will dwell with you in this place,"[18] so that the promise was that Yahweh would continue to dwell among his people in the temple. The use of *this place* to denote the temple is known elsewhere. Thus in 7:12 the reference is to the house of Yahweh at Shiloh. The *place (māqôm)* where Yahweh chose to set his name occurs in several passages in Deuteronomy (e.g., 12:11; 14:23), but also elsewhere (e.g., 1 K. 8:29–30, 35). In support of the second interpretation are statements made some years later by Ezekiel, that Yahweh later departed from the temple because of the multitude of evils perpetrated there (Ezek. 10:4, 18–19; 11:22–23). Whichever view is followed, one point is clear, that Yahweh was in no way obligated either to guarantee the inviolability of the temple and the city of Jerusalem, or to remain among his people if they continued to reject his sovereignty and his covenant demands. His ancient promises belonged only to a nation which kept his commandments faithfully (cf. Deut. 7:12–15). The popular idea that Yahweh was in some way bound to Zion was therefore wrong. His presence in the temple was an act of pure grace. The temple was, no doubt, a means by which God could show his grace among his people; but the temple in itself was of no value if God no longer manifested his grace among the people. As a concomitant to such thinking it is implicit that the temple was not essential to the fellowship between the man of Israel and his God. It would appear that in the days of Jeremiah the time for such an understanding had not yet come. It was important for now that the worship of the temple and the attitude of the worshippers should

17. Cf. J. Bright, *Jeremiah,* p. 52, "Reform the whole pattern of your conduct."
18. See textual note.

have their focus in God and not on a mere building. Certainly in some other passages in Jeremiah it seems clear that the prophet treated the temple and its rituals with veneration, for Yahweh might minister blessing to an obedient people by such means (cf. 17:24–26).[19] The oracles referring to the days of restoration seem to imply the existence of the temple (31:6, 12, 23; 33:11).

4 We find here a clear expression of the "temple theology" of the deluded priests and national leaders (2:6, 8, 26) and also of the ordinary citizens. They would argue that God had chosen Zion as his earthly dwelling place (cf. Ps. 132:13–14) and had promised to David and his descendants a kingdom for ever (2 Sam. 7:12–13).[20] In the light of such promises it seemed to be a natural conclusion that God would not allow either his dwelling place (the temple) or his chosen ruler to come to any harm. The temple was a symbol of inviolability which led the people to declare, *This is Yahweh's temple, Yahweh's temple, Yahweh's temple.* But it is a meaningless recitation of a formula, and the people of Judah are urged not to *put your trust in the words of The Lie (haššeqer).* One wonders whether Jeremiah may not have been making use here of the expression *The Lie* to describe some pagan deity like Baal, and to be asserting that the formula which the people were reciting gave no grounds for trust or confidence because it was merely the words of "The Deceiver."[21] Perhaps the triple repetition had some superstitious or magical significance in the popular mind.

5–6 The conditions under which Yahweh would continue to dwell among his people or allow them to continue in Jerusalem are now stated in unmistakable terms in a series of conditional sentences:

> *If you truly reform your way of life and your actions,*
> *If you really act justly with one another,*[22]
> (If you) *do not oppress the resident alien, the orphan, and the widow,*
> (If you) *shed no innocent blood in this place,*
> (If you) *do not run after other gods to your own ruin. . . .*

The first conditional is general and is repeated from v. 3. The other four conditionals lay stress on important moral, ethical, and religious

19. See the Introduction, "Jeremiah and the Cultus," pp. 67–71.
20. See J. Bright, *Covenant and Promise,* ch. 2, pp. 49–77.
21. For possible parallels see 5:31; 13:25.
22. The verbal expression in Hebrew in these two phrases is a strong one in which the finite verb is strengthened by the addition of the so-called infinitive absolute in front of it—"if in very fact you do. . . ."

principles, all of which may be understood as essential elements of the total covenant demand.

One of the inevitable consequences of any rejection of Yahweh's sovereignty over his covenant people was that they neglected their obligations to one another. In the Decalog (Exod. 20; Deut. 5) the first group of commandments deals with Israel's obligations toward Yahweh and the second with their obligations toward their fellow Israelites. With the abandonment of the first group of obligations the abandonment of the second follows inevitably, and injustice, oppression, and judicial killings result. We are dealing here with the strong ethical principles which characterized the prophets both before and after Jeremiah (7:23; Isa. 1:17; 11:1–5; Hos. 2:19; 10:12; Amos. 5:7, 10–15, 24; 8:4–6; Mic. 2:1–3; 3:1–3; Hab. 1:3–4). Yahweh required his people to practice justice (*mišpāṭ*) the one toward the other.[23] He also had a deep concern for the *resident alien (gēr),*[24] the *orphan (yāṯôm),* and the *widow ('almānâ),* who should not be oppressed (Deut. 10:18; Isa. 1:23; Ps. 10:14, 18; 68:6 [Eng. 5]; 146:9, etc.). Nor could Yahweh tolerate the judicial murders [25] which broke out from time to time in Israel and were evidently perpetrated also during the reign of Jehoiakim (26:23), when *innocent blood (dām nāqî)* was shed. All these social evils were rampant in Jeremiah's time. The list given in vv. 5–6 is no doubt merely representative. The profound concern for human welfare which comes to powerful expression in the Mosaic legislation (cf. Deut. 14:29; 24:19–21, etc.)

23. For a useful discussion on the point see E. W. Heaton, *The OT Prophets* (1961), pp. 90–123.

24. The noun *gēr,* "resident alien," derives from the root *gwr,* which denotes "to dwell" (KB, p. 192). In OT references it denotes someone who because of war, famine, plague, blood-guiltiness, or other misfortunes had to leave his original home or tribe and seek shelter at another place. In Israel he was accorded a wide range of civil rights in real property, marriage, justice, etc. He was expected to share in certain religious duties like the observance of the sabbath (Exod. 20:10), and fasting on the day of atonement (Lev. 16:29). He could offer sacrifices (Lev. 17:8, 22:18), and take part in religious festivals (Deut. 16:11, 14). He could celebrate the Passover provided he was circumcised (Exod. 12:48–49). Many of these must have been assimilated into Israel. They were of special concern to Yahweh along with the fatherless and the widows. See R. de Vaux, *Ancient Israel,* pp. 74–76.

25. The reference is to the execution of people found guilty of capital offenses in the courts of law. The inference is that many of these people were put to death for political purposes and on trumped up charges when there was no proven case, or where the case was not properly a capital one. At times of apostasy in Israel there seems to have been an outbreak of this evil. The killing of the prophet Uriah for prophesying against Jerusalem was a case in point (26:23). To execute such people was to shed "innocent blood" (*dām nāqî*). See 7:6; 22:3; 26:15. Cf. Deut. 19:10; 21:8f.; 1 Sam. 19:5; 2 K. 21:16; 24:4.

was ignored. But this was the consequence of the breach of the covenant attendant upon the rejection of Yahweh's sovereignty.

The explicit statement (If you) *do not run after other gods* spells out the source of Judah's social ills. The people had rejected the sole and complete sovereignty of Yahweh and had sought to share their allegiance with *other gods*. That course of action was a profound denial of the covenant by which Israel was bound utterly to Yahweh. There could be no shared allegiance. "Thou shalt have no other gods before me." The covenant bond was given expression in the statement "Your God—my people." The basis of all moral and social corruption in the nation was to be found in Israel's attempt to hold two sets of values side by side. Hence, if the people were to make legitimate claims upon Yahweh for the benefits (blessings) of the covenant, a thoroughgoing reformation at the deepest level of their lives was a fundamental requirement. The conditionals of vv. 5–6 were presented to the people of Jerusalem by Jeremiah as the *sine qua non* for Yahweh's continued protection of his people and for his continued presence among them. Anything less would lead to the people's *own ruin*.

7 What then was the promise that Yahweh made to his people through his servant Jeremiah? Simply that if the people fulfilled the demands of this extended conditional statement in vv. 5–6, then the apodosis would follow, namely, that Yahweh would dwell with them (or let them remain)[26] *in this place (māqôm), in the land that I gave to your fathers of old for all time*. The ambiguity in regard to the term *place* remains. Was it the land, the city Jerusalem, or the temple? Perhaps the ambiguity was intended. The place where Yahweh chose to set his name, or to which he laid claim,[27] was, in the nature of things, in the land promised to the fathers. Both stood or fell together. In fact, once the land of Judah fell to the forces of Nebuchadrezzar, the temple was destroyed (2 K. 25). But it was Jeremiah's belief that such a calamity could have been avoided if Judah had remained true to her covenant with Yahweh. The actions spelled out in vv. 5–6 are clear breaches of the covenant, the consequence of which would be judgment. The promise made to the *fathers* is referred to many times in the OT (e.g., Gen. 13:14–17; 15:18–21; 17:8; 24:7; Exod. 3:7–8; 12:25; Deut. 1:8, 35; 7:8; 8:1;

26. See textual note for 7:3 above.
27. The expression "to set one's name" can carry the sense of "to lay claim to." See J. A. Thompson, *Deuteronomy* (1974), p. 166.

11:9, 21; Judg. 2:1). In fact, God made a promise of both land and descendants. Each was important to the other. A people without a land was as unnatural a condition as a land without a people. So close was the link between these two that when the people sinned the land suffered.

8–11 Once again Jeremiah asserts, *But look, you are putting your trust in the words of The Lie* (v. 8).[28] It was simply not true that the presence of the temple in Jerusalem made the city and the people inviolable. Then, as if to strengthen the charges of vv. 5–6, the specific sins of which Judah was guilty are spelled out in v. 9. The crimes that are listed bear very close resemblance to the commandments given at Sinai, that is, the covenant stipulations. The precise vocabulary is repeated in the case of the first four sins, *steal (gānaḇ,* Exod. 20:15), *murder (rāṣaḥ,* Exod. 20:13), *commit adultery (nā'ap̱,* Exod. 20:14), *swear falsely* (Exod. 20:16, note the noun *šeqer);* in the case of the other two sins the reference to *Baal* and *other gods* is reminiscent of Exod. 20:3–5. The other gods are described as *gods which you have not known.* The reference may be to the fact that in former times such gods were not acceptable to Yahweh's people, although, to be sure, Israel's declension from Yahweh was quite ancient. But there may be a significant overtone in the verb "know" *(yāḏa')* used here. It is used frequently in the OT to denote the relationship that exists between two people at a deep level of mental, emotional, and volitional commitment, as between a husband and wife. Yahweh had never *known* any other people so intimately as he had known Israel (cf. Amos 3:2). Nor were those intimate commitments available to Israel with other gods. Only Yahweh could provide such a complete union of a people with their God. In all, commandments one, two, six, seven, eight, and nine are represented here. The implications are clear. Judah had rejected the covenant stipulations in her daily life. The hypocrisy of the people is clearly apparent in that, despite such an open breach of the covenant, they *come and stand before me in this house which bears my name.*[29] The expression *stand before ('āmaḏ lᵉp̄ānay)* carries overtones of submission and surrender for service. The secular parallel is of a vassal standing before his overlord in acknowledgment of the overlord's sovereignty and in submission to his overlord for whatever the overlord lays upon him. The very presence

28. Cf. v. 4.
29. See comment on v. 7 above.

of the vassal in the palace of the suzerain was filled with deep significance. It was unthinkable that a rebel vassal should go through such a form in the absence of complete allegiance.[30] The discovery of any hypocritical display of allegiance would lead to severe punishment. The hypocrisy of the people of Judah was that, despite having breached the covenant stipulations, they appeared in the presence of Yahweh their sovereign Lord and asserted their own inviolability—*We are safe!* (v. 10). They deluded themselves into thinking they were safe to continue breaking the covenant and committing the evils referred to in vv. 5–6, 9 and also referred to in v. 10 as *abominable things (tô'ēḇôṯ)*.

The result of such reckless disregard of Yahweh was that the temple (*this house*) came to be regarded as a *robbers' cave (mᵉ'āraṯ pāriṣîm)* (v. 11). The figure is an apt one. Robbers and bandits who sally forth for robbery and plunder secure for themselves a hideout in some secluded area, to which they retire for protection and safety away from the eyes of the authorities until the hue and cry dies down, only to issue forth again when the pursuit ceases, to commit fresh robberies. Yahweh's people too are law-breakers, i.e., covenant-breakers. Their misdeeds merit divine judgment. They flee to the temple for protection, thinking to be safe there, believing that participation in the formal rituals of the cult would somehow deliver them from the Judge. But the temple was no sheltering place for covenant-breakers. There was no security there from the searching eyes of Yahweh. Yahweh declares, *I myself have seen.* He was not blind; the temple would not shelter covenant-breakers. It was, in any case, not inviolable as the next verse shows.

12 At this point in his "sermon" Jeremiah introduced a vivid illustration of the fact that God is not bound either to a particular locality or to a particular structure. It was evidently a fact well known to the people of Jeremiah's day that the town of Shiloh which once housed the building where the Ark was kept was a deserted ancient site and certainly no longer the authorized place of worship. In the days of Eli the priest the worship of Yahweh was centered in Shiloh (1 Sam. 1–4). To this place people came to offer sacrifices to Yahweh, to worship, and to pray (1 Sam. 1:3), for here

30. Note that some of the Egyptian vassals in Palestine in the Amarna period (14th century B.C.) made great protestations of loyalty in letters to the pharaoh when, in fact, they were grossly disloyal, as a perusal of the Amarna correspondence will show. See *ANET,* pp. 483–490. In that case the Egyptian ruler was too weak to take action. Normally action was swift and severe in such cases.

stood the sanctuary (*hêkāl*) of Yahweh (1 Sam. 1:9), the "house of the Lord" (1 Sam. 1:24). But the place was destroyed by the Philistine army about 1050 B.C. (1 Sam. 4), a fact that has now become clear from archeological evidence.[31] That Yahweh had once *established a dwelling place for* his *name* in what was some sort of a sanctuary (*my place*) did not in any way guarantee the inviolability of the town or the sanctuary when there was *wickedness (rāʿâ)* among his people. The people of Jeremiah's day thus had before them a powerful proof that God could dispense with the Jerusalem temple in the same way he dispensed with the Shiloh temple. However valuable Ark and temple, sacrifice and psalm may be as aids to worship, these could never be accepted as a substitute for loyal obedience to Yahweh. It was a fundamental aspect of his recognition of Yahweh as sovereign Lord that the man of Israel, the man of the covenant, would observe and meticulously carry out the stipulations of the covenant. Failing that, "aids to worship" were meaningless and could be set aside. The affirmation of this principle must have seemed heresy of the worst kind to Jeremiah's hearers that day at the temple. Little wonder that the people rose up in angry protest (26:7–11).

13–15 If the wickedness of the people in Eli's day brought destruction to the sanctuary, what would happen to the people of Jeremiah's day who had *done all these things?* It was not that they had not been warned by Jermiah and a long line of prophets before him. The appeal came frequently and earnestly, but the people did not hear.[32] Yahweh called to his people but there was no answer. All loyal response seems to have been stifled.

The typical secular treaty of the time contained a brief historical resumé of past relations between the parties, with particular emphasis on the activities which the great king had undertaken for the welfare of the vassal. In gratitude for such beneficial activity on his behalf the vassal accepted the treaty stipulations, promising future obedience in gratitude for past favors. In a far more complete and wonderful way Yahweh once delivered his people from the bondage of Egypt. That was the supreme reason for Israel's response to Yahweh. At Sinai the people responded, "All that Yahweh has spoken we will do." But the descendants of that first generation

31. H. Kjaer, "The Excavation of Shiloh 1929," *JPOS* 10/2–3 (1930), pp. 87–174; W. F. Albright, "The Danish Excavations at Shiloh," *BASOR* 9, pp. 10–11.

32. The sense here of the root *šmʿ* seems to be not simply "hear" but "hear and heed," *listen*.

had so completely forgotten the saving acts of Yahweh that there was no strong motivation to obedience. Although the prophets reminded them of Yahweh's acts of redemption (cf. 2:1–3, 6–8; etc.) and of the obligations resting on each new generation (Deut. 5:3), they were met with flinty faces, deaf ears, and stubborn wills (1:8, 19; Ezek. 2:3–8; etc.). It was for this reason that Jeremiah declared that the temple (*bayiṯ, house)* in which they trusted would become like the sanctuary at Shiloh (v. 14), while the people themselves would be sent into exile, cast out of Yahweh's sight in the same way that the northern kingdom (Ephraim) had been cast out (cf. 3:6–10).

To judge from 26:1–6, the Temple Sermon ended at this point, for the material of 7:16–34 is lacking in ch. 26. For the consequences that followed on Jeremiah's startling declaration see 26:7–19.

(ii) The Cult of the Queen of Heaven (7:16–20)

16 *"And as for you, do not pray for this people, and do not offer on their behalf any entreaty or prayer, or intercede with me, for I will not listen to you.*

17 *Don't you see what they are doing in the cities of Judah and in the streets of Jerusalem?*

18 *Children gather wood, fathers kindle the fire, and the women knead dough to make cakes for the Queen of Heaven; and they pour out libation offerings to other gods in order to provoke me.*

19 *Is it me they are provoking?—Yahweh's word. Is it not their own selves, to their own shame?*

20 *Therefore, this is what the Lord Yahweh has said: See! my anger and my fury will be poured out on this place, on man and beast, on the trees of the field and the produce of the ground; and it shall burn and not be quenched."*

The short prose segment 7:16–20 is addressed to Jeremiah by Yahweh forbidding the prophet to pray for the people and drawing his attention to the worship of the Queen of Heaven which was going on in Judah. This would lead to severe judgment.

As the text now stands we have Yahweh's word addressed to Jeremiah, not to the people. This is an added reason for not including these verses in the Temple Sermon. On the other hand it is not difficult to see why these verses might have been included here since the whole of the chapter is concerned with the various activities in which Israel was involved in her "worship." But none of these was acceptable to God. The people of God, having rejected Yahweh's sovereignty, were open to every kind of compromise.

16 The oracle on the Queen of Heaven has a direct bearing on the strong rejection of sacrifice which we meet in 7:21–28. Yahweh here calls upon Jeremiah not to pray for the people, a call that was made at other times (11:14; 14:11). Such a call comes as a surprise to the reader. Presumably, the people in their deep apostasy stood in very great need of deliverance from this particular evil. It would seem from the passages we have referred to that Jeremiah went on praying, since the call to cease praying was repeated. But possibly the passage is intended to emphasize that the possibility of repentance was so remote that prayer would no longer avail. Persistent idolatry could only bring upon Judah, as a consequence, the curses of the covenant. That time had now arrived. If such was the case, Judah was in dire straits indeed. The form in which the prohibition to pray comes is very strong. *Do not pray (hiṯpallēl) for this people, and do not offer on their behalf any entreaty (rinnâ) or prayer (tepillâ), or intercede with me, for I will not listen to you.* If Jeremiah conveyed to the people anything of the seeming finality of such an instruction, it does not seem to have moved them to any response.

17–18 The evil practices which provoked such an instruction are now spelled out. In the cities of Judah and in the streets of Jerusalem the cult of the Queen of Heaven was being practiced. The reference is to the Assyro-Babylonian Astarte (Ishtar, cf. 44:17). The worship of Astarte along with other Mesopotamian gods was popular in Judah in the days of Manasseh (2 K. 21; 23:4–14). In Mesopotamia this goddess was known precisely as the Queen of Heaven (*šarrat šamē*) or the Mistress of Heaven (*bēlit šamē*). The name was still in use in the fifth century B.C. in Egypt, as the Aramaic papyri from the Jewish colony at Elephantine testify. Astarte was an astral deity, and her worship was practiced in the open (19:13; 32:29; cf. 2 K. 23:12; Zeph. 1:5). There were local expressions of her cult in Mesopotamia, Canaan, and Egypt. Perhaps, indeed, the cult of Astarte was identified with that of some Canaanite goddesses. Some aspects of the cult practices are referred to here. The children gathered wood and the fathers kindled fires while the mothers prepared cakes (*kawwānîm*[1]) to offer to the Queen of Heaven. A reference to the same practices in 44:19 indicates that the cakes bore the image of Ishtar. The offering of a *libation* or drink offering (*neseḵ*) was also part of the cult.

1. Cf. Akk. *kawānu, kamānu*. See Amos 5:26.

That the worship of the Queen of Heaven was old in Israel is clear from Amos 5:26, but one wonders whether the worship of Ishtar or some expression of the fertility goddess may not go back to Israel's earliest days (cf. 2:4–8). Whatever may have been the official religion of Israel, the women had indulged in a peculiarly women's kind of worship for centuries. Since such practices could be observed in the homes, they were not overt enough to come under condemnation. In any case the stress on the role of children and fathers (cf. 44:19) may point to the fact that all along the men connived in a practice which was in open defiance of all that Israel's official religion stood for. Apparently Josiah's enforced reformation did not reach to the women's quarters in the homes. Such worship could remain hidden by its very nature, requiring only a pinch of incense, a libation, or a cake in the shape of a woman, crescent moon, or star (all symbols of Ishtar). There is a hint that libations were poured out to *other gods* also (v. 18). All this provoked Yahweh to anger. Such practices indicate either the short-lived influence of Josiah's reform, or more likely that it had never reached to the grass roots of Israel's life.

19–20 The cult of the Queen of Heaven was a rejection of Yahweh's sole sovereignty as the supreme Lord of the covenant. Such a rejection was a provocation, but it was not only Yahweh himself who was provoked or spited (*hiḵ'îs*). The people were spiting themselves by such practices, to their own confusion. The end result would be judgment, the pouring out of Yahweh's hot anger on *this place (māqôm),* that is, on the temple in which they trusted (cf. vv. 4, 14) and upon the whole nation, man and beast, the trees of the field, the produce of the ground. Yahweh's hot anger would burn and never be quenched.

Nothing could have brought out the insincerity, the insensibility, and the incorrigibility of the nation more clearly than this alternative allegiance to which the people were devoted in a massive way. So deep-dyed were they in this evil that they had already passed beyond the possibility of repentance, a point made clear by the failure even of the destruction of Jerusalem by Nebuchadrezzar to turn them back to Yahweh in repentance. Those who fled to Egypt, taking Jeremiah with them, continued to worship the Queen of Heaven (ch. 44). It was for precisely this reason that Yahweh forbade Jeremiah to pray for the people, and in that prohibition the certainty of judgment was made clear. In the light of 7:16–20 it is easy to understand the oracle that follows in vv. 21–28.

(iii) *Obedience rather than Mere Sacrifice (7:21–28)*

21 *This is what Yahweh of Hosts, the God of Israel, has said: "Add your whole burnt offerings to your sacrifices and eat the flesh!*
22 *For in the day when I brought your fathers out of the land of Egypt I did not speak to them or give them a command concerning the details of burnt offering and sacrifice.*
23 *But this I commanded them: 'Obey my voice, and I will be your God and you shall be my people. You must live in the way I commanded you so that it may go well with you.'*
24 *But they did not listen and did not pay attention*[1] *but followed the counsel of their stubbornly wicked heart,*[2] *and went backward and not forward.*[3]
25 *From the day when your forefathers came out of the land of Egypt until this day I persistently sent*[4] *to you all my servants the prophets again and again;*[5]
26 *yet they did not listen to me and paid no heed, but were obstinate*[6] *and more evil than their fathers.*
27 *And when you say all these things they will not listen to you. You will call to them but they will not answer.*
28 *Then you will say to them, This is the nation that would not obey the voice of Yahweh its God nor accept correction.*[7]
Faithfulness has perished,
It has gone from their lips."

The oracle preserved here is an example of the so-called "prophetic indictment" of the sacrificial institutions (cf. 6:20; 1 Sam. 15:22; Ps. 51:18–19 [Eng. 16–17]; Isa. 1:4–15; Hos. 6:6; Amos 5:21–24; Mic. 6:6–8). As the material is arranged in ch. 7 there is a certain logical development in the argument. The temple in which the people trusted was a mere cover for every kind of ethical and legal misde-

1. Lit. "did not turn their ears."
2. The Hebrew text seems to include two variant readings: "They walked in the counsels of, in the stubbornness of their wicked heart." The LXX reads "they walked in the counsel of their wicked hearts" and omits "stubbornness." See A. Rahlfs, *Septuaginta* (1952), *ad loc.*
3. MT reads "They were (or with a few mss., "they went") backward and not forward." J. Bright, *Jeremiah,* pp. 54, 57, proposes "they got worse instead of better," a neat, dynamic equivalent.
4. Lit. "rising early and sending"; cf. 25:4; 26:5; 29:19.
5. MT has one word, "today." Syr. repeats the word, "day day," i.e., "daily" or "regularly."
6. Lit. "they hardened their neck."
7. "This is the nation . . . correction" is lacking in Syriac.

meanor and would therefore be destroyed (vv. 1–15). Alongside the temple practices was the deep-rooted worship of the Queen of Heaven which demonstrated a fundamental insincerity in the nation (vv. 16–20) and was a symptom of the people's refusal to accept the sovereignty of Yahweh and his will. In such circumstances, the whole sacrificial system had become meaningless to Yahweh (vv. 21–28). It was never his intention that either the temple or the sacrifice should become an empty form.

The logic of this argument, however, does not necessarily mean that we have before us here a continuous sermon. Rather we have an arrangement in which the theme of cultic abuses provides a basis for collecting several separate oracles together into a single literary unit. It may be that the separate oracles were delivered in the same general period. But they were brought together subsequently into what appears to be a continuous address. It is not impossible that Jeremiah himself may have done a certain amount of rearranging or coalescing of his messages (36:32). But it is just as likely that editors after his death undertook a lot of this work.

21 It is *Yahweh of Hosts, the God of Israel* who makes the startling pronouncement: *Add your whole burnt offerings to your* (other) *sacrifices and eat the flesh.* The *burnt offerings ('ōlôṯ)* were entirely burned on the altar of sacrifice. The noun is a derivative of the verb *'ālâ,* "go up," and provides a vivid description of an offering ascending as smoke and flame from the altar (Lev. 1, etc.). The other *sacrifices (zeḇaḥ),* or parts of them, were eaten by the worshippers (Lev. 3; 7:11–18; 22:18–23, 27–30; etc.). But the command here treats all sacrifices the same, since God does not care any longer which way the ritual is carried out. He rejects whole burnt offerings and other sacrifices alike (cf. 6:20). The essential ingredient of any and every sacrifice, namely, an attitude of obedience to Yahweh's covenant on the part of the worshippers, was lacking. The point is developed in the verses that follow.

22–23 The reference point is the time of the Exodus when, following Yahweh's mighty acts of deliverance from Egypt, Israel accepted him as their sovereign Lord, entered into his covenant, and accepted the covenant obligations with the words, "All that Yahweh has spoken we will do" (Exod. 19:8). A reading of Exod. 19:3–8 makes it clear that the first step in the covenant ceremony was Yahweh's demand for the unconditional acceptance of the covenant. The Decalog is spelled out in Exod. 20:1–17, but at no point is the narrative concerned with cultic details. It was only after the covenant had been ratified (24:1–8) that the cultic details of the tabernacle, the priesthood, and the sacrifices were declared. The last part of v. 22 and the first part of v. 23 both contain the noun *dāḇār* in a kind of poetic parallelism. The passage is in prose, but prose and poetry are very close to one another in elevated language. The repetition of *dāḇār* may have been deliberate, in which case the phrase in v. 22 *'al diḇrê 'ôlâ wāzāḇaḥ* may be translated *concerning the details of burnt offerings and sacrifice*. That was to come later. But the passage does not amount to a rejection of sacrifice as such. Jeremiah was really indicating that the order of revelation was indicative of the relative value of obedience and cultic observances. What he was telling his contemporaries was that God was indifferent to the way Israel brought their sacrifices, even if they committed the cultic enormity of eating the whole burnt offering as though it were a peace offering. Where the basic requisite of obedience was lacking, God refused to regard what went on in the temple as a true sacrifice. Here then is the divine demand *obey my voice*. The Hebrew for *obey* is *šāma' bᵉ*, "hear into." There is a small group of verbs in Hebrew which require the preposition *bᵉ* before the following noun.[8] The preposition may be regarded as emphasizing the personal commitment of the subject to the object. One may "hear" a voice in a purely physical sense or one may commit oneself to what is heard, that is, *obey*. God required of Israel deep personal commitment to his voice. Israel was commanded: *Obey my voice, and I will be your God and you shall be my people* (cf. Deut. 26:16–19). The condition which made possible the profound relationship *your God . . . my people* was obedience. All else was secondary.

Comparison should be made between this passage and other OT passages like Isa. 1:10–17; Hos. 6:6; Amos 5:21–25; Mic. 6:1–8. It is unlikely that any one of these passages is to be understood as a clear rejection of the sacrificial system as such or as a statement that Israel did not practice sacrifice in the wilderness. Rather, such statements served to stress the point that God's essential demand was the keeping of the covenant stipulations and not the performance of rituals. Any hope of God's blessing for the future depended on their walking in the way that God *commanded* them, that is, the blessings of the covenant were available only to those who walked

8. Among these are "hear" (*šāma' bᵉ*); "choose" (*bāḥar bᵉ*); "be attached to" (*ḥāšaq bᵉ*); "take pleasure in" (*ḥāp̄ēṣ bᵉ*); "cling to" (*dāḇaq bᵉ*); "wish" (*rāṣâ bᵉ*).

(conducted themselves) in accordance with the demands of the covenant.

24 A further historical memory is brought to the argument. The people did not obey Yahweh despite their declaration at Sinai, but they followed their own counsels and their own stubborn wills. As a result *they went backward and not forward,* that is, "they grew worse instead of better" (Bright). Deliberate rejection of the covenant obligations by one who rejects the covenant and the Lord of the covenant inevitably leads to deterioration.

25–26 The concern of Yahweh that Israel should be faithful to him and be obedient to the covenant obligations is now declared. Hardly had the forefathers of Jeremiah's contemporaries accepted the covenant than they began to be disobedient. In Jeremiah's view disobedience was as old as the Exodus and no new thing in Israel. Yahweh sent his servants the prophets with urgency and persistence (lit. "rising early and sending"). It was all in vain, for Israel did not heed Yahweh nor pay attention, but with willful obstinacy (lit. RSV "they stiffened their neck") they outdid their fathers in wickedness. The people of Jeremiah's generation were thus the inheritors of a long tradition of disobedience. Little wonder that Jeremiah declared the imminence of divine judgment.

27–28 The divine word had been given. It was Jeremiah's responsibility to declare it. It was part of his understanding, and certainly part of his experience, that the people might not listen (1:8, 17–19). Prophets before and after him had the same experience (cf. Ezek. 2:3–8; 3:4–11). But an audience that had already rejected the covenant would neither hearken nor respond (*answer*). Jeremiah's description of Israel as a *nation (gôy)*[9] *that would not obey (šāma' b*^{e}*) the voice of Yahweh its God nor accept correction* is an apt and succinct description of covenant-breakers. The oracle concludes with a poetic phrase:

Faithfulness ('^{e}*mûnâ) has perished,*
It has gone from their lips.[10]

The term *'*^{e}*mûnâ, faithfulness,* is a characteristic of men who keep the covenant. Jeremiah's contemporary Habakkuk urged the people to exercise this quality in the face of the Chaldean menace (Hab. 2:4). Jeremiah had been commanded earlier to search for a man who

9. Hardly a complimentary title since it was used more commonly of non-Israelite peoples.
10. Lit. "it has been cut off from their lips."

showed this quality (5:1, 3). His conclusion here is that this quality has *perished ('āḇaḏ).*

With these significant words Jeremiah concludes his comments on the theme that Yahweh's primary demand was obedience, not sacrifice. The point has been often discussed and the proposal has been made that we have here, and in the parallel passages in Amos, Hosea, Micah, Isaiah, and elsewhere, a categorical rejection of the sacrificial system. Such a view would seem to be an extreme one. The exilic and postexilic prophets looked for reforms in the administration of the rituals of sacrifice but did not teach that it was to be abandoned. Ezekiel looked for a restoration of the temple and its cultic officials and rituals (Ezek. 40–47). Haggai, Zechariah, and Malachi spoke of the temple and its officials, although Malachi was distressed about the attitudes of the priests and expressed the opinion that it would be better to close the doors of the temple (Mal. 1:10). However, the prophetic acceptance of the sacrificial system was not limited to postexilic times. The preexilic prophets, like Jeremiah, denounced a perverted kind of worship in which the liturgy had ceased to give the covenantal setting of worship its proper place. Where Yahweh was acknowledged as Israel's sovereign Lord, cultic practices were part of Israelite covenantal worship.[11] That there was a long tradition of sacrificial worship closely allied to the covenant is clear from the book of Deuteronomy, where the central sanctuary played an important role (e.g., Deut. 12).[12] Moreover, the attempts made to reform the practices in the temple and to eliminate Canaanite practices point to a concern to maintain the purity of a form of worship which had ancient authority. Thus a strong critic of the current system, Hosea, nevertheless includes among his list of the judgments that would befall Israel the following:

> They shall not pour libations of wine to Yahweh,
> And they shall not please him with their sacrifices.
> (Hos. 9:4)

These words at least suggest that Hosea believed that the loss of

11. See W. Brueggemann, *Tradition for Crisis* (1968). Note ch. 4, "The Prophets and the Covenant Institution," pp. 91–105, for a helpful discussion of the point.

12. It is now widely acknowledged that Deuteronomy has behind it an ancient covenantal tradition reaching back to the days of Moses. See discussion in J. A. Thompson, *Deuteronomy* (1974), pp. 35–42, 47–68, 76f. Even if the final date of compilation was as late as the seventh century, the book was accepted as the book of the law of the Lord. Much of its content had ancient roots.

libations and sacrifices was in the nature of divine judgment, not because Yahweh disapproved of these, but because he approved of them. Zephaniah (3:10) sees the dispersed ones coming to bring offerings (*minḥâ*). These are, to be sure, not sacrifices but gifts, but they were part of a total system. Jeremiah himself seems to give approval to the bringing of sacrifices when he discusses the consequences of obedience in the matter of keeping the sabbath. "People will come from the cities of Judah and from round about Jerusalem . . . bringing burnt offerings and sacrifices, cereal offerings and incense, and bringing also thank offerings to the house of Yahweh" (17:26). Similarly the promise is made that when the righteous Branch springs forth for David, there will never lack a Levitical priest to offer burnt offerings, burn cereal offerings, and make sacrifices (33:18). Isaiah likewise had a vision of the day when Egypt would worship with sacrifices and burnt offerings and make vows to the Lord (Isa. 19:21).

It would seem, therefore, that to affirm that the prophets rejected the whole sacrificial system is to go beyond the evidence. It was not the system as such that was rejected but the operation of the system, which divorced sacrifices from obedience and took them out of the covenantal setting in which they found their whole rationale.

(iv) *Sinful Deeds in the Valley of Hinnom (7:29–34)*

29 *"Cut off your hair and throw it away,*
Take up a lament on the heights;
For Yahweh has rejected
And abandoned the generation with which he is angry."

30 *"For the people of Judah have done what is evil in my eyes—Yahweh's word. They have placed their detestable cult objects*[1] *in the house that bears my name and have defiled it.*

31[2] *They have built the high place*[3] *of Topheth in the valley of Ben-hinnom in order to burn their sons and daughters in the fire—something I never commanded nor did it ever enter my thoughts.*

32 *Therefore, look, days are coming—Yahweh's word—when it shall no longer be called Topheth or the valley of Ben-hinnom, but the valley of Slaughter, for they will bury in Topheth till there is no room left.*

33 *Then the corpses of this people will become food for the birds of the air and the wild beasts, with no one to scare them away.*

1. Heb. *šiqqûṣ*.
2. Verses 31–33; cf. 19:5–7.
3. MT has plur. *bāmôṯ* but LXX and Targ. have singular.

34 *I will banish the sounds of joy and gladness, the voice of the bride and bridegroom from the cities of Judah and the streets of Jerusalem, for the land will become a desolate waste."*

Jeremiah's attack on other false cults continues in this section dealing with false religion in Judah. Some commentators see 7:29–8:3 as a single unit.[4] Others regard it as comprising two oracles,[5] and still others regard it as a collection of several short utterances of Jeremiah.[6] Certainly as we have it in its final form it is woven into one piece, which constitutes an attack on further cultic disorders and announces the shame of Judah and the awful judgment that is coming.[7] The words are addressed to Judah as a whole, personified as a woman.[8] A problem of translation occurs here, namely, whether to regard the verb forms as referring to a more distant past or to a nearer past. If the reference is to the more distant past, then it could go back to the time of Manasseh when detestable cult objects (*šiqqûṣîm*) were placed in the temple. In that case the translation would be "They placed their abominations in the house."[9] On the other hand if the practice was more recent, representing a resurgence of earlier apostasies in the days of Jehoiakim, the translation would be "They have placed their detestable cult objects in the house."[10] If this latter translation is accepted, then Jeremiah was a witness to unholy practices in the Hinnom Valley in his own day. There is certainly evidence for such practices in the days of Manasseh (2 K. 21:5–6; 23:10). Josiah's reform cleared out cult objects which remained from those days (2 K. 23:4–20). It would appear that some pagan practices were current in Jehoiakim's day although the books of Kings and Chronicles do not refer to them. But Ezek. 8 provides a picture of such activities in the days of Zedekiah. The cult practices referred to in 7:29–34 form part of the whole disgraceful picture of Judah's rejection of her covenant with Yahweh. In a time of relaxation under Jehoiakim, when people openly indulged in the cult of the Queen of Heaven (vv. 16–20 above), the heart of the

4. H. L. Ellison, "The Prophecy of Jeremiah, part XIII," *EQ* 34/2 (1962), p. 98; W. Rudolph, *Jeremia,* p. 55.
5. J. Bright, *Jeremiah,* p. 58.
6. G. P. Couturier, "Jeremiah," *JBC,* p. 310.
7. The imperatives in 7:29 are 2nd fem. singular.
8. AV and RV add the expression "O Jerusalem" in 7:29. The words are not in the Hebrew text and tend to give a wrong idea.
9. So H. L. Ellison, *loc. cit.,* p. 97.
10. As in AV, RV, RSV; W. Rudolph, *Jeremia,* p. 54; A. Weiser, *Das Buch des Propheten Jeremia,* p. 74.

people was shown to be rebellious still, and the generation of Jeremiah merely shared in the sin and the guilt of their forefathers. Hence the nation as a whole was under judgment. The forefathers and the living generation were joined together, at least symbolically, in the judgment Jeremiah proclaimed.

29[11] For their sins the people must *take up a lament (qînâ)*. The cutting off of the hair was a symbol of grief (Job 1:20; Mic. 1:16). The Hebrew text reads literally "Cut off your crown (*nezer*)." The hair was looked on as, in a sense, a diadem. To cut off the hair was to bring down Israel's pride. But there may be here an overtone of something else. The long hair of the Nazirite was a sign of his consecration to Yahweh (Num. 6:2–8). The removal of the hair signified an abandonment of his consecration (Judg. 16:15–22). In Jeremiah's view, Israel, now represented only by Judah and Jerusalem, had abandoned her consecration to Yahweh and was not worthy to wear the crown of her long hair. That the lamentation was to be made on the bare heights where so many of Israel's evils had been committed (2:20; 3:2, 21; etc.) was appropriate. Yahweh had *rejected (mā'as)* and *abandoned (nāṭaš)* the brood (*generation*) of people who had merited his wrath. The reasons for this are delineated in the verses that follow.

30–31 The placing of abominations *(šiqqûṣîm)—detestable cult objects*—in *the house that bears my name,* the temple, was a supreme act of defiance and a gross gesture of sacrilege, whether this had been done recently or in earlier years. The act could only serve to defile (*ṭammē'*) the temple and deny the sole sovereignty of Yahweh, Israel's sovereign Lord (cf. 32:34). It is of some interest that the word "abomination" *(šiqqûṣ),* which occurs some twenty-eight times in the OT, refers in most cases to some kind of object or cult image, although in some passages the term may refer to the whole cultic activity which included overt acts performed in the associated worship. Clearly, such objects were not mere ornaments but carried with them associated rituals, many of which were linked with such things as ritual prostitution and other fertility rites. Israel has revealed her deep degradation by introducing into the house of her God such unspeakable offenses to Yahweh's holiness and to her own consecration (Exod. 19:5, 6).

11. Verse 29 is poetry in contrast to the rest of the material which is prose. For this reason it has sometimes been regarded as a brief oracle of mourning which once had an independent existence but was woven in here, appropriately enough.

But there were other practices than those which Jeremiah found in the temple. In the *valley of Ben-hinnom,* which lay just south of the city, they built a *high place of Topheth.* The name Topheth may derive from an Aramaic word *tĕpaṯ,* "fireplace," while the name Ben-hinnom may derive from a former owner of the valley. The Hebrew vocalization of *Tĕpaṯ* into *Tōpeṯ*[12] was probably a deliberate change in which the vowels of the word *bōšeṯ,* "shame," were transferred to other consonants in order to emphasize the shameful character of the altar in question. This high place was the scene of pagan rites, which included human sacrifices, during the reign of Manasseh (2 K. 23:10). The practice of human sacrifice was known among the Amorites and others and was one of the principal rites in the worship of the god Molech. It was forbidden under the Mosaic Law (Lev. 18:21; 20:2–5). The suggestion seems to be conveyed in the last clause of v. 31 that the people imagined that such human sacrifices were acceptable to Yahweh (cf. Mic. 6:7). To be sure, all the first-born were to be consecrated to Yahweh (Exod. 13:2; 22:29b; 34:19; Num. 3:13; 8:17), but not by offering up children as human sacrifices. Yahweh had *never commanded* this evil thing.

32–34 For such evil deeds the people themselves, and not merely their children, would be slaughtered by the invading enemy. No longer would they speak of Topheth or the valley of Ben-hinnom, but of the *valley of Slaughter (gê' hah^{a}rēgâ).* In that day Topheth would be so full of corpses that many bodies would not be buried at all but would lie in the open for the scavengers of the air and the earth to dispose of. For the body to remain unburied and to become food for carrion birds and scavenging beasts was an unspeakable horror. Even a criminal's corpse was to be buried (Deut. 21:23). It was an unthinkable thing for a man to die without someone to bury him (14:16; Ps. 79:3). There are numerous OT passages which show that men were "buried with their fathers" (1 K. 14:31; 15:24; 22:50; etc.). The tragic irony of Jeremiah's picture is that the site of Judah's illegal sanctuary was to become the place either of their burial or of the desecration of their corpses.

A natural consequence of all this would be that all signs of normal life, the sounds[13] of mirth and gladness and the voices of

12. LXX has *Tapheth.* See also on 19:6.

13. Heb. *qôl* means either "sound" or "voice"; in v. 34 it is used in both senses. Cf. Gen. 3:8, "They heard the sound (*qôl*) of God walking in the garden."

bride and bridegroom, would disappear, and the land would be a *desolate waste* (*ḥorbâ*).[14]

(v) Astral Worship and its Awful Punishment (8:1–3)

1 *"At that time—Yahweh's word—they will take the bones of the kings of Judah and the bones of officials, together with the bones of the priests and prophets and the citizens of Jerusalem, from their graves.*
2 *And they will spread them out before the sun and the moon and all the heavenly host whom they loved and served and followed after and consulted, and before whom they bowed in worship. They will not be buried but will become dung on the ground.*
3 *And death will be preferred to life by all the survivors that are left out of this evil family in every place*[1] *to which I have driven them—the word of Yahweh of Hosts."*

There is evidence in these verses of one other act of apostasy, the worship of astral deities. The practice was common in the days of Manasseh (2 K. 21:3; cf. 23:4) but seems to have attracted the attention of the people of Israel both before and after Manasseh's time (cf. Ezek. 8:16).

1–2 In the day of judgment, the bones of those who were fortunate enough to be given burial would be removed from their graves and spread abroad.[2] The invaders who brought divine judgment would add insult to military defeat by opening the graves of kings, nobles (*śārîm*), priests, prophets, and ordinary citizens, and throwing their bones out *before the sun and the moon and all the heavenly host* (stars). The language of the prophet is derisive. These astral deities whom the people *loved and served,* whom they *followed after,* whom they *consulted* and worshipped, would look down on their scattered bones with cold indifference and unconcern. But because the exile of the population of Judah was part of the total picture of judgment, there would be few if any survivors to return to the scene to gather up the bones for burial. In such a case the bones would lie as *dung* (fertilizer, Heb. *dōmen*) on the surface of the ground.

14. Cf. Horeb in the Exodus story, Exod. 3:1; 17:6; Deut. 1:6, 4:10; 5:2; 9:8; etc. In these passages the reference is to a place without settled inhabitants or agricultural or urban activities. The picture is not of a desert waste. In fact, there were nomadic peoples in the area.

1. MT repeats "that are left." Omit with LXX and Syriac.

2. Even in modern times, the opening up of graves and the throwing about of the bones of the departed is practiced as a mark of extreme contempt. In recent wars in the Middle East such desecration and insult were perpetrated.

3 The final touch in this grim portrayal is that such survivors as remained from *this evil family*[3] in the various places to which they had been driven as exiles would deem death preferable to life, either because circumstances were so bad in foreign lands, or because the memory of those last days of Judah's downfall was too much to bear. The lot of survivors would be even more miserable than the fate of those who perished (2 K. 25:5–7; cf. Ps. 137).

2. AN INCORRIGIBLE PEOPLE AND THEIR FATE (8:4–10:25)

(i) *Blindly Complacent and Heading to Ruin (8:4–12)*

4 *"And you shall say to them: This is what Yahweh has said:*
Does one fall down and not get up?
Does one turn aside and not turn back?
5 *Then why does this people turn away*[1]
In perpetual backsliding?
They cling to deceit,
They refuse to return.
6 *I listened carefully;*[2]
They did not speak in such terms.[3]
No one is sorry for his wickedness
And says, 'What have I done?'
Every one of them turns away in headlong career
Like a horse storming into battle.
7 *Even the stork in the sky*
Knows her seasons.
The dove, the swallow, and the thrush
Observe the time for migration;
But my people do not know
The law of Yahweh.
8 *How can you say, 'We are wise;*
We have the law of Yahweh'?
But look, the deceiving pen of the scribes
Has turned it[4] *into a falsehood.*

3. That is, Judah, who at this stage represented all that remained of the former Israel.

1. Read *šôḇāḇ hā'ām hazzeh,* omitting the final *h* of *šôḇᵉḇâ* as a dittography. Also omit "Jerusalem" on the next line with LXX. There may have been a variant "Why has Jerusalem turned back?"
2. MT uses two verbs, "I paid attention and I heard." LXX suggests two imperatives, "Pay attention and listen."
3. MT *kēn,* "thus," is taken to mean: "(they did not speak) in terms of returning."
4. Vocalize MT *'āśâ* as *'āśāh,* "has made it."

9 *The wise are put to shame,*
They are stunned and trapped.
For look! they have rejected the word of Yahweh,
So what sort of wisdom is there?
10 *Therefore I will give their wives to others,*
Their fields to new owners.
For from the least to the greatest[5]
Everyone is greedy for gain.
The prophet and the priest,
Each one of them practices fraud.
11 *They dress the fracture of my daughter—my people*
Superficially and say 'All is well!
All is well!' There is nothing well.
12 *Are they ashamed that they have practiced abominations?*
No! They are not in the least ashamed.
They don't know how to blush.
Therefore they will fall among those who fall;
In the day of their reckoning they will be brought down[6]*—*
Yahweh has spoken."

One of the literary questions that is raised by the book of Jeremiah is that of the structure. On what basis did the editors arrange the material? Some blocks of material are relatively easy to isolate because of a unified theme, e.g., the chapters which gather together the oracles against the nations (chs. 46–51), or the section 21:11–23:8 dealing with the royal house of Judah.[7] But the section 8:4–10:25 seems to be a miscellaneous collection, although the twin themes of Israel's stubborn and incurable rebellion, and the inevitable doom which will befall her, appear again and again. The section is mostly poetic in form and is therefore generally accepted as authentic. The material can be generally dated to the early years of Jehoiakim's reign, that is, about 605 B.C. Commentators have striven to separate out the individual poems or complexes of poems, the fragmentary sayings or the more complete units.[8] This can be done with some degree of assurance if we hold the view that a group of verses which focus on a particular topic constitute a single unit. That may or may not be true, since speakers and writers are always at liberty to move from topic to topic within one given utterance.

5. LXX lacks the material from this line up to v. 12.
6. Lit. "they will be stumbled."
7. See the Introduction, "The Book of Jeremiah: Structure," pp. 27–32.
8. Compare the units proposed by the following: J. Bright, *Jeremiah,* pp. 60–80; G. P. Couturier, "Jeremiah" in *JBC,* p. 303; W. Rudolph, *Jeremia,* pp. 55–71; the Jerusalem Bible; R. K. Harrison, *Jeremiah and Lamentations,* pp. 88–94; etc.

But the materials of these chapters have clearly been edited and presented with the editor's unity imposed on them.

4–5 Jeremiah used the device of dwelling on the irrational conduct of Israel in several passages. At times he contrasted the behavior of Yahweh's people with that of the nations (2:10–11). In the present passage the prophet finds a contrast in nature. He takes up again the verb *šûḇ,* "turn" or "return."

These verses provide a good example of the "disputation" form (cf. 2:32; 3:1–5; 13:23; 18:14–15). There is a triple sequence of questions introduced respectively by the particles *ha-, 'im,* and *maddûa',* followed by an accusation.[9]

The question is raised as to whether it is possible for a people to turn aside from their God and never repent. In v. 7 it will be stated that this is entirely possible. Normally when men fall they rise. When they *turn aside (šûḇ)* they *turn back (šûḇ)* again. People in life learn from their mistakes. It would seem to be a built-in, intuitive response in many situations.[10] The point is demonstrated in many areas of nature (cf. vv. 6b, 7).

Now the question is asked, *Why does this people turn away (šōḇēḇ) in perpetual backsliding (mᵉšuḇâ)?* The affirmation is here made that Israel's backsliding is, in fact, permanent. In a rebellious and obstinate fashion the people *cling to deceit (tarmîṯ)* and *refuse to return.* Three times in this verse derivatives of the root *šûḇ* are used.

6 Although Jeremiah listened closely (lit. "gave heed and listened") there was not a man who uttered words of repentance for his evil or expressed regret for what he had done. It is the picture we have seen in 5:1–3. In willful fashion each man *turns away (šûḇ) in headlong career like a horse storming*[11] *into battle.* The headlong plunge is no gentle turning aside but a deliberate and vigorous action—a vivid picture.

7 Here Jeremiah turns to nature for a powerful illustration. God has built into the birds of nature an intuitive knowledge of *seasons* (*mô'ᵃḏîm*) and their *time* (*'ēṯ*), and they respond automati-

9. See B. O. Long, "The Stylistic Components of Jeremiah 3:1–5," *ZAW* 88 (1976), pp. 386–390.

10. Amos condemned the surrounding peoples for acting contrary to certain basic, universally valid rules of life known even among those whom Israel would call the heathen. See Amos 1:3–2:3.

11. Heb. *mᵉrûṣâ* derives from the verb *rûṣ,* "run," and denotes the place to which a man runs. J. Bright, *Jeremiah,* p. 60 aptly translates "Each of them plunges ahead."

cally to the movements of nature. By contrast Israel did not know the *law (mišpāṭ:* rule, ordinance, regulation[12]) *of Yahweh.* Yahweh had an order for his people; but Israel, unlike the birds of nature, was insensitive and unresponsive to that order. The tragedy was that while birds followed faithfully their instinctive urges to migrate, the people of Israel refused to respond to the promptings of Yahweh's covenant love. There are some problems in the identification of the birds of v. 7. The *ḥᵃsîḏâ* is the *stork,* the *tōr* the *dove* or turtle-dove, the *sîs* the *swallow* or swift, and the *'āḡûr* possibly a crane or a *thrush.*[13] But this uncertainty makes no difference to the main point at issue. It was an incredible thing that God's covenant people could behave so unnaturally toward their Creator, the sovereign Lord of the covenant.

The verb *know (yāḏa')* carries a deeper significance than that of intellectual knowledge. There is something of personal commitment at the emotional and volitional level as well. All the prophets unite in indicating that Israel was aware of her covenant relationship with Yahweh. That was written into her history and her traditions. Even her cry in 7:4, "The temple of Yahweh, the temple of Yahweh, the temple of Yahweh," bore witness to that. That being so, her present course could only have been due to her willful unfaithfulness to Yahweh and her rejection of the covenant.

The discussion about Israel's unnatural and incomprehensible behavior leads directly into a short comment about Israel's claim to be wise. Though it is linked in thought with 8:4–7 it may have been originally a separate piece addressed to the spiritual leaders of the nation.

8 The cultic officials in Jerusalem maintained that they were *wise (ḥāḵām)* and that the *law of Yahweh* was with them. Such a claim was made in the face of men like Jeremiah who brought another word from the Lord, which they rejected. The *law of Yahweh,* which was in their possession and of which they claimed to be the legitimate interpreters, was no doubt some written law, possibly a form of the book of Deuteronomy or some form of the ancient

12. The term *mišpāṭ* has a variety of meanings. In 1 Sam. 10:25 Samuel referred to the rights *(mišpāṭ)* and duties of kingship. He spoke also of the ways *(mišpāṭ)* of the king that the people were seeking (1 Sam. 8:11). A *mišpāṭ* is anything decreed by God, whether the instincts of migratory birds or the guidance provided for human beings, particularly for Yahweh's people.

13. The various lexicons should be consulted. Many of the biblical terms for birds, animals, plants, etc., are of uncertain meaning.

covenant law, which seems to have been the book found in the temple (2 K. 22:8–13). But perhaps other bodies of written law were in existence. Their confidence in the written page prevented them from accepting the word of Yahweh spoken through the prophets. The reference to *scribes (sôpēr)* is of particular interest. This is the first reference in the OT to scribes as a special class. According to 1 Chr. 2:55 these seem to have been organized on the basis of families or guilds. They were active in the time of Josiah, according to 2 Chr. 34:13. However, they may have been active at a much earlier date. How otherwise could the official records of the kingdoms of Israel and Judah have been kept and how could the Torah, or such parts of it as existed at the time, have been written? It would seem from the present verse that the scribes already had some kind of teaching function, since their *deceiving pen* (*'ēṭ šeqer*) had turned the law of God *into a falsehood (laššeqer)*.

9 The contrast is now drawn sharply. *The word of Yahweh* is set over against the law of Yahweh. The law of Yahweh was shut up within a document, which no doubt held within it the word of Yahweh also. But the word of Yahweh was a living thing, and was ongoing. God's servant Jeremiah brought other aspects of the word of Yahweh which the wise men rejected. To imagine that the full knowledge of Yahweh's will was locked up in the law could only result in the wise men being brought to shame, and being dismayed and trapped. Of what use was the wisdom claimed by Israel's wise men?

10–12 There are a number of parallels between these verses and 6:12–15.[14] This suggests either that Jeremiah had a number of well-tried phrases or that we have represented here some well-known material that was current among preachers of Jeremiah's type. In the coming judgment the people's *fields* (*śāḏeh*) would be taken by others and their wives would be given to other men. The wickedness that was rampant was to be found in every class, young or old, ordinary citizens, prophets, and priests. Greed characterized them all. The spiritual leaders, the prophets, and the priests dealt in *fraud (šeqer),* and had nothing to offer a broken people but empty assurances that all was well when the nation was sick. And were they ashamed that they acted thus? Not at all, for they neither felt shame nor knew how to blush. It was the end. The question had been

14. See commentary at 6:12–15. This pericope is missing at this point in LXX. The repetition here may be due to the key word *hōḇîšû* in vv. 9 and 12.

answered. Could men reach a stage of apostasy where they would never repent? Yes they could, and Judah had reached that point. Now they would fall among the fallen[15] and go down on the day of Yahweh's visitation.

(ii) No Grapes on the Vine (8:13–17)

13 *"I would have gathered their harvest*[1]*—Yahweh's word—*
But there are no grapes on the vine,
Not a fig on the fig tree.
Even the leaves have withered."[2]
14 *"Why are we sitting still?*
Band together! Let us run
To the fortified towns;
Let us perish there,
For Yahweh our God has condemned us to perish;
He has given us poison to drink
Because we have sinned against him.
15 *We hoped for peace,*
No good came;
For a time of healing,
But see, it is terror.
16 *From Dan the snorting of his horses is heard.*
At the sound of the neighing of his stallions
The whole land quakes.
They have come to devour the whole of our land,
City and citizens alike."

15. The expression which refers to the fallen reads lit. "They shall fall among the falling ones." The reference is to those who fall in battle. In the day of divine judgment (which turned out to be the fall of Jerusalem before Nebuchadrezzar) men would be slain and fall down in the battle for Jerusalem. Jeremiah's threat here is that the wise men, the prophets, and the priests who unashamedly held out false hope to the people would be caught up in the holocaust and would fall before the conqueror's sword in the same way as the warriors.

1. MT reads *'āsōp̱ '^{a}sîp̱ēm.* By revocalizing we preserve the consonantal text to read *'e'^{e}sōp̱ '^{a}sîp̱ām,* "I will gather their harvest" (cf. LXX), or *'āsōp̱ 'ōs^{e}p̱ēm,* "I will thoroughly harvest them," or *'^{e}sōp̱ '^{a}sîp̱ām,* "gather their harvest."
2. The last colon, omitted here, is obscure. MT reads lit. "And I gave to them. They shall pass them by." LXX omits. RSV has "What I gave them has passed away from them"; GNB "Therefore I have allowed outsiders to take over the land." If we take "gave" to mean "allowed" or "permitted" and regard the 3rd person plur. of the verb as referring to some attacking foe, we may be near to a solution. The Jerusalem Bible translates, "I have brought them ravagers to ravage them." Cf. W. Rudolph, *BHS, ad loc.* This is based on a metathesis of consonants and proposed haplography. He reads *m^{e}ḇa'^{a}rîm ûḇi'^{a}rûm.* There is no textual support for this. Many mss. read *ya'aḇ^{e}rûm,* "they destroyed them." We have not attempted a translation.

17 *"Watch out! I am sending among you*
Poisonous snakes
That cannot be charmed away.
They will bite you and you will not recover[3]*—Yahweh's word."*

In vv. 13–17 we have a composite unit with a brief reference to the foe from the north (v. 16) and a soliloquy spoken by the people (vv. 14–15). Yahweh's words (vv. 13 and 17) enclose the soliloquy.

The deep tragedy of the whole situation is spelled out in vivid pictures drawn from agriculture. The failure of crops and the arrival of poisonous snakes among the people were apt symbols of divine judgment for a predominantly agricultural people.

13 Yahweh goes forth among his people to gather his harvest (cf. 5:10; 6:9). But like an unproductive farm neither grapes nor figs appear on the plants but only withered leaves. The image of the vine, which appeared first in 2:21 where a choice vine is pictured as becoming a degenerate, wild vine, and appeared again in 6:9 where Jeremiah is pictured as gleaning the vine as a grape-gatherer, now appears a third time. But by now the vine has become completely fruitless. Such is the natural progression of a people who reject their covenant. The text at the close of the verse is uncertain.[4]

14–16 The possible reference to an attacking foe in v. 13 seems to find support from the description in v. 14 of the reaction of the people: *Why are we sitting still? Band together! Let us run to the fortified towns; Let us perish there.* It is the cry of men in desperation. Even though the men of Judah proposed steps for self-protection, it would be in vain. Yahweh had determined doom for them, symbolized as a draught of poisoned water. The reason was that they had sinned against their sovereign Lord. The empty words of v. 11, "Peace, peace," prove false. What use to hope for peace when no good came of it, or for healing when terror struck them? All they heard was the din of rumbling chariots in the distance. The end was at hand.

Here we meet the foe from the north, already encountered several times in earlier chapters. *Dan* lay at the most northerly limit of Israel near the headwaters of the Jordan (1 K. 4:25). Armies coming from the east would descend from the hills above the Jordan (the

3. This latter phrase is transferred from v. 18 (*BHS*). The difficult *maḇlîḡîṯî* is revocalized and slightly emended to *mibbᵉlî gᵉhōṯ,* "without recovery," with LXX.
4. See textual note.

modern Golan Heights) not far from Dan, so that Dan would be the first town to announce the arrival of an enemy force. In recent years the site of Dan has been excavated. Among other important finds was evidence for some kind of sanctuary with an altar (cf. 1 K. 12:29; 2 K. 10:29; Amos 8:14).[5] The impression is conveyed that the foe is numerous, for the very *snorting of his horses* and the *neighing of his stallions* causes the whole land to quake. Their purpose is clear—to devour the whole land, its towns and its inhabitants.

17 As in v. 13 we have a word from Yahweh. The words of the people (vv. 14–16) are bracketed by vv. 13 and 17, the first using the picture of crop-harvesting, and v. 17 referring to the coming judgment as the arrival of *poisonous snakes*[6] which cannot be charmed away. There may be a reminiscence here of Num. 21:6–9, where fiery serpents were sent by Yahweh to bring judgment on his people. However, although there was deliverance from serpents in the days of Moses, there would be none on this occasion.

(iii) The Prophet's Passionate Grief over Jerusalem (8:18–23 [Eng. 9:1])

18 *Grief has overwhelmed me,*[1]
I am sick at heart.
19 *Listen! hark! the cry of my daughter—my people*
From throughout the land.[2]
"Is Yahweh not in Zion?
Is her king no longer there?"
"Why do they provoke me with images
And their futile foreign gods?"
20 *"The harvest is past,*
The summer is over,
But we have not been saved."
21 *I am broken*[3] *because of the breaking of my daughter—my people;*
I mourn; dismay has seized me.[4]

5. A. Biran, "Tel Dan," *BA* 37/3 (1974), pp. 26–51, esp. pp. 40–43 and figs. 11–13.
6. Lit. "serpents (*neḥāšîm*), vipers (*ṣip'ōnîm*)."

1. The first word in the verse is added to v. 17. Then *'alê yāgôn 'ālay* may be read as *'ālâ* (or *ya'aleh*) *yāgôn 'ālay,* "Grief has come up upon me."
2. MT suggests the land of exile, "from afar," whereas the sense seems to require a cry from all over their own land. The phrase *marḥaqqîm* in Isa. 33:17 means "stretching afar."
3. Lacking in LXX and Syriac.
4. LXX adds "pangs as of a woman in labor" as in 6:24.

22 *Is there no balm in Gilead?*
Is there no physician there?
Then why has no new skin
Grown over their wound?
23(9:1) *Would that my head were water,*
My eyes a fountain of tears,
That day and night I might weep
For the slain of my daughter—my people!

Jeremiah was never a dispassionate observer of his nation's suffering, but entered into the anguish of the people and suffered with them. It is an open question whether the prophet is here projecting himself into the midst of a disaster about to overtake the people, or whether these words were uttered by the prophet at the time the disaster struck. Either view is possible, although the intensity of this agonized lament would lend support to the view that Jeremiah was experiencing either the invasion of 598/7 B.C. or the violent disturbances in the days preceding the invasion (35:11; 2 K. 24:2) when the whole land was being ravaged by guerrilla attacks.

This anguished sharing of the people's suffering was not peculiar to Jeremiah among the prophets. Men like Amos and Ezekiel entered deeply into the sufferings of Israel. The problem of these men was that they were bearing a message of divine judgment while at the same time sharing the sufferings of the people either in vision or in fact. But they were men torn asunder between God and the people, to both of whom they were bound with deep ties. This combination of love and anguish is nowhere seen more clearly than in Jeremiah. In the present section of the book we have two independent oracles 8:18–23 (Eng. 9:1) and 9:1, 2 (2, 3), the first of which shows Jeremiah mourning for Israel, and the second his desire to leave them for ever.

18–19 Jeremiah's unswerving loyalty to Yahweh and his commands, coupled with deep love for his own people and his own land, tore his heart apart so that he cried out, *I am sick at heart.*

Throughout the land the anguished cry of the people under judgment rose up. Jeremiah here uses the term *my daughter—my people*[5] again (cf. v. 21; 4:11), a poetic and endearing personification of the people. The noun *cry (šawᵉʿâ)* in other passages denotes a cry for help which echoed up and down the land. The cry is poignant,

5. See J. Bright, *Jeremiah,* p. 32 on 4:11.

Is Yahweh not in Zion? Is her king no longer there? In the synonymous parallelism of these phrases Yahweh is here called *king,* a comparatively rare appellation for Yahweh in the OT although the idea of the kingship of Yahweh is writ large in its pages. Interrogations such as these are well known in laments elsewhere in the OT (cf. Ps. 44:25–27 [Eng. 24–26]; 73:25–28; etc.). But Jeremiah himself was fond of the form in which pathos and surprise are mingled together (2:14, 31; 8:4–5, 19, 22; 14:19; 22:28; 49:1). The three questions here are quite in keeping with Jeremiah's method elsewhere. In the context, the first two questions are asked by the people while the third is introduced as Yahweh's own question, as though to say, "Yes, Yahweh is in Zion. Yes, Israel's king is there. But why have the people vexed (*hiḵ'îs*)[6] me with their images and with their foreign vanities?" It is as though the people had reached a point in their apostasy where they did not know Yahweh nor recognize his voice (cf. 9:2 [Eng. 3]). The cry for help continues in v. 20, but a significant sentence is inserted between the first part of the cry and its closing phrases. The insertion interrupts the plaint of the people and has sometimes been regarded as a gloss by commentators.[7] Such a view is not necessary. The words represent an interruption of the lament by Yahweh to explain why he has forsaken Jerusalem (cf. Ezek. 9:3; 10:18; 11:23). The people have provoked him with their idols and their *futile foreign gods.* Such an invasion of Yahweh's territory, such an encroachment on his sole sovereignty over Israel, and such a rejection of his covenant with Israel could have but one outcome, the operation of the curses of the covenant and the alienation of Yahweh from his people. Contrary to the opinions of some commentators, therefore, there are good reasons for retaining this phrase as part of the original and not regarding it as a gloss. It is arguable that Jeremiah intended this interruption precisely to add particular stress to the whole oracle. The style and word usage are in any case Jeremianic.[8]

20 The anguished cry of the people continues. The *harvest (qāṣîr),* that is, the wheat harvest, was past and the time for the

6. See W. L. Holladay, "Style, Irony, and Authenticity in Jeremiah," *JBL* 81 (1962), pp. 44f.; "The so-called 'Deuteronomic Gloss' in Jer. 8:19b," *VT* 12 (1962), pp. 494-98.
7. J. P. Hyatt, "Jeremiah," *IB* V (1956), p. 87; W. Rudolph, *Jeremia,* p. 54.
8. J. Bright, "The Date of the Prose Sermons of Jeremiah," *JBL* 70 (1951), pp. 15–35.

ingathering of the summer fruits (*qāyiṣ*) had gone.[9] Harvest lasted from April to June. If the wheat harvest failed, the people might look forward to the yield of grapes, figs, olives, etc. But if these fruits also failed, famine faced the people. It would appear that we have here a popular proverb used in daily life when men encountered a hopeless situation from which no deliverance or escape seemed possible. Jeremiah pictured the people of Judah as having passed by one opportunity after another to repent of their rebellious ways and so be delivered or *saved* (Heb. *nôša'*) from coming judgment. Setting aside the insertion, the brief poignant cry of the people gathers up two facts—the sense of being forsaken by Yahweh and the awareness that all hope of deliverance is gone:

Is Yahweh not in Zion?
Is her king no longer there?
The harvest is past,
The summer is over.
But we have not been saved.[10]

21–23(9:1) Now Jeremiah's passionate grief is brought to light. That cry of hopelessness reached his heart. If Yahweh's people *(my daughter—my people)* are broken, the prophet too is broken. He is overcome by mourning and dismay and even at that late stage searches for a remedy. For the wounds of the people's flesh there was relief in the soothing balsam (*ṣᵒrî*) of Gilead or from the attentive care of a doctor (*rōpē'*). Gilead on the eastern side of the Jordan River was famous already in patriarchal times for its healing balsams (Gen. 37:25).[11] The *balm of Gilead* was evidently one such healing substance. On the physical level there was healing to be found. But Gilead's balm and the doctor's care would not suffice for the deep wound inflicted on Jeremiah's own people. There could be no regeneration of Judah's health when her spirit remained rebellious and

9. H. L. Ellison, *EQ* 25/1 (1963), p. 5, translates "The harvest is past, the autumn is ended," and adds a note to the effect that the traditional rendering "summer" or "ingathering of summer fruits" obscures the significance for those unfamiliar with the climate of Palestine. The barley harvest came in March-April; the wheat harvest in May-June; grapes, figs, and olives ripened and were picked in July-August. Then, with September-October came the autumn and the time for ploughing to prepare for the sowing of wheat and barley in October and November. There were, in fact, still the maize and pomegranate harvests to be gathered in August-September, but after that, no more harvests. Once autumn had begun, and certainly when it had passed, there was nothing till the next barley harvest in the spring.

10. See J. Bright, *Jeremiah,* p. 62.

11. See J. D. Douglas, *NBD,* p. 129 on "Balm"; R. K. Harrison, *Healing Herbs of the Bible* (1966), pp. 17f.; Winifred Walker, *All the Plants of the Bible* (1957), p. 28.

unregenerate. The deep tragedy of it all led to Jeremiah's anguished cry that his very head might be water and his eyes a veritable fountain of tears that he might weep day and night for the slain of *my daughter—my people.*[12]

But that was one side of the painful inner tension. Jeremiah could mourn over the sufferings of his people because of his sympathy and love for them; yet his very message spoke doom to them. This strange paradox arising out of painful inner conflicts becomes clear in the so-called confessions of Jeremiah.[13] There follows immediately in 9:1–2 (Eng. 2–3) a brief oracle which is altogether different in character, in which Jeremiah, disgusted at all he found in his people, sought to escape from the corruption and degradation he saw about him to some wilderness refuge. In that desire he was sharing the mind of Yahweh, who had turned aside from his people and would presently forsake the temple.

(iv) A Depraved People and Yahweh's Judgment (9:1–8 [Eng. 2–9])

1(2) *Oh that I could find in the desert*
A wayfarer's lodge,
That I might leave my people
And get away from them;
For they are all adulterers,
A mob of traitors.
2(3) *They bend their tongue like a bow;*
Falsehood and not faithfulness prevail in the land.[1]
They run from evil to evil,
But they do not know me—Yahweh's word.[2]
3(4) *Be on your guard each one against his fellow,*
And do not trust any brother;
For every brother is a persistent cheater,[3]
And every friend peddles slander.

12. This key expression *baṯ-ʿammî* occurs four times in this short section (vv. 19, 21, 22, 23 [Eng. 9:1]).
13. See the Introduction, "The 'Confessions' of Jeremiah," pp. 88–92.

1. MT reads lit. "They bend their tongue, their bow is falsehood. And not for truth are they strong in the land." Our translation follows LXX broadly by redividing the cola, supplying *like* before *bow,* and reading the last verb as singular. The *l* before *'ᵉmûnâ (faithfulness)* is an emphatic *lameḏ;* cf. F. Nötscher, "Zum emphatischen Lamed," *VT* 3 (1953), p. 380.
2. *Yahweh's word* is lacking in LXX. It is possible that we have an abbreviation in *wᵉ'ōṯî* for *wᵉ'eṯ y(hwh),* "and Yahweh (they do not know)."
3. Heb. *ʿāqôḇ yaʿqōḇ,* infinitive absolute strengthening the verb, lit. "will indeed act craftily."

4(5) *Everyone cheats his neighbor;*
They never speak the truth.
They have trained their tongues to speak falsehood;
They act perversely, they weary themselves turning about;[4]
5(6) *Wrong follows wrong, deceit follows deceit.*
They refuse to acknowledge me[5]*—Yahweh's word.*[6]
6(7) *Therefore, this is what Yahweh of Hosts has said:*
"Look! I am their refiner and will assay them,
But how shall I act toward my daughter—my people?[7]
7(8) *Their tongue is a deadly arrow,*
Deceit they speak in their mouth.[8]
One speaks amicably to his neighbor,
But inwardly he is laying a trap for him.
8(9) *Shall I not judge them for these things?—*
Yahweh's word.
Shall I not avenge myself
On a nation such as this?"

The material of ch. 9 follows on 8:4–23 automatically. Jeremiah in one of his soliloquies had expressed his despair at this people's dishonesty and in his agony expressed a desire to flee from them (vv. 1–5 [2–6]). Yahweh announced judgment, returning to the figure of assaying and refining metal in vv. 6–8 (7–9) (cf. 6:27–30). These verses 1–8 (2–9) might well have come from early in Jehoiakim's reign, even before any disaster was imminent, although Jerusalem was doomed (vv. 9–10 [10–11]). It is possible that the largely prose comment of vv. 11–15 (12–16) may represent later editorial comment, although it is thoroughly in keeping with Jeremiah's thoughts. A dirge over Jerusalem perhaps uttered on the eve of the siege and exile (vv. 16–21 [17–22]), a brief oracle concerning man's proper

4. The translation of this and the following line (v. 5) results from a redistribution of the consonants as well as some revocalization: *he'^{e}wû nil'û šûḇ* (v. 5), *tôḵ b^{e}ṯôḵ* (cf. LXX). MT seems to require some such change. It reads *ha'wēh nil'û* (v. 5) *šiḇt^{e}ḵā b^{e}ṯôḵ mirmâ, b^{e}mirmâ mē'^{a}nû . . . :* "To act perversely they weary themselves from sitting in the midst of deceit. Through deceit they refuse. . . ." See further the commentary.
5. We may have another abbreviation here in *'ôṯî = 'eṯ y(hwh).*
6. Lacking in LXX.
7. The last part of the line seems awkward. The problem lies with *baṯ 'ammî*. LXX implies *rā'aṯ baṯ 'ammi,* "because of the wickedness of my people," which would suggest that a word has dropped out.
8. There are textual problems here also. MT reads "Deceit he speaks with his mouth." In that case who is the subject? There is also a shift from the 3rd masc. suffix in the previous colon, though this is not unknown in Hebrew. If "people" is regarded as a collective which reverts to its singular sense in the second colon the MT will pass, although in English we need to smooth out the translation.

boast (vv. 22–23 [23–24]), and a further prose comment (vv. 24–25 [25–26]) bring the chapter to a close.

It is not easy to reconstruct the chronology of the various elements in this chapter. There are some grounds for arguing that 9:21 (22) develops quite easily into 10:17–25,[9] leaving 9:22–23 (23–24) and 10:1–16 as a collection of miscellaneous sayings. Certainly the broad sweep of 9:1–21 (2–22) is concerned with Judah's depravity and inevitable ruin whatever the date of the separate literary elements.

1–2(2–3) However deeply Jeremiah may have entered into the impending agony of Judah's suffering (8:18–23 [9:1]), he did not attempt to hide the people's great wickedness. This was so deep that escape to a wilderness refuge seemed preferable to the degradations of Jerusalem. The simplest accommodation[10] in an uninhabited area[11] would enable the prophet to be free from the sights which thrust themselves upon him day by day in Jerusalem, where men were all *adulterers (mᵉnāʾēp̄)*, a company of *traitors (bōḡᵉḏîm)*. Their true character is spelled out in the following lines, but unfortunately the text seems to have been poorly transmitted.[12]

3–5(4–6) In his soliloquy Jeremiah addresses the people:

Be on your guard each one against his fellow,
And do not trust any brother;
For every brother is a persistent cheater,
And every friend peddles slander.

Cheating, lack of *truth (ʾᵉmeṯ)*, speaking *falsehood (šeqer)*, and perversion have led to a state of affairs where all strength of purpose to bring about a change has gone. The text at this point is difficult and has been variously translated, although the general sense is clear. The people are so deep in their sins that they are incapable of repentance, unable to retrace their steps[13] (cf. 5:3). They had literally worn themselves out with wicked perversion. The climax of Jeremiah's exposure of the apostasy of the people is: *They refuse*

9. See J. Bright, *Jeremiah*, pp. 70, 73.

10. *Wayfarer's lodge*—Heb. *mᵉlôn ʾōrᵉḥîm*, "accommodation for travellers," may have been little more than a shelter without a resident host.

11. *Desert* — Heb. *miḏbār* denotes an uninhabited area, but not necessarily a sandy desert waste.

12. See textual notes on v. 2 (3).

13. See textual note on v. 4 (5). RSV has "they . . . are too weary to repent." We have suggested *they weary themselves turning about;* cf. LXX *ou diélipon tou epistrépsai.*

to acknowledge me.[14] The verb *yāḏa',* "know," denotes much more than intellectual knowledge but rather that deep intimate knowledge that follows on the personal commitment of one life to another, which is at its deepest in the commitment of a man to God. Over a century earlier Amos had singled Israel out from the nations, declaring Yahweh's word to them: "you only have I known of all the families of the earth" (Amos 3:2). Amos had seen in the rejection of that special divine choice of Israel by Yahweh the seeds of judgment: "Therefore I will punish you for all your iniquities." In Judah's wanton rejection of Yahweh as the Lord of the covenant and the One who once took her from Egypt to lead her to a fair land, Jeremiah too saw the seeds of judgment, and like Amos made use of the verb *pāqaḏ,* "call to account" (v. 8 [9]). The breach of the covenant was the occasion for the operation of the curses of the covenant.

6–8(7–9) Reverting to a metaphor he had used earlier (6:27–30), Jeremiah takes up the picture of the refining crucible. God will refine and test (*bāḥan*) them. The crucible of suffering may succeed where all else had failed. The question *But how shall I act?* points up the legal aspects of breach of covenant. The simple fact was that their tongue was a deadly arrow, their mouth filled with deceit. In the daily life of the city, men greeted their neighbors amicably, but their inward intention was to do them harm (lit. "lay an ambush"). For such misdeeds Yahweh would punish or *judge (pāqaḏ)* the people (cf. 5:9, 29) and avenge himself on such a nation (*gôy*). The use of the term *gôy* for Israel may represent the transfer to Israel of a term which was regularly used of non-Israelite peoples. Its use here suggests that Jeremiah had come to regard the people as no different in their behavior from the *gôyîm,* the peoples outside the covenant. Certainly, whatever they might claim, there was nothing about them to suggest that their covenant with Yahweh had produced in them ethical responses which would mark them out from others around them. It was a sad decline for a people whom Yahweh had "known" uniquely among all the families of the earth. The term *avenge myself* should not be understood to mean that Yahweh was vengeful in the human sense. Judgment was the inevitable consequence of breach

14. See textual notes on v. 5 (6). Especially in the light of LXX the object of *acknowledge* could be Jeremiah, though we prefer to understand it as Yahweh.

of covenant, but in Yahweh's intention it was with a view to repentance and restoration.

(v) Jerusalem's Ruin (9:9–15 [Eng. 10–16])

9(10) *"For the mountains will I take up weeping and wailing,*
For the desert pastures I will utter a dirge;
For they are dried up places through which no one passes.
The lowing of the cattle they do not hear;
The birds of the sky and the beasts
Have fled away and are gone.
10(11) *I will make Jerusalem a heap of ruins,*
A dwelling place for jackals;
And the cities of Judah I will make a desolation
Where no one dwells."
11(12) *What man is wise enough to explain[1] this? And who is he to whom Yahweh's mouth has spoken that he may proclaim it?*
Why is the land become devastated,
Dry as the desert where nobody travels?
12(13) *And Yahweh said: "Because they forsook my law which I set before them, and did not listen to my law nor live in accordance with it,*
13(14) *but they followed after their own stubborn inclinations[2] and went after the Baals as their fathers had taught them,*
14(15) *therefore this is what Yahweh of Hosts, the God of Israel, has said:*
Look! I will feed this people with wormwood
And give them poison water to drink!
15(16) *I will scatter them among the nations*
Which neither they nor their fathers knew.
I will send the sword after them
Until I have made an end of them."

This segment is composed partly of poetry and partly of prose. Following a short lament (v. 9 [10]) and an oracle of judgment upon Judah and Jerusalem (v. 10 [11]), there is a commentary partly in prose and partly in verse. There is disagreement about the extent of the prose segment.[3] It has often been pointed out that the passage is written in the characteristic prose style of the Deuteronomic literature. Further, the literary form of the passage, with a question (v. 11 [12]), the answer and the explanation (vv. 12–13 [13–14]), and the statement of the judgment (vv. 14–15 [15–16]), is similar to the pattern which is found in 5:19; 16:10–13; 22:8–9, all of which are

1. Take the verb *w^e yāḇēn* as Hiphil, "cause to understand."
2. Lit. "hearts."
3. NEB, RSV, and GNB regard the whole of vv. 11–15 as prose; J. Bright takes vv. 11b and 14b as poetic. We propose that vv. 11b, 14b, and 15 are poetry.

in prose also. The theme that the land would be devastated because Israel had forsaken Yahweh's law (v. 13) follows the Deuteronomic view of the history of Israel (cf. 2 K. 17:13–23, 34–41). These points raise a question as to the nature of this segment. In the view of some writers the prose passage shows the hand of the Deuteronomic editor[4] and presupposes the devastation of 587 B.C.[5] While the particular literary form used here is well enough known in Deuteronomic literature, one would need to know whether it was used in other literature too. It is also possible that Jeremiah knew and used the form. As for the threat of devastation, this does not necessarily require that the destruction of 587 B.C. had already taken place. Other Near Eastern documents, particularly the political treaties, spoke of devastation as one of the consequences of a breach of treaty. There are too many imponderables to allow us to be dogmatic about the nature and origin of the prose material here or elsewhere in Jeremiah. In any case, the prose may be more limited in extent than the translations or even the Hebrew itself suggests.

9(10)[6] The calamity about to come upon an apostate nation hurrying on to divine judgment stirs Jeremiah's emotions, and he breaks into a lament *(qînâ)*[7] in which he reflects on the widespread destruction of life and property about to befall the land. The mountains and the pastures of the steppeland (Heb. *miḏbār*)[8] on which *beasts (miqneh)* graze will be ravaged. The lowing of the cattle will no longer be heard, and even the birds will have disappeared (cf. 4:25). The conjunction of Israel's sin with wide-ranging national disasters is a common theme in the prophets (cf. Amos 4; Mic. 6:10–16; Hag. 1:9–11; etc.).

10(11) These words seem to be an independent oracle distinct from the lamentation of v. 9.[9] Here Jerusalem is singled out as destined to become a heap of ruins and a haunt of *jackals (tannîm).*

4. E. W. Nicholson, *Preaching to the Exiles,* pp. 61–63.
5. E. W. Nicholson, *Jeremiah 1–25,* p. 94.
6. There is a slight textual problem at the start of v. 9. MT reads "I will take up," whereas LXX, Latin, and Syr. have the imperative "Take up." Since Jeremiah is the speaker, MT seems preferable. MT uses two nouns, "a weeping and a wailing," whereas LXX uses only one. MT may have included both of two variants.
7. The Qinah measure is commonly used in lamentations, though not exclusively. It consists of poetic lines with three stresses in the first colon and two in the second, i.e., a 3:2 pattern.
8. The term *miḏbār,* often translated "wilderness," does not denote a barren wasteland but rather uninhabited lands which nevertheless offered pasture to flocks (cf. Exod. 3:1).
9. See J. Bright, *Jeremiah,* p. 73.

The picture of jackals (or wolves) making their lair amid the ruins of devastated cities must have been familiar to Jeremiah and his contemporaries (cf. 10:22; 49:33; 51:37). Judah's towns would become an awesome waste without inhabitants.[10] The link between national apostasy and natural disasters was held to be a very close one.

11–15(12–16) These verses are clearly designed to offer an explanation of the judgment referred to in vv. 9–10 (10–11). They are often regarded as being the work of the Deuteronomic editors of Jeremiah's biography and preaching, who, during exile, were able to offer this kind of explanation. But if this were the case, the explanation is hardly other than what Jeremiah himself would have given. It was always his view that breach of the covenant would lead to precisely this kind of destruction. If an explanation was needed, it was simply that Yahweh's people had forsaken Yahweh's covenant and given their allegiance to other gods. That kind of explanation is offered in poetic sections which are undoubtedly from Jeremiah (e.g., 4:7–8, 20, 23–26; 5:17; 6:6, 8).

The answer to the pressing question as to why the land was devastated was: *Because they forsook (ʿāzaḇ) my law (tôrâ) which I set before them, and did not listen to my voice nor live in accordance with it* (v. 12 [13]). The reference to the covenant is clear. We are taken back to Exod. 19:4–8 when Israel accepted Yahweh's covenant and acknowledged his sovereignty. Obedience was very much in focus (Exod. 19:5). This was a demand to which Jeremiah returned again and again (cf. 7:23–26). While the call to obedience was stressed in Deuteronomy it was also strong in Jeremiah, who was probably strongly influenced by Deuteronomy. But whatever the source of his thinking, Jeremiah linked the destruction of Judah with disobedience to Yahweh's law. The people followed *their own stubborn inclinations* (lit. "the stubbornness of their hearts," *šᵉrirûṯ libbām)* as well as the *Baals,*[11] according to attitudes which their forefathers had taught them.

In theory the head of the Canaanite pantheon was El. Alongside him was his consort Athirat (Asherah). According to Canaanite

10. In 51:37 similar language is used of Babylon, and in 49:33 Hazor is similarly described. Cf. 2:15; 4:26; 34:22; 44:2–6.

11. For a discussion of the deities of the Canaanites and the characteristics of each of them see J. Gray, *The Legacy of Canaan,* SVT V (1965), pp. 152–192. See also H. Ringgren, *Religions of the Ancient Near East* (E.T. London, 1973), pp. 124–154.

mythology the offspring of these two deities was Baal, the fertility-god par excellence, who in practice was the active head of the pantheon. In the OT and in other Near Eastern texts the name Baal appears as the first element in a number of names of local deities, like Baal-hazor, Baal-peor, Baal-sidon, Baal-lebanon, Baal-haram, Ba'alat-gebal (mistress of Byblos). One interesting example in the OT is Baal-berith, "the lord of the covenant" (Judg. 9:4). The Baals with accompanying names are probably local forms of Baal in his character of tutelary deity of a city or an area. It is clear from a reading of the religious and legendary texts of Ugarit that many of the cultic practices associated with Baal and the fertility cult were heavily orientated toward sexual activity. These practices had an appeal for many Israelites over the centuries, and more than one of the prophets raised indignant protests against Israel's involvement in them (1 K. 18:20–40; Hos. 2:10–15, 18–22 [Eng. 8–13, 16–20]; Zeph. 1:4). But any such participation in the worship of another deity was a rejection of the lordship of Yahweh and could only lead to judgment, described here metaphorically as feeding the people with *wormwood (la'ᵃnâ)* and giving them *poison (rō'š)*.

The threat by Yahweh to scatter the people among nations which neither they nor their fathers had known, and to pursue them with the sword until he had made an end of them, is taken by some commentators to be an exilic comment. While it is possible that later editorial comment would use such an expression, exile was not unknown in Israel even well before Jeremiah's day (cf. 2 K. 5:2; 15:29; 17:6, 24). The mere fact that there is a reference to exile as one of the aspects of divine judgment does not therefore necessarily require an exilic date for this prose insertion. Nor does the fact that these verses seem to offer an explanation of why Yahweh had allowed his country to be destroyed point necessarily to an exilic date for their composition. To be sure, similar answers were given during the exile (e.g., Lamentations); but Isaiah spoke of divine judgment resulting from breach of covenant (Isa. 1:4–9, etc.), Amos threatened exile to the women of Samaria (Amos 4:1–3), and Micah referred to dire judgment on Jerusalem (Mic. 3:12). Threats of exile occur also in the remarkable list of curses in Deut. 28 (note vv. 64–68). Hence, although it is not impossible that vv. 11–15 (12–16) represent an exilic editorial comment, the grounds on which such a proposition are made need to be more secure than those which have sometimes been advanced.

The main thrust of these verses, then, is that Israel has forsaken the law of Yahweh and broken his covenant in disobedient stubbornness of heart. Failing genuine heart repentance, the only outcome was judgment.

(vi) A Dirge over Jerusalem (9:16–21 [Eng. 17–22])

16(17) *This is what Yahweh of Hosts has said: "Consider and*[1]
Call for the wailing women to come;
Send for the skilled women[2]
17(18) *To come quickly*[3] *and raise a lament over us,*
That our eyes may run with tears
And our eyelids stream with water.
18(19) *Listen! Weeping is heard from Zion:*
'How great our ruin! How great our shame!
For we have left the land,
Our homes have been torn down.' "[4]
19(20) *Now listen, you women, to Yahweh's word,*
That your ears may receive the word of his mouth.
Teach your daughters a lament,
Each woman a lamentation to her friend,
20(21) *For Death has come up through our windows,*
Has entered our strongholds,
To cut down a child in the street
And young men in the marketplaces.
21(22) *Speak! "This is the word of Yahweh:*[5]
'The corpses of men lie
Like dung on the surface of the fields,
Like sheaves behind the reaper
Which no one gathers.' "

1. But the first line is lacking in LXX, both the introductory phrase and the verb "consider." This latter word may suggest that it once commenced an oracle which is now lost, unless it be that the hearers (or readers) are called upon to consider what follows. The Hebrew text reads "consider and." Both words are lacking in LXX and in any case seem to add unnecessary weight to the colon.

As to the expression *This is what Yahweh of Hosts has said,* it normally introduces an oracle of some kind but sometimes it acts as an editorial link between a preceding section and new material. If the present passage 9:16–21 (17–22) is an independent oracle placed here by an editor, such a linking phrase would be normal since both the material in the preceding verses and the new material are concerned with judgment.

2. Lit. "wise women," i.e., professional mourners.

3. Lit. "Let them come, let them hasten."

4. MT reads "They have cast down our homes." LXX reads "We must cast aside (abandon) our homes," apparently vocalizing the verb as a Hophal, *hošlaḵnû mimmišk^enôṯênû.*

5. LXX, Syr. omit this line. Some Greek mss., Theodotion, and Latin have "Death," which may have read *deḇer,* "pestilence," instead of *dabbēr, Speak!* Some commentators and translators omit, (e.g., J. Bright, GNB), but RSV, NEB retain.

The lament which characterized the earlier part of this chapter (vv. 9–10 [10–11]) is resumed after the prose section. The general theme is the destruction of Jerusalem, but the death of her citizens at the hands of the grim reaper is the main concern of the mourner (v. 21 [22]).

16–19(17–20) After a brief oracular introduction[6] a call goes out to the *mourning women (m^{e}qôn^{e}nôṯ)* to come. The reference is to professional mourners. In the Middle East even today, on the occasion of deaths or calamities, mourning is carried out by professional women who follow the funeral bier uttering a high-pitched shriek.[7] Some of the Egyptian tomb paintings depict boatloads of professional mourners with their hair and garments disheveled accompanying a corpse on its way to a burial.[8] Jeremiah urges these professional mourners to hasten to their task, thus conveying a note of urgency. These women are to take up a *lament (nehî)*[9] till the eyes of the citizens of Jerusalem flow with tears and their eyelashes are wet with weeping (v. 17 [18]). The words of the loud lamentation peal out from Zion:

How great our ruin! How great our shame!
For we have left the land,
Our homes have been torn down.[10]

But it is not merely that the professional mourners are called upon to sing their dirge and their lament. They are to teach their tragic refrain to their daughters and their friends, for the days will be tragic enough to demand a multitude of mourners. It would seem that the prophet was hinting that the professional mourners themselves would enter into the experience of personal grief.

20–21(21–22) The picture of Death climbing in through the window and entering the *strongholds*[11] of the people is a vivid one. Jeremiah spread the net wide. It was *our windows* and *our strongholds* that Death would invade to claim his victims in Judah, without respect for age or sex. He would cut down children in the streets and young men in the open places.

6. See textual note.
7. See *NBD,* p. 171.
8. *Ibid.*
9. The term here, *nehî,* occurs in v. 9 but there it is associated with *qînâ,* "lament," as in v. 19.
10. See textual note.
11. Or "palaces," Heb. *'arm^{e}nôṯ.*

The idea that Death might come through the windows has a significant parallel in Canaanite mythology.[12] Baal had to win his kingship by battle with the god Yamm, but having won the victory he built a palace of enormous proportions and lavish splendor. The architect proposed that a window be included. Baal resisted the idea for a time but at last agreed. It was his undoing, for through the window came misfortune in the person of the god Mot, the god of infertility, death, and the underworld. There is possibly a reflection of this Canaanite myth in these verses. Jeremiah was suggesting that in the day of judgment it would be as if the god of death had entered the homes of the people and stalked through their streets. However, despite the apparent closeness of the parallel it may be no more than a coincidence arising from Jeremiah's personification of death.[13]

The ultimate horror would be that the corpses of men would fall and lie like dung in the fields, like sheaves behind the reaper, but no one would gather them up for burial, presumably because the reaper had done his work so completely. This was a possibility which evidently worried Jeremiah, for he referred to it several times.[14] The prophet's anguish at the coming disaster is here laid bare.

At this point in the book the theme changes completely. The dirge gives place to some reflections on wisdom,[15] although the dirge motif returns in 10:17. For this reason some commentators add 10:17–25 after 9:21 in order to complete the lament.[16] Certainly as the book stands after the editorial processes, there is no direct textual connection between 9:21 and 10:17. But we are dealing with an anthology of Jeremiah's utterances which an editor has brought to-

12. See Legend of Baal in C. H. Gordon, *Ugaritic Textbook* (1965), Text 51, pp. 169–174. Note v, ll. 120–27, p. 172; vi, ll. 1–9, p. 172; vii, ll. 15–27, p. 173. In English translation see J. B. Pritchard, *ANET* (1955), pp. 134–35. Note II AB, (v), ll. 120–27, p. 134; (vi), ll. 1–9, p. 134; (vii), ll. 15–27, p. 135.

The parallel between the picture in v. 20 ab and the Baal myth, though suggestive, is not proven. Cassuto, Albright, Ginsberg, and Driver have argued that Baal's objection to the window was that Mot (Death) might climb in, although a specific statement to this effect does not seem to occur in the Baal texts. See J. Gray, *The Legacy of Canaan*, SVT (^{2}1965), p. 51, n. 3.

13. Cf. Job 28:22; Ps. 49:15 (Eng. 14); Isa. 28:15–18; Hos. 13:14; Hab. 2:5; etc.

14. 8:2; 16:4, 6; 20:6; 25:33.

15. See the next section.

16. J. Bright, *Jeremiah*, pp. 70ff., esp. 73.

gether according to his own scheme, and it is not always possible for us now to discern his thought processes or the logic of his arrangements.

(vii) Man's Only Grounds for Boasting (9:22–23 [Eng. 23–24])

22(23) *This is what Yahweh has said:*
"Let not the wise man boast of his wisdom,
Let not the valiant man boast of his valor,
Let not the rich man boast of his riches;
23(24) *But let the man who boasts, boast of this,*
That he understands and knows me.
For I am Yahweh who acts in steadfast loyalty,
Justice, and right upon the earth;
For in these things I delight—Yahweh's word."

These comments on the nature of true wisdom seem to interrupt a sad lament and, as noted above, have sometimes been taken as an independent oracle placed here by the one who edited Jeremiah's utterances.[1] Be that as it may, there is a certain logic in placing the verses here, for they make the point that in such critical days the only hope for men lies in the faithfulness, justice, and integrity of Yahweh. Such thinking is in agreement with the central emphasis of Jeremiah's thought elsewhere, namely, that the wise men, the warriors, and the rich men of Judah had forgotten Yahweh in the midst of concentrating on their own achievements and activities.

The verses before us constitute a beautiful *logion* on true wisdom which is in the best tradition of wisdom literature. The theme of the true knowledge of God which stands apart from even the best of human thinking is one to which Jeremiah returned again and again.[2] The prophet Hosea in the previous century made the same point.[3] Both Hosea and Jeremiah believed strongly that true religion consists in a personal and existential knowledge of God, and in a commitment to those qualities displayed by Yahweh himself—unfailing loyalty, justice, and right dealing.

1. It needs to be recalled again that Jeremiah himself undertook a certain amount of editorial work.
2. Cf. 2:8; 4:22; 9:2–5 (Eng. 3–6); 22:16; 24:7; etc.—all poetry.
3. Hos. 4:1, 6; 5:4; 6:6; 8:2.

The brief passage is pregnant with theological meaning. In particular three significant words are used, *ḥeseḏ, mišpāṭ,* and *ṣᵉḏāqâ,* each of which is so wide-ranging in its connotation as to pose great difficulty in translation.

The first word *ḥeseḏ* has no exact equivalent in English. In occurs some 245 times in the OT.[4] In the great majority of cases the noun denotes in a general way that inner aspect of character which prompts God or man, quite apart from any constraint of law, to show kindness, friendship, and magnanimity to another, whether or not such consideration is expected or deserved. Such a quality of character lies at the foundation of all true community and all true fellowship. It is the virtue that knits society together.[5] When the term is used of God it denotes that deep commitment of God to his people that reaches out beyond the mere demands of reciprocal obligation such as those specified by law or custom. In an attempt to give definition to this beautiful but elusive concept, translators have used such terms as "loyalty," "covenant loyalty," "loving kindness" (AV, RV), "steadfast love" (RSV), "unfailing devotion" (NEB), "kindness" (Jerusalem Bible), "merciful love," "mercy" (AV), etc. Some small apprehension of this divine quality should be the pursuit of the wise man according to Jeremiah. It was a quality which Yahweh might have expected to find to some degree in his people but which, alas, was often lacking.[6] God's covenant faithfulness is here emphasized because the divine activity was in such striking contrast to the infidelity of his people.

The second term, *mišpāṭ,* likewise gathers up a wide range of ideas. In the Semitic world the root *špṭ* and its derivatives covered a wide variety of action which both accompanied and followed court proceedings. Not only was a verdict pronounced but a sentence was carried out. That is, the exercise of "justice" has a strong dynamic aspect. But there was more. It was important in society to establish a state of affairs where right-doing was encouraged and made possible. At times this involved the protection of citizens from those who would harm them and in some cases deliverance from oppressors. Yahweh as Judge[7] sought out both the wrongdoer to restrain

4. KB, p. 320a.
5. W. R. Smith, *The Prophets of Israel*², p. 408.
6. 16:5; 31:3; contrast 2:2. Compare Hos. 2:21–22 (Eng. 19–20); 4:1; 6:4, 6; 10:12; 12:7 (Eng. 6).
7. Gen. 18:25; Judg. 11:27; Ps. 94:2; etc.

him or to punish him, and the righteous man to deliver him and to vindicate him. His judgment would stand up to the utmost scrutiny, for it conformed perfectly to the principles he had laid down for men.[8] For that reason those who were oppressed in society appealed to him,[9] and men in Israel called upon him to judge between them.[10] He would perfectly establish the rights of every man, that is, he would establish *mišpāṭ.*

The third significant term used in this passage is *ṣ^e^ḏāqâ.* It has been variously translated "righteousness" (RSV, AV, RV), "right" (NEB), "integrity" (Jerusalem Bible). The root *ṣdq* gives rise to a range of derivatives the predominant usage of which suggests that it is concerned with what was regarded as "right," "standard," "normal" in various contexts—social, legal, ethical, and religious. In each case there was a definition of what was normal or standard. The man of Israel was involved in many relationships—family, clan, nation, economic, social, political, religious. Over and above all these lay the relationship offered to him by Yahweh, that of being a member of the covenant family. It was this that gave the deepest significance to his life and thought. The nouns deriving from this root are closely associated in the OT with the noun *mišpāṭ,* which in one important aspect of its meaning denotes the establishment of the rights and duties of parties to a relationship. Where "righteousness" *(ṣ^e^ḏāqâ)* obtained, "justice" *(mišpāṭ)* was enjoyed and the claims of everyone in the covenant community were properly safeguarded. In the establishment of *ṣ^e^ḏāqâ* two kinds of activity were necessary. Positively, "right" had to be restored to those who had been deprived of it, and negatively, offenders had to be punished. Yahweh could act to restore his people's "right" whether by "righteous acts" *(ṣ^e^ḏāqôṯ)* in history[11] or by the defense of the weak, the oppressed, the poor, and the defenseless.[12] Indeed, the term "righteousness" is synonymous with "deliverance" or "salvation" in several passages.[13]

8. See H. H. Rowley, *The Faith of Israel* (1956), p. 65.
9. Ps. 7:10 (Eng. 9); 10:18; 69:33 (Eng. 32); 109:31; etc.
10. Gen. 16:5; 1 Sam. 24:15; cf. Gen. 31:49.
11. Judg. 5:11; 1 Sam. 12:7; Dan. 9:16; Ps. 103:6; Mic. 7:9.
12. Isa. 11:4; Ps. 34:7 (Eng. 6); 35:10; 69:34 (Eng. 33); 72:2, 12; 107:41; 132:15; etc. Cf. Isa. 25:4; 29:19; 41:17; 66:2.
13. 5:1; Isa. 5:7; 28:17; Hos. 2:21 (Eng. 19); 10:12.

Yahweh looked for a similar quality in his people. A particular way of life was right and fitting for them. The norm was not merely social custom, but rather the character and will of the God of the covenant. Nothing less than the "righteousness of Yahweh" would suffice.[14] Yahweh's ultimate purpose was that his "righteousness" should prevail over the whole earth among his own people and among the peoples of the world as well. In that day the ideal ruler would govern with *mišpāṭ* and with *ṣᵉḏāqâ* (Isa. 9:6). At its deepest, the concept of *ṣᵉḏāqâ* connoted a loyalty manifested in the concrete relationships of a religious community, the covenant community.

In this brief statement therefore we have a succinct summary of the religion of Israel at its highest. Wisdom, strength, and riches, however valuable they may be when properly used, are altogether subordinate to the knowledge of God. True religion consists in acknowledging the complete sovereignty of God in life and allowing him to fill life with those qualities of steadfast faithfulness, justice, and righteousness which he possesses, in which he delights, and which he desires to find in his people.

(viii) The Worthlessness of Circumcision (9:24–25 [Eng. 25–26])

24(25) *"Look! days are coming—Yahweh's word—when I will punish all who are circumcised physically:*
25(26) *Egypt, Judah, Edom, Ammon, Moab, and all those whose temples are shaved who live in the steppelands, for all these nations are uncircumcised—and all the house of Israel is uncircumcised in heart."*

This short segment has no obvious connection with the preceding verses, unless it is that Jeremiah wished to point to one particular area of religious performance, namely circumcision, which was a futile ritual unless associated with an inward obedience to Yahweh. There was, in fact, a group of nations which practiced circumcision as well as Israel.[1] Each of those mentioned by Jeremiah had had at some stage in its history some contact with Israel, generally of a hostile kind. At one point, however, they were united. Yahweh would punish *(pāqaḏ)* them all. They were all *circumcised physically* (lit.

14. Isa. 46:12, 13; 51:1, 5, 8; 56:1.
1. W. Rudolph, *Jeremia* (1958), p. 65; R. de Vaux, *Ancient Israel* (1961), pp. 46–48.

"circumcised as to the foreskin"), but such a ritual performance could not deliver them from a divine visitation upon them for their evil deeds. The suggestion has been made that the particular combination of nations here represents an anti-Babylonian coalition under the leadership of Egypt, which is named first. Although such a coalition is otherwise unknown, it would seem from the context that Egypt, Judah, Edom, Ammon, and Moab as well as certain Arab groups were claiming that they all practiced circumcision, whereas others, like the Babylonians, did not. The proposal, though plausible, remains unproven. What is clear is that Yahweh rejects the boast of any nation to be circumcised, for circumcision in the flesh which was not linked to obedience from the heart was not acceptable to him. The members of the covenant family were ideally circumcised in their flesh as witness that they above all other nations acknowledged the sovereignty of Yahweh and obeyed his laws (Gen. 17:9–14). For Jeremiah, circumcision of the flesh did not amount to true circumcision. The "uncircumcised heart" was a heart that did not understand (4:4). The "uncircumcised ear" was an ear that did not listen (6:10). Hence Judah, which neither understood nor obeyed, was classed with the uncircumcised because she was *uncircumcised in heart.*

The reference to those with shaved temples who lived in the desert (v. 25 [26]) has in view certain Arab tribes who trimmed their hair away from the temples (cf. 25:23; 49:32). The practice was forbidden by Hebrew law (Lev. 19:27).[2] Plausibility may be added to the theory of a coalition of anti-Babylonian peoples in that the Babylonians conducted campaigns against the Arabs (49:28–33). The Babylonian Chronicle refers to one such campaign in 599/8 B.C. which Jeremiah may well have known about.[3]

We may associate the protest in these two verses with other protests of Jeremiah in 7:1–8:3, where a whole range of cultic abuses is passed in review.[4] The total picture indicated that Judah was no better than the pagan nations that surrounded her. Hence she could only expect to be punished.

2. Herodotus *Hist.* iii.8.
3. D. J. Wiseman, *Chronicles of Chaldaean Kings* (1956), pp. 31, 71.
4. See commentary above.

(ix) *A Satire on Idolatry: Yahweh and the Idols (10:1–16)*

1 *Hear the word which Yahweh has spoken to you,*
O house of Israel.
2 *This is what Yahweh has said:*
"Do not learn the practices[1] *of the nations,*
And do not be in awe of heavenly omens,
Though the nations are in awe of them.
3 *For the religion of the peoples*[2] *is a delusion,*[3]
For it is a tree one cuts down from the forest,
The handiwork of an artisan with an adze.
4 *With silver and gold they beautify it,*
With hammer and nails they make it sturdy
So that it does not topple over.
5 *They*[4] *are like a scarecrow in a cucumber patch;*
They do not speak;
They have to be carried
Because they cannot walk.
Do not fear them; they do not harm,
And they lack the power to do good."
6[5] *Where is one like thee, O Yahweh?*
Thou art great and great the might of thy name.
7 *Who should not fear thee, King of the nations,*
For this is thy due?
For among all the wise men of the nations
And in all their domains,
Where is one like thee?
8 *One and all they are stupid;*
The religion of idols is foolish.[6]

1. Heb. *dereḵ,* "way."
2. MT reads *ḥuqqôṯ hā'ammîm,* "the statutes of the peoples," which may refer to their religious laws (cf. Lev. 18:3). A suggested emendation is *ḥittaṯ hā'ammîm,* "the fear of the peoples," i.e., what the people fear. Another proposal is *mûsar hā'ammîm,* "the instruction (teaching) of the peoples." The word *mûsar* occurs in v. 8b. But probably MT makes good enough sense. See further the commentary.
3. Heb. *heḇel,* "wind," "emptiness," etc. The word occurs frequently in Ecclesiastes, "Vanity, vanity, all is vanity."
4. MT uses the 3rd plur. here and throughout v. 5, which represents a change from the sing. in v. 4. There is no need for the emendations suggested in *BHS;* it is common enough in the OT to move from the particular (sing. or collective) to the general (plur.).
5. Verses 6–8 are lacking in LXX. The *m* of *mē'ên* may be a dittography from the previous word; cf. v. 6b. Alternatively we might read following Theodotion *mē'ayin,* "from where" (so NEB).
6. MT reads "the instruction of 'nothings' is wood," a difficult phrase. Some interpreters abandon the colon and do not translate, e.g., J. Bright, p. 76, who asks whether the colon is a variant of v. 3a since both have the words *heḇel, hû',* and *'ēṣ.* The context suggests that the wise men of the nations know only what the wood (idol) teaches them, which is nothing. NEB proposes "learning their nonsense from a log of wood." R. K. Harrison, *Jeremiah and Lamentations* (1973), p. 93, suggests

9[7] *It is wood. Beaten silver is brought from Tarshish*
And gold from Ophir,[8]
The work of a craftsman and of the goldsmith's hands.
Violet and purple are their garments,
They are all the work of skilled men.
10 *But Yahweh is God in truth;*
He is a living God and an everlasting king.
At his wrath the earth quakes,
The nations cannot endure his fury.
11[9] *(You shall say this to them: "The gods who*
made neither the heavens nor the earth shall perish from
the earth and from under these heavens.")
12 *By his power he made the earth;*
He established the world by his wisdom
And by his understanding he stretched out the skies.
13 *At the thunder of his voice the waters in the heavens are amazed.*[10]
He brings up clouds from the ends of the earth;
He provides lightning flashes[11] *for the downpour*
And sends out the wind from his storehouses.

"An instruction of vanities is the tree itself." Another suggestion is that we have two haplographies and must restore *m* before *'ēṣ* and *h* after, to give *mûsar h^{a}ḇālîm mē'ēṣâ hû',* "The instruction of idols (vanities) is apart from counsel," i.e., it is foolish. Yet another proposal is to separate the first two verbs into two separate cola, "one and all they are stupid" and "the instruction of idols (nothings) is foolish." The last two words in the line are then transferred to v. 9 and understood to be a description of the idol. *BHS ad loc.* proposes two haplographies, the final *m* of *h^{a}ḇālîm,* and the initial *h* of *hû'*. If these are restored we obtain a word *mē'ēṣâ,* that is, *min* partitive, plus *'ēṣâ,* "counsel." The word then means "away from counsel," that is, "without counsel" or "foolish." Then to carry the haplography further, the MT *'ēṣ hû'* is repeated—"It is wood." See P. R. Ackroyd, "Jeremiah x:1–16," *JTS* N.S. 14/2 (1963), pp. 385–390, esp. p. 388, n. 8.

7. Some commentators transfer v. 9 to between v. 4a and 4b in order to keep the material about the decking out of the idol together; so J. Bright, p. 76.

8. Read *mē'ôp̱îr* with Syr. in place of MT *mē'ûp̱āz,* "from fine gold." See further the commentary below.

9. The verse is an Aramaic gloss.

10. The text may be defective; it reads "At the sound of his giving forth, tumult of waters in the heavens," but the verb has no object. LXX reads only "And much water in heaven." The words are repeated in 51:16 (51:15–19 repeat 10:12–16) where LXX reads them also. One possibility is that some words have fallen out. For MT *l^{e}qôl tittô h^{a}môn*, NEB proposes *l^{e}qôlô yiṯm^{e}hûn*, "at the thunder of his voice the waters in heaven are amazed." *BHS* suggests a metathesis *l^{e}ṯittô qôl,* "when he gives forth his voice," i.e., when he thunders. We propose a combination of *BHS* and NEB, *l^{e}ṯittô qôl yiṯm^{e}hûn.*

11. NEB proposes *b^{e}ḏāqîm,* "rifts," for MT *b^{e}rāqîm, lightning flashes,* and translates "he opens rifts for the rain." This is based on a possible confusion of *r* and *d* which is common enough. We retain MT.

14 *All mortals are stupid and ignorant,*
Every goldsmith is disillusioned[12] *by his idol;*
His images[13] *are a fraud,*
There is no breath in them.
15 *They are nonentities, a work of delusion;*
At the time of their reckoning they will perish.
16 *Not like these is the Portion of Jacob,*
For he is the maker of all things,
And Israel is the tribe of his inheritance;
Yahweh of Hosts is his name.

This poem is a scathing and satirical attack on idols. Because of striking similarities to Isa. 40:18–20; 41:7; 44:9–20; and 46:5–7 it has sometimes been regarded as a postexilic addition to the book of Jeremiah.

The text of the passage presents a number of problems. The Hebrew differs from LXX in a number of places. Verses 12–16 occur again in 51:15–19. Verse 11 is in Aramaic. As a result of textual problems commentators have been ready to rearrange the verses into what appears to them to be a more logical and consistent pattern. Such rearrangements are always open to question. Ancient Hebrew logic was not always the same as that of our time; and while there may be some virtue in rearranging the material for the purpose of explaining the passage to a modern audience, we are in danger of destroying an ancient pattern which has its own peculiar emphasis.[14] In view of the great variety of attempts to rearrange Jer. 10:1–16 it may be wise to ask whether such attempts are really the right procedure. It may be far better to attempt to make sense of what lies before us in the given text. Apart from the unusual Aramaic insertion in v. 11 it is possible to discern a reasonable pattern in which alternating assertions are made about idols and Yahweh.[15] After an introductory segment (v. 1), we have (i) a warning against idols (vv. 2–5), (ii) the supremacy of Yahweh (vv. 6–7), (iii) the fu-

12. Lit. "put to shame."
13. For MT *niskô,* "his image," read *n*^{e}*sāḵāw, his images,* to suit the context.
14. Among the more usual rearrangements we may note that of J. Bright, *Jeremiah,* pp. 76f. where v. 9 is inserted between v. 4a and 4b and v. 11 is omitted as a gloss; A. Weiser, *Das Buch des Propheten Jeremia,* pp. 85f. inserts v. 9 between v. 4a and 4b, places vv. 6–7 before v. 10, and follows the order 4a, 9, 4b, 5, 8, 11, 6, 7, 10; W. Rudolph, *Jeremia,* pp. 64–66 has 4a, 9, 4b, 5, 8, 10, 12–16, 6, 7, 11. Incidentally LXX places vv. 6–7 after v. 16 but omits vv. 8 and 10; it has the order 1–5a, 9, 5b, 11–16.
15. The treatment of P. R. Ackroyd in his article "Jeremiah x:1–16," *JTS* 14/2 (1963), pp. 385–390 seems to the writer to be altogether reasonable.

tility of idols (vv. 8–9), (iv) the reality and creative power of Yahweh (vv. 10–13, with v. 11 a gloss), (v) the idols and their makers to be judged (vv. 14–15), (vi) final acknowledgment of Yahweh's supremacy (v. 16). Seen in this way the whole passage has coherence and order. It is not unthinkable that the passage may have had a parallel in some liturgical form which was used in the temple, in which a contrast was drawn between Israel's true God, Yahweh, and the worthless idols to which some in Israel showed overdue respect. That there are parallels in thought and even in wording with some passages in Psalms and in Isaiah may indicate no more than that there was a traditional language of worship in Israel which was in use for a long period of time.

Theologically these verses are of great significance, for they set Yahweh apart from every other object of worship. There is none like him (v. 6). He is the true, living God (v. 10), the creator of the heavens and the earth (v. 12), the controller of the clouds and the rain (v. 13), the one who alone is worthy of the reverence of all men (v. 7). Moreover, he claims Israel as his own (v. 16). As Lord of the covenant Yahweh demanded total unswerving loyalty from his subjects. Any attempt to share allegiance to him with another merited judgment, for it amounted to a rejection of the covenant. In that case the curses of the covenant became operative.

It is not difficult to envisage Jeremiah giving utterance to such ideas as find expression in 10:1–16. He had witnessed at first hand the evil consequences of the Canaanite influence in the religious practices of many in Judah, and with his own strong awareness of the reality of Yahweh, Israel's covenant God, every idol seemed to be an empty sham and an insult to Yahweh. But whether or not this passage represents some liturgical form with which he was familiar, there is much in the poem which is in the spirit of Jeremiah, and one wonders just how valid is the complete rejection of Jeremianic authorship made by some writers.

1–2a A short prose introduction introduces the poem. The preposition *'al* may be translated "against." The ensuing poem may be regarded as a direct attack on the practice of some in Judah of giving credence to the lifeless idols of the nations.

2 There are some difficulties in translating the verse, although the meaning is clear. Israel is instructed not to learn the way of the nations. The reference seems to be to the religious ways or practices of the nations surrounding Israel, and the verb *learn* (Heb.

tilmādû) may have overtones of "becoming a disciple." Hence one translation is, "Do not be disciples of the religion of the nations."[16] As the poem develops it is evident that the central issue was idol-worship. One significant aspect of ancient Near Eastern religions was their attention to astral deities, sun, moon, and stars. This practice was a concern of Amos a century earlier than Jeremiah (Amos 5:25–26). In Manasseh's day (687–642 B.C.) the practice was rife (2 K. 21:5) and was one of the targets of Josiah's reform (2 K. 23:5, 11, 12). The nations held celestial phenomena in *awe* (Heb. *ḥāṯat),* particularly abnormal phenomena like comets and eclipses. Such awe was improper in Israel since it was the true God, the living God, the everlasting King (v. 10) who controlled these heavenly phenomena (Gen. 1:14; Hab. 3:4, 11; etc.).

3–4 A delineation of idol-worship commences at this point. A difficult Hebrew word confronts us immediately in *ḥuqqôṯ,* "statutes." The Hebrew text reads literally "the statutes of the peoples are a delusion."[17] If "statutes" is understood to refer to "religious ordinances" or simply "religion," the passage may be translated *the religion of the peoples is a delusion* (cf. Lev. 18:3). However, since the general context seems to refer in the second half of the line to something in the singular, it has been proposed to emend the plural *ḥuqqôṯ* to the singular *ḥittaṯ,* "an object of fear," that is, an idol[18] (cf. Gen. 35:5). In that case the passage would develop the sense of v. 2. Certainly the second half of the line refers to *a tree one cuts down from the forest* (or expressed in the passive, "a tree which is cut from the forest"). The description of the idol follows similar descriptions in other parts of the OT (Ps. 115:4; 135:15; Isa. 2:20; 31:7; 40:18–20; 41:7; 44:9–20; 46:5–7; Hab. 2:19).

It is probable that there was a range of aphorisms which were used in Israel over many centuries to describe the lifeless, futile idols to which men turned for help. In the passages in Jer. 10 and Isa. 40, 44, and 46 several of these are brought together. There is no necessity to insist with many writers that a passage like this represents a postexilic insertion into Jeremiah, even though such insertions were possible.

16. P. R. Ackroyd, *art. cit.,* pp. 386, 388; cf. W. Rudolph, *Jeremia,* p. 67. Note that the preposition *'el* has been taken by most commentators as the accusative marker *'eṯ;* cf. 12:16.
17. See textual notes.
18. See J. Bright, *Jeremiah,* p. 78. The Jerusalem Bible *ad loc.* translates "the Dread"; cf. W. Rudolph, *Jeremia,* p. 64. NEB translates in the plural, "the carved images."

The character of the tool referred to (*ma'ᵃṣāḏ*) is not clear. It has been variously translated as "chisel" (NEB), "axe" (RSV), "carver" (Jerusalem Bible), "billhook" (Ackroyd), "graving tool" (Bright). The idol was in any case a purely human production, carved from wood, beautified[19] with silver and gold overlay, and finally made sturdy with nails and a hammer to prevent it from toppling over (cf. 1 Sam. 5:1–4). Some commentators insert v. 9 after the first half of v. 4 because it seems to complete the description of the idol. But v. 9, as we shall see, fits very easily into the context of vv. 10–13.

5 The immobility of the completed idol is now described under two images. It is like an immobile and speechless scarecrow in a patch of cucumbers. It has to be carried about because it lacks even the power to move from one place to another.

Here is powerful irony. Idol-worship tried to capture in material objects what is a spiritual experience. As a result it encouraged the absurd practice of people venerating their own impotent creations. Jeremiah's appeal to the people here is not to *fear*[20] such lifeless inventions, which can do neither good nor evil.

6–7 In contrast to the idols stands the supremacy of Yahweh. Having made the contrast in these two verses with the picture in vv. 2–5, Jeremiah returns to ridicule in vv. 8–9.

The incomparability of Yahweh is a theme that is writ large in the OT.[21] He is incomparable, great in himself and great in his name (or character). Whereas idols derive their status and authority solely from human sources, Yahweh derives his position and authority from himself alone. He stands unique. That being so, the prophet can say, *Who should not fear thee, King of the nations, for this is thy due?*

The affirmation that Yahweh is *King of the nations* is significant. A king both deserves[22] and commands allegiance, and Yahweh is king over all. "Thine is the Kingdom." In order to stress the uniqueness of Yahweh further, the prophet now declares that Yahweh

19. Heb. *yᵉyappēhû;* cf. the adjective *yāp̄eh,* "beautiful." Targ. and Syr. suggest a verb *yᵉṣappēhû,* "overlay," although this may be an interpretation of MT.
20. Heb. *yārē'* means rather "to reverence."
21. See C. J. Labuschagne, *The Incomparability of Yahweh* (Leiden, 1966).
22. *Thy due*—The verb *yā'āṯâ* is impersonal, "it is becoming, fitting," and is preceded by "to you." Some commentators have seen in this phrase an Aramaizing influence; cf. Syr. *yā'ē'*. See J. Paterson, "Jeremiah" in *Peake's Commentary* (1962), p. 546.

is incomparable both among the wisest men[23] of the nations and among all their rulers.[24] It is possible in the context that comparison is being made not so much between Yahweh and human beings, the wise and great men of the nations, but between Yahweh and those other beings for whom the nations claim wisdom and royal dignity.[25] The poem now returns to a further description of the idols.

8–9 The prophet enlarges the picture already given in vv. 2–5. Men who claim wisdom and royalty for figments of their imagination are described as stupid men whose religion is foolish because it is tied to the lifeless objects of human handiwork. The Hebrew text at this point is difficult, as pointed out in the textual note above; but the sense is clear. Instruction received from idols is as valueless as the idol itself. The two verbs are separated, giving in the first phrase, *One and all they are stupid,* that is, the nations who worship idols, while in the second phrase we have "The instruction (*religion*) of 'nothings' *(idols)* is *foolish.*"[26] The last two words in the line (*It is wood*) can be read with the next verse; and there is no need to transfer v. 9 to a position between vv. 4a and 4b once the pattern of alternating statements about Yahweh and the idols becomes clear. The idol is only wood overlaid with gold and silver and decked out with fine garments. The gold and silver may have come from distant lands like Tarshish and Ophir, but this does not change the facts of the case. The idol remains a lifeless, speechless production of human hands. *Tarshish* was probably the western limit of the ancient world, perhaps Tartessus in Spain, which exported silver, lead, iron, and tin to Tyre (Ezek. 27:12). The situation of *Ophir* is unknown. Uphaz—the MT reading—is also unknown, and although some commentators have identified it with Ophir there is no evidence for this. There is another possibility. It may be that we do not have place references here at all but rather a reference to the metallurgical processes by which the silver and gold were prepared. The noun *taršîš* has recently been translated "refinery,"[27] so that "silver from *taršîš* may mean "refined silver." If this is correct, the next phrase

23. The expression *among all the wise men* may be taken as a superlative, "among the wisest," as in NEB.
24. Theodotion in his Greek translation reads "among all their kings."
25. See P. Ackroyd, *art. cit.,* p. 388 where he refers to W. Rudolph, *Jeremia,* p. 68.
26. See P. Ackroyd, *art. cit.,* pp. 387f.
27. W. F. Albright, *Archaeology and the Religion of Israel* (^{3}1953), p. 136; "New Light on the Early Phoenician Colonization," *BASOR* 83 (Oct. 1941), pp. 14–22, esp. pp. 21f.

may well mean "gold, even fine gold."[28] Thus the description of the idol is that it is only wood, refined silver and fine gold, the work of a craftsman coming from the hands of the goldsmith. The violet and purple garments are likewise the work of human craftsmen. Despite all its finery the idol remains an idol.

10 Three affirmations are made about Yahweh: he is a genuine[29] God, he is a living God, he is an eternal[30] king. Each of these stands in sharp contrast to similar affirmations which could be made about the idols, which represent a false deity, a lifeless deity, and a deity that exists only for a limited time. Moreover, it lies in the power of Yahweh to shake the earth in his wrath. Before his judgment the *nations (gôyîm)* cannot endure.

11 Presumably this Aramaic verse, which interrupts the flow of vv. 10, 12, 13, represents a scribal comment. It is not impossible that it was a well-known saying. That it is in Aramaic is no necessary argument for a late date, since Aramaic was widely known in Western Asia and among people on Israel's borders. Even so, it may represent a marginal note added later by an Aramaic speaker. The thought is in any case not inconsistent with Jeremiah's outlook.

12 The description of Yahweh is resumed. It is he who makes the earth by his own *power (kōaḥ)*, establishes the world by his wisdom, stretches out the skies by his understanding. The power, wisdom, and understanding of Yahweh are set in striking contrast to the weakness, foolishness, and witless character of the idols. Yahweh alone stands sovereign over the whole created universe (cf. Isa. 40:12–17). Because some of these phrases in vv. 12b and 13c occur in Ps. 65:7 (Eng. 6); 93:1; and 135:7 they are omitted by some commentators.[31] The omission seems to be quite arbitrary.

13 Attention is now focused on the activity of Yahweh in the thunder, the lightning, and the rain. The Hebrew text seems to have suffered in transmission;[32] clearly, though, a storm is depicted.

28. MT *mē'ûpāz* may be revocalized to read *me'ûpāz*, a Hophal participle from a conjectured root *pzz* as in 1 K. 10:18.
29. Taking *'emeṯ* in an adjectival sense.
30. There are some grounds for treating the root *'lm* in *'ôlām* as giving rise to a meaning "wise," relating it to Arabic and Ugaritic models. See J. A. Thompson, "The Root *'-l-m* in Semitic Languages and Some Proposed New Translations in Ugaritic and Hebrew," *Festschrift for A. Vööbus* (1977), pp. 301–308.
31. W. Rudolph, *Jeremia,* p. 66 under comments on vv. 12, 13.
32. See textual notes.

Thunder (his voice), lightning, rain,[33] and wind all follow the divine movement in the skies. There are interesting insights into the meteorology of Jeremiah's day in this verse. God brings up clouds from the distant horizons, he sets the waters of the heavens in a tumult, he makes flashes of lightning to accompany the rain, and releases the wind from his storehouse. These are not mere natural phenomena, nor are they the work of deities like Baal and Hadad. It is all the work of Yahweh.

The poem closes with a final exposure of the futility of idols and a striking description of Yahweh.

14 The man who lacks "knowledge," probably here the knowledge of God, is now described as brutish. The context seems to draw very sharply the contrast between those who know God and those who do not. It was the divine intention that Israel should "know" Yahweh. In a later chapter Jeremiah looked ahead to the day when "all shall know me from the least of them to the greatest" (31:34). The prophets often referred to such lack of knowledge (Isa. 1:3; Hos. 4:1, 6; Mic. 4:12; cf. Amos 3:2). If we understand by the "knowledge of God" that deep personal commitment of the whole person to God, intellectually, emotionally, and volitionally, we catch something of the meaning of the prophet here. Men who lack such knowledge are stupid and will have recourse to all kinds of stupid and shameful things. Every goldsmith will be put to shame by his idol, which is a mere *fraud (šeqer)* without life.

15 Three succinct phrases describe the idols. They are a nonentity *(heḇel), a work of delusion;* at the time of their *reckoning (pᵉquddâ)* they will perish. It is a final devastating demolition of these worthless things.

16 To conclude the poem the writer makes a strong affirmation of the creatorship of Yahweh and his special relationship to Israel, and states one of the important names of Yahweh.

Yahweh is set in contrast to the idols. He is *not like these.* He is the *Portion of Jacob (ḥēleq ya'ᵃqōḇ)* A similar phrase occurs in many of the Psalms (e.g., Ps. 16:5; 73:26; 119:57) and elsewhere in the OT (e.g., Deut. 32:9; Lam. 3:24). A man's "portion" referred to some possession that belonged to him, an area of land (2 K. 9:10, 21, 25–26; Ezek. 45:1, 4, 7), a share in some gift (Lev. 6:17; 1 Sam. 1:5), booty shared after battle (Gen. 14:24; Isa. 53:12), a share in the spirit of another (2 K. 2:9), etc. In the present context Yahweh the *maker (yôṣēr) of all things* is declared to be the one who

33. Heb. *māṭār,* the downpour which accompanies the storm.

had chosen Israel as the *tribe of his inheritance,* that is, "his very own tribe."[34] The correlate of this wonderful fact was that Yahweh was *the Portion of Jacob,* that is, of Israel.[35] Israel and Yahweh were bound together in a deep and intimate personal relationship in which Yahweh would extend unfailing love, care, and protection to Israel and in which Israel might offer her gratitude, obedience, and love. In such a relationship Israel had no cause to fear any other god, and certainly had no right to offer her worship to another god. The title *Yahweh of Hosts* may originally have had in mind the Lordship of Yahweh over the stars and the heavenly beings, but eventually it became an epithet for God's might and power, as here.[36] On this striking note this carefully structured poem with its remarkable unity and coherence of thought closes. It must have brought a deep challenge to those who first encountered it.

(x) The Coming Exile: Lament and Intercession (10:17–25)

17 *Pick up*[1] *your bundle from the ground,*
You who are living under siege,
18 *For thus has Yahweh spoken:*
"Look, I am about to throw out
Those who dwell in the land
At this very time,[2]
And I will press hard upon them[3]
And squeeze them dry."[4]

34. J. Bright, *Jeremiah,* p. 77.
35. Jacob and Israel were one and the same. After Jacob the deceiver had encountered God near the Jabbok, his name was changed to Israel (Gen. 32:22–32; note esp. v. 28). The names Jacob and Israel are frequently interchangeable in the OT (Num. 23:7, 10; 24:17, 19; Deut. 32:9; 33:10; Isa. 10:21; 14:1; 41:8, 14; 45:4; 48:20; Hos. 10:11; 12:3 [Eng. 2]; etc.).
36. See *NBD,* p. 480.

1. Lit. "Gather together." The imperative is fem. because it is addressed to Israel. The line can also be read "Gather your bundle! Out of the land!" See the commentary below.
2. LXX reads "those who are dwelling in this land" and omits *bappa'am* ("at the time"). See *BHS in loc.*
3. LXX reads "in trouble" in place of this line.
4. MT reads "I will press upon them (root *ṣwr*) so that they may find," which does not seem to suit the context. Various emendations have been suggested. A feasible solution is to replace MT *yimṣā'û* (from *māṣā',* "find") with *yimmāṣē'u* (a Niphal from *māṣâ,* "squeeze out"), i.e., "so that they may be squeezed out (drained)." See G. R. Driver, "Linguistic and Textual Problems: Jeremiah," *JQR* 28 (1937/38), p. 107. The verb is used of Gideon's action of squeezing out of the fleece (Judg. 6:38).

19 *Oh, this wound of mine,*
My injury is incurable.
But I said: Surely this is my[5] *affliction,*
I must endure it.
20 *My tent is ruined,*
All my tent ropes are snapped!
My sons have left me,
They are no longer here;[6]
There is no one to pitch my tent again,
To hang up my curtains.
21 *The shepherds have been stupid,*
They have not consulted Yahweh,
So they do not prosper
And all their flock is scattered.
22 *Listen! A report has come,*
A tremendous uproar from the northern land,
To make Judah's cities a desolation,
A haunt for jackals.
23 *I know,*[7] *O Yahweh,*
That a man's way is not in his control;
It belongs not to mortal[8] *man to direct his own steps.*
24 *Correct us,*[9] *O Yahweh, but with justice;*
Not in anger lest thou bring us to nought.
25 *Pour out your wrath upon the nations*
Who do not acknowledge you,
And upon tribes which do not invoke your name;
For they have devoured Jacob;
Yes, they have devoured him[10] *and made an end of him,*
And laid waste his pasture land.

Some commentators have proposed that these verses originally followed immediately after 9:17–22 but became separated by the in-

5. MT reads simply *ḥ^olî,* "affliction," whereas the versions have "my affliction." We may have a case of haplography since *ḥ^olî* ends in *y* and the 1st person possessive pronoun would require a second *y.*
6. LXX reads "my sons and my flocks are no more," based on some such text as *bānay w^eṣō'nî 'ênām.*
7. MT reads *yāḏa'tî,* "I know." W. Rudolph proposes in *BHS* that the final *y* may be a dittography with the first letter of the next word *yhwh,* so that the phrase would read "you know, O Lord."
8. Lit. "to a man who walks."
9. Read with LXX. MT "correct me" may, of course, be understood as the cry of each individual in Israel and therefore as having a collective sense. The same holds for the next line, where MT has "lest thou bring me to nought."
10. MT repeats "they have devoured him," which is omitted in LXX and the parallel Ps. 79:7.

sertion of other material. Editorial processes are seldom easy to follow, and the particular logic which caused an editor to arrange the text as we have it today often escapes us. Whatever the redactional situation may be, the theme of impending doom is now taken up again. Perhaps added emphasis was provided in inserting the poem in 10:1–16 before the final declaration set out in 10:17–25. The long-predicted catastrophe was now at the very gates of Jerusalem and the state of Judah was in imminent danger of destruction.

After a brief oracle (vv. 17–18) which depicts people preparing for flight, there is a solemn soliloquy and lament (vv. 19–21) in which Jeremiah gives expression to his own grief and reflects upon the stupidity of the rulers (shepherds) who brought the calamity to pass. This leads (v. 21) to an anguished cry that the foe is at hand. The section closes with a prayer for mercy (vv. 23–25). The final verse occurs also in Ps. 79:6–7 and may be an editorial comment.

17 The words are addressed to people who are under siege, probably the siege which preceded the fall of Jerusalem before the Babylonian armies in 597 B.C. The atmosphere is similar to that of 9:9–21 (Eng. 10–22). The verb "gather" *('āsap̱)* occurs both here and in 9:21. The people are to "gather up" (RVS) or *pick up*[11] their *bundle (kᵉnā'â)*, the few possessions they could carry for a journey. Assyrian bas-reliefs depict several scenes of captives carrying bundles on their heads. Such exiles were well known over a long period in the ancient Middle East.

18 There is a vividness in the first verb in this verse *(qāla')*, which is used of hurling with a sling. It is Yahweh himself who is pictured as casting out the inhabitants of Judah *at this very time.*[12] On other occasions he had been patient and forbearing; but now the hour of judgment had come.[13] The time for pleading and weeping had passed. The translation "I will press them hard and squeeze them dry" (NEB) depends on a minor textual change.[14] Both pic-

11. J. Bright, *Jeremiah,* p. 70. The force of *mē'ereṣ* is not clear. If it is an independent word in a staccato utterance, the sense may be "Gather together your bundle. Out of the land." Hence NEB "Put your goods together and carry them out of the country."

12. J. Bright, *Jeremiah,* p. 70 vividly translates "Now, right now."

13. The view that Yahweh made use of human agents or sometimes of the forces of nature to fulfil his purpose is common in the OT. Cf. Isa. 10:5; 44:28; etc.

14. See textual note. RSV adheres to MT with "I will bring distress on them, that they may feel (find) it."

tures are vigorous and lay stress on Yahweh's final decisive act of judgment.

19–21 The simplest way to understand these verses is to see in them the anguished cry of Jeremiah, who is so deeply identified with his people that his own lament can be equated with the lament of the nation.[15] Judah has suffered hurt. Her wound is incurable. Her reaction to her calamity is portrayed in the language of tent dwellers whose tent has been uprooted. This was an affliction and she must bear it. Like the nomad, her *tent* (Jerusalem) is ruined, all the tent ropes have been snapped, her *sons* (citizens) have left her, and no one remains to set up the tent again and to hang its curtains.

Continuing the symbolism, reference is made to shepherds and their flock. The *shepherds* were Judah's leaders, in the first instance perhaps the kings, although the term may include other leaders, political and religious (cf. 2:8). These are described as *stupid* ("mere brutes," NEB), men who do not seek after Yahweh, that is, they conduct themselves without reference to Yahweh's covenant and its laws and commandments, and without that sincere seeking after his mind and will which would arise out of an attitude of submission and obedience. Little wonder they did not prosper. It is they who are ultimately responsible for the plight of the whole nation. *All their flock is scattered.* This image of "stupid shepherds" and a "scattered flock" was taken up by Ezekiel in a lengthy allegory (Ezek. 34). Both Jeremiah and Ezekiel held the view that the kings through their sacred anointing were Yahweh's representatives to guard the covenant and lead the people. It was their task as national leaders to continue the work of Moses and the charismatic judges. All this is implied in the verb "seek" *(dāraš),* which often means "consult." Some commentators[16] regard the term *shepherd* as a metaphor for prophets, whose task it was to "inquire of the Lord" (cf. 21:2; 2 K. 22:13–14, etc.). But whomever Jeremiah had in mind, kings or prophets, when these were more interested in playing politics than in carrying out the will of Yahweh, the whole nation would suffer. Jeremiah had some notorious examples before him of such wanton rejection of the divine intention by a king in Israel, in the

15. See pp. 88–92.
16. W. L. Holladay, *Jeremiah: Spokesman Out of Time*, pp. 57f.

persons of Manasseh and his great-grandson Jehoiakim, who was ruling at the time of the oracle.[17]

22 A brief ejaculation announces the arrival of the foe from the north. The reference here is to the Babylonians, who were coming with a *tremendous uproar*[18] (cf. 1:13–15). They were intent on laying waste the cities of Judah and turning them into a refuge for wild beasts. As it turned out, following Nebuchadrezzar's second invasion in 587 B.C. destruction was widespread. Modern archeological investigation has shown a uniform picture. Many towns were destroyed at the beginning of the sixth century B.C. and never again occupied. Others were destroyed at the time and partly reoccupied at some later date. Still others were destroyed and reoccupied only after a long period of abandonment. There is no known case of a town in Judah proper which was continuously occupied through the exilic period.[19] The particular phrases used in the latter part of this verse seem to have been part of the literary language used to describe the destruction of cities (51:37; Zeph. 2:13–15; etc.).

23 Was there still some plea that Jeremiah could make on behalf of his nation? His deep concern for his own people compelled him to plead with God to the end, even while he pronounced Yahweh's judgment on them. Perhaps God would respond to the plea that there was an important extenuating factor, namely, the basic inability of men to control their own destiny. His argument with God was: "A man's course is not in his own control, nor is it in his power as he goes his way to direct his own steps." The exact import of these words is not clear. On the one hand Jeremiah may have been referring to a fundamental moral weakness in men which made them unable to resist evil consistently and to walk uprightly all their days. Such a view would find an echo in other places in Jeremiah's oracles (e.g., 17:9).[20]

Alternately the reference may be to the destiny of man, which is outside his control however much he may imagine in his pride that it lies in his own power.[21] God had purposes for Judah, and

17. See R. de Vaux, *Ancient Israel,* pp. 110–14 for a discussion on the Israelite view of kingship. Cf. S. Mowinckel, *He that Cometh* (Oxford, 1956), pp. 21–95.
18. The word *ra'aš* is commonly used for "earthquake" (e.g., 1 K. 19:11).
19. W. F. Albright, *The Archaeology of Palestine,* pp. 141f.
20. The view is accepted by R. K. Harrison, *Jeremiah and Lamentations,* p. 94.
21. The view is accepted by E. W. Nicholson, *Jeremiah 1–25,* p. 105; G. P. Couturier, "Jeremiah," *JBC,* p. 312.

there was no resisting the divine intention. After all, God was the potter and Judah the clay. The shape of the vessel lay in the mind of the potter. The allegory is worked out by Jeremiah in ch. 18 (cf. Isa. 45:9–13).

The particular vocabulary of this verse with its reference to *way (dereḵ)* and *steps (ṣaʿaḏ)* is well known in wisdom literature (cf. Ps. 37:23; Prov. 16:9; 20:24). There seems to have been a group of wise men in Jeremiah's day (cf. 18:18) who may have influenced such thinking. For the wise man the *way* was the sum of rules leading to a happy and successful life. But this lay in God's hands, who had control over all his creation, which included man.

Which of these views is correct in the context may be open to conjecture. There is a certain feasibility in both of them. But on either view Jeremiah, speaking on behalf of the people, offered this argument to God as a plea for mercy. The following verse constitutes a prayer offered from Jeremiah's lips but representing the prayer of the people.

24 It might well be asked what was the import of these words originally. The people may have been arguing that although God had often commanded them to walk uprightly (e.g., 6:16), they were not really responsible for their actions (v. 23); and although, perhaps, they deserved punishment, God should punish them with restraint. The verb translated *correct (yissar)* is used in many places in the OT for educational or corrective punishment.[22] There may well have been in the view of the people two possibilities of judgment. The one was punishment according to the gravity of the crime, that is, in strict *justice (mišpāṭ)*. That way lay destruction, and hence the plea, "not in anger lest thou bring us almost to nothing" (NEB). The other was correction according to their weakness. God was being asked to show mercy and patience with his people, correcting their behavior but sparing them from destruction (cf. 46:28).

The pages of the OT contain examples of both kinds of judgment. The view expressed in the words "Whom the Lord loveth he correcteth" (Prov. 3:12) is set in contrast with the view expressed in other passages (e.g., Prov. 19:28, 29; Ezek. 30:14). Corrective

22. In this sense the verb and the corresponding noun are common in Wisdom Literature, e.g., Job 5:17; Ps. 6:2 (Eng. 1); 38:2 (Eng. 1); Prov. 15:10; 29:17.

judgment and punitive judgment are both part of the OT.[23] Clearly here the people fear the latter. Hence they pray that the divine judgment will be applied without undue severity. On the other hand the people felt no restraint in asking God to pour out his wrath upon Israel's foes.

25 It was a commonly held view in ancient Israel that the *nations (gôyîm)* were the proper recipients of divine judgment, for they were not only outside the covenant, where God's mercy was especially operative, but they had attacked and preyed upon God's people down through the years. Israel was holy to the Lord, and upon all who harmed her evil would surely come (2:3). Their misdeeds are listed here. They *devoured*[24] *Jacob* (Israel), made an end of him, and laid waste his *pasture land (nāweh).* The reference is to the many invaders of the land over the centuries—Egyptians, Assyrians, Edomites, Syrians, etc. It was such as these who merited the *wrath (ḥēmâ)* of Yahweh. Moreover, these peoples did not *acknowledge (yāḏa',* "know") Yahweh and did not call upon his name. Jeremiah well knew that many in Judah did not know Yahweh in that intimate sense of personal committal which was of the essence of knowing the Lord (cf. 2:8). Many others, even if they called on him at times, did not call upon him exclusively but called also to a tree and a stone (2:26, 27; 10:1–16; etc.). Hence, if judgment was meted out on those who did not know Yahweh and did not call upon his name, then the people of Israel must share such a judgment with the nations (*gôyîm*).

In that lay Jeremiah's dilemma. His heart told him to plead for divine mercy; but logic pointed to the inevitability of judgment on Judah also (cf. Amos 5:18–20). That Israel also should need to be punished in the way prescribed for the Gentiles was the tragic result of centuries of unrestrained apostasy and the rejection of Yahweh's covenant and its demands. It was simply not true that Yahweh would overlook sin and rebellion in his own people, however

23. For a more complete discussion of the theme of judgment in the OT see some of the theologies of the OT such as W. Eichrodt, *Theology of the OT,* I (London, 1960), pp. 457–471. Eichrodt's emphasis is on "covenant breaking and judgment." See also G. von Rad, *OT Theology,* II (London, 1965), pp. 66ff., 156, 231, 283, 340, etc. The remarks of J. Lindblom, *Prophecy in Ancient Israel* (1962) are useful. See index.
24. See textual note.

much they reasoned that they lay beyond divine judgment simply because he once chose them to be his people. Jeremiah offered the people a theology for disaster before it struck. The weight of his words was not fully appreciated till many years after his death.

C. WARNINGS AND JUDGMENT (11:1–15:9)

1. THE BROKEN COVENANT AND WARNINGS OF JUDGMENT (11:1–13:27)

(i) The Broken Covenant (11:1–17)

1 *The word that came to Jeremiah from Yahweh:*
2 *"Listen*[1] *to the terms of this covenant. Repeat them*[2] *to the men of Judah and to the citizens of Jerusalem.*
3 *Tell them: This is what Yahweh the God of Israel has said: Cursed be the man who does not observe the terms of this covenant,*
4 *which I commanded your fathers in the day when I brought them out of the land of Egypt, out of the iron furnace, and said: 'Obey my voice and do exactly as I command you. Then you will be my people, and I in my turn will be your God.'*
5 *In this way I will perform the oath which I swore to your fathers, to give them a land flowing with milk and honey—as it obtains today." Then I answered, "Amen, Yahweh!"*
6 *Then Yahweh said to me, "Proclaim all these terms in the cities of Judah and in the streets of Jerusalem and say, Hear the terms of this covenant and carry them out!*
7[3] *For I solemnly warned your fathers in the day when I brought them up from the land of Egypt; even to this day I have warned them persistently:*[4] *Obey my voice!*
8 *But they have not obeyed, nor paid attention to me,*[5] *but each one followed the wicked obstinacy of his own heart. So I brought them all the penalties*[6] *of this covenant which I commanded them to perform but which they did not carry out."*
9 *Then Yahweh said to me, "A conspiracy exists among the men of Judah and among the citizens of Jerusalem.*

1. MT reads the plur. verb in "Hear the words of this covenant," although Jeremiah is addressed in vv. 1–3.
2. MT has another plur. in *wᵉdibbartām,* "You shall speak." LXX and Syr. read sing. *dabbēr.*
3. Most of vv. 7 and 8 are lacking in LXX. Only the last phrase of v. 8 is preserved, "and they did not obey."
4. Lit. "rising early and warning."
5. Lit. "they did not turn their ear."
6. Lit. "the words," but the reference seems to be to words of judgment or cursing.

10 *They have turned back to the iniquities of their earliest ancestors who refused to listen to my words. They themselves have followed other gods and worshipped them. The house of Israel and the house of Judah have broken my covenant which I made with their fathers.*

11 *Therefore these are the words of Yahweh: Look, I am about to bring upon them a disaster which they cannot escape; and though they cry out to me I will not hear them.*

12 *Then the cities of Judah and the citizens of Jerusalem will go and cry for help to the gods to which they have burnt sacrifices; but these will not in any way save them in their hour of disaster.*

13[7] *For your gods are as numerous as your cities, O Judah! And you have erected as many altars to the Shameful Thing*[8] *as there are streets in Jerusalem, altars to burn sacrifices to Baal.*

14 *So, for your part, do not pray for this people! Raise no entreaty or prayer on their behalf, for I will not listen when they call to me in the hour*[9] *of their distress.*

15[10] *What right has my beloved in my house,*
Working out clever schemes?
Can fat beasts and consecrated flesh
Turn away from you the calamity that threatens you?[11]
Can you by these escape?

7. There are some grounds for regarding vv. 13 and 14 as poetry. A possible arrangement is:

13 For-the-number-of-your'-cities are' your'-gods O-Judah,'
The number-of-the-streets'-of-Jerusalem you-have-set-up'
altars' to-the-Shame'ful-Thing,
Altars' to-sacrifice' to-Ba'al

The stress arrangement is 4:4:3.

14 But-you,' do-not-pray' for-the-people' this,'
Do-not-raise-up' for-them' entreaty' or-prayer,'
For-I-will'-not lis'ten at-the-time'-of-their-calling
To-me' in-the-time-of'-their-distress.

The stress arrangement is 4:4, 3:2.

In both verses there is a good measure of parallelism. The Jerusalem Bible recognizes the poetic form of v. 13.

8. The phrase *altars to the Shameful Thing* is lacking in LXX. It may be a gloss or a variant of "to burn offerings to Baal."

9. Many mss. and the Versions read *b^{e}'ēṯ* for MT *b^{e}'aḏ*, which may be a dittography from the preceding clause.

10. The verse has a number of textual problems. In line 1 read *mê lîḏîḏî b^{e}ḇēṯî 'āś^{e}ṯâ zimmâ*. In line 2 MT *hārabbîm*, "the many," seems unsuitable. NEB suggests *hābb^{e}rî'îm,* which becomes *habb^{e}riyyîm,* "fat offerings." Other suggestions are *han^{e}ḏārîm,* "vows," or *haḥ^{a}lāḇîm,* "fat." Also in line 2, for MT *ya'aḇ^{e}rû* (Qal) read the Hiphil *ya'^{a}ḇîrû mē'ālāyiḵ rā'āṯēḵî*, with LXX omitting *kî* as a dittography. The final *y* on *rā'āṯēḵî* is an old feminine ending. The phrase then means "will they turn away your disaster from upon you." Line 3 is difficult. MT *āz ta'^{a}lōzî,* "then you will exult," seems out of place. Various proposals have been made. LXX seems to point to a text *'im 'al zō'ṯ ta'ûzî,* "will you by these escape?" But NEB transfers the phrase to v. 16 after *š^{e}mēḵ,* "but you will feel sharp anguish."

11. Lit. "your calamity."

16 *A leafy olive tree, lovely to behold,*[12]
Was Yahweh's name for you.
But with the roar of a great tempest
He sets its foliage[13] *on fire,*
He consumes its branches.
17 *The Lord of Hosts who planted you has decreed disaster for you, because of the wickedness which both the house of Judah and the house of Israel have committed in provoking me to anger by burning sacrifices to Baal."*

The character of Jer. 11:1–17 has been the subject of a great deal of discussion. Three main issues are involved: (i) The question of the relationship between chs. 11 and 12 (and perhaps 13 also). There are some grounds for thinking that these two or three chapters form an editorial unit, even though they may comprise materials that are heterogeneous in character. The principal emphasis is on the broken covenant.[14] (ii) The prose material in ch. 11 raises the question of authorship. Was this authentically from Jeremiah? Or was it a free composition of later editors, perhaps the so-called Deuteronomic editors, who either made use of authentic material which stemmed from Jeremiah, or even wrote the prose themselves in an endeavor to capture the spirit of Jeremiah's preaching in a later day?[15] (iii) The meaning of the expression *this covenant* in vv. 3 and 8. Does *this covenant* refer to that made under Josiah (2 K. 23:1–3) following the discovery of the book of the law (2 K. 22:8) which added strength to Josiah's reform, or is the reference to the ancient Mosaic covenant? There may not be a great difference between the two since Josiah's covenant was regarded as a re-proclamation of the Mosaic covenant. Jeremiah was certainly concerned with obedience to the ancient covenant demands, which was more important than the performance of rituals in the temple.[16] Fortunately the main theological thrust of this section is not materially altered by the view adopted on any one of these issues.

1 The question is at once raised as to whether the prose material that follows is a verbatim report of Jeremiah's words. As

12. MT reads "fair of fruit, of form." LXX omits "fruit." *BHS* suggests *y^e^pêpēh*, "beautiful"; cf. also 46:20.

13. MT reads *'āleyhā,* "upon her." Read *b^e^'ālēhû,* "to its leaves." The context requires masculine. The picture is of a tree struck by lightning.

14. J. Bright, *Jeremiah,* p. 88; H. L. Ellison, "The Prophecy of Jeremiah," *EQ* 34/3 (July-Sept. 1962), pp. 154f.

15. See the Introduction, "The Book of Jeremiah: Composition," pp. 33–50.

16. See the Introduction, "Jeremiah and the Covenant," pp. 59–67.

with other prose segments in the book the material has been variously understood. There is no necessity to hold the view that we have here the exact words of Jeremiah. The material would have a high degree of authenticity if it could be regarded as based upon some original utterance of Jeremiah. It has often been pointed out that the language is as "Deuteronomic" as any in the book, and perhaps the most markedly Deuteronomic in the whole book[17] both in its words and the phrases and in the literary form, consisting of (i) the proclamation of God's law (vv. 3–7), (ii) a statement of Israel's disobedience (vv. 8–10), (iii) the announcement of God's rejection of and judgment upon Israel (vv. 11–17). The passage can be understood as explaining why disaster would befall Israel. Other prose passages were designed to give some hope for the future as well. It seems that part of the problem of this and other passages lies in whether Jeremiah sometimes preached in prose, and if he did, in what kind of prose? Might he not have inherited, as did the Deuteronomists, the prose style of the age?[18] And might Jeremiah not have used the same literary forms in his prose as the Deuteronomic authors, since they were both children of an age? Further, it would seem beyond doubt that the very things the Deuteronomists hoped to achieve by their writing, namely, to explain the cause of the calamity that befell Judah and to give some hope in the hour of despair, were strongly characteristic of Jeremiah's own preaching. Thus, it is arguable that the prose passages in Jeremiah, while not necessarily his *ipsissima verba,* represent strongly the teaching of the prophet and are, to an extent, couched in the language and form of a man of the late seventh and early sixth century B.C. There are two further points. It is arguable that Jeremiah himself had a strong personal conviction that he stood in the succession of Moses.[19] It did not need the activity of Deuteronomic editors to point that out. Further, if more weight is to be attached to poetry than prose in determining the authentic parts of the book of Jeremiah, it should be noted that there is probably more poetry in 11:1–17 than has been generally allowed. Verses 15–16 are accepted as verse by all commentators. We have argued that vv. 13–14 also have some claim to be recog-

17. E. W. Nicholson, *Jeremiah 1–25,* pp. 107f.
18. So J. Bright, "The Date of the Prose Sermons of Jeremiah," *JBL* 70 (1951), p. 26.
19. W. L. Holladay, "The Background of Jeremiah's Self-Understanding," *JBL* 83 (1964), pp. 153–164; "Jeremiah and Moses: Further Observations," *JBL* 85 (1966), pp. 17–27.

nized as verse. Indeed, one wonders whether there may not be snatches of rhythmic language in other areas despite their otherwise prosaic character.

A further question concerns the date at which the message was preached. The passage provides no direct clue. However, if there is any sort of chronological arrangement in the whole book, ch. 11 is subsequent to ch. 7, which can be dated to Jehoiakim's time (26:1), so that we may propose the reign of Jehoiakim rather than that of Josiah, that is, some years *after* Josiah's reform when the reform movement had lost its momentum and people had returned to their old ways.[20]

2–5 The MT of v. 2 is difficult. The Hebrew begins the verse with a plural verb, *Listen,* which does not suit the context where Jeremiah personally is addressed. A feasible proposal[21] is to translate: *Listen to the terms of this covenant.* (You [singular] are to) *repeat them to the men of Judah and to the citizens of Jerusalem. Tell them. . . .* If we translate v. 2 in this way the phrase *Listen to the terms of this covenant* becomes a heading to the whole section for which *this covenant* (vv. 2, 3, 6) is the key phrase. While at first sight the reference may seem to be to the Josianic covenant which was so prominent in the minds of Jeremiah's hearers, we should probably look to something more fundamental than that. The pronoun *this* points forward to vv. 4–5, which deal with the Sinaitic covenant at the beginning of Israel's history.[22] The moment we are freed from the necessity of linking this passage with Josiah's law book and covenant based on it, we are under no obligation to regard the passage as coming from the days of Josiah.

This brings us to the heart of a covenant. Significant words meet us at once—*cursed ('ārûr), observe* (hear or obey, *šāma'), terms* (words, *d^e^ḇārîm),*[23] *covenant (b^e^rîṯ).* The covenant comprised terms or covenant stipulations, curses and blessings and witnesses, and was accepted under an oath in which the subject promised obedience. Obedience to the covenant stipulations brought blessing,

20. J. Bright, *Jeremiah,* p. 89; H. L. Ellison, "The Prophecy of Jeremiah," *EQ* 34/3, pp. 155f. But cf. R. K. Harrison, *Jeremiah and Lamentations* (1973), p. 84; *Introduction to the OT* (1970), p. 805.

21. A. Weiser, *Das Buch des Propheten Jeremia* (1960), p. 93.

22. J. Skinner, *Prophecy and Religion* (1922), pp. 91–102.

23. The use of the word *dāḇār,* "word," is consistent with the Near Eastern treaties where the covenant or treaty stipulations are called words *(awātu).* See J. A. Thompson, *The Vocabulary of Covenant in the OT* (Unpub. Ph.D. thesis, University of Cambridge, 1963), pp. 203f.

breach of covenant brought a curse.[24] The covenant to which the passage refers is defined clearly in v. 4.[25] The covenant obligations are those which Yahweh commanded the forefathers of the present generation when he delivered them from Egypt, from the iron furnace (Deut. 4:20; 1 K. 8:51; Isa. 48:10). In those days the command was *obey (šāma' bᵉ) my voice and do exactly as I command you.* A promise is added: *You will be my people, and I . . . will be your God* (7:23; 24:7; 32:38; cf. Exod. 19:5–6). Such obedience would result in a blessing according to Yahweh's own covenant *oath (šᵉḇû'â)* which he swore to the forefathers.[26] Part at least of the promised blessing was *a land flowing with milk and honey.*[27] In fact, that promise had been fulfilled, as the people of Jeremiah's day well knew.[28]

Jeremiah's response to Yahweh's command was *Amen,* a standard response to a covenant.[29]

That then was the covenant Jeremiah was to declare. Judah needed to be recalled to the historic Sinai event when God promised to supply the material and spiritual needs of his people in their infancy as a nation, in return for their undivided worship and obedience. That way lay life. The way of disobedience was the way of death (cf. Deut. 30:15–20).

6–8 While vv. 7–8 are missing from LXX except for the phrase *which they did not carry out*[30] (the covenant stipulations), they may nevertheless have formed part of the original Hebrew text. Verse 6 raises an interesting question. Was Jeremiah in any sense an itinerant prophet, since according to this passage he was instructed to proclaim the covenant stipulations *in the cities of Judah and in the streets of Jerusalem*? Certainly the record does not preserve any reference to such a ministry. The impression we gain is that Jeremiah preached in Jerusalem and particularly in the temple area until he was forbidden (36:5). It was there that he clashed with Hananiah in the days of Zedekiah (28:1). It was there he preached

24. See Lev. 26:14–39; Deut. 27:15–26; 28:15–69 (Eng. 29:1).
25. Exod. 19:1–8; 20:1–17. The *words* of the Decalog are the covenant stipulations.
26. The promise ran back to Abraham (Gen. 15) and was renewed to Isaac and Jacob and later to the people of the Exodus (Deut. 7:8; 8:18; 9:5).
27. The phrase *milk and honey* was a description of fertility that was known in other documents in ancient Near Eastern literature, e.g., Tale of Sinuhe, *ANET,* p. 19. Cf. Exod. 3:8, 17; 13:5; 16:31; 33:3; Deut. 6:3; 11:9; 26:9, 15; 27:3; 31:20.
28. Cf. Deut. 2:30; 4:38; 6:23; 8:18.
29. Cf. Deut. 27:15–26; Exod. 19:8; 24:7.
30. Heb. *wᵉlō' 'āśû.*

the Temple Sermon (7:2). Shemaiah assumed that the high priest could contact him in the temple precincts (29:24–26). However, these verses could suggest such an activity, and it may be that under Jehoiakim, when it became clear to Jeremiah that the whole nation was apostate at heart, he undertook brief and unconventional visits to other cities. Such a possibility would provide a link between vv. 6–8 and vv. 9–14 where there is a reference to conspiracy (*qešer*) in the country as well as in the capital.

The demand presented by Jeremiah on Yahweh's behalf was *Hear the terms* (words) *of this covenant and carry them out!* (v. 6). Then in a wide-ranging review of Israel's past history the prophet spoke of the solemn warnings[31] issued during the centuries up to their own day without avail. The call was *Obey my voice*. But there was no obedience and no one paid attention. Rather did the people follow their own stubbornly wicked inclinations, which led them to share their allegiance with false gods (2:28). The breach of covenant was complete and judgment was inevitable. The theme of the false gods is developed in the following verses, which are thus closely linked to vv. 6–8.

9–14 An interesting term (Heb. *qešer*) is introduced at this point which has been variously translated *conspiracy,* "mutiny" (Moffatt), "revolt," as though there was a formal uniting of the people of Judah against Yahweh. The term is a metaphor. There was no deep-laid plot, no secrecy behind the apostasy that Jeremiah witnessed, although religiously Judah displayed all that a carefully organized plot would achieve.[32] The metaphor is a pointed one. The net result of the apostasy was the renunciation of Yahweh's lordship and of the nation's covenant obligations.

The verb *šûḇ,* which is used again and again in Jeremiah,[33] appears here in the sense of "turning back" (v. 9). The apostasy of Judah was a turning back of the people to the *iniquities ('ᵃwōnōṯ)* of their earliest forefathers, who refused to listen to Yahweh's covenant demands. This led them to follow other gods and to serve (or

31. The expression "rising early and warning" (Heb. *haškēm wᵉhā'ēḏ)* conveys a sense of urgency and of taking pains. Elsewhere in Jeremiah similar combinations occur like "rising early and speaking" (7:13; 35:14) and "rising early and sending" (7:25; 25:4; 26:5; 29:19; 35:15; 44:4).

32. The derivatives of the root *qšr* have a political significance in some cases. See P. Ackroyd, "The Verb Love—*'āhēb* in the David-Jonathan Narratives—a Footnote," *VT 25* (1975), pp. 213f.

33. See the Introduction, pp. 76–81, and W. L. Holladay, *The Root šûbh in the OT* (1958).

worship) them. Such an act constituted a breach of covenant[34] (v. 10) and would result in the operation of the curses of the covenant, from which there is no escape (v. 12). The repetition of 2:28 in v. 13 is presumably intended to imply that things under Jehoiakim were as they were in the early days of Jeremiah's ministry, that is, the reform of 621 B.C. had made no difference. In v. 14 there is a reiteration and slight expansion of 7:16. Renewed apostasy, bearing witness to the lack of any genuine repentance in Judah, made intercession useless.

If vv. 13 and 14 are, in fact, poetic, and if the poetic material is more likely to point to a genuine Jeremianic utterance, the content of these verses is unusually significant. They deal with the great number of altars set up for offering sacrifices to Baal (v. 13) and the instruction to Jeremiah not to pray for the people since Yahweh would not listen to them when they called on him in the hour of their distress. A similar prohibition to pray occurs in 7:16 and 14:11, both prose passages, while there are references to altars, *mizbeḥôt,* in 17:1, 2, also a prose passage.

15–17 The situation described in the preceding verses is summed up in a short oracle which has suffered severely in its textual transmission; any reconstruction is conjectural.[35] The picture of Israel as the beloved *(yāḏîḏ)* of Yahweh occurs also in 12:7 and in Isa. 5:1. *My house* is a reference to the temple in Jerusalem. It was there that Judah was carrying out *clever schemes,* a reference, it seems, to the meaningless rituals carried out there day by day. This is clear from the next line in the poem with its reference to fat beasts and the flesh of sacrifices. But these would not avail to turn disaster away from Judah. Once again the emptiness and futility of ritual sacrifices without faithfulness and obedience to Yahweh is stressed. The mere offering of a sacrifice in the belief that Yahweh was thereby satisfied reduced religion to little more than superstition.

There are more textual problems in v. 16 but the sense is clear.[36] Time was when Yahweh saw in Israel a leafy olive tree, beautiful to behold. Alas, that beautiful tree now appears to the prophet's vision with its foliage set on fire and its branches burning—a grim picture of the doom about to engulf Yahweh's people. It was he, Yahweh of Hosts, who had *planted* Israel,[37] but he had

34. The expression *hēpēr berîṯ* is standard for breaking a covenant.
35. See textual notes.
36. See textual notes.
37. Heb. *nāṭa'*. Cf. 1:10; 2:21; 18:9; Isa. 5:2.

pronounced evil (*disaster*) against her because of her evil (v. 17). There is a play on the term *rāʿâ,* which is used here for both evil and its consequences. The verb used for burning a sacrifice (*qiṭṭēr*) seems to have formed a significant element in the vocabulary of the book of Jeremiah.[38]

There is nothing in this oracle that does not appear in earlier oracles except that there is here a certain sense of the imminence of coming doom. Such language would certainly provoke the kind of reaction we find in 11:18–12:6, where we are told of a plot against Jeremiah's life in his own village.

(ii) A Plot against Jeremiah's Life (11:18–12:6)

18 *Yahweh informed me and so I knew it.*
Then it was you opened my eyes[1] *to their evil deeds.*
19 *And I, for my part, was like an innocent lamb*
Led to the slaughter,
Not knowing that it was against me
They had hatched plots.
"Let us destroy the tree while the sap is in it,[2]
Let us cut him off from the land of the living,
And let his name be remembered no more."
20 *O Yahweh of Hosts, who art a righteous judge,*
Who tests the heart[3] *and mind,*[4]
Let me see thy vengeance upon them,
For to thee I have committed[5] *my cause.*
21 *Therefore this is what Yahweh said concerning the men of Anathoth who seek your life*[6] *and say, "Do not prophesy in the name of Yahweh or we will kill you."*[7]

38. 1:16; 7:9; 11:12–13, 17; 18:15; 19:4, 13; 32:29; 44:3, 5, 8, 15, 17–19, 21, 23. Of these 1:16 and 18:15 are in poetic passages, which may indicate that Jeremiah himself used the verb. This lends weight to the possibility that the prose has preserved Jeremiah's words here, and perhaps also in many other places.

1. LXX reads "I saw."
2. MT *beḷaḥmô,* "with its bread," understood by AV, RSV as "with its fruit." Emend to *beḷēḥô,* "in its sap." It is possible that there is an enclitic *m* between the noun and the suffix which was misunderstood. See M. J. Dahood, "Ugaritic Studies and the Bible," *Gregorianum* 43 (1962), p. 66.
3. Heb. *kelāyôṯ,* "kidneys."
4. Lit. "heart."
5. MT *gillîṯî,* "I have revealed," is here revocalized to *gallôṯî,* "I have rolled upon," i.e., "entrusted" or "committed"; cf. Ps. 22:9 (Eng. 8); 37:5.
6. LXX "my life."
7. Lit. "that you do not die by our hand."

22 *Therefore this is what Yahweh of Hosts says:*[8] *"Look, I will punish them; their young men shall die by the sword, their sons and their daughters shall die by famine;*
23 *and they will leave no remnant. For I will bring calamity upon the men of Anathoth, the year of their doom."*
12:1 *O Lord, thou art in the right*
When I dispute with thee.
Yet there are cases I would argue with thee.
Why does the way of wicked men succeed?
Why are all treacherous men at ease?
2 *Thou hast planted them, and they take root,*
They grow and bear fruit.
Thou art near in their mouths,
But far from their hearts.[9]
3 *But thou, O Lord, knowest me, dost see me,*[10]
Dost examine my thoughts[11] *toward thyself.*
Drag them off like sheep to the slaughter house,[12]
And set them apart for the day of slaughter.
4 *How long must the land mourn*
And the green grass of every field wither
Because of the wickedness of those who dwell in it?
Both beasts and birds have perished
Since they have said, "He[13] *will not see what we are doing."*[14]
5 *"If you have raced with men on foot*
And they have wearied you,
Then how will you compete against horses?
And if in country that is safe
You are complacent,[15]
Then how will you fare in the thicket of the Jordan?
6 *For even your brothers and your kinsmen,*
Even they have betrayed you,
Even they are in full cry after you.
Do not trust them
Even though they speak fair words to you."

A plot against Jeremiah's life instigated by his own family at Anathoth is discovered by the prophet. This came as a shock to

8. This introduction is lacking in LXX; it may have been thought redundant because similar words appear in v. 21.
9. Lit. "their kidneys."
10. The last verb is lacking in LXX.
11. Lit. "my heart."
12. This colon is lacking in LXX.
13. LXX has "God."
14. MT reads "our end," *'aḥ^{a}rîṯēnû.* LXX reads "our ways," *'orḥôṯênû;* so NEB.
15. MT *bôṭēaḥ,* "trusting," "unsuspecting," "feeling secure" as in Judg. 18:10; Isa. 32:9–10; Amos 6:1. RSV "fall down" understands a root *bṭḥ* II as in KB[3]; others emend to *bôrēaḥ,* "fleeing."

Jeremiah and led him to some deep reflection on his own mission and on the meaning of human existence in general. The sequence of events in the present narrative is not easy to follow, and some commentators have sought to make the logic clearer to the modern reader by various rearrangements of the material. As the passage now stands, it begins abruptly. In terms of Western logic we might have expected that 12:6 with its details about the plot against Jeremiah would precede 11:18 since the plot was in fact prior in time to Jeremiah's discovery of it. But there is a variety of textual problems also, as we shall see in the exegesis. Perhaps therefore we should allow for some disturbance in the text.[16]

The section raises another interesting question, for we meet here the first of Jeremiah's so-called confessions, or dialogs, in which he gave expression to complaints against God.[17]

There remains the problem of the date of this incident. The editorial arrangement of the book may have placed the incident here in order to indicate that preaching of the kind we meet in 11:1–17 caused Jeremiah to be persecuted even by his relatives and fellow townsmen. Some commentators have attempted to place the "confessions" in chronological order. On one view 12:1–6 was one of the early confessions and came perhaps early in the reign of Jehoiakim.[18]

18 In vv. 18–23 we have the prophet's lament and plea (vv. 18–20) followed by God's response (vv. 21–23). Jeremiah begins by lamenting the treachery plotted against him and describing the intentions of his adversaries (cf. Ps. 3:2–3 [Eng. 1–2]). There is no prior hint about *their evil deeds*. The information comes suddenly,

16. J. Bright, *Jeremiah,* pp. 83ff., places 12:1–6 after 11:17 and then picks up 11:18–23. G. P. Couturier in "Jeremiah," *JBC*, p. 313, art. 42, is content merely to transpose 12:6 after 11:18 in the interest of logic. The problem arises from the fact that in 11:18–23 Jeremiah already knows of his kinsmen's treachery against him while in 12:6 he has just been informed. For this reason 12:1–5 is placed before 11:18–23. E. W. Nicholson, *Jeremiah 1–25,* p. 112, suggests another possibility, namely that 11:18–23 is, to some extent, the work of a Deuteronomic editor in which he took up some of Jeremiah's own words (vv. 18–20) and added interpretative comments (vv. 21–23). These show traces of the style and phraseology of the Deuteronomist and serve to explain what Jeremiah had said in his "confession." Jeremiah's words are seen in the light of 12:6 as a reference to his brothers and kinsmen in Anathoth. If this is so, then the original confession was vv. 18–20, with vv. 21–23 as an explanatory insertion.
17. See the Introduction, "The 'Confessions' of Jeremiah" (pp. 88–92) and compare exegesis at 15:10–12, 15–18; 17:5–8, 9–10; 20:7–12.
18. Introduction, p. 91.

and we must wait till v. 21 before the picture becomes clear. Nor are we informed how Yahweh made it known to him. A sympathetic relative who brought the news may well have been Yahweh's informant. Only then did Jeremiah "see through their foul deeds."[19]

19 Christians of a later age saw in this description, *an innocent lamb led to the slaughter,* a picture of the betrayal of Christ to his death.[20] The words are also reminiscent of Isa. 53:7. It seemed to Jeremiah that his relationship to the people of Anathoth was that of an animal which was completely unaware of the intentions of its owner as he took it and led it to slaughter. The verse suggests that Jeremiah was aware of some schemes afoot in the village, but was altogether unaware that it was against him that they were hatching plots,[21] to take his life while it was still in its prime.[22] There may also be a hint that since Jeremiah was unmarried and had no children, his early death would prevent progeny like him being born. His name would be forgotten, a tragic end for a man of Israel, for whom descendants demonstrated the divine blessing on his life.

For any man of Israel, rejection by his society was a great grief. It was the price Jeremiah was called upon to pay for being true to his call from Yahweh.[23] The village, which gave him his basic social and psychological security, turned against him; and he was alone, cut off from those with whom he grew up and unable to count on the support which was normally available to a villager. Little wonder that he fled to God in dismay and despair.

20 At least Jeremiah did not lose his confidence in God who vindicated the cause of the innocent (Ps. 17:1–9). God knew all and could judge aright.[24] He tested the motives and the thoughts of all men.[25] Jeremiah's plea was that since he himself could not cope with the enormity of his problem—his whole village had turned against him—he could only ask God to intervene. He would stand

19. So J. Bright, *Jeremiah,* p. 18, following LXX. He asks whether MT *hir'îṯanî* may be a conflate of *rā'îṯî* (I saw) with *hir'anî* (he showed me). The noun *ma'ᵃlāl* often means simply *action, deed,* but here there is something sinister about the deeds.
20. Acts 8:32.
21. Heb. *ḥāšᵉḇû maḥᵃšāḇôṯ,* lit. "thinking thoughts," although the phrase often conveys this more sinister sense.
22. See textual note.
23. See W. L. Holladay, *Jeremiah: Spokesman Out of Time* (1974), pp. 75f.
24. MT *šōp̄ēṭ ṣeḏeq,* "judges aright," or perhaps, *a righteous judge.*
25. MT *kᵉlāyôṯ wālēḇ,* "kidneys and heart." Internal organs were conceived of as the seat of thought and affections.

aside and witness God's judgment *(n^{e}qāmâ, vengeance)* on them.[26] That was not an unusual cry for oppressed men in Israel to utter (cf. Ps. 17:13–14; 99:8; 149:7; Isa. 34:8; 35:4; etc.). In the hour of oppression from which the godly man in Israel could find no escape he could only commit his *cause (rîḇ)* to God. This word *cause* or "case" has a legal connotation in many places in the OT and is used in the sense of a legal case. At times Israel herself is called into Yahweh's presence to answer his case against her (Mic. 6:1; cf. Jer. 12:1).

21–23 The reason for Jeremiah's complaint in vv. 18–20 is now made clear. It was the men of Anathoth (see 1:1), Jeremiah's own village, who plotted murder against him. There would have been some strong reason why Jeremiah's fellow citizens took such strong action against him, although such actions are not unknown even today in the Middle East. Sometimes members of a family will set out to kill a kinsman who has brought disgrace on the family. The story told in the NT in John 8:3–6 is one that would have many parallels in the Near East over the centuries. Why did the men of Anathoth plot against Jeremiah's life? Some commentators[27] have suggested that it was because he supported Josiah's reformation, which led to the suppression of local sanctuaries and deprived local priests of their livelihood. But it is not at all clear that Jeremiah openly supported Josiah's reform even if he gave it tacit support. Perhaps it was Jeremiah's strong criticism of the whole of Judah's religious and social life that resulted in the plot to kill him. Neither Josiah nor his advisers nor the people in general had any idea of the fundamentally wrong and even dangerous perspectives that were represented in the religion of the day. The powerful denunciation of Israel's past and present failure to please God was quite incomprehensible to the men of Anathoth; and Jeremiah, who denounced the nation's sins, had brought serious disgrace upon the village which gave him birth and shelter. Such a man was worthy of death.[28] The

26. An alternative suggestion has been offered by G. E. Mendenhall, who would translate "Thy deliverance from them" rather than "thy vengeance from them." The preposition *min* in *mēhem,* "from them," gives a certain plausibility to the proposal. See J. Bright, *Jeremiah,* p. 87.

27. R. K. Harrison, *Jeremiah and Lamentations* (1973), p. 96.

28. Another view is that the citizens of Anathoth viewed Jeremiah as something of a traitor because he advocated surrender to Babylon and even claimed that God had delivered Judah over to Babylon (cf. 27:1–11). Anathoth would not wish to harbor such a dangerous man. See E. W. Nicholson, *Jeremiah 1–25,* p. 115.

exact reason for the plot is not known, but the threat was serious enough for the Lord to inform Jeremiah (v. 18). For their part the men of Anathoth forbade Jeremiah to *prophesy in the name of Yahweh* under threat of being killed by their hands.

Yahweh's reaction to such evil plots against his servant was decisive. He would visit them with judgment. *Calamity (rā'â)* was determined for the men of Anathoth, for the *year of their doom (p^e quddâ)* had arrived. The descriptive phrases of vv. 22–23 point to the outcome of a military invasion with war *(sword)* followed by famine, and no survivors *(remnant, š^e'ērîṯ)*. Threats from the men of Anathoth did not silence Jeremiah any more than a night in the stocks (20:1–3), or confinement in the cistern (38:6) or in the court of the guard (38:13). The call of God and the divine assurance of help was enough (1:5–10). The manner in which Yahweh's word against Anathoth was fulfilled is not known, but according to Ezra 2:23 a hundred and twenty-eight men of Anathoth returned from the exile, presumably to build again in a village that had been destroyed by the Babylonians. The site of ancient Anathoth has not been excavated so that we have no archeological information about any destruction in 587 B.C.

12:1 In 12:1–6 we have one of Jeremiah's "confessions," a brief self-revelation in which a man lays bare some of his own deep questionings and intimate feelings.[29] Here he speaks in his own name. The *I* is not Yahweh, as in the oracles, but the prophet himself in soliloquy. The problem raised is the age-old question of why the wicked should flourish. They were God's creatures. It lay in his power to bring them to judgment. But they pursued their evil ways unchecked and caused innocent men to suffer. Why, for example, should Jeremiah, God's servant, called to declare his word to disobedient Israel, be subjected to the treacherous plots of the men of his own village? Like Job and some of the psalmists Jeremiah believed in God and stood under his sovereignty but found his ways hard to comprehend.

There is no question that Yahweh is *in the right (ṣaddîq)*. The Hebrew adjective used here has a variety of nuances and is not always easy to translate. In the present text it is translated "righ-

29. These include 11:18–12:6; 15:10–11, 15–21; 17:14–18; 18:18–23; 20:7–13, 14–18. Certain other passages like 4:19–21; 5:3–5; 8:18–23 (Eng. 9:1) present Jeremiah speaking in the 1st person and giving vent to his anguish or revealing his thoughts. See the Introduction, "The 'Confessions' of Jeremiah," pp. 88–92.

teous'' (RSV), ''just'' (NEB and Bright), ''right'' (Jerusalem Bible). The corresponding noun *(ṣeḏeq* or *ṣeḏāqâ)* has a central significance in the OT for the relationship between a man and God and also between a man and his fellows. The predominant usage of the noun is concerned with what was regarded as ''right,'' ''standard,'' or ''normal'' in various contexts—social, legal, ethical, and religious. The righteous man *(ṣaddîq)* was the man who was faithful to all his obligations of whatever kind. In the legal sphere, as in the present context where Jeremiah is conducting a debate with Yahweh on the rights and wrongs of the prosperity of the wicked, the term *saddîq* takes on a meaning consistent with the context. When it comes to a legal debate with Yahweh, Jeremiah cannot win, since Yahweh is in the right. The verb used here for *dispute (rîḇ)* occurs often in the OT in reference to legal disputation (e.g., 50:34; 51:36; Isa. 1:17; 51:22; Lam. 3:58; Mic. 6:1). No legal complaint can be brought against Yahweh since he is innocent of all charges. Yet there were some specific *cases (mišpāṭîm)* of ''right'' that Jeremiah wished to discuss, namely, cases where the wicked prosper.

An alternative approach to the first part of v. 1 has been suggested by W. L. Holladay,[30] who translates *ṣaddîq* as ''innocent,'' the verb *rîḇ* as ''file a complaint,'' and the phrase *dibbēr mišpāṭ* as ''pass sentence'' (cf. 1:16; 4:12; 39:5). The following translation results:

Innocent art thou, O Lord,
When I file a complaint against thee.
Yet I would pass judgment against thee.

If this sense is followed, Jeremiah was charging God with failure to defend and protect him. God has sued Israel for breach of her covenant contract, but he stood guilty of breach of contract also. Jeremiah would take the place of the judge and declare God guilty. The language is reminiscent of the law-court language in the book of Job (9:15–16, 19–22).

The specific complaint of Jeremiah was:

Why does the way of wicked men succeed?
Why are all treacherous men at ease?

2 Part of the problem lay in that it was God who had *planted* such men, and they had taken root and were growing and producing

30. See *Jeremiah: Spokesman Out of Time,* pp. 92f.; cf. ''Jeremiah's Lawsuit with God,'' *Interpretation* 17 (1963), pp. 280–87.

fruit. Sentiments like these recall the words of Ps. 1:3–4.[31] Indeed it is possible to argue that these words in Jeremiah are a variation of the words in Ps. 1:3–4, as are the words in 17:5–8. The psalm suggests that good people are strengthened and prospered by God while evil people have no stability and soon perish. That was not Jeremiah's experience, nor Job's. Rather did the wicked whom God planted take firm root and bear fruit. And yet, although God's name was in the mouth of wicked men, he was far from their heart. The wicked, says Jeremiah, may talk about God but they have no concern for him.

3 Instead of the wicked, who in Jeremiah's view might well have been punished, it was Jeremiah, the man called by God and the faithful servant of God, who was suffering. And God knew the whole story. He knew *(yāḏa')*[32] him and saw him, and had tested his devotion.[33] According to the generally accepted view it was Jeremiah who should have been spared. Hence the question, *Why do the wicked prosper?*[34] The answer to that question belongs to the mystery of evil in God's creation, which has puzzled men of faith in every age. All that Jeremiah could propose was:

Drag them off like sheep to the slaughterhouse,
And set them apart for the day of slaughter.

Jeremiah's lament and plea ended on no more confident a note than we find in Habakkuk and Job. That there might be some divine purpose served through his suffering or that it might prove a means to a deeper knowledge of God does not seem to have been clear to the prophet, or if it was, he did not declare it.

4–6 God's response to Jeremiah's complaint really comes in vv. 5–6. Instead of the conventional answer of 11:21–23 that God would punish these evildoers, the unexpected and surprising answer of vv. 5–6 is given. But v. 4 poses some special problems. It is difficult to see how it can be connected with the argument. It turns

31. Many commentators assume that Ps. 1 was written after Jeremiah's time, e.g., W. R. Taylor, *IB* IV, p. 18; J. P. Hyatt, *IB* V, pp. 950f. on 17:5–8. W. L. Holladay, *Jeremiah: Spokesman Out of Time,* pp. 93, 98f. argues that Ps. 1 is earlier than Jeremiah since he offers two variations on the theme.

32. The verb *yāḏa'*, "know," carries a stronger sense than intellectual knowledge. It includes emotional and volitional elements as well, and implies a deep and intimate interpersonal relationship.

33. Lit. "You have tested my heart (mind, thoughts) in regard to yourself." Cf. 6:27, where Jeremiah was called upon to assay (test) the people. Here God "assays" Jeremiah.

34. The question was asked by Habakkuk (1:2–4), the psalmists (Pss. 37, 49, 73), Job, and others.

aside to discuss the effects of a severe drought and would fit admirably into some such context as 14:1–6.[35] It may be, of course, that we in our time simply fail to understand the editorial processes of the men who long ago collected Jeremiah's sayings. The verse does give expression to ideas that Jeremiah might have used and the idea that nature is disturbed when men behave wickedly (cf. Amos 4:6–10). Here was another of Jeremiah's questions—*How long must the land mourn and the green grass of every field wither because of the wickedness (rāʿâ) of those who dwell in it? Both beasts and birds have perished. . . .* The latter part of v. 4 on the other hand would fit into the same context as v. 3, and many commentators propose that it belongs there.[36] There is a textual problem in its final words, as discussed above in a textual note. Whatever reading is correct, God is regarded as being indifferent to their activities. Such men as these are, in Jeremiah's view, to be set aside for the day of slaughter.

With v. 5 we have God's unexpected reply to the prophet's complaint, as though God would suggest that if Jeremiah found his present lot a tough one, there was worse to come. This is presented under vigorous metaphors.

The first metaphor is concerned with athletic prowess. If running a footrace had worn the prophet out (Heb. *lāʾâ),* how would he hope to vie[37] with horses? In this context running with men seems to refer to Jeremiah's encounters with other prophets. There is a significant statement in 23:21: "I did not send the prophets, yet they ran." The other prophets, false prophets in Jeremiah's eyes, seem to have given him a "good run" and to have provided strong opposition (cf. 2:8; 5:13; 23:9–22; 28:1–17; 29:15–28; etc.). But he had yet to compete with *horses.* Here there is probably a thinly veiled reference to the military might of Babylon (cf. 4:13; 8:16). Local opposition from the people of Judah, of which he had already experienced a little, and which he was about to experience again in the plot of the citizens of his own village Anathoth, and then more and more as the months passed, was modest by comparison with the opposition yet to be experienced from a foreign foe. Or to put the matter another way: if Jeremiah was unsuspecting, feeling secure in a country that was peaceful, that is, he was too complacent and had not formed the habit of being on his guard, how would he behave

35. See W. Rudolph, *Jeremia,* p. 78.
36. J. Bright, *Jeremiah,* pp. 83, 87; W. Rudolph, *Jeremia,* p. 78.
37. *Compete*—Heb. *t^{e}ṯaḥ^{a}reh*, 2nd sing. future, an unusual derivative *(Tiphal)* of *ḥārâ*, "to burn," "glow with anger." Here it conveys a sense of zealous rivalry.

in the *thicket (gā'ôn,* "pride," "splendor") of Jordan? The region surrounding the Jordan was a place of jungle growth, the lair of lions (cf. 49:19; 50:44). Here too is a thinly veiled comparison between the relative peace of Judah now, when men could afford to be unsuspecting and complacent, and the fearful conditions that would prevail in that peaceful land when Nebuchadrezzar and his armies arrived. But even before that day came, the unsuspecting Jeremiah, like a sheep led obediently to the slaughter (11:18), was the subject of the dastardly plot of the men of Anathoth, including his brothers and kinsmen, who acted treacherously (Heb. *bāgaḏ)* toward him, and were even then in full cry after him as though he were a hunted animal. There could be no complacency in regard to such a company even though they spoke fine words.

God's words to Jeremiah then were a warning to him both to be on his guard and to prepare for more severe trials yet to come. This was nothing other than he might have expected from his initial call to fulfil the kind of ministry that was his (1:17–19). Jeremiah's place was to keep faith and courage in his present sufferings, which were negligible in comparison with those that lay ahead.

(iii) Yahweh Laments His Ravaged Inheritance (12:7–13)

7 *"I have forsaken my house,*
I have abandoned my heritage;
I have delivered my dearly beloved[1]
Into the power of her enemies.
8 *My heritage has become*
Like a lion in the forest to me;
She has given out her roar against me;
Therefore I hate her.
9 *Is my very own heritage a speckled bird of prey?*
Are the birds of prey against her on every side?[2]
Go, gather together every wild beast;
Bring them to the feast.
10 *Many shepherds have laid waste my vineyard,*
They have trampled down my field,
They have reduced my pleasant inheritance
To a desolate wilderness.
11 *They have left it a wasteland;*
Wasted, it mourns before me;
The whole land is laid waste,
But no man lays it to heart."

1. Lit. "The beloved of my soul."
2. See the commentary below on the text and translation.

12 *Destroyers have come*
Over all the bare heights in the wilderness;
The sword of Yahweh devours
The land from end to end;
No living thing has peace.
13 *They sowed*[3] *wheat and reaped thistles;*
They have tired themselves out for nothing;
They are disappointed at their harvest,
Because of the anger of Yahweh.

No indication is given of the historical incident that might have given rise to the lament expressed in these verses. But it was an occasion when Yahweh forsook his people. It would suit the time when marauding bands of Babylonians, Arameans, Moabites, and Ammonites were overrunning the land in 602 B.C. just prior to the Babylonian attack of 598/7 B.C. (cf. vv. 9–10, 12; 35:11; 2 K. 24:2). It would appear that the destruction was fairly considerable even if we allow some hyperbole in the expression. To underline the sadness of the occasion the poem is written in the Qinah measure[4] evidently regarded as appropriate to lamentations.

7 Israel is described as *my house, my heritage, my dearly beloved,* strong words to describe the attitude of Yahweh to his people. By contrast, the verbs *I have forsaken, I have abandoned, I have delivered,* all stress that Yahweh himself has brought about this judgment on the people. The reference to *house* is not to the temple but to the people.[5] *My house* is parallel to *my heritage* (inheritance), a familiar designation for the people of Israel in the OT (Deut. 9:29; Joel 2:17; 3:2; etc.). Israel is also known elsewhere in the OT as the *beloved* of Yahweh (11:15; Isa. 5:1). The pain occasioned to Yahweh as he delivers over his beloved people to their foes is strongly expressed here.

8 But Yahweh's heritage had acted like a lion in the forest, "roaring defiance"[6] at her Lord. One senses that the response of Israel is like that of a lion disturbed in the forest and ready for attack. Such a reaction is hateful to Yahweh, and such lions have to be destroyed.

9 The verse is difficult to translate since the versions differ

3. LXX renders this and the next verb as imperatives.
4. This is a poetic form in which the beat of the words is arranged into a 3:2 pattern in line after line. A good example is to be found in Lamentations.
5. Cf. Hos. 8:1.
6. So J. Bright, *Jeremiah,* p. 85. The Hebrew reads lit. "she raises her voice *(nāṯᵉnâ ʿālay bᵉqôlāh* against me."

in places from the Masoretic Text. Heb. *ṣāḇûa'* may be taken as a passive participle meaning "colored" or *speckled*[7] and the first part of the verse translated: *Is my very own heritage a speckled bird of prey? Are the birds of prey against her on every side?*—that is, Israel with her proud plumage has attracted the attention of birds of prey (enemies) who move in to attack her. An alternative translation arises from rendering *ṣāḇûa'* as a noun, "hyena," which is possible.[8] This understanding of the word combined with the LXX substitution of the word "cave" for "bird of prey" leads to the translation:

Is this land of mine a hyena's lair
With birds of prey hovering all around it? (NEB)[9]

The picture that results is of a hyena's lair with vultures hovering around waiting to swoop down on what is left of a carcass after the hyena has eaten. In either case the people and land are under attack from foes. There is a feast prepared for all the wild beasts (lit. "beasts of the field"). The destruction of Judah will provide pickings for all.

10–11 The metaphor changes. *Many shepherds,* that is, rulers of foreign countries, have ravaged the vineyard of Yahweh (cf. 2:21; 5:10; Isa. 5:1–7; etc.), trampled down his *field (ḥelqâ),*[10] and made his heritage a wasteland. It is an archeological fact that some of the cities of Judah show two levels of destruction at the end of the seventh century, e.g., Lachish, so that Jeremiah may well have had in mind some serious attack that was already over when these words were written.

The Hebrew text plays strongly on the word *waste* in vv. 10 and 11. It is impossible to capture the strong assonance in English,[11] but the effect in Hebrew is striking. There is a sense of completeness and finality about the words.

12 The *destroyers* (or brigands)[12] have swarmed over the heights. But it is the *sword of Yahweh* that is operating. Foreign and pagan nations would become tools in Yahweh's hand to fulfil his

7. See W. Rudolph, *Jeremia,* p. 78.
8. See KB, p. 741. LXX reads *spēlaion*, "cave," for "bird of prey"; see *BHS, ad loc*.
9. See G. R. Driver, "Birds in the OT—II," *PEQ* (1955), pp. 139f.
10. MT uses *ḥelqâ* here, a different word from the *naḥ^alâ* of vv. 7, 8, 9. A few mss. use the latter word here also. See *BHS, ad loc.*
11. *Desolate* (v. 10), *š^emāmâ; have laid waste* (v. 11), *śāmāh* (or *śāmuhā,* cf. Syr., Targ., Vulg.) *lišmāmâ; wasted, š^emēmâ; is laid waste, nāšammâ; no man lays, 'ên 'îš śām.*
12. So J. Bright, p. 85.

purposes of judgment. Among such were Nebuchadrezzar (34:2, 3) and the Assyrians (Isa. 10:5–6). When Yahweh acts in judgment there is no peace for anyone. One of Jeremiah's contemporaries, Habakkuk, having been made aware that God would raise up the Chaldeans for judgment, pleaded with Yahweh to remember mercy in the hour of his wrath (Hab. 3:2).

13 This verse is best understood as a simple statement that as the result of the invasion of Judah by the Chaldeans, the people would be prevented from caring for their crops so that the weeds choked out the grain. Foreign armies often destroyed crops as well. This was understood in OT times to be part of the total judgment (Lev. 26:16; Deut. 28:38; Hos. 8:7; Mic. 6:15; etc.). The "foe from the north" is described in these verses as "vultures," "beasts of the field," "shepherds," "destroyers."

(iv) *Yahweh's Conditional Promise of Death or Life for Israel's Neighbors (12:14–17)*

14 *This is what Yahweh has said: "Concerning all my evil neighbors who encroached on the heritage which I gave to my people Israel as an inheritance, See! I will pluck them from their lands, but the house of Judah I will pluck from their midst.*

15 *Then after I have plucked them up I will again have compassion on them and will restore them, each man to his heritage, and each man to his land.*

16 *Then, if they will take the trouble to learn the religious practices of my people and swear by my name, 'as Yahweh lives,' just as they (once) taught my people to swear to Baal, then they will prosper among my people.*

17 *But if they will not listen,*[1] *then I will completely pluck up the nation and destroy it—Yahweh's word."*

The final segment of ch. 12 is in prose, and poses a number of questions. Israel's neighbors, who had formerly attacked her (vv. 7–13) as instruments of Yahweh's judgment, are seen in vv. 14–17 as Yahweh's enemies. The passage takes up a number of words which are familiar from other parts of Jeremiah but notably in ch. 1, namely, "heritage" *(naḥ^a^lâ),* "pluck up" (or uproot, *nāṯaš,)* "build" (prosper, v. 16, *bānâ,* Niph.), "destroy" *('abbēḏ).* Such a collection of terms would seem to point to an authentic oracle of Jeremiah even

1. LXX reads "If they will not turn." *BHS* proposes "if they will not swear," cf. v. 16.

if it has undergone some editorial reworking.[2] The passage lacks the normal clichés of the Jeremiah prose and is not readily identifiable as Deuteronomic prose. Another feature of the passage is the universalist note that is struck, namely, that although Israel's neighbors are condemned to exile and destruction, there is hope of deliverance for them if they turn to Yahweh, accept his sovereignty, and join Israel, accepting his covenant demands and living by them (cf. Isa. 2:1–4; 19:16–25; 56:6–8; 60:11–14; Mic. 4:1–3; etc.). That such universalist ideas are common in later times has led some writers to assign the passage to an exilic or postexilic editor. It is arguable, however, that universalist ideas are not confined entirely to the postexilic period (cf. Gen. 12:1–3)[3] and that Jeremiah may have been capable of such thinking.

14a–c The wicked neighbors would include all those who at some time spoiled the land that Yahweh had given to his people. Among these were the Egyptians, Assyrians, Edomites, Moabites, Amorites, Arameans, and Babylonians. The term *heritage* or "inheritance" *(naḥ^a^lâ)* occurs both here and in v. 15. Yahweh caused his people to inherit *(hinḥîl)* the land as an inheritance. Any who *encroached on (nāga')* that inheritance would be guilty of a great evil (cf. 2:3) and would be plucked up from their own land, that is, exiled. Such a threat was not peculiar to Israel. Numerous ancient Near Eastern texts include the threat of exile among the lists of curses designed for evildoers, especially treaty-breakers.[4] Verses 14d–15 turn aside to speak of the future of the people of Judah, who themselves had suffered exile at the hands of their hostile neighbors. The passage returns at v. 16 to the evil neighbors.

14d–15 There appears to be a change of subject in the last part of v. 14, where, as though in an afterthought or in a parenthesis after the comments about Israel's neighbors, reference is made to Judah—*But the house of Judah I will pluck from their midst.* An important historical question arises. Does this reference to a res-

2. Some writers (e.g., E. W. Nicholson, *Jeremiah 1–25,* pp. 26, 119), however, have argued that since terms like these occur only in the prose of Jeremiah and never in the poetry, they may be the work of the later Deuteronomic editors. W. Rudolph, *Jeremia,* p. 83, regards these verses as being based on an authentic oracle of Jeremiah which was thoroughly reworked during the Exile.

3. In M. Noth, *A History of Pentateuchal Traditions* (E.T. 1972, p. 38), Gen. 12:1–4a is allotted to the J source, which was certainly preexilic. Whatever the correct translation of Gen. 12:3, the verse refers to all the families of the earth who wish to share in the blessing of Abraham.

4. See *ANET(S)*, p. 534 in the Treaty of Esarhaddon with Baal of Tyre.

toration after exile presuppose the exile of 587 B.C. as is assumed by many modern commentators?[5] It has become almost axiomatic to assign references to exile to an exilic or postexilic date. But there is no necessary reason to reject such references as we find here as necessarily preexilic. The possibility of exile in the ancient Near East was an ever present one. In Israel, with a strong faith in Yahweh's ultimate good purposes for his people, even though they may need to pass through judgment, exile was not the end.

Yahweh's ultimate purpose for his people, or rather, for the remnant of his people, was to display compassion toward them once again[6] and to restore each man to his heritage and to his land. The promise of restoration like this occurs in numerous places in the OT, including several passages in the book of Jeremiah (16:15; 23:3; 24:6; 27:22; 29:10, 14; 30:3; 32:37; 33:10–11, 26; etc.). Although these are in prose sections, we need not deny that Jeremiah has a strong hope of future restoration.[7] Despite questions about the authenticity of prose passages it seems inconceivable that Jeremiah was completely lacking in any hope of a divine restoration for his people after judgment was past.

16 The verse commences with a strong conditional clause—*if they will take the trouble to learn.*[8] The sense of the Hebrew noun "ways" *(darᵉḵê),*[9] here as well as at 10:2, etc., seems to be *religious practices,* or simply "religion." The condition for the inclusion of these hostile neighbors within the ambit of God's care is that they follow Israel's religion, worship Israel's God Yahweh, and *swear by* his *name*. To affirm an oath with the words *as Yahweh lives* implies that the person making the oath worships Yahweh. The name of the deity was regularly invoked by men who were entering into an agreement or covenant (e.g., Gen. 31:51–53). For the nations to invoke Yahweh's name would mean a profound reversal of religious allegiance. Formerly they sought to lead Israel astray and to teach

5. E.g., E. W. Nicholson, *Jeremiah 1–25,* p. 120; W. Rudolph, *Jeremia,* p. 83; G. P. Couturier, "Jeremiah," *JBC,* p. 314; etc.

6. Heb. reads lit. "I will turn, I will have compassion on them," that is, "I will have compassion on them once again." This verse shows Jeremiah's love of the root *šûḇ,* which he exploits in various ways. The second usage occurs in the verb *restore.* See the Introduction, pp. 76–81.

7. See the Introduction, "The Message of Jeremiah" under "The Future Hope," pp. 112f.

8. The finite verb is strengthened by the so-called infinitive absolute.

9. LXX has singular, *tḗn hodón.*

them to invoke the name of Baal in their oaths. But granted such a profound reorientation of their thinking and the acceptance of Yahweh as their sovereign Lord and God, they would grow[10] and develop in the midst of God's people. Such a comment has a remarkably universal character. There was hope of redemption even for Israel's worst enemies, but it was available only to those who accepted Yahweh's sovereignty.

17 The alternative to redemption was complete uprooting[11] and destruction.[12] Rejection of Yahweh's sovereignty whether by Israel or by any other nation could only end in disaster. Not even Israel, the beloved of Yahweh, could escape that possibility.

(v) The Linen Waistcloth: A Symbolic Act (13:1–11)

1 *This is what Yahweh said to me: "Go and buy a linen girdle and put it around your waist, but do not let it come near water."*
2 *So I bought the girdle as Yahweh had said, and I put it around my waist.*
3 *Then the word of Yahweh came to me a second time:*[1]
4 *"Take the girdle which you have bought and which is about your waist, and go at once to Perath*[2] *and hide it there in a crevice among the rocks."*
5 *So I went to hide it in Perath as Yahweh commanded me.*
6 *Then after a lapse of many days Yahweh said to me, "Go at once to Perath and take the girdle which I commanded you to hide there."*
7 *So I went to Perath and dug, and took the girdle from the place where I had hidden it. The girdle was spoiled and no good for anything.*
8 *Then the word of Yahweh came to me as follows:*
9 *"This is what Yahweh has said: Thus will I destroy the pride of Judah and the great pride of Jerusalem.*
10 *This wicked people has refused to listen to my words and follows the stubbornness of their own heart.*[3] *They have gone after other gods, serving them and bowing down to them, and have become like this girdle which is no good for anything.*

10. *They will prosper*—lit. "they will be built." The root *bānâ* means "to build"; cf. Gen. 12:5 where Abraham is said to have "made *('āśâ)* souls" in Haran, that is, he developed a family. The sense of "produce progeny" for *bānâ* occurs in 31:4; Gen. 16:2; 30:3.
11. *I will completely pluck up*—Again the finite verb is strengthened by the infinitive absolute: "I will uproot this nation, uprooting and destroying. . . ."
12. Heb. *'abbēḏ* (Piel). Cf. 1:10, Hiphil *ha'ᵃḇîḏ*.

1. LXX lacks *a second time*.
2. Aquila reads "Pharan."
3. LXX lacks *and follows . . . heart*.

11 *For just as the girdle clings to a man's waist, so I made the whole house of Israel and the whole house of Judah cling to me—Yahweh's word—that they might be my people, a source of renown,*[4] *and praise and glory to me. But they would not listen."*

Chapter 13 contains a variety of elements, two parables in prose (vv. 1–11, 12–14) and several segments in poetry (vv. 15–17, 18–19, 20–27). First is an account of the symbolic act of the linen waistcloth (vv. 1–11) set out in autobiographical style (vv. 1–7), with a short oracle from Yahweh explaining the significance of Jeremiah's action (vv. 8–11). It was not unusual for Jeremiah to perform symbolic actions which were in the nature of parables.[5] Evidently the people of Israel were used to such performances from the prophets[6] and knew how to expect a word from Yahweh through them. The general purport of the symbol was that the nation's pride would be destroyed (v. 9) by her impending removal from her home territory, that is, by the exile that was soon to take place.

As in the case of all parables it is wrong in principle to search for a meaning in every detail. Such a procedure only leads to allegorism, which is fraught with danger and is a hindrance to sound exegesis and proper interpretation.

1–2 There remains some doubt about the garment that Jeremiah bought. Heb. *'ēzôr* has been variously translated *girdle* (AV, NEB), "waistcloth" (RSV, J. Bright), "loincloth" (Jerusalem Bible). The normal civilian of the times was dressed in a long tunic, to judge from Assyrian bas-reliefs.[7] If Jeremiah wore the traditional prophetic garb he would have been clothed in a fairly tight tunic of coarse material with a hair cloak over it. A linen girdle around his waist, such as was worn by priests and the rich nobility, would have made him something of a spectacle. This view is rejected by some commentators, who propose that *'ēzôr* means waistcloth,[8] that is, a short skirt worn wrapped about the hips and reaching about halfway down the thighs. Of more importance than the exact nature of

4. Lit. "a name."
5. See chs. 19, 27–28. Note the Introduction, "Symbolic Actions in Jeremiah," pp. 71–76.
6. See Isa. 20:2–6; Ezek. 4:1–13; 5:1–4.
7. E.g., the Israelite men who brought tribute to Shalmaneser of Assyria depicted on the Black Obelisk. See *The Ancient Near East,* ed. J. B. Pritchard (Princeton, 1958), photo 100B.
8. So J. P. Hyatt, "The Book of Jeremiah," *IB* V, pp. 922f.; J. Bright, *Jeremiah,* pp. 91, 94.

the garment was that it was made of *linen,* the material used for priestly garments (Lev. 16:4); for Judah was a priestly nation. Evidently the symbolism of the act required that the linen item should be placed around Jeremiah's waist as it came from the merchant, without touching water. This would serve to rule out any possibility of previous damage. It was the clean, dry, freshly purchased linen that was to be placed around the prophet's waist. Jeremiah complied with the divine instructions.

3–5 The second instruction from Yahweh was that Jeremiah should take the girdle, which he had some time before placed new and clean about his waist, and hide it in a crevice in the rocks at *Perath.* The exact nature of Jeremiah's action cannot be understood without knowing the meaning of *Perath.* The same word is used elsewhere in the OT for the Euphrates River, which lay some 350 miles northeast of Anathoth (Gen. 2:14; 15:18; Deut. 1:7; 11:24; 2 K. 23:29; 24:7; Jer. 46:2, 6; 51:63). These numerous occurrences of *Perath* in the sense of Euphrates have led generations of commentators to picture Jeremiah making two round trips (vv. 4, 6) each of some 700 miles.[9] A three months' disappearance by the prophet would have caused a stir in Anathoth, and his return without the girdle would have been cause for much comment. His second journey would have been understood as his going to find the abandoned garment. Moreover, the hiding of the girdle in the region of the Euphrates may have carried with it some implication about the Chaldean invasion. It would be the Chaldeans who would "spoil" Judah. There may have been an alternative inference that it was influences from the Euphrates direction, that is, from Assyria and Babylon, that had spoiled Judah, in particular the worship of astral deities (Amos 5:26–27). Certainly under Ahaz and Manasseh these influences were considerable (2 K. 16:10–16; 21:3–8). Perhaps Jeremiah was declaring that there would be no salvation because there was nothing left to save.

But what of the location of *Perath?* A number of commentators[10] have argued that *Perath* was none other than the spring from which the Wadi Farah arose. There is an abundant supply of water in 'Ain Farah about 4 miles northeast of Anathoth (cf. Josh. 18:23). Since, in any case, the whole action was symbolic, the

9. In Ezra 7:9 the journey from Persia to Jerusalem, about 800 miles, took about 100 days.
10. J. Bright, *Jeremiah,* p. 96; George Adam Smith, *Jeremiah,* p. 184.

spring Farah could have suggested the Euphrates, which was adequate for the purpose of the prophet's parable.

There is another possibility, namely, that we are here dealing with a visionary experience, a view proposed by another group of commentators.[11] Alternately the story was a parable supported by some token journey (such as to the 'Ain Farah).

Clearly there is no uniformity of opinion among scholars. Fortunately, uncertainty about the exact location of Perath, whether in fact or in vision, need not prevent us from understanding what Jeremiah meant. Presumably his contemporaries well understood his meaning.

6–7 Yahweh's third command to the prophet was to go and recover the girdle that he had hidden at Perath. The need to dig (Heb. *ḥāpar)* is understandable. In hiding the girdle Jeremiah doubtless covered it with dirt. But in any case fallen material would have covered it in the period between his visits. There was, no doubt, special symbolism in that the dirt of the "Euphrates" area had spoiled the girdle and rendered it unfit for use.[12]

8–11 The interpretation of the act is provided for the prophet by Yahweh. Just as the linen girdle had been spoiled, so also would the gross pride of Judah and the gross pride of Jerusalem be destroyed. The girdle represented the people of God, pure and untarnished at the time of their call (2:2, 3). As a girdle clings to a man's waist, so the entire house of Israel and the entire house of Judah once clung to Yahweh that they might be his people, his source of renown and praise and glory. But they had become tarnished and spoiled by contact with Mesopotamia. Jeremiah had denounced any alliance with Mesopotamia (Assyria) as a betrayal of their covenant (2:18). Such alliances facilitated the corrupting influence of foreign gods (v. 10) and brought about the contamination of God's people.

The date of this acted parable, like many passages in Jeremiah, cannot be determined with complete certainty. One possibility[13] is that some recent close contact with the Babylonians may have given rise to the incident. The change in Jehoiakim's allegiance from Egypt to Nebuchadrezzar after the battle of Carchemish (605 B.C.) may

11. See W. Rudolph, *Jeremia*, pp. 85ff.; A. Weiser, *Das Buch des Propheten Jeremia*, p. 112; A. S. Peake, *Jeremiah,* I (1910), p. 193; M. Cunliffe-Jones, *Jeremiah* (1960), p. 111.

12. Heb. reads lit. "It will not succeed for anything."

13. See J. P. Hyatt, "The Book of Jeremiah," *IB* V, pp. 817, 922.

have seemed to open up unlimited possibilities of further political and religious corruption for Judah by such a servile submission. But perhaps there is insufficient detail to enable exact dating since the main thrust of the parable is more general, namely, the contamination of Judah religiously and politically over a considerable period.

The last two verses (10–11) have been regarded by some commentators as an editorial expansion and interpretation of the preceding symbolic act in the style of later Deuteronomic editors.[14] The phraseology is said to link these verses unmistakably with other passages in Jeremiah which derive from later editors.[15] Here we touch again on the whole nature of the prose of Jeremiah.[16] Later editorial expansions and interpretations are by no means to be ruled out, but they are not always easy to identify with certainty.[17] One purpose they could serve would be to strengthen an interpretation already implied.

There is no necessity to see in v. 9 a reference to the Exile. But if an exile is implied the verse is not necessarily exilic or postexilic. Jeremiah was well able to think in terms of an exile. His world and the whole world of the ancient Near East knew only too well the possibility of such an eventuality. An exile to Babylonia was certainly within the range of possibility. This would destroy the pride of Judah and Jerusalem. There is no expression of hope here for an ultimate return. That was left for another occasion (e.g., 29:10–14). No prophet declares his whole theology in every utterance.

(vi) *The Parable of the Wine Jars (13:12–14)*

12 *"And you will repeat this saying to them:[1] 'This is the word of Yahweh the God of Israel. Every wine jar is to be filled with wine.' They will reply[2] to you, 'Don't we know quite well that every wine jar should be filled with wine!'*

14. *Ibid.*, p. 922; E. W. Nicholson, *Jeremiah 1–25*, pp. 122f.

15. Thus v. 11 is compared with Deut. 26:19, and the expression "which has followed the promptings of its stubborn heart" (in NEB) has a "Deuteronomic ring." The phrase is lacking in LXX. This may not be significant, however, since there are many areas in Jeremiah where LXX has a shorter reading. See the Introduction, "The Text," pp. 117–120.

16. See the Introduction, "The Book of Jeremiah: Composition," pp. 33–50.

17. E. W. Nicholson, *Preaching to the Exiles: A Study of the Prose Tradition*, works out in some detail the theory of Deuteronomic editors. See also *Jeremiah 1–25*, pp. 10–16.

1. LXX reads "you will say to this people." MT then adds "This is the word of Yahweh the God of Israel," which is lacking in LXX.

2. LXX reads "If they reply." The *'im* may have been lost by haplography.

13 *Then you will say to them, 'This is what Yahweh has said: Look! I am about to fill all the inhabitants of this land—the kings who sit on David's throne, the priests, the prophets,*[3] *and all the citizens of Jerusalem—until they are drunk;*[4]

14 *and I will dash them one against another, fathers and sons alike—an oracle of Yahweh; neither compassion nor pity nor mercy will restrain me from destroying them.' "*

The editor of Jeremiah's oracles evidently felt that the brief oracle in 13:12–14 fitted well in juxtaposition to 13:1–11 even though the two passages do not appear to us today to form a unity and may have been originally independent. The link may be that both of them refer to judgment on the people for some failure or neglect. Both the linen girdle and the jars were to be destroyed. Verses 12–14 like 1–11 are in prose.

12 Jeremiah seems to have taken up a popular proverb in *Every wine jar is to be filled with wine*. The people regarded Jeremiah as uttering a truism. The LXX reading "And if they say to you"[5] may suit the context better than the Hebrew "and they will say to you." The reply was derisive—"But of course, that's what wine jars are for."[6] We may have here a drinker's joke at a carousal. It was the proper function and intended use for a wine jar to fill it up!

The wine jar in question (Heb. *nēḇel)* was a jar of earthenware as may be seen from v. 14; 48:12; Isa. 30:14; Lam. 4:2, since it could be smashed, although at times the word may have been used for a wineskin.[7]

13–14 Jeremiah now suggests a grim use for Judah. The function for which she was intended has not been fulfilled. She was, as Yahweh's people, to be a source of renown and praise and glory for him (v. 11). Now she is fit for nothing but destruction. Using the imagery offered by a well-known proverb Jeremiah announced that God would fill the people with the *wine* of his wrath, and just as wine jars about which the people joked were smashed by dashing them one against another, so God would destroy his people. The judgment would fall without respect of persons, gathering in kings,

3. LXX adds "and Judah. . . ."
4. Lit. "drunkenness," i.e., "fill them with drunkenness."
5. See textual note.
6. See W. Rudolph, *Jeremia,* pp. 87f.
7. E.g., 1 Sam. 1:24; 10:3; 25:18; 2 Sam. 16:1; Job 38:37. The root of *nēḇel* does not demand a skin. Nor does it demand that it should have been a wine vessel. Water was regularly carried and stored in earthenware jars.

priests, prophets, and citizens. Revellers may think of themselves as jugs who mean to be filled with wine. But Yahweh will fill the whole nation with drunkenness, rendering them powerless to act in their own defense in the critical hour. The phrase *fathers and sons* may be a reference to old and young.[8] It is a tragic picture of destruction coming upon Judah mercilessly, relentlessly, pitilessly.[9]

Once the glory had departed from Israel the people were empty jars serving no purpose. It is clear that Israel had no claim upon Yahweh merely because he once chose them. Privilege always involves responsibility. An irresponsible Israel could not expect Yahweh's favor. Judah went to her fate because of her own disobedience and unfaithfulness and because of the arrogance and apostasy of the whole nation rather than because of any deliberate policy of the invading Chaldeans.

(vii) A Plea and a Last Warning (13:15–17)

15 *Hear and give heed: Do not be proud,*
For Yahweh has spoken.
16 *Give glory to Yahweh your God*
Before he brings darkness,
And before your feet stumble on the darkening hills,
And the light you had hoped for
He turns to deepest shadow
And changes it to thick darkness.
17 *But if you will not listen*
Then I will weep in secret for your pride.[1]
My eyes will weep bitterly and stream with tears,
For Yahweh's flock has been carried away into captivity.

This short piece seems to be an independent fragment, but it is not difficult to see why it was placed after the two parables of vv. 1–11 and 12–14 since it spells out the outcome of Judah's apostasy. There is a direct link also through the word *pride* (vv. 9, 17).[2] The segment

8. As in J. Bright, *Jeremiah,* p. 92.
9. So Jerusalem Bible.

1. There is a problem about where to place the noun *mistārîm,* "hidden places," "hiding places," in the line. If it is taken with the first verb we may render "If you will not listen in these deep glooms" (NEB). Alternately, we may take the word with the second phrase and translate, "In secret my soul (i.e., I) will weep" (RSV). We have decided on the second of these proposals.

The second problem is the word *gēwâ, pride.* Syr. reads *'qt',* Heb. *ṣārâ,* "distress." *BHS* proposes *gōlâ,* "exile"; cf. v. 17b.

2. Two different words are in fact used, *gā'ôn* (v. 9) and *gēwâ* (v. 17). Even if *gēwâ* in v. 17 is emended (see previous note), the idea of pride is contained in the verb *gāḇah* of v. 15.

is in poetry and therefore, according to some scholars, is more likely to be an authentic utterance of Jeremiah. The underlying imagery is probably of a shepherd or some other watcher, guarding his flock on the hillsides by night and awaiting the dawn. The historical occasion could have been the deportation of Jehoiachin in 597 B.C. (2 K. 24:8–17). But that was as twilight compared with the darkness of 587 B.C. when Jerusalem was destroyed and the state of Judah lost its independence.

15 The two verbs *hear (šāma')* and *give heed (he'ᵉzîn)*[3] strengthen one another since they are virtually synonyms. Here is something of a final plea to a self-willed, proud people who had treated with contempt the word of Yahweh brought to them by the prophets down the centuries. Once again Yahweh speaks. Let Judah not be too proud to listen.

16 Men who wait on the hillsides for the dawn to break know full well that although they may stumble in the darkness, the night will pass and their feet may tread securely. But for Judah the present twilight will not be the herald of dawn but will lead on into deep darkness.[4] This change in nature's order (metaphorically) will be brought about by the direct activity of Yahweh himself. *The light you had hoped for he turns to deepest shadow and changes it to thick darkness.* Only a sincere response to Yahweh's word would withhold the calamity and allow light to shine over the land. Otherwise the whole land would be cast into darkness, the symbol both of the invasion and the coming exile (cf. Isa. 5:20; 8:21–23 [Eng. 9:1]; Amos 8:9).

17 Jeremiah gives further expression to his own deep sorrow over the fate of his people. Despite translation problems[5] the main thrust of the verse is clear. Jeremiah, in the full awareness of the consequences of Israel's coming doom, can only weep in deep sorrow over the fate of his people (cf. 4:19–20; 8:18–19, 23 [Eng. 9:1]). *Yahweh's flock has been carried away into captivity*—The statement may well be one of historical reality against the background of partial captivity after Nebuchadrezzar's first attack on Jerusalem

3. The cognate noun is *'ōzen,* "ear."
4. The noun *ṣalmāwet,* lit. "shadow of death," denotes deep darkness. It appears in Ps. 23:4 and elsewhere in the OT. The proposal to translate the word in Ps. 23:4 as "deepest shadow" instead of "shadow of death" at the time when a new translation of the Psalms in the Book of Common Prayer was undertaken gave rise to animated protests and scholarly articles. See D. Winton Thomas, "*Ṣalmāwet* in the OT," *JSS* 7 (1962), pp. 191–200.
5. See textual note.

(2 K. 24:8–17). The following fragment (vv. 18, 19) referring to the queen mother and young king supports this view.

(viii) A Lament over the King and the Queen Mother (13:18–19)

18 *Say to the king and to the queen mother,*[1]
"Take a lowly seat,[2]
For your beautiful crown[3]
Has fallen from your heads."[4]
19 *The towns of Negeb are besieged;*
No one can break through.
All Judah has been taken into exile,
Completely exiled.[5]

This brief poem is in the Qinah measure composed of a line of three beats and two beats. The shorter second half may have conveyed some sense of a catch in the throat. It refers to the exile of Jehoiachin and his mother in 597 B.C. (see also 22:26; 29:2). According to 2 K. 24:8–17 Jehoiachin became king at the age of eighteen after the death of his father Jehoiakim, but after a three-month reign was exiled to Babylon. He was released many years later in 562 B.C. but was never permitted to return home (52:31–34; 2 K. 25:27–30).

18 We may well ask whether Jehoiachin ever heard these words, for he was taken to exile. They were addressed to the absent king and his mother Nehushta (2 K. 24:8) in faraway Babylonia. Their crown had fallen from their heads and their reign was over. They must now occupy a lowly place, their beautiful crown taken away, no doubt as part of the booty. The mention of the queen mother indicates her importance in Judah. She would have had a profound influence over her young son, to be sure, but the queen mother as such seems to have had some official status in Judah. Indeed 1 K. 2:19 suggests that she had a throne adjacent to the king.

1. LXX has "and to the warriors." But MT *g*[e]*ḇîrâ,* lit. "the high lady," is a clear reference to the queen mother.
2. Lit. "make low and sit," a hendiadys.
3. Lit. "crown of your beauty," another hendiadys.
4. MT has an unusual form *mar'*[a]*šôṯêḵem.* Most scholars follow LXX and Versions and read *mērā'šêḵem,* "from your heads." M. J. Dahood revocalizes as *mērā'šôṯêḵêm* and sees in it a plural of *rašt,* "head," attested in Ugaritic. This would make the emendation unnecessary. See M. J. Dahood, "Two Textual Notes on Jeremiah," *CBQ* 23 (1961), p. 462.
5. The Versions have the expression in Amos 1:6, "an entire exile," for the final phrase. MT reads *hoglāṯ š*[e]*lômîm* with a fem. sing. and a masc. plur. falling together. Some emendation seems to be called for, such as *gālûṯ š*[e]*lēmâ.*

The care with which the mothers of most of the kings of Judah are mentioned in the books of Kings gives support to the idea that the queen mother was of considerable significance in Judah. Her influence was so powerful and so pernicious in Asa's day that he had her removed (1 K. 15:13).

19 A glimpse is taken at the towns in southern Judah under siege (shut up) so that relief was not possible. The term *Negeb* refers strictly to the large, sparsely watered area south of Judah. In the present context it seems to be used loosely for southern Judah where towns existed. The expression *All Judah has been taken into exile* is poetic. There were many Jews who did not leave the land in 597 B.C. In any case King Nebuchadrezzar appointed Jehoiachin's uncle Zedekiah, a young man of twenty-one, to rule (2 K. 24:18). Equally hyperbolic is the last phrase, *completely exiled.*

(ix) Jerusalem's Incurable Sickness and Punishment (13:20–27)

20 *"Lift up your eyes and see*[1]
Those who are coming from the north.
Where is the flock that was entrusted[2] *to you,*
Your beautiful flock?
21 *What will you say*
When he appoints[3] *over your leaders,*
Those whom you yourself have taught,
To be your head?[4]
Will not pangs seize you
Like those of a woman in travail?
22 *And if you say to yourself,*[5]
'Why has all this happened to me?'
It is for the greatness of your iniquity
That your skirts are lifted up
And your limbs are treated violently.
23 *Can the Cushite change his skin,*
Or the leopard his spots?
Then you also can do good,
You who are trained to do evil.
24 *I will scatter you*[6] *like chaff*
on the desert wind.

1. The imperatives are 2nd fem. singular. LXX adds "O Jerusalem."
2. Lit. "given."
3. LXX has plur., "they appoint." It is a question of whether Yahweh or the invaders make the appointment. But it may be impersonal, "when one appoints."
4. MT reads "and you have taught them, over you as leaders, as head." Transfer *'allupîm, leaders,* to the second colon.
5. Lit. "in your heart."
6. The context requires *you* in place of MT "them."

25 *This is your lot, the portion measured out for you.*[7]
This comes from me, Yahweh's word,
You who have forgotten me
And trusted The Lie.
26 *So I myself have lifted up your skirts as high as your face*
And exposed your shame.
27 *Your adulteries! Your lustful neighing!*
Your lewd harlotries!
On the hills, in the fields,
I have seen your foul deeds.
Ah, woe to you, Jerusalem, you are unclean!
How much longer will this go on?"[8]

This poem about the approaching judgment of Jerusalem fits in with the theme of the earlier poems in vv. 15–17, 18–19 and with the parables in vv. 1–11 and 12–14. Although each of these segments may have been originally independent, there is a certain logic in grouping them together even though they may not be contemporary. Compilers of prophetic material were often more interested in themes than in chronology. We, however, need to make some attempt to date each literary element in the interests of exegesis. The passage before us portrays the onward march of the foe from the north. Jerusalem does not appear to have fallen yet. Hence a date prior to 597 B.C. would be suitable. Possibly the background to the poem is the defeat of the Egyptians at Carchemish in 605 B.C.[9] Nothing seemed to stand in the way of the victorious Babylonian armies, whose entry into Judah seemed only a matter of a very short time. The Babylonian armies did move south, ravaging towns on the Philistine plains (47:2–7) and taking captives from Ashkelon. Jerusalem was on the mountains and more difficult to reach. Jehoiakim transferred his allegiance to Nebuchadrezzar and became his vassal (2 K. 24:1). Then in August of 605 B.C. Nebuchadrezzar, hearing of his father's death, hastened home to assume the throne, and did not return till a year later. But the times were anxious ones in Judah (5:15–17; 6:22–26; Hab. 1:5–11). A background such as this could account for the present passage.

7. LXX suggests *meryēḵ,* "the rebel," hence NEB "the portion of the rebel." MT reads *middayiḵ,* so that the consonantal change is from MT *mdyk* to *mryk;* in Hebrew *d* and *r* look very similar and are easily confused.
8. MT is awkward and reads "afterward when still." NEB proposes a rearrangement of the three words and a slight emendation, from MT *'aḥ^arê māṯay 'ōḏ* to *'aḏ māṯay t^e'aḥērî,* "how long will you delay?"
9. See the Introduction, "Jeremiah in His Historical Setting," pp. 9–22.

20 The imperatives are feminine and would appear therefore to be addressed to the city of Jerusalem. The foe from the north, which featured so much in earlier poems (1:13–14; 4:6–8; 6:1–8, 22–26; etc.), reappears here. If the historical setting we have proposed is correct, the southward movement of the Babylonian armies had already begun. Jerusalem is pictured as a shepherdess, guardian of her flock *('ēḏer),* her beautiful flock *(ṣō'n).* But she is powerless to protect her people, Yahweh's flock.

21 Although there are many difficulties in translating this verse, so that some commentators even declare that the verse cannot be translated with any assurance,[10] some attempt should be made to deal with the text.[11] The general sense seems clear. Jerusalem and Judah had cultivated those who were now to become their rulers, that is, the Chaldeans. Pangs of consternation like the pangs of childbirth would seize them.

22 It is often the way of self-righteous and complacent men to ask, "Why should this happen to me?" What the dulled conscience could not realize was that because of its *iniquity ('āwôn)*, judgment had fallen. In other OT passages it is Israel's enemies and the passers-by who ask the reason for Israel's destruction (22:8–9; Lam. 2:15–16; Ezek. 5:14–15; etc.). Jeremiah himself answers the question elsewhere in terms of Israel's breach of covenant—"Because they forsook the covenant of Yahweh their God and worshipped other gods and served them" (22:9). In the present verse such behavior is spoken of as *the greatness of your iniquity.*

The judgment that had befallen Judah is likened to the exposure of the limbs. In a culture where it was gross evil to expose one's body, a most vivid metaphor for national destruction was the naked and ravished body. This exposure was considered particularly offensive in the case of women. Jerusalem, often spoken of as Yahweh's daughter, is here threatened with "the lifting up of her skirts" and with "suffering violence to her limbs." The expression "lift up the skirt" is a euphemism for sexual attack both here and elsewhere in the OT (Lev. 18:6–19; 20:17; Deut. 23:1 [Eng. 22:30]; 27:20; Isa. 47:3; Nah. 3:5; etc.). The second phrase, literally "your heels have suffered violence," is probably a euphemism also.[12] "Your

10. J. Bright, *Jeremiah,* p. 95. The translations offered in RSV, NEB, and Jerusalem Bible are all different.
11. See textual notes.
12. Cf. "feet" in Deut. 28:57; 1 Sam. 24:3; Isa. 6:2; etc.

heels" may represent "your body" (or genitals) and "suffer violence" may refer to sexual attack. The two phrases are thus vivid metaphors for the outrage that Jerusalem would suffer when the divine judgment fell upon her.

NEB treats the verse somewhat differently and translates, "For your many sins your skirts are torn off you, your limbs uncovered." There may be an allusion here to the practice of stripping an adulterous woman of her garments (Isa. 47:2–3; Hos. 2:5 [Eng. 3]). Judah is a prostitute because of her idolatrous practices and as such will be exposed nude.

23–24 The "disputation" form occurs here in v. 23. Two questions are first posed and are followed by the accusation (cf. 2:32; 3:1–5; 8:4–5; 18:14–15).[13] A negative answer must be given to the question of whether a *Cushite* (Nubian, or Ethiopian) can change his black skin or a leopard his spotted skin. In the case of Judah, deep-seated wickedness caused by centuries of schooling and repeated excursions into idolatry had made evil virtually a fixed feature of her life and behavior. She had set herself in a permanent state of rebellion and breach of covenant. Like chaff from the threshing floor driven along by the desert wind, so Judah would be driven out by Yahweh.

25–26 The point is made again that the coming judgment was not a chance thing. It was Judah's *lot,*[14] and it came from Yahweh himself. The reason was that Israel had *forgotten (šāḵaḥ)* Yahweh and trusted *The Lie*. Some commentators understand by Heb. *šeqer,* "lie," a reference to another god, probably Baal.[15] The view that some common terms like *šeqer* are used often in the OT euphemistically has been advocated by a number of scholars in recent years.[16] This attachment of Judah to *The Lie* was in itself a great shame, an act of adultery. It was Yahweh's own doing to strip off her skirts (or, snatch her skirt up over her face) so that Judah's *shame (qālôn)* might be laid bare.

27 In three striking phrases Judah's wickedness is de-

13. B. O. Long, "The Stylistic Components of Jeremiah 3:1–5," *ZAW* 88 (1976), pp. 386–390.
14. Heb. *gôrāl,* the regular word for a lot that is cast.
15. See J. Bright, *Jeremiah,* p. 95.
16. Notably M. Dahood, *Psalms I, II, III* (Anchor Bible), especially with reference to terms used euphemistically for Sheol. See the index to each volume.

scribed—*Your adulteries (ni'up̱îm), your lustful neighing* (or "rutting," *miṣhālâ), your lewd harlotries* (wanton affairs, *zimmaṯ zᵉnûṯ).* All these are an abomination *(foul deeds, šiqqûṣîm)* to Yahweh. They were perpetrated, as was the practice, on the hills and in the open fields. The general reference is to the cultic practices of the pagan gods and the immoral rites associated with them. It was these evils that Josiah had sought to root out in his reform movement of 621 B.C. (2 K. 23:1–20; 2 Chr. 34:1–7). But whatever there was of temporary success in these reforms was soon dissipated, and Josiah failed in the end as did other reformers like Asa (1 K. 15:9–15) and Hezekiah (2 K. 18:1–6) before him. External reforms can never reach the hearts of men, and when total life commitment is lacking no external pressure can avail to bring about a change in outlook. The tragic thing was that the same people of whom v. 27 could be uttered were frequenters of the temple, and mouthed formulas like "The temple of Yahweh, the temple of Yahweh, the temple of Yahweh" (7:4).

How much longer . . . ?—It almost seems that when Jeremiah became persuaded that the day of doom was at Judah's door there remained a lingering hope and a devout wish that it might be otherwise. He lived to see the day when the judgment fell. His hope had to rest then in the promise of a future day of restoration (31:31–34).

2. LAMENTS IN A TIME OF DROUGHT AND NATIONAL DEFEAT (14:1–15:9)

(i) Lament, Supplication, and Divine Response in a Time of Drought (14:1–16)

1 *The word of Yahweh which came to Jerusalem concerning the drought:*
2 *"Judah mourns, her cities[1] languish;*
Men sink to the ground, Jerusalem's cry goes up;
3 *Their nobles send their servants for water;*
They come to the pools but find no water.
They return with their vessels empty;
Ashamed and dismayed,
They cover their heads.[2]

1. Lit. "her gates."
2. The last two cola are lacking in LXX.

4 *The produce of the ground has failed,*[3]
For there has been no rain in the land.
The farmers are dismayed;
They cover their heads.
5 *Even the doe in the field*
Calves and forsakes (her young)
Because there is no grass.
6 *The wild asses stand on the bare heights;*
They sniff the wind like jackals;[4]
Their eyes are glazed because there is no grass."
7 *"Even though our iniquities accuse us,*
Act, O Yahweh, for thy name's sake,
For our defections[5] *have been many;*
We have sinned against thee.
8 *O hope of Israel,*[6] *its savior in time of trouble,*
Why art thou like an alien in the land,
Like a traveller who turns to spend the night?
9 *Why art thou like a man caught by surprise,*
Like a warrior who is unable to save himself?[7]
But thou, O Yahweh, art in our midst;
We are called by thy name; do not forsake us!"
10 *This is what Yahweh has said concerning this people:*
"They love to wander in this way;
They do not restrain their steps:
So Yahweh does not accept them.
But now he will remember their iniquity
And will punish their sins."[8]
11 *And Yahweh said to me: "Do not pray for the welfare of this people.*
12 *When they fast I will not listen to their cry, and when they offer a burnt offering and a cereal offering I will not accept them, but I will consume them by the sword, by famine, and by pestilence."*
13 *Then I said, "Ah, my Lord Yahweh, the prophets say to them, 'You shall not see the sword, you will not have famine, but I will give you enduring peace in this place.' "*

3. LXX reads "Tilling the soil has ceased," suggesting a Heb. text *ʿᵃḇôḏaṯ hāʾᵃḏāmâ ḥāḏᵉlâ.* MT reads "Because of the ground (which) is dismayed." By reading *baʿᵃḇûrāh (h* lost by haplography) we can translate "Because of it (i.e., the drought) the soil is dismayed." Some commentators (e.g., P. Volz, F. Nötscher) transfer *farmers* to this colon from the next line to read: "on account of the soil the farmers were dismayed," and read v. 4b as the last colon of v. 3 which it resembles. Indeed, LXX omits the last colon of v. 3. NEB reads simply *ʿᵃḇûr hāʾᵃḏāmâ*, "the produce of the land" (has failed because there is no rain), and omits the final *hāʾāreṣ* with LXX. We follow NEB.
4. LXX lacks *like jackals.*
5. Heb. *mᵉšûḇôṯ,* "backslidings," from *šûḇ.*
6. Some mss. and LXX add "O Yahweh."
7. MT has *lᵉhôšîaʿ,* "to save." NEB revocalizes to read a Niphal *lᵉhiwwāšēaʿ, to save himself,* which we accept although there is no textual support.
8. LXX lacks this last colon.

14 *But Yahweh replied to me, "The prophets are prophesying falsehood in my name. I have not sent them, I have not commissioned them, I have not spoken to them. They are prophesying to you a lying vision, worthless divination, and the delusions of their own hearts."*
15 *Therefore this is what Yahweh has said: "As regards the prophets who prophesy in my name although I did not send them, and who say, 'Sword and famine shall not come to this land,' those prophets will meet their end by sword and famine,*
16 *and the people to whom they prophesy shall be cast out into the streets of Jerusalem, victims of famine and sword, with no one to bury them—them or their wives, or their sons, or daughters. I will pour out upon them their judgment."*

These verses comprise an opening poem to a longer section (14:1–15:4) which has as its central theme some severe drought that had struck the nation. The passage is in the form of a lament. After the editorial heading (v. 1) there is a graphic picture of the drought and the suffering caused by it (vv. 2–6), a cry of penitence (v. 7), a plaintive question addressed to Yahweh asking why he delays in saving his people (vv. 8–9a), an expression of confidence, and an appeal to Yahweh to deliver his people (v. 9b). The poem closes with a reply from Yahweh (v. 10), who declares that because of the continued unfaithfulness of his people he will not answer their prayers.

The short prose passage of vv. 11–16 follows the lament of vv. 1–10. The normal oracle of assurance which is found in a lament is replaced by an oracle of doom (v. 10). Verses 11–16 are an extension of Yahweh's response in v. 10 written in an autobiographical style, in which Jeremiah tells how he had been forbidden to pray for his people. He tried to excuse the people by blaming the false prophets who had led them astray; but such an excuse was not acceptable to Yahweh, since blame must be attached to those who reject the covenant for whatever cause. Their judgment is inevitable.

Some scholars hold the view that the prose passage (vv. 11–16) is a Deuteronomic addition. In support of this it is argued that the whole segment 14:1–15:4 was given its present shape by the compiler(s). In structure 14:1–10 is a lament followed by a prose section in 14:11–16. Then 14:17–22 is another lament followed by a second prose discourse 15:1–4. In each case the prose portion arises out of the lament and is properly understood only in connection with it, for it is the response of Yahweh to the lament, not with assurance but with judgment. It is argued then that since 15:1–4 evinces a deep interest in Manasseh, who was singled out as the major cause of Yahweh's judgment on Judah (2 K. 21:11–17; 23:26–27; 24:3), and since the passage has two Deuteronomic expressions (15:3; cf. Deut. 28:25–26), the whole segment is due to Deuteronomic prose editors. This means that 14:11–16 is also a Deuteronomic prose segment, which gives expression to the concern of the Deuteronomists with the problem of false prophecy.[9]

There need be no question about the literary arrangement of the materials at the hand of some editor(s) or other. The important question is whether Jeremiah himself held the views here expressed and whether Jeremiah wrote prose something like what we have here. It is undoubtedly Jeremiah who complains elsewhere in the book (in poetic sections) about the false prophets (2:8; 4:9; 5:13; 6:13), which indicates that this was an authentic concern of his, although similar complaints occur also in prose (23:16–40; 29:15–23). There are no poetic passages which contain a reference to Manasseh, although it is unthinkable that Jeremiah should not have had a full knowledge of the evils of Manasseh and his baneful influence on the whole of national life. Whoever arranged the materials in the book of Jeremiah at this point was not introducing anything new, and it may well have been persons closely linked to Jeremiah during the period following 587 B.C. But the possibility that Jeremiah himself produced prose has been too readily ruled out by modern scholars. Two voices which have been raised in protest are John Bright and W. L. Holladay.[10]

1 The introductory formula is unusual. Literally it reads, "What was the word of Yahweh to Jeremiah." The same formula appears at 46:1; 47:1; and 49:34. From its content it would appear that the passage is not so much an oracle from Yahweh as Jeremiah's description of a drought.

2 In four brief staccato utterances the scene is portrayed. The word translated *her cities* (lit. "her gates") is a common usage in the OT in which a part of the city stands for the whole (Deut. 12:12, 15, 17, 18; 14:21; 15:7; etc.). In Jerusalem a ringing cry of grief goes up from the people. We are here introduced to a national lament in a time of national disaster, which often began with a description of the particular plight, plague, drought, enemy attack, defeat, etc.

9. E. W. Nicholson, *Preaching to the Exiles*, pp. 87, 101, 102.
10. See the Introduction, "The Book of Jeremiah: Composition," pp. 33–50.

(cf. 24:4–8). Some commentators see in the poem in vv. 2–9 a liturgical lament rather like some of the laments in the Psalms (Pss. 74, 70; cf. Joel 1–2). Whether Jeremiah actually heard such a liturgy recited in the temple on some national day of fasting is impossible to prove. The poem may have been a literary fragment composed by Jeremiah and placed in the mouth of the people of Judah (cf. Hos. 6:1–3). It is filled with deep emotion, and represents the profound concern of a man who was closely identified with the tragedy of his people.

3 Following the regular practice the men of influence *('addîr)* sent their young men *(ṣā'îr)* for water. But the cisterns *(gēḇ)* were empty and the young men returned with empty vessels. While it was no fault of these servants of the great ones of the land that the cisterns had dried up, they covered their heads in shame in a gesture of grief (cf. 2 Sam. 15:30). This latter picture comes at the end of the verse and is very similar to the last phrase of v. 4. It has sometimes been regarded as a doublet of v. 4b, partly because it is omitted in LXX. However, the repetition of phrases is common enough in Hebrew poetry and the expression here may be original.

4–6 The picture changes to the farmers and the beasts, the ones who feel a drought more severely than most.

The animals in the fields suffer. In particular the wild doe gives birth to her calf but has to abandon it because there is no grass for her to enable her to produce milk. The wild asses *(pere')* likewise, roaming the bare hillsides, sniff the wind (for moisture) like jackals, their eyes glazed[11] for want of grass.

The total picture is a graphic one touching on the most pathetic aspects of nature in a time of drought: empty pools, dried up pasture lands, and wild animals at the point of starvation and death.

7 Jeremiah, identifying himself with his people and acting as their spokesman, pleads with God for help and deliverance as he confesses the nation's past and present misdeeds. He calls upon God to *act ('āśâ)* despite the nation's *iniquities ('āwôn)* and *defections (m^e^šûḇâ)*, and despite their having *sinned (ḥāṭā')*. We have here an assemblage of words for breach of covenant. While it may be too much to argue that Jeremiah intended to define the kinds of failure,

11. The verb *kālâ* means "to be completed," "be at an end," "fail." The picture is of eyes that have become virtually motionless because death is near.

the terms do, in fact, suggest a range of misdeeds. The noun *'āwôn* suggests "turning away," "being perverse" (verb *'āwâ);* the noun *m^e^šûḇâ* derives from the verb *šûḇ,* "to turn," here "turn away"; the verb *ḥāṭā'* suggests "to miss the mark." This is a suggestive range of words.[12] The only reason offered for Yahweh's action is that his reputation and honor are at stake. He must act for the sake of his name (cf. Josh. 7:9; Ps. 23:3; 25:11; 31:4 [Eng. 3]; 79:9; 106:8; 109:21; 143:11; Isa. 48:9–11; Ezek. 20:9, 14, 22, 44; etc.). There may be something else. The noun *name (šēm)* in Hebrew often suggests the essential character of the person. Hence Jeremiah may be making a plea to Yahweh as the covenant-keeping God of Israel to act toward his people as befits his character as a God of mercy (cf. vv. 20, 21). The appeal is a powerful one, and touches on the important theological question of whether Yahweh would really act contrary to his character if he brought judgment on a rebellious Israel. It is arguable that judgment is as much a facet of the divine character as mercy, and perhaps Yahweh was just as much God of the covenant when he allowed the curses of the covenant to operate as when he allowed the blessings of the covenant to operate.

8–9 Supplication follows confession, a proper sequence. Yahweh is addressed as Israel's *hope (miqwēh)* and her *savior (môšîa') in time of trouble.* The two nouns *hope* and *savior* are significant ones in the OT. While the idea of hope features in many contexts, a few texts describe Yahweh[13] as the *hope of Israel* (50:7; Ps. 71:5; Joel 3:16). The term *savior* likewise has a number of uses. In some of these the reference is to a political deliverer (Judg. 3:9; 2 K. 13:5; Neh. 9:27; Obad. 21), but in a number of cases Yahweh is described as savior (2 Sam. 22:3; Ps. 106:21; Isa. 43:3, 11; 45:15; 49:26; 60:16; Hos. 13:4). In general, Yahweh acts as savior in times of trouble and distress. Some of the theological overtones of the word which occur in the NT are not evident in the OT. The real need of Judah in Jeremiah's day was physical deliverance from impending disaster occasioned by the approach of the Chaldean armies. But Yahweh seemed aloof, like a stranger in the land, or like a wayfarer who had stopped merely to spend a night, one who had no permanent interest in the land. Judah could only ask why Yahweh

12. Cf. the range of words in Ps. 51:4–7 ([Eng. 2–5],) which is even more extensive.
13. MT omits the name Yahweh at the start of v. 8, but it is found in LXX and in various mss. The name is, in any case, implied.

acted so, why he had behaved like a man who was terrified, or like a warrior who was unable to save himself or anyone else. It was a strange response from a nation that had neglected their God, rejected his sovereignty, and disobeyed his commandments. Could such people expect a favorable divine response? If God were merciful to them it would only be as a result of his own forgiving character. The sense of estrangement they experienced lay in their own neglect and resulted from a guilty conscience. In theory they could say, *Thou, O Yahweh, art in our midst; we are called by thy name; do not forsake us*. But the awareness of the divine presence is given only to those who are in fellowship with him. Backsliders are aware only of their aloneness.

There is an interesting expression here in Hebrew, literally "Your name is called upon us" (cf. 7:10, etc.). The phrase denotes ownership and might be translated "We belong to thee."[14]

The three verses 7–9 reveal several characteristics of the lament. After a description of the calamity (cf. Ps. 74:4–8) it was common to address a plaintive question to God. Has God forsaken his people completely? Why has he brought disaster upon his people? Surely he who delivered them in times past will deliver them again (cf. Ps. 44:24–25 [Eng. 23–24]). Supplication follows. The nation cries out to God for deliverance in their present disaster (cf. Ps. 44:27 [Eng. 26], etc.).

10 The reply of Yahweh follows. In this case it is a statement of judgment. In some laments some assurance of deliverance is given (e.g., Ps. 12:4 [Eng. 3]; 60:8–10 [Eng. 6–8]; 91:14–16). Some scholars have postulated a liturgical background to at least some of the OT laments, where the closing reply would be uttered by a priest or other official such as a cultic prophet. In the present lament there is no promise of deliverance and no ground for hope. Yahweh's reply was simple: *They love to wander in this way; they do not restrain their steps: so Yahweh does not accept them. But now he will remember their iniquity and will punish their sins*.[15] The verse is reminiscent of Hos. 8:13 and part of Hos. 9:9, and may be a question. Alternately it is a liturgical formula.

It would seem that this whole lament gives expression to Jeremiah's final conviction that judgment was at last inevitable.

14. A modern English idiom is "my name is on it," that is, "it belongs to me."
15. Verse 10 picks up two of the roots in v. 7, *iniquity* (*ʿāwôn*) and *sins* (*ḥaṭṭāʾṯ*).

11–12 The evil of which the people were accused is described as a restless wandering (v. 10), probably an allusion to the many idolatrous sanctuaries in the land or perhaps to the frequent attempts to enter into foreign alliances. As on other occasions Yahweh forbade Jeremiah to pray for the people (7:15; 11:14). That this injunction not to pray is here repeated for the third time may suggest that Jeremiah did not heed Yahweh's command. In a sense, prayer was futile in the circumstances since nothing in the book suggests any serious inclination to repentance. A theological question is raised as to whether it is ever proper to give up praying for anyone. Perhaps one may pray for them to come to repentance by way of divine judgment, but breach of covenant leads unerringly to divine judgment. Beyond judgment there may well be repentance. The NT injunction "Pray without ceasing"[16] seems to be a sound one for practical religion, which can seldom handle the complexities of theological reasoning. Jeremiah was hardly a theologian, but he was a man with a vital practical religion. His own deep involvement with his people could not permit him to give up praying for them.

The futility of religious exercises is again stressed. Fasting, burnt offerings *('ōlâ),* and cereal offerings *(minḥâ)*[17] are not acceptable to Yahweh in the absence of obedience (cf. 6:20; 7:21–28; 11:15). For such people intercession would be in vain.

The three items *sword (ḥereḇ), famine (rā'āḇ),* and *pestilence (deḇer)* were the regular accompaniment of war and are referred to several times in the OT (5:12; 14:15; 27:8; 29:18; 2 Sam. 24:13; Isa. 51:19; etc.). These three calamities constitute a classical trio all too well known over many centuries in the ancient Middle East, and not merely at the time of the fall of Jerusalem in 587 B.C. They always consumed *(killâ)* the people.

13–14 Jeremiah's plea centers on the influence of the false prophets who had sought to persuade the people that they would not experience sword and famine but would enjoy *enduring peace,* or lasting prosperity.[18] But it was typical of the prophets who op-

16. 1 Thess. 5:17.
17. The term refers to offerings of grain, flour, cakes (see Lev. 2). But possibly it refers more generally here to sacrificial gifts of various kinds.
18. MT reads *šᵉlôm 'ᵉmeṯ,* lit. "peace of (or in) truth." A few mss. read *šālôm we'ᵉmeṯ,* either "peace and security" or a hendiadys with no change in meaning from MT.

posed Jeremiah to paint too optimistic a picture of the future (cf. 27:16–17; 28:2–4; etc.). The facts would be quite otherwise. The prophets showed a profound misunderstanding of the nature of the covenant if they imagined that continual and wanton breach of the covenant would not result in the operation of the curses of the covenant.

Yahweh declared his mind about the utterances of the false prophets. They had preached in the name of Yahweh, but what they preached was a lie, a fraudulent vision, a worthless divination, the deceitful invention of their own hearts. The difference between a true prophet like Jeremiah and the false prophets had never been so clear (cf. 23:9–40).

15–16 Such deceivers, who claimed divine authority although Yahweh had never commissioned them, would be the first to encounter the judgment of sword and famine. But they would be followed by the gullible and faithless people who gave heed to them and who would be hurled out into the streets of Jerusalem with no one to bury them. To lie unburied was one of the most dreadful fates that could overtake the man of Israel. Even in modern times the desecration of graves is held to be the grossest of contemptuous insults to those who have died. There are echoes in several places in the OT of this awful sense of calamity when a corpse lay unburied (14:16; Ezek. 6:5; 37:1; Amos 2:1; etc.). But men and women, young and old would die and lie unburied on the streets of Jerusalem.

I will pour out upon them their judgment—literally "wickedness" *(rā'â)*. The term serves a double purpose, meaning either the moral evil of the people or the consequences of their evil, that is, the judgment or the doom that would befall the people because of their evil deeds.

Clearly Yahweh did not accept the plea of Jeremiah. It was the responsibility of any man in Israel to discern as false a prophet who undermined the authority of Yahweh or sought to weaken Israel's observance of the obligations of the covenant. Any attempt by a so-called prophet to lead people into a breach of the covenant relationship marked him out as false, and his words should have been rejected at once.

(ii) A Further Lament and Supplication in a Time of Defeat and Famine (14:17–15:4)

17 *"You shall speak this word to them:*
'Let my eyes overflow with tears night and day,
And let them not cease,
For my daughter—my people[1] *is broken in pieces*
With a very cruel blow.
18 *If I go out to the field,*
Then look—men slain by the sword.
If I enter the city,
Then look—the ravages of famine.
Prophet and priest alike
Roam the land, plying their trade,
And have no rest.' "[2]
19 *"Hast thou utterly rejected Judah?*
Dost thou[3] *loathe Zion?*
Why hast thou stricken us
So that there is no healing for us?
We hoped for peace—
No good came;
For a season of healing—
But instead, terror.
20 *We acknowledge, Yahweh, our rebellion,*
The perverseness of our fathers,
For we have sinned against thee!
21 *Do not spurn us, for thy name's sake!*
Do not dishonor thy glorious throne!
Remember and do not break thy covenant with us.
22 *Can any of the false gods of the nations bring rain?*
Or can the heavens bring showers?
Art thou not our God, O Yahweh?
We hope in thee,
For it is thou who hast made all these things."

1. LXX omits "virgin" before *bat–'ammî* and translates this phrase as elsewhere "daughter of my people." See J. Bright, *Jeremiah,* pp. 32, 99, and cf. 4:11; 8:11, 19, 21, 22; 8:23; 9:6 (Eng. 9:1, 7).
2. MT reads "have roamed to a land and they do not know." The verb *sāḥ*ª*rû* means "roam," "travel about," generally in pursuit of a livelihood, and hence "do business," "trade," as in Gen. 23:16; 37:28, where the participle *sōḥēr* means "merchant." See E. A. Speiser, "The Verb *SḤR* in Genesis and Early Hebrew Movements," *BASOR* 164 (1961), pp. 23–28; W. F. Albright, "Some Remarks on the Meaning of the Verb *SḤR* in Genesis," *ibid.*, p. 28.

The last verb *yāḏā'û* can be seen as deriving from a root *yd'* meaning "rest." See D. Winton Thomas, "A Note on *w*ᵉ*lō' yāḏā'û* in Jer. 14:18," *JTS* 39 (1938), pp. 273f.

The conjectured emendation in *BHS* from *saḥ*ª*rû* to *nisḥ*ª*ḇû (n* lost through haplography), and deleting *waw* from *w*ᵉ*lō'* with many mss., gives "(they) are dragged off to a land they do not know." Cf. 15:14.
3. Heb. *nap̄šeḵā,* RSV "thy soul."

15:1 *Then Yahweh said to me, "Even if Moses and Samuel stood before me my heart would not be moved in regard to this people. Send them from my presence and let them go.*
2 *When they ask you, 'Where shall we go?' say to them, 'This is what Yahweh has said:*

Those who are for death, to death,
Those who are for the sword, to the sword,
Those who are for famine, to famine,
And those who are for captivity, to captivity.'

3 *I will ordain for them four kinds of destroyers—Yahweh's word: the sword to kill, the dogs to tear, the birds of the air and the wild beasts to devour and to destroy.*
4 *And I will make them a sight to horrify all the kingdoms of the earth because of what Manasseh son of Hezekiah king of Judah did in Jerusalem."*

The segment 14:17–15:4 has a unity of its own which resembles in structure that of 14:1–16. It comprises the description of the plague (14:17–18); a collective national lament (14:19–22) addressed to Yahweh, asking why he has brought such an affliction on his people (v. 19), confessing sin (v. 20), and appealing to Yahweh for help (v. 21), for their trust is in him and in no other (v. 22); and then Yahweh's answer (15:1–4), largely in prose but with a brief poetic segment (v. 2b).[4] The background to the section seems to be a military defeat followed by a famine.

17–18 Following an editorial line the poem describes the plight of Judah (cf. 14:1–6), which has suffered a shattering blow in war. The nation is personified as a young woman mortally wounded (cf. 8:21; 10:19). She is described as *my daughter—my people*,[5] whose suffering makes the eyes of the prophet overflow with tears ceaselessly day and night. Wherever he turns he sees corpses, or people suffering the pangs of starvation, in the town and the field. The historical background to the section is possibly the first Babylonian invasion of Judah in 597 B.C. which resulted in severe destruction and partial exile (2 K. 24:10–17).

19 After the description of the calamity some questions are directed to Yahweh (cf. 14:8–9a). The last part of the verse repeats 8:15 and seems to have been a refrain. The response of the people to the calamity is to ask whether Yahweh has completely rejected[6]

4. See A. Weiser, *Das Buch des Propheten Jeremia* (1960), pp. 120f.
5. See textual note.
6. Heb. infinitive absolute plus perfect, an emphatic construction.

Judah and has a loathing for Zion. If not, why has he stricken them with wounds which cannot be healed? The paradox was, of course, that it was the people themselves who had rejected Yahweh and brought the troubles on themselves. In their complacency they thought that peace would be their continuing experience. Their prophets spoke of "peace" in false encouragement. But events proved otherwise, and hence their plaintive questions addressed to God.

20 The confession expressed in this verse is typical of the lament. It comes from Jeremiah, who identified himself with the nation and confessed guilt on their behalf (cf. 14:7). He admits to their own *rebellion (riš'â),* the *perverseness ('āwôn)*[7] of their forefathers, and their own sinning *(ḥāṭā')*[8] against Yahweh. The three terms used to describe the people's misdeeds provide a picture of three different kinds of evil-doing (cf. Ps. 51:3–6 [Eng. 1–4]).

21–22 It is characteristic of laments to follow the description of the plight of the people and the confession with a petition or supplication in which some features of God's character are made the point of appeal. Yahweh is urged to deliver Judah for his *name's sake,* that is, because of his reputation and his honor. The nations knew him to be Judah's God, and any withdrawal of his help now would not be to his credit. Moreover, the destruction of Jerusalem would involve the destruction of the temple, his glorious throne (cf. 3:17; 17:12). Yahweh was thought of as enthroned in the temple, which was regarded as a guarantee of the nation's safety (cf. 7:2–15). If he allowed calamity to touch his people or Jerusalem and its temple, this would cast a reflection on his power. Besides, he had a *covenant (b^e^rîṯ)* with the people which must surely have involved him in the most profound of obligations to deliver them from their enemies. There is a strange inconsistency in this plea, since it lays stress on Yahweh's obligations and overlooks the strong obligations of Israel to Yahweh. Finally, appeal is made to Yahweh as the one who had brought rain and showers to the land, something neither the false gods of the nations nor even the heavens[9] themselves could

7. The verb *'āwâ* to which this noun is related means "act perversely," "turn aside."
8. The root denotes "missing the mark"; cf. vv. 7, 10, etc.
9. There may well be a reference to deities associated with the heavens here. Astral worship was widely practiced all over the East, and the Bible makes reference to the sun, the moon, and the hosts of heaven which the people of Israel loved and served (7:2; 8:2; 43:13; Deut. 4:15, 19; 17:3; 2 K. 21:4, 11; 23:5, 11: Job 31:26, 27, 28; Ezek. 8:16). One of the names of Baal was *Ba'alšāmēm*, "the Baal of heaven,"

do. Yahweh was their God, the one in whom they placed their hope, and the one who had brought about their present troubles. Sin confessed and Yahweh's character acknowledged, the people waited for his word of deliverance. But what they heard was Yahweh's rejection of their hollow confession and empty plea.

15:1 Yahweh's final answer is given in 15:1–4. Two of the great intercessors of Israel's history were taken as illustrations. In his day Moses had pleaded with God for rebellious Israel (Exod. 32:11–14, 30–32; Num. 14:13–19; Deut. 9:13–29). On that occasion Moses' intercession was heard. Later, Samuel pleaded with God for Israel (1 Sam. 7:8–9; 12:19–25). Again God answered. Since those days, however, God's people had declined so far from their covenant that not even the prayers of Moses and Samuel, much less those of Jeremiah, could avail to turn Yahweh's heart toward the people, so deep was their sin and so irrevocable was Yahweh's judgment. They would be sent away from his presence.

The reference to Moses and Samuel was particularly significant for Jeremiah. It would seem that he saw in these two a pattern for his own ministry. He was in the succession of prophets "like Moses" (cf. Deut. 18:9–33).[10]

2–3 Verse 2 contains a poetic segment which indicates four possibilities for Judah. These are announced in four brief phrases each carrying three beats. The effect of the verse on the hearers must have been dramatic. Plague, sword, starvation, captivity were the regular accompaniments of war throughout the centuries. The reference to these is not, in itself, a sufficient ground to assign the passage to a postexilic writer.[11] The theme is developed in v. 3 with

---

presumably because of his connection with storms, thunder, and rain. The same deity is mentioned in Phoenician inscriptions as well as in Aramaic inscriptions down to the Hellenistic period. Whether as a specific object of worship or as the locus of the object of false worship the prophet here in 14:22 sets "the heavens" parallel to "false gods." Neither of them is able to bring rain to the land in a time of famine, but Yahweh has the power to do so.

10. See the Introduction, "The Life of Jeremiah," pp. 94–106; W. L. Holladay, "The Background of Jeremiah's Self-Understanding," *JBL* 83 (1964), pp. 153–164; "Jeremiah and Moses: Further Observations," *JBL* 85 (1966), pp. 17–27.

11. Some writers accept v. 2 as the original response to the lament in 14:17–22, e.g., E. W. Nicholson, *Jeremiah 1–25*, p. 135. Verses 1, 3, and 4 in this section, which are prose, are regarded as the work of later Deuteronomic authors; but see our comments elsewhere on the questions associated with the prose portions of Jeremiah, esp. the Introduction.

a reference to some of the gruesome details of what would happen to the corpses of the slain, with dogs, wild beasts, and carrion birds all sharing in their dismemberment. The picture of vultures and wild animals feeding on the corpses of the slain is paralleled by one of the curses in the vassal treaties of Esarhaddon.[12]

4 The responsibility of Manasseh son of Hezekiah, king of Judah, for at least some of Judah's apostasy is referred to. Various passages in 2 Kings refer to the wickedness of this king (2 K. 21:10–15; 23:26; 24:3). The phraseology employed in vv. 3–4 is reminiscent of Deut. 28:25–26 and has sometimes been understood as either an adaptation of Jeremiah's thought among his followers,[13] a gloss,[14] or a Deuteronomic comment.[15] Manasseh was the most syncretistic of all the Davidic kings and had a profound influence on the nation (2 K. 21). The impending doom is here seen as a divine judgment on the most dreadful king. The people of Judah would be *a sight to horrify all the kingdoms of the earth.* Such a perspective need not be denied to the prophet Jeremiah himself, even if the passage does not preserve his exact words but only a free rendering of them.

(iii) *Jerusalem's Terrible Fate (15:5–9)*

5 "*Who will take pity on you, O Jerusalem;*
Who will console you?
Who will turn aside
To ask about your welfare?

6 *It was* you *who deserted* me *—Yahweh's word—*
And turned your back.
I stretched out my hand against you and destroyed you;
I was weary of relenting.

7 *I have winnowed them with a winnowing fork*
Through the cities[1] *of the land;*
I brought bereavement on them, I destroyed my people;
They did not turn from their ways.

12. See D. J. Wiseman, *The Vassal Treaties of Esarhaddon,* ll. 425–27.
13. See J. Bright, *Jeremiah,* p. 102.
14. G. P. Couturier, "Jeremiah," *JBC,* Part 48, p. 35.
15. E. W. Nicholson, *Jeremiah 1–25*, p. 135. But see remarks above, pp. 43–50.
1. Lit. "the gates"; cf. 14:2; Deut. 5:14; 12:12, 17, 18; 14:21, 27–29; Judg. 5:8; etc.

8 *I have made widows among them more numerous*
Than the sands of the sea;
On the mother of young warriors[2]
I brought a destroyer at noonday;
Suddenly I let fall upon her
Anguish and terror.

9 *The mother of seven sons grew faint,*
She gasped for breath;[3]
Her sun went down while it was yet day;
She was ashamed and distraught.
And the remnant of them I gave to the sword
Before their foes—Yahweh's word."

Verses 5–9 comprise a poem describing the terrible fate of Jerusalem. Whatever the original setting may have been, it was aptly placed by the compiler after vv. 1–4, for it continues the same theme. The verbs are here translated in the past because it is assumed that they refer to an event already past in which Judah experienced a great tragedy. The imagery points to the ravages of invasion and war and probably reflects the Babylonian invasion of 597 B.C. (2 K. 24:10–17).

5 Yahweh is the speaker lamenting the terrible fate of Jerusalem. The three questions suggest that there is no one to pity or to console, or to turn aside to ask about Jerusalem's welfare. We are reminded of the despairing tone of the book of Lamentations, which reflects the greater tragedy of 587 B.C. (Lam. 1:1, 12, 21; 2:13, 20).

6 The pronouns are emphatic here: "It was *you* who deserted *me*." The Hebrew expression *'āḥôr tēlēḵî* may perhaps be translated "you kept going backward," which may be a reference to the worsening moral condition of Judah.[4] If we translate with NEB "you turned your backs on me," the emphasis on Judah's deliberate rejection of Yahweh's authority is still strong. Such a

2. MT reads "to them, upon the mother of the youth"; LXX omits "to them." NEB rearranges the consonantal text and revocalizes; MT *lāhem 'al 'ēm bāḥûr* thus becomes *'*^{a}*lēhem l*^{e}*'ōm maḥ*^{a}*rîḇ,* "upon them a destroying people." There is support for *'*^{a}*lēhem* in Syr. and Targ. G. R. Driver, "Linguistic and Textual Problems: Jeremiah," *JQR* 28 (1937–38), p. 113, proposes *'*^{a}*lēhem 'al maḥ*^{a}*rîb,* "against them for laying waste."

3. Heb. *nepeš* sometimes means "throat" in the OT (cf. 4:10). The same usage occurs in Ugaritic. It is not a case here of gasping out her *nepeš* in the sense of dying, since the next lines show that she is alive. Here the expression may mean "she fainted," "she sank into a swoon" (NEB).

4. So J. Bright, *Jeremiah,* pp. 105, 109.

breach of covenant will at last bring into operation the curses of the covenant. In mercy Yahweh will relent *(niḥam)* for so long, but finally he will grow weary of relenting.

7 The figure here would be well understood by the people of Judah, who annually gathered their harvest onto the threshing floors of the land and, after cutting the stalks to pieces with the threshing sledge, would toss the mixture of chaff and grain into the air with large wooden forks to let the wind winnow the grain. The chaff would be blown aside and the grain would remain. So God, in his winnowing of Israel, had tossed the people and scattered them. The historical reference is not clear, but it may be the partial exile brought about by the first Babylonian attack on Jerusalem in 597 B.C. Perhaps there was a more distant reference to the exile from Northern Israel in 722 B.C. One of the results of Nebuchadrezzar's attack on Jerusalem was that some people fled to other towns and others were taken to distant cities like Babylon. In either case the bereavement and destruction of many of the people did not lead those who remained to abandon their ways. National calamities might well have led people with some remaining shreds of conscience to reflect on the cause of the calamity and to return to Yahweh. But it was no different in the seventh century from what it was in the eighth (see Amos 4:6–11) when Yahweh tested the people with national physical disasters: "Yet you did not return to me" was the cry of Amos.

8–9 One of the results of war is that women are *made widows* through the death of their husbands. The events of 597 B.C. had left many widows, it seems. The destroyer came at noonday and did not need to seek the protection of the dawn, the twilight, or the night because of the weakness and unpreparedness of Judah.

The mother of seven sons seems to be a reference to the wiping out in battle of the whole of the male offspring of some houses. To be a mother of seven sons was to enjoy a great blessing (Ruth 4:15; 1 Sam. 2:5). But this would become a curse when *her sun,* that is, this group of sons, was taken away at noonday. Before the life of these young men was half spent, in their noonday and in the full strength of manhood, they were lost in battle, leaving the household with no future heir.[5] But, as if such a tragedy as this particular one were not enough, any remaining men of Judah would

5. The story of the mother in 2 Maccabees 7:1–41 provides a moving illustration of the kind of tragedy that can happen when cruel invaders enter a land.

perish by the sword at the hands of their enemies. It was a grim picture of the fate that had already befallen Jerusalem the mother-city of Judah.

D. CONFESSIONS, SYMBOLIC ACTS, AND PREACHING (15:10–25:38)

1. SOME PERSONAL TRIALS AND MISCELLANEOUS SAYINGS (15:10–20:18)

(i) Jeremiah's Inner Struggle and Yahweh's Answer (15:10–14)

10 *Alas, my mother, that you bore me,*
A man to accuse and to indict the whole land.
I have not loaned nor have I borrowed,
Yet all men curse me.[1]
11[2] *Yahweh said: "Surely*[3] *I have made an enemy for you for good;*
Surely I have laid on you,
In a time of evil and in a time of distress,
The enemy.[4]
12 *Will iron and bronze break iron from the north?*
13 *Your wealth and your treasures I will give away as spoil for no payment*
For all your sins throughout your country.
14 *I will cause you to serve*[5] *your enemies in a land you do not know,*
For in my anger a blazing fire is kindled
Which shall burn for ever."[6]

The text seems to have been disturbed in transmission. Verses 13–14 are a variant of 17:3–4; the text of vv. 11–12 is very uncertain and the translation difficult. In vv. 10 and 15–18 Jeremiah is seen

1. Supply *kî, yet,* which was lost by haplography, and redivide the consonants to read *kull*^{e}*hem qil*^{e}*lûnî,* "all of them curse me." See *BHS ad loc.*
2. The text presents several problems. LXX has *'āmēn* for MT *'āmar* as the first word, hence "So be it, Yahweh, if I did not. . . ." But it is arguable that MT *'āmar* is older than LXX and should remain. See further the commentary on vv. 11–12.
3. Heb. *'im lō',* "if not." This expression is often used in the OT to introduce oaths of the kind, "So may it happen to me *if* I do *not* do so and so . . . ," which means that the speaker intends to act in a particular way. One way to capture the idea in English is to translate, "I swear that. . . ."
4. For the same construction of *pāga'* Hiphil with *b*^{e} and *'eṯ,* cf. Isa. 53:6.
5. Read *w*^{e}*ha'*^{a}*ḇaḏtî* or *w*^{e}*ha'*^{a}*ḇaḏtîḵā,* which have the support of some mss. and of the parallel in 17:4. MT *ha'*^{a}*ḇartî* would give "I have caused your enemies to pass through to a land you do not know." See E. Gerstenberger, "Jeremiah's Complaints: Observations on Jer. 15:10–21," *JBL* 82 (1963), pp. 395f. Jeremiah seems, however, to have been persuaded that the full weight of divine judgment would fall on Judah.
6. Reading *'ad-'ôlām* with several mss. for MT *'*^{a}*lêḵem,* "upon you"; cf. 17:4.

protesting that although he has been faithful to Yahweh in discharging his responsibility, this has only led to anguish and loneliness. Verses 10–12 can be seen as an outburst of Jeremiah (v. 10) followed by Yahweh's response (vv. 11–12). Then vv. 15–18 (below) comprise a further lament and complaint from Jeremiah, with a response from Yahweh in vv. 19–21. Yahweh's word urges Jeremiah to discard his self-pity and to press on with his task. In that case divine assistance will be his.

10 We are here permitted to catch a glimpse into the inner anguish of the prophet. In a burst of powerful emotion the prophet wishes he had never been born (cf. 20:14–18; Job 3:3–10). His call dated from his mother's womb (1:5), and to curse the day of his birth was tantamount to a rejection of his very mission. His complaint here is that he was for ever involved in legal wranglings with his people, pointing out to them their breaches of the covenant and their disobedience to the laws of Yahweh. The two words *rîḇ* and *māḏôn* are used of legal strife and legal contention. Jeremiah seems like a man who is for ever taking his people to court.[7] That was, of course, what Yahweh intended him to be (1:10). Any persecution he may have suffered was a result of his proclamations, not a result of any misdeeds. On lending or borrowing for interest (or usury), cf. Deut. 23:19. Jeremiah had not engaged in borrowing or lending of any kind that might have caused tensions between him and others; even so they all cursed him. He longed for some relief.

11–12 The text has proved difficult to interpret and a variety of solutions have been offered. If we read *'āmēn* with LXX instead of *'āmar* with MT, we may see in the words of v. 11 a kind of oath in which Jeremiah responds to the curses of the people (v. 10), "I swear that I have served thee with good intent (well)."[8] The manner in which Jeremiah had served Yahweh was in interceding for the foe[9] in the time of his (the enemy's) trouble and woe. It was the trouble and distress of Jeremiah's persecutors which led him to intercede for them. On several occasions Jeremiah was forbidden to pray for the people. But it is clear that he was closely attached to

7. Hence J. Bright translates, "You bore me to accuse and to indict the whole land" (*Jeremiah,* p. 106). We have followed his proposal in our translation.
8. Reading *šērattîḵā*, "I have served thee," for the difficult MT *šērîṯiḵā*. See *BHS*.
9. On this view the expression *'eṯ hā'ōyēḇ,* "the foe," is transposed from the end of the verse. Hence read "I have served thee well in respect to the foe." This is the view of J. Bright, *Jeremiah,* pp. 106, 109.

them in his spirit and prayed for them, particularly when some disaster descended on them.

However, if we follow MT and read *Yahweh said,* we obtain a somewhat different translation. One possibility is represented by NEB, which reads:

The Lord answered,
But I will greatly strengthen you;[10]
In time of distress and in time of disaster
I will bring the enemy to your feet.[11]
Can iron break steel from the north?

According to another suggestion, which seems an attractive one, the root of the first verb in v. 11 should be taken as *šrr.*[12] The participle of the simple verb *šôrēr* means *enemy* and occurs five times in the OT. The verb here has a causative sense,[13] "to make an enemy." Hence we may translate, *I have made an enemy for you for good.* But the possible renderings of this verse are manifold, and it was difficult to choose one rather than another.

Verse 12 is likewise elusive. Literally it reads, "Will iron break iron from the north, and bronze?" By a slight rearrangement we can read, *Will iron and bronze break iron from the north?*[14] In the context, Jeremiah is shown the nature of the foe that is soon to descend on Judah. Any confidence on Judah's part was self-delusion, for no effort of their will, though it be iron and bronze, would be a match for the powerful foe *from the north.* In such circumstances Jeremiah's concern for his own troubles was hardly warranted (cf. 12:1–6; note vv. 5–6).

Perhaps there is a reference here to the fine quality of iron from the north, from the Black Sea region. Judah's feeble weapons were no match for such armaments. In the hour of invasion Judah had no hope of repelling the powerful Babylonian armies.

13–14 Although these verses are a partial duplicate of 17:3–4, they are hardly to be regarded as simply an intrusion into the text but may be seen as a significant part of the total picture. Following upon Jeremiah's complaint in v. 10, the succeeding verses may be looked on as follows: Jeremiah's own lament of v. 10 is answered by Yahweh's word of rebuke in vv. 11–12. In that context vv. 13–14

10. NEB reads *šārôṯīḵā*, "I will strengthen you greatly (lit. for good)."
11. Lit. "I will (an oath) cause the enemy to touch you."
12. Cf. W. L. Holladay, *Jeremiah: Spokesman Out of Time*, p. 90.
13. It is the Piel, *šērēr*.
14. RSV, however, reads "Can one break iron, iron from the north, and bronze?"

follow quite naturally. If Jeremiah bemoaned his own birth, God replied that he knew exactly what he was doing. He was in full control of the situation. There was an enemy at hand. Jeremiah should turn his attention away from personal and local troubles to the larger conflict ahead, when the stubborn people of Judah would have to confront the military might of Babylon. We are reminded of the response of Yahweh in 12:5–6 to the self-pitying complaints of Jeremiah in 12:1–4.

On these two verses see further the commentary on 17:3–4.

(ii) A Further Inner Struggle and the Divine Answer (15:15–21)

15 *"Ah, but thou art aware!*
Remember me, Yahweh; take note of me!
Take vengeance for me on my persecutors;
In thy patience take me not away;
Consider that I bore reproach for thy sake.
16 *When thy words were found I ate them;*[1]
Thy word[2] *became my delight*
And the joy of my heart.
For thou hast named me thine,
O Yahweh, God of Hosts.
17 *I have not sat with the company of roisterers making merry.*
With thy hand upon me I sat alone.
Because thou didst fill me with indignation.
18 *Why is my pain unending,*
My wound incurable, refusing to be healed?
Truly thou art to me like a deceitful brook,
Like waters that have failed."
19 *Therefore this was Yahweh's answer:*
"If you will turn back I will take you back
And you shall stand before me.
If you utter what is noble and not what is cheap
You shall be my spokesman.
Let them turn again to you,
But you must not turn to them.

1. LXX suggests for the verb *nimṣᵉʾû* a noun and a preposition *minnōʾᵃṣê,* "from the despisers of (thy words)"; for MT *wāʾōḵᵉlēm* ("and I ate them") NEB suggests a form of the root *klm,* "suffer." Hence NEB translates "I have to suffer those who despise thy words." LXX, however, takes the first words with the last sentence, thus "Consider how I bore reproach for thy sake from the despisers of thy words. Consume them and let thy word be my delight."
2. MT reads plur. "words," although the Qere and mss. and Versions read singular.

20 *And I will make you before this people*
An impregnable wall of bronze.
They will attack you but they will not prevail over you,
For I am with you to deliver you
And to save you—Yahweh's word.
21 *I will deliver you from the grasp of the wicked,*
And from the clutch of the ruthless I will rescue you."

There is a further "confession" of Jeremiah in vv. 15–18, and Yahweh's reply in vv. 19–21. Again Jeremiah cries out that he has been faithful in the discharge of his task despite the loneliness and the hatred that were his lot. Yahweh's reply again was something of a rebuke. He was urged to rid himself of self-pity if he would continue his office. However, divine aid was promised.

15 Jeremiah's plea was that Yahweh was well aware of what he was going through. The verb *yāḏa'*, "know," sometimes carries the sense of "being aware of." Yahweh is called upon to *remember (zāḵar).* Israelite "remembering" was not mere recollection. It was a recapturing of the past in a way that led to action in the present. Thus Jeremiah was asking Yahweh to call up from the past what he knew of Jeremiah and do something active on his behalf. What he asked was that Yahweh *take note* of him. The verb *pāqaḏ,* literally "visit," has a wide range of meanings. At times it denotes a visitation that brings judgment. Sometimes the visitation brings approval or deliverance. It is, in any case, an active idea. Jeremiah was concerned that Yahweh should act to restrain those who persecuted him.[3] The action Jeremiah sought was that Yahweh would *take vengeance (nāqam).* This verb has a special sense. The enemies in question are, in the final analysis, not Jeremiah's personal enemies but God's enemies. The persecutors who would seek to harm Jeremiah were really seeking to harm God's spokesman and therefore to harm God. The hour called for a display of Yahweh's sovereignty over those who persecuted his servant. It is not a case of a petty vendetta waged against Jeremiah's persecutors, but rather a display of Yahweh's positive action to restrain the evildoers and to enable his servant to continue the task to which Yahweh had called him. It was, after all, for Yahweh's sake that the prophet suffered the rebuffs of his persecutors; and in the light of Yahweh's known qualities of patience and forbearance Jeremiah asked that he not be taken away, that is, lose his life. There is a boldness about such words

3. The verb *rāḏap* means "pursue."

which only those in a very close relationship with Yahweh may show. In effect he was saying: "O Lord, you are surely aware of what is going on. Take active notice of me in my plight and obtain satisfaction from my persecutors for my sake. Do not be inactive but act now on my behalf, for it is for your sake that I am suffering their rebuffs."

16 Jeremiah accepted the divine instructions gladly once they were presented.[4] Ezekiel spoke in similar terms of his own acceptance of the divine word (Ezek. 2:8–3:3) in which he ate a scroll containing Yahweh's word. Both Jeremiah and Ezekiel found that having accepted Yahweh's word, which at first seemed unpalatable, it became acceptable, to Jeremiah a joy *(śāśôn)* and a delight to his heart, and to Ezekiel "as sweet as honey." There is a possibility, however, that the words in Jeremiah should be attached to the next phrase and the sentence should be read:

It was my joy and my heart's delight
That I bore thy name,
O Yahweh, God of Hosts.[5]

The expression *thou hast named me thine* reads literally "Thy name was called upon me." The phrase seems to denote ownership (cf. 7:10–11). It is reminiscent of passages in Deuteronomy which refer to the central sanctuary, or indeed to any sanctuary which Yahweh approved. The expressions "the place which Yahweh your God will choose to put his name and make his habitation there" (Deut. 12:5), "the place which Yahweh your God will choose to make his name dwell there" (Deut. 12:11, etc.), denote Yahweh's claim to ownership. Jeremiah, too, belonged to Yahweh and was available for his service.

In 2 K. 22:13 and 23:2 the expression "the words of the book (of the covenant) which had been found" occurs. Hence in 15:16 we may have a poetic reference to the finding of the scroll in the temple in 621 B.C.[6] In that case the phrase *I ate them* in 15:15 may refer to Jeremiah's own acceptance of God's call (cf. 1:9). Such a view would place the call of Jeremiah after the finding of the scroll in 621 B.C. and not before, that is, not in 627 B.C.[7]

4. *Thy words were found*—The verb *nimṣāʾ* often means "be present, in existence." The same word occurs in 2:34; 5:26.
5. Cf. J. Bright, *Jeremiah,* pp. 100, 110.
6. W. L. Holladay, *Jeremiah: Spokesman Out of Time,* pp. 22, 97.
7. See the Introduction, pp. 50–56.

17 Jeremiah's special role separated him from the normal social relations enjoyed by others. He was isolated by the grim task that was his to perform. This verse spells out the cost of his ministry to the prophet. Comparison with Ps. 26:3–5 is striking:

For thy constant love is before my eyes
And I live in thy truth.
I have not sat among worthless men,
Nor do I mix with hypocrites;
I hate the company of evildoers,
And will not sit among the ungodly.[8]

The first line of v. 17 reads literally, "I have not sat in the company of the merry makers and (did not) rejoice." The words "and rejoice" may once have introduced a separate colon. LXX is no help because its reading is somewhat different. The reason why Jeremiah *sat alone* was because of Yahweh's *hand,* that is, he was under divine constraint for his special task.[9] The nature of his task is indicated by the sentence *thou didst fill me with indignation,* that is, indignation at the grievous sins of his people.

18 Here is a characteristic plaintive question from one of God's servants under persecution. The question is followed by a cry expressing a sense of having been abandoned by God (cf. Ps. 22:2 [Eng. 1]). It seemed to the prophet that his pain was unending, his wound desperate and incurable. God seemed to be like a *deceitful brook ('akzāḇ,* cf. Mic. 1:14), that is, a stream that goes dry in summer and cannot be depended on for water. Time was when Jeremiah thought of Yahweh as a "fountain of living water" (2:13). But now he seems like *waters that have failed.*[10] The picture of a dry wadi was a familiar one. Indeed, in Palestine many wadis contain water only after heavy rainfalls. Travellers who approach a wadi in search of water are often disappointed.

19 Yahweh's response to Jeremiah's lament and complaint was startling. It began with an implied rebuke. Jeremiah had often called on his people to repent *(šûḇ)* and return to God. Now Yahweh calls upon Jeremiah himself to repent.

"If you will turn back to me I will take you back
And you shall stand before me." (NEB)[11]

8. Cf. Ps. 1:1–2.
9. Cf. 1 K. 18:46; 2 K. 3:15; Isa. 8:11; Ezek. 1:3; 3:14, 22; 37:1; 40:1.
10. Heb. *mayim lō' ne'ᵉmānû,* lit. "waters (that) have not proved trustworthy."
11. J. Bright, *Jeremiah,* p. 107, translates "If you repent, I'll restore you."

The words seem to mean, "If you turn (from such talk as is found in vv. 15–18), then I will turn you (that is, restore you) to the prophetic office." There is a play on the verb *šûḇ,* "turn." The bitterness of the prophet's experiences had almost closed his mouth and brought him close to losing sight of his divine commission and his confidence in the one who had commissioned him. He had almost renounced his calling (cf. 20:7–9). Yahweh now bids him to "turn back" to God and to renew his trust in God.

The expression *stand before (ʿāmaḏ lip̱nê)* is used frequently in the OT of those who serve God or kings (Num. 16:9; 27:21; Deut. 10:8; 1 K. 1:2; 10:8; 12:8; 17:1; Dan. 1:5; etc.). Repentance and restoration would enable Jeremiah to continue his special ministry.

The same idea is expressed in other words in the second line, literally: "if you bring forth (i.e., separate) the precious from the worthless," or, "if you bring forth (i.e., utter) what is precious without the worthless, you will be as my mouth," that is, "you will be my mouthpiece" (cf. 1:9–10). Perhaps God was telling the prophet that he had been overconcerned about what people thought and said about him when his one concern should have been to heed God's word and proclaim it. Any lesser attitude pointed toward a need for repentance on Jeremiah's part. Once restored, Jeremiah could become again a strong bronze wall (v. 20) according to the original promise to him (1:18–19).

The last line in this verse takes up the root *šûḇ* again with two more nuances of "turn." It is variously translated "They shall turn to you, but you shall not turn to them" (RSV); "Let them come over to you, don't you go over to them" (Bright), or "This people will turn again to you, but you will not turn to them" (NEB). The main thrust of the line is clear. The people are dependent on Jeremiah to hear God's word, but Jeremiah has no need to heed anything they say to him.

20–21 The words of v. 20 are strongly reminiscent of 1:8, 18–19, which describe Jeremiah's original call. The promise of deliverance is expressed in three significant OT verbs of deliverance, namely *hôšîaʿ,* "save," *hiṣṣîl,* "deliver," and *pāḏâ,* "redeem" or "rescue." They are found in such significant passages as the Exodus story, although they have more general application. The total picture of deliverance is many-sided and each verb provides a different emphasis. Thus *hôšîaʿ,* "save," and its related nouns lay stress on the bringing out of those under restraint into a broad place.[12] The verb *hiṣṣîl,* "deliver," pictures the activity of one who snatches his prey from the grasp of a powerful possessor.[13] By extension of the physical idea Israel thought of deliverance from death, the grave, sins, trouble, fear, etc. The verb *pāḏâ* was normally used in reference to liberation from the possession of another by the giving up of a ransom. It is used of the Exodus,[14] although by a metaphorical use it came to refer to acts of deliverance in daily life, including the rescue of Israel from sins and the fear of the grave. The richness of the picture in vv. 20 and 21 is thus evident. If Jeremiah was aware of the vast range of meaning attaching to such ideas, as no doubt he was, the encouragement to him must have been enormous.

Here then was a summons to turn again to renewed service for Yahweh accompanied by a reaffirmation of Yahweh's promise made to him at the time of his call. It was this strong assurance that enabled Jeremiah to continue his service for Yahweh down the years.

Some commentators have proposed that v. 21 has a more particular reference to specific individuals who troubled him, possibly Jehoiakim and his counsellors (ch. 36).[15] The idea is possible, although a more general application is just as likely.

(iii) Jeremiah's Life, a Mirror of His Message of Judgment (16:1–13)

1 *The word of Yahweh came to me as follows:*[1]
2 *"You shall not take a wife for yourself,*
Nor shall you have sons (and daughters in this place).[2]
3 *For this is what Yahweh has said:*
Against[3] *the sons,*
And against the daughters born in this place,
And against their mothers who bore them,
And against their fathers who begot them in this land:

12. Eng., Exod. 14:30; Ps. 106:8, 10, 21; Hos. 13:4. The noun *y^e^šû'â,* "salvation," occurs in Exod. 15:2; 1 Sam. 14:45; 2 Chr. 20:17; etc.
13. Exod. 3:8; 5:23; 6:6; 12:27; 18:4, 8–10; Judg. 6:9; 1 Sam. 10:18; etc.
14. Deut. 7:8; 9:26; 13:6 (Eng. 5); 15:15; 21:8; 2 Sam. 7:23; 1 Chr. 17:21; Mic. 6:4; etc.
15. See E. W. Nicholson, *Jeremiah 1–25,* p. 141.

1. The introductory words in vv. 1, 3, 5, and 9 are not part of the poetic scheme.
2. In an attempt to restore an original poetic form to these verses we could omit *and daughters* as a dittography from v. 3, and also *in this place* for the same reason. Wife and children *(bānîm)* would provide good parallelism.
3. The preposition *'al* occurs four times in this verse, each time marking out a group under judgment. This is balanced by a fourfold use in v. 7. Compare the tenfold use of *'al* in Isa. 2:12–16, two in Amos 3:1, and three in Jer. 23:30–32.

4 *They shall die of deadly diseases;*
They will not be lamented, nor will they be buried;
They shall become dung on the surface of the ground.
They shall perish by the sword and by famine,
And their corpses shall be food
For the birds of the sky and for the beasts of the earth.
5 *For this is what Yahweh has said:*
Do not enter[4] *a house where there is mourning,*
And do not go to lament
And do not grieve for them.
For I have taken away my peace from this people—Yahweh's word—
My[5] *steadfast love*
And my compassion.
6 *And they shall die both small and great (in this land).*[6]
They shall not bury and they shall not lament for them,
And they shall not cut themselves[7] *or shave their heads for them.*
7 *They shall not break bread*[8] *for mourning*
To comfort anyone for the dead;
Nor shall they give anyone the cup of consolation to drink
For his father or for his mother.
8[9] *You shall not enter the house of feasting*
To sit with them,[10]
To eat and to drink.

4. The prohibitions here are introduced by *'al* rather than *lō'*, and are thus simple warnings and not commandment-prohibitions. There are three of these. These three verbs are structurally balanced by the three nouns at the end of the verse.
5. In our translation we have *my peace, my steadfast love,* and *my compassion,* although only the first has the suffix. We assume that we have here an example of a suffix which serves a triple duty. See M. Dahood, *Psalms I: 1–50* (Anchor Bible), p. xxxiv. RSV and Bright follow this view although the Versions and many commentators have not so understood it.
6. We may omit this last phrase from the original poem so that the first colon here balances the first colon in v. 4. Then the first three cola of v. 4 balance the first three cola of v. 6.
7. We accept the proposal of W. L. Holladay, "The Recovery of Poetic Passages of Jeremiah," *JBL* 85 (1966), pp. 401–435, esp. p. 418, that MT *yqbrw* should be vocalized *yiqbᵉrû*, "they shall bury," i.e., as Qal rather than Niphal, since the verse is concerned with the activities of survivors and not with those who have died (cf. v. 4). The other verbs in the sentence are vocalized as Qal in MT. The last two verbs are here taken as plural with the Versions; see *BHS*.

The four verbs in question provide an interesting pattern of sounds. The first two contain the sounds *q-r* and *d* and the phrase closes with *lāhem;* the second two contains the sounds *d* and *q-r* and the phrase closes likewise with *lāhem*. There is a kind of assonantal chiasmus. See W. L. Holladay, *art. cit.*, p. 418.
8. MT reads *lāhem,* perhaps influenced by the previous line, but several mss. and LXX read *leḥem,* which seems to be required by the context.
9. This verse balances v. 5 and also refers back to the marriage motif of v. 3. Moreover, the infinitives *eat* and *drink* here correspond to "bread" and "cup" in v. 7.
10. Read *'ittām (with them)* instead of MT *'ōṯām* (accusative).

9 *For this is what Yahweh of Hosts the God of Israel has said:*
See, I am about to bring to an end
From this place,[11]
From before your[12] *eyes,*
And in your days,
The sound of mirth,
The sound of gladness,
The voice of the bridegroom,
And the voice of the bride.
10 *And when you tell the people all these things and they say to you, 'Why has Yahweh pronounced against us all this great misfortune? What is our iniquity and what is the sin that we have committed against Yahweh our God?'*
11 *then you will say to them, 'Because your fathers forsook me—Yahweh's word—and followed after other gods and served and worshipped them, and abandoned me and did not keep my law;*
12 *and you for your part have done worse than your fathers, for look, each one of you follows the stubbornness of his own evil heart, not listening to me,*
13 *I will throw you out of this land into the land which neither you nor your fathers have known, and you will there serve other gods day and night who will show you no favor.' "*[13]

The segment vv. 1–13 is here shown as partly poetic (vv. 1–9) and partly prose (vv. 10–13). The passage 16:1–9 has been taken as prose by most of the commentators. John Bright refers to its pedestrian style[14] and understands it as prose although he suspects a poetic original. For him the material is "unquestionably authentic." Writers like Giesebrecht, Nötscher, Rudolph, and Hyatt take the passage as prose, as do NEB, RSV, and GNB. Duhm regarded vv. 5–7 as poetry, and Weiser accepted v. 9 as poetic.[15] Mowinckel assigned all of vv. 1–13 to the poetic oracles of his Source A.[16]

The basis on which the passage is assigned to the prose segments of the book is the use of the following phrases: "they will not be lamented, nor will they be buried" (vv. 4, 6; cf. 8:2; 25:33); "they

11. *From this place* here balances "in this place" of v. 3, and the cessation of marriage festivities echoes the ban on Jeremiah's marriage in v. 2. The banning of joyful sounds is an ancient curse. Cf. D. Hillers, *Treaty-Curses and the OT Prophets*. Biblica et Orientalia 16 (1964), pp. 57f.

12. The fate of the people was announced in the 3rd person in v. 4, but in v. 9 it is in the 2nd person.

13. On the text and translation of the final phrase see the commentary below.

14. J. Bright, *Jeremiah*, p. 112.

15. See the commentaries and Versions *in loc.*

16. See the Introduction, "The Book of Jeremiah: Composition," pp. 33–50; cf. S. Mowinckel, *Zur Komposition des Buches Jeremia* (1914), pp. 39f.

shall become dung on the surface of the ground" (v. 4; cf. 8:2; 25:33); "their corpses shall be food for the birds of the sky and for the beasts of the earth" (v. 4; cf. 7:33; 19:7; 34:20); "the sound of mirth, the sound of gladness, the voice of the bridegroom and the voice of the bride" (v. 9; cf. 7:34; 25:10; 33:11). These passages occur elsewhere in the "prose" segments of Jeremiah.

Against the assignment of the passage to the prose sections of Jeremiah we should note the unusual vocabulary of vv. 5, 7, and 8 with a catalog of funeral customs unparalleled elsewhere in the book of Jeremiah. It should be noted that some of the so-called prose passages have their own inner parallelism. Even if such phrases are stereotyped in other passages in Jeremiah, they may well be drawn into poetic structures at times. W. L. Holladay has undertaken a detailed study of this passage[17] (and several others), and has demonstrated a quite remarkable system of balances and parallels in vv. 1–9 which makes it very difficult to deny to these verses a poetic form, "an extended unit of authentic poetry" making the passage "worthy to be placed alongside the call in 1:4–10 as a central testimony by the prophet in his own self-understanding."[18]

The unit may be seen as follows:

Introduction	Verse 1
Yahweh's commandment to Jeremiah: Not to marry	Verse 2
Yahweh's statement about the people: List of children and parents	Verse 3
Yahweh's statement about the people: Death and burial	Verse 4
Yahweh's prohibition to Jeremiah: Not to attend funerals	Verse 5
Yahweh's statement about the people: Survivors shall not mourn	Verse 6
Yahweh's statement about the people: No one to mourn, even for parents	Verse 7
Yahweh's prohibition to Jeremiah: Not to attend weddings	Verse 8
Yahweh addresses the people: No joyful sound, no weddings	Verse 9

17. "The Recovery of Poetic Passages in Jeremiah," *JBL* 85, pp. 401–435. The treatment of these verses in the present commentary owes a great deal to Holladay's discussion.
18. *Ibid.*, p. 420.

In vv. 2–9, using J to designate those verses addressed to Jeremiah and P those about the people, the symmetrical pattern JPPJPPJP emerges. Verse 9 also shows a remarkable set of balances with the rest of the poem.[19]

The whole section vv. 1–13[20] is in an autobiographical style and tells how Jeremiah was forbidden to marry and to participate in the normal joys and sorrows of his people. These deprivations made his life a picture of the terrible fate that awaited the nation. The passage fits well here because it is in close proximity to 15:10–18, which stresses the loneliness of Jeremiah's life. Perhaps, also, the reference to sword and famine in v. 4 provided a link with 14:1–18 and 15:1–4.

1–2 The prophetic word came not only by direct preaching and symbolic action, but at times through events in the life of a prophet or of his family. Hosea's unhappy marriage (Hos. 1–3), Isaiah's family (Isa. 7–8), the death of Ezekiel's wife (Ezek. 24:15–27), and Jeremiah's call to remain unmarried are all examples of the proclamation of the word through family events. But the call here to a life of celibacy is unique in the OT. In the ancient Near East, and therefore in Israel, a large family betokened divine blessing (Gen. 22:17; Ps. 127:3–4; etc.). Sterility and barrenness, on the other hand, were regarded as a curse (Gen. 30:1; 1 Sam. 1:6–8, etc.), and virginity was regarded as a cause for mourning (Judg. 11:37). An old Sumerian proverb curses celibacy.[21] Hence it was altogether unusual for a young man in Israel like Jeremiah to remain unmarried, and the point Jeremiah makes of his celibacy seems to suggest that it was not his choice to remain unmarried.[22] He could do so

19. *Ibid.*, pp. 419f.

20. It is commonly held that these verses are all in the typical Deuteronomic phraseology, but notably vv. 10–13, which are regarded as a Deuteronomic composition rather akin to 9:11–15 (Eng. 12–16); Deut. 29:22–28; 1 K. 9:8–9, where there is a pattern of question, answer and explanation, and a restatement of the circumstances which prompted the question. See E. W. Nicholson, *Preaching to the Exiles*, pp. 59–61.

21. W. G. Lambert, "Celibacy in the World's Oldest Proverb," *BASOR* 169 (1963), 63f.

22. M. D. Goldman, "Was Jeremiah Married?" *Australian Biblical Review* 2/1–2 (1952), pp. 42–47, argued that Jeremiah had once been married and that what he was forbidden to do was to marry *in this place,* that is, in Anathoth. His argument turns on 3:1; 8:10; 11:15; 12:7–10, which he thinks indicates that Jeremiah once had a wife

only because of a strong conviction that the single state might convey one aspect of his message to his people in powerful terms. That he abstained from marriage and children was a powerful sign that the end of Judah was at hand. People would die in the land before many days were past. Jeremiah, who never had a wife or children, was as those would be who had married and had produced children but would lose them all in the calamity that would befall Judah. The command to Jeremiah came in a peculiarly emphatic form. The negative used was *lō'* instead of the more usual *'al*. The use of *lō'* denoted something permanent and indicated that never, in any circumstances, was the prophet to marry. A similar usage occurs in the Ten Commandments. In a sense, Jeremiah was given his own special commandment.

3–4 Some of the grim consequences of war and famine are spelled out here. Sons and daughters, mothers and fathers would alike perish in the coming calamity. Jeremiah without a wife and family would be spared the sadness of his fellows who had a wife and children. With no surviving members of a family there would be no one to lament *(sāp̄aḏ)* them. But worse, burial would be denied to people of all classes, a state of affairs which the people of the ancient Near East regarded as a curse.[23] Jeremiah gave expression to his own horror of its possibility in several places (7:33; 8:2; 9:20 [Eng. 21]; 14:12; 15:3). Lacking burial, the corpses would lie unattended to be devoured by carrion birds (*birds of the sky)* and wild beasts *(beasts of the earth)*.[24]

The causes of the deaths would be varied but all would be associated with the war and its aftermath, *sword, famine,* and the *deadly diseases* of epidemic proportions which were associated with decomposing corpses.

Verse 3 shows some interesting poetical features. The people are mentioned in the order, male, female, female, male, that is, in a chiasmus.[25] Then *in this place* is parallel to *in this land,* both expressions forming part of a legal phraseology (cf. Deut. 26:9). The first phrase is masculine and the second is feminine. The root *yld*

---

who proved adulterous and made him see in private and public life treachery, adultery, and mistrust. It was a projection of this sad experience from his personal life into national life which was responsible for his whole estimate of Judah. The argument has not been generally taken up by others. Cf. W. Rudolph, *Jeremia,* p. 102, n. 1.

23. Cf. Deut. 28:26. See Hillers, *Treaty-Curses and the OT Prophets,* pp. 68f.

24. See commentary on 7:33. The wild beasts may have been roaming dogs.

25. The term refers to a statement of items in a particular order, which is then reversed.

(born, bear, beget) is used three times and the accusative *'ôṯām, them,* twice.

A feature of v. 4 is the sword-famine-pestilence motif. The "pestilence" element is represented here by "death" *(môṯ);* significantly, in 15:2 and 18:21 Jeremiah uses the same terms as a substitute for "pestilence," which is not followed in the prose sections and does not occur in this sense elsewhere in the OT.[26]

5 Jeremiah's solitary lot extended into other areas of life. He was forbidden to join in the normal practices associated with mourning, the mourning gatherings for the deceased, which was a further mark of his withdrawal from normal life, and a reminder that Yahweh had withdrawn from the life of his people.

The main thrust of this verse seems to be that in the shadow of impending national disaster mourning for the loss of a loved one was out of place. The word *mourning (marzēaḥ)* probably refers to a mourning feast as in Aramaic. All lamenting *(sāp̱aḏ)* and condoling *(nûḏ)* was inappropriate. Yahweh had "gathered up" *('āsap̱),* that is, withdrawn, his peace *(šālôm).* The term *peace* is rich in meaning and describes in its widest sense the totality of well-being. But that had been withdrawn as had his steadfast love and his compassion. The trio of terms *šālôm, ḥeseḏ,*[27] and *raḥ^a mîm, peace, steadfast love,* and *compassion,* provides a profound picture of Yahweh's deep commitment to his people. But now, says Jeremiah, these have been withdrawn. Only disaster remains. It is the ultimate calamity, the curse, which results from a breach of covenant. Ezekiel saw a comparable meaning in the death of his wife (Ezek. 24:15–27).

6 A number of items commonly associated with mourning rituals are referred to here, among which the first two were expressly forbidden in Israel presumably because of their pagan associations (Lev. 19:27–28; 21:5; Deut. 14:1). These are rites of self-mutilation, in which the mourners cut or gashed themselves and shaved the head and beard. They seem to have been widely practiced in Israel (41:5; 47:5; 48:37; Isa. 15:2–3; 22:12; Ezek. 7:18; Mic. 1:16; etc.) even though they were forbidden.[28] We will better

26. See W. L. Holladay, "Prototype and Copies," *JBL* 79 (1960), pp. 351–367, esp. p. 355.
27. The term *ḥeseḏ* has a rich connotation. It denotes that quality of character in the light of which a person is utterly faithful to his commitments inside a covenant relationship. The idea extends, however, beyond mere obligation and legal requirements into the area of sheer unmerited favor. The term occurs over 250 times in the OT and has to be translated by a variety of terms.
28. R. de Vaux, *Ancient Israel* (1961), p. 59.

understand the nature of these practices when the character of the religion of the peoples surrounding Israel is known. Possibly the OT opposition to these practices is connected with the worship of the Canaanite god Mot (cf. Deut. 26:14; Ezek. 8:14).

7 The two features referred to seem to have been aspects of a funeral meal, although the exact meaning is variously understood. Some commentators relate them to the ritual uncleanness of the house of one who had died, which prevented food from being prepared there. In that case neighbors would bring in food and drink for the relatives of the deceased (2 Sam. 3:35; Ezek. 24:17; Hos. 9:4). Alternately the *bread* and the *cup of consolation* were given to the mourners who were related to the deceased on the completion of their fast (Deut. 26:14; Ezek. 24:17, 22; Hos. 9:4). In later Judaism the consoling cup was a special cup of wine drunk by the chief mourner. The apocryphal book Tobit speaks clearly of food offered to the deceased (Tobit 4:17). Excavated tombs show that at least sometimes food was placed in the grave with the departed. According to the present verse, the bread and the cup brought *comfort* and *consolation* to the mourner.

In any case, Jeremiah was commanded not to join such mourning gatherings as a sign that Yahweh had withdrawn from his people (v. 5).

8 Joyful gatherings too were to be avoided by the prophet. The houses where men ate and drank are probably to be related to marriage celebrations. *The sound of mirth, the sound of gladness, the voice of the bridegroom and the voice of the bride* seem to allude to the happy festivities which followed the marriage ceremonies (cf. 7:34; 25:10; 33:11). Perhaps the Song of Songs represents a collection of songs suitable for such occasions. The banning of Jeremiah from such festive occasions further stresses the fact that Yahweh had withdrawn from the total life of his people. In the balance of the poem v. 8 is to be compared with v. 5, where Jeremiah is forbidden to attend funerals; here he is forbidden to attend weddings, which represents a return to the marriage motif of v. 2.

9 We reach the climax to the whole poem in a series of short, staccato cola. God addresses the people directly. The oracles of doom refer to the wiping out of all weddings, which is an echo of the private prohibition of Jeremiah's own marriage. The second person address to Jeremiah in vv. 5 and 8 is paralleled here by a second person address by Yahweh to the people. The pictures of death, lack of burial, and absence of mourning in vv. 4 and 6 are matched by the contrast of "no wedding" of v. 9. This closing verse of the poem thus draws together in a climactic statement the themes of vv. 2–8. The whole section is such a closely woven and carefully constructed poetic piece that it must certainly be regarded as an authentic poem by Jeremiah himself.

The total picture that emerges from vv. 1–9 is that Jeremiah was to be deprived of many of the normal activities of his fellows, marriage, family, and participation in the joys and sorrows of their common life. He was someone apart from his fellows. The strangeness of such isolation no doubt provoked many questions and provided Jeremiah with the opportunity to declare his word of judgment to a sinful and covenant-breaking people. His own separateness was a powerful testimony to the separateness of Yahweh as his people turned away from him. Something of the character of their apostasy becomes clear in vv. 10–13.

10–13 As ever, men whose conscience has been deadened through sin, far from discerning their own evil-doing, in the face of coming calamity ask why they are being judged or what evil they have done. One of the best examples of this blindness in the OT occurs in the prophet Malachi (Mal. 1:6–7; 2:17; 3:7–8, 13). It was a peculiarly odd response to Jeremiah's severe words and to the powerful testimony of his own deprivation to ask *Why has Yahweh pronounced against us all this great misfortune (rā'â)?* and *What is our iniquity* (or crime, *'āwôn) and what is the sin (ḥaṭṭā'ṯ) that we have committed (ḥāṭā') . . . ?* The answer to such blind and insensitive questioning comes in terms of the broken covenant. The fathers, and subsequently they themselves, had forsaken *('āzaḇ)* Yahweh. The meaning of this is made clear from the five phrases that follow. Instead of acknowledging the supreme and only sovereignty of Yahweh the Lord of the Covenant, the people had gone after other gods, served them, worshipped them, forsaken Yahweh, and failed to keep his law *(tôrâ)*. The verbs are all significant elements in the distinctive vocabulary for breach of covenant. The expression "follow after these gods" has its parallels in the secular ancient Near Eastern treaties, where vassals were forbidden to turn toward or to follow after other kings than the great king to whom they were bound by their treaty.[29] The verb "serve" *('āḇaḏ)* is re-

29. D. Hillers, *Covenant: The History of a Biblical Idea* (1969), p. 31. Cf. W. L. Moran, "The Ancient Near Eastern Background of the Love of God in Deuteronomy," *CBQ* 26 (1963), p. 83, n. 35.

lated to the noun "servant" or "slave" or "vassal" *('eḇeḏ)*. In the religious sense, religious service is worship. The verb "worship" *(hištaḥ^a wâ)* means literally "prostrate oneself toward"[30] and is used in the secular world of a vassal falling in obeisance before his overlord. The expression "keep the law" has its parallel in the observance of the treaty obligations in a secular setting. It is a comprehensive picture, the import of which could not have been missed by Jeremiah's hearers. Added emphasis was given by the further statement, *You for your part have done worse than your fathers*. Ultimately their rebellion arose from the *stubbornness* (*š^e rirûṯ*) of their own evil heart, and they followed inward promptings rather than obey Yahweh. So there were ample grounds for the imminent doom which would soon befall them. Yahweh would *throw (hēṭîl)*[31] them out (or, fling them headlong) from their own land to a land unknown where they would *serve ('āḇaḏ)* other gods. If they did not care to serve (or worship) Yahweh, they would be compelled to worship other deities all the time (lit. *day and night*).[32]

Who will show you no favor — This last phrase is variously read. The syntax would lead us to expect a verb relating to *other gods* who would not show favor to the people, and this sense is given in LXX. However, MT has the reading *'ettēn,* "I will give," apparently picking up the first person at the beginning of the verse. Either sense is possible but the theological thrust differs. The question remains. Who is it who will show no favor *(ḥ^a nînâ)* to the outcasts, Yahweh who cast them out, or the deities in the land to which they were sent? Some uncertainty remains for the modern reader.

Verses 10–13 comprise a short lament in the form of questions (v. 10) followed by a short oracle of judgment upon the people of Judah (vv. 11–13), all in prose. It bears some resemblance both in form and content to 5:19; 9:11–15 (Eng. 12–16) and 22:8–9. The literary forms are known elsewhere (e.g., Deut. 29:21–27 [Eng. 22–28]; 1 K. 9:8–9) and contain three elements—(a) a question asking why judgment has fallen, (b) an answer and explanation attributing the destruction to God's judgment because of the people's apostasy, and (c) a statement of the calamity which prompted the question.

30. C. Gordon, *Ugaritic Textbook,* Glossary, p. 395, No. 847.
31. The verb was evidently intended to convey a vigorous reaction on Yahweh's part.
32. The expression is lacking in LXX.

Here we have the questions (v. 10), the answer (vv. 11–12), and the restatement and description of the judgment (v. 13).

(iv) A New Exodus (16:14–15)

14 *"Therefore see! Days are coming—Yahweh's word—when it will no longer be said, 'As Yahweh lives who brought the Israelites up from the land of Egypt,'*

15 *But, 'As Yahweh lives who brought back the descendants of Israel from a northern land and from all the lands to which he had driven them'; and I will bring them back to the land which I gave to their forefathers."*

These verses are an almost exact equivalent of 23:7–8, where they appear to fit neatly into a context. At first sight they appear to interrupt an argument which is concerned with the judgment that will fall on the people of Judah in their land. Because these verses refer to a future restoration to the land and envisage a new exodus, not this time from Egypt but from lands to the north to which the people have been exiled, many commentators have regarded them as exilic in origin but inserted here by a later editor to indicate the outcome of the promised judgment of earlier verses.[1] While this view cannot be ruled out on any *a priori* grounds, it is probably wise to recognize that a reference to exile by no means requires that an exile had taken place. Exile was recognized at an early date as one of the possibilities that followed an invasion. Over a century earlier the northern kingdom had known a partial exile. For those already in exile a return from foreign soil was always hoped for, and it is not impossible that some exiles had returned. Hence some degree of caution is proper in making the statement that these verses are exilic and late. In any case, we ought not to deny to Jeremiah the expression of a hope that even if exile took place, it was not the end. There would be a return to the land.

The phrase *As Yahweh lives (ḥay YHWH)* occurs at the beginning of an oath. Yahweh is invoked as the guarantor of the oath. The verb *yēʾāmēr* (lit. "*let it be said*")[2] probably refers to the act of taking an oath. The verb "bring up" *(heʿᵉlâ)* occurs often in ref-

1. E.g., E. W. Nicholson, *Jeremiah 1–25*, p. 144; J. P. Hyatt, "Jeremiah," *IB* V, p. 947; *et al.*
2. The Niphal form of the verb. But LXX implies *yōʾmᵉrû*, "they will say," as in 23:7.

erence to the Exodus from Egypt (Exod. 3:8, 17; 17:3; 32:1, 4, 6, 7, 8, 23; etc.). The use of this term provides a setting for another exodus from lands to the north, when once again Israel would be redeemed and restored to her land. It was a theme taken up by the exilic prophet who proclaimed the words which occur in Isa. 43:16–20; 48:20–21; 51:9–11, although for him the new exodus from Babylon would surpass the ancient exodus from Egypt.

(v) A Further Saying of Judgment (16:16–18)

16 *"Look! I am sending for many fishermen—Yahweh's word—and they will fish for them. And after that I will send for many hunters, who will hunt them out from every mountain and hill and from the crevices of the rocks.*
17 *For my eyes are on all their ways; they are not hidden from my sight*[1] *and their iniquity is not concealed from my eyes.*
18 *I will make them pay*[2] *the equivalent of their sinful iniquity, because they have polluted my land with the corpses of their detestable idols and they have filled my heritage with their abominations."*

Verses 16–18 continue the description of Judah's sins already set out in vv. 11–12, although, as we have seen, vv. 10–13 form a small unit in themselves. It seems that vv. 16–18 may have been an oracle of doom preached by Jeremiah in another context but placed in its present setting to form a new unit which was built up from several fragments. The announcement of judgment in vv. 1–13 is continued in this passage with a similar intensity and severity.

16–17 The imagery of calling for fishermen to fish out the people of Judah occurs also in Ezek. 12:13; 29:4–5; Amos 4:2; Hab. 1:14–17. The figure was evidently well known and was an ancient one. Habakkuk's description of an enemy catching his prey in a net and offering sacrifice and burning incense before his net is a vivid one, although the practice is not attested for the Babylonians.

The figure of a hunter, hunting out quarry from rock crevices, was likewise a well-known image. A thorough and complete search for the hunted animals is depicted. A similar picture occurs in Amos 9:1–4. The total impression is of a judgment that would be both severe and complete. It would be little use to attempt to escape by

1. The clause *they are not hidden from my sight* is lacking in LXX.
2. MT reads "I will first repay." We omit "first" with LXX. It seems to be a gloss to explain that before the restoration of vv. 14–15 there will need to be a repayment.

hiding, for the eyes of Yahweh were upon them. Moreover, no evil deed and no iniquity was hidden from him.

18 The appearance of the word "first" in MT and its absence in LXX raises the question of the shorter and longer texts of Jeremiah. We are never certain whether LXX was following a variant Hebrew text at a particular point (and there were such variant texts),[3] or whether it was making a paraphrase of the Hebrew text. It would be easy to argue that the word "first" was inserted by an editor who wanted to indicate that the judgments pronounced by Jeremiah would be followed by a renewal. Indeed the previous vv. 14–15 refer to a restoration. If "first" is omitted the first part of v. 18 reads literally, "I will pay (recompense) double (or, the equivalent) of their iniquity *('āwôn)* and their sin." But even in so short a sentence[4] a number of possibilities are available. We may decide to omit "first." The verb may be understood as a causative, "I will cause them to pay" or "make them pay." The noun *mišnēh,* usually translated "double," can possibly be understood as *equivalent,* since a similar word has been found in cuneiform documents at Alalakh in Syria carrying this sense.[5] Then, if we see in the expression "their iniquity and their sin" a hendiadys[6] we may translate *their sinful iniquity.* Hence we may translate the whole as *I will make them pay the equivalent of their sinful iniquity,* and thus avoid the charge that God is "unreasonable and unjust."[7] A similar understanding of *mišnēh* may be possible in Deut. 15:18 and Isa. 40:2. In each case the judgment was equivalent to the offense.

By their *sinful iniquity* the people of Judah had defiled or *polluted (ḥll)*[8] Yahweh's land with their idols and abominations. The expression *the corpses of their detestable idols (niḇlaṯ šiqqûṣêhem)* is a suggestive one. The idols which were used in worship were lifeless, and seemed to Jeremiah like so many corpses defiling

3. The Hebrew text of Samuel found in the Qumran caves is much closer to LXX than to MT, to judge from the extant fragments. See the Introduction, "The Text," pp. 117–120.

4. Five words in Hebrew.

5. D. J. Wiseman, *NBD,* p. 67; *The Alalakh Tablets* (1953), pp. 31f. The noun *mištannu* in AT3 is possibly the equivalent of *mišnēh* here. In Deut. 17:18 *mišnēh hattôrâ* is a copy of the law; with respect to money and possessions, however, the word normally means "twofold," e.g., Gen. 43:12, 15 (cf. vv. 21–22); Job 42:10.

6. With J. Bright, *Jeremiah,* p. 108.

7. M. Tsevat, "Alalakhiana," *HUCA* 29 (1958), pp. 125f.

8. The verb is in its Piel form.

Yahweh's land (cf. Lev. 26:30). He uses a parallel expression, almost in the style of a poet.[9]

They have polluted my land with the corpses of their
detestable idols;
They have filled my heritage with their abominations.

The two expressions *my land* and *my heritage* provide an interesting insight into the understanding that Israel had of the land in which they lived. It was *their* land and *their* heritage, but behind that belief lay the view that it was Yahweh's land and Yahweh's heritage. The former land of Canaan was the heritage of Yahweh in a particular way (Exod. 15:17; Josh. 22:19; Ps. 79:1), although he was the God of the whole earth (Ps. 47:3 [Eng. 2]; etc.). It was for this reason that Israel was able to enjoy the land as their heritage.

The presence of idols and abominations in the land was an affront to Yahweh's sovereignty and a clear indication of the breach of the covenant, for these represented alternative sovereignties. They had the effect of polluting (*ḥillēl*) the land. The same verb is used frequently with the nouns "temple," "sabbath," "my holy name," "my house," "covenant," "altar," etc. In every case the item that was profaned was the peculiar property of Yahweh but others had encroached upon his sovereign rights. Unclean things like corpses, people outside the covenant, idols, or anything that did not display the peculiar holiness of Yahweh had the effect of polluting that which was holy. Nor could that which was holy confer holiness on anything it touched, but itself became polluted (Hag. 2:10–14). A land that was polluted could only experience the judgment of Yahweh upon it. In the present context the pollution of the land made the coming judgment all the more certain. The character of that judgment is presented in other terms in Isa. 47:6, where Yahweh is depicted as speaking to Babylon:

"I was angry with my people;
I profaned (*ḥillēl*) my heritage (*naḥ^{a}lâ);*
I gave them into your hand;
You showed them no mercy."

The cause of the heritage being profaned was the presence of idols; but it was Yahweh who brought judgment in the form of the Chaldean armies, further profaning his heritage by allowing the unclean foreigner to destroy the temple and devastate the whole land.

9. It is not impossible that one of Jeremiah's poetic oracles lay behind vv. 16–18, since there are a number of parallelisms here. See below.

A closer look at these verses suggests that they may have had a poetic original, which may have looked something like the following:

"I am sending for many fishermen, and they will fish for them;
I will send for many hunters, and they will hunt them out
From every mountain and hill,
From the crevices of the rocks.
For my eyes are on all their ways;
They are not hidden from my sight;
Their iniquity is not concealed from my sight.
I will make them pay the equivalent of their sinful iniquity,
Because they have polluted every land with the corpses of their detestable idols,
And they have filled my heritage with their abominations."

If some commentators show a tendency to allow that poetic sections are genuinely Jeremianic while prose passages are doubtful, the recognition of a poetic original here may point to the genuineness of the oracle.[10]

(vi) The Conversion of the Nations (16:19–21)

19 *O Yahweh, my strength and my stronghold,*
My refuge in the day of trouble,
To thee shall nations come
From the ends of the earth, and say,
"Our fathers have inherited a mere lie,
An idol in which there is no profit.
20 *Can mortal man make gods for himself?*[1]
They would be no gods!"
21 *"Therefore I am teaching them,*
Right now I will teach them
My power and my might,
And they shall learn that my name is Yahweh."

Chapter 16 concludes with a short poetic oracle which speaks of the future conversion of the nations to the worship of Yahweh. The abrupt introduction of such a theme has been taken by some commentators as evidence that the segment is a later insertion which

10. Some commentators, e.g., J. P. Hyatt, *IB* V, p. 948; W. Rudolph, *Jeremia,* p. 103, regard v. 18 as an editorial note to conclude the section comprising vv. 1–13, 16–17.

1. MT reads "Does one make for himself gods?" The sense seems to require some reference to mankind making his own deities.

may have been influenced by exilic preaching such as we find in Isa. 45:20, 24. Such a conclusion should not be readily allowed.[2] The passage has a number of phrases and terms which occur elsewhere in Jeremiah. The idea of the turning of the nations to Yahweh occurs in a variety of preexilic Psalms (e.g., Ps. 2), and has echoes in Jeremiah's own poetry (e.g., 4:1–2) and in other preexilic literature (e.g., 1 K. 8:41–43). There are good reasons to retain the passage as a genuine oracle of Jeremiah. It has been grouped with other material in ch. 16 for a reason best understood by the editor. One possible reason is that the reference to idols introduced into the land by Israel (v. 18) led the editor to add vv. 19–21 so as to provide the contrasting statement of v. 20 and the powerful example of those nations who reject their idols and come to worship Yahweh.

19–20 There is a superb grouping together here of titles for Yahweh, *my strength ('ōz), my stronghold (mā'ôz)*, and *my refuge (mānôs)*. These terms occur often in the Psalms (e.g., 18:3–4 [Eng. 2–3]; 28:1, 7–8; 59:11, 18–19 [Eng. 10, 17–18]) and elsewhere in the OT to express the confidence of Israel in God. Jeremiah needed to sense this kind of support behind him.

That the nations (*gôyîm*) would turn to Yahweh one day was part of Israel's belief in both preexilic and postexilic times (4:2; Isa. 2:1–3; Zech. 8:20–23; 14:16–17; etc.). In a number of OT passages the idea that the nations would come from the ends of the earth provides a sort of "universal" note. This was certainly common in exilic and postexilic writings (Isa. 42:4; 49:6; Zech. 8:20–23; 14:16–17). The best thought in ancient Israel regarded the mission of Israel to be worldwide (cf. Gen. 12:1–3).

Part of the conversion process would be that those who once worshipped idols would come to realize that an idol was a worthless thing. It was an inheritance from the past which was only a sham (or *lie, šeqer),* an empty thing *(heḇel).* This reflection leads to the significant line in v. 20:

Can mortal man make gods for himself?
They would be no gods!

One is reminded immediately of other OT passages which reflect on the vanity of idols (e.g., 2:11; 5:7; 10:1–16; 12:14–17; Isa. 40:19–20;

2. See A. Weiser, *Das Buch des Propheten Jeremia,* pp. 141f.

42:8; 45:14–25). Clearly, if there was ever to be a universal response to the God of Israel there would need to be a recognition of the unreality of all other gods. The nations would come to that recognition only after adequate instruction.

21 Yahweh himself would undertake the task of *teaching*[3] the nations, no doubt through his servants, and ideally through his servant Israel (Isa. 42:4; 49:6). The specific things Yahweh would teach the nations were his *power* (lit. "hand," *yāḏ*) and his *might (g*^{e}*ḇûrâ)*. In that way the nations would come to know that his name was Yahweh. But a name denoted one's character, and the very name Yahweh denoted a wide range of attributes not least of which was his power to save and deliver oppressed people from the nations (cf. Exod. 3:13–17). The Exodus from Egypt originally required a display of great power which Yahweh was able to exercise. The nations would one day come to understand the rich connotation that attached to the name Yahweh. But then they would understand that he was the sovereign Lord not merely of Israel, but of the whole earth.

As the modern reader takes a comprehensive look at the editor's handiwork in ch. 16 a number of things stand out.

The divine demand on Jeremiah was a severe one. Any member of a village was closely knit to the whole village in normal circumstances. When one of the villagers stood aloof from significant events like weddings or funerals, behaved oddly in that he did not seek marriage, embarrassed his village by exposing the national life as Jeremiah did, then he forfeited that basic social and psychological security which was the lot of every villager. Cut off from the support system which was available to members of a village, he was alone in the world. God was his sole support. Little wonder that when Jeremiah became convinced in his own mind that God was neglecting him, he laid his complaints against God in his "confessions."[4]

A second feature of the present chapter is the statement about coming judgment. The reasons for this are set out in terms of a rejection of Yahweh and a turning to other gods. The point at issue is a breach of covenant. Jeremiah's experience of withdrawal from

3. The verb is the Hiphil of *yāḏa'*, "to know," thus "cause to know," "teach."
4. See the Introduction, "The 'Confessions' of Jeremiah," pp. 88–92.

village life was a picture of Yahweh's withdrawal from his people. That prospect was a deep grief to Jeremiah and it created a tension for him. He was called to declare judgment on a covenant-rejecting people, but he hoped and prayed for their restoration. He was later to speak about a new covenant written in men's hearts (31:31–34).

The third theologically significant feature is the reference to the conversion of the nations *(gôyîm)*. But the basis of any conversion for them would be their willingness to cast away their idols and acknowledge the complete and only sovereignty of Yahweh, Israel's God, a position that Jeremiah's own people had abandoned.

(vii) Miscellaneous Sayings (17:1–13)

(a) Judah's guilt that cannot be erased (17:1–4)[1]

1[2] *"Judah's sin is engraved*
With an iron tool;
It is carved with a diamond point
On the tablet of their heart,
And on the horns of their[3] *altars.*
2 *As evidence against them*[4]
Their altars and their sacred poles
(Stand) beside spreading trees,
Upon the high hills,

1. The whole of vv. 1–4 is lacking in LXX for a reason that is not now clear. The Qumran fragment from ch. 17 commences only at v. 8 and is therefore no help in deciding whether LXX follows another Hebrew text which seems to be true in other parts of Jeremiah. In general, the Qumran Jeremiah text seems to follow the shorter LXX text, so it seems likely that these verses were lacking in the Qumran text also.

2. J. Bright, *Jeremiah,* p. 114, attempts a poetic rendering as follows:
Etched is Judah's sin
With iron pen,
With diamond point engraved
On the plaque of their heart
And the horns of their altars
(As evidence against them).

3. MT has "your altars," although many mss. and Versions have *their altars.* The next line reads *mizbᵉḥôṯām, their altars,* which we accept as the correct form. MT is not, however, impossible and could be understood as a sudden switch to the 2nd person plur. as Jeremiah faced an audience.

4. There is a question of where to attach the first two words of v. 2. One proposal is to attach them to the end of v. 1 as in NEB and to read the consonants *kzkrn bhm* instead of MT *kzkr bnhm,* which involves merely the transfer of the consonant *n* from the second word to the first. The sense would then be "as a remembrance (record, witness) against them." Alternately MT is left as it is and reads "while their children remember" (so J. Bright, p. 114).

3 *On the mountains*[5] *in the open country.*
Your wealth and[6] *all your treasures*
I will give away as spoil
As the price[7] *of your sin*
Throughout all your country.
4 *You will lose possession*[8] *of your inheritance*
Which I gave you.
I will make you serve your enemies as slaves
In a land you do not know;
For in my wrath a fire is kindled[9]
Which will burn for ever."

Despite textual uncertainties, the profound guilt of Judah is here underlined.[10]

1 Judah's sin is deeply ingrained. It is compared to an inscription carved with an iron tool into some rock face which cannot be erased. Heb. *'ēṭ,* often translated "pen" (AV, RSV), is hardly a writing pen but an engraver's tool. Nor can the verbal noun *keṯûḇâ* be translated as "written" (its normal sense) but must be rendered as *engraved* or "etched," as the parallel word in the next line suggests. We may have information here about the process of engraving an inscription in stone from the reference to the *diamond point (ṣippōren šāmîr).* The medium upon which such tools operated was normally stone, but the figure is strongly presented here because the medium into which the sin of Judah was *carved (ḥarûšâ)* was the *tablet of their heart.* The picture is consistent with much of Jeremiah's preaching. Judah's rebellion was deep-rooted and ineradicable unless a deep change such as is described later in the book (31:31–34) took place. Only when God wrote his law on his people's heart could obedience replace rebellion.

But Judah's sin was etched into their cultic practices, here represented by their *altars.* The *horns* of the altar were projecting carved stone pieces which were set on the top of the altar at each of the four corners to hold in place the timber for the fire and the

5. Reading *harărê* with Theodotion in place of MT *hărārî,* "my mountain." See *BHS.*
6. *And* is added following 15:13 in many mss. and Versions.
7. MT *bāmōṯeyḵā*, "your high places," is lacking in Syr.; read *bimḥîr* with 15:13.
8. MT is difficult. A widely accepted suggestion is to read *yāḏeḵā* for *ûḇeḵā,* i.e., "you will let drop your hand," hence *you will lose possession.*
9. Reading *qāḏeḥâ* for MT *qeḏaḥtem*, "you have kindled." Cf. 15:14.
10. J. Bright, *Jeremiah,* p. 117 proposes that 17:1–4 may have been the original conclusion to the poem and liturgy in time of drought in 14:1–10, 19–22.

sacrificial beast. Such altars have been discovered *in situ* in a number of excavations in recent years, but notably in Arad and Tel Sheba.[11] The present allusion seems to touch on the fact that when a sacrifice was offered, some of the blood was smeared on the horns of the altar. The true intention of an offering was related to some act of atonement where the blood of the sin-offering served as a covering for sin. But Jeremiah saw even in the offering of such sacrifices an affront to God. The sprinkled blood seemed but an engraving of Judah's sin on the horns of the altar as well as on the hearts of the people (cf. 7:21–26; Amos 4:4–5).

2 Although there have been a number of suggestions about how to handle v. 2 and the first words of v. 3, it seems clear that we have here a further reference to the prevalence of Canaanite worship throughout the land with its *altars, sacred poles,* and other paraphernalia of the cult. The *sacred poles* (Asherim, Heb. *'ᵃšērîm*) were objects of wood, perhaps wooden poles representing the goddess Asherah.[12]

The section emphasizes that while the people of Judah offered sacrifices to Yahweh they continued to be involved in the worship of the Canaanite deities, a clear rejection of the sole sovereignty of Yahweh the Lord of the covenant by the people of Judah. Little wonder that Jeremiah saw Judah's guilt as something deeply engraved on their hearts.

3–4 These verses are very similar to 15:13–14. Indeed we are able to restore some of the corrupt words in these two verses by reference to the earlier passage, and vice versa.[13] The picture portrays the nation being robbed of its wealth and treasures, presumably by an invader. Precisely this happened in 587 B.C. (2 K. 25:13–17). Another aspect of the coming judgment was to be that Judah would lose to the invader the patrimony which Yahweh gave to her, as well as her wealth. The last element in the judgment was exile. Judah would be forced to serve her enemies in an unknown land.

As a final statement to this brief oracle of judgment it is asserted that the fire of Yahweh once kindled would burn for ever.

11. See Y. Aharoni, "Arad: Its Inscriptions and Temple," *BA* 31/1 (1968), pp. 18–32; "The Horned Altar of Beersheba," *BA* 37/1 (1974), pp. 2–6.
12. See R. de Vaux, *Ancient Israel,* pp. 285–87.
13. See textual notes.

There could be no escaping the fiery wrath of Yahweh once it burst forth.

(b) A personal affirmation: trust in God rather than in man (17:5–8)

5 *This is what Yahweh has said:*
"Cursed is the man who trusts in mankind
And makes mortal flesh his strength
While his heart turns aside from Yahweh.
6 *He is like the desert shrub:*
When good comes he shall not see it;
He shall inhabit the parched places in the wilderness,
A salt land where no man lives.
7 *Blessed is the man who trusts in Yahweh;*
Yahweh will be his confidence;
8 *He is like a tree that is planted near water,*
That thrusts out its roots toward the stream.
When the heat comes it has nothing to fear;
Its leaves remain luxurious.
In a year of drought it is not troubled
And does not cease to bear fruit."

This short poem contrasting the righteous man and the wicked man is strongly reminiscent of Ps. 1, and has therefore often been explained as a piece of wisdom literature.[1] An alternative view, and one that seems to be more convincing, is to regard the section as one of Jeremiah's confessions,[2] a sort of personal affirmation.[3]

5–6 The brief introduction, which represents an editorial transition, is lacking in LXX. The *man (geḇer)* who trusts in *mankind ('āḏām)* is *cursed ('ārûr)*. Presumably Jeremiah referred here to the man of Israel who stood in a covenant relationship with Yahweh. In that case his only source of confidence should have been the Lord of the covenant and not mankind. In the poetic style *mankind* is set in parallel with *flesh (bāśār)* and the verb *trusts (bāṭaḥ)* is parallel to *makes his strength* (lit. "sets as his arm"). The noun *z*^{e}*rōa'*, "arm," often denotes *strength* or "might" in the OT and is often used for the strength of Yahweh (Exod. 6:6; 15:16; Ps. 79:11; 89:11 [Eng. 10]; Isa. 33:2; 51:9; 53:1; etc.). Such a man is described

1. J. Bright, *Jeremiah,* p. 119; G. P. Couturier, "Jeremiah," *JBC* (1969), p. 316; A. S. Peake, *Jeremiah,* I (1910), p. 221, etc.; J. P. Hyatt, "Jeremiah," *IB* V, pp. 950f.
2. W. L. Holladay, *Jeremiah: Spokesman Out of Time* (1974), pp. 98f.
3. Some commentators deny the poem to Jeremiah. See E. W. Nicholson, *Jeremiah 1–25,* p. 148. We accept it as genuine.

as one whose heart *turns aside (sûr)* from Yahweh, a verb almost synonymous with the verb *šûḇ* which is used so frequently by Jeremiah. To turn away from Yahweh was to reject his sovereignty and his covenant. In such a context the use of *cursed ('ārûr)* is appropriate.

The figure of a *shrub ('ar'ār)*[4] in the *desert ('ᵃrāḇâ)* is a vivid one. When *good* (perhaps in this case rain, cf. Deut. 28:12) comes he does not see it, for it passes him by. He remains dry and useless. His dwelling place is in the parched places and in the uninhabited salt lands.

7–8 In contrast stands the man who is *blessed (bārûḵ)* because he *trusts (bāṭaḥ)* Yahweh, that is, he acknowledges Yahweh as the Lord of the covenant and surrenders to him. The noun we have translated *confidence* is *miḇṭaḥ,* a cognate of the verb for "trust." Yahweh is the focal point of his confidence. The figure that develops differs somewhat from that in Ps. 1:3, where the man who is blessed is likened to a tree planted by rivers of water that produces fruit. There is another dimension here which is more active and dynamic. This tree actively *thrusts out*[5] its roots toward the stream and is not dismayed when heat and drought come. Its leaves remain green and it continues to bear fruit.

There is a difference between the shrub of v. 6 and the tree of v. 8. Both of them experience the drought, but the shrub has no deep rootage whereas the tree does. So the tree outlasts the drought and continues to produce its fruit.

These verses are a reflection of Jeremiah's own experience. He had known the drought experience when Yahweh seemed to him like a deceitful brook, like waters that failed when sought by a thirsty man (15:18). In that hour he discovered Yahweh had not forsaken him, but called him strongly to repent from his bitterness and his sense of being abandoned, for this had only led to despair and to cursing the day he was born. Those were worthless words. There were more precious things to utter (15:19). He needed to repent (turn, *šûḇ*). In 17:5–8 we see a man who has repented from foolish thoughts of despair and consternation before the powerful pressure of public opinion. He had learned to trust Yahweh rather than the opinions of men. The present passage is to be understood as his personal affirmation that he has survived his dry period. Indeed

4. The meaning of the Hebrew noun is uncertain. NEB translates "juniper."
5. The verb form is Piel and denotes an intensive and vigorous action.

these verses constitute a response to Yahweh's call to repentance in 15:19–21.[6]

Since Jeremiah offers two variations on the theme of Ps. 1, here in 17:5–8 and also in 12:1–2, it seems possible that Ps. 1 was available to the prophet.

(c) God knows the heart and rewards justly (17:9–11)[1]

9 *The heart is the most deceitful of all things,*
And it is desperately sick.[2]
Who can understand it?
10 *"I, Yahweh, explore the heart*
And test its hidden depths,
Requiting[3] *each man according to his ways*
And as his actions deserve."[4]
11 *Like a partridge gathering into its nest*
Eggs which it has not laid,
So is the man who amasses riches unjustly.
Before his days are half over they will leave him,
And in the end he will prove to be a fool.

This segment has links with the preceding verses. The word *heart (lēḇ)* occurs in both vv. 9 and 10. The human *heart* is deceitful (v. 9) but Yahweh knows it (v. 10). Verse 9 was possibly a well-known proverb. So also was the first half of v. 11, and the mention of *requiting each man according to his ways* (v. 10) links with *unjustly (lō' ḇᵉmišpāṭ)* in v. 11. The three verses are thus linked together in thought. Underlying them all is a guarantee to Jeremiah that Yahweh knows all, assesses *(bōḥēn,* v. 10) all, and judges all. If the fruit of Jeremiah's deed is good, he is in Yahweh's safe care.

9–10 The *heart* of man *(lēḇ)* in the psychology of OT times refers frequently to the mind, the source of a man's thinking and action.[5] It is here described as *deceitful* above all.[6] A picturesque

6. See W. L. Holladay, *Jeremiah: Spokesman Out of Time,* pp. 98f., whose argument has been followed here.

1. W. L. Holladay, *Jeremiah: Spokesman Out of Time,* pp. 99f., takes 17:9–10 as one of Jeremiah's confessions but rather in the nature of puzzlement than anything else.
2. The adjective *'ānuš* means *sick,* "weak," and gives better sense than "wicked" (AV) or "corrupt" (RSV). Cf. 15:18, where the word means "incurable."
3. Lit. "give."
4. Lit. "according to the fruit of his actions."
5. A. R. Johnson, *The Vitality of the Individual in the Thought of Ancient Israel* (1949), pp. 77-82.
6. The root *'qb* appears in the verbs "deceive" and "take by the heel," and also in the proper name Jacob. LXX reads "deep" *('āmōq)* but MT seems satisfactory. The same word in Isa. 40:4 is used of uneven or bumpy ground.

translation is "The heart is rougher than anything and incurable; who understands it?"[7] It is certainly a mystery to mankind, who does not *understand (yāḏa')* it. Yahweh, however, "explores" or searches *(ḥāqar)* the human heart.

A second word is here set in parallel to *heart,* literally, "kidneys" *(k^e^lāyôṯ), hidden depths.* These, Yahweh assays or "tests" *(bāḥan,* cf. 6:27; 11:20; 12:2; etc.). This term has sometimes been understood to refer to the seat of the emotions just as the heart is the seat of thought and will. Whether in fact this was so may be open to doubt, but the two terms "heart" and "kidneys" cover the range of hidden elements in man's character and personality. Nothing is hidden from Yahweh, either in the case of Jeremiah his servant or in the case of the people of Judah (cf. 11:20). When Yahweh comes to reward each man, it will be according to his *ways* (conduct) and *as his actions deserve* (cf. Isa. 11:3b, 4).

There is assurance in vv. 9–10 for a man who has determined to trust in Yahweh (v. 7) rather than in man (v. 5).

11 Further assurance comes from a consideration of yet another proverb, which seems to have been based on a popular belief that the *partridge (qōrē')*[8] hatches out eggs which were not its own[9] and which it had not *laid (yālaḏ).*[10] Like this bird is the man who *amasses riches,* but *unjustly* (not in justice). As the young birds of the deceiver grow up and recognize in the "parent" a different breed they fly off. So too, ill-gotten wealth is soon gone and the man who amasses it dishonestly is shown to be a *fool (nāḇāl) in the end.* The prosperity of the wicked is merely a passing delusion. The link with previous verses comes through the recognition of deceivers who, under test, are exposed both in nature and in the sight of Yahweh. Even if the material in vv. 1–11 appears to be heterogeneous,[11] it has been woven into a reasonably unified statement and is brought to a climax in vv. 12–13.

7. W. L. Holladay, *Jeremiah: Spokesman Out of Time,* p. 100.

8. The precise species of bird is uncertain. The *qōrē'* may not be specifically the partridge (*genera,* Alectoris and Ammoperdex), but could refer to some variety of sand grouse (Pteroclididae). Cf. G. R. Driver, *PEQ* (1955), p. 133.

9. The verb *dāḡar* means to gather and hatch (cf. Isa. 34:15). LXX has "gathers" here. In Aramaic the root *dgr* means "gather."

10. The verb *yālaḏ* normally means "bear, give birth to." Here it must mean "lay (an egg)."

11. So J. Bright, *Jeremiah,*, p. 119.

(d) Yahweh, the hope of Israel (17:12–13)

12 *A throne of glory, exalted*[1] *from the beginning,*
Is the place of our sanctuary.
13 *O Yahweh, the hope of Israel,*
All who forsake thee shall be put to shame;
Those who turn aside[2] *from thee shall be written*[3] *in the earth;*
For they have forsaken[4] *the fountain of living water.*

Jeremiah had complained in 15:18 of his unceasing pain and incurable wounds, refusing to be healed. Yahweh was a deceitful brook whose waters had failed. Now his whole tone has changed. Yahweh is the hope of Israel, the fountain of living water. Verse 12 is thus a confession that the opinion expressed in 15:18 was in error. Yahweh is to be trusted (v. 7). It is mankind upon whom men should never impose their confidence. Thus vv. 12–13 may be seen as a fitting climax to the whole argument which is developed in vv. 5–13. Whether the present arrangement is the work of Jeremiah or of a skillful compiler of fragments of Jeremiah's oracles, the whole hangs together in a remarkably logical fashion.

12 The phrase *throne of glory* (or glorious throne) is a reference to the temple where Yahweh's presence was known among his people. That glorious throne was exalted from the beginning. Yahweh was enthroned above the sacred Ark in the temple (Ps. 80:3 [Eng. 2]), here referred to as *our sanctuary (miqdāš)*. The focus is thus on the temple and on Yahweh the sovereign Lord of Israel. Comparison of this verse with a passage like 7:1–15 may seem at first sight to reveal a contradiction. But it was not the temple as such, nor the deep belief in Israel that God's presence was associated with

1. Reading with LXX *mûrām* in place of MT *mārôm*.
2. The sense requires "And those who turn aside from thee," *w*^{e}*sûrêḵā,* since the words are addressed to Yahweh. MT in its Qere suggests *y*^{e}*sûray,* "those who turn aside from me" (my rebels).
3. The text is difficult. MT here reads *yikkāṯēḇû*, "they will be written down." Between this verb and the first participle lies the phrase "in the land," which may be taken with either verb. Two meanings are possible: "those who turn aside from thee in the land," or "they will be written down in the earth" (J. Bright). The latter expression may mean that the apostates will be recorded in the dust and their record will soon be erased and forgotten. Alternately, the word "earth" has been taken to denote the underworld, that is, apostates will be listed for death (M. J. Dahood, *Biblica* 40 [1959], pp. 164–68, on the basis of Ugaritic evidence). But two other proposals have been made. Either read with Latin and Targ. *yikkārēṯû,* "they will be cut off," or read *yikkālēmû,* "they shall be ashamed."
4. MT adds "Yahweh" after the verb *have forsaken*. It is probably a gloss, though a correct one. Cf. 2:13.

the temple, that Jeremiah condemned in 7:1–15, but rather an attitude of mind, verging on blasphemy, which led the citizens of Jerusalem and Judah to believe that an association with the temple and its rituals was the sole demand that Yahweh made upon them. Clearly they had lost their way. A temple and a ritual were meaningful only for people who acknowledged the God who was worshipped in the temple. The complete sovereignty of Yahweh over their lives and their full obedience to the covenant demands were a *sine qua non* for acceptance by Yahweh of any who worshipped in the temple. But apart from that the temple had no meaning and could be destroyed as the earlier shrine at Shiloh had been (7:14). This emphasis becomes clearer in v. 13.

13 The significant word *hope (miqwēh) of Israel* occurs here (cf. 14:8; 50:7). Not merely in that particular hour of crisis but always, the one solid ground on which Israel might rest her hope was Yahweh. Hence those who forsook *('āzaḇ)* him stood under condemnation,[5] for they had rejected the covenant. The verb is taken up again in the next line, where Judah's offense is described as having *forsaken the fountain of living water (mᵉqôr mayim ḥayyîm)* (cf. 2:13). Despite textual difficulties[6] the main thrust of the verse is clear. Covenant-breakers who reject the lordship of Yahweh are guilty and will be brought to judgment.

(viii) Another Lament (17:14–18)

14 *Heal me, Yahweh, and I shall be healed;*
Save me and I shall be saved;
For thou art my praise.
15 *Look! they say to me, "Where is the word of Yahweh?*
Let it come then."[1]
16 *But I have not pressed for the day of evil,*[2]
Nor did I desire the day of disaster.
Thou knowest what has passed my lips;
It lies open before thee.

5. The verb *bôš,* generally translated *put to shame,* sometimes has reference to someone who is guilty before the law. Cf. J. W. Olley, "A Forensic Connotation of *bôš*," *VT* 26 (1976), pp. 230–34.
6. See textual notes.

1. *Then* is an attempt to capture the enclitic *nā'*.
2. MT reads "As for me I did not press from being a shepherd *(mērō'eh)* after thee." The sense is not clear and some emendation is suggested. The Versions understood the text to refer to "evil" or "disaster": Aquila and Symmachus *mērā'â,* "from evil"; Syr. *bᵉrā'â,* "in evil" or "with evil." Thus NEB reads "It is not the thought of disaster that makes me press after thee." Some commentators have proposed

17 *Do not become a terror to me,*
Thou, my refuge in the day of distress.
18 *May my persecutors be brought to shame, not I;*[3]
May they be terrified—not I.
Bring upon them the day of disaster;
Destroy them, destroy them utterly.[4]

This passage is yet another of Jeremiah's "confessions," this time presented as an individual lament opening with a petition and an expression of confidence and praise, followed by a statement of his trial and finally a prayer for personal deliverance and for judgment on his enemies. There is no answering word from Yahweh in this case.

14 Jeremiah had earlier spoken of his pain that refused to be healed (15:18). Again the fact of his wounds and pain comes forward. If Yahweh will but *heal (rāp̄ē')* him, then he will indeed be healed. If Yahweh will *save (hôšîa')* him, then he will indeed be saved. There is an underlying confidence in Yahweh here. Yahweh is described as his *praise (tᵉhillâ)* or perhaps his hope *(tôḥeleṯ)*.[5]

15 Jeremiah goes on to quote his scoffers who ask, probably sarcastically, for some evidence of God's action. It was imperative that Yahweh should show his hand one way or another, either in deliverance for Jeremiah or in judgment on the scoffers or both (cf. Isa. 5:19). The scoffers throw back at Jeremiah the claim he often made that he was delivering the *word of Yahweh.* That word was at times joy and happiness to him (15:16), but at times it brought trouble upon him (20:8). The prolonged lack of confirmation of his message exposed him to ridicule and filled him with despair.

16 Jeremiah now insists that he took no personal pleasure in the bad news he brought to his people. He did not press Yahweh to bring trouble *(rā'â)*[6] on the day of disaster. It was a simple matter always of delivering the message God had laid on his heart. There

---

lᵉrā'â, "for evil," i.e., "I did not press (strive) after thee for evil (or disaster)." Possibly the consonants *'ṣtymr'h* conceal the words *yôm rā'â, the day of evil* (cf. v. 18, and *yôm 'ānûš* in the next colon). Hence read *lō' 'aṣtî (lᵉ)yōm rā'â*, "I did not press for the day of evil." The phrase "after thee" is omitted. But the whole expression is admittedly difficult.

3. MT reads lit. "May my persecutors be put to shame,
And let me not be put to shame."
Similarly in the next line, "May they be terrified,
May I not be terrified."

4. Lit. "Destroy them with double destruction."

5. With the 1st person possessive the difference is slight, *thlty* or *tḥlty*.

6. See textual note.

was not the remotest element of sadism in the prophet's mind; and that, God knew full well. Hence Jeremiah protested his innocence, although the charge made by the scoffers was valid enough and Jeremiah had to live with it. Considering this along with his own deep inner doubts and turmoil, it is clear that he had a heavy burden to bear.

17 Jeremiah merely requests that Yahweh should not be a *terror (m^{e}ḥittâ)* to him, but rather be his *refuge (maḥseh)* in the day of disaster. The verb *ḥāsâ,* "to take refuge," and the cognate nouns played an important part in the devotional vocabulary of ancient Israel (cf. Isa. 14:32; 30:2; 57:13; Ps. 2:12; 5:12 [Eng. 11]; 7:2 [Eng. 1]; 11:1; 16:1; 17:7; 18:3, 31 [Eng. 2, 30]; etc.). But Jeremiah's response was not always so trusting (cf. 20:7–12). This expression of confidence in God who vindicates the cause of the innocent occurs in several psalms of lament (e.g., Ps. 17:1–8).

18 The cry for vengeance upon one's enemies is typical of psalms of lament (Ps. 17:13–14; cf. Jer. 20:12). What Jeremiah asked for was that his *persecutors (rōḏ^{e}pîm)* should be *brought to shame* (or, proven guilty) and filled with terror, and that the *day of disaster (rā'â)* should fall upon them and break them completely.

It would be normal for Yahweh to reply to such an utterance,[7] but this time there was no response.

(ix) Keeping the Sabbath (17:19–27)

19 *Yahweh spoke to me thus: "Go and stand in the People's Gate*[1] *through which the kings of Judah go in and out, and in all the gates of Jerusalem,*

20 *and say to them: 'Hear the word of Yahweh, you kings of Judah, and all Judah, and all you citizens of Jerusalem who enter these gates.*

21 *This is what Yawheh has said: Take care, as you value your lives, that you do not carry any burden on the sabbath day or bring it through the gates of Jerusalem.*

22 *You shall in no circumstances*[2] *carry out a burden from your houses on the sabbath day, or do work of any kind, but you shall keep the sabbath day as holy, as I commanded your forefathers.*

7. Cf. 11:21–23; 12:5, 6; 15:13–14, 19–21.

1. MT reads *b^{e}ša'ar b^{e}nê ?ā'ām*, with a consonant lacking before the third word. Qumran also lacks the consonant. LXX reads *laou sou,* "of your people." RSV emends to "the Benjamin gate," which is known elsewhere in Jeremiah (37:13; 38:7). But this would hardly have been misunderstood, hence it seems preferable to follow MT "the gate of the people" even if such a gate is otherwise unknown. The text may be corrupt in any case.

2. The emphatic negative *lō'* is used here in place of the more usual *'al*. The same emphatic negative occurs in the Ten Commandments.

23 *Yet they did not obey or pay attention, but stubbornly refused*[3] *to hear and to accept instruction.*
24 *Now if you will really listen to me—Yahweh's word—and bring no burden through the gates of this city on the sabbath day, and keep that day holy by doing no work on it,*
25 *then there shall pass through the gates of this city kings*[4] *who shall sit on David's throne, riding in chariots and on horses—they and their princes, and the people of Judah and the citizens of Jerusalem; and this city shall be inhabited for ever.*
26 *And people will come from the cities of Judah and from round about Jerusalem, the land of Benjamin, from the Shephelah, from the hill country and the Negeb, bringing whole-offerings, and sacrifices, cereal offerings and incense, bringing also thank offerings to the house of Yahweh.*
27 *But if you will not listen to me by keeping the sabbath day holy, and not carrying any burden or coming with it through the gates of Jerusalem on the sabbath day, then I will set fire to those gates, and the fire will consume the palaces of Jerusalem and will not be put out.' "*

This passage is in prose and is concerned only with the keeping of the sabbath. Some of the prose sermons in Jeremiah deal more generally with obedience to the covenant law (7:1–15; 11:1–17), but some sections, as here, single out a specific law for particular emphasis (cf. 34:8–22). In form, this sermon consists of an introduction, a proclamation of the law, a promise of blessing for those who obey, and a threat of judgment for those who are disobedient.

The passage raises all the questions that have been raised about the prose passages in Jeremiah,[5] and the question has been asked whether this section comes from Jeremiah at all.[6] But there is a contrary view that the passage is not necessarily to be regarded as very late judging either from its style or its content. Jeremiah must certainly have held the sabbath in high respect since he held the covenant law as binding on Israel. Even though Jeremiah does not appear as a legalist, he must have regarded sabbath-breaking as a serious offense, and would have been unlikely to exempt sabbath-keeping from the covenant law. Hence it is altogether likely that

3. Lit. "hardened their necks."
4. MT adds "and officials." Since only kings sit on David's throne, it is probably a dittography from later in the verse *(princes)*.
5. See the Introduction, "The Book of Jeremiah; Composition," pp. 33–50.
6. G. P. Couturier, "Jeremiah," *JBC,* p. 317, art. 56; J. P. Hyatt, "The Book of Jeremiah," *IB* V, pp. 958f.; W. Rudolph, *Jeremia,* p. 109, although he allows that a basic saying of Jeremiah gave rise to the passage.

Jeremiah made some comments on the keeping of the sabbath. On the other hand it is not impossible that some comments of his on the sabbath were expanded and further developed at the hands of an editor or by someone who knew Jeremiah's thinking.

An interesting feature of this section is the conditional nature of prophecies of doom. These can be revoked if there is repentance. Jeremiah made it clear that the people of Judah held their destiny in their own hands.

19–20 The precise place where Jeremiah spoke about the sabbath is not clear. MT refers to "the gate of the sons of the people," which is not attested elsewhere. The proposal that the passage originally referred to the Benjamin Gate which is known in other passages (37:13; 38:7), though plausible, has no textual support.[7] The gate seems to have been in the north wall of the city and led out to the region of Benjamin. It is further described as the gate by which *the kings of Judah go in and out.* The phrase *kings of Judah* may refer to the ruling king along with the royal princes. The gate in question, although not identifiable, was evidently a significant one where an audience might be expected to gather.

The final reference may be a generalizing statement instructing Jeremiah to proclaim the message everywhere. Otherwise he was required to go to each gate in turn preaching. The words were addressed to the rulers *(you kings of Judah),* to *all Judah,* and to the *citizens of Jerusalem.* They were thus intended for the whole nation from the highest to the lowest, since all of them were under covenant obligation to Yahweh.

21–23 The injunction is serious and is expressed strongly—"Take care with your lives," i.e., *as you value your lives* (cf. Deut. 4:15; Josh. 23:11).[8] The prohibition here stated, not to carry a burden on the sabbath (cf. Neh. 13:15–22), was not new in Jeremiah's day. It is clearly stated in the Decalog (Exod. 20:8–11; Deut. 5:12–15). It is altogether likely that if Jeremiah knew about careless observance of the sabbath he would have spoken out. The sabbath was to be kept *holy* (cf. Exod. 20:8, 11; Deut. 5:12),[9] that is, set apart as a day separate from other days. It was an ancient command, given to Israel's ancestors. But the sad fact was that Israel's ances-

7. See textual note.
8. J. Bright, *Jeremiah,* p. 117.
9. The verb here—*qiddēš*—derives from the root *qdš,* which in many of its derivatives denotes setting apart for God's use or service.

tors did not obey or pay attention[10] but like their descendants *stubbornly refused* either to hear or to accept instruction. Several of the phrases in these verses are strongly reminiscent of phrases in the Decalog where the sabbath law is formulated, e.g., not to do any work on the sabbath, to keep the sabbath day holy. It would seem that profanation of the sabbath had become commonplace—a further demonstration of Israel's rejection of the covenant law.

24 The covenant blessings are introduced by the conditional clause "if you will obey." The protasis is introduced by a strongly emphatic expression: *If you will really listen to me*[11]—*Yahweh's word.* The two conditions, which are aspects of the one covenant demand, are *bring no burden through the gates of this city,* and *keep that day holy by doing no work on it.* At first sight Jeremiah appears to be asserting that the nation's very existence was conditional upon observing the sabbath law to the letter. This has led some commentators to propose that such thinking could hardly have come from Jeremiah but reflects the strong emphasis on the sabbath law in postexilic Judaism (cf. Neh. 13:15–22).[12] But such a view is not necessary. Jeremiah stood as close to the ancient covenant traditions as any prophet. Even when he spoke of the New Covenant he still thought of the law, though one written upon men's hearts (31:33). In the present passage particular emphasis is placed on one aspect of the Decalog; but a similar statement might have been made for any one of the commandments of the Decalog. More generally Jeremiah was equally capable of saying, "If you will indeed keep the covenant" (cf. 7:23–26; 11:6–8; etc.), that is, the whole of the covenant demands, or any one of them. The open and defiant breach of one of the covenant demands was symptomatic of a rejection of the covenant as a whole. If the sabbath law is specifically mentioned here, other laws are referred to elsewhere as in 4:4; 7:5–9. Jeremiah's castigation of his people for multifarious breaches of the covenant demands is writ large in his preaching. No doubt the sabbath law became of great significance in postexilic times. But it was not the only law that became significant during those centuries. A degree of caution seems necessary, therefore, in regarding this passage as "reflecting the more intense significance and importance attached to the Sabbath which appears to have emerged among the exiles in

10. Lit. "turn their ears."
11. The normal verb is strengthened by the preceding infinitive absolute or *nomen verbi,* "if hearing you will hear."
12. See E. W. Nicholson, *Jeremiah 1–25,* p. 153.

Babylon to become one of the dominant characteristics of post-exilic Judaism."[13]

25 The apodosis of the conditional clause is given expression in a particularized form in these verses. It is expressed in terms of a restoration of Judah's sovereignty under its own king, and of the restoration of Jerusalem and of the cities of Judah, and of the temple with its rituals. These can be regarded as representing the blessings of the covenant bestowed by Yahweh on his obedient people (cf. Deut. 28:1–14; etc.). But in the present context these blessings are conditional upon keeping the sabbath. It is proposed that we have here a *pars pro toto* and that the sabbath law is representative of the whole covenant. It is when God's people keep the covenant that the blessings of the covenant are bestowed.

Whoever the *princes (śārîm)* were, they occupied a significant place alongside the king in the administration of the affairs of the kingdom.[14] These officials are referred to in one of the Lachish ostraca, where a complaint is made that their communications to the people of Lachish had had a demoralizing effect. "The words of the *śārîm* are not good but weaken our hands."[15] It was these officials who were later to demand the death of Jeremiah (38:4). Fortunately the king did not heed their demands.

Two concepts of special significance are expressed here—the throne of David and the permanent status of Jerusalem. Harking back to 2 Sam. 7, Jeremiah both here and in other passages (23:5–6; 30:9; 33:15) affirms the ancient belief that David's throne would persist. If it was temporarily suspended it would be restored, even though some of the kings were unworthy of that honor (22:30). Jerusalem, likewise, was the place where God had chosen to place his royal throne, and even if it were destroyed it would be restored and *inhabited for ever* (cf. Zech. 2:6–16 [Eng. 2–12]; 8:3, 15; 14:11). The security of the state would be guaranteed to the people if they kept the covenant.

26 Another aspect of the blessing which would be bestowed on an obedient people was that this people would come from all over the land—from the territory *round about Jerusalem;* from the area of *Benjamin* to the north; from the *Shephelah,* the foothills away to the west; from the mountain areas or *hill country;* and from the

13. *Ibid.*
14. R. de Vaux, *Ancient Israel,* pp. 69–71, 229f.
15. See *ANET,* p. 322, Lachish Ostracon VI.

Negeb away to the south—to worship God in the temple *(the house of Yahweh)* in Jerusalem. Here is a graphic description of the geography and topography of Judah so well known to those who are familiar with the area to this day. The range of offerings which would be brought is familiar from Leviticus, *whole-offerings ('ôlâ), sacrifices (zeḇaḥ), cereal offerings (minḥâ), incense (leḇônâ)* and *thank offerings (tôḏâ).*[16]

These three elements—the *throne of David,* the *temple,* and *the city Jerusalem*—comprised the basic aspects of the national and religious life of the people of the covenant. Loyalty to the Lord of the covenant and obedience to the covenant demands were fundamental to the enjoyment of the blessings of the covenant.

27 The other side of the picture is now given. Disobedience and breach of covenant could only lead to the operation of the curses of the covenant, represented here in terms of an unquenchable fire which would consume the *palaces ('armenôṯ)* (cf. 9:20 [Eng. 21]; 49:27; 50:32; Amos 1:3–2:5). In that case the throne, temple, and city would all be swept away.

(x) The Parable of the Potter's Vessel (18:1–12)

1 *The word which came to Jeremiah from Yahweh:*
2 *"Go down at once*[1] *to the potter's house, and there I will tell you what I have to say."*[2]
3 *So I went down to the potter's house, and there he was busy at work on the wheel.*
4 *Whenever a vessel he was making from the clay*[3] *was spoiled in the potter's hands, he would turn around and fashion it into another vessel according to his liking.*
5 *Then the word of Yahweh came to me:*
6 *"Can I not deal with you, O house of Israel, as this potter does?—Yahweh's word. See, like clay in the potter's hands, so are you in my hand, O house of Israel.*
7 *At one moment I may threaten to uproot a people or a kingdom,*[4] *to break it down and to destroy it;*

16. See R. de Vaux, *Ancient Israel,* ch. 10, pp. 415–423.

1. Lit. "Arise and go down."
2. Lit. "I will cause you to hear my word."
3. Latin and many mss. follow MT, but some mss. suggest *kaḥōmer,* "as clay," in place of *baḥōmer.* This would require a different translation: "Whenever a vessel that he was working on would turn out poorly, as clay (sometimes will) in the potter's hand . . ." (J. Bright, p. 121). The word is lacking in LXX.
4. Lit. "At one moment I may speak concerning a nation or concerning a kingdom, to uproot. . . ."

8 *but if the nation against which I have spoken*[5] *should turn back from its evil way, then I would think better of the evil which I had in mind to do to it.*
9 *At another moment I may declare my intention to build or to plant a nation or a kingdom;*
10 *but if it should do evil in my sight and not obey my voice, I would think better of the good things that I said I would do for it.*
11 *Now then, say to the men of Judah and to the inhabitants of Jerusalem, 'This is what Yahweh has said:*[6] *Look! I am shaping evil against you, laying plans against you. Turn back then every one of you from his evil course; reform your ways and your doings.'*
12 *But they will reply, 'It is no use! We will follow our own plans, and each of us will carry out the stubborn intentions of his evil heart.'"*

It is not difficult to see why these verses are placed immediately after 17:19–27, since each passage is concerned with a condition. The present prose passage is in an autobiographical style and describes a visit of Jeremiah to the potter's shop. There is nothing unusual in such a story. Pottery making was a common activity in the Near East, and Jeremiah would readily have appreciated the lessons to be learned from the potter. Commentators accept the story as authentic even though some would regard the passage as containing editorial expansions of an original incident.[7] As the story stands, Jeremiah is described as noticing that as the potter worked he rejected some of his pots, perhaps because the clay was not of the correct quality for the vessel he had planned. In such cases the potter reshaped the clay to make another vessel. Yahweh explained that Israel was like clay in his hands, for which he was free to change his original purpose. This theme is expanded in detail in vv. 7–12. It is this latter segment which some commentators have regarded as editorial.

There is no indication of a date for the incident, although the fact that the disaster Jeremiah had spoken of seems still to be avoidable would suggest that the incident was relatively early, perhaps during the first years of Jehoiakim's reign before the judgment of 598/7 B.C. fell, and certainly before the judgment of 587 B.C.

1–3 It was a regular feature of the prophetic ministry to find the word of Yahweh in the simple events of daily life. Jeremiah was

5. The phrase *against which I have spoken* is lacking in LXX, Syr., Latin.
6. LXX lacks *This is what Yahweh has said.*
7. Thus E. W. Nicholson, *Jeremiah 1–25,* p. 155, would consider vv. 1–6 as original and vv. 7–12 the prose expansion of a Deuteronomic editor. Cf. G. P. Couturier, *JBC,* p. 317.

in that tradition, and heard a word from Yahweh in an almond shoot (1:11–12), in a boiling pot (1:13–14), or in a potter at work with his clay. The divine command to go to the potter's house was a prelude to the declaration of Yahweh's word.

The potter's wheel is described here in tantalizing terms. The potter was working *on the wheel,* literally "at the two stones *('oḇnāyim).*" Presumably there were two stone wheels on a vertical axis, the lower of which was spun by kicking with the feet and the upper of which carried the clay which the potter shaped (cf. Eccl. 38:29–30).[8] Modifications of this apparatus are still in use today, although the two discs are generally made of wood.

4 The making of pottery was an essential trade in ancient Israel. Vast quantities of sherds, and in some cases complete vessels, are found in modern excavations, where they provide an important means of dating. The finds of the archeologist are important in determining the character of the many pottery vessels referred to by name in the OT (e.g., *baqbuq* in 19:1).[9] The particular vessels referred to in ch. 18 are not indicated by a specific name. The reference in v. 4 is simply to a *vessel* (k^e*lî*).

The precise meaning of this verse is crucial to the interpretation. It is commonly held that the work of the potter was an illustration of the fact that Yahweh would work patiently with his people to make of them the "vessel" he intended them to be. But the inference to be drawn from the verse, and from the more specific application in vv. 7ff., is clearly that the particular clay that lay on the wheel at the time was not suitable for the vessel the potter had designed, that is, the quality of the clay determined what the potter could do with it. He could make something else from the same clay, but not the particular vessel he had hoped for. The clay could thus frustrate the potter's original intention and cause him to change it. Yahweh the potter was dealing with a clay that was resistant to his purpose. The quality of the people in some way determined what God might do with them.

The point is well illustrated in ch. 17. People who were loyal to Yahweh and to his covenant could be taken up into Yahweh's purposes, which are described in 17:24–26 in terms of the Davidic king, the temple, and the city of Jerusalem. But people who broke

8. R. H. Johnston, "The Biblical Potter," *BA* 37/4 (1974), pp. 86–106.
9. J. Kelso, *The Ceramic Vocabulary of the OT* (Suppl. Stud. Nos. 5–6 to *BASOR,* 1948).

the covenant and rejected Yahweh's sovereignty were not material through whom the purposes of Yahweh could be fulfilled.

We should probably understand the verbs in v. 4 in an iterative sense, i.e., Jeremiah apparently saw the potter return the clay to the wheel more than once while he watched.

5–6 The symbolism is now spelled out. Yahweh is the potter *(yôṣēr)*. The idea is ancient in Israel (cf. Gen. 2:7) and is known also in Mesopotamia and Egypt. The verb *yāṣar,* "to fashion, shape," can also mean "create." A similar symbolism occurs in such passages as Isa. 29:16; 45:9; and 64:8 to express the creatureliness of man. In contrast to Yahweh the potter, man is the clay, an idea which is known elsewhere in the ancient Near East. Yahweh behaves toward his clay as the potter does. Israel is like clay in his hand. The interpretation of the passage depends on one's understanding of what went on in the potter's shop. Pliable clay can be fashioned into a desired shape but unpliable clay has to be used for something else.

7–8 In order to clarify and emphasize the point that the character of the clay determines what the potter can do with it, two illustrations are given, although of a rather general type. The reference is to any *people (gôy)* or *kingdom (mamlāḵâ),* and it takes up ideas which are mentioned in 1:10. There are from time to time peoples and kingdoms which merit divine judgment. These Yahweh threatens to *uproot (nāṯaš),* to *break down (nāṯaṣ),* and to *destroy ('āḇaḏ)*. See the commentary on 1:10 for this terminology.

The verb here translated *think better of (niḥam)* is translated in AV and RSV as "repent." It is hardly to be understood in the human sense; rather, because of a change in attitude in the people or nation, Yahweh is able to modify his action toward them. Thus it is not so much a change of mind as a change of treatment because of modified behavior.

Evildoers may *turn back (šûḇ)* from the *evil way (rā'â)* they have followed. The particular nuance attaching to the verb *turn* here is given by the use of the preposition *from (šûḇ min).*[10] The prophet has in mind the act of turning from evil.

The double use of the noun *rā'â* is of interest. If a nation turns back from its evil *(rā'â),* then Yahweh will think better of the evil *(rā'â),* that is, the judgment, he had thought to bring upon it.

9–10 The counter-example concerns Yahweh's intention *to*

10. See W. L. Holladay, *The Root šûbh in the OT* (1958), pp. 79f., 137, 139.

build up (bānâ) and *to plant (nāṭa')* a nation or kingdom.[11] But if that nation determined to do evil *('āśâ hārā'â)* and not to *obey* his *voice (šāma' beqôl),* such a clear change in behavior would result in a change in treatment on Yahweh's part.

The illustrations are pointed toward Israel. Several things are clear. It was not to be assumed that Yahweh would bless Israel automatically. Any possibility of the divine building up or planting was related to a nation's obedience to the divine commands, so that the nation did what was right and not what was evil in Yahweh's sight. The picture of the covenant is well to the fore, with its overtones of covenant stipulations, covenant sanctions, blessing and cursing. Israel would enjoy Yahweh's blessing only on the basis of obedience to his covenant. The term "blessing" as such is not used here, but it is implied in the expression *good things (ṭôḇ).*

11–12 The main thrust of the preceding verses is now made clear. Jeremiah was speaking at Yahweh's command to all the men of Judah and the citizens of Jerusalem. The expression *so now ('attâ)* occurs frequently in the OT to introduce the conclusion to an argument (Exod. 19:5; Deut. 4:1; etc.). In the present context Jeremiah's pronouncement in v. 11 is the logical conclusion of the argument in vv. 1–10. Yahweh was the one who was *shaping*[12] *evil (rā'â)* against his people and *laying plans* (lit. "thinking thoughts") against them, because the cast of their life was such as to demand judgment and the calling into operation of the curses of the covenant. Only a radical modification in the people's behavior could avert that calamity. Jeremiah brings into use once again the root *šûḇ, turn,* but this time with the sense of "turn from an evil way." This required that the people *reform* (lit. "make good," *hêṭîḇ)* their *ways (derāḵîm)* and their *doings (ma'alālîm)*. Alas, they had gone too far in following the *stubborn intentions* of their evil hearts, and could only reply, *It is no use (nô'āš)! We will follow our own plans.* In such circumstances they were like the refractory clay which sometimes came into the potter's hands. They could not be fashioned into the noble shape the potter had intended, at least in their present frame of mind. Only the refining influences of judgment could avail to make them amenable again to the potter's touch. See the commentary on v. 4.

Here is a sad reflection on the end result of evil-doing and of

11. See commentary on 1:10.

12. The word *yôṣēr* occurs several times in vv. 2–6 in the nominal sense of "potter," the one who shapes or fashions the clay. Here it assumes the verbal sense.

continuous breach of covenant. A state is reached where all desire and hope of repentance is lost and men are content to follow the uninhibited promptings of their own rebellious and wicked hearts. At that point judgment is inevitable. It came for Judah with the overthrow of the nation by Nebuchadrezzar. But for Jeremiah there was hope in the future when Yahweh would make a new covenant (31:31–33). The divine grace was equal to every demand of despair, hopelessness, and profligate abandonment of the covenant.

(xi) Israel's Unnatural Behavior and its Consequences (18:13–17)

13 *"Therefore this is what Yahweh has said:*
Inquire among the nations: Who has heard the like of this?
The virgin Israel has committed a most horrible offense.
14 *Do flints depart from the field or snow from Lebanon?*[1]
Or do men forget flowing waters, running springs?[2]
15 *Yet my people have forgotten me.*
They burn sacrifices to a mere idol;
They have stumbled in their paths, the way of wisdom,[3]
To walk in bypaths, an unmade road.
16 *Their own land they lay waste,*
An object to be hissed at for ever.
All who pass by it will be horror-struck and shake their heads.

1. Some commentators associate the noun *śāḏay, field* (or "fields"), with Akk. *šadu,* "mountain," and translate *ṣûr śāḏay* as "the rock of the mountain" or "the mountain crags." Others take *śāḏay* as an error for *śiryôn,* the ancient name for Mt. Hermon (Deut. 3:9), and read with RSV "Does the snow of Lebanon leave the crags of Sirion?" NEB reads "Will the snow cease to fall on the rocky slopes of Lebanon?" An alternative is to read *ṣōr,* "flint" or "pebble," for *miṣṣûr* ("from the rock") and translate "Do flints forsake the fields?" (J. Bright, *Jeremiah,* p. 122 following W. F. Albright in *HUCA* 23 [1950/1], pp. 23f.; M. Dahood, "Philological Notes on Jer. 18:14–15," *ZAW* 74 [1962], pp. 207–209). This introduces yet another comparison. The fields of the land are filled with stones, as any visitor to these lands today well knows.

2. The verb *nāṯaš* normally means "root up" or "pluck up." If MT is accepted we might translate "foreign waters are plucked up." However, by transposing the consonants of the verb we may read *nāšaṯ* and translate "they are dried up." Again, by reading *zāḇîm, flowing,* for *zārîm,* "foreign," we may render the phrase *flowing waters* and hence translate "Will the flowing waters be dried up?" The last two words in the line, *qārîm nôzᵉlîm,* "cold flowing (streams)," may be understood differently. By recognizing a haplography of the *m* in the previous word we may propose *mqrm,* hence *mᵉqōrîm, springs,* for *qārîm,* "cold," and make the phrase mean *running springs.* Moreover, a derivative from *nāšâ, forget,* with an infixed *t* reflexive could explain the verb form *yinnāṯᵉšû* here. The same root occurs in 23:39 and Lam. 3:17. Hence we may translate, *Do men forget flowing waters?* MT *qārîm* may be altered to *qōrîm,* without a change to *mᵉqōrîm* as some propose. Both *qr* and *mqr* meaning "spring" or "source" occur in Ugaritic. The thinking harks back to 2:13.

3. See commentary below.

17 *Like a wind from the east I will scatter them before their enemies;*
On the day of their downfall I will show them my back and not my face."

In vv. 13–17 we have a short poetic piece which develops out of the theme of v. 12. Jeremiah attacks the unnatural apostasy of the people and contrasts it with the constancy of nature. The passage may be compared with 2:10–13, with which it has a number of similarities. It is therefore probably to be dated to the earlier part of Jehoiakim's reign or even earlier.

13 *Virgin Israel* (cf. 14:7) has committed a *most horrible offense (ša'ᵃrurit̲).* She should have kept herself chaste like an unmarried virgin awaiting her husband, but instead she tainted herself with the practices of pagan religion. There is probably a reference here to the sexually oriented practices of some of the Canaanite rituals vividly defined elsewhere as "playing the harlot." Covenant overtones are clear. Israel's loyalty to Yahweh was to be total and to be shared with no other. But her disloyalty was so unnatural and so gross that nothing like it was known *among the nations (gôyîm).* The words are strongly reminiscent of 2:10–13, which spell out the offense in more detail.

In vv. 14–15 we have a good example of the "disputation" literary pattern which comprises a sequence of rhetorical questions and an indictment. Here there are two questions introduced respectively by the normal question marker *ha-* and the particle *'im.* The indictment is directed to Israel and is based upon, but goes beyond, the comparisons implied in the questions.[4]

14 The nation's faithlessness and gross disloyalty are contrasted with the constancy of nature. In 8:7 Jeremiah had referred to the constancy of the birds as they followed unswervingly their ingrained instincts. Here the comparison is with the snows of Lebanon and the permanent gushing springs which were one of the miracles of a dry land (cf. 2:13).

All translations of this verse are conjectural;[5] but while certainty is not possible the main thrust of the passage is clear. Whereas nature behaves in a constant, dependable fashion, Israel's behavior was quite inconsistent and irrational, quite the opposite of what

4. See B. O. Long, "The Stylistic Components of Jeremiah 3:1–5," *ZAW* 88 (1976), pp. 386–390.

5. See textual notes. The Qumran text is no help since it lacks v. 14 completely and commences only in the third line of v. 15.

might be expected of a people bound to Yahweh by solemn covenant ties. Little wonder, therefore, that the judgment of v. 17 was about to befall them.

15 The apostasy is spelled out. Yahweh's people *(my people)* had *forgotten (šāḵaḥ)* him. They had burned sacrifices *(qiṭṭēr)* to a *mere idol (šāwᵉ')*, a synonym for some false god, perhaps Baal.[6] Either as a result of this or simply as a concomitant, *they have stumbled in their paths (dereḵ)*.[7] The *paths* in question are defined as "the ancient ways" *(šᵉḇîlê 'ôlām)*. Alternately, the noun *'ôlām* may be related to the root *'lm*, which carries the meaning "knowledge" or *wisdom* in Arabic and Ugaritic.[8] The way Israel should have gone was the way of loyalty to Yahweh and obedience to his covenant, which was "the good way" (6:16). Foreigners could understand and approve such a course of action since they understood that every people had its own god(s) (2:10, 11). To go another way was to follow *bypaths (nᵉṯîḇôṯ)* and an *unmade road (dereḵ lō' sᵉlûlâ)*.

16 One of the consequences of apostasy was that the land, the national inheritance, suffered natural disasters (cf. Amos 4:5–10; etc.). Their own land they turned into a *waste (šammâ), an object to be hissed at for ever.* The term *šᵉrîqōṯ*, "hissing" or "whistling," denotes that the land would become a spectacle so shocking as to cause passers-by to whistle in awe (cf. 19:8). The verse is remarkable for its striking assonance, with its *s*-sounds conveying the impression of hissing:

lāśûm 'arṣām lᵉšammâ
šᵉrîqōṯ 'ôlām
kōl 'ôḇēr 'āleyhā yiššōm
wᵉyānîḏ bᵉrō'šô.

Travellers passing by would shake their heads in astonishment at the people of Israel for their stupidity in forsaking their God Yahweh and the old covenantal paths for the worship of other gods, which were, in any case, fraudulent and nonexistent.

17 In a brief but powerful statement Yahweh's judgment on

6. Cf. J. Bright, *Jeremiah*, p. 124, "To the Fraud they burn offerings."

7. MT reads *wayyaḵšilûm*, "they have caused them to stumble." But "they" has no antecedent, and by regarding *m* as an enclitic and reading *wayyiḵšᵉlû* we may translate as above.

8. See J. A. Thompson, "The Root *'-l-m* in Semitic Languages and Some Proposed New Translations in Ugaritic and Hebrew" in *Festschrift for A. Vööbus* (1977), pp. 301–308.

a covenant-forsaking people is declared. Like the sirocco, the hot dry wind blowing from the eastern deserts (cf. 4:11; 13:34), Yahweh would come as an *east wind* (the Babylonian armies). He would *scatter them before their enemies,* a reference to the impending invasion of the Babylonians and the dispersion of many of the people into exile far to the east (Babylon). In that day, the day of their disaster, Yahweh would offer no help to deliver them, for he would show them[9] his back and not his face.[10]

(xii) *Jeremiah's Reaction to a Plot against His Life (18:18–23)*

18 *They said: "Come, let us lay plans against Jeremiah, for priestly instruction, the counsel of wise men, and the prophetic word will never cease. Come, let us bring charges against him and let us pay no attention to any of his words."*
19 *O Yahweh, give heed to me,*
And listen to the statement of my case![1]
20 *Should evil be given as payment for good?*
For they have dug a pit for me.
Remember how I stood before thee
To speak for their welfare,
To avert[2] *thy fury from them.*
21 *Therefore hand over their sons to famine,*
Hurl them down to the power of the sword.
Let their women be childless and widowed;
Let their men be the victims of death,
And their young men cut down by the sword in battle.
22 *Let a cry of terror be heard from their houses*
When thou bringest raiders upon them suddenly.
For they have dug a pit to catch me,
And snares for my feet they have set.
23 *But thou, O Yahweh, dost know*
All their plotting against me to kill me.
Do not cover over their wrongdoing
Nor wipe out their sin from thy sight,
But let them be brought down before thee;
Act against them at the time of thine anger.

9. MT has Qal *'er'ēm,* "I will look at them." Vocalizing with the Versions as Hiphil *'ar'ēm,* "I will cause them to see," the passage makes better sense.
10. The practice of turning one's back on someone who has offended in some way is worldwide in its application. When relations between parties are normal and happy the parties meet face to face, which is the normal posture for social intercourse. The turning of the back is a sign of rejection.

1. MT reads *y^erîḇāy,* "my adversaries," giving a sentence which, though possible, seems to be less suitable in the context: "listen to the voice of my adversaries." LXX and other versions read *rîḇî, my case.* The Qumran text reads *ryby.*
2. The verb here derives from the root *šûḇ,* "turn," but it is used with the preposition *min* and is in the Hiphil, "to cause to turn from."

This second poetic passage (vv. 19–23) is introduced by a short prose piece (v. 18) which provides the background. Verses 19–23 constitute one of Jeremiah's "confessions."[3] In literary form, v. 18 is a quotation in prose from the people, with Jeremiah's response recorded in poetry in vv. 19–23. After calling upon Yahweh to heed his plea (vv. 19–20), Jeremiah gives himself over completely to cursing formulas. As in the case of several of the other "confessions," Yahweh provides no answer (cf. 17:14–18; 18:18–23; 20:7–12, 14–18). We are reminded of another plot against Jeremiah's life in 11:18–23; 12:1–6. The two incidents are not necessarily the same. Certainly no details of the nature of the plot are given here; but it was a gross injustice from Jeremiah's point of view, and he responded with great bitterness, calling upon Yahweh to punish the offenders in a way that is not seen in any of the other confessions. There are no grounds for rejecting such utterances as unworthy of Jeremiah and therefore regarding them as a later scribal insertion. The prophet was allied too deeply with the offense caused to Yahweh by Israel's breach of covenant not to give expression to judgment. It was not so much Jeremiah that the people had rejected but Yahweh (cf. 1 Sam. 8:7).

18 The quotation from the people indicates that their attitude was that all the means of receiving the divine word would continue much as they had ever been, despite Jeremiah's predictions that they would be withdrawn (6:13–15; 23:9–40). Literally the word of the people was, "For instruction *(tôrâ)* will not perish from the priest, nor counsel from the wise man, nor a word from the prophet." From the viewpoint of the people Jeremiah's words were false, and, since he claimed to speak in the name of Yahweh, he deserved to be put out of the way for making such a false and blasphemous utterance. Jeremiah had been relentless in his condemnation of the three classes of officials referred to here, priests, wise men, and prophets. It is probably a fair inference that it was these men of the establishment who instigated the plot. *Come, let us bring charges against him* (lit. "let us smite him with the tongue"; cf. 9:7 [Eng. 8] "the tongue is a deadly arrow") *and let us pay no attention (hiqšîḇ) to any of his words.* That reply provided the background to Jeremiah's plea to Yahweh to pay attention *(hiqšîḇ, give heed)* to him. The response of complacent, conscience-blinded, blind leaders of the blind is in line with the words of 13:12, "It's no use. We will

3. See the Introduction, "The 'Confessions' of Jeremiah," pp. 88–92.

follow our own plans and will act each of us as his own stubbornly wicked inclinations direct." People and leaders alike were satisfied with things as they were and as they would continue. To disturb a complacent leadership or a misguided populace was only to invite serious repercussions. Human society in every age bears eloquent testimony to the fact.

There is an interesting variant in LXX, which omits the negative in the last sentence and reads, "Let us pay attention to his message" (lit. "his words"). If this represents the original text the immediate sense, though perhaps not the final result, is changed. The desire of those who wished to do Jeremiah harm was to gather evidence from his words in order to bring charges against him. The Qumran text does not support LXX at this point.

19 Jeremiah's response was to ask Yahweh to *give heed (hiqšîḇ)* to his servant, who had his own *case (rîḇ*, a legal term, perhaps "cause") to state. If Jeremiah's adversaries were collecting evidence to lay a charge against him, he too had something to say to Yahweh. He made a similar appeal to Yahweh in similar circumstances (11:20). On that occasion he also appealed to Yahweh to bring judgment on his opponents. See the commentary on 11:18–20.

20 Jeremiah's dilemma was poignant. He called upon Yahweh to remember how he had stood before him to plead for the *welfare (ṭôḇâ)* of his enemies against a background of threatened judgment. *Should evil be given as payment for good?* Jeremiah had pleaded with Yahweh for the good of his own people, beseeching him to turn away his wrath from them. Their only response was to dig a pit to kill him (cf. v. 22). Some commentators omit this latter phrase as a variant of v. 22.[4] Jeremiah's intercessory role on behalf of his people was not matched by gratitude from the people (cf. 17:16). It is at this point that Jeremiah gave himself over to the utterance of formulas which feature in many of the curses in the OT (cf. Ps. 109:1–20).

21–22 Commentators have often been struck by the vehemence of Jeremiah's words in these verses. They seem to be so much out of character with Jeremiah's other utterances that some commentators regard them as the work of an entirely different author. But Jeremiah's cries for vengeance are too constant a feature in the book to be so easily removed. They have to be seen in the

4. LXX has a divergent, expanded reading for this colon: *hóti synelálēsan rhḗmata katá tḗs psychḗs mou kaí tḗn kólasin autṓn ékrypsán moi.*

light of the long years of working and watching and waiting as the prophet delivered God's words to a people who seemed hopelessly deaf and utterly unresponsive. Oftentimes Jeremiah must have wondered where God's help was to be found.

Another aspect of the total picture is that it was not simply a matter of wounded pride demanding revenge but rather of Jeremiah's profound identification with Yahweh and the demands of the covenant. The attitude of the scoffers and the adversaries of the prophet was seen as a rejection of Yahweh. Jeremiah's concern was for the cause of Yahweh. It was not his own message that he was delivering but Yahweh's: if the people rejected him, it was really Yahweh they were rejecting. Jeremiah here calls upon Yahweh to allow the curses of the broken covenant to come into operation. One so steeped in covenant thinking would naturally see divine judgment as inevitable. The terms in which this is expressed in these verses are not unique but are found in other parts of the OT (e.g., Lev. 26; Deut. 28).

Famine, death by the sword in battle, bereavement, and screams of terror were all concomitants of an enemy invasion. Jeremiah had referred often to the foe from the north, which as time went by became more clearly delineated as the Chaldeans. In the impending disaster all would suffer, men, wives, young men, children (sons). The cry *(zᵉʿāqâ)* which would be heard from the houses (v. 22) was a "scream of terror" (NEB) as the raiding force *(gᵉḏûḏ)* broke into defenseless homes. The verb in v. 21 is a vivid one, *hurl them down (haggirēm)*. The people would be thrown down helpless, to be slaughtered (lit. *to the power*[5] *of the sword)*.

23 This was not the first time that Jeremiah had said, *But thou, O Yahweh, dost know (yāḏaʿ)* (cf. 12:3; 15:15). The verb conveys something deeper than a mere knowledge of an intellectual kind. There was hope and comfort for Jeremiah in the fact that Yahweh's knowledge of him was of a most profound kind so that he entered into Jeremiah's experiences with him. The prophet's adversaries entertained murderous plots (lit. "counsel against me for death"). Such *wrongdoing (ʿāwôn)* was not to be covered over *(kippēr)*, that is, forgiven. Such men should be *brought down*[6] in Yahweh's presence. Yahweh should deal with them *(act against them)* while he was angry *(at the time of thine anger)*. Such words may appear

5. Lit. "hand" *(yāḏ)*.
6. Heb. *mukšālîm*, Hophal participle, "be made to stumble."

strangely vindictive from one who had at times pleaded for the people's good and had besought Yahweh to turn away his wrath from them (v. 20). If there seems to be a paradox here, it arises from the fact that one who was human carried within himself an identification with the divine purposes, which burst forth at times in paradoxical fashion.

It is of interest that Yahweh made no reply to this vehement outburst of the prophet. Nor had there been an answer to the utterances of 17:14–18 and 18:18–23, although there had been a divine response to 11:20; 12:1–4; and 15:14–18. Clearly there was no obligation resting on Yahweh to respond to every utterance of his servant. When he did respond, it was sometimes with a word of encouragement (11:21–23) and sometimes with a word of rebuke (12:5–6; 15:19).

(xiii) The Symbolic Action of the Broken Jar (19:1–20:6)

1 *This is what Yahweh said:*[1] *"Go and buy a potter's earthenware jar,*[2] *and take with you*[3] *some of the elders of the people and some of the priests,*[4]
2 *and go out to the valley of Ben-hinnom which is at the entrance of the Potsherd Gate and proclaim there the words that I speak to you.*
3 *Say, 'Hear the word of Yahweh, you kings of Judah and citizens of Jerusalem. This is what Yahweh of Hosts the God of Israel has said: I am about to bring a disaster on this place which will make the ears of everyone who hears it ring.*
4 *For they have forsaken me and made this an alien place, and have offered up sacrifices to other gods which neither they nor their fathers nor the kings of Judah have known, and they*[5] *have filled this place with the blood of innocents.*
5 *They have built the high places of Baal in order to burn their sons in the fire as burnt offerings to Baal—a thing I did not ever command, nor did I ever speak of it, nor did it ever enter my mind.*
6 *Therefore, believe me, days are coming—Yahweh's word—when they will no longer call this place Topheth, or the valley of Ben-hinnom, but the valley of Slaughter.*

1. LXX, Syr., and Targ. add "to me."
2. The word *baqbuq* may be onomatopoeic and suggests a gurgling sound. For this reason the vessel has often been identified with the widely used "decanters" of the Iron II age. See J. L. Kelso, *The Ceramic Vocabulary of the OT* (Suppl. Stud. Nos. 5–6 to *BASOR,* 1948), p. 17 and fig. 20.
3. MT seems to require the insertion of the words *and take with you* as in Syr., Targ., and LXX (although LXX lacks *with you*).
4. MT reads "some of the elders of the people and some of the elders of the priests." We follow LXX.
5. LXX takes *the kings of Judah* as the subject of *have filled this place.*

7 *I will annul the plans of Judah and Jerusalem in this place, and I will cause them to fall by the sword before their enemies at the hands of those who seek their life, and I will make their corpses food for the carrion birds and the wild beasts.*
8 *I will make this city a scene of horror and something to be hissed at. Everyone who passes by it will be horror-struck and will hiss at all its wounds.*
9 *I will make them eat the flesh of their sons and their daughters; they will even eat one another's flesh under the pressure of the siege to which their enemies and those who seek their life*[6] *will subject them.'*
10 *Then you must shatter the jar before the eyes of the men who have come with you,*
11 *and say to them, 'This is what Yahweh of Hosts has said: In this way I will shatter this people and this city, as one smashes a potter's vessel, so that it cannot be mended again; and in Topheth they shall bury the dead till there is no room left.*[7]
12 *Thus will I do to this place—Yahweh's word—and to its inhabitants, making this city like Topheth.*
13 *The houses of Jerusalem and the houses of Judah's kings, and indeed all the houses upon whose rooftops men have burnt offerings to all the host of heaven and poured out libations to other gods, will be like the place of Topheth, unclean.' "*
14 *Then Jeremiah returned from Topheth*[8] *where Yahweh had sent him to prophesy, and stood in the court of Yahweh's house and said to all the people,*
15 *"This is what Yahweh of Hosts the God of Israel has said: 'Look, I am bringing on this city and on its towns*[9] *every disaster which I have declared against it because they have obstinately refused to listen to my words.' "*
20:1 *When Pashhur ben Immer the priest, the chief overseer in the house of Yahweh, heard Jeremiah prophesying these things,*
2 *Pashhur had Jeremiah the prophet beaten, and put him in the stocks which were in the Upper Benjamin Gate in the house of Yahweh.*
3 *The next morning Pashhur released Jeremiah from the stocks, and Jeremiah said to him: "Yahweh has called you not Pashhur, but Magor-missabib.*

6. The words *and those who seek their life* are lacking in LXX.
7. LXX lacks *and in Topheth . . . room left.*
8. Some commentators have proposed that the word Topheth here is a substitute for "the entrance (of the Gate)" (v. 2b) made when the Topheth material was inserted into the simple narrative. The text itself does not demand such a change, and it is certainly not necessary if the chapter was originally a unity. See W. Rudolph, *Jeremia,* p. 126; J. Bright, *Jeremiah,* p. 131; E. W. Nicholson, *Jeremiah 1–25,* p. 166.
9. Some commentators have proposed that the word *towns* (plur.) here is to be related to an Ugaritic word meaning "a blood-daubed stone" (NEB "blood-spattered altars"). MT reads lit. "this city and all its cities." Apparently "all its cities" refers to the other cities of Judah. There seems little reason to depart from MT. See E. W. Nicholson, "Blood-spattered Altars?" *VT* 27 (1977), pp. 113–16.

4 *For this is what Yahweh has said: Believe me, I will make you a terror to yourself and to all your allies. They will fall by the sword of their enemies and you will see it with your own eyes. And I will hand over all Judah to the king of Babylon, who will deport them to Babylon and put them to the sword.*
5 *I will give all the wealth of this city and all its possessions, all its valuables and all the treasures of the kings of Judah into the hand of their enemies, who will seize them as spoil, and carry them away and take them to Babylon.*
6 *And as for you, Pashhur, and all the members of your household, you will go into captivity. Yes, to Babylon you will go, and you will die there, and there you will be buried—you and all your allies to whom you have prophesied falsely."*

In literary form the passage 19:1–20:6 is a continuous prose narrative continuing the larger literary unit which includes chs. 18, 19, and 20, which are built around the "potter-pot" theme. These chapters contain examples of all the major types of literary material found in the book of Jeremiah—poetic oracles, confessions, prose discourses, and biography. The section is marked also by symbolic actions. Chapters 19–20 cover the second of the symbolic actions described in prose, with an appended poetic segment, one of Jeremiah's confessions.

The narrative recounts how Jeremiah was commanded by Yahweh to take an earthenware jar and proceed to a point outside the Potsherd Gate. There, before witnesses he had taken with him, he was to smash the vessel. As he did so he was to announce that Jerusalem too would be smashed beyond repair. The symbolic act was tantamount to a word from Yahweh. Even in the absence of words, the act would declare the mind of Yahweh and would be fulfilled. There is no need to see in the act the performance of some kind of magic. The act was also the divine word.[10]

On Jeremiah's return to the city he repeated the words of judgment and was arrested by Pashhur ben Immer, beaten, and placed in the stocks. He was released the following morning. He then pronounced judgment against Pashhur himself and prophesied his exile to Babylon where he would die.

There is no indication in the text of the date of this incident, but there are some grounds for placing it early in the reign of Jehoiakim. We may have a clue in that 29:26, which is dated to 594 B.C., contains a reference to another person in the position of over-

10. See the Introduction, "Symbolic Actions in Jeremiah," pp. 71–76.

seer *(pāqîḏ)*, one Zephaniah ben Masseiah. It is arguable that Pashhur was deported in the 597 B.C. invasion of Nebuchadrezzar. Jeremiah was, in any case, in hiding after about 605/4 B.C. (36:26). By about 600/599 B.C. he was moving freely again (ch. 35). It seems at least plausible to place the present incident in the period between 609/8 and 605 B.C.

Commentators have raised questions about the form of the present prose narrative in 19:1–20:6, and have argued that an original brief account was later expanded, either by the insertion of a wordy harangue describing the fate of the city because of the abominable rites which were practiced at the high place of Topheth in the valley of Ben-hinnom, or by the conflation of two separate narratives. One suggestion is that into an original narrative from Baruch's memoirs was interpolated an oracle on Topheth. The original narrative dealing with the broken flask is to be discerned in 19:1, 2b, c, 10–11a, 19:14–20:6, while the interpolated material on Topheth is seen in 19:2a, 3–9, 11b–13.[11] The proposal is not in itself impossible, since editorial activity was an important aspect of the compilation of a prophetic book. But there is a certain subjectiveness in some of the arguments offered to identify the editorial additions.[12] Thus the observation that in v. 1 "elders" and "priests" accompanied Jeremiah, while in vv. 3–9 the address is made to the "princes of Judah" and "the inhabitants of Jerusalem," and only in vv. 10–11a was the symbolic act performed in the sight of the men who came with Jeremiah, is no necessary argument that vv. 3–9 are an intrusion, since the judgment was to be directed not merely to the select group of elders and priests but to the whole nation. (See the commentary.)

Again it is argued that the content of vv. 1–2, 10–11a is different from that of vv. 3–9, 11b–13 where Topheth is referred to. It would not be unlikely, indeed it would be altogether likely, that as Jeremiah stood with witnesses overlooking the valley of Ben-hinnom, the scene of scandalous pagan rites, he would refer to the offensive practices perpetrated there. On more than one occasion he referred to the worship of Baal (2:20–28; 3:22–25; 18:15; etc.). It was this display of disloyalty that had brought about the threat of judgment.

A further point is made that whereas in vv. 1–2, 10–11a the

11. See J. Bright, *Jeremiah,* p. 133; E. W. Nicholson, *Jeremiah 1–25,* pp. 162f.; W. Rudolph, *Jeremia,* pp. 125f.; G. P. Couturier, "Jeremiah," *JBC,* p. 318.
12. See E. W. Nicholson, *ibid.*

emphasis is on the smashing of the jar, in vv. 3–9, 11b–13 the emphasis is on Topheth and the valley of Ben-hinnom as the place where Judah and Jerusalem are to be destroyed (v. 6), where those who perish will be buried for lack of burial space elsewhere (v. 11). The death and destruction which will take place there is evoked as an illustration of what would befall Jerusalem on the day of disaster (v. 12). But such distinctions are of little significance. The shattered vessel was only one metaphor for destruction. The search for additional burial space was another. And Jeremiah was not one to avoid using a variety of metaphors (e.g., 2:14–16, 20–22) to emphasize his point.

Again vv. 3–9 are said to be strongly Deuteronomic in style and phraseology and thus have the appearance of being an insertion. The whole argument turns on the identification of this Deuteronomic style and phraseology.[13] See below on vv. 6–7.

Having raised these questions we do not necessarily rule out the possibility that there may have been an original brief account of the incident expanded by material from another context and delivered on another occasion. This material is, however, not out of place in the mouth of Jeremiah, and even if it has been reported freely by "Deuteronomic editors" it did not obscure what Jeremiah had declared on some other occasion. In any case, the final editor felt it appropriate to bring together in this section the material that we now have. In a similar manner the poetic materials in vv. 7–13 and 14–18 were included in the present context even though they may have been originally independent. The editor, at least, felt that they provided an appropriate picture of Jeremiah's reaction to the experiences of 19:1–20:6. However, when all has been said there would seem to be good reason to regard 19:1–20:6 as a unified account of an incident in Jeremiah's life in which he delivered a message appropriate to the occasion. While the postulate of the conflation of material from two sources is possible, it does not seem necessary.

1 There are several minor textual variants here. LXX and other texts and versions add "to me" as in 13:12, which introduces another symbolic act. Some commentators would add "to Jeremiah" to conform to the biographical style that follows (cf. v. 14). The earthenware vessel, *baqbuq,* is probably to be identified with the narrow-necked water decanter which was very common in the

13. See the Introduction, "The Book of Jeremiah: Composition," pp. 33–50.

Iron II period in Palestine. Examples of these vessels found in excavations range in size from about four or five inches to about one foot in height. *The elders of the people and* (the elders of) *the priests* were taken as witnesses. It is something of a puzzle to know how Jeremiah, being so unpopular, could persuade such important people to accompany him. That they did may indicate that they were anxious to collect incriminatory utterances which they could use against him (cf. v. 18).

2 The scene of the acted parable was just outside the *Potsherd Gate*. The words *the valley of Ben-hinnom which is at* have been regarded as an explanatory editorial gloss by some commentators.[14] In fact, the location of the Potsherd Gate in ancient Jerusalem is unknown. It may have acquired its name from the fact that potters whose workshops were near the gate dumped their broken vessels beyond the gate. The Hinnom Valley, which falls away steeply on the south side of the city, may well have been the dumping place, so that the Potsherd Gate was on this side of the city. The place would have been ideal for the performance of the symbolic act described in vv. 10–11. The Jerusalem Targum identified the Potsherd Gate with the Dung Gate (cf. Neh. 2:13; 3:13–14; 12:31).[15] There is a certain redundancy in the phrase *to the valley of Ben-hinnom* since the fact that the Potsherd Gate led out there was well known.[16] But Hebrew writers were not averse to redundancy. The valley of Ben-hinnom, called at times valley of Hinnom *(gê' hinnōm,* cf. the later Gehenna), is the modern Wadi er-Rababi, which runs first of all in a southerly direction on the west side of Jerusalem and then turns sharply eastward on the south side of Jerusalem to join the Wadi Kedron at the southeast corner of the city. In this area the refuse of the city was burned or dumped. In the same wadi, from time to time, the worship of pagan gods was conducted.

3 The message of Jeremiah commences at this point and is addressed to *You kings of Judah and citizens of Jerusalem.* Difficulties have been seen in this phrase. The plural *kings* is unexpected. The address is a public one to the *citizens of Jerusalem,* whereas the actual audience (v. 1) is the elders and priests whom Jeremiah took with him. But the difficulties are only apparent. It was not unusual for Jeremiah or for other prophets to address the nation as a whole

14. J. Bright, *Jeremiah,* p. 131; E. W. Nicholson, *Jeremiah 1–25,* p. 163.
15. Heb. *ḥarsîṯ,* here translated *potsherd,* derives from *ḥeres,* "pottery."
16. J. Bright, *Jeremiah,* p. 131; E. W. Nicholson, *Jeremiah 1–25,* p. 163.

even if the immediate audience was small. Nor need the plural *kings* occasion any difficulty. Jeremiah addressed himself to the rulers of Judah as a whole. In any case Jeremiah lived through the reigns of four kings. On the present occasion he spoke in the name of *Yahweh of Hosts the God of Israel,* one of the fuller forms of the divine Name,[17] and referred to the coming *disaster (rā'â)* which would make the *ears ring* (RSV "tingle"), an expression used elsewhere in the OT to describe the reaction of people to a catastrophe of unheard-of severity (1 Sam. 3:11; 2 K. 21:12).

4–5 The reasons for the coming calamity are now given, although they amount to one reason. Yahweh's total sovereignty over the people inside the covenant relationship had been rejected. The people were sharing their allegiance with other deities. They had *forsaken ('āzaḇ)* Yahweh and *made this an alien place*. The verb *nikkēr,* "make alien," is a vivid and highly suggestive term. The place had been denationalized, so that it could not be recognized as Israelite. It is not certain what *this place* refers to, but it may have been the temple, where foreign religious practices were introduced from time to time. Ezekiel's vision in Ezek. 8 depicts a variety of pagan cult practices which seem to have been current at the time of Ezekiel's exile in 597 B.C. But the reference may be simply to Jerusalem as in v. 3. The whole expression occurs almost verbatim in 2 K. 21:12. In particular, the people were offering up sacrifices *qiṭṭēr)* to other gods which neither they nor their ancestors had known (cf. Deut. 13:6; 28:64).[18] It would appear that the people as a whole[19] were involved in filling the place with *the blood of innocents (dam nᵉqiyyîm)*. The reference is to a cultic practice in which children were offered in the fire as burnt offerings on high places *(bāmôṯ)*[20] built for Baal (cf. 7:31). Human sacrifice in one form or another was known in the Middle East but especially in Phoenicia and Canaan. It was condemned in Israel at an early stage (cf. Gen. 22:1–19); but it is heard of from time to time, as in the days of Ahaz (2 K. 16:3; cf. Mic. 6:7) and Manasseh (2 K. 21:6). The destruction of the sanctuary in the valley of Ben-hinnom in the days of Josiah is referred to specifically in 2 K. 23:10. Evidently the practice was revived

17. The expression occurs some 35 times, e.g., 7:3, 21; 9:14 (Eng. 15); 16:9; 19:3, 15; 23:16; 25:27; 27:19, 21.

18. The verb *yāḏa'* here may carry overtones of the deep and intimate commitment of one person to another that this verb often has.

19. See textual note.

20. P. H. Vaughan, *The Meaning of 'bāmâ' in the OT* (Cambridge, 1974).

under Jehoiakim, and it was to this that Jeremiah addressed himself.[21] It was a practice of which Yahweh did not approve—*a thing I did not ever command, nor did I ever speak of it, nor did it ever enter my mind.* It was an affront to Yahweh and a rejection of his sole and total sovereignty over his covenant people. Wanton rejection of their covenant Lord could only result in the operation of the covenant curses.

6–7 The curses of the covenant would operate in the cancellation of Judah's plans *('ēṣâ)* and the destruction of the city and its people. The proposal to treat vv. 3–9 as referring to a separate incident from that of the broken bottle is not merely unnecessary but destroys a certain element of dramatic suspense. The select audience that accompanied Jeremiah may well have wondered about the jar in his hand, though they no doubt expected it to be used in some symbolic act. The dramatic moment for shattering the jar came when Jeremiah spoke of shattering *(šāḇar)* the people and the city (vv. 10, 11). Jeremiah's first threat was that in a coming day the place would undergo a change of name from *Topheth* or *the valley of Ben-hinnom* to *the valley of Slaughter.* A change of name signified a change of function as so often in the OT (Gen. 17:5, 15).[22]

The name *Topheth (tōpeṯ)* may derive from another noun *tāp̄ā',* or Aram. *tēpaṯ,* meaning "hearth," "fireplace," or "burning place," with the vowels of the noun *bōšeṯ,* "shame," attached to the original consonants.[23] However, the precise derivation is not certain. The change of name from *gê' ben-hinnōm, valley of Ben-hinnom,* to *gê' hahᵃrēḡâ, valley of Slaughter,* must reflect a change of function. Did Jeremiah connect Hinnom with the assonant adverb *ḥinnām,* "gratuitously," "favorably," and contrast this with *hᵃrēḡâ,* "slaughter"?[24]

Further, Yahweh will cancel *(annul* or "destroy," *bāqaq) the plans ('ēṣâ) of Judah and Jerusalem in this place.* The reference seems to be to the overthrow of all the ideas and intentions which the people carried out in the land in every department of their life. The verb form used here—*baqqōṯî*—is evidently a play on the noun

21. See R. de Vaux, *Ancient Israel,* pp. 441–46.

22. One is reminded of the many references to throne names in 1 and 2 Kings, e.g., 2 K. 23:34; 24:17.

23. See W. Robertson Smith, *Lectures on the Religion of the Semites* (1889), p. 353; KB, p. 1038. LXX has *Tapheth.* See also on 7:31.

24. The suggestion comes from G. P. Couturier, "Jeremiah" in *JBC,* p. 319.

baqbuq, "vessel," in v. 1.[25] Did Jeremiah, even at this point, do something with his jar, such as empty it of its contents and thus make it void? The root *bqq* can mean "lay waste," "make void," etc. The agent in this destruction will be the invader, clearly defined as Babylon in 20:6. The rest of the verse refers to people falling by the sword before their enemy who comes to seek their life. Their corpses would be unburied, *food (ma'ᵃḵāl)* for *carrion birds* (lit. "birds of the heavens") and *wild beasts* (lit. "beasts of the field"). The same picture occurs in 7:33; 16:4; and 34:20, all in prose passages, as well as in Deut. 28:26, the only place outside Jeremiah where the phrase occurs. This is taken by some writers as evidence that the chapter owes its present form to a Deuteronomic editor.[26] It is possible that Jeremiah himself was deeply affected by Deuteronomy. The curse, in any case, is a gruesome one, but is matched by similar curses in the nonbiblical literature, notably in Near Eastern treaties.[27]

8 Jerusalem itself would suffer severely and become a scene of *horror (šammâ)* and a cause for hissing or whistling *(šᵉrēqâ),* i.e., a sight so shocking as to make men whistle as they passed by and observed its devastation (lit. "all her blows"). There is some powerful assonance here, as in 18:16, caused by the sibilants—*yiššōm wᵉyišrōq.* The picture of passers-by who whistled at the sight of devastation occurs elsewhere in the OT (1 K. 9:8; Lam. 2:15, 16; Ezek. 27:36; Zeph. 2:15).

9 The gruesome curses continue. Under the pressure of a siege (lit. "in the siege [*māṣôr*] and in the dire straits [*māṣôq*]") the inhabitants of Jerusalem will eat the flesh of their sons and daughters and then turn to devouring one another (cf. Lev. 26:29; Deut. 28:53; Ezek. 5:10). The nauseating practice is attested in the siege of Samaria during the Aramean wars (2 K. 6:26ff.), during the siege of Jerusalem in 587 B.C. (Lam. 2:20; 4:10), and in A.D. 70 when Jerusalem fell to the Romans.[28] It was widely known in the Middle East.[29] The complete expression *under the pressure of the siege to which their enemies and those who seek their life will subject them*

25. W. Rudolph, *Jeremia,* p. 109. NEB seeks to capture the play by translating *I will shatter as a jar is shattered.*
26. E. W. Nicholson, *Jeremiah 1–25,* p. 164.
27. D. J. Wiseman, "The Vassal-Treaties of Esarhaddon," *Iraq* 20 (1958), ll. 427, 449f., 572, 591f., etc.
28. Josephus, *Wars of the Jews* 6:3–4.
29. Wiseman, *art. cit., Iraq* 20 (1958), ll. 448ff., 547–550, 570–72.

is strongly reminiscent of Deut. 28:53, 55, 57, a further indication of Deuteronomic influence of one kind or another.

10–11 The time was now appropriate to smash the jar. This action, as we have argued, need not be regarded as something independent of the preceding discourse. Nor need we accuse Jeremiah of engaging in some kind of magic rites such as were performed by the Assyrians, Hittites, and Arameans, who broke jars to cast off a sickness or release a curse on those who broke their treaty, or like the smashing of bowls or figurines in ancient Egypt to release powerful curses on their enemies.[30] If Israel's remote ancestors ever practiced magic the practice had long since been rejected. For Jeremiah, the breaking of the jar was a symbolic act, just as much a word from Yahweh as any verbal messages he delivered. It mattered little whether Jeremiah declared verbally that Jerusalem would be destroyed or whether he declared the same by smashing a jar. The same view should be taken of the symbolic actions of other prophets in Israel. In fact, Jeremiah accompanied the spoken word (v. 11) by the powerful symbolic act. God's word of judgment spoken, set in motion the judgment it declared. God's word symbolized in act likewise set in motion the judgment it portrayed.[31]

The command to *shatter (šāḇar)*[32] the jar before the eyes of the men Jeremiah had brought with him in no way restricted the message to them. Its application was to all the inhabitants of Jerusalem and Judah. But these witnesses were sufficiently influential to noise abroad all Jeremiah said and did and to take appropriate punitive action. The breaking of the jar was a symbol of the breaking of the people and the city. It was parallel to the breaking of a vessel by a potter. A flask which proved useless was broken into fragments. Once broken it could not be mended. Jeremiah's action stated the judgment in its grimmest terms, although elsewhere he expressed hope for restoration after judgment, albeit in some future day (24:4–7; 31:31–33; 32:13–15; etc.). But for the present, a nation which had flagrantly violated God's purpose for his people was useless.

The exact sense of the last sentence in v. 11 is not clear.

30. See J. A. Wilson, *The Culture of Ancient Egypt* (1951), pp. 1956–58. Egyptians of the Twelfth Dynasty used the practice widely, and the famous Execration Texts now provide valuable information about the peoples in their sphere of influence, but notably about Amorite princes in Palestine. See *ANET* (1950), p. 328.

31. On the whole question of the symbolic act see the Introduction, "Symbolic Actions in Jeremiah," pp. 71–76.

32. We might have expected the Piel *šibbēr.* The use here of the Qal may indicate that the verb was powerful enough even in this form not to need the intensive Piel.

Some translations understand it to mean that corpses were buried in Topheth because there was no room to bury them elsewhere (NEB). On the other hand the expression *mē'ên māqôm* could mean that Topheth would become a burial ground until there was no room left there (cf. *mē'ên yôšēḇ,* "without inhabitant," in 4:7; 26:9; etc.). In that case Topheth was not a place to receive an overflow of corpses, but was one vast cemetery, so full that many bodies could not be buried at all. These would be food for carrion birds and wild beasts (cf. 7:33). The fact that the text now returns to Topheth is no necessary argument that vv. 11b–13 belong to a different context from the story of the broken jar. It is not difficult to see the narrative as a whole.

12–13 The presence of corpses in the city made it unclean (Lev. 21:1ff.; Num. 5:2; etc.). A further reason for uncleanness was the pollution caused by the pagan worship conducted on the rooftops of the houses, where burnt offerings were offered to the *host of heaven,* the Mesopotamian astral deities (cf. 7:16–20), and where libations were poured out to other gods (cf. 32:29). Among the astral deities Astarte (Ashtaroth) was especially important. Texts from Ras Shamra include a ritual which was used when offerings were made on rooftops to astral deities and celestial luminaries. Both Jeremiah and his contemporary Zephaniah (Zeph. 1:5) refer to the practice. Contact with a corpse defiled anything and everything. Evidently a similar view was held by those who followed pagan cults, for Josiah defiled the altars and high places at Bethel by scattering on them bones taken from tombs (2 K. 23:14–20). The whole picture is a grim one. In the day of judgment the whole city would be, like Topheth, *unclean (ṭāmē').*

14 On Jeremiah's return to the city from Topheth he proceeded to the court of the temple. From 19:14 to 20:6 the narrative is written in the third person in contrast to the section 19:1–13 which reports Yahweh's words to Jeremiah. If we follow MT and omit "to me" in v. 1, the whole segment 19:1–20:5 could be regarded as a straight narrative. The audience in the temple court was no longer a select group of elders and priests but *all the people.* The message was, however, the same, preserved here in a much abbreviated form.

15 The fuller name for Yahweh is used, *Yahweh of Hosts the God of Israel.* All the *disaster (rā'â)* of which the prophet had spoken on Yahweh's behalf would fall upon the city and its neighboring towns. The reason is plain: literally, "they have hardened their necks so as not to listen to my word."

20:1 Jeremiah's preaching in the temple courtyard was heard by Pashhur ben Immer, who is described as *the priest, the chief overseer (pāqîḏ nāgîḏ).* His function was evidently to maintain order in the temple and its precincts and to deal with troublemakers (cf. 29:26). Jeremiah himself at his call (1:10) was appointed as an overseer *(pāqîḏ)* of the nations. There is intense irony in that the overseer in God's temple is now about to take action against God's overseer. There are two officials named Pashhur in the book, the one mentioned here, who is possibly to be identified with the father of Gedaliah (38:1), and the other referred to in 21:1 and 38:1 as Pashhur son of Malchiah. The name was evidently fairly common (see v. 3). The banning of Jeremiah from the temple (36:5) would have been the work of Pashhur. On that occasion Jeremiah sent Baruch to read the scroll (ch. 36). Pashhur evidently went into exile in 597 B.C. as Jeremiah had prophesied (20:6), because the office was held by Zephaniah son of Maaseiah after 597 B.C. (29:24, 26, 29). The names Pashhur and Immer appear after the Exile as family names (Ezra 2:37–38; 10:20), although there may be no connection with the Pashhur ben Immer of 20:1. Jeremiah was punished for his *prophesying (nibbā').*

2 The punishment involved first of all beating. The text reads literally *Pashhur had Jeremiah the prophet beaten.* LXX reads "smote him." Perhaps, in fact, it was Pashhur who struck the prophet. Following the beating Pashhur put him in the stocks *(mahpeḵeṯ).* There is some difficulty with this word. The Targum has "prison." There is at least the possibility that Jeremiah was placed in a small confined room used for short detentions.[33] The root *hpk* means "turn over," which has given rise to the idea of *stocks.* But a confined room would just as well have kept a man in a crooked or confined position which would produce cramped muscles (cf. 29:26; 2 Chr. 16:10; this latter verse adds "in prison").

The place of confinement was in the *Upper Benjamin Gate,* which was evidently a gate to the temple precincts, different from the Benjamin Gate which was a gate in the city walls (37:13; 38:7). The Upper Gate of Benjamin was located between the old court and the new court referred to in 2 K. 15:35 and 2 Chr. 20:5 (cf. Ezek. 9:2).[34] The name suggests that it was on the north side of the temple area facing the territory of Benjamin.

33. M. Greenberg, "Stocks," *IDB* IV, p. 443.
34. J. Morgenstern, "The Gates of Righteousness," *HUCA* 6 (1929), p. 19, n. 42.

3 When Pashhur released Jeremiah the next morning, Jeremiah gave him the symbolic name *Magor-missabib,* "terror all around." The name had been used in 6:25 of the relentless enemy from the north. In Jeremiah the expression appears in v. 10 of the present chapter and also in 46:5; 49:29 and in Lam. 2:22 and Ps. 31:14 (Eng. 13). The name may well be a play on words which reverses the meaning of Pashhur, but this is not obvious.[35] Whether or not we can identify the play on words, the significance of a new name to mark a new status is clear. Pashhur will not be a temple overseer who metes out punishment to others, but one who will himself suffer the divine judgment when terror surrounds him and the nation.

4–5 Jeremiah now makes more explicit the meaning of the new name. Yahweh will make Pashhur a terror to himself and to all his *allies.*[36] His new name amounted to a curse upon him. He would be caught up in the terror which would descend on all Judah. He and his political allies would all suffer. He would see many fall by the sword and many handed over to the king of Babylon for depor-

35. We would expect that the name *māgôr missāḇîḇ* was in some way related to the name *pašḥûr* semantically. A pun has been conjectured.

The phrase *māgôr missāḇîḇ* occurs five times in Jeremiah (6:25; 20:3, 10; 46:5; 49:29) as well as in Ps. 31:14 and Lam. 2:22. The LXX does not connect the word *māgôr* with "fear, terror" in any of its translations but rather with *gwr,* "sojourn with," or in 20:10; 46:5 with "assemble, gather in upon." Only in the Targ. at 20:3 do we find the two ideas of "assemble" and "destroy" (hence, terror) associated. Possibly there are reflections also of the verb *māgar* in the Piel, "cast down, destroy," so that the two roots *gwr,* "sojourn with," and *mgr,* "cast down, destroy," might have been drawn together in such a noun as *māgôr.* But probably the sense of "destruction all around" received more support from the context than from such etymological exercises. In Lam. 2:22 and Ps. 31:14 the word is used in the context of a lack of survivors. In Jer. 6:25 the phrase occurs alongside "the enemy has a sword" and in 20:3–4 the phrase is in the same context as "they shall fall by the sword," that is, Pashhur's friends. Pashhur is here seen at the center of a work of extermination.

But the problem is to link the phrase with *pašḥûr.* The first three consonants of this name, *pšḥ,* may provide a clue since this root is used in Aram. (e.g., Targ. to 1 Sam. 15:33 and Ps. 7:4 [Eng. 3]) and in Heb. in the sense of "tear off," "strip away"; e.g., in Lam. 3:11 we have the words "he tore me to pieces *(pšḥ),* he has made me desolate." If we postulate an original expression *paššāḥ sᵉḥôr,* "destruction all about," which became abbreviated to *pašḥûr,* we have a possible explanation of Jeremiah's pun. In effect, the prophet was saying "He is not really *Pašḥûr* but *Māgôr missāḇîḇ*" henceforth, for *pašḥûr* really means "destruction round about." See A. M. Honeyman, "MĀGÔR MIS-SĀBÎB and Jeremiah's Pun," *VT* IV/4 (1954), pp. 424–26.

36. Heb. *'ōhēḇ,* "friend," often means political ally. See J. A. Thompson, "The Significance of the Verb *Love* in the David-Jonathan Narratives in I Samuel," *VT* 24 (1974), pp. 334–38.

tation. The foe from the north is no longer an enigma. It is specifically the king of Babylon and his armies. The prophecy was made before 597 B.C.[37] The extent of the booty that would be taken is indicated by the use of four different words—*wealth (ḥōsen), possessions (y^e^gîa'), valuables (yāqār),* and *treasures ('ôṣ^e^rôṯ);* and the effect is further heightened by the use of the three verbs "loot" *(bāzaz),* "take" *(lāqaḥ),* and "carry off to" *(hēḇî' b^e^).* There could be no mistaking the severity of the calamity.

6 Pashhur's personal judgment would be deportation with his family to a land where he would die and be buried along with all his *allies ('ōhēḇ)* to whom he *prophesied falsely.* Pashhur was not merely a priest but a prophet, one among those who had declared that no harm would befall the nation (14:13). This was a lie and worthy of death (cf. chs. 26, 28). The noun *šeqer,* "falsehood," was used many times by Jeremiah. There is, indeed, a significant line of thinking in its use.[38] Judah's leaders, prophets, priests, wise men, and king as well as the people themselves were involved in a profound conspiracy of falsehood.

(xiv) Jeremiah's Inner Struggle about His Calling (20:7–13)

7 *You seduced*[1] *me, Yahweh, and I was seduced;*
You laid hold on me and overcame me.
I have become a laughingstock all the day long;
They all make fun of me.
8 *Whenever I speak I cry out;*
"Violence and Robbery," I shout.
The word of Yahweh has become for me
A reproach and derision all the time.
9 *Whenever I say, "I will not call him to mind,*
I will not speak again in his name,"
Then it is in my heart like a burning fire
Imprisoned within me;
I am weary holding it in,
And I cannot.

37. A similar prophecy of doom was delivered by Amos to Amaziah the priest in Samaria (Amos 7:10–17).
38. See Thomas W. Overholt, *The Threat of Falsehood* (1970).

1. See S. J. DeVries, *Prophet Against Prophet* (1978), p. 44. Cf. Ezek. 14:9. The same verb (Piel of *pth*) is used in 1 K. 22:20 where Yahweh challenged Ahab's advisers to "deceive" or entice Ahab.

10 *I hear many whispering,*
"Magor-missabib—
Denounce him! Let us denounce him!"
All my friends were watching for a false step:
"Perhaps he may be tricked,[2] *then we shall have him in our power;*
We will catch him and take our revenge on him!"
11 *But Yahweh is on my side, like a dread warrior;*
Therefore my persecutors will stumble and not prevail.
They will be deeply disgraced when they do not succeed.
Their everlasting shame will not be forgotten.
12 *O Yahweh of Hosts, who dost test the righteous,*
Who dost see into hidden motives and thoughts,
Let me see thy vengeance upon them,
For to thee I have committed my cause.
13 *Sing to Yahweh; give praise to Yahweh:*
For he has rescued the life of poor men
From the power of those who would do them wrong.

The account of Jeremiah's persecution is followed by another of his "confessions" (20:7–13). The catchword *Magor-missabib,* which occurs both here in v. 10 and in v. 3, although in different senses, links the poem with the prose narrative preceding. In literary form this poem is much like the individual psalms of lament, and its application is quite general against the background of persecution that Jeremiah suffered over the years. It is possible that it was placed here by the editor as a suitable expression of Jeremiah's response to the Pashhur incident.

The section divides readily into two parts:

(a) God as Antagonist: Jeremiah's struggle with God and his sense of God's overpowering mastery which compels him to prophesy (vv. 7–10).

(b) God as Protagonist: Jeremiah's conviction that God is with him and will punish his persecutors (vv. 11–13).

These verses are strongly reminiscent of the individual lament with its address or call to Yahweh, the lament proper, the confession of trust or certainty of being heard, the petition, and often an element of praise. The address here is in v. 7aα, the lament in vv. 7–10, the confession of trust and the affirmation of the prophet's confidence that he will be heard in vv. 11–12a, the petition in v. 12bα with a return to trust in 12bβ and praise in v. 13 expressed here as an imperative. It would seem that vv. 7–13 were originally a complete unit, both because of the lament form and also because of a

2. See the preceding note.

number of internal thematic and logical linkages.[3] In fact, vv. 7–13 indicate that Jeremiah was moving or had moved from a situation of distress and rebellion to one of confidence. Here we have a confident appeal to Yahweh as his deliverer from mockery and persecution. The segment has been persuasively interpreted as a public affirmation that the word spoken by Jeremiah was not his but Yahweh's. The focus of the poem may not originally have had reference to an inner crisis of faith but was rather a public confrontation of the prophet with the people.[4] Originally there need not have been any logical or temporal link between vv. 1–6 and 7–13 despite a number of parallel phrases occurring in the two passages, for these are mostly common phrases occurring elsewhere. The juxtaposition of the two passages is due to a redactor and resulted in a heightening of the emotional intensity of the narrative, besides giving a new strength to vv. 7–13. Whatever their original setting, however, these verses are appropriate in the setting of the Pashhur episode since they provided a strong picture of Jeremiah's assurance that Yahweh was with him in all such crises, even if he lost heart momentarily at times.[5]

The passage, and the succeeding poem (vv. 14–18), provide unusual insights into Jeremiah's own inner conflicts. He was engrossed in controversy with Yahweh. His sensitive nature was deeply hurt by the ridicule and sarcasm with which his preaching was received by the people. But he could do no other because of his deep commitment to his prophetic vocation. He was under a profound compulsion to expose the nation's rejection of Yahweh and his covenant. Yet he loved his own people deeply. Little wonder that deep emotional tensions and conflicts arose within him which led him at times to give expression to the intense feeling which is found in these poems. Only one who walked intimately with God would dare to speak as Jeremiah did. But despite such strong words, he continued

3. E.g., the idea of "prevailing" or "having power" (Heb. *yāḵōl* in vv. 7, 9). The "enemy" -like quality of Yahweh is the source both of the prophet's complaint (v. 7) and of his confidence, because Yahweh will prevail over Jeremiah's enemies (v. 11); Heb. *pāṯâ,* "persuade," "entice," occurs in v. 7 in reference to Yahweh's action toward Jeremiah and in v. 10 in reference to the hope of the enemies that Jeremiah may be "tricked." For a valuable discussion on the point see D. J. A. Clines and D. M. Gunn, "Form, Occasion and Redaction in Jeremiah 20," *ZAW* 88 (1976), pp. 390–409.

4. *Ibid.,* pp. 398–402.

5. *Ibid.,* pp. 402–405.

his calling steadfastly to the end. Even after the fall of Jerusalem he continued to preach the same message in Egypt (ch. 44).

7 The confession begins in a startling way with an address to Yahweh: *You seduced me, Yahweh, and I was seduced.* The verb *seduce (pāṯâ)* occurs in Exod. 22:16 (cf. Judg. 16:5) in a law regarding sexual seduction. Jeremiah seems to be saying that he had understood his relationship to Yahweh to be something like a marriage bond but it was now clear that he had been deceived, enticed by Yahweh, who had used him and tossed him aside. The language verges on the blasphemous. He spoke of Yahweh in 15:18 as a deceitful brook, but not as a seducer. There may be another overtone to the verb used here. In the story in 1 K. 22:1–38, Micaiah the prophet of Yahweh, who took a stand contrary to the four hundred prophets, asserted that God intended to "seduce" (the verb is the same) Ahab (1 K. 22:20).[6] Micaiah had said "No" rightly, and the four hundred false prophets had said "Yes" wrongly, because God intended to "seduce" Ahab. Jeremiah in his day dared to say "No" rightly, while the prophets said "Yes" wrongly (23:26). But now, Jeremiah is forced to the conclusion that it was he himself who had been seduced. His outburst was tantamount to a questioning of the very validity of his call from God.[7] The lament proper commences here. Yahweh had seduced him, and he on his part had allowed it to happen.[8] But more than that, Yahweh had *laid hold on* ("overpowered," *ḥāzaq)* him and had prevailed over him *(yāḵōl).* Perhaps the sense is, "you forced me," carrying on the metaphor of seduction. The verb *ḥāzaq* is used of sexual seduction elsewhere in the OT (Deut. 22:25; 2 Sam. 13:11, 14; cf. Prov. 7:13).

The result was that Jeremiah became a continual laughingstock and a butt for the mockery of the people. Evidently he had thought that the word of Yahweh would lead the people to repentance. It was a shock to him that his message brought only calumny and abuse. Had he thought back to his call he might have remembered that something of what happened was implied then (1:7, 8, 16–19).

8 Jeremiah had been commissioned originally "to root up and tear down, to destroy and to demolish, to build and to plant" (1:10). Up to the present his words corresponded only to the de-

6. The verb is used elsewhere of false prophets, e.g., Ezek. 14:9.

7. The argument of this paragraph follows that of W. Holladay in *Jeremiah: Spokesman Out of Time,* p. 101.

8. J. Bright, *Jeremiah,* p. 129, translates: "You seduced me, Yahweh, and I let you."

structive aspects of the total message. He continually cried out, *"Violence (ḥāmās) and Robbery (šōḏ)."* The verbs *cry out (zā'aq)* and *shout (qārā')* convey the impression of a loud and aggressive proclamation. Little wonder he attracted persecution to himself. His constant reiteration of threats of ruin to Jerusalem and his denunciation of national crimes against the covenant, in the absence of any fulfilment of his prophecies, made him a constant target for reproach and derision. Had he been able "to build and to plant" as well, he might have been able to bear it. He had once referred to the "merrymakers" (15:17) whose company he avoided, but now the joking and the teasing were turned on him. To be sure, there was to be an element of hope in his preaching, but that was later. The present lament may have come early in his ministry before the Chaldean threat loomed on the horizon and before he was able to speak of a future hope.

9–10 In the face of persecution the simplest solution was to withdraw and remain silent and thus abandon his vocation. He would forget Yahweh, *not call him* (or perhaps "it," i.e., "the word") *to mind.* But that was no solution, for the word was a *fire* (cf. 5:14; 23:29)[9] which he could not keep bottled up (lit. "imprisoned in my bones"). In attempting to do so he was wearing himself out. In any case people whispered *Magor-missabib,* evidently an expression he used so often that it became a nickname. "There goes old Magor-missabib!" The name was turned against the prophet himself in derision and mockery (cf. Job 33:11; Ps. 56:6 [Eng. 5]; 71:10); and they cried out all the more, *Denounce him! Let us denounce him!* Even his *friends* (lit. "every person of my peace,"[10] that is, all who had to do with his welfare) were watching for him to make a false step. They said, "Perhaps he may be tricked, then we can catch him." The verb *tricked* is the same as the verb "seduce" *(pāṯâ)* in v. 7a. The total social and psychological support of his fellow villagers and kinsmen was denied to him.[11] It was a devastating experience.

These verses are significant for a study of the prophetic call. The urge was inescapable. Amos a century earlier than Jeremiah had sensed a similar divine compulsion (Amos 3:3–8). "The word of the Lord which had been an outward reproach now became an

9. Only Jeremiah applied the word *fire* to Yahweh's word. Yahweh himself is spoken of as a consuming fire in other places, e.g., Exod. 24:17; Deut. 4:24; 9:3; Isa. 33:14.
10. Heb. *šālôm* means "welfare, well-being" in the broadest sense.
11. See commentary on 11:19–23.

inward torture—Yahweh had brought him into a strait from which he can find neither exit nor retreat."[12]

11 Coming in the midst of a passage describing the prophet's depression, this verse has at times been thought to be out of context. But there may be deeper dimensions to be considered. In a psychological and spiritual crisis like Jeremiah's, logic does not always govern a man's thinking; he may be dominated by conflicting convictions.[13] Jeremiah's only resort now is to a rock-bottom affirmation of his faith. *Yahweh is on my side, like a dread warrior.* God is described in Ps. 24:8 as *gibbôr:* "Yahweh strong and mighty... mighty in battle." Jeremiah had once referred to his enemies as ruthless (*'ārîṣ,* 15:21). Here in v. 11 Jeremiah applies both words to God. He is a *warrior (gibbôr),* and "tyrant" *(dread, 'ārîṣ),* the mighty and ruthless one. That being so, his persecutors will not prevail over him *(yāḵōl)* even if God does (cf. v. 7). In the hour of crisis Jeremiah could recall Yahweh's promise of 1:18, 19. He had gone back to that promise on other occasions (cf. 15:20). In the midst of strong contradictions Jeremiah was able to return to his faith in Yahweh's faithfulness (11:20; 12:3; 15:15; 17:18; 18:21–23).

12 The verse repeats 11:20 with some variations as though deliberately to reaffirm once more what he had affirmed earlier. The expression we have translated *who dost see into hidden motives and thoughts* is literally "who sees into kidneys and heart." The kidneys *(k^e^lāyôṯ)* may be thought of as the seat of the affections and the hidden motives. The *heart* is the seat of the thought and will. As the One who "assays" *(bōḥēn)* the *righteous (ṣaddîq),* Yahweh may be trusted to visit the evildoers with judgment. The thought is expressed more than once in Jeremiah. Jeremiah committed his *cause (rîḇ)* to Yahweh. The noun *rîḇ* has legal overtones. Jeremiah's accusers were bent on collecting evidence against him (v. 10; cf. 18:18). When the trial came, Yahweh would be Jeremiah's defendant.

13 The verse is difficult to interpret, and has often been rejected as a late doxology because it appears to be at variance with the mood of the passage and to interrupt the flow of Jeremiah's most profound confession. Such a conclusion is by no means a necessary one. Psalms of lament frequently contain or end with an expression of confidence (e.g., Ps. 6:9–10 [Eng. 8–9]). Further, the vocabulary of the verse fits well with other utterances of Jeremiah.

12. J. Skinner, *Prophecy and Religion: Studies in the Life of Jeremiah,* p. 212.
13. Cf. W. Rudolph, *Jeremia,* pp. 131ff.

The expression "from the hand *(power)* of the wicked *(rā'îm)*" occurs in 15:21; 21:12; 23:14, while the exact expression "to deliver from the hands of the evildoer" *(hiṣṣîl miyyaḏ mᵉrē'îm)* occurs only here and in 23:14 but nowhere else in the OT.[14] That v. 13 is in the third person while v. 12 is in the second person does not affect the case. Sudden changes of speaker and mood are not uncommon in Jeremiah or, for that matter, in the OT in general. Hence there are good reasons to preserve this verse as an integral part of the whole poem. There is every reason why an inner experience of calm and of renewed confidence in Yahweh came to him in the hour of testing, when his mood fluctuated under the pressures caused by the inner turmoil of his spirit. At one moment he could be in despair, at another he could say, *Sing to Yahweh; give praise to Yahweh.*[15]

The *poor ('eḇyôn)* here does not have a sociological meaning but refers rather to religious men. It refers to the pious man, poor in the sense that he is the client of Yahweh, dependent on Yahweh for the support of his spiritual life. In the face of persecutors it is not wealth that a man needs but spiritual strength. The poor in spirit, that is the pious, receive such strength and Yahweh delivers them from their foes.[16] In several of the Psalms we find an appeal to worshippers to praise Yahweh who has cared for the poor (Ps. 22:24–25 [Eng. 23–24]; 35:9–10, 27–28; 140:12–13).

It is noteworthy that there was no divine answer to Jeremiah's outpouring,[17] although there was an answer to a similar cry at 11:20. Yahweh is not bound to answer his servants, and even when he does his answer may be totally unexpected (cf. 12:5, 6; 15:19–21).

(xv) The Depths of Despair (20:14–18)

14 *Cursed be the day when I was born,*
The day my mother bore me;
May it be for ever unblessed.
15 *Cursed be the man who brought the news to my father:*
"A child is born to you, a son."
(How it gladdened his heart!)

14. W. L. Holladay, "Style, Irony, and Authenticity in Jeremiah," *JBL* 81 (1962), pp. 52f.
15. Cf. Ps. 22 where v. 25 (Eng. 24) follows vv. 21–22 (Eng. 20–21). The treatment of D. J. A. Clines and D. M. Gunn in *ZAW* 88 (1976), pp. 390–409, is important.
16. See P. Humbert, "Le mot biblique ebyōn," *RHPR* 32 (1952), pp. 1–6; A. Gelin, *The Poor of Yahweh* (1953).
17. Cf. 17:14–18; 18:18–23, to which there was also no answer.

16 *Let that man be like the cities*
Which Yahweh overthrew without pity.
Let him hear a cry of alarm in the morning,
The shout of battle at noon,
17 *Because he did not kill me in the womb*[1]
So that my mother became my grave
And her womb for ever pregnant.
18 *Why is it that I came forth from the womb*
To see only sorrow and trial,
And that my days should end in shame?

In these verses Jeremiah plumbed the depths of bitterness and despair, revealing a depth of misery and agony surpassing any other cry of anguish recorded among his lamentations. There is no ray of light here as at the end of the previous lament (vv. 11–13). The passage is reminiscent of Job 3:3–12, which in the opinion of some commentators may have been influenced by Jeremiah's words.[2]

The literary history of this segment is probably complex. Originally it may have been used as a self-curse, a conventional utterance of distress accompanying a woe-oracle. But it was incorporated into its present context in ch. 20 by being linked with the Pashhur story (vv. 1–6) and the appeal to Yahweh (vv. 7–13). In that setting vv. 14–18 became an expression of the prophet's own personal anguish occasioned by the bitter experience of 20:1–6. This in turn affected the original sense of vv. 7–13, so that its climax of confident appeal and praise is reversed and the dominant mood of the whole composition (vv. 7–18) becomes one of distress and lament. The curse of vv. 14–18 is the sequel to vv. 7–13; but it serves also as the preface to chs. 21–24, which are a collection of judgment-speeches against Judah, so that the short segment forms a transition from the personal experiences of the prophet (chs. 19–20) to the collective experience of the people (chs. 21–24) in which the prophet was involved.[3]

14–15 Jeremiah's crisis had reached its peak. He had once before bemoaned the fact that his mother had given him birth (15:10), although he had not cursed the day but merely declared "Woe is

1. W. L. Holladay, *Jeremiah: Spokesman Out of Time,* p. 104; E. W. Nicholson, *Jeremiah 1–25,* p. 171. Cf. J. Bright, *Jeremiah,* p. 134; G. P. Couturier, "Jeremiah," *JBC,* p. 319.
2. MT reads *mēreḥem,* "from the womb," but with a revocalization and the same consonants we may read *m^e^ruḥḥam,* "enwombed," i.e., *in the womb.* See M. J. Dahood, "Denominative *riḥḥam,* 'to conceive, enwomb,'" *Biblica* 44 (1963), pp. 204f.
3. See Clines and Gunn, *art. cit.,* pp. 405–408.

me" (*'ôy lî*). To curse either God or one's parents was a capital offense in Israel (Lev. 20:9; 24:10–16). Jeremiah avoided both by merely cursing the day of his birth. But even that was to curse his call from God, who had called him before he was born (1:5). The *day* here seems almost to be personified, as having a character and entity of its own (cf. Ps. 19:3–5 [Eng. 2–4]).

Nor did Jeremiah curse his father, but only the man who *brought the news*[4] of his birth to his father. The announcement *A child is born to you, a son,* shows that the noun *ben* sometimes means merely *child,* the sex of which is defined here by *zāḵār,* "male" (cf. the sons of Israel, i.e., the whole nation, male or female). For the man of Israel the birth of a son was particularly significant since it guaranteed the perpetuation of the family line. Normally in the ancient Near East, the heir was a son who became the head of the family. Daughters could share in the inheritance (Num. 27:11), but the head of the family was a male. Hence Jeremiah's father would rejoice to learn of the birth of a son.

16–17 The verbs are here translated *Let that man be . . . let him hear,* following the versions. *The cities which Yahweh overthrew* are Sodom and Gomorrah and the other cities of the plain (23:14; Gen. 19:24–28; cf. Isa. 1:9). It is an odd twist to Jeremiah's despair that he could wish a judgment on the man who brought news of his birth to his father like that which fell on Sodom and Gomorrah, *without pity.* He expressed the hope that the whole day should be filled with fearful cries, *a cry of alarm* (*z^e'āqâ*) in the morning, an uproar (or *shout of battle,* *t^erû'â*) at noon, and all because he did not kill Jeremiah in the womb. Such an expression must owe more to literary convention than to actual hatred of an innocent man, but well shows the intensity of Jeremiah's despair. The final part of the line provides a startling picture, that of a mother providing a tomb for her unborn babe.

18 But Jeremiah was born to see only *sorrow* (*'āmāl*) and *trial* (*yāḡôn*) and to end his days in *shame* (*bōšeṯ*).

The whole poem in its final setting comes strangely from the lips of one who had taken his divine call so seriously. Rarely has the question "Why was I ever born?" been asked so tellingly. To his cry of distress and to this poignant question Yahweh gave no answer. But what answer could he give?

4. The verb *biśśar* is neutral and means merely "bring news," whether good or bad.

2. KINGS AND FALSE PROPHETS DENOUNCED (21:1–23:40)

Two significant groups of people in the nation came in for a good deal of castigation from Jeremiah. In the editorial process—when his utterances were collected—these were grouped together into one block. The denunciation of the monarchy is dealt with in 21:1–23:8, and the denunciation of the false prophets in 23:9–40. The oracles and sayings about the monarchy, some in prose and some in poetry, deal with the monarchy in general, and with the last five kings of Judah in particular. In 21:1–22:30 the theme is judgment on the monarchy. In 23:1–4 future renewal and restoration under kings is taken up with a reference to the ideal king who will reign in peace and righteousness, 23:5–6. Finally, in 23:7–8 an announcement is made of the future restoration of the exiles in a new and more wonderful exodus. The sayings come from different times and in some cases may be the result of the editorial treatment of some of Jeremiah's original sayings.

(i) Zedekiah's Inquiry and Jeremiah's Reply (21:1–10)

1 *The word that came to Jeremiah from Yahweh when King Zedekiah sent to him Pashhur ben Malchiah and Zephaniah ben Maaseiah, the priest, with the request.*
2 *"Nebuchadrezzar, king of Babylon, is making war on us. Inquire, please, of Yahweh on our behalf. Perhaps Yahweh will perform for us one of his mighty acts*[1] *and force him to withdraw from us."*[2]
3 *But Jeremiah said to them, "Speak thus to Zedekiah:*
4 *'This is what Yahweh, the God of Israel, has said: I will turn back your weapons of war*[3] *with which you are fighting the king of Babylon and*[4] *the Chaldeans who are pressing you hard outside the wall, and I will gather them*[5] *into the heart of this city.*
5 *And I myself will fight against you with an outstretched hand and a strong arm in anger, wrath, and great fury.*
6 *I will strike down those living in this city, both men and beasts; they shall die*[6] *of a great pestilence.*

1. Lit. "perform with us according to his mighty acts."
2. Lit. "cause him to go up from against us." The present section portrays Jeremiah acting in what might be seen as a seditious manner. Cf. 27:2–15; 34:1–7; 37:3–10; 38:17–18; etc. See the Introduction, under "The 'Seditious' Utterances of Jeremiah," pp. 92–94.
3. MT adds "which are in your hands," lacking in LXX.
4. LXX lacks "the king of Babylon and. . . ."
5. LXX lacks "and I will gather them."
6. LXX, Syr., Targ., and some mss. omit "they shall die."

7 *After that—Yahweh's word—I will hand over Zedekiah king of Judah, and his officials,*[7] *and such of the people of this city*[8] *as have survived the pestilence, the sword, and the famine, to Nebuchadrezzar the king of Babylon,*[9] *to their enemies, and to those who seek their lives. He will put them to the sword without pity, mercy, or compassion.'*[10]

8 *You shall say to this people: 'This is what Yahweh has said: I offer you a choice between the way of life and the way of death.*

9 *Whoever stays in this city will die by the sword, by famine, or by pestilence, but whoever goes out and surrenders to the Chaldeans who are besieging you will live; he shall at least save his life.*

10 *I have set my face against this city purposing evil and not good—Yahweh's word. It will be handed over to the king of Babylon and he will burn it with fire.' "*

The passage is in prose, and relates to an incident which took place when Jerusalem came under the Chaldean blockade in late 589 or early 588 B.C. After the disturbances of 594 B.C. (chs. 27, 28) nothing is recorded of Jeremiah's ministry till this incident. Then in 589 B.C. Zedekiah showed signs of rebellion against Nebuchadrezzar, encouraged by the promise of Egyptian help and urged on by his nobles. Nebuchadrezzar soon reacted, perhaps late in 589 B.C., and by January 588 (52:4) his armies were in Judah and had commenced operations against Jerusalem (2 K. 25) and against the cities of Judah. The campaign went on through the winter and spring of 588 B.C. By the end of that time the land was in a desperate plight. In these circumstances Zedekiah sought the advice of Jeremiah (cf. 37:3–10, 17–21; 38:14–28). In neither case was the king given much assurance of deliverance.

In the sections that follow in 21:11–23:8 the whole question of Judah's recent kings is discussed. Thus, the present segment 21:1–10 provides a picture of the endpoint of a sad process, which is reviewed immediately in 21:11–23:8.

For the present prose passage, as for other prose passages throughout the book with their characteristic prose style, the question of final authorship is raised.[11] There can be little doubt that

7. Heb. *'ᵃḇāḏîm,* lit. "servants."

8. Following LXX, which omits the *wᵉ'eṯ* which MT places between *hā'ām* and *hanniš'ārîm.*

9. LXX omits "into the hand of Nebuchadrezzar the king of Babylon."

10. The text has three verbal expressions here, *lō' yāḥûs* ("he will not show pity"), *lō' yaḥmōl* ("he will not show mercy"), *lō' yᵉraḥēm* ("he will not show compassion").

11. See the Introduction, "The Book of Jeremiah: Composition," pp. 33–50.

Jeremiah would have raised the very issues that are discussed here, in particular the inevitability of Yahweh's judgment upon his people. Hence it may be accepted that the passage does not distort Jeremiah's message even if its present shape is due to editors.

1 The *Pashhur ben Malchiah* here is not to be confused with Pashhur ben Immer of 20:1–6. The present Pashhur was bitterly opposed to Jeremiah and attempted later to have him executed for treason (38:1–13). *Zephaniah ben Maaseiah the priest* was a member of another delegation to Jeremiah later (37:3). He does not seem to have been hostile to the prophet. He is referred to in 29:25–26 as the "overseer" *(pāqîḏ)* who was accused of failing to discipline Jeremiah. Shemaiah, one of those deported in 597 B.C., laid the charge, complaining about Jeremiah's letter to the exiles (29:1ff.) and demanding suitable action by Zephaniah against him.

2 The verb *inquire (dāraš)* is regularly used for the process of discovering the mind of Yahweh. It is used in a variety of contexts in the OT (Gen. 25:22; Exod. 18:15; Deut. 4:29; 12:5; 1 Sam. 9:9; 1 K. 22:5, 7–8; 2 K. 3:11; 8:8; 22:13; Isa. 31:1; 55:6; 65:10; Hos. 10:12; Amos 5:4–6; etc.). Zedekiah had in mind a former occasion when Jerusalem was besieged by Sennacherib and the Assyrian armies in 701 B.C., more than a century earlier (2 K. 19:35–36; Isa. 37:36–37). On that occasion Yahweh performed one of his *mighty acts (nip̱lā'ôṯ)* and forced Sennacherib to withdraw. The present situation was much the same and called for another miracle. This time it was the Chaldeans and their king who were attacking Jerusalem. *Nebuchadrezzar* is the more correct form of the king's name (Akk. Nabu-kadurri-uṣur) and occurs several times in these chapters (21:2, 7; 22:25; 25:9). Elsewhere the name appears as Nebuchadnezzar (27:6, 8, 20; 28:3, 11, 14; 29:1, 3). He ruled in Babylon 605–562 B.C. and was the son and successor of Nabopolassar (626–605 B.C.), who was the first ruler of the neo-Babylonian empire.[12]

3–4 Yahweh's answer destroyed all hope. He would *turn back* (repel) Judah's feeble forces *(weapons)* which were attempting to stem the onrush of the powerful Chaldean armies (15:12), and would draw them back (lit. *gather*) into the city. The significance of *them* is not clear. On the surface it seems to refer to the *weapons*, that is, Judah's troops who, at this stage, were still able to operate outside the walls and harass the Chaldeans. But it could equally

12. See the Introduction, "Jeremiah in His Historical Setting," pp. 9–22.

well refer to the Chaldean armies who would be gathered into the city. In v. 4 the sentence is long and complex in Hebrew. LXX is shorter and gives a smoother text.[13] MT includes the expression "the weapons of war which are in your hands," that is, Judah's troops. The translation of *ṣārîm* can hardly be "besieging," since the context shows that the siege had not begun. Hence translate *pressing hard* or "blockading."

5 An interesting point here is that Yahweh says *I will fight* against you. But he would use the Chaldean armies as his agents. The expression *with an outstretched hand and a strong arm* occurs also in 32:21 but with the adjectives reversed (cf. 27:5; 32:17, where *kōaḥ,* "power," replaces "hand"). Similar expressions occur elsewhere in the OT, in Exod. 6:6 ("arm" alone), often in Deuteronomy (both "arm" and "hand," Deut. 4:34; 5:15; 7:19; 26:8; etc.), and elsewhere (1 K. 8:42; 2 K. 17:36). The picture is an ancient one and may go back to the Holy War idea.[14] Jeremiah may well have used such expressions, since he was as much an inheritor of ancient traditions as were the writers of the so-called Deuteronomic literature.[15] The general thrust of the expression is that Yahweh will act with irresistible force. The fury of the final assault on the city is expressed by the use of three nouns, *anger ('ap̱), wrath (ḥēmâ),* and *great fury (qeṣep̱ gāḏôl).*

6–7 Yahweh himself, through his agent, elsewhere called "Nebuchadrezzar my servant" (43:10; cf. Isa. 45:1), would strike down man and beast, who would die in a great plague *(deḇer).* The king, his courtiers, and those who survived the plague *(deḇer),* the sword *(ḥereḇ),* and starvation *(rā'āḇ),* would be handed over to Nebuchadrezzar, who would slay them without pity, mercy, or compassion. The building up of nouns in blocks of three which is characteristic of this passage (vv. 6, 7) adds vividness and emphasis to the grim picture. The *officials ('ᵃḇāḏîm)* who were to accompany Zedekiah were his "courtiers." The term (lit. "servants") often has a political sense. The picture in these verses accords with 2 K. 25.

13. See textual notes.
14. R. de Vaux, *Ancient Israel,* pp. 258–265.
15. In much modern discussion great emphasis is placed on the Deuteronomic literature and its editors. A recent discussion is that of E. W. Nicholson, *Preaching to the Exiles: A Study of the Prose Tradition in the Book of Jeremiah.* There is a need to ask questions about Jeremiah's own literary traditions. These may well be the same as or similar to the "Deuteronomic editors." There is a great danger of arguing in circles in the discussion about the prose of Jeremiah. See the Introduction, pp. 29–32.

Nebuchadrezzar was a typical Near Eastern potentate when it came to the brutal treatment of his conquered enemies.

8–10 A short statement addressed to the general population follows. It is similar to that in 38:2–3. No doubt Jeremiah gave the same advice on more than one occasion. He offered the people a choice, literally "I set before you *the way of life* or *the way of death.*" (No choice is given in 38:2–3 but merely a statement of the facts.) The expression is common in Wisdom Literature and elsewhere (cf. Deut. 30:15–20, where the choice concerned obedience to the terms of the covenant). It is of some interest that although the words here are in prose, they are regarded as genuinely from Jeremiah by some who argue strongly that much of the prose in this book comes from Deuteronomic editors.[16] Jeremiah's advice to the people to surrender to the Chaldeans has sometimes led to speculation on his political orientation. He was certainly regarded as a traitor (38:17–21), yet when the nation fell in 587 B.C. he chose to remain in the land to work for the future renewal of the nation (cf. 40:1–6; 42:7–22). His basic principle was simple. Yahweh had abandoned his people because of their infidelity and disloyalty and therefore Jerusalem's downfall was inevitable. When Jeremiah counselled surrender he called for the nation to accept God's judgment, which was the first step toward future renewal. On the pragmatic level, slaughter could be avoided only by nonresistance and peaceful surrender, but this was neither political nor military, nor was it out of any pro-Babylonian orientation. The judgment of Yahweh on the nation was inevitable and would be realized through the success of the Babylonians (cf. 27:1–22).

The last part of v. 9 is unusual. It reads literally "his life will be his for booty." The expression is a military metaphor, occurring also in 38:2; 39:18; and 45:5. Victorious armies normally brought home booty, but in defeat they could say that their only booty was their life. In Jeremiah's view, surrender to the Chaldeans would allow the people to escape with their lives at least. Yahweh had set his face against the city and the result would be disaster *(rā'â, evil)* and not deliverance *(ṭôḇâ, good)*. It would be destroyed by fire.

A further word to Zedekiah along similar lines comes in 34:1–7.[17]

16. See E. W. Nicholson, *Jeremiah 1–25,* p. 176.

17. J. Bright, *Jeremiah,* p. 214, who rearranges some of Jeremiah's material in the interests of chronology, places 34:1–10 immediately following 21:1–10 in his commentary, and treats 21:11–14; 22:1–30; 23:1–40 after ch. 20.

(ii) *The Duties of the King (21:11–12) and An Oracle against Jerusalem (21:13–14)*

11 *"And to the royal house of Judah: 'Hear the word of Yahweh;*
12 *O house of David! This is what Yahweh has said:*
"Administer justice every morning,
Rescue from the oppressor the man who is robbed,
Lest my wrath break out like fire
And burn unquenched
Because of your evil deeds.[1]
13 *Look, I am against you enthroned above the valley*
And the rocky plateau—Yahweh's word—
You who say, 'Who can descend upon us?
Who can enter our lairs?'
14 *I will punish you as your deeds deserve—Yahweh's word;*[2]
I will kindle fire in her forest,
And it will consume everything round about her." ' "

Two things are in view here: the royal house of Judah and the royal city, Jerusalem. The section 21:11–22:9 is a general address to the royal house outlining the duties of the king (21:12; 22:1–9) and making a brief remark about his capital. Throughout the section the word *house (bayiṯ)* occurs several times, but sometimes in the sense of "dynasty" and sometimes of "palace." In the following sections the kings Shallum, Jehoiakim, Jehoiachin, and Zedekiah are passed in review to provide a background to 21:1–10, where Zedekiah was advised that there was no hope of a miracle of deliverance because of the gross national evils of the years past.

11 The title *To the royal house of Judah* and its counterpart in 23:9a "To the prophets" suggest that these two segments once had an independent existence and that they were brought here by the editor in order both to preserve important words of Jeremiah and also to build up a neat literary form extending from 21:1 to 23:8. The word *house* means "dynasty."

12 *House* here too means "dynasty." The fundamental responsibility of a king to administer *justice (mišpāṭ)* is stated. The expression "in the morning" *(labbōqer)* means "daily" or "regularly" but draws attention to the custom of adjudicating cases in the morning in the city gate (cf. Amos 4:4; Ps. 59:17 [Eng. 16]; etc.). The administration of justice was one of the main duties of kings all over

1. This phrase is lacking in LXX.
2. The first line is lacking in LXX.

the Near East. The king was the guardian of justice. In Israel there is a constant stress on this obligation. Solomon in his prayer to Yahweh asked for an understanding mind to discern between good and evil (1 K. 3:9; 8:32). The story in 1 K. 3:16–28 shows how royal discernment worked in one particular case. Several of the royal psalms stress the importance of justice (Ps. 45:5–9 [Eng. 4–8]; 72:1–4, 12–14; etc.). The prophets raised the question of social injustice on many occasions and called on kings to exercise justice (Amos 5:11–13; Isa. 1:17; Mic. 3:9–12; etc.). It is clear from Deut. 17:14–20 that the essence of authentic kingship was faithfulness to the covenant. A copy of the law was to remain with the king to be read daily so that he might understand and keep the statutes and commandments of the covenant. Failure to keep the covenant would result in judgment (v. 14; Ps. 132:12). One of the striking features of the reign of the Messiah would be his care to administer justice (23:5–6; Isa. 9:6–7; 11:1–4; etc.). In his day he would rescue from the oppressor the man who had been robbed.

Yahweh's judgment is likened to an unquenchable fire. It was a common metaphor for divine judgment and was used often by Jeremiah (4:4; 17:4, 27; 21:12, 14; 43:12; 49:27; etc.). These last three phrases all occur also in 4:4.

13 The *you* of this section is second person singular, feminine, and must refer to the city Jerusalem.[3] Cities were the "mother" of their inhabitants, and the villages round about were "daughters." The word "fire" in the next verse provides a link between v. 12 and vv. 13–14 (see also 22:7). There are some topographical problems here. Jerusalem was surrounded on the west, south, and east by deep valleys. Only in the north did it need defense. The expression "inhabitant of the Valley" does not appear to suit the topography although no doubt some citizens dwelt in the valley. Heb. *yōšeḇeṯ hā'ēmeq* could have an analogy in *yōšēḇ hakkᵉruḇîm* ("enthroned on/above the cherubim," 1 Sam. 4:4; 2 Sam. 6:2; etc.). Hence Jerusalem could be thought of as *enthroned above the valley*. The next colon contains the expression *ṣûr hammîšōr,* translated in AV as "rock of the plain." The word *mîšôr* may also be translated "pla-

3. There are some unusual shifts in the person of address in vv. 12–14. In v. 12 we have 2nd masc. plur., in v. 13a 2nd fem. sing., in vv. 13b–14a 2nd masc. plur., and in v. 14b 3rd fem. singular. The points of reference can be explained, but the alternation is considerable within a very brief space. See the commentary.

teau, tableland," and hence the whole expression as *rocky plateau,* a reference to the relatively level area on which Jerusalem stood.[4] The question *who can descend (nḥt) upon us* and *enter our lairs (mᵉʿônôṯ)?* may have some precise topographical overtone, for invaders came down upon Jerusalem from the hill country to the north. On the other hand the expression may be very general.

14 The first line is lacking in LXX but the context requires something like this after v. 13b. The *you* here is second masculine plural and refers to the people of Jerusalem. The noun *forest (yaʿar)* raises a question. Some commentators have proposed that the reference is to the royal palace, which is called in 1 K. 7:2 the "House of the Forest of Lebanon" because of the considerable quantity of cedar used in its construction. In that case "surroundings" *(everything round about her)* may refer to the city. Certainly in Jerusalem itself there was no forest, although there may have been forests on the hills about.

(iii) The Duties of the King, continued (22:1–9)

1 *This is what Yahweh has said: "Go down to the palace of the king of Judah and there speak this word.*

2 *Say, 'Hear the word of Yahweh, O king of Judah, you who sit on the throne of David—you and your officials*[1] *and your people who enter these gates.*

3 *This is what Yahweh has said: Act justly and fairly,*[2] *rescue from the oppressor the man who has been robbed. Do not ill-treat or do violence to the resident alien, the orphan, or the widow, or shed innocent blood in this place.*

4 *For if you scrupulously carry out this commission,*[3] *then kings who sit on David's throne will enter the gates of this palace riding in chariots and on horses—they and their officials and people.*

5 *But if you do not listen to these words, I swear—Yahweh's word—that this palace will become a ruin.' "*

4. It is possible, of course, that stereotyped expressions were used which were broadly applicable though not perfectly correct. See expressions used of Moab in 48:8, 21, 28–29.

1. Heb. *ʿᵃḇāḏîm,* lit. "servants." The king's servants here, as regularly in such a context, were his *officials* or courtiers. LXX reads "your house," which may be a reference to the dynasty. The *people* denotes the citizens or subjects.

2. Lit. "Perform justice and right."

3. Lit. "word." The word *scrupulously* is an attempt to convey the force of the infinitive absolute construction.

6 *For this is what Yahweh has said concerning the palace of the king of Judah:*
"You are like Gilead to me
Or the heights of Lebanon,
Yet I swear[4] I will make you a wilderness with abandoned towns,
7 *I will commission against you destroyers,*
Each man with his weapons,
And they will cut down your choicest cedars
And bring them down in the fire."
8 *"And many foreign peoples will pass by this city and will say to one another: 'Why has Yahweh done such a thing to this great city?'*
9 *And they will answer, 'Because they forsook the covenant of Yahweh their God, and worshipped other gods and served them.' "*

The brief statement of the duties of the king begun in 21:11–12 now continues. It leads quite naturally into a discussion of the three kings Jehoahaz (Shallum), Jehoiakim, and Jehoiachin (Coniah), and to an expression of promises for the future of the Davidic dynasty and the people (23:1–8). The segment 22:1–5, 8 is in prose while vv. 6–7 are poetic. The prose segment in vv. 1–5 has been taken by many commentators as a Deuteronomic composition, perhaps an expansion of 21:11–12. It is seen as expressing the demand of these authors that kings should adhere to God's law (cf. Deut. 17:18–20).[5] It ought to be said that such a view was held by prophetic groups in Israel over the centuries. Jeremiah certainly held this view. The constant recourse of some commentators to the theory of Deuteronomic authorship whenever such views are expressed in prose seems to deny that others could have similar views.

1–2 The word *bayiṯ* here means *palace*. The king is addressed as *you who sit on the throne of David*. Judah's royal line was a Davidic line. It would be restored as such (23:5; Ezek. 34:23; etc.). The word is addressed also to the officials and the people. The passage suggests much coming and going through the palace gates each day, no doubt for affairs of state and for the administration of justice (21:12; cf. 17:24–27).

3 The demand on the king was to administer justice *(mišpāṭ)* and "fair dealing" *(ṣ^e^ḏāqâ)*. These were significant terms in ancient Israelite thinking and are often linked together in the OT. Both terms have a background in the covenant law, *mišpāṭ* having particular

4. Heb. *'im lō'*, lit. "if not." This was part of an oath formula which appears in such expressions as "The Lord do such and such to me *if* I do *not* do such and such."
5. E. W. Nicholson, *Jeremiah 1–25*, p. 181.

reference to the covenant laws and statutes which it was the duty of judges and kings to administer, and *ṣ^eḏāqâ* having to do with what was right and according to the norm. In meaning they often overlap. The *ṣaddîq* in Israel was the man who did what was right according to the norms and standards of Yahweh. The king, and indeed the whole nation, were required always to act in justice and in fairness, giving consideration to all the facts (cf. the ideal king in Isa. 11:3b–5). Part of the total task was to establish justice and fair play for others, particularly for those who could not defend themselves against the oppressor, *to rescue from the oppressor the man who has been robbed*. The *resident alien (gēr)*, the *orphan (yāṯôm)*, and the *widow ('almānâ)* were not to be ill-treated or treated violently *(ḥāmas)*, nor was *innocent blood* to be shed, possibly a reference to the nefarious practices in the valley of Ben-hinnom associated with false worship at Topheth[6] (7:31; 19:3–15). The protection of these three classes is part of the covenant stipulation (Exod. 22:21–26; 23:9; Lev. 19:33–34; Deut. 10:18–19; 24:17). The king was as much obligated to fulfil the demands of the Sinai Covenant as were the people. The Davidic covenant (2 Sam. 7) was no different in this respect from the Mosaic covenant.

4–5 The continuance of the royal house depended on a wholehearted acceptance of the commission Jeremiah laid before the king. Only then would the gates of the *palace (bayiṯ)* remain open for kings, officials, and people to pass to and fro. Failure to heed the words of the prophet would result in the palace becoming a *ruin (ḥorbâ)*. That was Yahweh's sworn word (lit. "I have sworn by myself").

6–7 A brief poetic section is inserted between two prose portions. The palace was as *Gilead* and *Lebanon* to Yahweh. Both places were renowned for their forests. The royal palace was built with timbers from these areas. Massive cedar pillars and beams supported the "House of the Forest of Lebanon" (1 K. 7:2–5; Isa. 22:8) and perhaps other buildings in the whole palace complex (cf. 22:14). But despite the grandeur of the palace, which was something like the grandeur of the forests of Gilead and Lebanon, Yahweh would make it a *wilderness (miḏbār)*, with *abandoned towns*. He would *commission (qiddēš*, lit. "sanctify, set apart")[7] destroyers equipped

6. It is not impossible that the reference is to judicial killings of people against whom unproven capital charges were laid.
7. See 6:4 where the same word "sanctify" is used in reference to preparing a battle.

with their weapons of destruction to cut down the *choicest (miḇḥar) cedars* and *bring them down* (fell them) *in the fire*. In a sense, therefore, the Babylonians were "woodcutters." Ps. 74 is a vivid poetic portrayal of the way the Babylonians destroyed the temple with axes, hatchets, and hammers.

8–9 Another short prose section closes the introductory comments before discussion is undertaken about the individual kings.[8] The particular way of describing the calamity is to be found in various parts of the OT. Many foreigners *(gôyîm)* passing by the city ask why Yahweh would do such a thing to this great city. The answer is simple. The people *forsook ('āzaḇ) the covenant (b^e rîṯ) of Yahweh their God, and worshipped* ("prostrated themselves before") *other gods and served them*. The breach of Yahweh's covenant is clearly in view. The terms "prostrate oneself before" *(hištaḥ^a wâ)* and "serve" *('āḇaḏ)* are also used repeatedly in reference to Yahweh. In terms of the secular picture of a vassal paying homage to his suzerain, the vassal prostrates himself before the suzerain and serves him. The secular picture provided a suitable and powerful metaphor to describe the relationship between Israel and Yahweh. Idolatry such as that depicted here is basically a breach of the covenant (Exod. 20:3; Deut. 5:7).

(iv) Concerning Jehoahaz (Shallum) (22:10–12)

10 *Weep not for the dead nor bemoan him;*
Weep rather for him who has gone away,
For he will never come back again,
Never again see his native land.
11 *For this is what Yahweh has said concerning Shallum ben Josiah, king of Judah, who succeeded his father Josiah on the throne. "He has gone away from this place. He will never return to it again.*
12 *In the place to which they have deported him he will die and will never see this land again."*

This is the first of the segments on the kings known to Jeremiah. Verse 10 is a poetic piece followed by a prose passage (vv. 11–12) which interprets it.

8. The form, language, and content are markedly Deuteronomic, similar to 1 K. 9:8–9 according to scholars who hold this view. See E. W. Nicholson, *Jeremiah 1–25*, p. 183. The fact of similar language being used in many parts of the OT is undisputed. What this means is a debatable question. See the Introduction, "The Book of Jeremiah: Composition," pp. 33–50.

10 The *dead* (singular) refers to Josiah, who was slain at Megiddo in 609 B.C. (2 K. 23:29–30). The one *who has gone away* is Jehoahaz his son, who succeeded Josiah on his death but was almost immediately deposed by Pharaoh Necho and deported to Egypt three months later (2 K. 23:31–35). Shallum was his personal name, Jehoahaz his throne name. According to 1 Chr. 3:15 Jehoahaz was Josiah's fourth son, who had been put on the throne "by the people of the land" (2 Chr. 36:1) after the death of his father. Some internal political conflict lay behind this. It is possible that Jehoahaz followed his father's reforming policy and was placed on the throne by a faction that supported the reform. This would have been anti-Egyptian in outlook. Jeremiah regarded the deportation of Jehoahaz as more serious than the death of Josiah, and would have the people transfer their mourning from Josiah to the exiled king.

The international picture helps in understanding events in Judah. The Babylonian Chronicle makes it clear that in 609 B.C. the last king of Assyria, Ashur-uballit, was under severe pressure in Haran with the Chaldean armies pressing in on him.[1] Egypt hurried to help him, evidently recognizing the danger of the Chaldean advance. This brought Necho into Palestine, and he quickly assumed control of Syria-Palestine and set up his headquarters at Riblah (the modern Rable) some 47 miles south of Hama. He called Jehoahaz to meet him there, then deposed him and sent him in chains to Egypt.[2]

11–12 The short prose passage vv. 11–12 may be taken as a parallel tradition which expresses the thoughts of the poem in more precise terms. Nothing more is heard of Jehoahaz, in contrast to Jehoiachin (see commentary on vv. 24–30).

(v) Concerning Jehoiakim (22:13–19)

13 "*Woe to him who builds his house without right*[1]
And his upper rooms without justice,[2]
Who makes his fellow work for nothing
And does not pay him any wage;

1. D. J. Wiseman, *Chronicles of Chaldaean Kings,* p. 63.
2. See J. Bright, *A History of Israel*², p. 303; M. Noth, *The History of Israel*², p. 279.

1. MT *ṣeḏeq*.
2. MT *mišpāṭ*.

14 *Who says, 'I will build a spacious house for myself*[3]
With airy roof-chambers.'
So he widens its windows,[4]
panels it with cedar,
And paints it bright red.
15 *Does that make you a king*
That you outdo everyone in cedar?[5]
Think of your father:[6] *he ate and drank*
And dealt justly and fairly—
All went well with him.[7]
16 *He dispensed justice to the poor and needy;*[8]
Is not this what it means to know me?
—Yahweh's word.
17 *But you have no eyes and no thought*
Except for personal gain,
For shedding innocent blood,
And for perpetrating acts of extortion and tyranny."
18 *So this is what Yahweh has said concerning Jehoiakim*
ben Josiah, king of Judah:[9]
"They will not lament for him,
'Ah my brother!' or 'Ah sister!'
They will not lament for him,
'Ah father!' or 'Ah mother!'[10]
19 *He will be buried with a donkey's burial,*
Dragged out and dumped
Outside the gates of Jerusalem."

3. LXX reads "you have built for yourself" and begins the direct address here, rather than at v. 15.
4. Read *ḥallônāw* for *ḥallônāy* (haplography?). The other verbs here may be read as infinitive absolute and translated as present tense, *sāpôn,* "panelling," and *māšôaḥ,* "painting." LXX reads passive participles in each case, "fitted with windows . . . panelled . . . painted. . . ."
5. MT reads lit. "Though you compete in cedar." Cf. NEB "if your cedar is more splendid" *(mᵉtaḥᵃreh).*
6. In the text one word appears, "Your father"; but for the sense we need to insert something else like "Think of . . . ," "Now what about. . . ."
7. MT reads *'āz ṭôḇ lô* at the end of v. 15, and *'āz ṭôḇ* after the first colon of v. 16. LXX omits these words in the second occurrence but has similar words before the phrase *and dealt justly and fairly,* that is, Josiah ate and drank, "and found pleasure in these" (it was pleasant for him), and yet he dealt justly and fairly.
8. MT adds "then it was well" (see previous note).
9. LXX inserts "Woe to this man" at the beginning of the judgment.
10. This translation of the last formula has been proposed by M. Dahood, "Two Textual Notes on Jeremiah," *CBQ* 23 (1961), pp. 462–64, taking *'āḏôn* in the sense of *father* and reading *hôrâ, mother,* for *hōḏōh,* "his majesty." The king was often spoken of in the ancient Near East as father, mother, brother to his people. Two important Phoenician documents demonstrate that it was the duty of the king to be father, mother, brother, and sister to his people.

This passage is almost completely poetic. It probably comprises two short oracles, the first condemning Jehoiakim for his injustice, avarice, and tyranny (vv. 13–17), and the second (vv. 18b, 19), introduced by a brief prose section (v. 18a), announcing a terrible judgment on him. Jehoiakim was condemned by Jeremiah more severely than any other king. He seems to have been a typical Oriental despot[11] who rejected Josiah's reforms. He must have been pro-Egyptian in his political policy, for Necho chose him to succeed his brother Jehoahaz (2 K. 23:34). Jeremiah contrasts him with his father Josiah and has no difficulty in showing that whereas Josiah approached the model of true kingship, Jehoiakim was far from that model. In reference to the high standards set out in 21:12 and 22:3, he was a failure and fell under Yahweh's condemnation. The date of this oracle is probably early in the reign of Jehoiakim.

13 Jeremiah's first attack is on the luxurious buildings erected by Jehoiakim. He stresses the terms *right (ṣeḏeq)* and *justice (mišpāṭ)* which feature so prominently in 21:12 and 22:3, but has to prefix these by *without (lō')*. NEB translates, "by unjust means" and "by fraud"; cf. RSV, "by unrighteousness" and "by injustice." Jehoiakim accomplished the work by making his fellows labor for nothing. There is a strong democratic note here in that the king is called the *fellow (rēa')* of his builder. The freedom and rights of the individual Israelite were supposed to be guarded by the king as well as by his subjects. It was one of Solomon's grave offenses that he forced many of his fellows to build for him in Jerusalem and elsewhere (1 K. 5:13–14; 12:3–4). Such slavery was an offense against covenant law (Lev. 19:13; Deut. 24:14–15). It was the king's duty to secure the observance of this law, but in fact he himself was guilty of its violation.

It is reasonable to ask what buildings might have been in view. Nothing is known archeologically about buildings in Jerusalem itself, which would have suffered severely from the many attacks on the city over the centuries. Excavations at Ramat Raḥel in recent years have brought to light evidence of some fine structures from the end of the seventh century which would illustrate the point made by Jeremiah and may well have been the work of Jehoiakim.[12] Level five of the excavation dates from about 600 B.C. Here stood a fortress

11. W. Rudolph, *Jeremia*, p. 121.
12. Y. Aharoni, "Excavations at Ramat Raḥel," *BA* 24 (1961), p. 118; W. F. Albright, "Some Recent Publications on the Archaeology of Palestine," *BASOR* 170 (1963), p. 67; "Chronique Archéologique," *RB* 70 (1963), p. 574.

of the late Israelite period with an exterior wall made of fine masonry, a gateway, and a large building inside. A significant collection of stamped jar handles was found, some bearing the two-winged royal sign and the letters *lmlk ḥbrn,* "belonging to the king. Hebron." The excavator draws attention to Jer. 22:13–19 in his report. One wonders where the king obtained funds to build his spacious buildings, since he was required to pay heavy tribute to his Egyptian overlord (2 K. 23:33–35). At least the labor cost him nothing, because his fellows worked for *nothing (ḥinnām)* and did not receive a *wage (pōʿal)* for their work. Jehoiakim, who was only twenty-five years old when he began to reign and only thirty-six when he died (2 K. 23:36), was evidently a thoroughly spoiled and self-indulgent young despot.

14 Jehoiakim wanted to build *a spacious house.* Some of the details given in this verse are capable of different translations. The verb *qāraʿ* in the second line generally means "rend" or "tear" and has often been translated as "cut out" (AV, RV, RSV). The same verb in 4:30 means "widen" or "enlarge" (cf. "enlarge" the eyes with paint), so perhaps we are right to translate *he widens its windows.*

Panelling with cedar and painting with bright red or vermillion *(šāšar)* was a regular method of ornamentation (cf. Ezek. 23:14).

15–16 The contrast with Josiah begins at this point. LXX differs widely from MT, and the translation is conjectural in some places (see textual notes on v. 15); but the main thrust is clear.

Jeremiah makes the point that display of this kind, outdoing everyone in cedar, does not make a man a king. *Think of your father* (Josiah). He lived as a king should, *he ate and drank* (i.e., he lived well), and yet he attended to the important kingly duties of justice *(mišpāṭ)* and right *(ṣeḏeq),* that is, he administered these fundamental aspects of national life. And *all went well with him;* he did not need to outdo other rulers of his day or even his predecessors in luxurious living to be a good king. He was no ascetic but lived as befitted his royal status. But he took his obligations of kingship seriously. In particular he dispensed justice for the *poor (ʿonî)* and *needy (ʾeḇyôn)* (cf. 22:3). This was the true knowledge of God. To *know (yāḏaʿ)* God was to enter into a deep relationship of personal commitment, and this involved a concern to obey the stipulations of the covenant. In Jeremiah's view Josiah displayed such a knowledge. Jehoiakim did not. Such a eulogy suggests that Jeremiah was sympathetic to a degree with Josiah's reform.

17 Here is a scathing exposure of Jehoiakim's evil ways. His only concern was for personal gain, for shedding innocent blood (2 K. 24:3–4), and for acts of extortion and tyranny (cf. 22:3). He was bent on rejecting the covenant law. One of the underlying motifs of ch. 36 is this wanton rejection of the word of God by Jehoiakim. In his day he had the prophet Uriah slain (26:20–23).

18 Dire judgment is pronounced on this impious ruler. It is "woe to this man."[13] The word "woe" *(hôy)* appears four times in the Hebrew text. Jeremiah made the point that the regular form of lament would not be used for this king (cf. 1 K. 13:30).

19 The final words referring to a *donkey's burial* raise some questions. According to 36:30 the dead body of Jehoiakim was to be cast out to the heat by day and the frost by night. But according to 2 K. 24:6 "he slept with his fathers," which suggests a normal burial. This, however, may have been merely a stereotyped formula used in Kings at the end of a reign. It would appear from the Babylonian Chronicle that Nebuchadrezzar marched on Jerusalem in December 598 B.C.,[14] by which time Jehoiakim was already dead and Jehoiachin was on the throne (2 K. 24:5–10). A ready solution is that as the Babylonian armies approached, the pro-Babylonian party in Jerusalem organized an assassination of Jehoiakim in a palace revolt. At the time Jehoiakim had rebelled against Nebuchadrezzar (2 K. 24:1). In that case an ignominious death may have been followed by an ignominious burial, although in such circumstances an official burial could easily have been described by Jeremiah as the burial of an ass *(qᵉḇûraṯ ḥᵃmôr)*.[15] The statement that he would be *dragged out and dumped outside the gates of Jerusalem* accords well with the statement in 36:30.

(vi) Jerusalem's Doom (22:20–23)

20 *"Go up to Lebanon and cry out!*
In Bashan raise your voice;
Cry aloud from Abarim,
For all your 'lovers' are broken.
21 *I spoke to you in your prosperity;*
You said 'I will not listen.'
But this has been your way from your youth,

13. LXX; lacking in MT.
14. D. J. Wiseman, *Chronicles of Chaldaean Kings,* p. 73.
15. See W. F. Albright, "King Joiachin in Exile," *BA* 5 (1942), p. 49; J. Bright, *A History of Israel,* p. 386; J. P. Hyatt, "New Light on Nebuchadnezzar and Judaean History," *JBL* 75 (1956), p. 279.

For you have never listened to my voice.
22 *All your shepherds the wind shall shepherd,*
And your 'lovers' shall go into exile.
Then you will be put to shame and disgraced
Because of all your wickedness.[1]
23 *You dwellers in Lebanon,*
Who make your nests among the cedars,
How you will groan[2] *when the pains come upon you,*
Pangs like childbirth!"

The poetic section vv. 20–23 refers to Jerusalem. Grammatically the verbs and suffixes are second person feminine. As is common, Jerusalem is personified as a woman. Whether this was once an independent oracle or not, its position here is appropriate. After the trenchant criticism of Jehoiakim, his own doom and the doom of his capital would seem inevitable. But a date of composition not far from 597 B.C., shortly before the fall of Jerusalem to Nebuchadrezzar and the deportation of the first group of Judeans to Babylon along with Jehoiachin, seems likely. The passage about Jehoiachin follows immediately in vv. 24–30.

20 Jerusalem is ordered to bewail her doom far and wide, away to the north in *Lebanon,* to the northeast in *Bashan* in Transjordan, and in *Abarim,* the mountain range in Moab overlooking the Dead Sea of which Mount Nebo was the main peak. Moses viewed the promised land from here (Num. 27:12; Deut. 32:49).

The *"lovers"* are her political allies,[3] who have been *broken* (cf. Hos. 8:9). The reference may be to Egypt, but perhaps to other minor groups such as those who staged the revolt referred to in ch. 27. Nebuchadrezzar routed all these after the collapse of Egyptian forces at Carchemish in 605 B.C. (46:2–12). Ashkelon followed (47:2–7). Areas in Transjordan were soon vassals of Nebuchadrezzar (cf. 2 K. 24:1–2). Jerusalem was deserted, isolated and alone.

21 The cause of Jerusalem's doom lay in the refusal of the people to obey Yahweh ever since their beginnings (cf. 2:31; 3:24; 7:24–25; 11:7–13). It was only a matter of time before the divine judgment would fall.

1. LXX reads "in the eyes of *(apó)* all your friends" (Heb. *rēʿa),* a possible vocalization enhanced by the context and by the preposition *min.*

2. M. Dahood, "Ugaritic Studies and the Bible," *Gregorianum* 43 (1962), pp. 55–79, refers to an Ugaritic root *nḥn,* "groan."

3. See J. A. Thompson, "The Significance of the Verb *Love* in the David-Jonathan Narratives in I Samuel," *VT* 24 (1974), pp. 334–38.

22 There is an unusual metaphor here: *Your shepherds (rō'îm) the wind shall shepherd (tir'eh),* that is, round them up and drive them away. The shepherds are the leaders and nobility of Jerusalem, who were, in fact, deported in 597 B.C. (2 K. 24:22–25:7). Then Jerusalem would be *put to shame*[4] and disgraced because of all her *wickedness (rā'â).* If alternative meanings are allowed we might translate "then you will be judged worthy of shame and be disgraced because of your calamities,"[5] that is, the very fact of the destruction of the city would be a proof that she had been adjudged worthy of shame.

23 *Lebanon* is here used figuratively for Jerusalem itself (cf. v. 6) and not as in v. 20 of the land of Lebanon. The *cedars* is a reference to the fine palaces and buildings, which used large amounts of cedar. There was so much cedar from Lebanon in Jerusalem that Jerusalem was a little Lebanon. Perhaps there was another facet to the metaphor. Jerusalem was compared to the high cedars of Lebanon. Ezekiel in particular applied the comparison to the Davidic dynasty in general (Ezek. 17). The metaphor of the female continues with that most characteristic of a woman's experiences, the *pains (ḥeḇel)* and *pangs (ḥîl)* of a woman in childbirth.

(vii) Concerning Jehoiachin (Coniah) (22:24–30)

24 *"As I live—Yahweh's word—Coniah ben Jehoiakim king of Judah shall not be the signet ring on my right hand. Yes, Coniah, I will pull you off,*
25 *and I will hand you over to those who seek your life and of whom you are afraid, (to Nebuchadrezzar king of Babylon and)*[1] *to the Chaldeans.*
26 *And I will hurl you and the mother who bore you into (another)*[2] *country, where neither of you was born, and you will die there.*
27 *To the land to which they desperately long to return they will never return."*

4. The verb *bôš,* especially in the Hiphil, sometimes has a judicial sense, i.e., "be judged worthy of shame," which may be the case here. See J. W. Olley, "A Forensic Connotation of *bôš*," *VT* 26 (1976), pp. 230–34.
5. The noun *rā'â,* "evil," sometimes has this latter sense, "disaster," e.g., Deut. 31:17. See also the textual note.

1. Omitted by LXX.
2. Omitted by LXX.

28 *Is this man Coniah a mere figurehead,*[3]
Or a vessel no one wants?
Why, then, are they thrown headlong,
He and his children, hurled
To a land they do not know?
29 *O land, O land, O land,*
Hear the word of Yahweh.
30 *This is what Yahweh has said:*
"Write down this man as childless,
A man who in his lifetime shall not prosper,[4]
Nor shall any offspring of his succeed
In sitting on David's throne
Or ruling in Judah again."

The passage 22:24–30 has been variously seen as either all prose, or partly prose (vv. 24–27) and partly poetic (vv. 28–30). The first part seems to have been uttered just prior to the king's deportation and the second just after. Both announce the deportation and declare that Jehoiachin will never return to his beloved land. The poetic piece mourns the fact that none of his descendants will ever succeed to David's throne. The historical record occurs in 2 K. 24:8–17. Jehoiachin was the son of the ill-fated Jehoiakim and naturally succeeded his father. He reigned a mere three months before Jerusalem fell in 597 B.C. The young eighteen-year-old king along with his household and other key personnel in Judah were exiled to Babylon, where he eventually died (52:31–34; 2 K. 25:27–30).

24–25 In the oath formula introduced by *As I live,* the *'im* may be rendered "even if," with a sense as in RSV, "though Coniah . . . were the signet ring on my right hand, yet I would tear you off." But in an oath *'im* may be understood as an "unthinkable" condition implying an (unstated) drastic apodosis, hence negatively: "Coniah will never be the signet ring. . . ." The shift to direct address *(you)*, marked by the second *kî,* may suggest a translation such as we have given.

I will pull you off from there, and *hand you over to those who seek your life and of whom you are afraid.* Chaldea was a strange land, far away, and naturally to be feared. An important part of any man's basic security was to live in his own land. A land and a people belonged together. Any separation of the two was a disaster. A land

3. Heb. *'eṣeḇ* derives from the verb *'āṣaḇ*, "to shape." The noun seems to denote something that is lifeless, a figurehead; hence NEB "puppet." On the text of this verse see the commentary.
4. This line is lacking in LXX.

needs a people and a people needs a land. Little wonder that Jeremiah referred to the desperate yearning ("lifting up the soul," *niśśē' 'eṯ nep̱eš)* to return. But there would be no return. They would die there.

The name *Coniah* is an abbreviation of the king's full name, Jehoiachin (52:31). The shorter form occurs only here (vv. 24, 28) and in 37:1. Another form is Jeconiah (24:1; 27:20; 28:4; 29:2). The *signet ring* was used to impress the owner's signature into a document. Earthenware jars used to collect grain and oil for taxation purposes carried the royal stamp with the two-winged symbol, the word *lmlk,* "belonging to the king," and the name of the town where the collection was made. The kings of Judah were regarded as Yahweh's official representatives who employed his signet ring. The signet ring was valuable and precious to its owner. The same figure was applied to Jehoiachin's grandson Zerubbabel (Hag. 2:23). But Coniah would be rejected as Yahweh's signet ring and would no longer operate as Yahweh's anointed king in Judah.

26–27 The queen mother had some official status in Judah, and may have worn a crown and sat on a throne next to the king (1 K. 2:19). The names of the mothers of kings appear regularly in the books of Kings. See the commentary on 13:18 and cf. 2 K. 24:11–12. Jehoiachin was eventually released in the days of Evil-merodach, although he had to stay in Babylon where he died (2 K. 25:27–30; Jer. 52:31–34).[5]

28 A short poetic oracle[6] commences with this verse; but there are a number of textual problems. There seems to be a picture here of a vessel despised and broken. The image recalls the story of the broken flask (19:1–13). Jeremiah applied it to Moab also. Hosea applied the same figure to Israel (Hos. 8:8, "a useless vessel"). But here a question is asked: "Is this man Coniah a vessel despised and broken, something no one wants?" LXX has a somewhat briefer version: "Is Coniah despised as a vessel for which there is no use?"[7] The longer Hebrew text seems to obscure the meter.

5. See Albright, *BA* 5, pp. 49–55; A. Bea, "König Jojachin in Keilschriften," *Biblica* 23 (1942), pp. 78–82.

6. Not all commentators recognize the poetry, e.g., E. W. Nicholson, *Jeremiah 1–25*, p. 288; but cf. J. Bright, *Jeremiah,* p. 139; RSV.

7. See *BHS ad loc.* J. Bright, *Jeremiah,* p. 139, translates:

> Is Coniah a castoff pot,
> A utensil no one wants?

In the latter part of the verse in LXX the verbs *thrown headlong, hurled,* and *know* are in the singular.

Probably the general sense of the text is clear. Coniah and his family have been cast out as something unwanted and sent to a land unknown. The parallel with the rejected flask of ch. 19 is clear enough.

29–30 Coniah will be recorded as *childless*. The sense is not that he will have no sons. In fact he had seven (1 Chr. 3:17–18), and receipts for the issue of oil to captives in Babylon bear testimony to at least five sons.[8] The eldest of his sons may have been born already when this prophecy was delivered. Jehoiachin was, however, childless as far as having a descendant to sit on the throne of David. Zerubbabel, his grandson (1 Chr. 3:19), returned after the Exile as a kind of High Commissioner but not as king. Jeremiah's statement came from his belief that it was Yahweh's plan not to allow a descendant of Jehoiachin to be king.[9] It is possible that Jeremiah's words were directed particularly toward those who held out the hope that Jehoiachin might return and restore the Davidic dynasty. Some in Judah would not accept the fact that Zedekiah had been appointed king.[10] Jeremiah cut short all such speculations by an unambiguous rejection of both Jehoiachin and his descendants. The word here translated *childless*, *ʿ^arîrî*, could also be translated "stripped of all honor." However, the rest of the verse has to do with his lack of an heir. He was a man who did not prosper in his own lifetime, nor through his offspring.

(viii) *Promises for the Future of the Dynasty and the People (23:1–8)*

1[1] *"Woe to the shepherds who destroy.*
Who scatter the sheep of my pasture—Yahweh's word."
2 *Therefore this is what Yahweh the God of Israel has said against the shepherds who shepherd my people.*[2]
"You have scattered my flock
And driven them away,
And have not paid attention to them.
See, I will pay attention to you
For the evil of your deeds—Yahweh's word.

8. See *ANET*, p. 308.
9. W. Rudolph, *Jeremia*, pp. 123–25.
10. M. Noth, "La catastrophe de Jérusalem en l'an 587 avant Jésus Christ et la signification pour Israel," *RHPR* 33 (1953), pp. 81–102; *Gesammelte Studien*, pp. 346–376.

1. See W. L. Holladay, "The Recovery of Poetic Passages of Jeremiah," *JBL* 85 (1966), pp. 401–435. As against many commentators Holladay proposes that vv. 1–4 are poetic.
2. This first part of v. 2 is probably prose; cf. *ibid.*, p. 422.

3 *And I myself will gather the remnant of my sheep*
From all the lands where I have driven them;
I will bring them back to the fold,
Where they will be fruitful and multiply.
4 *And I will appoint over them shepherds*
Who will shepherd them,
So that they shall not be afraid again
Nor be terrified;
And none of them will be missing—Yahweh's word."
5 *"Look, days are coming—Yahweh's word—*
When I will raise up a Righteous Branch from David's line.
A king will rule wisely
And maintain justice and right in the land.
6 *In his days Judah shall triumph,*
And Israel shall dwell in safety.
And this is the name they shall call him:
'Yahweh is our Righteousness.' "
7 *"Therefore, look, days are coming—Yahweh's word—when they will*
no longer say 'As Yahweh lives who brought up the Israelites from
the land of Egypt,'
8 *but 'As Yahweh lives who brought the descendants of Israel*[3] *back*
from the north country, and from all the lands to which he had driven
them, that they might live in their own land.' "

Following the review of the various kings of Judah we might have expected some word on Zedekiah. But the order of things is changed. The present passage comprises two sections, a mostly poetic segment vv. 1–6 (which comprises two pieces, vv. 1–4 and 5–6), and a short prose section vv. 7–8. Only the name of Judah's last king is mentioned, although even this is transformed in order to proclaim the coming messianic era. Zedekiah has not been neglected in this general review, for in 21:1–10 the account of his inquiry to Jeremiah occurs as the opening section. But now, the message of judgment which runs through chs. 21–22 turns to one of hope and the promise of restoration both for the nation and for the dynasty of David.

The first section (vv. 1–4) continues the condemnation of the kings (shepherds) who have corrupted God's "flock," Israel, and refers to the future restoration of the nation from exile and the appointing of true "shepherds" who would care for the flock. The short poetic piece (vv. 5–6; cf. 33:15–16) promises the coming of the ideal king, "a Righteous Branch" of David's line who will rule

3. MT "who brought up and led the seed of the house of Israel." See the commentary.

wisely. Finally, a short prose piece (vv. 7–8) promises a new exodus but one of greater dimensions than the first.

On the surface it appears that vv. 1–4 were uttered in Zedekiah's reign. The second saying (vv. 5–6) with its play on Zedekiah's name must also have been uttered during Zedekiah's reign. There is no indication of a date for vv. 7–8.[4]

1 The word *Woe* introduces an oracle of judgment. The *shepherds* are Judah's rulers, including King Zedekiah and the nobles who seem to have dominated him. But the term may be wider still and gather up a long list of inept, careless, and neglectful rulers for many years past. Certainly the last four kings of Judah were bad shepherds who caused the scattering of the sheep and brought about their dispersal.[5] So the blame is attached to the rulers themselves.

2 Shepherds should shepherd the flock and "watch over" *(pāqaḏ)* them, not cause them to scatter and disperse. The verb *pāqaḏ* is taken up a second time with a change in application and meaning. The verb has a range of meanings.[6] Among these the following are to be found: "look after," "go to see," "take care of," "long for," "pass in review," "muster," "commission," "appoint," "call to account," "ask for vindication," "avenge" (used with *'al*). Translators have made some endeavor to relate the two usages here. Thus NEB translates: "You have not watched over them,[7] but I am watching you to punish[8] you for your evil-doings." The translation of John Bright attempts something similar: "You have not attended to them . . . I am going to attend to you for your wicked deeds." At the time this oracle was delivered it is evident that bad shepherds were still active and Yahweh was already at work to bring them to judgment.

3 A gathering together of the flock after it has been scattered is in view. Yahweh would gather the remnant. By contrast with v. 1, Yahweh says that it is he who scattered the flock. There is no contradiction. Due to the nation's rebellion and rejection of the covenant they were sent to exile. But it was the shepherds who were respon-

4. See the commentary for more on dating the whole section.
5. The two verbs *destroy* and *scatter* are causative.
6. See KB, p. 773.
7. The verb *pāqaḏ* is followed by the sign of a direct accusative *'eṯ*. The meaning is "look after, care for."
8. The verb is *pāqaḏ 'al* plus the accusative sign *'eṯ* before "the evil of your deeds." The meaning is "call to account," "punish."

sible for the state of the national life which resulted in the operation of the covenant curses.

It has been suggested by some commentators that this verse presupposes the Exile and that it therefore comes from a Deuteronomic author during the Exile. Such a view is by no means necessary. The possibility of exile was an ancient threat and appears in the secular treaties as one of the curses which will fall on those who break their treaty obligations. The mere reference to an exile is not proof that the passage was produced in exile. The possibility of exile for covenant-breakers and of restoration from exile for those who obeyed the covenant was understood clearly in preexilic times. There is no reason why Jeremiah might not have given expression to such a hope (cf. 3:14–18, in poetry). The motif of fruitfulness and increase after exile was a common one in both preexilic and postexilic times (Amos 9:11–15; Hos. 2:21–23; Ezek. 36; Zech. 8:9–13; etc.).

There is a doctrine of a *remnant* (*šᵉʾērîṯ*) here also. The same theme occurs elsewhere in Jeremiah (chs. 24, 40–44) and in the preexilic prophets (Isa. 1:9; 37:4; Mic. 4:7; 7:18). The theme was not peculiar to the people of Israel. It occurs among the blessings of some of the ancient Near Eastern treaties.[9] It cannot be argued therefore that such an idea is necessarily a mark of a postexilic writer.[10]

4 The promise of a restoration to the same state of affairs that obtained before the Exile was hardly adequate. There was a better hope— *shepherds* appointed by Yahweh who would shepherd them faithfully and remove fear and terror from the land. The play on *pqd* continues in MT.[11] For this sense of the Niphal, *be missing,* see Num. 31:49. The sheep will be mustered and all accounted for.

5 The short poetic piece which is now introduced is full of important aspects of messianic thinking (cf. 33:15–16).

There is some debate about the meter of vv. 5–6a. Following MT it may be described as 3/4, 3/4, 3/3 or perhaps 3/2/2, 3/2/2, 3/

9. E.g., in the treaty of Šuppiluliumaš with Mattiwaza, among the blessings held out to those who kept the treaty was the promise that in case of exile the king and his family would return to the place they occupied before and would thrive and expand. See *ANET,* p. 206.

10. E. W. Nicholson, *Jeremiah 1–25*, p. 191.

11. LXX lacks the phrase *and none of them will be missing.* NEB follows LXX but RSV preserves the phrase, as does John Bright.

3. One suggestion[12] is that a redivision of the cola could produce the metric pattern as 3/3, 2/2, 2/2, 3/3.

Behold, days are coming
When I'll raise for David a Shoot,
A righteous one who will reign,
A king who will prosper.

The expression *days are coming* is very general and has no particular time reference. It is simply a way of calling attention to a solemn proclamation (cf. v. 7; 7:32; 9:25; 31:31; etc.). The announcement concerns the ideal king (Messiah)[13] of the Davidic line under whose just and victorious rule the dynastic hopes of Judah would be realized. The Royal Psalms gather up much of this idealism (Pss. 2, 44, 72, 89–110). The metaphor is of a shoot *(ṣemaḥ)* bursting forth from the Davidic tree (i.e., the dynasty), which, though cut off, is not dead. English versions have generally translated the word as *Branch.* In postexilic times the term became the classic technical one for the expected ideal king (Zech. 3:8; 6:12). The figure, though not expressed in the same terms, occurs in Isa. 11:1, "There shall come forth a shoot from the stump of Jesse, and a branch shall grow out of his roots" (RSV).

The precise description in Hebrew is a *ṣemaḥ ṣaddîq,*[14] which could mean a "Righteous Shoot," or "a true shoot" of David's line as distinct from one who pretended to be such. There was much in the representatives of the Davidic dynasty during Jeremiah's day which suggested that they were a sham, for they failed to demonstrate the true qualities of kingship (21:11–14; 22:1–3). But there may well be another sense to the expression *ṣemaḥ ṣaddîq.* Comparison with a very similar expression in Phoenician inscriptions and in Ugaritic texts suggests that the meaning may be "legitimate scion."[15]

A king will rule wisely—MT reads literally "And a king will rule and act wisely." Perhaps the point was being made that this

12. See reference to D. N. Freedman's proposal in J. Bright, *Jeremiah,* p. 144, and cf. *JBL* 72 (1953), p. xx.

13. The term Messiah in the sense of the ideal king is not used in the OT although the idea is present.

14. Targ. reads *mšyḥ (māšîaḥ),* "Messiah," for *ṣemaḥ.*

15. J. Swetnam, "Some Observations on the Background of *ṣaddîq* in Jeremias 23:5a," *Biblica* 46/1 (1965), pp. 29–40. This article suggests that there was a tension in Judah after the exile of Jehoiachin and the appointment of Zedekiah, and there were those who held that Jehoiachin was the legitimate king and not Zedekiah. Against this background Jeremiah delivered his messianic promise.

coming king would, in fact, reign as a *king* and not as a puppet like Zedekiah (cf. 22:28). The verb *hiśkîl* has the force of "act wisely" or "have success," hence NEB "a king who shall rule wisely."[16] And in contrast to the present representatives of the Davidic dynasty, he would *maintain justice (mišpāṭ) and right (ṣᵉḏāqâ) in the land.*

6 In both the OT and in the later rabbinic writings there were two facets of the doctrine of Messiah: teaching about the Messiah as a person, and teaching about the Messianic Age. We have these two aspects here with the person of the Messiah in v. 5 and the Messianic Age in v. 6 (cf. Isa. 11:1–5 and 6–16). *In his days* Judah will be "rescued," "delivered," "liberated," all possible translations of the verb *tiwwāša'*.[17] The precise force of the verb is difficult to translate since a range of ideas clusters round the root *yš'*. But Jeremiah looked forward to a day when Judah would be released from all restraints. No longer would external foes or internal tensions trouble her. She would be "kept safe" (NEB), "saved" (RSV), would "triumph" (J. Bright). But in that day the whole family of Israel would share in the rule of the ideal king. *Israel* here refers to the northern kingdom. She too would live in safety. The theme of coming salvation for all Israel occurs in chs. 30 and 31.

As in Isa. 9:6 a symbolic name is given to the coming king, *Yahweh ṣiḏqēnû, Yahweh is our Righteousness*. The interpretation of the name varies. It is probably a play on the name of Zedekiah, *ṣiḏqî-yāhû, My righteousness is Yahweh.* The noun *ṣeḏeq* was firmly anchored in the concept of kingship in Israel, and it would not be surprising for a king to take such a name as Zedekiah. If the king failed to live according to the symbolism of his name, "Yahweh is my righteousness," it would be appropriate for a prophet to draw the contrast as though to say: "but our Righteousness is Yahweh." In general the term *ṣeḏeq* denotes "what is right," "according to the norm," and hence, what is just. In some cases where Yahweh, or a king, sets about to establish the right, the word (or its feminine form *ṣᵉḏāqâ)* comes to mean the justice done in favor of someone, or vindication (Isa. 41:2, 10; 58:8; 62:1, 2). The plural *ṣᵉḏāqôṯ* means "saving acts" (Judg. 5:11; 1 Sam. 12:7; Isa. 45:24; Mic. 6:5; Ps. 103:6).[18] Hence the symbolic name could mean "Yahweh is the

16. J. Bright, *Jeremiah,* p. 140, "As king he shall reign—and ably."
17. Niphal, 3rd fem. sing. of *yāša'*, "to save."
18. See KB, p. 795.

vindication of our right"[19] or "Yahweh is our Justice." The term must be allowed to take on its full meaning, which includes the saving presence and activity of Yahweh. The name is different from Zedekiah's name in that the pronouns are different and the position of Yahweh is different. The name Zedekiah could mean "Yahweh is my vindication." A play on the name seems evident and the oracle can therefore be dated during the reign of that king. There is no convincing reason why the saying should not be regarded as authentic.[20]

Clearly the oracle was a solemn one and pointed to a new era. Probably Jeremiah had in mind an ideal ruler who was closely bound to history. The forthcoming age was not seen as something reserved for the eschatological era, but as coming at the end of a particular era that had been marked by a failure in the functioning of the kingship in the context of the covenant. When kingship was exercised in the light of the covenant, then the blessings of the covenant would be realized among God's people in the land of promise.

Through the centuries, in dark periods when kings were unfaithful to their covenant obligations, prophets looked to this noble ideal and promised its fulfilment in some historical future, using terms much like those which are found in this passage (Isa. 9:5–6; 11:1–9; Mic. 5:1–5; Amos 9:11; Hos. 3:5; etc.). Jeremiah stood in a strong tradition and looked for the restoration of David's dynasty, not merely on political grounds but more significantly on the level of the religious and moral obligations of the covenant.

7–8 These verses occur in 16:14–15 with minor variations. The saying is appropriate here whatever its function may have been there. LXX places these verses at the end of the chapter after v. 40, suggesting that there was some fluctuation in the tradition. The verses predict a return from exile of the northern kingdom. This fact is not, in itself, a sufficient reason to identify them as exilic or postexilic in origin and due to a Deuteronomic writer of that period. We have noted already that secular Hittite treaties reaching back into the middle of the second millennium B.C. include the promise of restoration after exile as a blessing that would attend those who would

19. So J. Bright, *Jeremiah,* p. 144.
20. See E. W. Nicholson, *Jeremiah 1–25,* p. 192.

be loyal to their treaty obligations.[21] It was an essential part of the total picture of the new age. Yahweh's people who were dispersed in other lands could hardly remain in exile when the ideal king began his reign. Hence, in an exodus which would surpass in grandeur the original Exodus from Egypt, the descendants of Israel would return from a northern land and from all the lands to which Yahweh had dispersed them. The picture of the gathering of the remnant to its homeland where divine blessing would be manifested occurs in such passages as Isa. 11 and Ezek. 34, 37. As so often in Jeremiah, LXX has some variants from MT. In v. 8 MT has an additional verb, "By the life of Yahweh who brought up and led Israel. . . ." This may point to a conflation of two originally distinct readings. Similarly MT "the seed of the house of Israel" may represent a conflation of different readings. We read *who brought the descendants of Israel back.* The lands of their dispersion were to the north and would include at least Assyrian areas, but others as well (2 K. 17:6), all of which were reached by an initial journey northward.

(ix) Denunciation of the Prophets (23:9–40)

(a) A land full of adulterers (23:9–12)

9 *To the prophets:*[1]
My heart is deeply disturbed[2] *within me;*
All my limbs are weak.
I have become like a drunken man,
Like a person overcome with wine,
Because of Yahweh,
Because of his holy words.
10 *For the land is full of adulterers,*[3]
And because of these[4] *the land is parched,*
The pastures of the steppeland have dried up.
The course they run is evil
And their power is illegitimate.
11 *"Ah, prophet and priest alike are alienated from God.*
In my own house I have discovered their evil deeds
—Yahweh's word.

21. See comments on v. 3 above and cf. *ANET*, p. 206.

1. See S. J. DeVries, *Prophet Against Prophet,* p. 142. Jeremiah provides a good illustration of DeVries' theme of prophet against prophet.
2. Lit. "is broken" (Heb. *nišbar*).
3. The line is lacking in LXX.
4. MT reads *'ālâ,* "a curse." We read with LXX, Syr., and some mss. *'ēlleh, these.*

12 *Therefore their own way shall become*
Like slippery paths in the darkness,
On which they will be driven and will fall.
For I will bring disaster on them
When the time of their reckoning comes
—Yahweh's word."

The passage 23:9–40 comprises five units, which were probably originally separate sayings delivered at different times but brought together here because of their common theme, embraced under the general heading in v. 9, *To the prophets*. Jeremiah was at very great odds with the other prophets of his day, whom he regarded as by and large false prophets, and he never ceased denouncing them (2:8; 4:9; 5:31; 6:13–15; 14:13–16; etc.). The sayings collected here concentrate on the problem of false prophecy and provide a good picture of why Jeremiah was opposed to them. The five units are vv. 9–12, 13–15, 16–22, all in poetic form, vv. 23–32 partly if not completely poetic, and vv. 33–40 often regarded as prose but arguably poetic also.

In the passage before us the national apostasy is seen as adultery, probably a reference to the participation of the people in Canaanite religious rites, which not only indicated Israel's attempt to share her allegiance with other gods (hence the term adultery), but sometimes involved the people in sexually oriented fertility rites. The leaders of this apostasy were the prophets and priests. In vv. 9–12 there is no direct address to the prophets.

9 The word *heart* here denotes the mind. Jeremiah was not so much heartbroken (AV, RSV) as *deeply disturbed* ("shattered") in his mind. He was affected physically and had no strength in his limbs, so that he was like a drunken man as he thought of Yahweh and his holy words and then looked upon the moral and religious condition of his people. Judah was altogether corrupt (5:1–6:30). Once before Jeremiah had wanted to flee away from it all (9:1–5 [Eng. 2–6]) because it pained him so (4:19).

10 The land was full of *adulterers* (*m*^{e}*nā'*^{a}*p̱îm*). The adulterous state of the land was demonstrated both by idolatry and moral depravity (5:7–8). The worship of Baal, the Canaanite fertility-god, far from producing the hoped-for fertility of the land, had produced the opposite effect. The land lay *parched*[5] and barren. Only Yahweh,

5. There are two verbs *'bl*, one meaning "mourn" (AV; RSV "the land mourns") and the second "dry up" (Akk. *abālu;* see KB, p. 6).

and not Baal, could guarantee the good of the land (Hos. 2:5–8; Amos 4:4–9). Heb. *miḏbār* here cannot be "wilderness" in the sense of an arid desert, but denotes uninhabited pasturage out on the steppes. In the last couplet *they* must be the "adulterers," who run on an evil *course (m^erûṣâ)* and exercise *illegitimate* (lit. "not right") power.

11 It is best to understand vv. 11–12 as being a word from Yahweh, who refers to both prophet and priest as *alienated from God (ḥānēp)*.[6] In that case *my own house* refers to the temple, which the priests had polluted with pagan and immoral practices (2 K. 21:3–7; 23:4–7). Despite the reform of Josiah in 621 B.C. whereby he rooted out pagan cults from the temple and its precincts, after his death in 609 B.C. there was a recurrence of these practices in the days of Jehoiakim, Jehoiachin, and Zedekiah. Ezekiel gives a good idea of what went on in the temple precincts during the last years of the state of Judah (Ezek. 8). It was this that troubled Jeremiah's mind and made him physically faint.

12 The perpetrators of such apostasy had embarked on a slippery pathway in the darkness, along which they were *driven* as though by some hidden impulse. But they would fall in it. Yahweh would bring disaster upon them in the year of their reckoning, which according to Jeremiah was fast approaching.

(b) The prophets as leaders of national apostasy (23:13–15)

13 *In the prophets of Samaria*
I saw an offensive thing:
They prophesied by Baal
And led my people Israel astray.
14 *And in the prophets of Jerusalem*
I have seen a horrible thing:
They commit adultery and go after The Lie.
They strengthen the hands of evildoers
So that none of them turns from his wickedness.
To me, they are all like Sodom
And her inhabitants like Gomorrah.
15 *Therefore this is what Yahweh of Hosts has said concerning the prophets:*
"Look, I will give them wormwood to eat,
And I will give them poison to drink,
For it is from Jerusalem's prophets
That godlessness has spread to all the land."

6. On this root *ḥnp* see KB, p. 317.

Jeremiah's more detailed words about the false prophets begin at v. 13. The first characteristic of these prophets is their debased moral conduct. The prophets of Northern Israel are shown to be apostate, a statement which would be acceptable to Jeremiah's hearers in Judah. But Jeremiah compares the northern prophets with those in Judah and thus underlines the enormity of the conduct of his own contemporaries.[1]

13 Jeremiah saw an *offensive thing (tiplâ)* in Samaria's prophets because they led Israel astray and spoke in the name of Baal, i.e., prophesied in Baal's name. In such conduct one could discern the false prophet. Any prophet was false who turned Israel away from her complete loyalty to Yahweh her covenant lord. The true prophet would know that his task was to encourage the nation to maintain total loyalty to Yahweh and to set before them the obligations of the covenant.

14 Jerusalem's prophets also committed adultery *(nā'ôp)* and followed The Fraud *(šeqer)*.[2] In their own lives they rejected the sole and complete sovereignty of Yahweh. But they also gave such encouragement to *evildoers (mᵉrēʻîm)* that these continued in their evil ways. The verb *šûb*, a favorite verb of Jeremiah, is used here with the preposition *min* in the sense of "turn from." A picture of defiant evil comes to the prophet's mind. They were all like Sodom, and Jerusalem's citizens like Gomorrah (Gen. 18, 19; cf. Ezek. 16).

Thus the false prophets are distinguished both by their false preaching and by their evil way of life.

15 The *wormwood* plant *(laʻᵃnâ)* has a bitter taste and is probably to be identified with the genus *Artemisia*[3] (see 9:14 [Eng. 15]). It is coupled here as elsewhere in the OT with *rō'š* ("gall" or bitter *poison*), a fatally poisonous herb. Yahweh's sentence on false prophets was bitterness and tragedy. The nation's *godlessness (ḥᵃnuppâ)* was seen as spreading out from them through the whole land. These verses provide a powerful indictment of Jeremiah's opponents.

1. The device of leaving the local scene till the last was well used by Amos, at least as the material is arranged in the present literary collection. See Amos 1:3–2:1 as an introduction to 2:4–8.
2. *The Lie*—probably a name for Baal. Cf. 18:15 where the noun is *šāwᵉ'*.
3. See W. Walker, *All the Plants of the Bible* (1957), p. 236.

(c) False prophets speak an unauthorized word from their own heart[1] *(23:16–22)*

16 *This is what Yahweh of Hosts has said:*
"Do not listen to the words of the prophets who prophesy to you;
They are deluding you.[2]
They report a vision of their own hearts;
It is not from the mouth of Yahweh.
17 *They keep on saying*[3] *to those who despise Yahweh's word,*[4]
'All will be well with you';
And to all those who follow their own stubborn wills,
'Disaster will not befall you.' "
18 *But who has stood in Yahweh's council*
And has seen and heard his word?
Who has paid attention to his word and obeyed?
19 *Look! the fiery storm of Yahweh has gone forth,*
A furious whirlwind;
It whirls about the heads of the wicked.
20 *The wrath of Yahweh will not turn back*
Until he has accomplished and fulfilled
His deep designs.
In days to come you will understand it clearly.
21 *"I did not send these prophets,*
Yet—they ran!
I did not speak to them,
Yet—they prophesied!
22 *If they had stood in my council*
They would proclaim my words to the people,
And they would turn them from their wicked way
And from their evil-doings."

Another way to recognize false prophets is from their message. They pander to popular wishes, always foretelling peace even if the days are evil. They are liars and victims of their own imagination. The whole section is poetic, and all commentators agree that it is a genuine oracle of Jeremiah. There seems to have been some disturbance in vv. 16–17 which has upset the meter. It is not possible to give a

1. E. Lipiński, "*bᵉ'aḥᵃrîṯ hayyāmîm* dans les textes préexiliques," *VT* 20 (1970), pp. 445–450 (esp. 448–450), proposes a very symmetrical stress pattern for this poem.
2. LXX is shorter, "Do not listen to the words of the prophets; they are deluding." The extra words in MT disturb the meter of the Hebrew poetry and should perhaps be omitted.
3. The participle followed by the infinitive absolute, as in MT, generally indicates repeated action. LXX has only the participle.
4. Following LXX; see the commentary.

date since the oracle is very general without any specific historical reference.

16 The false prophets report *a vision of their own hearts,* that is, a self-induced vision, something that originated in their own minds. They did not "wait upon the Lord"; rather their own understanding of God and of his relationship to the nation was their sole source of information. It was *not from the mouth of Yahweh.* This was a bold claim from Jeremiah since it implied that his own message came from Yahweh directly. The verb *deluding (mahbilîm)* is related to the noun *heḇel* which features prominently in Ecclesiastes: "Vanity *(heḇel),* vanity, all is vanity," that is, "emptiness" or "wind." The false prophets were thus declared to be "a bag of wind."

17 The suggestion in MT that the false prophets persisted in their utterances is probably an accurate picture. MT reads further "to those who despise me Yahweh has said" *(limna'ᵃṣay dibber . . .),* which may be revocalized without changing the consonantal text to give a reading *to those who despise Yahweh's word (limᵉna'ᵃṣê dᵉḇar yhwh),* which conforms to LXX. The attempt to lull people into a false sense of security was a common failing of prophets who worked only on the human level (6:14; 8:11; cf. Mic. 3:5). The complacent word may have arisen from the view that since God was committed to Israel he was obliged to sustain and defend the nation in the face of its enemies. Such a view fails to give weight to demands laid upon Israel because of the covenant, to acknowledge the sole and complete sovereignty of Yahweh over them and to live according to the demands of covenant law. Righteousness and holiness were fundamental qualities to be expected in a people who expected Yahweh to bring them deliverance. Prophets who cried "Peace *(šālôm),* peace" when sudden destruction was at hand and said *Disaster will not befall you* were clearly deluded. Jeremiah was unhesitating and uncompromising in his condemnation. The false prophets "walked in the stubbornness of their hearts," that is, followed *their own stubborn wills.*

18 A significant feature about the true prophet was that he *stood in Yahweh's council (sôḏ).* Elsewhere in Jeremiah *sôḏ* refers to the "company" of merrymakers from whom the prophet stood apart (15:17) and to the "bands" of young men who were deaf to his message (6:11). Here it is the circle of those who are privy to the deep purposes of Yahweh and are in his confidence. In present circumstances the mind of God is clear: the storm of Yahweh is about to break on the head of the wicked. It is a word of judgment and not peace that should be proclaimed by one who really knows the mind of Yahweh. But one needs to stand in Yahweh's council, see what goes on there, hear and pay attention to Yahweh's word and obey it, to give such a word.

19–20 These verses are repeated in 30:21–24 with slight variations. They seem to be only loosely connected with the context in ch. 30, where they were probably added to stress the judgment on Israel's foes referred to there. But in the present context they fit very easily after v. 18, calling attention to what was really spoken in Yahweh's council. The true word of Yahweh was not peace *(šālôm)* but a *fiery storm (s^e'ārâ)* and a furious whirlwind which whirls about the head of evildoers. That is what a prophet should have heard who stood in Yahweh's council.

Moreover, Yahweh's anger *('ap̱)* will not turn aside *(šûḇ)* until he has fulfilled his *deep designs* (lit. "designs of his heart," *m^{e}zimmôṯ libbô)*. Only when the judgment has taken place will the false prophets understand. They had shown continuous hostility to Jeremiah and his message, which they found both unacceptable and incomprehensible because it ran counter to all they believed and taught about the inviolability of Jerusalem and the people of God. MT reads "at the end of days" *('aḥ^{a}rîṯ hayyāmîm),* but the phrase is probably not eschatological but merely means "afterward," that is, when the judgment has taken place. The prophets should have begun to realize what Jeremiah meant in 597 B.C., but certainly after 586 B.C. Yet the prophets who went to exile in 597 B.C. continued their work in Babylon and do not seem to have comprehended what Jeremiah was saying (29:21–23). A radical reorientation was needed in their understanding of the purposes of God. This could be achieved only through the judgment about to befall the nation. There was a need for a new and a deeper relationship with God than they had ever understood. God had purposes for his people and through them for the world, but these could be realized only inside the covenant. Only after the judgment would the false prophets realize how shallow their preaching had been, and, incidentally, something of the depth of Jeremiah's preaching.

21–22 Yahweh's own word is given. These false prophets had not been sent *(šālaḥ,* cf. 1:6; Isa. 6:8; Ezek. 3:5; cf. Amos 7:14), yet they went in haste (lit. *they ran),* driven by some powerful human impulse, perhaps being strong adherents of the doctrine of the inviolability of Israel, the temple, and Jerusalem. Yahweh had not given them his word, yet they prophesied. Here lie two important features of the true prophet—the divine sending and the divine word. In the absence of these, prophets had no authority and no clear understanding of the purposes of God. Not having been in his council (cf. 14:14; 27:15; 29:9) they had no word to proclaim, nor could they turn the nation away from *(šûḇ min)* its evil course and its evil deeds. Indeed, they could not discern in their fellows the kinds of activities which were an offense to Yahweh. The task of the true prophet was to convict people of their sinfulness. To do that he himself would need to have a clear understanding of the nature of the covenant and its demands upon the people of God. The only acceptable response to their election and their high calling was in terms of holiness and righteousness and utter loyalty to Yahweh the sovereign Lord of the covenant.

(d) The dream and God's word contrasted (23:23–32)

23 *"Am I a God who is near—Yahweh's word—*
And not a God far off?
24 *Can a man hide in secret places*
And I do not see him?—Yahweh's word.
Am I not the one who fills heaven and earth?—Yahweh's word.
25 *I have heard what they have said, the prophets who preach lies in my name and say, 'I have had a dream! I have had a dream!'*
26 *How long (will this go on)? Is (my name)*[1] *in the mind of the prophets who preach lies and proclaim the deceitfulness of their own heart,*
27 *who think they will make my people forget my name by their dreams which they recount to one another, just as their fathers forgot my name because of Baal?*
28 *The prophet who has a dream,*
Let him tell the dream;
But he who has my word,
Let him faithfully speak my word.
What has chaff to do with wheat?—Yahweh's word.

1. The text is difficult. It reads lit. "How long? Is there in the heart of the prophets who prophesy falsehood and prophesy the deceit of their heart?" The expression *How long* is no problem since it seems to mean "How long will this continue?" But the second sentence has no subject. Rudolph proposes to supply "my name," which makes good sense but has no support otherwise (cf. v. 27). Another proposal is that the expression *'aḏ māṯay, How long?* may hide a third *ḥālamtî,* "I have dreamed," due to some confusion of the text. The verse would then begin with the question, "Is my name in the mind of the prophets who preach falsehood. . . ?" The threefold repetition of a word is known in 7:4 and 22:29; cf. Isa. 6:3.

29 *Are not my words like fire*[2]*—Yahweh's word;*
Like a hammer that shatters the rock?
30 *Therefore, Look! I am against the prophets—Yahweh's word—who steal my words from one another.*
31 *Look! I am against the prophets—Yahweh's word—who take up their own words, and proclaim a message.*
32 *Look! I am against the prophets*[3] *who preach lying dreams—Yahweh's word—and retail them and mislead my people by their falsehoods and their boasting. I did not send them, nor did I commission them, and they will be of no benefit at all to this people —Yahweh's word."*

At first sight this section appears to consist of a brief poetic introduction (vv. 23–24), with another brief poetic section in vv. 28–29, combined with two prose segments (vv. 25–27, 30–32). The prose portion has been understood as a Deuteronomic development of some genuine material of Jeremiah in the period of the Exile.[4] But a close reading of the text will reveal that there is a good deal of parallelism throughout the passage. The repetition of *Yahweh's word* in several places throughout the section, once in v. 23, twice in v. 24, once in v. 28, once in v. 29, once in each of vv. 30, 31, and 32, eight times in all, would seem to point to a poetic original, as would also the thrice-repeated expression *Look! I am against the prophets* in vv. 30, 31, and 32. It would appear that the material has suffered a good deal in transmission since there are numerous variants in LXX. If, in fact, despite the present disorder of the text it can be established that vv. 23–32 were originally poetic in form, the necessity of postulating an exilic development of a saying of Jeremiah seems to vanish.

The passage offers another criticism of the false prophets. They depend on dreams which in themselves have nothing in common with the Word of God. In the ancient Near East dreams were of great significance in discovering the will of the gods.[5] Because of their magical and uncertain character and the difficulty of interpreting them, they do not seem to have carried much weight in Israel

2. MT adds the word *kōh,* "thus," which is lacking in LXX. Some emend the word to *kōweh,* "burning." LXX has an additional line at the end of v. 28, and the word may be a relic of a missing line in the Hebrew text. Perhaps we might read, "Are not my words scorching, like fire?" (NEB).

3. LXX *the prophets* is lacking in MT.

4. E. W. Nicholson, *Jeremiah 1–25,* p. 199.

5. A. L. Oppenheim, *The Interpretation of Dreams in the Ancient Near East with a Translation of an Assyrian Dream Book.* Transactions of the American Philosophical Society 46/3 (1956).

and were generally rejected as a means of revelation (27:9; Deut. 13:1–2; Zech. 10:2). So far as we know, the classical prophets never received a divine revelation through dreams (as contrasted with visionary experiences). Perhaps in popular belief the dream was thought to be significant. In the book of Daniel both Nebuchadrezzar and Daniel had dreams which were interpreted by God's servant Daniel. In Num. 12:16 the possibility of divine communication through dreams is allowed, although in 1 Sam. 28:6 Saul was denied an answer by dreams, prophets, or the Urim.[6] As a general statement, revelation by way of a dream was inferior to revelation through a prophet.

23–24 These verses give expression to both the transcendence and the immanence of God. The questions are rhetorical and demand a negative answer. Yahweh is not a small local deity unaware of the doings of his creatures and from whom one might hide, but he is a transcendent God who knows and sees all. And yet he is at hand and can find men out where they are, that is, he is immanent. The thought is not unique to Israel. It occurs in the Egyptian Hymn to Aten: "Thou hast made the distant sky in order to rise therein, in order to see all that thou dost make."[7] LXX varies a little in v. 23 from MT; it omits the question and merely makes the statement "I am a God near at hand and not far away."

25–27 The validity of dreams as a means of divine revelation is now questioned. Jeremiah believed that the false prophets prophesied *(nibbā')*[8] *lies (šeqer)*[9] in the name of Yahweh. In these verses *name (šēm)* refers to the essential character of Yahweh, that is, who he is (cf. Exod. 3:13–14; Isa. 9:6; etc.). Once men forgot the character of Yahweh they could be persuaded to accept all kinds of doctrines. This had happened to the ancestors of Jeremiah's generation. As a result they accepted the pagan beliefs about Baal. It was important not to *forget (šākaḥ),* but to remember and to call to mind the character of Yahweh.

28–30 In Jeremiah's view the dream was *chaff (teḇen).* Yahweh's word delivered through his servant was *wheat (bar).* He clearly regarded dreams as very subjective experiences which had nothing to do with Yahweh's word. There was a difference. Let the

6. See I. Mendelsohn, "Dream," *IDB* I, pp. 868f.; J. G. S. S. Thomson, "Dream," *NBD,* p. 323.
7. *ANET,* p. 371, translation by J. A. Wilson.
8. The verb is Niphal from the root *nb'*. The same root appears in *nāḇî'*, "prophet."
9. See T. W. Overholt, *The Threat of Falsehood* (1970).

dreamer tell his dream if he wished, but it should be made clear that it was a dream and not a word from Yahweh.

The Word of God impinged powerfully on men's minds. It burned itself first of all into the minds of those who received it and proclaimed it, and subsequently made an impact on those who heard it from them, convicting the hearers of sin and demanding of them total obedience. The two metaphors of *fire* and a *hammer that shatters the rock* convey something of the powerful character of the Word of God. It was wheat. By contrast the anemic, powerless dream was chaff which could not move a man deeply at the moral and religious level.

Despite textual problems the general thrust of the verses is clear.[10] The false prophets were so devoid of personal inspiration, not having received a word personally from Yahweh, that they could only repeat what they had heard others say. They kept stealing a message, each one from his fellow.

31 There is a wordplay here which is difficult to capture in English, literally, "they take up (use) their (own) tongue and oracle an oracle." The phrase which occurs many times in Jeremiah and is translated as *Yahweh's word (n^{e}'um yhwh)* is related to the wordplay here, *yin'^{a}mû n^{e}'um,* "they oracle an oracle." The verb occurs only here. The meaning is that the message of the false prophets originated from themselves and was presented in their own words with something of a flourish as though it were a word from Yahweh.

32 A third time Yahweh declared *I am against the prophets,* this time for preaching "dreams of falsehood" (false or fraudulent dreams). These they repeat, and lead astray God's people with their falsehoods and their *boasting (paḥ^{a}zûṯ).* They have not been sent *(šālaḥ)* like the classical prophets nor commanded *(ṣiwwâ)* by Yahweh. Hence their preaching could be of no profit to Israel.

The condemnation of the false prophets was severe. They were seen as men of low moral standards (vv. 13–15), purveyors of a message of peace when judgment was imminent (vv. 16–17), men who had not stood in the council of Yahweh (vv. 18–22), men who depended on dreams for their message and who borrowed ideas from one another (vv. 23–32). Jeremiah stood in striking contrast to the false prophets. He was a man of high moral integrity. He preached judgment. He had stood in the council of Yahweh. He had no re-

10. See textual notes.

course to dreams but depended on a direct revelation from Yahweh himself.

(e) The burden of Yahweh (23:33–40)

33 *"And if this people, or a prophet or a priest, should ask you 'What is the burden of Yahweh?' you shall say to them, 'You are the burden,*[1] *and I will throw you down—Yahweh's word.'*

34 *And as for the prophet or the priest or one of the people who utters 'The burden of Yahweh,' I will punish that man and his household.*

35 *This is what you shall say every man to his fellow and every man to his brother: 'What has Yahweh answered?' and 'What has Yahweh spoken?'*

36 *You shall never again mention the expression 'The burden of Yahweh'; for 'the burden' will be for the man (to whom he entrusts) his word. Then you would pervert the words of the living God, Yahweh of Hosts, our God.*

37 *This is what you shall say to the prophet: 'What did Yahweh answer you?' or 'What did Yahweh say?'*

38 *And if you shall say 'The burden of Yahweh,' then this is what Yahweh has said: 'Because you have spoken this word "The burden of Yahweh," though I spoke to you and said, "You shall not say 'The burden of Yahweh,' "*

39 *therefore, look, I will indeed lift you up*[2] *and throw you down, you and the city which I have given to you and to your fathers, from my presence.*

40 *And I will bring upon you an everlasting disgrace, and everlasting humiliation which will not be forgotten.' "*

This final passage is apparently in prose but clearly has an underlying poetic basis because of the number of parallelisms which occur. The whole section is built around the word *maśśā'*, *burden*, which is used in different ways. A number of textual problems make the translation and understanding of the passage difficult. In general the main thrust of the passage is that the prophetic office is to be undertaken with great seriousness. Only those to whom Yahweh entrusts his word are entitled to proclaim it. Impostors and plagia-

1. MT reads *'eṯ-mah-maśśā'*. This text is dislocated, but by a simple rearrangement to read *'attem hammaśśā', You are the burden,* we obtain good sense (so LXX). Another possibility is to rearrange the consonants as *'ttmh mśś'*, "You are a burden." The pronoun *'attmh* is an ancient form of the 2nd masc. plur. pronoun; cf. P. Wernberg-Møller, "The Pronoun *'tmh* and Jeremiah's Pun," *VT* 6 (1956), pp. 315f.
2. MT obscures the continuing play on *burden* by using the verb **nāšâ,* "forget," for *nāśā'*, "to lift up, carry." A number of mss. and Versions suggest that the first verb should be *nāśîṯî* or *nāśā'ṯî,* "I lift up, carry." The second verb, lacking in LXX, would suit the context better if it were *nāśō'* (infinitive absolute), as in some mss., instead of *nāšō'*.

rists will incur divine judgment. The date of the section is not easy to determine. It would fit the period of Zedekiah's reign when the tension between Jeremiah and the prophets was severe. It is possible that an original poetic saying of Jeremiah was reworded by the later editor. But if we attempt a rough arrangement of the present material in verse form it will be clear that an original poem lies very close to the surface. A possible structure of the system of stresses is added in parentheses. The cola on the whole carry four beats, but there are variations of two and three beats.

33 "And if this people should ask, (4)
Or the prophet or the priest, (4)
And say 'What is the burden of Yahweh?' (4)
Then you will say to them: 'You are the burden, (4)
And I will thrown you down—Yahweh's word.' (4)
34 And as for the prophet or the priest or one of the people (3)
Who utters 'The burden of Yahweh,' (4)
I will punish that man and his household. (4)
35 Thus shall you speak (2)
Each man to his neighbor (2)
And each man to his brother: (2)
'What has Yahweh replied?' (2)
'What has Yahweh said?' (2)
36 But 'The burden of Yahweh' you shall not mention again, (4)
For 'the burden' will be for the man of his word. (4)
Then you would pervert the words of the living God, (4)
Yahweh of Hosts, our God. (3)
37 This is what you shall say to the prophet: (3)
'What did Yahweh answer you?' (3)
'What did Yahweh say?' (3)
38 But if you should say 'The burden of Yahweh' (4)
Then this is what Yahweh has said: (4)
Because you have spoken this word (4)
'The burden of Yahweh,' (2)
Though I spoke to you and said, (3)
You shall not say 'The burden of Yahweh,' (4)
39 Therefore, look! I will indeed lift you up (4)
And I will throw you down, and the city (3)
Which I gave to you and to your fathers, (4)
From before my face. (2)
40 And I will bring upon you an everlasting reproach, (4)
And endless shame which shall not be forgotten." (4)

The point may be made again (cf. vv. 23–32) that if we are dealing with a poetic piece there seems no good reason to deny the poem to Jeremiah.

33 The key word here and throughout vv. 33–40 is *maśśā', burden*. It derives from the same root as the verb *nāśā'*, "to lift, bear, carry," and hence the noun denotes a load or burden. From its usage in the OT it seems clear that it is an imposed burden, imposed by a master, an overlord, or a deity on beasts or men. Metaphorically it can mean a burden of leadership or of religious duty, and at times the heavy burden of God's judgment. Often in prophetic writings it suggests a judgment or a catastrophe. The same word appears at the heading of prophetic oracles; but there it has acquired a technical sense, "argument," "thesis," even though the content of the passage that follows preserves the original sense of the term.[3]

The question was posed by the people, or a prophet or a priest, *What is the burden of Yahweh?* By this they meant "What is the utterance of Yahweh?" Jeremiah replies by creating a pun on the word: "You are the burden, and I will cast you off—Yahweh's word." The two senses of *maśśā'* here are "oracle" and "burden." The note of judgment is then sounded, *I will throw you down* (cf. 1:10).

34–37 Again, if a prophet or priest or one of the people[4] should utter *The burden of Yahweh,*[5] then Yahweh would *punish (pāqaḏ 'al)* that man and his household. It was not for those who were not called by Yahweh to utter his word. All they were permitted to do was to ask among themselves "What did Yahweh answer?" or "What did Yahweh say?" (v. 35). It was not for such as these to give utterance to the burden of Yahweh at any time. That burden was for the man to whom Yahweh entrusted his word (lit. "the man of his word," *'îš d^eḇārô)*. If unauthorized people should utter Yahweh's word they would only *pervert* (*hāpaḵ,* lit. "overturn") *the words of the living God, Yahweh of Hosts, our God* (v. 36).

The people were restricted merely to questions directed to the prophet, *What did Yahweh answer you?* or *What did Yahweh say?* (v. 37, cf. v. 35).

38–40 The judgment on impostors was to be severe. They had been forbidden to claim to be uttering the burden of Yahweh.

3. P. A. H. de Boer, "An Enquiry into the Meaning of the Term *maśśa',*" *OTS* 5 (1948), pp. 197–214.

4. The text reads *hā'ām, the people,* but the context suggests *one of the people*.

5. Possibly the "burdensome utterance," combining both ideas in v. 33.

If they persisted in deceiving the people Yahweh himself would pick them up *(nāśā')* and throw them down like a "burden," and bring everlasting and unforgettable disgrace and humiliation upon them.

The whole argument comes to us as rather complex, probably because the pun is developed in such a sustained manner. The two senses of *maśśā'*, "prophetic utterance" and "burden," and the verb *nāśā'* occur a number of times. The *maśśā'* of Yahweh is that the people are a *maśśā'*.

3. TWO VISIONS AND A SUMMARY (24:1–25:38)

(i) The Two Baskets of Figs (24:1–10)

1 *Yahweh showed me, and there, two baskets of figs set down*[1] *in front of the temple of Yahweh. (This was after Nebuchadrezzar king of Babylon had deported from Jerusalem Jeconiah ben Jehoiakim, king of Judah, along with the officials of Judah, the artisans, and the smiths,*[2] *and had taken them to Babylon.)*

2 *In one basket the figs were very good like the early ripening figs. In the other basket the figs were very bad, so bad that they were not fit to eat.*

3 *And Yahweh said to me, "What do you see, Jeremiah?" And I said "Figs! The good figs are very good, the bad figs are very bad, so bad that they are not fit to eat."*

4 *Then the word of Yahweh came to me:*

5 *"This is what Yahweh, the God of Israel, has said: Like these good figs will I recognize for favor the exiles of Judah whom I have sent away from this place to the land of the Chaldeans.*

6 *I will watch over them to do them good, and I will bring them back to this land; I will build them up and not tear them down, plant them and not uproot them.*

7 *And I will give them a mind to know me, that I am Yahweh. They shall be my people and I will be their God, for they shall return to me with all their heart.*

8 *But like the bad figs which are too bad to eat—this is what Yahweh has said—I will treat Zedekiah king of Judah and his officials and the survivors of Jerusalem, both those who remain in this land and those who live in Egypt;*

1. The Hophal participle of *y'd (mû'āḏîm)* occurs only here and in Ezek. 21:16. Emendation to *mo'ºmāḏîm*, "placed," or *'ômeḏîm*, "standing," is not necessary. But perhaps the root goes back to *wd'* (Arabic *wada'a*, to put, to deposit, to place). See D. W. Thomas, "A Note on *mû'āḏîm* in Jeremiah 24:1," *JTS* N.S. 3 (Apr. 1952, p. 55).
2. Heb. *masgēr.* LXX has "prisoners" and adds "and the wealthy." The root *sgr* certainly suggests "prisoner" or even "hostage" (see Ps. 142:7; Isa. 24:22; 42:7). But the occurrence of the word alongside *artisans* here and at 29:2; 2 K. 24:14, 16 suggests craftsmen of some sort.

9 *I will make them a horrible sight for all the kingdoms of the earth, an insult, an example, a taunt, and a curse in all the places to which I drive them.*
10 *And I will send against them sword, famine, and pestilence until they are exterminated from the land which I gave to their fathers."*

The historical background of this vision is the first deportation of the people in 597 B.C. After the exile of Jehoiachin and the leading citizens of Judah (2 K. 24:10–17), those who remained seem to have been full of optimism for the future. The new king Zedekiah even became involved in a conspiracy with the surrounding peoples for further rebellion against Babylon (ch. 27). The false prophets spoke of a quick return of the exiles from Babylon (ch. 28). Jeremiah saw that the attitude of the king and his supporters in Judah was wrong. True, there would be a new day for Judah and the people of God, but the future lay with the exiles and not with Zedekiah and his supporters. The current optimism led Jeremiah into a more determined and even more relentless ministry. Judah was still to face a judgment which would be far more devastating than any that had hitherto befallen it.

The literary structure is simple—the vision, a question from Yahweh, and the explanation.

1 The vision of baskets of figs is reminiscent of 1:11–16 (cf. Amos 7:1–9; 8:1–3). The expression *Yahweh showed me* suggests a visionary experience. The figs were *set down*[3] in front of the temple. One thinks immediately of the presentation of the firstfruits (Deut. 26:5–11; see v. 2). In that case one would want to know why there were bad figs set down along with good ones. They may represent the shabby offerings of those who were not serious about the sovereignty of Yahweh (cf. Mal. 1:6–9). But perhaps the whole thing was a vision and symbolic of the fact that what was corrupt would be rejected (even the temple, which had been desecrated; cf. 7:1–2).

The historical note, which is syntactically a parenthesis, is accurate. The date then is post-597 B.C. *Jeconiah* is elsewhere called Coniah or Jehoiachin (see on 22:24). The term *śar* may not refer specifically to nobles but to members of the king's inner council. The term translated *smith (masgēr)* is of uncertain meaning.[4]

3. See textual note.
4. See textual note.

2 The Hebrew text reads literally "The one basket good figs . . . the one basket bad figs." The good figs are *bakkurôṯ,* "newly ripe," *early ripening,* and hence the suggestion of firstfruits.

3 The manner in which the prophet saw his vision is not clear. It must often have happened that a concrete experience was transformed in the mind into a symbolic meaning. But that is not unique to a prophet in Israel; it happens in our day.

4–7 The *good figs* are identified as the exiles already in Babylon which are recognized *for favor,* that is: Yahweh looks on these as the ones singled out for favor. The future lies with them.

Those who had been deported to Babylon in 597 B.C. were, in fact, the cream of the country's leadership: "All the officials, all the mighty men of valor, ten thousand captives, and all the craftsmen and the smiths; none remained except the poorest people of the land. And he carried away Jehoiachin to Babylon; the king's mother, the king's wives, his officials, and the chief men of the land . . ." (2 K. 24:14–15). Among these were "officials" who had intervened on more than one occasion on Jeremiah's behalf (chs. 26, 36). Those who were left probably lacked political skill and seem to have been hostile to Jeremiah, for he suffered severely in the period between 597 and 586 B.C. The verbs *build up (bānâ), plant (nāṭa'), tear down (hāras),* and *uproot (nāṯaš)* are first met in 1:10 and repeatedly mentioned in the book (cf. 12:14–17; 31:27–28). They cover the double themes of judgment and restoration, which according to Jeremiah's call were to be at the heart of his preaching. It was his great grief that the bulk of his preaching was about judgment. His references to renewal, by comparison, are few. It will be granted to the exiles to know Yahweh and to form the nucleus of the renewed Israel which will recognize Yahweh's sovereignty. They will *return (šûḇ)* to him with their whole heart. Heart renewal could evidently come only after judgment, so that judgment was the very means by which the new beginning for God's people was to be achieved—an encouraging doctrine for those in exile and for those who would follow in 586 B.C.

8–10 The *bad figs, too bad to eat,* comprised those who were left in the land or who had settled in Egypt. We are not told when people fled to Egypt, but those of pro-Egyptian sympathies may have settled there when Jehoahaz was taken there in 609 B.C. (2 K. 23:34) or when Jehoiakim became Nebuchadrezzar's vassal (*c*. 603 B.C.) or even when Nebuchadrezzar invaded Judah in 598/7 B.C. Certainly a group fled to Egypt later (chs. 43–44). But these words can hardly be used to support a post-587 B.C. date for the present passage.[5]

Verses 9–10 contain several terms that are found frequently in Jeremiah to describe the doom that was about to befall Judah (15:4; 21:7; 29:18; 34:17; Deut. 28:37; Ps. 44:15–16 [Eng. 14–15]). The Jeremiah passages are in prose, and once again the question of the character of the prose in this book is raised.[6]

(ii) A Concluding Summary (25:1–14)

1 *The word that came to Jeremiah concerning all the people of Judah in the fourth year of Jehoiakim ben Josiah, king of Judah (that is, in the first year of Nebuchadrezzar king of Babylon).*[1]

2 *This is what Jeremiah the prophet spoke to all the people of Judah and all the citizens of Jerusalem:*

3 *"From the thirteenth year of Josiah ben Amon king of Judah up to the present day, for thirty years (the word of Yahweh has come to me)*[2] *and I have spoken to you persistently. (But you have not listened.)*[3]

4 *Moreover, Yahweh has sent to you persistently all his servants the prophets, but you have not listened nor shown any inclination to listen.*[4]

5 *They said, 'Turn, now, each one from his evil way and from his wicked deeds, and live in the land which Yahweh gave*[5] *to you and to your fathers for ever.*

6 *Do not follow other gods, to serve them and to worship them! Do not provoke me to anger with the work of your hands. Then I will not do you harm.'*

7 *But you would not listen to me—Yahweh's word. (This was in order to provoke me to anger with the work of your hands to your own hurt.)*[6]

8 *Therefore, this is what Yahweh of Hosts has said: Because you have not listened to my word,*

5. See J. Bright, *Jeremiah,* p. 193, and cf. E. W. Nicholson, *Jeremiah 1–25,* p. 207.
6. See the Introduction, "The Book of Jeremiah: Composition," pp. 33–50.

1. The words in parentheses are lacking in LXX.
2. The words in parentheses are lacking in LXX.
3. Lacking in LXX.
4. Lit. "You have not inclined your ear to listen." The last word *to listen* is lacking in LXX.
5. LXX reads "which I gave."
6. This sentence is lacking in LXX.

9 *Look! I am sending to take all the clans of the north—Yahweh's word—that is, for Nebuchadrezzar king of Babylon, my servant.*[7] *I will bring them against this land and its citizens and against all these peoples round about. And I will devote them to wholesale destruction and make them a thing of horror, something to whistle at and an everlasting spectacle.*[8]

10 *I will banish from them sounds of joy and gladness, the voice of the bride and bridegroom, the sound of the handmill and the light of the lamp.*

11 *And this whole land shall be a desolate waste,*[9] *and these nations will serve the king of Babylon*[10] *for seventy years.*

12 *Then, when seventy years have passed, I will punish the king of Babylon and*[11] *that nation—Yahweh's word—for their iniquity, that is, the land of the Chaldeans,*[12] *and I will make it a desolation for ever.*

13 *And I will bring upon that land all the things I spoke against it, all that is written in this book, all that Jeremiah prophesied against all the nations.*[13]

14 *Many nations and great kings will enslave them, and I will repay them according to their deeds, according to what they have done."*

The passage is entirely in prose and includes many phrases and expressions that occur elsewhere in the prose passages in Jeremiah.[14] There are marked differences between MT and LXX. There are also places where the syntax is awkward (e.g., vv. 12–14). LXX is shorter, omitting direct references to Nebuchadrezzar and Babylon and ending with v. 13bα *(all that is written in this book).*[15] It is thus extremely difficult to determine what the original text of Jeremiah's utterance was. It was probably much briefer than its present form and may have been concerned only with Judah. *This book* (v. 13) was probably the scroll which contained the prophecies of Jeremiah in chs. 1–25. But as the collection was expanded by the inclusion of foreign prophecies there were modifications to the original content of these verses plus chs. 46–51 in LXX. Despite many

7. The words from *that is* are lacking in LXX.
8. Reading *ḥerpaṯ* with LXX for MT *ḥorᵉḇôṯ*, "desolations."
9. Lit. "a desolation and a waste."
10. LXX reads "and they will serve among the nations," omitting *the king of Babylon.*
11. The words *the king of Babylon and* are lacking in LXX.
12. The words *Yahweh's word—for their iniquity, that is, the land of the Chaldeans* are lacking in LXX.
13. The words *all that Jeremiah prophesied against all the nations* are lacking in LXX.
14. The discussion here follows J. Bright, *Jeremiah,* p. 163, which is a balanced and judicious attempt to solve the literary problems of this chapter.
15. See below on vv. 12–14.

valiant attempts to account for ch. 25 in its present form it would seem to be impossible to deny Jeremiah's hand completely.[16]

1–2 The fourth year of Jehoiakim's reign (605 B.C.) was the year in which Jeremiah dictated his prophecies to Baruch. The scroll Baruch wrote was read to the king (36:1–26). Although the king destroyed the scroll it was later rewritten and became, it would seem, the nucleus of the earliest collection of Jeremiah's prophecies (36:27–32). The passage before us (25:1–14) can be seen either as a superscription to the whole collection, or its epilog. According to one view it is the conclusion to the scroll.[17] On another view it is a prefatory speech composed to accompany the reading of the scroll.

The reference to *Nebuchadrezzar* is lacking in LXX, but even if it is a gloss, it is correct. Nebuchadrezzar (Akk. Nabu-kudurri-uṣur) ascended to the throne in September 605 B.C. but his first official regnal year began in April 604 B.C. Jehoiakim reigned from 609–598 B.C. so that 605 B.C. would be in Nebuchadrezzar's accession year.

3–5 The thirteenth year of Josiah's reign is given in 1:2 as the date at which Jeremiah began his ministry, that is, 627 B.C.[18] As a general statement Jeremiah spoke to the people incessantly and earnestly (lit. "rising early and speaking")[19] but they did not listen to him. But that had been the pattern with all Yahweh's servants the prophets. Yahweh sent them persistently and without interruption, but Israel paid no attention. The constant appeal of the prophets of Israel was that every man should *turn* from *(šûḇ min)* his evil way and from his wicked deeds. Their continued life in the land promised to their fathers depended on their loyalty to Yahweh and his covenant.

It has often been pointed out that v. 4 is virtually the same as 7:25b, 26a, and for that reason the section is sometimes omitted. Some commentators searching for Jeremiah's *ipsissima verba* omit

16. E. W. Nicholson, *Jeremiah 1–25,* p. 209, declares categorically, "there can be little doubt that this 'sermon' is a purely editorial composition written by a Deuteronomic author as a summary conclusion to the first major portion of the book"; G. P. Couturier, "Jeremiah," *JBC,* p. 322, believes the text, released of certain glosses, gives a logical and clear summary of Jeremiah's preaching.

17. A. Weiser, *Das Buch des Propheten Jeremia,* p. 216.

18. The exact significance of this date is not certain. Does it refer to the year he first delivered a message, or to the year of his appointment to preach "from his mother's womb," that is, the date of his birth? See the Introduction, "The Date of Jeremiah's Call," pp. 50–56.

19. The combination of *haškēm,* "rising early," with another verb occurs several times in Jeremiah, all in prose passages. See 7:13, 25; 11:7; 25:4; 26:5; 29:19; 32:33; 35:14, 15; 44:4.

the last part of v. 3 and vv. 4, 6, and 7b. By contrast LXX makes Yahweh the speaker of the whole of vv. 3–7. It would seem that it is a fruitless undertaking to attempt to discern Jeremiah's actual words here. In any case, expressions once used by Jeremiah could be used more than once, assuming as we do that Jeremiah sometimes spoke in prose.

6–7 Some specific prohibitions are given here. The expressions *follow other gods, serve ('āḇaḏ), worship* or "bow down to" *(hištaḥᵃwâ), provoke to anger (hiḵ'îs)* are found elsewhere in Jeremiah and are also frequently used in Deuteronomy.[20] *The work of your hands* (vv. 6, 7) is sometimes taken to mean "idols your hands have made" (NEB), but it may be a general reference to the actions of the people, that is, what they do (cf. v. 14). The expression is ambiguous. In 1:16 it is parallel to "other gods" and is used with the verb "worship," so that it means idols.

8–11 The judgment that would fall on Judah is now given in the name of *Yahweh of Hosts*. Yahweh will bring *all the clans of the north* against Judah and its citizens as well as against the nations round about. The specific identification of Nebuchadrezzar following the more general clans *of the north* is syntactically awkward, and looks like an explanatory note added during later editing of Jeremiah's original word designed to indicate how the prophecy was fulfilled.

The use of the term "families" or *clans (mišpāḥôṯ)* probably refers to a sub-unit within a wider political unit.

The reference to Nebuchadrezzar as *my servant ('eḇeḏ)* raises an interesting question. There is no evidence that the king of Babylon was ever a worshipper of Yahweh. The term *servant* here and also in 27:6 and 43:10 has another meaning. Clearly he was God's instrument for judgment on Judah (cf. Cyrus in Isa. 44:28–45:1, called "my shepherd," "my anointed"). The omission by LXX of this reference to Nebuchadrezzar may indicate that the translator objected to giving such a title and such a place of honor to a pagan king.[21] But the title is probably more directly related to a political concept. The term "servant" is widely used in the context of suzerain-vassal relationships in the ancient Near East and forms a regular part of treaty terminology. The vassal was obligated to place his army at the service of his overlord. Nebuchadrezzar is here seen

20. E.g., Deut. 8:2; 13:10; 25:6.
21. See textual notes for other differences between MT and LXX.

as the vassal of Yahweh, and as such he is summoned along with the tribes of the north to destroy Judah and its inhabitants for their rebellion against him.[22]

The nations *round about* who are to be punished along with Judah are not identified. If the section 25:1–14 was originally addressed to Judah (v. 1) either as a prologue or as an epilogue to Jeremiah's preaching to Judah, these words may represent an editorial gloss which was added when account was taken of the foreign prophecies (chs. 46–51) and to conform with the material in vv. 15–38.

The judgments to be meted out to Judah are expressed in terms which are known elsewhere in Jeremiah. They would be devoted *to wholesale destruction* (Heb. *heḥ^e^rîm).* The verb is related to the noun *ḥērem.* It occurs frequently in early narratives dealing with the holy war especially in Joshua (Num. 21:2–3; Deut. 2:34; 3:6; 7:2; 20:17; Josh. 2:10; 6:18, 21; 8:26; 10:1, 28, 35, 37, 39–40; 11:11–12, 20–21; Judg. 1:17; 21:11; etc.). In continuance of the ancient holy war symbolism those who opposed Yahweh in the fulfilment of his purposes were put to the ban, and totally (or partially) destroyed. Further, the people would become a *horror (šammâ), something to whistle at (š^e^rēqâ),* and a *spectacle* (reading *ḥerpâ* with LXX), all well-known terms in Jeremiah.[23] The cessation of joy (7:34; 16:9), the halting of the millstone, and the extinction of the lamp would all mark the close of life (cf. Eccl. 12:3–6 for similar examples pointing to the approach of death). At v. 11 LXX reads "they shall serve among the nations" with no reference to the king of Babylon. "They" here denotes the people of Judah (cf. v. 1). The present edited text seems to have expanded the original text by reference to *these nations* and *the king of Babylon.*

The expression *seventy years* is significant. Originally it may have meant merely a normal life-span, as extrabiblical texts demonstrate (cf. forty years, a generation).[24] The expression is also used in 25:11 for a long but definite period. It became the basis for considerable discussion in postexilic times (2 Chr. 36:21; Dan. 9:2; cf.

22. Z. Zevit, "The Use of *'eḇeḏ* as a Diplomatic Term in Jeremiah," *JBL* 88 (1969), pp. 74–77.

23. *Šammâ,* 25:11, 38; 42:18; 44:12; 46:19; 48:9; 49:13, 17; 50:23; *š^e^rēqâ,* 18:16; 19:8; 25:9, 18; 29:18; 51:37; *ḥerpâ,* 23:40; 24:9.

24. E. Vogt, "70 anni exsilii," *Biblica* 38 (1957), p. 236, refers to a statement in an inscription of Esarhaddon; cf. O. Plöger, "Siebzig Jahre," *Festschrift, Friedrich Baumgartel* (1959), pp. 124–130 (in Erlanger Forschungen).

Ezra 1:1) and has been the subject of many discussions over the centuries. In Zech. 1:12 it seems to denote the interval between the destruction of the temple in 587 B.C. and its rebuilding in 520–515 B.C. In 2 Chr. 36:20–23 it is the period between 587 and Cyrus' edict of 538 B.C. In Daniel it is used as a basis for demonstration that in the days of Antiochus Epiphanes the purpose of God would be fulfilled (Dan. 9). In fact, the figure turns out to be approximately correct: from the fall of Nineveh (612 B.C.) to the fall of Babylon (539 B.C.) was seventy-three years while from the accession of Nebuchadrezzar (605 B.C.) to the fall of Babylon was sixty-six years. There are some modern writers who take the number seventy literally.[25] Even so the figure is not exact. If we regard it as a symbol for "many" (Judg. 1:7; 8:14; 1 Sam. 6:19; 2 Sam. 24:15; Ps. 90:10; etc.), it will serve the purpose which Jeremiah probably intended.

12–14 Questions of interpretation continue. LXX concludes this section at v. 13bα with the words *in this book* and places here, though in a different order, chs. 46–51. One feasible suggestion is that the words *which Jeremiah prophesied against all the nations* are a heading for vv. 15–38. What Jeremiah's original prophecy was is difficult to determine, though it was against Judah (v. 1). It is not likely that LXX represents the original form of the text although it may have been closer to it than MT. The material in vv. 3–13a will at least give some indication of the scope of Jeremiah's summary, making allowance for what seem to be obvious expansions. The material may have ended with the words: "For seventy years this whole country shall be a scandal and a horror; I will bring upon this country all I have said, all that is written in this book."

(iii) Judgment on the Nations—Yahweh's Cup of Wrath (25:15–29)

15 *This*[1] *is what Yahweh the God of Israel said to me:*[2] *"Take from my hand this cup of the wine of wrath*[3] *and make all the nations to which I send you drink of it.*

16 *When they have drunk they will stagger and go mad because of the sword which I am sending among them."*

25. C. F. Whitley, "The Term Seventy Years Captivity," *VT* 4 (1954), pp. 60–72; "The Seventy Years Desolation—A Rejoinder," *VT* 7 (1957), pp. 416–18; A. Orr, "The Seventy Years of Babylon," *VT* 6 (1956), pp. 304–306. Whitley, reviving the view of Duhm, argues that the text in 29:20 refers to the seventy years of the duration of Babylon, 605–539 B.C., which is only four years short of seventy.

1. MT "For this. . . ."
2. LXX lacks *to me*.
3. LXX "this cup of foaming (fermenting) wine," reading *ḥemer* for *ḥēmâ*.

17 *So I took the cup from the hands of Yahweh and I made all the nations to whom Yahweh, God, sent me, drink it:*
18 *Jerusalem, the cities of Judah, its kings and officials, making them a desolation, a horror, something to whistle at, an object of ridicule (as it is this day);*
19 *Pharaoh king of Egypt and his courtiers, his officials,*
20 *and all his people and all his rabble of followers; all the kings of the land of Uz; all the kings of the land of the Philistines, Ashkelon, Gaza, Ekron, and what remains of Ashdod;*
21 *Edom and Moab and the Ammonites;*
22 *all the kings of Tyre; all the kings of Sidon and the kings of the coastlands which are beyond the sea;*
23 *Dedan, and Tema, and Buz, and all who clip the hair of their temples;*[4]
24 *all the kings of Arabia and all the kings of the mixed peoples*[5] *who live in the desert;*
25 *all the kings of Zimri, all the kings of Elam, all the kings of the Medes;*
26 *all the kings of the north near and far, one after another, and all the kingdoms on the face of the earth. And the king of Sheshak shall drink last of all.*
27 *"You shall say to them: 'This is what Yahweh of Hosts, the God of Israel, has said: Drink and get drunk and vomit; fall and do not rise, because of the sword which I am sending among you.'*
28 *And if they refuse to take the cup from your hand and drink, then say to them: 'This is what Yahweh of Hosts has said: You have to drink it!*
29 *For look! At the very city that bears my name I am beginning to bring disaster, and you, do you think you will be exempt? No, you will not be exempt, for I am invoking the sword against all the inhabitants of the earth—the word of Yahweh of Hosts.' "*

It is at once evident that vv. 15–39 are closely related to the oracles against the foreign nations in chs. 46–51. Jeremiah was originally commissioned to be a prophet to the nations (1:5), and it is to be expected that some of his utterances would concern nations other than Israel. Verses 15–28 are in prose, couched in the form of an address by Yahweh to the prophet (vv. 15–16, 27–29) followed by a list of the nations (vv. 17–26). Judgment is likened to a stupefying draught which the nations are compelled to drink.

The figure of the "cup of wrath" is used not only by Jeremiah in this general period (cf. 13:12–14) but also by Habakkuk (Hab. 2:16) and in Lamentations (Lam. 4:21). It was used again during the

4. See the commentary.
5. These two phrases are very similar in Hebrew and may be a dittography; LXX has only "and all the mixed peoples."

Exile (Ezek. 23:32–34; Isa. 51:17, 21–22). In the light of Jeremiah's call it would seem unreasonable to deny to Jeremiah as some writers do[6] the kind of utterance we have in vv. 15–39. Even if some expansion has taken place in the list of peoples (vv. 18–26), such a list would be expected in a summary of the prophet's activity in regard to the nations. The fact that LXX places this material at the end of foreign oracles[7] while MT places it at the beginning may only indicate some variations in the textual arrangement (cf. the different arrangement of the books of the OT). The Hebrew order with these verses as a summarizing introduction has much to commend it.

15–17 The intoxicating cup as a symbol of divine wrath is alluded to in 49:12 and 51:7. In the present chapter the theme is developed in vv. 27–29.[8] These verses report Yahweh's word to Jeremiah. The drinking of a potion was also one of the ordeal procedures for testing the innocence of a person, and the "cup of wrath" symbol may have had its origin in such procedures (Num. 5:11–31). Drunkenness is also a symbol for a sinful state which calls for judgment (13:12–14; Isa. 19:14; 28:7–13). In the present passage the cup of wine symbolizes the avenging wrath of Yahweh[9] which he requires those who have offended him to drink. Jeremiah takes the cup and delivers it to all the nations to whom Yahweh sends him. It is his appointed task.[10] The cup is the sword which Yahweh would send among them to make them stagger and go out of their minds (cf. v. 27). The list of nations follows. All the nations referred to in chs. 46–51 are included here except Damascus, but other nations are referred to besides those mentioned in the oracles there.

18 Yahweh's own people in Jerusalem and the cities of Judah will be the first to receive the divine judgment (cf. v. 29). The description of the judgment is in terms which are commonly used in the book of Jeremiah (cf. v. 9).[11] The last phrase *as it is this day* suggests that at the time of writing some aspects of this judgment, at least, were apparent.

19–20 The historical context in which we may set these verses is not easy to define. The word came to Jeremiah in the fourth year of Jehoiakim, in the first year of Nebuchadrezzar (v. 1),

6. E. W. Nicholson, *Jeremiah 1–25,* p. 213.
7. 25:15–38 in MT becomes 32:1–24 in LXX.
8. Cf. also Hab. 2:15, 16; Isa. 51:17–23; Lam. 4:21; Ps. 60:5 (Eng. 3); 75:9 (Eng. 8).
9. There are some minor textual variations from LXX; see textual notes.
10. Cf. 1:5–10.
11. 19:9; 29:18; 42:18; 44:12; 49:12, 17; 51:37; etc.

that is, 605 B.C., the year in which the Egyptian garrison was overwhelmed at Carchemish (46:2ff.) and the Egyptians fled south pursued by the Chaldean armies. In August 605 B.C. Nebuchadrezzar returned to Babylon on his father's death to assume the throne. By the end of 604 B.C. the Chaldeans were in the Philistine plain and had destroyed Ashkelon (47:5–7). Against the background of such swiftly moving events Jeremiah spoke to the people of Judah of their impending doom and of their seventy years of servitude in Babylon (v. 11). The cup of Yahweh's wrath was to be passed on to the nations in turn, and after they had drunk it would pass to Babylon (v. 26). It must have seemed to Jeremiah that one by one the nations were to suffer at the hands of Nebuchadrezzar.

Egypt now passes in review (cf. ch. 46)—the pharaoh with his officials and nobles, his people, and the mixed company[12] who live in Egypt. The latter group comprised the many foreigners who resided in Egypt under the rule of the pharaoh. *The land of Uz,* the home of Job (Job 1:1), probably lay to the east of Palestine. In Lam. 4:21 it is connected with Edom. The reference is lacking in LXX.

The Philistine area is represented by Ashkelon, Gaza, Ekron, and Ashdod (ch. 47). The fifth city, Gath, is not mentioned. Perhaps it had declined by this time (cf. Amos 1:6ff.). Modern archeology has done much to elucidate the story of Ashkelon, Gaza, and Ashdod. According to Herodotus (ii.157) Ashdod was conquered and destroyed by Pharaoh Psammeticus I (663–609 B.C.) after a long siege. The reference to *what remains* (*šᵉʾērîṯ*) of Ashdod may bear witness to this event.

21–22 The nations of Edom, Moab, and Ammon (48:1–49:22) and the kings of Tyre and Sidon and their colonies (the coastlands beyond the sea) opposed Babylon (27:1–3) and would suffer.

23–24 The kings of the desert areas, Dedan, Tema, and Buz in the northern part of the Arabian peninsula (cf. 49:28–33), are listed. The location of Buz is not known. The expression *qᵉṣûṣê p̱ēʾâ* (lit. "the cutting of the fringe") is ambiguous. Some translations take it as "those who cut the corners of their hair," a reference to a tribal custom among some desert Arabs. The alternative and perhaps more convincing translation is "those who roam the fringe of the desert" (NEB; cf. 9:25 [Eng. 26]; 49:32), referring to nomadic or seminomadic tribes or clans who lived on the desert

12. *rabble*—Heb. *ʿereḇ,* "mixture," "mixed company," occurs in Exod. 12:38 to describe the mixed multitude that came out of Egypt with the Israelites.

fringes. Verse 24 closes with the words *who live in the desert,* a summarizing clause for vv. 23–24.

25 The name Zimri is unknown and the phrase *all the kings of Zimri* is lacking in LXX. Some commentators have suggested the reading "Zimki," an Atbash[13] for Elam (49:34–39). In that case Elam would be mentioned twice.

26 There is a general command to gather up other kings not yet mentioned, *kings of the north near and far,* and *all the kingdoms on the face of the earth.* The last to drink the cup is the king of Sheshak (cf. 51:41), which is the name of Babylon written as an Atbash (see note on previous verse). For a discussion of the significance of this device see below on 51:1, 41.

27–29 The passage returns to the direct words of Yahweh to Jeremiah, who is instructed to proclaim that for none of the inhabitants of the earth is there any way of avoiding the cup of Yahweh's wrath, least of all for Jerusalem itself.

(iv) The Universal Judgment of Yahweh (25:30–38)

30 *"As for you, prophesy to them all these things and say to them,*
'Yahweh roars from on high,
From his holy abode he thunders.
He roars aloud against his fold,
He shouts like the grape-treaders.
31 *The tumult reaches the ends of the earth,*
To all the dwellers on earth.[1]
For Yahweh brings an indictment against the nations
And he goes to law[2] *with all mankind;*
The wicked he has given over to the sword—
Yahweh's word.' "
32 *This is what Yahweh of Hosts has said:*
"Look! disaster has gone forth
From nation to nation.
A great tempest has blown up
From earth's farthest bounds.

13. The Atbash is a device in which the letters of a name counted from the beginning of the alphabet are exchanged for letters counted from the end; Zimki would be *'Êlām* in the Hebrew alphabet, and *bbl* (Babel) would be *ššk* (Sheshak, v. 26). In these ciphers *aleph (')* is replaced by *taw (t), beth (b)* by *shin (š),* etc.

1. This colon occurs before the previous one, at the end of v. 30, in MT. LXX connects it to the first part of v. 31.

2. The verb *nišpāṭ* is Niphal in form and means "go to judgment," "enter into legal proceedings."

33 *On that day those whom Yahweh has slain will stretch from one end of the earth to the other; they will not be lamented or gathered up*[3] *or buried, but will be like dung over the ground.*
34 *Howl, you shepherds! Cry aloud!*
Roll in the dust, you lords of the flock!
For your time has come to be slaughtered,
And you shall fall like the pick of the rams.[4]
35 *There will be no way to flee for the shepherds,*
No escape for the lords of the flock.
36 *Hark! the cry of the shepherds,*
The howl of the lords of the flock!
For Yahweh is ravaging their pasture;
37 *The peaceful folds lie silent*[5]
Because of Yahweh's hot anger.
38 *Like a lion he has left his thicket;*
Their land has become a waste
Before the cruel sword,[6]
Before his fierce anger."

The theme of universal judgment continues in poetic form, but without reference to the specific countries referred to in the earlier prose section (vv. 17–26). The judgment is presented as a lawsuit *(rîḇ,* v. 31). Parts of the poem are composed of conventional expressions (vv. 30–31) which Jeremiah took up, but vv. 32, 34–38 have much that is characteristic of the prophet.[7]

30 Pictures of Yahweh roaring like a lion (Amos 3:8; Hos. 11:10) or making himself heard in the midst of thunder (Exod. 19:16), or in storm (23:19; Amos 1:2; Joel 3:16), lie behind this verse. His voice is heard from *his holy abode,* from on high, that is, from heaven (cf. Amos 1:2; Joel 3:16). To heighten the effect Yahweh's roar is compared with the shout of the grape-treaders. The din resounds to the ends of the earth.

31–32 The motif of the lawsuit *(rîḇ)* against the nations re-

3. LXX omits "they will not be lamented, they will not be gathered."
4. The last phrase of v. 34 is difficult. The first word *t^epôṣôṯîḵem* is lacking in LXX and is not intelligible in Hebrew. It may be related to the roots *pṣṣ* and *npṣ,* both of which mean "shatter." Two possible variants may be suggested: "I will shatter you like a choice vessel" or "you will fall, like choice rams." The latter, in a context of slaughtering, seems preferable (so LXX); it requires emending *kiḵ^elî* to *k^e'êlê.*
5. Or, "are destroyed," *dmh* III; see the lexicons.
6. So several mss. and Versions (LXX, Latin, Targ.), reading *ḥereḇ* for MT *ḥ^arôn,* "anger"; cf. 46:16; 50:16.
7. Many commentators nonetheless regard the poem as the work of a late author.

news the picture of ch. 2.[8] A second legal term is used here, "go to law" *(nišpāṭ)*. There are guilty men *(wicked, rᵉšā'îm)* to be handed over to the judgment of the sword. The *disaster (rā'â)* is vast, spreading from nation to nation like a mighty tempest blowing up from earth's farthest bounds.

33 A prose piece interrupts the connection between vv. 32 and 34. It is possibly a gloss to heighten the effect still further (cf. 16:4).

34 The *shepherds* or *lords of the flock* were the rulers of the various nations who are called upon to *howl, cry aloud,* and *roll in the dust* (or "scatter ashes upon yourselves") as a sign of mourning, grief, and humiliation as their time for the slaughter comes. They will fall like the finest rams brought for killing.[9]

35–38 There will be no escape for the rulers *(shepherds)* and kings *(lords of the flock)* of the nations (cf. vv. 27–29), nor for their peaceful pastures. The lion has gone forth from his lair, and their land has become a *waste (šammâ)* before the sword and Yahweh's blazing anger.

The entire pericope stresses that Yahweh's action is not restricted to Israel but extends to all the known nations.

8. J. Harvey, "Le 'Rîb-Pattern,' réquisitoire prophétique sur la rupture de l'alliance," *Biblica* 43 (1962), pp. 172–196; H. B. Huffmon, "The Covenant Lawsuit in the Prophets," *JBL* 78 (1959), pp. 285–295.
9. See textual note.

III. JEREMIAH'S CONTROVERSY WITH FALSE PROPHETS (26:1–29:32)

A. THE TEMPLE SERMON AND ITS CONSEQUENCES (26:1–24)

1 *At the beginning of the reign of Jehoiakim ben Josiah king of Judah this word came from Yahweh.*[1]

2 *"This is what Yahweh has said: Stand in the court of the house of Yahweh and speak to all the people who come from cities of Judah*[2] *to worship in the house of Yahweh everything that I command you to say to them. Do not hold back a word.*

3 *Perhaps they will listen and everyone will turn from his evil way. Then I will think better of the disaster which I am purposing to bring upon them because of their evil deeds.*

4 *Say to them, 'This is what Yahweh has said: If you will not listen to me and follow my law which I have set before you,*

5 *and listen to the words of my servants the prophets which I send to you with great urgency, though you have never listened,*

6 *then I will make this house like Shiloh and this city I will make an object of ridicule to all the nations of the earth.' "*

7 *Now the priests and the prophets and all the people heard Jeremiah speaking these words in the house of Yahweh.*

8 *And when Jeremiah had finished speaking all that Yahweh had commanded him to say to all the people, the priests and the prophets and all the people*[3] *seized him and said: "You must certainly die!*

9 *Why have you prophesied in the name of Yahweh saying that this house will become like Shiloh and this city will be devastated without an inhabitant?" And all the people thronged around Jeremiah in the house of Yahweh.*

1. Latin and Syr. add "to Jeremiah."
2. MT has simply "to all cities of Judah who come. . . ." LXX reads "to every one of (*hápasi*) the Judeans and to all who come. . . ."
3. *All the people* must be understood as "some of the people." It is a very general statement. Some commentators omit the words, e.g., J. Bright, *Jeremiah,* p. 169.

10 *But the court officials*[4] *of Judah heard all of this and came up from the royal palace to the house of Yahweh and took their seats at the entrance of the New Gate of Yahweh's house.*[5]

11 *Then the priests and the prophets said to the officials and to all the people: "A death sentence for this man! He has prophesied against the city as you have heard with your own ears."*

12 *Then Jeremiah said to all the princes and all the people: "Yahweh sent me to prophesy against this house and this city all the things which you have heard.*

13 *Now therefore reform your ways and your doings and heed the voice of Yahweh your God so that Yahweh may think better of the disaster with which he has threatened you.*

14 *As for myself, look, I am in your hands. Do to me whatever you consider right and proper.*

15 *Only, know for certain that if you put me to death, you are bringing upon yourselves and on this city and its inhabitants innocent blood. For in very truth Yahweh has sent me to you to say all these things in your hearing."*

16 *Then the officials and all the people said to the priests and the prophets: "There will be no death sentence for this man, for he has spoken to us in the name of Yahweh our God."*

17 *Then some of the elders of the land rose up and said to the assembled people:*

18 *"In the days of Hezekiah king of Judah, Micah of Moresheth was prophesying; and he said to all the people of Judah, 'This is what Yahweh of Hosts has said:*
Zion shall become a ploughed field,
Jerusalem a heap of ruins,
And the temple mount a wooded ridge.'

19 *Did Hezekiah king of Judah, or anyone in Judah put him to death?*[6] *Did he not fear Yahweh and entreat the favor of Yahweh? Then did not Yahweh think better of the calamity with which he had threatened them? And we are about to bring a great disaster upon ourselves."*

20[7] *There was, indeed, another man who prophesied in the name of Yahweh, Uriah ben Shemaiah from Kiriath-jearim. He prophesied against this city and against this land just as Jeremiah did.*

21 *And when King Jehoiakim and all his bodyguard and all the officers heard his words the king sought to kill him. When Uriah heard of it he was afraid, and fled and escaped to Egypt.*

4. Heb. *śārîm,* "princes," were not necessarily of royal blood. None mentioned in Jeremiah seems to have been a royal prince. They were rather ministers and high officials of the crown.

5. *House* is lacking in MT but is restored from many mss. and Versions; cf. 36:10.

6. The expression is a strong one in MT, where the infinitive absolute precedes the verb: "really put him to death" or "put him to death in truth."

7. LXX has several small, mostly unimportant omissions in vv. 20–23.

22 *But King Jehoiakim sent Elnathan ben Achbor with a company of men*[8] *to Egypt,*
23 *and they brought Uriah from Egypt and led him to the king, who had him put to death by the sword. And they cast his body into the burial ground of the common people.*
24 *Yet Ahikam ben Shaphan gave support to Jeremiah so that he was not handed over to the people to be put to death.*

The incident described in ch. 26 took place sometime between the king's accession to the throne, on the deportation of his brother Jehoahaz to Egypt in the autumn or late summer of 609 B.C., and the following New Year (about 608 B.C.). In Judah regnal years were counted from the month Nisan of the first full year of a king's reign.[9] This would make the narrative the first of the stories which Jeremiah's biographer has left to us. The chapter is in prose and consists of four sections: a summary of the Temple Sermon (vv. 2–6); Jeremiah's arrest and trial (vv. 7–16); the elders' plea (vv. 17–19, 24); the execution of Uriah, a contemporary prophet (vv. 20–23).[10]

The passage gives a glimpse into legal proceedings and brings before us significant groups of people—the prosecutors, priests and prophets, the judges, princes (or civil authorities), elders, and the accused man. Procedures take place at the gate to Yahweh's house, and there is prosecution and defense. The prosecution demanded the death penalty. Jeremiah conducted his own defense.

One significant aspect of the story is that it records the rejection of the word of God spoken by Jeremiah, one of Yahweh's "servants the prophets," and makes clear that this rejection would inevitably bring judgment on Israel. There are several chapters in this part of the book (chs. 26–36) where the same motif can be discerned. Jeremiah was in constant conflict with the false prophets who held out optimistic hopes that the Exile would soon be over.[11]

8. The name *Elnathan ben Achbor* is lacking in LXX. But both MT and LXX have the phrase "sent men to Egypt." MT may have combined two variants into a conflate reading. There is a problem of how to assign the material in vv. 20–23. It may represent further remarks by the elders, in which case it is placed within quotation marks, as here. If it is only a historical comment the quotation marks should be omitted.

9. E. R. Thiele, *The Mysterious Numbers of the Hebrew Kings* (rev. ed. 1965), pp. 16–38. See further below under v. 1.

10. Note the discussion of E. W. Nicholson, *Preaching to the Exiles,* pp. 52, 55f., 86, 106, etc.

11. See the discussion at the introduction to the next section, p. 528.

1 The first expression in MT, *rē'šîṯ maml^ekûṯ*, corresponds to Akk. *rēš šarrûti*, a technical term for the period between the king's accession and the beginning of the next full year (the New Year). In some systems of dating this part year was counted as one, in others it was ignored and only full years were counted in the length of a king's reign. Israel followed the non-accession year system but Judah varied. From the days of Amaziah, at the beginning of the eighth century, to the end, Judah used the accession dating system and counted a year even if it was only part of a year.[12] The period between about September 609 B.C. and April (Nisan) 608 B.C. was thus the accession year of Jehoiakim, but also the first year of his reign. The setting of Jehoiakim on the throne was probably due to a popular move among the people.

2 A resumé of the Temple Sermon (7:1–15) begins here. Broadly it declared that Yahweh would suspend judgment on the nation if the people repented and observed the covenant law.

The *court* where Jeremiah was to stand is probably one of the inner courts. In 7:2, where it is stated that he stood in the gate of the Lord's house, it has been conjectured that he stood near the junction of the outer and the inner courts where people gathered on fast days and festivals.

The expression *Do not hold back (gāra') a word* is a vivid one. The verb sometimes refers to clipping off a beard (48:37; cf. Isa. 15:2). Jeremiah, who must have realized that the people would show hostility and that there could be severe consequences, may well have been tempted to "cut off" some words at least.

3 There was always a hope that the people might listen and *turn from (šûḇ min)* their evil way. For the sense of the verb *niḥam, think better of,* see comments on 18:8. The noun *rā'â* means evil in the sense of *disaster.* But once again the nation is given an opportunity to repent.

4–6 The emphasis here is that Yahweh makes his will known through the ministry of true prophets—*my servants the prophets.* These Yahweh kept sending *with great urgency,* or "persistence" (lit. "rising early and sending").[13] The group of chapters (27–29) will demonstrate the profound contrast between a true prophet and a false prophet. The covenant demands are here summarized under

12. E. R. Thiele, *loc. cit.*
13. Cf. 7:25; 25:4; 29:19.

my law (tôrâ), whereas in 7:5–6, 9, specific laws are mentioned which the nation is called upon to obey (cf. 2 K. 17:15). Rejection of the word of Yahweh spoken by his servants the prophets, in this case Jeremiah, would bring judgment; but there were others like Uriah (vv. 20–24). The particular judgment intended for the temple was to make it like the ancient sanctuary at Shiloh (1 Sam. 1–4). Shiloh was evidently destroyed about 1050 B.C. by the Philistine incursion into the land referred to in 1 Sam. 4. There is archeological evidence to support this (cf. Ps. 78:60, 61). Shiloh may have been rebuilt later but was again destroyed. It was in ruins in Jeremiah's day[14] and constituted a vivid picture of the destruction that was intended for Jerusalem and the temple. The term translated *object of ridicule* is *q^e^lālâ,* related to the adjective *qal,* "light." The term is often translated "curse" (RSV). A man was cursed if people spoke ill of him, downgraded him, belittled him, that is, made him an object of ridicule. Such talk cut across accepted theological views about the inviolability of the temple and the city and was tantamount to blasphemy. The prophet's words provoked a general scandal and led to his being charged with blasphemy.

7–8 Part of the offense lay in the fact that Jeremiah dared to utter such things in the very temple precincts. The *priests and the prophets* who heard were the cultic personnel of the temple, and *all the people* represented the congregation gathered for worship. Jeremiah was seized and charged with a capital offense. The expression *môṯ tāmûṯ, you must certainly die,* is akin to *môṯ yûmaṯ,* "he shall be put to death," in several places in Exod. 21–23, e.g., 21:15ff.[15]

9 The charge was that Jeremiah had spoken in Yahweh's name when he declared that the temple would become like Shiloh and Jerusalem would become a waste and uninhabited. Jeremiah was a false prophet in the eyes of his accusers, who believed sincerely that such things were impossible. He was, in fact, a double blasphemer. He spoke in Yahweh's name and he prophesied something that could never happen. It would seem that the people crowded about Jeremiah. The verb *qāhal* normally refers to a gathering for religious purposes but it is also used for war (2 Sam. 20:14), or for hostile intentions (Num. 16:3). Such a scene in the temple precincts indicates how angry the people were.

14. See references at 7:12.

15. Cf. Hammurabi Code, *ANET,* pp. 166–180, many examples; Lev. 24:10–16; 1 K. 21:13.

10 Fortunately for Jeremiah the *court officials (śārîm)*[16] were on hand to conduct a proper legal inquiry. Either they heard the commotion and came or a messenger was sent to bring them. A court was convened to try Jeremiah as soon as the officials arrived from the royal palace and took their seats at the entrance of the *New Gate*. Court sessions were held normally at gates (Gen. 23:10–20; Ruth 4:1; Prov. 31:23). No more is known about this gate than that it was in the upper court (cf. 20:2).

11 The prosecution, consisting of priests and prophets, demanded the death penalty before the *officials* (*śārîm*) acting as judges. No doubt they retailed the charges in full.

12–13 Jeremiah's defense was that Yahweh had sent him to prophesy against the temple and the city in the terms they had all heard, that is, the words were not his but Yahweh's. He was a true prophet and not a false one (cf. 23:21). To kill him would be to shed innocent blood and run the risk of divine retribution. And true to his prophetic calling he appealed to them to *reform* (lit. "make good," *hêṭîḇ*) their ways. There was a conditional element which ought not to be forgotten. Only repentance could save them. That would make Yahweh *think better (niḥam)* of the disaster he intended to send upon them. The principle of conditionality is enunciated in 18:1–12. It was evidently well known and understood, though probably not believed.

14–15 Jeremiah pressed his point. At that moment he was powerless before the hostile crowd. But Yahweh had truly sent him, and for the people to kill him would be to invite divine judgment on themselves for spilling innocent blood.

16 The royal officials, backed by the people, accepted the prophet's defense and took a stand against the religious authorities. It was his own defense and not the later support of certain elders which gained the verdict. The judges were persuaded that Jeremiah had spoken in the name of Yahweh. He was not a false prophet nor a blasphemer. He was acquitted.

17–19 The subsequent observations of some of the elders recalling the parallel case of Micah of Moresheth (Mic. 1:1), who had once spoken in similar terms (Mic. 3:12), came after the verdict was given, although it was good support. King Hezekiah (716–687 B.C.) and the people at that time, far from rejecting Micah's words,

16. See R. de Vaux, *Ancient Israel*, pp. 69, 138; and the textual note above.

reverenced (feared, *yārē'*) Yahweh and entreated his favor.[17] The elders pointed out that by contrast, they were on the point of bringing a great calamity upon themselves.

The quotation of Mic. 3:12 shows that the oracles of the prophets were preserved and were well known.

20–23 The prophet Uriah who proclaimed a message rather like that of Jeremiah is not known elsewhere. Evidently Jeremiah was not alone. Uriah ben Shemaiah came from Kiriath-jearim some 8 miles northwest of Jerusalem. It is identified today with Tell el-Azhar (Abu Ghosh) and was one of the four Gibeonite cities (Josh. 9:17). It was also known as Kiriath-baal (Josh. 18:14), and Baalah (Josh. 15:9). The Ark was kept here after it was sent back by the Philistines, and it was taken from there to Jerusalem (1 Sam. 7:1–2; 2 Sam. 6). It was thus a place with ancient historical associations.

The fate of Uriah was less happy than that of Jeremiah. He was put to death for preaching against the city and the land. He fled to Egypt when King Jehoiakim and his *officers* (*śārîm*) and his *bodyguard* (*gibbôrîm*), having heard his prophesying, sought his life. A certain Elnathan was sent to extradite him. The extradition of political refugees was frequently inserted as one of the clauses in the treaties of the second millennium B.C.[18] We may conjecture that there was a suzerain-vassal treaty between Egypt and Judah since Necho placed Jehoiakim on the throne in 609 B.C. and required him to pay tribute (2 K. 23:34–35). Such extradition clauses were reciprocal, becoming part of international law.

Elnathan ben Achbor was among the officials who heard the scroll of Jeremiah read (36:11–13). He seems to have been the son of one of the reformers, Achbor ben Micaiah, one of Josiah's officials (2 K. 22:12, 14). He may have been the father of Nehushta, the mother of Jehoiachin king of Judah. He must have been acting under orders in the matter of Uriah. He certainly tried to stop Jehoiakim from destroying Jeremiah's scroll later (36:25). Evidently the name Achbor was common, for a seventh-century seal bears the name Achbor ben Ahikam.[19]

17. Heb. *ḥillâ pānîm* means lit. "to soften (smooth) the countenance" or "pat the cheek." The origin of this bold anthropomorphism is now lost. It may have been used in the pagan environment of Israel to denote some ceremony of touching the god's image (Exod. 32:11; 1 Sam. 13:12; 1 K. 13:6; 2 K. 13:4; Ps. 119:58; Zech. 7:2; 8:21–22; Mal. 1:9).

18. See *ANET,* pp. 200f., 203 in the treaty between Ramses II and Hattusilis III (*c.* 1275–1250 B.C.).

19. N. Avigad, "Two Newly Found Hebrew Seals," *IEJ* 13 (1963), pp. 322f.

When Uriah was brought to Jerusalem Jehoiakim had him executed[20] with the sword. The prophet Zechariah (2 Chr. 24:20–22) is the only other prophet whose execution is recorded in the OT. The persistent rejection by Israel of the preaching of the prophets sent by Yahweh, the suffering of men like Jeremiah, the death of Uriah and Zechariah, gave rise to the legends of martyrdom of many of the prophets (e.g., Isaiah).[21] Uriah's body was cast into *the burial ground of the common people* in the Kidron Valley, outside Jerusalem (2 K. 23:6).

It seems clear that the narrator included this incident (vv. 20–23) to stress the very great danger in which Jeremiah stood when he continued to preach in the way he did.

24 Fortunately for Jeremiah he had the friendly support of men like Ahikam ben Shaphan. Shaphan was the scribe (RSV "secretary") of Josiah's reform (2 K. 22:3–14). Jeremiah seems to have had good relations with this family. Another son Gemariah urged Jehoiakim not to burn Jeremiah's scroll (36:10, 25), and a third son Gedaliah took charge of Jeremiah after the fall of Jerusalem (39:14; 40:5–16). The support of such a family saved Jeremiah's life. The friendly relations which existed between them and Jeremiah suggest that Jeremiah had a positive and sympathetic attitude to Josiah's reform and to his general policy.

B. JEREMIAH AND THE FALSE PROPHETS (27:1–29:32)

The three chapters 27–29 provide information about Jeremiah's direct confrontation with false prophets. Chs. 27 and 28 belong together. They describe Jeremiah's reaction to a coalition formed between states in the Syria-Palestine area, including Judah, which led to the prophecy of Hananiah, one of the false prophets. In ch. 29 we meet similar prophets in Babylon preaching the same shallow message to the exiles. Jeremiah entered into controversy with these false prophets, whether in Judah or in Babylon. Chs. 27 and 28 deal with an incident, or a series of incidents, which occurred in the fourth year of Zedekiah (594/3 B.C.). Ch. 29 belongs probably to about the same time. In all these chapters the main theme is the

20. The Hiphil of *nkh* indicates a causative.
21. The NT passages Matt. 23:37; Luke 13:34 have this background.

same as that in ch. 20, namely, the conflict which arose when the word of Yahweh spoken by his true prophet Jeremiah was rejected by the false prophets. At the same time, the way in which Judah was misled by false prophets (cf. 14:11–16; 23:16–40) is clearly indicated.

(i) *Jeremiah Warns against a Coalition against Nebuchadrezzar (27:1–22)*

1 *At the beginning of the reign of Zedekiah*[1] *son of Josiah king of Judah, this word came to Jeremiah from Yahweh.*
2 *This is what Yahweh has said to me: "Make yourself thongs and a yoke-bar and put them on your neck.*
3 *Then send*[2] *to the kings of Edom, Moab, Ammon, Tyre, and Sidon through their ambassadors*[3] *who have come to Jerusalem to Zedekiah king of Judah.*
4 *Give them this charge for their masters: 'This is what Yahweh of Hosts, the God of Israel, has said: Say to your masters:*
5 *"It is I who have made the earth and mankind and the beasts that live on the earth by my great power and my outstretched arm, and I give it to whom I see fit.*
6 *And now it is I who have delivered all these lands into the hands of my servant Nebuchadnezzar king of Babylon. And I have also given him the wild beasts to serve him.*
7 *All nations shall be subject to him and his son and his son's son until the destined hour of his own country comes. Then many nations and great kings shall reduce him*[4] *to servitude.*
8 *But the nation or the kingdom that will not be subject to Nebuchadnezzar king of Babylon and will not place its neck*[5] *under the yoke of the king of Babylon, I will punish that nation by sword, by famine, and by pestilence—Yahweh's word—until I have delivered them*[6] *into his hand.*
9 *For your part, do not listen to your prophets, your diviners, your dreamers,*[7] *your soothsayers, and your sorcerers who keep telling you not to submit to the king of Babylon.*

1. MT reads "Jehoiakim"; v. 1 is lacking in LXX, and may be a recopying of 26:1. A few mss., e.g., Syriac Peshitta, read *Zedekiah.* See commentary. Cf. vv. 3, 12.
2. MT reads "send them"; LXX omits "them."
3. MT has simply *ambassadors*; LXX adds *their.*
4. Or "it," the country. The text is ambiguous: "They shall serve through/with/in him/it." The context suggests a change in status for Nebuchadrezzar from lord to servant.
5. LXX omits "will not be subject to Nebuchadrezzar king of Babylon" and refers only to placing the neck under the yoke of the king of Babylon.
6. See the commentary below.
7. MT reads "your dreams." Read *dreamers* with the Versions.

10 *They are prophesying a falsehood to you with the result*[8] *that you will be removed*[9] *far from your land; for I will drive you out and you will perish.*

11 *But the nation that brings its neck under the yoke of the king of Babylon and is subject to him I will leave in its own land—Yahweh's word—to cultivate it and live there." ' "*

12 *To Zedekiah king of Judah I said all this: "Bring your necks under the yoke of the king of Babylon and be subject to him and to his people, and you will live.*

13 *Why should you and your people die by sword, famine, and pestilence as Yahweh has threatened to the nation that will not submit to the king of Babylon?*

14 *Do not listen to the words of the prophets who keep telling you not to submit to the king of Babylon, for it is a falsehood that they are prophesying to you.*

15 *I have not sent them—Yahweh's word—but they keep prophesying falsely in my name, which will result*[10] *in my driving you out, and you will perish, you and the prophets who have been prophesying to you."*

16 *I spoke to the priests and all this people as follows: "This is what Yahweh has said: Do not listen to the words of the prophets who keep prophesying to you and saying: 'Look, the furnishings of the house of Yahweh will be returned from Babylon very soon now'; it is a falsehood that they are prophesying to you.*

17[11] *Do not listen to them! Submit to the king of Babylon and live! Why should this city become a ruin?*

18 *If they are prophets, and if they have a word from Yahweh, let them approach Yahweh of Hosts so that the furnishings which are left in Yahweh's house and in the palace of the king and in Jerusalem do not go*[12] *to Babylon.*

19 *For this is what Yahweh of Hosts has said concerning the pillars, the sea, the stands, and the rest of the vessels which are left in this city,*
20 *which Nebuchadnezzar king of Babylon did not take when he deported Jeconiah ben Jehoiakim king of Judah to Babylon with all the nobles of Judah and Jerusalem.*

21 *For this is what Yahweh of Hosts the God of Israel has said with regard to the furnishings which are in the house of Yahweh and in the palace of the king of Judah and in Jerusalem.*

8. Heb. *lᵉma'an* normally means "in order that" but frequently it indicates a result (cf. Gk. *hina*), as here.
9. Lit. "one will remove you afar. . . ."
10. See n. 4 on v. 10.
11. Verses 17–22 are very much shorter in LXX, which reads: "If they are prophets, if the word of Yahweh is in them, let them entreat me. For this is what Yahweh has said: Even the rest of the furnishings, which the king of Babylon did not take when he deported Jeconiah from Jerusalem, shall be taken to Babylon, says Yahweh." MT is an expanded version of the variant text on which LXX is based.
12. Read *bô'* (infinitive) instead of *bō'û* (imperative) by transposing the *waw,* or alternately *yāḇō'û* assuming the *y* was lost by haplography.

22 *They shall be taken to Babylon, and there they shall remain until the day when I give attention to them—Yahweh's word. Then I will bring them back and restore them to this place."*

Chapter 27 comprises three sections in prose: Jeremiah's warning to the foreign ambassadors (vv. 1–11), his appeal to Zedekiah the king (vv. 12–15), and his appeal to the priests and all the people (vv. 16–22). In the fourth year of Zedekiah's reign (594/3 B.C.), vassal states in the western parts of Nebuchadrezzar's empire began to explore the possibility of a rebellion, probably encouraged by disturbances to the east of Babylon in the previous year.[13] Jerusalem was the center to which representatives from neighboring states came to enlist Zedekiah's support.

The false prophets in Jerusalem had been promising the overthrow of Babylon and the return of Jehoiachin and the exiles together with national treasures which had been taken away. The time seemed ripe for revolt. But it was a brave man who dared to oppose public opinion. Jeremiah was that man.

Another of Jeremiah's symbolic actions (cf. 13:1–11; 19:1–13) provides the setting for his words to the foreign ambassadors.

There are considerable variations between MT and LXX, generally in the form of omissions by LXX.

1 The chronological note given in v. 1 seems to be a copy of 26:1. In vv. 3, 12, and 28:1 the king is not Jehoiakim but Zedekiah. The events of the chapter presuppose the exile of 597 B.C. after which Zedekiah was on the throne. Syriac, Arabic, and a few manuscripts read correctly Zedekiah (NEB, RSV). A further difficulty is that the heading refers to the beginning of the king's reign, while 28:1 refers the event to the fourth year and states that this was the same year in which the events of ch. 27 took place. The whole verse is lacking in LXX.

A further peculiarity is that here Jeremiah is referred to as *yirm^{e}yâ*. Elsewhere he is *yirm^{e}yāhû*.

2 Jeremiah's audiences were evidently used to symbolic actions (13:1–11; 19:1–13). He made use here of the ox yoke, a wooden bar or bars tied by leather thongs to the animal's neck. Jeremiah placed the yoke on his own neck and thereby proclaimed the word of Yahweh just as effectively as he would by preaching (see commentary on 19:10).

13. See the Introduction, "Jeremiah in His Historical Setting," pp. 9–22.

3 The historical background to the years 596/5–594/3 B.C. has been greatly illuminated by the Babylonian Chronicles.[14] In 596/5 B.C. Nebuchadrezzar was attacked by an unnamed enemy, possibly Elam. In 595/4 he had to deal with a revolt within his own borders. In 594/3 he led a military campaign into Syria. They were troubled times for Nebuchadrezzar, and small states in the west thought they saw an opportunity to revolt and throw off the yoke of Babylon. As it happened the plan was fruitless. Zedekiah became involved, as the present chapter shows. But in the same year, the fourth year of his reign, the king went to Babylon (51:59), either because he was summoned or perhaps to re-pledge his loyalty in the light of recent events in the west.

There is some ambiguity about precisely what Jeremiah did with the ambassadors. MT seems to imply that Jeremiah made a yoke for each king as well as for himself. He put each yoke on his own neck and then gave it to the appropriate ambassador to take to his king. Verse 2 does not require more than one yoke consisting of bars and thongs. At least one Greek text omits "them" and reads simply *send.*[15] Each ambassador would report to his ruler what he had seen and in that sense a yoke was placed on the neck of each ruler. The grouping of nations is a compact one. These nations had been involved in coalitions in the days of the Assyrians.[16] Their presence in Jerusalem seems to have been for the express purpose of forming a coalition against Babylon. One wonders whether Zedekiah was the leading spirit in the plot. In the end nothing was done, either because they could not agree on a plan or perhaps because they decided the risk was too great. Jeremiah's words were plain and uncompromising.

4–5 The message from Jeremiah to these neighboring kings began with an assertion of the sovereignty and lordship of Yahweh, Israel's God, over the whole earth, its people and its creatures, since it was he who made them all. But he was also the Lord of history

14. D. J. Wiseman, *Chronicles of Chaldaean Kings* (1956).
15. See textual note.
16. See *ANET,* p. 278, concerning a coalition in the days of Shalmaneser III (858–824 B.C.) involving Damascus, Israel (Ahab), Arabia, and others. Sennacherib's Annals (704–681 B.C.) lists vassals among whom were Israel, Sidon, Arvad, Byblos, Ammon, Moab, Edom. He subdued these during his third campaign in 701 B.C. Esarhaddon's vassal treaties (D. J. Wiseman, "The Vassal-Treaties of Esarhaddon," *Iraq* 20 [1958], pp. 1–100) show great concern about insurrection among vassals. See ll. 136–152, 302f., etc.

who had commissioned Nebuchadrezzar his *servant.*[17] Yahweh's power is described in strong terms—*my great power and my outstretched arm* (irresistible might). There may be an inference about the powerlessness and nonexistence of other gods. It was a bold assertion of Israel's belief despite the fact that already some of the people had been exiled in 598/7 B.C. But for Jeremiah that was no cause for consternation since he had preached judgment for many years.

6–7 Yahweh's lordship over history is spelled out. For a reason which only Yahweh himself knew, he had given all these lands into the hands of Nebuchadrezzar to fulfil his own purposes in all lands.[18] All nations would be subject to him and to his descendants after him, until Babylon in its turn would be brought into subjection (v. 7). The death knell of even Babylon was here sounded, impossible as that may have seemed to the ambassadors of these small states. But it was the way all great empires went. Assyria fell in 609 B.C., within the lifetime of Jeremiah, and Babylon's turn would come.

We have translated the verb *'āḇaḏ* as *be subject to* although it often means "serve." The expression *to him and his son and his son's son* is probably a very general one denoting Nebuchadrezzar and his successors.[19]

8 The consequence of rejecting Jeremiah's advice, which was really a rejection of Yahweh's word, was judgment by sword, famine, and plague—all pictures of a military invasion and its aftermath, well known and well understood since all of these small states had suffered over the years from the Assyrians.

17. See Z. Zevit, "The Use of *'eḇeḏ* as a Diplomatic Term in Jeremiah," *JBL* 88 (1969), pp. 74–77. The name here is *Nebuchadnezzar,* elsewhere more correctly Nebuchadrezzar (cf. note on 21:2).

18. There is a certain parallelism in thought here in which the areas of Nebuchadrezzar's dominion are described as "all these lands" and "the beasts of the field." A similar expression occurs at 28:14 (cf. Dan. 2:38). The latter expression may simply indicate the all-embracing extent of Yahweh's dominion. The earth, mankind, the beasts, the animate and the inanimate world which God has created (v. 5), he, as Creator and Lord, has handed over to his servant Nebuchadrezzar. Any reference to the beasts of the field as representative of the nations (cf. Dan. 4:12, 21) does not seem to be intended here.

19. Verse 7 is lacking in LXX. It has sometimes been taken as a late expansion (cf. 25:12, 14). But it is not impossible that it was original, but was dropped in the Hebrew text lying behind LXX because Nebuchadrezzar's son was superseded in 560 B.C. when his line ended, even though the reference to Nebuchadrezzar and his sons is simply a stereotyped formula, a figure of speech.

The Hebrew expression *'aḏ tummî 'ōṯām* is translated in RSV "until I have consumed it." The verb *tāmam* is never transitive, and either a word has dropped out, "until I have finished (. . .)ing them," or an emendation is needed. In the light of Jeremiah's frequent use of *nāṯan b^e yaḏ,* "to give into the hand of," we may propose *until I have delivered them . . .* (*'aḏ tittî 'ōṯām*).[20]

9–11 Under the circumstances it was foolhardy for these nations to believe in the liberation being predicted by those who professed to be able to discern the future. These practitioners are well known in the OT: *prophets, diviners,*[21] *dreamers,*[22] *soothsayers,*[23] *and sorcerers.*[24] They were all banned in Israel (Deut. 18:9–13). They were all peddlers of *falsehood (šeqer),* and the acceptance of their lies could only lead to judgment, exile, and destruction. There was no way out but to submit to the overlordship of Babylon. People who followed this counsel might have to pay tribute but they would be allowed to remain in their own land to *cultivate ('āḇaḏ) it and live there.*

Jeremiah spoke with assurance, but it was not that he judged the situation on political grounds. He had a strong conviction that Yahweh's guidance of world affairs led in this direction. To resist Nebuchadrezzar was to resist Yahweh, and that could only result in one's own destruction. Like Isaiah his predecessor, who set a time limit for the Assyrians (Isa. 10:5–12) which would end when they had fulfilled the purposes of Yahweh, Jeremiah strictly limited the commission of Babylon. Nebuchadrezzar was Yahweh's servant, and as long as he was needed he was irresistible. His service was confined to the destruction of the things in which Israel was placing a false confidence. One day Babylon would have fulfilled Yahweh's purpose of destroying all these things and of bringing exiles to repentance. Then he would be set aside. This was not shrewd political comment but something Jeremiah received as he stood in the council of Yahweh.[25]

20. There is support for this rendering in Syr., Targ.
21. *qôsēm,* 27:9; 29:8; Deut. 18:10, 14; Josh. 13:22; 1 Sam. 6:2; 28:8; 2 K. 17:17; Isa. 3:2; 44:25; Ezek. 13:9, 23; Mic. 3:6f., 11.
22. *ḥôlēm,* 23:23–28; Deut. 13:1–5.
23. *'ōnēn,* Lev. 19:26; Deut. 18:10, 14; Judg. 9:37; 2 K. 21:6; Isa. 2:6; 57:3; Mic. 5:11.
24. *kaššap,* Exod. 7:11; 22:17; Deut. 18:10; Mal. 3:5; Dan. 2:2.
25. Adam C. Welch, *Jeremiah: His Time and His Work* (1928), pp. 195–212, in his chapter entitled "Jeremiah's Political Attitude."

12–13 The message to the kings of the small states around Judah was repeated to Zedekiah. The presence of the name Zedekiah here suggests that it should appear also in v. 1 instead of MT Jehoiakim. The terms of the message were the same: "I spoke according to all these words: 'Submit to the king of Babylon and live. Why die by the sword, by starvation, and by disease?' "

The following verses show that Jeremiah was discouraging resistance to the Babylonians. Jeremiah may well have been seen as a traitor engaged in seditious activity. See the Introduction, under "The 'Seditious' Utterances of Jeremiah," pp. 92–94.

14–15 The warning is given about listening to prophets who prophesy *falsehood (šeqer).* No reference is made to diviners, dreamers, soothsayers, and sorcerers, although it is difficult to believe that people who had shown such an inclination to worship Baal and practice the cult of the Queen of Heaven (7:17–18) would not also have resorted to these forbidden practitioners (Deut. 18:9–13).

False prophets had been castigated many times (cf. 23:15–40). Their prophecies were contrary to those of Jeremiah. They were not sent by Yahweh, and Zedekiah's rejection of Yahweh's true word through Jeremiah in preference to the word of these false prophets spelled his banishment and destruction. This was, in fact, the fate of Zedekiah, who after his attempt to rebel against Nebuchadrezzar (2 K. 25:1) was captured in 587 B.C. Nebuchadrezzar blinded him after slaying his sons before his eyes, and took him in chains to Babylon, where he died (2 K. 25:3–7).

16–18 The same word was given to the priests and the people. Special mention is made of the vessels (*kᵉlî*) of the temple. Since many of the items carried off by conquerors could hardly be classed as vessels, some more comprehensive word like *furnishings* or "accessories" is needed (cf. v. 19). The false prophets had promised that all these would be *returned*[26] from Babylon *very soon.*[27] Verse 16 is joined to the end of v. 15 in LXX, beginning: "To you and to all this people and to the priests I spoke. . . ." LXX omits *very soon now* but adds "I did not send them" at the end of the verse.

The word of the prophets to which the priests and the people listened was a *falsehood* (*šeqer,* v. 16), and to accept it was to reject

26. The verb is *šûḇ,* Pual participle.
27. Heb. *'attâ mᵉhērâ,* lit. "now, quickly." The expression is lacking in LXX.

Yahweh's word and run the risk of judgment. The preaching of these men was a provocation to rebellion, although they may have been sincere in thinking that the end of the exile was near. It was not a feeling such as this that mattered, however, but only a word from Yahweh.

A test is proposed for the false prophets (v. 18). If they are true prophets, let them pray (lit. draw near, *approach, pāga'*) to Yahweh to protect the items of furniture in the temple and in the king's palace which were left behind when Jeconiah[28] was deported. But as Jeremiah understood the mind of Yahweh it was inevitable that the temple furnishings would be taken to Babylon (2 K. 25:13–17).

19–20 The list of items in v. 19 (not in LXX) was typical of those which were found in the temple. The term *meḵōnôṯ* may refer to the wheeled items referred to in 1 K. 7:27–37, translated in NEB as "trolleys."[29] The *pillars* (1 K. 6:15–22) and the (molten) *sea* (1 K. 7:23–26) are identifiable. Upon his first visit Nebuchadrezzar carried off some of the temple treasures (2 K. 24:13), but there were still temple accessories to carry off in 586 B.C. (2 K. 25:13–17). Some had been left behind in 597 B.C. and no doubt others had been made to replace important items used in the regular worship of the temple.

21–22 Yahweh's final word was that the accessories of the temple and the royal palace would be taken to Babylon despite the words of the false prophets (v. 16). There they would remain until the day when Yahweh would *give attention (pāqaḏ)* to them. Then they would be brought back and restored to their place. The chapter thus ends on a note of hope for the future. The nation stood under judgment, but beyond the judgment Yahweh promised restoration. Some commentators have argued that the prediction of restoration is out of place in an oracle of doom and represents a late addition.[30] The real question is whether Jeremiah had any message of hope to proclaim. If he did—and it is difficult to imagine that he was completely preoccupied with judgment—then some word of hope would be expected here, even though LXX makes no reference to it. The theme is certainly expressed elsewhere in the book.

28. Jeconiah is a shortened form of Jehoiachin. See on Coniah in 22:24.
29. G. E. Wright, "Solomon's Temple Resurrected," *BA* 4/2 (1941), pp. 17–31.
30. G. P. Couturier, "Jeremiah," *JBC*, p. 324; *et al.*

(ii) *Jeremiah against Hananiah: Prophecy against Prophecy (28:1–17)*

1 *In that same year,*[1] *the fourth year of Zedekiah king of Judah, in the fifth month, Hananiah ben Azzur the prophet from Gibeon spoke to me*[2] *in the house of Yahweh in the presence of the priests and all the people.*

2 *"This is what Yahweh of Hosts, the God of Israel, has said: I have broken the yoke of the king of Babylon.*

3 *Within two years I will bring back to this place all the furnishings of Yahweh's house which Nebuchadnezzar king of Babylon took from this place and carried off to Babylon,*

4 *and Jeconiah ben Jehoiakim king of Judah and all the exiles of Judah who have gone to Babylon I will also bring back to this place—Yahweh's word; for I will break the yoke of the king of Babylon."*[3]

5 *Then the prophet Jeremiah spoke to Hananiah the prophet in the presence of the priests and all the people who were standing in the house of Yahweh.*

6 *Jeremiah the prophet said, "Amen! May Yahweh do so! May Yahweh confirm the words that you have prophesied by bringing back to this place the furnishings of Yahweh's house and all the exiles from Babylon.*

7 *But please listen to this word that I am speaking in your hearing and in the hearing of all the people.*

8 *The prophets who were of old, before my time and yours, prophesied against many countries and great kingdoms war, disaster,*[4] *and pestilence.*

9 *The prophet who prophesies well-being, when the word of that prophet comes to pass, then it will be known that Yahweh has really sent him."*

10 *Then the prophet Hananiah took the yoke from the prophet Jeremiah's neck and broke it.*

1. MT begins "In that year, in the accession year of Zedekiah king of Judah, in the fourth year. . . ." There is evidently some confusion in the text. It was either the first year or the fourth year. The fourth year would have given Zedekiah time to organize the ambassadors of ch. 27 after the debacle of 597 B.C. It seems that 27:1 is not original. LXX omits it. But the words *in that same year* are correct since the incident of ch. 28 took place shortly after that of ch. 27. Jeremiah was still wearing the yoke (vv. 10–11).

2. The MT and Versions read *to me* (first person), whereas in the rest of the chapter Jeremiah is referred to in the third person. One conjecture that has been made to overcome the difference in persons is to treat *ly* as a misunderstanding of an abbreviation *l y(rmyh), to J(eremiah).* Much of this chapter is in the first person, and this may have influenced the writer. See J. Bright, *Jeremiah,* p. 197; *BHS ad loc.*

3. The text of vv. 3–4 is somewhat different in LXX, and much shorter. LXX reads: "Within two years I will bring back to this place the furnishings of the Lord's house and Jeconiah and the exiles of Judah; for I will break the yoke of the king of Babylon."

4. Many mss. read *rā'āḇ,* "famine," for MT *rā'â.*

11 *And Hananiah spoke in the presence of all the people as follows: "This is what Yahweh has said: In this way I will break the yoke of Nebuchadnezzar king of Babylon off the neck of all the nations within two years." And the prophet Jeremiah went his way.*
12 *After Hananiah the prophet had broken the yoke from off Jeremiah's neck, the word of Yahweh came to Jeremiah:*
13 *"Go and tell Hananiah: 'This is what Yahweh has said: You have broken wooden yoke-bars and have made yoke-bars of iron in their place.*
14 *This is what Yahweh of Hosts the God of Israel has said: I have placed an iron yoke on the neck of all these nations to be subjects of Nebuchadnezzar king of Babylon. And they will be his subjects. And I have given the wild beasts to him as well.' "*[5]
15 *Then Jeremiah the prophet said to Hananiah the prophet: "Listen now, Hananiah. Yahweh did not send you. But you for your part have led this people to trust a falsehood.*
16 *Therefore this is what Yahweh has said: Look! I will dispatch you from off the face of the earth. This very year you will die because you preached rebellion against Yahweh."*[6]
17 *And Hananiah the prophet died that year in the seventh month.*

The narrative is biographical in style and no doubt goes back to someone like Baruch. Chapter 28 is a sequel to ch. 27 and describes the confrontation[7] between Jeremiah and Hananiah, one of the false prophets, who took up Jeremiah's symbolic action with the wooden ox yoke. He removed the yoke from Jeremiah's neck and with great confidence performed his own symbolic act. He broke Jeremiah's yoke as a symbol that Nebuchadrezzar's power would be broken. The same point is made as in chs. 26 and 27 that rejection of Yahweh's word was an act of rebellion which called forth the divine judgment, whether on a whole nation or, as here, on an individual. It was the curse of the covenant operating for the covenant-breaker.

1 The chronological question is discussed above in the textual note. The incident happened in 594/3 B.C. shortly after Jeremiah's encounter with the ambassadors of the surrounding states. He was still wearing the yoke for Hananiah to break (v. 10).

Hananiah was from Gibeon in Benjamin, a town some 6 miles northwest of Jerusalem identified with the modern el-Jib. The an-

5. In v. 14 LXX reads: "For thus says the Lord: An iron yoke I have placed on the neck of all the nations to serve the king of Babylon."
6. LXX lacks the rest of this verse.
7. This confrontation is typical of other confrontations of prophets against prophets. See S. J. DeVries, *Prophet Against Prophet,* pp. 71f., 143f., 151.

cient site has been excavated in recent years.[8] It had a number of important historical associations. The Gibeonites had deceived the Israelites in Joshua's day (Josh. 9:1–15). It was the scene of a contest between Saul's men and David's men (2 Sam. 20:12–17). Here Joab killed Amasa (2 Sam. 20:8–10).

Hananiah's name means "Yahweh has been gracious." It was an appropriate name for a prophet who believed strongly, if mistakenly, that Judah's fortunes would soon be restored. He is otherwise unknown.

2–4 Hananiah's statement was a direct contradiction of what Yahweh had said. He declared that Yahweh's word to him was that the Babylonian yoke would be broken within two years. The reference to the broken yoke was suggested by the yoke that Jeremiah was still wearing. The sacred objects from the temple would be restored along with the king and the exiles. The expression of the hope that Jeconiah would soon return may indicate that a part of the population still regarded him as legitimate ruler. He is referred to as Jehoiachin king of Judah on some Babylonian receipts for oil found in the gateway of Babylon.[9] The discovery of seal stamps bearing the name "Belonging to Eliakim, the steward of Yaukin" in the late strata of Beth Shemesh, Tel Beit Mirsim, and Ramat Raḥel may provide additional support for such a hypothesis.[10]

5–6 Jeremiah's response was not necessarily a sarcastic retort to Hananiah's oracle. As a lover of Judah and a patriot he could wish that Hananiah's prophecy would be realized and could say sincerely: *Amen! May Yahweh do so! May Yahweh confirm the words that you have prophesied*. But he well knew that the truth was otherwise.

7–9 Jeremiah here sets up another mark of a true prophet. His prophecies have to be fulfilled (23:16–40; cf. Deut. 18:21–22). There was a strong argument against the possibility of Hananiah's prophecy being fulfilled. When he announced imminent prosperity and *well-being (šālôm)* for the nation he spoke in a manner contrary

8. See J. B. Pritchard's articles in *BA* 19/4 (1956), pp. 66–75; 23/1 (1960), pp. 23–29; 24/1 (1961), pp. 19–24; 26/1 (1963), pp. 27–30; "Gibeon's History in the Light of Excavation," SVT VII (1959), pp. 1–12; *Hebrew Inscriptions and Stamps from Gibeon* (University Museum, Philadelphia, 1959).

9. *ANET,* p. 308. Jehoiachin is referred to as: "Jaukin king . . . ," "Jaukin, son of the king of Judah," and reference is made to the five sons of the king of Judah.

10. W. F. Albright, "Some Recent Publications on the Archaeology of Palestine," *BASOR* 170 (1963), p. 67.

to all the great prophets who had preceded him and Jeremiah. Their message was always one of doom—war, disaster, and pestilence. If now Hananiah's prophecy, which was the very opposite of the message of the past prophets, proved to be true, he would establish himself as a true prophet of Yahweh. These verses should not be interpreted to mean that the entire message of all the prophets before Jeremiah was one of judgment. Jeremiah's meaning was that the usual message of the earlier prophets was one of doom, and that when he spoke of judgment he was more in the line of the predecessors than Hananiah, who spoke only of peace and prosperity (Deut. 18:20–22). It is the error of some modern commentators to excise all hopeful references in the earlier prophets as being secondary postexilic glosses.

Time would reveal that Hananiah's optimistic picture was false and Jeremiah's was correct. At the time of the confrontation it was impossible to discern who was true and who was false, for both men spoke in the name of Yahweh. But the real question was, which of them had "stood in the council of Yahweh" (23:18, 22)? Clearly, only one. Jeremiah saw that Yahweh demanded a response of obedience and holiness from Israel. Israel's election meant far more than mere privilege, which could neglect solemn obligations and responsibilities.

10–11 Hananiah with great confidence, and perhaps somewhat angered by Jeremiah's words, now performed his own symbolic act. He snatched the yoke from the neck of Jeremiah, broke it in the presence of the people, and declared as Yahweh's word: *In this way I will break the yoke of Nebuchadnezzar . . . within two years* (cf. Jeremiah's seventy years, 25:11; 29:10). His action gave great encouragement to those who planned for a rebellious coalition, and who hoped for the quick reinstatement of Jehoiachin and the return of the sacred objects to the temple and the treasured objects to the palace. Jeremiah seems to have been taken aback and *went his way* without immediate comment. Hananiah had proclaimed a message which he claimed was Yahweh's, both by word and symbolic act. If this word were true, then Jeremiah's own words were false.

12–14 Only after a period of time did the answer come. The true prophet was not a dreamer, nor a shrewd political observer, nor a victim of autosuggestion. His word came from Yahweh, but it was no different from what he had already delivered, though it was declared in stronger terms. If Hananiah had broken the symbolic wooden bars, the symbol needed to be of a kind that could not be broken. *You have broken wooden yoke-bars and have made yoke-bars of iron in their place.* The very act of breaking wood was in itself a symbol that there could be no breaking of Yahweh's yoke, which was of iron. Yahweh had placed an iron yoke on the neck of all these nations. We may wonder whether Jeremiah returned to the encounter with an iron yoke-bar in his hand to reenact the symbol. Hananiah's counter-prophecy was now countered by something stronger.

Nebuchadrezzar's authority was complete. He would exercise sovereignty not only over men but over the *wild beasts* as well. It was, as humans go, a total supremacy. Only Yahweh stood above him. But then he was Yahweh's servant (vassal) and derived his authority from Yahweh, even though he would never acknowledge that fact.

15–17 Finally Jeremiah condemned Hananiah as a false prophet. Yahweh had not sent (*šālaḥ*) him. He had caused the people *to trust*[11] in a *falsehood* (*šeqer*). He had uttered *rebellion* (*sārâ*) against Yahweh. The same charge was laid against false prophets in Babylon who were proclaiming the same false hopes at the same time (29:32). The same term *sārâ* is used in Deut. 13:6 (Eng. v. 5) for the dreamer who taught rebellion to Israel. For this evil deed Yahweh would *dispatch* ("send away," *šillaḥ*)[12] him. If Yahweh did not send Hananiah he would certainly send him away to his death. The sentence was in accord with the law in Deut. 18:20 that the man who prophesied falsely in Yahweh's name committed a capital offense. When Jeremiah's enemies tried to commit him to death on a similar basis their charge was dismissed by the judges (26:8–11, 16). Two months later (cf. v. 1) Hananiah died in fulfilment of the curse pronounced upon him by Jeremiah (cf. 2 K. 1:17; 7:19–20; 8:10–15). There is no indication of how he died. It may have been by some natural cause such as illness. But whatever the means, Jeremiah's status as a true prophet was vindicated (cf. vv. 5–7). He who predicted deliverance in two years (v. 3) died in two months. It was a telling authentication of Jeremiah's position as a true prophet.

11. Hiphil of *bāṭaḥ*.
12. The play on words is clear in Hebrew.

(iii) *Correspondence with the Exiles (29:1–32)*

1 *This is the text of the letter which Jeremiah the prophet sent from Jerusalem to the remaining elders among the exiles, to the priests, the prophets, and to all the people whom Nebuchadnezzar had deported from Jerusalem to Babylon*

2 *after Jeconiah the king, the queen mother, the palace officials, the officials of Judah and Jerusalem, the artisans, and the smiths had gone from Jerusalem.*

3 *(The letter was sent) by the hand of Elasah ben Shaphan and Gemariah ben Hilkiah, whom Zedekiah king of Judah sent to Babylon to Nebuchadnezzar king of Babylon. It said:*

4 *"This is what Yahweh of Hosts the God of Israel has said to all the exiles whom I have deported*[1] *from Jerusalem to Babylon:*

5 *Build houses and settle down, plant gardens and eat their produce.*

6 *Marry wives and beget sons and daughters; take wives for your sons and give your daughters in marriage so that they may have sons and daughters.*[2] *Increase there and do not decrease.*

7 *Seek the welfare of the city*[3] *to which I have deported you and pray for it to Yahweh, for on its welfare your welfare depends.*

8 *For this is what Yahweh of Hosts, the God of Israel, has said: Do not let your prophets and your diviners who are in your midst deceive you, and pay no heed to the dreams that they are dreaming,*[4]

9 *for it is a falsehood that they are preaching to you in my name. I did not send them—Yahweh's word.*

10 *For this is what Yahweh has said: When Babylon's full seventy years are completed I will take up your cause and fulfil my promise to you to bring you back to this place.*

11 *It is I who know the plans I have made for you*[5]*—Yahweh's word—plans for welfare and not for misfortune, to give you the future you hope for.*[6]

12 *And when you call on me and come*[7] *and pray to me I will hear you;*

13 *and when you search for me you will find me, when you search for me with all your heart.*

1. The change from 3rd to 1st person is common in the prophets. LXX agrees with MT but Syr. uses the passive "who have been deported."
2. The last clause is lacking in LXX.
3. LXX reads "land."
4. The Hebrew text is awkward. It reads "your dreams which you cause to be dreamed." The verb form *maḥlᵉmîm* is unusual and may be an error for *hēm ḥōlᵉmîm*. LXX reads "Your dreams which you dream." Verse 9 is in the 3rd person. Some conjectural emendation seems to be needed.
5. The phrase "I know the plans which" is missing in LXX.
6. Lit. "a future and a hope." LXX has simply "these things."
7. Syr. omits *come*. On LXX see next note.

14 *And I will let you find me*[8]*—Yahweh's word; and I will restore your fortunes and will gather you from all the nations and all the places to which I have driven you—Yahweh's word; and I will bring you back to the place from which I deported you.*

15 *Now, because you say 'Yahweh has raised up prophets for us in Babylon. . . .' "*

16[9] *This is what Yahweh has said concerning the king who sits on the throne of David and concerning all the people who live in this city, your fellow countrymen who did not go into exile with you.*

17 *This is what Yahweh of Hosts has said: "Look! I am sending among them the sword, the famine, and the pestilence, and I will make them like rotten figs too bad to be eaten.*

18 *I will pursue them with the sword, the famine, and the pestilence, and I will make them a repugnant sight to all the kingdoms of the earth, an object of execration and horror, a cause for whistling and reproach among all the nations where I have driven them,*

19 *because they paid no attention to what I said—Yahweh's word—when I sent them my servants the prophets with urgency and persistence.*[10] *But you did not listen—Yahweh's word.*

20 *Now, as for you, hear the word of Yahweh, all you exiles whom I sent from Jerusalem to Babylon. . . .*

21 *This is what Yahweh of Hosts the God of Israel has said concerning Ahab ben Kolaiah and Zedekiah ben Maaseiah who are prophesying falsehood to you in my name: Look! I am handing them over to Nebuchadrezzar king of Babylon, who will execute them before your very eyes.*

22 *And a curse will be derived from them for all the exiles of Judah who are in Babylon: 'May Yahweh make you like Zedekiah and Ahab whom the king of Babylon roasted in the fire'*

23 *because they committed a scandalous thing in Israel. They committed adultery with the wives of their fellows and spoke a lie in my name which I did not authorize. And for my part I know and am witness to it*[11]*—Yahweh's word."*

24 *To Shemaiah the Nehelamite you shall say:*

25 *"This is what Yahweh of Hosts, the God of Israel, has said: Because*[12] *you have sent letters in your own name to all the people who are in Jerusalem and to Zephaniah ben Maaseiah the priest and to all the priests*[13] *to this effect:*

8. LXX for vv. 12–14 reads: "And pray to me, and I will hear you; 13 and search for me, and you will find me, because you seek me with all your heart; 14 and I will appear (or, manifest myself) to you." The rest of v. 14 is lacking.

9. LXX omits vv. 16–20. This preserves a logical transfer from v. 15 to v. 21. Lucian has the order vv. 14, 16–20, 15, 21–23.

10. Lit. "rising early and sending"; cf. 25:4; 26:5; etc.

11. LXX reads only "And I am witness," omitting the first verb and *to it.*

12. Heb. *ya'an 'ᵃšer*; cf. vv. 31b–32, where the *ya'an* clause (v. 31b) is finally completed by a *lāḵēn* ("therefore") conclusion.

13. LXX lacks "all the people who are in Jerusalem" as well as "and to all the priests."

26 *'Yahweh has appointed you priest in place of Jehoiada the priest to be overseer*[14] *in Yahweh's house for the sake of every madman who sets himself up as a prophet, to put him into prison and into the pillory.*
27 *Then why have you not disciplined Jeremiah of Anathoth who takes it upon himself to prophesy to you?*
28 *For that reason he has even sent to us in Babylon and said, "It will be a long time! Build houses, and settle down; plant gardens and eat their produce." '"*
29 *Then Zephaniah the priest read this in the hearing of Jeremiah the prophet.*
30 *And the word of Yahweh came to Jeremiah:*
31 *"Send to all the exiles and say: 'This is what Yahweh has said to Shemaiah the Nehelamite: Because Shemaiah has prophesied to you, though I did not send him, and he has led you to trust a falsehood,*
32 *therefore this is what Yahweh has said: Look! I will punish Shemaiah the Nehelamite and his descendants. He will have no one living among this people to see the good that I will do for my people*[15]*— Yahweh's word—for he has preached rebellion against Yahweh.' "*

Chapter 29 is a long prose passage consisting basically of letters between Jerusalem and Babylon. It would seem that at least four letters are in view—one from Jeremiah to the exiles (vv. 1–15, 21–23), one from Shemaiah in Babylon to Zephaniah (vv. 25–28), one from Jeremiah to Shemaiah (v. 24), and a second letter to the exiles (vv. 31–32).

The setting of the correspondence is in the days following the downfall of Judah in 597 B.C. There is no precise date. Even v. 2 is very indefinite and seems to be an insertion based on 2 K. 24:12–16 (cf. 24:1). But the situation is parallel to that described in chs. 27 and 28. There was a period of unrest all over the Babylonian empire, and prophets both in Jerusalem and in Babylon were proclaiming the imminent ending of the Exile, evidently believing that Babylon was on the point of collapse. The Babylonian Chronicle hints at internal troubles in Babylon in 595/4 B.C.[16] in which some of the deported Jews seem to have been involved. At least two were executed by Nebuchadrezzar (29:21–22).[17] The fact that Jeremiah's letter was sent by official envoys from Zedekiah to Nebuchadrezzar fits well with a date of 594 B.C. when Zedekiah may have been obliged to report on recent events in Judah and to reaffirm his loyalty.

14. MT is plur., LXX and Targ. singular.
15. LXX ends here, with "to you" in place of MT *for my people.*
16. D. J. Wiseman, *Chronicles of Chaldaean Kings,* pp. 36, 73.
17. On the general history see the Introduction, pp. 9–22.

The chapter is, however, somewhat complex. Verses 16–20, lacking in LXX, interrupt the flow of Jeremiah's letter to the exiles from v. 15 to v. 21. The words addressed to Shemaiah (vv. 25–28) seem to be cut off abruptly. The text shows a number of variations from LXX and other Versions.

The essential historicity of the material cannot be doubted although there is uncertainty about how it assumed its present state. A common view is that it is based on the memoirs of Baruch.[18] Another view is that it was composed in the characteristic prose style of the book of Jeremiah by Deuteronomic editors in exile.[19] In such matters certainty is not possible.

1 The chapter begins "These are the words of the document," or perhaps more idiomatically *This is the text of the letter.* MT refers to "those who were left of the elders" or *the remaining elders*. The expression seems to indicate that some of the elders had died or been executed or imprisoned as a result of troubles hinted at in vv. 21–22, perhaps in the disturbances of 595/4 B.C.

2 The verse is a parenthesis perhaps based on 2 K. 24:12–16. It interrupts the flow between v. 1 and v. 3. The term *sārîsîm*, usually translated "eunuchs," may refer to palace officials of some sort (cf. 52:25; 1 Sam. 8:15; etc.). In Gen. 39:1 Potiphar is so designated, but he was married. There may have been some original function such as chamberlain for the women's quarters, but this was changed although the name was preserved. The term *śārîm* ("princes") probably refers to another group of *officials* which may have included royal princes. The meaning of the term *masgēr* is uncertain but it is generally translated *smiths* (see note on 24:1).

3 The letter went in the diplomatic mail bag! The envoys were *Elasah ben Shaphan*, who may have been the brother of Ahikam ben Shaphan (26:24), and Gemariah ben Hilkiah (36:10ff.); both were from priestly families that played an important part in Josiah's reform. They were friendly toward Jeremiah and may even have had sympathy with his preaching (26:24; 36:10, 25; etc.). Perhaps, too, Gemariah ben Hilkiah was a son of the famous high priest of Josiah's day (2 K. 22:4–14). Their mission to Nebuchadrezzar may have been more delicate than simply to carry the annual tribute. They may have been sent to assure Nebuchadrezzar of Zedekiah's loyalty after the abortive attempt to plan a revolt among the small states to the

18. G. P. Couturier, "Jeremiah," *JBC*, p. 324.
19. E. W. Nicholson, *Jeremiah 26–52*, p. 42.

west (ch. 27). Otherwise the men were conducting routine business between the vassal and his overlord (cf. 51:59). It is evident that there was a good deal of communication between comparatively distant places in these years. But diplomatic correspondence between overlords and vassals was common in the second millennium B.C., as the Amarna letters written from Palestine to the pharaoh indicate.

4 The claim is again made that it was Yahweh who deported the exiles, through the agency of his servant Nebuchadrezzar. The shift from third to first person is frequent in prophetic addresses.

5–6 The advice given by Jeremiah was revolutionary and altogether contrary to that being given by the prophets in Babylon. *Build* and *plant* were verbs that went back to Jeremiah's call (1:10), but their use is different. The people were to settle down. They were evidently free to do so, as the book of Ezekiel suggests. They had their own organization with elders (Ezek. 8:1; 14:1). Ezekiel could minister to them, as could other prophets. They no doubt had tasks to perform for the state but otherwise could lead a reasonably normal life. Farming, marrying, giving in marriage, were to be part of daily living. It was a far cry from the words of the optimistic prophets who declared that the Exile would be over in two years (cf. vv. 27, 28). As to their worship of Yahweh the inference is that this can continue outside their native land and in the absence of temple and sacrifices (7:1–15, 21–22). The whole proposal was provocative and calculated to produce the sort of reaction which is described in vv. 24–28.

7 More revolutionary still was the advice to *seek the welfare (šālôm)* of the Babylonian regime, to pray for its welfare and not its downfall. Jeremiah by these words cast the people completely adrift from all those things on which they depended and which they regarded as essential to their own well-being, a nation-state, kingship, an army, national borders, the temple. Without all these Yahweh could give the nation new perspectives and a new understanding of their calling. For the present the action lay in Babylon. Such advice would not have been easy to accept for people who had been carried off from their homeland by those for whom Jeremiah was asking them to pray. No doubt the advice was practical. Any other approach would result in deep resentment or leave the people open to the persuasion of false prophets who might provoke rebellion. Jeremiah could see the end, far off perhaps, but certain. God had plans of restoration in due course (vv. 10–14).

8–9 Some commentators feel that these verses fit better after v. 15 because here they interrupt the sequence between v. 7 and v. 10. But the proposal is not necessary since these verses provide strong reinforcement for the preceding verses. The false prophets had told the people that their stay would be short, and Jeremiah needed to assert that this was a *falsehood (šeqer)* propagated in the name of Yahweh who had not sent them. These prophets are like the prophets in Jerusalem of whom Hananiah was a representative (ch. 28). They were associates of diviners and dreamers (27:9). It becomes clear in later verses (vv. 21–23) that at least some of these prophets were working for revolt, which could only bring disaster. It was an attempt to speed up the divine purposes. But Yahweh will not be hurried in his plans for his people.

10 The divine purpose for Israel is now stated. When Babylon's seventy years are completed, Yahweh will act on behalf of his people and fulfil his promise to bring them back[20] home (see comment on 25:11). It is remarkable that Jeremiah was able to propose that the power of Babylon would last so brief a time.[21]

11–13 Yahweh's thoughts for his people were fixed. They were for their *welfare (šālôm)* not their hurt (*rā'â*), and for the future they hoped for.

The privilege of the people in that future would be to continue their relationship with Yahweh. It would appear that when Jeremiah wrote this letter there was resentment against Yahweh and a loss of confidence. It was therefore only when they came to him and prayed and sought for him with their whole heart that he could be found (cf. Amos 5:4–6; Hos. 2:16–20). Yahweh could not dispense the blessings of the covenant to rebellious people (cf. Ezek. 2:3–5; 33:17–20). Obedience, loyalty, and fellowship were fundamental. There would be hope for the people when they could say: "Our transgressions and our sins are upon us, and we waste away because of them; how then can we live?" (Ezek. 33:10). To such people Yahweh could say: "As I live, I have no pleasure in the death of the wicked but that the wicked may turn from his way and live; turn back, turn back from your evil ways; for why will you die, O house of Israel?" (Ezek. 33:11, 12). In Jeremiah's words: *When you call on me* . . .

20. The verb is *šûḇ*.

21. From the fall of Nineveh (612 B.C.) to the fall of Babylon (539 B.C.) was 73 years; from Nebuchadrezzar's accession (605 B.C.) to the fall of Babylon was 66 years. And yet originally Jeremiah probably intended only a round number. In 27:7 Babylon was to last to the third generation.

I will hear you, or "You will call . . . and I will hear." The force of *with all your heart* is hardly to be captured by a reference to the emotions. It has rather the sense of "with all your will and your energy."

14 Granted the response of v. 13, the blessings of the covenant would become available. Fortunes would be restored.[22] The exiles would be gathered together from the nations and lands where they were scattered and restored[23] to their homeland, to the place from which they had been deported. Their land was the land promised to their forefathers. But the condition of their occupancy of the land was obedience. There was nothing automatic and nothing permanent for those who rejected Yahweh and his covenant.

15 The natural development of the argument is from v. 15 to v. 21. As the text stands, vv. 16–19 are a digression which serves to stress the fact that Yahweh would complete the judgment of Judah before any attention would be given to restoration.

16–19 The discussion returns to the people in Judah who had not been exiled to Babylon. Yahweh had a word for these and for Zedekiah the king of David's line at that time. Although they escaped the judgment of 597 B.C. they still stood under judgment and their fate had yet to befall them. This would be similar to what befell the first group of exiles—*sword, famine, pestilence.* The expression *rotten (šŏʿārîm)*[24] *figs too bad to be eaten* links the passage with ch. 24, which is both a polemic against the people still living in Judah and an encouragement to those in exile after 597 B.C. The people who remained after 597 B.C. might have taken heed of what Yahweh had spoken through his servant and mended their ways. They did not, despite the urgency and persistence with which Yahweh spoke to them. So, for them too, judgment would come.

20 Attention is now redirected to the exiles. It would appear that v. 20 is picking up the thread temporarily dropped at v. 15. *Now, as for you, hear the word of Yahweh, all you exiles whom I sent from Jerusalem to Babylon. (15) Because you say "Yahweh has raised up prophets for us in Babylon," (21) this is what Yahweh of Hosts the God of Israel has said. . . .* This leads back to the main argument of Jeremiah's letter. The identity of the prophets whom "Yahweh had raised up in Babylon" is now made clear.

22. The meaning of Heb. *šûḇ šᵉḇûṯ.*
23. The root is *šûḇ.*
24. The adjective *šŏʿārîm* means "bruised," "burst open." See KB, p. 1002. The word occurs only here. In 24:2–3 the adjective is *rāʿâ,* "bad."

21–23 Ahab ben Kolaiah and Zedekiah ben Maaseiah were probably two of many false prophets among the people in Babylon. Optimistic assertions of welfare for Judah in the years before 697 B.C., in the face of Jeremiah's preaching, were in no way diminished despite Nebuchadrezzar's invasion. Such blind optimism dies hard. They were still prophesying *falsehood (šeqer)* in Yahweh's name. In addition their lives were evil (cf. 23:9–15). They committed *adultery (nā'ap)* with the wives of their fellows and committed a scandal (*n*ᵉ*ḇālâ*). For these offenses they were handed over to Nebuchadrezzar for punishment. Nebuchadrezzar would not have punished them merely for these offenses. There was something else. They seem to have been involved in some political offense such as encouragement of the people to revolt. Nebuchadrezzar had them executed by roasting *(qālâ)* in the fire, which was a punishment that was used in Babylon over a long period (Hammurabi Code, 25, 110, 157; Dan. 3:6). The death of these two false prophets would give rise to a formula for cursing (*q*ᵉ*lālâ*), "*May Yahweh make you like Zedekiah and Ahab whom the king of Babylon roasted in the fire.*"

The fact was known to Yahweh, who was a *witness ('ēḏ)* to it all.

24–25 Jeremiah's letter evoked some repercussions. A certain Shemaiah the Nehelamite, another false prophet, wrote a complaint to the temple overseer. Details of Jeremiah's reply are not given but only his own summary of Shemaiah's letter of complaint (vv. 25–28). Shemaiah is otherwise unknown. His place of origin, Nahlam, is also unknown; one proposal is that *Nehelamite* is derived from the word *ḥālam,* "to dream," and that the term defines the man as a "dreamer"[25] (cf. v. 8; 27:9; etc.). Jeremiah charges this man with sending a letter in his own name to Zephaniah ben Maaseiah the priest, who was also the overseer (*pāqîḏ*) in the temple in Jerusalem. It is not clear why it was an offense to write in his own name, unless Jeremiah was expressing the view that the letter did not have Yahweh's authority because he did not write in the name of Yahweh. The charge is repeated in v. 31, followed in v. 32 by the syntactical conclusion that here is left unstated.

26–29 The contents of Shemaiah's letter are now summarized. Zedekiah was now priest-overseer in the temple in the place

25. L. Yaure, "Elymas—Nehelamite—Pethor," *JBL* 79 (1960), pp. 297–314, esp. 306–309. The name is a Niphal participle of *ḥlm.* There are no parallels for such a usage in the OT, however.

of Jehoiada. A previous occupant of the position was Pashhur (20:1–6), who must have been taken to Babylon among the exiles in 597 B.C. There is no indication of his presence in Babylon in this chapter. He may have died (20:6). One of the duties of the overseer was to lay hold of madmen *(m^e^šuggā')* and self-styled prophets *(miṯnabbē')* and lock them up.[26] Despite all that had happened in confirmation of Jeremiah's earlier preaching he was still regarded as mad. This Zephaniah ben Maaseiah consulted Jeremiah twice on Zedekiah's behalf (21:1; 37:3). He is described as second priest in 52:24. He was finally taken prisoner in 587 B.C. after the fall of Jerusalem and executed (52:24–27; 2 K. 25:18–21).

The concern of Shemaiah was that Zephaniah had not fulfilled his duty by leaving Jeremiah of Anathoth free. As a *miṯnabbē'*, one who took it on himself to prophesy, he should have been locked up. The specific complaint was that Jeremiah had said that the exiles would be in Babylon a long time and that they should build houses, settle down, plant gardens, etc. (v. 28, cf. vv. 5ff.). Unfortunately, the rest of Jeremiah's letter to Shemaiah has not been transmitted to us. All we have is that Zephaniah read the letter to Jeremiah (v. 29). Whether he was sympathetic or intended merely to warn Jeremiah is not clear. In any case, Jeremiah was not *disciplined* (*gā'ar,* v. 27).

30–32 Jeremiah wrote to the exiles concerning the false prophet Shemaiah in terms similar to those with which he addressed Hananiah (28:15–16). He had prophesied a *falsehood (šeqer)* and led the people to trust it. He was not sent by Yahweh. Yahweh would *punish (pāqaḏ)* him and his descendants. None of them would live to witness the good things *(ṭôḇ)* Yahweh would yet do for the people. His chief offense was that he had spoken *rebellion (sārâ)* against Yahweh.

So the last of this series of chapters (26–29) closes. Each narrative records the consequences which attend the rejection of the word of Yahweh spoken by one of his "servants the prophets." In every case judgment followed. Rejection of Yahweh's total sovereignty over his people as a nation or as individuals and disobedience to the covenant demands are a breach of covenant. The curses of the covenant then operate.

26. For discussion on *mahpeḵeṯ* ("stocks," *prison*) see 20:6. The term *ṣînōq* means "collar" or *pillory.*

IV. THE BOOK OF CONSOLATION (30:1–33:26)

A significant collection of four chapters now begins. Chapters 30 and 31 are almost completely poetical,[1] while chs. 32 and 33 are mainly prose. The collection has been called "The Book of Consolation" because it gives expression to hopes for the future rather than judgment which characterizes earlier chapters. The introductory verses (30:1–3) sound a note of comfort. In the early parts of the book there are some references to a future hope (23:1–8; chs. 24, 29), but the theme is here developed in some detail. Hope was integral to Jeremiah's preaching. It was not easy for him to preach judgment and he shrank from the task at times (e.g., 20:7–18 and other "Confessions"). For him, however, judgment was never an end in itself but the means Yahweh used to bring Israel into a new and lasting relationship with himself. The high point of these chapters lies in 31:31–34.

Few portions of the book of Jeremiah have provoked so much discussion and disagreement among scholars in regard to date, authorship, and interpretation. Not only is there the perennial question of how the prose passages in the whole book relate to Jeremiah, but even some of the poetic pieces have been widely discussed. The fact that the style and content of some passages are very similar to those of the latter chapters of Isaiah has raised questions about the relationship between Jeremiah and Deutero-Isaiah. Again, since some of the passages seem to reflect conditions in exile, some commentators have questioned their allocation to Jeremiah.

A further question concerns the precise situation to which

1. Prose sections appear in 30:1–4, 8–9; 31:1, most of 23–34, 38–40. But see commentary on 30:8–9.

the poems were addressed. Some have argued[2] that much of the material in 30:1–31:22 was written early in Jeremiah's ministry and refers to Northern Israel. The appearance of *Judah* in 30:3–4 and *Zion* in 30:17 is due to a later updating of poems when it was realized that Judah had passed through similar experiences to those of Israel. The grounds for this view are that many of the geographical and personal names point to Israel (Samaria, Jacob, Ephraim, Ramah). The "lovers" who prevent Israel from turning to God, the healing of wounds, laments on the heights, perversity since the days of youth, suggest a strong Hosean influence. Hence it is argued that these passages are a message of consolation for Northern Israel suffering exile since 721 B.C. When Josiah shook off the Assyrian yoke and extended his influence to the north (2 K. 23:15–20), Jeremiah thought that her purification was complete and that she would soon return home. As it happened, this was not possible because Babylon superseded Assyria very quickly. But Jeremiah's hopes did not vanish. He extended the hope to Judah as well (31:23–40) and may himself have emended earlier poems to make them suitable for Judah also (30:3–4, 17).

Few scholars would deny that Jeremiah held out some hope for the future (32:1–15). Moreover, even the most radical scholars allow the genuineness of some, and perhaps a good deal, of the material in chs. 30–31 (e.g., 31:2–6, 15–22), which are clearly addressed to Northern Israel (Ephraim) and would fit into an early period of Jeremiah's career, perhaps while Josiah was carrying out his reform in areas formerly occupied by Northern Israel (2 Chr. 34:6–7). Similarities between Jeremiah and Deutero-Isaiah may arise because both drew on the same conventional forms, or are due to a borrowing from Jeremiah by Deutero-Isaiah,[3] or because these passages are a late insertion among the genuine oracles of Jeremiah. A safe conclusion amid the multitude of varying opinions is that chs. 30–31 contain genuine sayings of Jeremiah (perhaps to a greater extent than is generally realized), addressed to Northern Israel and uttered relatively early in his career (31:2–6, 15–22) together with other words of his spoken later in his career. Finally, the whole passed through the hands of an editor or editors who may have been responsible for some expansion or adaptation of Jeremiah's thought

2. W. Rudolph, *Jeremia* (1968), pp. 188f.; G. P. Couturier, "Jeremiah," *JBC*, p. 325.
3. G. P. Couturier, *JBC*, p. 325.

to a later situation. We ought not conclude too easily that there has been a distortion of Jeremiah's thought.

For the present, taking ch. 30 by itself, after the superscription (vv. 1–3) and a heading to the collection that follows (v. 4) we find the following units: (1) vv. 5–11, calling Israel not to despair; (2) vv. 12–17, referring to Judah's incurable wound and ending with a promise of healing; (3) vv. 18–22, dealing with the restoration of Jacob; (4) vv. 23–24, reminiscent of 23:19–20 but incorporated here perhaps as an introduction to ch. 31.

A. THE RESTORATION OF ISRAEL AND JUDAH (30:1–31:40)

(i) Superscription (30:1–3)

1 *The word that came to Jeremiah from Yahweh:*
2 *"This is what Yahweh, the God of Israel, has said: Write down in a book everything that I have said to you.*
3 *For look, the days are coming—Yahweh's word—when I will restore the fortunes of my people, both Israel and Judah—Yahweh has spoken—and I will restore them to the land which I gave to their fathers and they shall take possession of it."*

1–2 These verses are an editorial preface to the whole collection. They consist of a summary of the message of renewal and restoration in chs. 30–33.

The instruction to Jeremiah to commit his words to writing is illustrated by ch. 36 (36:2, 4, 17–18, 28–32). Baruch the scribe was his amanuensis. In a nation where Yahweh's word was rejected, it was important to preserve it in writing so that the fulfilment of the prophecies could be a vindication of the earlier oracles of judgment. The word translated *book (sēp̄er)* has a wider meaning, denoting a document of some kind. In any case Jeremiah's words were recorded on a roll (*mᵉgillâ,* 36:2, 4, 20, 21, 23, 28, 32).

3 In prophetic language the expression *days are coming* was commonly used for future events. These were not always of an eschatological character, although they sometimes were. Often the promise was fulfilled in a reasonably short time. The expression *restore the fortunes* or "reverse the fortunes" (*šûḇ šᵉḇûṯ,* lit. "turn the turning") occurs frequently in the OT. The translation "turn the captivity"[1] is incorrect and the phrase occurs at times where no captivity is in view (e.g., Job 42:10; Ezek. 16:53). What is in view here is either a reversal of the fortunes of Yahweh's people or a restoration of their fortunes. The superscription, by its use of *both Israel and Judah,* affirms that all Israel, both the northern kingdom (Israel) and the southern kingdom (Judah), is the subject of Yahweh's promise. If in fact much of ch. 30 originally referred to Northern Israel, it became clear that all exiles would be restored to the land Yahweh gave to their fathers. Although many people were deported from the northern kingdom in 722 B.C. and from Judah in 597 and 587 B.C., many of the people, perhaps the majority of them, did not leave the land at all. Jeremiah's words were partly an encouragement to the exiles. But more important was the fact that the exiles were the "good figs" with whom the future lay. Those who remained were "bad figs" (ch. 24). The true people of God in the future would be those in Israel and Judah who were to be restored to possess the land of promise after the refining processes of the exile had done their work.

(ii) Jacob's Distress and Deliverance (30:4–11)

4 *These are the words which Yahweh spoke concerning Israel and Judah;*[1]
5 *Indeed this is what Yahweh has said:*
"We have heard a cry of panic,
Of terror with no peace.
6 *Ask, pray, and see:*
Can a man bear a child?
Why, then, do I see every man
With his hands on his thighs like a woman in labor?[2]
Every face has changed;
They have turned pale.
7 *Ah,*[3] *but that day is great*
Beyond any comparison;
It is a time of anguish for Jacob;
But out of this he shall be saved."

1. The word *šᵉḇûṯ* goes back to *šwḇ,* "return," and not to *šāḇâ,* "to take captive." The AV and RV both assume the root *šāḇâ,* "to take captive," and translate "turn again the captivity." In practice, after the exile "to turn the captivity" and "to reverse the fortunes" came to mean much the same thing, but the context seems to the present commentator to require derivation from the root *šwb.*

1. In a passage which deals with Israel the inclusion of *Judah* must represent a later attempt to bring Judah into the picture.
2. *Like a woman in labor* is lacking in LXX.
3. MT begins with *hôy,* "Alas!" LXX reads *hāyû,* "they have become," as the last word of v. 6: "all the faces have become pale."

8 *"On that day—the word of Yahweh of Hosts—I will break the yoke*[4]
from off their neck[5] *and will snap their bonds; and foreigners will no longer hold them*[6] *in servitude.*
9 *But they shall serve Yahweh their God and David their king whom I will raise up for them."*
10 *"So then, fear not, my servant Jacob—Yahweh's word—*
Nor be dismayed, O Israel;
For look! I will save you from afar,
And your offspring from the land of their captivity;
And Jacob shall return and be at rest,
Secure and with none to make him afraid.
11[7] *For I am with you—Yahweh's word—to save you,*
And I will make an end of all the nations
Among whom I have scattered you;
But I will not make an end of you.
I will punish you as you deserve;
I will not exempt you completely."

4 The verse is the heading of a very complex collection of poetic material in vv. 5–24. It is in the style of many such headings in the book (7:1; 11:1; 14:1; 18:1; 21:1; 25:1; etc.).

Again the reference is to Israel and Judah. The inclusion of Judah in a poem that leads into material about Northern Israel may suggest that the whole collection was finally reedited, perhaps after 586 B.C. (and perhaps by Jeremiah himself), to make the collection relevant to Judah as well. By 586 B.C. the total of all the exiles was complete.

5–7 The phrase *Indeed this is what Yahweh has said* is a further heading. The words of the people (or the prophet) are first given. Yahweh replies directly in vv. 10–11.

There is little in the way of hope here except in the last line. It is only panic and terror, but no peace. The day is awful (lit. *great,* v. 7), that is, the Day of Yahweh (cf. Amos 5:18–20; Isa. 2:12–21; Zeph. 1:14–18). The picture of men clutching their thighs in anguish gives rise to the question *Can a man bear a child?* They behave like

4. LXX "his yoke" refers to the oppressor's yoke.
5. MT reads "your neck . . . your bonds," which may go back to Isa. 10:27. LXX has *their.* If "your" is read, the passage represents a direct address to Jacob (v. 10).
6. MT has "hold him." The reference is to Jacob. We translate in a collective sense with LXX, which reads "and they shall no longer serve foreigners."
7. Jer. 46:28, which is parallel to this verse, has an additional line at the beginning, "So then, fear not, O Jacob my servant—Yahweh's word," as in v. 10. J. Bright, *Jeremiah,* p. 270 adds the line also here in v. 11.

women in labor and their faces have turned pale. Pangs of childbirth symbolize great distress elsewhere in Jeremiah (4:31; 6:24; 22:23). But now, men are experiencing them. It was the wish of every attacking force that the enemy should become like women (50:37). There may be an overtone of such a curse here. It is, in any case, a vivid picture of powerlessness and panic in the face of an unequal battle.

The oracle ends in a striking way: *But out of this he shall be saved*. The question arises whether this is a statement of hope or an incredulous remark, "and out of *this* he shall be *saved*?!" with a touch of sarcasm, serving to stress the hopelessness of the situation already pictured in the earlier lines of the poem. But in the absence of modern punctuation marks in the Hebrew text there is a certain ambiguity. Coming as it does at the head of a collection of material on hope, it may have been interpreted in a different way by the editor who assembled the various poetic pieces of this chapter: "And out of *this* he shall be saved!"[8] Verses 10–17 after the prose section (vv. 8, 9) would reinforce this hopeful note.

8–9 The prose verses break the connection between vv. 5–7 and 10–11 and seem to be an editorial insertion from another context, although the verses may be authentic Jeremiah material. They deal with the whole people of Yahweh in messianic times. We have called these verses prose, but if parallelism and some indication of regular beats are a sign of verse, it is not difficult to arrange them in poetic form. A suggested system of beats is shown in parentheses:

In that day it shall happen— (3)
Word of Yahweh of Hosts— (3)
I will break his yoke from off your necks, (3)
And I will snap their bonds. (2)
Foreigners will no longer make him a servant, (4)
9 But they will serve Yahweh their God (3)
And David their king (3)
Whom I will raise up for them. (3)

The expression *that day* here denotes something different from v. 7 where it is associated with judgment. Here it is associated with deliverance, the removal of the oppressor's yoke, the breaking of the cords which bound the captives, and their release from servi-

8. W. Holladay, *Jeremiah: Spokesman Out of Time*, pp. 111f.

tude. But the other side to their liberty is their willing obedience to Yahweh (*they shall serve* him) and the raising up of the ideal king, here called David (as in Hos. 3:5; Ezek. 34:23–24; 37:24–25).

There is no hint here of nationalistic aspirations or of supremacy over the nations who had oppressed the people. The purpose of restoration was the nation's recognition of Yahweh—a recognition which had not obtained in her past history. A suitable date for such an oracle would be after the destruction of Judah and her monarchy. There is no reason why the passage should not be genuinely from Jeremiah.

10–11 There is a close parallel between these verses and 46:27–28 although they suit the present context admirably. LXX omits these verses here but has them in 46:27–28. Verse 10 resumes from v. 7, where salvation was promised in the time of Jacob's distress. Here for the first time Jacob is referred to as *my servant* and identified with *Israel*. There are some similarities with passages in Second Isaiah (41:8–10; 43:1–6; 44:2–5; etc.) and for this reason v. 10 is said by many writers to show unmistakably the influence of Deutero-Isaiah. The existence of parallel phrases is beyond dispute. What this means is not at all clear. Similar phrases occur in later oracles of undisputed authenticity, and it may be that Jeremiah influenced the later writer[9] or that both of them drew from the same conventional form of address.[10] Where writers accept the influence of Deutero-Isaiah on such passages they are dated late in the Exile.[11] Verse 11 on the other hand contains a number of expressions that are found elsewhere in Jeremiah, such as *I will not make a full end* (4:27; 5:10, 18; 30:11; 46:28); *The nations among whom I have scattered you* (9:16); *I will punish you as you deserve* (10:24); *I am with you to save you* (1:8; 15:20). Some writers accept vv. 10–11 as genuine words of Jeremiah despite problems.[12]

(iii) The Healing of Zion's Wounds (30:12–17)

12 *For this is what Yahweh has said:*
"Your hurt is past healing,
Your wound is incurable;

9. G. P. Couturier, "Jeremiah," *JBC*, p. 325.
10. J. Bright, *Jeremiah*, p. 285.
11. E. W. Nicholson, *Jeremiah 26–52*, p. 54.
12. W. L. Holladay, *Jeremiah: Spokesman Out of Time*, p. 112.

13 *There is no healing for your sore,*[1]
There is no restored flesh for you.
14 *All your lovers have forgotten you,*
They search for you no longer;
For I struck you down with the blow of an enemy,
A cruel chastisement,[2]
Because your wickedness is great and your sins are many.[3]
15 *Why do you cry over your hurt*
That your sore is incurable?
For the greatness of your guilt and your countless sins
I did all this to you.
16 *Yet*[4] *all who devour you will be devoured,*
And all your oppressors shall go into captivity.[5]
Those who plunder you shall be plundered,
And those who despoil you I will give up as spoil.
17 *I will cause new flesh to grow*
And I will heal your wounds—Yahweh's word—
Because they called you outcast,
Zion,[6] *whom no one seeks out."*

12–15 The hopeless mood appears again. Yahweh now speaks to the people in the way Jeremiah spoke of himself (15:18) or as the people once spoke (10:19). This segment begins in v. 12 with the phrase *Your hurt is past healing ('ānûš l^ešiḇrēḵ)* and ends with a similar phrase in v. 15, *your sore is incurable ('ānûš maḵ'ōḇēḵ)*. The sequence of words is noteworthy, "hurt," "past healing," "wound" (v. 12), "no healing," "sore," "no restored flesh" (v. 13), "hurt," "sore," "incurable" (v. 15).[7] It is a grim picture of some terrible judgment that had befallen the people, probably the calamity of 587 B.C., although it is not impossible that we have here a doom pronouncement of Jeremiah before the event. The expression in v. 12,

1. MT reads "no one who pleads your case; for (your) sore, medicine." The first phrase introduces a legal picture which seems out of place, unless the sense is "No one pleads the case for your healing; you have no restoring medicines." But if we omit "pleads your case" we obtain a well-balanced line.
2. MT reads "the chastisement of a cruel one." Revocalize *mûsār* as the absolute, not the construct form of the noun, and read "a cruel chastisement."
3. This phrase is repeated in v. 15b and is omitted here by many commentators. But LXX omits v. 15, although in some recensions v. 15b occurs in the middle of v. 16.
4. MT *lāḵēn,* "therefore." W. Rudolph in *BHS ad loc.* proposes *w^eḵol,* "And all," deleting *lk* as a dittography from the end of v. 15, and reading *waw* for final *nun.*
5. LXX reads "all your oppressors shall eat their flesh."
6. LXX reads "she is your (read "our") quarry," *ṣêḏēnû hî'* for *ṣiyyôn hî'*.
7. The imagery of wounds and healing occurs elsewhere in poetic sections in Jeremiah (8:22; 10:19; 14:17). We are reminded of Hosea's language (Hos. 5:13; 6:1; 7:1; 11:7).

l^ešibrēk, is probably an example of the use of *l^e* to emphasize the noun that follows, "*your* hurt" or "your particular hurt" (cf. 9:2 [Eng. 3], *le'^emûnâ,* "truth itself").[8] The seriousness of the calamity is vividly stated at the end of v. 13. The noun *t^e'ālâ* refers to the healing that takes place over new flesh, the forming of skin over a wound,[9] hence NEB "the new skin cannot grow."

The *lovers (m^e'ah^abîm)* of v. 14 are Judah's political allies,[10] who have forgotten her and no longer seek her out. Among these Egypt and Edom stand out (e.g., 27:3; Obad. 9–14). Egypt had encouraged Judah to rebel against her overlord on a number of occasions (37:5–7; 2 K. 18:19–21). Though an Egyptian army did meet the Babylonians in 588 B.C. it was routed and withdrew, and Jerusalem fell shortly after (37:1ff.). But finally it was Yahweh who had struck his people with *the blow of an enemy, a cruel chastisement.* The line *because your wickedness is great and your sins are many* is repeated in v. 15. It is regarded as redundant by many commentators. On the other hand it may be a kind of refrain.

16–17 There is a change in outlook here. The prophet sees beyond the gloom to the day when those who harmed Judah would be brought under judgment themselves. The figure of Judah's foes "devouring" her is found also in 2:3; 5:17; 8:16; 10:25. In the present context the promise of judgment for Judah's foes represents a sudden reversal in thinking. There is nothing in these verses, however, to suggest that they are not from Jeremiah himself. He was quite capable of moving from an announcement of judgment to one of salvation. The transition in Hebrew from v. 15 to v. 16 is not as awkward as it may appear, especially if we accept a slight emendation and commence v. 16 with *Yet all who devour you. . . .*[11] Jeremiah gives expression here to his view that God will use Nebuchadrezzar his servant to complete his work with Israel and then his time for judgment on the Chaldeans will come. Isaiah in the previous century had expressed the same view in reference to Assyria (see comment on 27:9–11).

When the time is ripe the "incurable" (vv. 12, 15) becomes curable (v. 17). This seems to be a paradox. But paradoxes were no problem to OT prophets. Yahweh could take a new direction without warning. "With men it is impossible, but with God all things are

8. See F. Nötscher, "Zum emphatischen Lamed," *VT* 3 (1953), pp. 372–380.
9. KB, p. 1036.
10. J. A. Thompson, "Israel's 'Lovers,' " *VT* 27 (1977), pp. 475–481.
11. See textual note.

possible."[12] While the verb *niḥam,* "think better of," does not occur here, the present passage affirms the same flexibility in Yahweh (cf. ch. 18). Yahweh could modify his intention in response to a change in attitude of the people (see 18:7–8). In that future day many things would work together—repentance on Israel's part accompanied by a recognition of Yahweh's sovereign rights and a willingness to obey the covenant demands, a new heart, the removal of the bonds of captivity and the punishment of Israel's captors, a return to their homeland in peace and prosperity. In that day Yahweh would *cause new flesh*[13] *to grow* although men had regarded Israel as the *outcast, Zion,*[14] *whom no one seeks out.* The giving of a meaningful name to Israelite children, so common in the prophets (Hos. 1:4, 6, 8; Isa. 8:1; 9:6), takes on a new turn here. It is the nations who are pictured as giving to Zion the name *outcast (niddāḥâ).*[15] It was Yahweh himself who had cast his people out.

(iv) The Restoration of Jacob (30:18–22)

18 *This is what Yahweh has said:*
"I will restore the fortunes of Jacob's tents[1]
And have compassion on his dwellings.[2]
A city shall be built on its mound,
And a mansion will stand where it belongs,
19 *And from them shall come thanksgiving*
And the sound of laughter.
I will increase them, they will not decrease;
I will raise them to an honored place and they will not be inferior.
20 *Their sons shall be as in former times*
And their community shall be established before me.
I will punish all their oppressors.

12. Mark 10:27.
13. Heb. *'ᵃrûḵâ* means "repair," "healing." It is used here and in 8:22 with the verb *'ālâ,* "to come up." Here the Hiphil is used meaning "I will cause healing to come up."
14. Scholars who believe that this poem was originally addressed to Northern Israel either delete *Zion* as having been added in a day when the poem was given a fresh application, even if it was originally addressed to Northern Israel, or they accept LXX, which points to an original "our quarry"—"She is our quarry for whom no one cares." A similar updating is proposed for 30:3–4, "and Judah."
15. The same root is used in reference to casting out Ammon in 49:5 and of Judah in the phrase "they will return from the place to which they had been driven" (40:12; 43:5).

1. Lacking in LXX, which reads simply "I will restore the fortunes of Jacob."
2. LXX reads "his captivity."

21 *Their prince shall be of their own number,*
Their ruler shall come from their midst;
I will bring him near and he shall approach me;
For who would otherwise be so bold
As to approach me?—Yahweh's word.
22[3] *So you will be my people*
And I will be your God."

18 Promises of renewal have been of a somewhat general nature up to this point. Now the promises are given a concrete form in terms of striking images: Yahweh will *restore the fortunes (šûḇ š^{e}ḇûṯ) of Jacob's tents.* By the term *tents* we should understand "clans," that is, people who dwell in tents. There may be a reference here to Num. 24:5–6, where the oracle of Balaam refers to Jacob's "tents" and "encampments" in a future day and continues with a rich picture of what Yahweh had "planted" for them. In these verses we learn of the rebuilding of a city on its tell and a mansion or stronghold in the place where it once stood.[4] The tell (Heb. *tēl*), or *mound,* resulted from the accumulation of the debris of many centuries of occupation, with periods of destruction and rebuilding of the town on the ruins of the past. All over the Middle East today one sees such tells. They provide the archeologist with his source-material. After Roman times most of these were abandoned, and many of them even earlier. The nouns *city* and *mansion* are probably to be understood as collectives referring to a general restoration of towns and fine houses. However, the possibility that the singular *city* refers to Jerusalem and *mansion*[5] refers to the royal palace ought not to be ruled out, especially in view of the statement in v. 21 that a "prince" and a "ruler" would arise. Each of these things, city, palace, prince, was a bond of unity for a restored nation and a restored community.

19–20 There will be a change in the life of the people with a sound of praise and merrymaking (lit. "the sound of them who laugh") in place of laments, an increase in population instead of a dwindling[6] caused by sickness and exile (cf. Amos 9:11–13; Ezek.

3. Lacking in LXX.
4. MT reads "according to its rights" (*'al mišpāṭô*). The sense is not clear. NEB understands "shall have its familiar household."
5. Heb. *'armôn,* "stronghold."
6. The verbs *increase (hirbâ)* and *decrease (mā'aṭ)* occur also in Jeremiah's letter to the exiles in 594 B.C. (29:6).

36:33–38; Zech. 8:4–13), honor in place of dishonor (cf. v. 17). Their *sons* (lit. "his sons," i.e., Jacob's) will be restored to their former state, and their *community* (*'ēḏâ*) will be reestablished before Yahweh. This latter term denotes the community assembled for either cultic or political purposes (cf. 1 K. 12:20). The exact sense is not clear. It certainly involved a restoration of political functions where the nation had its own king and its own political institutions, which had not functioned normally since the destruction of national life. But the character of the king is defined further in v. 21. When restoration came, Yahweh would punish (*pāqaḏ*) every oppressor who sought to upset the order.

21 At the top of the institutional structure was the king, here described as *prince* (*'addîr*) and *ruler* (*mōšēl*). The name "king" (*meleḵ*) is not used here partly because the term was reserved for the ideal king who was yet to come, and partly because experience over the centuries had shown that most of Israel's kings fell far short of the ideal (cf. Ezekiel's reference to a prince, *nāśî'*, rather than a king, Ezek. 45:7, 17). That ruler would not come from outside, from a foreign land like Assyria, Egypt, or Babylon as he had in the course of the past century, but he would be one of their own number, from their midst. The passage does not specifically mention the messianic king of David's line but only a native ruler at the head of a restored political community. But the fact that the nation was to be so wonderfully restored leads us to think that a restoration of the glorious era of David with its free and joyous life in the land of promise was in view. The passage has a peculiarly messianic ring (cf. Isa. 11). The latter part of the verse adds a deeper dimension. Yahweh will bring the ruler, and only thus shall he approach Yahweh. Then the comment is offered, reading literally: "For who is he who would give his heart in security . . . ," that is, would venture of himself or would gamble his life, to approach Yahweh. To enter the divine presence unbidden was to risk death. The ruler thus appears to be undertaking a sacral or priestly function rather than one that is specifically political. The picture is of a ruler-priest performing both political and priestly duties. Such a concept was well known in the Middle East for many centuries. But this may be to press the picture too far. The passage may mean simply that only one upon whom Yahweh had set his approval would dare to take up the onerous task of leading a nation in the days of restoration. He would need to be one who was utterly loyal to Yahweh personally and who administered the nation in conformity with the demands of the covenant. Only a handful of kings like Hezekiah and Josiah in Israel's past approached such a noble ideal.

22 This conventional covenantal formula, lacking in LXX, is not out of place here. It sums up the goal of all the promises of restoration that Israel would at last be bound to Yahweh in the way that he had always intended she should be. Her true calling was to be God's holy, elect people (Exod. 19:5, 6). The covenant correlate "Your God—my people" is referred to a number of times in the OT (Lev. 26:12; Deut. 7:26; Jer. 7:23; 11:4; Ezek. 36:28; etc.). It would be surprising if Jeremiah did not use the formula sometimes (cf. 31:33). He may, indeed, have used it much more than the book indicates.

(v) The Divine Judgment: A Fragment (30:23–24; 31:1)

23 *Look! the scorching wind of Yahweh has gone forth;*
A sweeping[1] *whirlwind,*
It will whirl around the head of the wicked.
24 *Yahweh's fierce anger will not turn back*
Till he has finished and accomplished
His deep purposes.
In days to come you will understand this.
31:1 *"At that time—Yahweh's word—I will become the God of*[2] *all the families of Israel, and they shall become my people."*

23–24 These verses occur also in 23:19–20 with minor variations. In that context they state the truth not known to the false prophets but known to one who has stood in Yahweh's council, namely, that the future does not hold peace but judgment. In the present context they seem to have been taken up again and used to add emphasis to the promise of judgment on Israel's foes spoken of in vv. 11, 16, 20c. The last line, *In the days to come you will understand this* (cf. 23:20), is an affirmation that the purposes of Yahweh are already determined but will be understood (*hiṯbônēn*) only when the day has come. But that day is in the not too distant future; it is not an eschatological concept.

31:1 The somewhat vague promise of 30:23–24 is given clearer definition here by linking these verses back to 30:22. *At that time* the promise of restoration and renewal will come to fruition when *all the families of Israel,* the people of Judah, will be restored

1. Several mss. and 23:19 read *miṯḥôlēl* in place of the uncertain *mitgôrēr.*
2. Lit. "I will become God to. . . ."

to their proper covenant relationship with Yahweh (cf. 30:3; Amos 3:1–2).

This verse thus performs a double function. It concludes the block of material in 30:1–24 and serves as a heading for the complex of poems in ch. 31.

Chapter 31 like ch. 30 is mostly verse but there are prose sections in vv. 23–34 and 38–40, although it is arguable that vv. 23–34 are partly poetic. The poetic passages vv. 2–6 and 15–22 are directed to Northern Israel and come from Jeremiah's early period before any exile had touched Judah. There is a certain ambiguity in vv. 2–6 because the term Israel there may refer to all Israel. Some verses concern Judah and Jerusalem (vv. 23–26, 38–40).

Many of the verses refer to both Northern Israel and Judah (vv. 2–6, 10–14, 27–30, 31–34, 35–37). It would appear that the chapter represents a collection of various fragments brought together because of their common reference to the restoration of the people of God. Widely varying views have been held about the date, authorship, and addresses of the separate segments.

Some scholars hold that 31:1–22 represents material addressed originally to Northern Israel early in Jeremiah's career, before the first exiles left Judah in 597 B.C., and that references to Judah (30:3–4), Zion (30:17), and to "all the families of Israel" (31:1) represent later additions to poems directed originally to Northern Israel to make them applicable to the whole people.[3] Most scholars, however, hold the view that while some of the material is early and was addressed to Israel, some of it was later and referred to the hope of the restoration of Judah as well as Israel after the fall of Jerusalem in 597 B.C. or even after 586 B.C. Some of the material may represent the application of Jeremiah's prophecies more directly to the exiles during the early days of the Exile.[4] We shall make some specific suggestions in the commentary.

A special question is raised in the case of passages that seem to reflect the language and thought of Second Isaiah.[5]

Finally the prose portions vv. 23–26, 27–30, 31–34, 38–40 call for brief comment. The first is partly prose and partly poetry

3. G. P. Couturier, "Jeremiah," *JBC,* p. 326.

4. J. Bright, *Jeremiah,* p. 285; E. W. Nicholson, *Jeremiah 26–52,* pp. 59, 60, 63, 66f., 70f.

5. See above, pp. 327f.

and may have been all poetry originally. There is little reason to deny it to Jeremiah. The other three all commence with *the time is coming*. Of these, vv. 27–30 play on the popular proverb about fathers eating sour grapes (Ezek. 18:2) and vv. 38–40 refer to rebuilding Jerusalem's walls. These need not be denied to Jeremiah since there is no reason to think that he could not have expressed the same ideas. The passage vv. 31–34 is concerned with the New Covenant. It represents one of the deepest insights in all prophetic literature and became of tremendous importance to early Christians (cf. Heb. 8:8–9:28; 2 Cor. 3:5–18). The passage has often been denied to Jeremiah because it is written in the characteristic prose style of the book of Jeremiah and for that reason is ascribed to the Deuteronomic author or authors. On the surface at least, it would seem extraordinary to deny it to Jeremiah, who was undoubtedly responsible for a great deal that was noble and far-reaching in its implications. The view that these verses do not come from Jeremiah is deservedly rejected by some influential scholars. Even if the passage does not preserve the *ipsissima verba* of Jeremiah it represents a high point in theological thinking of which he was the source.[6] It is at least as likely that a giant in theological thinking should rise to these heights as that his successors should. We shall argue in the commentary that the section is all but poetic in form and may have had a poetic original if, indeed, it is not in verse form as it is. In that case it is not prose, so that it would be wrong to speak of the characteristic prose style of the book of Deuteronomy.

(vi) Further Promises to Ephraim and Judah (31:2–6)

2 *This is what Yahweh has said:*
"A people that survived the sword
Found favor[1] *in the wilderness.*
Israel journeyed to find rest;
3 *From afar Yahweh appeared to him.*[2]
I have loved you with an everlasting love,
Therefore I have prolonged unfailing faithfulness to you.

6. J. Bright, *Jeremiah,* p. 287; W. L. Holladay, *Jeremiah: Spokesman Out of Time,* pp. 118–121.

1. MT has a singular verb to suit the singular *people*.
2. MT reads "to me" and follows this with "and" in the next clause. LXX reads *to him* (Heb. *lô,* with the consonants *lw*). It would seem that an original Heb. *lw* became in MT *lî* w^e.

4 *Once again I will build you,*
O virgin Israel,
And you shall be rebuilt.
Once again you will adorn yourself with timbrels
And go forth in the dance with merrymakers.
5 *Once again you will plant vineyards*
On the hills of Samaria
Which those who planted defiled.
6 *For a day is coming when watchmen will shout*
On Ephraim's hills,
'Up! Let us go to Zion
To Yahweh our God.'"

2 The reference is back to Israel's escape from Egypt in the days of the Exodus but particularly to the deliverance from Pharaoh's troops at the Red (reed) Sea (Exod. 14:5–23) and to Yahweh's gracious provision and care during the wilderness wandering. The phrase "find favor" (*māṣā' ḥēn*)[3] occurs five times in the narrative in Exod. 33:12–17.

The last phrase raises some textual problems. MT reads literally "going (infinitive absolute) to find rest for him, Israel"; NEB reads "Israel journeyed to find rest"; RSV "Israel sought for rest." The Versions provide a variety of readings. The sense seems to be that Israel escaped from Egypt, and was searching for the land promised to her forefathers (cf. Exod. 33:14; Deut. 28:65). The verb "seek for rest" has a parallel in 6:16 "rest for your souls."

The captivity of Israel (Northern?) is here described as a new wandering in the wilderness (cf. Hos. 2:14–15). It may be that the theme of the New Exodus was already current in Judah long before it was taken up by Second Isaiah (Isa. 40:3–4; 42:14–16; 43:18–21; 44:27; 48:21; etc.).

3 The appearance of Yahweh to Israel *from afar* may refer to the fact that the people were in a foreign land far away when he acted. But a feasible suggestion is that *from afar* may mean "long ago," in the theophany of Sinai. This interpretation fits the present context. There are two significant covenant terms here, *love* (both the verb *'āhēḇ* and the noun *'ahᵃḇâ*) and *faithfulness (ḥeseḏ).* The latter occurs in the OT 245 times, mostly in a covenant or treaty

3. W. F. Lofthouse, "Ḥen and Ḥesed in the OT," *ZAW* 51 (1933), pp. 29–35.

context.[4] On the translation *Therefore I have prolonged unfailing faithfulness to you*[5] cf. Ps. 36:11 (Eng. 10), "Prolong your kindness to those that know you." The thought is akin to that of Hos. 11:4. Jeremiah's dependence on Hosea is seen in a number of places.

4 Once again Yahweh will build his people securely, literally "I will build you so that you are built." It is the promise of 1:10 (note "plant" in v. 5). Commentators who argue that vv. 2–6 refer to Northern Israel stress the phrase *O virgin Israel* in comparison with virgin Zion elsewhere. The point is strengthened by the mention of Samaria and Ephraim in vv. 5 and 6. The reference to Zion is seen as a prophetic reference to days of reunification of the divided people. When that day comes, the happiness which was lost when the Exile came will be restored. *Timbrels*—adornment with small pieces that tinkled in the dance was common all over the Near East in ancient times and still is today. The description "the whirl of the merrymakers" captures the village dance of all ages.

5 The scene changes to agriculture. Vineyards destroyed by enemy invaders will be replanted (cf. *plant, nāṭa',* in 1:10). The latter part of the verse is difficult. It reads literally "The planters planted and will profane" (cf. Deut. 28:30b). The meaning of the phrase depends on the meaning of the verb *ḥālal,* which normally means to put to secular or ordinary use something that was set apart as holy (cf. Lev. 19:23–25; Deut. 20:6). The text is taken by some commentators to mean "Those who planted will enjoy the fruit."[6] LXX reads "plant and give praise" (*hll* for *ḥll*). The alternative translation is "vineyards which the planters who planted then defiled." The reference would then be, possibly, to the worship of Baal, the god of fertility who ensured the produce of field, flock, and herd. The picture in Hos. 2 is consistent with this (Hos. 2:7, 10–11, 14–15 [Eng. 5, 8–9, 12–13]).

6 Jeremiah here has a vision of a united people worshipping Yahweh in Jerusalem. The sentiments expressed here suggest that Jeremiah was not opposed to the worship in the temple in principle. It was the practice that he rejected. And presumably he was not

4. KB, p. 317. The term is difficult to translate. Some such range of words as "loyalty," "faithfulness," "devotion," "steadfast love," "kindness," suits most cases. Prefixing the adjective *unfailing* to these may capture the sense better still. See N. Glueck, *Ḥesed in the Bible* (1927; E.T. 1967); Lofthouse, *art. cit.*

5. The pronoun attached to the verb *prolong (māšak)* is used datively. See M. Dahood, "Ugaritic Studies and the Bible," *Gregorianum* 43 (1962), pp. 55–79, esp. 67.

6. J. Bright, *Jeremiah,* pp. 273, 281.

opposed to Josiah's reforms. Rival sanctuaries at Bethel and Dan (1 K. 12:25–33) were destructive of unity.[7] A concomitant of reunification would be that the old northern kingdom would once again acknowledge Zion (Jerusalem) as the legitimate sanctuary of Yahweh.

The *watchmen (nōṣ^{e}rîm)* were posted high on vantage points in time of war to warn of an approaching enemy (cf. 6:17). But here the watchman's call is for a nobler purpose, *Up! Let us go to Zion.*

(vii) Israel's Homecoming (31:7–14)

7 *Yes, this is what Yahweh has said:*
"Break into shouts of joy for Jacob,
Cry aloud for the first of the nations.
Sound forth! Give praise and say,
'Yahweh has saved his[1] people,
The remnant of Israel.'
8 *Look, I am bringing them*
From the northern land;
From the farthest horizons I will gather them,
The blind and the lame among them,
The pregnant and women in labor as well.
They will return a mighty throng.
9 *Look,[2] they will come with weeping,*
But with comfort[3] I will lead them;
I will lead them by flowing streams
On a smooth path where they will not stumble.
For I am Israel's father
And Ephraim is my firstborn son.
10 *Hear, you nations, the word of Yahweh;*
On the farthest shores proclaim it. Say:
'He who scattered Israel shall gather them again,
And shall guard them like a shepherd his flock.'
11 *For Yahweh has ransomed Jacob*
And has redeemed him from the clutch of one too strong for him.
12 *They shall come with shouts of joy to Zion's height,*
With faces aglow over the bounty of Yahweh,
The corn, the new wine, and the oil,
The young of flock and herd.
They themselves shall become like a well-watered garden;
They shall never languish again.

7. Archeological work has revealed rival sanctuaries in southern Judah as well, at Arad and Beersheba. The great altar at Dan has now been excavated.

1. MT has "your," LXX and Targ. *his*.
2. The last word in MT of v. 8 is added to v. 9 and revocalized from *hēnnâ*, "here," to *hinnēh*.
3. So with LXX, emending MT *taḥ^{a}nûnîm*, "supplications," to *tanḥûmîm*.

13 *Then the maidens shall dance with joy,*
And young men and old men as well.[4]
I will turn their mourning into gladness
And will give them comfort[5] *and make them happy in their grief.*
14 *I will satisfy the priests with fat things*
And my people shall be sated with my bounty—Yahweh's word."

7 The brief formula which introduces this verse suggests that we have here another independent oracle. However, the section that follows, vv. 7–22, probably contains three passages, vv. 7–9, 10–14, 15–22. The triumphal return envisaged in vv. 2–6 gives rise to shouts of joy, for Yahweh has *saved (hôšîa')* his people. The beneficiary is Jacob, *the first of the nations*. The latter expression was evidently a popular and proud term for Israel (cf. Amos 6:1). Reference to such shouts for joy occur in other parts of the OT (Isa 12:6; 14:7; 36:10; 44:23; 48:20; 49:13; 51:11; 54:1; 55:12; etc.). The verb "save" in MT is imperative; LXX *has saved* seems preferable. The people are called the *remnant (šᵉ'ērîṯ) of Israel,* probably a reference to the small number who escaped the calamity of 721 B.C. and were purified by the Exile to reconstitute the New Israel that would be faithful to Yahweh (cf. the "good figs" from Judah, ch. 24).[6] The term *remnant* had several meanings in the OT: (a) those who escaped some present danger (Amos 5:15; Isa. 37:30–31; Jer. 8:3; Ezek. 5:10; 11:13); (b) the New Israel restored to the land of promise to form the new covenant community (Isa. 4:2; 28:5; Mic. 5:6–7; cf. Isa. 35:10, and several references in Isa. 60–66); (c) the wider remnant comprising the spiritual Israel, and the converts of the nations (Isa. 11:11; 28:5).[7]

8–9 These verses have some striking similarities in style and thought to the latter chapters of Isaiah. The picture is of Yahweh gathering his people from the *northern land* and from the farthest horizons and leading them on a "New Exodus" march along a highway by flowing streams to their homeland (cf. Isa. 35; 40:3–5, 11; 41:18–20; 42:16; 43:1–7; 44:3–4; 48:20–21; 49:9–13). The *northern*

4. LXX reads "maidens shall be happy in the assembly of young men and old men shall be merry," reading *qᵉhal* for *māḥôl* and *yaḥdû* for *yaḥdāw*. RSV accepts the second change but not the first.
5. This clause is lacking in LXX.
6. R. de Vaux, "Le 'Reste d'Israel' d'après les prophètes," *RB* 42 (1933), pp. 527–539.
7. There are several references in the OT to converts from the nations coming to worship Israel's God; cf. Isa. 24:14–16; 45:14–15; 49:6; 56:3, 6–8; Zech. 8:9–23; 14:16.

land was Assyria where Northern Israel had been taken captive in 721 B.C., and the *farthest horizons* were represented by the land of the Medes (2 K. 17:6). These geographical definitions are, however, more general and might equally well refer to a captivity in Babylon. The power from the north referred to so often in the earlier chapters of Jeremiah (4:5–6; 6:22–26; etc.) was eventually identified with the Chaldeans. The way of exile was north from Judah by way of Riblah although it turned southeast eventually. The caravan of those returning would contain weak people, *the blind and the lame among them, the pregnant and women in labor* (cf. Isa. 40:11), a further sign of the miraculous nature of the event (cf. Isa. 35:5–10; 42:15). Though the people come weeping (cf. Ps. 126), Yahweh will lead them, will comfort them (Isa. 40:11), and guide them by flowing streams on a *smooth* (*yāšār,* "straight") way where they will not stumble. The *flowing streams* may be a contrastive allusion to the water from the rock of Exod. 17:1–7; Num. 20:1–13, where there was an intermittent flow. Now there will be water in flowing streams (*naḥal,* "wadi"). The "straight road" serves to accentuate the ease of the march, which will be so different from the first Exodus (cf. Isa. 20:4). The imagery of the verse is strongly reminiscent of Deutero-Isaiah, where the return from captivity in Babylon is depicted. But the event transcends the Exodus from Egypt in every way (Isa. 43:16–29; cf. Jer. 16:14–15).

The reference to *Israel's father* and to *Ephraim my firstborn son (b^e ḵôr)* is important. The term *father* is not used a great deal for God in the OT. In Deut. 32:6 it is used to describe the close bond between Israel and Yahweh. Hosea used the picture of a son as a symbol of Yahweh's favor toward Israel during the Exodus period (Hos. 11:1–6; cf. Exod. 4:22). Jeremiah's use of the term lies in this context. Israel is the firstborn, not because she is superior to Judah but because Yahweh will renew with her the same fatherly love he displayed in centuries past. The ideas accord well with vv. 2–6. At least some aspects of the thought of vv. 8–9 lay in Israel's tradition before the Exile.

10 A number of the words and expressions here are reminiscent of the latter chapters of Isaiah. Among these we note *farthest shores ('iyyîm),*[8] the address to the *nations (gôyîm,* Isa. 41:1; 49:1; etc.),[9] the shepherd of the flock (Isa. 40:11). The nations and distant

8. Jeremiah uses the word in 2:10; 25:22; 31.10; 47:4.

9. The combination with *mamlāḵâ* in 18:7–9; 27:8 seems to be peculiar to Jeremiah.

islands are invited to witness the marvellous event (Isa. 42:10; 49:1). But the themes are not exclusive to Isaiah. The symbolism of the shepherd and his flock occurs in Jer. 23:1–2, and Jeremiah refers often to the nations.[10]

11 Two redemption terms occur together here although they are concerned rather with physical liberation. The verb "ransom" (*pāḏâ*) in some contexts refers to freedom after paying off a ransom price. Originally it is a term of commercial law. It is not used in Deutero-Isaiah.[11] The verb "redeem" (*gā'al*) is used often in the context of family obligation. The kinsman was required to redeem the property of a family member, even avenge his death. The kinsman-redeemer (*gô'ēl*) is a significant figure in the OT. Jeremiah was required to redeem the field at Anathoth owned by his cousin Hanamel (ch. 32).

Both these words feature in the deliverance of Israel from Egypt (cf. Exod. 6:5; 15:13; Deut. 7:8; 9:26). The word "redeem" (*gā'al*) and the verbal noun *gô'ēl*, "redeemer," feature prominently in the latter chapters of Isaiah where the verb "redeem" refers to Yahweh's deliverance from Babylon, and Yahweh is the "redeemer" of his people, acting as their "kinsman" to secure their freedom. The verb and its derivatives occur some twenty times in this part of the OT.

12 So they come to Zion with *shouts of joy,*[12] to Zion *with faces aglow*[13] at Yahweh's *bounty (ṭûḇ).* The items listed refer to elements of the staple diet in ancient Israel (cf. Hos. 2:7, 10 [Eng. 5, 8]). A bountiful supply of these was an evidence of divine favor. Even the people themselves would be, metaphorically, like a *well-watered garden (gan rāweh;* cf. Isa. 58:11), never to *languish* again.

13 LXX with a touch of realism reads: "The maidens (*b^e^ṯûlâ*) will be happy in the company of young men and the old men shall be merry," which suits the context as well as MT.

The weeping of v. 9 is now turned to *gladness (śāśôn),* and Yahweh comforts them and gives them gladness for sorrow. The

10. The term *gôy* in one form or another occurs some 85 times in Jeremiah and is found in both prose and poetic sections. It is generally used of the nations other than Israel but in several places it is used of Israel, e.g., 5:9, 29; 7:28; 9:9.

11. Deut. 9:26; 13:5; 21:8; Hos. 7:13; 13:14; Mic. 6:4; Zech. 10:8; Ps. 25:22; 78:42; Neh. 1:10.

12. The verb *rinnâ* means "utter a joyful shout."

13. The verb *nāhar* means "shine." It occurs elsewhere in Isa. 60:5; Ps. 34:6 (Eng. 5).

range of their former grief is indicated by three words, weeping (*bᵉḵî,* v. 9), *mourning ('ēḇel),* and *grief (yāḡôn).*

14 The term translated *fat things (dešen)* applied strictly to the fat of the offering, which was burned as an offering to Yahweh. The priests shared only in certain sacrifices. The right thigh of the sacrificial beast was reserved for them (Lev. 7:32–36). The reference may suggest that with a return to proper worship these portions would be reserved once again for the priests. But probably *fat* is here a symbol for life and prosperity (Ps. 36:8; 63:5; Isa. 55:2). The priests, who otherwise enjoyed no inheritance (Num. 18:20–23; Deut. 10:9; 18:1–5), are promised a share in the same prosperity as the people, here described in terms of the commodities which were produced in Israel (v. 12). In lyrical terms Jeremiah declared that the people would be *sated (śāḇa')* with Yahweh's *bounty (ṭûḇ).*

(viii) The End of Rachel's Mourning (31:15–22)

15 *This is what Yahweh has said:*
"Listen! In Ramah, lamentation is heard,
Bitter weeping,
Rachel bewailing her sons.
She refuses to be comforted,
For they are no more."
16 *This is what Yahweh has said:*
"Cease your loud weeping,
Restrain your tears,
For there is a reward for your activity[1]*—Yahweh's word;*
They shall return from the enemy's land;
17 *There is hope for your future—Yahweh's word;*
Your sons will return to their homeland.[2]
18 *I have heard distinctly*
Ephraim bemoaning himself:
'Thou hast trained me, and I have been trained
Like an unbroken calf.
Restore me and let me return,
For thou art Yahweh my God.
19 *After I had turned away I repented,*
And after I was instructed
I smote on my thigh.
I am ashamed, I am humiliated,
For I bear the disgrace of my youth!'

1. The noun **pᵉ'ullâ* derives from *pā'al*, "to do, act." "Toil" is hardly appropriate, even though weeping may be hard work. We have proposed *activity* in an attempt to cover Rachel's continuous concern for her exiled sons.
2. Lit. "their borders."

20 *Is Ephraim my dear son?*[3]
A child in whom I delight?
For the more I speak of him
The more vividly I remember him.
My heart yearns[4] *for him,*
I am filled with pity for him—Yahweh's word."
21 *"Set up roadmarks for yourself,*
Make for yourself guideposts;
Set your mind on the highway,
The way you have come.
Come back, O virgin Israel,
Come back to these towns of yours.
22 *How long will you dart hither and thither,*
My backsliding daughter?
For Yahweh has created a new thing on earth:[5]
A woman shall encompass a man."

15 The brief formula *This is what Yahweh has said* introduces a new poem clearly intended originally for Northern Israel. Many commentators who hesitate to apply the earlier part of this chapter to Northern Israel agree that vv. 15–22 concerned the North rather than Judah. The poem announces the return of Northern Israel, who had been taken into exile in 721 B.C. Jeremiah imagined the spirit of *Rachel,* one of the wives of Jacob and the mother of Joseph and Benjamin and therefore ancestress of the Joseph tribes (Ephraim and Manasseh), who covered a large area of Northern Israel, weeping for her children who had been deported by the Assyrians a hundred years earlier. *Ramah* (lit. "a height") lay in the tribe of Benjamin (Josh. 18:25; Judg. 4:5) on the boundary between Israel and Judah. It is identified today with er-Ram about 5 miles (approximately 8 km.) north of Jerusalem. According to 1 Sam. 10:2–3 Rachel's tomb was near here. Another tradition, which is still accepted, placed the tomb near Bethlehem (Gen. 35:19; 48:7; 1 Sam. 10:2–3). The idea of Rachel, the personified Israel, weeping for her children was taken up in the NT (Matt. 2:18), where it was used in connection with Herod's slaughter of the children of Bethlehem after the birth of Jesus.

As the poem opens, Rachel is pictured as weeping bitterly, refusing to be comforted, for her children who have gone away and

3. LXX reads the indicative, "Ephraim is my dear son."
4. Lit. "My bowels rumble."
5. Or "in the land."

ceased to exist. At this point Yahweh speaks. The rest of the poem constitutes Yahweh's words.

16–17 MT reads literally "Withhold your voice from weeping, and your eyes from tears." Yahweh has a *reward (śāḵār)* for all Rachel's activity on behalf of her children. They will return from enemy lands.

In v. 17 the term *'aḥ^{a}rîṯ* is ambiguous. It may mean simply *future* (RSV) or it could mean the future of Israel as a people, that is, Rachel's "descendants"; hence NEB: "You shall leave descendants after you." In any case, the return of Rachel's sons to their own borders will guarantee the future of the nation.

18–19 These verses are really a penitential confession from Northern Israel. Yahweh hears plainly Ephraim (his people) "rocking in his grief" (NEB) as he looks back over the years and recalls his careful training of him (*yissar*) until he was trained.[6] He was like an untamed calf to begin. The image comes from Hos. 4:16; 10:11. Some take the verb in the alternative sense of chastening, e.g., "Thou hast chastened me, and I was chastened, like an untrained calf" (RSV).[7]

The cry of remorseful Ephraim was *Restore me and let me return.* Jeremiah uses the root *šûḇ* to good advantage. In the context, return from exile is the primary sense, and Yahweh has "caused the exiles to return." But the sense of repentance is here also. Ephraim would return to Yahweh if he were allowed (*and let me return*). He confesses, *After I had turned away I repented.*[8] As a physical demonstration of remorse he beat on his *thigh (yārēḵ).* This was a gesture of pain and lament—not only in Israel but all over the ancient Near East (Ezek. 21:17).[9] He was ashamed and humiliated. But the disgrace of the past reached back to Israel's origins, to her *youth (n^{e}'ûrîm),* a theme that is referred to elsewhere in Jeremiah and in other prophets (2:2; 3:24, 25; 22:21; 32:30; Ezek. 16:22; Isa. 48:8; 54:4; etc.).

6. NEB has "Thou hast trained me to the yoke like an unbroken calf,/And now I am trained."

7. J. Bright, *Jeremiah,* p. 282 suggests "Thou didst chasten me that I might be chastened." His final translation "For my training thou didst flog me, like a fractious young bull" seems rather free.

8. W. Rudolph, *BHS ad loc.,* proposes to insert *šaḇtî,* "I turned back," as having fallen out after *šûḇî* through haplography. Hence J. Bright's translation (p. 225): "Ah, after I'd strayed/I repented, was sorry." This is done in the interest of meter.

9. Cf. *ANET,* p. 108, The Descent of Ishtar to the Underworld. Examples are known also in Greek literature, e.g., *Iliad* 15:397–98; 16:125; *Odyssey* 13:198–99.

20 Yahweh's reply to a cry of repentance is to assure Ephraim of his deep longing that Ephraim should return to him. The thought of this verse is strongly reminiscent of Hos. 11:1–4, 8–9. The terms of endearment are different but the love is the same, *my dear son, a child in whom I delight* or "my darling child." Yahweh cannot utter his name (speak of him) without remembering him vividly. The Hebrew text in the last line reads literally "my bowels rumble for him" but has to be rendered *my heart yearns for him*. The very vivid anthropomorphism depicts God's stomach being churned up with longing for his son. Although ancient psychology is different from our own, the physical effects of human emotions are recognizably the same then as now.

21–22 The address now changes to second feminine singular to accommodate the virgin daughter Israel. The call comes to the people to set out for home. The picture of the highway leading home was later developed greatly by Deutero-Isaiah (Isa. 35; 40:3–5, 11; 41:18–20; 42:16; 43:1–7; 44:3–4; 49:9–13), but it was already used by Jeremiah. The picture of *roadmarks* or "cairns" (*ṣiyyûn*) and *guideposts (tamrûr)* to mark the way was a well-known one and obtains today.[10]

A welcome awaited the virgin Israel, who was called to *come back (šûḇ) to these towns of yours*. She had been away too long darting hither and thither.[11] She is addressed as a *backsliding (šôḇēḇ) daughter* (cf. 3:14, 22).[12] The last line of v. 22 introduces what is probably a proverbial saying. It is introduced by the comment: *Yahweh has created (bārā') a new thing on earth,* literally, *A woman shall encompass (teṣôḇēḇ) a man*. The exact meaning of the proverb is not clear. Several suggestions have been made. It was clearly intended to describe something very unusual or unexpected. Jerome in the fourth century believed it was a prophecy about the Virgin Mary's protecting embrace of the Christ child. Some have regarded it as a sign of great security such as is displayed by a mother protecting a child. Israel will know such security during her return and resettlement in Palestine. Another explanation is that the proverb is

10. For Jeremiah there was a strong hope for future restoration. In the present context this was a hope for Israel, the Northern Kingdom, which was urged to set her mind on the road by which she had journeyed into captivity and retrace her pathway following the same road signs. There seems to be a lively call here for the people to make all speed to return. Roadmarks and guideposts were in place for their use and they could travel without missing their way.

11. J. Bright, *Jeremiah,* p. 276 translates "How long will you dilly-dally (*hiṯhammēq*)?"

12. RSV "faithless"; NEB "wayward"; J. Bright "turn about."

symbolic. The "woman" personified Israel and the "man" personified Yahweh. The adulterous wife, Israel, who had to be divorced by Yahweh her husband, now returns to him and clings to him (Hos. 1–3; Jer. 2:20–21). This would be something new, something unheard of in all Israel's history.[13] LXX is little help since it has an entirely different meaning. A rather bold explanation is to see the proverb as having some powerful sexual overtones.[14] The word *sôḇēḇ* is found in Deut. 32:10, where it is said that Yahweh found Israel in a desert land and "encircled him" (*yᵉsōḇᵉḇenhû*) "cared for him," and "kept him as the apple of his eye." The word for *man* here in Jeremiah is *geḇer,* which sometimes refers to a vigorous and virile young man. The related word *gibbôr,* "warrior," indicates this sense of *geḇer.* In the verse before us the meaning seems to be, a female embraces a warrior or a virile young man (cf. 30:6 for the same word). There are two contrary images of a woman here. In the one the woman (*nᵉqēḇâ*) is feminine, endearing, vulnerable, innocent. This was the way prophets often thought of Israel or Zion, "virgin Israel" (v. 21), "daughter of my people," "daughter of Zion" (4:11, 31), that is, "my darling daughter," "darling Zion."[15] Israel in the wilderness, pursuing lovers, was behaving out of character, in a "giddy" fashion. The other image is that in 30:5–7 warriors become women, effeminate. Israel then is both feminine and effeminate. But things will change. Woman will take the initiative in war and in sex. In the context: Israel has been weak in the past, darting hither and thither (cf. Hos. 7:11; 8:9), her warriors demoralized and under a curse. But it will change. The virgin Israel shall arise, something of an Amazon, and do exploits. A woman (Israel) will take the lead.

(ix) The Restoration of Judah (31:23–26)

23 *This is what Yahweh of Hosts the God of Israel has said: "Once again will they use this expression in the land of Judah and in its towns when I have restored their fortunes:*
'May Yahweh bless you,
O Righteous Abode,
O Holy Mount,'
24 *And Judah and all its people shall live together there,*
The farmers and those who roam with the flocks,

13. So G. P. Couturier, "Jeremiah," *JBC*, p. 326.
14. W. Holladay, *Jeremiah: Spokesman Out of Time,* p. 117.
15. See J. Bright, *Jeremiah,* p. 32.

25 *For I will satisfy the weary ones*
And everyone that languishes I will give his fill."
26 *Then I awoke and looked about, for my sleep had been pleasant to me.*

The short oracle vv. 23–25 is a poetic piece framed between two brief pieces of prose. But even these so-called prose pieces can be seen as poetic without much difficulty.

Again they will speak this word (4)
In the land of Judah and in its towns (3)
When I restore their fortunes. (2 or 3)

Verses 23b–25 follow in poetic form. But v. 26 may also be viewed as poetry.

At this I awoke and looked about (3)
And my sleep had been pleasant to me. (3)

23 The longer introductory formula turns our attention to Judah. A short blessing is given for Judah in the style of Num. 6:24–26 and Ps. 128:5. It comes in the name of Yahweh, who is described as the Righteous One (*ṣeḏeq*) and the Holy One (*qōḏeš*). The temple mountain appears to be in view in the expressions the *Righteous* (or, True) *Abode* (the abode of the Righteous One) and the *Holy Mount* (the mountain of the Holy One). But the context seems to require that these phrases be used of Yahweh. Yahweh is Israel's true resting place and her impregnable refuge. Once again he would dwell in the midst of his people to bless them.

24–25 The farmers and shepherds in Judah also would once again go about their daily work. *There* refers to the land.

26 The significance of this verse is obscure. Even if it were a marginal comment it is difficult to explain it, unless it is seen as a comment by an editor who had worked over all the promises of the previous sections, none of which had been realized at the time, and could only remark that he had awakened from what was a pleasant dream. Another possibility is that the verse represents the remains of an editorial framework which has been incompletely preserved. This may have been a framework once imposed on this material in its present context or, more likely, one that belonged to some of the material in an earlier context from which it was borrowed.

(x) *Two Short Sayings (31:27–30)*

27 *"Look, days are coming—Yahweh's word—when I will sow the house of Israel and the house of Judah with the seed of men and the seed of beasts.*

28 *And as I watched over them to uproot and to tear down, to demolish, to destroy and to harm, so I will keep watch over them to build and to plant—Yahweh's word.*
29 *In those days they will no longer say,*
'The fathers have eaten sour grapes
And the children's teeth are set on edge,'
30 *but a man shall die for his own wrongdoing. Any man who eats sour grapes, his teeth shall be set on edge."*

27 The first saying refers to the restoration of Israel and Judah (vv. 27–28). It would appear that some scene of destruction lay behind such a prophecy. The aftermath of the Babylonian invasion in the south and the Assyrian invasion in the north would leave the land desolated with its population diminished and its flocks and herds greatly reduced. There was a need to repopulate and to replant with *the seed of men* (*'āḏām*, generic) and *the seed of beasts* (*b^ehēmâ*). Yahweh would *sow* (*zāra'*) again in coming days.

28 The verbs of 1:10 are taken up again. The destructive process illustrated by the verbs *uproot* (*nāṯaš*), *tear down* (*nāṯaṣ*), *demolish* (*hāras*), *destroy* (*he'^eḇîḏ*), and *harm* (*hēra'*) will now be changed to a process of reconstruction according to 1:10 when Yahweh will *build* (*bānâ*) and *plant* (*nāṭa'*). The verb *watch over* (*šāqaḏ*) which appears in 1:12 reappears here. Indeed, the whole terminology centers round the themes of judgment and renewal after judgment. Yahweh's watchful eye had been on the prophet's first mission. Now the time had arrived for his second mission, the creation of a new people.

29–30 The second saying takes up the question of personal responsibility. The proverb quoted here occurs also in Ezek. 18:2. It seems that the feeling was widespread that the nation was being punished for the sins of past generations and that Yahweh was unjust (Ezek. 18:25). In Israel and the ancient Near East in general as well as in many primitive cultures a sense of collective responsibility largely prevailed in areas like morality and law (cf. Exod. 20:5; Deut. 5:9; Num. 14:18). Both Jeremiah and after him Ezekiel, who probably depends on Jeremiah, quote the proverb only to reject it. Jeremiah merely affirmed that in that day people would no longer complain about the injustice implied in that proverb. It is clearly absurd in the strict terms of the proverb that children's teeth could be set on edge because their fathers ate sour grapes. Only the man who sinned could be expected to suffer for his sin. This doctrine was adumbrated in Deut. 24:16. That is not to deny that the wrongdoing of one man may have repercussions in his own family for many years to come so that sons suffered for the wrongdoing of their fathers. But the principle of individual responsibility was far more fundamental than a principle of collective responsibility.

The point extended to one's recognition of Yahweh's sovereignty. Originally the covenant was concluded with individuals like Abraham and Moses, but as representatives of the nation. Yet inside the national covenant men were to make their individual choice of commitment to Yahweh. Each new generation had to choose afresh (Deut. 5:3). But there are not wanting individuals throughout Israel's history who made a personal choice often in the face of national or family opposition: Abraham (Gen. 15:6), Moses, Joshua (Josh. 24:15), Elijah (1 K. 19:10), and a whole line of prophets and unnamed individuals (1 K. 19:18). So the principle of individual responsibility was by no means new with Jeremiah and Ezekiel. The doctrine was understood by at least some in Israel. These two prophets spelled it out. Society needed to understand the need for both collective and individual responsibility. In the days of the New Covenant Yahweh's law would be written on the heart of individual men and women.

(xi) The New Covenant (31:31–34)

31 *"Look, days are coming—Yahweh's word—when I will make a new covenant with the house of Israel and the house of Judah:*
32 *not like the covenant which I made with their fathers in the day when I took them by their hand to bring them out of the land of Egypt. But they on their part broke my covenant although I for my part was their Lord—Yahweh's word.*
33 *But this is the covenant which I will make with the house of Israel after those days—Yahweh's word: I will set my law within them and will write it on their hearts, and I will become their God and they, on their part, will become my people.*
34 *And no longer will a man teach his neighbor or his brother and say 'Know Yahweh!' for all of them shall know me from the least of them to the greatest—Yahweh's word; for I will forgive their wrongdoing and will remember their sin no more."*

31 This is the only reference to *a new covenant* in the OT. The short passage which develops from the simple announcement in this verse is one of the most important in the book of Jeremiah. Indeed it represents one of the deepest insights in the whole OT. It was taken up in later centuries by two different groups. The sectarians of Qumran understood themselves to be the men of the New Covenant. But the New Covenant for them was nothing more than the Mosaic Covenant with strong legalistic tendencies. The other group was the Christians, who saw the fulfilment of Jeremiah's words in the emergence of the Christian church, which was comprised of those who confessed Jesus as Lord (Luke 22:20; 1 Cor. 11:15; Heb. 8:8–9:28).

In the text as it has reached us, the new covenant would be made with Israel and Judah, that is, with the whole people of Israel.

The question of whether this section came originally from Jeremiah or whether it was the work of a Deuteronomic author is hotly debated. We accept the view that apart from some editorial reworking the passage goes back to Jeremiah. It may not preserve his *ipsissima verba,* but it would seem strange indeed if Jeremiah's remarkable theological insights did not lead him through to this point, especially in view of the fact that he was on the verge of stating the doctrine on a number of occasions.

32 The background to this announcement is the covenant inaugurated between Yahweh and Israel at Sinai (Exod. 19:1–24:11). Integral to that covenant was the concept of Yahweh as the sovereign Lord of the Covenant who laid upon those who accepted it the stipulations of the covenant. The continued existence of the covenant depended on the continuing recognition of Yahweh as Lord, and continuing obedience to the terms of the covenant (Jer. 11:1–8). Failure to obey these laws would result in judgment and the operation of the curses of the covenant. Obedience brought the covenant blessings.[1]

The history of Israel since the days of Moses was one of persistent failure to live according to the terms of the covenant. They had not merely refused to obey the law or to acknowledge Yahweh's complete and sole sovereignty, but were incapable of such obedience. Here was a crisis for Israel's faith which Jeremiah understood clearly. "Can the Nubian change his skin or the leopard its spots?" Jeremiah asked (13:23). Clearly not. And could Israel do

1. For details of the formal structure of a covenant document see the Introduction, pp. 63–67.

good when she had been taught evil (13:23)? It was a spiritual dilemma. A new covenant was needed because they broke the first one despite the fact that Yahweh had undertaken mighty acts of deliverance on their behalf, seizing them by the hand and leading them from Egypt, and despite the fact that he was their Lord.[2]

33 Yahweh himself proposes to bring about the necessary change in the people's inner nature which will make them capable of obedience. He will set his *law (tôrâ)* within them and write it on their hearts, that is, on their minds and wills. The old covenant was written on stone (Exod. 31:18; 34:28–29; Deut. 4:13; 5:22) or in a book (Exod. 24:7). The heart as a writing material is spoken of in 17:1 in relation to sin. There are parallels of a kind in Deut. 6:6; 11:18; 30:14. But there could be no obedience and no recognition of Yahweh's sovereignty as long as the covenant was externalized. It needed to touch the life deeply and inwardly in mind and will. Then the covenant correlative could be realized: *I will become their God and they, on their part, will become my people.* The formula was well known (7:23; 11:4; 24:7; 30:22; 31:1; 32:38; Ezek. 11:20; 36:28; etc.). Its actualization had escaped Israel.

34 The extent of the transformation *in those days* would be that intermediaries like Moses, priests, prophets, teachers, would no longer be needed to instruct people and say "Know Yahweh," because all of them shall *know (yāḏa')* him, young and old, from the least to the greatest. The verb *know* here probably carries its most profound connotation, the intimate personal knowledge which arises between two persons who are committed wholly to one another in a relationship that touches mind, emotion, and will. In such a relationship the past is forgiven and forgotten. *I will forgive (sālaḥ) their wrongdoing ('āwôn) and will remember (zāḵar) their sin (ḥaṭṭā'ṯ) no more.*

It was a noble picture adumbrated already in Deut. 30:5, 6: "Yahweh your God will circumcise your hearts and the hearts of your descendants so that you will love him with all your heart and soul and you will live." Jeremiah's picture is somewhat more detailed but essentially the same.

2. The verb *bā'altî* means "I was Lord (*ba'al*)"; it also means "I was a husband." The figure of Yahweh as the husband and Israel as the wife was known in prophetic teaching since the time of Hosea (Hos. 1–3) and Jeremiah used the figure in ch. 3. The translation *I was Lord* suits the covenant context better.

(xii) The Inseparable Bond between Yahweh and Israel (31:35–37)

35 *This is what Yahweh has said,*
He who gives the sun as a light by day,
The moon and the stars as a light by night,[1]
Who stirs up the sea so that its billows roar,
Yahweh of Hosts is his name:
36 *"If this fixed order should be upset*[2]
From before me—Yahweh's word—
Then the descendants of Israel might cease
To be a nation for ever in my sight."
37 *This is what Yahweh has said:*
"If the heavens above can be measured
Or earth's foundations beneath can be explored,
Then might I cast off the whole race of Israel[3]
Because of all they have done—Yahweh's word."

Two sayings, semi-proverbial in character, lie behind this brief passage, which declares the impossibility of Israel ever being forsaken again by Yahweh.

35 The verse harks back to Gen. 1:16, where the verb *nāṯan,* "give," is also used in reference to the sun, moon, and stars. The reference to the stirring up of the seas and the roaring of the waves is known elsewhere (cf. Isa. 17:12; 51:15; Ps. 46:3).

36 But it all operates according to Yahweh's *fixed order* or "decrees" (*ḥuqqîm*). If these should ever cease, which they will not, then the *descendants (zera')* of Israel will *cease (šāḇaṯ)* to exist. It is an *argumentum ad absurdum,* and the saying would have given strong confidence to a people so beset by troubles as Israel.

37 The second saying is based on a different figure but amounts to the same thing. No one (in those days) could measure the heaven above or explore earth's foundations. No more could Yahweh *cast off* ("refuse, spurn," *mā'as*) the whole people of Israel. He had done too much in past days for his people for all his work to be wasted.

There is no compelling reason to deny these verses to Jeremiah.

1. Omit the word *ḥuqqōṯ,* "ordinances," with LXX as a dittography from *ḥuqqîm* in v. 36.
2. Lit. "If these statutes should be removed."
3. LXX reads "the descendants of Israel" and omits "all"; it also reads v. 37 before vv. 35–36.

(xiii) The New Jerusalem (31:38–40)

38 *"Look, days are coming*[1]*—Yahweh's word—when Yahweh's city will be rebuilt from the tower of Hanamel to the Corner Gate.*
39 *The measuring line shall go straight out to the hill of Gareb and around to Goath.*
40 *And all the valley (that is, the place of*[2] *the corpses and the greasy ashes),*[3] *and all the cemeteries*[4] *above*[5] *the brook Kidron as far as the corner by the Horse Gate eastward shall be holy to Yahweh. It will never again be torn down or be destroyed for all time to come."*

38 A third pericope is introduced by the phrase *days are coming* (cf. vv. 27, 31). In the Hebrew text there is a strange gap, "Look, days . . ."; but there can be no doubt about the missing word. *Yahweh's city*[6] is Jerusalem devastated by the Babylonians. The extent of the rebuilding is of some interest since the places referred to seem to lie on the north and east sides. The *tower of Hanamel* was at the northeast corner of the city (cf. Zech. 14:10; Neh. 3:1; 12:39). The *Corner Gate* seems to have been on the northwest side of the city (cf. Zech. 14:10; 2 K. 14:13; 2 Chr. 26:9). King Uzziah in the previous century built towers here and elsewhere (2 Chr. 26:9).

39 The image of a measuring line is employed in Ezek. 40–48 and Zech. 2 also in reference to the future restoration of Jerusalem.

In each case the rebuilding of the city was a prominent feature in the hopes for the future of God's people. The two places mentioned here, *the hill of Gareb* and *Goath,* are not known; but since v. 38 is concerned with the northern limits of the city and v. 40 with the south and east it is a fair assumption that Gareb and Goath were on the west side.

1. The words *are coming* are lacking in MT but are supplied from the Versions.
2. *The place of* is supplied for a smooth translation.
3. The first part of this verse is lacking in LXX. The word *dešen* is used in Lev. 1:16; 4:12; 6:8–9; 1 K. 13:3, 5 of the burnt wood of the fire soaked in fat.
4. MT *šᵉrēmôṯ* is unknown, but by the textually supported emendation of *reš* to *daleṯ,* which are easily confused in Hebrew texts, we have *šᵉḏēmôṯ,* which can be understood as "fields of death" or *cemeteries*. See M. R. Lehmann, "A New Interpretation of the Term *šdmwt,*" *VT* 3 (1953), pp. 361–371; J. S. Croatto and J. A. Soggin, "Die Bedeutung von *šdmwt* im AT," *ZAW* 74 (1962), pp. 44–50, esp. p. 49; see further the commentary below.
5. MT has *'aḏ,* "up to, as far as." At least one ms. reads *'al, above,* a reading accepted by J. Bright.
6. MT lit. "The city to Yahweh," which could be "Yahweh's city" or a city rebuilt "in Yahweh's honour" (NEB).

40 This verse raises some difficult textual questions. The intention of the first phrase *all the valley* is not clear,[7] but some reference to the valley of Hinnom would be expected. The place was referred to more than once by Jeremiah (2:23; 7:31; 19:2ff.; cf. 2 K. 23:10) as the scene of heathen cult practices. The next phrase, literally *the corpses (peger) and the greasy ashes (dešen),* would suggest that a reference is being made to Hinnom. The greasy ashes, however, may refer to the fat-soaked ashes from the altar fires and have no reference whatever to pagan cult practices. NEB omits the phrase and accepts only *all the valley.*

The third difficulty is *haššᵉrēmôṯ.* The noun *šdmwt* occurs five or six times in the OT (31:40; Deut. 32:32–33; 2 K. 23:4; Isa. 16:8; Hab. 3:17) and also in Ugaritic.[8] It has been proposed[9] that the expression is to be compared with Ugar. *šd mt,* "field of Death" or "field of Mot" (the Canaanite god of death). This would correspond to Heb. *śᵉḏēh māweṯ,* a reading supported by Symmachus and the Vulgate. According to this proposal the "field of Mot" refers to the site where human victims, sacrificed in the valley of Hinnom, were finally buried.

If we accept the suggestion that Topheth is to be identified with "heap of ashes" (*'ašpōṯ*),[10] then human victims may have been sacrificed in Hinnom, cremated in Topheth, and buried finally in Kidron, which is really a kind of extension of Hinnom. But whatever the origin of the word, it seems to have taken on the more general significance of "fields that required cultivation." In any case, the whole area would be set apart (*holy*) for Yahweh when the day came for rebuilding Jerusalem.

There is some obscurity about the boundary of the east side. The preposition *'aḏ, as far as,* occurs twice in MT. The first of these is read as *'al* in some manuscripts and gives a translation *above the brook Kidron,* which would be acceptable topographically. Otherwise the translation is "as far as the brook Kidron." The other reference point is *the corner by the Horse Gate* (Neh. 3:28). Since both of these were on the east (*mizrāḥâ*) it is possible that the Horse

7. Lacking in LXX.
8. C. Gordon, *Ugaritic Textbook* (1965), p. 488.
9. Lehmann; Croatto and Soggin (see the references in n. 4 above).
10. See W. Robertson Smith, *The Religion of the Semites* (London, 1907), p. 377, where the noun *tōpeṯ* is related to *'ašpōṯ,* "dunghill," a noun whose root is *špt* but which has acquired a prosthetic aleph. The denominative verb *šāpaṯ* means "to set on a pot" and the related noun *'ašpōṯ* denotes a heap of ashes resulting from the fire on which the pot was heated.

Gate lay on the southeast corner of the city and led to the Kidron Valley.

Then, taking up verbs from 1:10, Jeremiah gave the promise that the city would never again be *torn down (nāṯaš)* or *destroyed (hāras).* One ought not too hastily deny such a statement to Jeremiah.

B. THE RESTORATION OF JUDAH AND JERUSALEM: A PROSE COLLECTION (32:1–33:26)

(i) Jeremiah's Purchase of Land at Anathoth (32:1–15)

1 *The word that came to Jeremiah from Yahweh in the tenth year of Zedekiah king of Judah, which was the eighteenth year of Nebuchadrezzar.*

2 *At that time the forces of the king of Babylon were besieging Jerusalem and Jeremiah the prophet was shut up in the court of the guard, in the palace of the king of Judah*

3 *where Zedekiah king of Judah had imprisoned him, saying, "Why have you prophesied: 'This is what Yahweh has said: Believe me, I will deliver this city into the hands of the king of Babylon and he will take it;*

4 *Zedekiah king of Judah will not escape from the hands of the Chaldeans but will certainly be handed over to the king of Babylon; he will speak face to face and look on him with his own eyes;*[1]

5 *and he will take Zedekiah to Babylon and there he will remain*[2] *until I attend to him—Yahweh's word; though you fight against the Chaldeans you will have no success.' "*

6 *Jeremiah said, "The word of Yahweh came to me in this way:*

7 *'Listen! Hanamel the son of Shallum your uncle is coming to you and will say: "Buy my field at Anathoth, for you have a kinsman's right to redeem it." '*

8 *And just as Yahweh said, Hanamel my cousin*[3] *came to me to the court of the guard and said, 'Buy my field at Anathoth in the territory of Benjamin, for*[4] *you have the right of possession and redemption as next of kin. Buy it for yourself!' Then I knew that this was Yahweh's word.*

1. J. Bright, *Jeremiah,* p. 235, renders: "confronted by him face to face, will be made to answer to him personally." The Hebrew idiom, lit. "and his eyes will see his eyes," is not the same as the English "see eye to eye" but rather describes an "eyeball to eyeball" confrontation. The general content of Jeremiah's words had a seditious ring. See the Introduction, pp. 92–94, "The 'Seditious' Utterances of Jeremiah."
2. The rest of the verse is lacking in LXX.
3. Heb. *hinnēh* is difficult to translate. "Behold" (AV, RSV) is archaic. John Bright uses a variety of alternatives such as "Just wait!"; "Believe me!"; "Look"; "Ah, look!"
4. LXX reads here "for yours is the right of purchase and you are the oldest."

9 *So I bought the field at Anathoth from Hanamel my cousin and weighed out the money to him, seventeen shekels of silver.*
10 *I put the deed of purchase in writing, sealed it and had witnesses witness it, and weighed out the money on scales.*
11 *Then I took the deed of purchase, the sealed copy containing the contract and the conditions*[5] *and the unsealed copy,*
12 *and gave the document of purchase*[6] *to Baruch ben Neriah Maḥseiah in the presence of Hanamel my cousin*[7] *and in the presence of all the Jews who were sitting in the court of the guard.*
13 *Then I charged Baruch before them all and said:*
14 *'This is what Yahweh of Hosts the Lord of Israel has said: Take these documents—that is, this deed of purchase, both the sealed one and this unsealed document, and place them in an earthenware jar so that they may last a long time.*
15 *For this is what Yahweh of Hosts, the God of Israel, has said: Houses and fields and vineyards shall again be bought in this land.' "*

With ch. 32 the second half of the "Book of Consolation" commences. It is entirely in prose and centers round the story of Jeremiah's purchase of his cousin's field at Anathoth at a time when the Babylonian armies had momentarily withdrawn from the siege of Jerusalem at the approach of an Egyptian army in the summer of 588 B.C. The whole event casts considerable light on Jeremiah's belief that Judah would be restored in the future. He bought the field at Anathoth as a symbol of Yahweh's promise (v. 15).

The chapter falls into two main parts, the purchase of the field (vv. 1–15) and a lengthy dialog between Jeremiah and Yahweh. The nature of the whole chapter has been the subject of a great deal of debate. After the story in vv. 1–15 Jeremiah began to pray. He first extolled Yahweh's great power and his favor toward his people (vv. 16–23) and then took up the matter of the impending siege and of Yahweh's instruction to him to buy the field when Jerusalem was about to be delivered up to the Chaldeans (vv. 24–25). Yahweh's reply begins at v. 26. Part of it reflects on the rebellion of Judah which led up to the Chaldean attack (vv. 28–35), and part on the glorious future awaiting Yahweh's people (vv. 36–40). The section vv. 17b–23 seems to be composed of very conventional expressions which may be found in a variety of places in the OT. Some writers

5. The words *the contract (miṣwâ) and the conditions (ḥuqqîm)* are lacking in LXX. The reference is presumably to the order transferring the property and the conditions of the sale.
6. MT reads "the deed, the purchase."
7. MT reads "my uncle" instead of "son of my uncle" (so LXX and Syr.; cf. vv. 7–9).

have no hesitation in attributing this section to a Deuteronomic author.[8] There is nothing in it which would have been foreign to Jeremiah, although its style and phraseology raise again the question of the prose in Jeremiah.[9] The segment vv. 28–35, which seems to be an oracle of a threatening nature, interrupts Yahweh's promise for the future and may have come here from another context.

1 The incident is dated and a synchronism with Babylonian and Judean chronology is attempted. Zedekiah's tenth year was 588/7 B.C. It synchronizes with Nebuchadrezzar's eighteenth year if Nebuchadrezzar's reign is counted from his accession year in 605 B.C. (cf. 25:1; 52:12; 2 K. 25:8). If the count follows his first regnal year (604/3) as in 52:29, then 588/7 B.C. was his seventeenth year. It was normal in Judah, where the first accession year was recognized, to count the years of non-Judean rulers in the same way.[10]

2 Verses 2–5 may be seen as an editorial parenthesis explaining how Jeremiah came to be in prison. The story belongs with chs. 37–38, where it is related how at the time when the Chaldeans withdrew from Jerusalem to deal with the approaching Egyptians, Jeremiah was arrested, accused of desertion by some of the royal officials, and placed in confinement.[11] Strictly therefore it was not Zedekiah who had him shut up, although no doubt the royal officials claimed royal sanction for their action. Initially Jeremiah was put into a cistern (*bôr*), from which he was removed at Zedekiah's command (37:17). He was later put into another cistern (38:6) where there was no water but only mud. It was one of the many ignoble features of Judean life.

3–5 Jeremiah's imprisonment is here said to be on account of his "seditious" utterances. Perhaps the charge that he was deserting to the Chaldeans was only subterfuge. Jeremiah had declared in Yahweh's name that Jerusalem would be handed over to the king of Babylon. Zedekiah the king would not escape but would certainly be captured and have a mouth to mouth and eye to eye confrontation with Nebuchadrezzar (cf. 2 K. 25:4–7). He would be taken to Babylon until the day came for Yahweh to attend to him.

8. E. W. Nicholson, *Jeremiah 26–52,* p. 79.
9. See the Introduction, "The Book of Jeremiah: Structure," pp. 27–32.
10. See E. R. Thiele, *The Mysterious Numbers of the Hebrew Kings* (1965), ch. 2, pp. 16–38.
11. J. Bright, *Jeremiah,* pp. 234f., places this story (32:1–15) after chs. 37–38 in his attempt to indicate the chronological order of events.

Precisely in what way Yahweh would *attend to him* is not clear. The verb *pqd* can have an ominous sense. It seems likely that Zedekiah did not receive the same favor as Jehoiachin, who was later released (52:31–34).

6 The verse resumes the introduction of v. 1 after the parenthesis of vv. 2–5. Yahweh's word commences in v. 7.

7 The setting is that Hanamel, Jeremiah's cousin from Anathoth, evidently despairing of the future and seeing only the present, was prepared to sell up and leave his village. Alternately, he had fallen into debt and was in danger of losing the land to a creditor. Perhaps both alternatives obtained. Hanamel had recourse to the ancient law of Lev. 25:25–31, according to which when a man became poor and sold part of his property his next of kin could redeem the property (cf. 31:11; Ruth 4:1–2) in order to keep the patrimony within the family. Hanamel supported his request for Jeremiah to buy his field with the observation "Yours is the right of redemption (*g^e'ullâ*) to buy." We know nothing about Jeremiah's family and the operation of the property and inheritance laws at the time. It is possible that others closer to Hanamel had refused to redeem the property and that Jeremiah as a more distant kinsman had to be called in (Ruth 3:9–13; 4:1–12). In such disturbed times few relatives would exercise their rights in this respect.

8 Hanamel's visit was not unexpected. It was a conviction that Jeremiah had from Yahweh. As so often happens, divine guidance comes in the midst of affairs of life in which men are involved. Perhaps Jeremiah was on his way to Anathoth about this very matter when he was arrested (37:11–14). His cousin succeeded in coming to him before the siege of Jerusalem was resumed. Hanamel's arrival at the court of the guard was the guidance Jeremiah needed. It was Yahweh's word to him.

9 The purchase of the field was carried out according to the legal procedures of the day. In days when there was no coinage, gold or silver was paid by weight. The price of seventeen shekels of silver tells us little since the size of the field is unknown. Since the shekel weighed about two-fifths of an ounce (about 11.5 grams) Jeremiah paid out seven ounces of silver (cf. Gen. 23:16).

10 Jeremiah *put the deed of purchase in writing* (lit. "I wrote in the document," i.e., wrote the deed out, or wrote my name on it), put his seal on it in the presence of witnesses, and paid the money (lit. silver). There is some ambiguity here. It would appear that a deed of purchase was prepared which Jeremiah sealed with his personal seal in the presence of the witnesses. If the practice was that of the Jewish community at Elephantine in Egypt in the late fifth century B.C., the contract was written out on papyrus and was then folded over several times, tied, and sealed. This was the closed official copy. An unsealed copy was attached to it for consultation. A similar practice was followed in Mesopotamia, where the official contract written on clay was enclosed in a clay envelope bearing the same contract and the seal impressions of the witnesses' cylinder seals.[12] The same practice obtained in Palestine in the fourth century B.C. Similar "tied deeds" have been discovered in the Judean desert.[13]

11–12 The deed of purchase *(sēp̱er hammiqnâ),* both the sealed copy and the open copy, were handed to Baruch in the presence of Hanamel and the witnesses for safekeeping according to normal business practice. It is odd that such a procedure should take place in the court of the guard. But the whole of the proceedings, combined with the unusual and even extraordinary character of the business, constituted a very powerful symbolic act.

13–15 The conclusion to this acted prophecy was the charge Jeremiah gave to Baruch. Both the legal documents were to be placed in an earthenware jar so that they might be preserved for a long time. A striking illustration of this procedure has come with the discovery of biblical and nonbiblical scrolls put away for safekeeping in tall jars in caves near the Dead Sea by the Jewish sectarians who lived during the first century B.C. and the first century A.D. at Qumran. The significance of Jeremiah's action was that it was intended to be a sign that the day would come when normal economic activity would be resumed. On that day these documents would be significant. It was a powerful and telling affirmation of hope for the future at the very hour when the Babylonian armies were poised for the final assault.[14]

12. R. de Vaux, "Mélanges," *RB* 45 (1936), esp. pp. 96–99. The seal of "Godliyah who was over the house" provides the first epigraphic evidence of the name of an official mentioned in the Bible; cf. 1 K. 4:6; 16:9; 2 K. 15:5; 19:2; 2 Chr. 28:7; Isa. 36:3.
13. Y. Yadin, "Expedition D—The Cave of Letters," *IEJ* 12 (1962), pp. 227–257, but note pp. 236–38.
14. See the Introduction, "The Message of Jeremiah," pp. 107–117.

(ii) Jeremiah's Prayer (32:16–25)

16 *"Then after I had given the document of purchase to Baruch ben Neriah I prayed to Yahweh:*
17 *'Ah, Yahweh my Lord! Behold, thou hast made the heavens and the earth by thy great might and with thy outstretched arm; nothing is impossible for thee.*
18 *Thou art faithful to thousands, and thou dost pay back the iniquity of the fathers into the bosom of their sons after them. O great and mighty God, whose name is Yahweh of Hosts,*
19 *great in purpose and mighty in deed, whose eyes are open to all the deeds of men to reward each man according to his ways and as his deeds deserve,*[1]
20 *who didst perform signs and wonders in the land of Egypt and even up to today, both in Israel and among all men,*[2] *and hast made a name for thyself that is thine today.*
21 *Thou didst bring thy people Israel out of the land of Egypt with signs and wonders, with a strong hand and with an outstretched arm and with terrible power.*
22 *Thou didst give them this land which thou didst promise with an oath to their forefathers, a land flowing with milk and honey.*
23 *But when they entered and took possession of it, they did not obey thy voice or follow thy law. Nothing that thou didst command them to do did they do. And so thou hast brought all this calamity upon them.*
24 *Look at the siege-ramps! They are coming against the city to take it! The city will be given into the hands of the Chaldeans who are attacking it because of sword, famine, and pestilence. The word thou hast spoken is fulfilled. Surely thou seest it.*[3]
25 *Yet thou, O Lord Yahweh, didst say to me: "Buy the field*[4] *for money and have witnesses to witness it," even though the city is given into the hands of the Chaldeans.' "*

16 The whole transaction was concluded with prayer.

As it stands the prayer has an interesting structure. It begins with a lengthy ascription of praise to Yahweh (vv. 17–23) and concludes by drawing Yahweh's attention to the enemy at the gates of

1. The last phrase is lacking in LXX.
2. M. Dahood has proposed that *ûḇā'āḏām* ("among mankind") might be better translated "and in the steppeland." See "Zacharia 9:1, *'ên 'āḏām*," *CBQ* 25 (1963), pp. 123f. Dahood argues that Hebrew possesses a masc. substantive *'āḏām* in addition to the fem. *'ᵃḏāmâ*, the masc. meaning "steppeland." This meaning makes good sense in Prov. 30:14b; Job. 36:28; Zech. 13:5 and here, and may be the semantic equivalent of *'ên hā'āreṣ* in Exod. 10:5, 15; Num. 22:5, 11.
3. This last sentence is lacking in LXX.
4. From this point LXX reads: "So I wrote the deed and sealed it and got witnesses," which follows MT for v. 10.

Jerusalem and expressing incredulity that Yahweh had asked him to purchase a field when the whole land was about to be overrun by the Chaldeans. It was one more of the puzzling things Yahweh had laid upon Jeremiah (cf. chs. 19–20).

It is no odd thing in biblical prayers that the first part of such prayers is taken up with an ascription of praise to Yahweh or sometimes with confession, before intercession begins.[5] In the final form Jeremiah's prayer no doubt owes something to editorial arrangement. One could imagine that such a segment as vv. 17–23 could have been taken from some other context, even from some liturgical context, in order to give the prayer an appropriate form. But it is not unthinkable that Jeremiah would at times in his own prayers dwell on the greatness of Yahweh before making his request.

17 The evidence of Yahweh's great power in creation makes it possible to say *Nothing is impossible* (lit. "extraordinary") *for thee*. The affirmation is taken up by Yahweh in v. 27.

18–19 Reference is now made to Yahweh's demonstration of his "steadfast loyalty" (*ḥeseḏ*) toward thousands,[6] and of his paying back *(šillam)* the sins of the fathers into the bosom of their children (NEB "requite . . . on the heads"). Yahweh's purposes (*'ēṣâ,* "counsel") are great and his deeds mighty, and no action of man escapes his notice. His judgments are according to a man's deeds.

20–21 The mighty acts of Yahweh in the deliverance of his people from Egypt are reviewed. The terms *signs ('ōṯôṯ)* and *wonders (mōp^eṯîm)* occur often in the OT. Such deeds had continued in Israel over the centuries and among mankind generally, and thereby Yahweh had won renown (lit. *a name, šēm*) which had remained down the years. The mighty acts of the Exodus were deeply inscribed in the literature and religion of Israel. The Pentateuch, the historical books, the prophets, and the writings refer to them again and again; and the feasts, festivals, and songs of the temple constantly recalled them. The phraseology of v. 21 occurs in the Exodus

5. Cf. the prayers of Ezra (Ezra 9:6–15; Neh. 9:6–37) and Solomon (1 K. 8:22–53). Of these Neh. 9:6–37 is somewhat similar in nature to Jeremiah's prayer. In a particular historical context where Nehemiah needed to pray he gave time to praising God.

6. The expression *'āśâ ḥeseḏ,* "to perform *ḥeseḏ,*" goes back to Exod. 20:5–6, but is used many times in the OT. The rest of the verse recalls the expression in the Decalog in Exod. 20:5–6 and Deut. 5:9–10.

narrative and in many parallel passages. The final phrase *with terrible power,* or "with great terror" (*môrā' gāḏôl*), refers to the fear engendered in the hearts of the Egyptians and other peoples as Yahweh pressed ahead irresistibly in the performance of his purposes.

22 The entry of Israel to the land of promise is in view. Again the phraseology is well known elsewhere in the OT—the oath sworn to the fathers, the land flowing with milk and honey.

23 The theme of disobedience so often referred to by Jeremiah is mentioned. Here the terms are strong. "Everything you commanded them to do they did not do"; hence the present *calamity (rā'â).* The mention of *this calamity* leads directly to the thing that provoked the prayer, namely, the Chaldean attack on Jerusalem and Yahweh's strange request.

It should be obvious that while much in the prayer to this point is in the form of stereotyped phrases, several of the themes are well worked by Jeremiah elsewhere and are in no way out of place in one of his prayers.

24 At the time of the prayer the siege had been lifted, but it had been in progress some time before the Chaldean armies were pulled back to attack the advancing Egyptians. Jeremiah gives a picture of the conditions which assisted the attackers, the sword outside the city, starvation and disease inside. The whole sad story was to be repeated within a matter of weeks. Yahweh's word of judgment had been fulfilled.

25 And now the crux of the prayer—it was Yahweh who had instructed the prophet to buy the field in such extraordinary circumstances. We sense the bewilderment of Jeremiah as once again he obeyed the divine command (cf. 20:7–9).

(iii) Yahweh's Reply to Jeremiah (32:26–35)

26 *Then the word of Yahweh came to Jeremiah*[1] *as follows:*
27 *"Look! I am Yahweh the God of all flesh. Is anything impossible for me?*
28 *Therefore this is what Yahweh has said: Believe me, I will deliver this city*[2] *into the hands of the Chaldeans and into the hands of Nebuchadrezzar king of Babylon, who will take it.*

1. LXX reads "to me."
2. LXX reads "This city will surely be given. . . ." Cf. 34:2. LXX also omits *the Chaldeans and into the hands of Nebuchadrezzar* and thus has a shorter reading following v. 3b.

29 *And the Chaldeans who are attacking this city will enter and set fire to the city and burn it down, together with the houses on whose roofs they made offerings to Baal and poured out libation offerings to other gods, to provoke me.*
30 *Ah! from the earliest days the people of Israel and the people of Judah have been doing what is evil in my eyes.*[3] *Indeed the people of Israel have been provoking me by their actions—Yahweh's word.*
31 *For this city has so roused my anger and my wrath, from the day they built it until today, that I would destroy it out of my sight*
32 *because of the wickedness which the people of Israel and the people of Judah have done in order to provoke me, they, their kings, their officials, their priests, their prophets, the men of Judah, and the citizens of Jerusalem.*
33 *They have turned their backs to me and not their faces, though I took great trouble to instruct them:*[4] *but they did not hear or accept instruction.*
34 *They set up loathsome idols in the house which bears my name in order to defile it,*
35 *and built the high places of Baal*[5] *in the valley of Hinnom to surrender their sons and daughters to Molech—something I did not order nor did the performance of such an abomination enter my mind—in order to lead Judah into sin."*

26 A similar literary arrangement to that found in Jeremiah's prayer occurs here. Yahweh's reply appears to contain an insertion which is in the style of Deuteronomic composition. Opinions vary as to the extent of the insertion. One view is that the reply to Jeremiah's prayer is confined to vv. 27–29a and 42–44 while vv. 29b–41 are seen as a free composition inspired by a number of Jeremiah's prophecies.[6] Another view is that Yahweh's answer consists of vv. 27, 36–44, while vv. 28–35 are an editorial insertion.[7] A more extreme view is that the whole dialog vv. 16–44 is so thoroughly Deuteronomic in style, phraseology, and content that it is very improbable that it is based on anything deriving from Jeremiah.[8]

27 The verse replies to v. 17b ("Nothing is impossible for thee") with the assurance *Is anything impossible for me?* (lit. "is

3. The whole of the latter part of v. 30 is lacking in LXX. Both halves of the verse are very similar; but this may well be stylistic: note that both parts of v. 30 and the beginning of v. 31 are introduced by *kî,* "for, because."
4. LXX, Syr., and Vulg. read "I instructed them." MT uses the infinitive absolute, which must be read *'ᵃlammēḏ,* lst person, lit. "I instructed them rising early and instructing."
5. Syr. "in Topheth."
6. G. P. Couturier, "Jeremiah," *JBC*, p. 328.
7. J. Bright, *Jeremiah,* pp. 289–291, 298.
8. E. W. Nicholson, *Jeremiah 26–52*, p. 79.

anything extraordinary away from me?"). Yahweh is the *God of all flesh,* that is, of all the human race (and perhaps also the animals). The promise of the restoration of Judah after its collapse comes in vv. 36–44.

28–29 Jerusalem would be captured and burned by the Chaldeans. In the holocaust the houses where pagan worship was conducted would also be destroyed and thus the provocation of the past centuries would cease.

30 The provocation of Yahweh reached back to the days of Israel's youth *(n^{e}ʿurôṯ).* Jeremiah had once remarked on the faithfulness (*ḥeseḏ*) displayed by Israel in the days of her youth (*n^{e}ʿurîm,* 2:2). But it was short-lived, and through the centuries they had provoked (*hik̲ʿîs*) Yahweh by what they had done.[9]

31–32 Jerusalem itself had become the scene of so many evil practices, which began when it was built and had continued ever since, that Yahweh had resolved to destroy it. The Hebrew idiom cannot be reproduced in English: literally "Indeed this city has been to me upon my wrath and my anger" (cf. 52:3). The whole nation was involved in the evil—kings, officials, priests, prophets, and citizens.

33–35 Yahweh the Lord of the covenant had been ignored and rejected (*they have turned their backs to me and not their faces*), despite Yahweh's persistent attempts to instruct them. Then they gave their allegiance to Baal and Molech and set up *loathsome idols (šiqqûṣ)* in the very precincts of the temple (lit. *the house that bears my name*; note 2 K. 21:4–5; 23:4; Ezek. 8), thus defiling it (*ṭimmēʾ*). Out in the valley of Hinnom (cf. ch. 19) they built *high places (bāmôṯ)* to Baal and sacrificed their children to Molech. The verb *surrender* is literally "to cause to pass," that is, "to pass through the fire," "to devote." The cult of Molech involved child-sacrifice (2:23; 7:30—8:3; 19:5). It was unauthorized and calculated to lead Judah into sin.

(iv) Yahweh's Reply, continued (32:36–44)

36 *"Now therefore this is what Yahweh the God of Israel has said to this city of which you*[1] *say: 'Through sword, starvation, and disease it is delivered up to the king of Babylon.'*

9. There is ambiguity in the phrase "the work of their hands" (*maʿ^{a}śēh y^{e}ḏêhem*), which can mean *actions* or "handiwork," a possible reference to pagan idols.

1. MT has 2nd plur. *ʾattem,* which would suggest that the people of Jerusalem were speaking in these terms. LXX reads singular.

37 *Look! I will gather them from all the countries to which I have driven them in my anger, rage, and great indignation, and I will bring them back to this place and let them dwell there in safety.*
38 *They shall be my people and I will be their God.*
39 *I will give them one heart and one way of life,*[2] *to reverence me at all times, for their own good and the good of their children after them,*
40 *and I will make with them an everlasting covenant not to turn away from them, but to do them good; and I will put in their hearts reverence for me so that they do not turn aside from me.*
41 *And I will rejoice over them and over doing them good, and will faithfully plant them in this land with all my heart and soul.*
42 *For these are the words of Yahweh: Just as I have brought all this great disaster on this people, so I will bring upon them all the prosperity which I now promise them.*
43 *Fields shall be bought again in this land of which you say, 'It is desolate without man or beast; it is given up to the Chaldeans.'*
44 *They will buy fields for money, they will write documents (of purchase) and seal them, and witnesses shall witness (them) in the land of Benjamin, in the neighborhood of Jerusalem and in the towns of Judah, the towns of the hill country, the Shephelah, and the Negeb; for I will restore their fortunes—Yahweh's word."*

36 Yahweh's reply now turns to the promise of the future, which seems to be the answer to Jeremiah's implied question in v. 25. Jeremiah had spoken of the sword, starvation, and disease involved in the city's fall. That was all true. For her rebellion Israel had come under judgment. As a partner to the covenant she was guilty of breach of covenant and therefore liable to the curses of the covenant. But Yahweh was equal to the situation. With him nothing was impossible. There was another option.

37 Yahweh's purpose was to gather the exiles from the lands to which he had driven them, bring them back[3] home, and let them dwell[4] there in safety (cf. Deut. 30:1–5).

38–40 The restoration of the covenant is in view. The covenant correlative is stated, *my people . . . their God*. A change of heart is envisaged (*one*[5] *heart and one way of life*) which will lead

2. MT reads *one heart and one way* (cf. Ezek. 11:19); LXX reads "another way and another heart," Syr. "new heart, etc."; cf. "new heart" and "new spirit" in Ezek. 18:31; 36:26. As between MT and LXX the unvocalized "one" (*'ḥḏ*) and "another" (*'ḥr*) differ little since *d* and *r* are very easily confused in Hebrew texts.
3. Hiphil of *šûḇ*.
4. Hiphil of *yāšaḇ*. The assonance amounts almost to a play on words.
5. See textual note.

them to *reverence* (*yārē'*) Yahweh always for their own *good* (*ṭôḇ*) and the good of their children. Yahweh's intention to make an everlasting covenant with them is stated. The only difference between this promise and that of 31:31–34 is that the covenant is here declared to be *everlasting* (v. 40; cf. Isa. 55:3; Ezek. 16:60; 37:26) and in place of "the knowledge of Yahweh" (31:34) we have "reverence" of Yahweh in their hearts. Yahweh will not *turn away from* (*šûḇ min*) his people but will *do them good* (*hêṭîḇ*) and will *plant* (*nāṭa'*) them in the land. On the other hand Israel will not *turn aside* (*sûr*) from Yahweh.

41 For Yahweh's pleasure in his people on the day of restoration see Deut. 30:9; Isa. 62:5; 65:19; etc.

42–44 In direct reference to Jeremiah's query about buying a field, the affirmation is made that fields will be bought in a land that is now a desolation (*š^e māmâ*), without man or beast. The normal commercial activities will be renewed (v. 44) over the whole range of the land. Restoration is expressed here in geographical terms (cf. 17:26).

(v) *Jerusalem and Judah Restored (33:1–13)*

1 *The word of Yahweh came to Jeremiah a second time as follows, while he was still shut up in the court of the guard:*
2 *"This is what Yahweh has said—he*[1] *who made the earth and fashioned it so as to establish it—Yahweh is his name.*
3 *Call on me and I will answer you, and tell you of great and unsearchable*[2] *things which you do not understand.*[3]
4 *For this is what Yahweh the God of Israel has said concerning the houses of this city and the houses of the kings of Judah which have been torn down,*[4] *(concerning the siege ramps and the sword,*

1. So with LXX, which implies Heb. *'ōśeh 'ereṣ w^e yôṣēr 'ôṯāh.* MT "he who made it, Yahweh who shaped it" (*'ōśāh yhwh yôṣēr 'ôṯāh*) lacks the accusative "land," "earth."
2. MT *b^e ṣurôṯ* elsewhere means "inaccessible" and is used of a city or fortress. Some mss. have *n^e ṣurôṯ,* "hidden, guarded"; cf. Isa. 48:6.
3. Heb. *yāḏa'.*
4. From this point MT is difficult, at the end of v. 4 and the start of v. 5. It reads "to the siege ramps and to the sword, coming to fight the Chaldeans. . . ." LXX reads "ramparts" for "sword," omits "coming," but otherwise follows MT. We may suspect that words have fallen out. The words "and in order to fill them (LXX "it," i.e., the city)" are difficult to relate to the preceding text. The parentheses in our translation suggest uncertainty.

5 *those coming to fight against it, the Chaldeans,) and those who are filling them with the corpses of the men I have slain in my furious rage; on account of all their wicked deeds I have turned away*[5] *my face from this city.*

6 *See! I will bring health*[6] *and healing to her and I will cure them, and I will allow them to see true peace*[7] *as a crowning blessing.*[8]

7 *I will restore the fortunes of Judah and Jerusalem and will build them as they were at first.*

8 *I will cleanse them from all their evil deeds which they have committed against me, and will forgive all their transgressions which they have committed against me and their rebellion against me.*

9 *And Jerusalem*[9] *shall be a source of joy and praise and glory before all the nations of the earth, who shall hear of all the good things that I do for her,*[10] *and they shall fear and tremble at all the bounty and the prosperity which I provide for her.*

10 *This is what Yahweh has said: Once again there shall be heard in this place of which you say, 'It is a waste without man or beast,' that is, in the cities of Judah and in the streets of Jerusalem which are desolate, without a man or a beast,*[11]

11 *sounds of joy and gladness, the voice of the bridegroom and the bride, the voice of those who say, 'Give thanks to Yahweh of Hosts for he is good, for his steadfast love is everlasting,' as they bring a thank offering to Yahweh's house. For I will restore the fortunes of the land and make it as it was at first—Yahweh has spoken.*

12 *This is what Yahweh of Hosts has said: Once again there will be in this place, now laid waste without man or beast, and in all of its towns, pastures for shepherds who rest their flocks.*

13 *In the towns of the mountain areas, in the towns of the Shephelah and the Negeb, in the land of Benjamin, in the neighborhood of Jerusalem and in the towns of Judah, flocks will once again pass under the hands of the one who counts them—Yahweh has spoken."*

Chapter 33 contains two further complexes of sayings, vv. 1–13 and 14–26. The first links with ch. 32 by the note in v. 1 that the words came to Jeremiah while he was shut up in the court of the guard.

5. The verb *histartî* is often taken as the Hiphil of *sāṯar,* "to hide." We propose that it derives from *sûr,* "turn away," and is a verb form with an infixed *t* such as occurs in Ugaritic. See Cyrus Gordon, *Ugaritic Textbook,* in the grammar section, 9.32, p. 81, the so-called Gt form.

6. Lit. "I will cause to come up for her (i.e., Jerusalem) new skin."

7. Lit. "peace and truth," a hendiadys.

8. The word *'^{a}ṯereṯ* occurs only here. A word with a similar sound is *'aṭereṯ,* "crown, diadem," the basis of our reading. Some have emended to *'tdt*> *'^{a}ṯîḏôṯ,* "treasures."

9. MT reads "She shall be to me a name of joy (*lî l^{e}šēm śāśôn*)." LXX omits "to me a name" (*ly lšm*). The text seems to require a reference to Jerusalem and may represent a corruption of *yršlm l. . . .*

10. MT has "them" as a direct object; LXX omits. The context suggests *her* (*'ôṯāh*).

11. MT "without inhabitant" is omitted following LXX; cf. v. 12.

Much of the material resembles sayings in ch. 32 and deals with the general theme of peace and prosperity in the new age. The second block of material (vv. 14–26) is lacking completely in LXX. In the first block of material (vv. 1–13) three introductory phrases (1, 10, 12) suggest three separate units (vv. 1–9, 10–11, 12–13). In the second main section (vv. 14–26), which is lacking in the LXX, there are three brief sayings which stress Yahweh's promise to the line of David. The main emphasis of each is the promise of Yahweh to the line of David. The first (vv. 14–18) is a prose version of the poetic piece 23:5–6. The second (vv. 19–22) and third (vv. 23–26) develop the thought of the poetic piece 31:35–37. All three look beyond the devastation to a new beginning inaugurated by Yahweh. If their present form is due to editorial re-presentation, the basic thought is that of Jeremiah and reflects his belief in the restoration of the nation at Yahweh's hand.

1 The verse is a link attaching the complex of sayings in 33:1–13 to those in the preceding chapter. Yahweh spoke *a second time* in the court of the guard.

2 The titles of "maker" *('ôśeh)* and "fashioner" *(yôṣēr)* trace back to Gen. 1, where three verbs *'āśâ* ("make"), *yāṣar* ("fashion"), and *bārā'* ("create") are used of the creative activity of God. The verse links back to 32:17.

3 Presumably the people of Judah are invited to call upon Yahweh in this critical hour. He will answer and tell them of great things which are inaccessible to men. The context indicates that the inaccessible things concern the future, which was beyond their understanding at that time, but when the day came they would understand (cf. 30:24, etc.).

4–5 These verses are difficult and translations vary. The reference seems to be to the destruction of the houses[12] and palaces in Jerusalem through the agency of the Chaldeans with their siege

12. Something of the nature of the houses of the ordinary citizens of Jerusalem has been brought to light in important excavations on the eastern slope of the city overlooking the brook Kidron. It became clear that there were typical Iron Age houses built down the slope on terraces. Under the assault of the Chaldean army considerable areas of the terraces and the houses which rested on them collapsed and slid down the slope, leaving an unbelievable mass of fallen masonry which had to be cleared before the excavations could reach the structures that had been preserved (cf. Neh. 2:12–14). The size of the typical Jerusalem house of Jeremiah's day and the domestic vessels in common use can now be described in some detail. See K. M. Kenyon, *Digging up Jerusalem* (1974), pp. 82–84 and plates 46–48.

ramps and swords. The outcome was that the city was filled with the corpses of the slain.[13] Yahweh had turned away his face. Little wonder the people were in perplexity and could not understand.

6–8 The great and unsearchable things are now revealed. Yahweh will bring healing, peace, security, restoration, cleansing, and forgiveness. The promise of healing goes back to 30:17, where the same expression[14] occurs. As a crowning blessing true peace would be revealed and the people's fortunes would be restored. An important aspect of the day of restoration was cleansing from guilt and forgiveness for sins committed (cf. Ezek. 36:25–26). There is a collection of terms in these verses which between them cover several aspects of the idea of sin, "iniquity" (*'āwôn,* "straying from the path"), "sin" (*ḥāṭā',* "to miss the mark"), "rebel" *(pāša').* The passage rings the changes very effectively. In such a context the verbs *cleanse (ṭihar)* and *forgive (sālaḥ)* are appropriate.

9 In that day Jerusalem will be a source of joy and praise and honor for Yahweh before the nations whereas once she was a shame and a disgrace. There was universal significance in Israel's standing before Yahweh. All the nations of the earth, hearing of all the good things that Yahweh was doing for his people, would be fearful and tremble in the presence of such bounty and welfare. There is here an affirmation of Yahweh's universal dominion over the nations, which is by implication an affirmation of monotheism.

10–11 The sounds of joy and gladness and the voice of the bridegroom and of the bride would be heard again, in a reversal of Jeremiah's words of judgment in 7:34; 16:9; 25:10. And once again the joyful sounds of worshippers bringing their thank offerings to Yahweh would be heard. The refrain in v. 11 closely resembles refrains in Ps. 100:5; 106:1; 107:1; 136. Verse 10 links back to 32:43.

12–13 The geographical extent of the restoration is reminiscent of 17:26, as is the picture of citizens bringing offerings. Presumably the reference to flocks passing under the hand of one who counted them is a picture of the shepherd counting his flock as they returned to the fold at the close of the day, to see that none was missing. He may even have touched each one as it passed through the entrance.

13. See comment of J. Bright, *Jeremiah,* p. 296 on vv. 4–5.
14. See textual note, and n. 2 on p. 534.

(vi) The Dynasty of David and the Levitical Priests (33:14–26)[1]

14 *"Look! the days are coming—Yahweh's word—when I will fulfil the promise which I made to the house of Israel and the house of Judah.*
15 *In those days and at that time I will make a legitimate shoot*[2] *of David spring forth, who will execute justice and righteousness in the land.*
16 *In those days Judah will be rescued and Jerusalem will dwell in safety; and this is the name*[3] *by which it will be called: Yahweh Ṣiḏqēnû, 'Yahweh is our Righteousness.'*
17 *For this is what Yahweh has said. David will never lack a successor to sit on the throne of the house of Israel,*
18 *nor will the Levitical priests lack a man who will offer burnt offerings, bring grain offerings, and make sacrifices continually before me."*
19 *The word of Yahweh came to Jeremiah as follows:*
20 *"This is what Yahweh has said: If my covenant with the day and my covenant with the night should be broken, so that day and night did not function at their proper time,*
21 *then my covenant with my servant David might also be broken, so that no descendant of his should sit on his throne; so also (my covenant)*[4] *with the Levitical priests who serve me.*
22 *As the heavenly host is innumerable, and as the sand of the sea is immeasurable, so will I multiply the descendants of David my servant and the Levites who serve me."*
23 *The word of Yahweh came to Jeremiah as follows:*
24 *"Have you noticed what these people have been saying: 'The two families which Yahweh chose he has rejected'; and how they hold my people in contempt so that they are no longer a nation in their view?*
25 *This is what Yahweh has said: If my covenant with day and night (were) not (in effect),*[5] *and if I did not establish a fixed order in heaven and earth,*
26 *then I would also reject the descendants of Jacob and of my servant David, and would not take any of David's descendants as rulers over the descendants of Abraham, Isaac, and Jacob. But now I will restore their fortunes and have mercy on them."*

14 A small collection of messianic prophecies is gathered in these verses. There are parallels with other passages in the book as the commentary will show, although these are transformed somewhat.

1. This entire section is lacking in LXX.
2. A few mss., supported by some Greek texts, have *ṣaddîq* instead of *ṣᵉḏāqâ,* and many mss. add "and he shall reign as king and act wisely," as in 23:5. On the translation see the commentary below.
3. Omitted in MT but provided by Theodotion and Vulgate, and some Greek texts.
4. The word is not in MT but is added in translation. MT here reads "the Levites, the priests," reversing the normal order.
5. There is no verb in MT; the parenthetical words are supplied in translation.

We ought not to affirm too readily that they are merely a development of Jeremiah's beliefs by Deuteronomic authors. There are other possibilities.[6] The focus here is on the whole people, *Israel* and *Judah.* Yahweh will fulfil the *promise* (lit. "the good word") which he had made.

15–16 The passage is based on the poetic piece in 23:5–6 but there are slight differences in emphasis. In 33:16 it is Jerusalem that replaces Israel in 23:6; in 33:16 the city of Jerusalem is to be called *Yahweh Ṣiḏqēnû* whereas in 23:6 it is the ideal king. The problem of translating the phrase *ṣemaḥ ṣᵉḏāqâ* arises again. Traditionally this has been translated "Righteous Shoot" or "Righteous Branch" (AV, RSV, NEB), but there are some grounds for translating "legitimate scion"[7] or "legitimate ruler." He will be, in any case, the ideal King who will rule justly and rightly. Judah will be delivered (*tiwwāšaʿ*)[8] and Jerusalem will dwell in safety (cf. 23:6). The name *Yahweh is our Righteousness (Yahweh Ṣiḏqēnû)* is attached to the city. There has been some uncertainty about the text over the centuries. Some Greek texts, Theodotion, and the Vulgate insert *the name* in v. 16. A few manuscripts and the Syriac Peshitta text read "his name"; the Targum, to agree with the feminine Jerusalem, adds "her name." It is clear, however, that all texts attribute the name to Jerusalem. The inference is that Jerusalem would so manifest the qualities of justice and righteousness (in contrast to her past bad record) that she would be worthy of such a name and exemplify the divine order for all the cities and all the people in Israel.

It seems strange that modern translations leave vv. 15 and 16 in prose when they are as clearly poetic as are 23:5–6. One possible arrangement, with stresses in parentheses, is as follows:

15 In those days and at that time (4)
I will cause to spring forth a Righteous Branch for David, (4)
And he will execute justice and right in the land. (4)
16 In those days Judah shall be preserved (4)
And Jerusalem shall dwell in safety; (4)
And this is the name by which she will be called: (4)
Yahweh Ṣiḏqēnû.

6. See the Introduction, pp. 33–50.
7. See commentary on 22:5.
8. The root *yšʿ* appears in the verb "save" *(hôšîaʿ)*, the nouns "savior" *(môšîaʿ)*, "salvation" (*yēšaʿ* and *yᵉšûʿâ*), and the proper name *yᵉhôšûaʿ*.

An alternative arrangement of the colons and the stress would give a scheme 2/2/3; 3/2; 2/2/3; 3/2, which is quite symmetrical.[9] The fact that the segment follows 23:5, 6a and is apparently poetic must point to its originality with Jeremiah (allowing for minor changes, which could have been his also).

17 The "true shoot" or "true branch" seems to be seen in the verse as the progenitor of a continuing dynasty. The promise of Nathan to David in 2 Sam. 7:12–16 (cf. Ps. 89:36–38 [Eng. 35–37]) implied a throne that would be established for ever. Whether the present reference had the same intention is not clear. It may simply be a quotation to show that according to the promise there would always be a successor to David. In Jeremiah's day there was a king in Judah. He was saying that despite judgment the promise held. The fact that the line of Davidic kings was broken posed a problem for later religious leaders and strengthened the messianic idea. It is to be noted that here the king is to sit on *the throne of Israel.* The original Davidic dynasty had precisely that reference. The separation of the northern kingdom following Solomon's death was not merely a political rebellion against the house of David but a rebellion against a divinely ordained order for all Israel (cf. 1 K. 2:4; 8:25; 9:5; 2 Chr. 6:16; 7:18).

18 The Levitical priesthood, as well as the Davidic dynasty, is seen as sharing in the same promise. Successors in Yahweh's service in the temple would never be lacking, and *burnt offerings* (*'ôlâ*), "cereal" or *grain offerings* (*minḥâ*), and *sacrifices* (*zeḇaḥ*) would be offered continually. Jeremiah must have been aware of the possibility of the destruction of the temple and the dispersal of the priests. But he believed that it was only a temporary disaster. In fact this is the only reference in the book where the revival of the priesthood is mentioned. The text here refers to "the priests, the Levites,"[10] an expression which occurs often in Deuteronomy. The particular way of describing the priests here may be another way of referring to "legitimate priests." Jeremiah was as critical of the priests of his day as he was of the prophets (6:13; 19:1; 26:10–11). The need for

9. The discussion of F. M. Cross and D. N. Freedman, "A Royal Song of Thanksgiving: II Samuel 22–Psalm 18," *JBL* 72 (1953), pp. 15–34, provides some valuable insights into Hebrew poetic structures.

10. See R. de Vaux, *Ancient Israel,* pp. 362–64, for a succinct discussion on the nature of the Levitical priests.

a "legitimate" priesthood was as serious as was the need for a "legitimate" ruler.

19–21 Another argument similar to that in 31:36 is offered to prove the reliability and permanence of Yahweh's promises. The regular succession of day and night was established at creation (Gen. 1:5; 8:22). It was part of the nature of things. It is here described as Yahweh's *covenant (bᵉrîṯ)* with day and night which could never be *broken.*[11] If this were broken so that day and night did not function at the proper time, then one could expect Yahweh's covenant with his servant David and with the Levitical priests to fail. But the thought was absurd. David's son would sit on the throne, and the Levitical priests would *serve (šērēṯ)* Yahweh.

22 The promise of an innumerable posterity once given to the patriarchs (Gen. 13:16; 15:5; 22:17; etc.) is now applied to the descendants of David as well as of the priests.

23–26 The horizon is extended again. The promise of v. 22 is extended to include the whole nation. The two families—Israel and Judah—had suffered divine judgment and had been rejected (*mā'as*) even though Yahweh had once chosen (*bāḥar*) them. Israel's election had failed, and they held Yahweh's families (*mišpāḥôṯ*) in contempt also, not regarding them as a nation. There is no subject to the verb *hold in contempt (ni'ēṣ)*. It may refer to the non-Israelite nations about Israel or it may refer to those within Israel who had ceased to believe in Yahweh's election of his people. The argument is the same. Yahweh will no more reject the *descendants (zera')* of Jacob (Israel), or fail to select from David's descendants rulers for the descendants of Abraham, Isaac, and Jacob, than he would break the order of day and night. The future was assured. The fortunes of Israel would be restored and Yahweh would *have mercy (riḥam)* on them.

Many people after the tragedy of 597 B.C. and with the memory of 721 B.C. also before them must have believed that Yahweh had rejected his people. The events of 587 B.C. made their pessimism all the more severe. At what point Jeremiah began to expound the message of these verses is not known, but it would have been pos-

11. The root *prr* is used in the Hiphil *hēpēr* in many passages to describe breaking a covenant (11:10; 14:21; 31:32; 33:20; Gen. 17:14; Lev. 26:15, 44; Deut. 31:16, 20; Judg. 2:1; Isa. 24:5; 33:8; Ezek. 16:59; 17:15–16, 18; 44:7; Zech. 11:10).

sible to speak in such terms after 587 B.C., and no doubt he did. A fuller form of the message may have come in 587 B.C. That is not to say that the material of ch. 33 represents the prophet's *ipsissima verba*. But we ought not dismiss the chapters as being merely a composition of a Deuteronomic author.[12]

12. G. P. Couturier, "Jeremiah," *JBC,* p. 328 regards 33:14–26 as postexilic and makes comparisons with Isa. 56–66, Haggai, and Malachi; so also E. W. Nicholson, *Jeremiah 26–52,* p. 79.

V. INCIDENTS FROM THE DAYS OF JEHOIAKIM AND ZEDEKIAH (34:1–39:18)

(i) A Message to Zedekiah (34:1–7)

1 *The word which came to Jeremiah from Yahweh when Nebuchadrezzar king of Babylon and his entire army, together with*[1] *the kingdoms and peoples of the earth subject to his rule, were attacking Jerusalem and all her towns.*

2 *"This is what Yahweh the God of Israel has said: Go and speak to Zedekiah the king of Judah and say to him: 'This is what Yahweh has said: Believe me, I will give this city into the hand of the king of Babylon and he will burn it down.*[2]

3 *You yourself will not escape from his hand but will certainly be captured and be handed over to him. You will see the king of Babylon face to face and he will speak with you personally; and you will go to Babylon.'*

4 *But give heed to Yahweh's word, O Zedekiah king of Judah; this is what Yahweh has said about you: 'You shall not die by the sword;*[3]

5 *you shall die peacefully. And they will burn fires for you as they burned fires for your ancestors, the former kings who preceded you. They will bewail you, "Ah! lord!" Yes, I myself have made a promise'—Yahweh's word."*

6 *The prophet Jeremiah spoke all these words to Zedekiah king of Judah in Jerusalem,*

7 *while the forces of the king of Babylon were attacking Jerusalem and all the cities of Judah which were left, namely, Lachish and Azekah.*[4] *These were the only fortified cities left in Judah.*

Chapter 34 combines two different sections both of which refer to incidents that took place during the closing days of Judah's exis-

1. The phrase that follows is awkward in Hebrew. LXX omits *the kingdoms and peoples of*; MT may represent a conflate reading.
2. Lit. "he will burn it with fire."
3. This clause is lacking in LXX.
4. LXX reads "against Jerusalem and against all Judah, against Lachish and Azekah."

tence. Jerusalem was under siege by the Babylonian army, which had invaded Judah late in 589 B.C. The strategy of the invaders was to hold the capital under siege and reduce the outlying strongholds one by one during the next year. When only Lachish and Azekah remained (v. 7) it seemed that some hope of relief had at last appeared, as news of the approach of an Egyptian army under Pharaoh Hophra (44:30) reached the capital, probably in the late spring or early summer of 588 B.C. Lachish Letter III[5] mentions a visit to Egypt by an army commander named Coniah ben Elnathan. Its purpose may have been to seek help from the pharaoh.[6] The Babylonian army lifted the siege and went to meet the Egyptians. There was a respite for Jerusalem until the defeat of the Egyptians was achieved. The extent of that respite is not known, but important events took place at this time.

The first part of ch. 34 comprises a word sent to Zedekiah before relief came (vv. 1–7; so also 21:1–10). During the respite the incident described in 34:8–22 took place (as well as incidents described in 37:1–10, 11–21; 38:1–28; 39:15–18; 32:1–15). In literary form ch. 34 is almost entirely in prose, as are the other chapters that deal with these months.

Verses 1–7 of this chapter may in fact be poetry.[7] If we leave aside introductory phrases in vv. 1–2a, 4abα, and the prose conclusion in vv. 6–8, as well as words that are lacking in LXX in vv. 3 and 4bβ, it is possible to arrange the material in these verses in poetic form. The number of stresses is shown in parentheses.

2b "This is what Yahweh has said! (3)
Look! I am handing over this city (4)
Into the hands of the king of Babylon and he will burn it with fire. (4)
3–4 As for yourself, you will not escape from his hand; (4)
You will surely be captured and given into his hand, (4)
And your eyes will see the eyes of the king of Babylon; (4)
And you will go to Babylon where you will die in peace. (4)
5 And the fires like those of your ancestors, the former kings (4)
Which were before you, will burn for you. (4)
And they will bewail you, 'Ah lord!'— (4)
Yahweh's word." (2)

5. *ANET,* p. 322; see comments on v. 7.
6. See J. Bright, *A History of Israel,* p. 329; M. Noth, *The History of Israel,* p. 285.
7. E. Lipiński, "Prose ou poésie en Jer. xxxiv:1–7?" *VT* 24 (1974), p. 112.

Even if this proposed scheme should be defective in some respects, the fact of parallelism is clear and there is sufficient uniformity in the rhythm to suggest an underlying poetic structure. As such there are good grounds for regarding the piece as coming from Jeremiah himself, even though it shows signs of editorial expansion.

1 The picture is of a suzerain with contingents of troops from the vassal states. It was one of the terms of a treaty between a suzerain and a vassal that the vassal supplied troops to assist the overlord in a campaign against his enemies.[8] The attack on Jerusalem and the outlying towns of Judah was simultaneous. Judean forces were driven back into their fortified towns, which were captured one by one while Jerusalem was held under a tight blockade.

2–5 The threat of Jeremiah was made more than once (cf. 21:4–7). Zedekiah was slow to accept the fact, but he would have to face his suzerain as a rebellious vassal (Ezek. 17:11–21). It was to be expected that he would suffer severe punishment. The Hebrew idiom is very vivid, "Your eyes will look at the eyes of the king of Babylon[9] and his mouth will speak with your mouth." Such confrontations are well known in the extant documents of the ancient Near East. The encounter of Zedekiah with Nebuchadrezzar is referred to briefly in 2 K. 25:6, 7. The one reassuring feature was the promise that his life would be spared. As events proved, a harrowing fate awaited Zedekiah (39:4–7; 52:7–11) and in the end he died in Babylon, blind, hardly "in peace" (*bᵉšālôm*). It may be that Jeremiah was speaking conditionally (cf. 18:1–11). The victory of Nebuchadrezzar was certain. If Zedekiah surrendered at once, his own life would be spared and peace secured (cf. 21:8–10). Failure to surrender would ensure a tragic outcome for both the king and the people and the city. Jeremiah continued to urge Zedekiah to surrender to the end (cf. 38:17–18).[10]

The burning of fires and the placing of spices[11] on the coffin of a departed king is attested in 2 Chr. 16:14; 21:19, while the cry of lament *Ah! lord!* is mentioned in 22:18 (see comment).

6–7 Some details of the progress of the Babylonian campaign are given. The operations were being conducted against both Jerusalem and the provincial towns. The initial part of Nebuchadrezzar's campaign was well advanced since only Lachish and Azekah

8. *ANET,* p. 204, Art. 10 in the Treaty between Muršiliš and Duppi Teššub, etc.
9. LXX has simply "his eyes."
10. See Introduction, pp. 92–94, under "The 'Seditious' Utterances of Jeremiah."
11. Heb. *śārap* is translated in RSV "burn spices"; cf. J. Bright, *Jeremiah,* p. 214.

remained of the fortified provincial towns. Lachish is well known as Tell ed-Duweir some 23 miles southwest of Jerusalem, and Azekah is Tell ez-Zakariyah about 11 miles north of Lachish and 18 miles west-southwest of Jerusalem. An interesting glimpse into the contemporary situation in these towns comes from the Lachish Letters, twenty-one in all, written on pieces of broken pottery which were found in a room filled with ashes from the fire that destroyed the city in 587 B.C. They represent urgent messages from military commanders in outposts to the garrison commander at Lachish.[12] Letter IV in particular contains the words, "And let my lord know that we are watching for the signals of Lachish according to all the indications which my lord has given, for we cannot see Azekah." It would seem that Azekah had fallen.[13] If so, this letter was written shortly after Jeremiah spoke the words recorded in this chapter.

(ii) Treachery against Slaves (34:8–22)

8 *The word that came to Jeremiah from Yahweh after King Zedekiah had made a covenant with all the people in Jerusalem*[1] *to issue a proclamation of emancipation,*

9 *to the effect that every man should set free his Hebrew slave, male or female, so that no one in Judah should hold his fellow Jew in slavery.*

10 *And all the nobles and people who had entered into the covenant, to set free each man his male and female slaves so that they no longer served them, gave heed and set them free.*

11 *But later, they changed their minds and took back the male and female slaves whom they had set free, and forced them to become bondmen and bondwomen.*[2]

12 *Then the word of Yahweh came to Jeremiah from Yahweh as follows:*

13 *This is what Yahweh the God of Israel has said: "I made a covenant with your fathers in the day when I brought them out of Egypt from slavery,*[3] *and said,*

14 *'At the end of seven years each of you shall set free your fellow Hebrew who has sold himself to you and has served you for six years: you must set him free from your custody.' But your fathers did not heed me or pay any attention.*

12. See *ANET,* p. 324, for translation of the letters by W. F. Albright.

13. It is possible, of course, that it was obscured from the vision of the outpost. But in either case, the letters come from the first phase of the war sometime after Jan. 588 B.C. See J. Bright, *A History of Israel* (^{2}1972), pp. 308f.

1. LXX reads simply "with the people."

2. LXX is shorter in vv. 10–11: "And all the nobles and all the people who had entered into a covenant, to release every man his male servant and every man his female servant, turned around afterward and forced them to become slaves and slave women."

3. Heb. *mibbêṯ ʿaḇāḏîm,* lit. "from the house of slaves"; cf. the Decalog.

15 *You for your part recently[4] repented[5] and did what was right in my eyes by proclaiming emancipation, each man for his fellow, and you made a covenant before me in the house that bears my name.*
16 *But you turned about[6] and profaned my name, and have taken back every one of you his male and female slaves whom he had set free to go where they wished, and have compelled them once more to be your bondmen and bondwomen."*
17 *And so this is what Yahweh has said: "You have not obeyed me by proclaiming each one of you emancipation for his brother and his fellow. So, believe me, I will proclaim 'emancipation' for you—Yahweh's word—to the sword, disease, and starvation; and I will make you a sight to horrify all the kingdoms of the earth.*
18 *I will hand over the men who transgressed my covenant, who did not fulfil the terms of the covenant which they made in my presence when they cut the calf in two[7] and passed between the pieces,*
19 *that is, the officials of Judah and the officials of Jerusalem,[8] the palace officials, the priests, and all the people of the land who passed between the pieces of the calf.[9]*
20 *And I will give them into the hand of their enemies and into the hands of those who seek their life.[10] Their corpses will be food for the birds of prey and the wild beasts.*
21 *And Zedekiah king of Judah and his nobles I will deliver into the hands of their enemies and into the hands of those who seek their life,[11] and to the army of the king of Babylon which has withdrawn from you.*
22 *But I will give command—Yahweh's word—and I will bring them back to this city; they will attack it and take it and burn it down. As for the cities of Judah I will make them a desolation without inhabitants."*

8–9 The second event in this chapter is dated from v. 22 by the words "I will bring them back to this city," that is, the Babylonians who had withdrawn temporarily. This was in the late spring or early summer of 588 B.C.

4. Lit. "today."
5. The root *šûḇ* is used here also.
6. The root is *šûḇ*.
7. The Hebrew text is unusual. It reads ". . . in my presence, the young bull which they cut in two." Some emendation seems necessary. Some commentators insert *k^e*, "like," before "calf" and read "I will make the men . . . like the calf which they cut . . ." (*kā'ēgel* for *hā'ēgel*). Others simply transpose *the calf* after *they cut*, as here. LXX alters the last phrase in this verse, probably because the ceremony was not understood or was offensive.
8. LXX omits *the officials of Jerusalem*.
9. LXX has only "and the people," omitting the last part of this verse.
10. LXX reads only "I will give them to their enemies."
11. LXX is abbreviated as in v. 20.

During the siege, and before the temporary withdrawal, Zedekiah had entered into a solemn covenant with his nobles (*śār*) and the people in the beleaguered city of Jerusalem to liberate such of their slaves as were fellow Hebrews. It may have been a matter of convenience since slaves had to be fed and could no longer be used for work in the fields. Moreover, the men were needed for the defense of the city. Some owners may have had nobler motives and wished to comply with the law. The manner of making the covenant is given in vv. 18–19 (see comments). The slave-owners agreed to proclaim an emancipation (*d^erôr*).[12] Such proclamations were not unknown in Israel and indeed were enjoined in the law (Exod. 21:2–6; Deut. 15:12–18). But they were also known elsewhere in the ancient Near East.[13]

The intention of the proclamation was that every slave-owner should "send away (*šillaḥ*) free (*ḥop̱šî*),"[14] or release as a free individual, any male slave (*'eḇeḏ*) or female slave (*šip̱ḥâ*) which belonged to a Hebrew. The Hebrew text spells out the details as follows: "every man to send away free his male slave and every man his female slave, Hebrew or Hebrewess, so as not to keep in slavery a Jew, his brother." The term *Hebrew* (*'iḇrî*) is significant. In the OT it was not normally used by the people of Israel of themselves but appeared in periods in their history when they were in a condition of servitude, as in Egypt in pre-Exodus days, and at the time of the Philistine domination.[15] In the present context Israelites were in a state of bondage and may have been known technically by the term *'iḇrî*. The name is similar to that of the Habiru/Hapiru peoples who feature in ancient Near Eastern documents over many centuries and in many lands. These were wandering adventurers or dispossessed peoples who made themselves available for service in many countries. They had no specific ethnic identification.[16] That the people of Israel might be enslaved to their own countrymen was largely

12. MT reads "to proclaim for them (i.e., for themselves; or possibly the king issued a proclamation for them) emancipation."
13. *CAD* I/2 (1968), pp. 115ff. under *andurāru*.
14. The term *ḥop̱šî* is attested in numerous cuneiform texts from ancient Near Eastern contexts. See H. Cazelles, "Hebrew, Ubru et Hapiru," *Syria* 35 (1958), pp. 198–217; R. de Vaux, *Ancient Israel*, p. 88.
15. Valuable details about the use of the term *'iḇrî* in the OT are available in R. de Vaux, "Les patriarches Hébreux et les découvertes modernes," *RB* 55 (1948), pp. 321–347, but especially under "l'origine ethnique," pp. 337–347; J. Bright, *A History of Israel*, pp. 84–86.
16. See W. F. Albright, "Abraham the Hebrew," *BASOR* 163 (Oct. 1961), pp. 36–54.

a matter of economics. Men in debt might accept a status of servitude till their debt was liquidated (see comments on vv. 13–14).

10 The covenant proposed by Zedekiah was accepted by all the nobles and the people, and the slaves were released as free individuals. But it was a short-lived freedom for the slaves. When the siege was momentarily lifted (vv. 21, 22) they reversed their decision and forced their fellow Israelites back into slavery. It was a predictable response from people whom Jeremiah had exposed time and again as covenant-breakers. The whole exercise of proclaiming emancipation was abortive. The crisis led to an apparent repentance and a desire to obey Yahweh's law and to do what was just and right. But there was no depth of conviction, and a reversion to complacency and injustice was evident as soon as the crisis had passed. We might credit Zedekiah with sincerity since he wished to gain Yahweh's favor by returning to the covenant. In that way the nation might enjoy the blessings of the covenant, namely, liberation from her enemies and independence from Babylon.

12–14 Jeremiah's response to such perfidy was immediate and, as usual, set in the context of the covenant of Israel with Yahweh. Yahweh made the covenant[17] with his people when he delivered them from Egypt (Exod. 19:4–6). They too had been released from the "house of slaves" (*bêṯ ʿᵃḇāḏîm*).[18] Therefore a significant part of the covenant stipulations dealt with slaves in Israel. The relevant stipulation was (v. 14): "Every seven years[19] each of you shall set free your fellow Hebrew who has sold himself[20] to you. . . . You shall set him free from your custody." The law is formulated in Exod. 21:2–6 and Deut. 15:12–18. The former law is general and does not refer to female slaves, but Deut. 15:12 is quite specific. Jeremiah had the more specific law in mind. The reason that the release of slaves was stipulated in the seventh year was that it was the last year of the seven-year cycle and was thus the sabbatical

17. The expression "make (lit. "cut") a covenant" (Heb. *kāraṯ bᵉrîṯ*) has some support in nonbiblical sources. See W. F. Albright, "The Hebrew Expression for 'Making a Covenant' in Pre-Israelite Documents," *BASOR* 121 (1951), pp. 21f.; E. Vogt, "Vox *bᵉrîṯ* concrete adhibita illustratur," *Biblica* 36 (1955), pp. 565f.

18. The expression occurs repeatedly in the Pentateuch: Exod. 13:3, 14; 20:2; Deut. 5:6; 6:12; 8:14; 13:5; cf. Josh. 24:17; Judg. 6:8.

19. Lit. *at the end of seven years,* though it was actually at the end of six years as the passage makes clear. LXX emends (so also RSV), but Deut. 15:1, 12 uses "at the end of seven years." See M. David, "The Manumission of Slaves under Zedekiah," *OTS* 5 (1948), pp. 73–79.

20. The Niphal is used in a reflexive sense here.

year, which stood in relation to the previous six years as the seventh day stood to the previous six days in a week. The same principle applied in agriculture, where land was to lie fallow in the seventh year. Farmers were forbidden to till the fields or reap any produce which grew in that year (cf. Exod. 23:10–11; Lev. 25:3–7). On the wider view still Deut. 15:1–4 legislated for the remission of the debts of poor people every seven years. There was thus any amount of direct and indirect legislation for the release of slaves in Jerusalem. Jeremiah made the point that the forefathers of the present generation had paid scant attention to the law. They too were covenant-breakers.

15–16 There seemed to be for one brief period a change in attitude when the people of Jeremiah's own day repented and did what was acceptable to Yahweh (*what was right in his eyes*) and proclaimed emancipation for the slaves. This was all done in the temple (*the house that bears my name*). But it was a sham. The covenant undertaken in the name of Yahweh was soon breached when the people turned about and *profaned* (*ḥillēl*) his name. They were forbidden "to take the name of Yahweh as an empty thing," i.e., in their oath-taking, yet they quickly took back the slaves they had released *to go where they wished* (lit. "to their desire," *lenap̱šām,* cf. Deut. 21:14).

Some commentators[21] have speculated on the possibility that a more general ceremony of covenant renewal may have been involved here, such as that carried out in Josiah's day in 621 B.C. (2 K. 23:1–2) or in Nehemiah's day (Neh. 9:38). Zedekiah and the people in their extremity pledged themselves to serve Yahweh and to obey his laws, among which was the law concerning sabbatical release of slaves, which was remembered because it was the most spectacular evidence of covenant renewal. But the passage itself does not lead to such a conclusion.

17–20 Because of their perfidy in proclaiming a genuine emancipation for their slaves, Yahweh will proclaim an "emancipation" for them. They will be liberated from their disobedience and treachery and delivered over to the sword, disease, and starvation. By breaking the covenant they had called down upon themselves the curses of the covenant symbolically taken upon themselves in the covenant ceremony in the temple. A fascinating account of such a covenant ceremony is now described. As part of the cere-

21. E. W. Nicholson, *Jeremiah 26–52,* p. 96.

mony a young calf (*'ēgel*) was *cut* (*kāraṯ*) in two and the parties to the covenant passed between the two halves laid one over against the other (cf. Gen. 15:10, 17).[22] The meaning of the rite seems to have been that the parties to the covenant thereby called down an imprecation on themselves. The fate of the animal was a picture of the fate that would befall them if they broke the covenant. The rite has its parallel in the covenant ceremonies of the ancient Near East in which a beast was cut in pieces to serve as a symbol of the judgment that would befall the covenant-breaker. In the present instance judgment would be severe. The offenders would become a sight to *horrify* (*z*^{e}*wā'â*) the whole world; they would be handed over to their enemies and their corpses would lie about unburied as food for carrion birds and wild animals (7:33; 16:4; 19:7; Deut. 28:26). All grades of society who had slaves were included—the nobles of Judah and Jerusalem, the palace officials, the priests, and the people of the land.

21–22 Zedekiah the king would not be spared, for even if he initiated the covenant to release slaves he was guilty in many other respects. He would be handed over to the king of Babylon. We learn here specifically that the Babylonian army had broken off the siege (lit. "has gone up from against you"). But they would return because Yahweh had commanded it, and Jerusalem and all the provincial towns of Judah would be devastated and stripped of inhabitants. How complete that destruction was has become evident from archeological investigations in recent years.

> Many towns were destroyed at the beginning of the sixth century B.C. and never again occupied; others were destroyed at that time and partly reoccupied at some later date; still others were destroyed and reoccupied after a long period of abandonment, marked by a sharp change of stratum and by intervening indications of use for non-urban purposes. There is not a single known case where a town of Judah proper was continuously occupied through the exilic period.[23]

22. H. Cazelles, "Connexions et Structure de Gen. xv:1," *RB* 69 (1962), pp. 321–349, esp. p. 345; D. J. Wiseman, "Abban and Alalakh," *JCS* 12/4 (1958), pp. 124–29; M. Noth, "Das Alttestamentliche Bundschliessen im Lichte eines Mari Texts," *Gesammelte Studien,* pp. 142–154; *ARM* II, 37, 1.14f.; J. A. Fitzmyer, "The Aramaic Inscriptions of Sefire I and II," *JAOS* 81 (1961), pp. 181, 201. The Sefiré Treaty provides an eighth-century parallel from Aram. In D. J. Wiseman's publication of the treaty between Abban and Jarimlim (*op. cit.*) we have the phrase "Abban placed himself under oath to Jarimlim and had cut the neck of a sheep saying: Let me so die if I take back that which I gave thee" (ll. 40–42).
23. W. F. Albright, *Archaeology of Palestine* (1960), p. 160.

(iii) Jeremiah and the Rechabites (35:1–19)

1 *The word that came to Jeremiah from Yahweh in the days of Jehoiakim ben Josiah king of Judah:*

2 *"Go to the Rechabite community*[1] *and speak with them, and bring them to Yahweh's house to one of the chambers there and offer them wine to drink."*

3 *So I took Jaazaniah ben Jeremiah ben Habazziniah, together with his brothers and all his sons and the whole family of the Rechabites,*

4 *and I brought them to Yahweh's house, to the chamber of the sons of Hanan ben Yigdaliah, the man of God, who was next to the chamber of the officials, above the chamber of Maaseiah ben Shallum the keeper of the threshold.*

5 *And I placed before the members of the Rechabite community vessels full of wine and cups, and I said to them, "Drink some wine!"*

6 *But they said, "We will not drink wine, because Jonadab ben Rechab our ancestor commanded us, 'You shall not drink wine, neither you nor your sons forever.*

7 *You shall not build houses, you shall not sow seed, you shall not plant vineyards or own one, but you shall live in tents always, so that you may live long on the land where you are resident aliens.'*

8 *And we have obeyed the command of Jehonadab ben Rechab our forefather in everything he commanded, drinking no wine all our lives, we and our wives, our sons and our daughters,*

9 *and building no houses to live in. We have no vineyards, no fields, and no seed,*

10 *but have lived in tents and have heeded and carried out everything which Jonadab our father commanded us.*

11 *But when Nebuchadrezzar king of Babylon invaded our land we said, 'Come, let us go to Jerusalem, out of the way of the armies of the Chaldeans and the Arameans.' So we are living in Jerusalem."*

12 *Then the word of Yahweh came to Jeremiah as follows:*

13 *"This is what Yahweh of Hosts, the God of Israel, has said: Go and say to the men of Judah and the citizens of Jerusalem: Will you not accept correction and listen to my words?—Yahweh's word.*

14 *The commands of Jehonadab ben Rechab which he commanded his sons, never to drink wine, have been carried out; they have not drunk wine to this day, for they have heeded the command of their ancestor. I, on the other hand, have been at great pains to speak to you*[2] *and you did not obey me.*

1. Heb. *bêṯ hārēḵāḇîm,* lit. "the house of the Rechabites."
2. Lit. "rising early and speaking."

15 *I sent to you all my servants the prophets with urgency and persistence*[3] *to say to you, 'Turn now every one from your evil way, reform your life*[4] *and do not follow other gods to worship them. Then you will remain in the land which I gave to your fathers.' But you did not pay attention*[5] *or obey us.*

16 *The descendants of Jehonadab ben Rechab carried out the command of their ancestor which he commanded them, but this people does not obey me.*

17 *And so this is what Yahweh the God of Hosts, the God of Israel, has said: Believe me, I will bring upon Judah and upon all the citizens of Jerusalem all the calamity with which I have threatened them,*[6] *because they did not listen when I spoke to them nor answer when I called to them."*

18 *But to the Rechabite community Jeremiah said, "This is what Yahweh of Hosts, the God of Israel, has said: Because you have obeyed the command of Jehonadab your ancestor and have kept all his instructions and carried out all he told you,*

19[7] *therefore this is what Yahweh of Hosts, the God of Israel, has said: There will never be lacking a descendant*[8] *of Jonadab ben Rechab to stand before me for all time."*

The story is concerned with an event at the very end of Jehoiakim's reign. No precise date is given, but the mention in v. 11 of Chaldean and Aramean forces coming up against the land seems to suit 2 K. 24:2–4, when bands of Chaldeans, Arameans, and other vassal contingents were sent against Jehoiakim, once a vassal of Pharaoh Necho but now, out of convenience, a vassal of Nebuchadrezzar. After three years he rebelled, probably after the Egyptians inflicted heavy casualties on Nebuchadrezzar's army in 601 B.C. and forced his withdrawal. Unable to take decisive action against Judah at once, he sent contingents from the neighboring vassal states on nuisance raids which were enough to make unprotected groups like the tent-dwelling Rechabites seek the protection of the fortified city Jerusalem. The situation may be depicted in 12:7–13.

The theme of Israel's disobedience is again stressed. The contrast between the loyalty and obedience of the Rechabites to their founder and the disloyalty and disobedience of the nation to

3. Lit. "rising early and sending."
4. Lit. "make good your actions."
5. Lit. "You did not turn your ears."
6. LXX omits the rest of the sentence from this point.
7. LXX omits from "therefore" to "God of Israel."
8. Lit. "There shall not be cut off a descendant. . . ."

Yahweh was pointed to by Jeremiah through another of his symbolic acts.[9]

The narrative is in an autobiographical style and unquestionably derives from Jeremiah's own reminiscences. The main narrative (vv. 1–11) is followed by two prose oracles, one addressed to the people (vv. 12–17) and one to the Rechabites (vv. 18–19).

The chapter gives an interesting insight into an unusual reactionary group in the land at the close of the seventh century B.C. Another such group who shared some of the ideas of the Rechabites was the Nazirites (Num. 6; Judg. 13:4–7; 1 Sam. 1:11).

1 For the historical setting see above.

2–3 The "house" of the Rechabites was their "household" or *community;* consistent with their beliefs (see below) they may be presumed to have set up tents within the walls of Jerusalem. This passage provides the most extensive information available on this remarkable group. In 1 Chr. 2:55 there is a brief note which identifies their origin with the Kenites. Nothing is known about them till a certain Jonadab ben Rechab is mentioned in connection with Jehu's bloody extermination of the house of Ahab in 842 B.C. and his subsequent purge of the Baal-worshippers who had flourished under the patronage of Jezebel, Ahab's Tyrian wife (2 K. 10:15–17). From the notice in 1 Chr. 2:55 we have a link with the semi-nomadic Kenite clan which was friendly with Israel's ancestors in the days of the Exodus (Gen. 15:19; Num. 24:21, 22; Judg. 1:16; 4:11, 17; 5:24; 1 Sam. 15:6; 27:10; 30:29).

One of the distinctive features of the Rechabites was their belief in nomadism and opposition to all aspects of settled living; thus they refused to drink wine or to work at the cultivation of grapes (vv. 6, 7). It was a good test of obedience to the precepts of their founder to invite them to drink wine. So Jeremiah invited them to one of the many rooms off the temple courts which were used for the priests' residence and for storage (1 K. 6:5; 1 Chr. 28:12; 2 Chr. 31:11). The text seems to indicate that the whole of the Rechabite community in the city at the time was taken to the temple chamber for the symbolic action.

4 Nothing else is known about Hanan ben Yigdaliah. He is here called a *man of God.* In earlier periods "the man of God" was a title applied to a prophet, not merely the great prophets like Samuel (1 Sam. 10:6–10), Elijah (2 K. 1:9–13, etc.), and Elisha (2 K. 4–

9. See the Introduction, pp. 71–76.

13), but also to various nameless prophets (1 Sam. 2:27; 9:6, 8, 10; 1 K. 12:22; 13:1, 11, 12, 21, 26; 17:24; 20:28; etc.). The term occurs only here in Jeremiah, but it is not clear whether this title denoted a special person distinct from the prophet (*nāḇî'*). If Hanan was a prophet, or one of the cultic functionaries, the reference to *sons* may suggest that Hanan had disciples. He was, in any case, sympathetic to Jeremiah. His *chamber* (*liškâ*) was next to the chamber of the *court officials* (*śār*) and above the chamber of Maaseiah, the *keeper of the threshold (šōmēr hassap̱),* evidently an important priestly office (cf. 52:24; cf. 2 K. 12:9). Maaseiah may have been the father of the priest Zephaniah (21:1; 29:25; 37:3). In 2 K. 25:18 (cf. 52:24) three such priests are mentioned, possibly one for each of the principal entrances to the temple. It is clear that the Rechabites found themselves in the midst of very important officials all of whom, no doubt, knew what was going on. Jeremiah chose a significant setting for his symbolic act that day.

5 Jeremiah did not simply ask the Rechabites whether they would drink wine but set large bowls (*gāḇîa'*)[10] filled with wine before them and cups for drinking, and invited them persuasively, "Have some wine." It was a dramatic setting for Jeremiah's graphic declaration.

6–10 The Rechabites in justification of their refusal explained their origins and their way of life. Jonadab ben Rechab had forbidden them to drink wine, to build houses, to sow seeds, to plant vineyards or to own one. All these were strongly and permanently forbidden by the use of the negative *lō'* (instead of *'al*) before the verb (cf. the Decalog). They were to live for ever in tents in order to live in the land where they were *resident aliens (gārîm).* They were thus reactionaries whose Yahwism had fossilized at the nomadic stage. They had rejected a sedentary culture completely. For them Yahweh was a nomadic deity. Perhaps they had grounds for their outlook. When Israel settled in Canaan and began to live the sedentary life and to practice agriculture they encountered the Canaanite culture and religion; increasingly they were drawn to the fertility-god Baal, to whom the Canaanites turned to bless their crops and flocks, and were tempted to accept the religion of Canaan. The Rechabites identified sedentary life with a particular religion. To be sure some forms of civilization are dangerous to religion, but no religion can really be identified with a particular civilization. For

10. See KB, p. 166; L. Köhler, "Hebräische Etymologien," *JBL* 59 (1940), p. 36.

the Rechabites Yahweh was a nomadic God and Baal was a sedentary one. If some of the prophets recalled the period of wandering in the wilderness as an ideal (Jer. 2:2, 3), their reasons were not cultural.[11] But the Rechabites had obeyed the commands of Jonadab in every particular down the years. For two and a half centuries they had been faithful and obedient. They thus provided Jeremiah with a powerful illustration of obedience.

11 The Rechabites made it clear that although for the present they were in the city, this was not to be seen as a surrender of their principles. Military action had endangered their lives, and for the moment they had to live in Jerusalem.

12–16 Jeremiah could now draw his lesson, addressing the men of Judah and the citizens of Jerusalem with a stern rebuke: *Will you not accept correction (mûsār) and listen to my words?* The example of the Rechabites lay before them. This group had been scrupulous in their obedience to Jonadab their founder, but Israel, with much more reason to obey Yahweh, had never listened to him. Yahweh had taken great pains to send his prophets over long centuries, without avail. The people stood condemned by the Rechabite community. Jeremiah was not expressing approval for the nomadic type of life and religion practiced by the Rechabites. He was merely using their unswerving obedience to the commands of a human founder as an example of what obedience meant. It was obedience in the realm of religion and not at all in the realm of culture that was the issue. Such obedience had been enjoined by Jeremiah on many occasions (7:24–28; 11:1–17; 13:10; 25:4–8; 26:2–6; 29:17–29; etc.).

17 Disobedience in the face of repeated appeals could only result in judgment. By 601/600 B.C., the period of this incident, there was no sign of repentance in Israel and Jeremiah had virtually lost all hope of a present renewal. The *calamity* (*rā'â*) would come.

18–19 By contrast the community of the Rechabites would be assured of descendants down the years. The phrase "stand before Yahweh" is frequently used of men who serve Yahweh in some way but particularly in the priestly service in the temple (7:10; 15:19; Deut. 4:10; 10:8; 1 K. 17:1; 18:15; 2 K. 3:14). What service was envisaged for the Rechabites is not clear, although a later tradition held that the Rechabites became involved in the service of the tem-

11. R. de Vaux, *Ancient Israel*, pp. 13–15.

ple. According to the Mishnah[12] "the children of Jonadab son of Rechab" had a fixed day in the year for bringing wood for the altar of the temple. Other traditions refer to "water-drinking" sacrificers whose descent is traced to Jonadab.[13]

We do not know what happened to the Rechabites in the disaster of 587 B.C. and in the years that followed. A Malchijah ben Rechab was engaged in the repair of the Dung Gate in the days of Nehemiah (Neh. 3:14). He is described as a ruler of the district of Beth-hakkerem ("the house of the vineyard"!). Such details suggest that this man at least had forsaken the Rechabite rule of life. Perhaps force of circumstances compelled many of the Rechabites to abandon or modify their traditional way of life. It is a pattern that many exclusive and traditional groups have followed down the centuries. Such modification of a way of life need not mean abandonment of the basic principle of obedience to the law of God.

(iv) Jeremiah's Scrolls (36:1–32)

(a) The writing of the scroll: Yahweh's word recorded (36:1–8)

1 *In the fourth year of Jehoiakim ben Josiah king of Judah this word came to Jeremiah from Yahweh as follows:*
2 *"Take a scroll and write on it all that I have spoken to you concerning*[1] *Israel*[2] *and Judah and all the nations from the day I spoke to you—that is, from the days of Josiah until this day.*
3 *Perhaps the house of Judah will hear of all the calamity which I propose to do to them, so that every man will turn from his evil way; and then I will forgive their wrongdoing and their sin."*
4 *So Jeremiah called Baruch ben Neriah, and Baruch wrote on the scroll at Jeremiah's dictation all the words of Yahweh which he had spoken to him.*
5 *Then Jeremiah instructed Baruch as follows: "I am barred. I cannot enter the house of Yahweh.*

12. *Talmud, Ta'anîṯ* 4:5.
13. *Midrash Rabbah,* Gen. 98:10; *Sifre, Num.* 28:81; *Talmud, Ta'anîṯ* 4:2; 28a; 68a.

1. The preposition *'al* can also mean "against" (so W. Rudolph, *Jeremia,* p. 228). But this would presume that the scroll contained only oracles of woe, which is by no means certain. The more neutral term is preferable.
2. LXX$^{B,\aleph}$ read "Jerusalem" for MT *Israel,* and this has been adopted by B. Duhm; W. Rudolph, *Jeremia,* p. 228; and others. MT is to be preferred, since the second scroll probably contained much that was not in the first and this narrative represents the final story.

6 *So you must go and read all the word of Yahweh from the scroll which you have written at my dictation, in the hearing of the people there in Yahweh's house on a fast day. And you must also read them in the hearing of all the people of Judah who will be coming from their cities.*

7 *Perhaps their supplication will come before Yahweh and they will turn each one from his evil way; for Yahweh has spoken against this people in great anger and wrath."*

8 *And Baruch ben Neriah did exactly as Jeremiah the prophet had directed, namely, to read the words of Yahweh from the book in the house of Yahweh.*

There is much about ch. 36 that is noteworthy. The fourth year of Jehoiakim was the year 605/4 B.C. (Nisan to Nisan, that is, April to April). In the late spring or early summer of 605 B.C. Nebuchadrezzar had defeated the Egyptian forces at Carchemish on the Euphrates and had begun to move south into Syria, and eventually into Palestine. It must have seemed like a climax to Jeremiah and an appropriate time to read the contents of the scroll described here. There is no indication how long the scroll had been in preparation. It was not read in the temple until the ninth month of Jehoiakim's fifth year (v. 9), that is, December 604 B.C., the very month the Babylonian army attacked and sacked the city of Ashkelon on the Philistine plain.[3] At the time Judah was still nominally a vassal of Egypt, but it seemed clear that Egypt could no longer exercise any control over Judah and a decision had to be made about Judah's own stance in the light of present events. It has been suggested that the fast day (v. 6) was proclaimed at a time of national crisis. The gathering of a large crowd in Jerusalem seemed to provide an opportune occasion for Jeremiah to declare that the day of judgment he had spoken of over the years had arrived and the "foe from the north" was already at Judah's door.

Chapter 36 is also significant both for the insight it gives into the method of preparing such a scroll (vv. 17, 18, 32) and because it gives important information about the beginnings of the process by which Jeremiah's sayings were collected and given a fixed literary form. It also throws important light on some of the nobles who held high positions in the national government. At least some of them were concerned for the safety of Jeremiah and Baruch. They had earlier given their support to Josiah's reform and seem to have received Jeremiah's words sympathetically.

3. See D. J. Wiseman, *Chronicles of Chaldaean Kings,* p. 69.

The whole narrative is marked by a wealth of circumstantial detail suggesting that the story was told by an eyewitness or received from eyewitnesses. The narrative is believed by many to be the work of Baruch. It is not merely biographical, however, but displays a strong theological intent as well. The story concludes with the destruction of the scroll by the king, the nation's head. The rejection of God's word spoken by his prophet Jeremiah could only lead to judgment. The whole nation, the ordinary people, the priests, the prophets, the officials, and now the king had rejected Yahweh's sovereignty and had not heeded his word. The theme is a central one in many of the chapters in the book.

One further important observation should be made. While ch. 36 is, in a sense, an independent unit, it is at the same time the last segment in a "tradition complex" which begins at ch. 26, where Jeremiah is vindicated as a true prophet of Yahweh by Jerusalem's highest court and where the aim of his prophetic ministry is set out, and ends with ch. 36 where the continuing negative response of the people and of the king reaches a climax and the rejection of the nation is confirmed.[4] The history of the mediation of Yahweh's word by the faithful prophet Jeremiah concludes and another complex of chapters dealing with the prophet's sufferings follows in chs. 37–43. The picture of Yahweh's change of mind (*nḥm*) in Judah's favor as a result of the people's repentance is given in 26:3, but in ch. 36 there is no such suggestion. The focus is now on Judah's accumulated guilt and impending doom.

1 The year was somewhere between Nisan (April) 605 B.C. and Nisan 604 B.C. following Nebuchadrezzar's defeat of the Egyptians at Carchemish.[5] The "foe from the north" had by now been identified.

2 The scroll on which Baruch wrote was made of either papyrus or leather. The expression *m^e^gillaṯ sēp̄er* is unusual and occurs only here, and in Ps. 40:8 and Ezek. 2:9. The scroll is normally referred to as a *m^e^gillâ*. The length of such scrolls varied according to the content. There is some disagreement in the texts about the word *Israel* here. LXX has "Jerusalem" and NEB follows this reading. The witness of LXX is not unanimous, however, and MT is to be preferred. Jeremiah's usual expression is "Judah and

4. See M. Kessler, "Form-critical Suggestions on Jeremiah 36," *CBQ* 28 (1966), pp. 389–401.

5. See the Introduction, p. 22.

Jerusalem" and not vice versa. The reference to *the nations* suggests that Jeremiah had a broader perspective than Judah alone.

The contents of this scroll are not known. There have been many attempts to reconstruct the scroll but all are speculation.[6] All we can say is that it contained oracles of judgment proclaimed before 605 B.C. These are to be found for the most part in chs. 1–25 and 46–51, although there were, no doubt, subsequent editorial additions, alterations, rearrangements, etc. The scroll, in any case, cannot have been very long since it was read in a single sitting (vv. 10, 15, 21, 22).

Interesting questions arise about the reason why Jeremiah would be impelled to dictate a scroll. Theologically the answer may be that he was acting under divine instructions (v. 2). Circumstantially it could be argued that since Jeremiah was forbidden to speak this was the only way to communicate with the people (v. 5). Another factor was that the advent of the Babylonian armies seemed likely to destroy the nation, and the normal processes of oral transmission would be likewise destroyed. So long as Jeremiah was alive and so long as there was social continuity so that there were people to hear, all was well. But if Jeremiah's life were in danger, if he had no sons to carry on his word (16:2), if the nation and the whole fabric of society were about to collapse, then a scroll would preserve the message. There was a great precedent in the scroll discovered in the temple in 621 B.C.

3 The immediate concern was with the *house of Judah.* For this reason some commentators have accepted the LXX reading "Jerusalem" in place of *Israel* in v. 2. But even in the passages which refer specifically to Israel there is a warning for Judah (3:6–11). It would seem that up to the very last Jeremiah hoped for repentance. *Perhaps ('ûlay) the house of Judah will hear of all the calamity (rā'â) which I propose to do to them, so that every man will turn from his evil way; and then I will forgive their wrongdoing and their sin*—that is, even the threat of judgment was conditional (cf. 18:5–11). At any time a change in Judah's attitude could avert the divine judgment (cf. 26:3). The motif of repentance comes in the phrase *turn (šûḇ) from his evil way* (cf. v. 7 and 26:3).

4 The process of writing a scroll was for the prophet to dictate to a scribe who would write down his words. There is a slight ambiguity in the phrase *all the words of Yahweh which he had*

6. See the Introduction, pp. 56–59.

spoken to him. Does the text refer to the words which Yahweh had spoken to Jeremiah or to those which Jeremiah had spoken to Baruch? Perhaps the former sense is to be preferred. There is close cooperation between Jeremiah the prophet and Baruch the scribe, with Jeremiah taking the initiative (cf. vv. 2, 8; Exod. 4:16).

5 We are not told why Jeremiah was barred from the temple. The verbal noun *'āṣûr* sometimes means physical arrest (cf. 33:1; 39:15), and there may have been a danger of this once the king had heard the scroll read (cf. vv. 19, 26). But the probable sense here is that Jeremiah had been forbidden to enter the temple precincts after the events of 19:1–20:6 or after the Temple Sermon (7:1–15), or even more generally because he was suspect and would be prevented from speaking if he tried, in the light of his many utterances.

6 Jeremiah had to continue his ministry through his scribe, keeping his oracles in written form for future testimony. Baruch was to read Jeremiah's oracles on a *fast day*. Such fasts were not fixed occasions (v. 9) but were called in times of emergency. We are not told what the present emergency was, but it may have been the arrival of the Babylonian armies on the Philistine plains. The reading was done in December 604 B.C. How long before this Jeremiah gave instructions to Baruch is not stated. But it may have been some time before the next fast day when he could speak to a sizable audience composed of the citizens of Jerusalem and people from the outlying towns who had come into the city.

7–8 On such a fast day people made supplication to Yahweh for deliverance from the present trouble. Jeremiah's hope is expressed in the words, *Perhaps their supplication (t^eḥinnâ) will come before Yahweh and they will turn each one from his evil way,* that is, when Yahweh acts to deliver them, they will repent. Repentance was fundamental if the people were to avert the judgment which Yahweh had threatened in his great anger and wrath.

(b) The reading of the scroll: Yahweh's word heard (36:9–20)

9 *In the ninth month of the fifth year of Jehoiakim ben Josiah king of Judah they summoned all the people of Jerusalem, together with all the people coming from the cities of Judah to Jerusalem,*[1] *to a fast before Yahweh.*

1. LXX reads "all the people of Jerusalem and the house of Judah."

10 *Then Baruch read from the book the words of Jeremiah, in Yahweh's house in the chamber of Gemariah, son of Shaphan the state secretary,*[2] *in the upper court at the entrance of the New Gate of Yahweh's house, in the hearing of all the people.*
11 *When Micaiah, the son of Gemariah ben Shaphan, heard all the words of Yahweh out of the book,*
12 *he went down to the palace to the chamber of the state secretary, and there were*[3] *all the state officials in session, Elishama the secretary, Delaiah ben Shemaiah, Elnathan ben Achbor, Gemariah ben Shaphan, Zedekiah ben Hananiah, and all the other state officials.*
13 *And Micaiah told them everything that he had heard when Baruch read from the book in the hearing of all the people.*
14 *Then all the state officials sent Yehudi ben Nethaniah ben Shemaiah ben Cushi to Baruch with the command: "Take the scroll from which you have read in the hearing of all the people, and bring it with you." Then Baruch ben Neriah took the scroll and came to them.*
15 *And they said to him: "Sit down please and read it in our hearing." So Baruch read in their hearing.*
16 *When they heard everything they were perturbed and said to one another:*[4] *"We will certainly have to report all this to the king."*
17 *They asked Baruch, "Tell us please, how did you write down all these things? Was it at his dictation?"*[5]
18 *Baruch replied, "From his own mouth he*[6] *dictated all these words to me, and I wrote in the book with ink."*
19 *Then the state officials said to Baruch, "Go and hide, you and Jeremiah, so that no one knows where you are!"*
20 *Then they went into the court of the king having deposited the scroll in the chamber of Elishama the state secretary. And they reported everything to the king.*

9 The date when the fast was proclaimed was December 604 B.C., that is, the ninth month, when the weather was cold (v. 22). The

2. The Heb. term *sōpēr* is difficult to translate consistently. It derives from the root *spr* which denotes "to write," and the *sōpēr* is literally "a writer." The term is used in at least two ways in chs. 36, 37, and 38. It refers to one of the king's high officials in 36:10, 12, 20, 21; 37:15, 20, while in 36:26, 32 the reference is to Baruch. We propose to use the terms "state scretary" and "secretary" for the official, and "scribe" for Baruch, in order to distinguish between the two functions, although the word is *sōpēr* in each case.
3. Heb. *hinnēh-šām*.
4. MT reads "They were perturbed to one another and said to Baruch." LXX omits "to Baruch." It may be that "they said to one another" and "they said to Baruch" are variants and MT is a conflation.
5. MT reads "from his mouth"; LXX omits. MT anticipates the answer in v. 18. If we add an *h* lost by haplography and read *hᵃmippîw* we could translate as here, *Was it at his dictation?* (RSV).
6. LXX adds "Jeremiah."

translation of the sentence occasions some difficulty. The plural verb *they summoned* (*qārᵉʾû*) would seem to mean that the authorities summoned the people to a fast, since the people themselves had no such authority. Alternately, we might take the verb in another sense like "observed," with the people as subject.

10 The reading[7] of the scroll by Baruch in the chamber of Gemariah the son of Shaphan the state secretary has an interesting parallel in the story of the finding of the scroll in the temple in Josiah's day (2 K. 22:3–23:3), when Shaphan the father of Gemariah, the state secretary to Josiah, read the scroll (2 K. 22:3). Gemariah himself did not hold this high office (cf. v. 12). The fact that Baruch was able to use Gemariah's room indicates that the latter was well disposed toward Jeremiah.[8] The chamber from which Baruch read to the people was in the upper court (cf. 26:10). He was thus in a position overlooking the people gathered in the courtyards and could be seen and heard by everyone. Nothing is said about the response of the people except for Micaiah, son of Gemariah ben Shaphan.

11–13 The next step in the drama was that Micaiah the son of Gemariah reported the words to the *state officials* (*śārîm*) who were in session in the chamber of the state secretary, Elishama. Among these was Elnathan ben Achbor (v. 12, cf. 26:22). His father had figured in the narrative of the finding of the scroll in Josiah's day (2 K. 22:12). These similarities seem to have been noted deliberately by the writer of ch. 36 (possibly Baruch) to underline the similarity of the process by which the two scrolls were brought to the attention of the people. We are kept in suspense here too as to the response of the royal officials personally.

14–15 The state officials sent Yehudi to bring Baruch in person and have him read the scroll again in their hearing. It was the second reading that day. It is unusual to find the ancestry of an otherwise unknown person given in such detail to the third generation. The apparent courtesy with which the state officials treated Baruch indicates their friendly attitude, although it may be too that Baruch was of noble birth.

7. The verb "read" (*qārāʾ*) occurs seven times in vv. 9–32, in six of which it is used with the phrase "in the ears of" (*bᵉʾoznê*), which underlines the purpose for which the scroll was composed.

8. Another son of Shaphan, Ahikam, is mentioned in 26:24. He also was friendly to Jeremiah.

16–18 The importance of what was heard required that the whole matter should be brought to the king.[9] It was not a case of tale-bearing since these officials were concerned for Jeremiah's life, but the total impact of these oracles which had been delivered over a number of years was terrifying. But they first wanted to be assured that the material had come from the prophet of Yahweh and was not from Baruch himself. They heard the story of how Jeremiah dictated and how Baruch wrote down his words. It was the beginning of a long association between the two. Seventeen years later on the eve of the final fall of Jerusalem Jeremiah entrusted to Baruch the title deed to the field he bought in Anathoth (32:13, 16). Baruch finally went with Jeremiah to Egypt (43:6). During all those years it is reasonable to suppose that Baruch had abundant opportunity for undertaking editorial tasks on Jeremiah's words and activities. The contribution of Baruch to the final shape of the book of Jeremiah should not be underrated. Perhaps he, like others, was the inheritor of a prose style we have come to know as "the Deuteronomic prose style" and his hand should be recognized in prose passages in the book of Jeremiah.

19–20 The concern of these state officials for the safety of Jeremiah and Baruch is clear. Evidently they had little confidence that Jehoiakim would accept the prophet's message and anticipated some violent reaction. The king had already caused the prophet Uriah to be put to death after extraditing him from Egypt (26:20–24). When they went to report to the king they left the scroll in the chamber of Elishama for safety. It would be better to keep the scroll out of the king's hands.

(c) Jehoiakim destroys the scroll: Yahweh's word rejected (36:21–26)

21 *The king sent Yehudi to bring the scroll, and he brought it from the chamber of Elishama the secretary. Then Yehudi read it to the king and to all the officials who were in attendance on the king.*
22 *It was the ninth month.*[1] *The king was sitting in the winter apartment*[2] *and there was a brazier fire*[3] *burning in front of him.*

9. The Hebrew text is emphatic. The finite verb is supported by the infinitive absolute: *haggēḏ naggîḏ,* "we will assuredly tell."

1. Omitted by LXX. In MT it occurs after *winter apartment* and may be a gloss.
2. Heb. *bêṯ haḥōrep.* RSV has "winter house," but a winterized room or rooms in the palace (cf. 2 K. 23:7) may be meant.
3. MT reads *'eṯ,* the sign of the direct object; LXX reads *'ēš, fire.*

23 *And as Yehudi read three or four columns he cut them off with a penknife and cast them into the fire in the brazier, until the entire scroll was consumed in the fire which was in the brazier.*
24 *Yet neither the king nor any of his courtiers who heard all these words showed any fear or rent their clothes.*
25 *Elnathan, Delaiah, and Gemariah begged the king not to burn the scroll, but he would not listen to them.*[4]
26 *Then the king ordered Prince Jerahmeel, Seraiah ben Azriel, and Shelemiah ben Abdul*[5] *to arrest Baruch the scribe and Jeremiah the prophet. But Yahweh had hidden them.*[6]

21–22 It was in vain. The king sent for the scroll as he sat in the winter apartment of his palace. Certain rooms in large houses and palaces were built for the cold season (cf. Amos 3:15). They no doubt had special heating arrangements. Jehoiakim had a brazier fire burning in front of him.

23–25 For the third time now the scroll was read. That it was read three times that day certainly limits the length.[7] The scene that followed, with the king cutting (*qāraʿ*) three or four columns of writing from the scroll as they were read and burning them in the brazier, is in marked contrast to the scene in 2 K. 22:11–20, where Jehoiakim's father Josiah rent his clothes as he heard the Book of the Law read. The contrast is drawn out in v. 24 in the comment *yet neither the king nor his courtiers . . . showed any fear or rent (qāraʿ) their clothes* (cf. 2 K. 22:11). The cynical response of Jehoiakim to the word of Yahweh contrasts with the response of Josiah, who was afraid and called his people to repentance. It may even be that Jehoiakim believed that he would destroy the power of the prophetic word by destroying the recorded words in a kind of execrating act. He may have entertained some hope that his nominal Egyptian overlord might yet come to the aid of his vassal despite Jeremiah's prophecies about the foe from the north.

The *courtiers* (*ʿᵃḇāḏîm*) who were with the king seem to have been other than the state officials (*śārîm*) who called on the king that day. But although Elnathan, Delaiah, and Gemariah begged the king not to burn the scroll, it was completely destroyed.

4. The last phrase is lacking in LXX.
5. The last name is lacking in LXX.
6. LXX omits *Yahweh* and has "they were hidden" or "they had hidden themselves."
7. W. L. Holladay, *Jeremiah: Spokesman Out of Time*, pp. 155f., limits the first scroll to chs. 1–6. See the Introduction, pp. 56–59.

26 Jehoiakim's last scornful act was to send one of the royal princes (*ben hammeleḵ*)[8] and two others to arrest Jeremiah and Baruch. Having destroyed the scroll the king turned to destroy its authors. They were not to be found: *Yahweh had hidden them.*[9] What their fate might otherwise have been may be judged from 26:20–23. It is uncertain how long Jeremiah and Baruch remained in hiding; but Jehoiakim must have dropped the whole matter, for Jeremiah was able to move about freely later as the story about the Rechabites indicates (ch. 35).

The narrative in these verses seems to have been composed as a conscious parallel to 2 K. 22. In each case a scroll is brought before the king. First the scroll comes into the hands of a state official (2 K. 22:9–10; Jer. 36:10–11). Both narratives record the reaction of the king (2 K. 22:11–13; Jer. 36:23–26). Both narratives refer to an oracle that follows the king's response (2 K. 22:15–20; Jer. 36:28–31). In 2 K. 22:11 Josiah "rent his clothes"; in Jer. 36:24 Jehoiakim did not rend his clothes but rent the scroll.

(d) The scroll is rewritten: Yahweh's word preserved (36:27–32)

27 *After the king had burned the scroll with all that Baruch had written at Jeremiah's dictation, the word of Yahweh came to Jeremiah as follows:*

28 *"Now take another scroll and write on it all the words that were on the first scroll*[1] *which Jehoiakim king of Judah burned.*

29 *And regarding Jehoiakim king of Judah you shall say:*[2] *This is what Yahweh has said: 'You personally burned this scroll and said: "Why have you written here that the king of Babylon will surely come and will destroy this land and exterminate from it both man and beast?"*

30 *Therefore this is what Yahweh has said concerning Jehoiakim king of Judah: No descendant of his shall sit on David's throne! His dead body will be cast out to the scorching heat by day and to the frost by night.*

31 *I will punish him and his offspring and his servants for their iniquity, and I will bring upon them and upon all the citizens of Jerusalem and the men of Judah all the evil with which I have threatened them, but which they did not heed.' "*

8. The precise meaning of *ben hammeleḵ* is uncertain. Perhaps Jerahmeel was the king's "deputy" (NEB).
9. See textual note.

1. MT reads "all the former words which were on the former scroll"; LXX omits both adjectives.
2. See D. J. Wiseman, *Chronicles of Chaldaean Kings*, p. 69.

32 *So Jeremiah took another scroll and gave it to Baruch ben Neriah the scribe, who wrote in it at Jeremiah's dictation all the words of the book that Jehoiakim king of Judah had burned in the fire. And in addition many similar words were added to them.*

27–28 The burning of the scroll was not the end of Yahweh's word, however much Jehoiakim may have believed that he could annul the power of the Word by burning the words. Jehoiakim had merely registered his rejection of Yahweh's word; but the oracles of Jeremiah could be rewritten as a sign and witness to Yahweh's judgment against the nation. Yahweh's word would stand and be fulfilled whether written down or not. Baruch wrote a new edition of the scroll as before, at Jeremiah's dictation (v. 32).

29–31 The rewriting of the scroll was the occasion for a new oracle of doom against the king (cf. 2 K. 22:15–20). The king had *personally*[3] burned the scroll and questioned Jeremiah's right to speak as he had done. Therefore no descendant of his would sit on David's throne. This prophecy was only partially fulfilled, for Jehoiachin his son became king for a brief period of three months. He was deposed and later died in exile (2 K. 24:8, 9; 25:27–30). Jehoiakim would die an ignominious death (cf. 22:18–19) and would lie unburied, exposed to the scorching sun by day and the frost by night (v. 30). He who sat comfortably by the fire and burned Yahweh's word by throwing it (*hišlîḵ*) into the fire would himself be *cast out* (*hušlaḵ*) to the heat by day and the frost by night. A similar wordplay on the root *šlḥ* occurs in 28:15–16.

32 The second scroll was not merely a copy of the first but contained additional material described as *many similar words*. We have no means of knowing what this additional material comprised, but it was necessarily only material which referred to the period up to December 604 B.C., the date of the present incident, or perhaps shortly afterward.[4] Jeremiah was to utter many more oracles in the years 604–586 B.C.

(v) Zedekiah Consults Jeremiah: First Account (37:1–10)

1 *King Zedekiah son of Josiah, whom Nebuchadrezzar king of Babylon had set on the throne in the land of Judah, reigned in place of Coniah son of Jehoiakim.*

3. MT is emphatic, using the pronoun as well as the verb.

4. W. L. Holladay, *Jeremiah: Spokesman Out of Time,* p. 156, proposes that the additional material is to be found in chs. 8:14–9:9; 9:17–22; 10:17–25. See also *The Architecture of Jeremiah 1–20* (1976), esp. ch. 10, pp. 169–174. See the Introduction, "Jeremiah's First and Second Scrolls," pp. 56–59.

2 *Neither he nor his courtiers nor the people of the land listened to the words of Yahweh which he spoke through Jeremiah the prophet.*
3 *And King Zedekiah sent Jehucal ben Shelemiah and Zephaniah ben Maaseiah, the priest, to Jeremiah the prophet to say, "Pray now to Yahweh our God for us."*
4 *Jeremiah was free to move about among the people, for they had not yet put him in prison.*
5 *Meanwhile the army of Pharaoh had marched from Egypt, and the Chaldeans who were besieging Jerusalem*[1] *heard the news and withdrew from Jerusalem.*
6 *Then the word of Yahweh came to Jeremiah the prophet as follows:*
7 *"This is what Yahweh the God of Israel has said: This is what you will say to the king of Judah who has sent you to me to consult me: 'Listen! the army of Pharaoh which is advancing to your aid will return to Egypt, its own land,*
8 *and the Chaldeans will return to attack this city; they will capture it and set it on fire.*
9 *This is what Yahweh has said: Do not deceive yourselves and say, "The Chaldeans will surely go away*[2] *from us," for they will not go.*
10 *Even if you defeated the entire Chaldean army which is attacking you and there remained of it only wounded men, each one in his tent*[3] *would rise up and set this city on fire.' "*

It is clear from the text that the incident recorded here took place during the brief respite when the Babylonian siege of Jerusalem was lifted because of the approach of an Egyptian army. This was probably in the late spring or early summer of 588 B.C. During that interval the incident of the shameful and treacherous treatment of the slaves took place (34:8–22) as well as Zedekiah's two consultations with Jeremiah, the first (37:1–10) prior to Jeremiah's arrest conducted through messengers, and the second after his arrest. The further interview recorded in 38:1–28 is regarded by some commentators as a variant account of 37:1–10 (see discussion in the next chapter).

The commentator B. Duhm wrote some striking words about these interviews between Jeremiah and King Zedekiah:[4]

> The scene is just as moving as it is historically interesting; on the one hand is the prophet, disfigured by mistreatment, the prison atmosphere and privations, but firm in his predictions, without any

1. The words *who were besieging Jerusalem* are lacking in LXX.
2. The emphatic infinitive is used, *hālōḵ yēlᵉḵû,* so great was the people's foolish confidence.
3. LXX reads "in his place (*tópos*)."
4. B. Duhm, *Das Buch Jeremia* (1901), p. 301. The text we quote follows the translation of J. P. Hyatt, "Jeremiah," *IB* V (1956), pp. 73f.

> invective against his persecutors, without defiance, exaggeration or fanaticism, simple, physically mild and humble; on the other hand is the king who, obviously against his own will, had been led by his officials into the war venture, anxiously watching the lips of the martyr for a favorable word for himself, whispering secretly with the man whom his officials imprisoned for treason, weak, a poor creature but not evil, a king but much more bound than the prisoner who stands before him.

1–2 These verses provide a superscription to chs. 37–45 and serve as a transition from ch. 36, which deals with Jehoiakim's reign. It would seem that chs. 37–45 must have comprised a distinct unit which was taken into the book as a whole. The editor seems to have condensed the material in 2 K. 24:17–20 on Zedekiah. The point is made that after Zedekiah's appointment as king by Nebuchadrezzar (cf. 2 K. 24:17), he too, like his predecessors, ignored the word of Yahweh proclaimed by Jeremiah. The judgment may seem harsh since Zedekiah consulted Jeremiah at least twice and showed him some kindness. But he appears as a weak individual who was afraid of his officials (38:24–27) and *courtiers* (*ʿᵃḇāḏîm*), who themselves rejected Jeremiah's preaching. The phrase *the people of the land* seems to refer here to the people generally.[5]

3 Zedekiah's first approach to Jeremiah in his time of anxiety was indirect. He seems to have lacked the courage for a more open approach. Zephaniah was a member of an earlier delegation to Jeremiah at the start of the siege (21:1–10) and was the one to whom a letter came from Shemaiah the prophet in exile demanding that Jeremiah should be imprisoned (29:24–32). He is not listed among those who tried to have Jeremiah executed (38:1). His companion Jehucal and Pashhur his companion in 21:1, on the other hand, were among those who demanded Jeremiah's execution. The request was brief: *Pray now to Yahweh our God for us.* Perhaps Zedekiah hoped almost beyond all hope that Yahweh would repeat the miracle of 701 B.C. when he removed the Assyrian armies from Jerusalem in the days of Hezekiah (2 K. 19:32–37). Jeremiah had already foretold the fate of Zedekiah and the city at the commencement of the siege (34:1–7).

4 At the time Jeremiah *was free to move about among the people,* lit. "going in and going out" among them. The expression

5. The term has been widely discussed. See E. W. Nicholson, "The Meaning of the Expression *'am hā'āreṣ* in the OT," *JSS* 10 (1965), pp. 59–66.

is used in this sense in a number of places in the OT.[6] The verse leads up to vv. 13–14, where we are told of Jeremiah's arrest. After that he remained in prison till the downfall of the city in July 587 B.C.

5 In the summer of 588 B.C. the Egyptians moved into the Palestine area, possibly in response to an appeal from Zedekiah (Lachish Letter II refers to a visit to Egypt by the commander of Judah's army), but perhaps also in an attempt to stave off an invasion of Egypt. In any case the Babylonians were forced to lift their siege of Jerusalem to deal with the Egyptians.

6–10 The answer to Zedekiah was to the effect that the Egyptian army which had come to bring help would return to Egypt and the Chaldeans would return and destroy the city. Even if Nebuchadrezzar had only wounded soldiers fighting for him, he would win. Such rhetorical exaggeration served to portray in stark fashion the inevitability of Jerusalem's fall and destruction. The prophet's answer was as clear and stern as ever. His assurance about the outcome was greater than ever.

Such words, coming at a time when the morale of the people had been boosted by the Babylonian withdrawal, could only arouse bitter and violent antagonism against him. The account of his arrest and imprisonment which follows (vv. 11–21) is not surprising.

The expression *do not deceive yourselves* in the translation renders the idiomatic Hebrew expression "do not cause your souls to rise (lift up)."

(vi) Jeremiah's Arrest and Imprisonment (37:11–21)

11 *When the Chaldean army had withdrawn from Jerusalem at the approach of Pharaoh's army,*
12 *Jeremiah set out from Jerusalem to go to the land of Benjamin, to obtain his share from there among the people.*
13 *When he arrived at the Benjamin Gate, the officer of the guard there, whose name was Irijah ben Shelemiah ben Hananiah, seized Jeremiah the prophet and said, "You are deserting[1] to the Chaldeans!"*
14 *"It is a lie!" said Jeremiah; "I am not deserting to the Chaldeans." Irijah would not listen to Jeremiah, but arrested him and brought him to the state officials.*

6. It is used of normal moving about in Deut. 28:6; 2 K. 19:27; Ps. 14:8; of military movement in Deut. 31:2; Josh. 14:11; 1 Sam. 29:6; and of cultic ceremonies in Exod. 28:35; Lev. 16:17; Ezek. 46:10.

1. Lit. "falling" (Heb. *nōpēl*).

15 *The state officials were angry with Jeremiah. They flogged him and threw him into prison in the house of Jonathan the state secretary, which they had converted into a prison.*
16 *And Jeremiah went into the vaults in the cistern house and there he remained for some time.*
17 *King Zedekiah sent and took him.*[2] *The king questioned him secretly in the palace and said, "Is there any word from Yahweh?" Jeremiah replied, "There is!" and added, "You will be handed over to the king of Babylon."*
18 *Jeremiah said to King Zedekiah, "What sin have I committed against you or your courtiers or this people that you have thrown me into prison?*
19 *Where are your prophets who prophesied to you and said that the king of Babylon would not attack you or this country?*
20 *And now please listen to me, my lord the king! Let my entreaty come before you. Do not send me back to the house of Jonathan the secretary lest I die there."*
21 *Then King Zedekiah gave orders and they committed Jeremiah to the court of the guard house, giving him a loaf of bread daily from the Street of the Bakers until the bread in the city was all gone. So Jeremiah remained in the court of the guard house.*

11–12 The arrest of Jeremiah took place at some time during the interruption of the siege when there was a certain freedom for people to move about outside the city. Just how Jeremiah's projected visit to Anathoth is to be related to the purchase of the field of his cousin Hanamel (ch. 32) is not entirely clear. The transaction was arranged after Jeremiah had been imprisoned (32:1–2). The interpretation depends in part on the way we are to understand "the king of Babylon's army was then besieging Jerusalem" in 31:2. If this is a very general expression intended to mean that Jerusalem had been under siege and was still under threat, we can suppose that the cousin managed to get into Jerusalem before the siege was resumed. But Jeremiah was already in prison at that stage, having attempted to visit Anathoth himself (vv. 11, 12) and having been arrested as he set out. He may, of course, have known of the possibility of inheriting Hanamel's property and been on his way to Anathoth to arrange this when he was arrested. The Hebrew expression is obscure and its precise force is not clear—"to divide from there among the people" (*laḥ^{a}liq miššām b^{e}ṯôḵ hā'ām*).[3] It may be that the whole

2. The Hebrew expression probably means simply "Zedekiah had Jeremiah brought to him."

3. For *ḥālaq* as "obtain one's share" cf. 1 Sam. 30:24. Greek texts vary but in general read "to make a purchase," "to do business" (*agorásai*). See *BHS ad loc.*

question of the patrimony of Jeremiah's family was under discussion because of the Babylonian invasion and a family meeting had been convened to decide about the division. Jeremiah set out to attend this meeting but was arrested. Subsequently Hanamel decided to sell his share to Jeremiah. In that case Jeremiah had some knowledge of what was going on in the family before Hanamel called (32:6–8). We know too little about Jeremiah's family and about the operation of the laws concerning property and inheritance at the time to say precisely how Jeremiah was related to the issues.

13–16 The Benjamin Gate opened to the north and led to the Benjaminite territory where Anathoth was situated. The officer of the guard (*ba'al p^eqiḏuṯ*) arrested him thinking him to be a deserter. He had some grounds for thinking this, since Jeremiah had urged others to desert (21:9; 38:2) and in fact a number of Judeans did defect to the enemy (38:19; 52:15). Further, Jeremiah's message of certain victory for the Babylonians was well known. Hence Irijah's accusation was understandable if mistaken. Jeremiah was arrested and brought before the *state officials* (*śārîm*), who flogged him and confined him to an uncomfortable prison. It was a temporary prison in the house of Jonathan the state secretary. Why his house should have been used as a prison is not stated. Possibly other prisons were full, or perhaps the secretary's house was regarded as particularly secure. It would appear from the difficult Hebrew text that Jeremiah's place of confinement was an underground dungeon. It was in *the vaults in the cistern house*. In 38:6, 13 he is cast into a cistern (*bôr*). Here it is into the cistern house (*bêṯ habbôr*). It was, in any case, an unhealthy place where he would certainly have died before long (v. 20). Even so, he was there for some time. It was to this place that Zedekiah sent for him.

17 At the palace, secretly, Zedekiah asked the question he had asked before: *Is there any word from Yahweh?* Something of Zedekiah's character is revealed. The consultation was in secret because of the king's fear of his officials. The message was the same: the fate of the king was sealed. Jeremiah even in duress could not compromise the truth.

18–19 Jeremiah's counter-request concerned his own welfare. Before he made it he asked simply in what way he had sinned against the king and his *courtiers* (*'^aḇāḏîm*) and the people to be thrown into prison (*bêṯ hakkele'*),[4] particularly since his prophecies

4. This term is different from that in v. 15, *bêṯ hā'ēsûr.*

had come true whereas the prophets who had said that the king of Babylon would not attack the land had proved false. But he was in prison and they, despite their false words, were presumably free.

20 Jeremiah's plea was an earnest one. "Let me earnestly entreat you not to send me back to the house of Jonathan the secretary lest I die there."[5] It must have been a foul and dangerous place to be incarcerated.

21 The secret interview ended in a kindly gesture from the king. Jeremiah was taken from the cistern and committed to the court of the guard, where conditions were better. This was situated next to the palace (32:2; Neh. 3:25) and seems to have been used for men who did not require strict confinement. It was here that Jeremiah was able to conduct the business concerned with the purchase of his cousin's land in Anathoth (34:1–15). Moreover, there was some guarantee of food, at least as long as food lasted in a besieged city.[6] But as the siege was pressed, the predicted famine became a reality.

(vii) Zedekiah Consults Jeremiah: Second Account (38:1–28a)

(a) Arrest and imprisonment (38:1–6)

1 *Now Shephatiah ben Mattan, Gedaliah ben Pashhur, Jucal ben Shelemiah, and Pashhur ben Malchiah*[1] *heard the things that Jeremiah was saying to all the people.*

2 *"This is what Yahweh has said: Whoever remains in this city will die by the sword, by starvation, and by disease, but whoever goes out to the Chaldeans will live;*[2] *he will at least escape with his life and will survive.*[3]

3 *This is what Yahweh has said: This city will certainly be handed over to the army of the king of Babylon and he will capture it."*

4 *Then the officials said to the king, "This man must*[4] *be put to death because of the way he is weakening the morale*[5] *of the soldiers who are left in this city as well as of all the people by speaking such things to them. This fellow does not desire the welfare of this people but their ruin."*

5. J. Bright, *Jeremiah,* p. 225.

6. The reference to the *Street of the Bakers* gives some indication of the commercial organization of ancient Jerusalem. People engaged in the same trade were to be found in the same street, an arrangement that still obtains in Middle Eastern cities.

1. This last name is lacking in LXX, probably through error.

2. MT *yᵉḥāyâ* is here revocalized as *yiḥyeh,* "he will live."

3. MT lit. "his life will be his for booty"; see 21:9.

4. The emphatic particle *nā'* is used.

5. The words of Jeremiah seemed seditious. See the Introduction, pp. 92–94, under "The 'Seditious' Utterances of Jeremiah."

5 *And King Zedekiah said, "Very well, he is in your hands; the king can do nothing to oppose you."*[6]
6 *So they took Jeremiah*[7] *and threw him into the cistern of Prince Malchiah which was in the court of the guard, letting him down with ropes. There was no water in the cistern, only mud, and Jeremiah sank in the mud.*

Chapter 38 poses one major problem, namely, the relationship between the events recorded here and those narrated in 37:11–21. The two accounts have a great deal in common. In both narratives the prophet is arrested, referred to the state officials (*śārîm,* 37:14, 15; 38:1–4) on a charge of treason, and imprisoned in an underground cistern (*bôr*) where conditions were appalling (37:16; 38:6, 7, 9, 13). Both narratives tell of a subsequent release and private consultation with Zedekiah, who sent for the prophet (37:17; 38:14). There are exact parallels in the language used. The content of the conversation in each case is substantially the same. It deals with the inevitable destruction of Jerusalem. Subsequently, Jeremiah was not sent back to the cistern but was kept in the court of the guard (37:21; 38:28). Both accounts mention incarceration in the house of Jonathan the secretary (37:15, 20; 38:26).

There are points of difference too. Chapter 37 tells of Jeremiah's arrest but not ch. 38. The cistern house is located in the home of Jonathan the secretary in 37:15–16, while in 38:6 it is called the cistern of Prince Malchiah and is located in the court of the guard. This difference may not be significant because we do not know where the secretary's house stood in relation to the court of the guard, which was near the palace (32:2). It would be reasonable to think of a state secretary being close by. Chapter 38 tells of Jeremiah's rescue from the cistern in some detail and refers to the part played by Ebed-melech (vv. 7–13), but ch. 37 does not. The king's secret interview with Jeremiah is reported in greater detail in 38:14–26 than in 37:11–27 although the general tone is the same. In 37:21 we are told of a daily ration as long as the food supply lasted, while in 38:28a we learn only that he was kept in the court of the guard till the city fell. But the two statements are virtually the same since we know from 52:6ff. that the food supply ran out on the eve of the fall of the city.

6. MT reads "for the king is not one who is able to do anything with you"; LXX "for the king was not able against them."
7. LXX omits *they took Jeremiah.*

It is tempting to regard 37:1–21 and 38 as simply different accounts of the same course of events. This is not unknown elsewhere in Jeremiah.[8] Thus the account of the Temple Sermon is given in chs. 7 and 26. There seem to be two accounts of Jeremiah's release by the Babylonians, one represented by 38:28b; 39:3, 14 and the other by 39:11–12; 40:1–6.

1 Two of the persons mentioned here are referred to elsewhere as members of deputations sent to Jeremiah by the king. Jehucal (Jucal here) ben Shelemiah visited Jeremiah during the temporary withdrawal of the Babylonians (37:3), and Pashhur ben Malchiah was sent when Nebuchadrezzar began the siege of Jerusalem in January 588 B.C. (21:1).

2 The statement of Jeremiah here is the same as that in 21:9, which he made at the start of the siege before his arrest. There is no need to regard this as a gloss.[9] The state officials would be in possession of Jeremiah's utterances and would quote them as incriminating evidence when needed. The combination of terms "sword, famine, and pestilence" is frequent in Jeremiah.[10] The verb "go out to" probably bears the sense "desert to" or "give oneself to." Jeremiah's remarks seemed to be traitorous and to give the officials good grounds to arrest the prophet.

3 No less seditious was this second statement, the substance of which had been stated several times (21:7; 34:2, 22; 37:8; etc.). The point is made with some emphasis with the verb *be handed over* supported by the infinitive absolute. Jeremiah's message did not change. Jerusalem's fate was irrevocable.

4 The state *officials* (*śārîm*) asked for the death penalty. In the circumstances this seemed reasonable since Jeremiah's utterances were treasonable. They were "weakening the hands of the soldiers," that is, weakening their morale. A similar expression occurs in Lachish Letter VI.[11] The military commander there referred to certain defeatist elements among the officials in Jerusalem. However, the text is broken and it is impossible to decide who is being blamed. There is certainly not enough evidence to identify the of-

8. See the Introduction, p. 30.
9. W. Rudolph in *BHS*; E. A. Leslie, *Jeremiah* (1954), p. 246.
10. See 14:12; 21:7, 9; 24:10; 27:8, 13; 29:17, 18; 32:24; 34:17; 38:2; 42:17, 22; 44:13. All of these are in prose passages.
11. *ANET*, p. 322 (l. 6).

fender as Jeremiah[12] even though Lachish Letter III refers to a prophet who declares "Beware." If Jeremiah was regarded as a defeatist, there were evidently defeatists among the national leaders also.

5 The king's true position is here revealed, and he is his own critic. The real power lay with the officials who had Zedekiah under their control (cf. vv. 25–27). He was, of course, a puppet king, set up by Nebuchadrezzar after the exile of Jehoiachin and possibly not accepted by everyone in the nation as the true king. Many hoped for the return of Jehoiachin.

6 The final intention of the officials was to bring about Jeremiah's death without bloodshed (cf. Gen. 37:18–19). He could well die a slow and painful but bloodless death in a cistern (*bôr*). The Hebrew text describes the cistern as being in the court of the guard and as belonging to Malchiah the king's son, which seems to contradict v. 26 where Jeremiah after his rescue pleaded not to be returned to the house of Jonathan (cf. 37:15, 16). But these differences may be more apparent than real; see the discussion at the beginning of this chapter on the relation between the two accounts of the events recorded in chs. 37–38. There is no need to transpose 38:24–28a to the end of ch. 37 to avoid the appearance of Jonathan in ch. 38.[13]

The narrator eases the reader's concern by relating that there was no water in the cistern, only mud, which was unpleasant enough, for Jeremiah sank in it. He would not be able to survive for long there.

A typical cistern was dug out of limestone rock and consisted of a narrow neck perhaps three feet across and three or four feet in depth opening into a much longer bulbous cavity of varying depth. Water from catchment areas was directed to the opening. The whole land made considerable use of cisterns for storing water. Entrance to them was difficult, hence the reference to letting Jeremiah down with ropes and lifting him out by ropes (v. 13).

12. See R. de Vaux, "Les Ostraka de Lâchis," *RB* 48 (1939), pp. 181–206; D. Winton Thomas, *The Prophet in the Lachish Ostraca* (1946); *Festschrift Otto Eissfeldt* (1958), pp. 244–49.
13. See *BHS* at 37:21 (W. Rudolph).

(b) Jeremiah rescued from the miry cistern (38:7–13)

7 *But Ebed-melech the Ethiopian, a eunuch*[1] *who was in the palace, heard that they had put Jeremiah into the cistern. The king was sitting in the Benjamin Gate at the time.*[2]
8 *Ebed-melech came from the palace and spoke to the king as follows:*
9 *"My lord the king, these men have committed evil in all that they have done to Jeremiah the prophet, whom they have thrown into the cistern to die*[3] *down there*[4] *from hunger, when there is no more bread in the city."*
10 *Then the king ordered Ebed-melech the Cushite, "Take with you from here three*[5] *men and lift Jeremiah out of the pit before he dies."*
11 *And Ebed-melech took the men with him and went to the palace to the wardrobe storeroom,*[6] *and obtained from there old rags and worn-out clothes, and let them down by rope to Jeremiah in the cistern.*
12 *And Ebed-melech the Cushite said to Jeremiah, "Put these old rags and clothes under your armpits and under the ropes." Jeremiah did this.*
13 *Then they pulled Jeremiah up by the ropes and brought him up from the cistern; and he remained in the court of the guard.*

7–8 Jeremiah's rescue came from a kindly Ethiopian (Cushite) named Ebed-melech. The term *eunuch* (*sārîs*) frequently denotes a royal official of some kind.[7] This man took quick action to rescue Jeremiah from certain death. Jeremiah later promised him deliverance in the coming destruction of Jerusalem (39:15–18). Ebed-melech hastened to report to the king, who at the time *was sitting in the Benjamin Gate,* presumably, according to the custom, hearing complaints and adjudicating in law cases (cf. 2 Sam. 15:2–4). This gave Ebed-melech the opportunity to approach the king easily: he had a complaint.

9 The sentence is complex in Hebrew. The MT "and he has died," if it is not to be emended, may suggest that he was as good

1. LXX omits *a eunuch.*
2. *At the time* is added in the translation to mark contemporaneous action shown by the present participle.
3. MT *wayyāmoṯ* means "and he has died"; revocalize *w*[e]*yāmuṯ,* "that he may die."
4. Heb. *taḥtayw,* "under it," i.e., "in its depths."
5. Read *š*[e]*lōšâ* instead of *š*[e]*lōšîm* ("thirty"!).
6. Reading *'el meltaḥaṯ hā'ôṣār* in place of MT *'el taḥaṯ hā'ôṣār,* "to under the storeroom"; cf. 2 K. 10:22.
7. Cf. Akk. *ša rēsi šarri* (lit. "he who is of the head of the king"; see KB, p. 668), a court official; in Egypt, Gen. 37:36; 39:1; 40:2, 7; in Assyria, 2 K. 18:17; 20:18; in Babylon, 39:3, 13; Isa. 39:7; Dan. 1:3, 7–11; Persia, Esth. 1:10, 12; Jerusalem, 29:2; 34:19; 38:7; 41:16; 52:25; 2 K. 23:11; 25:19; etc. The name *Ebed-melech* itself means "servant (courtier) of the king."

as dead. The state officials may have intended to starve him to death if he did not die of exposure or suffocate in the mud first. The final comment in the verse to the effect that Jeremiah would die of hunger when the food ran out in the city seems to us superfluous, especially in the light of 52:6–7 where it is stated that the city's food supply did not run out till the eve of the fall of the city, which was still some time away (v. 28a). Some commentators omit the clause,[8] but this does not seem justified. Ebed-melech would not be expected to know when the city would fall or what was the state of food supplies in the city. Moreover, he would be anxious to make the case as urgent as possible. He would not be concerned, in a time of crisis, with matters of logic such as how getting Jeremiah out of the cistern would help him if there were no more food.

10 The king's response was immediate and practical. The "thirty men" of the Hebrew text should probably be read "three men" with one manuscript. If "thirty" is original, one wonders what they would all do, unless they were needed for protection.

11–13 Ebed-melech proved to be practical and resourceful. Ropes under the armpits to lift Jeremiah from the pit might cut into his flesh; hence he took with him from the wardrobe storeroom some worn-out and unwanted clothing to cushion the ropes. The narrative in 37:17–21 does not mention these details about Jeremiah's rescue, although both the present narrative and that in ch. 37 refer to Jeremiah's plea not to be sent back to the cistern in Jonathan's house (37:20; 38:26) and both state that he was kept in the court of the guard house (*ḥ*^{a}*ṣar hammaṭṭārâ*) (37:21; 38:13).

(c) Zedekiah's last interview with Jeremiah (38:14–28a)

14 *King Zedekiah sent and received Jeremiah the prophet at the third entrance of the house of Yahweh. And the king said to Jeremiah, "I am going to ask you for an oracle;*[1] *hide nothing from me."*

15 *Jeremiah said to Zedekiah, "If I were to tell you, would you not be certain to have me put to death? And if I were to advise you, you would not listen to me."*

16 *But King Zedekiah swore to Jeremiah secretly, "As Yahweh lives who gave us these lives of ours, I will not have you put to death, nor will I hand you over to these men who are seeking your life."*

8. J. Bright, *Jeremiah,* p. 237; W. Rudolph, *BHS ad loc.*

1. Lit. "I am asking you a word (*dāḇār*); do not keep hidden from me a word."

17 *Then Jeremiah said to Zedekiah, "This is what Yahweh the God of Hosts, the God of Israel, has said: If you will go out at once*[2] *to the officials of the king of Babylon, then you shall live and this city will not be burned in flames; you yourself and your family*[3] *will live.*

18 *But if you do not go out to the officers of the king of Babylon, then this city will be handed over to the Chaldeans, who will burn it in flames, and you yourself will not escape from their hands."*

19 *King Zedekiah said to Jeremiah, "I am afraid of the Judeans who have gone over to the Chaldeans lest I should be given into their hands and they should treat me roughly."*

20 *Jeremiah answered, "They will not give you up. Now give heed, I beg you, to the voice of Yahweh, to what I am telling you, that it may be well with you and so that you may live.*

21 *But if you refuse to go out, this is what Yahweh has shown me:*

22 *Look here! all the women who are left in the household of the king of Judah will be led out to the officers of the king of Babylon, and will say:*

> *'They misled you and prevailed over you*
> *These "friends" of yours.*
> *Your feet are sunk in the mire;*
> *They have turned away from you.'*

23 *All your women and your children they will bring out to the Chaldeans; and you yourself will not escape from their hands but you will be seized by the king of Babylon, and the city will be burned*[4] *in the flames."*

24 *Zedekiah said to Jeremiah: "Do not let anyone know about this conversation*[5] *and you will not be put to death.*

25 *If the state officials hear that I have spoken with you and come to you and say to you, 'Tell us now, what you said to the king and what the king said to you;*[6] *hide nothing from us and we will not put you to death,'*

26 *then say to them, 'I was presenting my petition to the king not to send me back to the house of Jonathan to die there.' "*

27 *And when the officials came to Jeremiah and questioned him, he told them exactly as the king had instructed him. So they stopped inquiring—no one had overheard what had been said.*[7]

28a *And Jeremiah remained in the court of the guard till the day that Jerusalem was taken.*[8]

2. The verb is strengthened by the infinitive absolute.
3. Heb. *bêṯ,* "house."
4. MT reads *tiśrōp,* "you will burn." Revocalize to *tiśśārēp* (fem. to agree with *city*).
5. Lit. "these words."
6. This last phrase lies at the end of the verse in MT but we transpose it here following Syr., for better sense.
7. Lit. "And they became silent from him, for the thing had not been heard."
8. We omit the latter part of v. 28 in MT with LXX.

14 The secret meeting between the king and Jeremiah which followed Jeremiah's rescue from the cistern has a parallel in 37:17; the relationship between ch. 37 and ch. 38 is discussed at the beginning of the present chapter. The secret place where the interview was held is here identified as *the third entrance,* a place not otherwise mentioned. It may have been the king's private entrance to the temple leading directly from the palace. Zedekiah's request for a "word" should be understood as a word from Yahweh or an *oracle* (cf. v. 17), as in 37:17.

15–16 Knowing the king's weakness of character and his subservience to his officials, Jeremiah recognized the futility of passing on to him any word from Yahweh. He had rejected Yahweh's word before and had cast Jeremiah into prison (32:1–5). But now things were more serious, and Zedekiah declared with an oath "by the life of Yahweh who made this life for us" that he would not put him to death or hand him over to the officials.

17–18 Jeremiah's message was the same (cf. 21:8–10; 38:2–3). The only hope for the king and the people was surrender. The die was cast. It was the message for which Jeremiah had been thrown into the cistern, but he had no other. There is a certain irony in the use of the same word for the Chaldean officials, *śārîm,* as is used for the Judean officials. Judean officials would take Jeremiah's life; Chaldean officials would spare it.

19 Once again Zedekiah's weakness of character shows up. There was a course of action to be followed which he knew to be right, but he lacked the courage to take it (cf. v. 5). He had another fear besides that of his officials. Already there were deserters, whether on Jeremiah's advice or on their own initiative (cf. 39:9; 52:15). Such people might feel animosity toward Zedekiah, perhaps for not surrendering to the Babylonians earlier.

20–23 Jeremiah assured Zedekiah that he need not fear the deserters. What he should fear was a refusal to give heed to Yahweh's word and to surrender to the Babylonians. Only in that way could his life be spared. Jeremiah painted a striking picture of the outcome of a refusal to surrender. It was a vision Yahweh had shown him. Women and children of the king's household would be led out to the Babylonian officials, chanting as they went what may have been a brief traditional song about being betrayed by friends (cf. 20:10; Ps. 41:9) and being deserted as you sank in the mud (cf. Ps. 69:14). The short song was appropriate to Jeremiah's own recent experience (v. 6), and also to the king himself. The "friends" (lit.

"men of your peace," 20:10; Obad. 7) had misled the king and prevailed over him (cf. 38:5 where the same verb *yāḵōl,* "to be able, prevail" is used negatively of the king). The fate of Zedekiah described in the second part of this poem is seen as a parallel to Jeremiah's fate in the cistern (v. 6). Yahweh had used Ebed-melech to rescue Jeremiah from the cistern (*bôr*) and from death, but there would be no rescue for Zedekiah. There may be a subtle overtone in the use of the word *bôr,* which occurs as a symbol for the place of the dead in some places in the OT. Only Yahweh can rescue from such a predicament (Ps. 28:1; Isa. 28:18).

24–26 We are not told how Zedekiah received this message. One senses that he knew that Jeremiah's advice was the only possible solution. All he could say was to request Jeremiah to remain silent. He was powerless to act (cf. v. 5). But in no circumstances must the officials (*śārîm,* v. 25) learn that he had conferred with Jeremiah about what to do in the face of the Babylonian siege. Should the officials find out and come to inquire, Jeremiah was to answer, *I was presenting my petition* (lit. "letting my supplication fall"; cf. 37:20) *to the king not to send me back to the house of Jonathan to die there.* Some commentators would read vv. 24–28a after 37:21 so as to complete the story there. Such a transfer is not necessary. We may regard both ch. 37 and ch. 38 as variants of the same story with each having preserved some independent details. For the complete story the two chapters have to be combined.

27–28 The officials heard of the visit of Jeremiah to Zedekiah and were told the one part of the total conversation which did not concern them greatly. In fact, Jeremiah had made a strong plea to be removed (37:20). This silenced the officials, and the more sensitive part of the interview was not reported. Jeremiah was allowed to remain in the court of the guard till Jerusalem fell, and Zedekiah returned to the palace to suffer the anguish of knowing what was right to do but lacking the courage to do it.

(viii) The Fall of Jerusalem (39:1–10)

1 *In the ninth year of Zedekiah king of Judah, in the tenth month, Nebuchadrezzar king of Babylon moved against Jerusalem with all his forces, and they laid siege to it.*
2 *In the eleventh year of Zedekiah, in the fourth month on the ninth day of the month, the city was breached.*

3 *And all the officers of the king of Babylon came and took their seats in the Middle Gate: Nergal-sharezer of Simmagar, Nebushazban the Rabsaris, Nergal-sharezer the Rabmag,*[1] *and all the other officers of the king of Babylon.*

4[2] *And when Zedekiah king of Judah and all the soldiers saw this*[3] *they fled, and they went out of the city by night by way of the king's garden, through the gate between the two walls, and went in the direction of the Arabah.*

5 *But the Chaldean forces pursued them and overtook Zedekiah in the steppeland near Jericho. They seized him and brought him up to Nebuchadrezzar king of Babylon at Riblah in the land of Hamath, and he passed sentence upon him.*[4]

6 *The king of Babylon executed the sons of Zedekiah at Riblah before his very eyes; the king of Babylon also executed all the nobles of Judah.*

7 *Then he blinded the eyes of Zedekiah, and he bound him in fetters to take him to Babylon.*

8 *The Chaldeans burned the royal palace, the temple,*[5] *and the houses of the people in the flames, and tore down the walls of Jerusalem.*

1. The same names are listed in 39:13 somewhat differently. MT attests to some confusion in the preservation of the Babylonian names—always a problem when one has to represent foreign names in one's own language, and especially so where there is a wide phonetic difference between the two languages, as here. The list here in v. 3 has been emended in accordance with that in v. 13. The name Nergal-sharezer is the Akk. *Nergal-šar-uṣur* (Nergal protects the king) who is described in v. 13 as Rabmag (Akk. *rab-mūgi*), a highly ranked officer whose function is not known. Some translators insert "Rabmag" here from v. 13. MT *Samgar* must represent the name *Sin-magir (Simmagar),* a district of which Nergal-sharezer was governor according to a contemporary inscription. It seems likely that Nergal-šar-uṣur is the Neriglissar who succeeded Nebuchadrezzar's son Amel-Marduk (562–560 B.C.) on the Babylonian throne, probably by a *coup d'état.* He was the Rabmag at the time of this event but was later to be king. He was a brother-in-law of Amel-Marduk.

The second Nergal-sharezer is not mentioned in v. 13, but the name was a common one and it is possible that there were two men of this name among Nebuchadrezzar's officials. Some commentators omit the second Nergal-sharezer and include his title with the first one: Nergal-sharezer, lord of Sin-magir the Rabmag. See J. Bright, *Jeremiah,* p. 243; J. A. Bewer, "Nergalsharezer Samgar in Jer. 39:3," *AJSL* 42 (1925/6), p. 130; W. Rudolph, *Jeremia,* pp. 224f.

In v. 13 we have mention of *Nebushazbān rab-sārîs.* The *Nebu sar-sekim* of v. 3 is taken as a corruption of this name. *Rab* and *Sar* are equivalent. The Rabsaris was a high military or diplomatic official.

2. LXX omits vv. 4–13, but this may have been due to homoioteleuton as the scribe's eye moved from the ending of v. 3 to the ending of v. 13.

3. MT reads "saw them." But the king did not wait until the officers of v. 3 took their seats at the gate but fled when the wall was breached (v. 2). Verse 3 seems to be out of context here; see further the commentary. If "them" is original it must mean Nebuchadrezzar and his army as they stormed into the city through the wall.

4. Lit. "he spoke judicial decisions with him."

5. MT here omits *the temple* but it is restored from 52:13 and 2 K. 25:9.

9 *Nebuzaradan the commander of the bodyguard deported to Babylon the rest of the people left in the city, and those who had deserted to him, and the rest of the artisans.*[6]
10 *Only some of the poor people who had nothing did Nebuzaradan the commander of the guard leave in the land of Judah, and he assigned to them vineyards and fields.*[7]

This chapter has raised a number of questions for commentators and has generally been regarded as an editorial weaving together of several originally separate pieces. Part of the problem for modern commentators is that they do not always understand the methods of the ancient compilers, who had their own ways of handling parentheses, of adding explanatory sentences, and of interrupting the flow of an argument. Some of our own attempts to unravel an ancient editor's work would seem quite unnecessary to him. Thus the view that "this pericope is a fine example of textual imbroglio"[8] would come as a surprise to the ancient editor. The further comment "We present only the obvious emendations" may have been no less a surprise. But with our own literary methods we seem to need to resort to some analysis of passages which have arisen from what to us are strange literary methods. We proceed then to our own analysis of this chapter. Thus there is a brief oracle addressed to Ebed-melech (vv. 15–18) which belongs with the Ebed-melech story in ch. 38. Verse 3 seems to be a variant of v. 13. The story of the fall of Jerusalem is told succinctly in vv. 1–2, 4–10. It seems to be based on 52:4–16 (cf. 2 K. 25:1–12), perhaps as an abridgement. The last words of 38:28 appear to be a dittography. They are lacking in LXX, Syriac, and some manuscripts and could probably be omitted. But many commentators transfer them to the start of 39:3 and regard 39:3 as the first part of one account of Jeremiah's release. In its context v. 3 is a parenthesis describing one of the things that was done soon after the fall of Jerusalem. Its true context is at v. 13, where it is inserted again in the first account of Jeremiah's release. The proposal to link 38:28b with 39:13, 14 as comprising this first account is plausible and widely accepted.[9] The account then reads:

6. Read *w^{e}'ēṯ yeṯer hā'āmôn* (or *hā'ommān*) as in 52:15 in place of MT *w^{e}'ēṯ yeṯer hā'ām*.
7. MT *y^{e}gēḇîm* is of doubtful meaning. Vulg. reads "cisterns" (*gēḇîm*). A parallel text in 52:16 reads "as vinedressers" (*kōr^{e}mîm*) and "husbandmen" (*yōg^{e}ḇîm*), which is followed by NEB here.
8. G. P. Couturier, "Jeremiah," *JBC,* p. 330.
9. J. Bright, *Jeremiah,* p. 245; E. W. Nicholson, *Jeremiah 26–52,* p. 126; W. Rudolph, *Jeremia,* pp. 225–237.

"When Jerusalem was captured, all the officials of the king of Babylon came in and took their seats in the Middle Gate: Nergal-sharezer of Simmagar, the Rabmag, Nebushazban the Rabsaris, and all the other officers of the king of Babylon. They sent and brought Jeremiah from the court of the guard and handed him over to Gedaliah ben Ahikam ben Shaphan to take him out to the Residence. And he remained among the people."

However, it is not difficult to see in vv. 11–14 a self-contained and consistent unit, and the great pains some modern commentators have taken to separate out 38:28b; 39:3, 14 as the original account seem to be unnecessary.

The second account of Jeremiah's release occurs in 40:1–6. It overlaps a little, notably at the point where Jeremiah's own wishes were to be sought. But this second account is more detailed in a number of respects. The two stories are not necessarily in conflict, for Nebuzaradan may have given a general amnesty to all friends of Babylon. Jeremiah was among these and was released after the trial scene of 28:13. But he may have been rounded up by soldiers as he wandered in the streets of Jerusalem, and taken to Ramah where he was again released. He finally found his way to Gedaliah at Mizpah.

1–2 This chronological note is to be linked with 52:4, which, however, adds "on the tenth day of the month." But 39:1–2 is an abridgement of 52:4–6. It was in July 587 B.C. (cf. 52:5ff.) that Jerusalem fell to the Babylonians. A month later (52:12ff.; 2 K. 25:8ff.) Nebuzaradan, commander of Nebuchadrezzar's bodyguard, arrived at the city. The siege had lasted from January 588 till July 587 B.C., with a brief interlude in the summer of 588. The years were counted from the Babylonian New Year in the spring (March/April), that is, from the month Nisan.

3 See textual footnotes. Verse 3 seems to be an intrusion or parenthesis which is relevant at v. 13. In the present context one would wonder why the king was not captured at once. MT suggests that Zedekiah saw "them," that is, the Babylonian officers, taking their seats at the Middle Gate and fled. The king would hardly wait for any kind of trial but would flee by night once the wall was breached. By removing v. 3 to v. 13 the narrative flows on to verse 4 easily. What Zedekiah saw was Nebuchadrezzar and his army (v. 1).

The *Middle Gate* is mentioned only here in the OT. It may refer to an opening in the wall separating two quarters of the city.

4–5 The path of flight is not known, but presumably there was a secret exit not known to the Babylonians. The term *Arabah* covered the Jordan Valley and extended to the area south of the Dead Sea. But here it refers to the Jordan Valley in the region of Jericho (cf. v. 5). The intentions of Zedekiah are not known. He was no doubt in a dilemma whether to hide or to flee further east across the Jordan. The Babylonians soon overtook the fleeing king in the *steppeland*[10] near Jericho, and took him as a prisoner to Nebuchadrezzar at *Riblah,* an ancient Syrian town to the south of Kadesh on the river Orontes. It was situated at a strategic point where military highways between Egypt and Mesopotamia met. Evidently Nebuchadrezzar remained at his headquarters in central Syria while his general pursued the war in Judah. Prisoners were brought to the king for judgment.

6–7 Zedekiah's fate was nothing short of horrific. Before his eyes were put out, the last sight he witnessed was his sons being executed in front of him.[11] It was a brutal judgment on a rebel. Execution was also the lot of the *nobles* (*ḥôr,* as distinct from *śārîm,* "officials"). The blinded Zedekiah was taken in fetters to Babylon. It was a grim fulfilment of the words of Jeremiah on several occasions. We know nothing of Zedekiah's end except that he died in Babylon (52:11), perhaps not long after the physical and mental tortures inflicted on him.

8 The text in 52:13 includes "the house of Yahweh" along with the king's palace and the houses of the people, although it is not mentioned here in the Hebrew text. Many commentators add the phrase to the text at this point. In any case this was the fact. The extent of the destruction of the private houses has been revealed by excavations on the eastern slope to the south of the present wall.[12] Nothing is yet known archeologically about the destruction of the temple and the palaces. The verb "pull down" (*nāṯaṣ*), used here of the wall, occurred in another connection in Jeremiah's call (1:10).

9–10 As on the occasion of the first fall of Jerusalem (2 K. 24:10–14) the Babylonian authorities rounded up and carried off the citizens of Jerusalem, especially the skilled artisans (see textual note), and deported them to Babylon. Nebuzaradan, the *com-*

10. Heb. *ʿarāḇôṯ,* the plural of *Arabah.*
11. No doubt this was done not by Nebuchadrezzar personally but by soldiers under his command.
12. See K. M. Kenyon, *Jerusalem: Excavating 3000 Years of History* (1967).

mander of the bodyguard,[13] undertook a systematic redistribution of the population. The poorer people, probably the peasants (*dallîm*), were assigned holdings of land in Judah to be worked as vineyards or farms (see textual note) for their support.

(ix) *Jeremiah's Release: First Account (39:11–14)*

11 *And Nebuchadrezzar king of Babylon gave Nebuzaradan the commander of the guard orders about Jeremiah:*
12 *"Take him," he said; "take special care of him.*[1] *Do him no harm but do for him whatever he asks."*
13 *So Nebuzaradan the commander of the guard, together with Nebushazban the Rabsaris, Nergal-sharezer the Rabmag, and all the chief officers of the king of Babylon,*
14 *sent and brought Jeremiah from the court of the guard and handed him over to Gedaliah ben Ahikam to take him out to the Residence, and he remained among the people.*

11–12 Special attention was paid to Jeremiah. Nebuzaradan had instructions from Nebuchadrezzar to care for him. How Jeremiah was known to the Babylonian authorities is not made clear, though very likely it was through the Judean deserters.[2]

13–14 It would appear from these verses in the Hebrew text that Nebuzaradan, Nebushazban the Rabsaris, Nergal-sharezer the Rabmag, and all the chief officials of the king of Babylon brought Jeremiah from the court of the guard and handed him over to Gedaliah, who had been appointed governor of the remnants of the population. Gedaliah then took him to the governor's residence (*habbāyiṯ*, "The House") and he continued to live among the people.[3]

But this account is somewhat different from the one in 40:1–6, where Nebuzaradan the commander of the guard found Jeremiah in fetters among a whole train of captives at Ramah, 5 miles north of Jerusalem, and having released him spoke with him of the options open to him. It is thus clear that the editor had two stories before him both of which were included in the book.

13. Lit. "the chief butcher," an ancient title retained after the functions of the holder had altered; cf. Gen. 40:2.

1. Lit. "Set your eyes upon him."
2. They can be expected to have been pressed for information for intelligence purposes, if they did not volunteer it readily.
3. The proposal of W. Rudolph in *BHS ad loc.* that the text might be read *lᵉhôṣî'ô wᵉlahᵃḇî'ô,* "to let him go out and come in" among the people, is an attractive one; cf. 37:4.

The story in vv. 11–14 reads as a straightforward, consistent narrative. We can only presume that after his initial trial he was set free but was picked up by soldiers, put in chains, and sent to the holding camp at Ramah for transport to Babylon via Riblah.

Jeremiah remained in the land no doubt because he knew that there was still work to be done there.

(x) Hope for Ebed-melech (39:15–18)

15 *The word of Yahweh came to Jeremiah while he was confined to the court of the guard:*
16 *"Go and tell Ebed-melech the Ethiopian: 'This is what Yahweh of Hosts the God of Israel has said: Look, I will fulfil my words against this city for evil and not for good,*[1] *and on that day they will be fulfilled before your eyes.*
17 *But I will rescue you on that day—Yahweh's word—and you will not be handed over to the men whom you fear.*
18 *For I will surely keep you safe, and you will not fall a victim to the sword; you will escape with your life because you trusted in me—Yahweh's word.' "*

This small unit belongs properly with the story of Ebed-melech in 38:1–13. Why it was placed in the present context is not clear unless it was that the editor wished to show that Ebed-melech (39:15–18), like Jeremiah himself (39:11–14), survived the fall of Jerusalem recorded in 39:1–10. We do not know, in fact, that he did survive the destruction of the city but may infer this because of the promise made by Jeremiah while he was still confined to the court of the guard. The promise of deliverance was made in emphatic terms—*I will surely keep you safe*. Ebed-melech *trusted* (*bāṭaḥ*) in Yahweh. He was evidently another person in contact with the king who sympathized with Jeremiah.

The instruction to Jeremiah, *Go and tell Ebed-melech,* could hardly have been carried out literally since Jeremiah was in confinement.

The men whom you fear may be a reference to the high officials mentioned in 38:1 who sought Jeremiah's death. It was a brave palace servant who would accuse such men of crime (38:9).

The phrase we have translated *You will escape with your life* reads literally "your life shall be yours for booty"; see the note on 21:9, and cf. 38:2; 45:5.

1. LXX omits the rest of this verse.

VI. JEREMIAH'S EXPERIENCES AFTER THE FALL OF JERUSALEM (40:1–45:5)

A. IN JUDAH (40:1–43:7)

(i) Jeremiah's Release: A Second Account (40:1–6)

1 *The word which came to Jeremiah from Yahweh after Nebuzaradan the commander of the guard had set him free at Ramah. When he found*[1] *him he was in fetters*[2] *along with the other captives of Jerusalem and Judah who were being deported to Babylon.*
2 *The commander of the guard took Jeremiah*[3] *and said to him, "It was Yahweh your God who threatened this place with this disaster;*
3 *and now Yahweh has brought it to pass and has done as he said he would. It was because you sinned*[4] *against Yahweh and did not obey his voice that this thing has happened to you.*[5]
4 *So now today I am taking away the fetters on your wrists. If you wish to come to Babylon with me, come, and I will take care of you;*[6] *but if it does not please you to come to Babylon with me, then don't.*[7] *The whole land lies before you. Go wherever seems good and right to you.*

1. The verb is the participle of *lāqaḥ,* "take." The sense in which this verb is read governs the translation. It is here understood to mean that Nebuzaradan was looking out for Jeremiah, and when inquiry showed he was with the captives in chains he took him away from them.
2. The circumstantial clause is lacking in LXX.
3. The use of *l*ᵉ instead of *'eṯ* before the proper noun Jeremiah looks like an Aramaic accusative marker.
4. This and the following verb are plural, as is the final pronoun, *to you*—not Jeremiah but the people of Israel.
5. LXX is shorter, "and Yahweh has done it because you sinned against him and did not listen to his voice."
6. LXX is shorter and omits the last part of the verse from this point. MT may represent a conflation of different traditions, in this verse and the last.
7. Lit. "desist!"

5[8] *If you wish to remain, then return to Gedaliah ben Ahikam ben Shaphan, whom the king of Babylon has made governor over the cities*[9] *of Judah, and stay with him among the people, or go to wherever seems proper to go." Then the commander of the guard gave him provisions and a present and sent him away;*
6 *and Jeremiah came to Gedaliah ben Ahikam at Mizpah and remained with him among the people who were left in the land.*

The present section really belongs with 39:11–18, which is concerned with Jeremiah's release. The next section in 40:7–44:13 deals with the community that remained in the land. 40:7–43:7 deal with the appointment of Gedaliah and the conspiracy that followed his appointment, his assassination, and the decision of many Jews to flee to Egypt in defiance of Yahweh's command through Jeremiah. 43:8–44:30 describe Jeremiah's ministry in Egypt to those who had defied Yahweh's word. Clearly the future did not lie with such rebels. As in ch. 24 and 29:16–20 the point is made that the future lay with the exiles who had been deported to Babylon. One may discern in the story in 40:7–44:30 not only historical narrative but the development of the theological theme that disobedience leads to judgment. The enthusiastic practice of idolatry in Egypt excluded such people from future participation in the restoration of the people and the land.

1 40:1–6 acts as a kind of introduction to the story about Gedaliah, who is here introduced as governor of the land of Judah (v. 5). It would appear that there was a staging area at Ramah, the modern Er-Ram some 5 miles north of Jerusalem. From here the deportees would set off for Babylonia (see note on 31:15). Jeremiah appeared with a group of other captives, all in fetters. There had been some mistake! Nebuchadrezzar had ordered considerate treatment for Jeremiah and he had been set free earlier (39:11–14). But an embarrassing mistake had been made by the soldiers responsible for rounding up the Jews in Jerusalem, and Jeremiah was brought in chains with the rest of the captives to Ramah. Nebuzaradan the

8. The text of v. 5 has suffered in transmission and can be made intelligible only by conjecture. The first phrase in MT reads "and he did not yet reply"; LXX reads "and if not, go your way and go back to . . . ," which links to v. 4a. LXX omits v. 4b. If we accept Rudolph's emendation in *BHS,* then we pick up "if it is good" (*'im ṭôḇ*) from v. 4a, omit v. 4b, and emend the first part of v. 5 to read "in your eyes to return, then return," i.e., "if you wish to remain, then return to Gedaliah. . . ."
9. LXX reads "the land."

captain of the guard promptly set him free. He had come to Jerusalem one month after its fall (cf. 2 K. 25:3, 8) to complete the destruction of the city and to organize the caravan train for the exiles. It was he who had set Jeremiah free on his arrival (39:11–14). Now he had to free him again.

The opening words of v. 1, *The word which came to Jeremiah from Yahweh,* would normally be the introduction to an oracle, which does not appear.[10] Verse 1b may be regarded as a parenthesis explaining the circumstances under which Jeremiah was found. The following verses, which are a resumé of what Jeremiah had preached, come from the lips of Nebuzaradan and may be regarded as the oracle we might have expected. In any case they depict Jeremiah's release and speak of his freedom to choose where he wished to go.

2–3 The Chaldean commander was evidently aware of what Jeremiah had been saying, for he took up his views in a brief summary in order to justify recent events. Jeremiah could only agree that the *disaster* (*rāʿâ*) that had befallen Jerusalem was not unexpected by him and that it was a divine judgment on the people for their sin and their disobedience.

4 Jeremiah's safety had been the intention of Nebuchadrezzar (39:12), who had evidently heard about the activities of the prophet. Did he know of Jeremiah's opposition to the false prophets referred to in 29:20–23? The generous treatment of Jeremiah, giving him a free choice of what he wanted to do, is an enlarged version of what appears in 39:12. He was treated as a "friend" of Babylon. No doubt he would have been just as unhappy about such an assumption of his loyalty as he had been when he was accused by the Jewish military authorities of going over to the enemy (38:13). He would not have found it any easier to explain his theological position to the Babylonians than to the people of Jerusalem and Judah.

5 The Hebrew text at the beginning of this verse is difficult. It appears to be saying "And he did not yet reply (return answer) and return (imperative)." NEB reads "Jeremiah had not yet answered when Nebuzaradan went on 'Go back. . . .' " We follow the emendation proposed by W. Rudolph.[11]

10. NEB translates, "The word which came from the Lord concerning Jeremiah." The next verses are evidently seen as a declaration of the mind of Yahweh about Jeremiah.
11. See textual note.

Jeremiah had a choice of options: return to Babylon with Nebuzaradan and under his special care; stay in the land and go wherever he wished; or join Gedaliah in Mizpah. We learn for the first time of the appointment of Gedaliah ben Shaphan (cf. 39:14) as governor of the province. The Babylonians turned to the descendant of an old noble family who feature often in the book of Jeremiah. Shaphan the grandfather was Josiah's secretary and carried the newly found scroll to the king (2 K. 22:3–13). One son, Ahikam, was part of the delegation Josiah sent to the prophetess Huldah (2 K. 22:12–14). Ahikam offered protection to Jeremiah after he had preached the Temple Sermon (26:24). It was Ahikam's son Gedaliah who was the new governor of the Babylonian province of Judah.[12] He may have had a good deal of administrative experience in Zedekiah's cabinet. A seal impression found at Lachish dating to the beginning of the sixth century B.C. bears the name "Belonging to Gedaliah, Over the House." The latter expression was used of the chief minister of the king.[13]

6 Gedaliah's administration was not set up in Jerusalem, which at this stage was uninhabitable (Lam. 2:13; 4:1), but in Mizpah, which is probably to be identified with the modern Tel en-Nasbeh some 8 miles north of Jerusalem.[14] The town had been a political and religious center over the centuries (Judg. 20:1–3; 1 Sam. 7:5–14; 10:17). No signs of the destruction of Mizpah at this period have been revealed by excavation,[15] in sharp contrast to Jerusalem and the cities of Judah.[16]

12. Another grandson of Shaphan was Micaiah, the son of Gemariah who brought the news of Baruch's reading of Jeremiah's scroll to King Jehoiakim (36:11). His father Gemariah tried to dissuade Jehoiakim from burning the scroll (36:25). A third son of Shaphan, Elasah, went with the delegation of Zedekiah to Babylon and carried Jeremiah's letter to the exiles (29:3). The family was a noble one and deeply involved in Jeremiah's affairs. The following table sets out the relationship between them.

Shaphan

Ahikam	Gemariah	Elasah
Gedaliah	Micaiah	

13. See R. de Vaux, "Mélanges: Le Sceau de Godolias, maître de Palais," *RB* 45 (1936), pp. 96–102. This is the first epigraphic attestation of a well-known title. Cf. 1 K. 4:6; 16:9; 2 K. 15:5; 19:2; Isa. 36:3.

14. It has been excavated in recent years by W. F. Badé. See *Tell en Nasbeh,* Vols. I and II (Berkeley, 1947).

15. See K. Kenyon, *Archaeology in the Holy Land* (London, 1960), p. 390.

16. W. F. Albright, *From the Stone Age to Christianity* (1946), p. 246; G. E. Wright, *Biblical Archaeology* (London, 1962), pp. 177–79.

(ii) Gedaliah and the Community in Judah after 587 B.C. *(40:7–12)*

7 *When the commanders of the troops who were in the countryside together with their men heard that the king of Babylon had appointed Gedaliah ben Ahikam governor of the land and had put him in charge of the men, women, and children belonging to the poorest people of the land who had not been deported to Babylon,*

8 *they came to Gedaliah at Mizpah: Ishmael ben Nethaniah, Johanan and Jonathan*[1] *sons of Kareah, Seraiah ben Tanhumeth, the sons of Ephai the Netophatite, Jaazaniah*[2] *the son of the Maacathite with their men.*

9 *And Gedaliah ben Ahikam ben Shaphan gave his oath to them and their men: "Do not be afraid of the Chaldean officials.*[3] *Stay in the land and be subjects of the king of Babylon and it will go well with you.*

10 *For my part I will remain in Mizpah to represent you before the Chaldeans when they come to us. What you should do is gather in the wine, summer fruits, and oil and store them in jars and live in the towns which you have taken over."*

11 *The Judeans who were in Moab, in Ammon, in Edom, and in other countries heard that the king of Babylon had left some survivors in Judah and had made Gedaliah ben Ahikam ben Shaphan governor over them.*

12 *Then all these Judeans returned from all the places where they were scattered to the land of Judah. They came to the land of Judah to Gedaliah at Mizpah and gathered in an abundant supply of wine and summer fruits.*

7–8 At first Gedaliah had some success in rallying the population that remained in the land, and many who had been in hiding reappeared to build up something from the ruins, once they were assured that the Babylonians had gone. These included groups of Judean troops and their commanders (*śar*) who had managed to escape the Babylonian forces. The terrain of the Judean hills provided numerous safe hiding places. Some of the commanders are named because it was these men who became involved in the trouble that soon arose, in particular Ishmael, a man of royal birth (41:1) who was to assassinate Gedaliah and commit other atrocities.

The great bulk of these Judeans were of the underprivileged classes (39:10), but there were others including some royal prin-

1. Jonathan is lacking in some mss., 2 K. 25:23, and LXX, which reads "Johanan son of Kareah." MT includes another individual Jonathan.
2. MT reads "Jezaniah" but we follow 2 K. 25:23 and some mss.
3. So LXX and 2 K. 25:24. MT reads "Do not be afraid to submit to the Chaldeans." The emendation required is minimal: MT *mēʿ^{a}ḇôḏ* becomes *mēʿaḇ^{e}ḏê*.

cesses (*b^e nôṯ hammeleḵ,* 43:6) as well as remnants of the Judean army who may have been engaged in guerrilla activity against the Chaldeans.

9 Gedaliah's first act was to pacify the guerrilla commanders and to gain their confidence by giving them the assurance (lit. "he swore to them") that they need not fear the Babylonian officials (cf. 2 K. 25:24). Their best course was to settle in the land and be subject to the king of Babylon.

10 The oath of v. 9 is not given verbatim but it may have involved the promise of v. 10, namely, that Gedaliah would act as a mediator between the Jews and the Chaldeans in the conduct of official affairs. He would, literally, "stand before the Chaldeans when they appeared in the land." The people would in return accept Gedaliah as governor and settle down to their agriculture. Summer fruits, wine, and oil were to be harvested, produced, and stored as formerly. Any future for the surviving group depended on a proper submission to the Babylonians. Even if Judah was now simply a Babylonian province, she could still preserve her identity. There is no literary evidence that the small territory was ever colonized by the Chaldeans the way Israel was after the Assyrian conquest in 721 B.C. (2 K. 17:24–27).

The *towns* referred to here are presumably those which had been destroyed in the Babylonian campaign but were subsequently occupied by the bands of troops that had escaped the Babylonian army.

11–12 Refugee Jews from Moab, Ammon, and Edom and other lands soon joined the *survivors (š^e'ērîṯ)* and farmed the desolate land to good profit, gathering in an abundant harvest of wine and summer fruits.

All was going well. Life resumed its normality and there was hope for the future. Then came the devastating plot and the assassination of Gedaliah.

(iii) The Assassination of Gedaliah (40:13–41:3)

13 *Then Johanan ben Kareah and all the commanders of the troops which were in the countryside came to Gedaliah at Mizpah*

14 *and said to him: "Surely you know that Baalis king of Ammon has sent Ishmael ben Nethaniah to assassinate you?" But Gedaliah ben Ahikam did not believe them.*

15 *Then Johanan ben Kareah spoke to Gedaliah secretly in Mizpah: "Just let me go and kill Ishmael ben Nethaniah and no one will know. Why should he assassinate you and thus cause all the Judeans who have gathered about you to be scattered and the remnant of Judah to perish?"*

16 *But Gedaliah ben Ahikam said to Johanan ben Kareah, "You shall not do this thing, for it is a falsehood that you are speaking about Ishmael."*

41:1 *In the seventh month Ishmael ben Nethaniah ben Elishama who was of the royal house, one of the chief officers of the king,*[1] *came to Gedaliah ben Ahikam at Mizpah accompanied by ten men. And as they were eating together*

2 *Ishmael ben Nethaniah and the ten men with him rose to their feet and struck down Gedaliah ben Ahikam ben Shaphan with the sword, and assassinated the man whom the king of Babylon had made governor of the land.*

3 *Ishmael also struck down all the Judeans who were with Gedaliah in Mizpah as well as the Chaldean soldiers who happened to be there.*

13–14 Johanan ben Kareah, one of the commanders who had joined Gedaliah, led a deputation to the new governor to warn him of a plot to assassinate him. Baalis king of Ammon had persuaded the royal prince Ishmael to take Gedaliah's life. It is not clear what the motives of Baalis were. He may have wished to carry on the plot of 594 B.C. (27:3) to overthrow or simply to harass the Babylonians. It would appear from Ezek. 21:18–32 that when Nebuchadrezzar planned a campaign in the west in 587 B.C. there was as much reason to attack Ammon as to attack Judah since probably both had offended him. It is possible that Zedekiah was trying to flee to Ammon when he was captured after the fall of Jerusalem (39:4–5).

Nor is it clear why Ishmael should have allowed himself to be implicated in the plot. Being a member of the royal house (41:1) he may have planned to seize power in Judah, but this seems unlikely since he fled to Ammon once the dastardly deed was done. So perhaps he too was motivated only by a desire to harass the Babylonians. He probably regarded Gedaliah as a collaborator.

Johanan found it incredible that Gedaliah was unaware of the plot: *Surely you know (h*^{a}*yāḏōa' tēḏa')*?[2] If Gedaliah did know he refused to believe what he had heard. He seems to have been of a

1. MT *w*^{e}*rabbê hammelek̠*, "and the chief officers of the king," should either be deleted with LXX and 2 K. 25:25 (cf. v. 2a) or read as here with RSV.

2. The Hebrew text included the interrogative phoneme *h*^{a} before *yāḏōa'*, so that the sense of the expression is "Do you certainly know," i.e., *Surely you know*, as in our translation.

magnanimous disposition and unable to believe evil of one whom he knew personally in the days when he was a state official and Ishmael was a royal prince.

15–16 Johanan was more aware of the dangerous consequences that would follow the assassination of Nebuchadrezzar's governor in Judah. The Jews so recently gathered about Gedaliah at Mizpah would be scattered and the *remnant* ($\check{s}^e$*'ērîṯ*) would perish. Clearly such a murderous act would prevent the establishment of a new nation founded upon the remnant of Judah left in the land. Better to slay Ishmael secretly than allow an evil train of events to be set in course.

Gedaliah could not accept the fact that others were less sincere than he was in his desire to reestablish a stable Judah. His sheer transparent magnanimity made him incapable of a critical assessment of people or of situations. This mistake, which many noble men in Israel and elsewhere both before and since have made, cost him his life.

41:1 In the seventh month, that is, October, Gedaliah was slain. The year is not stated but may have been the year of Jerusalem's fall (39:2 refers to the fourth month), which would still have given time to gather in the summer crops (40:12). On the other hand a lot of things had taken place (40:7–16) and the assassination may have occurred the next year or even after several years. Some commentators have even suggested that Gedaliah's murder may have been connected with the third deportation of Jews in 582 B.C. referred to in 52:30, some five years later. In the centuries that followed, the Jews were to observe a fast to commemorate this tragedy (Zech. 7:5; 8:19).

The deed was dastardly in the extreme. By customary law the host was bound to protect his guests while the guests were expected to act in good faith. Treachery was never expected. Gedaliah was caught off his guard and was defenseless. The fact that Ishmael was at Gedaliah's table may suggest that the two men knew one another and that Gedaliah was making a gesture of friendship. Ishmael violated all the laws of Oriental hospitality by his shocking act of perfidy. The act was, moreover, a gross offense against the Chaldeans who had appointed Gedaliah.

3 The first murder led to others. Some Judeans who were with Gedaliah were also slain. These must have been merely representatives of the Jewish population of Mizpah since others were later rounded up (v. 10). Finally the Chaldeans who were stationed at Mizpah, or such of them as happened to be at the meal, were slain. Clearly Ishmael would have needed to dispose of the whole Chaldean garrison there, but it may have been small and could have been eliminated in a surprise attack. The whole shameful incident was bound to encourage stern reprisals by the Babylonians.

(iv) Further Atrocities (41:4–18)

4 *The second day after the murder of Gedaliah, while no one knew of it,*
5 *eighty men arrived from Shechem, from Shiloh, and from Samaria with their beards shaved and their clothing torn, covered with self-inflicted gashes, and carrying cereal offerings and incense to take to the house of Yahweh.*
6 *Ishmael ben Nethaniah went out from Mizpah to meet them, weeping as he went. And when he met them he said to them, "Come to Gedaliah ben Ahikam."*
7 *As soon as they were inside the city, Ishmael ben Nethaniah and the men who were with him massacred them and threw them*[1] *into a cistern.*
8 *But there were ten men among them who said to Ishmael, "Don't kill us! We have a secret supply of wheat, barley, olive oil, and honey in the fields." So he spared them and did not kill them along with their companions.*
9 *Now the cistern into which Ishmael threw the corpses of the men he had slain was a large cistern,*[2] *one that King Asa had made (as a defense) against Baasha king of Israel. This, Ishmael ben Nethaniah filled with the slain.*
10 *Then Ishmael made prisoners of all the rest of the people who were in Mizpah*[3] *including the king's daughters whom Nebuzaradan the commander of the guard had entrusted to Gedaliah ben Ahikam. These, Ishmael ben Nethaniah took as prisoners and set out to cross over into the territory of Ammon.*
11 *When Johanan ben Kareah and all the military leaders who were with him heard of the dastardly thing which Ishmael ben Nethaniah had committed,*
12 *they took all their men and went to attack Ishmael ben Nethaniah. They found him by the great pool at Gibeon.*

1. The verb *threw* is lacking in MT. Syr. has the equivalent of *wayyašlīḵēm,* "and he threw them" (cf. v. 9). The verb has to be supplied both in English and in MT.
2. So LXX, implying *bôr gāḏôl* for MT *bᵉyaḏ gᵉḏalyāhû,* "by the hand of Gedaliah." However, *byd* is used in Ugaritic to mean "because of," which would suit well here: the men were slain "because of Gedaliah"; these new murders were to cover up the first. See M. Dahood, "Hebrew-Ugaritic Lexicography I," *Biblica* 44 (1963), pp. 300f.
3. MT repeats the phrase "and all the people left in Mizpah." Omit with LXX.

13 *When all the people who were with Ishmael saw Johanan ben Kareah and all the military leaders who were with him, they were overjoyed.*
14 *And all the people whom Ishmael had taken captive from Mizpah turned about and returned and hurried back to Johanan ben Kareah.*[4]
15 *But Ishmael ben Nethaniah escaped from Johanan with eight men and went to the land of Ammon.*
16 *Then Johanan ben Kareah and all the military leaders who were with him took all the rest of the people whom Ishmael ben Nethaniah had carried away from Mizpah*[5] *after he had slain Gedaliah ben Ahikam, men,*[6] *women, children, and eunuchs whom he had brought back from Gibeon.*
17 *And they set out and halted at Geruth-Kimham, near Bethlehem, on their way to Egypt*
18 *to get away from the Chaldeans, whom they feared because Ishmael ben Nethaniah had slain Gedaliah ben Ahikam whom the king of Babylon had made governor of the land.*

4–5 Two days after the murder of Gedaliah *no one knew of it.* Pilgrims from old Northern Israel cultic centers, Shechem, Shiloh, and Samaria, arrived at Mizpah on their way to Jerusalem to engage in worship, as is clear from the *cereal offerings* (*minḥâ*) and *incense* (*lᵉḇônâ*) they carried. It was the seventh month, which was the time of the great autumn feast and the cultic new year (as distinct from the civil New Year which fell in the spring at this period following the Babylonian Calendar). The fact that these pilgrims came from the north suggests that at least some in Northern Israel accepted and remained faithful to Josiah's reformation of 622 B.C. Presumably they were following the prescriptions of Deuteronomy which required centralization of worship in the central sanctuary, by that time fixed at Jerusalem (cf. Deut. 12:5–6, etc.; 2 K. 23). The custom had been securely established before the fall of Jerusalem. The pilgrims wore the signs of mourning and repentance, shaven beards, torn clothes, and gashed bodies (cf. 16:6; 48:37),[7] no doubt because the temple had been destroyed. Mourning for the temple was an important theme during the whole exilic period (Lamentations; Pss.

4. LXX is shorter than MT, lacking *they were overjoyed* in v. 13 and reading for v. 14 simply "and they turned about toward Johanan." A conflation of texts is probable in MT.
5. MT reads "whom he had rescued from Ishmael ben Nethaniah, from Mizpah"; cf. LXX. The present reading emends MT *hēšîḇ mē'ēṯ* to *šāḇâ 'ōṯām.*
6. Both MT and LXX add "soldiers" (Heb. *'anšê hammilḥāmâ*); but this may be a gloss inserted by someone who wanted to explain the consonants of *gᵉḇārîm,* "men," as *gibbôrîm,* "soldiers." It is unlikely that Ishmael would take warriors captive.
7. The verb *hiṯgôḏēḏ* sometimes refers to a cultic practice known among Baal-worshippers (Deut. 14:1; 1 K. 18:28; cf. Jer. 5:7 MT).

74, 79; Isa. 63:7–64:12). For some time at least, cultic worship in some form continued in Jerusalem after 587 B.C.

6–8 It was an act of sheer deceit and perfidy for Ishmael to meet the pilgrims with such a display of sympathy for them in their sorrow. By pretending himself to be overcome with grief, *weeping as he went,* he won their confidence. Equally deceitful was his welcome in the name of Gedaliah. The pilgrims were completely off their guard before a master of treachery who was ably supported by his henchmen. The corpses of the massacred pilgrims were thrown into a *cistern* (*bôr*), a favorite place for oppressors to dispose of their victims whether living or dead (cf. 37:6; 38:6). It is difficult to understand why Ishmael should so brutally murder pilgrims. He could still have kept his first dastardly act hidden and found an explanation for the absence of Gedaliah, to whom they would naturally come to pay their respects. One begins to picture Ishmael as a brutal murderer who enjoyed killing for its own sake. His having allowed ten men to escape (v. 8) in order to guarantee supplies meant that the story would be circulated sooner or later. But no doubt he was capable of first gaining the supplies from these men and then slaying them by another act of treachery. He evidently did not intend to remain in Judah and planned to flee almost at once to Ammon (v. 10). He would need the provisions for the journey, or else he may have intended to use such provisions on a future guerrilla raid into Judah. He remains a puzzling figure.

9 The cistern into which the bodies were cast was made by Asa, who according to 1 K. 15:22 undertook the building of a fortress at Mizpah three hundred years previously with material he had robbed from the fortress of Baasha of Israel at Ramah. Excavations at Tell en-Nasbeh may have brought the cistern in question to light.[8]

10 The reference to *the king's daughters* raises a question. It is strange that the Babylonians did not round up such politically significant people. The Chaldean garrison at Mizpah must have known about them if they were, indeed, the daughters of the exiled and blinded Zedekiah. Certainly there is no reference to them in the narrative in 2 K. 24:1–7 or in Jer. 39:1–7, and on the basis of these passages it could be argued that they escaped the dreadful fate of their father and brothers. We cannot be certain who they represent, whether Zedekiah's daughters or some other women of royal de-

8. C. C. McCown, *Tell en Nasbeh I, Archaeological and Historical Results* (Berkeley, 1947); J. C. Wampler, *Tell en Nasbeh II—The Pottery* (Berkeley, 1947).

scent, of whom there may have been quite a number from other branches of the royal family. It is interesting to observe that Jeremiah may have been among those whom Ishmael took prisoner since he was present with the group after their rescue and their flight to Bethlehem (42:2ff.). But this is not certain, for there were people absent from Mizpah at the time, for example, Johanan.

11–12 It would appear that Johanan was not immediately aware of the crime. Indeed, Ishmael, who was no doubt aware of Johanan's suspicions, probably waited for his absence from Mizpah to carry out his murderous act. Once he became aware of the fact he gave chase to Ishmael and caught up with him at the great pool of *Gibeon*. This important landmark was the scene of a bloody incident in the days of Saul and David when twelve of Abner's men fought twelve of Joab's men (2 Sam. 2:12–16). Recent excavations at el-Jib some 6 miles northwest of Jerusalem have revealed a large pit hewn out of the rock, some 82 feet deep, which had steps carved around its sides from top to bottom to enable people to reach the water stored there.[9]

If Mizpah is indeed Tell en-Nasbeh, then Gibeon lay a mere 3 miles southwest rather than to the east, which would have been in the direction of Ammon. It may be that Ishmael followed a roundabout route to throw off the pursuit, but in terms of distance from Mizpah he had not travelled far with his group of captives. His movements were probably observed by many people who were not actually in Mizpah.

13–15 Ishmael did not wait but fled with eight men to Ammon. The captives happily rejoined Johanan. The Hebrew text seems to be very repetitive; the Greek text by comparison is much shorter. Some translators omit parts of the Hebrew text without any loss (e.g., NEB). Others attempt some rearrangement of the text.[10]

16–18 The immediate result of Ishmael's treacherous murder of Gedaliah and some of the inhabitants of Mizpah was that Johanan and his fellow military commanders began to think of military reprisals from the Babylonians. The crime could only be interpreted by them as a new revolt against Babylon, and retaliation was expected (52:30). The only neighboring country which was free from Babylonian domination was Egypt. As a first step a group of

9. J. B. Pritchard, "The Water System at Gibeon," *BA* 19/4 (1956), pp. 66–75; "Gibeon's History," SVT VII (1960), pp. 1–12, esp. p. 9.
10. E.g., J. Bright, *Jeremiah*, pp. 249f.; see the textual note.

refugees set out southward and reached Bethlehem about 6 miles southwest of Jerusalem. The stopping place was Geruth-Kimham. The name Kimham is only known as a personal name in 2 Sam. 19:37, 38, 40. Kimham was a son of Barzillai, who gave help to David during the rebellion of Absalom, escorting David across the Jordan when Absalom returned to Jerusalem in triumph. David offered to reward him by making him a member of the royal household, but because of age he was unable to accept the offer. His son Kimham received the honor and was given a grant of land near Bethlehem, a kind of fief.[11] The location is unknown.

It was at this point that the refugees decided to consult Jeremiah (42:1). It is clear that Johanan and his fellow officers took Jeremiah from Mizpah with them. Refuge in Egypt seemed preferable to a return to Mizpah to face Babylonian reprisals. An oracle from Yahweh, however, would be an encouragement.

(v) The Flight to Egypt: Jeremiah's Warning Rejected (42:1–43:7)

(a) Jeremiah is consulted (42:1–6)

1 *Then all the military commanders and Johanan ben Kareah and Jezaniah ben Hoshaiah, together with all the people both small and great,*
2 *approached Jeremiah the prophet and said, "May our petition be acceptable to you. Pray to Yahweh our God for us and for this whole remnant (for only a few of us remain out of many, as you can see)*
3 *that Yahweh our God may tell us the way we ought to go and the thing we should do."*
4 *Then Jeremiah the prophet said to them, "I have heard. I will indeed pray to Yahweh your God as you request, and whatever answer Yahweh gives you I will tell you. I will keep nothing back from you."*
5 *Then they said to Jeremiah, "May Yahweh be a true and faithful witness against us if we do not do everything which Yahweh your God sends you to tell us.*
6 *Whether it pleases us or not we will obey the word of Yahweh our God to whom we are sending you, that it may be well with us. Yes, indeed, we will obey the word of Yahweh our God."*

Chapter 42 continues the story of the particular remnant left in Judah at Mizpah. Jeremiah is not mentioned in the narrative in 40:7–41:18 but he reappears to be consulted by this community in their perplexity following the crisis caused by Ishmael's treachery. The

11. A. Alt, *Kleine Schriften zum Geschichte des Volkes Israel,* pp. 364f., suggests that the word *gērûṯ* should be translated "the right of a resident alien," that is, a "fief."

reappearance of Jeremiah introduces us to the final phase of his prophetic activity, which was to end in Egypt. He played no part in the tragic incident surrounding the death of Gedaliah. If he did speak in that period, we are not informed. It is odd that so prominent a person escaped the bloodbath. But it must have been for him one of the most tragic events of his life, since it dashed for ever all hopes he may have had to end his days in his homeland, where Yahweh had promised one day to restore the national life of his people (32:1–15).

The passage 42:1–43:7 tells of the flight of Jeremiah and the remnant to Egypt. The people paid no more attention to Jeremiah there than they had in Judah.

The whole of the section 40:7–44:30 is in the characteristic prose style of the book.[1] The historicity of the events need not be questioned. Jeremiah's message remained relevant for people in exile whether in Egypt or in Babylonia. Idolatry and disobedience could never be tolerated by Yahweh. But it was clear that the future restoration of which Jeremiah spoke earlier was not to be enjoyed by those who went to Egypt.

1–3 The military commanders seem to have played an important role in these days. Johanan is still prominent. The other person referred to here is Jezaniah ben Hoshaiah, who appears in 43:2 as Azariah ben Hoshaiah.[2] The idiom "from the small to the great" indicates that the whole group was involved, people of every class, high and low (NEB). They approached Jeremiah the prophet as a whole community. The mention of Jeremiah indicates that he was with the group that fled from Mizpah after Johanan had rescued those whom Ishmael had taken. It is not clear whether Jeremiah was in the captive group or joined them after their return to Mizpah, although the text does not refer to others besides the survivors from Ishmael's evil adventure (41:16). The idiom "let our petition fall before you" occurs elsewhere (36:7; 37:20; 38:26; 42:9) and is used of petitioners to both men and God. It was evidently an indication of an urgent petition, to judge from the contexts in which it occurs. There was some degree of panic among the refugees as to what should be their next move. An oracle from Yahweh would cut short their perplexity. They seemed to be a mere handful of people out of the many who comprised the original nation.

1. See the Introduction, "The Book of Jeremiah: Composition," pp. 33–50.
2. LXX has Azariah in both places.

4 Jeremiah's cautious response suggests that he wanted to be sure that his answer would be accepted whatever it was. He knew enough about his people to realize that they might well reject whatever Yahweh might say, which is what they did. Perhaps their decision to go to Egypt was already final.

There is an interesting shift in the possessive pronoun used in vv. 2–6, *your God* (Jeremiah's, vv. 2, 3, 5), *your God* (the people's, v. 4), *our God* (everybody's, v. 6), although it may not have been significant.[3]

5–6 The people made a show of sincerity and pledged themselves to obedience. Yahweh was not merely a witness (*'ēḏ*) but a *true and faithful witness*. Three times they affirmed their intention to give heed to Yahweh's word. The expression *'im ṭôḇ wᵉ'im rā'*, "whether good or evil," is a common idiom: "We will obey his word whatever it is." The final *kî* in the verse has an emphatic value, *Yes, indeed!* These verses serve to heighten the subsequent disobedience of the people.

(b) Yahweh's answer to Jeremiah's prayer (42:7–22)

7 *Ten days later the word of Yahweh came to Jeremiah.*
8 *So he summoned Johanan ben Kareah and all the military commanders who were with him, and all the people both small and great,*
9 *and said to them: "This is what Yahweh the God of Israel to whom you sent me to present your petition has said:*
10 *If you are prepared to go on living*[1] *in this land, then I will build you up and not pull you down, and I will plant you and not uproot you; for I am grieved over the disaster which I have brought upon you.*
11 *Do not be afraid of the king of Babylon whom you fear, but fear him not—Yahweh's word—for I am with you to save you and to deliver you from his power.*
12 *I will show you mercy. He also will show you mercy and will let you return to your own land.*
13 *But if you say 'We will not remain in this land,' not obeying the word of Yahweh your God*
14 *and saying 'No! We will go to Egypt where we will see no war, nor hear the trumpet blast, nor starve for want of food, and will live there,'*
15 *then hear the word of Yahweh, you remnant of Judah! This is what Yahweh of Hosts the God of Israel has said: If you have really made up your mind*[2] *on going to Egypt to settle there,*

3. LXX reads "our God" in v. 4 and omits *your God* in v. 5.

1. An emphatic form with the infinitive absolute, *yāšôḇ tēšᵉḇû*. MT omits the first *y* but it is restored with LXX, Targ., and Vulgate.
2. Lit. "set your faces"; again the verb is strengthened by the infinitive absolute.

16 *then the sword which you fear will overtake you in the land of Egypt, and the famine you dread will follow after you to Egypt, and there you will die.*
17 *And all the men who have set their minds on going to Egypt to live there will die by the sword, and from starvation and disease; there will not be one survivor, not one who will escape from the disaster which I will bring upon you.*
18 *For this is what Yahweh of Hosts the God of Israel has said: Just as my anger and my wrath were poured out upon the citizens of Jerusalem, so will my wrath be poured out upon you when you go to Egypt; you will become an object of execration, of horror, of ridicule and reproach; you will never see this place again.*
19 *Yahweh has told you, you remnant of Judah: 'Do not go to Egypt.' You should know beyond all doubt and I warn you this day*
20 *that you are deceiving yourselves at your peril. For you yourselves sent me to Yahweh your God and said, 'Pray for us to Yahweh our God; tell us all that Yahweh our God says and we will do it!'*
21 *I have told you this day, but you have not obeyed the word of Yahweh your God in everything that he sent me to tell you.*
22 *So now you may know for certain that you will die by the sword, by starvation, and by disease in the place where you wish to go and settle."*

7–9 It was ten days before Yahweh's answer came. Such a delay only aggravated the situation and fear of Babylonian reprisals must have increased. But we have here a glimpse into the nature of prophecy. No doubt Jeremiah spent a lot of time in prayer and meditation in those days, but he needed to be sure that when he spoke finally it would be the word of Yahweh and not the promptings of his own heart. The true prophetic inspiration did not arise from human insight. Jeremiah needed to stand in the council of Yahweh (23:18). His own inclinations were, no doubt, to remain in his homeland. But such a course was not necessarily best for the people nor according to the will of Yahweh. Once before when Hananiah had confronted him he was momentarily speechless, and only later did he speak (28:10–12). Now when he was ready to speak he addressed the whole group.

10 In emphatic language, and using the verbs which took a prominent place in his call (1:10), he delivered Yahweh's response. If the people desired to be planted and not uprooted, built up and not torn down, they should remain in their land (cf. 31:28). This remnant, like the one in Babylon, was being offered the same promise of renewal and restoration. There was no unwillingness on Yahweh's part to allow any individual or group of individuals among his people to enjoy the blessings of the day of restoration. Had this group committed themselves to him and obeyed him, the promise could have been realized for them. But in a negative way it became clear, as it was declared positively elsewhere, that the future lay with the exiles in Babylon (chs. 24, 29) and not with those who fled to Egypt or those who remained in the land. The fulfilment of the promise was not possible since the judgment foretold by Jeremiah had fallen. Yahweh could declare *I am grieved for the disaster which I have brought upon you.* The verb translated "grieve for" (*niḥam*) should not be translated "repent" as in AV, RV, and RSV, as though Yahweh realized that he had made a mistake and was sorry for it. LXX translates "I relent with regard to,"[3] that is, the judgment that had already fallen had satisfied the divine demands resulting from the broken covenant. Nothing further was required and the future held hope of better things. The primary sense of the verb is "take a (deep) breath," which is the sense here, and the translation "grieve" (sigh sorrowfully) would suit the present context. "I am sorry for the hurt that I have had to inflict upon you."[4] The verb sometimes denotes a change in Yahweh's plans due to a change in Israel's behavior; see the commentary on 18:18.[5]

11–12 These verses touch on what was the basic cause of the proposed flight to Egypt—fear of reprisals. There would have been good reason for this, and if it happened the king of Babylon would punish everyone for the sin of the one man Ishmael. But such fears were declared to be unfounded. Yahweh would *save* (*hôšîaʿ*) and *deliver* (*hiṣṣîl*) them from his power. And if Yahweh showed mercy to his people, so would the king of Babylon. He would allow them to return to their homes in peace.[6] There is no evidence that Nebuchadrezzar avenged the governor's assassination; he did take more captives in 582 B.C. (52:30), but if this was a reprisal it was a very much belated one.

13–14 The mind of the refugees seemed to be made up. Their immediate fears could not be removed by Yahweh's promises.

3. Gk. *anapépaumai epí*, LXX 49:10; cf. Amos 7:3, 6; etc.

4. J. Bright, *Jeremiah*, p. 256. See KB, pp. 608f. for the semantic range of the root *nḥm*.

5. The verb is used in this sense also in 4:18; 18:8, 10; 26:3.

6. The fugitives had left their homes and were about to enter Egypt out of fear. The king of Babylon would let them return to their homes. There is no need to emend the text to read "he will let you stay on your own soil" (NEB). LXX reads 1st person throughout and refers the sentence to Yahweh: "I will let you return." This may understand the verb forms *riḥam* and *hēšîḇ* as infinitive absolutes, which would be possible and would also make good sense.

Egypt seemed far from war, the sound of the trumpet, and the shortage of food. They could dwell there in peace. Jeremiah anticipated their reply.

15–19 Yahweh's word to the remnant (*šᵉ'ērîṯ*) of Israel was clear. If they had really decided to go to live in Egypt, that would not achieve freedom from the sword, starvation, disease, and death. As though to contrast their experiences after the fall of Jerusalem and the murderous acts of Ishmael with what could now happen, the threat was that there would be no *survivor* (*śārîḏ*), and no *escape* (*pālîṭ*). Just as acts of disobedience against Yahweh's word brought his anger and his wrath on Jerusalem, so would his wrath be poured out on them in Egypt. Their end is described in terms used elsewhere in the book (e.g., 42:18; 44:12). Never would they return to *this place,* i.e., their own land.

20–22 The prohibition against going to Egypt was now stated emphatically. Jeremiah's warning was a strong one. They should know beyond all doubt[7] that they had deceived themselves[8] into thinking that their plan to flee to Egypt would win Yahweh's approval when they sent Jeremiah to Yahweh to pray for them. So sure were they that the answer would be in line with their own plans that they had promised to carry out all that Yahweh told him. Just as emphatically Jeremiah now declared that they would die in Egypt from the very causes which they imagined would fall upon them in their own land.

Some commentators propose to place 43:1–3 after 42:18, and the final verses of ch. 42 after 42:3,[9] in order to indicate that the people had their minds made up already and that Jeremiah's words in 42:19–22 are a reply to the arrogant words of 43:1–3. The suggestion is plausible but not necessary. The disobedience of the people is already anticipated in vv. 15–17, and Jeremiah's advice and warning were given in anticipation of their response before his words were rejected as a lie (43:2).

(c) Jeremiah and the community go to Egypt (43:1–7)

1 *When Jeremiah had finished telling all the people all the words which Yahweh their God had sent him to tell them,*[1] *namely all these words,*[2]

7. The verb is supported by the infinitive absolute, *yāḏōaʿ tēḏᵉʿû.*
8. Lit. "You have caused yourselves to wander."
9. J. Bright, *Jeremiah,* pp. 252, 256; G. P. Couturier, "Jeremiah," *JBC,* p. 332.

1. LXX is slightly shorter but the omissions are not significant.
2. Presumably the words in ch. 42.

2 *Azariah ben Hoshaiah and Johanan ben Kareah and all the other arrogant men said*[3] *to Jeremiah, "You are lying! Yahweh our God did not send you to tell us not to go to Egypt to live there.*
3 *No! Baruch ben Neriah has incited you against us in order to give us into the power of the Chaldeans, so that they may kill us or deport us to Babylon!"*
4 *So Johanan ben Kareah and the military commanders and all the people did not heed the word of Yahweh to remain in the land of Judah.*
5 *But Johanan ben Kareah and the military commanders took all the remnant of Judah who had returned from all the nations to which they had been scattered to dwell in the land of Judah,*[4]
6 *the men, the women, and children, the king's daughters, every person whom Nebuzaradan the commander of the guard had left with Gedaliah ben Ahikam ben Shaphan, as well as Jeremiah the prophet and Baruch ben Neriah.*
7 *And they came to the land of Egypt, disobeying the word of Yahweh, and arrived at Tahpanhes.*

1 The section 42:19–22 indicates that Jeremiah's words had been rejected, but the formal rejection comes here in 43:1–3. The lengthy remarks of Jeremiah in 42:15–19 seem repetitious to modern ears and they have often been understood as representing an expanded version of something Jeremiah said. While this is not impossible we ought to recognize that a Middle Easterner of every age is given to prolixity and repetitiveness. Jeremiah would be no exception. Even as Jeremiah delivered his repetitive remarks he could discern from his hearers' faces what their reply would be. He had failed to dissuade them from their set purpose of going to Egypt.

2–3 Azariah and his friends, afraid to attack Yahweh and his messenger directly, aimed their attack against the less dangerous Baruch, a third party. To be sure they accused Jeremiah of uttering a falsehood (*šeqer*). In their view Yahweh had not forbidden them to go to Egypt. Here is a good example of a man who was so persuaded that his own wrong views were right that his mind was completely closed to any other possibility—an age-old phenomenon. The narrator regarded Azariah, Johanan, and their friends as arrogant and self-willed.

Baruch shows up here in an interesting light. He is pictured as a man who, in addition to being Jeremiah's scribe, had some

3. Some emend *'ōmᵉrîm*, "saying," to *hammōrîm* ("rebellious"). LXX omits *arrogant.*
4. The Qumran fragment 4QJer^b on 43:3–9 has "land of Egypt." See J. G. Janzen, *Studies in the Text of Jeremiah* (1973), pp. 182–84.

thoughts of his own and exerted an influence on Jeremiah. A study of the contacts of Baruch with Jeremiah[5] would not lead to this conclusion, but his relationship continued over a considerable period and there may well have been some discussions between them. (See comment on 36:16–19.)

4–6 The extent of the *remnant* (*s*^{e}*'ērîṯ*) is difficult to judge. There must have been many Judeans left in the land after the fall of Jerusalem in 587 B.C., many of whom did not gather at Mizpah with Gedaliah. The reference must therefore be to the particular group that had fled as far as Bethlehem, among whom were some who had taken refuge in Transjordan and had recently returned to Judah (40:11–12). It is not even possible to say that all the Judeans in the vicinity of Mizpah joined the fleeing group. In the days when the exiles returned, there were certainly Judeans living in the former Judah. No doubt the writer of this account regarded this group as the significant group because it contained proven leaders and significant people like royal princesses, as well as Jeremiah and Baruch. There seemed little hope for the poor group left behind if one thought of future renewal. As for the group that fled, these comprised rebels against Yahweh's will and would be understood by the Babylonians as rebels against themselves. Thus in no way was there any hope for the future.

It is not clear whether Jeremiah and Baruch went voluntarily with the refugees or were forced. It seems unlikely that the prophet would have gone willingly, however, for that would have been to defy Yahweh's word. On the other hand we may wonder why the refugees would force Jeremiah to go, since their own past experience of him would show them that he could only be a source of aggravation as long as he lived. If he did go willingly it was out of undying faithfulness to the people and to the message of Yahweh that he felt compelled to bring them.

7 The refugees arrived at Tahpanhes, a frontier city in the eastern Delta probably to be identified with Tell Dafneh today (cf. Daphne of 2:16).

B. IN EGYPT (43:8–45:5)

(i) Nebuchadrezzar's Invasion of Egypt Foretold (43:8–13)

8 *The word of Yahweh came to Jeremiah in Tahpanhes as follows:*

5. 32:12, 13, 16; 36:4, 5, 8, 10, 13–19, 26, 27, 32; 43:6; 45:1, 2.

9 *"Take some large stones in your hand and bury them in mortar in the pavement*[1] *at the entrance to Pharaoh's palace in Tahpanhes, in the view of some of the men of Judah.*
10 *Then say to them: 'This is what Yahweh of Hosts the God of Israel has said: See! I will send and bring Nebuchadrezzar the king of Babylon my servant, and he*[2] *will place his throne on these stones which you*[3] *have hidden and spread out his canopy*[4] *over them.*
11 *He will come and smite the land of Egypt, killing those doomed to death, taking captive those marked for deportation, and putting to the sword those marked for the sword.*[5]
12 *He will set fire to the temples of the gods of Egypt and burn them or carry them away captive. He will pick the land of Egypt clean as a shepherd picks lice from his clothing, and will then depart from there in peace.*
13 *He will break the sacred pillars of Beth-shemesh in the land of Egypt and burn the temples of the gods of Egypt in flames.' "*

8 Almost at once Jeremiah reiterated his statement of 42:15ff. that the escape to Egypt would not guarantee safety from sword, famine, and disease. Here it becomes more specific. The agent of these judgments will be the Babylonians whom the refugees feared (42:11, 12).

9 Jeremiah resorted again to a symbolic act. The act in itself was a divine word and would be fulfilled. Jeremiah must have buried the stones some distance away from the actual building; it seems unlikely that a refugee Judean would be allowed to disturb a laid-out pavement. The words that accompanied the act merely added further definition. The meaning of the act is clear enough despite some textual difficulties. The large stones were symbolic of a pedestal on which Nebuchadrezzar would set up his throne as a sign of his conquest of Egypt. The word *meleṭ* ("clay," *mortar*), which occurs only here, is of uncertain meaning. The second word *malbēn* (*pavement*?) elsewhere denotes "brick-mold" or "brick-kiln" (2 Sam. 12:31; Nah. 3:14). The two words may be variants.[6] The "house of

1. On the text and translation see the commentary below.
2. So LXX, Syr. MT reads "I will place."
3. So LXX, Syr. MT has "I have buried."
4. The meaning of *šaprîr* is uncertain; it occurs only here. Among proposals are "carpet of throne," "state tent." See KB, p. 1006.
5. The Hebrew is very staccato, "He who is for death, to death; he who is for captivity, to captivity; he who is for the sword, to the sword."
6. LXX omits the phrase, but other Greek texts (Symmachus, Theodotion, Aquila) preserve the first as *krýphios* = Heb. *ballāṭ*. The Qumran fragment on 43:3–9 has a gap at this point which could accommodate the MT material.

Pharaoh" was not the royal palace as such but must have been a governor's residence or government building used by Pharaoh on his visits to the frontier town of Tahpanhes. On the southern frontier at Elephantine there was a "king's house" according to the Aramaic papyri found there.[7]

10 Jeremiah's explanation followed his prophetic act. Yahweh would bring his *servant* (cf. 25:8–9; 27:6), who would set up his throne over the very spot where the stones were hidden and spread his *canopy* (*šap̱rîr* or *šap̱rûr*) or perhaps his "carpet" over them. The exact meaning of the noun is not known.

11 The language of this passage is stereotyped. A part of the oracle repeats 15:2.

12–13 Nebuchadrezzar's activities would involve the humiliation of the temples of Egypt and their deities. The practice was well known in the ancient Near East. In Babylonia itself Nabonidus the last king of Babylon despoiled temples and carried off the images of their gods to Babylon. The Elephantine papyri bear witness to the havoc wrought on temples by Cambyses the Persian ruler when he conquered Egypt.[8] There is a homely picture here which is well understood by those who have travelled in some parts of the Middle East. The picking[9] of lice from one's clothing is used to describe Nebuchadrezzar's plundering activities when he finally invaded Egypt. The resistance offered by Egypt would be virtually negligible, for Nebuchadrezzar would depart *in peace,* that is, unmolested. Special mention is made of the *sacred pillars* (*maṣṣēḇôṯ*) in the temple of Beth-shemesh, the "House of the Sun." The reference is to Heliopolis (Hebrew On), situated about 5 miles northeast of Cairo. The city was well known for its temple of Re the sun-god, which was approached by two rows of obelisks, only one of which still stands. LXX adds "which are in On," a gloss making the point that the reference is not to the Beth-shemesh in Palestine.

Nebuchadrezzar did invade Egypt in his thirty-seventh regnal year (567/6 B.C.).[10] A fragmentary inscription[11] suggests that Nebuchadrezzar did not intend a permanent conquest but thought to

7. A. Cowley, *Aramaic Papyri of the Fifth Century B.C.* (1923), pp. 2–6, text No. 2.
8. See *ANET* (1955), "Nabonidus' Rise to Power," p. 311a; "Cyrus Cylinder," p. 316; "Elephantine Text recording a 'petition for authorization to rebuild the temple of Yaho' in 407 B.C.," p. 491.
9. Heb. *'āṭâ,* found otherwise only at Isa. 22:17, is here rendered by *phtheiriéō* and *phtheirízō,* "delouse," in LXX.
10. This corresponds roughly to the date given in Ezek. 29:17–20.
11. *ANET,* p. 388.

deter Egypt from meddling in Asia. Although the Pharaoh Amasis (570–526 B.C.) was defeated in battle he maintained his independence and thereafter seems to have preserved friendly relations with Babylon. Jeremiah's prophecy was not fulfilled literally—a good indication that it is genuine and not made *ex post facto*—but the very fact that Nebuchadrezzar came at all was sufficient to establish his reputation as an authentic prophet of Yahweh still further.

(ii) *Jeremiah's Last Known Words (44:1–30)*

(a) *No remorse for sin and no reverence for Yahweh (44:1–14)*

1 *The word that came to Jeremiah for all the Judeans living in Egypt, those living in Migdol, in Tahpanhes, in Noph, and in the land of Pathros:*

2 *"This is what Yahweh of Hosts, the God of Israel, has said: You yourselves have seen the whole calamity that I brought upon Jerusalem and all the cities of Judah. Look at them today lying in ruins and uninhabited*

3 *because of the evil which they did, provoking me to anger by going to sacrifice and to worship*[1] *other gods whom neither they, nor you, nor your fathers knew.*[2]

4 *And though I persistently sent to you all my servants the prophets to beg you, 'Do not do this*[3] *detestable thing which I hate,'*

5 *they*[4] *did not give heed or pay attention*[5] *by turning from their wickedness and ceasing to make sacrifices to other gods.*

6 *So my anger and wrath were poured out, and blazed up in the cities of Judah and in the streets of Jerusalem so that they became a desolation and an awesome waste, as they are today.*

7 *And now, this is what Yahweh, God of Hosts, the God of Israel has said: Why are you doing yourselves this great evil by cutting off from the midst of Judah man and woman, child and babe without leaving a remnant for yourselves?*

8 *Why do you provoke me to anger by the things you do, sacrificing to other gods in the land of Egypt where you have come to dwell, so that you cut yourselves off and become an object of ridicule and a reproach among all the nations of the earth?*

1. LXX lacks the verb *worship,* lit. "serve" (Heb. *'āḇaḏ*).
2. LXX has only "which you knew."
3. Lit. "saying, 'Do not, I pray you (Heb. *'al-nā'*), do this. . . .' "
4. A change in person does not always require emendation. Jeremiah saw Israel as a unity and could in the same sentence address the people before him and refer to their forefathers.
5. Lit. "tilt their ear."

9 *Have you forgotten the wicked deeds of your fathers, and the wicked deeds of the kings of Judah and their wives,*[6] *and your own*[7] *wicked deeds and those of your wives which they committed in the land of Judah and in the streets of Jerusalem?*
10 *To this day they have not humbled themselves*[8] *and have not shown reverence. They have not lived according to the law and the statutes which I set before you and before your fathers.*
11 *Therefore this is what Yahweh of Hosts, the God of Israel, has said: Look! I have made up my mind to bring calamity upon you*[9] *and to cut off the whole people of Judah.*
12 *I will take the remnant of Judah who have made up their minds to go to the land of Egypt to live there, and they will all perish. In the land of Egypt they will fall by the sword or perish from starvation. Both small and great shall die by the sword or by starvation, and become an object of execration, of horror, of ridicule and reproach.*
13 *I will punish those who live in Egypt as I punished Jerusalem, by sword, starvation, and disease.*
14 *There will not be any who escape or survive, from the remnant of Judah which came to live in the land of Egypt, to return to the land of Judah where they long desperately*[10] *to return and live. But they will not return, except (some) refugees."*

Chapter 44 consists basically of a long, repetitive prose discourse in which Jeremiah castigates the Judeans living in Egypt for their worship of other gods and warns them of the dire consequences of their action. The practice was not new among Yahweh's people, for it had been condemned in the Temple Sermon (7:16–20). But in spite of all that had happened in fulfilment of Jeremiah's warnings of judgment in the fall of Jerusalem, the refugees from Mizpah had learned nothing. Idolatry persisted. Only now it was openly defended by those who practiced it (vv. 15–19). Jeremiah condemned the people in vehement language (vv. 11–14, 24–30) and warned them again of the dreadful fate that awaited them. But none of those who had fled to Egypt to escape the kind of thing their fellows had passed through in 587 B.C. would survive, and not one would escape.

It has often been noted that the language here is much like that in other prose passages in Jeremiah, and some commentators

6. LXX reads "your officials."
7. Lacking in LXX.
8. Lit. "they were not crushed" (Pual of *dk'*), in the sense of being crushed in spirit as in Ps. 51:19 (Eng. 17); Isa. 19:10; 57:15. The text is uncertain, however, and the versions have different readings. See *BHS ad loc.* where W. Rudolph proposes *nik̲'û*, "they were afraid"; cf. Dan. 11:30.
9. Lit. "I have set my face against you for evil."
10. Lit. "lift up their souls."

see the passage as being freely composed by a Deuteronomic editor who wished to develop still further the declaration of judgment in 43:8–13.[11] Even if some expansion took place in transmission, however, there is no reason to question the essential historicity of the incident or of Jeremiah's reply. Jeremiah's own view of the disaster of 587 B.C. was totally different from that of those to whom he spoke. In the book of Jeremiah idolatry is considered one of the reasons why Yahweh brought judgment on the nation. The theme appears in both the poetic and prose parts of the book (2:8, 23; 9:13 [Eng. 14]; 19:5; 23:13; 32:29, 35; etc.). The people, by contrast, claimed that things went badly only when they failed to propitiate the Queen of Heaven. Perhaps they had in mind the long and relatively peaceful reign of Manasseh during which non-Yahwistic cults of all kinds were freely allowed. Only after Josiah forbade these practices did troubles come. For these people Josiah's reform was a retrograde step and led to the downfall of the state.

The narrative makes it clear that any hopes that might have arisen among the "remnant" after the catastrophe of 587 B.C. were short-lived. Nor did the future hold any hope for those who by wanton disobedience and apostasy had utterly rejected Yahweh and his covenant and had therefore forfeited Yahweh's promises for renewal and restoration.

1 It seems to be implied here that other Jewish colonies were in existence in Egypt when the refugees from Mizpah arrived. Over the centuries various groups from Israel probably found their way to Egypt. As long ago as the tenth century B.C. the Egyptian army under Shishak had conducted an extensive campaign in the land (1 K. 14:25, 26; 2 Chr. 12:9–12), and although captives are not mentioned it would be normal to take some. In the days of Pharaoh Necho, King Jehoahaz was taken to Egypt and no doubt others with him (2 K. 23:31–34). Others from Judah may have gone to Egypt for other reasons over the centuries.

Jeremiah's oracle was addressed to *all the Judeans living in Egypt.* Apart from Tahpanhes, which may already have had a Jewish colony, Migdol, Memphis, and Pathros are mentioned. *Migdol* (the name means "tower") is known in the Tel el-Amarna tablets from the fourteenth century B.C. as Ma-ag-da-li. It is mentioned again in

11. E. W. Nicholson, *Jeremiah 26–52,* p. 152; W. Rudolph, *Jeremia,* p. 239 think that the original words of Jeremiah come in vv. 2, 7–8, the remainder consisting of extracts from Jeremiah's sermons on related topics. See the Introduction, "The Book of Jeremiah: Composition," pp. 33–50.

the days of Exodus (Exod. 14:2; Num. 33:7) and also in Ezekiel's time (Ezek. 29:10; 30:6). The name is Semitic, probably borrowed by the Egyptians from the Canaanites. We do not know whether all these texts refer to the same place but they probably do. The place was located in the east of the Delta region, probably in the same general area as Tahpanhes. The exact site is unknown; Tel el-Her midway between Pelusium and Sele has been suggested.[12] *Noph,* a variant form of Moph, is the Hebrew name for Memphis, the chief city of Lower (northern) Egypt. It was situated some 13 miles south of modern Cairo. *Pathros* was the name of Upper Egypt, literally "land of the south."[13] The expression *land of Pathros* suggests a region. It is now known that a sizeable Jewish community was established at Elephantine, an island on the Nile in southern Egypt, during the fifth century B.C. Important Aramaic documents left by them have provided valuable information about their society.[14] How early this colony was founded is not known, but to judge from Jer. 44:1 it was there already just after the fall of Jerusalem in 587 B.C.

It seems unlikely that Jeremiah would have addressed directly all the Jews in Egypt. The text merely states that he delivered an oracle for all the Judeans living in the land. His actual audience may have comprised only those who had traveled with him, although it is not impossible that he delivered this oracle some time after his arrival when some of the Jews already living in Egypt came to see and to hear the newcomer. What Jeremiah had to say concerned them all.

2–3 The recent arrivals from Mizpah had seen with their own eyes *the whole calamity* which had befallen Jerusalem. Jews who were already living in Egypt had heard only of the judgment on Jerusalem. That noble city and the cities of Judah were in ruins and uninhabited. For Jeremiah the reason was plain: it was because of the idolatrous practices carried on in Judah that the calamity had come. The verb translated *sacrifice* (*qiṭṭēr*) is often translated "burn incense" (AV, RV, RSV); but although it has this latter meaning sometimes, it is often used of offering up burnt offerings of the fat of animals (1 Sam. 2:16; Lev. 1:9, 17; 3:11, 16; etc.) or of meal (Amos 4:5).

12. T. O. Lambdin, "Migdol," *IDB* III, p. 377.
13. The Hebrew is an attempt to transcribe the Egyptian name *p'-t'-rsy.*
14. A. Cowley, *Aramaic Papyri of the Fifth Century B.C.* (1923).

It is clear that Jeremiah addressed his remarks to all the Jews who were then living[15] in Egypt. The phrase at the end of v. 3, *neither they, nor you, nor your fathers,* needs to be understood in the context. The audience (or those to whom the words were directed) are addressed as *you.* Jerusalem and Judah are addressed as *they,* and are charged with idolatry, but the reference must be to the inhabitants of Judah and Jerusalem who were judged in the calamity that befell the city and the land. *They* had burned incense to other gods and served them. But those gods were strange gods, forbidden gods, the gods of the nations and by no means to become the focal point of the people's allegiance and devotion. In those idolatrous intentions the Jews living in Egypt were likewise involved, and they too were in danger of divine judgment. Yahweh alone should occupy the focus of their allegiance. To know God is to give him one's total allegiance, devotion, and worship and to live out one's life in obedience to his covenant demands (22:16; cf. Hos. 4:1; 6:6).

The expression *I persistently sent* (lit. "rising early and sending") occurs several times in prose passages in Jeremiah (7:25; 25:4; 26:5; 29:19; 35:15) in reference to Yahweh's *servants the prophets.* Their mission as successors of Moses was to proclaim Yahweh's law, and to exhort and admonish Israel to obey it and to be loyal to Yahweh and his covenant. In a sense they were the guardians of the covenant. Rejection of its words was tantamount to rejection of Yahweh's word and his sovereignty. But Jeremiah's theological outlook was quite different from that of the people (vv. 17–19). It was for wanton disobedience to Yahweh's word that Jerusalem and the cities of Judah were destroyed and were now a desolate and awesome waste.

7–10 Against the background of the judgment that had befallen Jerusalem and Judah the appeal is made to these refugees to heed the lesson and turn from their idolatry. The phrase *And now* (Heb. *wᵉʿattâ*) is frequently used in the OT when a conclusion to an argument is to be drawn (Exod. 19:5; Deut. 4:1; Josh. 24:14; 1 Sam. 8:9; etc.). The danger was that persistence in idolatry would lead to the destruction (*cutting off*) of the whole community, described as *man and woman, child and babe,* so that no remnant remained. The expression "the work of your hands" may denote

15. The Hebrew verb is the present participle (*yōšᵉḇîm*) and refers to both the Jews who were resident in Egypt when Jeremiah's group arrived and the newcomers as well.

either their handiwork (in the form of idolatrous images) or *the things you do.* Such a provocation of Yahweh would only result in their being cut off (destroyed) and becoming an *object of ridicule* (*qᵉlālâ*)[16] and a *reproach* (*ḥerpâ*) among every nation on earth. It was almost meaningless for Jeremiah to ask, *Have you forgotten the wicked deeds (rāʿôṯ) of your fathers? etc.,* because neither the fathers nor the present generation acknowledged their actions as wicked. Nor would any kind of repentance or reverence for Yahweh have been envisaged in the context of their own theological outlook. Once they rejected Yahweh's sovereignty it would follow automatically that they would not live according to (lit. "walk in") the law and the statutes he had set before them. Israel's disobedience to the *law* (*tôrâ*) of Yahweh and his covenant *statutes* (*ḥuqqôṯ*) is a central theme in Jeremiah and lies at the basis of several passages (cf. 7; 11; 17:19–27; 34:8–22).[17]

11–14 The judgment upon these Judeans would be complete and final. If the people had made up their minds to go to Egypt, and also to continue their idolatry, Yahweh had made up his mind to visit them with judgment (*pāqaḏ, punish,* v. 13). The terms are strong. *Calamity* (*rāʿâ*) would befall them; Yahweh would *cut* them *off* (*hak-rîṯ*); they would all *perish* (*tāmam*); they would fall by the sword or perish from starvation, both small and great; they would become an object of execration and horror, of ridicule and reproach; not one would survive or escape from the remnant that fled from Mizpah. The stubborn determination of the people to have their own way would be met by Yahweh's determination to have his way. In the end it would be Yahweh's word that would stand, not theirs (vv. 28–29). It is not clear whether *the remnant of Judah* who were determined to live in Egypt (v. 12) included "all the Judeans who were living in Egypt" in v. 1. If it does, all the Judeans fall under the one judgment. Perhaps the point is being made again that Israel's future lay with the exiles in Babylon (cf. chs. 24, 29).

The final comment in the verse *except refugees* seems to contradict the strong language of earlier verses and may be a later gloss.

16. The noun *qᵉlālâ* is related to the adjective *qal,* "light." When someone spoke disparagingly to another person so as to "make light" of him, to downgrade him or ridicule him, the remarks were regarded almost as a curse.

The term was used by Jeremiah in combination with *ḥerpâ,* also in 42:18. It is used with *šammâ* ("horror") in 42:18 and here in vv. 12 and 22, with *ḥōreḇ* ("waste") in 49:13, and with *šᵉrēqâ* (an "object of whistling") in 25:18. All these occur in prose passages.

17. The noun *tôrâ* occurs also in 2:8; 6:19; 8:8; 18:18; *ḥoq* also in 5:22.

If a very few return to their homeland it will be so few as merely to emphasize the extent of the judgment on the community in Egypt; cf. v. 28 below.

(b) Idolatry in Egypt (44:15–19)

15 *Then all the men who knew that their wives were burning sacrifices to other gods, and all the women who stood by, a big crowd,*[1] *and all the people who were living in Egypt in Pathros,*[2] *answered Jeremiah:*
16 *"We will not listen to the word which you have spoken to us in the name of Yahweh.*
17 *But we intend to do*[3] *everything that we have undertaken; we will offer sacrifice to the Queen of Heaven and pour out libations to her as we and our fathers, our kings and our state officials,*[4] *have done in the cities of Judah and in the streets of Jerusalem; for then we had plenty of food, we were prosperous, and experienced no misfortune.*
18 *But from the time when we ceased sacrificing to the Queen of Heaven and pouring out libations to her,*[5] *we have lacked everything and we have died by the sword and by famine."*
19 *And the women added,*[6] *"We will continue to burn sacrifices to the Queen of Heaven and to pour out libations to her. Has it been without the approval of our husbands that we have made crescent cakes to represent her*[7] *and poured out libations to her?"*

15–16 The response of the people to Jeremiah's words reflects a completely different theological outlook. It was an understandable response. After Josiah's reforms in the years 621 B.C. and following, a series of disasters hit Judah beginning with the death of Josiah himself (609 B.C.). In close sequence Judah witnessed the deposition of King Jehoahaz after an Egyptian occupation, the appearance of the Babylonian armies following the defeat of Egypt at Carchemish in 605 B.C., an uneasy change in the allegiance of Jehoiakim from Pharaoh Necho to Nebuchadrezzar, the raids of 601 B.C. (2 K. 24:1),

1. LXX reads "with a great voice," i.e., "aloud," reading MT *qāhāl (qhl)* as *qôl (qwl)*.
2. The last clause *and all the people . . . in Pathros* is omitted by many commentators because it seems to be merely tacked on to a complete sentence in the Hebrew text. Such "afterthoughts" are not unknown elsewhere in the OT.
3. The verb *do* is emphasized by the infinitive absolute.
4. Heb. *śārîm*, which can also mean "princes."
5. This latter phrase is lacking in LXX.
6. The Lucianic Greek text adds this phrase because the women are now the speakers; similarly Syriac. The following participle *m^eqaṭṭ^erîm, burn sacrifices,* though grammatically masculine must be taken as feminine. If this introductory phrase is omitted, the passage should be interpreted as indicating what the people did as a whole although it was the women who performed these acts.
7. The verb *ha'^aṣîḇ* (root *'ṣb,* "to shape") means "to make an image."

the first Babylonian attack on Jerusalem in 598/7 B.C. and the deportation of Jehoiachin, the disaster of 587 B.C., and finally the assassination of Gedaliah. All of this might have been interpreted as due to the neglect by the Jews of the Queen of Heaven (vv. 17ff.). Jeremiah's counterexplanation was unacceptable.

In v. 15 there is an interesting collection of people who supported the opposite view to that of Jeremiah, namely, the Jews who knew that their wives were sacrificing to other gods, the women themselves, and the Jews from Pathros in Upper Egypt (see 44:1). If the latter part of the verse is authentic, then the reaction of these Jews in southern Egypt must have reached Jeremiah. There was, in short, an all but universal rejection of Jeremiah's words even though they were given in the name of Yahweh.

17–18 The argument is plausible. As long as the people acknowledged the Queen of Heaven there was food, prosperity, and no disaster. The *Queen of Heaven* at this period was probably the Assyrian-Babylonian goddess Ishtar, who was known by this title. This goddess is probably to be identified with Astarte (Ashtoreth), the Canaanite goddess of fertility.[8] An Egyptian text refers to the worship of Anat, a Canaanite fertility-goddess in Egypt.[9] Whatever the exact identity, the Queen of Heaven seems to have been a fertility-goddess. We have referred to the determined policy of these Jews in Egypt to adhere to their allegiance to the Queen of Heaven. Certainly the later Elephantine documents (very late 5th century) give a clear indication of syncretism. There was even a goddess Anat-Yahu worshipped there, i.e., Anat of Yahweh.[10]

Verse 18 testifies to the effectiveness of Josiah's reform, at least temporarily. Long-established and deeply rooted cultic practices such as this one would have been impossible to wipe out, and any relaxation of control would see an outbreak of the same practices. Evidently the controls had remained long enough to enable people to claim the truth of their assertion in v. 18. The collapse of the reform movement and of the movement for national independence which were active at the same time, following the death of

8. See M. J. Dahood, *Revista Biblica* 8 (1960), pp. 166–68, who identifies the goddess with Shapash.

9. See *ANET,* p. 491, last line in col. 1. However, the translation here expresses the view that the peculiar combination Anatbethel in this text may refer to a male deity. But note *ANET,* p. 250, col. 1, reference to the fact that Anath and Astarte were popular in Egypt during the 18th dynasty. See bibliography provided.

10. E. G. Kraeling, "Elephantine," *IDB* II, pp. 83–85.

Josiah at Megiddo in 609 B.C. (2 K. 23:28–30), led to disillusionment and a reversion to practices which were approved by kings and officials as well as the ordinary populace.

19 The women were the practitioners of the ritual. It was they who burnt the sacrifices and poured out the libations, and they would continue. Their husbands well knew that they were making special *crescent cakes* (*kawwān*) which were stamped with the image of the goddess.[11] Further details of this cult in 7:17–19 indicate that the whole family was involved: children gathered wood, fathers kindled the fire, and women kneaded dough to make cakes for the Queen of Heaven. The offering of grain, bread, and cakes to deities was widely known in the ancient Near East.

One of the features of the worship involved the making of vows (v. 25), and according to the law (Num. 30:7–16) women had to have their husband's consent. It was a strange syncretistic mixture.

(c) Jeremiah's final condemnation (44:20–30)

20 *Then Jeremiah spoke to all the people and against the men and the women, that is, all the people who answered him this way. He said:*
21 *"The sacrifices that you and your fathers, your kings, your state officials, and the people of the land offered in the cities of Judah and in the streets of Jerusalem, did Yahweh not remember them? It came to his notice,*[1]
22 *and he could no longer tolerate the wickedness of your behavior and the abominable things you did. Your land became a desolation, a waste, an object of horror with no inhabitants, as it is today.*
23 *It was because you offered sacrifices and sinned against Yahweh, and did not heed the word of Yahweh or live according to his law, his statutes, and his covenant stipulations that this disaster has befallen you as it has now."*[2]
24 *Then Jeremiah said to all the people and to the women: "Listen to the word of Yahweh, all you of Judah who are in the land of Egypt.*
25 *This is what Yahweh of Hosts, the God of Israel, has said: You women!*[3] *You have spoken with your mouths and with your hands you have fulfilled your promise*[4] *by saying, 'We will diligently perform the vows that we have made to offer sacrifices to the Queen of Heaven and to pour out libation offerings to her.' Go ahead and fulfil your vows, and by all means perform them.*[5]

11. Cf. Amos 5:26.

1. Lit. "It came upon his heart (mind)."
2. LXX lacks this final phrase.
3. So LXX. MT reads "You and your wives."
4. Lit. "you have fulfilled." The implied object is added in translation.
5. The verb *hēqîm,* "establish, fulfil," is made emphatic by the infinitive absolute, as is the second verb *'āśâ,* "do, perform."

26 *But hear Yahweh's word, all you of Judah who live in the land of Egypt. Believe me, I have sworn by my great name—Yahweh has spoken—that never again shall my name be invoked by the mouth of any man in the whole land of Egypt by saying 'As the Lord Yahweh lives.'*

27 *Believe me, I am watching over them to bring evil and not good; all the men of Judah who are in the land of Egypt shall perish by the sword and by famine until they are annihilated.*

28 *Such fugitives from the sword as return from the land of Egypt to the land of Judah shall be very few indeed.*[6] *Then all the remnant of Judah that came to Egypt to settle there shall know whose word stands, mine or theirs.*

29 *This shall be a sign to you—Yahweh's word—that I will punish you in this place, so that you may know that any pronouncements of evil against you will definitely stand.*

30 *This is what Yahweh has said: Look! I will hand over Pharaoh Hophra king of Egypt to his enemies and to those who seek his life, just as I handed over Zedekiah king of Judah to Nebuchadrezzar king of Babylon, his enemy who sought his life."*

20–23 It was those very sacrifices, so dear to the people, which Yahweh remembered. The whole people, high and low, were involved. Some commentators have proposed that the phrase *the people of the land* sometimes refers to the landed gentry, but here it seems to refer to the people in general.[7] It was precisely this apostasy and idolatry which brought the divine judgment on the people. A covenant people cannot play fast and loose with the covenant and the covenant stipulations without running the danger of suffering the curses of the covenant. The reference to his law, his statutes, and his covenant stipulations (*'ēḏûṯ*) takes us into the heart of covenant thinking. Breach of covenant results in judgment (curses). The argument of the people in vv. 15–19 was thus refuted.

24–28 The rest of the chapter comprises a final statement of judgment on the Judeans now resident in Egypt. In the development of the theme it is clearly the women who were being addressed (vv. 25ff.), and many scholars would delete *to all the people* in v. 24, as well as following LXX in v. 25, so that the words are addressed to the women only. It was they who had promised unreservedly to fulfil their vows to sacrifice to the Queen of Heaven. In terms reminiscent of 7:21 Yahweh declares, *Go ahead and fulfil*

6. Lit. "men of a number," i.e., able to be counted.

7. See E. W. Nicholson, "The Meaning of the Expression *'am hā'āreṣ* in the OT," *JSS* 10 (1965), pp. 59–66.

your vows, and by all means perform them. But in this case he has sworn by his own name[8] that never again will Jews in Egypt invoke his name in their oaths.[9] The reason follows. Yahweh is *watching over* (*šōqēḏ*) the people to bring evil and not good (cf. 1:12; 31:28). The end would be virtual annihilation by sword and famine. Such fugitives as returned to the land would be few. Whether indeed any were repatriated we have no information.

29–30 Finally Yahweh gave a sign (*'ôṯ*) that he intended to punish (*pāqaḏ*) the people *in this place,* that is, in Egypt. In that way the people would understand that it was Yahweh's word that would prevail and not the word of the people. The sign was that Pharaoh Hophra, named Apries (589–570 B.C.), would be handed over to his enemies. He was the pharaoh who promised support to Zedekiah in the revolt against Nebuchadrezzar in 588 B.C. and sent a military force into Judah (cf. 37:5). Jeremiah did not specify that Hophra would fall into the hands of Nebuchadrezzar but merely into the hands of his enemies; just as Zedekiah lost his life so would Pharaoh Hophra. In fact, in 570 B.C. toward the end of his reign there was a rebellion against him among some sections of the army on the occasion of a war in Libya. General Amasis was sent to quell the revolt, but Amasis was proclaimed king and reigned alongside Hophra. After three years Hophra was executed.[10] It is not known whether Jeremiah lived to see these events. As for Nebuchadrezzar, he did not appear in Egypt after these troubles in 568/7 B.C. The statement in v. 30 is very general. The proposal that ch. 44 is a free composition in the Deuteronomic style composed during the period of the exile and that this reference to Hophra's death is a "prophecy after the event,"[11] does not necessarily follow from v. 30. There is nothing in the text to indicate the nature or time of Hophra's death. The statement is couched in very general terms. Jeremiah would let the future unfold the truth. But he was persuaded in his own mind that such would be the course of events, and he could use it as a sign to warn the Jews in Egypt.

8. Men made their oaths in the name of a deity. Yahweh would swear by no other but undertook his oath in his own great name (22:5; 32:22; 44:26; 49:13; 51:14).

9. Heb. *'im* introduces a negative oath. It is part of a longer formula represented in such an oath as "The Lord do so to me and more also *if* I do such and such," i.e., I will *not* do such and such.

10. See Herodotus *Hist.* ii.161–63, 169; iv.159.

11. See E. W. Nicholson, *Jeremiah 26–52,* p. 160. We may compare such general statements as that the "foe from the north" would bring judgment on Israel, or that the Chaldeans would return to attack Jerusalem after withdrawing (37:6–10).

(iii) A Parenthesis: Baruch's Despair and Consolation (45:1–5)

1 *The word that Jeremiah the prophet spoke to Baruch ben Neriah when he wrote these words in a scroll at Jeremiah's dictation in the fourth year of Jehoiakim ben Josiah king of Judah:*
2 *"This is what Yahweh the God of Israel has said concerning you, Baruch:*
3[1] *You have said 'Woe is me, for Yahweh has added grief to my suffering. I am worn out with my sighing and find no respite.'*
4 *This is what Yahweh has said: Look! What I have built I am about to tear down, and what I have planted I am about to uproot. (And so it will be with the whole earth.)*[2]
5 *For your part, you seek great things for yourself. Seek them not. For look! I am about to bring disaster upon all flesh—Yahweh's word; but you will preserve your life wherever you may go."*

The passage is a kind of appendix that belongs with ch. 36, and is valuable for the insight it gives into Baruch's own life. He too could be beset by despair as was Jeremiah, and could say "Woe is me" (v. 3). It may be that as he dictated Jeremiah's words of judgment, and knew in his heart that they were true and would certainly come to pass, he became depressed at it all and was filled with foreboding about his own future. He was deeply involved in Jeremiah's affairs. He wrote down his oracles for the first and second scrolls in 605/4 B.C. He certainly continued to record the prophet's sayings thereafter and went with him to Egypt, where he probably continued his work as a scribe. It is not impossible that Baruch eventually returned to Judah or even journeyed to Babylon to join the exiles there, and was able to relate what took place in Egypt, although there is no evidence one way or the other. At times he was associated with Jeremiah in dangerous situations (36:19, 26; 43:3). Much of the present book of Jeremiah must go back either directly or indirectly to him.[3]

1 The occasion was the writing of *these words in a scroll* (*sēp̄er,* "book") at Jeremiah's dictation in the fourth year of Jehoiakim, i.e., 605/4 B.C. (see ch. 36).

2–3 Evidently Baruch in despair revealed his state of mind to Jeremiah, who had troubles of his own (20:7–18). Baruch declared that Yahweh had added sorrow to his suffering. He was worn out with sighing and found no respite. Only here do we have an oppor-

1. LXX adds "for," suggesting that *k* was lost by haplography.
2. This last sentence is lacking in LXX.
3. See the Introduction, "Jeremiah's First and Second Scrolls," pp. 56–59.

tunity to discover the cost to Baruch of being the scribe of a man like Jeremiah. The implications both personal and national of Jeremiah's words led to this outburst of despair.

4 Jeremiah had to remind Baruch of God's own sorrow at what was to happen. The words of Jeremiah's call in 1:10 provide a picture of Yahweh's grief. Yahweh had built (*bānâ*) something and was about to destroy it (*hāras*). He had planted (*nāṭaʿ*) and was about to uproot it (*nāṯaš*). The reference is presumably to his planting and building of Israel in the land of promise (1:10; 2:21; 31:5; etc.). Had they obeyed the covenant, they might have become a very great nation, but all those hopes lay in ruins. That was Yahweh's great sorrow. The judgment would touch the whole earth.[4] But such a calamity was inevitable in the light of Israel's willful disobedience and apostasy. She was intended to fulfil a noble calling as Yahweh's elect covenant people. She was planted a choice vine. She had degenerated and become a wild vine (2:21).

5 In the judgment that would befall Israel Baruch would be spared. Yahweh would "give him his life as booty." The expression occurs in 21:9 (see note *in loc.*); 38:2; 39:18; the figure is of a soldier barely escaping with his life after a defeat in battle. Such a promise would relieve any concern Baruch might have about his life when Yahweh brought *disaster* (*rāʿâ*) upon all flesh. But there was another side to Baruch's despair. He had sought *great things* for himself. Baruch was an educated man, qualified as a secretary, whose brother (51:59) was an officer of high rank under Zedekiah. He may have entertained hopes of some distinction in the nation. But whatever "great things" he sought for himself were forfeited by his loyal support of Jeremiah. Now, in the hour of disaster, all that mattered was his own life. Ironically, the very suffering through which Baruch passed because of his loyalty to Jeremiah gained him honor beyond anything he could have anticipated.

The narrative is chronologically out of order, but this may have arisen because ch. 44 contained some severe threats against the Jews in Egypt, among whom was Baruch (43:35). In order to avoid any misunderstanding about Baruch the editor took this promise to Baruch from its original position and inserted it after ch. 44 to show that he was exempted from those threats.[5]

4. So MT but not LXX. The argument really turns on the uprooting and destruction of Israel. She would, of course, be caught up in a much wider conflagration.
5. O. Eissfeldt, *The OT: An Introduction* (E.T. 1965), p. 354.

VII. ORACLES AGAINST THE NATIONS (46:1–51:64)

(i) Egypt (46:1–28)

(a) The defeat of Egypt at Carchemish (46:1–12)

1 *The word of Yahweh that came to Jeremiah the prophet concerning the nations.*
2 *About Egypt:*
Concerning the army of Pharaoh Necho, king of Egypt, which was at Carchemish on the river Euphrates when Nebuchadrezzar king of Babylon defeated (it) in the fourth year of Jehoiakim ben Josiah king of Judah.
3 *"Make ready shield and buckler!*
Advance to battle!
4 *Harness the horses!*
Riders mount!
Stand ready, your helmets on, your lances burnished!
Put on your coats of mail!
5 *But what do I see?*
They are terrified;
They turn back.
Their warriors are panic-stricken;
They turn to flight;
They do not look backward.
Everywhere panic—Yahweh's word.
6 *Let not the swift run away,*
Let not the warrior escape!
In the north, by the river Euphrates,
They stumble and fall.
7 *Who is this that rises like the Nile,*
Like streams whose waters surge?
8 *It is Egypt that rises like the Nile,*
Like streams whose waters surge.

He says: I will rise and cover the earth,
I will destroy both its cities and its peoples.[1]
9 *Charge, you horses! Roll on, you chariots!*
Forward, you warriors!
Men of Cush and of Put carrying shields,[2]
Lydians grasping their bows.[3]
10 *That day belongs to the Lord, Yahweh of Hosts;*[4]
A day of vengeance, to be avenged of his foes.
The sword shall devour and be sated,
And drink its fill of their blood,
For the Lord Yahweh of Hosts holds a feast
In the northern land, by the river Euphrates.
11 *Go up to Gilead and bring back balm,*
O virgin daughter Egypt!
In vain do you multiply remedies;
There is no healing for you.
12 *The nations have heard your cry,*[5]
The earth is filled with your screams,
When warrior stumbled against warrior
And both have fallen together."

Chapters 46–51 consist entirely of oracles addressed to the nations. They form a distinct unit in the book of Jeremiah.[6] In LXX these chapters come after the title in 25:13a and conclude with 25:15–38 (= LXX ch. 32). This suggests that the block of oracles circulated for a time as an independent unit which was woven into the whole book in different ways. In the other major prophets, Isaiah and Ezekiel, the oracles against the nations are inserted between oracles directed against Israel and oracles dealing with Israel's restoration. The order here is different in Hebrew and Greek. The Hebrew text follows a geographical pattern moving from west to east, while LXX appears to arrange the nations in order of political importance.

The authenticity of the material in this section has been de-

1. The nouns are sing. but may be collectives. LXX omits *cities.*
2. Lit. "Cush and Put, bearers of a shield."
3. The three words describing the Lydians present some problems. MT reads *tōpᵉśê dōrᵉḵê qāšeṯ,* lit. "handlers of, benders of, a bow." The first word occurs in the preceding line and may be merely redundant. J. Bright, *Jeremiah,* p. 302, translates "good shots with the bow," which is a dynamic equivalent if not an exact translation.
4. LXX is shorter, "that day (belongs) to the Lord our God."
5. MT has *qᵉlônēḵ,* "your shame," which does not suit the parallelism; read *qôlēḵ* with LXX. It may be too that there was a noun *qālôn,* a development of *qôl,* "voice," "cry," since endings in *n* are common. In late medieval and modern Hebrew *qôlān* denotes a "crier," "one who makes a loud noise."
6. See the Introduction, "The Book of Jeremiah: Structure," pp. 27–32.

bated at length. Nineteenth- and early twentieth-century critical scholars were prepared to reject much of it and place it considerably later than Jeremiah. Such a position is no longer possible with the discovery of a good deal of historical evidence about the late seventh and sixth centuries B.C. Each oracle has to be considered separately. It would be strange, in any case, if Jeremiah had remained silent about the nations. There is no good reason for not accepting many of the utterances as coming from Jeremiah himself. At the same time there may be sayings of anonymous origin which were preserved by those who collected Jeremiah's words. Even so there seems little reason to date any of the material later than the couple of decades after the fall of Jerusalem in 587 B.C.

Prophecies against the nations were one aspect of the prophetic ministry. Isaiah, Jeremiah, Ezekiel, Amos, Nahum, and Obadiah all have considerable sections devoted to the theme, while other prophets generally mention the nations. Such prophecies indicate Israel's view that Yahweh was not merely the God of Israel but was Lord over all the nations of the world, whose destiny lay in God's hands. The theme is important in the overall theology of the OT.

Chapter 46 is devoted entirely to Egypt apart from vv. 27–28 which refer to the future restoration of Israel. There are two reasonably long poems, the first (vv. 3–12) dealing with the defeat of the Egyptian forces at Carchemish, and the second (vv. 14–24) depicting the Egyptian terror at the approach of Nebuchadrezzar. Two short fragments, vv. 25–26 and 27–28, close the chapter.

All commentators agree that the poem in vv. 3–12 was composed by Jeremiah. The poem in vv. 13–24 has been much disputed but many commentators accept it as coming from Jeremiah without question. The two fragments have also been questioned but may be attributed to Jeremiah without much difficulty.

1 The verse stands as a superscription to the entire collection (chs. 46–51). The formula is unusual but occurs also at 14:1; 47:1; and 49:34.

2 The specific title is brief—*About Egypt.* The year is given as *the fourth year of Jehoiakim ben Josiah,* i.e., 605 B.C. The background is the defeat of Pharaoh Necho at *Carchemish on the river Euphrates* (Heb. *p*^{e}*rāṯ*) at the hands of Nebuchadrezzar. During most of the second millennium Egypt controlled the area of Syria-Palestine, but she lost undisputed control after the collapse of the Nineteenth Dynasty (c. 1200 B.C.) and never regained it, although she made an incursion into the area under Pharaoh Shishak (1 K. 14:25–26) just before 900 B.C., and was involved in intrigues and even launched attacks in the days of the Assyrians, Babylonians, and Persians who controlled the area in turn. In 609 B.C. Pharaoh Necho II (610–594 B.C.), who had succeeded his father Psammetichus, marched north to assist the Assyrians, now in their last throes, to recapture Haran. The assault on Haran failed, but Necho remained in the area with a center at Carchemish (the modern Jerablus in the upper Euphrates). When the Babylonian armies were ready, however, they launched an all-out attack on Carchemish and sent the Egyptian forces fleeing headlong. The words of the poem vv. 3–12 were composed either just before or just after Nebuchadrezzar had humiliated the Egyptians.

3–4 The poem commences at v. 3. The poetry is among the most vivid in all the OT and is certainly unsurpassed in the book of Jeremiah. It is reminiscent of Nah. 3:1ff. It depicts the Egyptian armies preparing for battle. We hear the commands of the Egyptian officers in sharp staccato terms. In v. 3 the infantry is given its instructions: "Ready—bucklers and shields! Forward! Close combat!"[7] In v. 4 the charioteers make ready and at the same time the infantry put on their armor and sharpen their weapons. "Harness—horses! Riders—mount! Fall in—with helmets! Whet—lances! On—full armor!"[8] The weapons are well known. The *shield* (*ṣinnâ*) was heavier and longer than the *buckler* (*māḡēn*); cf. 1 K. 10:16–17. Helmets, lances, and body armor have been found in excavations. Chariots and war horses are depicted on bas-reliefs.

5–6 A sudden change comes over the battlefield, dramatically introduced by the question *What do I see?* Terrified troops breaking ranks and turning to flight, a scene of demoralization. But every way of escape is cut off. It is a striking scene of warriors fleeing in disarray and confusion. The phrase *they stumble and fall* is picked up in v. 12, "warrior stumbled against warrior." The expression *everywhere panic (māḡôr missāḇîḇ)* appears in 6:25 concerning the "foe from the north," in 20:3 as a name for Pashhur, Jeremiah's persecutor, in 20:10 of those who plot against Jeremiah, and in Ps. 31:13 of the psalmist's enemies. It was well known and probably a proverbial curse formula.

7–8 The resurgence of Egypt under Pharaoh Necho and her

7. So J. Bright, *Jeremiah,* p. 301. In the poem the stress pattern is 3:2.
8. *Ibid.* The stress pattern is 2:2; 2:2; 2:2.

reappearance in strength in the Syria-Palestine area is likened to the Nile in flood. Like Egypt of old, the resurgent Egypt fancies herself as covering the earth and destroying cities and people. The Nile during the summer begins to rise slowly but eventually bursts its banks and becomes a rushing torrent, its waters spreading out over the surrounding land. So will Egypt *rise and cover the earth* (cf. Isa. 8:7–8 where the same metaphor is used of Assyria).

9 The scene changes to the mercenary troops in the service of the pharaoh. Still the staccato orders come. Whether this represents a second wave of troops or is simply a further glimpse of the Egyptian army is not clear. Horsemen, chariots, and warriors are involved. *Cush* was Ethiopia in the region of the Nile south of Egypt proper. The identification of *Put* is disputed. It was probably the *Punt* of Egyptian literature and lay along the east coast of Africa in the region of modern Somaliland. Alternately it was part of Libya.[9] *Lud* is variously understood. Some regard Lud as Lydia in Asia Minor referred to in Isa. 66:19 along with Javan (Greece) and the coastal islands. In that passage Lydians are associated with the Egyptian army. Psammetichus I (663–609 B.C.) was given help by Gyges king of Lydia to resist Ashurbanipal's domination. From that time Greek influence on Egypt was significant.[10] Alternately Lud refers to a land in North Africa (cf. Gen. 10:13). Another proposal is to read "Libyans"[11] as in Nah. 3:9, where Put and the Libyans are allied with Cush and Egypt in a losing cause.

10 The motif of *vengeance* (*n*ᵉ*qāmâ*) is introduced. The reason for the vengeance is not given, but Jeremiah was grieved over the death of Josiah at the hands of Necho in 609 B.C. (2 K. 23:29, 30) and the defeat of Necho enabled Yahweh to be avenged for the death of his servant. The picture of a wild beast devouring people and drinking his fill of blood is a common symbol for the sword in the OT.[12] The defeat of the Egyptians is seen as a sacrificial *feast* (*zeḇaḥ*) which Yahweh holds (cf. Isa. 34:5–7; Zeph. 1:7).

11–12 Egypt seeks healing ointments for her wounds. Gilead was a place where men might find *balm* (*ṣ*ᵒ*rî;* cf. 8:22; 46:11; 51:8; cf. Gen. 37:25). The association of balm with Gilead may be linked to the fact that caravans from the east bearing supplies of

9. See T. O. Lambdin, "Put," *IDB* III, p. 971.
10. E. Drioton, J. Vandier, *L'Égypte* (²1952), pp. 575–584.
11. Emending *lûḏîm* to *lûḇîm*.
12. Deut. 32:42; note *l*ᵉ*pî ḥereḇ,* "to the mouth of the sword," in Num. 21:24; Josh. 11:10; 1 Sam. 15:8; "a sword with two mouths," Judg. 3:16; etc.

balm passed through Gilead. The identity of the plant which produced the aromatic resin known as balm is not certain.[13] The name *virgin daughter Egypt* is reminiscent of "virgin Israel" (18:13; 31:4, 21) or "virgin daughter of my people" (14:17). For her present hurt there was no remedy (**rᵉpû'â*), and *no healing* for her wounds.[14] Her piteous cry and her screams were heard among the nations.

(b) Nebuchadrezzar's conquest of Egypt (46:13–24)

13 *The word which Yahweh spoke to Jeremiah the prophet when Nebuchadrezzar king of Babylon was coming to attack the land of Egypt:*

14 *"Announce it in Egypt, proclaim it in Migdol,*
Declare it in Noph and Tahpanhes.
Say: 'Stand ready! Be prepared!
For the sword shall devour round about you.'
15 *Why has Apis fled?*[1]
Your bull did not stand his ground
Because Yahweh has driven him away.
16 *Your multitude stumbled and fell.*[2]
Each man said to his fellow,
'Up! Let us return to our people,
To the land of our birth,
Away from the sword of the oppressor.'
17 *Give Pharaoh king of Egypt a name:*[3]
'A big noise, who let the appointed time pass by.'
18 *As I live—the word of the King,*
Yahweh of Hosts is his name—
He will come like Tabor among the mountains,
Like Carmel by the sea.
19 *Make ready your baggage for exile,*
You inhabitants of Egypt,[4]
For Noph shall become a waste,
Ruined and uninhabited.

13. Herodotus *Hist.* ii.84 refers to the widespread practice of medicine in Gilead.
14. The noun *tᵉ'ālâ,* related to the verb *'ālâ,* "to come up," is used of the fresh skin that grows over a wound when it heals. The same combination of nouns occurs also in 30:13.

1. MT reads "Why was he swept away (*nisḥap*)?" But if the word is divided into *ns ḥp* and vocalized *nās ḥap̱* we can read, "Why did Haf flee?" Haf is Apis. In this way we match LXX.
2. The text is difficult. MT reads lit. "He increased, one stumbling, also a man fell on his fellow and they said. . . ." LXX reads "your multitude" (*rubbᵉḵâ,* or *'erbᵉḵâ,* "your mixed multitude," 25:20) for "he increased" (*hirbâ*). Also *kšl* may be vocalized as *kāšal*, "he stumbled," instead of *kôšēl*, "stumbling."
3. MT reads "They cried there, 'Pharaoh is . . .' " (*qārᵉ'û šām*). LXX suggests *qirᵉ'û šēm,* "Call a name."
4. Lit. "Inhabitress, daughter of Egypt." The expression is feminine, which is common to denote the inhabitants of a land. It must have a collective sense here.

20 *A beautiful[5] heifer is Egypt,*
But a gadfly from the north has come upon her.[6]
21 *The mercenaries, too, in her midst*
Were like fatted calves,
But they too turned and fled;
Not one stood his ground;
For the day of their calamity has come upon them,
The time of their reckoning.
22 *Her cry is like a snake gliding away,[7]*
For they have come in strength,
And with their axes they fall upon her
Like men cutting down trees.
23 *They cut down her forest—Yahweh's word—*
Since it cannot be searched.[8]
They are more numerous than locusts,
Beyond counting.
24 *Shamed is the Daughter of Egypt;*
She is delivered into the power of a northern people."

13 After Carchemish, Nebuchadrezzar advanced toward Egypt. The prophet now summoned Egypt to prepare for imminent disaster in a poem which is as vivid in its staccato phrases as the first poem. There is no reason to deny it to Jeremiah. There must have been an interval between the two poems. In August 605 B.C. Nabopolassar the father of Nebuchadrezzar died and his son hurried back to Babylon to take the throne. However, the Babylonian advance on Egypt was soon resumed and by the end of 604 B.C. the Babylonian army captured and sacked Ashkelon (47:2–9). With Nebuchadrezzar's forces pressing on toward Egypt, Jeremiah composed the oracle of vv. 14–24.

14–16 For details about Migdol, Noph, and Tahpanhes see 2:16; 44:1. Egypt is commanded to stand to and make ready before the devouring sword (cf. v. 10). But she was forsaken by her god Apis (Heb. *hap̱*), who fled. The parallelism of the verse sets Apis

5. Many mss. combine the uncertain *yᵉp̄ēh-piyyâ* into one word, *yᵉp̄êhp̱iyyâ*, "beautiful."

6. MT *bā' ḇā'*, "has come, has come," is read as *bā' ḇāh,* "has come on her," with many Gk. and Syr. mss.

7. MT reads "Her sound is like a snake as it goes (*yēlēḵ*)." The verb is very close to the last verb in the line *yēlēḵû* and dittography seems possible. LXX reads "hissing" (*šôrēq*). Although this emendation is widely accepted, the text as it stands is clear.

8. Heb. *yēḥāqēr.* Modern translators propose such renderings as "it is impenetrable" (RSV; Bright), "it flaunts itself no more" (NEB).

alongside *'abbîr,* young *bull*[9] (champion). Apis was the sacred bull revered as the incarnation of the god Ptah and worshipped in Noph (Memphis) from early times. The bull was a symbol for fertility deities all over the ancient Near East (cf. Hos. 8:5–6). In later times Apis became associated with Osiris the god of vegetation and regeneration. The priests of the cult of Apis had the care of a special live bull as the representative of the god. These bulls were buried in a special mortuary at death, each bull in its own huge sarcophagus.

Under the threat of invasion the mixed multitude of mercenaries and Egyptian troops fled headlong.

17 Pharaoh Hophra (Apries), who boasted greatly of what he would do but in the critical hour was unable to carry it out, is branded with an uncomplimentary name which was probably a pun on his own name; the Hebrew verb *he'ᵉḇîr*, "let pass," is similar to the Egyptian name Apries, *w'ḥ-ib-r'*. It is not easy for us today to appreciate the pun, although the device was common enough then (cf. 20:3). It is not entirely clear whether Jeremiah had in mind the recent success of Pharaoh Hophra in the Palestine-Syria area, or whether he may have had in mind the promise made to help Zedekiah during the final siege of Jerusalem (37:5–6). Perhaps both events were representative of numerous braggart actions. Hophra was a big noise who seemed adept at missing the appointed time.

18 The real king speaks, Yahweh of Hosts. The title *King* is applied to Yahweh in a number of places in the OT and is implied in many other passages.[10] The word of the true King is that Nebuchadrezzar will come. His irresistible might is likened to two striking landmarks in the land of Israel. The first is Tabor, which rises some 1800 feet as an isolated mountain in the plain of Jezreel in northern Israel. It creates the impression of considerable height with its steep slopes and is certainly a striking landmark over a wide area. The second is Mount Carmel by the sea, which rises at its maximum height to some 1700 feet and at its western edge falls away sharply to the Mediterranean Sea. It was the scene of Elijah's contest with the prophets of Baal (1 K. 18:19–40). Both seemed to Jeremiah to depict Nebuchadrezzar, who towered over Egypt in his might like lofty mountains towering over a plain.

9. The word is plural in the text, perhaps the plural of majesty.
10. 8:19; 10:7, 10: 48:15; 51:57; Num. 23:21; Deut. 33:5; Isa. 6:5; 33:22; 41:21; 44:6; Zeph. 3:15; Zech. 14:9; Mal. 1:14; Ps. 5:2; 10:16; 24:7–10; 29:10; 44:4; 47:2; 68:24; 74:12; etc.

19 Jeremiah, so recently reminded of the outcome of a Babylonian invasion which sent his own people with their baggage to exile in Babylonia, advised the Egyptians to prepare for such an eventuality. Egypt is addressed as "Inhabitress, Daughter of Egypt." The phrase is reminiscent of a similar phrase applied to Judah's citizens, "My daughter—my people" (4:11; 6:26; 8:11, 19, 21–33; 14:17). Another vivid memory for Jeremiah was a devastated, depopulated Jerusalem, the capital of Judah. Noph (Memphis), the capital of Egypt, would become a *waste* (*šammâ*), an uninhabited ruin.[11]

20 A metaphor well known in agricultural communities is used, that of the large fly which buzzes loudly and stings cattle, leaving a wound. Egypt is pictured as a young, healthy heifer (feminine, for a land) attacked by this fly from the north. The metaphor of a young heifer may be a passing ironical reflection on the fact that one of Egypt's deities was Apis the sacred bull.

21 The *mercenaries* (lit. "hired ones") in her midst were evidently well cared for (*fatted calves*) but useless in the hour of danger. Jeremiah may have had another agricultural picture in mind, that of calves fattened for killing.

22–24 A third picture is drawn from rural life, that of a snake driven from its hiding place by woodcutters and unable to do more than hiss at them. The snake hides in the forest, and since the woodcutters cannot search the forest to find it, they cut the forest down. The metaphor is an apt one since the snake was important in Egyptian religion and featured on royal insignia. The invading force is pictured as a horde of locusts. Jeremiah often made use of rural and agricultural imagery. It was very much part of the daily life of the people of Judah of his day.

Finally Egypt is brought to shame. The reference is possibly to her exposure as she was delivered into the hands of a people from the north. It was an exposure that Jeremiah had witnessed when Jerusalem fell and the girls and women became objects to satisfy the lust of the Babylonian troops. He makes a point of this possibility in language similar to what he had used to warn his own people long before the collapse of Judah and Jerusalem (6:12; 38:23; etc.). The exposure was complete and involved the carrying off by the invaders of people and goods alike (2 K. 24:12–16; 25:13–21).

11. The noun *niṣṣᵉṯâ* is used of Jerusalem in 9:11 (Eng. 12) and the verb in 2:15 of the cities of Judah and its pasture lands.

(c) *Two fragments: Egypt humiliated; Israel delivered (46:25–28)*

25 *Yahweh of Hosts the God of Israel has said:*
"Look! I will punish Amon of No,[1]
Egypt and its gods and kings,
Pharaoh and those who trust in him.
26 *I will deliver them into the power of those who seek their lives,*
Into the power of Nebuchadrezzar king of Babylon and his officers;
Afterward they shall dwell as in former times—Yahweh's word."

27 *"As for you, fear not, Jacob my servant,*
Be not dismayed, O Israel.
For see! from afar I will save you,
Your offspring from the land of captivity,
And Jacob will find rest once more,
Secure with none to disturb.
28 *And so you, my servant Jacob, fear not—Yahweh's word—*
For I am with you.[2]
I will make an end of all the nations
Among whom I scattered you,
But I will not make an end of you;
I will punish you as you deserve;
By no means will I exempt you."

25–26 This fragment is regarded as prose by some translators[3] but it is almost poetic and is printed as poetry in NEB. If it is taken as verse it follows a different stress pattern from the earlier poems. In any case it may be regarded as a separate unit which represents Jeremiah's final oracle against Egypt.

Amon was the chief deity of *No* (Thebes), the capital of Upper Egypt. Amon was later merged with Re to become Amon-Re, the king of the gods and peculiarly the god of the rulers of Egypt. The reference to Thebes shifts the scene from Memphis in the north to Thebes in the south, thus pushing the conquest of Nebuchadrezzar well to the south. There is no historical evidence of this. But the text suggests that Yahweh was punishing rather than destroying Egypt, so that later she could continue as in the past. This promise of restoration is repeated for other nations (48:47; 49:6, 39).

1. MT inserts "Pharaoh" after *No,* but the name occurs again so that one of the occurrences is redundant. LXX omits *Egypt and its gods and kings, Pharaoh.* We omit the first "Pharaoh" (cf. NEB).
2. Cf. 30:11 where "to deliver you" is added.
3. RSV; J. Bright, *Jeremiah,* pp. 304f.

Verse 26 is lacking in LXX and is regarded by some commentators as a later gloss.[4]

27–28 These verses occur with minor differences in 30:10–11. See commentary *ad loc.* An earlier saying of Jeremiah was used again by the editor to set the future of Israel alongside the promise of Egypt's eventual restoration. LXX omits these verses from ch. 30, which according to the LXX order would be their second occurrence. But the proper and original context of these verses is ch. 30.

(ii) The Philistines (47:1–7)

1 *What came as the word of Yahweh to Jeremiah the prophet concerning the Philistines, before Pharaoh attacked Gaza.*
2 *"This is what Yahweh has said:*
Look! waters are rising from the north
And becoming like a river in flood;
They will flood the land and all that is in it,
Cities and their citizens.[1]
Men will cry out,
And all who dwell in the land will howl
3 *At the noise of the stamping of the hooves of his chargers,*
The din of his chariots and the rumbling of their wheels.
Fathers turn not back for their children
Because of enfeebled hands,
4 *Because the day has come to destroy all the Philistines,*
To cut off from Tyre and Sidon all surviving help;[2]
For Yahweh will destroy the Philistines,
The remnant of the isle of Caphtor.
5 *Baldness has come to Gaza,*
Ashkelon is struck dumb.
Remnant of their strength,[3]
How long will you gash yourself?
6 *Ah, sword of Yahweh,*
How long before you desist?[4]
Return to your scabbard,
Rest and be quiet.
7 *How can it rest*
When Yahweh has given it orders?
Against Ashkelon and the seacoast
He has given it an appointment."

4. G. P. Couturier, "Jeremiah," *JBC, ad loc.*

1. Lit. "City and those who dwell in her," here understood collectively.
2. Lit. "every survivor, helper."
3. MT "their valley"; LXX "the Anakim"; see commentary below.
4. Lit. "Until when will you not be quiet (rest)?"

The chapter is written in verse in a vivid style similar to that found in ch. 46. There is no reason to deny it to Jeremiah. It is difficult, however, to be certain about its historical setting. In LXX (ch. 29), v. 1 reads simply "Concerning the Philistines," so that the comment about Pharaoh and Gaza may be treated separately. The rest of the chapter seems clearly to point to the Babylonians "from the north" and can probably be linked to the events following the defeat of the Egyptians at Carchemish in 605 B.C. Jeremiah's prophecy could well have been given after the battle of Carchemish when the prophet became convinced that the Babylonians would move through to the conquest both of Judah and the surrounding nations.

The reference to Gaza in MT v. 1 may refer to a quite separate incident, as for example an attack on Gaza by Egypt in late 601 B.C. after Necho had met Nebuchadrezzar in a pitched battle and mauled him badly, so that he had to retire to Babylonia to reequip his army. During that interval Necho may have attacked and captured Gaza. But our records are inadequate and we cannot be entirely certain.[5]

1 For the introductory formula see 14:1; 46:1; 49:34. The verse is a chronological notation giving the date of the oracle that follows in vv. 2–7. It seems to indicate that the main oracle was delivered before the pharaoh attacked Gaza. Although LXX omits most of this verse and reads only "concerning the Philistines," the rest need not for that reason be regarded as an erroneous interpolation. No doubt it was an editorial expansion, but it may be taken as factually correct. Our problem today is to identify the occasion when the pharaoh captured Gaza. We have argued that it was associated with Pharaoh Necho's battle with Nebuchadrezzar in 601 B.C., referred to in the Babylonian Chronicle.

To be sure, there are other proposals. One is that the Egyptian attack on Gaza is to be linked with the campaign of Pharaoh Necho in 609 B.C. as he moved north to defeat and slay Josiah at Megiddo (2 K. 23:29, 30) and then went on to assist Assyria at Haran. Some support for this view comes from Herodotus,[6] who states that Necho conquered the city of Kadytis (identified with Gaza) after his defeat of Josiah in 609 B.C. In that case Jeremiah must have prophesied that all this would be reversed as the Baby-

5. D. J. Wiseman, *Chronicles of Chaldaean Kings (626–556 B.C.)*, pp. 23ff., 67ff. See further the commentary below.
6. *Hist.* ii.159.

lonian armies would presently move south.[7] But in that case the attack on Gaza was before the events of 605/4 B.C.

The matter is finally not certain. If the main oracle is to be dated to the period following 605 B.C., then the attack on Gaza must be dated post-605 B.C. if the chronological note in v. 1 is to be taken seriously.

2 The reference to waters rising in the north is clearly to the Babylonians, a metaphor used by Isaiah of the Assyrians (Isa. 8:7–8). The comparison with the Nile was probably not far from Jeremiah's mind, but there was the difference that the annual Nile flood brought fresh supplies of alluvium and water to the land after the dry summer whereas the Babylonian flood would make the Philistines cry out and howl.

3 The language is vivid and staccato, conveying the impression of an army advancing with all speed to the attack, horses' hooves pounding and chariot wheels rumbling. Terror strikes deep and men flee, forsaking even their children, and powerless to fight "from the weakness of their hands." This verse has a counterpart in v. 5a, which describes the effects of the attack of the enemy from the north.

4 Philistines and Phoenicians are associated here. Whether or not there was an alliance between the two, the story of the past showed that the great powers all attacked the persistently rebellious (cf. 27:3) Phoenician seaport towns first of all before descending on Philistia.[8] With Tyre and Sidon destroyed to the last defender, the despoiling of Philistia normally followed. Jeremiah described the Philistines as *the remnant of the isle of Caphtor.* According to Amos 9:7 Caphtor was their original home. It is usually identified with Crete but may denote more generally Crete and the Aegean isles from which the Philistines and other groups of sea peoples came in the twelfth and eleventh centuries B.C. They were halted at the frontier of Egypt by Ramses III in about 1188 B.C., but many of them settled along the coastal plains of Palestine.

5 As the oracle developed, Jeremiah saw the ruin of Gaza and Ashkelon. Three of the common signs of mourning were shaving the head, silence, and inflicting gashes on oneself (cf. 16:6; 41:5). These two towns were seen as the last remnants of the strength of

7. For a variation of this view see A. Malamat, "The Historical Setting of Two Biblical Prophecies on the Nations," *IEJ* 1 (1950/51), pp. 154–59.

8. Sennacherib in his first campaign did precisely this. See *ANET,* pp. 287–88.

the Philistines. The Hebrew noun *'ēmeq,* if translated "valley" as normally, gives a very strange expression "remnant of their valley." It is probably to be connected with Ugaritic *'mq* meaning *strength.*[9] The LXX reading "Anakim" seeks to link the people of Gaza and Ashkelon with the race of giants that inhabited Canaan before the arrival of the Israelites (Num. 13:22–23; Deut. 1:28). According to Josh. 11:22 remnants of these were to be found in Gaza, Gath, and Ashdod.[10] The first of these proposals seems to be more acceptable.

The proposal that the name Ashdod has dropped out of the list is plausible. An expression "O Ashdod, last of their strength" would suit the context (cf. Zeph. 2:4). Haplography seems a possibility since Ashkelon and Ashdod both commence with the consonants *'š.* However, textual evidence is completely lacking.

6–7 Any attempt to restrain the sword of Yahweh till its work is finished is futile, for it was commissioned against Ashkelon and the seacoast. In fact, the prophecy was fulfilled in 604/3 B.C. when Nebuchadrezzar appeared on the coastal plain and overran Ashkelon after a siege.[11] A letter found at Saqqara (Memphis) and written in Aramaic by Adon king of Ashkelon to the pharaoh advises that Babylonian troops had advanced to Aphek. Adon besought help from Pharaoh Necho.[12] Receipts discovered at Babylon refer to sons of the king, seamen, and others from Ashkelon. Other receipts in the same batch refer to Yaukin (Jehoiachin) of Judah and his sons.[13] At some undefined period, therefore, captives were taken from Ashkelon. At Ashdod, not far away, excavations have revealed a layer of destruction at the end of the seventh century and may point to the same campaign.[14]

As we have seen (comments on ch. 36), it was the sacking of Ashkelon that caused King Jehoiakim to proclaim a fast in Jerusalem. The fast provided the opportunity for Baruch to read Jeremiah's scroll.

9. G. R. Driver, "Difficult Words in the Hebrew Prophets," *Studies in OT Prophecy* (ed. H. H. Rowley), p. 61; C. H. Gordon, *Ugaritic Textbook* (1965), Glossary, p. 457, No. 1873.

10. The LXX reading is accepted in RSV and by G. P. Couturier, "Jeremiah," *JBC,* p. 334.

11. D. J. Wiseman, *Chronicles of Chaldaean Kings*, p. 69.

12. J. Bright, "A New Letter in Aramaic Written to a Pharaoh of Egypt," *BA* 12 (1949), pp. 46–52; H. L. Ginsberg, "An Aramaic Contemporary of the Lachish Letters," *BASOR* 111 (1948), pp. 24–27.

13. *ANET,* p. 308.

14. D. N. Freedman, "The Second Season at Ancient Ashdod," *BA* 26 (1963), pp. 134–39, note p. 139.

(iii) Moab (48:1–47)

(a) The destruction of Moab (48:1–10)

1 *Concerning Moab:*
This is what Yahweh of Hosts the God of Israel has said:
"Alas for Nebo! She is laid waste;
Kiriathaim is put to shame[1] *and captured;*
The fortress[2] *is reduced to shame and shattered.*
2 *The glory of Moab is gone;*
In Heshbon they plotted evil against her:
'Come! let us cut her off from being a nation.'
With a loud voice shall Madmen weep;[3]
The sword will pursue you.
3 *Hark! a cry from Horonaim:*
'Desolation! Great destruction!
4 *Moab is broken!'*
Their cry is heard as far as Zoar![4]
5 *Along the road up to Luhith*
With weeping they ascend it.[5]
On the way down from Horonaim
Men hear the cry of destruction:[6]
6 *Flee! Escape for your lives!*
You will be like a wild desert ass[7]

1. The verb "shamed" is lacking in LXX and may be a dittography of the same word in the next line.
2. NEB takes *miśgāḇ* as a place name, "Misgab"; but no such place is known and most translations understand it as *fortress,* that is, the fortress of Kiriathaim.
3. Following M. Dahood, "Ugaritic Studies and the Bible," *Gregorianum* 43 (1962), pp. 55–79, note p. 70: Ugar. *gm* means "in a loud voice"; Heb. *gam* here may well mean the same. Cf. A. Kischke in *Verbannung und Heimkehr. Festschrift W. Rudolph* (1961), p. 185. See further the commentary below. For *dmm* II, "wail," see Isa. 23:3; Lam. 2:10.
4. MT reads "Her little ones (Qere: *ṣᵉʿîreyhā*) make a cry heard," which is followed by GNB, "Listen to the children crying." LXX reads *eis Zogora,* which implies Heb. *ṣōʿᵃrāh;* cf. Isa. 15:5. The consonantal text is the same for either reading.
5. MT repeats *bᵉḵî,* "weeping," at the end of the line, which seems to be a dittography since the next line begins with *kî.* Read *bô,* "on it," following Isa. 15:5 of which this verse is a variant.
6. MT reads "the distresses of the cry of . . ." (*ṣārê ṣaʿᵃqaṯ* . . .); LXX and Isa. 15:5 omit *ṣārê.*
7. The verse poses textual problems. MT reads "And you (fem. pl.) will be like Aroer in the desert." The feminine form of the verb could be taken as representing the nation, which is feminine in Hebrew (or as 2nd person masculine with energic ending). But "Aroer" poses some questions. In Isa. 15:5 *yᵉʿōʿērû*, "they raise a cry," appears. The text here may be a corrupted variant of this. LXX reads "like a wild ass (*ʿārôḏ*)." Vulg. suggests *ʿarʿār*, "a desert shrub," perhaps a juniper as in 17:6. The translation "like Aroer" is possible but its significance escapes us; see further the commentary below.

7 *Because of your trust*
In your own works and your wealth.[8]
You too will be captured,
And Kemosh will go into exile,
His priests and his officials with him.
8 *A destroyer shall fall upon every city,*
No city shall escape;
The valley shall be laid waste,
The plateau shall be destroyed,
As Yahweh has said.
9 *Provide salt*[9] *for Moab,*
She shall surely be laid in ruins;[10]
Her cities shall become waste places
Without an inhabitant.
10 *Cursed is the man who does Yahweh's work casually, and*
cursed is the man who withholds his sword from bloodshed."

In literary form the chapter is almost completely in verse; there seem to be prose segments at vv. 10, 21–24, 34–36, 38–40, 47, but even these may have been poetic originally.

There are numerous parallels with Isa. 15–16 although the meaning of this is not clear. It has been suggested that someone with the creative genius of Jeremiah would hardly have felt the need to borrow so extensively from an earlier source[11] even though he may have adapted earlier material or taken it up again to make some point. On the other hand there may have been behind both passages anonymous sayings about Moab which were quite old, since Moab was a traditional enemy of Israel and hostility between the two nations went back to the days of the Exodus.

That Jeremiah himself uttered oracles against Moab need not be questioned (cf. ch. 27). That he was capable of taking up and adapting older material must also be allowed. But a place must be allowed also for the work of the compiler or compilers of Jeremiah's material, who may have added historical, geographical, or theological comments in much the same way modern editors do. The pres-

8. MT makes good sense; cf. LXX "in your strongholds," suggesting one word like *mā'ōz* or *m*[e]*ṣuḏâ*.
9. Following W. L. Moran, "Ugaritic *ṣîṣûma* and Hebrew *ṣiṣ*," *Biblica* 39 (1958), pp. 69–71. On the significance see the commentary below. LXX reads "Give a sign to Moab," probably reading *ṣiyyûn,* "cairn."
10. MT *nāṣō' tēṣē'* seems to be another way of writing *nāṣōh tiṣṣeh* (from *nṣh,* "to fall in ruins"). A final ' and final *h* are sometimes interchanged. Some have proposed a reading *yāṣô' tēṣē'* and translate "she will surely surrender." The verb *yṣ'* is used in this sense in 1 Sam. 11:3; Isa. 36:6. See W. L. Moran, *ibid.*
11. E. W. Nicholson, *Jeremiah 26–52,* p. 177.

ent chapter is probably too complex to enable a commentator to identify precisely what sections were completely original with Jeremiah, what were adaptations of older material, and what are the work of the editors.

When we come to give a precise setting for the prophecy, the case is equally difficult. Part of the problem lies in that the history of Moab is not well known.[12] A further problem arises because older material which had reference to a former situation is here reapplied to another situation, namely, to events concerning Moab in the period of Jeremiah or shortly after. We may suspect that Moab like Judah submitted to the Babylonians after Carchemish in 605 B.C. Moab did not revel in the 600–598 B.C. period, when Jehoiakim and Judah were in revolt and Moab provided mercenaries to quell Judah (2 K. 24:2). She did contemplate revolt in 594 B.C. (27:3) but nothing came of the plot. In 589–587 B.C. when Judah rebelled, Moab was not involved. The general picture was one of noncooperation with Judah, which had been the case in the days of Isaiah in the eighth century and earlier. There was little love lost between the two nations, a fact which is attested by foreign prophecies directed against Moab by Isaiah (chs. 15–16), Amos (2:1–3), Zephaniah (2:9), Jeremiah, and Ezekiel (25:8–11). The end of Moab as an independent nation seems to have come in 582 B.C. when Nebuchadrezzar, no doubt because of a rebellion, marched against Moab and Ammon.[13] In the same year a third deportation from Judah took place (52:30). Not long after this the small states in Transjordan were overwhelmed by an Arab invasion and ceased to exist as a nation. We should probably view this prophecy in Jer. 48 as having relevance to these years, no later than the end of the first quarter of the sixth century, that is, not far away from 580 B.C. The earlier judgment on Moab from which she recovered provided a pattern for a further judgment.[14]

The chapter is noteworthy also for the great number of place names it contains, making it an invaluable source of information about the geography of ancient Moab. Several of the sites are known

12. See A. H. van Zyl, *The Moabites* (1960), for a succinct account of our knowledge up to 1960. There has been some progress since then but not a great deal.

13. According to Josephus *Antiquities* x.9.7.

14. In the middle of the seventh century an invasion of Arab tribes overran Moab and adjacent lands and probably provided the background to Isa. 15–16. See W. F. Albright, in a review of R. H. Pfeiffer's *Introduction to the OT, JBL* 61 (1942), p. 119. This is not to rule out the possibility that such a poem as Isa. 15–16 contained still older material referring to occasions of which we are ignorant; cf. Num. 21:25–30.

and some have been excavated in part, but there are a number whose location is uncertain and which are otherwise unknown.[15]

The division of the chapter into several sections is somewhat artificial and is intended only as a means of breaking a long poem into shorter segments for comment.

1 Moab lay on the eastern side of the Dead Sea, bounded on the south by the river Zered, on the north by the river Arnon, on the west by the Dead Sea, and on the east by the desert. At times the small kingdom extended north beyond the Arnon. Several of the towns mentioned in this poem lie north of the Arnon and were Moabite towns in periods of expansion. The total area of the kingdom varied during the centuries. In the days of the Exodus, according to Num. 21:21–31, these areas just to the north of the Arnon were under Sihon king of the Amorites. The area was occupied by the tribes of Reuben and Gad (Num. 32:33–38). In the days of Mesha king of Moab (mid-ninth century B.C.) Moab regained these areas from Israel. Moab proper was a plateau with many rich, cultivable areas.

In the opening part of the poem destruction for Moab is announced. So far as we can judge from our limited knowledge of the geography of ancient Moab, the invading power moved from the north to the south, obliging the Moabites to seek refuge in the desert (v. 6).

Nebo was a city of Reuben (Num. 32:3, 38) and became a city of Moab.[16] Its exact location is uncertain, although it may have been near Mount Nebo some 12 miles east of the northern tip of the Dead Sea. *Kiriathaim* was also a city of Reuben (Josh. 13:19) and is identified on the Moabite Stone as a Moabite city.[17] It is possibly the modern el-Qereiyat, about 5 miles northwest of Dibon (cf. Gen. 14:5).

2 *Heshbon* was the capital of the Amorite king Sihon (Num. 21:25–30). It was assigned to Reuben (Num. 32:37; Josh. 13:17), but in Josh. 13:26 it is listed as a city of Gad. The Moabite Stone refers to the men of Gad in this area.[18] There is a wordplay in Hebrew in the phrase *In Heshbon they plotted (bᵉḥešbôn ḥāšᵉḇû).* The particular historical reference is not clear. Excavations have revealed an

15. Y. Aharoni, *The Land of the Bible* (E.T. 1966); W. Rudolph, *Jeremia*, pp. 245–47.
16. *ANET*, pp. 320f., Moabite Stone, l. 15.
17. *Ibid.*, l. 10.
18. *Ibid.*

Iron Age city as the site of modern Heshbon. The ancient tell lies on the edge of the town.[19] The verb "cut off" often means "destroy, annihilate." The picture is of a plot to destroy the nation of Moab.

Madmen, another town, cannot be identified. There is a further play on words, in a difficult text where MT has *gam maḏmēn tiddōmmî.* The name may be a play on Dimon (Isa. 15:9; cf. the figure in Isa. 25:10). LXX, Syriac, and Vulgate all read instead of *Madmen* the infinitive absolute of the next verb *dmm,* hence "you will certainly become silent." It is also possible that the initial *m* is a dittography from the first word so that we are left with *dmn,* "Dimon," after all. On our tentative translation see the textual note. If a town Madmen is to be read it may be identified with Khirbet Dimneh 2 miles northwest of Rabbah.

3–4 *Horonaim* is mentioned on the Moabite Stone[20] as Hauronen, but its location is uncertain. The cry of Moab is heard at *Zoar,* one of the "cities of the plain" (Gen. 13:10ff.). The site is probably to be located at the southern end of the Dead Sea. It was, in any case, in the Arabah, the great rift valley in which the river Jordan and the Dead Sea lie, some 2000 feet below the plateau of Moab. The picture is a vivid one. Cries from the mountain regions reached down to the plains.

5 Verse 5 is almost identical with the latter part of Isa. 15:5, which helps in restoring the text (see textual notes). *Luhith* is unknown, but it may have been located between Zoar and Rabbath-Moab.

6 See textual note. The MT seems to contain a reference to *Aroer,* an ancient fortified site on the northern side of the river Arnon, perched at the very edge of the gorge ("Aroer which is on the edge of the valley Arnon," Deut. 2:36). Recent excavation[21] has revealed some Iron Age occupation followed by an abandonment. If the MT is followed, the reason for mentioning Aroer is not now clear, unless it is that only a place that stood isolated in the wilderness could hope to survive. We have translated following LXX, but MT might prove acceptable if we knew all the facts.

7 Moab trusted in her works and in her wealth, which were no protection against her foes. Nor would her god Kemosh (RSV

19. S. Horn, "The 1973 Season of Excavations at Tell Hesban," *ADAJ* 19 (1974), pp. 151–56; L. T. Geraty, "Excavations at Tell Hesban, 1976," *ASOR News Letter* No. 8 (Jan. 1977).
20. Lines 32, 33.
21. E. Olivarri, "Sondages à 'Arô'er sur l'Arnon," *RB* 72 (1965), pp. 77–94.

Chemosh) and his priests and officials be of help to her. The powerlessness of the gods of the nations is a well-worked theme in the OT. Kemosh, the god of the Moabites, is referred to on the Moabite Stone as Ashtar-Kemosh. Ashtar in Canaan was the god of the morning star, so that Kemosh may have been associated with astral deities. Solomon built a "high place" for Kemosh (1 K. 11:7) for the use of the Moabite women in his harem. The carrying off of statues of the gods into exile was common in the ancient Near East (cf. Amos 5:25; Isa. 46:1, 2).

8 Moab was a place of valleys (*'ēmeq*) and plateaus (*mîšōr*). All would be destroyed before the spoiler. But the reference may be wider. The spoiler may have been concerned with more lands than Moab, *the valley* may refer to the Jordan valley, that is, the region below Moab, and *the plateau* to the Transjordan highland from the Arnon north to Heshbon.

9 The first half of this verse is difficult. English versions have normally translated "give wings to Moab that she may fly away." But the noun *ṣîṣ* normally means "blossom," "ornament," and only in later Hebrew does it mean "wing."[22] On the translation *Provide salt,* based on Ugaritic, see the textual note. The idea of sowing cities with salt as a sign of their destruction is well known in the ancient Near East (cf. Judg. 9:45).[23]

10 The verse appears to be an editorial comment. It is generally understood as prose but is almost poetic. As a comment it probably refers to the work of the destroyer and despoiler of Moab, who is looked upon as Yahweh's agent to carry out his work faithfully.

(b) Moab's complacency ended (48:11–17)

11 *"Moab has been at ease from his youth,*
Settled on his lees,
Never emptied from vessel to vessel.
He has never gone into exile,
So he retains his taste,
And his flavor is unchanged.
12 *Therefore days are coming—Yahweh's word—*
When I will send tilters who will tilt him.
They will empty his vessels
And smash his jars.

22. See W. L. Moran, "Ugaritic *ṣîṣûma* and Hebrew *ṣîṣ*," *Biblica* 39 (1958), pp. 69–71.
23. See S. Gerwitz, "Jericho and Shechem: A Religio-Literary Aspect of City Destruction," *VT* 13 (1963), pp. 52–62.

13 *Then Moab will be disillusioned*[1] *with Kemosh*
As Israel was disillusioned by Bethel,
The one in whom they trusted.
14 *How can you say, 'We are warriors,*
Men who are valiant in battle'?
15 *The destroyer of Moab and her cities has come up.*[2]
His finest young men have gone down to the slaughter.
(The word of the King, Yahweh of Hosts is his name.)[3]
16 *Moab's disaster is close at hand;*
Disaster rushes swiftly upon him.
17 *Mourn for him, all you his neighbors*
And all who know his name;
Say, 'Alas, the mighty scepter is broken,
The glorious staff.' "

11–12 These verses refer to the fact that Moab had never suffered exile like Judah. She may have been subject to Israel for a time and been defeated in battle but she had never suffered the deep anguish of exile. She lay outside the normal route of the invaders of the Middle East and was rarely disturbed. Moab is here compared with wine which has been allowed to settle down with its dregs and sediment to age and mature and improve its flavor. It had settled quietly on its lees and had never been disturbed by being poured from vessel to vessel. The picture is one of complacency. But this would soon change. The comparison of Moab with wine is an apt one, for Moab was renowned for its vineyards (cf. vv. 32–33; Isa. 16:8–11). Even in later times the area produced good wine.[4]

The metaphor continues in v. 12, which refers to those who will come and *tilt* (*ṣāʿâ*) the wine jars, empty the vessels, and smash the jars. The wordplay is difficult to capture in English. *Tilters* refers to men in a wine cellar who decant the wine.

13 The verse is sometimes regarded as a prose insertion,[5] but it is not difficult to see a poetic structure in it as the translation shows (cf. NEB). Moab was *disillusioned* (Heb. *bōš*) by Kemosh. Time was when the Moabites claimed that Kemosh had saved them

1. Lit. "be ashamed."
2. MT reads "Moab is destroyed (*šuddaḏ*); and to her cities he has come up." LXX reads "Moab is destroyed (with) his city." By reading *šōḏēḏ*, "destroyer" (with the same consonants), and *bᵉʿārayw*, "against his cities," we may read as here; cf. NEB "The spoiler of Moab and her cities has come up."
3. The sentence is lacking in LXX and is omitted by some translators.
4. A wine seal has been found bearing the pre-Masoretic, unvocalized text of v. 11. See W. A. Irwin, "An Ancient Biblical Text," *AJSL* 48 (1931), p. 184.
5. J. Bright, *Jeremiah,* p. 320.

from all the kings and let them see their desire upon their adversaries.[6] In the coming disaster Kemosh would be powerless.

The parallel to Kemosh in Moab is given as *Bethel* in Israel, a place name that must also have been either the name of a deity or a divine epithet. It was in use at the Jewish colony at Elephantine in the fifth century B.C.[7] It may have been a substitute name for Yahweh in the cult in Northern Israel as practiced at Bethel.

14–15 In the prophetic vision of the writer the so-called "heroes" and "valiant warriors," the "choicest of her young men," would be struck down. On Yahweh as *King* see comments on 46:18.

16–17 The nations around Moab are united to bemoan the downfall of the nation. The expressions *mighty scepter* and *glorious staff* refer back to the days when Moab was able to exert some influence in the neighboring areas (27:3; 2 K. 1:1; 3:4–5; 24:2). Certainly after about 580 B.C. Moab lost her independence for ever. The language of v. 16 is reminiscent of Deut. 32:35.

(c) Catastrophe for Moab's cities (48:18–28)

18 *"Come down from your place of honor,*
Sit on the dry ground,[1]
You inhabitress of Dibon,
For Moab's destroyer has fallen upon you
And destroyed your strongholds.
19 *Stand by the road and watch,*
You that live in Aroer.
Question him who flees and her who escapes;[2]
Ask, What has happened?
20 *Moab is put to shame, for it is destroyed.*
Howl and cry!
Proclaim along the Arnon
That Moab lies waste."
21 *Judgment has come to the tableland: to Holon, Jahzah, and Mephaath,*
22 *to Dibon, Nebo, and Beth-diblathaim,*
23 *to Kiriathaim and Beth-gamul and Beth-meon,*
24 *to Kerioth and Bozrah, and to all the cities of the land of Moab both far and near.*

6. Moabite Stone, l. 7.
7. See *ANET,* p. 491; J. P. Hyatt, "The Deity Bethel and the OT," *JAOS* 59 (1939), pp. 81–98; W. Albright, *Archaeology and the Religion of Israel* (1946), pp. 168–175; A. Cowley, *Aramaic Papyri of the Fifth Century B.C.* (1923), p. 72, col. vii.

1. MT reads *baṣṣāmā',* "in thirst," which can be vocalized *baṣṣāmē',* "on the parched ground" (RSV, cf. Isa. 44:3). Syr. implies *baṣṣō'â,* "in excrement (filth)."
2. The Versions read both participles as masculine, hence "the fleeing refugee."

25 *"Moab's horn is cut off,*
His arm is broken—Yahweh's word.
26 *Make him drunk, for he has*
Acted proudly against Yahweh.[3]
Moab will overflow with his vomit[4]
And become an object of derision himself.
27 *Was not Israel an object of derision to you?*
Was he found in company with thieves,
So that whenever you spoke of him[5]
You would shake your head?
28 *Abandon your cities! Make your home in the cliffs,*
You who dwell in Moab!
Become like a dove that makes its nest
In the rockface at the mouth of a cavern."

18 The symbolism of proud rulers being caused to sit in the dust (*'āpār*) is known elsewhere (e.g., Isa. 47:1). The word here is not "dust," however, but "thirst" (*ṣāmā'*), which is unusual and often emended; see the textual note. The call is addressed to "her who lives as the daughter of Dibon (or daughter-Dibon[6])." The phrase is difficult and may mean simply "You that live in Dibon" (cf. v. 19). A similar expression "inhabitress daughter-Egypt" occurs in 46:19, where it is a poetic personification of Egypt's population. Jeremiah uses the phrase "my daughter—my people" to personify the inhabitants of Judah. The destroyer has come upon this city too. *Dibon* is the modern Diban, 4 miles north of the Arnon and 13 miles east of the Dead Sea. It was an impressive walled city throughout the Iron Age, as modern excavation has shown.[7] It was here that the Moabite Stone was found in 1868.[8] There is a specific reference to Dibon in the inscription.[9]

3. Lit. "He has become great against Yahweh."
4. The verb *sāpaq* normally means "clap" the hands (Num. 24:10; Lam. 2:15) or the thighs (Jer. 31:19) in rage, disgust, or remorse, thus lit. "Moab shall clap in his vomit," conveying a picture of a man vomiting and writhing in violent spasms. Or possibly the word may relate to Aram. *s^e^pēq,* "overflow," "empty out"; cf. RSV "wallow," and cf. Heb. *śāp̄aq* in 1 K. 20:10; Isa. 2:6 (?). See G. R. Driver, "Difficult Words in the Hebrew Prophets," *Studies in OT Prophecy* (ed. H. H. Rowley) (1950), p. 61.
5. MT *d^e^ḇāreyḵā*, "your words," can be revocalized to *dabberêḵā*, "your speaking."
6. J. Bright, *Jeremiah,* pp. 320f. LXX omits "daughter" (haplography?).
7. *The Excavations at Dibon (DHĪBÂN) in Moab;* Part I, The First Campaign, 1950–1951, F. V. Winnett; Part II, The Second Campaign, 1952, W. L. Reed. *Annual of the American Schools of Oriental Research*, 36–37 (1964).
8. *ANET,* p. 320.
9. *Ibid.,* ll. 1, 21, 28.

19 *Aroer,* situated southeast of Dibon, lay on the southern boundary of the old Amorite kingdom, the Wadi Arnon (Judg. 11:18–19). See further comments on v. 6. Aroer is pictured as standing by the roadside and asking the fleeing refugees what has happened.

20–24 These verses appear to be the reply to the question posed in v. 19. At first sight they seem to be in prose, but it would not be difficult to see in them a poetic structure with each colon containing three beats. Of the towns referred to, Jahzah (Jahaz, v. 34), Beth-diblathaim, Beth-meon, Kerioth, and Bozrah are mentioned on the Moabite Stone. The locations of *Holon* and *Kerioth* are not known and that of *Jahzah* (the Jahaz of Josh. 21:36) is uncertain. *Mephaath,* a Levitical city (Josh. 21:37), may be modern Tell Jawah some 6 miles south of Ammon; *Beth-gamul* is probably the modern *Khirbet el Jemeil* 8 miles east of Dibon; *Beth-meon* was the Baal-meon of Num. 32:38 some 5 miles southwest of Medeba; *Kerioth* is referred to in Amos 2:2; *Bozrah* is perhaps the Bezer of Deut. 4:43; Josh. 20:8; and 21:36 rather than the Edomite city referred to later in Jer. 49:13, 22.[10]

25 The nouns *horn* and *arm* are both metaphors for strength in the OT.

26–27 The imagery of drunkenness is another well-known OT picture. It is often associated with the drinking of the cup of Yahweh's wrath which makes men stagger. The imagery was used by Jeremiah in 25:15–29 where a list is given of all those who would drink from the cup. Moab appears in that list (25:21). These verses are sometimes regarded as a prose insertion,[11] but they fall quite easily into a poetic form (NEB).

The picture of a drunken man doubled over by vomiting is both disgusting and likely to provoke derision. Once Moab had laughed at Israel as she drank the cup of Yahweh's wrath, regarding her as a laughingstock and treating her as a thief who has been punished.

28 The tables are turned. Moab is an object of derision as she must flee from her cities and go to live in places of refuge in the high mountains.[12]

10. For further details about these cities see A. H. van Zyl, *The Moabites;* W. Rudolph, *Jeremia,* pp. 245–47; Y. Aharoni, *The Land of the Bible.*
11. RSV, J. Bright.
12. There are other examples of such behavior in biblical history. David hid in caves. So did the Maccabees, and later on the men of Qumran.

(d) A lament over Moab (48:29–39)

29 *We have heard of Moab's pride—*
Very proud indeed—
Of his haughtiness, his arrogance, his boastfulness
And lofty conceit.
30 *"I myself know his arrogance—Yahweh's word;*
His idle talk is not well founded,
His deeds will not last.
31 *Therefore I will wail for Moab,*
For the whole of Moab I will cry out."
For the men of Kir-heres will he mourn.[1]
32 *"O fountain of Jazer, I will weep for you;*
O Sibmah's vine,
Whose tendrils spread out to the sea,
And extend as far as Jazer.[2]
The despoiler has fallen on your summer fruit and on your grapes.
33 *Gladness and joy are taken away*[3]
From the fruitful land of Moab;[4]
I have stopped the wine from the winepresses,
The grape-treader does not tread,
No glad shout goes forth."[5]
34 *The people of Heshbon and Elealeh cry out,*[6]
As far as Jahaz the cry is heard,[7]
And from Zoar as far as Horonaim and Eglath-shelishiyah;[8]
For even the waters of Nimrim have become a desolate waste.

1. The context seems to require the first person, and *BHS ad loc.* proposes to change to the first person. But the MT can stand and the line may be understood either as a quotation from a snatch of familiar material, or as a kind of antiphonal response of the people something in the manner of a Greek chorus. The speaker starts again at v. 32.
2. Omit the second reference to the "sea" (*yām*) with some mss. and Isa. 16:8.
3. Lit. "have been gathered."
4. Lit. "from the fruitful land (*karmel*) and from the land of Moab." LXX preserves only the second phrase and Isa. 16:10 the first, so that MT seems to be a conflation.
5. NEB attempts a translation "nor shall shout follow shout from the harvesters, not one shout!" RSV "no one treads them with shouts of joy; the shouting is not the shout of joy." In MT *hêḏāḏ,* "shout," occurs three times in these two lines; for our translation we emend the first of these to *haddōrēḵ,* "the one treading," as in the parallel Isa. 16:10 and with some versional and ms. support.
6. MT reads "At the cry of Heshbon as far as Elealeh." Isa. 15:4 reads "Heshbon and Elealeh cry out" (cf. RSV, NEB). LXX conforms to MT. One of the problems for the textual critic is that it must not be assumed that the text of Isaiah is in every case superior. Jeremiah's text may have its own value.
7. Lit. "they give forth their voice (sound)."
8. RV, RSV, NEB following LXX take this as a proper name. Cf. AV "heifer of three years old."

35 *"In Moab I will bring to an end the offering of burnt offerings on the high places*[9] *and the making of sacrifices to their gods—Yahweh's word.*
36 *So my heart wails for Moab like a reed pipe, yes, wails for the men of Kir-heres like a reed pipe, because the remainder of his work has perished."*
37 *"For every head is shaved,*
Every beard is cut off,
On every hand are gashes,
On every[10] *waist sackcloth."*[11]
38 *"On all the rooftops of Moab, and in his broad streets, there is nothing but lamentation; for I have smashed Moab like an unwanted vessel*[12]*—Yahweh's word."*
39 *"How shattered he is! Cry aloud!*
How Moab turns his back in shame!
Moab becomes an object of derision,
And an object of terror to all his neighbors."[13]

Moab's arrogant pride may have been the subject of popular sayings (cf. Isa. 16:5; 25:10–11; Zeph. 2:8–11). It was an empty pride which would rebound on the nation. The whole section vv. 29–39 has many resemblances to Isa. 15–16.

The translation given above with its frequent use of quotation marks is based on the suggestion that in vv. 29–39 we have to do with a series of utterances by Yahweh each followed by an antiphonal response from an audience. We would propose that such responses may be recognized in vv. 31c, 34, 37, and 39. We may have here a deliberate rhetorical device of a type which is known in the Greek chorus. A careful study of other passages in the Old Testament and also in Jeremiah may uncover many occurrences of this device. I owe this suggestion to John W. De Hoog.

29–30 Jeremiah here piles up a number of synonymous terms designed to emphasize Moab's pride: *pride* (*gā'ôn*), *proud* (*gē'eh*), *haughtiness* (*gāḇōah*), *arrogance* (*gā'ôn*), *boastfulness* (*ga'ᵃwâ*), *lofty conceit* or "loftiness of heart" (*rûm lēḇ*), *arrogance* (*'eḇrâ*).

NEB translates as follows:

"We have heard of Moab's pride, and proud indeed he is,

9. MT "offering (on the) high place" (*ma'ᵃleh ḇāmâ*) is probably an abbreviation of *ma'ᵃleh 'ōlâ 'al habbāmâ*, "offering burnt offerings on the high places" (sing. nouns used collectively).
10. MT lacks *every* but LXX and versions insert it.
11. Verse 37 may be understood as another antiphonal response.
12. Lit. "a vessel in which is no desire."
13. Verse 39 is interpreted as another antiphonal response.

Proud, presumptuous, overbearing, insolent.
I know his arrogance, says the Lord;
His boasting is false, false are his deeds."

31 *Kir-heres* (lit. "city of potsherds") is the "Kir-hareseth" of 2 K. 3:25; Isa. 16:7, but it appears in Isa. 16:11 also as Kir-heres. It is probably to be identified with el-Kerak some 17 miles south of the river Arnon and 11 miles east of the Dead Sea. If we allow a confusion of *r* and *d* which is fairly common in Hebrew texts, the original name may have been "Kir-hadesheth" (lit. "the new city"). It may have been the same city as *QRḤH* in the Moabite Stone (l. 3), built by Mesha.

32–33 These verses resemble Isa. 16:8–10. *Jazer* was further north and was originally in the area of the Ammonites, but it was evidently conquered by Moab along with other towns. Jazer does not appear in the Moabite Stone but is probably to be identified with a site 10 miles north of Heshbon, originally in the territory of Sihon.[14] It was captured by Israel from the Amorites (Num. 21:32).

Sibmah probably lay 3 miles northwest of Heshbon and likewise belonged to Sihon. The whole region was an area of vineyards, hence the phrase *Sibmah's vine (gepen)*[15] and the references to *summer fruit, grapes, winepresses, grape-treader, shout* (of the harvesters). But all this will be taken away. The shout that is heard is not the glad shout of the treaders of grapes, but the noise of warriors bent on destruction (cf. 25:30; 51:14).

34 Verses 34–39 (except v. 37) appear to be prose, but a poetic structure behind them would not be difficult to reconstruct. There are many parallels to Isa. 15–16; cf. v. 34 with Isa. 15:4–6; v. 36 with Isa. 16:11; 15:7; v. 37 with Isa. 15:2, 3; v. 38 with Isa. 15:3.

Elealeh is the modern *el-'Al* about 2 miles north of Heshbon; *Jahaz* was further southwest, and *Zoar* and *Horonaim* were in southern Moab. There was a place Zoar in the valley below the south end of the Dead Sea (Gen. 14:2; 19:22), but this was evidently a different town since the places listed here are all in Moab. *Eglath-shelishiyah* (lit. "the third Eglath") may have been the third of three places known as Eglath. The location is unknown. The *waters of Nimrim* may refer to either the Wadi en-Numeirah which flows into

14. G. M. Landes, "The Fountain of Jazer," *BASOR* 144 (1956), pp. 30–37, who proposes Khirbet es-Ṣîreh 2 km. northeast of Khirbet Ṣār.
15. See comment on vv. 11–12.

the Dead Sea about 10 miles from its southern end, or the Wadi Nimrim which enters the Jordan about 8 miles from the northern end of the Dead Sea.

35–36 All that Moab cherished was about to perish, her religion and her achievement in material things alike. A wailing like the sound of a *reed pipe* (*ḥālîl*) is raised. The pipe in question was probably the common reed pipe known all over the ancient (and modern) Middle East and used to express both joy and sorrow.

37 The features referred to were common among those who mourned. See comment on 41:5.

38–40 In private homes and in public on the streets, lamentation is heard. The phrase *an unwanted vessel* is used of Jehoiachin in 22:28. The arrogant Moab will become a laughingstock and an object of terror to all her neighbors.

(e) Moab's doom—and final mercy (48:40–47)

40 *Yes, this is what Yahweh has said:*
"Look! like an eagle he swoops down
And spreads his wings over Moab.
41 *The towns are taken,*
The strongholds are seized,
The courage of Moab's warriors becomes on that day
Like the courage of a woman in labor.
42 *Moab shall be destroyed, no longer a nation,*
Because he acted proudly against Yahweh.
43 *Terror, the pit and the trap*
Are upon you, O inhabitant of Moab—Yahweh's word.
44 *The man who flees from the terror*
Falls into the trap;
The man who climbs up out of the pit
Is caught in the trap.
Ah, this I will bring upon Moab
In the year of their reckoning—Yahweh's word.
45 *In the shadow of Heshbon*
Fugitives stand helpless,
For fire has gone forth from Heshbon
And a flame from the city[1] *of Sihon;*
It devours Moab's forehead,
And the crown of the sons of tumult.

1. MT reads "from between (*mibbên*) Sihon." Greek Theodotion and Syr. read *mibbêṯ,* "from the house (palace)," i.e., the capital city, cf. Num. 21:28 *miqqiryaṯ,* "from the city"; also the Assyrian name for Samaria was "house of Omri." However, MT is not impossible with much the same meaning, "from the midst of."

46 *Alas for you, O Moab!*
The people of Moab have perished,
For your sons are taken away captive
And your daughters into exile.
47 *Yet in days to come I will restore the fortunes of Moab—*
Yahweh's word."
Thus far is the judgment of Moab.

40–42 LXX omits all of these verses except the heading and the first half of v. 41, for which it reads "Akkarioth is captured, the strongholds taken." The omitted material is, however, repeated with slight variations in 49:22 and it is common in LXX not to repeat duplicate passages. The image of the *eagle* is reminiscent of the picture in Ezek. 17:3–5 where the eagle Babylon swoops down and takes away the top of the cedar, or Ezek. 17:7–8 where the eagle is Egypt. In v. 40 the eagle is not defined (cf. Deut. 28:49; Jer. 40:22). Ultimately Moab will cease to exist as a nation.

43–44 There is some good assonance in v. 43, *paḥaḏ wā-paḥaṯ wāpāḥ, terror, the pit, and the trap.* For comparable imagery see Amos 5:19. These verses occur with slight variations in Isa. 24:17–18, but they are not necessarily taken from Isaiah. Both may have been conventional material some of which was applied to Moab (e.g., Isa. 25:10–12).

45–46 These verses are lacking in LXX, which inserts the material on the cup of fiery wine (25:25–29) at this point. It would appear that these verses consist of a free quotation from the old song of Heshbon which occurs in Num. 21:28–29 and also from Num. 24:17.[2]

We may see in these words a claim that Balaam's oracle against Moab was about to be enacted. *Sihon* was the Amorite ruler of lands north of the river Arnon in the days of Moses (Num. 21:21–30). His capital was Heshbon.

47 Despite predictions of death and destruction, the prophet looks to a future day when Yahweh would restore the fortunes (*šāḇ šᵉḇûṯ*) of Moab. Similar prophecies of judgment on Israel and Judah are accompanied by promises of restoration.

2. Cf. v. 45b and Num. 21:28a; v. 45c and Num. 24:17c; v. 46 and Num. 21:29.

(iv) Ammon (49:1–6)

1 *Concerning the Ammonites:*
This is what Yahweh has said:
"Has Israel no sons?
No heir at all?
Why has Milcom[1] *taken possession of Gad*[2]
And his people inherited its towns?
2 *Look, therefore! Days are coming—*
Yahweh's word—
When I will make Rabbath-Ammon[3] *hear*
The shout of battle,
And she will become a desolate mound,
Her villages[4] *will be burned in flames.*
Then Israel will disinherit those who disinherited him—
Yahweh has spoken.
3 *Howl, Heshbon! for Ai*[5] *is laid waste.*
Cry out, villages of Rabbah!
Put on sackcloth! Lament!
Rush to and fro in confusion,[6]
For Milcom is going into exile,
His priests and his officials with him.
4 *Why do you boast of your strength,*
Your diminishing strength,[7]
O faithless daughter,
Who trusts in her treasures
And says,[8] *'Who will come against me?'*

1. MT has *malkām,* "their king," but LXX, Syr., Vulg., read *Milcom;* so also in v. 3.
2. LXX reads "Gilead."
3. Lit. "Rabbath of the sons of Ammon." LXX omits *b^{e}nê 'ammôn* and reads simply "Rabbath."
4. LXX reads "her high places" *(bāmōṯeyhā);* but cf. v. 3, which also has *b^{e}nôṯ,* "daughters," i.e., "villages."
5. MT and the versions follow this reading. No site Ai is known in Ammon and emendations are proposed. See the commentary below.
6. MT *bagg^{e}ḏērôṯ,* "among the sheep pens," is difficult. LXX omits the whole phrase. Some commentators follow 48:37 with *big^{e}ḏuḏôṯ,* "with gashes," i.e., showing signs of mourning. This involves a change of *r* to *d* in the second to last consonant, a common problem in Hebrew. We have translated "in confusion" rather by way of a paraphrase. Whether or not the people of Ammon rushed to and fro "among the sheep pens" "with gashes on their bodies," there must have been confusion among them. J. Bright, *Jeremiah,* p. 324, leaves a blank in his translation but expresses general support for a translation "Rush to and fro (covered) with gashes," that is, in mourning. Cf. 48:37.
7. See the commentary on 47:5. RSV reads "Why do you boast of your valleys?"
8. *And says* is supplied in translation.

5 *Believe me, I will bring upon you*
Terror from all around you—
Word of the Lord, Yahweh of Hosts.[9]
Every one of you will be driven headlong[10]
With no one to gather the fugitives.
6[11] *But afterward I will restore the fortunes of the Ammonites—*
Yahweh's word."

Chapter 49 contains several shorter oracles directed at a number of neighboring areas: Ammon, Edom, Damascus, Arab tribes, and Elam. The first of these is Ammon, and it appears to reflect a similar political situation to that of Moab.

Israel's relations with Ammon were generally unfriendly. In the days of the Exodus, Ammon was bypassed as were Moab and Edom, and only the Amorite kingdoms of Sihon and Og were taken over (Deut. 2:37); but thereafter there was intermittent war between Israel and Ammon. Jephthah, in the days of the Judges, defeated them (Judg. 11:4–33). Nahash opposed Israel in Saul's day (1 Sam. 11:1–11). David sought peace but his servants were insulted, and despite Aramean help Ammon was punished (2 Sam. 10). Solomon held them in check (1 K. 4:13–19). Amos commented on their cruel activities in the area of Gilead in the eighth century B.C. (Amos 1:13–15). The deportation of part of the Israelite population of Transjordan by Tiglath-pileser III of Assyria in 733 B.C. (2 K. 15:29) and the subsequent collapse of Israel enabled the Ammonites to annex part of the territory of Gad (v. 1). During the seventh century B.C. Ammon was a prosperous semiautonomous kingdom like Judah, but nominally a vassal of Assyria.[12] Ammon must have suffered somewhat from the Arab invaders who attacked Moab in the mid-seventh century.[13] But with the collapse of Assyria at the end of the century Ammon was again independent. We have no information about any activities of Josiah in the area in the late seventh century,

9. The Hebrew line is broken up with the last part inserted between "terror" and "on every side." LXX has only "says the Lord."
10. Lit. "each man before him (*lᵉpānāyw*)."
11. LXX omits the verse.
12. G. M. Landes, "The Material Civilization of the Ammonites," *BA* 24 (1961), pp. 66–86, gives a convenient summary of the history and culture of Ammon.
13. W. F. Albright in *JBL* 61 (1942), p. 119 points out that when Ashurbanipal of Assyria was fighting his brother Shamashumukin during the years 652–648 B.C. Arab hordes flooded into East Syria and Palestine, from Zobah east of Anti-Lebanon to Seir in the South. Moab is expressly mentioned in the Rassam Cylinder, col. viii, l. 112.

but with the rise of the Chaldeans and the advance of Nebuchadrezzar into Palestine after Carchemish (605 B.C.) in 605/4 B.C. she probably submitted to the Chaldeans. When Judah rebelled in 600–597 B.C. Nebuchadrezzar was able to send contingents of Arameans, Moabites, and Ammonites to subdue Judah (2 K. 24:2). Ammon was implicated in the proposed rebellion of 594 B.C. (27:3), and in the 589/7 B.C. period she showed disloyalty to Babylon (Ezek. 21:18–32). Her king Baalis was implicated in the assassination of Gedaliah (40:13–41:15). Perhaps because of these acts of rebellion Nebuchadrezzar conducted a campaign of reprisal against Ammon as well as against Moab and Judah in 582 B.C. (52:30). Thereafter Ammon fell victim to the Arab invasions that destroyed Moab and Edom, and before the middle of the sixth century B.C. Ammon had ceased to exist as an independent nation.

The present prophecy (49:1–6) may have been delivered any time before the fall of Judah and Ammon, perhaps after the raids of 601–600 B.C. (2 K. 24:2). It was probably fulfilled in part in the visit of Nebuchadrezzar in 582 B.C. but more completely in the middle of the sixth century at the time of the Arab invasion.

1 On *the Ammonites* (lit. "sons of Ammon") see the introductory notes. Their territory normally comprised areas to the east of the Wadi Jabbok. Its boundaries to the north and south were flexible and it expanded to the west from time to time. Elsewhere it bordered the Syrian desert. *Milcom* (Molech)[14] was the national deity of Ammon. The name means "the king." The influence of this religion was felt in Israel (32:35; Lev. 18:21; 20:2, 3, 4, 5; 1 K. 11:5, 7, 33; 2 K. 23:10, 13; Amos 5:26). The reference to Milcom disinheriting[15] Gad is probably a reminiscence of Ammon's expansion to the west after Tiglath-pileser's campaigns of 734 B.C. had removed Israelite people from Transjordan. Ammon moved into the weakened area and occupied the territory of Gad.[16]

2 *Rabbath-Ammon* was the capital of Ammon and is to be identified with modern Amman, the capital of Jordan today. Excavations have brought to light the citadel area of Rabbath-Ammon.[17] Some important inscriptions in ancient Ammonite have been found.

14. See W. F. Albright, *Archaeology and the Religion of Israel,* pp. 162–64.
15. The verb *yāraš,* "inherit," "possess," can also mean "disinherit," "dispossess." One can hardly possess lands without dispossessing the inhabitants.
16. Mentioned in the Moabite Stone, l. 10.
17. Fawzi Zayadine, "Recent Excavations on the Citadel of Amman," *ADAJ* 17 (1973), pp. 17–53.

The modern archeological term *tell* occurs in the phrase *a desolate mound (tēl šᵉmāmâ)*. The *villages* (lit. "daughters," *bᵉnôṯ*) were the other towns of Ammon. These too were destroyed in the course of military campaigns, normally by burning them down. How Israel would repossess these areas is not clear. Historically this did not take place. The expression is a stereotyped one.

3 *Heshbon* was normally under Moab's control (48:2) although it may have belonged to Ammon at the time (cf. Judg. 11:26). It lay on the border. The mention of *Ai* (lit. "ruin") raises a question. It cannot be the Ai of Israelite territory and we must suppose that there was another town of that name. The location is not known. The exile of a people along with the images of their gods was common practice (cf. 48:7; Amos 5:26). One difficult phrase occurs in this verse, *Rush to and fro in confusion*. The last noun in the Hebrew text means "among the sheep pens," which is possible. It conjures up a picture of people darting about in open areas. The emendation to "gashes" (see textual note) suggests a picture of people gashing themselves in mourning. The first is a pastoral scene; the second, a cultic picture, is probably to be preferred (cf. 41:5; 48:37).

4–5 We follow the suggestion made in 47:5 and translate *strength* in place of "valley" (RSV). The connotation is not certain. It may refer to economic as well as strategic and military strength, as suggested by *treasures*. But it was a diminishing strength soon to be sapped away. Ammon was complacent and said, *Who will come against me?* But when Yahweh's judgment struck, men would flee, each for his own safety with no thought for stragglers. The phrase *terror from all around you (paḥaḏ mikkol sᵉḇîḇāyiḵ)* is a variant of "terror all around" (*māḡôr missāḇîḇ*), used several times by Jeremiah in different settings (6:25; 20:3, 4, 10; 46:5; 49:29).

6 This prose comment is to be compared with the promise to Egypt in 46:26 and to Moab in 48:47. In Persian times Tobiah was a local governor of Ammon (Neh. 2:10, 19; 4:7). It is of some interest that there was a revival of Moabite fortunes later. In the second century B.C. the Tobiad family was still ruling and in the first century B.C. Judas Maccabeus fought against the Ammonites (1 Macc. 5:6).

(v) Edom (49:7–22)

7 *Concerning Edom:*
This is what Yahweh of Hosts has said:
"Is wisdom no longer in Teman?
Has counsel departed from the understanding?
Has their wisdom become putrid?

8 *Flee! Turn about!*
Dwell in a remote area,
You who live in Dedan!
For I will bring Esau's disaster upon him,
The time of his reckoning.
9 *When grape-gatherers come to you*
Do they not leave gleanings?
If thieves (come) in the night
They take what they want.[1]
10 *But I, I have stripped Esau;*
I have uncovered his hiding places,
And he is not able to conceal himself.
His offspring are destroyed,
His kinsmen and his neighbors;
Not one is left (to say)[2]
11 *'Leave your orphans; I will take care of them.*
Your widows may trust in me.' "
12 *Yes, this is what Yahweh has said: "Look! If they who were not legally*
bound to drink the cup had to drink it, are you to go unpunished?[3]
No, you will not go unpunished, you will certainly drink.
13 *I have sworn by myself—Yahweh's word—that Bozrah shall become*
a horror, a reproach, a desolation,[4] *a cause for ridicule, and all her*
cities shall be desolate wastes for ever."
14 *I have heard a report from Yahweh,*
An envoy has been sent to the nations,
"Gather together and march against her,
Rouse yourselves for battle!
15 *Look here! I will make you the least of the nations*
Despised among men.
16 *Your pride*[5] *has deceived you,*
Your arrogant heart,
You who dwell in the clefts of the rocks
And grasp the lofty height;
Though your nest is as high as the eagle
I will bring you down—
Yahweh's word.

1. Lit. "They will destroy their sufficiency."
2. MT *wᵉ'ênennû,* "and they are not," is meaningful enough; but some, including J. Bright, p. 328, feel that the reported speech of the next line requires an introduction and following Symmachus and Lucian emend to read *wᵉ'ên 'ōmēr,* "and no one says."
3. Cf. 25:29.
4. LXX omits *lᵉḥōreḇ,* perhaps by haplography of *lᵉḥorᵉḇôṯ* in the next clause.
5. The word *tipleṣeṯ* occurs only here and is of uncertain meaning. Traditionally it has been translated "terribleness," "terror." J. Bright (p. 331) suggests the word may have been *mipleṣeṯ* (1 K. 15:13), "terrible idol." See further the commentary below.

17 *Edom shall become a thing of horror. Every one who passes by her*
will be shocked and will whistle at all her wounds.
18 *Like the overthrowing of Sodom and Gomorrah and her neighbors—*
Yahweh has spoken—
No man shall live there,
No human shall dwell there.
19 *Look! Like a lion coming up*
From Jordan's thicket to the perennial pastures,
So[6] *will I suddenly*[7] *chase them away*[8] *from her*
And select the choicest of her rams.[9]
For who is like me? Who will summon me?
What shepherd can stand before me?
20 *Therefore, listen to the plan that Yahweh has devised against Edom*
and the purposes he has proposed against the inhabitants of Teman.
The young ones of the flock shall surely[10] *be dragged away*
And their flock shall be appalled because of them.
21 *The earth quakes at the sound of their fall,*
Their cry is heard at the Sea of Reeds.[11]
22 *Look! Like an eagle he soars up and swoops*[12]
And spreads his wings over Bozrah.
And the heart of Edom's warriors shall be on that day
Like that of a woman in labor."

The prophecy against Edom is mostly in verse. Even the apparently prose insertions at vv. 12–13 and v. 20 may have been poetic at one stage, as they suggest an underlying poetic structure. There are close parallels between vv. 9–10 and Obad. 5–6, and between vv. 14–16 and Obad. 1–4. Some verses have parallels elsewhere in the book of Jeremiah (see comments). The question is therefore raised as to whether the passage comes in its entirety from Jeremiah or whether editors gathered originally anonymous sayings and used them along with genuine utterances of Jeremiah in a prophecy against Edom. It is not impossible, of course, that Jeremiah himself took up phrases he had used on other occasions as well as other traditional phrases which Obadiah, his contemporary, had also used. The prophecy in

6. The *kî* here is asseverative and serves to emphasize the statement.
7. The first verb has an adverbial force; it means lit. "I will do in a moment."
8. MT lit. "I will cause him to run." The translation *them* instead of "him" follows LXX and other versions; cf. 50:44 which has "them" in a similar context.
9. MT *ûmî bāḥûr 'ēleyhā,* "And who is chosen? Over him (I will place)," with a very slight change can be emended to *ûmiḇḥar 'êleyhā*, "and from the choicest of her rams."
10. On the strong, oath-like idiom used here see the commentary below.
11. The final word in MT, *qôlāh,* "her voice," is omitted with LXX and 50:46. It may be a gloss or a variant of *their cry.*
12. LXX and 48:40 omit the first verb.

its present form reflects the bitter hatred which the Jews felt toward the Edomites in the days following the fall of Judah in 587 B.C.

There was a long story of opposition between Judah and Edom reaching back to the days of the Exodus (Num. 20:14–21; Judg. 11:17). The people were on one occasion forbidden to ill-treat the Edomites (Deut. 23:7–8), who were their brothers. David brought them under his control (2 Sam. 8:13–14). Solomon had trouble with Hadad, who fled to Egypt (1 K. 11:14–22). In the days of Jehoshaphat there was a Judean deputy in Edom (1 K. 22:47), and in a retaliatory war against Moab the people of Edom supported Judah and Israel (2 K. 3:9). Edom revolted in the days of Joram (2 K. 8:20–22) when Judah was attacked by Israel and Aram. Edom broke free from Judah (2 K. 16:5, 6). Amaziah defeated them in battle (2 Chr. 25:14; 2 K. 14:7) in the eighth century B.C. Uzziah extended his boundaries into Edom (2 K. 14:22). Edom won back much of its territory at the time of Ahaz (2 K. 16:6). She paid tribute to Tiglath-pileser III at Damascus[13] and remained a vassal of Assyria for the next century. Probably the Edomites paid tribute to Nebuchadrezzar after 605 B.C., but like Ammon and Moab they plotted rebellion in 594 B.C. When Judah felt the weight of Nebuchadrezzar's attack in 589–587 B.C. Edom not only gave no assistance but seems to have collaborated with the Babylonians (Ezek. 25:12–14; Ps. 137:7; Obad.; Lam. 4:21). With the advent of Arab groups from the eastern deserts the Edomites moved into southern Judah and eventually reached a point north of Hebron. The area occupied was later known as Idumea. By the end of the sixth century B.C. Edom was occupied by Arab tribes and sedentary occupation came to an end.

The prophecy in 49:7–22 reflects an early phase of the series of events which began at the start of the sixth century, but in the background lay the memory of many earlier clashes between Judah and Edom which may have given rise to anonymous oracles which were taken up by prophets like Jeremiah and Obadiah.

7 The kingdom of Edom lay south of the Dead Sea and extended for about 100 miles between the Wadi Zered and the Gulf of Aqabah. Like Moab it was a high mountainous area which fell away steeply to the west into the Arabah. It had cultivable areas (Num. 20:17, 19), and straddled the King's Highway (Num. 20:14–18) which passed along the eastern plateau of Edom to the north.

13. *ANET,* p. 282.

Teman (lit. "south") was either a district or a city of Edom, but here it is a poetic name for Edom (cf. v. 20). Traditionally Edom was famous for wisdom although the basis for this is not clear. At the time of the prophecy, sound counsel (*'ēṣâ*) and wisdom (*ḥoḵmâ*) had departed from them.

8 The oasis of *Dedan* lay in northwest Arabia, to the southeast of Edom, and may have been part of Edom. Alternately a clan of Dedanites may have settled in Edom. It is often identified with the oasis of el-'Ulâ and the surrounding area.[14] Dedan is warned to flee and hide in the face of the coming disaster in Edom, here referred to as Esau. According to Gen. 36, Esau the brother of the patriarch Jacob (Israel) was the ancestor of Edom. The name Esau is here a poetic name for the Edomites in much the same way as Jacob or Israel was for the people of Palestine.

9–11 The verses are to be compared with Obad. 5–6 where they formulate a question, and are treated as such here. The metaphor is a vivid one. Whereas men picking grapes leave some gleanings and thieves who raid the crop take only what they need, Yahweh would strip Edom bare and destroy his offspring, kinsmen, and neighbors. The words in v. 11 seem to refer to the words spoken by a kindly survivor promising to help widows and orphans.

12 The verse takes up the theme of drinking the cup of Yahweh's wrath (25:15–29). The figure is applied specifically to Edom.

13 *Bozrah* was the chief city and capital of Edom to be identified with the modern Buseira about 25 miles southeast of the Dead Sea. It is different from the Moabite Bozrah (48:24). Although the verse is read as prose, the poetic form lies very close to the surface and there is good parallelism.

14–16 These verses are closely parallel to Obad. 1–4. They predict a sharp declension in Edom's stature. Edom was remarkable for her strongholds hidden away in mountain fastnesses, one of the most famous being Umm el Biyara lying behind the later Petra[15] (2 K. 14:7). The unusual noun in v. 16, *tipleṣeṯ,* may be a derogatory substitute for one of Edom's deities.[16]

14. W. F. Albright, "Dedan" in *Geschichte und Altes Testament* (Festschrift A. Alt) (1953), pp. 1–12.
15. W. H. Morton, "Umm el Biyara," *BA* 19/2 (1956), pp. 26–36.
16. Cf. the name Molech as a substitute for Milcom, by revocalizing the consonants *mlk* with the vowels of *bōšeṯ,* "shame." See also the textual note.

17 The verse occurs with minor variations in 19:8. The theme is common in Jeremiah.

18 The verse occurs with variations in 50:40, while the small poetic piece reappears in v. 33b as a kind of refrain. The overthrow of Edom is likened to that of Sodom and Gomorrah and the two neighboring towns of Admah and Zeboiim (Gen. 18, 19; Deut. 29:23–25). The former destruction was complete.

19–20 These verses and the following appear with variations in 50:44–46. Yahweh is likened to a lion in search of food coming out of the jungle-like thickets in the region of the Jordan to seize one of the sheep which were grazing in the evergreen pastures of the Jordan valley. The *thicket (gā'ôn)* of the Jordan (cf. 12:5) was the Zor, one of the three physical zones of the Jordan Valley; it was the haunt of the Asiatic lion and other wild animals in earlier biblical times (Amos 5:19). In a similar way Yahweh, through his agent the enemy of Edom, would suddenly chase Edom's sheep (i.e., her people) and select the choicest of her rams to devour them. No shepherd in Edom will be able to summon him to explain his actions or stand before him. He would be as irresistible to shepherds and sheep alike as any jungle lion, for he had plans to carry out in regard to Edom which would bring about their destruction.

The *young ones (ṣā'îr)* of the flock will be dragged away,[17] and the *flock (nāweh)* will be appalled because of what happened to them. These last two cola are each introduced by *'im lō'*, "If not . . . ," as in the common oath formula "God do so to me and more if I do not do . . ."; they are thus very strong statements of Yahweh's firm resolve regarding Edom.

21 Howls of anguish are heard at the Reed Sea (*yam-sûp̱*), the place of the Exodus crossing, not identifiable but near the northeastern frontier of Egypt. The effect is heightened by reference to a rocking of the earth (cf. Ps. 114:3–6).

22 The verse is parallel to 48:40–41. The enemy is likened to an eagle swooping down on his prey, a well-known phenomenon in Middle Eastern lands. See comments on 48:40–41. The image of a warrior (*gibbôr*) whose heart was like that of a *woman in labor ('iššâ meṣērâ)* is a picture of helplessness and fear.

17. Lit. "they will drag (them) away."

(vi) Damascus (49:23–27)

23 *Concerning Damascus:*
"Hamath and Arpad are dismayed,
For they have heard news of disaster;
Their heart dissolves with anxiety,[1]
It cannot be still.
24 *Damascus has become faint,*
She turns to flee;
Panic has seized her,
Anguish has gripped her,[2]
Pangs like a woman in childbirth.
25 *How utterly forsaken she is,*[3]
A city of joyful song,[4]
A town of gladness![5]
26 *Therefore her young men shall fall in her squares,*
And all her warriors lie silent.
In that day—the Word of Yahweh of Hosts—
27 *I will kindle a fire at the wall of Damascus*
Which will consume the strongholds of Ben-hadad."

Three short oracles are gathered together at the end of ch. 49. The first concerns Damascus but refers also to Hamath and Arpad, two smaller Aramean city-states in central and northern Syria which appear often in Assyrian texts of the eighth century and earlier. All three states fell to Tiglath-pileser, Arpad and Hamath before 738 B.C. (cf. Isa. 10:9; 36:19; 37:13) and Damascus in 732 B.C. (2 K. 16:9). Sargon II had to crush a rebellion in Damascus in 720 B.C. It would seem that they lost their independence before the end of the eighth century B.C. but probably regained a measure of independence when Assyria collapsed in 609 B.C. They would have become

1. MT reads *nāmōḡû bayyām d*^{e}*'āḡâ,* "they meet; in the sea is anxiety." The expression is a strange one, and various emendations are proposed. RSV reads *kayyām dā'*^{a}*ḡû*, "they are troubled like the sea." Some suggest *nāmôḡ libbām midd*^{e}*'āḡâ*, "their heart dissolves with worry" (J. Bright, p. 333). NEB reads "They are tossed up and down in anxiety, like the unresting sea."

2. To obtain a metrical form two words are transposed. MT reads "anguish and pangs have gripped her as of one in childbirth." LXX omits.

3. MT *lō'-'uzz*^{e}*bâ* would mean "How is she not deserted!" and is an expression not otherwise attested in Hebrew. It may be an error arising from an original emphatic *lameḏ*. See F. Nötscher, "Zum emphatischen Lamed," *VT* 3 (1953), pp. 372–380.

4. Heb. *t*^{e}*hillâ*, "song of praise" (cf. the heading of Ps. 145, e.g.), may have the extended meaning "praise, renown," hence RSV "famous city."

5. MT "town of my gladness." Omit "my" with several versions; see *BHS*. It is possible that the *y* is an archaic genitive ending.

nominal vassals of Egypt but submitted to Nebuchadrezzar after the battle of Carchemish in 605 B.C.

All three of these Aramean states, but especially Damascus, played their part in the history of the Syria-Palestine region during much of the period of the kings of Israel, and their kings Hazael, Ben-hadad, and Rezin feature in biblical history in wars that were waged over possession of the northern parts of Transjordan (1 K. 20; 22; 2 K. 5; 9:14–15; 10:32–33; 12:17–18; 14:23–29; 16:5–9; etc.). Most of this activity concerned Israel, the northern kingdom, which theoretically held large areas of Transjordan under her control. In Nebuchadrezzar's day Aramean troops were sent with others on a punitive expedition to Judah (2 K. 24:2). As a general rule the Arameans did not affect Judah directly. This makes it a little difficult to account for the inclusion of an oracle in Jeremiah directed to people who did not concern Judah greatly. Amos in the eighth century directed an oracle against Damascus for their cruelty in the Transjordan areas (Amos 1:3–5). Jeremiah may well have taken up an older anonymous oracle from the eighth century and applied it to Damascus in connection with some events in the late seventh or early sixth century relating to Nebuchadrezzar, or even events of which we are ignorant at present. Although the precise historical background is not clear, there is no reason not to accept the oracle as having come from Jeremiah.

23 Damascus was situated as it is today a short way from Mount Hermon. Hamath was on the river Orontes in central Syria near the modern Hama some 110 miles north of Damascus. It was an important town on the main trade route connecting Asia Minor with the south. Arpad is probably the modern Tell Erfad, or Tell Rifa'ad, about 20 miles northwest of Aleppo. The two northern states were dismayed at the news they had heard of the *disaster (rāʿâ)* which had befallen Damascus.

24–25 The once powerful city which knew joy and gladness, the former leader of Aramean coalitions (Isa. 7:8), was forsaken. The cause of this may have been the Assyrians who brought the independence of Damascus to an end in 732 B.C. and incorporated the area into the Assyrian province of Hamath. Verse 25 may be understood as the remark of a citizen of Damascus about the once celebrated city.

26–27 The *young men (baḥûrîm)* and the *warriors* (lit. "men of war") are identical. They would fall in the city streets and lie silent on the day of judgment. Damascus was a walled city like many of those mentioned in the OT. Normally conquerors beat down the walls and set fire to the entire city. The kindling of a fire at[6] the wall, which would burn the city, may be a reference to the flame-throwers which were a regular feature of siege warfare. The name *Ben-hadad* (lit. "son of [the deity] Hadad") was borne by some of the kings of Damascus in the ninth and eighth centuries B.C., two and perhaps three of whom are mentioned in the books of Kings (1 K. 15:18; 20:1–34; 2 K. 6:24; 8:7; 13:3, 24). Hadad was the storm-god worshipped by the Arameans, the equivalent of the Canaanite Baal. There is an interesting parallel to this verse in Amos 1:4: "I will send fire into the palace of Hazael, and it will devour the strongholds of Ben-hadad." The expression seems to have been a stereotyped one (cf. Amos 1:4, 14; 2:2, 5).

(vii) Arab Tribes (49:28–33)

28 *Concerning Kedar and the chieftains of Hazor whom Nebuchadrezzar king of Babylon defeated:*
This is what Yahweh has said:
"Rise up! Advance on Kedar!
Plunder the People of the East!
29 *Carry off their tents and their flocks,*
Their tent curtains and all their equipment.
Take their camels from them,
And shout against them 'Terror is all around!'
30 *Flee! Run away quickly!*
Hide yourselves well,
You who dwell in Hazor—Yahweh's word.
For Nebuchadrezzar[1] *king of Babylon has laid a plan against you,*
And has devised a scheme against you.
31 *Rise up! Advance on a nation at ease,*
Living in security—Yahweh's word[2]*—*
With neither gates nor bars,
That dwells alone.
32 *Their camels shall be booty,*
Their countless herds plunder;
I will scatter to the winds
The people who cut the corners of their hair.
From every side I will bring disaster—
Yahweh's word.

6. Translating b^e as *at*.

1. Lacking in LXX.
2. Lacking in LXX.

33 *And Hazor shall become a haunt of jackals,*
A desolation for ever;
No one shall live there,
No human being shall dwell in her."

This short prophecy is directed to certain Arab tribes located in the Syrian desert region east of Palestine. Nomadic Arab groups were likely at any time to make incursions into settled areas to carry off plunder. It was the perennial struggle between the Desert and the Sown (cf. Judg. 6:1–6). The Assyrians conducted campaigns against these desert Bedouin Arabs on more than one occasion.[3] One of the most serious incursions came in the middle of the seventh century when lands in the Transjordan and southern Syria were invaded by Arabs and Ashurbanipal undertook vigorous punitive raids (see comments under 49:1–6). With the collapse of Assyria the Arabs troubled Nebuchadrezzar and in 599/8 B.C., the year prior to his attack on Judah, he conducted a punitive raid against the Arabs.[4] This occasion may well provide the background for the present prophecy.

28 *Kedar* was an important Arab tribe frequently referred to in the OT (2:10; Gen. 25:13; Isa. 21:16, 17; 42:11; 60:7; Ezek. 27:21; etc.). The center of the Kedar tribes seems to have been the oasis of el-'Ulā[5] in the northern Hedjaz. The men of Kedar were known in OT times as sheep-breeders (Isa. 60:7), traders with Phoenicia (Ezek. 27:21), and skilled archers (Isa. 21:16–17). Kedar is associated in the OT with Dedan and Tema (Isa. 21:13–14) and various other Arab areas. The name Dedan as a designation for Semitic nomads goes back a thousand years before the earliest biblical allusion, although the use of Dedan as a place name in proto-Arabic inscriptions comes after the sixth century B.C.

The name *Hazor* poses a question. It is not the well-known city to the north of Galilee which was an important strategic town for some centuries, but rather a place in the eastern desert. It would seem to have been a specific place—to judge from vv. 30, 33—but may have denoted the name of a collection of unwalled villages. The noun *ḥāṣēr* is very close to *ḥāṣôr* in form. The plural *ḥ^{a}ṣērîm* is

3. Sargon II (721–705 B.C.), Sennacherib (704–681 B.C.), and Esarhaddon (680–669 B.C.) all record campaigns among the Arabs to take booty and to carry off their gods, which were then used as a bargaining point. See *ANET,* pp. 286, 291, 292.
4. D. J. Wiseman, *Chronicles of Chaldaean Kings*, pp. 31f., 71.
5. W. F. Albright, "Dedan," *Geschichte und Altes Testament* (Beiträge zum Historischen Theologie 16) (1953), pp. 1–12.

used in Isa. 42:11 of small unwalled villages where Arab tribes settled.[6] It is possible that the region where such *ḥᵃṣērîm* were concentrated was known as *Hazor.* The associated noun *mamlᵉḵôṯ,* normally translated "kingdoms," has an alternative usage, "kings" or *chieftains.*[7] Hence, a possible translation here is "village chieftains." A third group, the *People of the East (bᵉnê qeḏem),* is known in other parts of the OT. These people are associated with Midianites and Amalekites in Judg. 6:3, nomadic groups who raided Israelite territory in the days of the Judges (cf. Gen. 29:1; Judg. 5:33; 7:12; 8:10; 1 K. 4:30; Isa. 11:14; Ezek. 25:4; Job 1:3).

29 The items referred to, *tents, flocks, tent curtains, camels,* are characteristic of nomads rather than of settled peoples. The cry *Terror is all around (māḡôr missāḇîḇ)* is used several times in Jeremiah (6:25; 20:3, 4, 10; 46:5). It is here used to denote the shout of raiders as they advance on the camps of the Bedouin.

30 The verse is difficult metrically. The omission of *Nebuchadrezzar* with LXX gives a simple 3:3/3:3 pattern.

31–32 The phrase *qᵉṣûṣê pē'â* (lit. "the cutting of the fringe") is ambiguous; see comments on 25:23 and cf. NEB "the fringe of the desert." Such defenseless communities were no match for the well-equipped Babylonian armies. Verse 31 resembles Ezek. 38:11 but there is no reason to think that either is dependent on the other.

33 All the expressions used here, *haunt of jackals* (9:10; 10:22; 51:37), *a desolation* (4:27; 6:8; 9:11; 10:22; 12:10, 11; 32:43; 44:6; 49:2, 33; 50:13), *no one shall live there* (4:7, 29; 9:11; 26:9; 33:10; 44:22; 46:19; 51:29, 37), *no human being shall dwell in her,* are conventional and are used more than once by Jeremiah as well as by other prophets. The first part of the verse resembles 9:10 and 10:22, and the latter part is identical with v. 18b. Jeremiah had many expressions he used over and over again.[8]

(viii) Elam (49:34–39)

34 *What came as the word of Yahweh to Jeremiah the prophet concerning Elam, at the beginning of the reign of Zedekiah king of Judah.*

6. Cf. Gen. 25:16; Exod. 8:9; Josh. 13:23; Isa. 42:11; Neh. 11:25; 12:2–3; 1 Chr. 9:16.
7. See W. F. Albright, "The Oracles of Balaam," *JBL* 63 (1944), p. 218, n. 70; "A Catalogue of Early Hebrew Lyric Poems (Psalm LXVIII)," *HUCA* 23 (1950/51), p. 34; Z. S. Harris, *A Grammar of the Phoenician Language* (1936), p. 118.
8. See S. R. Driver, *An Introduction to the Literature of the OT* (9th ed. 1913), pp. 247–277.

35 *This is what Yahweh of Hosts has said:*
"Look! I will break the bow of Elam,
The mainstay of their might.
36 *And I will bring upon Elam four winds,*
From the four quarters of heaven.
And I will scatter them before all these winds,
And there will be no nation
To which the fugitives of Elam shall not come.
37 *I will terrify Elam before their foes,*
Before those who seek their life.
I will bring disaster upon them,
My furious anger—Yahweh's word.
I will send the sword to pursue them,
Until I have made an end of them;
38 *And I will set my throne in Elam,*
And will destroy from thence the king and his officers—
Yahweh's word.
39 *But in days to come, I will restore the fortunes of Elam—*
Yahweh's word."

The final prophecy in ch. 49 is dated to the accession year of Zedekiah, 597 B.C. Elam lay to the east of Babylon in the southwest of modern Iran. In ancient times it was a significant nation in the politics of lower Mesopotamia. After many years of conflict in Assyria, Elam was finally conquered by Ashurbanipal about 640 B.C. when Ashurbanipal destroyed the capital Susa. In 612 B.C. Cyaxares, the Medean ruler, helped Nabopolassar of Babylon destroy Nineveh the Assyrian capital, and presumably this meant freedom for Elam once again. But it may have become independent a little earlier, perhaps around 626/5 B.C.[1] A broken text in the Babylonian Chronicle may indicate a clash between Nebuchadrezzar and Elam in 596/4 B.C. to prevent an Elamite advance into Babylonia.[2] If the interpretation of the fragmentary text is correct, Jeremiah's date of 597 B.C. (the accession year of Zedekiah) would predate this event. Jeremiah's prophecy added weight to earlier prophecies about a long exile for the captive Judeans (cf. v. 29). The present oracle cut short any hope of an early return, for it indicated that Elam would be overwhelmed herself in the will of Yahweh.

34 The same introductory formula occurs at 46:1; 47:1. Je-

1. D. J. Wiseman, *Chronicles of Chaldaean Kings*, pp. 8–10, 51.
2. *Ibid.*, p. 73

rusalem fell according to the Babylonian Chronicle on the second of Adar 597 B.C., which was March 16th by modern reckoning. The next month was Nisan, when the New Year began. Zedekiah's accession year lasted only a month.

35 The reference to the *bow of Elam* suggests that the Elamites were famous for their archers (cf. Isa. 22:6), who comprised the mainstay of their might. Elam was absorbed into the Persian Empire after 539 B.C., and during Persian times one of the features of the Persian army was a strong body of bowmen. Landowners were required to furnish the king with a bowman or pay him a sum of money to hire one.[3]

36–37 The picture of four winds to represent military might is known elsewhere in the OT (Ezek. 37:9; Dan. 8:8; Zech. 6:1–8). The terms are general here. Yahweh will bring military powers upon Elam to destroy it as a nation. The latter part of v. 37 is repeated from 9:16b. The expressions are conventional ones used by Jeremiah and others.

38 The picture of a conquering king setting up his throne in the land he has defeated is used by Jeremiah in 1:15; 43:8–13. It is a symbol of conquest and subjugation.

39 A prose comment is added which promises restoration (cf. 46:26; 48:47; 49:6). The comment is often attributed to a later editor. Jeremiah certainly looked for days of restoration for Judah and Israel, and perhaps he had some hopes for the day when Yahweh would be acknowledged in other lands with a consequent restoration of their fortunes too. Certainly the doctrine is not developed in Jeremiah, so that the origin of such a comment is uncertain.

(ix) Babylon (50:1–51:64)

(a) Babylon's fall and Israel's release (50:1–10)

1 *The word that Yahweh spoke concerning Babylon, concerning the land of the Chaldeans through the prophet Jeremiah.*[1]

3. Documents from Nippur show that Jews in this center were among those who paid bow tenure in the days of Artaxerxes I (464–424 B.C.) and Darius II (424–405 B.C.).

1. This verse is abbreviated in LXX to "The word of Yahweh which he spoke concerning Babylon."

2 *"Declare among the nations and proclaim!*
Give the signal! Proclaim![2]
Don't keep it a secret! Say:
'Babylon is taken,
Bel is put to shame.
Marduk is dismayed;
Her idols are put to shame,
Her disgusting images are dismayed.'[3]
3 *For a nation from the north has fallen upon her*
That will make her land a desolate waste
With no one living there.
Both man and beast have fled and gone away.[4]
4 *In those days and at that time—Yahweh's word—*
The people of Israel shall come,
They and the people of Judah as well,
And weeping as they go,
They shall seek Yahweh their God.
5 *They shall ask the way to Zion,*
Their faces toward her;
And they shall come[5] *and join themselves to Yahweh*
In an everlasting covenant that will not be forgotten.
6 *My people were lost sheep,*
Their shepherds led them astray;
They turned them out on the mountains,
They wandered from mountain to hill;
They forgot their fold;
7 *Whoever found them devoured them.*
Their enemies said, 'We are not guilty
Because they sinned against Yahweh,
The true pasture and hope of their fathers.'
8 *Flee from the midst of Babylon,*
From the land of the Chaldeans!
Go forth and be as he-goats leading the flock!
9 *For look! I will stir up*
And bring against Babylon
A horde of mighty nations
From a northern land.
They will line up against her
And she will be taken from the north.[6]
Their arrows are like a skilled[7] *warrior*
Who never returns empty-handed.

2. The line is lacking in LXX.
3. The last two lines are lacking in LXX.
4. For the last two lines LXX reads "Neither man nor beast lives there."
5. MT has the imperative "come." We emend with LXX.
6. Lit. "from there."
7. MT reads *maškîl* but it must be *maśkîl*.

10 *And Chaldea shall be plundered;*[8]
All her plunderers will be sated—Yahweh's word."

Jeremiah's final prophecy against the nations concerns Babylon. Almost as much space is devoted to Babylon as to all the other nations together. This gives some indication of the tremendous importance of Babylon to the whole of western Asia at the close of the seventh and during the early decades of the sixth century. Several of the other foreign prophecies make reference to Babylon directly or by implication (46:2, 13, 25; 49:28–33). From Judah's point of view the nation had gone to exile at the hands of the Chaldeans, who were the archenemy of the people of Yahweh. Little wonder that so much space is given to Babylon.

The analysis of the lengthy prophecy is not easy. It would seem that a lot of material was brought together into one large block. For convenience the commentary will be broken into several smaller segments. Clearly this is quite artificial and different commentators propose different schemes.

The central theme is the overthrow of Babylon and the restoration of the Jews to their homeland. It would be reasonable to assume that the section was compiled from several shorter poems which have been drawn together into one whole, with a number of prose sections interspersed. But it is impossible to decide at this point of time what were the original poems, how much of the material was genuinely from Jeremiah, how much is editorial comment, and how much comprises anonymous oracle material uttered in prophetic circles during the exilic period. There is no good reason to place any of the material in the post-exilic period. None of the material shows any awareness of the fact that Cyrus finally captured Babylon without destroying the city, but rather these chapters speak in terms of the devastation of Babylon by its enemies. No reference whatever is made to the Persians.

That Jeremiah himself delivered oracles against Babylon and that he expected the ultimate overthrow of Babylon is not open to question (e.g., 27:7; 29:10; 51:59–64). Words spoken by Jeremiah himself on other occasions may have been taken up again and applied to Babylon (e.g., 50:41–43). But it is impossible to speak dogmatically. It would be a fair question to ask frequently as one studies these chapters whether Jeremiah could possibly have written a par-

8. Lit. "shall be for spoil."

ticular segment. Certainly these poems reflect a period prior to Cyrus' overthrow of the Medean king Astyages in 550 B.C., but they might suit a period even earlier so that the time of compilation might be rather earlier than 550 B.C. If we take the references to Nebuchadrezzar in 50:17 and 51:34 as indicating that Nebuchadrezzar was still alive, these chapters are to be dated before 562 B.C., the date of his death.

After the death of Nebuchadrezzar in 562 B.C. the neo-Babylonian power had just over twenty years to run. His son Amel-Marduk (Evil-Merodach) was assassinated in 560 B.C. by his brother-in-law Neriglissar (560–556 B.C.). His son Labashi-Marduk reigned a matter of months and was supplanted by Nabonidus (556–539 B.C.). The rise of the Persians under Cyrus (550–530 B.C.) and their emergence as rulers of the East is not even hinted at here.

1 This verse is the superscription of the whole prophecy in chs. 50 and 51. The *Chaldeans (kaśdîm)* were descended from a seminomadic tribe which was settled to the south of Ur. From the tenth century B.C. their land *Kaldu* is known in inscriptions. In the ninth century some of the Chaldean chiefs were vassals of the Assyrian ruler Adadnirari III (811–784 B.C.). The father of Nebuchadrezzar, Nabopolassar, was a native Chaldean who took the throne of Babylon in 626 B.C. and gave rise to the neo-Babylonian period which lasted till 539 B.C. Nebuchadrezzar was the most illustrious and longest reigning of these kings.

2 All commentators agree that vv. 2 and 3 are clearly poetic in form. Babylon's gods are to be put to shame. The prophecy refers to the day when Babylon will be captured and her protective deities will be humiliated. *Bel* (lit. "lord") was the title of the storm-god Enlil, the chief god of Nippur. *Marduk* (Merodach) was the chief god of Babylon and head of the Babylonian pantheon. Bel became an appellation for Marduk, and here Bel and Marduk are the same as the poetic parallelism demonstrates. Marduk was the creator-god of the Babylonian Creation Epic who emerged as "king of the gods." The *idols (ʿaṣabbîm)* and the *disgusting images (gillûlîm)* refer to representations of the deities in statue form. The word *gillûlîm* is indelicate, meaning "balls of excrement." It is applied to pagan idols in Lev. 26:30; Deut. 29:17; 1 K. 15:12; 21:25; etc. Ezekiel used the word some thirty-eight times. The term may be related to the word *'elîlîm*, "nothing," a pun on *'ēlîm* or *'elōhîm*, "gods." Perhaps *gillûlîm* is another pun but with a rather crude association. Jeremiah was fond of puns (cf. 2:5, 8, 11; etc.). The habit of speaking disparagingly of pagan gods is known in several places in the OT. One of the most sustained pictures occurs in Isa. 44:9–17.

3 The *nation from the north* is not defined. The expression is a favorite of Jeremiah (1:14; 4:6; 6:1; 13:30; 15:12; 46:20; 47:2; 50:41; 51:48). Although the meaning is obscure in earlier chapters it is eventually defined as Babylon. Here the term has become indefinite again (cf. Ezek. 38:1–3). The reference at this stage is hardly to the Persians who came from the east, although the strategic line of attack was roughly from the north. But although the meaning is vague and undefined, for Babylon it meant the destruction and desertion of the city by man and beast. This did not happen when Cyrus took the city.

4–5 The section vv. 4–7 is regarded as prose in RSV, NEB, and other versions, but there is strong parallelism throughout these verses and good reason to regard them as poetic.[9] A total Israel, *the people of Israel* and *the people of Judah as well,* seek Yahweh with weeping and come to join themselves to Yahweh again in an everlasting covenant (cf. 32:40). As in the Book of Consolation (chs. 30–33), the future restoration of Yahweh's people includes the unity of the people, repentance, and renewal of the covenant, which will not be broken again (cf. 31:31–33; 32:40).

6 The *shepherds* who led them astray included all their leaders, kings, priests, and prophets. The present context points to the religious leaders who encouraged apostasy and the worship of Baal on the high hills (2:20; 3:2; etc.) so that they forgot their own *fold,* that is, the place where they were cared for and nurtured by Yahweh their true shepherd. The breach of covenant envisaged in v. 6 is set over against the renewal of their everlasting covenant in v. 5.

7 This verse is reminiscent of 2:3, where it was declared that in the days of her youth, when her covenant was newly made and when she displayed love and loyalty, she was holy to Yahweh, and all who devoured her were held to be guilty. But in her apostasy enemies who devoured her could claim *We are not guilty.* In her state of apostasy she was not holy to Yahweh. She had *sinned (ḥāṭā')* against him who was her *true pasture*[10] and the *hope of their fathers.*

9. See J. Bright, *Jeremiah*, pp. 339f.
10. Heb. *nᵉwēh ṣeḏeq*. The verbs *'āḵal* ("eat, devour") and *'āšam* ("be guilty") occur both here and in 2:3.

8 But Babylon's end was at hand and captive Israel was due for release. The picture is a pastoral one. Once the sheepfold was opened the male goats would rush to leave the enclosure first. So Judah would be in the forefront of captive peoples breaking loose from Babylon to return home.

9–10 As Babylon once invaded and ravaged Judah and Jerusalem, so *a horde of mighty nations from a northern land* would line up in battle array against Babylon. Another "foe from the north," another destroyer, would come, but this time against Babylon. That foe in relation to Babylon would be just as invincible as Babylon was against Judah. The word translated *skilled (maśkîl)* can also mean "successful," i.e., victorious. The picture is of a warrior skilled at his art returning from every battle with booty. To such warriors Babylon would become spoil (*šālāl*) to such a degree that those who despoiled her would be sated. Their arrows would have found their mark.

(b) Babylon's fall (50:11–16)

11 *"Though you rejoice, though you exult,*
You plunderers of my patrimony,
Though you paw the ground like a young heifer at pasture[1]
And neigh like stallions,
12 *Your mother will be deeply ashamed,*
And she who bore you will be disgraced.
Look (at her)! the least[2] *of the nations,*
A wilderness dry and barren!
13 *Through the wrath of Yahweh she will be uninhabited,*
She will become a complete desolation.
All who pass by Babylon shall be appalled
And shall whistle at all her wounds.
14 *Draw up battle lines against Babylon on every side,*
All you that bend the bow!
Shoot[3] *at her! Spare no arrows,*
Because she has sinned against Yahweh![4]

1. MT reads *k^e'eglâ dāšâ,* "like a heifer threshing"; but LXX suggests *k^e'eglê baddeše'*, "like heifers in the grass," which is in keeping with the rest of the verse.
2. Lit. "the last."
3. Reading *yārû* for *y^eḏû*.
4. Lacking in LXX and omitted by some commentators because it disturbs the logical flow.

15 *Raise the war cry against her from all sides!*
She has thrown up her hands!
Her bulwarks[5] *have fallen,*
Her walls are demolished;
This is the vengeance of Yahweh—
Take vengeance on her!
Do to her as she has done!
16 *Cut off the sower from Babylon,*
And the one who reaps with his sickle at harvest-time.
Before the dreadful sword
Every man turns toward his own people,
Every man flees to his homeland."

There is a note of vengeance running through these verses, and indeed through the whole of chs. 50–51. There is nothing here that would require a late date. The material is very general and not different from the kind of thing Jeremiah might well have uttered. It seems unnecessary to assume that the setting is in the context of the Exile, with Babylon on the verge of downfall and the exiles soon to return home.[6] We are certainly in the context of exile in the mind of the writer, since some Jews are already there. And he certainly gives expression to his belief that Babylon will fall and the exiles will return, but all this is a projection into the future and a transfer to Babylon of the sufferings of the people in Judah and Jerusalem caused by the Babylonians.

11 Verse 11 is the protasis (*kî, though*) of a conditional sentence which finds its apodosis in v. 12. The verbs are to be read as second masculine plural. The passage takes a backward glance at Babylon's treatment of Judah and Jerusalem. She plundered Yahweh's *patrimony (naḥ^{a}lâ),* and rejoiced and exulted over her deed. In ancient Israel a man's patrimony was the land inherited from his ancestors. The land of Israel is here pictured as Yahweh's patrimony. The term is a favorite one with Jeremiah and is variously used of the land as Israel's patrimony (3:18–19; 12:14, 15) and as Yahweh's patrimony (2:7; 16:18; 50:11), but also in the sense that Yahweh himself is Israel's patrimony (10:16; 51:19), while Israel is Yahweh's patrimony (12:7, 8, 9).

The two pastoral images, of young heifers running free in

5. The word is unclear; *'āšwiyyōṯ* occurs only here. The parallelism requires a word like "wall" in the second half of the line.
6. G. P. Couturier, "Jeremiah," *JBC,* p. 335.

pastures and of neighing stallions, strengthen the picture of Babylon's delight at her capture of Jerusalem and Judah.

12–13 The mother referred to is the city of Babylon, personified as the mother of the inhabitants. Powerful Babylon the chief of the nations will be reduced to a minor status, the least of the nations. In former times cities that had been destroyed by Babylon, in particular Jerusalem, were turned into a dry and barren wilderness, uninhabited, a complete waste which caused passers-by to be appalled and to whistle at the sight of their wounds. The language of this verse appears several times in Jeremiah's oracles and was evidently conventional language (cf. 6:8; 9:10; 12:10–11; 18:16; 19:8; 34:22; 44:6; 49:17, 33; etc.). But in the day of Yahweh's wrath the same expressions would be used of Babylon.

14–15 Instructions are issued to the attacking forces to press the attack on every side (*sāḇîḇ*). Then comes the great reversal. It is now Babylon who throws up her hands as a sign of surrender (cf. 1 Chr. 29:24; 2 Chr. 30:8).[7] Babylon had once breached the walls of other cities (2 K. 25:4, 10) and destroyed their defenses. Now her turn has come. The poet notes that Babylon's defeat is Yahweh's *vengeance (nᵉqāmâ)* on the proud and erstwhile ruthless city, and cries out, *Take vengeance on her! Do to her as she has done!*

16 As Babylon had destroyed the farms and killed the farmers in her campaigns, the poet now asks that this may happen to Babylon.

The last part of the verse is reminiscent of Isa. 13:14b. With the fall of Babylon, captured peoples like the Jews would take the opportunity to flee to their own homelands and to their own people (cf. 46:16) lest the dreadful sword overtake them.

(c) Israel's return (50:17–20)

17 *"A scattered flock*[1] *is Israel;*
Lions scatter him.[2]
First the king of Assyria devoured him,
And now[3] *Nebuchadrezzar king of Babylon has gnawed his bones.*[4]

7. In Chronicles the expression is the same as we find here, *nāṯan yāḏ*, lit. "to give a hand."

1. Heb. *śeh*, "sheep," is singular but the word has a collective sense.
2. The verb in MT lacks a suffix; LXX and Vulg. read masc. singular.
3. Heb. *wᵉzeh hā'aḥᵃrôn,* "after this," in conjunction with *hāri'šôn* in the previous clause seems to be an emphatic construction, perhaps: "First it was thus, and now, on top of that" or "the final degradation."
4. LXX lacks the name Nebuchadrezzar. The verb *'iṣṣēm* (gnaw the bones) is a Piel derived from *'eṣem* (bone).

18 *Therefore this is what Yahweh of Hosts the God of Israel has said:*
Look! I will punish the king of Babylon and his country
As I have punished the king of Assyria.
19 *And I will bring Israel back to his pasture;*
And he will graze on Carmel and in Bashan,
And on the hills of Ephraim and Gilead shall he eat his fill.
20 *In those days, and at that time—Yahweh's word*[5]*—*
Israel's guilt shall be sought,[6] *but there shall be none,*
And Judah's sin, but it is not to be found;
For I will forgive those whom I leave as a remnant."

Verses 17–20 cover two ideas both of which relate to Israel. In the first (vv. 17–19), Babylon's judgment and Israel's consequent restoration are declared. In the second (v. 20), the emphasis is on Yahweh's complete forgiveness of Israel. Opinions vary about the literary form of these verses. RSV regards them as prose. NEB takes only v. 20 as prose. In our view they are all poetic. A further section on Israel occurs at vv. 33–34.

17 Israel is introduced as a scattered flock chased by lions, that is, enemy nations, defined as Assyria and Babylon. Assyria first fed on Israel when they invaded and destroyed Northern Israel in 722 B.C. and took many into captivity (2 K. 17:1–6). Then more recently Babylon gnawed the bones of Israel by destroying the southern kingdom and taking many captive (2 K. 24).

18 At the time the poem was written, Assyria had been punished. In fact, Assyria fell before the Babylonian onslaught in the years 612–609 B.C. This poem must date after 609 B.C., although how much later is not known. But there was a strong assurance that Babylon too would be punished (cf. Isa. 10:5–19).

19 Yahweh is pictured as a Shepherd who will bring his flock Israel back to its pasture (*nāwēh*) so that it grazes (*rā'â*) again on the rich pastures of Carmel and Bashan, and on the hills of Ephraim and Gilead.

20 One of the important features of the days of restoration is spiritual renewal with its concomitant of forgiveness. The doctrine is here expressed in noble form. The forgiveness of the remnant will be such that their *guilt ('āwôn)* and their *sins (ḥaṭṭō'ṯ)* will be com-

5. Lacking in LXX.
6. The Pual (passive) of *bqš* is here used with what appears to be a direct accusative. See *GK*, ([28]1910), art. 121, a, b, pp. 387f.

pletely obliterated (cf. 31:34; 33:8; 36:3). It was a theme that other OT writers spoke about (Mic. 7:18, 19; Ezek. 33:10–20; 36:26–29; Ps. 103:12). If the people carried in their memory a sense of guilt and despair such as that which is depicted in Ezek. 33:10–11 ("Our transgressions and our sins are upon us and we waste away because of them; how then can we live?"), they may be assured that the dark shadow of guilt that had dominated their thinking would be taken away, never to threaten them again.

(d) God's judgment on Babylonia (50:21–40)

21 *"(March) against*[1] *the land of Merathaim,*
March against her
And against the people of Pekod,
Slay[2] *and devote every one of them to destruction*[3]*—Yahweh's word—*
And do whatever I command you."
22 *Listen! There is battle in the land!*
Great destruction![4]
23 *Look how the hammer of all the earth*
Is broken in pieces and shattered,
How Babylon has become
A horror among the nations.
24 *O Babylon, you set a snare*[5] *for your own gain.*[6]
But you have been trapped without knowing it.
You were found out. You are held fast
Because you have challenged[7] *Yahweh.*
25 *Yahweh has opened his armory*
And brought forth the weapons of his wrath,
For the Lord, Yahweh of Hosts, has work
In the land of the Chaldeans.

1. MT has simply "against the land of Merathaim." A verb seems to be required such as that in the second half of the line, *'ᵃlēh.* This could have been dropped through haplography; cf. Syriac.
2. The first verb *ḥrb* normally means "be dry." In the context one would expect a verb like "kill." It is possible that here and in v. 27 we have a verb form of *ḥereḇ,* "sword."
3. MT follows the second verb with *'aḥᵃrêhem,* "after them," which is lacking in LXX. Targ. reads the equivalent of *'aḥᵃrîṯām,* "the last of them." J. Bright, *Jeremiah*, p. 342 suggests an original text of *heḥᵉrîm haḥᵃrēm,* the verb plus the infinitive absolute, "devote them to utter destruction."
4. LXX reads: "The din of battle, a mighty crash, in the land of Chaldeans."
5. Read 2nd fem. singular. Cf. *BHS*. The *y* may be an old poetic ending.
6. Translating *lāḵ* as a dative of advantage.
7. Heb. *hiṯgārâ,* "engage in a contest."

26 *"Enter from every side!*[8]
Open her granaries!
Heap her up[9] *like heaps of grain, devote her to destruction,*
Let no survivor remain.
27 *Put all her warriors*[10] *to the sword,*[11]
Let them go to the slaughter.
Woe to them for their day has come,
The time of their reckoning."
28 *Listen! Fugitives and refugees from the land of Babylon*
Announcing in Zion the vengeance of Yahweh our God,
Vengeance for his temple.
29 *"Summon archers*[12] *against Babylon,*
All who draw a bow!
Lay siege to her on every side
So that no one escapes!
Repay her according to her deeds!
For she has acted insolently against Yahweh
The Holy One of Israel.
30 *Therefore her young men shall fall in her streets*
And all her warriors shall lie silent on that day—
Yahweh's word.
31 *Look! I am against you, insolent city—*
Word of the Lord, Yahweh of Hosts.
Yes,[13] *your day has come, the time of your reckoning,*
32 *And 'Insolence' shall stumble and fall,*
And no one shall lift him up.
I will kindle fire in his towns[14]
Which will consume everything around him."
33 *This is what Yahweh of Hosts has said:*
"The people of Israel are oppressed
And the people of Judah too.
All their captors hold them fast;
They refuse to release them.

8. The sense of *miqqēṣ* is uncertain. NEB translates "Her harvest time has come to her," reading *qēṣ* as "harvest." But the expression *miqqāṣeh,* "from all sides," occurs in 51:31; Gen. 19:4; etc., and possibly we have here an abbreviation, "from end (to end)."
9. The same verb is used of the heaping up of the waters in Exod. 15:8.
10. Lit. "bulls" (*pārîm*).
11. See note 2 above.
12. MT reads *rabbîm,* which LXX understands as "many" but which may be revocalized as *rōḇîm* (cf. Gen. 21:20), *archers* (participle of *rbh*).
13. Here *kî* is asseverative.
14. LXX reads "forests" (*b^eya'^{a}rô* for MT *b^e'ārāyw*).

34 *But their Redeemer is strong;*
Yahweh of Hosts is his name;
He will himself[15] *plead their cause.*
He will bring rest to the earth,
But bring unrest to the people of Babylon.
35 *A sword on the Chaldeans—*
Yahweh's word—
On the people of Babylon,
Her officials and her men of wisdom.
36 *A sword on the false prophets,*[16] *who are made fools;*
A sword on the warriors, who are terrified;
37 *A sword on her horses and her chariots,*[17]
And against all the hired soldiers within her;
They shall become like women.
A sword against her treasures; they shall be plundered.
38 *A sword against her waters; they shall dry up.*
For it is a land of images;
They are made foolish by their terrifying idols.
39 *Therefore demons and evil spirits*[18] *shall live there,*
And desert owls shall inhabit her.
Never again will people live there,
Nor shall anyone dwell there for ages to come.
40 *As when God overthrew Sodom and Gomorrah and their neighbors—*
Yahweh's word—
No man shall live there,
No mortal shall settle there."

In vv. 21–32 the theme is judgment on Babylon. The note of vengeance is struck several times (e.g., v. 28). Babylon is depicted as the personification of insolence (v. 31). In the midst of this picture of judgment Israel's deliverance is again mentioned (vv. 33–34). A sustained graphic description of the destruction of Babylon, its people, its leaders, its army, its wealth, is given in vv. 35–38 where the phrase "A sword against . . . ," that is, "death to . . . ," occurs five times. No doubt these verses represent a gathering together of several originally independent oracles now woven into one and linked to the preceding and following verses.

15. The verb is strengthened by the infinitive absolute: "He will surely plead their cause." There is a strong assonance in the Heb. *rîḇ yārîḇ 'eṯ-rîḇām*.
16. The term *baddîm,* "boasters," may be a pun on *bārîm.* The *bāru*-priests practiced divination by liver reading (hepatoscopy). See H. B. Huffmon, "Prophecy in the Mari Letters," *BA* 31/4 (1968), pp. 101–124. They were well known in Babylon (cf. Isa. 44:25).
17. There is a change of pronoun in MT to "his." This line is lacking in LXX.
18. J. Bright, *Jeremiah,* p. 355 translates "goblins and ghouls."

21 It seems possible that this announcement of the destruction of glorious Babylon was to proclaimed in Jerusalem (v. 28). The call goes out to the enemy from the north (vv. 9, 41) to come up against *the land of Merathaim* and *the people of Pekod*. Both areas are well known. *Merathaim* was the region of *Mat Marratim* at the head of the Persian Gulf where the Tigris and Euphrates rivers meet. It was known as *nār marrūti*. But there is a play on words here, for the root *mrh* means "to rebel" and the form of the word is a dual, meaning "(land of) double rebellion," or "twofold rebel," that is, "rebel of rebels." The second region Pekod (cf. Ezek. 23:23) is the Akkadian *Puqudu* which lay in eastern Babylonia. But the root *pqd* means "to punish." Hence the land of Pekod is the "land of doom."

The verb *devote to destruction (heḥ^{e}rîm)* is a denominative verb from the noun *ḥērem,* something devoted to destruction.[19] In the context of the holy war everything captured in battle, the total city and its inhabitants and their property, belonged to Yahweh, whose right it was to distribute it or to retain it. Where he retained it, it was destroyed completely. In the overthrow of Babylon there was a good reason to withhold from Israel the idolatrous city and its associated wealth which might taint Israel. In that case Babylon was to be "devoted to destruction." When Yahweh's retribution came, the entire city was to be placed under the ban (cf. Josh. 8:26).

Presumably the command of v. 21 is addressed to the attacking forces.

22–24 The poet senses the din of war and the massive destruction in the land of Chaldea. He saw that Babylon, the hammer that had pounded the whole earth into submission when at the zenith of its power, was now to be broken and shattered. Once, Judah and Jerusalem had become a *horror (šammâ).*[20] Now Babylon herself would become a horror among the nations.

Like a hunter who trapped birds, Babylon had set traps (*yāqōš*) and had trapped nations, including Judah. But she was now trapped herself, and all unaware. The point is made elsewhere in the prophets that Yahweh may appoint a nation to fulfil a purpose as his servant. But this does not absolve such a nation from the conse-

19. 50:21, 26; 51:3; Num. 21:2–3; Deut. 2:34; 3:6; 7:2; 13:16; 20:17; Josh. 2:10; 6:18, 21; 8:26; 10:1, 28, 35, 37, 39–40; 11:11–12, 20–21; Judg. 1:17; 21:11; 1 Sam. 15:3, 8–9, 15, 18, 20; 30:17; etc.

20. The word was frequently on Jeremiah's lips, generally in reference to Judea: 2:15; 4:7; 5:30; 18:16; 19:8; 25:9, 11, 18, 38; 29:18; 42:18; 44:12, 22; 46:19; 48:9; 49:13, 17; 50:3; 51:29, 37, 41, 43.

quence of guilty acts or an insolent attitude. If Isaiah made the point in reference to the Assyrians (Isa. 10:5–19) in the eighth century B.C., Jeremiah was to reiterate the point in the sixth century.[21] Theologically, Yahweh's purposes for mankind were closely linked to his purposes for Israel and no great power could frustrate the divine intention. In order to bring about the release of the exiles, Babylon's power had to be broken. Jeremiah had the strong assurance that this would happen.

25 The work of overthrowing Babylon was Yahweh's.

The Lord, Yahweh of Hosts, has a work
In the land of the Chaldeans.

The weapons of his wrath which he brought out from his armory were none other than those of the Persian conqueror spoken of in Isa. 44:28–45:1 as his shepherd and his anointed one.

26–27 The end of Babylon is likened to the breaking open of granaries and the piling up of looted grain for destruction.

The verb *devote to destruction* is again used. The destruction of Babylon is to be complete (cf. 25:9; 50:21; 51:3). No survivors (*šᵉʾērîṯ*) are to be left. The Babylonian soldiers are here spoken of figuratively as "bulls," the strong ones of the nation (cf. Isa. 34:6, 7).

28 As the picture unfolds, fugitives escaping from the land of Babylon carry the message to Jerusalem that Yahweh's vengeance has been wreaked on Babylon. The fugitives are probably to be thought of as Jewish fugitives who have fled the city and reached Zion to declare the news that Israel's hated oppressor has been overthrown (cf. 46:10; 50:15; 51:6). Though the words *vengeance for his temple* are lacking in LXX, they represent an appropriate comment and should not necessarily be taken as secondary (cf. 51:11). The temple was Israel's central sanctuary, the divinely appointed place to which the people brought their sacrifices and offerings and where Yahweh's presence was tabernacled. It was an act of blasphemous insolence to desecrate it. Such an act called for the vengeance of Yahweh. With delight refugee Jews would declare that they who had destroyed the temple were now the subjects of divine retribution.

29–32 The poet returns to the attacker of Babylon. Archers are prominent in the assault. This was normal, as the Assyrian bas-reliefs show. Sloping ramps were thrown up on which battering rams

21. Adam C. Welch, *Jeremiah: His Time and His Work* (1928), pp. 195–212.

were run up. Archers protected by large shields generally carried by other warriors showered the walls with arrows, while sappers sought to undermine the walls as the battering rams approached under the protection of the arrows.[22] The walled city is surrounded by the encampments of the invaders who have laid siege to the city. The author of these lines was well aware of the methods of siege warfare. Jeremiah himself had passed through the experience twice in his lifetime. The present assault was a repayment for Babylon's many attacks on cities, but in particular for her attack on Jerusalem. Her case was all the worse because she had insulted (*zāḏâ*) Yahweh (cf. v. 24). She was, indeed, *Insolence* (*zāḏôn,* v. 32) personified. She had acted presumptuously and rebelliously against Yahweh, Israel's God, as though he were powerless and of no consequence. Yahweh is here called the *Holy One of Israel* (v. 29), a favorite expression of Isaiah and Second Isaiah[23] but which occurs only here in Jeremiah. But now "Insolence" is to be struck down with no one to raise him up when he stumbles and falls. His towns will be destroyed by fire as formerly he destroyed the capitals and lesser towns of the states he subdued, but notably Jerusalem and the smaller towns of Judah. Verse 30 is repeated *verbatim* from 49:26 where the words apply to Damascus.

33–34 Once again Israel is brought into focus. It is all Israel that is in view, the people of Israel together with the people of Judah, emphasizing the concept of a united Israel that will enjoy the days of restoration. Taking up an ancient picture of the oppression of Israel in Egypt, the prophet describes Israel in Babylonia in similar terms. Neither in Egypt nor in Babylonia did there seem to be hope of release. Those who oppressed them refused to release them. The verb *release (šillāḥ)* occurs also in Exod. 7:14; 9:2, 13; 10:3; etc. But as in the days of the first Exodus Yahweh had redeemed (*gā'al*) Israel from Egypt (Exod. 6:6; 15:13), so would he redeem them from Babylon. Israel's *Redeemer (gô'ēl),* Yahweh of Hosts, was *strong* (see comments on 31:11). The redeemer or advocate in normal life was a kinsman who took it upon himself to avenge the murder of a kinsman, to protect him, or to secure his freedom or the release of his property (cf. Lev. 25:25, 47–55; Num. 35:21; etc.). These ideas found their parallel in the redemption of Israel from

22. See R. Barnett, *Assyrian Reliefs,* Plates 23, 38, 40, 44, etc.
23. Isa. 1:4; 5:19, 24; 10:20; 12:6; 17:7; 29:19; 30:11–12, 15; 31:1; 37:23; 41:14, 16, 20; 43:3, 14; 45:11; 47:4; 48:17; 54:5; 60:9, 14.

Babylon. If Yahweh once brought Israel out of Egypt by a "strong hand," he was still strong to bring his people out of Babylon.

Yahweh is also pictured as a strong and successful advocate for Israel's defense in a court of law. Once Yahweh was depicted as both plaintiff and counsel for the prosecution as he brought a charge against his own people (2:9). But now Yahweh will act as advocate for Israel against those who have wronged them (cf. 51:36). In that lawsuit he will be successful and Israel's persecutors will be brought to judgment (cf. 25:31). On that day Yahweh will *bring rest* (*rāga'* Hiph.) to the earth but *bring unrest* (*rāgaz* Hiph.) to the inhabitants of Babylon.

35–38 These verses comprise a short poetic piece in which the phrase *A sword on . . .* recurs several times in a frenetic judgment on Babylon's citizens and her civilization. All of them will experience the wrath of Yahweh. The classes of people listed are the Chaldeans and the citizens of Babylon, her officials and wise men, her false prophets, her warriors and her mercenaries. When divine retribution falls, Babylon's religious system typified by her false prophets will become foolish, her warriors will be terrified, and her mercenary troops will behave like women. Her treasures, many of them plundered from lands the Babylonians had subdued (e.g., Judah, 2 K. 24:13; 25:13–17), would be looted. The waterways on which she depended for irrigation and agriculture would be dried up through neglect. Babylonia's idols would be useless in that hour. They would only make the worshippers look foolish.

39–40 Once Babylon was destroyed it would become a habitation of desert creatures. The terms *ṣiyyîm* and *'iyyîm* are sometimes regarded as animals, but there was something uncanny about creatures who inhabited ruined cities and the terms *demons* and *evil spirits* would seem to be more appropriate.[24] In any case even if the original intention was to refer to animals, these are of a less reputable character such as jackals, rodents, or hooting owls. No self-respecting creatures would live there, much less human beings. The description was designed to heighten the utter desolation of Babylon. These verses have a parallel in Isa. 13:19–22. In fact, much of the imagery of Isa. 13, which is an oracle concerning Babylon, has its counterpart in Jer. 50–51.

The ultimate picture of destruction was the overthrow of

24. See KB, pp. 35, 801; C. C. Torrey, *The Second Isaiah* (1928), pp. 289f. on Isa. 34:13–14.

Sodom and Gomorrah and the neighboring cities (cf. 49:18). In that case the destruction was complete, for Yahweh rained brimstone and fire on the cities, obliterating them and all the valley around, the inhabitants of the cities and what grew on the ground (Gen. 19:24–25).

(e) The agony of Babylon (50:41–46)

41 *"Look! a nation coming from the north,*
A mighty nation,
And many kings stirred up
From earth's farthest bounds.
42 *Armed with bow and blades*
They[1] *are cruel and merciless,*
With a noise like the roaring of the sea.
They ride on horses
Arrayed like men for battle
Against you, daughter Babylon!
43 *The king of Babylon has heard news of them;*
His hands hang limp;
Anguish has gripped him,
Pangs like a woman in labor.
44 *Look! Like a lion coming up*
From the thicket of Jordan to perennial pastures,
I will suddenly chase them away from her
And select the choicest of her rams.
For who is like me? Who is my equal?
What shepherd can stand before me?
45 *So, hear the plan that Yahweh has devised against Babylon,*
The schemes that he has schemed against the land of the Chaldeans.
The young ones of the flock shall be dragged away,
And their flock will be appalled because of them.
46 *At the shout 'Babylon is taken!'*
The earth is shaken,
The cry is heard among the nations."

This brief passage has an interesting thrust. It is the culmination of statements about a foe from the north (vv. 3, 9), but whereas in an earlier day Babylon constituted the "foe from the north" for Judah (e.g., 6:22–24) which invaded and destroyed Israel, now Babylon herself was to suffer a similar fate from an equally ruthless foe from the north (vv. 41–43; cf. 6:24). We have here a reapplication of

1. MT reads plural. LXX has singular as in 6:23. See also the verb "they are merciless."

earlier prophetic sayings to a new situation. There is nothing in these verses which Jeremiah may not have uttered, and it is entirely possible that it was he who adapted an earlier saying to this new situation.

41–43 These verses repeat 6:22–24 with minor changes. The *many kings* (cf. 51:27) refer to vassal kings assisting their overlord. It was normal for the kings of Assyria, Babylonia, Persia, etc. to call on vassal kings to send contingents of troops to help them in their enterprises. Indeed, it was a normal part of a suzerain-vassal treaty.[2] At the time Jeremiah composed this oracle he could not have known the composition of the invading force. In fact it was Cyrus the Persian, whose army contained a variety of vassal contingents. They came from lands far from Babylon, *from earth's farthest bounds.* The advance of such an army with infantry, horses, and chariots was, no doubt, accompanied by a great deal of noise. Small wonder that the Babylonian king, used to being the victor, is now petrified with fear as the potential victim.

44–46 These verses repeat substantially the oracle against Edom in 49:19–21. See comments there. The question *What shepherd can stand before me?* is addressed to earthly rulers. None of these, however powerful, can resist Yahweh or prevent the fulfilment of his purposes, which concern both the overthrow of Babylon and the release of Yahweh's people. The cry *Babylon is taken* would bring delight to peoples in many lands. To the people of Israel in particular, the dawn of a new day was at hand.

In the historical context, of course, the people in exile had little hope of deliverance when these words were uttered. Only those who believed Yahweh's word about a future restoration had hope. Yet such a word as this was designed to give hope to a people that had lost hope. At first the exiles were angry and unwilling to acknowledge their sin and iniquity which had brought them to their present plight. It was Ezekiel's special ministry to persuade them that Yahweh had acted justly (Ezek. 1–24). Once despair set in (Ezek. 33:10), Ezekiel took the opportunity to declare that the way of Yahweh was just (Ezek. 33:10–20). After the fall of Jerusalem (Ezek. 33:21) he began to preach a message of restoration (Ezek. 34–48). The exiles who cared to listen had much to give them hope

2. D. J. Wiseman, "The Vassal-Treaties of Esarhaddon," *Iraq* 20 (1958), Part I. See *ANET(S)*, pp. 534ff. Note section 4, p. 535.

in the words of Ezekiel and Jeremiah and later, as time drew on, in the preaching of Second Isaiah (Isa. 40–55).

The oracle against Babylon continues in ch. 51.

(f) Again—the judgment of Babylon (51:1–14)

1 *This is what Yahweh said:*
"Look! I am arousing against Babylon,
Even against those who live in 'Leb-kamai,'[1]
A destroying wind.
2 *I will send winnowers*[2] *to Babylon*
And they will winnow her and lay waste her land.
Truly[3] *they will come against her*[4] *from all sides*
On the day of disaster.
3 *Let the bowman draw his bow against her,*
Let him rise up in his armor against her.[5]
Do not spare her young men!
Destroy her entire army!
4 *They shall fall down wounded in the land of Chaldea,*
Thrust through in her streets.
5 *Israel and Judah have not been 'widowed'*
By their God, Yahweh of Hosts,
Though their[6] *land was filled with guilt*
Against the Holy One of Israel.

1. *Leb-kamai* is an Atbash (see note on 25:25) for Chaldea (so LXX) using the consonants *lbqmy* for *ksdym*.
2. MT *zārîm* is revocalized to *zōrîm* to match the following verb, with Aquila, Symmachus, Vulg., and most commentators.
3. The emphatic use of *kî*.
4. Read *kî yihyû,* restoring a *y* lost through haplography. The emendation to *kî yaḥᵃnû* proposed by Rudolph in *BHS* is ingenious but not entirely necessary, i.e., "They will set up camp against" or "they will attack"; cf. Syr., Vulgate.
5. The text is quite difficult, and the Versions evidently found it so. See *BHS*. MT reads "Unto (against), let bend, let bend, the bowman, his bow; unto (against), let him rise up in his mail." Syr., Targ., Vulg., and many mss. write *'al* negative for *'el* (unto) in both cases. The Qere and many mss. and Versions omit the second "let bend," which indeed is left unvocalized in MT. The sense is then that the Babylonians are not to be given time to string their bows or put on their armor. Alternately, if *'el* is omitted with LXX, or better, if it is read *'ēlêha,* "against her," with LXX^{L} and some other mss. and Targ., we are able to read as in our translation. An attempt to follow MT is made by R. K. Harrison, *Jeremiah and Lamentations* (1973), p. 186: "Against him who bends (his bow), let the bowman bend his bow, and (also) against him who puts on his armour." This is somewhat awkward although it gives the sense that attacking bowmen prevent the defending bowmen from acting. Any translation is at best a conjecture.
6. We take this as referring to the land of the Chaldeans; cf. RSV, NEB. J. Bright, p. 346, refers the phrase to Israel.

6 *Flee from the midst of Babylon!*
Every man for himself!
Do not be slain for her iniquity,[7]
For it is the time of Yahweh's vengeance;
He will pay her full recompense.
7 *Babylon was a golden cup*
In the hand of Yahweh
To make the whole earth drunk;
The nations have drunk of her wine,
Thereupon the nations have gone mad.
8 *Suddenly Babylon fell and was broken.*
Howl over her!
Take balm for her wound;
Perhaps she will be healed.
9 *We wanted to heal Babylon,*
But she would not be healed.
Leave her! Let us go every one to his own country;
For her judgment has reached the heavens
And has been carried up to the skies.
10 *Yahweh has brought to view our vindication.*[8]
Come! Let us announce in Zion
What Yahweh our God has done.
11 *Sharpen the arrows!*
Make ready the shields![9]
(Yahweh has aroused the spirit of the king[10] *of the Medes, for his purpose concerning Babylon is to destroy it. The vengeance of Yahweh is the avenging of his temple.)*
12 *Give the signal to attack Babylon's walls!*
Strengthen the guard!
Post a watch!
Place men in ambush!
For Yahweh has both planned and carried out
What he threatened against the inhabitants of Babylon.

7. I.e., do not be caught up in her punishment. The noun *'āwôn, iniquity,* may also be translated "punishment." It is a common enough feature of the OT that the various nouns for "sin" denote both the sin and the consequences of the sin.
8. The noun is plural in MT but LXX and Aquila read singular, *tó kríma*. Syr. and some Targ. mss. also have singular.
9. The force of both the verb and the noun is not clear. The verb *ml'* normally means "fill" and the noun *šᵉlāṭîm* seems to mean "shields" in 2 Sam. 8:7; 2 K. 11:10. An alternate proposal is that the noun refers to some kind of dart. See Y. Yadin, *The Scroll of the War of the Sons of Light against the Sons of Darkness,* p. 134. It may be that the use of the verb is a technical one here (cf. 2 Sam. 23:7; Zech. 9:13), meaning "fill up with," "arm oneself with," "take up." The LXX reading is "fill the quivers."
10. MT has plural. LXX and Syr. are singular, which seems to suit the context unless "kings" refers to all the participants in the battle.

13 *You who dwell by many waters,*
Rich in treasures,
Your end has come,
Your life's thread is cut.[11]
14 *Yahweh of Hosts has sworn by himself:*
'I will surely fill[12] *you with men like locusts,*
And they will sing a song of triumph over you.' "

The judgment on Babylon continues with a brief announcement of Israel's restoration (v. 5). The passage shows an awareness of siege warfare and returns to the symbol of the cup of Yahweh's fury and the call for men to flee from Babylon (v. 6). It would be hard to argue that Jeremiah was incapable of writing such poetry. That it speaks of the impending fall of Babylon does not necessarily point to a date of composition near 539 B.C. Similar words might have been used of any city that was being attacked. Here one verse that requires an exact knowledge of events is v. 11, where specific mention is made of the Medes, about whose rise neither Jeremiah nor the people in exile could have had any inkling until about 560 B.C. Hence v. 11 may be regarded as a later gloss. The reference seems to be prose and it interrupts the flow of thought from v. 11a to v 12.

1–4 The use of the Atbash to disguise the identity of the adversary would, in the context of the Exile, and particularly in the earlier period of the Exile, seem to make historical sense. But one would wonder why a writer would introduce the device at this point when Babylon has been referred to already. NEB substitutes *kambul*[13] for the unusual word and proposes that a district in Babylon was intended. No such district is, in fact, known. The expression *lēḇ qāmāy* itself means "heart of my adversaries" and as such does not appear to make sense. Judging from the use of the Atbash in Jeremiah (cf. Sheshak at 25:26 and 51:41) it is mainly a literary device, possibly insulting or with some other emotional overtones, but possibly, too, used by the Babylonians themselves (cf. below on v. 41).

The symbol of the destroying wind is known in other parts of the OT, often as an east wind (the sirocco).[14] It suits the picture

11. Lit. "the cubit of your being cut off." See the commentary below.
12. See the commentary below.
13. This involves considerable adjustment of MT and has no textual support.
14. Gen. 41:6, 23, 27; Job 15:2; 27:21; 38:24; Ps. 78:26; Isa. 27:8; Hos. 12:1; 13:15. The word is *qāḏîm*.

of winnowing in v. 2 (cf. 49:32, 36). It is possible, however, that the reference is to "the spirit of a destroyer" (cf. v. 11). In either case the result is the same.

Verse 3 has several textual difficulties (see textual notes), but it seems to convey a picture of the complete inability of the defenders of Babylon to ward off the strength of the attack on Babylon. The attack would come so quickly that the Babylonians would be unable to offer resistance.

Yahweh's instructions to the attackers were that they were not to spare the young warriors but to devote the entire Babylonian army to destruction.[15] Jeremiah no doubt had in mind a picture of the last days of Jerusalem when the defenders were powerless to ward off the Babylonian onslaught. The young warriors of Judah had fallen, thrust through by Babylonian weapons in the streets of Jerusalem. The judgment on Babylon would be in similar terms.

5–6 In that hour Israel would be spared. All Israel is in view, both northerners and Judeans. They would not be left *widowed ('almān)* as they had been in a former day (cf. Isa. 54:4–8). The sense of v. 5b is not clear since the expression *their land* seems at first sight to belong to Israel. On the other hand, if a contrast is being drawn between Israel's fortune and that of Babylon the sense may be, "but *their* land," i.e., the land of the Chaldeans, was filled with guilt against Yahweh, the Holy One of Israel.[16] Because of her guilt (*'āšām*), judgment would fall upon her. Hence the people, and probably the reference is to the people of Israel, were urged to flee, *every man for himself,* lest they be caught up in the judgment intended for Babylon. As so often in the history of the human race, innocent bystanders become involved in national judgments. It was the day of Yahweh's *vengeance (n^{e}qāmâ)* on Babylon when he would recompense her to the full. The note of vengeance which occurs several times in these two chapters is in evidence again (50:15, 18, 28, 29; 51:24, 36, etc.).

7–8 The theme of the cup of Yahweh's wrath is given a slightly different twist here although the imagery is similar to that in 25:15ff. Babylon is pictured as a golden cup in Yahweh's hands. In a former day she had been Yahweh's instrument of wrath which

15. The verb is the Hiphil of *ḥrm*. It occurs often in narratives concerned with the holy war in the days of Joshua and the judges. See note on 50:21.
16. See note on 50:29–32.

was poured out on the nations, but in particular, on Judah and Jerusalem (13:12ff.; cf. Isa. 51:17). But the cup of Yahweh's wrath was passed on to others, e.g., Edom (49:12–13), and it was Babylon who gave them the cup to drink. But in the day of her own visitation Babylon would drink the cup (25:15–29). The cup is depicted as a *golden cup* because of Babylon's great wealth. The effect of drinking the potion was to make those who drank it behave like madmen. Now the golden cup from which so many had drunk would be smashed suddenly. Babylon would suddenly fall. But though Israel's wounds could be treated and healed by balm from Gilead (cf. 8:22; 46:11) so that the flesh would be restored (cf. 30:17; 33:6), there would be no healing for Babylon's wound. Her fate was absolute.

9 It is not clear whether the intention of the writer was to suggest that it was Israel, who had known great suffering and severe wounds, who wished to bring healing to Babylon. It would have been a magnanimous gesture. Certainly in v. 10 Israel is the subject. But the divine judgment was absolute and final. It was time for men to forsake Babylon and return home, for Babylon's judgment was complete. The expression *Her judgment has reached the heavens and has been carried up to the skies* is proverbial and like many such expressions in the OT indicates that the judgment was of vast proportions (cf. Num. 13:28; Deut. 1:28).

10 Clearly the subject of this verse is the fugitive remnant making its way back to Zion (cf. 50:28). By bringing his judgment on Babylon Yahweh had brought vindication[17] (*ṣᵉḏāqâ*) to his own people. They could now emerge from captivity to a new life in their homeland. The words of the prophet Jeremiah were thus fulfilled. He had spoken of a return after seventy years and of wonderful days of restoration. Chapters 50 and 51 reiterate that claim. The liberated remnant would yet declare what Yahweh had done (lit. "the action of Yahweh our God"). But there was a more important aspect of Babylon's fall. It was a *vindication* of Israel. Not that she was guiltless or that she did not deserve the divine judgment herself. But she had now received from Yahweh's hand adequate compensation for all her iniquity (Isa. 40:2). Now she would be reinstated and shown to be what she really was, Yahweh's elect nation (Exod. 19:5, 6).

17. The root *ṣdq* in Hebrew has a subtle range of meanings. See J. J. Scullion, "ṢEDEQ-ṢEDAQAH in Isaiah cps. 40–66," *Ugarit-Forschungen* 3 (1971), pp. 335–348.

Nebuchadrezzar might scoff and say that he was not guilty because Israel had sinned against Yahweh (50:7). That was true enough, but not the whole truth. But it would need some massive vindication of Israel on Yahweh's part to persuade Babylon that in dealing with Israel he was dealing with the elect of Yahweh.

11 The oracle returns to the attack on Babylon. The enemy is exhorted to press on with his task. *Sharpen the arrows! Make ready the shields!*

The logical sequence to this exhortation is v. 12 so that the next part of v. 11 seems to be an explanatory comment, possibly an editorial gloss. The reference to the king of the Medes being roused up calls for some explanation. The Medes lived in northwest Iran in the general region of the modern Iranian Kurdistan. Their capital was Ecbatana and one of their greatest kings was Astyages (585–550 B.C.). Their history before Cyrus is somewhat obscure, but something is known. Shalmaneser III of Assyria (859–824 B.C.) in the ninth century B.C. encountered their chiefs and destroyed many towns in the region of Lake Urmia. Tiglath-pileser (745–727 B.C.) had campaigns against Urartu and pillaged the lands of the Medes. One of their leaders, Rusas, stirred up intrigue among the tribes against Assyria. Sargon II (721–705 B.C.) encountered the Mannai southeast of Lake Urmia, and the Medes in the same general area during the late eighth century B.C. It is people of this type who appear in v. 27—Ararat (Urartu), Minni (Mannai), and Ashkenaz (Ashguzai)—along with the Medes.[18]

In 550 B.C. Cyrus the Persian ruler invaded the region and subjugated it. The MT refers to the "kings" of the Medes in the plural, which may mean only that the leader of the Medes is seen as being associated with a number of vassal rulers. If the term Medes is to be taken at face value, these lines must have been written at a time when the Medes were powerful enough to be considered a potential destroyer of Babylon. There is some evidence that about 561–560 B.C. an invasion of Babylon by the Medes was expected. We have no historical evidence of any outcome.[19] On the other hand the term Medes may be a general one. It is known that the mother

18. Note the discussion in *Cambridge Ancient History* III, *The Assyrian Empire* (1927), pp. 26, 34, 51, etc.

19. Note the discussion of D. J. Wiseman, *Chronicles of Chaldaean Kings (626–556 B.C.)*, p. 38.

of Cyrus the Persian was a Mede, and the Medes and Persians are linked together several times in the book of Daniel (e.g., Dan. 5:28; 6:8, 12, 15). In that case the reference here may be to Cyrus, but the matter is still open to debate (cf. Isa. 13:17).

The purpose of Yahweh in stirring up the spirit of the kings of the Medes is stated as the destruction of Babylon and as an act of vengeance designed to avenge the destruction and pillaging of the temple by the Babylonians (cf. 52:12–13, 17–23; 2 K. 24:13; 25:13–17).

12 The exhortation to attack Babylon is resumed, with some attention to aspects of the final assault on a beleaguered city. A strong guard needed to be posted and a watch kept to block possible sorties (cf. 2 K. 25:4) from the city; and an ambush had to be placed in position (*Place men in ambush*) to catch those who escaped, or even to launch some attack, for example, on the gate, when some diversion caused by a sortie took place. When all such matters were attended to, the signal to attack Babylon's walls was given. By a carefully planned assault on the city the attackers would fulfil Yahweh's plan against Babylon.

13–14 Babylon is addressed now as the one who dwelt by many waters and was rich in treasures, whose end had come. The description of the city as one who dwelt *by many waters* is a reference to her situation on the Euphrates River (cf. Ps. 137:1). Numerous canals in the area provided water and irrigation for her environs. There was, moreover, a system of artificially made ditches and lakes which could be filled with water to add strength to the defenses of the city. There may also be an allusion to one of the mythological beliefs which were held in the city, so that the "many waters" referred to the great subterranean ocean which was the source of the streams that watered the earth.[20] Babylon's fabulous treasures had been gathered from the temples and treasuries of the Near East (cf. 52:12–13, 17–23; 2 K. 24:13; 25:13–17; Dan. 5:2–4). But her end had come, her life's thread was cut. The last figure in v. 13 is a metaphor from weaving. It likens Babylon to a measure of cloth cut from the loom, which was a figure for death (cf. Isa. 38:12). Now the enemy will swarm into the city like a cloud of

20. H. G. May, "Some Cosmic Connotations of *mayim rabbîm*, 'Many Waters,' " *JBL* 74 (1955), pp. 9–21.

locusts. Yahweh's oath is introduced in standard fashion.[21] The invaders would chant the conqueror's triumph song. The noun *hēḏaḏ* occurs in 25:30 and 48:33 for the grape-treader's song. The entry of warriors into Babylon has about it something of the quality of grape-treaders trampling the grapes when the harvest has been taken in. The crushed grapes produce wine for men to drink. Perhaps there is an overtone here of the preparation of wine for Yahweh's cup of wrath.

(g) *A hymn of praise to God (51:15–19)*

15 *By his power he makes the earth,*
He established the world by his wisdom,
And by his understanding he stretches out the heavens.
16 *When he utters his voice there is a tumult of waters in the heavens,*[1]
And he brings up the clouds from the ends of the earth.
He provides lightning flashes for the rain,
And sends out the wind from his storehouses.
17 *All mortals are stupid and ignorant,*[2]
Every goldsmith is put to shame by his idol.
His images are a fraud,
There is no breath in them.
18 *They are nonentities, a work of delusion;*
At the time of their reckoning they will perish.
19 *Not like these is the Portion of Jacob,*
For he is the maker of all
And Israel[3] *is the tribe of his inheritance;*
Yahweh of Hosts is his name.

These verses are virtually a repetition of 10:12–16. See comments there. The one question we have to answer is why the poem was used again. There are many examples of doublets in Jeremiah where phrases, sentences, or whole passages are re-used in a different context.[4] That is not surprising since writers in every age take up

21. The expression *kî 'im* points to a formula "May Yahweh do so to me if I do not (*kî 'im*) . . . ," which amounts to a strong affirmation, "I will do so and so"; cf. 2 K. 5:20. An alternative translation is obtained by a slight rearrangement of the consonants to *kî 'im mālē'ṯ kᵉāḏām,* "even if you were filled with people as with locusts (in number), yet. . . ."

1. The text is unusual and possibly defective. See textual note on 10:13.
2. Lit. "apart from knowing."
3. MT and LXX both omit *Israel* although it is present in many other mss., Lucian, Targ., Vulg., and in the parallel 10:16.
4. S. R. Driver, *An Introduction to the Literature of the OT* ([9]1913), p. 277.

again and again expressions which they have found valuable in presenting their point of view. From our point in time we might think that some of Jeremiah's expressions are more suitable in one context than another. But the choice was his, or in some cases, the choice of editors. The particular relevance of this passage in its present context seems to be that whereas in her hour of emergency Babylon's gods were impotent (v. 17), there was no impotence in Yahweh, who was the creator and sustainer of the universe (vv. 15–16) and had the power and the authority to carry through his purposes in the destruction of Babylon and the release of Israel, his very own "tribe." The expression *the Portion (ḥēleq) of Jacob* is a reference to the God of Jacob. In human affairs a man's portion was the inheritance he received from his father. It was his by legal and moral right. So Yahweh was peculiarly the proper inheritance of Israel. As Yahweh had chosen Israel as his very own tribe, *the tribe of his inheritance,* so Israel had Yahweh as her very own possession, her *Portion.* There was an intimate relationship between Yahweh and his people which could never exist between the idols and fraudulent images made by smiths and the people of Babylon.

(h) Yahweh's hammer and its end (51:20–26)

20 *"You are my hammer,*
My weapon of war;
With you I shatter nations,
With you I destroy kingdoms.
21 *With you I shatter horse and rider,*
With you I shatter chariot and driver.[1]
22 *With you I shatter man and woman,*
With you I shatter an old man and a boy,
With you I shatter a young man and a maiden.
23 *With you I shatter a shepherd and his flock,*
With you I shatter a farmer and his team;
With you I shatter governors and high officials.
24 *But I will repay Babylon and the people of Chaldea*
For all the evil which they did
Before your very eyes in Zion—
Yahweh's word.

1. MT reads "chariot and rider." By revocalizing *wᵉrōḵᵉḇô* to *wᵉrakkāḇô* we can translate "charioteer" or *driver.*

25 *See! I am against you, O destroying mountain*[2]*—Yahweh's word—*
You who destroy the whole earth.
I will stretch out my hand against you,
And I will roll you down from the rocky heights
And make you a burnt-out mountain.
26 *They will never take from you a cornerstone,*
Nor a foundation stone,
But you will be for ever a waste—Yahweh's word."

This section comprises two originally independent poems, vv. 20–23 and 24–26, which are nevertheless related in that the first deals with Babylon as Yahweh's hammer, and the second describes the end of Babylon.

20–23 The first short poem is very different in character from the hymn in praise of Yahweh (vv. 15–19). It is addressed to some unnamed power that is described as Yahweh's hammer. In the context it seems to refer to Babylon since at the time of Jeremiah the only power in view that had shattered nations and destroyed kingdoms was Babylon. The theme of Yahweh's hammer appeared already in 50:23 where Babylon is clearly named as such.

The thought is consistent with the view of the prophets that Yahweh could and did call into his service people of all kinds. Thus Isaiah saw Assyria as Yahweh's "rod" (Isa. 10:5–19), and in Jeremiah's view Nebuchadrezzar was Yahweh's "servant" (27:4–11). At a later date Second Isaiah would refer to Cyrus as Yahweh's "shepherd" and "anointed one" (Isa. 44:28; 45:1). In the present passage Babylon is addressed as Yahweh's *hammer* soon to be brought to judgment herself. This concept found expression in Isaiah's day. Assyria the "rod" of Yahweh's anger and the "staff" of his fury was nevertheless arrogant, proud, and cruel, and declared "By the strength of my hand I have done it" (Isa. 10:13). When Yahweh had finished all his work on Mount Zion and on Jerusalem he would punish the arrogant boasting of the king of Assyria and his haughty pride (Isa. 10:12). He was an axe which vaunted itself over him who hewed with it, a saw which magnified itself against him who wielded it (Isa. 10:15). So too the insolent (50:29, 31) and

2. Lit. "mount of the destroyer." J. Bright, *Jeremiah,* pp. 348, 357 translates "Mountain of Raiders"; he refers to the use of *mašḥîṯ* in some passages to denote a detachment of troops engaged in pillage (1 Sam. 13:17; 14:15) and suggests a mountain which harbors robber bands who sally forth to loot and plunder. However, the expression may be idiomatic with overtones that escape us, perhaps of a mythological character in which "the Destroyer" is the god of death and the underworld. Such views were current in Babylon.

mighty Babylon and the inhabitants of Chaldea would be repaid for all the evil they had committed in Zion (v. 24).[3] The note of vengeance appears again.

24–26 The poem about Yahweh's hammer ends at v. 23. Verse 24[4] provides a transition to vv. 25–26 which refer to the destruction of Babylon. Verse 24 takes a backward look at the destruction of Jerusalem, which is regarded as being unnecessarily violent and destructive and associated with a vast display of evil which the people of Judah had witnessed. She would be repaid (cf. Amos 1:3–2:16).

The character of the *mountain* in v. 25 has been variously understood. At least one interpretation of the context is to see a reference to Babylon, which in her prime towered over the nations. There is ambiguity and ambivalence in v. 25. Babylon is the mountain but she is also seized and rolled down from the mountain. In the end she is a burnt-out mountain (lit. "a mountain of burning"). She will be so completely burned that thereafter her stones will be useless as cornerstones or foundation stones. The figure is a striking one.

The fact that historically Cyrus entered Babylon without any appreciable resistance and left the city intact is quite contrary to the description of devastation that appears in v. 26, so that the verses, as well as others in chs. 50 and 51, must come from a period before the conquest of Babylon by Cyrus. The terms, though vivid, are very general, and these verses might well have come from Jeremiah himself.

(i) The nations ally against Babylon (51:27–33)

27 *"Raise a signal in the land!*
Sound the trumpet among the nations!
Consecrate the nations against her!
Summon kingdoms against her,
Ararat, Minni, and Ashkenaz!
Appoint a commander-in-chief against her!
Bring up horses like bristling locusts!

3. The view that vv. 15–19 refer to Cyrus seems to ignore the total context and the specific reference in 50:23. NEB translates the passage neither in the past nor in the present but in the future, apparently with Cyrus in mind. See E. W. Nicholson, *Jeremiah 26–52*, p. 216, who regards the NEB translation as preferable. He refers to v. 11 of the present chapter and to Isa. 41:2–4 in this connection.

4. J. Bright, *Jeremiah,* pp. 348, 357 and RSV regard v. 24 as prose; NEB prints it as poetry.

28 *Consecrate the nations against her: the king*[1] *of the Medes, his governors and his officials, and all the land of his domain."*
29 *The land trembled and writhed,*
For Yahweh's designs against Babylon stand,
To make the land of Babylon
A desolation and uninhabited.
30 *Babylon's warriors have ceased to fight;*
They remain in the strongholds;
Their courage has failed,
They act like women.
Her houses are burning,
The bars of her gates are broken down.
31 *Runner comes running to meet runner,*
Messenger to meet messenger,
To tell the king of Babylon
That his city has been taken on all sides.
32 *The river crossings are seized,*
The reedy swamps[2] *set on fire,*
And the warriors gripped with panic.
33 *For this is what Yahweh of Hosts, the God of Israel, has said:*
"Daughter Babylon is like a threshing floor
At the time when it is trodden down.
In a short time
Her harvest time[3] *will come."*

The account of Babylon's fall is taken up yet again, but this time several nations are announced as participants in her downfall. At the time this poem was composed it would appear that these nations were subjects of the Medes.

27 Babylon's enemies are again summoned to prepare their troops for attack, to raise the signal and sound the trumpet. The nations are now consecrated (*qiddēš*) against Babylon. The verb has a wide usage in the OT for anything that is set apart for sacred or ritual use, including persons, places, days.[4] Here the nations which Yahweh would use in the overthrow of Babylon were, from his point of view, "consecrated." But they themselves probably had their own rituals of consecration for battle (cf. 6:4; 22:7). Three groups

1. LXX and Syr. have singular. MT has "kings" and "her," i.e., Medea's, governors and officials, but "his domain."
2. The word *'ᵃgammîm* probably refers to the swamps (cf. *'agmōn,* "swamp grass, reeds") which formed part of the city defenses.
3. LXX, Syr., and Targ. omit *time,* which in MT may be a dittography from the first half of the line. If omitted, the verb should be *ūḇā'* instead of *ūḇā'â.*
4. A useful analysis of the various forms and meanings of *qdš* is given in KB, p. 825. See 17:22, 24, 27; cf. Exod. 19:23; 28:3, 41; 29:1, 36–37, 44; 30:29; Deut. 5:12; 1 K. 8:64; 2 K. 10:20; Joel 1:14; 2:15; 4:9.

are specified, all of which were to be found in the area of present-day Armenia. Each is known in Assyrian cuneiform texts, Urartu, Mannai, and Ashguzai in the neighborhood of Lake Van and Lake Urmia. The *Ashkenaz* *(Aš-ku-za)* were allies of the Mannai in a revolt against the Assyrians in the seventh century B.C. They were conquered by the Medes and later by the Persians and provided contingents of troops in the Persian army that took Babylon in 538 B.C. The *commander-in-chief* *(ṭip̱sār)* was a high-ranking military officer[5] appointed to lead these "nations." The army so mustered was pictured as a vast one whose horses were like a plague of locusts (cf. v. 14). The term *yeleq sāmār* is of uncertain meaning, but it is thought to refer to the locust at a very destructive stage in its life-cycle when the wings were covered with a rough, horny casing, hence *bristling locusts*. The picture is thus one of vast numbers of people, led by a commander, probably riding on horses and well protected with armor, and very destructive.

28 Cf. v. 11. The introduction of the term *Medes* at this point in a brief prose segment suggests that we are dealing with a gloss inserted to explain that the Medes with their governors and officials were leaders of the three nations referred to. The citing of the phrase *consecrate the nations against her* from v. 27 in the manner of a commentary strengthens the impression of a gloss.[6]

29 The trembling and writhing of the earth at the approach of Yahweh in war against his foes is a well-known motif in the OT (e.g., Judg. 5:4; Nah. 1:2–6; Hab. 3:1–15). There will be no thwarting of his plans to make Babylon an uninhabited waste. Similar expressions are used elsewhere in Jeremiah in reference to the state of Judah after Nebuchadrezzar had completed his destructive work (4:7; 44:22). Similar words were used of Egypt (46:19) and Moab (48:9). What Babylon had done to others would now happen to her.

30 The utter collapse of Babylon's warriors is referred to several times in these chapters (50:30, 36, 37, 43; 51:30, 32). Several descriptive phrases are piled up here: they *have ceased to fight; they remain in the strongholds; their courage has failed, they act like women*.

5. The Hebrew term derives from Akk. *ṭupšarru*, "tablet writer." The same Hebrew word occurs in Nah. 3:17 where it is used in connection with locusts.

6. J. Bright, *Jeremiah*, p. 357, asks whether the material of the poem in vv. 27–33 may not have been preexilic with v. 28 added to make it applicable to a time when the Medes controlled areas to the north and east of Mesopotamia prior to the absorption of Medea into the Persian empire in 550 B.C.

31–32 In the conduct of warfare in the ancient world specially trained runners brought news from the scene of battle to the king (cf. 2 Sam. 18:19–19:1 [Eng. 18:33]).[7] Babylon's runners were renowned, and it was these men who came running from every direction to announce to the king that the city had fallen. The first news seems to refer to the collapse of the defenses outside the city. These were vast. In addition to the two massive walls surrounding the heart of Babylon, an inner one some 21 feet thick and an outer one over 12 feet thick, there were great walls thrown up at intervals beyond the city together with a chain of fortresses north and south of the city. The Euphrates River gave protection, and a variety of waterways and large depressions flooded with water all combined to create the impression of an impregnable city.[8] But the fords across the rivers and waterways were seized and the reedy swamps were set on fire. The burning of the swamp reeds would deprive refugees of a place to hide and would flush out any who might have escaped there already. Such news threw the warriors into a panic.

33 Yahweh's word was topical and well understood all over the ancient Near East. When villagers prepared for harvest they pounded down and levelled the flat area or *threshing floor (gōren)* where the threshing and winnowing were carried out. The farmers would tramp their beasts round and round on the stalks of grain while they sat on the small threshing sledge beneath which were sharp blades or stones to cut up the stalks. That completed, they threw up the material with broad winnowing forks on a windy day. The grain dropped and the chaff was blown aside. At harvest time the dross was removed and the solid grain preserved. Babylon was a threshing floor to be levelled to the ground. It would be trodden down in preparation for the harvest which was to come. Although the overthrow of Babylon may have lain several decades in the future, the whole scene is depicted as though it were taking place at the time of the prophecy.[9]

7. In the classical world the runner who reported the defeat at Marathon in Athens gave his name to the modern long distance race.

8. H. W. F. Saggs, *The Greatness that was Babylon* (1962), p. 144; A. Parrot, *Babylon and the OT* (1958), pp. 23f.

9. This fact does not necessarily argue for a date of these prophecies just before the collapse of Babylon. Other prophets too depicted the future in terms that made their prophecy seem to be very close at hand.

(j) Judah's complaint against Babylon and Yahweh's requital (51:34–40)

34 *"Nebuchadrezzar king of Babylon devoured me*
And threw me into confusion.[1]
He set me down an empty vessel,
Like a monster he gulped me down.
He filled his belly with my delicacies[2]
And rinsed me out.[3]
35 *On Babylon be the violence done to my flesh!"*[4]
Let Zion's mistress say;
"And my blood be upon the citizens of Chaldea!"
Let Jerusalem say.
36 *Therefore this is what Yahweh has said:*
"Look! I will plead your cause,
I will take vengeance on your behalf;
I will dry up her sea
And make the source of her water go dry.
37 *Then Babylon shall become a heap of ruins,*
A haunt of jackals,
A scene of horror, a cause of whistling,
Where nobody dwells.
38 *Like lions they roar together,*
Like the cubs of a lioness they growl.
39 *While they are excited I will prepare their banquet.*
I will make them drunk so that they may be stupefied.[5]
Then they will sleep a perpetual sleep
And never awake—Yahweh's word.
40 *I will drag them like lambs to the slaughter,*
Like rams and he-goats."

1. The sense of the verb *hmm* here is not clear. Normally it means "confuse, throw into confusion"; see KB, p. 237. LXX suggests "he divided me," i.e., cut me up. The context seems to require a verb akin to "eat up." NEB has "sucked me dry." Throughout this verse the verbs in the Ketib have *-anû,* "us," but the Qere suggests *-anî, me*.
2. MT has *mēʿaḏānāy,* "from my delights." By revocalizing to *maʿaḏannāy* we may translate with J. Bright, p. 350, "tit-bits." Cf. *BHS*.
3. Some commentators revocalize from *heḏîḥānî* to *hiddiḥānî,* "he thrust me out, expelled me"; hence NEB "spewed me up." MT makes sense since an empty dish is rinsed afterward. But the emended reading is possible. Gluttonous animals after gulping food sometimes vomit it up.
4. The text is difficult. MT reads lit. "My violence and my flesh be upon Babylon." The first phrase "my violence" means "the violence done to me" (cf. Gen. 16:5). The second phrase "my flesh" may be understood as referring to the end-point of the violence. LXX though confused keeps the two nouns, and in any case the noun *flesh* has a parallel in the next line in *my blood*.
5. MT lit. "in order that they may rejoice (*yaʿalōzû*)," perhaps meaning "in order that they may be merry" or "be tipsy." LXX *hópōs karōthōsin* suggests *yeʿullāpû,* the basis of our reading; similarly Syr., Targ., Vulgate.

These verses commence with the complaint of Jerusalem against Nebuchadrezzar and Babylon, whom she held responsible for all her sufferings. The people of Zion virtually call down on Babylon the fate that Babylon had afflicted on them (vv. 34–35). Yahweh's reply (vv. 36–40) is that he will plead his people's cause and bring Babylon to judgment.

34–35 Nebuchadrezzar is compared with a gluttonous man devouring Jerusalem and setting her aside as one does an empty vessel whose contents have been quaffed. In a more vigorous figure still, Nebuchadrezzar is compared to a monster gulping down food, filling its belly with food that delights it and then vomiting it up. Such gluttony left torn flesh and spilt blood behind. For such unspeakable viciousness Jerusalem calls for vengeance upon her captors.

36–37 Yahweh her God would take up her case, plead her cause (*rîḇ*), and take vengeance on her behalf, that is, obtain a requital. The term *rîḇ* points to a legal process and is used in several contexts in Jeremiah. Israel herself was the subject of a legal process when Yahweh conducted his case against her (2:9). Jeremiah pleaded his cause to Yahweh (12:1; 20:12). Yahweh conducted a case against the nations (25:31). Here, Yahweh pleads Israel's cause as he conducts his case against Babylon (cf. 50:34). Jeremiah, when he was the subject of a plot by the men of Anathoth, committed his cause to Yahweh and left requital with him (11:20). In the present passage it is Yahweh who promises that he will take vengeance on Jerusalem's behalf. In the outworking of that requital Babylon's sea and water supply would be dried up. Her very life depended on her rivers and canals, and this surface water was believed to well up from the underground ocean (cf. comments on v. 13). Moreover, Babylon would become an appalling waste, literally "a scene of horror and whistling," i.e., something at which men whistled in horror as they passed by (cf. 9:9 [Eng. 10]; 10:22), and devoid of inhabitants. All this was a striking reversal of what she was formerly, a vast city, wealthy beyond reckoning, the focus of an empire, the center of Marduk-worship, with a large population both within the main city and in the extensive and prosperous surrounding area.

38–40 The Babylonians were likened to lions and lion cubs growling in anticipation of their meal. In their hunger they became *excited.*[6] Appetites are aggravated and they are ravenous for food.

6. The verb means "become heated" (*ḥmm*).

Yahweh prepares a banquet. The central feature of the banquet is the drinking that would take place. We are once again led into the theme of the cup of Yahweh's wrath (cf. 25:15ff.). As they drink, they will become drunk and stupefied, for the cup of Yahweh's wrath is a deadly potion which causes them to fall into a perpetual sleep, never to awake. The lions will be as sacrificial lambs, rams, and goats led to the slaughter.

(k) Babylon's fate (51:41–48)

41 *"How Sheshak*[1] *is taken;*
The pride of all the earth has been captured!
How Babylon has become
A horror among the nations!
42 *The sea has surged over Babylon;*
She is covered by its roaring waves.
43 *Her towns have become a horrifying sight,*
A dry and desert land.
Not a soul lives in them,[2]
No human being passes by them.
44 *I will punish Bel in Babylon*
And make him bring up what he has swallowed.
No more shall nations stream to him.
The wall of Babylon has fallen!
45 *Come out of her midst, my people!*
Let every man escape for his life,
From the heat of Yahweh's anger.
46 *Now, let not your hearts grow faint,*
Nor be fearful because of the rumor heard in the land,
The rumor which comes one year,
And the rumor after it, in another year:
Violence in the land, ruler against ruler.
47 *For believe me, days are coming*
When I will punish the idols of Babylon,
And her whole land will be put to shame,
And all her slain shall lie fallen in her midst.
48 *Heaven and earth and all that is in them*
Will shout for joy over Babylon,
For destroyers from the north shall come upon her—
Yahweh's word."

Further aspects of the coming destruction of Babylon are brought before the reader. The final overthrow of Babylon was so significant

1. Sheshak is an Atbash for Babylon; see on v. 1 and on 25:25–26. LXX omits.
2. Omit "land" with LXX. The noun is resumed in the word *bāhēn, in them*.

in the thought of Jeremiah and his editors that scene after scene was brought before the people. To judge from the length of chs. 50–51 Jeremiah had a strong assurance that mighty Babylon would at length be laid low.

41 The name *Sheshak* is an Atbash for Babylon (see note on 25:26). The proposal that this name was used as a substitute for Babylon in a day of political danger seems to be overruled, at least in chs. 50 and 51, by the frequent reference to Babylon. Another possibility is that the Babylonians themselves made use of the Atbash and that Sheshak was an alternate name. There is some evidence that this was so.[3] The absence of the name from the LXX text suggests that its presence here may have been a gloss. Babylon would become a *horror (šammâ)* among the nations in the same way as she had turned others into a horror.[4] Terms that were used to describe the results of Babylon's ruthless campaigns were taken up again and turned back on her own head.

42 The reference is hardly to the Euphrates, nor to any literal sea. The Persian Gulf is a long way from Babylon. There is probably an allusion here to the mythological chaotic waters of the primeval ocean (Tiamat) which, according to the Babylonian myth of creation, were overthrown by the god Marduk when he fought against Tiamat and destroyed her. The fall of Babylon would be of such gigantic proportions that it would appear as nothing less than a reversal of that primeval victory. Babylon's foes would surge over her like the chaotic waters of the primeval ocean with their roaring waves, a vivid symbol indeed.

43 Several of the terms used here are used elsewhere in the book of Jeremiah for Judah and Jerusalem, and also for other lands devastated by Babylon: a *horrifying sight (šammâ),* a *dry (ṣiyyâ)* and *desert land (ʿ^{a}rāḇâ),* no inhabitants, no passers-by. The gathering together of such expressions in reference to Babylon and her cities seems to have been deliberate, to show that Babylon would eventually suffer the same fate she had meted out to others.

44 The name *Bel* (lord) was an appellation for Marduk, who was the "lord" of the gods. See comment on 50:2. The verse harks

3. E. W. Nicholson, *Jeremiah 26–52,* pp. 222f.

4. The term is used frequently in Jeremiah. It occurs no fewer than 24 times in the book, generally in association with other terms depicting destruction: 2:15; 4:7; 5:30; 8:21; 18:16; 19:8; 25:9, 11, 18, 38; 29:18; 42:18; 44:12, 22; 46:19; 48:9; 49:13, 17; 50:3, 23; 51:29, 37, 41, 43.

back to v. 34 where Nebuchadrezzar is pictured as a monster gulping down Jerusalem. The verb "gulp down" (*bāla'*) occurs also in v. 34, and the noun *bela'*, "what is gulped down," occurs here. Bel will be compelled to bring it up (disgorge it). The picture of nations streaming to Babylon covers many aspects of Babylon's political life. Vassal kings and diplomats with their entourage frequented the capital, traders moved in and out of the city, and captive peoples were brought in droves to the land. But all that would cease. The collapse of Babylon's walls in itself would be a startling phenomenon. The city wall proper was of double construction. The outer component was 12 feet thick and lay 23 feet from the inner wall which was 21 feet thick, so that is was wide enough to allow several chariots to drive abreast along the walls. Towers were set into the walls at intervals of about 60 feet. Outside the walls lay a ditch lined with bricks and bitumen and kept filled with water from the Euphrates.[5]

45 A further appeal is made to the exiles of Israel to flee the city, not merely to escape from the burning anger of Yahweh, but to bring to fulfilment the promise that Israel would be restored (cf. 50:8; 51:6).

46–48 The exiles are exhorted to take courage in days of confusion and of rumors of victory and defeat. The Babylonian Empire was never so stable that it was free at any time of some local disturbances. The book of Jeremiah witnesses to several plots among subject peoples hoping to break free from Babylon's power (27:1–7; 29:20–23, 29–32). Both of the attacks on Jerusalem were in response to a local rebellion. Then there were the exploratory probes of Elamites, Medes, Egyptians, and others into the confines of the Babylonian Empire. In court circles there were feuds and revolts. Nebuchadrezzar's son Amel-Marduk (Evil-merodach) was assassinated in 560 B.C. by his brother-in-law Neriglissar (560–556 B.C.). Neriglissar's heir, Labashi-Marduk, reigned only a few months and was supplanted by Nabonidus (556–539 B.C.). It is not possible to link v. 46 with any particular set of events, but the continuing instability of the empire must have given rise to many rumors. The whole scene was calculated to make the exiles lose heart and to grow fearful. If ever they had premature hopes of release, those

5. See H. W. F. Saggs, "Babylon," in *Archaeology and OT Study*, ed. D. Winton Thomas (Oxford, 1967), pp. 39–56. Note p. 42.

hopes were quickly dashed. Babylon's might always seemed to be adequate to cope with rebels.

But Yahweh had other plans. Babylon would one day be overthrown, her idols discredited, the whole land would be put to shame, and her mighty warriors would lie slain in her midst. The whole universe, *heaven and earth and all that is in them,* would send out a ringing cry of triumph over fallen Babylon. The agents for that destruction would be *destroyers (šōḏᵉḏîm)*[6] *from the north.* These are not further identified and were probably not precisely known at the time of the original oracle. The references to the Medes and their allies in vv. 11 and 28 appear, as we noted, to be later glosses.

Babylon's downfall was certain. That was Yahweh's word.

(l) Yahweh's message to the exiles in Babylon (51:49–53)

49 *"Babylon herself must fall for*[1] *Israel's slain*
Even as the slain of the whole world have fallen for Babylon.
50 *You who have escaped from her sword,*
Go![2] *Do not linger!*
Remember Yahweh from afar,
Let Jerusalem come to your mind."
51 *"We have been put to shame, for we have heard reproaches;*
Our faces are covered with confusion;
Aliens have entered the sanctuary[3] *of Yahweh's house."*
52 *"Therefore, believe me, days are coming—*
Yahweh's word—
When I will punish her idols.
And throughout her land the wounded shall groan.
53 *Though Babylon should ascend to the heavens,*
And though she should make her high fortress inaccessible,
Yet destroyers from me would come to her—
Yahweh's word."

Once again the note of vengeance on Babylon for her cruel deeds against Israel is struck. There is a brief dialog in vv. 49–53. Yahweh

6. The word is used frequently in Jeremiah: 6:26; 12:12; 15:8; 25:36 refer to a destroyer against Israel; 47:4 against the Philistines; 48:8, 18, 32 against Moab; 51:48, 53, 56 against Babylon.

1. *For (lᵉ-)* is supplied, having dropped out through haplography.
2. The regular imperative of *hālaḵ,* "go," in the plural is *lᵉḵû* and not *hilᵉḵû* as here. A redivision of the consonants would give *mḥrbh lk*, thus *mēḥarbāh lᵉḵû,* "You escaped from her sword. Go!"
3. LXX and Vulg. read *miqdᵉšēnû,* "our sanctuary," in place of *miqdᵉšê,* "sanctuaries of"; cf. Syr., Targum. Another possibility is to read *mqdšy* as *mqdš y(hwh),* "the sanctuary of Yahweh," where *y* is an abbreviation. In that case *bêṯ yhwh* would be a doublet.

has a message to the exiles in Babylon (vv. 49, 50) to which they reply (v. 51). In response Yahweh speaks again, assuring them of Babylon's doom (vv. 52, 53).

49–50 Yahweh's word to Israel is that Babylon herself must fall as a compensation for Israel's slain. It was the operation of the *lex talionis*. The exiles who had escaped death when the Babylonians had slain their fellows should not linger in the day of Babylon's judgment. Two things are enjoined upon her: *remember Yahweh from afar,* and *let Jerusalem come to your mind.* The term *remember (zāḵar)* generally involves something more than mere mental recall. The act of remembering involves an active identification of one's whole being with the object of remembering. Thus to remember the day when Israel came out of Egypt was to become personally involved in that far-off event in such a way as to participate in all the wonder and challenge of the event and to live in humble gratitude to Yahweh thereafter. In the present context the people are urged to *remember Yahweh,* that is, to put their trust in him and become personally involved in his purposes. The phrase *from afar* may mean from the distant land of Babylon, separated by a great distance from Yahweh's temple. The phrase may also have a time reference, "from the days long past." In either case, the refugees were exhorted to sense the nearness of Yahweh's presence both for their encouragement and as a source of strength. The second thing they were to do was to let Jerusalem come to mind. Jerusalem was not finished for ever but had a glorious future.

51 The exiles' reply is in terms of the shame they have suffered, the reproaches they have borne, and the fact that aliens had entered the sanctuary of Yahweh. The implication of the reply may be that Yahweh was powerless to deliver his people or his sanctuary. That kind of despair and lack of faith must have been one of the most anguishing experiences of exile. We catch a glimpse of this in Ezek. 33:10 where the exiles, doubting that the way of Yahweh was just, could say, "Our transgressions and our sins are upon us, and we waste away because of them; how then can we live?" Part of Ezekiel's task was to give hope to the exiles and to assure them of Yahweh's loving concern for them and of the glory of Israel's future. The dialog in the verses before us gives another glimpse into the profound questionings and deep perplexities that possessed the minds of the exiles. In that context the exiles needed reassurance that Yahweh was in control and that Babylon would fall in due course.

52–53 Yahweh's reply to the exiles took up the question of the apparent supremacy of Babylon and her gods. *Days are coming when I will punish her idols.* Nor was her army, whose troops had desecrated the temple of Yahweh, invincible. Her warriors would be wounded throughout her land. Yahweh would send despoilers (*šôḏᵉḏîm*) to overrun her. If aliens (*zārîm*) had overrun the temple of Yahweh in Jerusalem, marauders would break through Babylon's lofty and inaccessible fortresses to lay her low. Under Nebuchadrezzar an extensive program of building was carried out in the city of Babylon. The walls were strengthened, vast buildings were erected, temples extended, etc. Nebuchadrezzar's building inscriptions provide valuable information about the extent of this program.[4]

The "high towers" (NEB; Heb. *mᵉrôm ʿōz*, lit. "height of strength") of v. 53 may be the ziggurats, described as *inaccessible* (*bṣr* Piel). But whether ziggurats or palaces or some other fortified areas, they were neither inaccessible nor impregnable and would soon collapse in ruins (cf. 45:16; Isa. 14:13–15). That promise came with Yahweh's own assurance, Yahweh's word.

(m) Babylon is finally repaid in full (51:54–58)

54 *Hark! a plaintive cry from Babylon,*
A mighty crash from the land of Chaldea!
55 *For Yahweh is despoiling Babylon,*
Silencing for ever its loud clamor.
Their billows roar like mighty waters,
Their noisy clamor resounds.[1]
56 *For a destroyer has marched upon Babylon herself;*
Her warriors are captured,
Their bows are broken;
For Yahweh, a god of recompense,
Will repay in full.[2]
57 *"I will make her princes and her wise men drunk,*
Her governors, her prefects, and her warriors;
They will sleep a perpetual sleep
And will never awake—the word of the King,
Yahweh of Hosts is his name."

4. An interesting collection of these occurs in W. H. Lane, *Babylonian Problems* (1923), pp. 177–194.

1. Lit. "the noise of their voice is given forth."
2. The verb is strengthened by the infinitive absolute.

58 *This is what Yahweh of Hosts has said:*
"The broad wall[3] *of Babylon*
Shall be razed to the ground,
And her lofty gates
Shall be set on fire.
'Nations toil for nothing,
Peoples weary themselves[4] *only for the flames!' "*

54–55 The sound of cries for help and a mighty crash in Babylon announce the end. Yahweh himself is the wrecker who silences (lit. "destroys violently") its clamorous din (lit "mighty voice"). But in fact, it is the enemy from the north who comes with his invading army which is likened to the sea rolling over Babylon with a mighty roar. There may be a further use here of the metaphor already met in v. 42. So tremendous will be the onslaught of the foe that it can best be likened to the release of the chaotic waters of the primeval ocean.

56–58 In terms of human personnel, when the destroyers marched on Babylon the warriors would be captured and their weapons of war destroyed. The symbolism of the cup of the wrath of Yahweh appears again. Princes and wise men would be made drunk and governors, prophets, and warriors would sleep the sleep of death. A succinct theological statement of the fact of retribution comes in the words *Yahweh is a God of recompense who will repay in full.* In terms of the physical existence of Babylon, those massive defenses in which she trusted, her broad wall and her massive gates, would be razed and burned. Taking up a popular saying which appears also in Hab. 2:13:

Nations toil for nothing,
Peoples weary themselves only for the flames,

the writer declares that it was by the toil and wearying exertions of captive peoples that Babylon's city was built. In this particular case, and in general, the work of nations is all for nothing; their efforts go up in flames.

3. MT reads "the walls of broad Babylon" (cf. NEB). Many mss., LXX, and Vulg. read *hômaṯ,* "wall of," which makes it possible to translate in keeping with the archeological facts.

4. Read *yîʿāpû* (impf.) as in Hab. 2:13, of which the last two cola are a very close parallel, perhaps a quotation, or more likely it was a commonly known proverb. MT reads *wᵉyāʿēpû,* perf. with conjunction.

(n) A symbolic action against Babylon (51:59–64)

59 *The instructions which the prophet Jeremiah gave Seraiah ben Neriah ben Mahseiah when he went to Babylon with*[1] *Zedekiah king of Judah in the fourth year of his reign (Seraiah was the quartermaster*[2]*).*
60 *Jeremiah wrote on a single document all the evil that would befall Babylon, that is, all these things that are written concerning Babylon.*
61 *And Jeremiah said to Seraiah, "When you arrive in Babylon make certain that you read all these words aloud,*
62 *and say 'O Yahweh, it is thou who hast said that thou wouldst destroy this place so that no one would live in it, man or beast, and that it would become a desolate waste*[3] *for ever.'*
63 *Then, when you have finished reading this document tie a stone to it and throw it into the Euphrates,*
64 *and say, 'Just so shall Babylon sink to rise no more after the disaster which I shall bring upon her.' "*[4] *Thus far the words of Jeremiah.*

This final segment of ch. 51 provides a further example of Jeremiah's penchant for the symbolic[5] (chs. 13, 19, 27–28). An oracle concerning Babylon's collapse was written on a document (scroll), which was taken to Babylon and cast into the river Euphrates. Both the written document and the symbolic act were a "word" from Yahweh. A third "word" was added by Jeremiah, "So shall Babylon sink to rise no more after the disaster which I shall bring upon her."

This fragment is chronologically misplaced. But the reason may be that the saying of Jeremiah quoted here was seen against the background of the threats in the long passage 50:1–51:58 in order to show that the possibility of such a disaster for Babylon had been anticipated by Jeremiah somewhat earlier.[6]

59 The incident is dated in the fourth year of Zedekiah, i.e., in the year 594/3 B.C. This was the year of the plot to rebel against Babylon recorded in ch. 27. Zedekiah seems to have been implicated in the plot. Although the plot was abortive, Nebuchadrezzar's "intelligence" got wind of it and some explanation was needed. It is

1. LXX has "from Zedekiah," i.e., on his orders.
2. Lit. "officer of the resting place (*m*ᵉ*nûḥâ*)," i.e., "officer responsible for overnight stops on a journey." LXX reads "officer of the (tribute) gifts (*m*ᵉ*nāḥôṯ*)."
3. MT has plural, the versions singular. The plural may be a plural of majesty designed to heighten the picture. The ruin would be as many ruins.
4. MT adds *w*ᵉ*yā'ēpû*, "and they shall weary themselves." The expression is omitted with LXX. Rudolph in *BHS* suggests plausibly that it is a misplaced corrective gloss to v. 58 (*q.v.*).
5. See the Introduction, "Symbolic Actions in Jeremiah," pp. 71–76.
6. See O. Eissfeldt, *The OT: An Introduction*, p. 354.

altogether likely that Zedekiah was summoned in person to explain, although he may have gone on his own initiative to pledge his loyalty and to present his annual tribute. Jeremiah's letter of ch. 29 seems to have been sent earlier by different envoys. On that occasion also Zedekiah may have sent a message to assure Nebuchadrezzar that the people of Judah were in no way implicated in the disturbances referred to in 29:21–23.

When Zedekiah went in person, Jeremiah seized the opportunity to entrust to Seraiah, who was possibly the brother of Baruch (32:12),[7] the written oracle referred to in v. 60 and to ask him to carry out the symbolic act referred to in vv. 61–64. Seriah was one of the officials in the caravan whose task was to secure suitable billets for overnight stops, or perhaps (LXX) to supervise the tribute (see textual note).

60 The document on which Jeremiah wrote was probably a scroll of some kind. It is referred to specifically as *a single document (sēp̱er 'eḥāḏ),* which may suggest that it was a fairly succinct statement.[8] Even if it contained all the material of chs. 50–51—and there is no evidence of this—the bulk would not be great. But it must have declared that disaster (*rā'â, evil*) would befall Babylon, and perhaps some details were added.

61–62 The audience that heard the reading is not specified. It was probably some of the exiles since it would be extremely imprudent to declare such things openly in Babylon even if the event was some distance in the future. Jeremiah on another occasion had assured the exiles that the downfall of Babylon was a long way off and that they had to settle down there (ch. 29).

63–64 The complete "word" of Yahweh comprised the word that came to Jeremiah which he wrote in the scroll, the word declared to the audience in Babylon, and the act of sinking the written oracle in the Euphrates. It was a powerful combination, a threefold reiteration of the same word.

The final note *Thus far the words of Jeremiah* is significant for a study of the process of compilation. In fact, this editorial note did not mark the end of the book since ch. 52 follows it as a historical appendix, which is for the most part parallel to 2 K. 24:18–25:30 but differs from it in certain respects as we shall see.

7. They are both described as "ben Neriah ben Maḥseiah."

8. J. Bright, *Jeremiah,* p. 207 translates "a single sheet."

VII. APPENDIX—THE FALL OF JERUSALEM (52:1–34)

(i) The Fall of the City and the Capture of Zedekiah (52:1–16)

1 *Zedekiah was twenty-one years old when he became king, and he reigned in Jerusalem for eleven years; his mother's name was Hamutal, daughter of Jeremiah of Libnah.*
2 *He did what was wrong in the eyes of Yahweh according to all that Jehoiakim had done.*
3 *Indeed, in Jerusalem and Judah Yahweh's wrath was provoked so that he banished them from his sight;*[1] *and Zedekiah rebelled against the king of Babylon.*
4 *In the ninth year of his reign, in the tenth month, on the tenth day of the month, Nebuchadrezzar, king of Babylon, with his entire army moved against Jerusalem, set up camp, and erected siege-works against it on all sides,*[2]
5 *and the city was under siege until the eleventh year of King Zedekiah.*
6 *In the fourth month,*[3] *on the ninth day of the month when famine had gripped the city and there was no food for the people,*[4]
7 *the city was breached. When the king*[5] *and all the warriors saw this they fled*[6] *and left the city by night, by way of the gate between the two walls near the king's garden; and the Chaldeans were all around the city. They went in the direction of the Arabah;*
8 *but the Chaldean army pursued the king and overtook Zedekiah in the plains of Jericho; and all his troops were scattered.*

1. The syntax of this verse seems to 20th-century readers awkward and is to be compared with that in 32:31. The verse reads lit. "Indeed, according to the wrath of Yahweh, it was in Jerusalem and Judah, until he cast them from his sight." In 32:31 the Hebrew reads "Indeed, this city has been to me according to my wrath and my anger from the day they built it unto this day, to remove it from my sight."
2. 39:1 reports only that they "came against Jerusalem and besieged it."
3. Lacking in LXX. Syr. reads "the fifth month."
4. The detail about the famine is not given in 39:1–10.
5. *When the king . . . saw this* is restored here from 39:4 although it is lacking in both Kings and LXX; cf. vv. 8ff. where the king is very much involved.
6. The verb is lacking in LXX.

9 *They seized the king and brought him to the king of Babylon at Riblah in the land of Hamath, and he passed sentence on him.*
10 *The king of Babylon executed Zedekiah's sons before his eyes and in addition he executed all the officials of Judah at Riblah.*
11 *Then he blinded the eyes of Zedekiah and bound him with fetters of bronze, and the king of Babylon brought him to Babylon where he committed him to prison until the day of his death.*
12 *In the fifth month, on the tenth day of the month, that is, in the nineteenth year of the reign of Nebuchadrezzar king of Babylon, Nebuzaradan, commander of the king's bodyguard, one of the servants of*[7] *the king of Babylon in Jerusalem, came*
13 *and set fire to the house of Yahweh and the king's palace, and all the houses of Jerusalem, including the houses of every important person.*[8]
14 *All the Chaldean forces who were with the commander of the guard pulled down all the walls of Jerusalem on all sides.*
15 *Then Nebuzaradan the commander of the guard deported*[9] *such of the people as were left in the city together with those who had deserted to the king of Babylon,*[10] *along with the rest of the skilled artisans.*[11]
16 *The commander of the guard left as vinedressers and laborers*[12] *some of the poorest people of the land.*

This concluding chapter to the book of Jeremiah is based on 2 K. 24:18–25:30 with the exception of 25:22–26, which is the story of Gedaliah's assassination, already recorded in some detail in chs. 40 and 41. The section from Kings was probably included to show how

7. MT reads "he stood before the king of Babylon." Revocalize *'āmaḏ* to *'ōmēḏ*, "he who stands." The expression in 2 K. 25:8 is "the servant of the king," which means the same. J. Bright, *Jeremiah*, p. 364 translates "a member of the king's personal entourage," which is an extended paraphrase but conveys the sense well.
8. The consonants of "great," *gdl*, are very close to those of Gedaliah, *gdlyh.* NEB translates the phrase as "including the mansion of Gedaliah." There is no independent textual evidence for NEB.
9. The inclusion here in MT of "some of the poorest of the people" is difficult to account for. The phrase is lacking in 39:9 and 2 K. 25:11 and seems to have been picked up by accident from the next verse. All three accounts report that this group was left behind.
10. Lit. "the falling (away) ones who had fallen (away) to the king of Babylon."
11. MT *hā'āmôn* means "architect," "builder." It differs from 2 K. 25:11—*hehāmôn,* "the crowd." The reading in 39:9—*hā'am,* "the people"—hardly suits the context, where the reference seems to be to skilled craftsmen. One proposal is to revocalize the MT to read *ha'ommān* (cf. Akk. *ummānu*), which means more specifically "artist," "craftsman." But the point need not be pressed since the Chaldeans would have been as much interested in architects and builders as in craftsmen. In either case the noun is singular grammatically, although the sense may be collective.
12. The word *yōgᵉḇîm* may mean "field laborers," i.e., agricultural workers; cf. 39:10 and note there. The parallel Arabic noun *wajbat* means "compulsory labor," and one wonders whether such a meaning adheres to the Hebrew word as well.

Jeremiah's prophecies were fulfilled. He had reiterated many times that Jerusalem would be destroyed and Judah sent into exile, and things happened as he had foretold. The other aspect of Jeremiah's preaching was the promise of restoration. In the release of Jehoiachin recorded in 52:31–34 the first sign of hope for the future was given.

Chapter 52 divides into four sections: The fall of the city and capture of Zedekiah (vv. 1–16), the sacking of the temple (vv. 17–23), the numbers deported to Babylon (vv. 24–30), and the release of Jehoiachin from prison (vv. 31–34).

1–3 Zedekiah was the throne-name of Mattaniah (2 K. 24:17), who was appointed to rule in Judah by Nebuchadrezzar after the deportation of his nephew Jehoiachin. The assessment of his reign is that *he did what was wrong in Yahweh's eyes*. The syntax of v. 3 seems awkward although it resembles that of 32:31 (see textual note). The passage should not be interpreted as meaning that the divine anger was the cause of the iniquity that was rampant in Judah. It was quite the reverse. The divine anger was the result of Judah's iniquity. The sense is that things in Judah were of such a character as to provoke Yahweh's wrath ("according to the wrath of Yahweh"). Then, to cap it all, Zedekiah rebelled against the king of Babylon (2 K. 24:29).

4–6 The *ninth year* of Zedekiah's reign, i.e., 589/8 B.C., was counted from the Babylonian New Year, the month of Nisan, which was March/April. The siege began on the tenth month and the tenth day of the month, approximately the beginning of January 588 B.C. No doubt Nebuchadrezzar had undertaken a good deal of preliminary work before that, perhaps for some time before the end of 589 B.C. The character of the *siege-works (dāyēq)* may be judged from a study of Assyrian reliefs since the methods of warfare had not altered much. Such works included siege walls, encampments, engines of war like battering rams, and mobile towers from which missiles or burning tar could be hurled. The siege continued till the fourth month of the eleventh year of Zedekiah, about July 587 B.C. (The month is not given in 2 K. 25:3 or LXX.) The siege thus lasted about eighteen months.

7 The text in this chapter makes no reference to the escape of the king although it is clear from later verses that the king had escaped (see textual note). It is possible that the gate by which

Zedekiah escaped was known as "Between the Two Walls."[13] It is not otherwise known and cannot now be identified. How Zedekiah and his entourage managed to penetrate the tight cordon thrown round Jerusalem by the Chaldeans is hard to imagine. But Zedekiah and his men must have known the area intimately and could therefore penetrate lines set by foreigners. Throughout the centuries Jewish guerrillas have been more than a match for invading forces, slipping through their lines in both directions. This feature is lacking in 39:1–10.

8 The scattering of Zedekiah's troops is a detail absent from 39:1–10. What is meant by the scattering of the troops is not clear. It may mean that in the dark the company was not able to keep together. Alternately the meaning may be that Zedekiah's troops fled as they saw the Chaldeans approaching. This incident may be alluded to in Lam. 4:19–20.

9–11 The capture of Zedekiah and his sons and his officials is recorded in 39:5–7 and 2 K. 25:5–7. Nebuchadrezzar was awaiting the outcome of the campaign at *Riblah in the land of Hamath,* an ancient Syrian town south of Kadesh on the Orontes River. It was the meeting point of several military roads between Egypt and Mesopotamia and a strategic base of Nebuchadrezzar. The sentences passed by the king of Babylon were severe and ruthless (see comments on 38:5–7). The statement that *all the officials of Judah* were executed at Riblah must refer to such of the officials as were there. The story of Gedaliah's assassination in chs. 40–41 refers to some other officials who seem to have escaped the Chaldean net (cf. 41:1). This detail is lacking in 2 K. 25:6–7 but is given in Jer. 39:6. Since time must have elapsed before these prisoners reached Riblah, their execution took place some weeks after the fall of Jerusalem. The detail about committing Zedekiah to prison in Babylon is not mentioned in 39:7. One wonders how long he survived after the physical and mental suffering through which he passed in the weeks before and after the fall of Jerusalem and particularly in the experience at Riblah.

12–13 Nebuzaradan, appointed as Nebuchadrezzar's special representative in Jerusalem,[14] arrived in the fifth month, i.e., August. The breach had been made in the walls (v. 7) in the fourth

13. Heb. *bên-haḥōmōṯayim*. Cf. the name of the Persian satrapy known as "Across the River," *ʿaḇar-nahărâ*.
14. See textual note.

month (July). A month later Nebuzaradan came to supervise the destruction of the city. The exact day is not known for certain since 2 K. 25:8 gives the seventh day, and v. 12 the tenth day. The city fell just as food ran out, although there had been a severe shortage before that. The year is given as the nineteenth year of Nebuchadrezzar. The year 587 B.C. is counted from the date of his actual accession to the throne in 605 B.C. and is reckoned according to the method used in Judah, which counted the accession year, however brief or long the period of reign, as one year (but cf. vv. 28–30 which follow Babylonian reckoning).

Nebuzaradan was charged with burning the city. Important buildings like the temple (house of Yahweh), the king's palace, and other important houses and buildings would be the first to be destroyed. Thereafter the flames spread to the whole city.

14 Nebuzaradan also undertook the dismantling of the walls of the city. Just how complete this dismantling was has been revealed by excavations on the eastern side of the city overlooking the Kidron Valley.[15] The verb "pull down" (*nāṯaṣ*) occurs several times in the book of Jeremiah. Yahweh had appointed the prophet to pull down kingdoms (1:10). Yahweh himself might pull down a kingdom (18:7). He had pulled Israel down (31:28). Thus the use of the verb "pull down" in reference to the walls carries with it some significant overtones.

15–16 In reference to the citizens of Jerusalem the passage tells us that Nebuzaradan deported those who were left in the city along with deserters who had been rounded up and the skilled artisans[16] who might be useful in Babylon. However, he did leave behind the insignificant members of the populace (the weak ones) to undertake agricultural tasks as *vinedressers (kōrᵉmîm)* and *laborers (yōgᵉḇîm)*. That these are referred to as "poor" or "weak" people (*dallôṯ*) suggests a low estimate of the significance of farm workers.[17] Perhaps the Chaldeans had a surplus of captives to do this work and had no need of more. They did, however, need skilled artisans. It is clear from chs. 40–41 that the community at Mizpah had some significant leadership both civil and military. The refer-

15. K. Kenyon, *Digging Up Jerusalem* (1974).
16. See textual note.
17. See A. Baumann in G. J. Botterweck and H. Ringgren, eds., *Theological Dictionary of the OT* (TDOT), III (E.T. 1978), pp. 225–29. This work is a translation of the German volume *Theologisches Wörterbuch zum Alten Testament* (Band 2, Lieferungen 1–4, 1974–75).

ence to the *poorest people of the land* in v. 16 is thus not easy to understand. It may refer only to the people in Jerusalem but it is not impossible that the words express the view that only the exiles were "good figs" (ch. 24). Those left behind were "bad figs," "the poorest people."

(ii) The Sacking of the Temple (52:17–23)

17 *The Chaldeans smashed the bronze pillars which belonged to Yahweh's house, the wheeled stands and the bronze seas that were in Yahweh's house, and they transported all the bronze*[1] *to Babylon.*

18[2] *They took away also the pots, the shovels, the snuffers, the basins, the incense bowls, indeed all bronze vessels which were used in the temple service.*

19 *In addition the commander of the guard took away the small bowls,*[3] *the firepans, the basins, the pots, the lampstands, the incense bowls, and the libation bowls, both those that were made of gold and those that were made of silver.*[4]

20 *As for the two pillars, the one sea, the twelve bronze bulls that were under the sea,*[5] *the ten*[6] *wheeled stands which King Solomon made for Yahweh's house, the bronze that was in all these things was beyond weighing.*

21 *As for the pillars, the height of each pillar was eighteen cubits and the circumference was twelve cubits;*[7] *it was hollow and its thickness was four fingers.*[8]

22 *It had a capital of bronze five cubits high, and all around the capital was a network with pomegranates all of bronze. The second pillar with its pomegranates was like it.*[9]

1. The word *bronze* is lacking in LXX and 2 K. 25:13.
2. The text of vv. 18 and 19 is longer than in LXX or 2 K. 25:14, 15.
3. MT reads *sippîm;* LXX transliterates a text *sappôṯ*. The meaning is probably the same in either case. The singular *sap̱* (Akk. *šappu*) has alternative plurals *sippîm* and *sippôṯ*. The meaning is simply "basin," "bowl." Our translation "small bowls" is an attempt to distinguish these temple items from some of the very large bowls or craters. But there must remain a degree of uncertainty about the exact size of the bowls referred to here. See KB, p. 633; J. L. Kelso, *The Ceramic Vocabulary of the OT* (Suppl. Studies Nos. 5–6 to *BASOR,* 1948), pp. 13, 27f. and figs. 11, 12 on p. 48.
4. Lit. "which were gold, gold, and which were silver, silver." The expression has a distributive sense and is to be applied to each of the items in v. 19. In fact, most of them are referred to in 1 K. 7:49–50 or Exod. 25:29ff. as being made of gold.
5. MT lacks *the sea,* but it is restored with LXX. Cf. 1 K. 7:25. The whole phrase referring to the bronze bulls is lacking in 2 K. 25:16.
6. In MT *'eśer, ten,* may have dropped out before *'ašer;* 1 K. 7:27 refers to ten stands.
7. Lit. "a line of twelve cubits would surround it."
8. Lacking in 2 K. 25:17.
9. The text seems to have been disturbed; cf. 2 K. 25:17 which begins the sentence with "on the network" and breaks off (and omits the present v. 23 altogether). LXX reads "eight pomegranates to the cubit for the twelve cubits." Our translation smooths out a difficult text. See NEB.

23 *And there were ninety-six pomegranates evenly spaced.*[10] *In all, there were one hundred pomegranates on the network all around.*

These verses indicate that the Babylonians looted the temple before destroying it and then carried off the temple utensils of bronze, silver, and gold. It was the second time they had done this. After the capture of Jerusalem in 597 B.C. they carried away various utensils (27:16; cf. 2 K. 24:13). That there were more vessels to be carried off again in 586 B.C. suggests that the people had manufactured new ones. Jeremiah had warned the people in 27:19–22 that objects left after the first invasion in 597 B.C. would eventually be carried off. The same story is told in 2 K. 25:13–17 but it is somewhat briefer than here. The accounts of the temple equipment given in Exod. 25:30 and 1 K. 6–7 are of help in elucidating some of the problems in the present text. Archeological work has contributed somewhat to our understanding of the text as well. Even so, some of the identifications are uncertain.

17–18 The items in v. 17 are referred to in 1 K. 7:15–37. The pillars are there named Jachin and Boaz and details of their ornamentation are given[11] (1 K. 7:15–23). The sea is mentioned in 1 K. 7:23–26 and the wheeled stands or trolleys in 1 K. 7:27–37. The purpose of the two pillars is not certain but they may have served as cressets or fire-altars. Such columns were common in the first millennium B.C. in temples of Syrian design.[12] The sea was used for ritual washing and the wheeled stands were used to move small lavers from one place to another in the temple. According to 2 Chr. 4:6 the small lavers were used to bring the water in which the instruments used in the burnt offerings were washed, while the big laver was used by the priests in performing their own ritual washings. The size of these items was quite considerable. The bronze

10. Heb. *rûḥâ* is of uncertain meaning. It may be related to the root *rwḥ* which occurs in the noun *rewaḥ*, "space," "interval" (cf. Gen. 32:17) and hence mean *evenly spaced;* so J. Bright, *Jeremiah,* p. 365. NEB reads "exposed to view," i.e., open to the wind (*rûaḥ* with *he locale*). Rudolph in *BHS* thinks the text is corrupt but offers no suggestions. The versions translate variously; Syr. omits.

11. J. Gray, *I and II Kings* (^{2}1970), pp. 183ff., has a detailed discussion of the various items in the temple of Solomon.

12. W. F. Albright, *Archaeology and the Religion of Israel,* pp. 139, 144, 147, 155; "Two Cressets from Marisa and the Pillars of Jachin and Boaz," *BASOR* 85 (1942), pp. 18ff.; R. B. Y. Scott, "The Pillars of Jachin and Boaz," *JBL* 58 (1939), pp. 143ff.; D. J. Wiseman, "Jachin and Boaz," *NBD*, p. 593; H. G. May, "The Two Pillars Before the Temple of Solomon," *BASOR* 88 (1942), pp. 19–27; S. Yeivin, "Jachin and Boaz," *PEQ* 1959, pp. 6–22.

sea was some 15 feet in diameter and 7½ feet high, all in cast bronze of 3 inches thickness. The pillars were some 27 feet high with a thickness of "four fingers" (v. 21). The wheel stands and their lavers were large enough to contain twenty baths of water each. The total quantity of bronze in each of these large items was enormous and was clearly valuable enough to be transported to Babylon.

We are in a good position today to understand the appearance of some of these items because of modern excavation.[13] A model of a wheeled stand and base was discovered at Megiddo.[14] Several finds throw light on the nature of some of the smaller items (vv. 18, 19).[15] The items in this list present some problems of interpretation.[16] The *pots (sirôṯ)* may have been used for removing fat and ashes from the altar. The *shovels (yāʿîr)* were probably used to remove the ashes from the altar and place them in the pots. The *snuffers (mᵉzammᵉrôṯ)* were used to trim the wicks of the lamps. The *basins (mizrāqôṯ)* were bowls used to dash the blood of the sacrifices against the altar, to judge from the verb *zāraq,* "to throw (blood)." The *incense bowls* or "ladles" (*kappôṯ*) were probably vessels shaped in the form of a human palm (*kap̱*). Small vessels with hands carved on their backs have been found in excavations in strata from the period 1000–600 B.C.[17] Some of these show traces of carbon on the hollow side and may have been used for burning incense. All these vessels were very much smaller than the items of v. 18 but, being bronze, they too could be melted down and the bronze re-used.

19 Several of the items in this verse are mentioned in v. 18, but the present reference is to vessels of gold and silver. The items mentioned here and not already mentioned in v. 19 are the *small bowls* or cups (*sippîm*)[18] used for holding the blood of the sacrifices (Exod. 12:22, 23) into which the hyssop bush was dipped, and perhaps also for pouring out libations; the *firepans (maḥtôṯ),* used for carrying live coals to and from the altar but possibly used also as

13. A useful account of the temple furnishings is given in G. E. Wright, *Biblical Archaeology* (rev. ed. 1962), pp. 137–146. Several plates are included and some discussion about the symbolism of some of the items. Linguistic details are given in J. Gray, *I and II Kings*, pp. 191ff. Note also A. Parrot, *The Temple in Jerusalem* (1957); G. A. Barrois, "The Temple," *IDB* IV, pp. 541f.

14. See J. B. Pritchard, *The Ancient Near East in Pictures* (²1969), plate 587.

15. See G. E. Wright, *Biblical Archaeology,* pp. 137–146. Note fig. 95.

16. J. L. Kelso, *The Ceramic Vocabulary of the OT* (Suppl. Stud. Nos. 5–6 to *BASOR*, 1948), provides some valuable linguistic and archeological material on many of the terms used here.

17. *Ibid.*, Fig. 95.

18. See J. Gray, *I and II Kings,* p. 200.

censers; the *lampstands (mᵉnōrôṯ),* used as stands for the lamps to light up the holy place; and the *libation bowls (mᵉnaqqiyyôṯ),* used for pouring out libations (Exod. 25:29). It is of some interest that here by contrast with 1 K. 7:49–51 and Exod. 25:29–39 these vessels are said to be made of gold and silver. The other texts refer to them as vessels of gold.

20 This verse returns to the bronze items made by Solomon. Reference to *the twelve bronze bulls that were under the sea* is lacking in 2 K. 25:16, but this is not a ground for deleting the phrase here. The bronze bulls had been removed in Assyrian times a century earlier and sent to the Assyrian king Tiglath-pileser (2 K. 16, 17). However, it is likely that the bulls were replaced since they were a regular part of the temple equipment and in any case the sea had to be supported on some kind of stand. The point is made that *the bronze in all these things was beyond weighing.* Clearly the amount of bronze in the temple was of great interest to the Chaldeans.

21–23 Some attempt is made in these verses to describe the decoration of the pillars and their capitals. There are some textual variants, however. The height of the pillars is given as *eighteen cubits* (cf. 1 K. 7:5), whereas LXX and 2 Chr. 3:15 have thirty-five cubits. This latter figure seems difficult to accept since the temple itself was only thirty cubits high (1 K. 6:21) and we have no evidence that the pillars stood up beyond the roof of the temple unless, of course, they stood outside the entrance, which is possible. It may be, however, that the figure in LXX and Chronicles represents the total length for both pillars. The circumference was twelve cubits, i.e., about 18 feet since one cubit is approximately 18 inches. According to 1 K. 7 these pillars were cast by the artisan Hiram from Tyre, in clay of the Jordan valley (1 K. 7:46). The method was similar to one used by the Assyrians for massive casting.[19] The thickness of the metal in the hollow pillars was *four fingers,* that is, one quarter of a hand-breadth, rather less than one inch.[20]

Details of the decoration on the capitals are given in 1 K. 7:16–20.[21] Pomegranates feature prominently in the decoration. This kind of decoration appears also on the high priest's robe (Exod. 28:33) but is known in other areas of the Near East besides Israel, e.g., a laver found at Ras Shamra had metal pomegranates hanging

19. *ARAB* II, 1927, p. 169.
20. See *NBD,* p. 1322 where an approximation of 0.73 inch is given.
21. For textual problems see textual notes.

from the stand.[22] According to 1 K. 7:20, 42 each capital had two hundred pomegranates around it in two rows.

The material in ch. 52 is thus merely a summary, and it is not surprising that it is not always possible to match this account with that in 1 K. 7. The aim was not to give a detailed technical account but rather to stress two facts, first, that there was a very considerable amount of bronze (vv. 18, 20–23), and second, that the pillars were very beautiful, which made their destruction all the more tragic.

(iii) The Numbers Deported to Babylon (52:24–30)

24 *The commander of the guard took Seraiah*[1] *the chief priest and Zephaniah*[2] *the second priest, and the three keepers of the threshold;*
25 *and he took from the city*[3] *a certain official who was in charge of the warriors, seven*[4] *men of the king's personal advisers who happened to be in the city, the assistant to the army commander who mustered the people of the land for war, and sixty men from the ordinary people who were still in the city.*
26 *Nebuzaradan the commander of the guard seized them and went to the king of Babylon at Riblah.*
27 *And at Riblah in the land of Hamath the king of Babylon had them tortured*[5] *and put to death. So Judah went into exile from their own land.*
28[6] *This is the count of the people whom Nebuchadrezzar deported in the seventh year,*[7] *three thousand and twenty-three men of Judah;*
29 *in Nebuchadrezzar's eighteenth year, eight hundred and thirty-two people from Jerusalem;*
30 *in Nebuchadrezzar's twenty-third year, Nebuzaradan the commander of the guard deported seven hundred and forty-five men of Judah— all told four thousand and six hundred persons.*

The future lay with these exiles. The compiler of the book was able to bring the lists up to date although we are not certain how the count was made. The sentence *So Judah went into exile from their*

22. See G. E. Wright, *Biblical Archaeology,* p. 143, fig. 94.

1. Lacking in LXX.
2. Lacking in LXX.
3. Lacking in LXX.
4. 2 K. 25:19 has "five."
5. The root *nkh* is difficult to translate. The Hiphil is often translated "smite," but it can mean "wound, hurt, torture, flog," etc. On the other hand the verb may be used here for emphasis, "he smote them and had them slain." The second verb is lacking in LXX, which ends this section here and resumes at v. 31.
6. 2 K. 25 and LXX omit vv. 28–30.
7. Syr. adds "of his reign." The suggested emendation in *BHS* to "seventeenth year" is historically incorrect and without support.

own land (v. 27 MT) appears to single out this particular group as though those left behind did not matter. Here was Judah, going to exile. With this group Israel's future lay.

24 Nebuzaradan was selective in the people he rounded up for execution. *Seraiah the chief priest* was the grandson of Hilkiah, Josiah's chief priest (1 Chr. 6:13–15). His son was Jehozadak, who was the father of Joshua the high priest when the temple was rebuilt after the Exile (Ezra 5:2; Hag. 1:1; etc.). Five high priests spanned the period between Josiah and the Restoration. *Zephaniah* is possibly the person referred to in 29:24–32 and 37:3. The *keepers of the threshold* were high-ranking priests, perhaps custodians of the temple.

25 The *official (sārîs) who was in charge of the warriors* may have been a civilian official whose duty it was to act as overseer (*pāqîd*) of the men of war, perhaps as minister of defense. The group of seven *personal advisers* were men who had access to the king's presence and were in his confidence (lit. "those who saw the king's face"). The *assistant* (*sōp̱ēr,* "scribe," "secretary") *to the army commander* was responsible for personnel. All these were key government officials. The sixty ordinary citizens may have been representatives of the general populace singled out from the conscripted soldiers for exemplary punishment. The term *'am hā'āreṣ* seems to have the force of *the ordinary people* here although in some parts of the OT it may have another sense.[8]

26–27 This carefully selected group was taken to Riblah where King Zedekiah was also taken, and there they were executed, possibly after being tortured or flogged (see textual note).

28–30 Three groups of exiles are mentioned, the first in 598/7 B.C., the second in 587/6, and the third in 582/1.

The first was in Nebuchadrezzar's seventh year. In this case the year count was according to the Babylonian system of reckoning, which omitted the first partial year and began counting the regnal years from the New Year of 604 B.C. The figure given here of 3,023 is very different from that in 2 K. 24:14, 16, where it is 10,800. The difference may be that the latter figure represents the whole population while the smaller figure represents the exact count of adult males.

The second deportation came in Nebuchadrezzar's eighteenth year according to Babylonian reckoning, i.e., 587/6 B.C.; ac-

8. E. W. Nicholson, "The Meaning of the Expression *'am hā'āreṣ* in the OT," *JSS* 10 (1965), pp. 59–66.

cording to the reckoning of 2 K. 25:8 it was the nineteenth year. The figure again seems small and may represent the males, a mere 832. But on that occasion many were slain in the siege, the final assault, and subsequent punitive actions.

The third deportation in the twenty-third year of King Nebuchadrezzar, i.e., 582/1 B.C., is not so easy to identify,[9] but it may have been associated with a further revolt, or have been a belated punitive raid for the assassination of Gedaliah.

A total of 4600 in these deportations, even if this represents only the males, seems small. Even allowing for females and children the total may not amount to more than 15,000 to 20,000. Many of these may have died on the way to Babylonia. Even so, this select group was the stuff of the restored Israel. Perhaps the editor wanted to make the point that Yahweh could build a new future out of a mere handful of people. The exactness of the figures 3,023, 832, and 745 suggests an authentic recording of the numbers of some kind.

(iv) The Release of Jehoiachin from Prison (52:31–34)

31 *In the thirty-seventh year of the exile of Jehoiachin king of Judah, in the twelfth month on the twenty-fifth day*[1] *of the month, Evil-merodach king of Babylon in his succession year showed favor*[2] *to Jehoiachin king of Judah and released him from prison.*

32 *He addressed him kindly and gave him a position*[3] *above that of the kings who were with him in Babylon.*

33 *So Jehoiachin changed his prison garments and ate regularly in the king's presence as long as he lived.*

34 *And for his support, a regular allowance was given to him by the king of Babylon, on a daily basis as long as he lived until the day of his death.*

31 The thirty-seventh year of the exile of King Jehoiachin was 561 B.C. By that time Nebuchadrezzar had died and his son Evil-merodach was king. His Akkadian name was Awel (Amel)-Marduk ("man of Marduk"). It is possible that the name in Hebrew is due not merely to the problems of transliteration between the two languages but to deliberate corruption since *'ᵉwil* means "a stupid (foolish) person." This man ruled for only a short time, 561–560 B.C., before

9. See the Introduction, "Jeremiah in His Historical Setting," pp. 9–22.

1. LXX reads "the twenty-fourth," 2 K. 25:2 "the twenty-seventh." It is impossible to decide which is correct.
2. Lit. "lifted up his head."
3. Lit. "a seat."

being assassinated by his brother-in-law Neriglissar (560–556 B.C.). The present text suggests that Awel-Marduk released Jehoiachin in his succession year, which is entirely possible since it was an occasion for acts of favor. It was also an occasion for vassals to renew their allegiance to the new king, and Jehoiachin may have done this. By then it was some thirty-five years since his exile from Judah in 597 B.C. so that an affirmation of allegiance would mean little. Things had changed greatly in Judah. He may, of course, still have been regarded by some in Judah as the legitimate ruler, and there is some evidence to support this view.[4] Certainly in the early days of his exile this was so, and it was popularly believed that Jehoiachin and the exiles would soon return (28:1–4). He was known as "king of Judah" in Babylon, to judge from receipts for oil, etc., issued in the name of "Yaukin king Judah" and his sons, found in excavations in Babylon.[5] The character of his imprisonment is not known. He may have been well treated.

32–34 The king of Babylon addressed him kindly (lit. "spoke good things with him") and gave him a special place among the other kings who were in exile in Babylon. The phrase *the kings who were with him* is ambiguous. It may refer to Jehoiachin's associates, or alternately to all the kings who were with Awel-Marduk. The special nature of the favor is spelled out in terms of his change from prison clothes, his privilege of dining in the king's presence, and his regular allowance. The latter was no doubt for the support of his family, for according to the receipts referred to above, he had five sons at least. The record states that this continued to the day of his death. Presumably the usurper Neriglissar continued those favors, as did the other rulers up till the day of Jehoiachin's death. We have no other information on the matter.

There is considerable theological significance in these four verses. The fact that Jehoiachin lived on long after the exile and that he was finally released from prison may have seemed like the first signs of the fulfilment of Jeremiah's promise of a day of restoration. To the last, the future of Israel is seen as lying with the exiles in Babylon and not with those in Egypt or in their old homeland.

4. See above, pp. 482–85; cf. W. F. Albright, "King Joiachin in Exile," *BA* 5 (1942), pp. 49–55.
5. *ANET*, p. 308.

I. INDEX OF SUBJECTS

II. INDEX OF AUTHORS

III. INDEX OF PERSONS AND PLACES

IV. INDEX OF SCRIPTURE REFERENCES

V. INDEX OF NONBIBLICAL TEXTS

MAPS

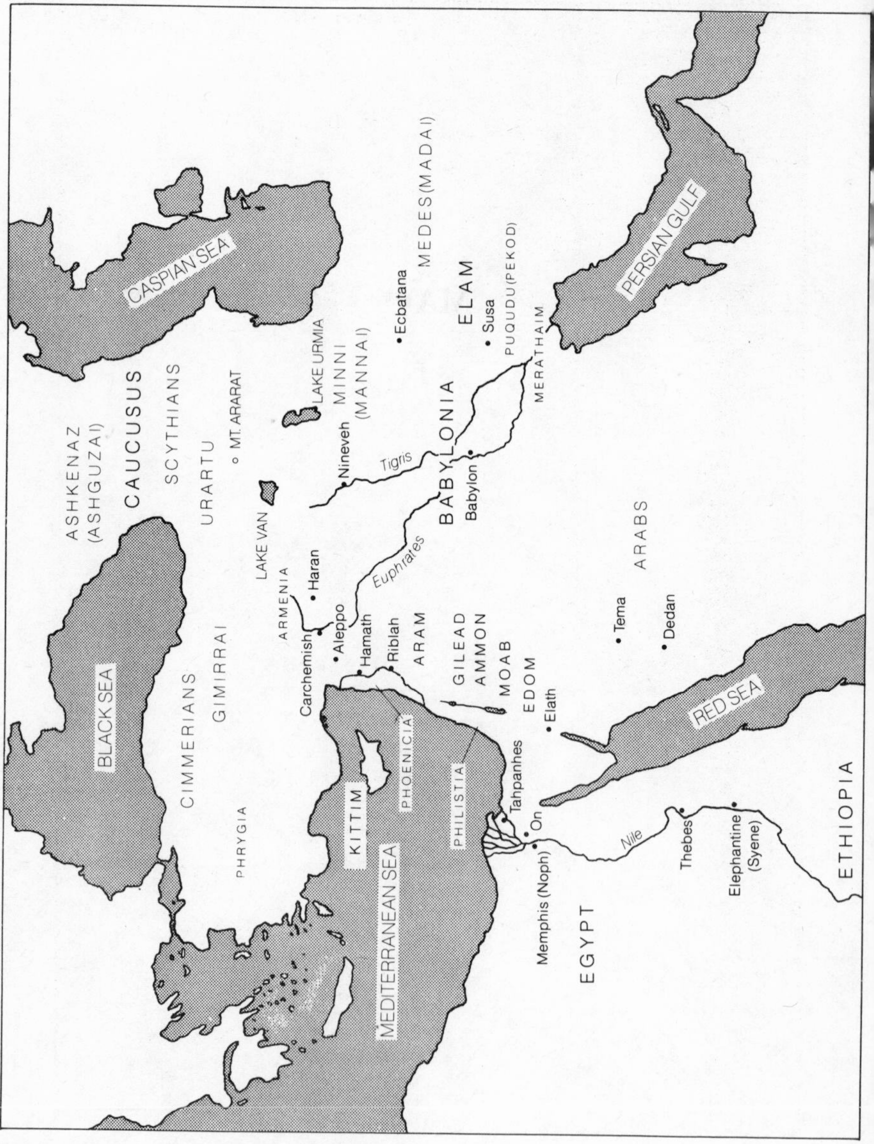
CASPIAN SEA
BLACK SEA
PERSIAN GULF
RED SEA
MEDITERRANEAN SEA
ASHKENAZ
(ASHGUZAI)
CAUCUSUS
SCYTHIANS
URARTU
MT. ARARAT
LAKE VAN
LAKE URMIA
MINNI
(MANNAI)
MEDES (MADAI)
Ecbatana
ELAM
Susa
PUQUDU (PEKOD)
MERATHAIM
BABYLONIA
Babylon
Nineveh
Tigris
Euphrates
ARMENIA
Haran
Carchemish
Aleppo
Hamath
Riblah
ARAM
GILEAD
AMMON
MOAB
EDOM
Elath
ARABS
Tema
Dedan
CIMMERIANS
GIMIRRAI
PHRYGIA
KITTIM
PHOENICIA
PHILISTIA
Tahpanhes
On
Memphis (Noph)
Nile
Thebes
Elephantine
(Syene)
EGYPT
ETHIOPIA

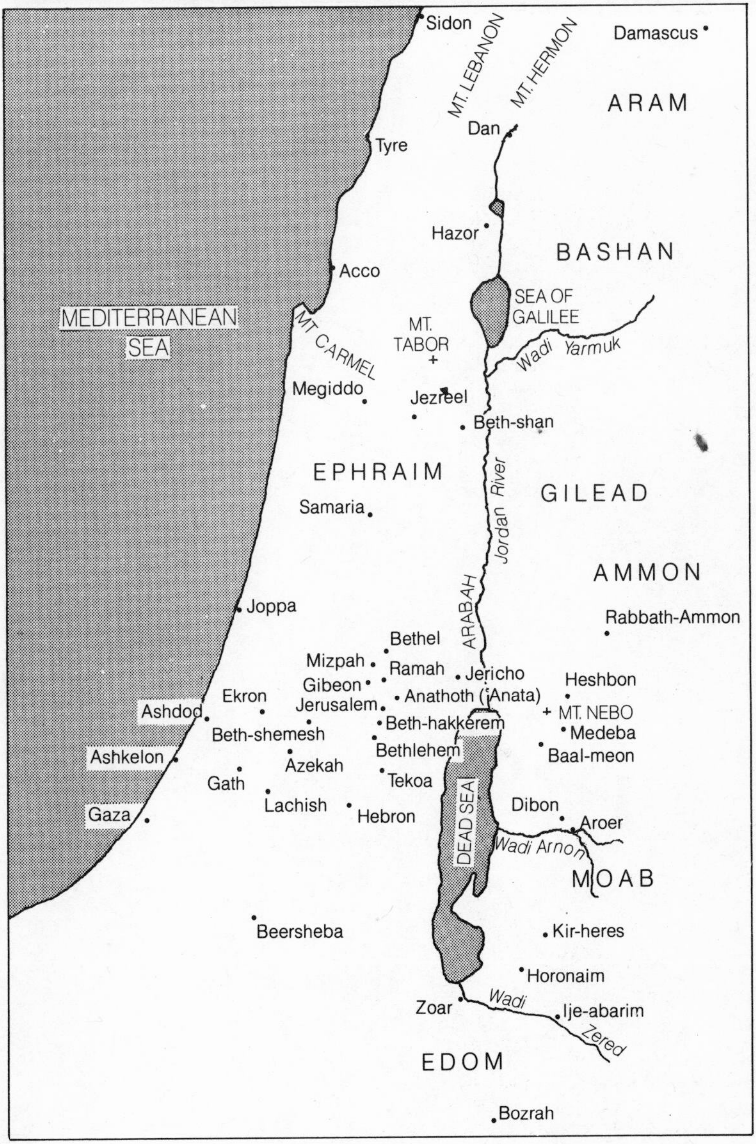
Sidon
MT. LEBANON
MT. HERMON
Damascus
ARAM
Dan
Tyre
Hazor
BASHAN
Acco
SEA OF GALILEE
MEDITERRANEAN SEA
MT CARMEL
MT. TABOR
Wadi Yarmuk
Megiddo
Jezreel
Beth-shan
EPHRAIM
Jordan River
GILEAD
Samaria
AMMON
ARABAH
Joppa
Rabbath-Ammon
Bethel
Mizpah
Ramah
Jericho
Heshbon
Gibeon
Anathoth (Anata)
Ekron
Jerusalem
MT. NEBO
Ashdod
Beth-hakkerem
Medeba
Beth-shemesh
Bethlehem
Baal-meon
Ashkelon
Azekah
Gath
Tekoa
DEAD SEA
Dibon
Lachish
Hebron
Aroer
Gaza
Wadi Arnon
MOAB
Beersheba
Kir-heres
Horonaim
Zoar
Wadi Zered
Ije-abarim
EDOM
Bozrah